THE
PUBLIC GENERAL ACTS
AND GENERAL SYNOD MEASURES
1984

[IN FOUR PARTS]

PART II
(Chapters 31-49)

with
Lists of the Public General Acts
Local Acts and an Index

LONDON
HER MAJESTY'S STATIONERY OFFICE
1985
£180·00 net

HMSO publications are available from:

HMSO Publications Centre
(Mail and telephone orders only)
PO Box 276, London SW8 5DT
Telephone orders (01) 622 3316
General enquiries (01) 211 5656

HMSO Bookshops
49 High Holborn, London, WC1V 6HB   (01) 211 5656 (Counter service only)
258 Broad Street, Birmingham, B1 2HE   (021) 643 3757
Southey House, 33 Wine Street, Bristol, BS1 2BQ   (0272) 24306/24307
9–21 Princess Street, Manchester, M60 8AS   (061) 834 7201
80 Chichester Street, Belfast, BT1 4JY   (0232) 234488
13a Castle Street, Edinburgh, EH2 3AR   (031) 225 6333

HMSO's Accredited Agents
(see Yellow Pages)

And through good booksellers

ISBN 0 11 840244 7

THIS PUBLICATION
relates to
the Public General Acts
and General Synod Measures
which received the Royal Assent in 1984
in which year ended the THIRTY-SECOND
and began the THIRTY-THIRD YEAR
of the Reign of HER MAJESTY
QUEEN ELIZABETH THE SECOND
and
ended the First Session
and began the Second Session
of the Forty-ninth Parliament of the
United Kingdom of Great Britain
and Northern Ireland.

d

Produced in England by W. J. SHARP, CB
Controller and Chief Executive of Her Majesty's Stationery Office
and Queen's Printer of Acts of Parliament

e

CONTENTS

PART I

PART II

PART III

PART IV

TABLE I

Alphabetical List of
the Public General Acts of 1984

TABLE II

Chronological List of
the Public General Acts of 1984

* Consolidation Act

* Consolidation Act

TABLE III

Alphabetical List of
the Local and Personal Acts of 1984

TABLE IV

Chronological List of
the General Synod Measures of 1984

There were no Measures passed by the General Synod of the Church of England during the year 1984.

Rating and Valuation (Amendment) (Scotland) Act 1984

1984 CHAPTER 31

An Act to amend the law of Scotland as regards rating, valuation and local government finance and for connected purposes. [26th June 1984]

B E IT ENACTED by the Queen's most Excellent Majesty, by and with the advice and consent of the Lords Spiritual and Temporal, and Commons, in this present Parliament assembled, and by the authority of the same, as follows:—

PART I

RATING AND LOCAL GOVERNMENT FINANCE

1.—(1) In Part I of Schedule 1 to the Local Government (Scotland) Act 1966 (which among other things relates to the apportionment of the needs element of rate support grants), after paragraph 3 there shall be inserted the following paragraph—

Basis of apportionment of needs element of rate support grants.
1966 c. 51.

"3A. Without prejudice to sections 5 and 5A of this Act or to the generality of paragraphs 1 and 3 above, the Secretary of State may, in prescribing a basis for apportionment under either of those paragraphs or in providing for apportionment under paragraph 3 above, have regard to the extent to which, in his opinion, either or both—

(*a*) the actual expenditure of an individual authority has conformed (whether or not in the year for which the amount of the needs element is payable),

Part II   A

(*b*) the estimated expenditure of such an authority conforms,

with any guidance issued by him, before the start of the
year to which the expenditure relates, as to what that
expenditure ought to be.".

(2) Schedule 1 to the said Act of 1966 is set out as amended
by this section in Schedule 1 to this Act.

Procedure
under section 5
of the Local
Government
(Scotland) Act
1966.
1966 c. 51.

2.—(1) In section 5 of the Local Government (Scotland) Act
1966 (reduction in certain circumstances of rate support grant
and rates), after subsection (5) there shall be inserted the following subsection—

" (5A) A report under subsection (1) above may relate
to more than one local authority and, if a report so relating
is approved by a resolution of the Commons House of Parliament, subsections (4) and (5) above shall, with the necessary modifications, apply in relation to the report.".

(2) Sections 2 to 7 of the said Act of 1966 are set out as amended by this section in Schedule 1 to this Act.

Power of
Secretary of
State to
control rates.
1973 c. 65.

3. After section 108A of the Local Government (Scotland)
Act 1973 there shall be inserted the following sections—

" Power of
Secretary of
State to
control
rate levels.

108B.—(1) The Secretary of State may, as respects the rates to be determined under section 108
of this Act by local authorities in respect of any
financial year, by order prescribe—

    (*a*) the maximum amount by which those rates
        may be greater than ; or

    (*b*) the minimum amount by which those rates
        shall be less than,

the rates so determined in respect of the immediately preceding financial year.

(2) Any amount prescribed under subsection (1)
above—

    (*a*) may be expressed as a percentage ;

    (*b*) shall be prescribed in relation to one or
        more of the following classes of rate, that
        is to say—

           (i) the regional rate ;

           (ii) the general rate ;

           (iii) the district rate.

(3) The Secretary of State may, under subsections (1) and (2) above, prescribe differently in respect of the different classes of rate specified in the said subsection (2).

(4) Nil may be the amount prescribed under subsection (1) above.

(5) The Secretary of State shall, before making an order under this section, consult such associations of local authorities as appear to him to be concerned.

(6) A statutory instrument containing an order under this section shall not have effect until approved by a resolution of the Commons House of Parliament.

(7) If—

(a) an order under this section has effect in relation to a local authority ; and

(b) the authority have not, by the date prescribed under section 108(1) of this Act, determined their rate in accordance with the order,

then the authority shall be deemed to have, on that date, determined the rate at which the maximum or, as the case may be, the minimum amount referred to in the order is exactly complied with.

(8) A reference in this Act (except section 108(1)) or in any other enactment, whether passed or made before or after the passing of this Act, to such rates as are determined under the said section 108 shall be construed as including such rates as are deemed to have been determined under subsection (7) above.

Derogations from rates control under section 108B.

108C.—(1) The Secretary of State may, on the application of a local authority, direct that nothing in an order under section 108B of this Act specified in the direction shall apply to the local authority.

(2) A direction under subsection (1) above may be made subject to such conditions as may be specified in it.

(3) An application under subsection (1) above shall be in such form and be accompanied by such information as the Secretary of State may direct.

A 2

PART I

(4) A direction made under this section may be revoked or amended by a further direction so made.".

Consultation with non-domestic ratepayers.

1973 c. 65.

4. In section 108 of the Local Government (Scotland) Act 1973 (determination of rates) there shall be inserted after subsection (2) the following subsections—

" (3) Before determining a rate under this section, a local authority shall, in accordance with such procedure as the Secretary of State may direct—

(*a*) make available to the persons mentioned in subsection (4) below such information as he may direct ; and

(*b*) consult those persons on that information and on the rate which the local authority propose to determine.

(4) The persons referred to in subsection (3) above are—

(*a*) those liable to pay rates in respect of lands and heritages other than dwelling-houses (construed in accordance with section 7(3) of the Local Government (Scotland) Act 1966) ; and

1966 c. 51.

(*b*) bodies appearing to the local authority to be representative of persons so liable.

(5) A direction made under subsection (3) above may be revoked or amended by a further direction so made.

(6) The duty under subsection (3) above does not apply in relation to the determination of a rate under section 108A of this Act or section 5(4)(*b*) of the Local Government (Scotland) Act 1966 or in relation to a deemed determination of a rate under the proviso to the said section 5(4)(*b*) or under section 108B of this Act.".

1966 c. 51.

Premises qualifying for rates relief for institutions for the disabled.

1978 c. 40.

5.—(1) In section 5 of the Rating (Disabled Persons) Act 1978 (rate rebates for institutions for the disabled)—

(*a*) in subsection (1) for the words from " and are " onwards there shall be substituted the following—

" if half or more of the floor area of so much of any building or, where there are more than one, those buildings as is comprehended in the lands and heritages is used exclusively for one or more of the purposes specified in subsection (2) below or purposes ancillary thereto, or is available so to be used." ;

(*b*) for subsection (5) there shall be substituted the following subsections—

" (5) The rebate under this section in respect of any lands and heritages shall be so much of the rates chargeable on the lands and heritages as is attributable to so much of the lands and heritages as is used exclusively for one or more of the purposes specified in subsection (2) above or purposes ancillary thereto or is available so to be used ; and, where the lands and heritages qualify for rebate for part of a rebate period, the rebate shall be proportionately reduced.

(5A) For the purposes of calculating the rebate under this section, the assessor shall certify what amount of rateable value is attributable to so much of the lands and heritages as is used as mentioned in subsection (5) above or is available so to be used and, subject to subsection (7) below, the assessor's certificate shall be conclusive." ;

(*c*) after subsection (6) there shall be inserted the following subsection—

" (7) An appeal shall lie in respect of a certificate under subsection (5A) above and a complaint may be made about such a certificate in either case to the valuation appeal committee ; and the provisions of the previous Valuation Acts relating to application to the assessor for redress, to appeals and complaints to the valuation appeal committee and to appeals from that committee to the Lands Valuation Appeal Court shall, with the necessary modifications, apply for the purposes of this subsection.".

(2) In section 6 of the said Act of 1978 (administration and appeals)—

(*a*) after subsection (5) there shall be inserted the following subsection—

" (5A) A person who has been granted a rebate under section 5 of this Act but is nevertheless dissatisfied with the amount of rebate may appeal to the sheriff ; and if the sheriff allows the appeal he may give the rating authority such direction as respects the matters mentioned in subsection (5) of that section as he thinks fit." ; and

(*b*) in subsection (6) after the word " (5) " there shall be inserted the words " or (5A) ".

PART I
Relief of
rates in
respect of
lands and
heritages
partly
occupied
for a short
time.
1947 c. 43.

6. After section 243 of the Local Government (Scotland) Act 1947 there shall be inserted the following section—

" Relief of
rates in
respect of
lands and
heritages
partly
occupied
for a short
time.

243A.—(1) If it appears to the rating authority that part of any lands and heritages included in the valuation roll is unoccupied but will remain so for a short time only, the authority may request the assessor to apportion the rateable value between the occupied and unoccupied parts and on being thus requested the assessor shall apportion the rateable value accordingly.

(2) As from whichever is the later of the following—

> (a) the date upon which lands and heritages the rateable value of which has been apportioned under section (1) above became partly occupied ;

> (b) the commencement of the financial year in which the request under that subsection relating to those lands and heritages was made,

until whichever of the events specified in subsection (3) of this section first occurs, the value apportioned to the occupied part of the lands and heritages shall be treated for rating purposes as if it were the rateable value ascribed to the lands and heritages in the valuation roll.

(3) The events mentioned in subsection (2) above are—

> (a) the reoccupation of any of the unoccupied part ;

> (b) the end of the financial year in which the request was made ;

> (c) a further apportionment of the value of the lands and heritages taking effect under subsection (1) above.

(4) Notwithstanding paragraph (b) of subsection (3) above, if it appears to the rating authority that the part of the lands and heritages which was unoccupied at the date of an apportionment of the rateable value thereof under subsection (1) above has continued after the end of the financial year referred to in that paragraph to be unoccupied but will remain so for a short time only, the authority may direct that the apportionment shall continue to have effect for the next financial year ; and subsections (2)

and (3)(*a*) and (*c*) above shall have effect in relation
to that year accordingly.

(5) In this section, "financial year" has the
meaning assigned to it by section 96(5) of the Local 1973 c. 65.
Government (Scotland) Act 1973.

(6) This section shall have effect as if it had come
into force on 1st April 1984.".

7. After section 243 of the Local Government (Scotland) Relief of
Act 1947 there shall be inserted the following section— rates in
respect of non-
" Relief of   243B.—(1) For the purposes of— domestic
rates in   lands and
respect of   (*a*) section 243 of this Act, lands and heritages to heritages not
non-   which this section applies shall be treated as in active use.
domestic
lands and   unoccupied and unfurnished ; 1947 c. 43.
heritages
not in   (*b*) section 243A of this Act and sections 24 to 27
active use.   of the Local Government (Scotland) Act 1966 c. 51.
                             1966 (rating of unoccupied property), lands
                             and heritages to which this section applies
                             shall be treated as unoccupied,

if, apart from this section, they would fall to be
treated as occupied (or, as the case may be, occupied
or furnished) by reason only of there being kept on
the lands and heritages plant, machinery or equipment—

(i) which was last used on the lands and heritages
when they were last in use ; or

(ii) which is intended for use on the lands and
heritages.

(2) This section applies to lands and heritages
which are not a dwelling-house, a private garage or
private storage premises ; and in this subsection—

(*a*) " private garage " means a building having
a floor area not exceeding 25 square
metres which is used wholly or mainly for
the accommodation of a motor vehicle ;
and

(*b*) " private storage premises " means lands
and heritages which are used wholly in
connection with a dwelling-house or dwelling-houses and wholly or mainly for the
storage of articles of domestic use (including bicycles and similar vehicles) belonging to persons residing there.

(3) For the purposes of subsection (2) of this
section lands and heritages that are not in use shall

A 4

nevertheless be treated as a dwelling-house, a private garage or private storage premises if it appears that, when next in use, they will be lands and heritages of that description.".

Power of Secretary of State to limit estimated rate fund contributions to housing revenue account.

1972 c. 46.

8.—(1) After section 23 of the Housing (Financial Provisions) (Scotland) Act 1972 there shall be inserted the following section—

" Power of Secretary of State to limit estimated rate fund contributions to housing revenue account.

23A.—(1) The Secretary of State may by order impose, as respects a local authority or class thereof specified in the order, a limit to the amount of contribution out of their general fund which the authority or, as the case may be, an authority of the class may estimate that they will carry to the credit of their housing revenue account for the year specified in the order ; and it shall be the duty of the local authority so to estimate that amount as not to exceed that limit.

(2) The limit referred to in subsection (1) above may be expressed in whatever way the Secretary of State thinks fit.

(3) An order under this section shall be made by statutory instrument which shall be subject to annulment in pursuance of a resolution of either House of Parliament.

(4) Every local authority shall, during the year 1984-85 and each of the subsequent years, submit to the Secretary of State an estimate of the income and expenditure an account of which they are obliged, under section 23 of this Act, to keep in their housing revenue account for the year next following.

1973 c. 65.

(5) In subsection (1) above, " general fund " means the fund maintained by a local authority under section 93 of the Local Government (Scotland) Act 1973.".

Separate accounts of expenditure by local authorities under section 83 of the Local Government (Scotland) Act 1973.

9. In section 83 of the Local Government (Scotland) Act 1973 (power of local authorities to incur expenditure for certain purposes not otherwise authorised) after subsection (6) there shall be inserted the following subsection—

" (7) The accounts kept under section 96 of this Act by a local authority shall include a separate account of any expenditure incurred by the authority under this section.".

10.—(1) For subsection (1) of section 101 of the Local Government (Scotland) Act 1973 there shall be substituted the following subsection—

" (1) At each audit under this Part of this Act of a local authority's accounts, any persons interested may inspect the accounts to be audited and all books, deeds, contracts, bills, vouchers and receipts relating thereto and make copies of all or any part of the accounts and those other documents.".

(2) In section 105(1)(*d*) of that Act (regulations as to the period in which accounts may be inspected and as to informing persons about their rights of inspection and objection) for the words " abstract and accounts " there shall be substituted the words " accounts and other documents ".

PART II
Inspection
of local
authorities'
accounts.
1973 c. 65.

PART II

VALUATION

11. In section 3 of the Local Government (Scotland) Act 1975 (appeal against entry in valuation roll) after subsection (2) there shall be inserted the following subsections—

" (2A) Where a person becomes the proprietor, tenant or occupier of lands and heritages which are included in the valuation roll he shall thereupon have the same right of appeal under subsection (2) above as he would have had if there had been sent to him the notice referred to in that subsection, except that the last date for lodging an appeal by virtue of this subsection shall be the last day of a period of six months beginning with the day upon which the person became the proprietor, tenant or occupier and all other time limits prescribed under the Valuation Acts in that regard shall have effect accordingly.

(2B) The right of appeal conferred by subsection (2A) above may be exercised whether or not any previous proprietor, tenant or occupier of the lands and heritages had reached agreement with the assessor as mentioned in section 2(3) of this Act or had appealed or obtained redress under subsection (2) above.".

Right of
appeal on
change of
owner, tenant
or occupier.
1975 c. 30.

12.—(1) In section 1 of the Lands Tribunal Act 1949 (which amongst other things provides as to the jurisdiction of the Lands Tribunal for Scotland), after subsection (3) there shall be inserted the following subsections—

" (3A) The Lands Tribunal for Scotland may also determine any appeal or complaint under the Valuation Acts (within the meaning of section 37(1) of the Local Government (Scotland) Act 1975) referred to it by a valuation appeal committee.

Jurisdiction in
valuation
matters of
Lands Tribunal
for Scotland.
1949 c. 42.

(3B) The jurisdiction conferred by subsection (3A) of this section includes power, in relation to an individual appeal or complaint, to decline with reason stated to proceed to determine it.

(3C) The provisions of the said Valuation Acts with regard to appeal to judges of the Court of Session shall, with any necessary modifications, apply in relation to determinations of the Lands Tribunal for Scotland under subsection (3A) of this section as they apply in relation to decisions of valuation appeal committees.

(3D) The Secretary of State may by order made by statutory instrument repeal or amend any enactment (including this Act) to the extent necessary to give full effect to this section.

(3E) A statutory instrument containing an order under subsection (3D) above shall have no effect until approved by resolution of each House of Parliament.".

1963 c. 12.

(2) In section 15 of the Local Government (Financial Provisions) (Scotland) Act 1963 after subsection (2) (regulations as to valuation appeal committees) there shall be inserted the following subsection—

" (2A) The Secretary of State may make regulations governing—

(a) the circumstances and manner in which an appeal or complaint may be referred to the Lands Tribunal for Scotland in pursuance of subsection (3A)

1949 c. 42.

of section 1 of the Lands Tribunal Act 1949 (jurisdiction of the Tribunal to determine valuation cases referred to it) ; and

(b) the consideration of the appeal or complaint by a valuation appeal committee in a case where the Tribunal have declined under subsection (3B) of that section to proceed to determine it.".

Constitution of lands valuation appeal court.

1867 c. 80.

1879 c. 42.

13.—(1) In section 8 of the Valuation of Lands (Scotland) Amendment Act 1867 and in section 7 of the Valuation of Lands (Scotland) Amendment Act 1879 (which sections, construed as originally enacted, provide, amongst other things, that appeals in valuation matters shall lie to two judges of the Court of Session), for the words " any two " there shall be substituted the words " a judge or (in a case in relation to which the judge to whom it was submitted has directed that it be heard by three judges or where the appeal is against a determination of the Lands Tribunal for Scotland under section 1(3A) of the Lands Tribunal Act 1949) three ".

(2) In the proviso to the said section 8, after the word " said " there shall be substituted the words " judge or, as the case may be,".

(3) In the said section 7—

    (*a*) for the word " judges ", where secondly and thirdly occurring, there shall be substituted the words " judge or, as the case may be, judges " ; and

    (*b*) for the word " their ", in each place where it occurs, there shall be substituted the words " his or, as the case may be, their ".

(4) Section 7(2) of the Local Government (Scotland) Act 1908 1908 c. 62. (which provides for the construction of the said section 8 and section 7 as if the references to two judges were references to three judges) shall cease to have effect.

14. After subsection (8) of section 3 of the Rating (Caravan Sites) Act 1976 (valuation and rating of caravan sites) there shall be inserted the following subsection— *Separate entry in valuation roll of pitches for static caravans.* *1976 c. 15.*

    " (8A) Where—

        (*a*) a caravan site is treated under subsection (1) above as a single unit of lands and heritages ;

        (*b*) a caravan pitch on that site would be taken as including, as part of lands and heritages, the caravan for the time being on it ; and

        (*c*) the caravan pitch is separately occupied by a person other than the site operator,

the assessor shall, on the application of that person, omit the pitch from the single unit and enter it separately in the valuation roll.".

15. After section 3 of the Rating (Caravan Sites) Act 1976 there shall be inserted the following section— *Percentage derating of static caravans.* *1975 c. 15.*

    " *Percentage derating of static caravans.* 3A.—(1) The Secretary of State may by order provide that the rateable value of a caravan site to which this section applies shall be the sum of the following amounts—

        (*a*) the amount produced by deducting from the aggregate net annual value of the caravan pitches on the site, which are caravan pitches to which this section applies, such percentage of that aggregate value as may be specified in the order ;

    (*b*) the amount of the net annual value of so much of the site as does not consist of those pitches.

(2) This section applies to any caravan site which is treated under section 3(1) above as a single unit of lands and heritages.

(3) This section applies to caravan pitches—

    (*a*) each of which when taken under section 3(5) above, as including the caravan for the time being on it, would constitute a dwelling-house for the purposes of section 7 of the Local Government (Scotland) Act 1966 (reduction of rates on dwellings by reference to the domestic element);

    (*b*) each of which is separately occupied by a person other than the site operator; and

    (*c*) none of which has been entered separately in the valuation roll under section 3(8A) above.

(4) An order under this section shall be made by statutory instrument which shall be laid before the Commons House of Parliament and shall not have effect until approved by a resolution of that House.".

Exemption of
reed beds
from rates.
1956 c. 60.

16.—(1) In subsection (2) of section 7 of the Valuation and Rating (Scotland) Act 1956 (valuation of agricultural lands and heritages), in the definition of " agricultural lands and heritages ", after the word " orchards " there shall be inserted the words ", reed beds ".

(2) In subsection (3) of the said section 7 after the words " agricultural lands and heritages ", where secondly occurring, there shall be inserted the words " (other than agricultural lands and heritages being lands and heritages used as reed beds) and on and after the first day of April nineteen hundred and eighty four have effect in the case of agricultural lands and heritages being lands and heritages used as reed beds ".

(3) After the said subsection (3) there shall be inserted the following subsection—

    " (3A) Any reference in the valuation roll to any lands and heritages used as reed beds shall, as from 1st April 1984, be of no effect ".

17. After section 8 of the Valuation and Rating (Scotland) Act 1956 there shall be inserted the following section—

PART II
Common
parts of
shopping
malls not to
be entered
separately in
valuation roll.
1956 c. 60.

"Common parts of shopping malls not to be entered separately in valuation roll.   8A. There shall not be entered separately in the valuation roll any part of a covered shopping mall, being a part the sole or main purpose of which is to serve two or more of the lands and heritages comprised in the mall.".

18. After section 8 of the Valuation and Rating (Scotland) Act 1956 there shall be inserted the following section—

Exemption
from
valuation
and rating
of certain
moorings.

"Exemption from valuation and rating of certain moorings.   8AA.—(1) For the purpose of ascertaining the net annual value of any lands and heritages no account shall be taken of any mooring to which this section applies.

(2) This section applies to any mooring—

> (*a*) used or intended to be used by a boat or ship ; and
>
> (*b*) equipped only with a buoy attached to an anchor, weight or other device—
>
>> (i) which rests on or in the bed of the sea or any river or other waters when in use ; and
>>
>> (ii) which is designed to be raised from that bed from time to time.".

19. At the end of subsection (1) of section 15 of the Local Government (Financial Provisions) (Scotland) Act 1963 (comparison with other lands and heritages) there shall be inserted—

Comparison
with
hereditaments
in England
and Wales.
1963 c. 12.

" or, in accordance with subsections (1A) to (1C) below, on hereditaments in England and Wales.

(1A) It shall be competent to found, by way of comparison, on hereditaments in England and Wales only if—

> (*a*) there is no evidence available as to lands and heritages in Scotland comparable to those which are the subject of the proceedings ; or
>
> (*b*) such evidence as is available in that regard is not adequate to enable the committee or, as the case may be, the Lands Tribunal for Scotland to draw conclusions as to the rent at which the lands and heritages which are the subject of the proceedings might reasonably be expected to let from year to year in the circumstances mentioned in section 6(2) or, as the case may be, 6(8) of the Valuation

Part II

and Rating (Scotland) Act 1956 (ascertainment of gross and net annual values by reference to expected rent).

1967 c. 9.

(1B) The net annual value ascribed in the valuation list maintained under the General Rate Act 1967 to a hereditament in England and Wales shall, for the purposes of subsections (1) and (1A) above, be treated as equal to the rent at which the hereditament (as at the date as at which its net annual value was ascribed to it) might reasonably be expected to let from year to year if the tenant undertook to pay all usual tenants' rates and taxes and to bear the cost of the repairs and insurance and the other expenses, if any, necessary to maintain the hereditament in a state to command that rent.

(1C) A valuation appeal committee or the Lands Tribunal for Scotland shall, in considering a hereditament in England and Wales by way of comparison in pursuance of this section, make such adjustment as is, in their opinion, necessary—

(*a*) to its rent as established by the evidence, so as to take account of (amongst any other things) the date at which that rent became payable ;

(*b*) to its rent as established under subsection (1B) above, so as to take account of (amongst any other things) the date as at which, under that subsection, that rent is to be treated as payable.".

Alteration of "material change of circumstances".

1975 c. 30.

20. In section 37(1) of the Local Government (Scotland) Act 1975, in the definition of " material change of circumstances "—

(*a*) the word " and ", where fourthly occurring, shall be omitted ; and

(*b*) for the words from " but " onwards there shall be substituted the words " and any decision of that Court, committee or Tribunal which alters the gross or net annual value or rateable value of any comparable lands and heritages ; ".

Part III

General

Amendments and repeals.

21.—(1) The enactments specified in Schedule 2 to this Act shall have effect subject to the amendents specified in that Schedule.

(2) The enactments specified in Schedule 3 to this Act are PART III
hereby repealed to the extent specified in column 3 of that
Schedule.

22. There shall be paid out of moneys provided by Parlia- Financial
ment— provisions

(a) any administrative expenses of the Secretary of State
under this Act ; and

(b) any increase attributable to the provisions of this Act in
the sums payable out of moneys so provided under any
other Act.

23.—(1) This Act, which may be cited as the Rating and Citation,
Valuation (Amendment) (Scotland) Act 1984, shall come into commence-
force as follows— ment and
extent.

(a) sections 1, 2 and 4 and this section shall come into force
on the day this Act is passed ;

(b) sections 7, 9 to 13, 17 to 19 and paragraphs 9, 12
to 15 and 17 of Schedule 2 shall come into force on
1st April 1985 ;

(c) the other provisions shall come into force at the end of
the period of two months beginning with the day on
which this Act is passed.

(2) This Act applies to Scotland only.

SCHEDULES

SCHEDULE 1

SECTIONS 2 TO 7 OF THE LOCAL GOVERNMENT (SCOTLAND) ACT 1966 SET OUT AS AMENDED

Rate support
grants.

2.—(1) Subject to the provisions of this Part of this Act, the Secretary of State shall, for each year, make grants to local authorities in Scotland in accordance with this section ; and any grants made in pursuance of this subsection shall be known as " rate support grants ".

(2) For the purpose of fixing the estimated aggregate amount of the rate support grants for any year the Secretary of State shall determine—

(*a*) the aggregate amount which he estimates is to be available for the payment out of moneys provided by Parliament of grants (other than housing subsidies) to local authorities in respect of their relevant expenditure for that year ; and

(*b*) the portion of that amount which the Secretary of State estimates will be allocated to grants in respect of such services as the Secretary of State may determine ;

and the amount remaining after deducting that portion from the aggregate amount aforesaid shall, subject to sections 3 and 4 of this Act, be the estimated aggregate amount of the rate support grants for that year.

(3) Before determining the amount and the portion mentioned in paragraphs (*a*) and (*b*) of subsection (2) above, the Secretary of State shall consult with such associations of local authorities as appear to him to be concerned and shall take into consideration—

(*a*) the latest information available to him as to the rate of relevant expenditure ;

(*b*) any probable fluctuation in the demand for services giving rise to relevant expenditure so far as the fluctuation is attributable to circumstances prevailing in Scotland as a whole which are not under the control of local authorities ;

(*c*) the need for developing those services and the extent to which, having regard to general economic conditions, it is reasonable to develop those services ; and

(*d*) the current level of prices, costs and remuneration and any future variation in that level which in the opinion of the Secretary of State will result from decisions which appear to him to be final and which will have the effect of increasing or decreasing any particular prices, costs or remuneration.

(4) After consultation with such associations of local authorities as appear to the Secretary of State to be concerned, the estimated aggregate amount of the rate support grants for any year shall be divided by the Secretary of State into three parts (to be known respectively as " the needs element ", " the resources element " and " the domestic element ") and the amounts of needs element and the domestic element and the estimated amount of the resources element shall be such as may be prescribed ; and the provisions of Schedule 1 to this Act shall, subject to sections 4 and 5 of this Act, have effect with respect to the determination of the amounts payable to any local authority in respect of those elements for any year and with respect to the other matters there mentioned.

(5) Payments in respect of elements of rate support grants shall be made to any local authority at such times as the Secretary of State may, with the consent of the Treasury, determine and shall be made in aid of the revenues of the authority, generally.

(6) Subject to subsection (7) below, the Secretary of State may—

(a) defray any expenditure incurred in any year in the provision of services for local authorities by any body specified in regulations made by the Secretary of State ; and

(b) deduct from the aggregate amount of the needs element for that year such amount, not exceeding the total of the expenditure so defrayed, as appears to him to be appropriate.

(7) Before exercising his powers under subsection (6) above, the Secretary of State shall consult with such associations of local authorities as appear to him to be concerned.

(8) In this section—

" housing subsidies " means such grants to local authorities out of moneys provided by Parliament for housing as may be determined by the Secretary of State to be housing subsidies for the purposes of this section ;

" relevant expenditure ", in relation to any year, means the sum of the following amounts as estimated by the Secretary of State—

(a) the amount of expenditure for that year falling to be paid out of the rates of a local authority, and

(b) an amount equal to the amount receivable by the local authority for that year as grants (within the meaning of section 2(2)(a) of this Act) and as payments under Part V of the Local Government Act 1948,

1948 c. 26.

reduced by the amount estimated as aforesaid, in whole or in part, of such payments relating to housing and of such payments of other descriptions falling to be made for that year as the Secretary of State may determine.

3.—(1) The estimated aggregate amount of the rate support grants determined (or redetermined) in accordance with subsection (2) of section 2 of this Act for any year and the matters which under that section or Schedule 1 to this Act are to be prescribed shall be fixed and prescribed by an order made by the Secretary of State after consultation with such associations of local authorities as appear to him to be concerned and with the consent of the Treasury (hereafter in this Act referred to as a " rate support grant order ").

(2) Any rate support grant order shall be laid before the Commons House of Parliament together with a report of the considerations leading to the provisions of the order, including considerations leading to the determination of the amount and the portion mentioned in section 2(2)(*a*) and (*b*) of this Act, and shall not have effect until approved by a resolution of that House.

(3) Subject to section 4 of this Act, rate support grant orders shall be made in advance for successive periods of two years ; and a rate support grant order may, as respects any matter to be fixed or prescribed by the order, make different provision for different years.

4.—(1) The Secretary of State may, at any time after the estimated aggregate amount of the rate support grants has been fixed for any year redetermine, under section 2(2) of this Act, that amount for that year.

(2) A rate support grant order made by virtue of subsection (1) above with respect to any year may vary matters prescribed by the rate support grant order which first fixed the estimated aggregate amount of the rate support grants for that year.

(3) A rate support grant order may, if the Secretary of State considers it practicable that it should do so, relate both to an estimated aggregate amount of the rate support grants determined, and to such an amount redetermined under section 2(2) of this Act.

Reduction in
certain
circumstances
of rate support
grant and rates.

5.—(1) Subject to subsections (1A)(*b*) and (3) below, if the Secretary of State is satisfied—

(*a*) that a local authority or a joint board have failed to achieve or maintain a reasonable standard in the discharge of any of their functions, regard being had to the standards maintained by other authorities and boards which are, in the opinion of the Secretary of State, of a similar type to the local authority or, as the case may be, joint board concerned ; or

(*b*) that the expenditure of any local authority or joint board has been excessive and unreasonable, regard being had to the financial and other relevant circumstances of the area or areas concerned ; or

(*c*) subject to subsection (1A)(*b*) below, that in respect of any local authority the total estimated expenses mentioned in section 108(2) of the Local Government (Scotland) Act 1973 are excessive and unreasonable, regard being had to the financial and other relevant circumstances of the area of the authority ;

and is of opinion that by reason of the failure or the excessive and unreasonable expenditure or estimated expenses a reduction should be made in the amount of any element of rate support grant payable to the local authority or a constituent authority of the joint board, as the case may be, he may, after affording to the local or constituent authority in question an opportunity of making representations, make and cause to be laid before Parliament a report stating the amount of and the reasons for the proposed reduction and setting out any representations made by the authority with respect to the proposed reduction.

(1A) In determining, for the purposes of paragraph (c) of subsection (1) above, whether, in relation to any year, total estimated expenses of a local authority are excessive and unreasonable the Secretary of State—

    (a) may (in addition to the matters to which in terms of that paragraph regard must be had) have regard—

        (i) to expenditure or estimated expenses, in that or any preceding year, of other local authorities which the Secretary of State is satisfied are closely comparable (or as closely comparable as is practicable) with the local authority concerned ;

        (ii) to general economic conditions ; and

        (iii) to such other financial, economic, demographic, geographical and like criteria as he considers appropriate ; and

    (b) may leave out of account such categories of estimated expenses as he thinks fit ; and different such categories may be left out of account according to whether the proposed reduction under this section is of a rate or of the amount of an element of rate support grant.

(2) The Secretary of State may make regulations, subject to annulment in pursuance of a resolution of either House of Parliament, for prescribing standards and general requirements in relation to any function of a local authority ; and in determining for the purposes of subsection (1) of this section whether there has been such a failure as is there mentioned, regard shall be had to any such regulations and any other standards or requirements imposed by or under any enactment.

(3) Where the Secretary of State is satisfied as is mentioned in paragraph (c) of subsection (1), as read with subsection (1A), above, he may in his report under the said subsection (1), instead of or in addition to proposing a reduction in the amount of an element of rate support grant, propose a reduction in the rate determined by the local authority ; and the provisions of the said subsection (1) shall apply to the amount of, reasons for and representations with respect to, the proposed reduction in rate as they apply to a proposed reduction in the amount of such element.

(4) If a report under subsection (1) above is approved by the Commons House of Parliament and contains a proposal—

    (a) to reduce an element of rate support grant, the Secretary of State may reduce that element by an amount not exceeding the amount of the reduction proposed ;

(*b*) that there should be a reduction in the rate determined by the authority to which the report relates, the authority shall forthwith determine under this paragraph a new rate less, by the proposed reduction in the rate or by such smaller amount as the Secretary of State may agree, than the rate determined by them under section 108 of the Local Government (Scotland) Act 1973 :

Provided that where, for any reason whatsoever, by the twenty-eighth day after the approval under this section of a report an authority have not made a determination required, in relation to that report, by paragraph (*b*) above the authority shall be deemed to have determined on that day a rate under the paragraph such that the reduction proposed under subsection (3) above by the Secretary of State is effected.

(5) If an authority determine a rate under paragraph (*b*) of subsection (4) above, or are deemed by virtue of the proviso to that subsection to have determined such a rate, that rate and not the rate determined under the said section 108 shall be their regional, general or district rate, as the case may be, for the financial year and shall be levied (and the rights and liabilities of ratepayers shall be construed) accordingly.

(5A) A report under subsection (1) above may relate to more than one local authority and, if a report so relating is approved by a resolution of the Commons House of Parliament, subsections (4) and (5) above shall, with the necessary modifications, apply in relation to the report.

(6) The Secretary of State may by order under this subsection repeal or amend any enactment (including this Act) in so far as that enactment relates to the determination, levy or payment of a regional, general or district rate and such determination, levy or payment is affected by a determination (or deemed determination) under paragraph (*b*) of subsection (4) above.

(7) An order made under subsection (6) above shall have not effect until approved by resolution of each House of Parliament.

(8) A reference in this Act (except this section) and in any other enactment (except subsection (1) of the said section 108) whether passed before or after the passing of this Act, to such rates as are determined under the said section 108 shall be construed as including a reference to such rates as are determined, or are deemed to have been determined under paragraph (*b*) of subsection (4) above.

(9) Section 19 of the Local Government (Miscellaneous Provisions) (Scotland) Act 1981 (which among other things empowers the Secretary of State to make certain estimates where a local authority fail to supply him timeously with information) shall apply for the purposes of such of the Secretary of State's functions under this section as do not relate to rate support grants as it applies for the purposes of those which do.

5A.—(1) Subject to subsections (2) and (3) below, where an element of rate support grant payable to a local authority has been reduced under section 5 of this Act, the Secretary of State may—

    (*a*) restore to the local authority some or all of the reduction if he considers that their subsequent conduct has been such as to merit such restoration ;

    (*b*) in respect of the year to which the failure or the excessive and unreasonable expenditure or estimated expenses relates, determine by order that an amount not greater than the reduction shall be distributed—

        (i) on such basis ; and

        (ii) among such other local authorities,

as he thinks fit, by means of an increase in the needs element payable to each of those other authorities:

Provided that, in a case where an amount is restored under paragraph (*a*) above, an amount distributed under this paragraph shall not exceed the difference between the reduction and the amount so restored.

Sch. 1

Redistribution and restoration of amounts by which rate support grant reduced.

(2) An order under subsection (1) above shall be subject to annulment in pursuance of a resolution of the Commons House of Parliament.

(3) After the Secretary of State has, under regulation 9(3) of the Rate Support Grant (Scotland) Regulations 1975, (or any regulation making like provision), made and given due notification of a conclusive calculation of amounts which include the amount reduced—

    (*a*) no restoration relating to the reduction shall take place under paragraph (*a*) of subsection (1) above ; and

    (*b*) no order, under paragraph (*b*) of that subsection, so relating shall be made, amended or (until spent) revoked.

6.—(1) The Secretary of State may make regulations for carrying the foregoing provisions of this Act into effect and, without prejudice to the generality of this provision,—

Supplemental.

    (*a*) for determining the manner in which any calculation or estimate is to be made for any of the purposes of those provisions and, in particular, for determining—

        (i) the manner in which and the time as at which road mileages, population, the numbers of persons of any specified description and any other relevant elements for any area are to be ascertained,

        (ii) the descriptions of roads which are to be taken into account in calculating road mileages,

        (iii) the authority or person by or to whom any information required for the said purposes is to be given and the time at which and the form in which it is to be given,

        (iv) the adjustments to be made for any abnormal treatment of income or expenditure in accounts ;

(*b*) for providing that the calculations or estimates by reference to which any payments are made may be treated as either conclusive or provisional or conclusive for some purposes and provisional for other purposes and, in so far as they are treated as provisional, for the making of further calculations or estimates based on information not previously available and for adjusting, in the light thereof, any payment already made ;

(*c*) for modifying the operation of the foregoing provisions of this Act in relation to any authority if and in so far as any modification is required in relation to that authority in consequence of any alterations or combinations of authorities or alterations of boundaries ;

and regulations under this subsection may make different provisions for different circumstances.

(2) The Secretary of State may, if he thinks fit, determine that any sea route between two places in the area of any local authority, being a sea route served by a ferry or by public transport vessels and specified in the determination, shall be treated for the purposes of regulations made under this section as if it were a road in that area ; and any such determination may be varied or revoked by the Secretary of State.

(5) References in this section to the foregoing provisions of this Act include references to Schedule 1 to this Act.

(6) Any statutory instrument containing regulations made under this section shall be subject to annulment in pursuance of a resolution of either House of Parliament.

Reduction of rates on dwellings by reference to the domestic element.

7.—(1) Subject to section 24 of this Act, every rating authority shall reduce the amount of the rate levied by the authority for any year on dwelling-houses in their area by the amount in the pound prescribed for that year for their area in pursuance of paragraph 1 of part III of Schedule 1 to this Act. In this subsection the words " the amount of the rate ", in relation to a regional council, mean the aggregate amount of the regional rate and the district rate.

(2) Where lands and heritages are a dwelling-house during part only of a year, the reduction to be made in pursuance of the foregoing subsection shall be made for that part of the year only.

(3) In this section " dwelling-house " includes premises entered in the valuation roll as such by virtue of section 16(3) of the Water (Scotland) Act 1949 and premises which would have been so entered if domestic water rate had been leviable in respect of them.

1949 c. 31.

(4) For the purposes of this section the gross annual value and rateable value attributable to the last mentioned premises shall in accordance with the provisions of section 6 of the Valuation and Rating (Scotland) Act 1956, be determined by the assessor for the area in which the premises are situated and shall be entered in the valuation roll ; any such determination shall be subject to appeal under the Valuation Acts and shall accordingly be notified to the

1956 c. 60.

occupier of the premises and to the rating authority concerned within
the times for the issue of notices set out in Schedule 2 to the said
Act of 1956.

Schedule 1
To the Local Government (Scotland) Act 1966
Set Out as Amended

Rate Support Grants

Part I

The Needs Element

Apportionment

1. The amount of the needs element of rate support grants payable
for any year, or such part thereof as may be determined by the
Secretary of State, shall be apportioned to all regions, islands areas
and districts on such basis as may be prescribed.

2.—(1) Notwithstanding the provisions of paragraph 1 above, the
Secretary of State may, as respects any year, make provision for
the apportionment of a prescribed part of the needs element among
authorities incurring extraordinary expenses, by reference to so much
of the estimated extraordinary expenses of each such authority as he
may determine to be appropriate to be taken into account for the
purposes of this paragraph.

(2) In this paragraph " extraordinary expenses " means expenses of
such categories and for such purposes as the Secretary of State, after
consultation with such associations of local authorities as appear to
him to be concerned, may determine should be supported by an
apportionment under this paragraph ; and in determining the amount
of the estimated extraordinary expenses of an authority to be taken
into account for any year, the Secretary of State—

  (a) shall have regard to the expected income of that authority
      for that year ; and

  (b) may have regard to the extent by which the extraordinary
      expenses for a previous year exceeded or fell short of the
      estimated extraordinary expenses of the authority for that
      year.

3. Notwithstanding the provisions of paragraph 1 above the Secretary of State may, as respects any year, make provision for the
apportionment of the needs element or any part thereof among such
classes of local authorities and on such basis as may be prescribed
or of a prescribed amount of the needs element to such classes of
authorities or to any such authority as may be prescribed.

3A. Without prejudice to sections 5 and 5A of this Act or to the generality of paragraphs 1 and 3 above, the Secretary of State may, in prescribing a basis for apportionment under either of those paragraphs or in providing for apportionment under paragraph 3 above, have regard to the extent to which, in his opinion, either or both—

(a) the actual expenditure of an individual authority has conformed (whether or not in the year for which the amount of the needs element is payable) ;

(b) the estimated expenditure of such an authority conforms,

with any guidance issued by him, before the start of the year to which the expenditure relates, as to what that expenditure ought to be.

Adjustment of the needs element payable to local authorities

5.—(1) The needs element for any year shall be subject to adjustment, in accordance with regulations made under this paragraph, in respect of expenditure to which this paragraph applies.

(2) The Secretary of State may after consultation with such associations of local authorities as appear to him to be concerned by regulations subject to annulment in pursuance of a resolution of either House of Parliament, provide for ascertaining the aggregate of such expenditure for the year in question of all local authorities, for apportioning the aggregate among such classes of local authority as may be specified in the regulations, and for giving effect to the apportionment by means of increases or decreases in the needs element payable to such authorities as may be so specified of such amounts as may be ascertained in accordance with the regulations.

(3) This paragraph applies to such expenditure incurred as may be specified in regulations made under this paragraph.

PART II

THE RESOURCES ELEMENT

1. No payment in respect of the resources element shall be made to a local authority for any year unless in that year the product of a rate of one penny in the pound for the authority's area is less than the standard penny rate product for the area.

2. Subject to any provision made by virtue of section 4(5) of this Act and to paragraph 3 below, the amount of the resources element payable to a local authority for any year shall be the product of—

(a) the number of pence in the pound of the regional, general or district rate, as the case may be or, where the Secretary of State is, as regards the local authority, satisfied—

(i) that they have fixed a rate higher than that required to provide the sufficient moneys mentioned in section 108(2) of the Local Government (Scotland) Act 1973 ; or

  (ii) as is mentioned in subsection (1)(*c*), as read with subsection (1A), of section 5 of this Act,

 such lesser number of pence in the pound of that rate as the Secretary of State considers appropriate, and

 (*b*) the difference between the rate products mentioned in paragraph 1 above.

3.—(1) If, after the amount of the resources element payable to a local authority for any year has been determined under paragraph 2 above—

 (*a*) the rateable values of lands and heritages in the authority's area are reduced with effect from a date on or before that which is relevant for determining the product of a rate of one penny in the pound for the authority's area for that year ; and

 (*b*) the effect of that reduction is to produce a reduction in the said product which is of such a magnitude that, expressed as a percentage of the initially ascertained figure, it exceeds such percentage as may be specified for the purposes of this paragraph in regulations made by the Secretary of State ; and

 (*c*) the authority by notice in writing request the Secretary of State to give a direction under this paragraph ;

the Secretary of State shall direct that the amount of the resources element payable to the authority for that year shall be recalculated in accordance with the following provisions of this paragraph and a further payment on account of that element shall be made to the local authority accordingly.

(2) Where sub-paragraph (1) above applies—

 (*a*) the product of a rate of one penny in the pound for the local authority's area for the year concerned shall be recalculated by treating the initially ascertained figure as reduced by the amount of the excess referred to in sub-paragraph (1)(*b*) above.

 (*b*) subject to any provision made by virtue of section 4(5) of this Act, paragraph 2 above shall have effect accordingly for the purpose of determining the amount which, on the basis of that recalculation, would have been payable to the authority for that year.

(3) The further payment referred to in sub-paragraph (1) above shall be an amount equal to the difference between the amount previously paid to the authority for the year concerned on account of the resources element and the amount determined as mentioned in sub-paragraph (2)(*b*) above.

(4) In this paragraph " the initially ascertained figure ", in relation to any year, means the product of a rate of one penny in the pound ascertained for the purposes of paragraph 2 above.

(5) The provisions of this paragraph shall have effect notwithstanding that the actual aggregate amount of the resources element

SCH. 1   for the year concerned may have been specified in an order under section 4(1) of this Act, and if any amount has been so specified it shall be treated as having been increased to such amount as may be necessary to provide for any further payment made to a local authority under this paragraph.

PART III

THE DOMESTIC ELEMENT

1. There shall for each year be prescribed, for the purposes of section 7 of this Act, an amount in the pound which in the opinion of the Secretary of State corresponds to the amount of the domestic element prescribed for that year in pursuance of section 2(4) of this Act and different amounts in the pound may be so prescribed for the areas of different rating authorities.

2. The amount of the domestic element payable to a rating authority for any year shall be determined in the manner provided by regulations made by the Secretary of State after consultation with such associations of local authorities as appear to him to be concerned.

Any statutory instrument containing regulations made under this paragraph shall be subject to annulment in pursuance of a resolution of either House of Parliament.

3. Any amounts payable to a rating authority in respect of the domestic element shall be taken into account for the purposes of this and any other Act as if they were payable on account of rates and in computing the product of a new penny rate ; and any reduction made in pursuance of section 7 of this Act shall be disregarded in computing the product of a new penny rate for those purposes.

Section 21

SCHEDULE 2

AMENDMENTS OF ENACTMENTS

Lands Valuation (Scotland) Act 1854 (*c.* 91)

1975 c. 21.   1. In section 7 of the Lands Valuation (Scotland) Act 1854 (which, as read with section 289G(4) of the Criminal Procedure (Scotland) Act 1975, provides for the levels of penalty for failure to provide the assessor with certain particulars)—

(*a*) after the word " liable ", in both places where it occurs, there shall be inserted the words " on summary conviction " ;

(*b*) for the words " level 2 " there shall be substituted the words " level 3 " ; and

(*c*) for the words " of level 3 " there shall be substituted the words " not exceeding level 3 ".

2. In section 24 of the Lands Valuation (Scotland) Act 1854 (giving of notice of valuation to public undertakings)—

(*a*) after the words " copy of " there shall be inserted the words " so much of " ; and (*b*) after the word " 1975 " there shall be inserted the words " as relates to the valuation of the lands and heritages of the company ".

3. For section 26 of the Lands Valuation (Scotland) Act 1854 (power of assessor of railways and canals to obtain information) there shall be substituted the following section—

" Power of Assessor of Public Undertakings (Scotland) to obtain information.   **26.**—(1) For the purpose of valuing any lands and heritages which he is obliged under any enactment to value, the Assessor of Public Undertakings (Scotland) may—

    (*a*) require the undertaking occupying such lands and heritages to provide him with such information as he may need ;

    (*b*) require the attendance of any official of the undertaking for examination.

(2) Where any such undertaking or official thereof refuses or unreasonably delays to comply with a requirement under subsection (1) above, that undertaking shall not be entitled to appeal against or object to the Assessor's valuation in respect of which such refusal or delay occurred.".

Rating and Valuation (Apportionment) Act 1928 (c. 44)

4. In subsection (5) of section 9 of the Rating and Valuation (Apportionment) Act 1928 after the word " heritages " where it first occurs there shall be inserted the words " (other than lands and heritages in respect of which the rateable value is prescribed or determined by or under an order under section 6 of the Local Government (Scotland) Act 1975) ". 1975 c. 21.

5. In subsection (14) of section 9 of the Rating and Valuation (Apportionment) Act 1928 (which subsection, as read with section 289G(4) of the Criminal Procedure (Scotland) Act 1975, provides for the level of penalty for refusing to admit or obstructing the assessor in the exercise of his powers under that subsection) for the words " level 2 " there shall be substituted the words " level 3 ".

Local Government (Scotland) Act 1947 (c. 43)

6. In section 238(1) of the Local Government (Scotland) Act 1947 (fixing of dates for lodging and hearing of appeals against rates) at the beginning there shall be inserted the words " In respect of each rate levied by them ".

7. In section 243 of the Local Government (Scotland) Act 1947 (rating of unoccupied and unfurnished property) after subsection (2) there shall be inserted the following subsections—

" (2A) The Secretary of State may by regulations provide in relation to lands and heritages which are unoccupied and unfurnished for any period in a financial year less than 3 months that rates shall not be payable for that period in respect of such descriptions of those lands and heritages and in such circumstances as may be prescribed ; and he may make different provision for lands and heritages of different descriptions and for different circumstances.

(2B) Regulations under subsection (2A) above shall be made by statutory instrument which shall be subject to annulment in pursuance of a resolution of either House of Parliament.".

Rating and Valuation (Scotland) Act 1952 (*c.* 47)

8. In section 3(1) of the Rating and Valuation (Scotland) Act 1952 (giving of notice to local authorities of proposed valuations of public undertakings)—

(*a*) after the words " copy of " there shall be inserted the words " so much of " ; and

(*b*) for the words " relating to " there shall be substituted the words " as relates to the valuation of ".

Local Government (Financial Provisions) (Scotland) Act 1963 (*c.* 12)

9. In section 15(1) of the Local Government (Financial Provisions) (Scotland) Act 1963 (proceedings in valuation appeals) after the word " committee " there shall be inserted the words " or, under section 1(3A) of the Lands Tribunal Act 1949, before the Lands Tribunal for Scotland ".

Local Government (Scotland) Act 1966 (*c.* 51)

10. In subsection (3) of section 18 of the Local Government (Scotland) Act 1966 (determination of question whether premises are situated on operational land) at the end there shall be added the words " and section 9(1) of the Local Government (Scotland) Act 1975 (which provides for restricted rates to be payable pending determination of an appeal) shall apply to the payment of rates during the period where such an application is pending as if that application were an appeal under the Valuation Acts.".

11. Section 25(4) of the Local Government (Scotland) Act 1966 (which, before its repeal by the Local Government (Miscellaneous Provisions) (Scotland) Act 1981, enabled the Secretary of State to provide that rates which would otherwise be payable on certain unoccupied property under section 24 of the said Act of 1966 would not be payable in such cases as he prescribed) is hereby revived.

Tribunals and Inquiries Act 1971 (*c.* 62)

12. In section 13 of the Tribunals and Inquiries Act 1971 (appeals from certain tribunals) after paragraph (*b*) of subsection (6) there shall be inserted the following paragraph—

" (*bb*) subsection (1) of this section shall not apply in relation to proceedings before the Lands Tribunal for Scotland which advise under section 1(3A) of the Lands Tribunal Act 1949 (jurisdiction of the Tribunal in valuation matters).".

Local Government (Scotland) Act 1975 (*c.* 30)

13. In subsection (1) of section 2 of the Local Government (Scotland) Act 1975 (alterations to be made in the valuation roll)—

(1) in paragraph (*a*) there shall be added at the end the words " or which, being still in existence, have been erroneously deleted from the roll under paragraph (*h*) below " ;

(2) after paragraph (*e*) there shall be inserted the following paragraph—

" (*ee*) to give effect to any decision following upon an appeal or complaint under the Valuation Acts ; " ; and

(3) at the end there shall be inserted the words " and may so alter the roll to give effect to any change in the proprietorship, tenancy or occupancy of any lands and heritages.".

14. In subsection (2) of section 2 of the Local Government (Scotland) Act 1975 (date of effect of alteration in the valuation roll) after paragraph (*c*) there shall be inserted the following paragraph—

" (*cc*) made under subsection (1)(*ee*) above following upon an appeal by virtue of section 3(2A) of this Act by a person who has become the proprietor, tenant or occupier of lands and heritages shall have effect only as from the date when he became such proprietor, tenant or occupier ; ".

15. In section 2(3) of the Local Government (Scotland) Act 1975 (procedure following upon agreement between the parties to a valuation appeal) after the word " committee " there shall be inserted the words " or by the Lands Tribunal for Scotland ".

16. In the proviso to subsection (2) of section 5 of the Local Government (Scotland) Act 1975 (valuation of public undertakings) after the word " 1963 " there shall be inserted the words " or the doing of anything under Schedule 2 to the Local Government (Scotland) Act 1966 c. 51. 1966 (valuation of water undertakings) or under any order under section 6 of this Act ".

17. In section 37(1) of the Local Government (Scotland) Act 1975, in the definition of " material change of circumstances ", after the words " are situated " there shall be inserted the words " or the Lands Tribunal for Scotland under section 1(3A) of the Lands Tri- 1949 c. 42. bunal Act 1949 ".

18. In Schedule 1 to the Local Government (Scotland) Act 1975 (lands and heritages the valuation of which may be prescribed or determined by formula under section 6 of that Act) there shall be added after paragraph 4 the following paragraph—

" 4AA. Any lands and heritages which are, or form part of, premises occupied by a private generator or supplier for or in connection with the generation or supply of electricity other than—

(*a*) lands and heritages occupied and used as a dwelling house ;

Sᴄʜ. 2

(*b*) a shop, room or other place occupied and used wholly or mainly for the sale, display or demonstration of apparatus or accessories for use by consumers of electricity:

Provided that in determining whether any such shop, room or other place is so occupied and used, use for the receipt of payments for electricity consumed shall be disregarded ;

(*c*) lands and heritages held by a private generator or supplier under a lease for a period not exceeding 21 years ; or

(*d*) premises which are—

(i) occupied by a private supplier ;

(ii) used wholly or mainly as an office or for office purposes ; and

(iii) situated on land which, in respect of its nature and situation, is comparable rather with land in general than with land used for the purpose of the generation or supply of electricity.

In this paragraph " private generator or supplier " has the same meaning as in section 5 of the Energy Act 1983.".

1983 c. 25.

Section 21.

SCHEDULE 3

Rᴇᴘᴇᴀʟs

Chapter	Short title	Extent of repeal
17 & 18 Vict. c. 91.	Lands Valuation (Scotland) Act 1854.	Sections 37 and 38.
8 Edw. 7. c. 62.	Local Government (Scotland) Act 1908.	Section 7(2).
10 & 11 Geo. 6. c. 43.	Local Government (Scotland) Act 1947.	The proviso to section 238(1).

London Regional Transport Act 1984

1984 CHAPTER 32

An Act to make provision with respect to transport in and around Greater London and for connected purposes. [26th June 1984]

BE IT ENACTED by the Queen's most Excellent Majesty, by and with the advice and consent of the Lords Spiritual and Temporal, and Commons, in this present Parliament assembled, and by the authority of the same, as follows:—

PART I

LONDON REGIONAL TRANSPORT

Constitution and general functions of London Regional Transport

1.—(1) Parts I and II of the 1969 Act (which made provision with respect to transport in and around Greater London and, in particular, established the London Transport Executive to run London transport services subject to the overall control of the Greater London Council) shall cease to have effect on the appointed day.

London Regional Transport.

(2) Notwithstanding the repeal by this Act of the provisions of the 1969 Act under which the Executive was established, the Executive shall continue to exist, but shall be known, as from the appointed day, as London Regional Transport.

(3) London Regional Transport shall continue to be a body corporate; and Schedule 1 to this Act has effect with respect to the constitution and proceedings of London Regional Transport and the other matters there mentioned.

(4) In this Act " the appointed day " means such day as the Secretary of State may by order appoint for the purposes of this section.

Provision of passenger transport services for Greater London.

2.—(1) It shall be the general duty of London Regional Transport, in accordance with principles from time to time approved by the Secretary of State and in conjunction with the Railways Board, to provide or secure the provision of public passenger transport services for Greater London.

(2) In carrying out that duty London Regional Transport shall have due regard to—

(a) the transport needs for the time being of Greater London; and

(b) efficiency, economy and safety of operation.

(3) It shall be the duty of London Regional Transport and the Railways Board, either acting directly, or acting indirectly through subsidiaries of theirs, to co-operate with one another in the exercise and performance of their respective functions for the purpose—

(a) of co-ordinating the passenger transport services provided by, or by subsidiaries of, those authorities respectively; and

(b) of securing or facilitating the proper discharge of London Regional Transport's duty under subsection (1) above;

and to afford to one another such information as to their services as may reasonably be required for those purposes.

(4) For the purposes of the co-operation required of them under subsection (3) above London Regional Transport and the Railways Board shall have power to enter into such arrangements with one another with respect to the exercise and performance of their respective functions on such terms as may appear to them to be expedient.

(5) London Regional Transport's duty under subsection (1) above is subject to their financial duty under section 15 of this Act and their duty under section 16(5) of this Act to conduct their affairs with a view to achieving any financial objectives determined for them by the Secretary of State under section 16.

(6) This section is not to be read as imposing, either directly or indirectly, any form of duty or liability enforceable by proceedings before any court.

(7) The reference in subsection (2)(*a*) above to the transport needs of Greater London is a reference to the needs of Greater London with respect to public passenger transport services for persons travelling within, to or from Greater London, including persons who are disabled.

3.—(1) London Regional Transport shall have power to form, General promote and assist, or join with any other person in forming, powers. promoting and assisting, a company for the purpose of carrying on any activities which London Regional Transport have power to carry on.

(2) London Regional Transport shall have power to enter into and carry out agreements with any person for the carrying on by that person, whether as agent for London Regional Transport or otherwise, of any activities which London Regional Transport have power to carry on (and, in particular, for the provision by that person of any public passenger transport services which London Regional Transport have power to provide).

(3) The duty of London Regional Transport and the Railways Board under section 2(3) of this Act to co-operate for the purpose mentioned in paragraph (*a*) of that subsection shall extend to any public passenger transport services provided by any person other than a subsidiary of London Regional Transport under an agreement entered into by London Regional Transport by virtue of subsection (2) above; and any such agreement shall include such provision as appears to London Regional Transport to be appropriate—

    (*a*) for securing the proper discharge of their general duty under subsection (1) of that section; and

    (*b*) for the purposes of the co-operation with the Railways Board required of them by subsection (3)(*a*) of that section.

(4) Without prejudice to subsection (3) above, any agreement entered into by London Regional Transport by virtue of subsection (2) above may in particular provide for—

    (*a*) combined services for the through carriage of passengers or goods to be provided by London Regional Transport or any of their subsidiaries and any other party to the agreement, the quoting of through rates and the pooling of receipts and expenses in respect of such services;

    (*b*) securing efficiency, economy and safety of operation is the provision of any public passenger transport services in pursuance of the agreement;

    (*c*) the exercise by London Regional Transport, in accordance with the agreement, of control over fares in respect of any such services and their routes and frequency of operation and over charges in respect of any other facilities provided in pursuance of the agreement ; and

(*d*) the making of payments by London Regional Transport to any other party to the agreement.

(5) Where—

(*a*) a company has been formed in the exercise of the powers conferred by subsection (1) above (whether by London Regional Transport alone or by London Regional Transport jointly with some other person) ; or

(*b*) London Regional Transport have entered into an agreement with any person in exercise of their powers under subsection (2) above ;

London Regional Transport may, with the consent of the Secretary of State, enter into arrangements with that company or person for the transfer from London Regional Transport to that company or person, in such manner and on such terms (including payments by any of the parties to the arrangements to any of the other parties) as may be provided for by the arrangements, of any property, rights or liabilities of London Regional Transport relevant to the purpose for which the company was formed or (as the case may be) to the performance by that person of his obligations under the agreement.

(6) Without prejudice to subsections (3) and (4) above, London Regional Transport shall have power to enter into and carry out agreements with—

(*a*) any subsidiary of theirs ; or

(*b*) any person with whom they have entered into an agreement by virtue of subsection (2) above ;

providing for London Regional Transport to give assistance to the other party to the agreement by making available to that party any services, amenities or facilities provided by, or any works or land or other property belonging to, London Regional Transport, on such terms (including the reciprocal provision by that other party of similar assistance for London Regional Transport) as may be agreed between them.

(7) Without prejudice to the preceding provisions of this section, London Regional Transport and the Railways Board shall each have power to enter into and carry out agreements with the other and with any subsidiary of the other—

(*a*) for the use by one party to the agreement of any amenities or facilities provided by the other ;

(*b*) for the management, working and use by one party to the agreement of works (whether within paragraph (*a*) above or not) or land or other property belonging to the other ; and

(c) with respect to the rendering of services and the pooling of receipts or expenses.

(8) The power—

(a) of London Regional Transport under subsection (2) or (7) above ; and

(b) of the Railways Board under subsection (7) above ;

to enter into an agreement as there mentioned is exercisable notwithstanding that the agreement involves the delegation of the functions of London Regional Transport or (as the case may be) of the Railways Board under any enactment relating to any part of their undertaking.

(9) Schedule 2 to this Act has effect for conferring further powers on London Regional Transport for the purpose of the exercise and performance of their functions under this Act and with respect to the other matters there mentioned.

Organisation of undertaking

4.—(1) Before the end of such period as the Secretary of State may specify for the purposes of this subsection in a direction given to London Regional Transport, London Regional Transport shall submit to the Secretary of State for his approval written proposals for the formation by them of a company for the purpose of providing public passenger transport services by bus for Greater London.

Duty to establish companies to run London bus and underground services.

(2) Before the end of such period as the Secretary of State may so specify for the purposes of this subsection, London Regional Transport shall submit to the Secretary of State for his approval written proposals for the formation by them of a company for the purpose of providing public passenger transport services by underground railway for Greater London.

(3) Any proposals submitted to the Secretary of State under this section must provide for the company to which the proposals relate to be a company limited by shares and registered under the Companies Act 1948.

1948 c. 38.

(4) The objects of each company formed in pursuance of this section shall be such as appear to London Regional Transport to be necessary or appropriate in view of the purpose for which that company is established ; and any proposals submitted to the Secretary of State under this section shall include a draft of the memorandum and articles of association of the company to which the proposals relate.

(5) The Secretary of State may approve any proposals submitted to him under this section either without modifications or with such modifications as, after consultation with London Regional Transport, he thinks fit.

PART I

1948 c. 38.

(6) Where the Secretary of State approves any such proposals London Regional Transport shall form the company to which the proposals relate in accordance with the proposals as approved by the Secretary of State, and secure the registration of that company under the Companies Act 1948, within such period as the Secretary of State may, in giving his approval, specify.

(7) Together with any proposals submitted to the Secretary of State under this section London Regional Transport shall submit to the Secretary of State for his approval a scheme providing for the transfer to the company to be formed in pursuance of those proposals of any property, rights and liabilities of London Regional Transport relevant to the carrying on of any activities which London Regional Transport have power to carry on and which are within the scope of the objects of that company as set out in those proposals.

(8) A scheme under this section may be framed as providing for an immediate transfer of any property, rights and liabilities to which it relates on the assumption that the company which is to take the transfer will be formed before the scheme takes effect.

(9) Section 27 of this Act applies to a scheme under this section.

Redistribution of property among London Regional Transport and subsidiaries.

5.—(1) London Regional Transport may, as occasion seems to them to require it, make schemes for the transfer, between London Regional Transport and a subsidiary of theirs or between one such subsidiary and another, of any property, rights and liabilities of theirs or of any such subsidiary.

(2) Section 27 of this Act applies to a scheme under this section.

Obligation to invite tenders.

6.—(1) London Regional Transport shall, in the case of such activities carried on by them as they may determine to be appropriate, invite other persons to submit tenders to carry on those activities for such period and on such basis as may be specified in the invitation to tender.

(2) London Regional Transport shall exercise their control over any subsidiary of theirs so as to require any such subsidiary, in the case of such activities carried on by that subsidiary as London Regional Transport may determine to be appropriate, to invite other persons to submit tenders to carry on those activities for such period and on such basis as may be so specified.

(3) London Regional Transport—

    (*a*) shall accept a tender invited by them in pursuance of this section ; and

    (*b*) shall exercise their control over any subsidiary of theirs so as to cause that subsidiary to accept a tender invited by that subsidiary in any case within subsection (2) above ;

if it appears to them that to do so would result in the relevant activities being carried on in a satisfactory manner and at less cost to them or (as the case may be) to that subsidiary than if they or that subsidiary were to continue to carry on those activities.

(4) Every annual report of London Regional Transport under section 34 of this Act shall contain a statement showing the steps which London Regional Transport have taken in the accounting year to which the report relates to comply with the requirements of subsections (1) and (2) above.

(5) For the purposes of any reference in this or any other Act to an agreement entered into by virtue of section 3(2) of this Act, any agreement concluded by London Regional Transport under this section shall be taken to be within that reference.

Planning and co-ordination

7.—(1) It shall be the duty of London Regional Transport to prepare, in accordance with this section, statements setting out in general terms—

    (*a*) the policies they intend to follow with a view to the discharge of their general duty under section 2(1) of this Act ; and

    (*b*) any action they have taken or propose to take for the purpose of carrying those policies into effect during the period to which the statement relates.

Planning of passenger transport services for Greater London.

(2) Any statement prepared under this section shall in particular deal with the following, that is to say—

    (*a*) the policies and plans of any subsidiaries of theirs, including (in the case of any such statement other than the first) any major changes or developments of any such policies and plans since the last statement so prepared ;

    (*b*) any current or proposed arrangements between London Regional Transport and the Railways Board under section 2(4) of this Act ; and

    (*c*) any agreements which London Regional Transport have made or propose to make with the Railways Board or any other person in exercise of their powers under section 3 of this Act.

(3) Any statement prepared under this section shall deal with the financial prospects of London Regional Transport and any subsidiaries of theirs for the period to which the statement relates, having regard to any financial objectives determined for them by the Secretary of State under section 16 of this Act which, at the time when that statement is prepared, apply in relation to that period or any part of it.

(4) In preparing any statement under this section London Regional Transport shall consult with—

(a) the Railways Board ;

(b) the local authorities concerned ;

(c) the Passengers' Committee ; and

(d) such other persons (if any) as London Regional Transport may think fit ;

and shall have regard to any considerations to which the Secretary of State may from time to time draw their attention (including, in particular, considerations of national or regional transport policy) and to the development plan for any district which appears to London Regional Transport to be affected by any policies, proposals or plans which they propose to set out in the statement.

(5) London Regional Transport—

(a) shall submit any statement prepared under this section to the Secretary of State ; and

(b) shall cause any such statement to be published in such manner as appears to them to be appropriate for informing persons appearing to them to be likely to be concerned.

(6) In the exercise and performance of their functions under this Act with respect to any matter dealt with by a statement prepared under this section, London Regional Transport shall take into account any observations the Secretary of State may make with respect to that matter following the submission to him of that statement in accordance with subsection (5)(a) above.

(7) The first statement required by subsection (1) above shall be prepared, and shall be submitted to the Secretary of State and published in accordance with subsection (5) above, before the end of the period of one year beginning with the appointed day.

(8) Each subsequent statement shall be prepared, and shall be so submitted and published, before the end of the period of three years beginning with the date on which the last statement prepared under this section was so published.

(9) For the purposes of subsection (4)(*b*) above, the local Part I authorities concerned are—

(*a*) the Greater London Council ;

(*b*) the councils of the London boroughs ;

(*c*) the Common Council ; and

(*d*) the council of any county or district any part of whose area appears to London Regional Transport to be affected to a significant degree by any policies, proposals or plans which they propose to set out in the statement ;

and the reference in that subsection to the development plan for any district shall be construed in accordance with section 20 of the Town and Country Planning Act 1971. 1971 c. 78.

8. It shall be the duty of London Regional Transport to Co-ordination exercise their control over any subsidiaries of theirs and their of fares, powers under this Part of this Act so as to determine— services and
charges under

(*a*) the general level and structure of the fares to be charged control of for public passenger transport services provided by London
Regional London Regional Transport or any subsidiary of theirs Transport. or by any other person in pursuance of any agreement entered into by London Regional Transport by virtue of section 3(2) of this Act ;

(*b*) the general structure of routes of such services and the general level of provision to be made with respect to their frequency of operation ; and

(*c*) the general level of charges to be made for other facilities provided as mentioned in paragraph (*a*) above.

Powers of disposal

9.—(1) Without prejudice to their powers of disposal under Powers of Schedule 2 to this Act, London Regional Transport shall have disposal. power, subject to subsection (2) below, to provide for the disposal, in such manner as they think fit, of—

(*a*) any securities of one of their subsidiaries which are held by London Regional Transport or by another of their subsidiaries ; or

(*b*) the whole or any part of the undertaking of any of their subsidiaries.

(2) London Regional Transport may not exercise their powers under subsection (1)(*a*) above except with the consent of the Secretary of State.

(3) In exercising those powers London Regional Transport may, with the consent of the Secretary of State, provide for employees' share schemes to be established in respect of any of their subsidiaries ; and any such scheme may provide for the transfer of shares without consideration.

(4) In this section " employees' share scheme " means a scheme for encouraging or facilitating the holding of shares or debentures in a company by or for the benefit of—

(a) the bona fide employees or former employees of the company or of a subsidiary of the company ; or

(b) the wives, husbands, widows, widowers or children or step-children under the age of eighteen of such employees or former employees.

(5) London Regional Transport may exercise their powers under section 3 of this Act—

(a) to form companies ; and

(b) to transfer property, rights and liabilities to companies formed by them ;

for the purpose of facilitating the eventual disposal under subsection (1) above of any part of their undertaking or of the whole or any part of the undertaking of any of their subsidiaries.

(6) London Regional Transport may also, for that purpose, make schemes for the transfer, between London Regional Transport and a subsidiary of theirs or between one such subsidiary and another, of any property, rights and liabilities of theirs or of any such subsidiary.

(7) Section 27 of this Act applies to a scheme under subsection (6) above.

Power of Secretary of State to require exercise of powers of disposal, etc.

10.—(1) The Secretary of State may give directions to London Regional Transport requiring them to exercise their powers under section 9 of this Act, and their powers under section 3 of this Act so far as applicable by virtue of subsection (5) of section 9, for such purposes and in such manner as may be specified in the directions.

(2) Before giving any direction under this section the Secretary of State shall consult with—

(a) London Regional Transport ; and

(b) in the case of a direction requiring London Regional Transport to exercise their powers under section 9(1) of this Act in relation to any of their subsidiaries, every council to which this paragraph applies in whose area that subsidiary provides public passenger transport services.

(3) Subsection (2)(*b*) above applies to county and district councils, the Greater London Council, the councils of the London boroughs, and the Common Council.

(4) It shall be the duty of London Regional Transport to give effect to any directions given to them by the Secretary of State under this section notwithstanding any of their other duties under this Act.

11.—(1) The powers of London Regional Transport under section 3(6) of this Act shall be exercisable in relation to any related company as they are exercisable in relation to any subsidiary of London Regional Transport.

(2) In this Act " related company " means any company as respects which London Regional Transport have, or at any time have had, a beneficial interest (either directly or through nominees or subsidiaries) in not less than twenty per cent. of its issued ordinary share capital.

Financial provisions

12.—(1) The Secretary of State may, with the consent of the Treasury, make grants to London Regional Transport for any purpose and on such terms and conditions as the Secretary of State thinks fit.

(2) Subject to any such terms or conditions, it shall be the duty of London Regional Transport to apply sums received by way of grants under this section—

(*a*) in aid of capital investment or operating costs in respect of public passenger transport services provided by them or any of their subsidiaries ; or

(*b*) in making payments to any other person providing such services in pursuance of any agreement entered into by London Regional Transport by virtue of section 3(2) of this Act in aid of his capital investment or operating costs in respect of those services ;

in such manner as appears to them to be appropriate for the purpose of the discharge of their general duty under section 2(1) of this Act.

(3) Where sums so received are applied by London Regional Transport in making any such payments as are mentioned in subsection (2)(*b*) above, London Regional Transport shall secure that the relevant agreement—

(*a*) provides for the manner in which those payments are to be applied ; and (*b*) includes terms appearing to London Regional Transport to be appropriate for securing that those payments are applied in accordance with the agreement.

(4) In relation to any services, references in subsection (2) above to operating costs in respect of those services include any provision for the depreciation or renewal of assets employed in or in connection with the operation of those services.

Contribution from London ratepayers to expenditure on grants under section 12.

13.—(1) The Secretary of State may in respect of any year make a levy on the rating authorities for all rating areas comprised in Greater London for the purpose of recovering a contribution from the ratepayers of Greater London towards his estimated expenditure in that year on grants under section 12 of this Act.

(2) Subject to the following provisions of this section, for the purpose of raising the levy under this section in respect of any year the Secretary of State may issue a demand for payments in respect of that year to the rating authorities mentioned in subsection (1) above.

(3) Any such demand—

(*a*) shall require each of those rating authorities to levy, as part, or as an additional item, of the rate, a rate of the required amount in the pound ; and

(*b*) shall state the date or dates on or before which payments are required to be made on account of the rate levied in pursuance of the demand, and the amount of each such payment.

(4) The reference in subsection (3)(*a*) above to the required amount in the pound is a reference to such amount in the pound as may be specified by an order made by the Secretary of State in respect of the year to which the demand relates.

(5) The amount in the pound to be specified in an order made by the Secretary of State under subsection (4) above in respect of any year shall be such as appears to the Secretary of State to be sufficient, if a rate of that amount in the pound is levied by each rating authority mentioned in subsection (1) above in pursuance of a demand issued under subsection (2) above in respect of that year, to raise the appropriate contribution for that year from the ratepayers of Greater London.

(6) For any year, that contribution is such a proportion, not exceeding a maximum of two-thirds, of the Secretary of State's estimated expenditure in that year on grants under section 12 of this Act, as it appears to the Secretary of State appropriate to recover from the ratepayers of Greater London.

(7) An order under subsection (4) above shall set out the
factors taken into account and the method of calculation employed in determining the amount in the pound specified in the
order.

(8) The Secretary of State may by order substitute for the
maximum proportion specified in subsection (6) above (whether
as originally enacted or as modified by a previous order under
this subsection) such maximum proportion as he thinks fit.

(9) No order may be made under this section unless a draft
of the order has been laid before, and approved by a resolution of, the Commons House of Parliament.

(10) Any sums received by the Secretary of State in pursuance
of a demand issued under subsection (2) above shall be paid
into the Consolidated Fund.

14.—(1) Subject to subsection (2) below, section 12 of the Provisions
General Rate Act 1967 (provision as to precepts by certain auth- supplementary
orities) shall apply to a demand issued under section 13(2) of to section 13.
this Act by the Secretary of State as it applies to a precept issued 1967 c. 9.
by any of the authorities mentioned in section 12(1) of that
Act.

(2) In that section, as applied by this section—
  (a) subsections (1), (2) and (10) shall be omitted;
  (b) references to the precepting authority shall be read as
      references to the Secretary of State;
  (c) the reference in subsection (4) to that section shall be
      read as a reference to section 13 of this Act;
  (d) subsection (4) shall apply as if for the words " 1st Feb-
      ruary " there were substituted the words " 1st Nov-
      ember "; and
  (e) the reference in subsection (11) to subsection (2) of that
      section shall be read as a reference to section 13(3)
      of this Act.

(3) References to precepts and precepting authorities in—
  (a) section 5(1)(e) of that Act (information as to amounts
      levied for the purposes of rating authorities and pre-
      cepting authorities to be included in demand notes for
      rates); and
  (b) section 14(2) of that Act (information to be supplied
      by precepting authorities for the purposes of section
      5);
shall be read respectively as including any demand under section
13(2) of this Act and as including, in relation to any such
demand, the Secretary of State.

(4) References to section 12 of that Act—

   (*a*) in section 14(1) of that Act ; and

   (*b*) in any rules made under section 113 of that Act for the purposes of section 12 of that Act ;

shall be read as including section 12 as applied by this section ; and any such rules shall have effect, in their application by virtue of this section, with any further modifications necessary in consequence of this section.

(5) Where in accordance with section 12 as applied by this section any amount is payable to the Secretary of State in pursuance of a demand issued to a rating authority under section 13(2) of this Act, and the Secretary of State is satisfied—

   (*a*) that the rating authority have refused or through wilful neglect or wilful default failed to raise that amount by a rate ; or

   (*b*) that, having raised the amount by a rate, the rating authority have refused or through wilful neglect or wilful default failed to pay the amount due under the demand (determined in accordance with section 12 as so applied) ;

the provisions of section 15 of that Act (power for securing payment of precepts) shall apply (subject to subsection (6) below) as they apply where the Secretary of State issues a certificate to the effect mentioned in subsection (1) of that section (which makes provision with respect to the amount due under a precept corresponding to the provision made above in this subsection).

(6) The provisions of section 15 apply with the omission of subsection (2) ; and in those provisions, as applied by subsection (5) above, references to the precepting authority and to the precept shall be read respectively as references to the Secretary of State and to the demand.

1982 c. 32.

(7) Section 4 of the Local Government Finance Act 1982 (proceedings in respect of rates and precepts) shall apply to a demand under section 13(2) of this Act as it applies to a precept.

1967 c. 9.

(8) Expressions used in this section or section 13 of this Act to which a meaning is given for the purposes of the General Rate Act 1967 have the same meaning as in that Act.

Financial
duty.

15.—(1) London Regional Transport shall so perform their functions as to ensure so far as practicable that the combined revenues of London Regional Transport and any subsidiaries of theirs are not less than sufficient to meet their combined charges properly chargeable to revenue account, taking one accounting year with another.

(2) In respect of each accounting year of London Regional Transport, London Regional Transport shall charge to revenue account, and secure that any subsidiary of theirs so charges, all charges which are proper to be made to revenue account, including, in particular, proper provision for the depreciation or renewal of assets.

(3) The Secretary of State may from time to time, after consultation with London Regional Transport and with the approval of the Treasury, give to London Regional Transport directions—

    (a) requiring London Regional Transport to allocate to reserve for a particular purpose, or to cause any of their subsidiaries so to allocate, either a specified amount or such amount as London Regional Transport consider adequate;

    (b) with respect to the transfer of any amount from one reserve to another; or

    (c) with respect to the application by London Regional Transport or any of their subsidiaries of amounts allocated to reserve.

(4) Directions under subsection (3) above requiring the allocation of any amount to reserve may provide for it to be so allocated either at a specified time or during the course of a specified period.

(5) Subject to subsection (6) below, London Regional Transport may, with the consent of the Secretary of State given with the approval of the Treasury, make charges to capital account representing interest on expenditure of a capital nature (including expenditure of a capital nature incurred before the appointed day).

(6) The interest on expenditure represented by charges made under subsection (5) above must be interest for a period which ends on or before the end of the accounting year of London Regional Transport in which the project or scheme to which the expenditure relates is in the opinion of the Secretary of State completed.

(7) If in respect of any accounting year there is an excess of the revenues of London Regional Transport over the total charges properly chargeable by them to revenue account, the Secretary of State may, with the approval of the Treasury, require that excess, so far as it appears to him, after consultation with London Regional Transport, to be surplus to the requirements of London Regional Transport, to be paid over to the Secretary of State.

(8) Any sums received by the Secretary of State under subsection (7) above shall be paid into the Consolidated Fund.

(9) For the purposes of subsections (1) and (7) above, the revenues of London Regional Transport are to be taken as including any sums received by them by way of grants under section 12 of this Act which are entered in their revenue account ; but where any sums so entered are applied in making payments which London Regional Transport have power to make (under that section or otherwise) to a subsidiary of theirs or to any other person, those payments are charges properly chargeable to their revenue account for the purposes of those subsections.

(10) For the purposes of subsection (1) above, the revenues of any subsidiary of London Regional Transport are to be taken as including any such payments from London Regional Transport as are mentioned in subsection (9) above which are entered in that subsidiary's revenue account.

(11) A company which would not otherwise be a subsidiary of London Regional Transport shall not be treated as such for the purposes of this section by virtue of section 62 of this Act.

Control by
Secretary of
State of
financial
objectives.

16.—(1) The Secretary of State may from time to time determine, as respects such period as he may determine, the financial objectives which, having regard to the duty imposed on London Regional Transport by section 15 of this Act, he considers it is reasonable for London Regional Transport to achieve in that period (whether as regards their own business or that of any of their subsidiaries).

(2) Different determinations may be made by the Secretary of State under this section for different periods and in relation to different assets and different activities of London Regional Transport or (as the case may be) of any of their subsidiaries.

(3) A determination under this section—

(a) may relate to a period beginning before the date on which it is made ; and

(b) may contain incidental and supplemental provisions.

(4) A determination under this section in respect of any period may be varied or revoked by a further determination under this section.

(5) London Regional Transport shall conduct their affairs during any period in respect of which a determination has been made under this section, or (as the case may be) secure that any subsidiary of theirs conducts its affairs, with a view to achieving the financial objectives specified by the determination as for the time being in force.

(6) The Secretary of State may not make a determination under this section except with the approval of the Treasury and after consultation with London Regional Transport.

(7) The Secretary of State shall give notice in writing to London Regional Transport of any determination under this section.

17.—(1) London Regional Transport may give or lend money Financial to or, with the consent of the Secretary of State, give a guarantee support for for the benefit of any of their subsidiaries. subsidiaries, contractors,

(2) For the purpose of enabling any person (other than a etc. subsidiary of theirs) with whom they have entered into an agreement by virtue of section 3(2) of this Act to carry out that agreement, London Regional Transport may give money to or, with the consent of the Secretary of State, lend money to or give a guarantee for the benefit of that person.

(3) London Regional Transport may, with the consent of the Secretary of State, and for the purposes of their business, lend money to, or give a guarantee for the benefit of, any person for the purposes of an undertaking carried on by him or, where that person is a body corporate, any undertaking carried on by a subsidiary of that body corporate.

(4) Subsections (1) and (2) above are without prejudice to any other power of London Regional Transport under this Act to make payments to their subsidiaries or to any person with whom they have entered into an agreement by virtue of section 3(2) of this Act.

18.—(1) London Regional Transport may borrow temporarily, Borrowing by way of overdraft or otherwise, either from the Secretary of powers. State or, with the consent of the Secretary of State, from any other person, such sums as may be required for meeting the obligations or discharging the functions of London Regional Transport or any of their subsidiaries.

The aggregate of the amounts outstanding in respect of any temporary loans raised by London Regional Transport under this subsection shall not exceed such limit as may for the time being be imposed for the purposes of this subsection by a direction given to London Regional Transport by the Secretary of State.

(2) London Regional Transport may borrow, otherwise than by way of temporary loan—

    (a) in sterling from the Secretary of State ; or

    (b) with the consent of the Secretary of State and the approval of the Treasury, in sterling or a currency other than sterling from a person other than the Secretary of State ;

such sums as may be required by London Regional Transport or any of their subsidiaries for all or any of the purposes mentioned in subsection (3) below.

(3) Those purposes are—

(a) meeting any expenses incurred by London Regional Transport or any of their subsidiaries in connection with any works the cost of which is chargeable to capital account;

(b) the provision of working capital required by London Regional Transport or any such subsidiary;

(c) acquiring an undertaking or part of an undertaking;

(d) subscribing for or acquiring securities of a body corporate otherwise than by way of investment;

(e) promoting or participating in promoting the formation of a company;

(f) the payment of interest charged to capital account under section 15(5) of this Act;

(g) repayment of any money borrowed by London Regional Transport or any of their subsidiaries and repayment of any sums issued by the Treasury in fulfilment of a guarantee under section 20 of this Act;

(h) making any loan, or fulfilling any guarantee given, in pursuance of the powers conferred on London Regional Transport by this Act;

(i) any purpose for which capital moneys are properly applicable, whether or not specified in any of the preceding paragraphs of this subsection.

(4) London Regional Transport shall not have power to borrow money, otherwise than from a subsidiary of theirs, except in accordance with this section.

(5) References in this section to borrowing do not include the receipt of money by London Regional Transport solely for the purpose of making payments into or out of a pension fund established for the purposes of a pension scheme in which employees of London Regional Transport or a subsidiary of theirs participate.

Loans from
Secretary of
State.

19.—(1) The Secretary of State may, with the approval of the Treasury, lend to London Regional Transport any sums which London Regional Transport have power to borrow under section 18(1) or (2) of this Act.

(2) Any loans which the Secretary of State makes under this section shall be repaid to him at such times and by such methods, and interest on any such loans shall be paid to him

at such rates and at such times, as he may, with the approval of the Treasury, from time to time direct.

(3) The Treasury may issue out of the National Loans Fund to the Secretary of State such sums as are necessary to enable him to make loans under this section.

(4) Any sums received under subsection (2) above by the Secretary of State shall be paid into the National Loans Fund.

(5) The Secretary of State shall, as respects each financial year, prepare in such form and manner as the Treasury may direct, an account of—

(*a*) sums issued to him under subsection (3) above ;

(*b*) sums to be paid into the National Loans Fund under subsection (4) above ; and

(*c*) the disposal by him of those sums respectively ;

and send it to the Comptroller and Auditor General not later than the end of November following the year ; and the Comptroller and Auditor General shall examine, certify and report on the account and lay copies of it, together with his report, before each House of Parliament.

20.—(1) The Treasury may guarantee, in such manner and on such conditions as they may think fit, the repayment of the principal of, the payment of interest on and the discharge of any other financial obligation in connection with, any sums which London Regional Transport borrow from a person other than the Secretary of State in exercise of their powers under section 18 of this Act.

Treasury guarantees.

(2) Immediately after a guarantee is given under this section the Treasury shall lay a statement of the guarantee before each House of Parliament ; and where any sum is issued for fulfilling a guarantee so given the Treasury shall, as soon as possible after the end of each financial year, beginning with that in which the sum is issued and ending with that in which all liability in respect of the principal of the sum and in respect of interest on the sum is finally discharged, lay before each House of Parliament a statement relating to that sum.

(3) Any sums required by the Treasury for fulfilling a guarantee under this section shall be charged on and issued out of the Consolidated Fund.

(4) If any sums are issued in fulfilment of a guarantee given under this section, London Regional Transport shall make to the Treasury, at such times and in such manner as the Treasury may from time to time direct, payments, of such amounts as the Treasury may so direct, in or towards repayment of the

PART I   sums so issued and payments of interest on what is outstanding
for the time being in respect of sums so issued at such rate as
the Treasury may so direct.

(5) Any sums received under subsection (4) above by the
Treasury shall be paid into the Consolidated Fund.

Control over
financial
commitments
of subsidiaries.

21. London Regional Transport shall exercise their control
over their subsidiaries so as to ensure that a subsidiary of theirs
does not—

(a) except with the consent of the Secretary of State, lend
money to or give any guarantee for the benefit of any
person other than London Regional Transport or any
other subsidiary of London Regional Transport; or

(b) except with the consent of the Secretary of State and
the approval of the Treasury, borrow money from any
such person.

Limit on
financial
commitments
of London
Regional
Transport
group.

22.—(1) The aggregate amount outstanding, otherwise than by
way of interest, in respect of—

(a) money borrowed by any member of the London
Regional Transport group otherwise than from another
member of the group;

(b) money borrowed by any person other than a member
of the London Regional Transport group subject to a
guarantee given by a member of the group which
applies to repayment of that money; and

(c) sums issued by the Treasury in fulfilment of guarantees
under section 20 of this Act;

shall not at any time exceed £100 million or such other sum as
the Secretary of State may from time to time by order specify.

(2) The Secretary of State may, with the approval of the
Treasury, from time to time give directions as to the method
of calculation to be used, and the date to be taken, in determining for the purposes of subsection (1) above the value in sterling
of any amount outstanding in respect of money borrowed in a
currency other than sterling.

(3) In this Act "the London Regional Transport group"
means London Regional Transport and their subsidiaries.

(4) No order shall be made under subsection (1) above unless
a draft of the order has been laid before, and approved by a
resolution of, the Commons House of Parliament.

Accounts.

23.—(1) London Regional Transport shall keep proper accounts and proper records in relation to the accounts.

(2) London Regional Transport shall prepare in respect of each accounting year—

    (*a*) a statement of accounts with respect to their own affairs, and

    (*b*) such statement or statements of consolidated accounts dealing with the affairs of London Regional Transport and any one or more other members of the London Regional Transport group as the Secretary of State may, with the approval of the Treasury, from time to time direct (whether generally or as respects any particular accounting year of London Regional Transport).

(3) The statement of accounts prepared in accordance with paragraph (*a*) of subsection (2) above shall give a true and fair view of the state of affairs and profit or loss of London Regional Transport; and any such statement prepared in accordance with paragraph (*b*) of that subsection shall give a true and fair view of the state of affairs and profit or loss of the members of the London Regional Transport group dealt with by that statement as a whole.

(4) Every statement of accounts prepared by London Regional Transport in accordance with this section shall comply with any requirements imposed by directions given by the Secretary of State, with the approval of the Treasury and after consultation with London Regional Transport, with respect to—

    (*a*) the information to be contained in the statement;

    (*b*) the manner in which that information is to be presented; and

    (*c*) the methods and principles according to which the statement is to be prepared.

(5) The accounts of London Regional Transport shall be audited by an auditor or auditors appointed in respect of each accounting year by the Secretary of State after consultation with London Regional Transport.

(6) A person shall not be qualified to be appointed to audit the accounts of London Regional Transport unless he is a member, or is a firm in Scotland in which each of the partners is a member, of one or more of the following bodies—

    The Institute of Chartered Accountants in England and Wales;

    The Institute of Chartered Accountants of Scotland;

    The Association of Certified Accountants;

    The Institute of Chartered Accountants in Ireland;

    Any other body of accountants established in the United Kingdom and for the time being recognised for the purposes of section 161(1)(a) of the Companies Act 1948 by the Secretary of State.

(7) As soon as the accounts of London Regional Transport have been audited in accordance with this section, London Regional Transport shall send to the Secretary of State—

(a) a copy of the statement of accounts prepared in accordance with subsection (2)(a) above ; and

(b) a copy of any statement of accounts prepared in accordance with subsection (2)(b) above ;

together with a copy of the report made by the auditor or auditors on that statement or (as the case may be) on each of those statements.

(8) A copy of every such statement and report shall be included in the annual report of London Regional Transport with respect to the accounting year in question which the Secretary of State is required by section 34 of this Act to lay before each House of Parliament.

Exclusion of National Audit Act 1983.

1983 c. 44.

24. London Regional Transport shall not be subject to investigation by the Comptroller and Auditor General under section 7 of the National Audit Act 1983 (examinations into the economy, efficiency and effectiveness with which bodies mainly supported by public funds use their resources in discharging their functions) ; and accordingly, in Schedule 4 to that Act (which lists authorities and bodies exempt from investigation under that section) the words " London Regional Transport " shall be inserted at the appropriate place in alphabetical order.

Pensions

Pensions and orders about pensions.

25.—(1) Sections 73 and 74 of the 1962 Act (which relate respectively to the powers of the Boards as regards pensions and pension schemes and the power of the Secretary of State to make orders about pensions) shall have effect as if—

(a) the expression " Board " in each of those sections included London Regional Transport ;

(b) the references in section 74(1)(a)(ii) to the Commission included references to the London Board ; and

(c) the reference in section 74(2)(a) to a pension scheme in which employees of the Commission or a subsidiary of the Commission participated before the date there mentioned included a reference to any pension scheme in which employees of, or of a subsidiary of, the London Board participated before the vesting date within the meaning of the 1969 Act and to any scheme or fund to which subsection (2) below applies in which employees of, or of a subsidiary of, London Regional Transport participated before the appointed day.

(2) This subsection applies to—

(a) any pension scheme or pension fund established under section 6(1)(k) of the 1969 Act (powers of Executive with respect to pensions and pension funds) ; and

(b) any superannuation fund maintained by a local authority.

(3) In section 74(2)(a), as it applies by virtue of subsection (2)(b) above in relation to a superannuation fund, the reference to payments under that fund shall be read as including a reference to payments under any agreement or arrangements with respect to the participation in that fund of employees of, or of a subsidiary of, London Regional Transport made by virtue of section 6(1)(k) of the 1969 Act.

(4) Without prejudice to section 74(4), in section 74(2)(a) as it applies by virtue of this section, references to employees of London Regional Transport shall be read as including any persons who immediately before the appointed day were participating, as members or former members of the Executive, in any scheme or fund to which subsection (2) above applies.

(5) Where by virtue of any provision made under section 74, as it applies for the purposes of this section, any member of London Regional Transport—

(a) continues to participate in any such scheme or fund ; or

(b) is admitted to participate in any pension scheme established under that section ;

paragraph 6(1)(b) of Schedule 1 to this Act shall not apply to him.

26.—(1) The Secretary of State may make such orders under Pensions for section 74 of the 1962 Act in relation to related companies as employees of he may make by virtue of section 25 of this Act in relation to related subsidiaries of London Regional Transport. companies.

(2) In exercising with respect to any pension scheme the powers conferred by this section, the Secretary of State shall take into account any representations made by the persons administering the scheme.

(3) Except on the application of a related company which is not a subsidiary of London Regional Transport, no order shall be made by virtue of this section which has the effect of placing the related company or any of its subsidiaries in any worse

position; but for the purposes of this subsection a related company or a subsidiary shall not be regarded as being placed in a worse position because an order provides that any changes in a pension scheme are not to be effected without the consent of the Secretary of State.

(4) An order such as is mentioned in subsection (3) above which is made otherwise than on the application of the related company shall not be invalid because it does not have the effect of securing that the related company and its subsidiaries are not placed in any worse position, but except in so far as the related company approves the effect of the order the Secretary of State shall as soon as may be make the necessary amending order.

(5) Subsections (3) and (4) above have effect only in relation to orders made after such day as may be appointed for the purposes of this section by order made by the Secretary of State and different days may be so appointed in relation to different related companies.

(6) Where an order (the " first order ") applying to a related company has been made under section 74 and at the time when it was made the related company was a subsidiary of London Regional Transport, the order shall not apply to the related company when it ceases to be such a subsidiary except where an order made by virtue of this section (whether before or after the related company ceases to be such a subsidiary) provides for the first order to continue to apply to the related company.

(7) An order made by virtue of this section may, in particular, authorise London Regional Transport or any subsidiary of London Regional Transport—

    (*a*) to transfer liabilities and obligations under a pension scheme in relation to some (but not all) of the participants in that scheme to another pension scheme ; and

    (*b*) to divide or apportion a pension fund held for the purposes of the first-mentioned scheme between that scheme and the other scheme.

Miscellaneous and supplemental

Supplementary provisions with respect to transfer schemes.

27.—(1) This section applies to any scheme under section 4, 5 or 9(6) of this Act (referred to below in this section as a transfer scheme).

(2) A transfer scheme may define the property, rights and liabilities to be transferred by the scheme—

    (*a*) by specifying the property, rights and liabilities in question ; or (*b*) by referring to all the property, rights and liabilities comprised in a specified part of the transferor's undertaking ;

and may contain such supplementary, incidental and consequential provisions as may appear to London Regional Transport to be necessary or expedient.

(3) Without prejudice to section 47 of this Act and subject to subsection (4) below, a transfer scheme may provide that any functions of the transferor under any statutory provision shall be transferred with the property, rights and liabilities affected by the scheme, if and so far as that statutory provision—

(*a*) relates to the part of the transferor's undertaking, or to property, to be transferred by the scheme ; or

(*b*) authorises the carrying out of works designed to be used in connection with that part of the transferor's undertaking or the acquisition of land for the purpose of carrying out such works.

(4) Subsection (3) above does not apply to any function of London Regional Transport, or of London Regional Transport or any subsidiary of theirs, under any provision of this Act or any other statutory provision specifically amended by any provision of this Act.

(5) A transfer scheme may define any functions of the transferor to be transferred by the scheme in accordance with subsection (3) above—

(*a*) by specifying the statutory provisions in question ;

(*b*) by referring to all the statutory provisions (except those mentioned in subsection (4) above) which relate to the part of the transferor's undertaking, or to property, to be transferred by the scheme or authorise the carrying out of works designed to be used in connection with that part of the transferor's undertaking or the acquisition of land for the purpose of carrying out such works ; or

(*c*) by referring to all the statutory provisions within paragraph (*b*) above, but specifying certain excepted provisions.

(6) A transfer scheme shall not come into force until it has been approved by the Secretary of State or until such date as the Secretary of State may, in giving his approval, specify ; and the Secretary of State may approve a transfer scheme either without modifications or with such modifications as, after consultation with London Regional Transport, he thinks fit.

(7) On the coming into force of a transfer scheme the property, rights and liabilities affected by the scheme shall, subject to sub-section (8) below, be transferred and vest in accordance with the scheme.

(8) Subject to subsection (9) below, Schedule 4 to the 1968 Act (supplementary provisions as to certain transfers of property, rights and liabilities) shall apply to any transfer under subsection (7) above ; and subsection (7) above shall have effect subject to the provisions of that Schedule.

(9) In Schedule 4 as it applies by virtue of subsection (8) above—

(*a*) any reference to a transfer by or a vesting by virtue of that Act shall be read as a reference to a transfer by or a vesting by virtue of the transfer scheme in question ; and

(*b*) the reference in paragraph 13(5) to the relevant provis-ions of that Act shall be read as including a reference to the relevant provisions of this Act.

28.—(1) London Regional Transport shall have power to enter into and carry out agreements with—

(*a*) the council of a London borough ;

(*b*) the Common Council ;

(*c*) any urban development corporation established for an area in Greater London under Part XVI of the Local Government, Planning and Land Act 1980 ; or

(*d*) the council of any district ;

with respect to the provision or continued provision by London Regional Transport, and the financing, on such terms as may be agreed between the parties, of public passenger transport ser-vices and facilities which would not be available apart from any such agreement.

(2) The council of a London borough, the Common Council and the council of any district shall each have power to enter into and carry out agreements with London Regional Transport with respect to the matters mentioned in subsection (1) above.

29.—(1) It shall be the duty of London Regional Transport in each accounting year to prepare, and cause to be published in such manner as they think fit, a plan containing their pro-posals with respect to the conduct of their undertaking and the businesses of their subsidiaries during the period to which the plan relates.

(2) Subject to subsection (3) below, the plan shall give such information relevant to their proposals, and deal with such other matters, as London Regional Transport consider appropriate for presenting their proposals in the context of the past and current performance and policies of themselves and their subsidiaries.

(3) In preparing the plan London Regional Transport shall have regard to any guidance given by the Secretary of State as to the form and content of the plan and the period to which it is to relate.

30.—(1) It shall be the duty of London Regional Transport in each year to inform the local authorities concerned and the Passengers' Committee of their current plans with respect to—

Information and publicity with respect to plans as to services and fares.

> (a) the general level of transport services and facilities to be provided by them, by subsidiaries of theirs or by other persons in pursuance of any agreement entered into by them by virtue of section 3(2) of this Act, and the general structure of routes of those services ; and

> (b) the general level and structure of the fares to be charged for those services, and the general level of charges to be made for those facilities.

(2) For the purposes of subsection (1) above, the local authorities concerned are—

> (a) the Greater London Council ;

> (b) the councils of the London boroughs ;

> (c) the Common Council ; and

> (d) the council of any county or district any part of whose area appears to London Regional Transport to be affected to a significant degree by the plans mentioned in that subsection.

(3) London Regional Transport shall cause particulars of the general level and structure of the fares referred to in subsection (1)(b) above as they apply for the time being to be published in such manner as they think fit.

31. The Railways Board shall in each year consult with London Regional Transport as to—

Duty of Railways Board to consult London Regional Transport as to fares and services in London.

> (a) the general level and structure of the fares to be charged for the carriage of passengers by the Board's railways on journeys wholly within Greater London ; and

> (b) the general level of the provision to be made for such journeys.

32.—(1) In addition to any power of the Secretary of State under any other provision of this Act to give directions to London Regional Transport with respect to any matter, the Secretary of State may, after consultation with London Regional Transport, give to London Regional Transport directions of a general character as to the exercise and performance by them of their functions (including the exercise of rights conferred by the holding of interests in companies).

(2) London Regional Transport shall, in framing and carrying out proposals involving substantial expenditure of a capital nature by London Regional Transport or a subsidiary of theirs, act on lines settled from time to time with the approval of the Secretary of State.

(3) London Regional Transport shall, in formulating policies and plans for the general conduct of their undertaking and the businesses of their subsidiaries, act on lines settled from time to time with the approval of the Secretary of State.

(4) If it appears to the Secretary of State to be desirable to do so for the purpose of obtaining information not otherwise available, he may at any time cause a review to be carried out (whether by London Regional Transport or by any persons appointed by him for the purpose) of the organisation of the undertaking of London Regional Transport and the businesses of their subsidiaries, with a view to determining whether any occasion arises for the exercise by him of any of his powers under this Part of this Act in relation to London Regional Transport.

(5) Without prejudice to the preceding provisions of this section or section 10 of this Act, but subject to subsection (6) below, the Secretary of State may, after consultation with London Regional Transport, direct London Regional Transport to take, or to exercise their control over any subsidiary of theirs so as to require that subsidiary to take, any of the following actions, that is to say—

(a) to discontinue any activities ;

(b) to dispose of any assets ;

(c) to call in any loan ;

(d) to exercise any power London Regional Transport or (as the case may be) that subsidiary may possess to revoke any guarantee.

(6) The Secretary of State shall not give any direction under subsection (5) above unless he is satisfied that the carrying on of the activities or the retention of the assets or the continuance of the loan or guarantee (as the case may be) is unnecessary for

the proper discharge by London Regional Transport (whether directly or by acting through the subsidiary in question) of their duties under this Act.

(7) Without prejudice to the preceding provisions of this section or section 10 of this Act, the Secretary of State may give directions to London Regional Transport requiring them to exercise their powers under section 3 of this Act—

(*a*) to form companies ; and

(*b*) to transfer property, rights and liabilities to companies formed by them ;

for such purposes (other than the purpose of facilitating the eventual disposal under section 9 of this Act of any part of their undertaking or of the whole or any part of the undertaking of any of their subsidiaries) and in such manner as may be specified in the directions.

(8) If it appears to the Secretary of State that there is any action which London Regional Transport ought in the interests of national defence—

(*a*) to have power to take ; or

(*b*) to be required to take ;

and that it would be consistent with the duties imposed on London Regional Transport by this Act, he may authorise or direct London Regional Transport to take that action.

(9) No limitation on the powers of London Regional Transport contained in this Act or in any local enactment shall prevent London Regional Transport from taking any action they are authorised or required to take by a direction under subsection (8) above.

(10) London Regional Transport shall furnish the Secretary of State with such information as he may specify in writing and London Regional Transport have or can reasonably be expected to obtain with respect to such matters relating to—

(*a*) London Regional Transport or any subsidiary of theirs ; or

(*b*) their activities (past, present or future), plans or property ;

as the Secretary of State may so specify.

(11) Information required under subsection (10) above shall be furnished in such manner and at such times as the Secretary of State may specify in writing.

Part I
Further
provision
with respect
to control of
subsidiaries.

33. London Regional Transport shall exercise their control over their subsidiaries so as to ensure that a subsidiary of theirs—

    (*a*) does not engage in activities in which London Regional Transport have no power to engage (including activities in which London Regional Transport have no power to engage because the consent of the Secretary of State has not been obtained);

    (*b*) does not do anything which the Secretary of State has directed London Regional Transport not to do; and

    (*c*) does not, except with the consent of the Secretary of State, raise money by the issue of shares or stock to any person other than London Regional Transport or any other subsidiary of London Regional Transport.

34.—(1) Without prejudice to section 32(10) of this Act, London Regional Transport shall, as soon as possible after the end of each accounting year of London Regional Transport, make to the Secretary of State a report on the exercise and performance by them of their functions during that year.

(2) The report shall deal with the activities of any subsidiaries of London Regional Transport, so far as relevant to the performance by London Regional Transport of their functions during the year in question.

(3) The report made under this section in respect of any accounting year of London Regional Transport shall—

    (*a*) include such information as the Secretary of State may from time to time specify in writing with respect to any matter the report is required to deal with by virtue of subsection (1) or (2) above;

    (*b*) include a statement of any action taken during that year by London Regional Transport and any subsidiaries of theirs in relation to, or for the purpose of securing, provision for disabled persons in the public passenger transport services and facilities provided for Greater London (whether by London Regional Transport or any subsidiary of theirs or by any other person);

    (*c*) include a statement of any action taken during that year by London Regional Transport and any subsidiaries of theirs for the purpose of co-ordinating the public passenger transport services provided by, or by any subsidiary of, the Railways Board and those provided by London Regional Transport, any subsidiary of London Regional Transport, or any other person under an agreement entered into by London Regional Transport by virtue of section 3(2) of this Act;

(*d*) set out any directions given by the Secretary of State to London Regional Transport under this Act during that year, unless the Secretary of State has notified to London Regional Transport his opinion that it is against the interests of national security to do so ; and

(*e*) include a statement of the salaries or fees and of the emoluments of each of the members of London Regional Transport during that year. PART I

(4) The Secretary of State shall lay a copy of every report under this section before each House of Parliament.

35.—(1) This section applies to any business carried on by London Regional Transport or any subsidiary of theirs which is a business of providing services for the carriage of passengers by road which do not require authorisation by a road service licence and would not require such authorisation even apart from the exemption given to London Regional Transport and any subsidiaries of theirs by section 43(1) of this Act. Inclusion in annual report of information with respect to contract and express carriage business.

(2) In the case of any business to which this section applies, the annual report of London Regional Transport under section 34 of this Act for any accounting year shall include a statement of—

(*a*) the amount, as determined by London Regional Transport, of the turnover of London Regional Transport or (as the case may be) of the subsidiary in question for that year in respect of that business ;

(*b*) the extent or approximate extent (expressed in either case in monetary terms) to which, as so determined, the carrying on of that business contributed to, or restricted, the profit or loss of London Regional Transport or of that subsidiary for that year before taxation ; and

(*c*) the method by which any determination for the purposes of paragraph (*a*) or (*b*) above was arrived at.

PART II

THE LONDON REGIONAL RAIL PASSENGER NETWORK

36.—(1) The Secretary of State may by order provide that sections 37 and 38 of this Act shall apply, as from such day as may be specified in the order (referred to below in this section as the operative date), for the purpose of conferring or imposing on London Regional Transport certain functions in relation to the provision by the Railways Board of railway passenger services and in relation to services so provided. Provision for additional functions of London Regional Transport as to railway services.

(2) Those sections are to be read, accordingly, as applying only as from the operative date.

Part II

(3) In those sections, references to the London regional rail passenger network are references to such railway passenger services as may be determined from time to time by the Secretary of State, after consultation with London Regional Transport and the Railways Board.

(4) An order under subsection (1) above may contain such supplementary, incidental and consequential provisions as may appear to the Secretary of State to be necessary or expedient, including provisions modifying sections 37 and 38 of this Act or any other enactment (whether contained in this Act or not).

(5) Any order under subsection (1) above shall cease to have effect (without prejudice to its earlier revocation) at the end of the accounting year of London Regional Transport current at the expiry of the period of eight years beginning with the operative date, unless before the end of that period of eight years it is confirmed by order made by the Secretary of State for the purposes of this subsection.

(6) An order under subsection (1) above specifying a day for the application of sections 37 and 38 of this Act may not be varied before the end of the period of eight years mentioned in subsection (5) above, except with respect to any such provisions as are mentioned in subsection (4) above ; and no order under subsection (1) above may be varied or revoked after it has been confirmed in accordance with subsection (5) above.

(7) No order shall be made—

    (a) under subsection (1) above specifying a day for the application of sections 37 and 38 of this Act or revoking a previous order under that subsection specifying such a day ; or

    (b) confirming any order under that subsection for the purposes of subsection (5) above ;

unless a draft of the order has been laid before, and approved by resolution of, each House of Parliament.

(8) An order under subsection (1) above varying a previous order under that subsection shall be subject to annulment in pursuance of a resolution of either House of Parliament.

Responsibility for London regional rail passenger network.

1974 c. 48.

37.—(1) London Regional Transport shall be the competent authority of Great Britain in relation to the Railways Board for the purposes of the relevant transport regulations within the meaning of the Railways Act 1974, so far as relates to the operation of any services for the time being comprised in the London regional rail passenger network ; and, accordingly, for subsections (1) to (3) of section 3 of that Act (functions of the Secretary of State in relation to the Railways Board under those regulations) there shall be substituted the following subsections—

" (1) The competent authority of Great Britain in relation to the Railways Board for the purposes of the relevant transport regulations shall be—

    (*a*) in relation to any services comprised in the railway passenger system of the Board other than services within paragraph (*b*) below, the Secretary of State ; and

    (*b*) in relation to any services for the time being comprised in the London regional rail passenger network, London Regional Transport ;

and references below in this section, in relation to the competent authority, to services within the competence of that authority, are references to the services mentioned in paragraph (*a*) or (*b*) above (as the case may require).

(2) The competent authority may give directions to the Board imposing on them obligations of a general nature with respect to the operation of the whole or any part of their railway passenger system, so far as relates to services within the competence of that authority or any matter affecting those services.

(3) It shall fall to the competent authority to make any payments which are required to be made to the Board by any provisions of the relevant transport regulations in respect of services within the competence of that authority or any matter affecting those services, and that authority may, subject to and in accordance with the provisions of those regulations, determine the manner of calculating, and the conditions applicable to, those payments.

(3A) Any direction given under subsection (2) above may be varied or revoked, so far as relates to any services or any matter affecting any services, by a subsequent direction so given by the competent authority in relation to those services (whether or not that authority was the authority which gave the earlier direction).".

(2) In subsections (4) and (6) of that section, for the words " subsection (1) above " there shall be substituted the words " subsection (2) above ".

(3) In section 4 of that Act (the Board's duties in relation to policies, plans and information)—

    (*a*) after subsection (2) there shall be inserted the following subsection—

        " (2A) In relation to—

            (*a*) expenditure in respect of any services for the time being comprised in the London regional rail passenger network ; and

> (*b*) policies and plans for the conduct of the undertaking of the Board and the businesses of their subsidiaries, so far as relates to any services so comprised ;

> subsections (1) and (2) above shall apply with the substitution, for references to the Secretary of State, of references to London Regional Transport." ;

(*b*) after subsection (3) there shall be inserted the following subsection—

> " (3A) In relation to information with respect to any services for the time being comprised in the London regional rail passenger network, references in subsection (3) above to the Secretary of State shall include London Regional Transport." ; and

(*c*) in subsection (5) the following paragraph shall be inserted after paragraph (*a*)—

> " (*aa*) set out any directions given to the Board under section 3(2) above during that year ; "

> and in paragraph (*b*), for the words from " section 3 of " to " above " there shall be substituted the words " or section 3 of the Transport Act 1981 ".

1981 c. 56.

(4) Any direction given by the Secretary of State under section 3(1) of that Act before the operative date within the meaning of section 36 of this Act shall be treated for the purposes of sections 3 and 4 of that Act, as they have effect by virtue of this section, as given under section 3(2) as substituted by subsection (1) above.

(5) In section 10(2) of that Act (interpretation), after the definition of " the 1968 Act " there shall be inserted the following definition—

> " ' London regional rail passenger network ' has the meaning given by section 36(3) of the London Regional Transport Act 1984 ; ".

Application and modification of Part I.
1974 c. 48.

38.—(1) In exercising their functions under sections 3 and 4 of the Railways Act 1974, as those sections apply by virtue of section 37 of this Act, London Regional Transport shall have due regard to their general duty under section 2(1) of this Act with respect to the provision of public passenger transport services for Greater London.

(2) Section 2(3) and (4) of this Act shall not apply, but London Regional Transport and the Railways Board shall continue to have power to enter into such arrangements as are mentioned in section 2(4) where those arrangements appear to London Regional Transport to be appropriate for the discharge of

their general duty under section 2(1) of this Act in relation to the provision by the Railways Board of services for the time being comprised in the London regional rail passenger network.

(3) Any statement prepared by London Regional Transport under section 7 of this Act shall deal with—

(a) any current or proposed arrangements between London Regional Transport and the Railways Board under subsection (2) above ; and

(b) any action London Regional Transport have taken or propose to take in exercise of their powers under section 4(1) and (2) of the Railways Act 1974 (settlement of guidelines as to capital expenditure, policies and plans of Railways Board), so far as relevant to carrying into effect the policies mentioned in section 7(1) of this Act during the period to which the statement relates.

1974 c. 48.

(4) London Regional Transport may apply sums received by way of grants under section 12 of this Act in making any payments which fall to be made by them to the Railways Board in accordance with section 3(3) of that Act.

(5) The duty of London Regional Transport under section 30(1) of this Act to inform the persons there mentioned of their current plans with respect to the general level of transport services to be provided as mentioned in paragraph (a) of that subsection shall apply to their current plans with respect to the general level of provision of services for the time being comprised in the London regional rail passenger network.

(6) Section 31 of this Act shall apply in relation to any journeys, whether wholly within Greater London or not, by way of services for the time being comprised in that network ; and the Railways Board shall inform London Regional Transport in advance of any proposals for changes in substance in any fares to be charged for the carriage of passengers by the Board's railways on such journeys or in the level of provision to be made for such journeys.

39. This Part of this Act shall cease to have effect—

(a) if no order is made under section 36(1) of this Act before the end of the period of eight years beginning with the date on which this Act is passed, at the end of that period ;

(b) if an order made under section 36(1) specifying a day for the application of sections 37 and 38 of this Act ceases to have effect by virtue of subsection (5) of that section, or is revoked before the end of the period of eight years mentioned in that subsection, on the date when that order ceases to have effect or (as the case may be) is revoked.

PART III

MISCELLANEOUS AND GENERAL

Consultation with passengers

The London Regional Passengers' Committee.

40.—(1) There shall be established in accordance with this section a body to be known as the London Regional Passengers' Committee.

(2) The Committee shall consist of a chairman appointed by the Secretary of State, and such other members (not exceeding thirty) as the Secretary of State may appoint after consultation with such bodies as appear to him to be representative of the interests of persons likely to be significantly concerned with matters within the competence of the Committee.

(3) The Secretary of State may appoint one or more members of the Committee to be deputy chairman or (as the case may be) deputy chairmen of the Committee.

(4) Subject to subsection (6) below, it shall be the duty of the Committee to consider and, where it appears to them to be desirable, make recommendations with respect to any matter affecting the services and facilities provided—

> (a) by London Regional Transport or any subsidiary of theirs ; or
>
> (b) by any other person in pursuance of an agreement entered into by London Regional Transport by virtue of section 3(2) of this Act ; or
>
> (c) by the Railways Board or any subsidiary of theirs ;

which falls to be considered by the Committee in accordance with subsection (5) below.

(5) A matter falls to be considered by the Committee if—

> (a) it has been the subject of representations (other than representations appearing to the Committee to be frivolous) made to the Committee by or on behalf of users of any services or facilities so provided ; or
>
> (b) it has been referred to the Committee by the Secretary of State, by London Regional Transport or by the Railways Board ; or
>
> (c) it otherwise appears to the Committee to be a matter to which consideration ought to be given ;

and, in the case of any matter affecting services or facilities provided by the Railways Board or any subsidiary of theirs, those services or facilities are within the competence of the Committee by virtue of section 41(7) of this Act.

(6) Without prejudice to section 41 of this Act, the Committee may not by virtue of subsection (4) above consider the charges made for any service or facility or any question relating to—

>   (*a*) the discontinuance by London Regional Transport or any subsidiary of theirs of all railway passenger services from any station or on any line on their railways ; or

>   (*b*) the discontinuance or reduction of railway services provided by the Railways Board or any subsidiary of theirs.

(7) Copies of the minutes, conclusions and recommendations of the Committee with respect to any matter shall be sent—

>   (*a*) in the case of any matter affecting services and facilities provided as mentioned in subsection (4)(*a*) or (*b*) above, to London Regional Transport ;

>   (*b*) in the case of any matter affecting services and facilities provided as mentioned in subsection (4)(*c*) above, to the Railways Board ; and

>   (*c*) in the case of any matter referred to the Committee by the Secretary of State, to the Secretary of State.

(8) Where the Secretary of State receives a recommendation under subsection (7) above he may give to London Regional Transport or (as the case may require) to the Railways Board such directions as he thinks fit with respect to matters dealt with in the recommendation which concern them or a subsidiary of theirs ; but before giving any such direction to London Regional Transport the Secretary of State shall consult with London Regional Transport.

(9) On reaching a decision with respect to matters dealt with in any recommendation received by them or him under subsection (7) above, London Regional Transport, the Railways Board or (as the case may be) the Secretary of State shall give notice in writing of that decision to the Passengers' Committee.

(10) The Committee shall make an annual report to the Secretary of State, and the Secretary of State shall lay a copy of the report before each House of Parliament.

(11) A company which would not otherwise be a subsidiary of London Regional Transport or the Railways Board shall not be treated as such for the purposes of this section by virtue of section 62 of this Act.

(12) Schedule 3 to this Act has effect with respect to the Committee.

PART III
Operation of
the
Passengers'
Committee as
an Area
Transport
Users'
Consultative
Committee.

41.—(1) The Passengers' Committee shall be treated as one of the Area Transport Users' Consultative Committees (referred to below in this section as " Area Committees ") for the purposes of the provisions of section 56 of the 1962 Act mentioned in subsection (2) below—

(a) in substitution for the Area Committee whose area comprises Greater London immediately before the appointed day ; and

(b) subject to any directions given by the Secretary of State under subsection (1)(b) of that section as it applies by virtue of subsection (2)(a) below, for the same area as the area of that Area Committee at that time ;

and that Area Committee shall accordingly cease to exist, and the persons who are for the time being its members shall cease to hold office, on the appointed day.

(2) The provisions of section 56 referred to in subsection (1) above are—

(a) subsection (1)(b) (Area Committees to be established for all parts of Great Britain) ;

(b) subsection (2), so far as relates to the constitution of the Central Transport Consultative Committee for Great Britain (referred to below in this section as the " Central Committee ") and the attendance of a chairman of an Area Committee at a meeting of the Central Committee ; and

(c) subsections (7) to (10) and (13) (which relate to railway closures) ;

and the power of the Passengers' Committee under paragraph 9(4) of Schedule 3 to this Act to determine their own procedure is subject to subsection (13) of that section as applied by this section.

(3) Without prejudice to section 40(7) of this Act, copies of the minutes, conclusions and recommendations of the Passengers' Committee with respect to any matter affecting services or facilities provided by the Railways Board or any subsidiary of theirs shall be sent to the Central Committee.

(4) The Passengers' Committee shall be treated as an Area Committee within the meaning of section 56 of the 1962 Act for the purposes of section 54(5) of the 1968 Act (reference to an Area Committee of any matter affecting the provision of alternative services in case of a railway closure).

(5) The Central Committee may from time to time make general recommendations to the Passengers' Committee with respect to any matter affecting the functions of the Commitee—

(a) under section 40 of this Act, so far as relates to services or facilities provided by the Railways Board or any subsidiary of theirs ; or

(b) under section 56 of the 1962 Act or section 54(5) of the   PART III
   1968 Act;

or the procedure of the Committee in exercising or performing
any of those functions.

(6) The annual report of the Central Committee under section 56(15) of the 1962 Act shall not deal with the exercise and
performance of the functions of the Passengers' Committee except in so far as relates to matters affecting services or facilities
provided by the Railways Board or any subsidiary of theirs.

(7) Services or facilities so provided are within the competence
of the Passengers' Committee for the purposes of section 40 of
this Act if they are provided within the area for which the
Passengers' Committee act as an Area Committee by virtue of
this section.

Railway closures in and around Greater London

42.—(1) The former functions of the London Board in rela- Application
tion to railway closures continue to be exercisable by London of provisions
Regional Transport; and the following provisions of this section and 1968 Acts
have effect for the purpose of—   relating to
                                                                railway
   (a) extending those functions to any subsidiary of London closures.
      Regional Transport; and

   (b) making amendments consequential on the provisions
      of this Act in the provisions of the 1962 and 1968
      Acts relating to such closures.

(2) In section 54(1) of the 1962 Act (advance information
about railway and shipping closures), for the references to the
Executive substituted by paragraph 1 of Schedule 3 to the 1969
Act for express references to the London Board there shall be
substituted references to the appropriate authority in relation
to the services in question.

(3) In section 56(7) of that Act and section 54(1) of the 1968
Act (provisions with respect to proposals for railway closures),
for the express references to the London Board which fell by
virtue of section 25(1) of the 1969 Act to be construed as
references to the Executive there shall be substituted references
to the appropriate authority in relation to the services in question.

(4) In section 54(5)(d) of the 1968 Act (power of Secretary
of State to give directions in connection with a railway closure
which was exercisable before the coming into operation of the
1969 Act in relation to the London Board), after the words
" the Railways Board or " there shall be inserted the words
" (as the case may be) to London Regional Transport or, in

C 3

relation to services provided by a subsidiary of London Regional Transport, to that subsidiary, and ".

(5) In consequence of the amendments made above in this section, references (however expressed) in section 56(7) to (9) and (13) of the 1962 Act and in section 54(1) of the 1968 Act to a Board shall be read, in relation to railway services provided by London Regional Transport or any subsidiary of theirs, as references to the appropriate authority in relation to the services in question.

(6) For the purposes of this section, the appropriate authority in relation to any railway services is—

> (a) where those services are provided by London Regional Transport, London Regional Transport ; and
>
> (b) where those services are provided by a subsidiary of London Regional Transport, that subsidiary.

Regulation of services by public service vehicles in and around London

43.—(1) A road service licence is not required for the provision—

> (a) by London Regional Transport or any subsidiary of theirs ; or
>
> (b) by any other person in pursuance of any agreement entered into by London Regional Transport by virtue of section 3(2) of this Act ;

of any bus service operated wholly as a London bus service.

(2) Where a road service licence is granted in respect of a bus service—

> (a) provided as mentioned in paragraph (a) or (b) of subsection (1) above ; but
>
> (b) operated in part only as a London bus service ;

no condition shall be attached to the licence with respect to the carriage of passengers who are both taken up and set down in Greater London.

(3) Where—

> (a) London Regional Transport or any subsidiary of theirs propose to provide a new bus service which is to be operated wholly or in part as a London bus service or to vary a bus service currently provided by them which is being so operated ; or
>
> (b) London Regional Transport propose to enter into an agreement by virtue of section 3(2) of this Act for the provision of such a new bus service by any other per-

son or to agree to a variation in any bus service currently provided in pursuance of any such agreement which is being so operated ;

then, before deciding on, or on the provisions to be contained in any such agreement with respect to, or on any variation affecting, any relevant aspects of that service London Regional Transport shall, so far as the service is or is to be provided in Greater London, consult with the commissioner or commissioners of police concerned, with the local authorities affected, with the Passengers' Committee and with any other person they think fit.

(4) In subsection (3) above—

(a) references to a new bus service are references to a bus service which has not been provided continuously since before the appointed day (disregarding, in the case of a bus service operated during certain periods of the year only, any period other than one during which the service is due to be operated) ;

(b) the reference to relevant aspects of the service is a reference to the route of the service, a terminal point, a point at which passengers may or may not be taken up or set down, or a place at which, or street by the use of which, vehicles used for the service may turn at a terminal point ; and

(c) " commissioner of police " means, in relation to the metropolitan police district, the Commissioner of Police of the Metropolis and, in relation to the City of London, the Commissioner of Police for the City of London ;

and for the purposes of that subsection the local authorities affected are the Greater London Council and any of the following councils, that is to say, the councils of the London boroughs and the Common Council, in whose area any part of the route in question or (as the case may be) the point, place or street in question is situated.

(5) Where—

(a) London Regional Transport or any subsidiary of theirs propose to discontinue a bus service currently provided by them which is being operated wholly or in part as a London bus service ; or

(b) London Regional Transport propose not to renew any agreement entered into by them by virtue of section 3(2) of this Act for the provision by any other person of any bus service which is being so operated or to agree to the discontinuance of any such bus service currently provided in pursuance of any such agreement ;

PART III

then, before any decision is taken to that effect, London Regional Transport shall, so far as the service is provided in Greater London, consult with the Greater London Council, with any of the following councils, that is to say, the councils of the London boroughs and the Common Council, in whose area any part of the route of the service is situated, with the Passengers' Committee and with any other person they think fit.

(6) Where an agreement entered into by London Regional Transport by virtue of section 3(2) of this Act for the provision of a bus service relates to such a service part only of which is operated as a London bus service, any provision contained in that agreement with respect to the carriage of passengers other than those who are both taken up and set down in Greater London shall be of no effect if or so far as it is inconsistent with any condition for the time being attached to any road service licence under which the bus service is provided.

(7) In this section—

" bus service " means a service for the carriage of passengers by road for which a road service licence is required, or would but for subsection (1) above be required, other than an excursion or tour within the meaning of the Public Passenger Vehicles Act 1981 ; and

1981 c. 14.

" London bus service " means a bus service which is, or so far as it is, a service on which passengers may be taken up and set down at different places within Greater London, whether or not any passengers on that service may also be taken up or set down outside Greater London.

Provisions consequential on section 43.

44.—(1) The provisions of the Public Passenger Vehicles Act 1981 are subject to section 43 of this Act, but, except as provided by that section, apply for regulating the provision of stage carriage services (within the meaning of that Act) within Greater London as well as elsewhere.

(2) The following provisions of this section have effect for the purpose of making amendments of that Act consequential on section 43 of this Act (which supersedes provisions of the 1969 Act which, in effect, gave control over all such stage carriage services in Greater London to the Executive).

(3) In subsection (1) of section 30 (road service licences required for operation of stage carriage services), for the words " section 23 of the Transport (London) Act 1969 " there shall be substituted the words " section 43 of the London Regional Transport Act 1984 ".

(4) In section 35 (grant of road service licences for certain excursions or tours) for subsection (1)(*a*)(ii) there shall be substituted the following sub-paragraph—

" (ii) any London bus service within the meaning of section 43 of the London Regional Transport Act 1984 which, by virtue of subsection (1) of that section, does not require a road service licence ; ".

(5) In subsection (2) of section 42 (use of certain vehicles by educational and other bodies) the words from " and section 23(2) " to " services) " (which refer to the provisions of the 1969 Act mentioned in subsection (2) above) shall be omitted.

(6) In section 45(5) (which makes special provision with respect to community bus services provided in whole or in part in Greater London)—

(*a*) for the words from " section 23 " to " of a road service licence) " there shall be substituted the words " section 43 of the London Regional Transport Act 1984 (which exempts London bus services under the control of London Regional Transport from the requirement of a road service licence) " ; and

(*b*) the words from " but where " to the end of the subsection shall be omitted.

45.—(1) The following section shall be inserted in the Public Passenger Vehicles Act 1981 immediately after section 35 (grant of road service licences for certain excursions or tours)—

" Excursions and tours with stopping places in Greater London.

35A.—(1) If, in the case of any application for a road service licence made to the traffic commissioners for the Metropolitan Traffic Area—

(*a*) the traffic commissioners are satisfied as mentioned in section 35(1) of this Act ; and

(*b*) they are also satisfied that the proposed service involves the use of any place in Greater London as a stopping place ;

the following provisions of this section shall apply in relation to the application and to any licence granted on it instead of section 35(1).

(2) In this section " stopping place " means, in relation to any service, a point at which passengers are taken up or set down in the course of that service.

(3) Section 33 of this Act shall not apply in relation to any application for a road service licence to which this section applies or in relation to any licence granted on any such application, and sections 31 and

32 of this Act shall so apply subject to the modifications provided by the following provisions of this section.

(4) The interests of the public falling to be considered under any provision of section 31 or 32, as that provision applies by virtue of this section, shall be confined to the interests of the public in securing that only places which are suitable for use as such are used as stopping places for the service in question in Greater London.

The reference above in this subsection to the service in question is a reference to the proposed service or the service provided under any road service licence granted on an application to which this section applies (as the case may require).

(5) For the purposes of this section a place is to be regarded as not being suitable for use as a stopping place for any service if the traffic commissioners are satisfied that its use as such would be prejudicial to the safety or convenience of the public.

(6) Section 31 shall apply with the omission of—

(*a*) paragraphs (*a*) and (*b*) of subsection (3); and

(*b*) subsection (4);

and subsection (3)(*c*) of that section shall apply only in relation to objections or representations made by the commissioner or commissioners of police concerned or by any of the local authorities affected.

(7) In subsection (6) above " commissioner of police " means—

(*a*) in relation to the metropolitan police district, the commissioner of police of the metropolis ; and

(*b*) in relation to the City of London, the Commissioner of Police for the City of London ;

and for the purposes of that subsection the local authorities affected are the Greater London Council and any of the following councils, that is to say, the councils of the London boroughs and the Common Council of the City of London, in whose area any stopping place for the proposed service is situated.

(8) Section 32 shall apply with the omission of subsections (1) and (2), but the traffic commissioners in granting a licence on any application to which

this section applies may attach to the licence such conditions of a description within section 32(1)(*c*) as they think fit, having regard to any objections or other representations that fall to be considered in relation to that application by virtue of section 31(3)(*c*) as it applies by virtue of this section, for securing that only places which are suitable for use as such are used as stopping places for the proposed service in Greater London.

(9) Any condition attached to a road service licence under subsection (8) above shall be treated for the purposes of the references in sections 30(7) and 32(5) of this Act to a condition attached under section 32 as having been attached to the licence under that section.

(10) Subsections (2) and (3) of section 35 of this Act shall apply in relation to a road service licence granted in pursuance of section 31, as section 31 applies by virtue of this section, as those subsections apply in relation to a road service licence granted in pursuance of section 35."

(2) In section 35(1) of that Act, at the beginning there shall be inserted the words " Subject to section 35A of this Act ".

(3) In section 54(4) of that Act (procedure of the traffic commissioners in certain cases)—

(*a*) in paragraph (*a*), after the word " Act " there shall be inserted the words " or (as the case may be) as mentioned in section 35(1) of this Act and also as mentioned in section 35A(1)(*b*) of this Act " ; and

(*b*) in paragraph (*b*), for the words " so satisfied " there shall be substituted the words " satisfied as mentioned in section 34(1) or 35(1), other than an application in the case of which they have determined that they are also satisfied as mentioned in section 35A(1)(*b*) ".

(4) Nothing in this section shall apply in relation to an application for a road service licence made before this section comes into force.

Transfers to and from the Railways Board, etc.

46.—(1) London Regional Transport and the Railways Board, acting jointly, may make schemes for the transfer, between any member of the London Regional Transport group and any member of the Railways Board group, of—

(*a*) any specified property, rights or liabilities ; or

(*b*) all property, rights and liabilities comprised in a specified part of the transferor's undertaking ;

PART III
and any such scheme may contain such supplementary, incidental and consequential provisions as may appear to London Regional Transport and the Railways Board to be necessary or expedient.

(2) A scheme under this section shall not come into force until it has been approved by the Secretary of State or until such date as the Secretary of State may, in giving his approval, specify; and (subject to subsection (3) below) the Secretary of State may approve a scheme either without modifications or with such modifications as, after consultation with London Regional Transport and with the Railways Board, he thinks fit.

(3) Without prejudice to his powers under section 47 of this Act, the Secretary of State shall not approve a scheme under this section which makes provision for a transfer of any property, rights or liabilities which it appears to him would materially prejudice the proper discharge by London Regional Transport or the Railways Board of their respective functions.

(4) On the coming into force of a scheme under this section the property, rights and liabilities in question shall (subject to subsection (6) below) be transferred and vest in accordance with the scheme.

(5) Subject to any order under section 74 of the 1962 Act (power of Secretary of State to make orders about pensions in the nationalised transport industry) which takes effect on or at any time after the transfer date for the purposes of any transfer under subsection (4) above, any person who, on that date—

(a) ceases to be employed by any member of one or other of the London Regional Transport group and the Railways Board group and becomes employed by a member of the other group; or

(b) is employed by a company which immediately before that date was a subsidiary of London Regional Transport or (as the case may be) of the Railways Board but on that date becomes a subsidiary of the other of those authorities;

shall not in consequence cease to be eligible to participate in any pension scheme in which he was a participant immediately before that transfer date.

(6) Subject to subsection (7) below, Schedule 4 to the 1968 Act (supplementary provisions as to certain transfers of property, rights and liabilities) shall apply to any transfer under subsection (4) above; and subsection (4) above shall have effect subject to the provisions of that Schedule.

(7) In Schedule 4 as it applies by virtue of subsection (6)
above—

(*a*) any reference to a transfer by or a vesting by virtue
of that Act shall be read as a reference to a transfer
by or vesting by virtue of the scheme in question;
and

(*b*) the reference in paragraph 13(5) to the relevant provisions of that Act shall be read as including a reference to the relevant provisions of this Act.

(8) In this section and section 47 of this Act, references to
the Railways Board group are references to the Railways Board
and their subsidiaries.

47.—(1) Subject to the following provisions of this section, the Orders for
Secretary of State may by order— transfer of
functions, etc.,
(*a*) make provision for the transfer, between any members within London
of the London Regional Transport group, or between Regional
any member of that group and any member of the Transport
Railways Board group, of any functions of the trans- group and
feror in connection with the carriage of passengers; group and
and Railways
Board group.
(*b*) make any such provision with respect to either party
to the transfer of functions as is mentioned in section
46(1) of this Act.

(2) An order under this section may, for the purpose of any
transfer of functions made by the order, amend any of the
enactments relating to those functions.

(3) Any such order may contain such supplementary, incidental and consequential provisions as may appear to the Secretary
of State to be necessary or expedient.

(4) The power to make orders under this section shall not be
exercisable so as to cause all or substantially all of the functions
of the London Regional Transport group to become functions
of, or of subsidiaries of, the Railways Board.

(5) Before making any order under this section the Secretary
of State shall consult with—

(*a*) London Regional Transport;

(*b*) the Railways Board;

(*c*) the Passengers' Committee; and

(*d*) such other persons (if any) as the Secretary of State may
think fit.

PART III

(6) In the case of an order under this section making such provision as is mentioned in section 46(1) of this Act, the property, rights and liabilities in question shall, subject to subsection (8) below, be transferred and vest in accordance with the order on such date as may be appointed by the order for that purpose.

(7) Section 46(5) of this Act shall apply in relation to a transfer under subsection (6) above as it applies in relation to a transfer under subsection (4) of that section.

(8) Subject to subsection (9) below, Schedule 4 to the 1968 Act shall apply to any transfer under subsection (6) above ; and subsection (6) above shall have effect subject to the provisions of that Schedule.

(9) In Schedule 4 as it applies by virtue of subsection (8) above—

    (*a*) any reference to a transfer by or a vesting by virtue of that Act shall be read as a reference to a transfer by or a vesting by virtue of the order in question ; and

    (*b*) the reference in paragraph 13(5) to the relevant provisions of that Act shall be read as including a reference to the relevant provisions of this Act.

(10) No order shall be made under this section unless a draft of the order has been laid before, and approved by a resolution of, each House of Parliament.

Compensation for loss of employment, etc.

Compensation for loss of employment, etc.

48.—(1) The Secretary of State may by regulations provide for the payment, by such persons as may be prescribed by or determined under the regulations, in such cases and to such extent as may be so prescribed or determined, of pensions, allowances or gratuities by way of compensation to or in respect of persons who have suffered loss of employment or loss or diminution of emoluments by reason of—

    (*a*) the disposal under section 9(1) of this Act of any part of the undertaking of London Regional Transport or of the whole or any part of the undertaking of any of their subsidiaries ;

    (*b*) any transfer of property, rights or liabilities under section 27, 46 or 47 of this Act ; or

    (*c*) any preparatory steps taken (after the making of the scheme or order in question) for the purposes of any such transfer which does not in fact take place, or taken for the purposes of any action required by a direction under section 10 of this Act which ceases to be so required before the action is taken.

(2) Regulations under this section may—

(a) include provision as to the manner in which and the person to whom any claim for compensation is to be made, and for the determination of all questions arising under the regulations ;

(b) make different provision as respects different classes of persons and different circumstances and make or authorise the Secretary of State to make exceptions and conditions ; and

(c) be framed so as to have effect from a date earlier than the making of the regulations ;

but regulations having effect from a date earlier than the date of their making shall not place any individual who is qualified to participate in the benefits for which the regulations provide in a worse position than he would have been in if the regulations had been so framed as to have effect only from the date of their making.

(3) Regulations under this section may include all or any of the following provisions, namely—

(a) provision authorising the payment, without probate or other proof of title, of any sum due under the regulations in respect of a person who has died to his personal representatives or such other persons as may be prescribed by the regulations ;

(b) provision rendering void any assignment of or charge on, or any agreement to assign or charge, any benefit under the regulations, and provision that on the bankruptcy of a person entitled to such a benefit no part of it shall pass to any trustee or other person acting on behalf of the creditors except in accordance with an order made by a court in pursuance of any enactment specified in the regulations ; and

(c) such incidental, supplementary, consequential and transitional provisions as appear to the Secretary of State to be necessary or expedient.

(4) Without prejudice to the preceding provisions of this section, regulations under this section may, in relation to any compensation required to be paid under the regulations by any person (" the person primarily liable "), specify persons who are to be liable to contribute towards that person's liability in accordance with subsections (5) and (6) below (" contributories ").

(5) Where contributories have been so specified in relation to any compensation, the contributories may arrange to make to the person primarily liable in respect of that compensation payments by way of contribution towards that person's liability.

(6) If the person primarily liable in respect of any compensation satisfies the Secretary of State that any contributory has not made proper contribution towards that person's liability, whether by payment of money or by finding employment for persons to or in respect of whom the compensation has become payable, the Secretary of State may require that contributory to make such payment to the person primarily liable as appears to the Secretary of State to be just.

(7) Regulations under this section shall be subject to annulment in pursuance of a resolution of either House of Parliament.

Grants by Greater London Council for initial year

Grants by Greater London Council for year including appointed day.

49.—(1) The Secretary of State may by a direction given to the Greater London Council require that Council to pay to London Regional Transport, in the financial year in which the appointed day falls (referred to below in this section as "the initial year"), such an amount by way of grant as the Secretary of State may determine, not exceeding the aggregate of—

(a) the revenue grants under section 3(1)(a) of the 1969 Act determined in respect of that year for the Executive ; and

(b) the sum of £170 million ;

less any sums which the Secretary of State is satisfied that the Council have paid to the Executive by way of grants under section 3(1)(a) in that year before the appointed day.

(2) Subject to subsection (3) below, references in subsection (1) above to the revenue grants under section 3(1)(a) of the 1969 Act determined in respect of the initial year for the Executive are references to any grants under that paragraph in aid of the revenues of the Executive (including grants in respect of reductions in fares for children) which the Greater London Council have determined, in accordance with section 4(1) of the Transport Act 1983, are to be made by them to the Executive in the initial year.

1983 c. 10.

(3) Any amount of the revenue grants so determined which is referable to provision for depreciation or renewal of assets shall be disregarded for the purposes of subsection (1) above.

(4) A direction under subsection (1) above may require that the amount to which it relates shall be paid in instalments of such amounts as may be specified in the direction ; and any amount payable by virtue of any such direction shall be due on such date as may be so specified in relation to that amount.

(5) If any amount so payable is not paid on or before the date so specified, interest on that amount shall be payable to London Regional Transport at the rate for the time being applicable for

the purposes of section 12(8) of the General Rate Act 1967
(interest on amounts due under precepts). 1967 c. 9.

(6) The Secretary of State may by notice in writing to London Regional Transport make the application by London Regional Transport of any sums received by them by virtue of this section subject to such terms and conditions as the Secretary of State thinks fit.

(7) Sections 12(2) to (4) and 15(9) and (10) of this Act shall apply in relation to sums so received as they apply in relation to sums received by way of grants under section 12 of this Act (taking the reference in section 12(2) to any such terms and conditions as a reference to any terms and conditions applicable by virtue of subsection (6) above).

(8) Any reference in—

(*a*) Article 1 of the Capital Allowances (Relevant Grants) S.I. 1969/1541.
   (No. 2) Order 1969, as it has effect by virtue of paragraph 4 of Schedule 5 to this Act ; and

(*b*) section 83(4)(*d*) of the Capital Allowances Act 1968, 1968 c. 3.
   as substituted by paragraph 4 of Schedule 6 to this Act ;

to a grant made under section 12 of this Act shall be read as including a reference to a grant made under this section.

(9) As respects the period beginning with the appointed day and ending with 31st March 1985, paragraphs 25B(*a*) and 29A of Schedule 2 to the London Government Act 1963 shall have effect 1963 c. 33. as if for references to the Executive there were substituted references to London Regional Transport.

(10) In this section " financial year " means a period of twelve months beginning with 1st April.

Travel concessions

50.—(1) Subject to subsection (4) below, any local authority, Travel or any two or more local authorities acting jointly, may enter concessions on into arrangements with London Regional Transport under journeys in which— and around Greater London.

(*a*) London Regional Transport grant, or arrange with some other person for that other person to grant, such travel concessions as may be provided for by the arrangements to any persons eligible to receive them in accordance with subsection (7) below ; and

(*b*) that local authority (or, as the case may be, those local authorities in such proportions respectively as they may agree among themselves) reimburse the cost incurred in granting those concessions.

(2) Any London authority may contribute to any cost incurred by a local authority within the meaning of the Public Service Vehicles (Travel Concessions) Act 1955 in granting travel concessions under that Act.

(3) Subject to subsection (4) below, any London authority, or any two or more London authorities acting jointly, may make, with any independent transport service operator or with the Railways Board, arrangements under which—

  (a) that operator or (as the case may be) the Board grant such travel concessions as may be provided for by the arrangements to any persons eligible to receive them in accordance with subsection (7) below ; and

  (b) that authority (or, as the case may be, those authorities in such proportions respectively as they may agree among themselves) reimburse the cost incurred in granting those concessions.

(4) The concessions that may be provided for by any arrangements under subsection (1) or (3) above are concessions on journeys—

  (a) between places in Greater London ;

  (b) between such places and places outside but in the vicinity of Greater London ; or

  (c) between places outside but in the vicinity of Greater London.

(5) Any arrangements entered into by a local authority under subsection (1) or (3) above may include provision for the performance of functions in connection with the travel concessions in question by the local authority or local authorities concerned.

(6) Any London authority making contributions under subsection (2) above may enter into arrangements with the authority to whom those contributions are paid for the performance by that London authority of functions in connection with the travel concessions in respect of which the contributions are paid.

(7) The persons eligible to receive travel concessions under arrangements made under subsection (1) or (3) above are persons mentioned in any of the following paragraphs, or any description of such persons, that is to say—

  (a) men over the age of sixty-five years and women over the age of sixty years ;

  (b) blind persons, that is to say, persons so blind as to be unable to perform any work for which sight is essential ;

  (c) persons suffering from any disability or injury which, in the opinion of the local authority or any of the local

authorities by whom the cost incurred in granting the   PART III
concessions falls to be reimbursed, seriously impairs
their ability to walk.

(8) In this section—

(*a*) " independent transport service operator " means any
person operating a public service vehicle undertaking
or a tramcar or railway undertaking other than—

  (i) a local authority within the meaning of the
  Act of 1955 mentioned above ;

  (ii) London Regional Transport, the Railways
  Board or any subsidiary of either of those authorities ;
  or

  (iii) any person providing public passenger transport services in pursuance of an agreement entered
  into by London Regional Transport by virtue of
  section 3(2) of this Act ;

and any person whose use of a motor vehicle (within
the meaning of the Public Passenger Vehicles Act 1981)   1981 c. 14.
is covered by an authorisation under section 48 of that
Act (use of passenger vehicles in experimental areas) ;

(*b*) " local authority " means the council of a county or
district and any London authority ;

(*c*) " London authority " means the Greater London Council, the council of any London borough and the Common Council ; and

(*d*) " tramcar " has the same meaning as in the Public Passenger Vehicles Act 1981.

(9) In this section and sections 51 to 53 of this Act " travel
concession " means the reduction or waiver of a fare or charge
either absolutely or subject to terms, limitations or conditions.

51.—(1) If immediately before 1st January in any accounting   Reserve free
year of London Regional Transport it appears to London   travel scheme
Regional Transport that there are not for the time being in   for London
force arrangements under section 50(1) of this Act for travel   residents.
concessions for London residents which—

(*a*) meet the requirements of section 53 of this Act as to
scope and uniformity ; and

(*b*) will apply throughout the next following accounting
year of London Regional Transport ;

the following provisions of this section (referred to below in this
section and in section 52 of this Act as the free travel scheme)
shall apply to the next following accounting year.

(2) In any accounting year to which the free travel scheme applies it shall be the duty of London Regional Transport to grant, or (as the case may be) to exercise their control over any subsidiaries of theirs and their powers under Part I of this Act so as to secure that there are granted, the travel concessions for eligible London residents required by this section.

(3) In this section and sections 52 and 53 of this Act—

(*a*) references to eligible London residents are references to persons resident in Greater London who are eligible in accordance with section 50(7) of this Act to receive travel concessions under arrangements under subsection (1) of that section ;

(*b*) references to categories of such residents are references to the categories of persons so eligible mentioned in paragraphs (*a*), (*b*) and (*c*) of section 50(7) ;

(*c*) "travel concession permit" means, in relation to a travel concession under any such arrangements or under this section, a document in any form indicating that the person to whom it is issued is a person entitled in accordance with those arrangements or (as the case may be) under this section to receive the concession in question ;

(*d*) "relevant journey" means any journey of a description within section 50(4)(*a*), (*b*) or (*c*) of this Act; and

(*e*) references to any services under the control of London Regional Transport are references to any public passenger transport services provided by London Regional Transport or any subsidiary of theirs or by any other person in pursuance of any agreement entered into by London Regional Transport by virtue of section 3(2) of this Act.

(4) The travel concession required by this section in the case of all eligible London residents in the blind persons' category is the waiver, on production of a travel concession permit issued to any such resident under section 52 of this Act, of any fare otherwise payable by the person to whom it was issued for any relevant journey on a service under the control of London Regional Transport.

(5) The travel concession required by this section in the case of all eligible London residents in any other category is the waiver, on production of such a permit, of any fare otherwise payable by the person to whom it was issued for any such journey beginning—

(*a*) at any time on a Saturday or Sunday or on any day which is a bank holiday in England and Wales under the Banking and Financial Dealings Act 1971 ; or (*b*) in the daytime, evening or late-night period on any other day. PART III

(6) Subject to subsection (7) below, for the purposes of paragraph (*b*) of subsection (5) above—

(*a*) the daytime period is the period from 9.30 a.m. until 6.30 p.m. ;

(*b*) the evening period is the period from 6.30 p.m. until midnight ; and

(*c*) the late-night period is the period from midnight until 1.00 a.m.

(7) The daytime, evening or late-night period for the purposes of subsection (5)(*b*) above may be altered from time to time by London Regional Transport by notice published in such manner as they think fit, specifying the new period or periods and the effective date of the alteration.

(8) A notice under subsection (7) above may not specify an effective date for the alteration of a period to which it applies falling earlier than three months after the date of publication of the notice ; and before publishing any such notice London Regional Transport shall consult with all London authorities (within the meaning of section 50 of this Act) and with the Passengers' Committee.

52.—(1) The following provisions of this section apply for the purposes of the operation of the free travel scheme in relation to any accounting year of London Regional Transport to which the scheme applies (referred to below in this section as the relevant accounting year). Supplementary provisions with respect to the free travel scheme.

(2) As soon as the requirements for the application of the free travel scheme to the relevant accounting year are met, London Regional Transport shall notify all London borough councils and the Common Council (referred to below in this section as issuing authorities) that the scheme will apply to that accounting year.

(3) London Regional Transport shall from time to time supply to each issuing authority such travel concession permits as appear to London Regional Transport to be required by that authority for issue to eligible London residents in accordance with the following provisions of this section.

(4) Subject to subsection (5) below, an issuing authority shall issue a travel concession permit supplied by London Regional Transport under this section to any eligible London resident who applies for one and is resident in the area of that authority.

(5) The issue of such a permit by any issuing authority shall be subject to such terms, limitations or conditions as the authority

may, with the approval of the Secretary of State, from time to time determine as respects any category of eligible London residents.

(6) Before 1st February in the accounting year immediately preceding the relevant accounting year London Regional Transport shall give written notification to each issuing authority of the charge to be paid to them under this section by the issuing authority, for each quarter of the relevant accounting year, in respect of a travel concession permit issued under this section to an eligible London resident of each category which is valid on the first day of that quarter.

(7) The charges payable by issuing authorities under this section—

(a) shall be fixed by London Regional Transport with a view to securing that the costs of the operation of the free travel scheme are met from the proceeds of those charges (taking one accounting year to which the scheme applies with another, where the scheme applies to two or more consecutive accounting years) ; and

(b) may differ for different quarters of an accounting year.

(8) The reference in subsection (7)(a) above to the costs of the operation of the free travel scheme is a reference, in relation to any accounting year of London Regional Transport taken into account in fixing any charges under that subsection, to the aggregate of—

(a) the revenue by way of fares which London Regional Transport estimate they and any subsidiaries of theirs have lost or will lose in that year in consequence of the provision of free travel under the scheme ; and

(b) any other costs which London Regional Transport have incurred or estimate that they will incur in that year in connection with providing or for the purpose of securing the provision of free travel under the scheme (including any payments London Regional Transport have made or propose to make for that purpose to any person with whom they have entered into an agreement by virtue of section 3(2) of this Act).

(9) Before the end of the first month of each quarter of the relevant accounting year, each issuing authority shall—

(a) pay to London Regional Transport, in respect of each travel concession permit issued by that authority and valid on the first day of that quarter, the charge fixed by London Regional Transport under this section for that quarter which is applicable to that permit ;

(*b*) provide London Regional Transport with a written statement giving the particulars required by subsection (10) below with respect to the travel concession permits supplied to the authority by London Regional Transport under this section ; and

(*c*) if required to do so by London Regional Transport, return to London Regional Transport all such permits which have not been issued by the authority before the beginning of that quarter.

(10) The particulars required by this subsection in any statement under subsection (9)(*b*) above with respect to any quarter of the relevant accounting year are—

(*a*) the number of such permits issued to eligible London residents of each category which are valid on the first day of that quarter ;

(*b*) the number of such permits so issued (if any) which expired or were surrendered to the authority during the last preceding quarter ; and

(*c*) the number of such permits supplied for issue to eligible London residents of each category which have not been issued by the authority before the beginning of the quarter for which the statement is required.

(11) In the application of section 50(7)(*c*) of this Act for the purposes of the free travel scheme and this section, the reference to the opinion of the local authority or any of the local authorities there mentioned shall be read, in relation to persons resident in the area of an issuing authority, as a reference to the opinion of that authority.

(12) The annual report of London Regional Transport under section 34 of this Act with respect to the relevant accounting year shall contain a statement of—

(*a*) the manner in which the charges fixed under this section in respect of each quarter of that year were calculated ; and

(*b*) the aggregate of the amounts paid to London Regional Transport during that year by the issuing authorities under this section.

53.—(1) Arrangements under section 50(1) of this Act for travel concessions for London residents meet the requirements of this section as to scope if they provide for the grant of travel concessions to all eligible London residents on relevant journeys on all services under the control of London Regional Transport (subject to any terms, limitations or conditions with respect to the particular journeys on any such services on which any such

Requirements as to scope and uniformity of arrangements for travel concessions under section 50(1).

concession is available to eligible London residents of any category).

(2) Arrangements under section 50(1) of this Act for travel concessions for London residents meet the requirements of this section as to uniformity if they—

> (a) make the same provision, for all eligible London residents of the same category, with respect to the benefit of any travel concession granted to those residents under the arrangements and the periods during which it is available ;
>
> (b) make the enjoyment of the benefit of any travel concession granted under the arrangements conditional on the production, by any person seeking to travel under that concession, of a travel concession permit issued to him in accordance with the arrangements ; and
>
> (c) make the same provision with respect to the period of validity of all travel concession permits issued in accordance with the arrangements to eligible London residents of the same category ;

whether or not, in any other respects, the arrangements make different provision for different cases to which they apply.

(3) References in subsection (2) above to the benefit of a travel concession are references to the waiver or reduction of any fare or charge to which the arrangements in question apply, as distinct from any terms, limitations or conditions applicable to that waiver or reduction in accordance with the arrangements.

(4) Where individual arrangements under section 50(1) made between a particular local authority or local authorities and London Regional Transport apply to certain eligible London residents only, all arrangements so made shall be considered together for the purpose of determining whether subsections (1) and (2) above are satisfied.

Penalty fares

Penalty fares.   **54.**—(1) This section and the three next following sections have effect in relation to—

> (a) travel on a bus service to which this section applies ; and
>
> (b) travel on a train service to which this section applies ;

if an order under section 58 of this Act is for the time being in force with respect to the service in question.

(2) Subject to subsection (4) below, if at any time during his journey on any bus service to which this section applies on which fare tickets are issued in return for fares paid by persons travelling on that service a person so travelling fails, on being required

to do so by an authorised person, to produce any necessary fare ticket for his journey on that service, he shall be liable to pay a penalty fare in respect of that journey.

(3) Subject to subsection (4) below, if a person travels on any such bus service on which fare tickets are not so issued without paying the fare (if any) properly payable for his journey on that service, or for any part of his journey on that service, he shall be liable to pay a penalty fare in respect of that journey.

(4) A person shall not be liable to pay a penalty fare—

   (a) in a case within subsection (2) above, if he had no reasonable opportunity to obtain any necessary fare ticket before the time when he was required to produce such a ticket ;

   (b) in a case within subsection (3) above, if he had no reasonable opportunity to pay the fare in question before the time when he was found to have failed to pay it.

(5) Subject to subsection (6) below, if at any time during his journey on any train service to which this section applies a person travelling on that service fails, on being required to do so by an authorised person, to produce any necessary fare ticket for his journey on that service, he shall be liable to pay a penalty fare in respect of that journey.

(6) A person shall not be liable to pay a penalty fare by virtue of subsection (5) above if he had no reasonable opportunity to obtain any necessary fare ticket, or a deferred fare authority applicable to his journey or to any relevant part of his journey, at the time when he started to travel.

(7) A penalty fare payable by any person under this section in respect of any journey shall be an amount equal to—

   (a) the minimum penalty ; or

   (b) the default fare for the journey multiplied by the multiplier ;

whichever is the greater ; and any such penalty fare shall be payable to the person providing the service in question within the period of twenty-one days beginning with the day following the date on which the journey was completed.

(8) In subsection (7) above—

   (a) " the minimum penalty " means £5 or such other (lower or higher) sum as the Secretary of State may by order prescribe ; and

   (b) " the multiplier " means ten or such other (lower or higher) figure as the Secretary of State may by order prescribe.

(9) In any case within subsection (2) or (5) above the default fare for the journey mentioned in subsection (7)(*b*) above is—

> (*a*) where the whole of the distance travelled on that journey was not covered by any fare ticket produced by the person in question or by any deferred fare authority or other valid authority to travel, an amount equal to the full fare for the whole of that distance;
>
> (*b*) where any part (but not the whole) of the distance so travelled was not so covered, an amount equal to the full fare for that part of that distance;
>
> (*c*) where the whole or any part of the distance so travelled was covered by a fare ticket so produced showing payment of a fare appropriate in the case of another category of traveller but lower than the fare properly payable by the person in question for that journey or for the relevant part of that journey, an amount equal to the difference between the fare shown on the ticket and the full fare for that distance or (as the case may be) for that part of that distance; and
>
> (*d*) where both paragraphs (*b*) and (*c*) above apply, the aggregate of the amounts applicable under each of those paragraphs.

(10) In any case within subsection (3) above the default fare for the journey mentioned in subsection (7)(*b*) above is an amount determined by applying subsection (9) above, taking references (however expressed) to a fare ticket produced by the person in question and the fare shown on any such ticket as references to a fare paid by that person.

(11) In this section " full fare " means, in relation to the whole or any part of the distance travelled by any person on a journey on any bus or train service to which this section applies, the single ordinary fare payable by an adult for travelling on that service for that distance or (as the case may be) for that part of that distance on a journey corresponding to the one actually taken (but treated, where it covers part only of the distance travelled on that journey, and also where the whole of the distance so travelled formed part of a journey made partly by way of another service, as a separate journey).

(12) The liability of any person under this section to pay a penalty fare in respect of any journey is subject to section 57 of this Act.

55.—(1) Section 54 of this Act applies to any bus or train service provided by London Regional Transport or any subsidiary of theirs or by any other person in pursuance of any agreement entered into by London Regional Transport by virtue of section 3(2) of this Act which provides that that section is to apply to services provided in pursuance of that agreement.

(2) In this section and the three next following sections " the penalty fares provisions " means section 54, this section and the two next following sections.

(3) In the penalty fares provisions—

" authorised person " means a person authorised by the person providing the service in question ;

" authority to travel " means any ticket (other than a fare ticket), permit, voucher or other document authorising the person to whom it is issued to travel on any bus or train service to which section 54 applies, whether or not subject to any terms, limitations or conditions as to its use ;

" bus journey " means a journey on a bus service to which that section applies ;

" bus service " has the meaning given by section 43(7) of this Act ;

" deferred fare authority " means an authority to travel subject to a condition requiring payment of the fare applicable in the case of the person using that authority for the whole or any part of any journey on which it is used at the conclusion of that journey or otherwise as provided by any terms applicable to its use (whether or not it is also subject to any other terms, limitations or conditions) ;

" deferred fare " means the fare payable for a journey authorised by a deferred fare authority ;

" fare ticket " means a ticket showing payment of a fare for travelling on a bus or train journey and authorising the person to whom it is issued to travel on any such journey for the distance covered by that fare, whether or not subject to any terms, limitations or conditions as to its use ;

" train journey " means a journey on a train service to which section 54 of this Act applies ; and

" train service " means a service for the carriage of passengers by rail.

(4) References in the penalty fares provisions to the fare properly payable for a person's journey on any bus or train service to which section 54 applies are references to the fare so payable excluding any deferred fare for the journey ; that is to say, the fare payable by a person of the category to which he belongs for travelling on that service for the whole of the dis-

tance travelled on that journey, or for such part of the distance so travelled as is not covered by any deferred fare authority or other valid authority to travel that applies to his journey on the occasion in question.

This subsection applies in relation to references in those provisions to the fare properly payable for part of a person's journey as it applies to references to the fare properly payable for a person's journey.

(5) References in those provisions to any necessary fare ticket for a person's journey on any such bus or train service are references to a fare ticket required for his journey on the occasion in question which—

(*a*) applies to his journey on that occasion ; and

(*b*) shows payment of the fare properly payable for that journey.

(6) For the purposes of those provisions, no fare is properly payable for a bus journey and no fare ticket is required for a bus or train journey if the person travelling on that journey has a deferred fare authority or other valid authority to travel that applies to the whole of his journey on the occasion in question.

Supple-
mentary
provisions
with respect
to penalty
fares.

56.—(1) In any action for the recovery of a penalty fare payable under section 54 of this Act it shall be for the plaintiff to show that any relevant exception provided by subsection (4) or (6) of that section does not apply.

(2) It shall be the duty of London Regional Transport to secure that the requirements of the following provisions of this section with respect to warning notices are met in the case of every bus or train service to which section 54 applies.

(3) In the case of a bus service, a warning notice meeting the requirements of subsection (4) below shall be posted in every vehicle used in providing that service or, where any such vehicle has more than one deck, on each deck of that vehicle, in such a position as to be readily visible to persons travelling on the vehicle.

(4) A warning notice posted in pursuance of subsection (3) above shall state—

(*a*) in the case of a bus service within section 54(2) of this Act, that persons travelling on that service who cannot produce a ticket showing payment of the correct fare for their journey, or for any part of their journey not otherwise authorised, may be liable to a penalty fare ; and

(*b*) in the case of a bus service within subsection (3) of that section, that persons who travel on that service without paying the correct fare for their journey, or for any part of their journey not otherwise authorised, may be liable to a penalty fare.

(5) In the case of a train service, a warning notice meeting the requirements of subsection (6) below shall be posted—

　(a) in every station at which persons may start to travel on that service, in such a position as to be readily visible to prospective passengers ; and

　(b) in every carriage of every train used in providing that service.

(6) A warning notice posted in pursuance of subsection (5) above shall state that persons travelling on that service who cannot produce a ticket showing payment of the correct fare for their journey, or for any part of their journey not otherwise authorised, may be liable to a penalty fare.

(7) Every warning notice posted in pursuance of this section shall state the amount of the current minimum penalty (within the meaning of section 54(7) of this Act) and indicate that a penalty fare may be higher.

(8) Any order under subsection (8) of that section shall be subject to annulment in pursuance of a resolution of either House of Parliament.

57.—(1) Where a person has become liable under section 54 of this Act to pay a penalty fare in respect of any bus or train journey (" the relevant journey "), no proceedings may be brought against him for any of the offences specified in subsection (2) below before the end of the period mentioned in subsection (7) of that section ; and no such proceedings may be brought after the end of that period if either— *Exclusion of double liability.*

　(a) he has paid that fare to the person providing the service before the end of that period ; or

　(b) an action has been brought against him for the recovery of that fare.

(2) The offences mentioned in subsection (1) above are—

　(a) any offence under section 5(3)(a) or (b) of the Regulation of Railways Act 1889 (travelling without paying the correct fare with intent to avoid payment) arising from the relevant journey ; *1889 c. 57.*

　(b) any offence under byelaws made under section 67 of the 1962 Act (byelaws for railways, etc.) involving a failure to obtain or produce a fare ticket or authority to travel for the relevant journey ; and

　(c) any offence under section 25(3) of the Public Passenger Vehicles Act 1981 of contravening or failing to comply *1981 c. 14.*

with any provision of regulations for the time being having effect by virtue of that section by failing to pay the fare properly payable for the relevant journey or any part of it.

(3) If proceedings are brought against any such person for any such offence he shall cease to be liable to pay the penalty fare and, if he has paid it, the person to whom it was paid shall be liable to repay to him an amount equal to the amount of that fare.

Operation of
the penalty
fares
provisions.

58.—(1) The Secretary of State may by order provide that the penalty fares provisions shall have effect, as from such day as may be specified in the order, with repect to—

(*a*) bus services to which section 54 applies ; and

(*b*) train services to which that section applies ;

and different days may be specified under this section with respect to bus services and train services.

(2) Any such order is referred to below in this section as an order activating the penalty fares provisions.

(3) The revocation by the Secretary of State of an order activating the penalty fares provisions shall be without prejudice to the power of the Secretary of State to make further orders under this section activating those provisions.

(4) An order activating the penalty fares provisions may provide that any provision of a local Act specified in the order (being a provision which appears to the Secretary of State to be unnecessary having regard to the penalty fares provisions so far as they have effect by virtue of the order) shall be suspended while that order has effect ; and any such provision shall accordingly be treated, so long as that order has effect, as if it had been repealed.

(5) Without prejudice to subsection (4) above, any order activating the penalty fares provisions, and any order revoking any such order, may contain such supplementary, incidental and consequential provisions (including transitional provisions) as may appear to the Secretary of State to be necessary or expedient.

(6) No order activating the penalty fares provisions may be made except at the request of London Regional Transport.

Miscellaneous

Provision of
extra
transport
services and
facilities by
Railways
Board.

59. The council of a London borough and the Common Council shall each have power to enter into and carry out agreements with the Railways Board with respect to the provision or retention and financing of public passenger transport services and facilities which would not be available apart from any such agreement.

60.—(1) No direction may be given by the Greater London Council to the Executive under section 20(1) of the 1969 Act (power of Council to direct preparation of proposals for transfers of functions, etc.) after the passing of this Act.

(2) Where before the passing of this Act the Greater London Council have directed the Executive under section 20(1) to give effect to any proposals submitted to that Council in accordance with a previous direction under that provision, subsection (1) above is without prejudice to the duty of the Executive under section 41 of that Act to comply with that direction.

(3) During the period between the passing of this Act and the appointed day the Executive shall not make any alteration in the general level or structure of the fares to be charged for the time being for the carriage of passengers by the Executive or any subsidiary of theirs, unless their proposals for that alteration have been submitted to and approved by the Secretary of State.

61.—(1) Any approval or consent of the Secretary of State under any provision of this Act—

   (*a*) shall be given in writing ;

   (*b*) may be given for any case or description of cases specified in the approval or consent, or may be general ; and

   (*c*) may be given subject to conditions.

(2) Nothing done by London Regional Transport shall be unlawful on the ground that it was done without the approval or consent of the Secretary of State and that under this Act it required his approval or consent.

(3) If it appears to the Secretary of State that London Regional Transport propose to do anything, or have done anything, without the approval or consent of the Secretary of State which in his opinion requires his approval or consent under this Act, he may, after consultation with London Regional Transport, give to London Regional Transport such directions as appear to him to be appropriate.

(4) The directions which the Secretary of State may give under subsection (3) above in a case where London Regional Transport have already done anything without the Secretary of State's approval or consent may, in particular, require London Regional Transport to discontinue any activity or to dispose of any assets, and directions may be given to that effect notwithstanding that they make it necessary for London Regional Transport to dispose of assets at a loss or incur liability to other persons.

(5) Any direction given by the Secretary of State under this Act shall be in writing; and (without prejudice to section 10(4) of this Act) it shall be the duty of London Regional Transport or of any other person to whom the Secretary of State gives a direction under this Act to give effect to any such direction.

Joint
subsidiaries

62.—(1) Subsection (2) below applies to the following authorities, that is to say, London Regional Transport and the Railways Board.

(2) Where a company of which both those authorities are members would, if those authorities were a single body corporate, be a subsidiary of that body corporate, then, whether or not that company is apart from this subsection a subsidiary of one of those authorities, that company shall be treated for the purposes of this Act (subject to any express provision to the contrary) as a subsidiary of each of those authorities.

(3) Section 51(5) and (6) of the 1968 Act shall continue to apply to London Regional Transport and to have effect accordingly as if London Regional Transport were one of the Boards, but in the application of those provisions in relation to any company in any case where the authorities concerned include London Regional Transport—

    (*a*) subject to subsection (4) below, subsection (5) (joint wholly owned subsidiary of two or more authorities to be treated for purposes of 1962 Act and provisions of 1968 Act other than Parts V and VI as a wholly owned subsidiary of each authority) shall have effect as if the words " wholly owned " (in each place where they occur) were omitted; and

    (*b*) subsection (6) (duty of individual authority to control subsidiary superseded by joint duty in case of joint subsidiaries) shall have effect as if the reference to section 25(1) of the 1962 Act included a reference to sections 21 and 33 of this Act.

(4) Subsection (3)(*a*) above shall not affect the application of section 51(5) for the purpose of determining whether the company in question is to be treated for the purposes mentioned in section 51(5) as a wholly owned subsidiary of the authority or authorities concerned other than London Regional Transport.

Orders and
regulations.

63. Any power to make an order or regulations conferred on the Secretary of State by any provision of this Act shall be exercisable by statutory instrument.

Stamp duty.
1973 c. 51.

64.—(1) Stamp duty shall not be chargeable under section 47 of the Finance Act 1973 in respect of the formation by London Regional Transport of a company in pursuance of section 4 of this Act, if the formation of that company is certified by the Treasury—

    (*a*) as being effected in pursuance of section 4 ; and

    (*b*) as satisfying the requirements of subsection (5) below.

(2) Stamp duty shall not be so chargeable in respect of—

    (*a*) the formation of a company (otherwise than in pursuance of section 4 of this Act) ; or

    (*b*) any increase in the capital of a company ;

if the transaction concerned is certified by the Treasury as satisfying the requirements of subsections (3) to (5) below.

(3) A transaction satisfies the requirements of this subsection if it relates to a public transport company and—

    (*a*) in a case within subsection (2)(*a*) above, the company will on its formation be owned by London Regional Transport ; or

    (*b*) in a case within subsection (2)(*b*) above, the company is owned by London Regional Transport immediately before and immediately after the increase in its capital takes effect.

(4) A transaction satisfies the requirements of this subsection if it is effected solely for the purpose—

    (*a*) of facilitating such an eventual disposal as is mentioned in section 9(5) of this Act ; or

    (*b*) of complying with a direction given by the Secretary of State under section 10(1) of this Act.

(5) A transaction satisfies the requirements of this subsection if it is entered into solely in connection with a relevant transfer, takes place on or before the transfer date and does not give rise to an excess of capital.

In this subsection, " relevant transfer " means—

    (*a*) in a case within subsection (1) above, a transfer to be effected in pursuance of a scheme made under section 4 of this Act ;

    (*b*) in a case within subsection (2) above, a transfer to be effected in pursuance of a scheme made under section 9(6) of this Act.

(6) For the purposes of subsection (5) above a transaction gives rise to an excess of capital if—

    (*a*) in a case within subsection (1) or (2)(*a*) above, the total issued capital of the company exceeds, on the transfer date, the total value of the assets less liabilities transferred ; or

    (*b*) in a case within subsection (2)(*b*) above, the aggregate amount of the increase in issued capital of the company exceeds, on that date, that total value ;

D

PART III

and in this subsection " issued capital " means issued share capital or loan capital.

(7) Stamp duty shall not be chargeable on any instrument which is certified to the Commissioners of Inland Revenue by London Regional Transport as having been made or executed in pursuance of Schedule 4 to the 1968 Act as it applies—

(*a*) by virtue of section 27 of this Act to a transfer in pursuance of a scheme made under section 4 of this Act or to a transfer made in pursuance of a scheme made under section 9(6) of this Act in compliance with a direction given by the Secretary of State under section 10 of this Act ; or

(*b*) by virtue of section 47 of this Act to a transfer in pursuance of an order made by the Secretary of State under that section ;

1891 c. 39.

but no such instrument shall be treated as duly stamped unless it is stamped with the duty to which it would but for this subsection be liable or it has, in accordance with the provisions of section 12 of the Stamp Act 1891, been stamped with a particular stamp denoting that it is not chargeable with any duty or that it is duly stamped.

(8) For the purposes of subsection (3) above—

(*a*) " public transport company " means a company whose objects include the provision of public passenger transport services ; and

(*b*) a company is to be treated as owned by London Regional Transport at any time when more than half in nominal value of that company's issued share capital is held by London Regional Transport or by nominees on their behalf.

Inquiries by Secretary of State.

1919 c. 50.

65. The Secretary of State may hold inquiries for the purposes of his powers under this Act as if those purposes were purposes of the Ministry of Transport Act 1919, and section 20 of that Act shall apply accordingly.

Construction of powers of London Regional Transport.

66.—(1) Each of the powers conferred on London Regional Transport by the provisions of this Act is in addition to, and not in derogation of, any other power conferred on London Regional Transport by this Act or by any other enactment.

(2) It is declared that the provisions of this Act conferring powers on London Regional Transport relate only to the capacity of London Regional Transport as a statutory corporation and nothing in those provisions is to be read as authorising the disregard by London Regional Transport of any enactment or rule of law.

67.—(1) Without prejudice to the effect of any other provision PART III
of this Act in relation to any functions exercisable before the General
coming into operation of the 1969 Act by the London Board, provision
the functions transferred to the Executive or (as the case may be) with respect
to the designated company (within the meaning of that Act) by to former
or under section 17 of or Schedule 3 to that Act (the London London
Board's statutory functions) continue to be exercisable (subject functions.
to the provisions of this Act) by London Regional Transport or
(as the case may be) by that company.

(2) Without prejudice to subsection (1) above, Schedule 4 to
this Act has effect for the purpose of replacing (with certain
modifications) the provisions of Schedule 3 to the 1969 Act
(so far as not spent, irrelevant to the operations of London
Regional Transport or superseded by any other provisions of this
Act) with provisions referring to London Regional Transport
or (as the case may be) to London Regional Transport and
any subsidiary of theirs.

(3) Schedule 4 to this Act also has effect for the purpose of
substituting, for references to the Executive in enactments relating to the functions mentioned in subsection (1) above contained
in Acts passed after the passing of the 1969 Act, references to
London Regional Transport or (as the case may be) to London
Regional Transport and any subsidiary of theirs.

68. In this Act— Interpretation.

" the 1962 Act " means the Transport Act 1962 ; 1962 c. 46.

" the 1968 Act " means the Transport Act 1968 ; 1968 c. 73.

" the 1969 Act " means the Transport (London) Act 1969 ; 1969 c. 35.

" accounting year " means, subject to paragraph 1 of Schedule 5 to this Act, a period of twelve months beginning with 1st April ;

" the appointed day " has the meaning given by section
1(4) of this Act ;

" the Boards " (unless the context otherwise requires) means
the Boards established under section 1 of the 1962 Act
other than the London Board, and references to a Board
shall be construed accordingly ;

" the Bus Company " means the National Bus Company
established under section 24 of the 1968 Act ;

" charges " includes fares, rates, tolls and dues of every
description ;

" the Common Council " means the Common Council of the
City of London ;

" the Executive " means the London Transport Executive
established under section 4 of the 1969 Act ;

D 2

" functions " includes powers, duties and obligations;

" goods " includes animals, parcels and mails;

" Greater London " means the administrative area of Greater London as for the time being constituted;

" hovercraft " has the same meaning as in the Hovercraft Act 1968;

" land " includes buildings and other structures, land covered by water and any interest or right in, over or under land;

" liability " includes an obligation;

" the London Board " means the London Transport Board established under section 1 of the 1962 Act;

" London bus service " has the meaning given by section 43(7) of this Act;

" the London Regional Transport group " has the meaning given by section 22(3) of this Act;

" participant ", in relation to a pension scheme, means—

> (a) in relation to a scheme under which benefits are or will be receivable as of right, a person who has pension rights under the scheme (whether he has contributed or not); and

> (b) in relation to a scheme under which benefits are not or will not be receivable as of right, a person who (whether he is referred to in the scheme as a member, contributor or otherwise) has contributed under the scheme and has pension rights under it;

and " participate " and " eligible to participate " shall be construed accordingly;

" Passengers' Committee " means the body established under section 40 of this Act;

" pension ", in relation to a person, means a pension, whether contributory or not, of any kind whatsoever payable to or in respect of him, and includes a gratuity so payable and a return of contributions to a pension fund, with or without interest on or any other addition to those contributions, and any sums payable on or in respect of the death of that person;

" pension fund " means a fund established for the purposes of paying pensions;

" pension rights " includes, in relation to any person, all forms of right to or liability for the present or future payment of a pension, and any expectation of the accruer of a pension under any customary practice, and includes a right of allocation in respect of present or future payment of a pension:

" pension scheme " includes any form of arrangement for the payment of pensions, whether subsisting by virtue of an Act of Parliament, trust, contract or otherwise ;

" public service vehicle " has the same meaning as in the Public Passenger Vehicles Act 1981 ;

" the Railways Board " means the British Railways Board established under section 1 of the 1962 Act ;

" related company " has the meaning given by section 11(2) of this Act ;

" road service licence " has the same meaning as in the Public Passenger Vehicles Act 1981 ;

" securities ", in relation to a body corporate, means any shares, stock, debentures, debenture stock and any other security of a like nature of a body corporate ;

" statutory provision " means a provision, whether of a general or of a special nature, contained in, or in any document made or issued under, any Act, whether of a general or special nature ;

" subsidiary " (subject to section 62 of this Act) means, in relation to any body corporate, a body corporate which is a subsidiary of the first-mentioned body corporate as defined by section 154 of the Companies Act 1948 (taking references in that section to a company as being references to a body corporate) ;

" vehicle " includes a hovercraft ; and

" wholly owned subsidiary " means a subsidiary all the securities of which are owned by a body of which it is a subsidiary, or by one or more other wholly owned subsidiaries of that body, or partly by that body and partly by any wholly owned subsidiary of that body.

69. There shall be paid out of money provided by Parliament— Expenses.

(*a*) any expenses incurred by the Secretary of State under or in consequence of the provisions of this Act ;

(*b*) any increase attributable to any of the provisions of this Act in the sums so payable under any other Act.

70.—(1) Subject to the following provisions of this section, Initial the chairman and any other person who is a member of membership the Executive immediately before the appointed day shall con- Regional tinue in office in accordance with the terms of their appointment Transport. (taking references in those terms to the Greater London Council as references to the Secretary of State) and be treated for the purposes of Schedule 1 to this Act as if appointed by the Secretary of State in pursuance of the provisions of that Schedule.

(2) At any time during the period of three months beginning with the appointed day the Secretary of State may remove any

PART III

such person from office, without notice and without assigning cause.

(3) If a person ceases to be a member of London Regional Transport, otherwise than on the expiration of his term of office, at any time within the period mentioned in subsection (2) above, London Regional Transport shall pay to that person compensation of such amount, and on such terms, as the Secretary of State may, with the approval of the Treasury, determine.

(4) The Secretary of State shall remove a member of London Regional Transport from office in pursuance of this section in the manner provided by paragraph 7(4) of Schedule 1 to this Act.

Further transitional provisions, savings, amendments and repeals.

71.—(1) If an order has been made under section 36(1) of this Act specifying a day for the application of sections 37 and 38 of this Act and either—

> (a) the period of eight years mentioned in subsection (5) of section 36 has expired without the order having been confirmed by order made under that subsection; or
>
> (b) before the expiry of that period a further order has been made under subsection (1) of that section for the purpose of revoking the order;

the Secretary of State may by order make such transitional and consequential provision (including provision modifying any enactment contained in this or any other Act) as appears to him to be necessary or desirable in consequence of the expiry of Part II of this Act by virtue of section 39(b) of this Act.

(2) The transitional provisions and savings in Schedule 5 to this Act shall have effect.

(3) Subject to those transitional provisions and savings—

> (a) the enactments mentioned in Schedule 6 to this Act shall have effect subject to the amendments specified in that Schedule, being minor amendments and amendments consequential on the provisions of this Act; and
>
> (b) the enactments mentioned in Schedule 7 to this Act (which include enactments which were spent or of no practical utility at the passing of this Act) are repealed to the extent specified in the third column of that Schedule.

(4) For any reference in any statutory provision (other than one specifically amended by any provision of this Act) to the Executive there shall be substituted a reference to London Regional Transport.

(5) Subsection (4) above—

> (a) applies to any reference, however worded, whether express or implied, and including a reference made

by means of a general reference to a class of persons
of which the Executive are one, without the Executive
themselves being specifically referred to ; and

(b) is without prejudice to the effect in relation to London
Regional Transport of any provision of any agreement
or of any provision of any other document (not being
a statutory provision) which refers (in whatever words
and whether expressly or by implication) to the Executive.

(6) No statutory provision excluded by section 24(4) of the
1962 Act from applying to any of the Boards (statutory provisions
relating to accounts, statistics and returns to be kept by railway
companies, etc.) shall apply to London Regional Transport or
any subsidiary of theirs.

(7) Any order under subsection (1) above shall be subject to
annulment in pursuance of a resolution of either House of
Parliament.

72.—(1) This Act may be cited as the London Regional
Transport Act 1984.

*Short title,
commence-
ment and
extent.*

(2) Subject to the following provisions of this section, this Act
shall come into force on the appointed day.

(3) The following provisions of this Act, that is to say—

(a) this section ;

(b) sections 60, 68, 69 and 71(2) (so far as that subsection
relates to the provisions of Schedule 5 mentioned in
paragraph (c) below) ; and

(c) in Schedule 5, paragraph 7 and sub-paragraphs (1) to (5),
(9) and (10)(a) of paragraph 8 ;

shall come into force on the passing of this Act.

(4) Without prejudice to section 13 of the Interpretation Act
1978, section 40(1) to (3) and (12) of, and Schedule 3 to, this Act
shall come into force on the passing of this Act for the purpose
of enabling the Passengers' Committee to exercise and perform
their functions with full effect as from the appointed day.

1978 c. 30.

(5) Section 45 of this Act shall come into force at the end of
the period of two months beginning with the day on which this
Act is passed.

(6) The repeals made by this Act in Schedule 2 to the London
Government Act 1963 (and the related repeal of paragraph 9
of Schedule 13 to the Local Government, Planning and Land
Act 1980) shall come into force on 1st April 1985.

1963 c. 33.

1980 c. 65.

(7) This Act, except—

(a) paragraph 8 of Schedule 1 ; and

(b) paragraph 13 of Schedule 3 ;

does not extend to Scotland or to Northern Ireland.

D 4

SCHEDULES

SCHEDULE 1

CONSTITUTION AND PROCEEDINGS OF LONDON REGIONAL TRANSPORT

Preliminary

1. References below in this Schedule to the Corporation are references to London Regional Transport.

Constitution

2.—(1) The Corporation shall consist of—

   (*a*) a chairman appointed by the Secretary of State ; and

   (*b*) not less than four nor more than eleven other members appointed by the Secretary of State after consultation with the chairman of the Corporation.

(2) The Secretary of State may, after consultation with the chairman of the Corporation, appoint a member of the Corporation to be deputy chairman of the Corporation.

Status

3. The Corporation shall not be regarded as the servant or agent of the Crown, or as enjoying any status, immunity or privilege of the Crown, or (subject to any express provision of this Act) as exempt from any tax, duty, rate, levy or other charge whatsoever, whether general or local ; and the Corporation's property shall not be regarded as property of, or property held on behalf of, the Crown.

Members

4.—(1) The chairman and other members of the Corporation shall be appointed by the Secretary of State from among persons who appear to him to have had wide experience of, and shown capability in, transport, industrial, commercial or financial matters, administration, applied science, or the organisation of workers.

(2) A member of the Corporation shall hold and vacate his office in accordance with the terms of his appointment and shall, on ceasing to be a member, be eligible for re-appointment.

(3) A member may at any time by notice in writing to the Secretary of State resign his office.

5.—(1) Before appointing a person to be a member of the Corporation the Secretary of State shall satisfy himself that that person will have no such financial or other interest as is likely to affect prejudicially the exercise and performance by him of his functions as a member of the Corporation, and the Secretary of State shall also satisfy himself from time to time with respect to every member of the Corporation that he has no such interest ; and a person who is, or whom the Secretary of State proposes to appoint to be, a member of the Corporation shall, whenever requested by the Secretary of State so to do, furnish to him such information as the Secretary of State considers necessary for the performance by the Secretary of State of his duties under this paragraph.

(2) A member of the Corporation who is in any way directly or indirectly interested in a contract made or proposed to be made by the Corporation, or in a contract made or proposed to be made by a subsidiary of the Corporation which is brought up for consideration by the Corporation, shall disclose the nature of his interest at a meeting of the Corporation ; and the disclosure shall be recorded in the minutes of the Corporation, and the member shall not take any part in any deliberation or decision of the Corporation with respect to that contract.

(3) For the purposes of sub-paragraph (2) above, a general notice given at a meeting of the Corporation by a member of the Corporation to the effect that he is a member of a specified company or firm and is to be regarded as interested in any contract which may, after the date of the notice, be made with the company or firm shall be regarded as a sufficient disclosure of his interest in relation to any contract so made or proposed to be so made.

(4) A member of the Corporation need not attend in person at a meeting of the Corporation in order to make a disclosure which he is required to make under this paragraph if he takes reasonable steps to secure that the disclosure is made by a notice which is brought up and read at the meeting.

6.—(1) The Corporation—
  (a) shall pay to the members of the Corporation such salaries or fees, and such allowances, as the Secretary of State may determine ; and
  (b) as regards any member in whose case the Secretary of State may so determine, shall pay such pension, allowance or gratuity to or in rspect of him or make such payments towards the provision of such a pension, allowance or gratuity as may be so determined ;

and, if a person ceases to be a member of the Corporation and it appears to the Secretary of State that there are special circumstances which make it right that that person should receive compensation, the Secretary of State may require the Corporation to pay to that person a sum of such amount as the Secretary of State may determine.

(2) The Secretary of State may not make a determination or impose a requirement under this paragraph without the approval of the Treasury.

(3) So much of sub-paragraph (1) above as requires that the pensions (if any) which are to be paid in the case of members of London Regional Transport are to be determined by the Secretary of State shall not apply in relation to any pension payable apart from the provisions of that sub-paragraph.

7.—(1) If the Secretary of State is satisfied that a member of the Corporation—

(*a*) has been absent from meetings of the Corporation for a period longer than three consecutive months without the permission of the Corporation ; or

(*b*) has become bankrupt or made an arrangement with his creditors ; or

(*c*) is incapacitated by physical or mental illness ; or

(*d*) is otherwise unable or unfit to discharge the functions of a member ;

he may remove that member from office.

(2) The terms of appointment of a member of the Corporation may provide for his removal from office (without assigning cause) on notice from the Secretary of State of such length as may be specified in those terms, subject (if those terms so provide) to compensation from the Corporation ; and in any such case the Secretary of State may remove that member from office in accordance with those terms.

(3) Where a member whose terms of appointment provide for compensation on his removal from office in pursuance of sub-paragraph (2) above is removed from office in pursuance of that sub-paragraph, the Corporation shall pay to him compensation of such amount, and on such terms, as the Secretary of State may with the approval of the Treasury determine.

(4) The Secretary of State shall remove a member of the Corporation from office in pursuance of this paragraph by declaring his office as a member of the Corporation to be vacant and notifying that fact in such manner as the Secretary of State thinks fit ; and thereupon the office shall become vacant.

8. Part II of Schedule 1 to the House of Commons Disqualification Act 1975 (which specifies certain commissions, tribunals and other bodies all members of which are disqualified under that Act) shall be amended by inserting the words " London Regional Transport " at the appropriate place in alphabetical order.

Proceedings

9. The validity of any proceedings of the Corporation shall not be affected by a vacancy amongst the members of the Corporation or by a defect in the appointment of a member.

10. The quorum of the Corporation shall be three ; and, while a member is disqualified from taking part in a decision or deliberation of the Corporation with respect to a matter, he shall be disregarded for the purpose of constituting a quorum of the Corporation for deciding, or deliberating on, that matter.

11. Subject to the preceding provisions of this Schedule, the Corporation shall have power to regulate their own procedure.

Staff

12. The Corporation shall appoint a secretary of the Corporation and may appoint such other employees as they may determine.

Application of seal and proof of instruments

13. The application of the seal of the Corporation shall be authenticated by the signature of the secretary of the Corporation or of some other person authorised, either generally or specially, by the Corporation to act for that purpose.

14. A certificate signed by the secretary of the Corporation that an instrument purporting to be made or issued by or on behalf of the Corporation was so made or issued shall be conclusive evidence of that fact.

15. Every document purporting to be an instrument made or issued by or on behalf of the Corporation and to be duly executed under the seal of the Corporation, or to be signed or executed by the secretary of the Corporation or a person authorised by the Corporation to act in that behalf shall be received in evidence and be treated, without further proof, as being so made or issued unless the contrary is shown.

SCHEDULE 2

OPERATING POWERS OF LONDON REGIONAL TRANSPORT

Carriage and storage

1.—(1) London Regional Transport may carry passengers by any form of land or water transport (including in either case hovercraft) within, to or from Greater London.

(2) London Regional Transport may carry passengers as mentioned in sub-paragraph (1) above between places outside Greater London, in so far as they consider it requisite to do so—

  (*a*) in connection with the exercise of their powers under that sub-paragraph ; or

  (*b*) in order to avoid an interruption of services provided by the Executive before the appointed day in exercise of their powers under section 6(1)(*b*)(ii) of the 1969 Act (provision of services outside Greater London to avoid interruption of services formerly provided by the London Board).

(3) London Regional Transport may also carry luggage and other goods, but only in any vehicle or vessel used for the carriage of passengers in pursuance of sub-paragraph (1) or (2) above or in another vehicle drawn by or with, or propelled with, any vehicle so used.

2.—(1) London Regional Transport may enter into arrangements with any person providing passenger transport services by air for the provision of such services between places in Greater London or between such places and places outside Greater London.

(2) Without prejudice to their powers under section 3 of this Act, London Regional Transport may enter into arrangements with any person operating a business of providing passenger vehicles for hire (whether with or without the services of a driver, and whether under private hire arrangements or by way of plying for public hire), for that person to make passenger vehicles operated by him available for hire, or for use in accordance with the arrangements, on such terms and in such manner as may be provided for by the arrangements, in or between places in Greater London or between such places and places outside Greater London.

(3) Any arrangements under this paragraph may include provision for the making of payments by London Regional Transport to the other party to the arrangements.

3. London Regional Transport may store within Greater London or in any premises of theirs outside Greater London goods which have been or are to be carried by London Regional Transport or a subsidiary of theirs and, so far as any premises provided for the purposes of that or any other part of their business are not required for those purposes, may use those premises to provide facilities for the storage of other goods.

Incidental amenities and facilities

4. London Regional Transport may provide amenities or facilities, and construct works, for the purpose of making those amenities, facilities or works available for the use of any other person in pursuance of any agreement under section 3(6) or (7) of this Act.

5.—(1) In places where those using the services and facilities provided by London Regional Transport or any of their subsidiaries may require them, London Regional Transport may provide both for them and for other persons facilities for the purchase and consumption of food and drink, places for refreshment and such other amenities and facilities as appear to London Regional Transport appropriate.

(2) Without prejudice to their powers under sub-paragraph (1) above, London Regional Transport may provide car parks and amenities or facilities for persons using them at any place convenient for prospective users of—

    (*a*) any services or facilities provided at another place by them, by any of their subsidiaries, or by any other person in pursuance of any agreement entered into by London Regional Transport by virtue of section 3(2) of this Act ; or

    (*b*) any other London passenger services or London connecting services.

(3) London Regional Transport may provide facilities for the parking or keeping of any public service vehicles used in the provision of any London passenger service or London connecting service at any place convenient for persons providing any such service.

(4) In this paragraph—

" London passenger service " means any service for the carriage of passengers within, to or from Greater London (whether or not provided by London Regional Transport, by any subsidiary of theirs, or by any such other person as is mentioned in sub-paragraph (2)(*a*) above) ; and

" London connecting service " means any service for the carriage of passengers to or from any place outside Greater London but convenient for prospective users of London passenger services or for persons seeking to transfer from London passenger services to services for the carriage of passengers to destinations further afield (including destinations outside the United Kingdom).

6.—(1) Where by virtue of any provision of paragraph 4 or 5 above London Regional Transport have power to provide any amenities or facilities (including any amenities or facilities of a particular description specifically mentioned in any such provision), they may enter into arrangements for the provision (including the management or operation) or (as the case may be) for the management or operation of any such amenities or facilities by any other person.

(2) Any arrangements under this paragraph may include provision for the making of payments by London Regional Transport to, or, with the consent of the Secretary of State, for the giving of guarantees or any other financial assistance by London Regional Transport for the benefit of, the other party to the arrangements.

(3) References in this Act to amenities or facilities provided by London Regional Transport include amenities or facilities provided, or managed or operated, by any other person in pursuance of arrangements under this paragraph.

Charges for services and facilities

7.—(1) London Regional Transport may make (or waive) such charges for their services and facilities, and make the use of those services and facilities subject to such terms and conditions, as they think fit.

(2) London Regional Transport's power under sub-paragraph (1) above is subject only to the provisions of this Act and to any local enactment so far as that local enactment expressly provides for freedom from charges or otherwise prohibits the making of any charge (as distinct from limiting the discretion of persons carrying on any particular undertaking as to the charges of any description to be made by them).

(3) Neither London Regional Transport nor any subsidiary of theirs shall be regarded as a common carrier by rail or inland waterway.

(4) No local enactment passed or made with respect to any particular undertaking so far as it imposes on persons carrying on that undertaking—

    (*a*) a duty to connect, or afford facilities for the connection of, any siding to a railway ; or

(b) a duty to permit privately owned railway wagons to be used on a railway owned or operated by them ; or

(c) a duty (otherwise than to a named person, or to the successor of a named person, or for the benefit of specified lands) to provide or maintain any other railway services or facilities (including the provision of stations, sidings or carriages and of any services, facilities or amenities connected with stations, sidings or carriages) ;

or so far as it otherwise makes provision corresponding to any of the repealed enactments, shall apply to London Regional Transport.

(5) The reference in sub-paragraph (4) above to the repealed enactments is a reference to the following enactments, that is to say—

1845 c. 20.   section 76 of the Railways Clauses Consolidation Act 1845 ;

1845 c. 33.   section 69 of the Railways Clauses Consolidation (Scotland) Act 1845 ;

1854 c. 31.   sections 2 and 7 of the Railway and Canal Traffic Act 1854 ;

1921 c. 55.   sections 16 and 39 of the Railways Act 1921 ;

1933 c. 14.   section 30 of the London Passenger Transport Act 1933 ;

1933 c. 53.   section 39 of the Road and Rail Traffic Act 1933 ; and

1953 c. 13.   section 22 of the Transport Act 1953 ;

all of which made provision with respect to transport charges and facilities and were repealed by the 1962 Act.

Other activities

8.—(1) London Regional Transport may develop their land in such manner as they think fit.

(2) London Regional Transport may in particular—

(a) develop for use by other persons land belonging to them which is not required for the purposes of their business ; and

(b) where the use of their land for the purposes of their business can be combined with its use by other persons, develop the land by constructing or adapting buildings on it for use wholly or partly by other persons ;

with a view to the disposal of any right or interest in the land or (as the case may be) the buildings or any part of the buildings, after the development is carried out.

(3) London Regional Transport shall not incur any substantial item of expenditure in developing their land for use for purposes which are not the purposes of their business without the consent of the Secretary of State ; and the Secretary of State may from time to time give directions to London Regional Transport indicating what is to be treated for the purposes of this paragraph as a substantial item of expenditure.

(4) Subject to sub-paragraph (5) below, where London Regional Transport propose under this paragraph to develop any land for

use otherwise than for the purposes of their business they may, with the consent of the Secretary of State, acquire by agreement adjoining land for the purpose of developing it together with the other land.

(5) The consent of the Secretary of State is not required to a proposal by London Regional Transport to acquire land in exercise of the power under sub-paragraph (4) above in any case where the Secretary of State has under sub-paragraph (3) above consented to the incurring by London Regional Transport of a substantial item of expenditure in developing their land as mentioned in sub-paragraph (3) which includes expenditure in carrying out that proposal.

9.—(1) London Regional Transport may manufacture and repair any spare parts and components or other supplementary machinery or equipment required for the purpose of the operation or repair of any existing vehicles or other equipment of theirs or of any subsidiary of theirs.

(2) London Regional Transport may repair any vehicles or other equipment, whether owned by them or any subsidiary of theirs or by any other person, and for the purpose of repairing any vehicle or equipment not belonging to them may supply any necessary parts and components for that vehicle or equipment.

(3) The exercise of any of London Regional Transport's powers under sub-paragraphs (1) and (2) above is subject to any directions given by the Secretary of State ; and, in addition, London Regional Transport shall from time to time submit to the Secretary of State for his approval proposals as to the manner in which—

(a) any activities of manufacture authorised by sub-paragraph (1) above ; or

(b) any activities authorised by sub-paragraph (2) above, so far as relates to repair of vehicles or equipment not belonging to them or any subsidiary of theirs ;

are to be carried on by them or any such subsidiary, and shall carry on or (as the case may be) exercise their control over that subsidiary so as to ensure that the subsidiary carries on, those activities in accordance with the approval of the Secretary of State.

(4) The Secretary of State may approve any proposals submitted to him by London Regional Transport under sub-paragraph (3) above with such modifications or subject to compliance with such conditions as he thinks fit.

(5) The Secretary of State may at any time, after consultation with London Regional Transport, direct London Regional Transport to discontinue or (as the case may be) to exercise their control over any of their subsidiaries so as to require the subsidiary to discontinue, any of the activities which London Regional Transport or the subsidiary are carrying on in accordance with the approval of the Secretary of State given under this paragraph.

(6) In this paragraph—

(*a*) references to manufacture include references to construction and production ; and

(*b*) references to repair include references to maintenance.

10. London Regional Transport may let passenger vehicles on hire with or without other vehicles drawn by or with, or propelled with, those passenger vehicles for the carriage of goods.

11.—(1) London Regional Transport may do anything which appears to them to be practicable and desirable for the purpose of promoting—

(*a*) research on lines settled from time to time with the approval of the Secretary of State into matters affecting, or arising out of, the exercise of the functions of London Regional Transport or any subsidiary of theirs ; and

(*b*) the exploitation of the results of any research into any such matter (whether or not promoted by London Regional Transport) and of anything resulting from any idea affecting, or arising out of, the exercise of any of those functions.

In paragraph (*b*) above " exploitation " means the doing of any work requisite to enable the results or (as the case may be) the thing in question to be turned to account.

(2) London Regional Transport may exercise their powers under sub-paragraph (1) above by carrying out any research or work for that purpose themselves or by arranging for it to be carried out or done by some other person with or without assistance (including financial assistance) from London Regional Transport.

(3) Nothing in this paragraph authorises London Regional Transport to do themselves, either directly or through a subsidiary, any work which London Regional Transport would not have power to do apart from this paragraph.

12.—(1) London Regional Transport may provide for any person technical advice or assistance, including research services, as respects any matter in which London Regional Transport have skill or experience.

(2) London Regional Transport may, on the request of any person for whom they are providing advice or assistance under sub-paragraph (1) above, establish for that person an undertaking carrying on any business in which London Regional Transport have skill or experience and manage it on his behalf.

13.—(1) In this paragraph—

(*a*) " relevant passenger service " means any London passenger service or London connecting service within the meaning of paragraph 5 above which is provided by any form of land or water transport (including, in either case, hovercraft) ; and (*b*) " independent service " means any relevant passenger service provided otherwise than by London Regional Transport or the Railways Board or by any subsidiary of either of those authorities.

(2) London Regional Transport may—

(*a*) provide information, in such manner and form as they think fit, with respect to any relevant passenger services ; and

(*b*) make such charges as they think fit with respect to the provision by them of information with respect to any independent services.

(3) London Regional Transport may enter into arrangements with any person providing independent services for the reciprocal provision, on such terms as may be provided for by the arrangements, of ancillary services by each party to the arrangements in respect of any relevant passenger services provided by the other.

(4) In sub-paragraph (3) above, " ancillary services " means, in relation to any relevant passenger services, the sale of tickets for the carriage of passengers on those services and the reservation of seats in vehicles used in the provision of those services.

Acquisition of land

14.—(1) Subject to paragraph 16 below, London Regional Transport may acquire land for the purposes of their business (including the rehousing of the occupiers of dwellings acquired or to be acquired by London Regional Transport).

(2) Where London Regional Transport propose to dispose of any of their land they may acquire by agreement adjoining land for the purpose of disposing of it together with the other land.

(3) London Regional Transport shall not incur any substantial item of expenditure under sub-paragraph (2) above without the consent of the Secretary of State ; and the Secretary of State may from time to time give directions to London Regional Transport indicating what is to be treated for the purposes of this paragraph as a substantial item of expenditure.

15.—(1) Subject to the following provisions of this paragraph and paragraph 16 below, the Secretary of State may authorise London Regional Transport to purchase compulsorily any land which they require for the purposes of their business or that of any subsidiary of theirs.

(2) The Acquisition of Land Act 1981 shall apply to any compulsory purchase by virtue of sub-paragraph (1) above.   1981 c. 67.

(3) Activities carried on by London Regional Transport by virtue of paragraph 12 above shall not be treated as forming part of the business of London Regional Transport for the purposes of sub-paragraph (1) above.

SCH. 2

(4) This paragraph does not authorise London Regional Transport to purchase compulsorily land which they have power to acquire by agreement under paragraph 8(4) or 14(2) above.

(5) Subject to sub-paragraph (6) below, the power of purchasing land compulsorily in this paragraph includes power to acquire an easement or other right over land by the creation of a new right.

(6) Sub-paragraph (5) above does not apply to an easement or other right over land which forms part of a common, open space or fuel or field garden allotment within the meaning of section 19 of the Acquisition of Land Act 1981.

1981 c. 67.

16. Except as provided by paragraph 8(4) or 14(2) above, London Regional Transport do not have power to acquire land for purposes which are not related to any of the activities of London Regional Transport or any of their subsidiaries other than the development of land.

Welfare and efficiency of employees

17.—(1) London Regional Transport may do anything they think fit for the purpose of advancing—

(a) the skill of persons employed by them or by any subsidiary of theirs ;

(b) the efficiency of the equipment of London Regional Transport or of any subsidiary of theirs or of the manner in which that equipment is operated ;

including providing, or assisting others in providing, facilities for training, education and research.

(2) London Regional Transport may provide houses, hostels and other similar accommodation for persons employed by them or by any subsidiary of theirs.

(3) London Regional Transport may make housing loans to persons employed by them or by any subsidiary of theirs to assist them to acquire housing accommodation and may guarantee loans made by building societies and other bodies to such persons for housing purposes.

Power to promote and oppose Bills

18. London Regional Transport may, with the consent of the Secretary of State, promote Bills in Parliament and may oppose any Bill in Parliament.

Other powers

19. London Regional Transport may do anything necessary for the purpose of fulfilling a contract to which the Executive was a party immediately before the appointed day, notwithstanding that apart from this paragraph London Regional Transport would not have power to do that thing.

20. London Regional Transport may acquire any undertaking or part of an undertaking if the assets comprised in the undertaking or the part of the undertaking are wholly or mainly assets which London Regional Transport require for the purposes of their business.

21. For the purposes of their business, London Regional Transport may, with the consent of the Secretary of State, subscribe for or acquire any securities of a body corporate.

22.—(1) London Regional Transport may dispose (whether absolutely or for a term of years) of any part of their undertaking or any property which in their opinion is not required by them for the purposes of their business and, in particular, may dispose of any interest in, or right over, any property which, subject to that interest or right, is retained by London Regional Transport.

(2) London Regional Transport may supply to any person spare parts and components for passenger road vehicles disposed of by London Regional Transport in the exercise of their powers under sub-paragraph (1) above, or by a subsidiary of London Regional Transport, as being no longer required for the purposes of their business.

23. London Regional Transport may—

   (a) invest any sums not immediately required for the purposes of their business ; and

   (b) turn their resources to account so far as not required for those purposes.

24. London Regional Transport may do all other things which in their opinion are necessary or expedient to facilitate the proper carrying on of their business.

Supplementary

25. If London Regional Transport engage, either directly or through a subsidiary, in any activities authorised by paragraph 8(2) or

Sch. 2   (4) or 10 above, they shall in carrying on those activities act as if they were a company engaged in a commercial enterprise or (as the case may be) shall exercise their control over that subsidiary so as to ensure that the subsidiary in carrying on those activities acts as a company so engaged.

26. Any specific power conferred on London Regional Transport by or by virtue of any provision of this Act to make any loan or give any guarantee or to subscribe for or acquire any securities shall not affect the power of London Regional Transport—

    (*a*) to lend money by way of investment or to subscribe for or acquire securities by way of investment ; or

    (*b*) to leave outstanding any loan made or guarantee given, or to retain any securities acquired, before the appointed day by the Executive or any predecessor in title of theirs.

Section 40 (12).

SCHEDULE 3

The London Regional Passengers' Committee

The chairman

1. If the Secretary of State so determines, there shall be paid to the chairman of the Committee such remuneration as the Secretary of State may determine.

2. If the Secretary of State so determines in the case of a person who has been remunerated under paragraph 1 above, a pension shall be paid to or in respect of that person, or payments towards the provision of a pension to or in respect of that person shall be made, in accordance with the determination.

3. If a person in receipt of remuneration under paragraph 1 above as chairman ceases to hold that office, and it appears to the Secretary of State that there are special circumstances which make it right that that person should receive compensation, he shall be paid by way of compensation a sum of such amount as the Secretary of State may determine.

Administration, personnel, etc.

4. The Committee may, subject to the approval of the Secretary of State as to numbers, appoint such officers as appear to the Committee to be requisite for the performance of their functions.

5.—(1) The Secretary of State shall provide the Committee with funds with which to pay—

   (a) to their members, such travelling and other allowances as the Secretary of State may determine ; and

   (b) to their officers, such remuneration and such travelling and other allowances as the Committee may with the approval of the Secretary of State determine.

(2) The Secretary of State shall provide the Committee with funds with which to defray such other expenses in connection with the Committee's functions as the Secretary of State may determine to be appropriate.

6. The Secretary of State may make arrangements for the Committee to be provided with office accommodation.

7.—(1) There shall be paid such pensions, or arrangements shall be made for the payment of such pensions, as the Secretary of State may determine to or in respect of such persons who are or have been officers of the Committee as the Secretary of State may determine.

(2) The Secretary of State shall provide the Committee with funds with which to pay any such pension or to finance any such arrangements.

Constitution and procedure

8.—(1) The persons appointed to be members of the Committee shall hold and vacate office in accordance with the terms of their respective appointments and shall, on ceasing to be members of the Committee, be eligible for re-appointment.

(2) Any person so appointed may at any time by notice in writing to the Secretary of State resign his office.

9.—(1) The Committee shall meet—

   (a) at least twice a year ; and

   (b) whenever convened by the chairman.

(2) Without prejudice to the discretion of the chairman to call a meeting whenever he thinks fit, he shall call a meeting when required to do so by any three members of the Committee.

SCH. 3   (3) Minutes shall be kept of the proceedings of every meeting of the Committee.

(4) Subject to the preceding provisions of this paragraph, the Committee shall determine their own procedure (including the quorum at meetings of the Committee).

10. The Committee may delegate the exercise and performance of any of their functions to such sub-committees of the Committee as they think fit.

11. The validity of any proceedings of the Committee shall not be affected by any vacancy amongst the members or by any defects in the appointment of a member.

Amendment of other Acts

1970 c. 44.   12. In section 14(1) of the Chronically Sick and Disabled Persons Act 1970, after the words " Transport Users' Consultative Committees " there shall be inserted the words " the London Regional Passengers' Committee ".

1975 c. 24.   13. In Part III of Schedule 1 to the House of Commons Disqualification Act 1975, there shall be inserted at the appropriate place in alphabetical order—

" Chairman in receipt of remuneration of the London Regional Passengers' Committee ".

Supplementary

14. The consent of the Treasury shall be required for any determination or approval by the Secretary of State under this Schedule.

15. Any payment to be made under paragraphs 1 to 3 above shall be made by the Secretary of State.

Section 67(2), (3).

SCHEDULE 4

OPERATION OF ENACTMENTS RELATING TO FORMER LONDON BOARD FUNCTIONS

PART I

PROVISIONS REFERRING TO THE LONDON BOARD OR THE EXECUTIVE

1.—(1) In the provisions specified in sub-paragraph (2) below, for any reference to the Executive substituted by paragraph 1 of Schedule

3 to the 1969 Act for a reference to (or a reference falling to be construed as a reference to) the London Board, there shall be substituted a reference to London Regional Transport and any subsidiary of theirs (within the meaning of this Act).

Sch. 4

(2) The provisions referred to in sub-paragraph (1) above are—

(a) the London Passenger Transport Act 1933 and the London Passenger Transport Acts 1933 to 1947 (provisions originally referring to the London Passenger Transport Board) ; 1933 c. 14.

(b) the provisions of Parts I and III of Schedule 2 to the 1962 Act amending section 44(1)(b) of the Post Office Act 1953, section 40 of the British Transport Commission Act 1954 and section 66 of the British Transport Commission Act 1957 (by substituting references to certain of the Boards for references to the Commission) ; 1953 c. 36.
1954 c. lv.
1957 c. xxxiii.

(c) section 13(3)(c) of the Lee Valley Regional Park Act 1966 (provision or operation of passenger transport services by the Regional Park Authority) ; and 1966 c. xli.

(d) section 3(3) of the London Cab Act 1968 (restrictions on the parking of cabs). 1968 c. 7.

2.—(1) In section 67 of the 1962 Act (byelaws for railways and railway shipping services)—

(a) in subsection (1), for the words from first " and " to " may each " there shall be substituted the word " may " and in paragraph (e) for the word " Boards " there shall be substituted the word " Board " ;

(b) after subsection (2) there shall be inserted the following subsection—

" (2A) London Regional Transport shall have the like power to make byelaws as is conferred on the Railways Board by subsections (1) and (2) of this section (taking the reference in subsection (2) to ships as including hovercraft within the meaning of the Hovercraft Act 1968) ; and accordingly, references in this section, as it applies to London Regional Transport, to " a Board " or " the Board " shall be read as references to London Regional Transport." ; and 1968 c. 59.

(c) in subsections (15) and (16), for the references to the Executive substituted by paragraph 5(1) of Schedule 3 to the 1969 Act for express references to the London Board there shall be substituted references to London Regional Transport.

(2) In paragraph 4 of Schedule 16 to the 1968 Act (which extends the power to make byelaws under section 67 of the 1962

Act), for sub-paragraph (5) (extension as to premises, etc., of subsidiaries) there shall be substituted the following sub-paragraph—

> " (5) For the purposes of the said section 67, railways, railway premises, or officers and servants of, or ships (or hovercraft) operated by, a wholly owned subsidiary of the Railways Board or the Scottish Group or any subsidiary of London Regional Transport shall be deemed to be railways, railway premises, or officers and servants of, or ships (or hovercraft) operated by, that Board or Group or (as the case may be) by London Regional Transport.".

(3) In section 24(2) of the London Transport Act 1975, for the words " the Executive " there shall be substituted the words " London Regional Transport ".

3.—(1) In section 32(1) of the General Rate Act 1967 (rating of railway or canal premises) and paragraph 1 of Schedule 5 to that Act, for the words " the London Transport Board " (in those provisions as originally enacted) there shall be substituted the words " London Regional Transport ".

(2) In section 162 of the 1968 Act (which contains provisions affecting the operation of section 32 of the Act of 1967 mentioned above), in subsection (1), for the reference to the Executive substituted by virtue of paragraph 1(2)(*j*) of Schedule 3 to the 1969 Act for an express reference to the London Board there shall be substituted a reference to London Regional Transport.

(3) Accordingly, in section 32 of and Schedule 5 to the Act of 1967 mentioned above and section 162 of the 1968 Act, references (however expressed) to a Board or Boards shall be read as, or as including, references to London Regional Transport where London Regional Transport are the authority, or one of the authorities, concerned ; but in the application in relation to London Regional Transport—

> (*a*) of subsection (4)(*c*) of the former section, as inserted by subsection (5) of the latter section ; and
>
> (*b*) of subsection (3) of the latter section ;

the references to any powers conferred by section 48 or section 50(1) to (7) of the 1968 Act shall be read as references to any powers conferred on London Regional Transport by paragraph 9(2) or 12(1) of Schedule 2 to this Act.

4.—(1) In sections 116 to 119 of the 1968 Act (duties of Boards with respect to bridges and highways on bridges), for any reference to the Executive substituted by virtue of paragraph 1(2)(*l*) of Schedule 3 to the 1969 Act for an express reference to the London Board there shall be substituted a reference to London Regional Transport.

(2) In section 121 of that Act (application of the preceding sections of Part VIII of that Act to undertakers other than the Boards), for the reference in subsection (1) to the London Board there shall be substituted a reference to London Regional Transport.

(3) Accordingly, in the sections of the 1968 Act mentioned above in this paragraph, references (however expressed) to a Board or

Boards shall be read as, or as including, references to London Regional Transport where London Regional Transport are the authority, or one of the authorities, concerned.

5. In section 144 of the 1968 Act (transfer and disposal of historical records and relics)—

(a) in subsections (3) and (7), for the references to the Executive substituted by virtue of paragraph 1(2)(n) of Schedule 3 to the 1969 Act for express references to the London Board there shall be substituted references to London Regional Transport;

(b) in the former of those subsections, after the words "that is to say", there shall be inserted the words "London Regional Transport";

(c) in the latter of those subsections, the following paragraph shall be inserted at the end—

"In relation to any document or object in the possession of London Regional Transport, references above in this subsection to the Board concerned are references to London Regional Transport."; and

(d) after that subsection there shall be inserted the following subsection—

"(7A) Neither subsection (4) nor subsection (7) above shall apply to a transfer by London Regional Transport of any record or relic or (as the case may be) of any document or object to any subsidiary of theirs; but in relation to any such record, relic, document or object for the time being in the possession of a subsidiary or former subsidiary of London Regional Transport—

(a) references to a relevant authority in subsections (5) and (6) of this section and references to London Regional Transport in subsection (7) of this section (except in the reference to an agreement between London Regional Transport and the Secretary of State) shall be read as including that subsidiary or former subsidiary; and

(b) the foregoing provisions of this subsection shall apply for the purposes of subsection (4) of this section (as it applies by virtue of subsection (5)) and for the purposes of subsection (7) of this section as if the reference to a transfer by London Regional Transport to any subsidiary of theirs were a reference to a transfer by the subsidiary or former subsidiary in question to any subsidiary of London Regional Transport.".

Part II

Provisions referring to the Boards

6.—(1) The provisions specified in sub-paragraph (2) below shall continue to have effect as if "the Boards" included London Regional Transport.

(2) The provisions referred to in sub-paragraph (1) above are—

 (a) sections 52(4) and 83(7) of the 1962 Act (exclusion of the Boards from the definition of independent railway undertakings) ;

 (b) the provisions of Parts I and III of Schedule 2 to the 1962 Act (amendments of enactments referring to bodies superseded by the London Board) specified in sub-paragraph (3) below ;

 (c) the provisions of Part IV of that Schedule applying enactments contained in the Railways Clauses Acts there mentioned to the Boards ;

 (d) Schedule 6 to the 1962 Act (distribution of Commission's undertaking), except paragraph 2(3) ; and

 (e) section 125 of the 1968 Act (powers of inspectors of railways as respects persons other than railway companies).

(3) The provisions of Schedule 2 to the 1962 Act referred to in sub-paragraph (2)(b) above are those amending the following enactments, that is to say—

1905 c. 11.   (a) section 2 of the Railway Fires Act 1905 ;

1949 c. 74.   (b) paragraph (c) of the proviso to sections 5(4) and 8(4) of the Coast Protection Act 1949 ;

1954 c. 64.   (c) section 13(1) of the Transport Charges &c. (Miscellaneous Provisions) Act 1954 ;

4 & Eliz. 2
c. 16.   (d) section 11(2) of the Food and Drugs Act 1955 ;
1949 c. xxix. (e) sections 54, 55, 56, 57 and 59 of the British Transport Commission Act 1949 ; and

1953 c. xlii. (f) section 52 of the British Transport Commission Act 1953.

(4) Paragraph 7(1) of Schedule 16 to the 1968 Act (references to be substituted in certain enactments by Schedule 2 to the 1962 Act to include references to any wholly owned subsidiary of any of the Boards) shall continue to have effect as if " the Boards " included London Regional Transport ; but for the purposes of its application to London Regional Transport, that sub-paragraph shall have effect as if the words " wholly owned " were omitted.

(5) The provisions mentioned in sub-paragraph (2)(a) and (c) above, and those specified in sub-paragraph (3)(b) above, shall also have effect, as from the appointed day, as if " the Boards " included any subsidiary of London Regional Transport.

7.—(1) Section 86 of the 1962 Act and section 141 of the 1968 Act (application of the Town and Country Planning Acts) shall each continue to have effect as if " the Boards " included London Regional Transport.

(2) For the purposes of its application to London Regional Transport, section 86 shall have effect as if the powers referred to in subsection (1)(a) included the powers conferred by paragraph 8 of Schedule 2 to this Act.

(3) For the purposes of its application to London Regional Transport, section 141 shall have effect as if—

    (*a*) in subsection (2)(*a*) the words " wholly owned " (referring to a wholly owned subsidiary) were omitted ; and

    (*b*) the powers referred to in paragraphs (*a*) and (*c*)(ii) of sub-section (3) included the powers conferred by paragraph 14(2) of Schedule 2 to this Act.

Part III

Further Provisions derived from Schedule 3 to the 1969 Act

8.—(1) The provisions specified in sub-paragraph (2) below, which confer functions on, or otherwise have effect in relation to, the Executive or (as the case may be) the designated company (within the meaning of the 1969 Act) shall continue to apply in relation to London Regional Transport or (as the case may be) in relation to that company, as they applied, and with respect to any area with respect to which they applied, immediately before the appointed day.

(2) The provisions referred to in sub-paragraph (1) above are—

    (*a*) sections 104 and 109 of the London Passenger Transport Act 1934 ;   1934 c. xcvi.

    (*b*) sections 64 and 68(1) of the London Passenger Transport Act 1937 ;   1937 c. xc.

    (*c*) section 65 of the London Passenger Transport Act 1938 ;   1938 c. xcii.

    (*d*) section 57 of the British Transport Commission Act 1949 ;   1949 c. xxix.
    and

    (*e*) section 15 of the British Transport Commission Act 1951.   1951 c. xxxix.

(3) Those provisions shall also apply in relation to any subsidiary of London Regional Transport as they apply in relation to London Regional Transport ; and section 104 of the Act of 1934 mentioned above (power to erect shelters, etc.) shall also apply (with any necessary modifications) with respect to the routes of any public passenger transport services operated by any person in pursuance of any agreement entered into by London Regional Transport by virtue of section 3(2) of this Act as it applies with respect to the routes of such services operated by London Regional Transport or any subsidiary of theirs.

(4) The functions of the Executive under—

    (*a*) section 69 of the Act of 1937 mentioned above ; and

    (*b*) section 25 of the London Transport Act 1969 ;   1969 c. 1.

shall continue to be functions of London Regional Transport, exercisable with respect to any area with respect to which they were exercisable immediately before the appointed day.

(5) For the purposes of section 69 of the Act of 1937 mentioned above—

    (*a*) tramcars, trolley vehicles or public service vehicles of any subsidiary of London Regional Transport shall be treated as tramcars, trolley vehicles or public service vehicles of London Regional Transport ; and

    (*b*) proceedings brought by any such subsidiary shall be treated as brought by London Regional Transport.

(6) For the purpose of section 25 of the London Transport Act 1969—

(*a*) road transport garages, depots, bus stations, shelters or other road transport premises belonging to, leased to or worked by, and any officers and servants of, any subsidiary of London Regional Transport shall be treated respectively as road transport garages, depots, bus stations, shelters or other road transport premises belonging to, leased to or worked by, and officers and servants of, London Regional Transport ; and

(*b*) any such subsidiary may exercise the power under subsection (3) of that section in any case where the premises (within the meaning of that section) in relation to which the danger, annoyance or hindrance there mentioned arises are premises of that subsidiary and (in the case of any hindrance) the hindrance in question is hindrance to that subsidiary in the lawful use of those premises.

9.—(1) The provisions of this paragraph shall have effect in relation to London Regional Transport in place of paragraph 5 of Schedule 16 to the 1968 Act (agreements by the Railways Board to make available the services of the transport police) ; and any agreement made under that paragraph, as it applied to the Executive, which is in force immediately before the appointed day shall have effect as if made under this paragraph.

(2) The Railways Board may make an agreement with—

(*a*) London Regional Transport ; or

(*b*) any related company ;

for making available to London Regional Transport or any subsidiary of theirs or (as the case may be) to that company, for such period, to such extent and on such terms as may be specified in the agreement, the services of the British Transport Police Force.

(3) Where such an agreement has been made with any related company members of the British Transport Police Force shall, notwithstanding the provisions of any other enactment but subject to the terms of the agreement, have the same powers to act as constables—

(*a*) in relation to any premises of that company which have at any time been premises belonging or leased to, or worked by, London Regional Transport ; and

(*b*) in relation to matters connected with or affecting that company or its undertaking ;

as they would have if those premises belonged to London Regional Transport, or (as the case may be) if those matters were connected with or affected London Regional Transport or their undertaking.

(4) The functions exercisable immediately before the appointed day by the Executive under the British Transport Police Force Scheme shall continue to be exercisable by London Regional Transport.

(5) Section 70(5) to (7) of the 1962 Act shall continue to have effect as if " the Boards " included London Regional Transport.

(6) Section 25 of the British Railways Act 1978 (which amends provisions of section 53 of the British Transport Commission Act 1949 as to the appointment and powers of members of the British Transport Police Force) shall continue to have effect in relation to London Regional Transport as one of the Boards ; and accordingly, in subsection (1), for the words " the London Transport Executive " there shall be substituted the words " London Regional Transport ". 1978 c. xxi.
1949 c. xxix.

(7) In section 25(4) of the Act of 1978 mentioned above, as it applies in relation to London Regional Transport, for the reference to a wholly owned subsidiary there shall be substituted a reference to any subsidiary (whether wholly owned or not) of London Regional Transport (within the meaning of this Act).

(8) The provisions of sub-paragraphs (4) to (7) above are subject to any agreement made under paragraph 5 of Schedule 16 to the 1968 Act or under this paragraph.

(9) In this paragraph —

(a) " the British Transport Police Force Scheme " means the Scheme set out in the Schedule to the British Transport Police Force Scheme 1963 (Approval) Order 1964 made under section 69 of the 1962 Act ; and S.I. 1964/1456.

(b) " the British Transport Police Force " means the force established by that Scheme.

10.—(1) Paragraph 5(2) and (4) of Schedule 16 to the 1968 Act shall continue to apply to the Bus Company, for the purposes only of any transferred premises, as they apply to the Scottish Transport Group.

(2) The functions exercisable immediately before the appointed day by the Bus Company under the British Transport Police Force Scheme shall continue to be exercisable by the Bus Company, for those purposes only.

(3) Section 70(5) to (7) of the 1962 Act shall continue to have effect as if " the Boards " included, for those purposes only, the Bus Company.

(4) The provisions of sub-paragraphs (2) and (3) above are subject to any agreement made under paragraph 5 of Schedule 16 to the 1968 Act and to any adaptations made under sub-paragraph (4) of that paragraph.

(5) In this paragraph and in paragraph 11 below, references to transferred premises are references to premises transferred under section 16(2) of the 1969 Act.

(6) In this paragraph " the British Transport Police Force Scheme " has the same meaning as in paragraph 9 above.

11.—(1) For the purpose only of applying section 54 of the British Transport Commission Act 1949 (powers of search and arrest) to

SCH. 4   transferred premises, the Bus Company shall continue to be treated
as one of the Boards.

1982 c. v.   (2) In section 20 of the London Transport Act 1982 (which
continues section 54 in force as it applies, by virtue of paragraph
6 above, to London Regional Transport)—

> (*a*) the reference to the Executive shall be construed in accord-
> ance with sub-paragraph (4) below ; and
>
> (*b*) the reference to paragraph 1(2)(*g*) of Schedule 3 to the 1969
> Act shall be read as a reference to paragraph 6 above.

(3) In any enactment passed after this Act which provides for section 54 to continue in force for a further period in its application to
London Regional Transport, any reference to London Regional
Transport shall be construed in accordance with sub-paragraph (4)
below.

(4) Any reference which falls to be construed in accordance with
this sub-paragraph shall be read as a reference—

> (*a*) to London Regional Transport and any subsidiary of London
> Regional Transport ; and
>
> (*b*) for the purpose mentioned in sub-paragraph (3) above but
> for that purpose only, to the Bus Company and any wholly
> owned subsidiary of the Bus Company.

Section 71(2).   SCHEDULE 5

TRANSITIONAL PROVISIONS AND SAVINGS

Accounts

1. The first accounting year of London Regional Transport shall
be the period beginning with 1st January 1984 and ending with
31st March 1985.

Annual report

2. In relation to the first accounting year of London Regional
Transport, the reference in section 34(3)(*d*) of this Act to directions
given by the Secretary of State under this Act shall be read as
including a reference to directions given by the Greater London
Council or by the Secretary of State under the 1969 Act.

Revenue grants

3. So far as relates to the first accounting year of London Regional
Transport, section 15(9) and (10) of this Act shall apply in relation
to sums received by the Executive by way of grants under section
3(1)(*a*) of the 1969 Act in aid of the revenues of the Executive
(including grants made under that paragraph in respect of reductions
in fares for children) as they apply in relation to sums received by
way of grants under section 12 of this Act which are entered in the
revenue account of London Regional Transport.

Capital allowances

4. Notwithstanding the substitution by paragraph 4 of Schedule 6
to this Act of a new paragraph (*d*) for the paragraph (*d*) inserted in

section 83(4) of the Capital Allowances Act 1968 by section 3(2)   Sch. 5
of the 1969 Act, the Capital Allowances (Relevant Grants) (No. 2) 1968 c. 3.
Order 1969 (which was made under section 83(4) by virtue of the S.I. 1969/1541.
original paragraph (*d*))—

  (*a*) shall continue in force as if so made by virtue of the new
      paragraph (*d*) ; and

  (*b*) shall have effect with the substitution, for the reference in
      Article 1 of that Order to a grant made under section 3 of
      the 1969 Act, of a reference to a grant made under section
      12 of this Act.

5. Any reference in—

  (*a*) Article 1 of the Order mentioned in paragraph 4 above,
      as it has effect by virtue of that paragraph ; and

  (*b*) section 83(4)(*d*) of the Capital Allowances Act 1968, as
      substituted by paragraph 4 of Schedule 6 to this Act ;

to a grant made under section 12 of this Act shall be read as
including a reference to a grant made under section 3 of the 1969
Act.

Pensions and pension schemes

6. Any order made under section 74 of the 1962 Act (orders about
pensions), as applied by section 18 of the 1969 Act, if and in so
far as—

  (*a*) it is still in force immediately before the appointed day ;
      and

  (*b*) it would not by virtue of section 17(2)(*b*) of the Interpretation 1978 c. 30.
      Act 1978 (which saves subordinate legislation on repeal
      and re-enactment of a provision if it could have been made
      under the provision as re-enacted) have effect as if made
      under section 74 as applied by section 25 of this Act ;

shall continue in force notwithstanding the repeal by this Act of
section 18 of the 1969 Act.

7.—(1) Without prejudice to section 13 of the Interpretation Act
1978 (anticipatory exercise of powers), orders may be made under
section 74 of the 1962 Act, as it applies by virtue of sections 25 and
26 of this Act, before sections 25 and 26 come into force.

(2) Any orders so made shall come into force on the appointed
day.

The Passengers' Committee

8.—(1) In this paragraph and paragraph 9 below—

  " the consultative body " means the body established by the
      Greater London Council under section 14 of the 1969 Act
      (users' consultative body) ; and

  " the Area Committee " means the Area Transport Users'
      Committee referred to in section 41(1)(*a*) of this Act.

(2) For the purpose of preparing for the transition from the law
in force immediately before the appointed day to the provisions of
sections 40 and 41 of this Act—

  (*a*) the consultative body shall send to the Executive ; and (*b*) the Area Committee shall send to the Railways Board ; copies of any relevant representations or reference pending before them at the passing of this Act or made to them on or after the passing of this Act.

(3) For the purpose mentioned in sub-paragraph (2) above, where in relation to any relevant representations or reference so pending or made that body or Committee determine that it is not desirable to make any recommendation under section 14(1) of the 1969 Act or (as the case may be) under section 56(4) of the 1962 Act, that body or Committee shall send to the Executive or (as the case may be) to the Railways Board written notification of that determination.

(4) In this paragraph " relevant representations " means—

(*a*) representations made to the consultative body as mentioned in section 14(1)(*a*) of the 1969 Act ; and

(*b*) representations made to the Area Committee as mentioned in section 56(4)(*a*) of the 1962 Act ;

other than representations which that body or Committee have determined not to consider as being representations appearing to them to be frivolous.

(5) In this paragraph " relevant reference " means any reference made—

(*a*) to the consultative body by the Greater London Council or by the Executive under section 14(1)(*b*) of the 1969 Act ; or

(*b*) to the Area Committee by the Secretary of State or by the Railways Board under section 56(4)(*b*) of the 1962 Act.

(6) London Regional Transport and the Railways Board shall each send to the Passengers' Committee—

(*a*) copies of any representations of which copies have been sent to them in pursuance of sub-paragraph (2) above which are pending before the consultative body or (as the case may be) the Area Committee at the appointed day ; and

(*b*) copies of any relevant reference pending before the consultative body or (as the case may be) the Area Committee at the appointed day.

(7) Any representations of which a copy is sent to the Passengers' Committee in accordance with sub-paragraph (6)(*a*) above shall be treated for the purposes of section 40(5)(*a*) of this Act as having been made to that Committee as there mentioned.

(8) Any reference of which a copy is sent to the Passengers' Committee in accordance with sub-paragraph (6)(*b*) above shall be treated for the purposes of section 40(5)(*b*) of this Act as having been made to that Committee and (where it was made by the Greater London Council) as having been so made by London Regional Transport.

(9) For the purposes of this paragraph, any representations or reference made to the consultative body or (as the case may be) to the Area Committee before any relevant time are to be regarded

as pending before that body or Committee at that time if that body or Committee have not before that time—

(a) made, and sent to the Executive under section 14(1) of the 1969 Act or (as the case may be) to the Railways Board under section 56(4) of the 1962 Act, any recommendation with respect to the matter which is the subject of the representations or (as the case may be) of the reference ; or

(b) determined that it is not desirable to make any such recommendation with respect to that matter and, in the case of any such determination on or after the passing of this Act, sent written notification of that determination to the Executive or the Railways Board in accordance with sub-paragraph (3) above.

(10) In sub-paragraph (9) above " relevant time " means—

(a) for the purposes of sub-paragraphs (2) and (3) above, the passing of this Act ; and

(b) for the purposes of sub-paragraph (6) above, the appointed day.

Compensation for chairmen of bodies superseded by the Passengers' Committee

9. Where a person ceases to hold office (otherwise than on the expiration of his term of office)—

(a) as chairman of the consultative body by virtue of the repeal by this Act of section 14 of the 1969 Act ; or

(b) as chairman of the Area Committee by virtue of the dissolution of that Committee by section 41(1) of this Act ;

the Secretary of State shall pay to that person compensation of such amount, and on such terms, as the Secretary of State may, with the approval of the Treasury, determine.

London bus services

10.—(1) Notwithstanding any repeal made by this Act, sections 23A and 23B of the 1969 Act (right of appeal where Executive refuses to make or vary an agreement authorising a London bus service)—

(a) shall continue to apply in relation to any appeal made in accordance with section 23A which has not been determined or withdrawn before the appointed day and in relation to any appeal under section 23B from the decision of the Secretary of State on any such appeal under section 23A ; and

(b) subject to sub-paragraph (2) below, shall continue to authorise appeals to be brought on or after that day against a refusal or failure on the part of London Regional Transport to enter into an agreement to vary the terms of an agreement made under section 23(2) of that Act for the time being subsisting between any person and London Regional Transport.

(2) Sub-paragraph (1)(*b*) above only applies to any agreement under section 23(2) which is in force immediately before the appointed day or is entered into by London Regional Transport in pursuance of any order made by the Secretary of State on any appeal to which sub-paragraph (1)(*a*) above applies.

(3) Notwithstanding any repeal made by this Act, but subject to sub-paragraph (4) below, paragraphs 4 to 13 of Schedule 4 to the 1969 Act (provisions with respect to consents for London bus services continued in force or granted under that Schedule) shall continue to apply in relation to—

    (*a*) any consent continued in force or granted under that Schedule which is in force immediately before the appointed day ; and

    (*b*) any application for the grant of a consent under paragraph 4 or 5 of that Schedule (consents as of right for certain successors in title) which has not been determined before the appointed day and any consent granted (or deemed by virtue of paragraph 6 of that Schedule to have been granted) in pursuance of any such application.

(4) A consent continued in force or granted under Schedule 4 to the 1969 Act may not be renewed under paragraph 8(1) of that Schedule except on an application made before the appointed day.

(5) Where on the date when any agreement to which sub-paragraph (1)(*b*) above applies would apart from this sub-paragraph expire there is pending in relation to that agreement any such appeal as is mentioned in that sub-paragraph, that agreement shall not cease to be in force until the appeal is determined or withdrawn.

(6) Where on the date when any consent within sub-paragraph (3)(*a*) or (*b*) above would apart from this sub-paragraph expire there is pending in relation to that consent—

    (*a*) any appeal under paragraph 7 or 9 of that Schedule (including paragraph 9 as applied by paragraph 10) ; or

    (*b*) any appeal under paragraph 12 of that Schedule against the cancellation of that consent under that paragraph ;

that consent shall not cease to be in force until the appeal is determined or withdrawn.

(7) In any provision of the 1969 Act which by virtue of this paragraph continues to apply for any purpose after the appointed day, references to the Executive shall be read as references to London Regional Transport.

(8) So far as relates to the purposes of section 23A of the 1969 Act as that section applies by virtue of this paragraph, section 248 of the Road Traffic Act 1960 (power of Secretary of State to hold inquiries) shall have effect as if the repeal made by this Act of words referring to section 23A had not been made.

11.—(1) This paragraph applies to—

    (*a*) any agreement under section 23(2) of the 1969 Act to which paragraph 10(1)(*b*) above applies ; and

    (*b*) any consent within paragraph 10(3)(*a*) or (*b*) above.

(2) Subject to sub-paragraph (3) below, any agreement or consent to which this paragraph applies shall be treated for the purposes of this paragraph as remaining in force for an additional period of one month beginning with the day immediately following the date on which it expires (whether according to its terms or as extended by virtue of paragraph 10(5) or (6) above).

(3) Sub-paragraph (2) above does not apply where in a case within paragraph 10(6)(*b*) above the cancellation of the consent takes effect on the determination of the appeal.

(4) So long as any agreement or consent to which this paragraph applies remains in force, any person providing a London bus service in accordance with that agreement or consent shall be treated for the purposes of any reference in this or any other Act to any service or services provided in pursuance of an agreement entered into by virtue of section 3(2) of this Act (except the references in sections 8(*a*), 30(1)(*a*), 40(4)(*b*), and 51(3)(*e*) of this Act) as providing that service in pursuance of such an agreement (and shall accordingly be exempt by virtue of section 43(1) of this Act from the requirement of a road service licence in respect of that service and by virtue of subsection (2) of that section from the application to any such licence held by him which is within that subsection of any such condition as is there mentioned).

(5) Subject to sub-paragraph (6) below, where at any time before any agreement or consent to which this paragraph applies ceases to be in force any person providing a London bus service in accordance with that agreement or consent applies to the metropolitan traffic commissioners for a road service licence in respect of that service, those commissioners shall grant that person a road service licence in accordance with paragraph 12 below.

(6) Sub-paragraph (5) above does not apply in relation to a person providing a London bus service in accordance with a consent to which this paragraph applies where—

(*a*) that consent has been cancelled under paragraph 12 of Schedule 4 to the 1969 Act ; but

(*b*) the cancellation has not yet taken effect.

(7) Where an application is made under sub-paragraph (5) above for a road service licence, as respects any period between the date on which the agreement or consent in question expires or (if later) the date of the application and the date of the grant of a road service licence in pursuance of the application—

(*a*) a road service licence in the form applied for shall be regarded as having been granted to the applicant on the date of the making of the application ; and

(*b*) sub-paragraph (4) above shall not apply to the agreement or consent in question.

(8) In this paragraph " metropolitan traffic commissioners " means the traffic commissioners for the Metropolitan Traffic Area.

12.—(1) Subject to the following provisions of this paragraph, a road service licence granted on an application under paragraph 11(5)

Sch. 5

above in respect of a London bus service (referred to below in this paragraph as a concessionary licence) shall authorise the continuation of that service on the same terms and conditions as applied under the agreement or consent in question immediately before the date of that application.

(2) Any terms or conditions as to fares, or the minimum or maximum fares, which might be charged for that service under that agreement or consent shall not apply to the licence.

1981 c. 14.

(3) The provisions of the Public Passenger Vehicles Act 1981 with respect to, and with respect to applications for and the grant of, road service licences are subject to the following provisions of this paragraph as they have effect in relation to, and in relation to an application for and the grant of, a concessionary licence.

(4) Sections 31(2) to (4), 34 and 35 of that Act (considerations as to initial grant of licence) shall not apply in relation to an application for a concessionary licence.

(5) Section 32(1) of that Act (attachment of conditions on granting licence) shall not apply on the grant of a concessionary licence, but any terms or conditions attached to any such licence by virtue of sub-paragraph (1) above may be altered or removed in accordance with that section and shall be treated for the purposes of subsection (5) of that section as attached under that section.

(6) No condition as to fares shall be attached under section 33 of that Act to a concessionary licence at the time when it is granted.

(7) The traffic commissioners granting a concessionary licence may not under section 37(2) of that Act determine that it shall continue in force only up to and including an earlier date than the one which would apply under that subsection apart from any such determination.

Compensation for loss of employment, etc.

13.—(1) Any regulations made under section 37 of the 1969 Act, if and in so far as they are in force immediately before the appointed day —

(a) shall continue in force notwithstanding the repeal by this Act of that section ; and

(b) may be varied or revoked by regulations made under section 48 of this Act as if they had been made by reason of any such transfer of property, rights or liabilities as is mentioned in section 48(1)(b).

(2) Section 48(5) and (6) shall apply in relation to any such regulations as if—

(a) that one of the relevant authorities required by those regulations to pay compensation under the regulations were the person primarily liable ; and

(b) the other two authorities were contributories.

(3) In sub-paragraph (2) above " the relevant authorities " means London Regional Transport, the Railways Board and the Bus Company.

Travel concessions

14. Arrangements made under section 138 of the 1968 Act by virtue of section 40 of the 1969 Act (which extended section 138 to the Executive and to local authorities in London) shall be treated as made under section 50 of this Act.

Commitments to pay grants

15.—(1) Where before 2nd December 1983 the Greater London Council have entered into any commitment (whether legally enforceable or not)—

 (a) to make any payment to any person (other than the Executive) under section 56(2) of the 1968 Act (grants by local authorities towards capital expenditure on public passenger transport facilities) ; or

 (b) to make any grant to the Railways Board under section 3(1)(b) of the 1969 Act (grants in respect of passenger transport services, amenities or facilities required to meet the needs of Greater London) ;

that commitment shall have effect, so far as relates to anything falling to be done in accordance with it on or after the appointed day, as if entered into by London Regional Transport.

(2) London Regional Transport shall be entitled to recover from the Greater London Council an amount equal to any expenditure incurred by them in the initial year in making payments in pursuance of any such commitment.

(3) In sub-paragraph (2) above, " the initial year " has the same meaning as in section 49 of this Act.

16. Any obligation of the Greater London Council—

 (a) to make any payment to the Executive under section 56(2) of the 1968 Act ; or

 (b) to make any grant to the Executive under section 3(1)(a) of the 1969 Act ;

shall cease to have effect.

Provisions as to transfer under 1969 Act

17. Notwithstanding any repeal made by this Act, the provisions of Schedule 2 to the 1969 Act, as they had effect immediately before the appointed day, continue to apply for the purpose of determining the effect of or giving effect to, or making any provision consequential on or incidental to, any transfer under section 16 of that Act.

Continuity of powers

18.—(1) Anything done by the Executive under a superseded enactment, so far as that thing is still in force, subsisting or effective immediately before the appointed day, shall be treated for the purposes of this Act —

 (a) as done ; and

 (b) if properly done under the superseded enactment, as properly done ;

E 3

SCH. 5   by London Regional Transport under the corresponding enactment in this Act.

(2) For the purposes of sub-paragraph (1) above a thing is properly done under an enactment if it is done with any approval or consent required by that enactment for the doing of that thing.

(3) So far as relates to anything done before the appointed day under a superseded enactment, references in this Act to the approval or consent of the Secretary of State shall be read as references to any approval or consent required by the superseded enactment.

(4) In this paragraph, " superseded enactment " means an enactment which —

    (*a*) is repealed by this Act or ceases to apply to London Regional Transport by virtue of any repeal made by this Act ; and

    (*b*) is replaced by an enactment in this Act which re-enacts it, with or without modification.

Construction of references to London Regional Transport

19. To avoid doubt, it is declared that any reference (express or implied) to anything done by or to, to the employment of, or to any agreement or other thing subsisting in relation to or otherwise affecting London Regional Transport—

    (*a*) in this Act ; or

    (*b*) in any statutory provision amended by this Act ;

is to be read, in relation to anything occurring before the appointed day, as a reference to anything done by or to, to the employment of, or (as the case may be) to any agreement or other thing subsisting in relation to or otherwise affecting London Regional Transport under their former name.

Section
71(3)(*a*).

SCHEDULE 6

MINOR AND CONSEQUENTIAL AMENDMENTS

PART I

PUBLIC GENERAL ACTS

1875 c. 17.

The Explosives Act 1875

1.—(1) Section 35 of the Explosives Act 1875 (byelaws for regulating the conveyance, loading and unloading of explosives by railway and canal companies) shall not apply to any subsidiary of London Regional Transport which is a railway company within the meaning of that Act ; but the duty to make byelaws under that section shall apply in relation to London Regional Transport as if any railway of any such subsidiary were a railway of theirs.

(2) Without prejudice to their application by virtue of that section apart from this paragraph, byelaws made under that section by London Regional Transport shall also apply to any railway, and to the agents and servants, of any such subsidiary of London Regional Transport, and to the persons using any such railway or the premises connected with any such railway and occupied by or under the control of any such subsidiary.

(3) Any byelaws made under that section which are in force and apply to the railways of the Executive immediately before the appointed day shall also apply as mentioned in sub-paragraph (2) above, and in those byelaws—

(*a*) for references to the Executive there shall be substituted references to London Regional Transport or any such subsidiary (as the context may require) ; and

(*b*) references to London Transport railways shall be read as references to the railways of London Regional Transport and of any such subsidiary.

(4) If London Regional Transport cease to be a railway company within the meaning of that Act, section 35 shall nevertheless continue to apply to them as if they were such a railway company, so far as relates to the making of byelaws to apply as mentioned in sub-paragraph (2) above in relation to any subsidiary of theirs which is such a railway company.

The Regulation of Railways Act 1889

1889 c. 57.

2. Section 6 of the Regulation of Railways Act 1889 (chargeable fare to be printed or written on the face of passenger tickets issued by railway companies) shall not apply to passenger tickets issued by London Regional Transport or by any subsidiary of London Regional Transport in respect of any railways of London Regional Transport or (as the case may be) of that subsidiary.

The Finance Act 1965

1965 c. 25.

3. In section 92 of the Finance Act 1965 (grants to operators of bus services towards duty charged on bus fuel), for subsection (8) there shall be substituted the following subsection—

" (8) In this section—

' bus service ' means a stage carriage service within the meaning of the Public Passenger Vehicles Act 1981 which is available to the general public and is neither an excursion or tour within the meaning of that Act nor a service as regards which the condition specified in section 2(3)(*a*) of that Act (long journeys only) is satisfied ;

1981 c. 14.

' operator ', in relation to a bus service, means—

(*a*) the holder of the road service licence under which the service is provided ; or

(*b*) if the service is provided otherwise than under a road service licence by, or by a subsidiary of—

(i) London Regional Transport ; or

(ii) the Executive for a designated area within the meaning of section 9(1) of the Transport Act 1968 ;

1968 c. 73.

London Regional Transport or (as the case may be) that Executive or that subsidiary ;

(c) if the service is provided otherwise than under a road service licence by a person—

 (i) in pursuance of an agreement under section 3(2) of the London Regional Transport Act 1984 ; or

 (ii) in pursuance of an agreement under section 19(2) of the Transport Act 1968 or under a consent granted under Schedule 6 to that Act ;

that person ;

(d) if and to the extent that the service operates within a trial area (within the meaning of the Public Passenger Vehicles Act 1981), the person by whom the service is provided ;

'subsidiary' has the same meaning as for the purposes of the Transport Act 1968.".

The Capital Allowances Act 1968

4. In section 83(4) of the Capital Allowances Act 1968 (grants relevant for the purpose of the withholding or withdrawal of investment and initial allowances), for the words inserted at the end of paragraph (c) by section 3(2) of the 1969 Act there shall be substituted the words " or

 (d) a grant made under section 12 of the London Regional Transport Act 1984 ".

The Transport Act 1968

5. In section 138 of the 1968 Act (travel concessions)—

(a) at the beginning of subsection (3) there shall be inserted the words " Subject to subsection (3A) below " ; and

(b) after that subsection there shall be inserted the following subsection—

 " (3A) Arrangements may not be made by a local authority under subsection (3) of this section with London Regional Transport or any subsidiary of theirs, or with any person in respect of journeys on services provided by that person in pursuance of any agreement entered into by London Regional Transport by virtue of section 3(2) of the London Regional Transport Act 1984.".

The Post Office Act 1969

6. In section 7(1A) of the Post Office Act 1969 (powers of the Post Office to perform services for other bodies)—

(a) in paragraph (b) the words " the London Transport Executive and " shall be omitted ; and

(b) at the end of paragraph (f) (wholly owned subsidiaries of bodies within paragraphs (a) to (e)) there shall be inserted the words " or any subsidiary (whether wholly owned or not) of London Regional Transport (within the meaning of the London Regional Transport Act 1984) ".

The Income and Corporation Taxes Act 1970   SCH. 6

7. In section 272(6) of the Income and Corporation Taxes Act 1970 c. 10.
1970 (Passenger Transport Executives treated as companies for the
purposes of provisions of Chapter II of Part XI of that Act about
groups of companies)—

  (a) the words " the London Transport Executive and " shall be
    omitted ; and
  (b) for the words " each of those Executives " there shall be
    substituted the words " that Executive ".

The Finance Act 1970   1970 c. 24.

8. In Schedule 3 to the Finance Act 1970 (application of Corporation Tax Acts in relation to Public Transport Authorities in
London)—

  (a) in paragraph 1, in the definition of " the transferee ", for
    the words " the Executive " there shall be substituted the
    words " London Regional Transport " ; and
  (b) paragraph 8(2) (which amends section 272(6) of the Income
    and Corporation Taxes Act 1970 and is superseded by
    paragraph 7 above) shall be omitted.

The Town and Country Planning Act 1971   1971 c. 78.

9. In section 223(2)(b) of the Town and Country Planning Act
1971 (exception from rule that certain land is not to be treated as
operational land), after the words " the Transport Act 1968 " there
shall be inserted the words " or the Transport (London) Act 1969 ".   1969 c. 35.

The Road Traffic Act 1972   1972 c. 20.

10. In section 144(2) of the Road Traffic Act 1972 (exceptions
from requirement of third-party insurance or security) paragraph
(e) (exception for the Executive) shall be omitted.

The Local Government Act 1974   1974 c. 7.

11. In Schedule 1 to the Local Government Act 1974 (existing
grants for highways and public transport)—

  (a) in paragraph 8(1)(a), for the words " the London Transport
    Executive " there shall be substituted the words " London
    Regional Transport " ;
  (b) in paragraph 9(1)(a), the words " or the London Transport
    Executive " shall be omitted ; and
  (c) in paragraph 9(3), the words from " and " to the end of the
    paragraph shall be omitted.

The Land Drainage Act 1976   1976 c. 70.

12. In section 112(3) of the Land Drainage Act 1976 (railway
bridges, etc., not to be interfered with without consent), for the
words " the London Transport Executive " there shall be substituted
the words " London Regional Transport ".

The Agricultural Holdings (Notices to Quit) Act 1977

13.—(1) In section 1(3) of the Agricultural Holdings (Notices to Quit) Act 1977 (tenancies excepted from requirements about length of notice to quit), for the words " the London Transport Executive " (in each place where they occur) there shall be substituted the words " London Regional Transport ".

(2) After that subsection there shall be inserted the following subsection—

" (3A) Subsection (3) above shall have effect in relation to a subsidiary of London Regional Transport (within the meaning of the London Regional Transport Act 1984) as it has effect in relation to London Regional Transport, so far as relates to land transferred to London Regional Transport as there mentioned and subsequently transferred to that subsidiary by a scheme made under section 4 or 5 of that Act.".

1978 c. 55.

The Transport Act 1978

14. In section 21 of the Transport Act 1978 (travel concessions for transferred employees), for the words " the London Transport Executive " there shall be substituted the words " London Regional Transport ".

1980 c. 21.

The Competition Act 1980

15.—(1) In section 11(3) of the Competition Act 1980 (persons who may be the subject of a reference to the Monopolies and Mergers Commission)—

1969 c. 35.

    (*a*) in paragraph (*b*), for the words " the Transport (London) Act 1969 " there shall be substituted the words "the London Regional Transport Act 1984 " ; and

    (*b*) after that paragraph there shall be inserted the following paragraph—

        " (*bb*) any person who provides a railway passenger service in pursuance of an agreement entered into by London Regional Transport by virtue of section 3(2) of the last-mentioned Act ; or ".

(2) In subsection (4) of that section, after the words " subsection (3)(*b*) " there shall be inserted the words " or (*bb*) ".

(3) In subsection (5) of that section—

    (*a*) after the words " subsection (3)(*b*) " there shall be inserted the words " or (*bb*) " ; and

    (*b*) for the words " that subsection " there shall be substituted the words " either of those paragraphs ".

1980 c. 66.

The Highways Act 1980

16. In section 115H(4) of the Highways Act 1980 (council not to exercise certain powers in relation to certain highways maintained by other authorities without obtaining the consent of those authorities)—

    (*a*) for the words " the London Transport Executive " there shall be substituted the words " London Regional Transport or any subsidiary of London Regional Transport (within the meaning of the London Regional Transport Act 1984) " ; and

(*b*) for the words " the Executive " there shall be substituted the words " London Regional Transport or that subsidiary of London Regional Transport ".

17. In section 115J(8) of that Act (payment of arbitrator's expenses and remuneration), for the words " the London Transport Executive " there shall be substituted the words " London Regional Transport or any subsidiary of London Regional Transport (within the meaning of the London Regional Transport Act 1984) ".

18. In section 157(5) of that Act (schemes for repair and improvement works in Greater London), for the words " the London Transport Executive " there shall be substituted the words " London Regional Transport ".

19. In section 169(6) of that Act (exceptions to provisions controlling scaffolding on highways), for the words " the London Transport Executive " there shall be substituted the words " London Regional Transport or any subsidiary of theirs (within the meaning of the London Regional Transport Act 1984) ".

20. In section 219(4)(*i*) of that Act (exceptions to requirements that owners of new buildings pay for street works) in sub-paragraph (i)—

(*a*) for the words " the London Transport Executive " there shall be substituted the words " London Regional Transport " ;

(*b*) the word " or " (in the first place where it occurs) shall be omitted ; and

(*c*) at the end there shall be added the words " other than London Regional Transport, or any subsidiary (whether wholly-owned or not) of London Regional Transport (within the meaning of the London Regional Transport Act 1984) ".

21. In section 329(4) of that Act (construction of references to property of certain undertakers), in the second paragraph—

(*a*) for the words " the London Transport Executive " there shall be substituted the words " London Regional Transport " ;

(*b*) the word " or " (in the first place where it occurs) shall be omitted ; and

(*c*) at the end there shall be added the words " other than London Regional Transport, or any subsidiary (whether wholly-owned or not) of London Regional Transport (within the meaning of the London Regional Transport Act 1984) ".

The Public Passenger Vehicles Act 1981

22. In section 27(3) of the Public Passenger Vehicles Act 1981 (duty to make certain returns not to apply to the Railways Board or the Executive), for the words " the London Transport Executive " there shall be substituted the words " London Regional Transport or to any subsidiary of London Regional Transport (within the meaning of the London Regional Transport Act 1984) ".

The Animal Health Act 1981

23. In section 38(2) of the Animal Health Act 1981 (food and water for animals to be provided at railway stations)—

(a) in paragraph (b), for the words " the London Transport Executive " there shall be substituted the words " London Regional Transport " ; and

(b) in paragraph (i), after the word " include " there shall be inserted the words " in the case of those mentioned in paragraph (a) " and at the end there shall be added the words " and in the case of London Regional Transport, any subsidiary (whether wholly-owned or not) of London Regional Transport (within the meaning of the London Regional Transport Act 1984) ".

The Transport Act 1981

24. In paragraph 31(4) of Schedule 3 to the Transport Act 1981 (public transport authorities with whom Associated British Ports may co-operate) for the words " the London Transport Executive " there shall be substituted the words " London Regional Transport ".

The Local Government (Miscellaneous Provisions) Act 1982

25. In section 41(12)(c) of the Local Government (Miscellaneous Provisions) Act 1982 (exceptions to provisions about lost property), for the words from " the London Transport Executive " to the end of the paragraph there shall be substituted the words " or under the control of London Regional Transport or of any subsidiary of London Regional Transport (within the meaning of the London Regional Transport Act 1984) ".

The Local Government Finance Act 1982

26. In section 31 of the Local Government Finance Act 1982 (passenger transport executives and their subsidiaries)—

(a) in subsection (1) the words " and the London Transport Executive " shall be omitted ;

(b) subsection (2)(b) and the word " and " immediately preceding it shall be omitted ; and

(c) in subsection (3) the words from first " and " to " 1969 " shall be omitted.

The Criminal Justice Act 1982

27. In section 39(1)(b)(ii) of the Criminal Justice Act 1982 (certain special cases excepted from the general increase of fines under section 38 of that Act), the reference to section 12(1) of the London Transport Act 1977 shall be read as including section 12(1) as extended by Part II of this Schedule.

The Transport Act 1983

28. In section 1 of the Transport Act 1983 (interpretation of Part I)—

(a) the following provisions shall be omitted, that is to say—
(i) the definition of " the Act of 1969 " ;

(ii) in the definitions of " Executive " and " Authority ", paragraph (*b*) and the word " and " immediately preceding it ; and

(iii) in the definition of " revenue grants ", the words from " or section " to " 1969 " ; and

(*b*) for the words (in the last-mentioned definition) " those provisions " there shall be substituted the words " that section ".

29. In section 2 of that Act (financial duty of Executive)—

(*a*) in subsection (4), for the words from " under Part II " to " 1969 " there shall be substituted the words " or under Part II of the Act of 1968 " ; and

(*b*) in subsection (5), the words from " and the " to the end shall be omitted.

The Food Act 1984

1984 c. 30.

30.—(1) In section 11(4)(*a*) of the Food Act 1984 (vehicles whose detention by an officer of a council is not authorised under that section), for the words from " Boards " to " subsidiaries " there shall be substituted the words " transport authorities mentioned in subsection (4A) ".

(2) The following subsection shall be inserted after section 11(4)—

" (4A) The transport authorities referred to in subsection (4)(*a*) are—

(*a*) the Boards established by the Transport Act 1962 and any wholly owned subsidiary of any of those Boards ; and

(*b*) London Regional Transport and any subsidiary (whether wholly owned or not) of London Regional Transport (within the meaning of the London Regional Transport Act 1984). ".

1962 c. 46.

31. In Schedule 11 to that Act (repeals and revocations), after the entry relating to the Health Services and Public Health Act 1968 there shall be inserted the following words—

1968 c. 46.

| " 1968 c. 73. | Transport Act 1968. | In Schedule 16, paragraph 7(2)(*d*)." |

PART II

LOCAL ACTS

The London Transport Act 1965

1965 c. xli.

32. In section 34 of the London Transport Act 1965 (increase of penalties under enactments relating to railways)—

(*a*) for the words " the Board " (in the first place where they occur) there shall be substituted the words " London Regional Transport or any subsidiary of theirs (within the meaning of the London Regional Transport Act 1984) " ; and (*b*) for those words (wherever else occurring) there shall be substituted the words " London Regional Transport or any such subsidiary ".

The Greater London Council (General Powers) Act 1969

33. In section 18A(2)(*c*) of the Greater London Council (General Powers) Act 1969 (definition of apparatus for purposes of exception from prohibition on use of vehicles on walkways)—

(*a*) for the words " the London Transport Executive " there shall be substituted the words " London Regional Transport or any subsidiary of theirs (within the meaning of the London Regional Transport Act 1984) " ; and

(*b*) for the words " they are " there shall be substituted the words " London Regional Transport or (as the case may be) that subsidiary is ".

The Greater London Council (General Powers) Act 1970

34. In section 15(5) of the Greater London Council (General Powers) Act 1970 (exemption from requirement of a licence to erect scaffolding), for the words " or the London Transport Executive " there shall be substituted the words " London Regional Transport or any subsidiary of London Regional Transport (within the meaning of the London Regional Transport Act 1984) ".

The London Transport Act 1971

35. In section 26(1)(*a*) of the London Transport Act 1971 (arrest without warrant on suspicion of contravention of byelaw), for the words " the Executive " there shall be substituted the words " London Regional Transport ".

36. In section 27(2) of that Act (extension of power to place advertisements on shelters, etc.) for the words " the Executive " there shall be substituted the words " London Regional Transport or any subsidiary of theirs (within the meaning of the London Regional Transport Act 1984) ".

The Greater London Council (General Powers) Act 1974

37. In sections 14(7)(*c*) and 15(7)(*b*) of the Greater London Council (General Powers) Act 1974 (definition of apparatus for the provisions to which they respectively apply)—

(*a*) for the words " or the London Transport Executive " there shall be substituted the words " London Regional Transport or any subsidiary of London Regional Transport (within the meaning of the London Regional Transport Act 1984) " ; and

(*b*) for the words " they are " there shall be substituted the words " that Board or (as the case may be) London Regional Transport or that subsidiary is ".

38. In section 21 of that Act (removal of vehicles for street cleansing), in the definition of " vehicle " in subsection (7), for the words

" the London Transport Executive or " there shall be substituted the
words " London Regional Transport or any subsidiary of theirs (within the meaning of the London Regional Transport Act 1984) or by ".

The London Transport Act 1976 1976 c. xxxvii.

39. In section 17(2) of the London Transport Act 1976 (effect of certain regulations about public service vehicles in relation to the Executive), for the words " the Executive " there shall be substituted the words " London Regional Transport or any subsidiary of theirs (within the meaning of the London Regional Transport Act 1984) ".

40. In section 18 of that Act (microfilming of documents—

(a) for the words " the Executive " (wherever occurring) there shall be substituted the words " London Regional Transport " ; and

(b) at the end there shall be added the following subsection—

" (6) This section applies in relation to documents of any subsidiary of London Regional Transport (within the meaning of the London Regional Transport Act 1984) as it applies in relation to documents of London Regional Transport ; and, accordingly, references in subsections (1) to (5) above to London Regional Transport shall be read as including references to any such subsidiary.".

The London Transport Act 1977 1977 c. xii.

41. In section 12(1) of the London Transport Act 1977 (increase of fines under enactments relating to railways)—

(a) for the words " the Executive " (in the first place where they occur) there shall be substituted the words " London Regional Transport or any subsidiary of theirs (within the meaning of the London Regional Transport Act 1984) " ; and

(b) for those words (in the second place where they occur) there shall be substituted the words " London Regional Transport or of any such subsidiary ".

The Greater London Council (General Powers) Act 1979 1979 c. xxiii.

42. For paragraph (b) of the proviso to section 5(2) of the Greater London Council (General Powers) Act 1979 (consent required for advertisements, etc., in streets) there shall be substituted the following paragraph—

" (b) the British Railways Board, London Regional Transport or (as the case may be) any subsidiary of London Regional Transport (within the meaning of the London Regional Transport Act 1984) in the case of any street which belongs to or is repairable by that Board, by London Regional Transport or by that subsidiary.".

The London Transport Act 1980 1980 c. xxxii.

43. In section 24 of the London Transport Act 1980 (distance markers) subsections (1) and (2) shall apply to any subsidiary of

London Regional Transport as they apply to London Regional Transport ; and accordingly—

> (*a*) in subsection (1), for the words " the Executive " there shall be substituted the words " London Regional Transport or any subsidiary of theirs (within the meaning of the London Regional Transport Act 1984) " and
>
> (*b*) in subsection (2)—
>
>> (i) for the words " The Executive " (in the first place where they occur) there shall be substituted the words " London Regional Transport or any such subsidiary " ; and
>>
>> (ii) for those words (in the second place where they occur) there shall be substituted the words " London Regional Transport or (as the case may be) of that subsidiary ".

1845 c. 20.

44. In section 25 of that Act (increase of fines under sections 24 and 103 of the Railways Clauses Consolidation Act 1845)—

> (*a*) for the words " the Executive " (in the first place where they occur) there shall be substituted the words " London Regional Transport or any subsidiary of theirs (within the meaning of the London Regional Transport Act 1984) " ; and
>
> (*b*) for those words (in the second place where they occur) there shall be substituted the words " London Regional Transport or of any such subsidiary ".

1982 c. v.

The London Transport Act 1982

45. In section 19 of the London Transport Act 1982 (lost property)—

> (*a*) for the words " the Executive " (in the first place where they occur) there shall be substituted the words " London Regional Transport or any subsidiary of theirs (within the meaning of the London Regional Transport Act 1984) " ; and
>
> (*b*) for those words (wherever else occurring) there shall be substituted the words " London Regional Transport ".

46. In Schedule 2 to that Act (further provisions with respect to lost property), for the words " the Executive " (wherever occurring) there shall be substituted the words " London Regional Transport ".

1982 c. xxi.

The London Transport (General Powers) Act 1982

47. In section 15(2) of the London Transport (General Powers) Act 1982 (under which the rules of the pension scheme established by the London Transport (Male Wages Grades Pensions) Order 1966 may be changed), for the words " the Executive " there shall be substituted the words " London Regional Transport ".

SCHEDULE 7

Section 71(3)(*b*).

ENACTMENTS REPEALED

Chapter	Short title	Extent of repeal
1933 c. 14.	The London Passenger Transport Act 1933.	Section 19(2). Section 24.
1937 c. xc.	The London Passenger Transport Act 1937.	Section 68(2).
1939 c. lxxxix.	The London Passenger Transport Act 1939.	Section 49.
1960 c. 16.	The Road Traffic Act 1960.	In section 248, the words " or section 23A of the Transport (London) Act 1969 ".
1962 c. 46.	The Transport Act 1962.	Section 67(14). Section 68. In Part I of Schedule 2, the entry relating to the London Passenger Transport Act 1933. In Part II of Schedule 2, the entry relating to the London Passenger Transport Acts of 1934 to 1947.
1963 c. 33.	The London Government Act 1963.	Section 72(2)(*h*). In Schedule 2, in paragraph 25B, the words from " (*a*) " to " (*b*) ", and paragraph 29A.
1968 c. 73.	The Transport Act 1968.	In section 56(6)(*b*) the words " the Greater London Council ".
1969 c. 1.	The London Transport Act 1969.	Section 26.
1969 c. 35.	The Transport (London) Act 1969.	Parts I to IV. Sections 37 to 41. Section 44. In section 45(1) all the definitions except the following, that is to say, the definitions of " the Act of 1967 ", " appointed day ", " charges ", " the Common Council ", " the Council ", " Greater London ", " liability " and " the Minister ". In section 47(3), paragraphs (*a*) and (*b*). Schedules 1 to 4.
1969 c. 48.	The Post Office Act 1969.	In section 7(1A)(*b*), the words " the London Transport Executive and ".
1970 c. 10.	The Income and Corporation Taxes Act 1970.	In section 272(6) the words " the London Transport Executive and ".
1970 c. 24.	The Finance Act 1970.	In section 16(1), the words " or of the London Transport Executive " and paragraph (*b*). In Schedule 3, paragraph 8(2).

Chapter	Short title	Extent of repeal
1972 c. 20.	The Road Traffic Act 1972.	Section 144(2)(*e*).
1972 c. xlii.	The London Transport Act 1972.	Sections 21 and 22.
1972 c. 70.	The Local Government Act 1972.	Section 81(3A). In section 140(4), the words from " local authority " to " expression ".
1974 c. 7.	The Local Government Act 1974.	In Schedule 1, in paragraph 9(1)(*a*) the words "or the London Transport Executive", and in paragraph 9(3) the words from " and " to the end of the paragraph. In Schedule 6, paragraph 23. In Schedule 7, paragraph 11.
1975 c. ix	The London Transport (Additional Powers) Act 1975.	The whole Act.
1978 c. 44.	The Employment Protection (Consolidation) Act 1978.	In Schedule 16, paragraph 7.
1979 c. xxiii.	The Greater London Council (General Powers) Act 1979.	Section 4.
1980 c. 34.	The Transport Act 1980.	Section 35. Section 62(1). In Part II of Schedule 5, the entry relating to the Finance Act 1965.
1980 c. xxxii.	The London Transport Act 1980.	Section 23.
1980 c. 65.	The Local Government, Planning and Land Act 1980.	In section 4, in subsection (4), paragraph (*f*) and in subsection (5), paragraph (*b*) and the word " and " immediately preceding it. In Schedule 13, paragraphs 9 and 10.
1980 c. 66.	The Highways Act 1980.	In section 219(4)(*i*), in subparagraph (i), the word " or " where it first occurs. In section 329(4), the word " or " where it first occurs.
1981 c. 14.	The Public Passenger Vehicles Act 1981	In section 42(2), the words from " and section 23(2) " to " services ". In section 45(5), the words from " but where " to the end of the subsection. In Schedule 7, paragraphs 3 and 11.
1982 c. 12.	The Travel Concessions (London) Act 1982.	The whole Act.

Chapter	Short title	Extent of repeal
1982 c. 32.	The Local Government Finance Act 1982.	In section 31, in subsection (1) the words " and the London Transport Executive ", in subsection (2) paragraph (*b*) and the word " and " immediately preceding it, and in subsection (3) the words from first " and " to " 1969 ". In section 33(4)(*b*), the words " and the London Transport Executive ". In Schedule 5, paragraph 4.
1982 c. 49.	The Transport Act 1982.	In section 3(5), the definition of " county council ".
1983 c. 10	The Transport Act 1983.	In section 1, the definition of " the Act of 1969 ", in the definitions of " Executive " and " Authority ", paragraph (*b*) and the word " and " immediately preceding it, and in the definition of " revenue grants ", the words from " or section " to " 1969 ". In section 2(5), the words from " and the " to the end. In section 3(3), the words " or section 5(1) of the Act of 1969 ". In section 4(6), the words from " or sections " to the end. In section 6, in subsection (6), paragraph (*b*) and the word " and " immediately preceding it, and in subsection (7) the words " or section 11(2)(*d*) of the Act of 1969 ". In section 7, in subsection (2), the words " or section 15 of the Act of 1969 " and in subsection (3) the words " or section 11(6) of the Act of 1969 ". In section 8, in subsection (5), the words " or section 15 of the Act of 1969 ", and subsection (6). In section 9, subsections (4) and (5). In section 10(1), in paragraph (*a*), the words from " section 9(1) " to " 1969 " and the words " to (5) ", and in paragraph (*b*), the words from " section 9(1) " to " 1969 ".

Chapter	Short title	Extent of repeal
1983 c. 55.	The Value Added Tax Act 1983.	In section 20(3)(*d*), the words " the London Transport Executive and ".
1984 c. 27.	The Road Traffic Regulation Act 1984.	In Schedule 13, paragraph 8.
1984 c. 30.	The Food Act 1984.	In Schedule 10, paragraph 16.

Rates Act 1984

1984 CHAPTER 33

An Act to enable the Secretary of State to limit the rates made and precepts issued by local authorities; to require local authorities to consult representatives of industrial and commercial ratepayers before reaching decisions on expenditure and the means of financing it; to make provision for requiring additional information to be given to ratepayers; to require notice of the rates payable in respect of a dwelling-house to be given to any occupier not in receipt of a demand note; and to make other amendments relating to rates.

[26th June 1984]

BE IT ENACTED by the Queen's most Excellent Majesty, by and with the advice and consent of the Lords Spiritual and Temporal, and Commons, in this present Parliament assembled, and by the authority of the same, as follows:—

PART I

SELECTIVE LIMITATION OF RATES AND PRECEPTS

1.—(1) The Secretary of State may, in accordance with the provisions of this Part of this Act, prescribe a maximum for the rate made or, as the case may be, the precept issued for any financial year by an authority to which this Part of this Act applies and which is designated by him in relation to that year in accordance with those provisions.

(2) Where an authority is designated as aforesaid in relation to a financial year its powers and duties in respect of the making of a rate or issuing a precept for that year shall have effect subject to the provisions of this Part of this Act.

Power to prescribe maximum rates and precepts.

PART I   (3) This Part of this Act applies to—

(*a*) the council of a county or district;

(*b*) the Greater London Council, the council of a London borough and the Common Council of the City of London;

(*c*) the Inner London Education Authority; and

(*d*) the Council of the Isles of Scilly.

(4) A maximum prescribed under this section for a rate shall apply to the rate exclusive of any part made for giving effect to—

(*a*) a precept issued to the rating authority by another authority to which this Part of this Act applies or by the Receiver for the Metropolitan Police District; or

1984 c. 32.   (*b*) a levy made on the rating authority under section 13 of the London Regional Transport Act 1984.

(5) In the case of the Inner London Education Authority the power to prescribe a maximum under this section shall be construed as a power to prescribe a maximum for such part of any precept issued by the Greater London Council as is attributable to expenditure of the Authority; and any maximum prescribed under this section in the case of the Greater London Council shall apply only to such part of any precept issued by the Council as is not attributable to such expenditure.

Designation of authorities.   **2.**—(1) The authority or authorities in whose case a maximum is to be prescribed under section 1 above for any financial year shall be designated by the Secretary of State in a report laid before the House of Commons in the preceding financial year; and on laying any such report the Secretary of State shall serve on the authority or, as the case may be, each of the authorities designated in it a notice stating that the authority has been so designated.

(2) The Secretary of State shall not in a report laid under subsection (1) above in any financial year designate an authority unless it appears to him from the best information available to him that its total expenditure in that year is likely—

(*a*) to exceed its grant-related expenditure for that year or £10 million, whichever is the greater; and

(*b*) to be excessive having regard to general economic conditions.

(3) If the total of relevant expenditure as estimated for the purposes of the Rate Support Grant Report for any financial year (other than the first) in which this section is in force is greater or smaller than the total of relevant expenditure as

estimated for the purposes of the Rate Support Grant Report
for the previous financial year, the Secretary of State shall by
order substitute for the amount for the time being specified in
subsection (2)(*a*) above (whether £10 million or an amount previously substituted under this subsection) an amount which is
proportionately greater or smaller except that any substituted
amount may be rounded to the nearest £100,000.

(4) The power to make an order under subsection (3) above
shall be exercisable by statutory instrument subject to annulment
in pursuance of a resolution of the House of Commons.

(5) The power to designate an authority shall be exercised
in accordance with principles determined by the Secretary of
State and, in the case of an authority falling within any of the
classes specified in subsection (6) below, those principles shall
be the same either for all authorities falling within that class or
for all of them which respectively have and have not been
designated under this section in the previous financial year.

(6) The classes referred to in subsection (5) above are—
   (*a*) councils of metropolitan counties ;
   (*b*) councils of non-metropolitan counties ;
   (*c*) councils of metropolitan districts ;
   (*d*) councils of non-metropolitan districts ;
   (*e*) councils of inner London boroughs ; and
   (*f*) councils of outer London boroughs.

(7) Any report under subsection (1) above shall contain a
statement of the principles in accordance with which the authority or authorities included in the report have been designated.

(8) Separate reports and orders may be made under this section
in relation to England and Wales respectively.

(9) References in the following provision of this Part of this
Act to a designated authority are to an authority designated
under this section.

3.—(1) For the purpose of enabling the Secretary of State to Expenditure
prescribe a maximum under section 1 above for the rate made levels.
or precept issued by a designated authority the Secretary of
State shall determine a level for its total expenditure in the
financial year for which the maximum is to have effect.

(2) The power to determine a level for the total expenditure of a designated authority shall be exercised in accordance with principles determined by the Secretary of State and, in the case of an authority falling within any of the classes specified in subsection (6) of section 2 above, those principles shall be the same either for all authorities falling within that class or for all of them which respectively have and have not been designated under that section in the previous financial year.

(3) The Secretary of State shall serve on each designated authority a notice stating the level determined by him in the case of that authority.

(4) Any authority on which a notice is served under subsection (3) above may, within the period specified in the notice, apply to the Secretary of State for a re-determination of the level stated in the notice at a greater amount ; and any such application shall be accompanied by such information in such form as the Secretary of State may require.

(5) Where an application is made in accordance with subsection (4) above the Secretary of State may, after considering the information submitted with it, any additional information furnished by the applicant and any other matters that he thinks relevant, either confirm his original determination or re-determine the level at a greater or smaller amount ; and in making any such re-determination the Secretary of State may depart from the principles referred to in subsection (2) above.

(6) Where under subsection (5) above the Secretary of State re-determines a level at a greater amount he may impose on the authority in question such requirements relating to its expenditure or financial management as he thinks appropriate ; and it shall be the duty of the authority to comply with any such requirements and to report to the Secretary of State whenever he so directs on the extent to which those requirements have been complied with.

(7) The duties of an authority under subsection (6) above shall be enforceable at the suit of the Secretary of State ; and where an authority fails to comply with any such duty the Secretary of State may designate the authority under section 2 above in relation to a subsequent financial year without regard to subsection (2) of that section.

(8) The Secretary of State's decision under subsection (5) and any requirements imposed by him under subsection (6) above shall be stated in a notice served by him on the authority concerned.

(9) In making a decision under subsection (5) above the Secretary of State shall have regard to the extent (if any) to which the authority's proposed expenditure is to consist of con-

tributions to charities registered, or excepted from registration, under section 4 of the Charities Act 1960.

4.—(1) As soon as practicable after the Rate Support Grant Report for any financial year has been laid before Parliament the Secretary of State shall serve on each designated authority a notice stating the maximum which he proposes to prescribe under section 1 above for the rate made or precept issued by that authority for that year.

(2) The Secretary of State shall determine that maximum by reference to—

> (*a*) the level of expenditure determined or re-determined by him for the authority under section 3 above ;
>
> (*b*) the block grant (if any) which he estimates will become payable to the authority in question ; and
>
> (*c*) in the case of an authority affected by a scheme under section 66 of the London Government Act 1963 (equalisation of rates), any contribution to be made by or to the authority in pursuance of the scheme ;

and in determining that maximum the Secretary of State may take into account any financial reserves available to the authority.

(3) If—

> (*a*) the proposed maximum stated in a notice served on a designated authority under subsection (1) above is accepted by the authority within the period specified in the notice ; or
>
> (*b*) a designated authority and the Secretary of State agree on a different maximum,

the power of the Secretary of State to prescribe a maximum under section 1 above in the case of that authority for the financial year in question shall be exercised by specifying in a direction in writing served on the authority a maximum equal to that stated in the notice or agreed with the authority, as the case may be.

(4) In any other case the power of the Secretary of State to prescribe a maximum under section 1 above shall be exercised by specifying by order a maximum equal to or greater than that stated in the notice served on the authority in question.

(5) The power to make an order under subsection (4) above shall be exercisable by statutory instrument and no such order shall be made unless a draft of it has been laid before and approved by a resolution of the House of Commons.

(6) An order under subsection (4) above may relate to two or more authorities.

5.—(1) If in the case of any designated authority no maximum has been prescribed under section 1 above before the relevant date, the Secretary of State may prescribe an interim maximum under this section by a direction in writing served on the authority.

(2) For the purposes of subsection (1) above the relevant date in relation to a maximum under section 1 above for any financial year is—

    (*a*) in the case of a rate, 1st March ; or

    (*b*) in the case of a precept, 15th February,

in the preceding financial year.

(3) An interim maximum shall have effect until replaced by a maximum prescribed under section 1 above (a " final maximum ") ; and where an interim maximum is prescribed in the case of any authority the Secretary of State shall as soon as reasonably practicable replace it with a final maximum.

(4) If an authority makes a rate or issues a precept by reference to an interim maximum and the final maximum is higher—

    (*a*) a substituted rate or precept complying with the final maximum may be made or issued by the authority under section 3 of the Local Government Finance Act 1982 without regard to subsection (2) of that section (which limits the estimated product of a substituted rate or precept by reference to the estimated product of the rate or precept for which it is substituted) ; and

    (*b*) that subsection shall not prevent a substituted rate being made by any other authority in pursuance of subsection (4)(*a*) of that section for giving effect to a precept substituted in accordance with paragraph (*a*) above.

(5) Section 1(4) and (5) above shall apply to an interim maximum as they apply to a final maximum.

6.—(1) Any maximum prescribed under this Part of this Act for a rate shall be expressed as a limit on the amount in the pound of the rate exclusive of any such part as is mentioned in section 1(4) above ; and a rate shall be invalid if—

    (*a*) the amount in the pound of the rate (exclusive of any such part) exceeds a limit applicable to it by virtue of any such maximum ; or

    (*b*) any part of the rate is made for giving effect to a precept which is invalid under subsection (2) below.

(2) Any maximum prescribed under this Part of this Act for a precept or, in a case within section 1(5) above, for part of a precept shall be expressed as a limit on the amount in the pound of the precept or part; and a precept shall be invalid if the amount in the pound of the precept or, as the case may be, of the relevant part of it exceeds a limit applicable to it by virtue of any such maximum.

(3) The Secretary of State may by order make provision with respect to the application of any such limit as is mentioned in subsection (1) or (2) above in cases where the rate or precept or, as the case may be, the relevant part of the rate or precept falls to be levied otherwise than at a uniform rate in the pound.

(4) The power to make an order under subsection (3) above shall be exercisable by statutory instrument subject to annulment in pursuance of a resolution of the House of Commons.

(5) Separate orders may be made under subsection (3) above in relation to England and Wales respectively.

7.—(1) Where a rate is subject to a maximum under this Part of this Act the notice of the rate given under section 4 of the General Rate Act 1967— Certificates of compliance. 1967 c. 9.

   (a) shall include a statement by the proper officer of the rating authority to the effect that the rate complies with the maximum; and

   (b) shall (without prejudice to any other method of publication allowed by that section) be published in a newspaper circulating in the area of the authority;

and a statement to the same effect by the proper officer of the authority shall be included in every demand note on which the rate is levied.

(2) Where a precept is subject to a maximum under this Part of this Act the precept shall include a statement by the proper officer of the precepting authority to the effect that the precept complies with the maximum.

(3) Where a rate gives effect to a precept which is subject to a maximum under this Part of this Act, then—

   (a) if the rate falls within subsection (1) above, the statements required by that subsection shall include a statement to the effect that the precept complies with the maximum; and

   (b) if the rate does not fall within that subsection, the requirements of that subsection shall apply to the notice of the rate and the demand notes on which it is levied with the substitution for the reference to the rate in paragraph (*a*) of that subsection of a reference to the precept.

(4) Subsection (1) above shall apply to the City of London with the substitution for the reference to section 4 of the said Act of 1967 of a reference to section 20(1) of the City of London (Union of Parishes) Act 1907.

(5) The statements required by subsections (2) and (3) above in a case within section 1(5) above shall be to the effect that the relevant part or parts of the precept comply with the maximum applicable to that part or, as the case may be, each of those parts.

Information.

8.—(1) A designated authority shall furnish the Secretary of State with such information as he may require for the purpose of exercising his powers under this Part of this Act ; and if any such information is not furnished within such time as he may require he may exercise those powers on the basis of such assumptions as he thinks appropriate.

1967 c. 9.

(2) For the purpose of enabling him to prescribe a maximum for a precept under this Part of this Act the Secretary of State may require each rating authority to which the precept can be issued to furnish him with an estimate of the amount, calculated in the manner prescribed under the General Rate Act 1967, which would be produced in the year in question by a rate of a new penny in the pound levied in its area or any part of it ; and if any such estimate is not furnished within such time as the Secretary of State may require he may himself make the estimate for that purpose.

1972 c. 70.
1980 c. 65.

(3) The Secretary of State may use for the purpose of exercising his powers under this Part of this Act any information obtained by him under section 168 of the Local Government Act 1972 (local financial returns), section 65 of the Local Government, Planning and Land Act 1980 (information for purposes of block grants) or under any other enactment.

Part II

General Limitation of Rates and Precepts

Power to introduce general control.

9.—(1) Subject to the provisions of this section, the Secretary of State may make an order bringing sections 10 and 11 below into force on such date as may be specified in the order.

(2) Before making an order under this section the Secretary of State shall consult such associations of local authorities as

appear to him to be concerned and any local authority with PART II
which consultation appears to him to be desirable.

(3) No order shall be made under this section unless a draft
of the order has been laid before and approved by a resolution
of each House of Parliament.

10.—(1) Section 2 above shall not apply after the date on Authorities
which this section comes into force and, subject to subsections subject to
(2) and (5) below, the other provisions of Part I of this Act shall general
have effect as if every authority to which that Part applies were a control.
designated authority in relation to each financial year beginning after that date.

(2) If in any financial year it appears to the Secretary of
State from the best information available to him that an authority—

> (*a*) has in each of the three preceding financial years com-
> plied with subsection (3) below and is likely to comply
> with that subsection in that financial year ; or

> (*b*) has in each of the three preceding financial years com-
> plied with subsection (4) below and is likely to comply
> with that subsection in that financial year,

he shall by a notice in writing served on that authority exempt
it from the operation of subsection (1) above in relation to the
next financial year.

(3) An authority complies with this subsection in a financial
year if it has not been designated in relation to that year under
section 2 above and its total expenditure in that year does not
exceed its grant-related expenditure for that year.

(4) An authority complies with this subsection in a financial
year if it has not been designated in relation to that year under
section 2 above and complies in that year with guidance issued to
it for the purposes of section 59(6)(*cc*) of the Local Government, 1980 c. 65.
Planning and Land Act 1980.

(5) If in a case to which subsection (2) above does not apply
it appears to the Secretary of State from the best information
available to him that the total expenditure of an authority in
any financial year is not likely to exceed such amount as may
be prescribed by an order made by him for the purposes of
this subsection, he may by a notice in writing served on that
authority exempt it from the operation of subsection (1) above
in relation to the next financial year.

(6) The power to make an order under subsection (5) above
shall be exercisable by statutory instrument subject to annulment in pursuance of a resolution of the House of Commons.

PART II
Expenditure
levels and
variation of
maximum.

11.—(1) Before determining levels of total expenditure under section 3 above for the authorities treated as designated by virtue of section 10 above the Secretary of State shall consult such associations of local authorities as appear to him to be concerned.

(2) Section 5 above shall not apply in the case of an authority treated as designated by virtue of section 10 above but any maximum prescribed in the case of such an authority by an order under section 4(4) above may be—

(*a*) increased by a direction in writing served by the Secretary of State on that authority ; or

(*b*) reduced by an order made by the Secretary of State.

(3) If an authority has made a rate or issued a precept by reference to a maximum which is subsequently increased under subsection (2)(*a*) above—

1982 c. 32.

(*a*) a substituted rate or precept complying with the higher maximum may be made or issued by the authority under section 3 of the Local Government Finance Act 1982 without regard to subsection (2) of that section ; and

(*b*) that subsection shall not prevent a substituted rate being made by any other authority in pursuance of subsection (4)(*a*) of that section for giving effect to a precept substituted in accordance with paragraph (*a*) above.

(4) The power to make an order under subsection (2)(*b*) above shall be exercisable by statutory instrument and no such order shall be made unless a draft of it has been laid before and approved by a resolution of the House of Commons.

(5) An order under subsection (2)(*b*) above may relate to two or more authorities.

Supple-
mentary
provisions.

12.—(1) Separate orders may be made under this Part of this Act in relation to England and Wales respectively ; and if an order under section 9 above is made in relation to only one of those countries the reference in section 10(1) above to the authorities to which Part I of this Act applies shall be construed as a reference to such of those authorities as are in that country.

(2) Section 8 above shall apply to the powers of the Secretary of State under this Part of this Act as it applies to his powers under Part I of this Act.

PART III

OTHER PROVISIONS RELATING TO RATES AND PRECEPTS

13.—(1) Every authority to which Part I of this Act applies Duty to shall in each financial year consult persons or bodies appearing consult to it to be representative of industrial and commercial ratepayers industrial and in its area about its proposals for expenditure and the financing ratepayers. of expenditure in the next financial year.

(2) The duty under subsection (1) above shall be performed by an authority in each financial year before it determines for the purposes of section 2 or 11 of the General Rate Act 1967 the 1967 c. 9. amount of its total estimated expenditure for the next financial year.

(3) In performing that duty an authority shall have regard to any guidance issued by the Secretary of State concerning—

    (*a*) persons or bodies to be regarded for the purposes of this section as representative of industrial and commercial ratepayers ; and

    (*b*) the timing and manner of consultation under this section.

(4) An authority shall make available to the representatives whom it proposes to consult under this section such information concerning its past and proposed expenditure and financing of expenditure as may be prescribed by regulations made by the Secretary of State.

(5) The power to make regulations under subsection (4) above shall be exercisable by statutory instrument subject to annulment in pursuance of a resolution of either House of Parliament.

(6) For the purposes of this section the area of the Inner London Education Authority is the Inner London Education Area.

14.—(1) Rules under section 113 of the General Rate Act Provision of 1967 may require a rating authority to serve with any demand information to note for a rate a notice containing information— ratepayers.

    (*a*) as to the past or proposed expenditure of—

        (i) the rating authority ; or

        (ii) any authority by which a precept has been issued to the rating authority,

    and as to the financing of that expenditure ; and

    (*b*) as to any increase or reduction in the rates made by the rating authority or in the precepts issued to it.

PART III

(2) Rules under that section may require an authority having power to issue precepts to serve notices on ratepayers in its area containing information—

(a) as to its past or proposed expenditure and as to the financing of that expenditure ; and

(b) as to any increase or reduction in the precepts issued by the authority.

(3) Rules made by virtue of this section may make different provision for different cases ; and any notice required to be served by rules made by virtue of this section shall be in such form (if any) as the rules may prescribe.

(4) An authority having power to issue precepts to a rating authority shall supply that authority with such information as is reasonably necessary for enabling it to comply with any requirements imposed by rules made by virtue of subsection (1) above ; and a rating authority shall supply an authority having power to issue precepts to it with such information as is reasonably necessary for enabling the precepting authority to serve any notices required by rules made by virtue of subsection (2) above.

Notice of rates payable in respect of dwelling-house.

15.—(1) Every rating authority shall within three months after a rate is made serve a notice under this section on each occupier of a dwelling-house in its rating area, being an occupier to whom this section applies.

(2) This section applies to an occupier—

(a) to whom the rating authority has not issued and does not intend to issue a demand note for the rate ; and

(b) who does not occupy the dwelling-house jointly with another person to whom the rating authority has issued or intends to issue such a demand note.

(3) A notice under this section shall contain or be accompanied by—

(a) such information as may be prescribed concerning the rate and the amount of it chargeable in respect of the dwelling-house ; and

(b) such additional information (if any) as has been or will be included in or sent with demand notes for the rate issued or to be issued by the authority to occupiers of dwelling-houses.

1967 c. 9.

(4) The General Rate Act 1967 and this section shall have effect as if this section were contained in that Act.

Miscellaneous amendments and repeals.

16.—(1) The enactments mentioned in Schedule 1 to this Act shall have effect subject to the provisions of that Schedule.

(2) Schedule 2 to this Act shall have effect with respect to the PART IV rating of moorings.

(3) Section 170 of the Local Government Act 1972 (schemes 1972 c. 70. for equalisation of rates in metropolitan counties) is hereby repealed.

PART IV

SUPPLEMENTARY

17. There shall be paid out of moneys provided by Parliament Expenses. any administrative expenses incurred by the Secretary of State in consequence of this Act and any increase attributable to this Act in the sums payable out of such moneys under any other Act.

18.—(1) The first financial year for which a maximum may be Commence-prescribed under Part I of this Act shall be the year beginning ment. on 1st April 1985.

(2) The first financial year in which consultation is required to take place under section 13 above shall be the financial year beginning on 1st April 1984.

(3) Section 15 above shall have effect in relation to any rate made after the passing of this Act.

(4) The provisions of Schedules 1 and 2 to this Act shall come into force as provided in those provisions respectively.

19.—(1) This Act may be cited as the Rates Act 1984. Short title, interpretation

(2) In this Act— and extent.

" financial year " means a period of twelve months begin-ning with 1st April ;

" grant-related expenditure ", " Rate Support Grant Re-port " and " total expenditure " have the same meaning as in Part VI of the Local Government, Planning and 1980 c. 65. Land Act 1980 and " relevant expenditure " has the meaning given in section 54 of that Act ;

" the proper officer " shall be construed in accordance with section 270(3) of the Local Government Act 1972 ;

" rate " means the general rate except that in the case of the City of London it includes the poor rate.

(3) This Act extends to England and Wales only.

Part II   F

SCHEDULES

SCHEDULE 1

MISCELLANEOUS AMENDMENTS AND REPEALS

Interpretation

1. In this Schedule " the principal Act " means the General Rate Act 1967.

Assessment of rateable value of premises

1. In this Schedule " the principal Act " means the General Rate be added the words " and section 23 of this Act ".

(2) In subsection (1) of section 23 of that Act for the words " section 19 of this Act the gross value " there shall be substituted the words " section 19(2) or (3) of this Act the gross value or, as the case may be, the net annual value " ; and in subsections (3) and (4) of that section after the words " gross value " there shall be inserted the words " or net annual value ".

(3) This paragraph shall have effect for any rate period beginning on or after the first date after the passing of this Act on which new valuation lists come into force under section 68(1) of that Act.

Valuation of public houses

3.—(1) In section 20(2) of the principal Act the words after " hereditament " in the third place where it occurs are hereby repealed.

(2) Subject to sub-paragraph (3) below, sub-paragraph (1) above shall come into force on the first date after the passing of this Act on which new valuation lists come into force under section 68(1) of that Act.

(3) The reference to " relevant factors " in section 19A(2)(*b*) of that Act shall be construed as if sub-paragraph (1) above had come into force on the passing of this Act.

Parts of hereditaments temporarily unoccupied

4.—(1) In subsection (1) of section 25 of the principal Act for the words from " until " to " subsection " there shall be substituted the words " until whichever of the events specified in subsection (1A) of this section first occurs ".

(2) After that subsection there shall be inserted—

" (1A) The events mentioned in subsection (1) of this section are—

(*a*) the reoccupation of any of the unoccupied part ;

(*b*) the ending of the rate period in which the request was made ;

(*c*) a further apportionment of the value of the hereditament taking effect under that subsection.

(1B) Where an apportionment of the value of a hereditament under subsection (1) of this section has taken effect in a rate period and, in that or a subsequent rate period, it appears to the rating authority that the part of the hereditament which was unoccupied at the date of the apportionment has continued to be unoccupied but will remain so for a short time only, the rating authority may give further effect to the apportionment by making a determination under this subsection in relation to a specified rate period.

(1C) From the commencement of the rate period to which a determination under subsection (1B) of this section relates until whichever of the events specified in subsection (1D) of this section first occurs the value apportioned to the occupied part shall be treated for rating purposes as if it were the value ascribed to the hereditament in the valuation list.

(1D) The events mentioned in subsection (1C) of this section are—

   (*a*) the reoccupation of any of the unoccupied part ;

   (*b*) the ending of the rate period to which the determination relates ;

   (*c*) a further apportionment of the value of the hereditament taking effect under subsection (1) of this section."

(3) In subsection (2) of that section for the word " subsection " there shall be substituted the word " subsections ".

(4) This paragraph shall have effect for any rate period beginning on or after 1st April 1984 ; and any apportionment which has taken effect under subsection (1) of section 25 of the principal Act before this paragraph comes into force shall cease to have effect on 31st March 1985, unless it has previously ceased to have effect under that subsection or it is the subject of a determination made by virtue of this paragraph in relation to a rate period beginning after that date.

Rating of transport Boards

5. The following sections shall be substituted for section 32 of the principal Act—

" Transport Boards— exemption and notional hereditaments.

   32.—(1) Subject to sections 32A and 32B(1) of this Act and without prejudice to subsection (2) of this section, no premises which are or form part of premises occupied by the British Railways Board, London Regional Transport or the British Waterways Board (each of which is referred to in this section and in section 32A of this Act as a " transport Board ") shall be liable to be rated or to be included in any valuation list or in any rate.

F 2

(2) For the purposes of the making and levying of rates for any rate period a transport Board shall be treated as occupying in any designated rating area during that period a hereditament of a rateable value calculated in accordance with the provisions of an order under section 19 of, and paragraph 2 of Schedule 3 to, the Local Government Act 1974.

(3) The hereditament which a transport Board are to be treated as occupying in a designated rating area by virtue of subsection (2) of this section shall be taken not to be situated in any part of that area in which there are leviable, as an additional item of the rate in that area, expenses which are not leviable in the area taken as a whole.

(4) In this section a " designated rating area ", in relation to a transport Board, means a rating area of such a description as the Secretary of State may by order specify in relation to that Board.

Transport Boards— rateable premises.

32A.—(1) Section 32(1) of this Act shall not apply—

(a) to premises occupied as a dwelling, hotel, shop, museum or place of public refreshment ;

(b) subject and without prejudice to paragraph 8 of Schedule 5 to this Act, to office premises occupied by a transport Board which are not situated on operational land of that Board ;

(c) to premises so let out as to be capable of separate assessment ;

(d) subject and without prejudice to subsection (3) of this section, to premises occupied for any of the purposes specified in subsection (2) of this section.

(2) The purposes mentioned in paragraph (d) of the foregoing subsection are—

(a) purposes of any of the parts of the undertaking of a transport Board which are—

(i) concerned with the carriage of goods or passengers by road transport or sea transport or with harbours ; or

(ii) subsidiary or incidental to any such part of an undertaking so concerned ;

(b) purposes of the supply of electricity to an Electricity Board within the meaning of section 34 of this Act, including the generation of electricity so supplied ;

(c) purposes of the exercise—

(i) by the British Railways Board or the British Waterways Board of any powers conferred by section 48 or 50(1) to (7) of the Transport Act 1968 ; or

(ii) by London Regional Transport of any
powers conferred by paragraph 9(2) or 12(1)
of Schedule 2 to the London Regional Transport Act 1984.

(3) For the purpose of determining whether premises
fall within paragraph (*d*) of subsection (1) of this section,
services performed by a transport Board in connection
with the collection and delivery of parcels, goods or mer-
chandise conveyed or to be conveyed by rail or inland
waterway shall be deemed not to be performed in
carrying on a part of the Board's undertaking concerned
with the carriage of goods by road transport, or with any
activity which is subsidiary or incidental to the carriage
of goods by road transport.

(4) Where a hereditament consists of premises other
than premises falling within paragraphs (*a*) to (*c*) of subsection (1) of this section, and the premises are occupied
by a transport Board partly for any of the purposes specified in subsection (2) of this section and partly for
other purposes, there shall be ascribed to the hereditament under section 19 of this Act such net annual value
as may be just having regard to the extent to which it is
occupied for the purposes specified in the said subsection
(2) ; and if under any scheme for the time being in force
such as is mentioned in section 117(7) of this Act any
deduction falls to be made from the net annual value
of the hereditament in arriving at its rateable value, that
deduction shall be calculated with regard only to those
purposes.

(5) This section and section 32 of this Act apply to a
subsidiary of a transport Board as they apply to that
Board, and references in either section to a transport
Board include references to a subsidiary of it.

(6) In this section—

" harbour " means any harbour, whether natural or
artificial, and any port, haven, estuary, tidal
or other river or inland waterway navigated by
sea-going ships, and any dock, including any
pier, jetty or other place at which ships can ship
or unship goods or passengers ;

" inland waterway " includes any such waterway,
whether natural or artificial ;

" office premises " means any hereditament used
wholly or mainly as an office or for office purposes ;

" office purposes " includes the purposes of administration, clerical work and handling money ; and
" clerical work " includes writing, book-keeping,
sorting papers, filing, typing, duplicating, punch-
ing cards or tapes, machine calculating, drawing and the editorial preparation of matter for
publication ;

F 3

          " operational land ", in relation to any body, means land which is used for the purpose of the carrying on of the body's undertaking, not being land which, in respect of its nature and situation, is comparable rather with land in general than with land which is used for the purpose of the carrying on of statutory undertakings within the meaning of the Town and Country Planning Act 1971 ;

          " road transport " includes transport by light railway or tramway, if the light railway or tramway is laid wholly or mainly along a public highway and is used wholly or mainly for the carriage of passengers ;

          " subsidiary ", in relation to a body corporate, means a body corporate which is a subsidiary of the first-mentioned body corporate as defined by section 154 of the Companies Act 1948 (taking references in that section to a company as being references to any body corporate).

    (7) The supplementary provisions contained in Schedule 5 to this Act shall have effect for the purposes of this section.

    32B.—(1) The Secretary of State may by order vary any provision of section 32 or 32A of this Act in its application to any premises of a description specified in the order.

    (2) Before making an order under this section or section 32 of this Act the Secretary of State shall consult with such associations of local authorities or of persons carrying on undertakings as appear to him to be concerned and with any local authority or person carrying on an undertaking with whom consultation appears to him to be desirable.

    (3) An order under this section or section 32 of this Act shall not have effect unless approved by a resolution of each House of Parliament."

    6.—(1) In section 28(6) of the principal Act for the words from " railway " to the end there shall be substituted the words " premises occupied by a transport Board, within the meaning of section 32 of this Act, other than premises such as are mentioned in section 32A(1) of this Act.".

    (2) In sections 33(7)(c) and 34(5)(d) of that Act for " 32(8) " there shall be substituted " 32A(6) ".

    (3) In section 68(4) of that Act for paragraph (d) there shall be substituted—

        " (d) in the case of any premises occupied by a transport Board, within the meaning of section 32 of this Act,

partly for any of the purposes specified in section   Sᴄʜ. 1
32A(2) of this Act and partly for other purposes, a change
in the extent to which they are occupied for any of the
purposes so specified.".

(4) In section 69(2)(c) of that Act for "32(3)" there shall be
substituted "32(1)".

(5) In paragraph 8 of Schedule 5, paragraph 12 of Schedule 6
and paragraph 15 of Schedule 7 to that Act for "32(2)(b)", in each
place where it occurs, there shall be substituted "32A(1)(b)".

(6) In Schedule 3 to the Local Government Act 1974 for para- 1974 c. 7.
graph 2 there shall be substituted—

> "2. Any hereditament which a transport Board, within the
> meaning of section 32 of the principal Act, are to be treated
> as occupying by virtue of subsection (2) of that section.".

(7) The following provisions are hereby repealed—

(a) paragraphs 1 to 7 of Schedule 5 to the principal Act ;

(b) section 162(1), (3), (4)(a) and (5) of the Transport Act 1968 c. 73.
1968 ; and

(c) paragraph 3 of Schedule 4 to the London Regional Transport 1984 c. 32.
Act 1984.

(8) This paragraph and paragraph 5 above shall come into force
on such day as the Secretary of State may by order made by statutory instrument appoint.

Rating of British Gas Corporation

7.—(1) In section 69(2) of the principal Act—

(a) paragraph (a) is hereby repealed ;

(b) in paragraph (b) for the words "33(1)(a) or (b)" there shall
be substituted "33(1)" ;

and in section 80(4) of that Act for "33(1)(a)" there shall be substituted "33(1)".

(2) This paragraph shall be deemed to have come into force on
1st January 1973.

Rating of private generators or suppliers of electricity

8.—(1) After section 34 of the principal Act there shall be
inserted—

" Other   34A.—(1) The Secretary of State may by order pro-
generators   vide that, in such cases and subject to such exceptions
or suppliers   and modifications as may be prescribed by the order,
of   section 34 of and Schedule 7 to this Act shall apply
electricity.   to premises which are, or form part of, premises occupied by a private generator or supplier of electricity.

(2) In this section " private generator or supplier "
has the same meaning as in section 5 of the Energy 1983 c. 25.
Act 1983.

F 4

SCH. 1

(3) Any statutory instrument containing an order under this section shall be subject to annulment in pursuance of a resolution of either House of Parliament.".

1974 c. 7.

(2) In Schedule 3 to the Local Government Act 1974 (hereditaments to which section 19(1) of that Act applies) after paragraph 4 there shall be inserted—

" 4A.—(1) Any hereditament which a private generator or supplier is to be treated as occupying in a rating area by virtue of section 34(3) of the principal Act as applied by order under section 34A of that Act.

1983 c. 25.

(2) In this paragraph " private generator or supplier " has the same meaning as in section 5 of the Energy Act 1983.".

(3) This paragraph shall come into force at the end of the period of two months beginning with the day on which this Act is passed.

Non-domestic hereditaments not in active use

9.—(1) After section 46 of the principal Act there shall be inserted—

" Relief for non-domestic hereditaments not in active use.

46A.—(1) For the purposes of this Act a hereditament to which this section applies shall be treated as unoccupied if, apart from this section, it would fall to be treated as occupied by reason only of there being kept in or on the hereditament plant, machinery or equipment—

(a) which was used in or on the hereditament when it was last in use ; or

(b) which is intended for use in or on the hereditament.

(2) This section applies to a hereditament which is not a dwelling-house, a private garage or private storage premises ; and in this subsection—

(a) " private garage " means a building having a floor area not exceeding 25 square metres which is used wholly or mainly for the accommodation of a motor vehicle ; and

(b) " private storage premises " means a hereditament which is used wholly in connection with a dwelling-house or dwelling-houses and wholly or mainly for the storage of articles of domestic use (including bicycles and similar vehicles) belonging to persons residing there.

(3) For the purposes of subsection (2) of this section a hereditament that is not in use shall nevertheless be treated as a dwelling-house, a private garage or private storage premises if it appears that, when next in use, it will be a hereditament of that description."

(2) This paragraph shall have effect for any rate period beginning on or after 1st April 1985.

Domestic rate relief

10.—(1) In section 48(5) of the principal Act for the word " movable " there shall be substituted the words " two or more moveable " and in paragraph 3 of Schedule 13 to that Act before the word " moveable " there shall be inserted the words " two or more ".

(2) This paragraph shall be deemed always to have had effect.

Limits on payment by instalments

11.—(1) In section 50(1) of the principal Act for the words from " (not being a tenant " to " through the owner " there shall be substituted the words " is liable to pay any rates in respect of a hereditament " ; and for the words " any rates ", in both places where they occur, there shall be substituted the words " the rates ".

(2) Section 50(5) to (7) of that Act and section 34(1)(c) of the Local Government, Planning and Land Act 1980 are hereby repealed. 1980 c. 65.

(3) This paragraph shall have effect as respects rates for any rate period beginning on or after 1st April 1985.

Alterations of current valuation list

12.—(1) For section 70(2) of the principal Act there shall be substituted—

" (2) The owner or occupier of the whole or any part of a hereditament to which the proposal relates may, within twenty-eight days from the date on which a copy of the proposal is transmitted to the occupier under subsection (1) of this section, serve on the valuation officer notice in writing of objection to the proposal ; and where—

(a) the rating authority for the area in which the hereditament is situated are not entitled to object by virtue of the foregoing provisions of this subsection ; but

(b) the hereditament is of a class or description specified by the authority in accordance with subsection (6) of this section,

the authority may, within twenty-eight days from the date on which a copy of the proposal is transmitted to them under subsection (1) of this section, serve on the valuation officer notice in writing of objection to the proposal.

(3) Where the proposal was made otherwise than by the valuation officer, he shall, within twenty-eight days from the date on which a notice of objection is served on him under subsection (2) of this section, transmit a copy of it to the maker of the proposal.

(4) Where the proposal was made by the valuation officer or by any other person, not being the rating authority, and—

(a) a notice of objection is served on the valuation officer under subsection (2) of this section otherwise than by the rating authority ; and (*b*) the hereditament in question is of a class or description specified by the authority in accordance with subsection (6) of this section,

the valuation officer shall, within twenty-eight days from the date on which the notice is served on him, transmit a copy of it to the authority.

(5) The valuation officer shall, within twenty-eight days from the date on which a notice of objection is served on him under subsection (2) of this section, serve on the objector a notice in writing stating that unless—

(*a*) the proposal is withdrawn ; or

(*b*) all notices of objection to the proposal are unconditionally withdrawn ; or

(*c*) an agreement in respect of the proposal is reached under section 72 of this Act,

a copy of the proposal and of every notice of objection which has not been unconditionally withdrawn will be transmitted to the clerk of the local valuation panel in accordance with section 73 of this Act ; and the notice shall explain that the transmission of a copy of the proposal will have effect as an appeal by the maker of the proposal against every objection signified by a notice of which a copy is transmitted.

(6) A rating authority may from time to time serve on the valuation officer for their area a notice in writing specifying a class or description of hereditament in respect of which they wish subsections (2) and (4) of this section to apply to them ; and any such notice shall have effect in relation to any proposal made by or served on the valuation officer after the end of the rate period in which the notice is served.

(7) Where a notice served by a rating authority under subsection (6) of this section has effect in relation to a proposal of which a copy is transmitted to the authority under subsection (1) of this section and the authority do not serve a notice of objection to the proposal under subsection (2) of this section, the authority may serve on the valuation officer a notice in writing stating that they wish sections 72(2)(*e*) and 76(4)(*d*) of this Act to apply to them in respect of the proposal ; and any notice under this subsection shall be served—

(*a*) in the case of a proposal made by the valuation officer, within twenty-eight days from the date on which a copy of any notice of objection to the proposal is transmitted to the authority under subsection (4) of this section ; and

(*b*) in the case of any other proposal, within twenty-eight days from the date on which a copy of the proposal is served on the authority or from the date mentioned in paragraph (*a*) of this subsection."

13. The following provisions of section 71 of the principal Act are hereby repealed—

(*a*) in subsection (1)(*b*), paragraph (iii) together with the word " or " immediately preceding it ; and (*b*) subsection (2).

14. In section 72(2) of the principal Act for paragraph (*e*) there shall be substituted—

" (*e*) the rating authority for the area in which the hereditament is situated if—

(i) the authority are not included by virtue of paragraph (*b*), (*c*) or (*d*) of this subsection ; and

(ii) the authority have notified the valuation officer in accordance with section 70(7) of this Act that they wish this paragraph to apply to them.".

15. The following provisions of section 73(2) of the principal Act are hereby repealed—

(*a*) paragraph (*a*) ; and

(*b*) in paragraph (*b*) the words in brackets.

16. For section 74 of the principal Act there shall be substituted—

" 74.—(1) In the case of a proposal made under section 69 of this Act otherwise than by the valuation officer, the valuation officer may, at any time within the period of four months beginning with the date on which the proposal was served on him, give notice in writing to the maker of the proposal that the valuation officer is satisfied that the proposal is well-founded ; but no notice shall be given under this subsection if a notice of objection to the proposal has been served within the time limited by section 70(2) of this Act and has not been unconditionally withdrawn.

(2) If in the case of any proposal to which subsection (1) of this section applies the valuation officer does not give a notice under that subsection and the proposal is not withdrawn, the valuation officer—

(*a*) may at any time within the period mentioned in that subsection ; and

(*b*) shall not later than the end of that period,

transmit to the clerk to the local valuation panel constituted under section 88 of this Act from the members of which the local valuation court would fall to be constituted a copy of the proposal together with a statement that the valuation officer objects to the proposal and a copy of any notice of objection to the proposal which has been served under section 70(2) of this Act and has not been unconditionally withdrawn.

(3) Where, in accordance with subsection (2) of this section, the valuation officer transmits a copy of a proposal to the clerk to a local valuation panel, the transmission shall have effect as an appeal to a local valuation court, by the person who made the proposal, against the objection by the valuation officer and against every objection signified by a notice of which a copy is transmitted with the copy of the proposal.

(4) The valuation officer shall serve on the maker of every proposal to which subsection (1) of this section applies a notice in writing stating the effect of subsections (2) and (3) of this section.

(5) Where the date referred to in subsection (1) of this section falls before the first anniversary of the coming into force of the valuation list to which the proposal relates, that subsection shall have effect as if for the words " four months " there were substituted the words " six months ".".

17. In section 75(*b*) of the principal Act after " 73(2) " there shall be inserted the words " and 74(3) ".

18. In section 76(4) of the principal Act for paragraph (*d*) there shall be substituted—

" (*d*) the rating authority for the area in which the hereditament is situated if—

(i) the authority are not the appellant ; and

(ii) the authority have notified the valuation officer in accordance with section 70(7) of this Act that they wish this paragraph to apply to them ; and ".

19. Paragraphs 12 to 18 above shall have effect in relation to any proposal made by or served on the valuation officer on or after 1st April 1985, but where—

(*a*) a proposal is made by or served on the valuation officer before that date ; and

(*b*) a further proposal in respect of the same hereditament is made by or served on him on or after that date and before the first proposal has been settled,

those paragraphs shall not have effect in relation to the further proposal.

Rating records

20.—(1) For section 108 of the principal Act there shall be substituted—

" Inspection of documents.

108.—(1) Any ratepayer and any valuation officer may at all reasonable times without payment inspect and take copies of and extracts from—

(*a*) any valuation list whether prepared under Part V of this Act, under Part III of the Local Government Act 1948, or under the Rating and Valuation Act 1925 ;

1948 c. 26.
1925 c. 90.

(*b*) any notice of objection, proposal or notice of appeal with respect to the valuation list currently in force in a rating area or, subject to subsection (3) of this section, the immediately preceding valuation list ;

(c) minutes of the proceedings of any local valuation court with respect to the valuation list currently in force in a rating area or, subject to subsection (3) of this section, the immediately preceding valuation list ; and

(d) minutes of the proceedings of any rating authority during the preceding ten years or, where the valuation list currently in force in the rating area of an authority was transmitted to it under section 68(2) of this Act before the commencement of that period, during the period since the list was transmitted to the authority.

(2) Any person having custody of any such document who obstructs a person in the exercise of any right under this section to inspect or take copies of or extracts from the document shall be liable on summary conviction to a fine of an amount not exceeding level 3 on the standard scale, as defined in section 75 of the Criminal Justice Act 1982. 1982 c. 48.

(3) Where a valuation list currently in force in a rating area has been in force for more than ten years, paragraphs (b) and (c) of subsection (1) of this section do not apply to the immediately preceding valuation list.

(4) For the purposes of this section the expression " ratepayer " includes an occupier who pays a rent inclusive of rates, and also includes any person authorised by a ratepayer to act on his behalf under this section."

(2) This paragraph shall come into force on 1st January 1985.

Application of receipts

21.—(1) Section 112 of the principal Act is hereby repealed.

(2) This paragraph shall come into force on the passing of this Act.

Rebates for institutions for the disabled

22.—(1) In subsection (1) of section 2 of the Rating (Disabled Persons) Act 1978 for the words after " used " there shall be substituted the words " wholly or predominantly for a qualifying purpose ; and a hereditament is used for a qualifying purpose if it is used— 1978 c. 40.

(a) for one or more of the purposes specified in subsection (2) below ; or

(b) for one or more of those purposes and for purposes ancillary thereto.".

(2) For subsection (5) of that section there shall be substituted—

" (5) The rebate in respect of any hereditament—

(a) in the case of a hereditament used wholly for a qualify-

SCH. 1

ing purpose, shall be equal to the rates chargeable on the hereditament for the rebate period ;

(b) in the case of a hereditament used predominantly for a qualifying purpose shall be equal to the rates that would be chargeable on the hereditament for the rebate period if its rateable value were so much only of its rateable value as is attributable to the part or parts of it used for that purpose,

but where a hereditament qualifies for rebate for part only of a rebate period the rebate shall be reduced proportionally.

(5A) Where the rating authority give the valuation officer notice of a part or parts of a hereditament used for a qualifying purpose, the valuation officer shall certify what amount of rateable value is attributable to that part or those parts and, subject to subsection (5B) below, his certificate shall be conclusive.

(5B) An applicant for a rebate who is dissatisfied with the amount of rateable value certified under subsection (5A) above may appeal to the local valuation court by sending a notice in writing to the clerk of the local valuation panel constituted under section 88 of the General Rate Act 1967 ; and the court may, if they allow the appeal, alter the amount certified to any other amount which the valuation officer could have certified and which they think fit.

1967 c. 9.

(5C) Sections 76(2) and (4) and 77 of the said Act of 1967 (procedure of local valuation court and right of appeal to Lands Tribunal) shall, with the necessary modifications, apply to the proceedings and decision of a local valuation court under this section.".

(3) After subsection (6) of that section there shall be inserted—

" (7) For the purposes of this section, a hereditament shall be regarded as being used predominantly for a qualifying purpose if 50 per cent. or more of the floor area of any building comprised in the hereditament (or, if there is more than one such building, of all such buildings) is used, or is available for use, wholly for the qualifying purpose ; and in this subsection " building " includes a part of a building and " buildings " shall be construed accordingly.".

(4) For section 3(5) of that Act there shall be substituted—

" (5) An applicant for a rebate—

(a) whose application is refused by a rating authority ; or

(b) who is dissatisfied with any decision of the rating authority as to whether the hereditament is used wholly or predominantly for a qualifying purpose or as to whether any part of it is used for a qualifying purpose,

may appeal to the county court ; and if that court allows the appeal it may give the rating authority such directions in relation to the rebate or the application as it thinks fit.".

(5) This paragraph shall have effect as respects rates for any rate period beginning on or after 1st April 1985.

Adjustment of grant for disparities in rate revenue

23.—(1) For section 59(11)(c) of the Local Government, Planning and Land Act 1980 there shall be substituted— 1980 c. 65.

" (c) as if paragraph (e)—

(i) were omitted except in relation to any exercise of the power conferred by subsection (1) above for a purpose mentioned in subsection (6)(b) or (c) above ; and

(ii) in relation to any such exercise of that power, referred to two classes, namely, councils of inner London boroughs and councils of outer London boroughs.".

(2) This paragraph has effect in relation to any financial year beginning on or after 1st April 1983.

Substituted rates and precepts

24.—(1) After subsection (8) of section 3 of the Local Govern-ment Finance Act 1982 there shall be inserted— 1982 c. 32.

" (9) Where the original rate or precept has been quashed because it is insufficient to meet the expenditure required to be taken into account under section 2 or 11 of the said Act of 1967, subsection (2) above shall not prevent a substituted rate or precept being made or issued which is sufficient to meet that expenditure.

(10) Where, whether by virtue of this section or otherwise, a precept is issued to a rating authority after it has made a rate for the financial year to which the precept relates, sub-section (2) above shall not prevent a substituted rate being made by the authority for giving effect to the precept ; and a rating authority which makes a substituted rate by virtue of this subsection shall be entitled to recover from the precepting authority in question any increase in its administrative or rate collection expenses which is attributable to that rate."

(2) This paragraph shall have effect in relation to any financial year beginning on or after 1st April 1984.

SCHEDULE 2

RATING OF MOORINGS

Section 16(2).

PART I

EXEMPTION OF CERTAIN MOORINGS

1.—(1) No mooring to which this paragraph applies shall be liable to be rated or to be included in any valuation list or in any rate.

(2) This paragraph applies to any mooring—

(a) used or intended to be used by a boat or ship ; and

(b) equipped only with a buoy attached to an anchor, weight or other device—

(i) which rests on or in the bed of the sea or any river or other waters when in use ; and

(ii) which is designed to be raised from that bed from time to time.

SCH. 2   (3) This paragraph shall have effect for any rate period beginning on or after 1st April 1985.

PART II

RATING OF MULTIPLE MOORINGS

2.—(1) Where on any land there are two or more moorings and it appears to the valuation officer that the moorings are separately occupied, or are available for separate occupation, by persons other than the owner so as to form separate hereditaments for the purposes of rating within the meaning of the principal Act, the valuation officer, in preparing a new valuation list or in altering a current valuation list, may, if he thinks fit, treat as a single hereditament—

(*a*) all or any of the moorings ; or

(*b*) all or any of the moorings together with any adjacent moorings occupied by the owner or adjacent land so occupied.

(2) Where any moorings, or any moorings and land, are treated as a single hereditament under sub-paragraph (1) above, they shall, for the purposes of rating within the meaning of the principal Act, be deemed to be a single hereditament in the occupation of the owner.

(3) For the purposes of any proposal for the alteration of the valuation list made by the valuation officer by virtue of sub-paragraph (1) above—

(*a*) the hereditament shall be treated as in the occupation of the owner ; and

(*b*) in section 70(2) of the principal Act (which confers on certain persons the right to object to a proposal), the reference to any part of a hereditament shall be omitted.

(4) Where a valuation list is altered by virtue of sub-paragraph (1) above so as to include moorings, or moorings and land, as a single hereditament, any item comprised in that hereditament and separately entered in the list may be deleted from the list without any proposal being made to delete it ; and a deletion so made shall have effect as from the same date as the alteration of the list to include the single hereditament.

(5) Where moorings, or moorings and land, are treated as a single hereditament under sub-paragraph (1) above, or where the valuation officer has made a proposal for the alteration of the valuation list in order that they shall be so treated, a proposal to omit from the hereditament and enter separately in the valuation list a mooring occupied by a person other than the owner may be made by that person if the mooring would fall to be entered separately in the list but for this paragraph ; and sections 69(4) and (5) and 70 to 74 of the principal Act shall apply in relation to a proposal under this sub-paragraph as they apply to a proposal under section 69 of that Act.

3.—(1) Where by virtue of paragraph 2 above the valuation officer makes a proposal for the alteration of the valuation list so as to treat moorings, or moorings and land, as a single hereditament he shall, within twenty-eight days after the date on which the proposal is made, give the owner written notice of—

(a) the number and description of moorings which will be comprised in the hereditament ; and

(b) the proportion of the proposed rateable value of the hereditament which is attributable to each of those moorings.

(2) Where moorings, or moorings and land, are treated, or proposed by the valuation officer to be treated, as a single hereditament under paragraph 2 above, the owner shall, if so requested by the occupier of a mooring comprised or proposed to be comprised in the single hereditament, supply the occupier with particulars—

(a) of the matters specified in sub-paragraph (1)(a) and (b) above ; and

(b) of the amount in the pound at which the rate for the rating area in which the mooring is situated is currently charged.

(3) If the owner without reasonable excuse fails within twenty-eight days after the making of a request under sub-paragraph (2) above to comply with the request, he shall be liable on summary conviction to a fine of an amount not exceeding level 2 on the standard scale, as defined in section 75 of the Criminal Justice Act 1982. 1982 c. 48.

4.—(1) Subject to the following provisions of this paragraph, any alteration made in a valuation list by virtue of paragraph 2 above—

(a) shall, in relation to any rate current at the date when notice of the relevant proposal was served on the owner, be deemed to have had effect as from the commencement of the period in respect of which the rate was made ; and

(b) shall have effect for the purposes of any subsequent rate.

(2) Sub-paragraph (1)(a) above shall not apply if—

(a) any of the moorings which are treated as a single hereditament by virtue of the alteration was included as a separate hereditament in the valuation list immediately before the alteration was made ; or

(b) any of the moorings which are so treated has come into existence since the commencement of the period in respect of which the rate was made and was not so included before the alteration was made ;

but the alteration shall, in a case within (a) above, be deemed to have had effect as from the date when notice of the relevant proposal was served on the owner and, in a case within (b) above or within (a) and (b) above, be deemed to have had effect as from the date when the mooring came into existence or, if there are two or more moorings to which (b) above applies, as from the date when the most recent of them came into existence.

(3) In this paragraph " the relevant proposal ", in relation to an alteration in the valuation list, means the proposal in pursuance of which the alteration was made.

(4) Where—

(*a*) an alteration is made in a valuation list by virtue of paragraph 2 above so that moorings, or moorings and land, are treated as a single hereditament ; and

(*b*) any rate has been levied in respect of any item comprised in that hereditament,

so much (if any) of the amount of the rate levied as relates to the period after the alteration is deemed to have effect shall be repaid or allowed.

5.—(1) Where, after a valuation list has been altered so as to treat moorings, or moorings and land, as a single hereditament, it appears to the valuation officer that there is any other mooring—

(*a*) which could have been included with the moorings, or moorings and land, so treated ; or

(*b*) which could have been so included if it had been in existence at the time when the proposal to alter the list was made,

the valuation officer, in preparing a new valuation list or in altering a current valuation list, may, if he thinks fit, treat those moorings, or moorings and land, and that other mooring as a single hereditament.

(2) The provisions of paragraph 2(2) to (5) and paragraphs 3 and 4 above shall apply in relation to moorings, or moorings and land, treated as a single hereditament under this paragraph and in relation to any proposal or alteration made by virtue of this paragraph as they apply in relation to moorings, or moorings and land, treated as a single hereditament under paragraph 2 above and in relation to proposals and alterations made by virtue of that paragraph.

6. In this Part of this Schedule—

" the principal Act " means the General Rate Act 1967 ;

" owner ", in relation to a mooring, means any person for the time being receiving or entitled to receive the rack-rent of the mooring, whether on his own account or as agent or trustee for any other person, or who would so receive or be entitled to receive that rent if the mooring were let on a rack-rent,

and any other expression which is also used in the principal Act has the same meaning as in that Act.

7. No proposal for the alteration of a valuation list shall be made under this Part of this Schedule before the first rate period beginning after the passing of this Act.

Juries (Disqualification) Act 1984

1984 CHAPTER 34

An Act to make further provision for disqualification for jury service on criminal grounds.   [12th July 1984]

BE IT ENACTED by the Queen's most Excellent Majesty, by and with the advice and consent of the Lords Spiritual and Temporal, and Commons, in this present Parliament assembled, and by the authority of the same, as follows:—

1.—(1) The following paragraphs shall be substituted for the second paragraph of Part II of Schedule 1 to the Juries Act 1974 (persons disqualified for jury service)—

> " A person who at any time in the last ten years has, in the United Kingdom or the Channel Islands or the Isle of Man—
>
> > (*a*) served any part of a sentence of imprisonment, youth custody or detention; or
> >
> > (*b*) been detained in a Borstal institution; or
> >
> > (*c*) had passed on him or (as the case may be) made in respect of him a suspended sentence of imprisonment or order for detention; or
> >
> > (*d*) had made in respect of him a community service order.
>
> A person who at any time in the last five years has, in the United Kingdom or the Channel Islands or the Isle of Man, been placed on probation."

Disqualification for jury service of persons who have served or had imposed on them certain sentences.

1974 c. 23.

(2) This section shall not affect the qualification of any person to serve on a jury in pursuance of any summons to attend for jury service issued under the Juries Act 1974 before the commencement of this Act (whether by notice in accordance with section 2 of that Act or under section 6 of that Act).

Short title, repeal, commencement and extent.

1982 c. 48.

1974 c. 23.

2.—(1) This Act may be cited as the Juries (Disqualification) Act 1984.

(2) In Schedule 14 to the Criminal Justice Act 1982, paragraph 35(*b*)(ii) (which amends the second paragraph of Part II of Schedule 1 to the Juries Act 1974), and the word " and " immediately preceding it, are hereby repealed.

(3) This Act shall come into force on such day as the Secretary of State may by order made by statutory instrument appoint.

(4) This Act extends to England and Wales only.

Data Protection Act 1984

1984 CHAPTER 35

An Act to regulate the use of automatically processed
information relating to individuals and the provision
of services in respect of such information.

[12th July 1984]

BE IT ENACTED by the Queen's most Excellent Majesty, by and
with the advice and consent of the Lords Spiritual and
Temporal, and Commons, in this present Parliament
assembled, and by the authority of the same, as follows:—

PART I

PRELIMINARY

1.—(1) The following provisions shall have effect for the interpretation of this Act.

*Definition of
" data " and
related
expressions.*

(2) " Data " means information recorded in a form in which
it can be processed by equipment operating automatically in
response to instructions given for that purpose.

(3) " Personal data " means data consisting of information
which relates to a living individual who can be identified from
that information (or from that and other information in the
possession of the data user), including any expression of opinion
about the individual but not any indication of the intentions of
the data user in respect of that individual.

(4) " Data subject " means an individual who is the subject
of personal data.

(5) " Data user " means a person who holds data, and a person " holds " data if—

    (a) the data form part of a collection of data processed or intended to be processed by or on behalf of that person as mentioned in subsection (2) above ; and

    (b) that person (either alone or jointly or in common with other persons) controls the contents and use of the data comprised in the collection ; and

    (c) the data are in the form in which they have been or are intended to be processed as mentioned in paragraph (a) above or (though not for the time being in that form) in a form into which they have been converted after being so processed and with a view to being further so processed on a subsequent occasion.

(6) A person carries on a " computer bureau " if he provides other persons with services in respect of data, and a person provides such services if—

    (a) as agent for other persons he causes data held by them to be processed as mentioned in subsection (2) above ; or

    (b) he allows other persons the use of equipment in his possession for the processing as mentioned in that subsection of data held by them.

(7) " Processing ", in relation to data, means amending, augmenting, deleting or re-arranging the data or extracting the information constituting the data and, in the case of personal data, means performing any of those operations by reference to the data subject.

(8) Subsection (7) above shall not be construed as applying to any operation performed only for the purpose of preparing the text of documents.

(9) " Disclosing ", in relation to data, includes disclosing information extracted from the data ; and where the identification of the individual who is the subject of personal data depends partly on the information constituting the data and partly on other information in the possession of the data user, the data shall not be regarded as disclosed or transferred unless the other information is also disclosed or transferred.

The data protection principles.

2.—(1) Subject to subsection (3) below, references in this Act to the data protection principles are to the principles set out in Part I of Schedule 1 to this Act; and those principles shall be interpreted in accordance with Part II of that Schedule.

(2) The first seven principles apply to personal data held by data users and the eighth applies both to such data and to per-

sonal data in respect of which services are provided by persons carrying on computer bureaux.

(3) The Secretary of State may by order modify or supplement those principles for the purpose of providing additional safeguards in relation to personal data consisting of information as to—

(a) the racial origin of the data subject;

(b) his political opinions or religious or other beliefs;

(c) his physical or mental health or his sexual life; or

(d) his criminal convictions;

and references in this Act to the data protection principles include, except where the context otherwise requires, references to any modified or additional principle having effect by virtue of an order under this subsection.

(4) An order under subsection (3) above may modify a principle either by modifying the principle itself or by modifying its interpretation; and where an order under that subsection modifies a principle or provides for an additional principle it may contain provisions for the interpretation of the modified or additional principle.

(5) An order under subsection (3) above modifying the third data protection principle may, to such extent as the Secretary of State thinks appropriate, exclude or modify in relation to that principle any exemption from the non-disclosure provisions which is contained in Part IV of this Act; and the exemptions from those provisions contained in that Part shall accordingly have effect subject to any order made by virtue of this subsection.

(6) An order under subsection (3) above may make different provision in relation to data consisting of information of different descriptions.

3.—(1) For the purposes of this Act there shall be—

(a) an officer known as the Data Protection Registrar (in this Act referred to as " the Registrar "); and

(b) a tribunal known as the Data Protection Tribunal (in this Act referred to as " the Tribunal ").

(2) The Registrar shall be appointed by Her Majesty by Letters Patent.

(3) The Tribunal shall consist of—

(a) a chairman appointed by the Lord Chancellor after consultation with the Lord Advocate;

(b) such number of deputy chairmen appointed as aforesaid as the Lord Chancellor may determine; and (*c*) such number of other members appointed by the Secretary of State as he may determine.

(4) The members of the Tribunal appointed under subsection (3)(*a*) and (*b*) above shall be barristers, advocates or solicitors, in each case of not less than seven years' standing.

(5) The members of the Tribunal appointed under subsection (3)(*c*) above shall be—

> (*a*) persons to represent the interests of data users ; and

> (*b*) persons to represent the interests of data subjects.

(6) Schedule 2 to this Act shall have effect in relation to the Registrar and the Tribunal.

Part II

Registration and Supervision of Data Users and Computer Bureaux

Registration

Registration of data users and computer bureaux.   **4.**—(1) The Registrar shall maintain a register of data users who hold, and of persons carrying on computer bureaux who provide services in respect of, personal data and shall make an entry in the register in pursuance of each application for registration accepted by him under this Part of this Act.

(2) Each entry shall state whether it is in respect of a data user, of a person carrying on a computer bureau or of a data user who also carries on such a bureau.

(3) Subject to the provisions of this section, an entry in respect of a data user shall consist of the following particulars—

> (*a*) the name and address of the data user ;

> (*b*) a description of the personal data to be held by him and of the purpose or purposes for which the data are to be held or used ;

> (*c*) a description of the source or sources from which he intends or may wish to obtain the data or the information to be contained in the data ;

> (*d*) a description of any person or persons to whom he intends or may wish to disclose the data ;

> (*e*) the names or a description of any countries or territories outside the United Kingdom to which he intends or may wish directly or indirectly to transfer the data ; **and**

> (*f*) one or more addresses for the receipt of requests from data subjects for access to the data.

(4) Subject to the provisions of this section, an entry in respect of a person carrying on a computer bureau shall consist of that person's name and address.

(5) Subject to the provisions of this section, an entry in respect of a data user who also carries on a computer bureau shall consist of his name and address and, as respects the personal data to be held by him, the particulars specified in subsection (3)(*b*) to (*f*) above.

(6) In the case of a registered company the address referred to in subsections (3)(*a*), (4) and (5) above is that of its registered office, and the particulars to be included in the entry shall include the company's number in the register of companies.

(7) In the case of a person (other than a registered company) carrying on a business the address referred to in subsections (3)(*a*), (4) and (5) above is that of his principal place of business.

(8) The Secretary of State may by order vary the particulars to be included in entries made in the register.

5.—(1) A person shall not hold personal data unless an entry in respect of that person as a data user, or as a data user who also carries on a computer bureau, is for the time being contained in the register. Prohibition of unregistered holding etc. of personal data.

(2) A person in respect of whom such an entry is contained in the register shall not—

    (*a*) hold personal data of any description other than that specified in the entry ;

    (*b*) hold any such data, or use any such data held by him, for any purpose other than the purpose or purposes described in the entry ;

    (*c*) obtain such data, or information to be contained in such data, to be held by him from any source which is not described in the entry ;

    (*d*) disclose such data held by him to any person who is not described in the entry ; or

    (*e*) directly or indirectly transfer such data held by him to any country or territory outside the United Kingdom other than one named or described in the entry.

(3) A servant or agent of a person to whom subsection (2) above applies shall, as respects personal data held by that person, be subject to the same restrictions on the use, disclosure or transfer of the data as those to which that person is subject under paragraphs (*b*), (*d*) and (*e*) of that subsection and, as respects personal data to be held by that person, to the same restrictions as those to which he is subject under paragraph (*c*) of that subsection.

(4) A person shall not, in carrying on a computer bureau, provide services in respect of personal data unless an entry in respect of that person as a person carrying on such a bureau, or as a data user who also carries on such a bureau, is for the time being contained in the register.

(5) Any person who contravenes subsection (1) above or knowingly or recklessly contravenes any of the other provisions of this section shall be guilty of an offence.

Applications for registration and for amendment of registered particulars.

6.—(1) A person applying for registration shall state whether he wishes to be registered as a data user, as a person carrying on a computer bureau or as a data user who also carries on such a bureau, and shall furnish the Registrar, in such form as he may require, with the particulars required to be included in the entry to be made in pursuance of the application.

(2) Where a person intends to hold personal data for two or more purposes he may make separate applications for registration in respect of any of those purposes.

(3) A registered person may at any time apply to the Registrar for the alteration of any particulars included in the entry or entries relating to that person.

(4) Where the alteration would consist of the addition of a purpose for which personal data are to be held, the person may, instead of making an application under subsection (3) above, make a fresh application for registration in respect of the additional purpose.

(5) A registered person shall make an application under subsection (3) above whenever necessary for ensuring that the entry or entries relating to that person contain his current address; and any person who fails to comply with this subsection shall be guilty of an offence.

(6) Any person who, in connection with an application for registration or for the alteration of registered particulars, knowingly or recklessly furnishes the Registrar with information which is false or misleading in a material respect shall be guilty of an offence.

(7) Every application for registration shall be accompanied by the prescribed fee, and every application for the alteration of registered particulars shall be accompanied by such fee, if any, as may be prescribed.

(8) Any application for registration or for the alteration of registered particulars may be withdrawn by notice in writing to the Registrar at any time before the applicant receives a notification in respect of the application under section 7(1) below.

7.—(1) Subject to the provisions of this section, the Registrar shall as soon as practicable and in any case within the period of six months after receiving an application for registration or for the alteration of registered particulars notify the applicant in writing whether his application has been accepted or refused; and where the Registrar notifies an applicant that his application has been accepted the notification shall contain a statement of—

    (a) the particulars entered in the register, or the alteration made, in pursuance of the application; and

    (b) the date on which the particulars were entered or the alteration was made.

(2) The Registrar shall not refuse an application made in accordance with section 6 above unless—

    (a) he considers that the particulars proposed for registration or, as the case may be, the particulars that would result from the proposed alteration, will not give sufficient information as to the matters to which they relate; or

    (b) he is satisfied that the applicant is likely to contravene any of the data protection principles; or

    (c) he considers that the information available to him is insufficient to satisfy him that the applicant is unlikely to contravene any of those principles.

(3) Subsection (2)(a) above shall not be construed as precluding the acceptance by the Registrar of particulars expressed in general terms in cases where that is appropriate, and the Registrar shall accept particulars expressed in such terms in any case in which he is satisfied that more specific particulars would be likely to prejudice the purpose or purposes for which the data are to be held.

(4) Where the Registrar refuses an application under this section he shall give his reasons and inform the applicant of the rights of appeal conferred by section 13 below.

(5) If in any case it appears to the Registrar that an application needs more consideration than can be given to it in the period mentioned in subsection (1) above he shall as soon as practicable and in any case before the end of that period notify the applicant in writing to that effect; and in that event no notification need be given under that subsection until after the end of that period.

(6) Subject to subsection (8) below, a person who has made an application in accordance with section 6 above shall—

    (a) until he receives a notification in respect of it under subsection (1) above or the application is withdrawn; and (*b*) if he receives a notification under that subsection of the refusal of his application, until the end of the period within which an appeal can be brought against the refusal and, if an appeal is brought, until the determination or withdrawal of the appeal,

be treated for the purposes of section 5 above as if his application had been accepted and the particulars contained in it had been entered in the register or, as the case may be, the alteration requested in the application had been made on the date on which the application was made.

(7) If by reason of special circumstances the Registrar considers that a refusal notified by him to an applicant under subsection (1) above should take effect as a matter of urgency he may include a statement to that effect in the notification of the refusal; and in that event subsection (6)(*b*) above shall have effect as if for the words from " the period " onwards there were substituted the words " the period of seven days beginning with the date on which that notification is received ".

(8) Subsection (6) above shall not apply to an application made by any person if in the previous two years—

    (*a*) an application by that person has been refused under this section ; or

    (*b*) all or any of the particulars constituting an entry contained in the register in respect of that person have been removed in pursuance of a de-registration notice ;

but in the case of any such application subsection (1) above shall apply as if for the reference to six months there were substituted a reference to two months and, where the Registrar gives a notification under subsection (5) above in respect of any such application, subsection (6) above shall apply to it as if for the reference to the date on which the application was made there were substituted a reference to the date on which that notification is received.

(9) For the purposes of subsection (6) above an application shall be treated as made or withdrawn—

    (*a*) if the application or notice of withdrawal is sent by registered post or the recorded delivery service, on the date on which it is received for dispatch by the Post Office ;

    (*b*) in any other case, on the date on which it is received by the Registrar ;

and for the purposes of subsection (8)(*a*) above an application shall not be treated as having been refused so long as an appeal against the refusal can be brought, while such an appeal is pending or if such an appeal has been allowed.

8.—(1) No entry shall be retained in the register after the expiration of the initial period of registration except in pursuance of a renewal application made to the Registrar in accordance with this section.

(2) Subject to subsection (3) below, the initial period of registration and the period for which an entry is to be retained in pursuance of a renewal application (" the renewal period ") shall be such period (not being less than three years) as may be prescribed beginning with the date on which the entry in question was made or, as the case may be, the date on which that entry would fall to be removed if the renewal application had not been made.

(3) The person making an application for registration or a renewal application may in his application specify as the initial period of registration or, as the case may be, as the renewal period, a period shorter than that prescribed, being a period consisting of one or more complete years.

(4) Where the Registrar notifies an applicant for registration that his application has been accepted the notification shall include a statement of the date when the initial period of registration will expire.

(5) Every renewal application shall be accompanied by the prescribed fee, and no such application shall be made except in the period of six months ending with the expiration of—

    (*a*) the initial period of registration ; or

    (*b*) if there have been one or more previous renewal applications, the current renewal period.

(6) Any renewal application may be sent by post, and the Registrar shall acknowledge its receipt and notify the applicant in writing of the date until which the entry in question will be retained in the register in pursuance of the application.

(7) Without prejudice to the foregoing provisions of this section, the Registrar may at any time remove an entry from the register at the request of the person to whom the entry relates.

9.—(1) The Registrar shall provide facilities for making the information contained in the entries in the register available for inspection (in visible and legible form) by members of the public at all reasonable hours and free of charge.

(2) The Registrar shall, on payment of such fee, if any, as may be prescribed, supply any member of the public with a duly certified copy in writing of the particulars contained in the entry made in the register in pursuance of any application for registration.

Enforcement
notices.

Supervision

10.—(1) If the Registrar is satisfied that a registered person has contravened or is contravening any of the data protection principles he may serve him with a notice (" an enforcement notice ") requiring him to take, within such time as is specified in the notice, such steps as are so specified for complying with the principle or principles in question.

(2) In deciding whether to serve an enforcement notice the Registrar shall consider whether the contravention has caused or is likely to cause any person damage or distress.

(3) An enforcement notice in respect of a contravention of the fifth data protection principle may require the data user—

(*a*) to rectify or erase the data and any other data held by him and containing an expression of opinion which appears to the Registrar to be based on the inaccurate data ; or

(*b*) in the case of such data as are mentioned in subsection (2) of section 22 below, either to take the steps mentioned in paragraph (*a*) above or to take such steps as are specified in the notice for securing compliance with the requirements specified in that subsection and, if the Registrar thinks fit, for supplementing the data with such statement of the true facts relating to the matters dealt with by the data as the Registrar may approve.

(4) The Registrar shall not serve an enforcement notice requiring the person served with the notice to take steps for complying with paragraph (*a*) of the seventh data protection principle in respect of any data subject unless satisfied that the person has contravened section 21 below by failing to supply information to which the data subject is entitled and which has been duly requested in accordance with that section.

(5) An enforcement notice shall contain—

(*a*) a statement of the principle or principles which the Registrar is satisfied have been or are being contravened and his reasons for reaching that conclusion ; and

(*b*) particulars of the rights of appeal conferred by section 13 below.

(6) Subject to subsection (7) below, the time specified in an enforcement notice for taking the steps which it requires shall not expire before the end of the period within which an appeal can be brought against the notice and, if such an appeal is brought, those steps need not be taken pending the determination or withdrawal of the appeal.

(7) If by reason of special circumstances the Registrar considers that the steps required by an enforcement notice should be taken as a matter of urgency he may include a statement to that effect in the notice ; and in that event subsection (6) above shall not apply but the notice shall not require the steps to be taken before the end of the period of seven days beginning with the date on which the notice is served.

(8) The Registrar may cancel an enforcement notice by written notification to the person on whom it was served.

(9) Any person who fails to comply with an enforcement notice shall be guilty of an offence ; but it shall be a defence for a person charged with an offence under this subsection to prove that he exercised all due diligence to comply with the notice in question.

11.—(1) If the Registrar is satisfied that a registered person has contravened or is contravening any of the data protection principles he may—

De-registration notices.

(*a*) serve him with a notice (" a de-registration notice ") stating that he proposes, at the expiration of such period as is specified in the notice, to remove from the register all or any of the particulars constituting the entry or any of the entries contained in the register in respect of that person ; and

(*b*) subject to the provisions of this section, remove those particulars from the register at the expiration of that period.

(2) In deciding whether to serve a de-registration notice the Registrar shall consider whether the contravention has caused or is likely to cause any person damage or distress, and the Registrar shall not serve such a notice unless he is satisfied that compliance with the principle or principles in question cannot be adequately secured by the service of an enforcement notice.

(3) A de-registration notice shall contain—

(*a*) a statement of the principle or principles which the Registrar is satisfied have been or are being contravened and his reasons for reaching that conclusion and deciding that compliance cannot be adequately secured by the service of an enforcement notice ; and

(*b*) particulars of the rights of appeal conferred by section 13 below.

(4) Subject to subsection (5) below, the period specified in a de-registration notice pursuant to subsection (1)(*a*) above shall not expire before the end of the period within which an appeal

can be brought against the notice and, if such an appeal is brought, the particulars shall not be removed pending the determination or withdrawal of the appeal.

(5) If by reason of special circumstances the Registrar considers that any particulars should be removed from the register as a matter of urgency he may include a statement to that effect in the de-registration notice ; and in that event subsection (4) above shall not apply but the particulars shall not be removed before the end of the period of seven days beginning with the date on which the notice is served.

(6) The Registrar may cancel a de-registration notice by written notification to the person on whom it was served.

(7) References in this section to removing any particulars include references to restricting any description which forms part of any particulars.

Transfer prohibition notices.

12.—(1) If it appears to the Registrar that—

(*a*) a person registered as a data user or as a data user who also carries on a computer bureau ; or

(*b*) a person treated as so registered by virtue of section 7(6) above,

proposes to transfer personal data held by him to a place outside the United Kingdom, the Registrar may, if satisfied as to the matters mentioned in subsection (2) or (3) below, serve that person with a notice ("a transfer prohibition notice") prohibiting him from transferring the data either absolutely or until he has taken such steps as are specified in the notice for protecting the interests of the data subjects in question.

(2) Where the place to which the data are to be transferred is not in a State bound by the European Convention the Registrar must be satisfied that the transfer is likely to contravene, or lead to a contravention of, any of the data protection principles.

(3) Where the place to which the data are to be transferred is in a State bound by the European Convention the Registrar must be satisfied either—

(*a*) that—

(i) the person in question intends to give instructions for the further transfer of the data to a place which is not in such a State ; and

(ii) that the further transfer is likely to contravene, or lead to a contravention of, any of the data protection principles ; or

(*b*) in the case of data to which an order under section 2(3) above applies, that the transfer is likely to contravene or lead to a contravention of, any of the data protec-tion principles as they have effect in relation to such data.

(4) In deciding whether to serve a transfer prohibition notice the Registrar shall consider whether the notice is required for preventing damage or distress to any person and shall have regard to the general desirability of facilitating the free transfer of data between the United Kingdom and other states and terri-tories.

(5) A transfer prohibition notice shall specify the time when it is to take effect and contain—

(a) a statement of the principle or principles which the Registrar is satisfied are likely to be contravened and his reasons for reaching that conclusion ; and

(b) particulars of the rights of appeal conferred by section 13 below.

(6) Subject to subsection (7) below, the time specified in a transfer prohibition notice pursuant to subsection (5) above shall not be before the end of the period within which an appeal can be brought against the notice and, if such an appeal is brought, the notice shall not take effect pending the determina-tion or withdrawal of the appeal.

(7) If by reason of special circumstances the Registrar con-siders that the prohibition should take effect as a matter of urgency he may include a statement to that effect in the transfer prohibition notice ; and in that event subsection (6) above shall not apply but the notice shall not take effect before the end of the period of seven days beginning with the date on which the notice is served.

(8) The Registrar may cancel a transfer prohibition notice by written notification to the person on whom it was served.

(9) No transfer prohibition notice shall prohibit the transfer of any data where the transfer of the information constituting the data is required or authorised by or under any enactment or required by any convention or other instrument imposing an international obligation on the United Kingdom.

(10) Any person who contravenes a transfer prohibition notice shall be guilty of an offence ; but it shall be a defence for a person charged with an offence under this subsection to prove that he exercised all due diligence to avoid a contravention of the notice in question.

(11) For the purposes of this section a place shall be treated as in a State bound by the European Convention if it is in any territory in respect of which the State is bound.

Appeals

13.—(1) A person may appeal to the Tribunal against—

(*a*) any refusal by the Registrar of an application by that person for registration or for the alteration of registered particulars ;

(*b*) any enforcement notice, de-registration notice or transfer prohibition notice with which that person has been served.

(2) Where a notification that an application has been refused contains a statement by the Registrar in accordance with section 7(7) above, then, whether or not the applicant appeals under paragraph (*a*) of subsection (1) above, he may appeal against the Registrar's decision to include that statement in the notification.

(3) Where any such notice as is mentioned in paragraph (*b*) of subsection (1) above contains a statement by the Registrar in accordance with section 10(7), 11(5) or 12(7) above, then, whether or not the person served with the notice appeals under that paragraph, he may appeal against the Registrar's decision to include that statement in the notice or against the effect of the inclusion of the statement as respects any part of the notice.

(4) Schedule 3 to this Act shall have effect in relation to appeals under this section and to the proceedings of the Tribunal in respect of any such appeal.

14.—(1) If on an appeal under section 13(1) above the Tribunal considers—

(*a*) that the refusal or notice against which the appeal is brought is not in accordance with the law ; or

(*b*) to the extent that the refusal or notice involved an exercise of discretion by the Registrar, that he ought to have exercised his discretion differently,

the Tribunal shall allow the appeal or substitute such other decision or notice as could have been made or served by the Registrar ; and in any other case the Tribunal shall dismiss the appeal.

(2) The Tribunal may review any determination of fact on which the refusal or notice in question was based.

(3) On an appeal under subsection (2) of section 13 above the Tribunal may direct that the notification of the refusal shall be treated as if it did not contain any such statement as is mentioned in that subsection.

(4) On an appeal under subsection (3) of section 13 above the Tribunal may direct that the notice in question shall have effect as if it did not contain any such statement as is mentioned in that subsection or that the inclusion of the statement shall

not have effect in relation to any part of the notice and may make such modifications in the notice as may be required for giving effect to the direction.

(5) Any party to an appeal to the Tribunal may appeal from the decision of the Tribunal on a point of law to the appropriate court ; and that court shall be—

    (*a*) the High Court of Justice in England if the address of the person who was the appellant before the Tribunal is in England or Wales ;

    (*b*) the Court of Session if that address is in Scotland ; and

    (*c*) the High Court of Justice in Northern Ireland if that address is in Northern Ireland.

(6) In subsection (5) above references to the address of the appellant before the Tribunal are to his address as included or proposed for inclusion in the register.

Miscellaneous and supplementary

15.—(1) Personal data in respect of which services are pro- Unauthorised vided by a person carrying on a computer bureau shall not be disclosure by disclosed by him without the prior authority of the person for computer whom those services are provided. bureau.

(2) Subsection (1) above applies also to any servant or agent of a person carrying on a computer bureau.

(3) Any person who knowingly or recklessly contravenes this section shall be guilty of an offence.

16. Schedule 4 to this Act shall have effect for the detection Powers of of offences under this Act and contraventions of the data entry and protection principles. inspection.

17.—(1) No enactment or rule of law prohibiting or restricting Disclosure of the disclosure of information shall preclude a person from furn- information. ishing the Registrar or the Tribunal with any information necessary for the discharge of their functions under this Act.

(2) For the purposes of section 2 of the Official Secrets Act 1911 c. 28. 1911 (wrongful communication of information)—

    (*a*) the Registrar and his officers and servants ;

    (*b*) the members of the Tribunal ; and

    (*c*) any officers or servants of the Tribunal who are not in the service of the Crown,

shall be deemed to hold office under Her Majesty.

(3) The said section 2 shall not be construed as precluding the disclosure of information by any person mentioned in sub-

PART II

section (2)(*a*) or (*b*) above or by any officer or servant of the Tribunal where the disclosure is made for the purpose of discharging his duties under this Act or for the purpose of proceedings under or arising out of this Act, including proceedings before the Tribunal.

Service of notices.

18.—(1) Any notice or notification authorised or required by this Act to be served on or given to any person by the Registrar may—

    (*a*) if that person is an individual, be served on him—

        (i) by delivering it to him ; or

        (ii) by sending it to him by post addressed to him at his usual or last-known place of residence or business ; or

        (iii) by leaving it for him at that place ;

    (*b*) if that person is a body corporate or unincorporate, be served on that body—

        (i) by sending it by post to the proper officer of the body at its principal office ; or

        (ii) by addressing it to the proper officer of the body and leaving it at that office.

(2) In subsection (1)(*b*) above " principal office ", in relation to a registered company, means its registered office and " proper officer ", in relation to any body, means the secretary or other executive officer charged with the conduct of its general affairs.

(3) This section is without prejudice to any other lawful method of serving or giving a notice or notification.

Prosecutions and penalties.

19.—(1) No proceedings for an offence under this Act shall be instituted—

    (*a*) in England or Wales except by the Registrar or by or with the consent of the Director of Public Prosecutions ;

    (*b*) in Northern Ireland except by the Registrar or by or with the consent of the Director of Public Prosecutions for Northern Ireland.

(2) A person guilty of an offence under any provision of this Act other than section 6 or paragraph 12 of Schedule 4 shall be liable—

    (*a*) on conviction on indictment, to a fine ; or

    (*b*) on summary conviction, to a fine not exceeding the statutory maximum (as defined in section 74 of the Criminal Justice Act 1982).

1982 c. 48.

(3) A person guilty of an offence under section 6 above or the said paragraph 12 shall be liable on summary conviction to a fine not exceeding the fifth level on the standard scale (as defined in section 75 of the said Act of 1982).

PART II

(4) Subject to subsection (5) below, the court by or before which a person is convicted of an offence under section 5, 10, 12 or 15 above may order any data material appearing to the court to be connected with the commission of the offence to be forfeited, destroyed or erased.

(5) The court shall not make an order under subsection (4) above in relation to any material where a person (other than the offender) claiming to be the owner or otherwise interested in it applies to be heard by the court unless an opportunity is given to him to show cause why the order should not be made.

20.—(1) Where an offence under this Act has been committed by a body corporate and is proved to have been committed with the consent or connivance of or to be attributable to any neglect on the part of any director, manager, secretary or similar officer of the body corporate or any person who was purporting to act in any such capacity, he as well as the body corporate shall be guilty of that offence and be liable to be proceeded against and punished accordingly.

Liability of directors etc.

(2) Where the affairs of a body corporate are managed by its members subsection (1) above shall apply in relation to the acts and defaults of a member in connection with his functions of management as if he were a director of the body corporate.

PART III

RIGHTS OF DATA SUBJECTS

21.—(1) Subject to the provisions of this section, an individual shall be entitled—

Right of access to personal data.

(a) to be informed by any data user whether the data held by him include personal data of which that individual is the data subject; and

(b) to be supplied by any data user with a copy of the information constituting any such personal data held by him;

and where any of the information referred to in paragraph (b) above is expressed in terms which are not intelligible without explanation the information shall be accompanied by an explanation of those terms.

(2) A data user shall not be obliged to supply any information under subsection (1) above except in response to a request

PART III   in writing and on payment of such fee (not exceeding the prescribed maximum) as he may require ; but a request for information under both paragraphs of that subsection shall be treated as a single request and a request for information under paragraph (*a*) shall, in the absence of any indication to the contrary, be treated as extending also to information under paragraph (*b*).

(3) In the case of a data user having separate entries in the register in respect of data held for different purposes a separate request must be made and a separate fee paid under this section in respect of the data to which each entry relates.

(4) A data user shall not be obliged to comply with a request under this section—

> (*a*) unless he is supplied with such information as he may reasonably require in order to satisfy himself as to the identity of the person making the request and to locate the information which he seeks ; and

> (*b*) if he cannot comply with the request without disclosing information relating to another individual who can be identified from that information, unless he is satisfied that the other individual has consented to the disclosure of the information to the person making the request.

(5) In paragraph (*b*) of subsection (4) above the reference to information relating to another individual includes a reference to information identifying that individual as the source of the information sought by the request ; and that paragraph shall not be construed as excusing a data user from supplying so much of the information sought by the request as can be supplied without disclosing the identity of the other individual concerned, whether by the omission of names or other identifying particulars or otherwise.

(6) A data user shall comply with a request under this section within forty days of receiving the request or, if later, receiving the information referred to in paragraph (*a*) of subsection (4) above and, in a case where it is required, the consent referred to in paragraph (*b*) of that subsection.

(7) The information to be supplied pursuant to a request under this section shall be supplied by reference to the data in question at the time when the request is received except that it may take account of any amendment or deletion made between that time and the time when the information is supplied, being an amendment or deletion that would have been made regardless of the receipt of the request.

(8) If a court is satisfied on the application of any person who has made a request under the foregoing provisions of this section

that the data user in question has failed to comply with the request in contravention of those provisions, the court may order him to comply with the request; but a court shall not make an order under this subsection if it considers that it would in all the circumstances be unreasonable to do so, whether because of the frequency with which the applicant has made requests to the data user under those provisions or for any other reason.

(9) The Secretary of State may by order provide for enabling a request under this section to be made on behalf of any individual who is incapable by reason of mental disorder of managing his own affairs.

22.—(1) An individual who is the subject of personal data Compensation held by a data user and who suffers damage by reason of the for inaccuracy of the data shall be entitled to compensation from inaccuracy. the data user for that damage and for any distress which the individual has suffered by reason of the inaccuracy.

(2) In the case of data which accurately record information received or obtained by the data user from the data subject or a third party, subsection (1) above does not apply if the following requirements have been complied with—

  (a) the data indicate that the information was received or obtained as aforesaid or the information has not been extracted from the data except in a form which includes an indication to that effect; and

  (b) if the data subject has notified the data user that he regards the information as incorrect or misleading, an indication to that effect has been included in the data or the information has not been extracted from the data except in a form which includes an indication to that effect.

(3) In proceedings brought against any person by virtue of this section it shall be a defence to prove that he had taken such care as in all the circumstances was reasonably required to ensure the accuracy of the data at the material time.

(4) Data are inaccurate for the purposes of this section if incorrect or misleading as to any matter of fact.

23.—(1) An individual who is the subject of personal data Compensation held by a data user or in respect of which services are provided for loss or by a person carrying on a computer bureau and who suffers unauthorised damage by reason of— disclosure.

  (a) the loss of the data;

  (b) the destruction of the data without the authority of the data user or, as the case may be, of the person carrying on the bureau; or (*c*) subject to subsection (2) below, the disclosure of the data, or access having been obtained to the data, without such authority as aforesaid,

shall be entitled to compensation from the data user or, as the case may be, the person carrying on the bureau for that damage and for any distress which the individual has suffered by reason of the loss, destruction, disclosure or access.

(2) In the case of a registered data user, subsection (1)(*c*) above does not apply to disclosure to, or access by, any person falling within a description specified pursuant to section 4(3)(*d*) above in an entry in the register relating to that data user.

(3) In proceedings brought against any person by virtue of this section it shall be a defence to prove that he had taken such care as in all the circumstances was reasonably required to prevent the loss, destruction, disclosure or access in question.

24.—(1) If a court is satisfied on the application of a data subject that personal data held by a data user of which the applicant is the subject are inaccurate within the meaning of section 22 above, the court may order the rectification or erasure of the data and of any data held by the data user and containing an expression of opinion which appears to the court to be based on the inaccurate data.

(2) Subsection (1) above applies whether or not the data accurately record information received or obtained by the data user from the data subject or a third party but where the data accurately record such information, then—

    (*a*) if the requirements mentioned in section 22(2) above have been complied with, the court may, instead of making an order under subsection (1) above, make an order requiring the data to be supplemented by such statement of the true facts relating to the matters dealt with by the data as the court may approve ; and

    (*b*) if all or any of those requirements have not been complied with, the court may, instead of making an order under that subsection, make such order as it thinks fit for securing compliance with those requirements with or without a further order requiring the data to be supplemented by such a statement as is mentioned in paragraph (*a*) above.

(3) If a court is satisfied on the application of a data subject—

    (*a*) that he has suffered damage by reason of the disclosure of personal data, or of access having been obtained to personal data, in circumstances entitling him to compensation under section 23 above ; and

(b) that there is a substantial risk of further disclosure of or access to the data without such authority as is mentioned in that section,

the court may order the erasure of the data ; but, in the case of data in respect of which services were being provided by a person carrying on a computer bureau, the court shall not make such an order unless such steps as are reasonably practicable have been taken for notifying the person for whom those services were provided and giving him an opportunity to be heard.

25.—(1) The jurisdiction conferred by sections 21 and 24 above shall be exercisable by the High Court or a county court or, in Scotland, by the Court of Session or the sheriff.

(2) For the purpose of determining any question whether an applicant under subsection (8) of section 21 above is entitled to the information which he seeks (including any question whether any relevant data are exempt from that section by virtue of Part IV of this Act) a court may require the information constituting any data held by the data user to be made available for its own inspection but shall not, pending the determination of that question in the applicant's favour, require the information sought by the applicant to be disclosed to him or his representatives whether by discovery (or, in Scotland, recovery) or otherwise.

PART IV

EXEMPTIONS

26.—(1) References in any provision of Part II or III of this Act to personal data do not include references to data which by virtue of this Part of this Act are exempt from that provision.

(2) In this Part of this Act " the subject access provisions " means—

(a) section 21 above ; and

(b) any provision of Part II of this Act conferring a power on the Registrar to the extent to which it is exercisable by reference to paragraph (a) of the seventh data protection principle.

(3) In this Part of this Act " the non-disclosure provisions " means—

(a) sections 5(2)(d) and 15 above ; and

(b) any provision of Part II of this Act conferring a power on the Registrar to the extent to which it is exercisable by reference to any data protection principle inconsistent with the disclosure in question.

PART IV

(4) Except as provided by this Part of this Act the subject access provisions shall apply notwithstanding any enactment or rule of law prohibiting or restricting the disclosure, or authorising the withholding, of information.

National security.

27.—(1) Personal data are exempt from the provisions of Part II of this Act and of sections 21 to 24 above if the exemption is required for the purpose of safeguarding national security.

(2) Any question whether the exemption mentioned in subsection (1) above is or at any time was required for the purpose there mentioned in respect of any personal data shall be determined by a Minister of the Crown ; and a certificate signed by a Minister of the Crown certifying that the exemption is or at any time was so required shall be conclusive evidence of that fact.

(3) Personal data which are not exempt under subsection (1) above are exempt from the non-disclosure provisions in any case in which the disclosure of the data is for the purpose of safeguarding national security.

(4) For the purposes of subsection (3) above a certificate signed by a Minister of the Crown certifying that personal data are or have been disclosed for the purpose mentioned in that subsection shall be conclusive evidence of that fact.

(5) A document purporting to be such a certificate as is mentioned in this section shall be received in evidence and deemed to be such a certificate unless the contrary is proved.

(6) The powers conferred by this section on a Minister of the Crown shall not be exercisable except by a Minister who is a member of the Cabinet or by the Attorney General or the Lord Advocate.

Crime and taxation.

28.—(1) Personal data held for any of the following purposes—

(a) the prevention or detection of crime ;

(b) the apprehension or prosecution of offenders ; or

(c) the assessment or collection of any tax or duty,

are exempt from the subject access provisions in any case in which the application of those provisions to the data would be likely to prejudice any of the matters mentioned in this subsection.

(2) Personal data which—

(a) are held for the purpose of discharging statutory functions ; and

(b) consist of information obtained for such a purpose from a person who had it in his possession for any of the purposes mentioned in subsection (1) above, are exempt from the subject access provisions to the same extent as personal data held for any of the purposes mentioned in that subsection.

(3) Personal data are exempt from the non-disclosure provisions in any case in which—

(a) the disclosure is for any of the purposes mentioned in subsection (1) above ; and

(b) the application of those provisions in relation to the disclosure would be likely to prejudice any of the matters mentioned in that subsection ;

and in proceedings against any person for contravening a provision mentioned in section 26(3)(a) above it shall be a defence to prove that he had reasonable grounds for believing that failure to make the disclosure in question would have been likely to prejudice any of those matters.

(4) Personal data are exempt from the provisions of Part II of this Act conferring powers on the Registrar, to the extent to which they are exercisable by reference to the first data protection principle, in any case in which the application of those provisions to the data would be likely to prejudice any of the matters mentioned in subsection (1) above.

29.—(1) The Secretary of State may by order exempt from the subject access provisions, or modify those provisions in relation to, personal data consisting of information as to the physical or mental health of the data subject.

Health and social work.

(2) The Secretary of State may by order exempt from the subject access provisions, or modify those provisions in relation to, personal data of such other descriptions as may be specified in the order, being information—

(a) held by government departments or local authorities or by voluntary organisations or other bodies designated by or under the order ; and

(b) appearing to him to be held for, or acquired in the course of, carrying out social work in relation to the data subject or other individuals ;

but the Secretary of State shall not under this subsection confer any exemption or make any modification except so far as he considers that the application to the data of those provisions (or of those provisions without modification) would be likely to prejudice the carrying out of social work.

(3) An order under this section may make different provision in relation to data consisting of information of different descriptions.

PART IV
Regulation of
financial
services etc.

30.—(1) Personal data held for the purpose of discharging statutory functions to which this section applies are exempt from the subject access provisions in any case in which the application of those provisions to the data would be likely to prejudice the proper discharge of those functions.

(2) This section applies to any functions designated for the purposes of this section by an order made by the Secretary of State, being functions conferred by or under any enactment appearing to him to be designed for protecting members of the public against financial loss due to dishonesty, incompetence or malpractice by persons concerned in the provision of banking, insurance, investment or other financial services or in the management of companies or to the conduct of discharged or undischarged bankrupts.

Judicial
appointments
and legal
professional
privilege.

31.—(1) Personal data held by a government department are exempt from the subject access provisions if the data consist of information which has been received from a third party and is held as information relevant to the making of judicial appointments.

(2) Personal data are exempt from the subject access provisions if the data consist of information in respect of which a claim to legal professional privilege (or, in Scotland, to confidentiality as between client and professional legal adviser) could be maintained in legal proceedings.

Payrolls and
accounts.

32.—(1) Subject to subsection (2) below, personal data held by a data user only for one or more of the following purposes—

(a) calculating amounts payable by way of remuneration or pensions in respect of service in any employment or office or making payments of, or of sums deducted from, such remuneration or pensions ; or

(b) keeping accounts relating to any business or other activity carried on by the data user or keeping records of purchases, sales or other transactions for the purpose of ensuring that the requisite payments are made by or to him in respect of those transactions or for the purpose of making financial or management forecasts to assist him in the conduct of any such business or activity,

are exempt from the provisions of Part II of this Act and of sections 21 to 24 above.

(2) It shall be a condition of the exemption of any data under this section that the data are not used for any purpose other than the purpose or purposes for which they are held and are not disclosed except as permitted by subsections (3) and (4)

below ; but the exemption shall not be lost by any use or disclosure in breach of that condition if the data user shows that
he had taken such care to prevent it as in all the circumstances
was reasonably required.

(3) Data held only for one or more of the purposes mentioned
in subsection (1)(*a*) above may be disclosed—

    (*a*) to any person, other than the data user, by whom the
remuneration or pensions in question are payable ;

    (*b*) for the purpose of obtaining actuarial advice ;

    (*c*) for the purpose of giving information as to the persons
in any employment or office for use in medical research
into the health of, or injuries suffered by, persons engaged in particular occupations or working in particular places or areas ;

    (*d*) if the data subject (or a person acting on his behalf)
has requested or consented to the disclosure of the
data either generally or in the circumstances in which
the disclosure in question is made ; or

    (*e*) if the person making the disclosure has reasonable
grounds for believing that the disclosure falls within
paragraph (*d*) above.

(4) Data held for any of the purposes mentioned in subsection (1) above may be disclosed—

    (*a*) for the purpose of audit or where the disclosure is for
the purpose only of giving information about the data
user's financial affairs ; or

    (*b*) in any case in which disclosure would be permitted by
any other provision of this Part of this Act if subsection (2) above were included among the non-
disclosure provisions.

(5) In this section " remuneration " includes remuneration in
kind and " pensions " includes gratuities or similar benefits.

33.—(1) Personal data held by an individual and concerned Domestic
only with the management of his personal, family or household or other
affairs or held by him only for recreational purposes are exempt limited
from the provisions of Part II of this Act and of sections 21 purposes.
to 24 above.

(2) Subject to subsections (3) and (4) below—

    (*a*) personal data held by an unincorporated members' club
and relating only to the members of the club ; and

    (*b*) personal data held by a data user only for the purpose
of distributing, or recording the distribution of, articles
or information to the data subjects and consisting only

of their names, addresses or other particulars necessary for effecting the distribution,

are exempt from the provisions of Part II of this Act and of sections 21 to 24 above.

(3) Neither paragraph (*a*) nor paragraph (*b*) of subsection (2) above applies to personal data relating to any data subject unless he has been asked by the club or data user whether he objects to the data relating to him being held as mentioned in that paragraph and has not objected.

(4) It shall be a condition of the exemption of any data under paragraph (*b*) of subsection (2) above that the data are not used for any purpose other than that for which they are held and of the exemption of any data under either paragraph of that subsection that the data are not disclosed except as permitted by subsection (5) below ; but the first exemption shall not be lost by any use, and neither exemption shall be lost by any disclosure, in breach of that condition if the data user shows that he had taken such care to prevent it as in all the circumstances was reasonably required.

(5) Data to which subsection (4) above applies may be disclosed—

(*a*) if the data subject (or a person acting on his behalf) has requested or consented to the disclosure of the data either generally or in the circumstances in which the disclosure in question is made ;

(*b*) if the person making the disclosure has reasonable grounds for believing that the disclosure falls within paragraph (*a*) above ; or

(*c*) in any case in which disclosure would be permitted by any other provision of this Part of this Act if subsection (4) above were included among the non-disclosure provisions.

(6) Personal data held only for—

(*a*) preparing statistics ; or

(*b*) carrying out research,

are exempt from the subject access provisions ; but it shall be a condition of that exemption that the data are not used or disclosed for any other purpose and that the resulting statistics or the results of the research are not made available in a form which identifies the data subjects or any of them.

Other exemptions.   **34.**—(1) Personal data held by any person are exempt from the provisions of Part II of this Act and of sections 21 to 24 above if the data consist of information which that person is required by or under any enactment to make available to the

public, whether by publishing it, making it available for inspec-
tion or otherwise and whether gratuitously or on payment of a
fee.

(2) The Secretary of State may by order exempt from the
subject access provisions personal data consisting of information the disclosure of which is prohibited or restricted by or
under any enactment if he considers that the prohibition or
restriction ought to prevail over those provisions in the interests
of the data subject or of any other individual.

(3) Where all the personal data relating to a data subject
held by a data user (or all such data in respect of which a data
user has a separate entry in the register) consist of information in
respect of which the data subject is entitled to make a request to
the data user under section 158 of the Consumer Credit Act 1974   1974 c. 39.
(files of credit reference agencies)—

> (*a*) the data are exempt from the subject access provisions ;
> and
>
> (*b*) any request in respect of the data under section 21
> above shall be treated for all purposes as if it were a
> request under the said section 158.

(4) Personal data are exempt from the subject access provisions if the data are kept only for the purpose of replacing
other data in the event of the latter being lost, destroyed or im-
paired.

(5) Personal data are exempt from the non-disclosure provisions in any case in which the disclosure is—

> (*a*) required by or under any enactment, by any rule of
> law or by the order of a court ; or
>
> (*b*) made for the purpose of obtaining legal advice or for
> the purposes of, or in the course of, legal proceedings
> in which the person making the disclosure is a party
> or a witness.

(6) Personal data are exempt from the non-disclosure provisions in any case in which—

> (*a*) the disclosure is to the data subject or a person acting
> on his behalf ; or
>
> (*b*) the data subject or any such person has requested or
> consented to the particular disclosure in question ; or
>
> (*c*) the disclosure is by a data user or a person carrying on
> a computer bureau to his servant or agent for the pur-
> pose of enabling the servant or agent to perform his
> functions as such ; or
>
> (*d*) the person making the disclosure has reasonable grounds
> for believing that the disclosure falls within any of
> the foregoing paragraphs of this subsection.

(7) Section 4(3)(*d*) above does not apply to any disclosure falling within paragraph (*a*), (*b*) or (*c*) of subsection (6) above ; and that subsection shall apply to the restriction on disclosure in section 33(6) above as it applies to the non-disclosure provisions.

(8) Personal data are exempt from the non-disclosure provisions in any case in which the disclosure is urgently required for preventing injury or other damage to the health of any person or persons ; and in proceedings against any person for contravening a provision mentioned in section 26(3)(*a*) above it shall be a defence to prove that he had reasonable grounds for believing that the disclosure in question was urgently required for that purpose.

(9) A person need not comply with a notice, request or order under the subject access provisions if compliance would expose him to proceedings for any offence other than an offence under this Act ; and information disclosed by any person in compliance with such a notice, request or order shall not be admissible against him in proceedings for an offence under this Act.

Examination marks.

35.—(1) Section 21 above shall have effect subject to the provisions of this section in the case of personal data consisting of marks or other information held by a data user—

   (*a*) for the purpose of determining the results of an academic, professional or other examination or of enabling the results of any such examination to be determined ; or

   (*b*) in consequence of the determination of any such results.

(2) Where the period mentioned in subsection (6) of section 21 begins before the results of the examination are announced that period shall be extended until—

   (*a*) the end of five months from the beginning of that period ; or

   (*b*) the end of forty days after the date of the announcement,

whichever is the earlier.

(3) Where by virtue of subsection (2) above a request is complied with more than forty days after the beginning of the period mentioned in subsection (6) of section 21, the information to be supplied pursuant to the request shall be supplied both by reference to the data in question at the time when the request is received and (if different) by reference to the data as from time to time held in the period beginning when the request is received and ending when it is complied with.

(4) For the purposes of this section the results of an examination shall be treated as announced when they are first published or (if not published) when they are first made available or communicated to the candidate in question.

(5) In this section " examination " includes any process for PART IV determining the knowledge, intelligence, skill or ability of a candidate by reference to his performance in any test, work or other activity.

PART V

GENERAL

36.—(1) It shall be the duty of the Registrar so to perform his General duties functions under this Act as to promote the observance of the of Registrar. data protection principles by data users and persons carrying on computer bureaux.

(2) The Registrar may consider any complaint that any of the data protection principles or any provision of this Act has been or is being contravened and shall do so if the complaint appears to him to raise a matter of substance and to have been made without undue delay by a person directly affected ; and where the Registrar considers any such complaint he shall notify the complainant of the result of his consideration and of any action which he proposes to take.

(3) The Registrar shall arrange for the dissemination in such form and manner as he considers appropriate of such information as it may appear to him expedient to give to the public about the operation of this Act and other matters within the scope of his functions under this Act and may give advice to any person as to any of those matters.

(4) It shall be the duty of the Registrar, where he considers it appropriate to do so, to encourage trade associations or other bodies representing data users to prepare, and to disseminate to their members, codes of practice for guidance in complying with the data protection principles.

(5) The Registrar shall annually lay before each House of Parliament a general report on the performance of his functions under this Act and may from time to time lay before each House of Parliament such other reports with respect to those functions as he thinks fit.

37. The Registrar shall be the designated authority in the Co-operation United Kingdom for the purposes of Article 13 of the European between Convention ; and the Secretary of State may by order make parties to provision as to the functions to be discharged by the Registrar Convention. in that capacity.

38.—(1) Except as provided in subsection (2) below, a govern- Application ment department shall be subject to the same obligations and to government liabilities under this Act as a private person ; and for the departments purposes of this Act each government department shall be and police.

PART V treated as a person separate from any other government department and a person in the public service of the Crown shall be treated as a servant of the government department to which his responsibilities or duties relate.

(2) A government department shall not be liable to prosecution under this Act but—

(a) sections 5(3) and 15(2) above (and, so far as relating to those provisions, sections 5(5) and 15(3) above) shall apply to any person who by virtue of this section falls to be treated as a servant of the government department in question ; and

(b) section 6(6) above and paragraph 12 of Schedule 4 to this Act shall apply to a person in the public service of the Crown as they apply to any other person.

(3) For the purposes of this Act—

(a) the constables under the direction and control of a chief officer of police shall be treated as his servants ; and

(b) the members of any body of constables maintained otherwise than by a police authority shall be treated as the servants—

(i) of the authority or person by whom that body is maintained, and

(ii) in the case of any members of such a body who are under the direction and control of a chief officer, of that officer.

(4) In the application of subsection (3) above to Scotland, for the reference to a chief officer of police there shall be substituted a reference to a chief constable.

(5) In the application of subsection (3) above to Northern Ireland, for the reference to a chief officer of police there shall be substituted a reference to the Chief Constable of the Royal Ulster Constabulary and for the reference to a police authority there shall be substituted a reference to the Police Authority for Northern Ireland.

Data held, and services provided, outside the United Kingdom.

39.—(1) Subject to the following provisions of this section, this Act does not apply to a data user in respect of data held, or to a person carrying on a computer bureau in respect of services provided, outside the United Kingdom.

(2) For the purposes of subsection (1) above—

(a) data shall be treated as held where the data user exercises the control referred to in subsection (5)(b) of section 1 above in relation to the data ; and (*b*) services shall be treated as provided where the person carrying on the computer bureau does any of the things referred to in subsection (6)(*a*) or (*b*) of that section.

(3) Where a person who is not resident in the United Kingdom—

(*a*) exercises the control mentioned in paragraph (*a*) of subsection (2) above ; or

(*b*) does any of the things mentioned in paragraph (*b*) of that subsection,

through a servant or agent in the United Kingdom, this Act shall apply as if that control were exercised or, as the case may be, those things were done in the United Kingdom by the servant or agent acting on his own account and not on behalf of the person whose servant or agent he is.

(4) Where by virtue of subsection (3) above a servant or agent is treated as a data user or as a person carrying on a computer bureau he may be described for the purposes of registration by the position or office which he holds ; and any such description in an entry in the register shall be treated as applying to the person for the time being holding the position or office in question.

(5) This Act does not apply to data processed wholly outside the United Kingdom unless the data are used or intended to be used in the United Kingdom.

(6) Sections 4(3)(*e*) and 5(2)(*e*) and subsection (1) of section 12 above do not apply to the transfer of data which are already outside the United Kingdom ; but references in the said section 12 to a contravention of the data protection principles include references to anything that would constitute such contravention if it occurred in relation to the data when held in the United Kingdom.

40.—(1) Any power conferred by this Act to make regulations, rules or orders shall be exercisable by statutory instrument.

Regulations, rules and orders.

(2) Without prejudice to sections 2(6) and 29(3) above, regulations, rules or orders under this Act may make different provision for different cases or circumstances.

(3) Before making an order under any of the foregoing provisions of this Act the Secretary of State shall consult the Registrar.

(4) No order shall be made under section 2(3), 4(8), 29, 30 or 34(2) above unless a draft of the order has been laid before and approved by a resolution of each House of Parliament.

(5) A statutory instrument containing an order under section 21(9) or 37 above or rules under paragraph 4 of Schedule 3 to this Act shall be subject to annulment in pursuance of a resolution of either House of Parliament.

(6) Regulations prescribing fees for the purposes of any provision of this Act or the period mentioned in section 8(2) above shall be laid before Parliament after being made.

(7) Regulations prescribing fees payable to the Registrar under this Act or the period mentioned in section 8(2) above shall be made after consultation with the Registrar and with the approval of the Treasury ; and in making any such regulations the Secretary of State shall have regard to the desirability of securing that those fees are sufficient to offset the expenses incurred by the Registrar and the Tribunal in discharging their functions under this Act and any expenses of the Secretary of State in respect of the Tribunal.

General interpretation.

41. In addition to the provisions of sections 1 and 2 above, the following provisions shall have effect for the interpretation of this Act—

" business " includes any trade or profession ;

" data equipment " means equipment for the automatic processing of data or for recording information so that it can be automatically processed ;

" data material " means any document or other material used in connection with data equipment ;

" a de-registration notice " means a notice under section 11 above ;

" enactment " includes an enactment passed after this Act ;

" an enforcement notice " means a notice under section 10 above ;

" the European Convention " means the Convention for the Protection of Individuals with regard to Automatic Processing of Personal Data which was opened for signature on 28th January 1981 ;

" government department " includes a Northern Ireland
    department and any body or authority exercising statu-
    tory functions on behalf of the Crown ;

" prescribed " means prescribed by regulations made by the
    Secretary of State ;

" the Registrar " means the Data Protection Registrar ;

" the register ", except where the reference is to the register
    of companies, means the register maintained under
    section 4 above and (except where the reference is to a
    registered company, to the registered office of a com-
    pany or to registered post) references to registration
    shall be construed accordingly ;

" registered company " means a company registered under
    the enactments relating to companies for the time
    being in force in any part of the United Kingdom ;

" a transfer prohibition notice " means a notice under sec-
    tion 12 above ;

" the Tribunal " means the Data Protection Tribunal.

42.—(1) No application for registration shall be made until
such day as the Secretary of State may by order appoint, and
sections 5 and 15 above shall not apply until the end of the
period of six months beginning with that day.

Commence-
ment and
transitional
provisions.

(2) Until the end of the period of two years beginning with the
day appointed under subsection (1) above the Registrar shall not
have power—

   (a) to refuse an application made in accordance with section
       6 above except on the ground mentioned in section
       7(2)(a) above ; or

   (b) to serve an enforcement notice imposing requirements to
       be complied with, a de-registration notice expiring, or a
       transfer prohibition notice imposing a prohibition tak-
       ing effect, before the end of that period.

(3) Where the Registrar proposes to serve any person with an
enforcement notice before the end of the period mentioned in
subsection (2) above he shall, in determining the time by which
the requirements of the notice are to be complied with, have
regard to the probable cost to that person of complying with
those requirements.

(4) Section 21 above and paragraph 1(b) of Schedule 4 to
this Act shall not apply until the end of the period mentioned
in subsection (2) above.

PART V

(5) Section 22 above shall not apply to damage suffered before the end of the period mentioned in subsection (1) above and in deciding whether to refuse an application or serve a notice under Part II of this Act the Registrar shall treat the provision about accuracy in the fifth data protection principle as inapplicable until the end of that period and as inapplicable thereafter to data shown to have been held by the data user in question since before the end of that period.

(6) Sections 23 and 24(3) above shall not apply to damage suffered before the end of the period of two months beginning with the date on which this Act is passed.

(7) Section 24(1) and (2) above shall not apply before the end of the period mentioned in subsection (1) above.

Short title and extent.

43.—(1) This Act may be cited as the Data Protection Act 1984.

(2) This Act extends to Northern Ireland.

(3) Her Majesty may by Order in Council direct that this Act shall extend to any of the Channel Islands with such exceptions and modifications as may be specified in the Order.

SCHEDULES

SCHEDULE 1

Section 2(1).

THE DATA PROTECTION PRINCIPLES

PART I

THE PRINCIPLES

Personal data held by data users

1. The information to be contained in personal data shall be obtained, and personal data shall be processed, fairly and lawfully.

2. Personal data shall be held only for one or more specified and lawful purposes.

3. Personal data held for any purpose or purposes shall not be used or disclosed in any manner incompatible with that purpose or those purposes.

4. Personal data held for any purpose or purposes shall be adequate, relevant and not excessive in relation to that purpose or those purposes.

5. Personal data shall be accurate and, where necessary, kept up to date.

6. Personal data held for any purpose or purposes shall not be kept for longer than is necessary for that purpose or those purposes.

7. An individual shall be entitled—

    (*a*) at reasonable intervals and without undue delay or expense—

        (i) to be informed by any data user whether he holds personal data of which that individual is the subject ; and

        (ii) to access to any such data held by a data user ; and

    (*b*) where appropriate, to have such data corrected or erased.

Personal data held by data users or in respect of which services are provided by persons carrying on computer bureaux

8. Appropriate security measures shall be taken against unauthorised access to, or alteration, disclosure or destruction of, personal data and against accidental loss or destruction of personal data.

PART II

INTERPRETATION

The first principle

1.—(1) Subject to sub-paragraph (2) below, in determining whether information was obtained fairly regard shall be had to the method by which it was obtained, including in particular whether any person from whom it was obtained was deceived or misled as to the purpose or purposes for which it is to be held, used or disclosed.

(2) Information shall in any event be treated as obtained fairly if it is obtained from a person who—

(a) is authorised by or under any enactment to supply it ; or

(b) is required to supply it by or under any enactment or by any convention or other instrument imposing an international obligation on the United Kingdom ;

and in determining whether information was obtained fairly there shall be disregarded any disclosure of the information which is authorised or required by or under any enactment or required by any such convention or other instrument as aforesaid.

The second principle

2. Personal data shall not be treated as held for a specified purpose unless that purpose is described in particulars registered under this Act in relation to the data.

The third principle

3. Personal data shall not be treated as used or disclosed in contravention of this principle unless—

(a) used otherwise than for a purpose of a description registered under this Act in relation to the data ; or

(b) disclosed otherwise than to a person of a description so registered.

The fifth principle

4. Any question whether or not personal data are accurate shall be determined as for the purposes of section 22 of this Act but, in the case of such data as are mentioned in subsection (2) of that section, this principle shall not be regarded as having been contravened by reason of any inaccuracy in the information there mentioned if the requirements specified in that subsection have been complied with.

The seventh principle

5.—(1) Paragraph (a) of this principle shall not be construed as conferring any rights inconsistent with section 21 of this Act.

(2) In determining whether access to personal data is sought at reasonable intervals regard shall be had to the nature of the data, the purpose for which the data are held and the frequency with which the data are altered.

(3) The correction or erasure of personal data is appropriate only where necessary for ensuring compliance with the other data protection principles.

The eighth principle

6. Regard shall be had—

(a) to the nature of the personal data and the harm that would result from such access, alteration, disclosure, loss or destruction as are mentioned in this principle ; and (*b*) to the place where the personal data are stored, to security measures programmed into the relevant equipment and to measures taken for ensuring the reliability of staff having access to the data.

Use for historical, statistical or research purposes

7. Where personal data are held for historical, statistical or research purposes and not used in such a way that damage or distress is, or is likely to be, caused to any data subject—

(*a*) the information contained in the data shall not be regarded for the purposes of the first principle as obtained unfairly by reason only that its use for any such purpose was not disclosed when it was obtained ; and

(*b*) the data may, notwithstanding the sixth principle, be kept indefinitely.

SCHEDULE 2

Section 3(6).

THE DATA PROTECTION REGISTRAR AND THE DATA PROTECTION TRIBUNAL

PART I

THE REGISTRAR

Status

1.—(1) The Registrar shall be a corporation sole by the name of " The Data Protection Registrar ".

(2) Except as provided in section 17(2) of this Act, the Registrar and his officers and servants shall not be regarded as servants or agents of the Crown.

Tenure of office

2.—(1) Subject to the provisions of this paragraph, the Registrar shall hold office for five years.

(2) The Registrar may be relieved of his office by Her Majesty at his own request.

(3) The Registrar may be removed from office by Her Majesty in pursuance of an Address from both Houses of Parliament.

(4) The Registrar shall in any case vacate his office on completing the year of service in which he attains the age of sixty-five years.

(5) Subject to sub-paragraph (4) above, a person who ceases to be Registrar on the expiration of his term of office shall be eligible for re-appointment.

Salary etc.

3.—(1) There shall be paid—

(*a*) to the Registrar such salary, and

(*b*) to or in respect of the Registrar such pension,
as may be specified by a resolution of the House of Commons.

(2) A resolution for the purposes of this paragraph may either
specify the salary or pension or provide that it shall be the same as
that payable to, or to or in respect of, a person employed in a
specified office under, or in a specified capacity in the service of, the
Crown.

(3) A resolution for the purposes of this paragraph may take effect
from the date on which it is passed or from any earlier or later date
specified in the resolution.

(4) Any salary or pension payable under this paragraph shall be
charged on and issued out of the Consolidated Fund.

(5) In this paragraph " pension " includes an allowance or gratuity and any reference to the payment of a pension includes a reference to the making of payments towards the provision of a pension.

Officers and servants

4.—(1) The Registrar—

    (*a*) shall appoint a deputy registrar ; and

    (*b*) may appoint such number of other officers and servants as
    he may determine.

(2) The remuneration and other conditions of service of the persons
appointed under this paragraph shall be determined by the Registrar.

(3) The Registrar may pay such pensions, allowances or gratuities
to or in respect of the persons appointed under this paragraph, or
make such payments towards the provision of such pensions, allowances or gratuities, as he may determine.

(4) The references in sub-paragraph (3) above to pensions, allowances or gratuities to or in respect of the persons appointed under this
paragraph include references to pensions, allowances or gratuities by
way of compensation to or in respect of any of those persons who
suffer loss of office or employment.

(5) Any determination under sub-paragraph (1)(*b*), (2) or (3) above
shall require the approval of the Secretary of State given with the
consent of the Treasury.

5.—(1) The deputy registrar shall perform the functions conferred by this Act on the Registrar during any vacancy in that office
or at any time when the Registrar is for any reason unable to act.

(2) Without prejudice to sub-paragraph (1) above, any functions of
the Registrar under this Act may, to the extent authorised by him,
be performed by any of his officers.

Receipts and expenses

6.—(1) All fees and other sums received by the Registrar in the
exercise of his functions under this Act shall be paid by him into
the Consolidated Fund.

(2) The Secretary of State shall out of moneys provided by Parliament pay to the Registrar such sums towards his expenses as the
Secretary of State may with the approval of the Treasury determine.

Accounts

7.—(1) It shall be the duty of the Registrar—

(*a*) to keep proper accounts and other records in relation to the accounts ;

(*b*) to prepare in respect of each financial year a statement of account in such form as the Secretary of State may direct with the approval of the Treasury ; and

(*c*) to send copies of that statement to the Comptroller and Auditor General on or before 31st August next following the end of the year to which the statement relates or on or before such earlier date after the end of that year as the Treasury may direct.

(2) The Comptroller and Auditor General shall examine and certify any statement sent to him under this paragraph and lay copies of it together with his report thereon before each House of Parliament.

(3) In this paragraph " financial year " means a period of twelve months beginning with 1st April.

Pᴀʀᴛ II

Tʜᴇ Tʀɪʙᴜɴᴀʟ

Tenure of office

8.—(1) A member of the Tribunal shall hold and vacate his office in accordance with the terms of his appointment and shall, on ceasing to hold office, be eligible for re-appointment.

(2) Any member of the Tribunal may at any time resign his office by notice in writing to the Lord Chancellor (in the case of the chairman or a deputy chairman) or to the Secretary of State (in the case of any other member).

Salary etc.

9. The Secretary of State shall pay to the members of the Tribunal out of moneys provided by Parliament such remuneration and allowances as he may with the approval of the Treasury determine.

Officers and servants

10. The Secretary of State may provide the Tribunal with such officers and servants as he thinks necessary for the proper discharge of its functions.

Expenses

11. Such expenses of the Tribunal as the Secretary of State may with the approval of the Treasury determine shall be defrayed by the Secretary of State out of moneys provided by Parliament.

Pᴀʀᴛ III

Gᴇɴᴇʀᴀʟ

Parliamentary disqualification

12.—(1) In Part II of Schedule 1 to the House of Commons Disqualification Act 1975 (bodies whose members are disqualified) there shall be inserted at the appropriate place " The Data Protection Tribunal ". 1975 c. 24.

SCH. 2   (2) In Part III of that Schedule (disqualifying offices) there shall be inserted at the appropriate place "The Data Protection Registrar".

1975 c. 25.   (3) Corresponding amendments shall be made in Parts II and III of Schedule 1 to the Northern Ireland Assembly Disqualification Act 1975.

Supervision by Council on Tribunals

1971 c. 62.   13. The Tribunals and Inquiries Act 1971 shall be amended as follows—

(a) in section 8(2) after "paragraph" there shall be inserted "5A";

(b) in section 19(4) after "46" there shall be inserted the words "or the Data Protection Registrar referred to in paragraph 5A";

(c) in Schedule 1, after paragraph 5 there shall be inserted—

"Data protection.   5A. (a) The Data Protection Registrar;
                                (b) The Data Protection Tribunal."

Public records

1958 c. 51.   14. In Part II of the Table in paragraph 3 of Schedule 1 to the Public Records Act 1958 there shall be inserted at the appropriate place "the Data Protection Registrar"; and after paragraph 4(1)(n) of that Schedule there shall be inserted—

"(nn) records of the Data Protection Tribunal;".

Section 13(4).

SCHEDULE 3

APPEAL PROCEEDINGS

Hearing of appeals

1. For the purpose of hearing and determining appeals or any matter preliminary or incidental to an appeal the Tribunal shall sit at such times and in such places as the chairman or a deputy chairman may direct and may sit in two or more divisions.

2.—(1) Subject to any rules made under paragraph 4 below, the Tribunal shall be duly constituted for an appeal under section 13(1) of this Act if it consists of —

(a) the chairman or a deputy chairman (who shall preside); and

(b) an equal number of the members appointed respectively in accordance with paragraphs (a) and (b) of section 3(5) of this Act.

(2) The members who are to constitute the Tribunal in accordance with sub-paragraph (1) above shall be nominated by the chairman or, if he is for any reason unable to act, by a deputy chairman.

(3) The determination of any question before the Tribunal when

constituted in accordance with this paragraph shall be according to the opinion of the majority of the members hearing the appeal.

3. Subject to any rules made under paragraph 4 below, the jurisdiction of the Tribunal in respect of an appeal under section 13(2) or (3) of this Act shall be exercised ex parte by the chairman or a deputy chairman sitting alone.

Rules of procedure

4.—(1) The Secretary of State may make rules for regulating the exercise of the rights of appeal conferred by section 13 of this Act and the practice and procedure of the Tribunal.

(2) Without prejudice to the generality of sub-paragraph (1) above, rules under this paragraph may in particular make provision—

(a) with respect to the period within which an appeal can be brought and the burden of proof on an appeal ;

(b) for the summoning of witnesses and the administration of oaths ;

(c) for securing the production of documents and data material ;

(d) for the inspection, examination, operation and testing of data equipment and the testing of data material ;

(e) for the hearing of an appeal wholly or partly in camera ;

(f) for hearing an appeal in the absence of the appellant or for determining an appeal without a hearing ;

(g) for enabling any matter preliminary or incidental to an appeal to be dealt with by the chairman or a deputy chairman ;

(h) for the awarding of costs ;

(i) for the publication of reports of the Tribunal's decisions ; and

(j) for conferring on the Tribunal such ancillary powers as the Secretary of State thinks necessary for the proper discharge of its functions.

Obstruction etc.

5.—(1) If any person is guilty of any act or omission in relation to proceedings before the Tribunal which, if those proceedings were proceedings before a court having power to commit for contempt, would constitute contempt of court, the Tribunal may certify the offence to the High Court or, in Scotland, the Court of Session.

(2) Where an offence is so certified, the court may inquire into the matter and, after hearing any witness who may be produced against or on behalf of the person charged with the offence, and after hearing any statement that may be offered in defence, deal with him in any manner in which it could deal with him if he had committed the like offence in relation to the court.

SCHEDULE 4

POWERS OF ENTRY AND INSPECTION

Issue of warrants

1. If a circuit judge is satisfied by information on oath supplied by the Registrar that there are reasonable grounds for suspecting—

    (*a*) that an offence under this Act has been or is being committed ; or

    (*b*) that any of the data protection principles have been or are being contravened by a registered person,

and that evidence of the commission of the offence or of the contravention is to be found on any premises specified in the information, he may, subject to paragraph 2 below, grant a warrant authorising the Registrar or any of his officers or servants at any time within seven days of the date of the warrant to enter those premises, to search them, to inspect, examine, operate and test any data equipment found there and to inspect and seize any documents or other material found there which may be such evidence as aforesaid.

2. A judge shall not issue a warrant under this Schedule unless he is satisfied—

    (*a*) that the Registrar has given seven days' notice in writing to the occupier of the premises in question demanding access to the premises ;

    (*b*) that access was demanded at a reasonable hour and was unreasonably refused ; and

    (*c*) that the occupier has, after the refusal, been notified by the Registrar of the application for the warrant and has had an opportunity of being heard by the judge on the question whether or not it should be issued ;

but the foregoing provisions of this paragraph shall not apply if the judge is satisfied that the case is one of urgency or that compliance with those provisions would defeat the object of the entry.

3. A judge who issues a warrant under this Schedule shall also issue two copies of it and certify them clearly as copies.

Execution of warrants

4. A person executing a warrant issued under this Schedule may use such reasonable force as may be necessary.

5. A warrant issued under this Schedule shall be executed at a reasonable hour unless it appears to the person executing it that there are grounds for suspecting that the evidence in question would not be found if it were so executed.

6. If the person who occupies the premises in respect of which a warrant is issued under this Schedule is present when the warrant is executed, he shall be shown the warrant and supplied with a copy of it ; and if that person is not present a copy of the warrant shall be left in a prominent place on the premises.

7.—(1) A person seizing anything in pursuance of a warrant under this Schedule shall give a receipt for it if asked to do so.

(2) Anything so seized may be retained for so long as is necessary in all the circumstances but the person in occupation of the premises in question shall be given a copy of anything that is seized if he so requests and the person executing the warrant considers that it can be done without undue delay.

Matters exempt from inspection and seizure

8. The powers of inspection and seizure conferred by a warrant issued under this Schedule shall not be exercisable in respect of personal data which are exempt from Part II of this Act.

9.—(1) Subject to the provisions of this paragraph, the powers of inspection and seizure conferred by a warrant issued under this Schedule shall not be exercisable in respect of—

> (a) any communication between a professional legal adviser and his client in connection with the giving of legal advice to the client with respect to his obligations, liabilities or rights under this Act ; or

> (b) any communication between a professional legal adviser and his client, or between such an adviser or his client and any other person, made in connection with or in contemplation of proceedings under or arising out of this Act (including proceedings before the Tribunal) and for the purposes of such proceedings.

(2) Sub-paragraph (1) above applies also to—

> (a) any copy or other record of any such communication as is there mentioned ; and

> (b) any document or article enclosed with or referred to in any such communication if made in connection with the giving of any advice or, as the case may be, in connection with or in contemplation of and for the purposes of such proceedings as are there mentioned.

(3) This paragraph does not apply to anything in the possession of any person other than the professional legal adviser or his client or to anything held with the intention of furthering a criminal purpose.

(4) In this paragraph references to the client of a professional legal adviser include references to any person representing such a client.

10. If the person in occupation of any premises in respect of which a warrant is issued under this Schedule objects to the inspection or seizure under the warrant of any material on the grounds that it consists partly of matters in respect of which those powers are not exercisable, he shall, if the person executing the warrant so requests, furnish that person with a copy of so much of the material as is not exempt from those powers.

Return of warrants

11. A warrant issued under this Schedule shall be returned to the court from which it was issued—

    (a) after being executed ; or

    (b) if not executed within the time authorised for its execution ;

and the person by whom any such warrant is executed shall make an endorsement on it stating what powers have been exercised by him under the warrant.

Offences

12. Any person who—

    (a) intentionally obstructs a person in the execution of a warrant issued under this Schedule ; or

    (b) fails without reasonable excuse to give any person executing such a warrant such assistance as he may reasonably require for the execution of the warrant,

shall be guilty of an offence.

Vessels, vehicles etc.

13. In this Schedule " premises " includes any vessel, vehicle, aircraft or hovercraft, and references to the occupier of any premises include references to the person in charge of any vessel, vehicle, aircraft or hovercraft.

Scotland and Northern Ireland

14. In the application of this Schedule to Scotland, for any reference to a circuit judge there shall be substituted a reference to the sheriff, for any reference to information on oath there shall be substituted a reference to evidence on oath and for the reference to the court from which the warrant was issued there shall be substituted a reference to the sheriff clerk.

15. In the application of this Schedule to Northern Ireland, for any reference to a circuit judge there shall be substituted a reference to a county court judge and for any reference to information on oath there shall be substituted a reference to a complaint on oath.

Mental Health (Scotland) Act 1984

1984 CHAPTER 36

An Act to consolidate the Mental Health (Scotland) Act 1960.   [12th July 1984]

BE IT ENACTED by the Queen's most Excellent Majesty, by and with the advice and consent of the Lords Spiritual and Temporal, and Commons, in this present Parliament assembled, and by the authority of the same, as follows:—

PART I

APPLICATION OF ACT

1.—(1) The provisions of this Act shall have effect with respect to the reception, care and treatment of persons suffering, or appearing to be suffering, from mental disorder, to the management of their property and affairs, and to other related matters. Application of Act: "mental disorder".

(2) In this Act—

" mental disorder " means mental illness or mental handicap however caused or manifested ;

Part II   H

" mental impairment " means a state of arrested or incomplete development of mind not amounting to severe mental impairment which includes significant impairment of intelligence and social functioning and is associated with abnormally aggressive or seriously irresponsible conduct on the part of the person concerned ; and cognate expressions shall be construed accordingly ;

" severe mental impairment " means a state of arrested or incomplete development of mind which includes severe impairment of intelligence and social functioning and is associated with abnormally aggressive or seriously irresponsible conduct on the part of the person concerned ; and cognate expressions shall be construed accordingly ;

and other expressions have the meanings assigned to them in section 125 of this Act.

(3) No person shall be treated under this Act as suffering from mental disorder by reason only of promiscuity or other immoral conduct, sexual deviancy or dependence on alcohol or drugs.

PART II

MENTAL WELFARE COMMISSION

Mental
Welfare
Commission.

2.—(1) There shall continue to be a body called the Mental Welfare Commission for Scotland (in this Act referred to as " the Mental Welfare Commission ") who shall perform the functions assigned to them by or under this Act.

(2) The Mental Welfare Commission shall consist of no fewer than 10 commissioners (including at least 3 women) of whom one shall be chairman, at least 3 shall be medical practitioners (in this Act referred to as " medical commissioners "), and one shall be a person who has been for a period of at least 5 years either a member of the Faculty of Advocates or a solicitor.

(3) Five commissioners of whom at least one shall be a medical commissioner shall constitute a quorum of the Mental Welfare Commission.

(4) The commissioners shall be appointed by Her Majesty on the recommendation of the Secretary of State and shall hold and

vacate office under the terms of the instrument under which they are appointed, but may resign office by notice in writing to the Secretary of State.

(5) Before making a recommendation under subsection (4) of this section the Secretary of State shall consult such bodies as appear to him to be concerned.

(6) No person who for the time being is employed in the civil service of the Crown whether in an established capacity or not, and whether for the whole or part of his time, shall be appointed to the Mental Welfare Commission.

(7) The Mental Welfare Commission may—

    (*a*) pay to the said commissioners such remuneration ; and

    (*b*) make provision for the payment of such pensions, allowances or gratuities to or in respect of the said commissioners,

as the Secretary of State may, with the approval of the Treasury, determine ; and such determination may make different provision for different cases or different classes of case.

(8) The following provisions of the National Health Service (Scotland) Act 1978 shall apply to the Mental Welfare Commission as they apply to a Health Board, that is to say—

    (*a*) sections 85(1), (2A), (4) and (6) (which contain provisions as to expenditure being met by the Secretary of State) ;

    (*b*) sections 85A(1) and (3) (which impose financial duties) ; and

    (*c*) section 86 (which provides for the auditing and examination of accounts).

(9) The Secretary of State may provide for the Mental Welfare Commission such officers and servants and such accommodation as the Commission may require.

(10) The Mental Welfare Commission shall be a body corporate and shall have a common seal.

(11) The proceedings of the Mental Welfare Commission shall not be invalidated by any vacancy in the membership of the Commission or any defect in the appointment of any commissioner.

PART II
Functions and
duties of the
Mental
Welfare
Commission.

3.—(1) It shall be the duty of the Mental Welfare Commission generally to exercise protective functions in respect of persons who may, by reason of mental disorder, be incapable of adequately protecting their persons or their interests, and, where those persons are liable to be detained in hospital or subject to guardianship under the following provisions of this Act, their functions as aforesaid shall include, in appropriate cases, the discharge of such patients in accordance with the said provisions.

(2) In the exercise of their functions as aforesaid, it shall be the duty of the Mental Welfare Commission—

(a) to make enquiry into any case where it appears to them that there may be ill-treatment, deficiency in care or treatment, or improper detention of any person who may be suffering from mental disorder, or where the property of any such person may, by reason of his mental disorder, be exposed to loss or damage ;

(b) to visit regularly and, subject to paragraph (c) of this subsection, as often as they think appropriate, patients who are liable to be detained in a hospital or who are subject to guardianship and on any such visit to afford an opportunity, on request, for private interview to any such patient or, where the patient is in a hospital, to any other patient in that hospital ;

(c) in any case where—

(i) the authority for the detention of a patient—

(A) has been renewed for a period of one year under section 30 of this Act ; and

(B) is renewed for a further period of one year under that section ; and

(ii) the patient has not, during the period referred to in sub-paragraph (i)(A) of this paragraph—

(A) appealed to the sheriff under section 30(6) of this Act ; or

(B) been visited by the Mental Welfare Commission under paragraph (b) of this subsection,

to visit the patient before the expiry of the period of one year referred to in sub-paragraph (i)(B) of this paragraph, unless the patient has previously been discharged, and on any such visit to afford an opportunity, on request, for private interview to any such patient ;

(d) to bring to the attention of the managers of any hospital or of any local authority the facts of any case in which in the opinion of the Mental Welfare Commission it is desirable for the managers or the local authority to exercise any of their functions to secure the welfare of any patient suffering from mental disorder by—

(i) preventing his ill-treatment ;

(ii) remedying any deficiency in his care or treatment ;

(iii) terminating his improper detention ; or

(iv) preventing or redressing loss or damage to his property ;

(e) to advise the Secretary of State, a Health Board or a local authority on any matter arising out of this Act which has been referred to the Commission by the Secretary of State, the Health Board, or the local authority, as the case may be ;

(f) to bring to the attention of the Secretary of State, a Health Board, a local authority or any other body any matter concerning the welfare of any persons who are suffering from mental disorder which the Commission consider ought to be brought to his or their attention.

(3) Where, in the course of carrying out any of their functions, the Mental Welfare Commission form the opinion that any patient who is—

(a) liable to be detained in a hospital ; and

(b) either a restricted patient within the meaning of section 63 of this Act or a person mentioned in section 67(1) or (2) (persons treated as restricted patients) of this Act,

should be discharged, they shall recommend accordingly to the Secretary of State.

(4) On any visit by the Mental Welfare Commission in pursuance of paragraph (b) or (c) of subsection (2) of this section, the visitor shall be, or the visitors shall include, a medical commissioner or a medical officer of the Commission.

(5) For the purposes of subsection (2) of this section, the Mental Welfare Commission may interview, and a medical commissioner or a medical officer of the Commission may examine, any patient in private.

(6) A medical commissioner or a medical officer of the Mental Welfare Commission may require the production of and inspect the medical records of any patient.

(7) The Mental Welfare Commission shall in 1985 and in every year thereafter publish a report on their activities ; and copies of each such report shall be submitted by the Commission to the Secretary of State who shall lay copies before Parliament.

H 3

(8) Subject to the provisions of subsection (4) of this section, the Mental Welfare Commission may appoint—

(*a*) any commissioner or committee of commissioners to carry out any of the functions of the Commission, other than those relating to the discharge of patients, under this Act,

(*b*) a person, not being a commissioner—

(i) to make by himself ; or

(ii) to act as chairman of any committee of commissioners appointed under paragraph (*a*) of this subsection to make,

any enquiry which the Commission are obliged to make under subsection (2)(*a*) of this section

and where any committee is so appointed the Commission may fix a quorum for that committee and otherwise regulate its proceedings.

(9) A person appointed under subsection (9)(*b*) of this section shall be—

(*a*) an advocate ; or

(*b*) a solicitor,

of not less than 5 years standing.

(10) Any commissioner or committee or person appointed in pursuance of subsection (9) of this section shall exercise the functions so conferred in accordance with the directions of the Mental Welfare Commission.

Proceedings and evidence at enquiries under section 3.

4.—(1) For the purpose of any enquiry under section 3(2)(*a*) of this Act, the Mental Welfare Commission may, by notice in writing, require any person to attend at the time and place set forth in the notice to give evidence, but no person shall be required in obedience to such a notice to go more than 10 miles from his place of residence unless the necessary expenses of his attendance are paid or tendered to him.

(2) A person giving evidence at such an enquiry shall not be required to answer any questions which he would be entitled, on the ground of privilege or confidentiality, to refuse to answer if the enquiry were a proceeding in a court of law.

(3) The proceedings in any such enquiry shall have the privilege of a court of law.

(4) The chairman of, or person holding, the enquiry may administer oaths to witnesses and examine witnesses on oath, and may accept, instead of evidence on oath by any person, evidence on affirmation or a statement in writing by that person.

(5) Any person who refuses or wilfully neglects to attend in obedience to a notice under subsection (1) of this section or to

give evidence shall be guilty of an offence and liable on summary conviction to a fine not exceeding level 1 on the standard scale.

5.—(1) The Secretary of State shall afford the Mental Welfare Commission all facilities necessary to enable them to carry out their functions in respect of any patient in a hospital other than a private hospital.

(2) The local authority concerned and the guardian of any person subject to guardianship under this Act, shall afford the Mental Welfare Commission all facilities necessary to enable them to carry out their functions in respect of such a patient.

6. The Mental Welfare Commission may—

    (*a*) appoint officers and servants on such terms as to remuneration and conditions of service ; and

    (*b*) make provision for the payment of—

       (i) such remuneration to—

          (A) any person appointed under section 3(9)(*b*) of this Act ; and

          (B) any medical practitioner or other person appointed for the purposes of the provisions mentioned in section 97(2) of this Act ; and

       (ii) such pensions, allowances or gratuities to or in respect of any officers, servants, persons and medical practitioners appointed under paragraph (*a*) or as mentioned in paragraph (*b*)(i) of this section,

as the Secretary of State may, with the consent of the Treasury, determine ; and such determination may make different provision for different cases or different classes of case.

PART III

LOCAL AUTHORITY SERVICES

7.—(1) In relation to persons who are or have been suffering from mental disorder a local authority may, with the approval of the Secretary of State and shall, to such extent as he may direct, make arrangements for any of the following purposes—

    (*a*) the provision, equipment and maintenance of residential accommodation, and the care of persons for the time being resident in accommodation so provided ;

H 4

PART III

(b) the exercise by the local authority of their functions under the following provisions of this Act in respect of persons under guardianship (whether under the guardianship of a local authority or of any other person) ;

(c) the provision of any ancillary or supplementary services ;

(d) the supervision of persons suffering from mental handicap who are neither liable to detention in a hospital nor subject to guardianship.

(2) The reference in subsection (1)(a) of this section to the care of persons for the time being resident in accommodation provided by a local authority includes, in the case of persons so resident who are under the age of 16 years, the payment to those persons of such amounts as the local authority think fit in respect of their personal expenses where it appears to that authority that no such payment would otherwise be made.

Provision of after-care services.

8.—(1) A local authority shall provide after-care services for any persons who are or have been suffering from mental disorder.

(2) In providing after-care services under subsection (1) of this section a local authority shall co-operate with such health board or boards and such voluntary organisations as appear to the local authority to be concerned.

(3) The duty imposed by this section is without prejudice to any other power or duty which a local authority may have in relation to the provision of after-care services.

Appointment of mental health officers.

9.—(1) A local authority shall appoint a sufficient number of persons for the purpose of discharging in relation to their area the functions of mental health officers under this Act.

1973 c. 65.

(2) Any officer appointed by a local authority to act as a mental health officer after the date of coming into force of section 64(4) of the Local Government (Scotland) Act 1973 (that is to say, 16th May 1975) but before 16th August 1983 shall be deemed to have been appointed under subsection (1) of this section as if that subsection and section 64(5)(bb) of the said Act of 1973 had come into force on 16th May 1975.

(3) On and after a day appointed by the Secretary of State by order, no person shall be appointed to act as a mental health officer under subsection (1) of this section unless he is approved by the local authority as having competence in dealing with persons who are suffering from mental disorder ; and before

appointing a person to act as a mental health officer, a local authority shall—

(a) ensure that the person has such qualifications, experience and competence in dealing with persons suffering from mental disorder ; and

(b) have regard to such other matters,

as the Secretary of State may direct.

(4) No person appointed to act as a mental health officer before the appointed day shall continue so to act on or after the appointed day unless—

(a) he is approved by the local authority as having competence in dealing with persons who are suffering from mental disorder ; and

(b) the local authority are satisfied that he has such qualifications, experience and competence in dealing with persons who are suffering from mental disorder as the Secretary of State may direct.

10.—(1) The provisions of this section shall apply to any patient suffering from mental disorder who is— *Welfare of certain hospital patients.*

(a) a child or young person in respect of whom the rights and powers of a parent are vested in a local authority by virtue of—

(i) section 17 of the Social Work (Scotland) Act 1968 ; or *1968 c. 49.*

(ii) section 3 of the Child Care Act 1980 (which relates to the assumption by a local authority of parental rights and duties in relation to a child in their care) ; or *1980 c. 5.*

(iii) section 10 of the said Act of 1980 (which relates to the powers and duties of local authorities in England and Wales with respect to persons committed to their care) ;

(b) a person who is under the guardianship of a local authority under the following provisions of this Act or under the provisions of the Mental Health Act 1983 ; or *1983 c. 20.*

(c) a person the functions of whose nearest relative under this Act or under the Mental Health Act 1983 are for the time being transferred to a local authority.

(2) Where a patient to whom this section applies is admitted to any hospital or nursing home in Scotland (whether for treatment for mental disorder or for any other reason) then, without pre-

PART III   judice to their duties in relation to the patient apart from the provisions of this section, the authority having rights or functions in relation to him as aforesaid shall arrange for visits to be made to him on their behalf, and shall take such other steps in relation to the patient while in the hospital or nursing home as would be expected of a parent.

The training and occupation of the mentally handicapped.

11.—(1) Without prejudice to the operation of section 1 of the Education (Scotland) Act 1980 (which among other things imposes a duty on education authorities to provide educational facilities for pupils who suffer from disability of mind) it shall be the duty of the local authority to provide or secure the provision of suitable training and occupation for persons suffering from mental handicap who are over school age within the meaning of the Education (Scotland) Act 1980:

1980 c. 44.

Provided that this subsection shall not apply in the case of a person in a hospital.

(2) A local authority shall make such provision as they may think necessary for securing that transport is available for the conveyance of persons for the purpose of their training and occupation under this section; and accordingly section 45 of the National Health Service (Scotland) Act 1978 (which relates to the provision by the Secretary of State of ambulances and other means of transport), shall not have effect in relation to the conveyance of persons as aforesaid.

1978 c. 29.

(3) Where a local authority makes arrangements with any voluntary organisation for the performance by that organisation of any services in connection with the duties of the local authority under this section, the local authority may make contributions to the funds of that voluntary organisation.

PART IV

PRIVATE HOSPITALS

Registration of private hospitals.

12.—(1) Every private hospital within the meaning of this Act shall be registered and the following provisions of this Part of this Act shall apply to the registration, conduct and inspection of such hospitals.

(2) In this Act " private hospital " means any premises used or intended to be used for the reception of, and the provision of medical treatment for, one or more patients subject to detention under this Act (whether or not other persons are received and treated), not being—

(a) a hospital vested in the Secretary of State;

(*b*) a State hospital ; or

(*c*) any other premises managed by a Government department or provided by a local authority.

(3) Application for registration of premises as a private hospital shall be made in writing to the Secretary of State by or on behalf of the person proposing to carry on the hospital and the application shall be accompanied by a fee of £1.

(4) Subject to section 13 of this Act, the Secretary of State may register the premises named in the application as a private hospital and issue to the person proposing to carry on the hospital a certificate in that behalf (in this Act referred to as " a certificate of registration ").

(5) A certificate of registration shall specify the maximum number of persons who at any one time may receive care or treatment in the hospital to which the certificate relates, and such conditions as the Secretary of State may consider appropriate for regulating the category of patients who may be received into the hospital.

(6) A certificate of registration shall lapse on the expiration of a period of 5 years from the date of issue, but shall be renewable on a fresh application.

(7) A certificate of registration shall be kept fixed conspicuously in the hospital to which it relates and if this requirement is not complied with the person carrying on the hospital shall be guilty of an offence under this Part of this Act.

13.—(1) The Secretary of State shall not issue a certificate of registration unless he is satisfied— Pre-requisites of registration.

(*a*) that the person proposing to carry on the hospital is a fit person for this purpose, having regard to his age, conduct and any other relevant consideration ;

(*b*) that the premises are fit to be used for a private hospital ;

(*c*) that neither the hospital nor any premises to be used in connection therewith consist of or include works executed in contravention of section 12(1) of the Health Services Act 1976 ; 1976 c. 83.

(*d*) that the arrangements proposed for patients are suitable and adequate ; and

(*e*) that the medical and nursing staff proposed is adequate for the hospital and is suitably trained and qualified.

(2) Nothing in the foregoing provisions of this Part of this Act shall be construed as requiring the Secretary of State to issue a certificate of registration under section 12 of this Act.

PART IV
Control of private hospitals.

14.—(1) Any person carrying on a private hospital shall—

(a) keep the hospital open to inspection for the purposes of this section at all reasonable times ;

(b) keep such registers and records as the Secretary of State may from time to time by regulations prescribe, and keep such registers and records open to inspection ;

(c) ensure that any conditions specified in the certificate of registration are complied with ;

(d) afford to the Mental Welfare Commission all such facilities (including facilities for inspection of the hospital) as are necessary for the Commission to exercise their functions under this Act,

and any person who fails to comply with any requirement of this subsection shall be guilty of an offence under this Part of this Act.

(2) The Secretary of State shall ensure by regular inspection of any private hospital that that hospital is being properly carried on, and any person authorised in that behalf by the Secretary of State may, after producing, if asked to do so, some duly authenticated document showing that he is so authorised, enter any hospital for the purpose of any inspection in pursuance of this section and carry out that inspection.

(3) Any person authorised under subsection (2) of this section may interview any patient in private.

Cancellation and continuance in certain circumstances of registration.

15.—(1) Subject to the provisions of this section, the Secretary of State may, at any time, cancel a registration of a private hospital on any ground on which he might have refused an application for such a registration of that hospital, or on the ground that the person carrying on the hospital has been convicted of an offence under this Act.

(2) On the cancellation of a registration, the person who is or was carrying on the hospital shall forthwith deliver up the certificate to the Secretary of State, and if this requirement is not complied with the holder of the certificate shall be guilty of an offence under this Part of this Act.

(3) Where at the time of any cancellation of a registration under subsection (1) of this section any patient is liable to be detained on the premises concerned, the registration shall, notwithstanding the cancellation, continue in force until the expiration of a period of 28 days from the date of cancellation or until every such patient has ceased to be so liable, whichever first occurs.

16.—(1) If any person carries on a private hospital which is not registered under this Part of this Act, he shall be guilty of an offence and shall be liable on summary conviction to a fine not exceeding the statutory maximum or on conviction on indictment to a fine.

(2) Any person guilty of an offence under this Part of this Act other than the offence specified in subsection (1) of this section shall be liable on summary conviction to a fine not exceeding level 1 on the standard scale and in the case of a continuing offence to a further fine not exceeding two pounds in respect of each day on which the offence continues after conviction.

PART V

ADMISSION TO AND DETENTION IN HOSPITAL AND GUARDIANSHIP

Grounds for hospital admission

17.—(1) A person may, in pursuance of an application for admission under section 18(1) of this Act, be admitted to a hospital and there detained on the grounds that—

Patients
liable to be
detained in
hospital.

> (a) he is suffering from mental disorder of a nature or degree which makes it appropriate for him to receive medical treatment in a hospital ; and
>
>> (i) in the case where the mental disorder from which he suffers is a persistent one manifested only by abnormally aggressive or seriously irresponsible conduct, such treatment is likely to alleviate or prevent a deterioration of his condition ; or
>>
>> (ii) in the case where the mental disorder from which he suffers is a mental handicap, the handicap comprises mental impairment (where such treatment is likely to alleviate or prevent a deterioration of his condition) or severe mental impairment ; and
>
> (b) it is necessary for the health or safety of that person or for the protection of other persons that he should receive such treatment and it cannot be provided unless he is detained under this Part of this Act.

PART V

(2) Nothing in this Act shall be construed as preventing a patient who requires treatment for mental disorder from being admitted to any hospital or nursing home for that treatment in pursuance of arrangements made in that behalf without any application, recommendation or order rendering him liable to be detained under this Act, or from remaining in any hospital in pursuance of such arrangements if he has ceased to be so liable to be detained.

Procedure for admission of patients : hospital

Admission and detention of patients: hospital.

18.—(1) A patient may be admitted to a hospital and there detained for the period allowed by this Part of this Act in pursuance of an application in the prescribed form (in this Act referred to as " an application for admission ") approved by the sheriff and made in accordance with this Part of this Act.

(2) An application for admission shall be founded on and accompanied by 2 medical recommendations which shall be in the prescribed form and each such recommendation shall include the following statements, being statements of opinion, and the grounds on which each statement is based—

(*a*) a statement of the form of mental disorder from which the patient is suffering, being mental illness or mental handicap or both ; and

(*b*) a statement as to which of the grounds set out in section 17(1) of this Act apply in relation to the patient.

(3) An application for admission shall be of no effect unless the patient is described in each of the medical recommendations as suffering from the same form of mental disorder, whether or not he is described in either of those recommendations as suffering also from the other form.

General provisions as to applications: hospital.

19.—(1) Subject to the provisions of this section, an application for admission may be made either by the nearest relative of the patient or by a mental health officer ; and every such application shall be addressed to the managers of the hospital to which admission is sought.

(2) The nearest relative of the patient shall not make an application for admission unless he has personally seen the patient within the period of 14 days ending with the date on which the proposed application is submitted to the sheriff for his approval.

(3) A local authority shall, if so required by the nearest relative of a patient residing in their area, direct a mental health officer as

soon as practicable to take the patient's case into consideration with a view to making an application for admission in respect of the patient; and if in any such case that officer decides not to make an application he shall inform the nearest relative of his reasons in writing.

(4) A mental health officer shall make an application for admission in respect of a patient within the area of the local authority by whom that officer was appointed in any case where he is satisfied that such an application ought to be made and is of the opinion, having regard to any wishes expressed by relatives of the patient and to any other relevant circumstances, that it is necessary or proper for the application to be made by him.

(5) A mental health officer who proposes to make an application for admission shall—

(a) interview the patient within the period of 14 days ending with the date on which the proposed application is submitted to the sheriff for his approval and satisfy himself that detention in a hospital is, in all the circumstances of the case, the most appropriate way of providing the care and medical treatment which the patient needs; and

(b) take such steps as are reasonably practicable to inform the nearest relative of the patient of the proposed application, and of his right to object thereto in accordance with the provisions of section 21 of this Act.

(6) A mental health officer shall make an application for admission in respect of a patient where—

(a) he has received the 2 medical recommendations required for the purposes of such an application; and

(b) he has been requested to do so by a medical practitioner who gave one of the medical recommendations,

and the application shall include—

(i) a statement of the mental health officer's opinion as to whether or not the application should be granted; and

(ii) a statement of the grounds on which that opinion is based.

(7) An application under this section by a mental health officer may be made outside the area of the local authority by whom he is appointed.

20.—(1) The medical recommendations required for the purposes of an application for admission shall satisfy the following requirements—

(a) such recommendations shall be signed on or before the date of the application and shall be given by medical practitioners (neither being the applicant) who have personally examined the patient separately, in which case not more than 5 days must have elapsed between the days on which the separate examinations took place, or, where no objection has been made by the patient or his nearest relative, together ;

(b) one of the recommendations shall be given by a practitioner approved for the purposes of this section by a Health Board as having special experience in the diagnosis or treatment of mental disorder and the other recommendation shall, if practicable, be given by the patient's general medical practitioner or another medical practitioner who has previous acquaintance with him ;

(c) neither recommendation shall be given by a practitioner on the staff of the hospital named in the application where the patient is to be accommodated under section 57 or 58 of the National Health Service (Scotland) Act 1978 (which relates to accommodation for private patients) or in a private hospital and, subject to subsection (2) of this section, where the patient is to be accommodated otherwise one only of the recommendations may be given by such a practitioner ;

(d) such recommendations shall contain a statement as to whether the person signing the recommendation is related to the patient and of any pecuniary interest that that person may have in the admission of the patient to hospital.

(2) Notwithstanding the provisions of paragraph (c) of subsection (1) of this section, both medical recommendations may be given by practitioners on the staff of the hospital named in the application where—

(a) compliance with the said paragraph (c) would result in a delay involving serious risk to the health or safety of the patient or to the safety of other persons ;

(b) one of the practitioners giving the recommendations works at the hospital for less than half the time which he is bound by contract to devote to work in the health service ; and

(c) if one of the practitioners is a consultant, the other does not work (whether at the hospital or elsewhere) in a grade in which he is under that consultant's directions.

(3) For the purposes of this section a general practitioner who is employed part-time in a hospital shall not be regarded as a practitioner on its staff.

21.—(1) An application for admission shall be submitted to a sheriff of the sheriffdom—

    (a) within which the patient is resident at the time when the application is submitted ; or

    (b) where the patient is a resident patient in a hospital at the time when the application is submitted, within which the hospital is situated,

for his approval within 7 days of the last date on which the patient was examined for the purposes of any medical recommendation accompanying the application.

(2) Subject to the following provisions of this section and to section 113 of this Act, the sheriff, in considering an application submitted to him under this section—

    (a) may make such inquiries and hear such persons (including the patient) as he think fit ; and

    (b) where an application is the subject of objection by the nearest relative of the patient, shall afford that relative and any witness that relative may call an opportunity of being heard ; and

    (c) shall, where a mental health officer makes an application for admission in respect of a patient under section 19(6) of this Act and such application includes a statement of the mental health officer's opinion that the application should not be granted, afford the mental health officer an opportunity of being heard.

(3) The sheriff shall not withhold approval to an application submitted under this section without affording to the applicant and any witness the applicant may call an opportunity of being heard.

(4) Any proceedings under this section shall, where the patient or applicant so desires or the sheriff thinks fit, be conducted in private.

(5) The sheriff in the exercise of the functions conferred on him by this section shall have the like jurisdiction, and the like powers as regards the summoning and examination of witnesses, the administration of oaths, the awarding of expenses, and otherwise, as if he were acting in the exercise of his civil jurisdiction.

PART V
Effect of
applications:
hospital.

22.—(1) Where an application for admission has been approved by the sheriff, that application shall be sufficient authority for the removal of the patient to the hospital named in the application and, when the application has been forwarded to the managers of the hospital, for the admission of the patient to that hospital at any time within a period of 7 days from the date on which the sheriff approved the application and for his detention there in accordance with the provisions of this Act.

(2) Where a patient has been admitted to a hospital in pursuance of an application under this Part of this Act, it shall be the duty of the managers of the hospital to notify—

    (*a*) the Mental Welfare Commission ; and

    (*b*) the local authority for the area in which the hospital is situated (except where the admission is in pursuance of an application made by a mental health officer appointed by that authority),

of that admission together with a copy of the application and recommendations relating to the patient's admission within 7 days of its taking place.

(3) A local authority shall, on being notified under subsection (2) of this section, arrange for a mental health officer as soon as practicable and, in any event, not later than 7 days before the expiry of the period of 28 days beginning with the day on which the patient was admitted to a hospital—

    (*a*) to interview the patient whose admission has been notified to them ; and

    (*b*) to provide the responsible medical officer and the Mental Welfare Commission with a report on the patient's social circumstances,

unless the mental health officer has done so under section 26(5) of this Act within the previous 28 days.

(4) Where a patient has been admitted as aforesaid the responsible medical officer shall—

    (*a*) within the period of 7 days ending on the 28th day after the patient's admission—

        (i) examine the patient or obtain from another medical practitioner a report on the condition of the patient ; and

        (ii) consult such other person or persons who appear to him to be principally concerned with the patient's medical treatment ; and

(*b*) if he is satisfied, as a result of the examination or report,
that—

(i) the patient is not suffering from mental disorder of a nature or degree which makes it appropriate for him to be liable to be detained in a hospital for medical treatment ; or

(ii) it is not necessary for the health or safety of the patient or for the protection of other persons that he should receive such treatment,

order the discharge of the patient ; or

(*c*) if he does not order the discharge of the patient, so inform the Mental Welfare Commission, the nearest relative of the patient, the local authority and the managers concerned.

23.—(1) If within the period of 14 days beginning with the   Rectification day on which a patient has been admitted to a hospital in pursuance of an application for admission, the application, or any   of application and recommendations: hospital. medical recommendation given for the purposes of the application, is found to be in any respect incorrect or defective, the application or recommendation may, not later than 7 days after the expiration of the said period, with the approval of the sheriff, be amended by the person by whom it was signed ; and upon such amendment being made the application or recommendation shall have effect, and shall be deemed always to have had effect, as if it had been originally made as so amended.

(2) Without prejudice to the provisions of subsection (1) of this section, if within the period first mentioned therein it appears to the managers of the hospital, that one of the 2 medical recommendations on which the application for admission is founded is insufficient to warrant the detention of the patient in pursuance of the application, they may within that period give notice in writing to that effect to the applicant and to the sheriff ; and where any such notice is given in respect of a medical recommendation that recommendation shall be disregarded, but the application shall be, and shall be deemed always to have been, sufficient if—

(*a*) a fresh medical recommendation complying with the relevant provisions of this Part of this Act (other than the provisions relating to the time of signature and the interval between examinations) is furnished to the managers and to the sheriff ; and

(*b*) the sheriff is satisfied that that recommendation and the other recommendation on which the application is founded together comply with those provisions.

(3) **Where** the medical recommendations upon which an application for admission is founded are, taken together, insufficient to warrant the detention of the patient in pursuance of the application, a notice under subsection (2) of this section may be given in respect of either of those recommendations ; but this subsection shall not apply in a case where the application is of no effect by virtue of section 18(3) of this Act.

Emergency admission: hospital.

24.—(1) In any case of urgent necessity a recommendation (in this Act referred to as " an emergency recommendation ") may be made by a medical practitioner in respect of a patient stating that by reason of mental disorder it is urgently necessary for his health or safety or for the protection of other persons, that he should be admitted to a hospital, but that compliance with the provisions of this Part of this Act relating to an application for admission before the admission of the patient to a hospital would involve undesirable delay.

(2) An emergency recommendation shall not be made unless, where practicable, the consent of a relative or of a mental health officer has been obtained ; and the recommendation shall be accompanied by a statement that such a consent as aforesaid has been obtained or, as the case may be, by a statement of the reasons for the failure to obtain that consent.

(3) An emergency recommendation shall be sufficient authority for the removal of the patient to a hospital at any time within a period of 3 days from the date on which it was made and for his detention therein for a period not exceeding 72 hours from the time of his admission.

(4) An emergency recommendation shall be made only by a medical practitioner who has personally examined the patient on the day on which he signed the recommendation.

(5) Where a patient is admitted to a hospital in pursuance of this section, it shall, where practicable, be the duty of the managers without delay to inform the nearest relative of the patient, the Mental Welfare Commission and, except in the case of a patient referred to in section 25 of this Act, some responsible person residing with the patient.

(6) A patient who has been detained in a hospital under this section shall not be further detained under this section immediately after the expiry of the period of detention.

Detention of patients already in hospital.

25.—(1) An application for admission or an emergency recommendation may be made under this Part of this Act notwithstanding that the patient is already in a hospital ; and where the application or recommendation is made in such a case the patient shall be treated for the purposes of this Part of this Act as if he had been admitted to the hospital on the date on which the application was forwarded to the managers of the hospital, or, as the case may be, the recommendation was made.

(2) If, in the case of a patient who is already in a hospital receiving treatment for mental disorder and who is not liable to be detained therein under this Part of this Act, it appears to a nurse of the prescribed class—

   (*a*) that the patient is suffering from mental disorder to such a degree that it is necessary for his health or safety or for the protection of other persons for him to be immediately restrained from leaving the hospital ; and

   (*b*) that it is not practicable to secure the immediate attendance of a medical practitioner for the purpose of making an emergency recommendation,

the patient may be detained in the hospital for a period of 2 hours from the time when he was first so detained or until the earlier arrival at the place where the patient is detained of a medical practitioner having power to make an emergency recommendation.

(3) Where a patient is detained under subsection (2) of this section the nurse shall as soon as possible record in writing—

   (*a*) the facts mentioned in paragraphs (*a*) and (*b*) of the said subsection (2) ;

   (*b*) the fact that the patient has been detained ; and

   (*c*) the time at which the patient was first so detained.

(4) A record made by a nurse under subsection (3) of this section shall, as soon as possible after it is made, be delivered by the nurse, or by a person authorised by the nurse in that behalf, to the managers of the hospital ; and a copy of the record shall, within 14 days of the date on which the managers received it, be sent to the Mental Welfare Commission.

(5) A patient who has been detained in a hospital under subsection (2) of this section shall not be further detained thereunder immediately after the expiry of that period of detention.

(6) In subsection (2) of this section " prescribed " means prescribed by an order made by the Secretary of State.

26.—(1) Where a patient is admitted to a hospital in pursuance Short term of section 24 of this Act, he may be detained in that hospital after detention. the expiry of the period of 72 hours referred to in subsection (3) of that section if—

   (*a*) a report on the condition of the patient has been furnished to the managers of the hospital ; and

   (*b*) where practicable, consent to the continued detention has been given by the nearest relative of the patient or by a mental health officer.

(2) The report referred to in subsection (1)(*a*) of this section shall—

   (*a*) be given by a medical practitioner approved for the purposes of section 20(1)(*b*) of this Act who has personally examined the patient and shall include a statement that in the opinion of the medical practitioner—

      (i) the patient is suffering from mental disorder of a nature or degree which makes it appropriate for him to be detained in a hospital for at least a limited period ; and

      (ii) the patient ought to be so detained in the interests of his own health or safety or with a view to the protection of other persons ;

   (*b*) include, where consent to the continued detention has not been obtained, a statement of the reasons for not obtaining such consent ; and

   (*c*) contain a statement as to whether the person signing the report is related to the patient and of any pecuniary interest that that person may have in the admission of the patient to hospital.

(3) Subject to subsection (6) of this section, where a report is duly furnished under subsection (1) of this section the authority for the detention of the patient shall be thereby renewed for a further period of 28 days from the expiry of the period of 72 hours referred to in the said subsection (1).

(4) Where a patient is detained in a hospital in pursuance of this section, the managers of the hospital shall so inform—

   (*a*) the Mental Welfare Commission ;

   (*b*) where practicable, the nearest relative of the patient (except where the nearest relative has consented under subsection (1)(*b*) of this section) ; and

   (*c*) the local authority (except in a case where a mental health officer appointed by that local authority has consented under subsection (1)(*b*) of this section),

not later than 7 days after the patient was detained.

(5) A local authority, on being informed under subsection (4) of this section of the admission of a patient, shall arrange for a mental health officer as soon as practicable and in any event not later than 7 days before the expiry of the period of 28 days referred to in subsection (3) of this section—

   (*a*) to interview the patient ; and

   (*b*) to provide the responsible medical officer and the Mental Welfare Commission with a report on the patient's social circumstances.

(6) Any patient may, within the period for which the auth- Part V
ority for his detention is renewed by virtue of a report furnished
in respect of him under this section, appeal to the sheriff to order
his discharge and the provisions of section 33(2) and (4) of this
Act shall apply in relation to such an appeal.

(7) A patient who has been detained in a hospital under this
section shall not be further detained under this section nor
detained under section 24 of this Act immediately after the ex-
expiry of the period of detention under this section.

Care and treatment of patients : hospital

27.—(1) The responsible medical officer may grant to any Leave of
patient who is for the time being liable to be detained in a absence from
hospital under this Part of this Act leave to be absent from the hospital.
hospital.

(2) Leave of absence may be granted to a patient under this
section either on specified occasions or for any specified period
of not more than 6 months ; and where leave is so granted for
a specified period it may be extended for further such periods
as aforesaid.

(3) Where it appears to the responsible medical officer that
it is necessary so to do in the interests of the patient or for the
protection of other persons, he may, upon granting leave of
absence under this section, direct that the patient remain in
custody during his absence ; and where leave of absence is so
granted the patient may be kept in the custody of any officer
on the staff of the hospital, or of any other person authorised
in writing by the managers of the hospital, or, if the patient
is required in accordance with conditions imposed on the grant
of leave of absence to reside in another hospital, of any officer
on the staff of that other hospital.

(4) Where leave of absence is granted to a patient under this
section or where a period of leave is extended by further leave
and the leave or the extension is for a period of more than 28
days, it shall be the duty of the responsible medical officer to
inform the Mental Welfare Commission within 14 days of the
granting of leave or of the extension, as the case may be, of
the address at which the patient is residing and, on the return
of the patient, to notify the Commission thereof within 14 days.

(5) In any case where a patient is absent from a hospital in
pursuance of leave of absence granted under this section, and it
appears to the responsible medical officer that it is necessary so
to do in the interests of the health or safety of the patient or for
the protection of other persons, that officer may, subject to sub-

PART V

section (6) of this section, by notice in writing given to the patient or to the person for the time being in charge of the patient, revoke the leave of absence and recall the patient to the hospital.

(6) A patient to whom leave of absence is granted under this section shall not be recalled under subsection (5) of this section after he has ceased to be liable to be detained under this Part of this Act.

Return and re-admission of patients absent without leave: hospital.

28.—(1) Where a patient who is for the time being liable to be detained under this Part of this Act in a hospital—

(a) absents himself from the hospital without leave granted under section 27 of this Act ; or

(b) fails to return to the hospital on any occasion on which, or at the expiration of any period for which, leave of absence was granted to him under that section, or upon being recalled thereunder ; or

(c) absents himself without permission from any place where he is required to reside in accordance with conditions imposed on the grant of leave of absence under that section,

he may, subject to the provisions of this section, be taken into custody and returned to the hospital or place by any mental health officer, by any officer on the staff of the hospital, by any constable, or by any person authorised in writing by the managers of the hospital.

(2) Where the place referred to in subsection 1(c) of this section is a hospital other than the one in which the patient is for the time being liable to be detained, the references in that subsection to an officer on the staff of the hospital and to the managers of the hospital shall respectively include references to an officer on the staff of the first-mentioned hospital and to the managers of that hospital.

(3) A patient shall not be taken into custody under this section after the expiration of the period of 28 days beginning with the first day of his absence without leave and a patient who has not returned or been taken into custody under this section within the said period shall cease to be liable to be detained at the expiration of that period.

(4) A patient shall not be taken into custody under this section if the period for which he is liable to be detained is that specified in section 24(3), 25(2) or 26(3) of this Act and that period has expired.

29.—(1) A patient who is for the time being liable to be detained in a hospital by virtue of an application for admission under this Part of this Act may be transferred by the managers of that hospital, as follows—

(a) to another hospital with the consent of the managers of that hospital ; or

(b) into the guardianship of a local authority with the consent of that authority ; or

(c) into the guardianship of any person approved by a local authority with the consent of that person.

(2) Any transfer of a patient under the last foregoing subsection shall be intimated to his nearest relative and to the Mental Welfare Commission by the managers of the hospital to which the patient is transferred or, as the case may be, by the local authority concerned within 7 days of the date of transfer.

(3) Where a patient is transferred in pursuance of this section, the provisions of this Part of this Act (including this subsection) shall apply to him as follows, that is to say—

(a) where the patient, being liable to be detained in a hospital by virtue of an application for admission, is transferred to another hospital, as if the application were an application for admission to that other hospital, and as if the patient had been admitted to that other hospital at the time when he was originally admitted in pursuance of the application ;

(b) where the patient, being liable to be detained as aforesaid, is transferred into guardianship, as if the application were a guardianship application duly forwarded to the local authority at the time aforesaid.

(4) Where a patient is transferred to a State hospital under subsection (1)(a) of this section he or his nearest relative may within 28 days of the date of the transfer, appeal by way of summary application to a sheriff of the sheriffdom within which the hospital from which the patient was transferred is situated against the decision of the managers of that hospital to transfer the patient ; and on any such appeal the sheriff shall order the return of the patient to the hospital from which he was transferred unless he is satisfied that the patient, on account of his dangerous, violent or criminal propensities, requires treatment under conditions of special security, and cannot suitably be cared for in a hospital other than a State hospital.

Duration of authority for detention and discharge of patients:
hospital

30.—(1) Subject to the provisions of this Part of this Act, a patient admitted to a hospital in pursuance of an application for admission may be detained in a hospital for a period not ex-

PART V   ceeding 6 months beginning with the day on which he was so admitted, but shall not be so detained for any longer period unless the authority for his detention is renewed under the following provisions of this section.

(2) Authority for the detention of a patient may, unless the patient has previously been discharged, be renewed under this section—

>(a) from the expiration of the period referred to in subsection (1) of this section, for a further period of 6 months ;

>(b) from the expiration of any period of renewal under paragraph (a) of this subsection, for a further period of one year, and so on for periods of one year at a time.

(3) The responsible medical officer shall within the period of 2 months ending on the day when a patient who is liable to be detained in a hospital under this Part of this Act would cease to be so liable under this section in default of the renewal of the authority for his detention—

>(a) examine the patient or obtain from another medical practitioner a report on the condition of the patient; and

>(b) consult such other person or persons who appear to him to be principally concerned with the patient's medical treatment,

and thereafter assess the need for the detention of the patient to be continued ; and if it appears to him that the grounds set out in section 17(1) of this Act apply to the patient he shall furnish to the managers of the hospital where the patient is liable to be detained and to the Mental Welfare Commission a report to that effect in the prescribed form, along with the report first mentioned if such a report has been obtained.

(4) Subject to subsection (6) of this section and section 33(2) and (4) of this Act, where a report is duly furnished to the managers of a hospital under subsection (3) of this section, the authority for the detention of the patient shall be thereby renewed for the period prescribed in that case by subsection (2) of this section.

(5) Where a report under this section is furnished to them in respect of a patient, the managers of the hospital shall, unless they discharge the patient, cause him and his nearest relative to be informed.

(6) Any patient may within the period for which the authority for his detention is renewed by virtue of a report furnished in respect of him under this section appeal to the sheriff to order his discharge and the provisions of section 33(2) and (4) of this Act shall apply in relation to such an appeal.

31.—(1) If on the day on which, apart from this section, a patient would cease to be liable to be detained under this Part of this Act or within the period of one week ending with that day, the patient is absent without leave, he shall not cease to be so liable or so subject— PART V
Special
provisions as
to patients
absent without
leave:
hospital.

    (a) in any case, until the expiration of the period during which he can be taken into custody under section 28 of this Act, or the day on which he returns or is returned to the hospital or place where he ought to be, whichever is the earlier ; and

    (b) if he returns or is returned as aforesaid within the period first mentioned in the foregoing paragraph, until the expiration of the period of one week beginning with the day on which he is returned or returns as aforesaid.

(2) Where the period for which a patient is liable to be detained is extended by virtue of this section, any examination and report to be made and furnished under subsection (3) of section 30 of this Act may be made and furnished within that period as so extended.

(3) Where the authority for the detention of a patient is renewed by virtue of this section after the day on which, apart from this section, that authority would have expired under section 30 of this Act, the renewal shall take effect as from that day.

32.—(1) Where a patient who is liable to be detained in a hospital under this Part of this Act is detained in custody in pursuance of any sentence or order passed or made by a court in the United Kingdom (including an order committing or remanding him in custody) and is so detained for a period exceeding 6 months, he shall, at the end of that period, cease to be so liable. Special
provisions as
to patients
sentenced to
imprisonment
etc.:
hospital.

(2) Where any such patient is detained in custody as aforesaid for a period not exceeding 6 months, or for successive periods that do not in the aggregate exceed 6 months, then—

    (a) if apart from this subsection the patient would have ceased to be liable to be detained as aforesaid on or before the day he is discharged from custody, he shall not cease to be so liable until the end of that day ; and

    (b) in any case, sections 28 and 31 of this Act shall apply in relation to the patient as if he had absented himself without leave on that day.

33.—(1) Subject to the provisions of this and the next following section, a patient who is liable to be detained in a hospital under this Part of this Act shall cease to be so liable if an order in writing discharging him from detention (in this Act referred to as "an order for discharge ") is made in accordance with the following provisions of this section.

(2) An order for discharge may be made in respect of a patient by the responsible medical officer, the Mental Welfare Commission or, where an appeal has been taken under sections 26, 30 or 34 of this Act, by the sheriff:

> Provided that such an order shall not be made by the responsible medical officer in respect of a patient detained in a State hospital without the consent of the managers of the hospital.

(3) The responsible medical officer or the Mental Welfare Commission shall make an order for discharge in respect of a patient where he is or they are satisfied that—

(a) he is not suffering from mental disorder of a nature or degree which makes it appropriate for him to be liable to be detained in a hospital for medical treatment; or

(b) it is not necessary for the health or safety of the patient or for the protection of other persons that he should receive such treatment.

(4) Where an appeal is made to the sheriff by a patient under sections 26, 30 or 34 of this Act, the sheriff shall order the discharge of the patient if he is satisfied that—

(a) the patient is not at the time of the hearing of the appeal suffering from mental disorder of a nature or degree which makes it appropriate for him to be liable to be detained in a hospital for medical treatment ; or

(b) it is not necessary for the health or safety of the patient or for the protection of other persons that he should receive such treatment.

(5) Subject to the provisions of this section and section 34 of this Act, an order for discharge in respect of a patient may also be made by the managers of the hospital or by the nearest relative of the patient.

(6) An order for discharge made in respect of a patient by the managers of a hospital shall, with the consent of the responsible medical officer, take effect on the expiration of a period of 7 days from the date on which the order was made, and where the responsible medical officer does not so consent he shall furnish to the managers a report certifying that in his opinion the grounds set out in section 17(1) of this Act apply in relation to the patient.

34.—(1) An order for the discharge of a patient who is liable to be detained in a hospital shall not be made by his nearest relative except after giving not less than 7 days' notice in writing to the managers of the hospital; and if within that period the responsible medical officer furnishes to the managers a report certifying that, in his opinion, the grounds set out in section 17(1) of this Act apply in relation to the patient—

> (a) any order for the discharge of the patient made by that relative in pursuance of the notice shall be of no effect; and
>
> (b) no further order for the discharge of the patient shall be made by that relative during the period of 6 months beginning with the date of the report.

(2) In any case where a report under subsection (1) of this section is furnished in respect of a patient, the managers shall cause the nearest relative of the patient to be informed and that relative may, within the period of 28 days beginning with the day on which he is so informed, appeal to the sheriff to order the discharge of the patient and the provisions of section 33(2) and (4) of this Act shall apply in relation to such an appeal.

(3) An order for discharge in respect of a patient detained in a State hospital shall not be made by his nearest relative.

Appeals : hospital

35.—(1) Where an appeal lies to the sheriff in respect of a report on a patient under any of sections 26, 30 or 34 of this Act, the managers of the hospital where the patient is liable to be detained shall, when intimating that a report has been furnished in pursuance of any of the said sections, inform any person having a right so to appeal, whether the patient or his nearest relative or both, of that right and of the period within which it may be exercised.

(2) An appeal under any of the said sections shall be made by way of summary application to a sheriff of the sheriffdom—

> (a) within which the patient is resident at the time when the appeal is made; or
>
> (b) where the patient is a resident patient in a hospital at the time when the appeal is made, within which the hospital is situated.

(3) For the purpose of advising whether any appeal to the sheriff under any of the said sections should be made by or in respect of a patient who is liable to be detained under this Part of this Act, or of furnishing information as to the condition of a patient for the purposes of such an appeal or of advising the nearest relative of any such patient as to the exercise of any power to

order the discharge of the patient, any medical practitioner authorised by or on behalf of the patient or by the nearest relative of the patient, as the case may be, may, at any reasonable time, visit the patient and may examine him in private.

(4) Any medical practitioner authorised for the purposes of subsection (3) of this section to visit and examine a patient may require the production of and inspect any records relating to the detention or treatment of the patient in any hospital.

Grounds for reception into guardianship

Patients liable to be received into guardianship. 36. A person may, in pursuance of an application for reception into guardianship under section 37(1) of this Act, be received into guardianship on the grounds that—

(a) he is suffering from mental disorder of a nature or degree which warrants his reception into guardianship; and

(b) it is necessary in the interests of the welfare of the patient that he should be so received.

Procedure for reception of patients : guardianship

Reception of patients into guardianship. 37.—(1) A patient who has attained the age of 16 years may be received into guardianship for the period allowed by this Part of this Act, in pursuance of an application in the prescribed form (in this Act referred to as " a guardianship application ") approved by the sheriff and made in accordance with the provisions of this Part of this Act.

(2) The person named as guardian in a guardianship application may be—

(a) the local authority to whom the application is addressed ; or

(b) a person chosen by that authority ; or

(c) any other person who has been accepted as a suitable person to act in that behalf by that authority,

and any person chosen or accepted as aforesaid may be a local authority or any other person including the applicant.

(3) A guardianship application shall be founded on and accompanied by 2 medical recommendations in the prescribed form and a recommendation by a mental health officer in such form ; and

(a) each medical recommendation shall include—

(i) a statement of the form of mental disorder from which the patient is suffering being mental illness or mental handicap or both ; and

(ii) a statement that the ground set out in section 36(a) of this Act applies in relation to the patient, being statements of opinion, together with the grounds on which those statements are based ;

(b) the recommendation by the mental health officer shall include—

(i) a statement, being a statement of opinion, that the ground set out in section 36(b) of this Act applies in relation to the patient, together with the grounds on which the statement is based ; and

(ii) a statement as to whether he is related to the patient and of any pecuniary interest that he may have in the reception of the patient into guardianship.

(4) A guardianship application shall be of no effect unless the patient is described in each of the medical recommendations as suffering from the same form of mental disorder, whether or not he is described in either of those recommendations as suffering also from the other form.

38.—(1) Subject to the provisions of this section, a guardianship application may be made either by the nearest relative of the patient or by a mental health officer ; and every such application shall be addressed to the local authority for the area in which the patient resides.

(2) The nearest relative of the patient shall not make a guardianship application unless he has personally seen the patient within the period of 14 days ending with the date on which the proposed application is submitted to the sheriff for his approval.

(3) A local authority shall, if so required by the nearest relative of a patient residing in their area, direct a mental health officer as soon as practicable to take the patient's case into consideration with a view to making a guardianship application in respect of the patient ; and if in any such case that officer decides not to make an application he shall inform the nearest relative of his reasons in writing.

(4) A mental health officer shall make a guardianship application in respect of a patient within the area of the local authority by whom that officer was appointed in any case where he is satisfied that such an application ought to be made and is of the opinion, having regard to any wishes expressed by relatives of the patient and to any other relevant circumstances, that it is necessary or proper for the application to be made by him.

(5) A mental health officer who proposes to make a guardianship application shall—

(a) interview the patient within the period of 14 days ending with the date on which the proposed application is submitted to the sheriff for his approval ; and

PART V

(b) take such steps as are reasonably practicable to inform the nearest relative of the patient of the proposed application, and of his right to object thereto in accordance with the provisions of section 40 of this Act.

(6) An application under this section by a mental health officer may be made outside the area of the local authority by whom he is appointed.

Medical recommendations: guardianship.

39. The medical recommendations required for the purposes of a guardianship application shall satisfy the following requirements—

(a) such recommendations shall be signed on or before the date of the application and shall be given by medical practitioners (neither being the applicant) who have personally examined the patient separately, in which case not more than 5 days must have elapsed between the days on which the separate examinations took place, or, where no objection has been made by the patient or his nearest relative, together ;

(b) one of the recommendations shall be given by a practitioner approved for the purposes of this section by a Health Board as having special experience in the diagnosis or treatment of mental disorder and the other recommendation shall, if practicable, be given by the patient's general medical practitioner or another medical practitioner who has previous acquaintance with him ;

(c) such recommendations shall contain a statement as to whether the person signing the recommendation is related to the patient and of any pecuniary interest that that person may have in the reception of the patient into guardianship.

Approval of applications by the sheriff: guardianship.

40.—(1) A guardianship application shall be submitted to a sheriff of the sheriffdom—

(a) within which the patient is resident at the time when the application is submitted ; or

(b) where the patient is a resident patient in a hospital at the time when the application is submitted, within which the hospital is situated,

for his approval within 7 days of the last date on which the patient was examined for the purposes of any medical recommendation accompanying the application, together with a statement of the willingness to act of the guardian named in the application.

(2) Subject to the following provisions of this section and to section 113 of this Act, the sheriff, in considering an application submitted to him under this section may make such inquiries and hear such persons (including the patient) as he thinks fit, and, where an application is the subject of objection by the nearest relative of the patient, shall afford that relative and any witness that relative may call an opportunity of being heard.

(3) The sheriff shall not withhold approval to an application so submitted without affording to the applicant and any witness the applicant may call an opportunity of being heard.

(4) Any proceedings under this section shall, where the patient or applicant so desires or the sheriff thinks fit, be conducted in private.

(5) Every such application shall, after it is approved by the sheriff, be forwarded to the local authority for the area in which the patient resides.

(6) The sheriff in the exercise of the functions conferred on him by this section shall have the like jurisdiction, and the like powers as regards the summoning and examination of witnesses, the administration of oaths, the awarding of expenses, and otherwise, as if he were acting in the exercise of his civil jurisdiction.

41.—(1) Where a patient has been received into guardianship in pursuance of an application under this Part of this Act, the local authority concerned shall notify the Mental Welfare Commission of that reception together with a copy of the application and recommendations relating to the patient's reception within 7 days of its taking place.

Effect of applications: guardianship.

(2) Where a guardianship application has been approved by the sheriff and forwarded to the local authority concerned within a period of 7 days from the date on which the sheriff approved the application, the application shall, subject to the following provisions of this section and to regulations made by the Secretary of State, confer on the authority or person named in the application as guardian, to the exclusion of any other person, the following powers—

(a) power to require the patient to reside at a place specified by the authority or person named as guardian;

(b) power to require the patient to attend at places and times so specified for the purpose of medical treatment, occupation, education or training;

(c) power to require access to the patient to be given, at any place where the patient is residing, to any medical practitioner, mental health officer or other person so specified.

PART V

(3) Nothing in the provisions of subsection (2) of this section or of regulations made thereunder shall confer any power on a guardian in respect of a patient received into his guardianship to intromit with any property of that patient.

(4) No person who is appointed as a guardian of a patient under this Act shall administer corporal punishment to that patient, and any person who contravenes the provisions of this subsection shall be guilty of an offence and shall be liable on summary conviction to a fine not exceeding level 3 on the standard scale and the court shall intimate the conviction to the Mental Welfare Commission.

Rectification of application and recommendations: guardianship.

42.—(1) If within the period of 14 days beginning with the day on which a patient has been received into guardianship in pursuance of a guardianship application, the application, or any medical recommendation given for the purposes of the application, is found to be in any respect incorrect or defective, the application or recommendation may, not later than 7 days after the expiration of the said period, with the approval of the sheriff, be amended by the person by whom it was signed ; and upon such amendment being made the application or recommendation shall have effect, and shall be deemed to have had effect, as if it had been originally made as so amended.

(2) Without prejudice to the provisions of subsection (1) of this section, if within the period first mentioned therein it appears to the designated medical officer that one of the medical recommendations on which the guardianship application is founded is insufficient to warrant reception into guardianship in pursuance of the application, he may give notice in writing to that effect within that period to the applicant and to the sheriff ; and where any such notice is given in respect of a recommendation that recommendation shall be disregarded, but the application shall be, and shall be deemed always to have been, sufficient if—

(a) a fresh recommendation complying with the relevant provisions of this Part of this Act (other than the provisions relating to the time of signature and the interval between medical examinations) is furnished to the local authority concerned and to the sheriff ; and

(b) the sheriff is satisfied that that recommendation and the other recommendations on which the application is founded together comply with those provisions.

(3) Where the medical recommendations upon which an application under this Part of this Act is founded are, taken together, insufficient to warrant reception into guardianship in

pursuance of the application, a notice under subsection (2) of this
section may be given in respect of either of those recommendations; but this subsection shall not apply in a case where the
application is of no effect by virtue of section 37(4) of this Act.

Care and treatment of patients: guardianship

43.—(1) Subject to the provisions of this Part of this Act, the
Secretary of State may make regulations for regulating the exercise by the guardians of patients received into guardianship
under this Part of this Act of their powers as such, and for imposing on such guardians, and upon any local authority concerned, such duties as he considers necessary or expedient in the
interests of the patients.

(2) Regulations under this section may in particular make
provision for requiring the patients to be visited, on such
occasions or at such intervals as may be prescribed by the regulations, on behalf of such local authorities as may be so prescribed.

44.—(1) Where a patient who is for the time being subject to
guardianship under this Part of this Act absents himself without the leave of the guardian from the place at which he is
required by the guardian to reside, he may, subject to the provisions of this section, be taken into custody and returned to
that place by the guardian, by any officer on the staff of a local
authority, by any constable, or by any person authorised in writing by the guardian or a local authority.

Return of
patients
absent
without
leave:
guardianship.

(2) A patient shall not be taken into custody under this section
after the expiration of the period of 28 days beginning with the
first day of his absence without leave and a patient who has
not returned or been taken into custody under this section within
the said period shall cease to be subject to guardianship at the
expiration of that period.

45.—(1) A patient who is for the time being subject to the
guardianship of any person, including a local authority, by virtue
of a guardianship application may be transferred by the local
authority concerned into the guardianship of another such person with the consent of that other person; but no patient shall
be so transferred except with the consent of his guardian, or,
if that consent is refused, with the approval of the sheriff to the
transfer.

(2) Any transfer of a patient under the last foregoing subsection shall be intimated to his nearest relative and to the Mental

PART V

Welfare Commission by the local authority concerned within 7 days of the date of transfer.

(3) Where a patient is transferred under this section, the provisions of this Part of this Act (including this subsection) shall apply to him as if the person into whose guardianship he is transferred had been the person named in the guardianship application.

Transfer of guardianship in case of death, incapacity etc. of guardian.

46.—(1) If any person (other than a local authority) having the guardianship of a patient received into guardianship under this Part of this Act—

(*a*) dies ; or

(*b*) gives notice in writing to the local authority concerned that he desires to relinquish the functions of guardian,

the guardianship of the patient shall thereupon vest in the local authority concerned, but without prejudice to any power to transfer the patient into the guardianship of another person under section 45 of this Act.

(2) If any such person, not having given notice under subsection (1)(*b*) of this section, is incapacitated by illness or any other cause from performing the functions of guardian of the patient, those functions may, during his incapacity, be performed on his behalf by the local authority concerned, or by any other person approved for the purpose by that authority.

(3) Where the guardianship of a patient is transferred to a local authority or other person by or under subsection (1) of this section, section 45(3) of this Act shall apply as if the patient had been transferred into the guardianship of that authority or person in pursuance of that section.

Duration of authority for guardianship and discharge of patients

Duration of authority: guardianship.

47.—(1) Subject to the provisions of this Part of this Act, a patient received into guardianship in pursuance of a guardianship application, may be kept under guardianship for a period not exceeding 6 months beginning with the day on which he was so received, but shall not be so kept for any longer period unless the authority for his guardianship is renewed under the following provisions of this section.

(2) Authority for the guardianship of a patient may, unless the patient has previously been discharged, be renewed under this section—

(a) from the expiration of the period referred to in subsection (1) of this section, for a further period of 6 months;

(b) from the expiration of any period of renewal under paragraph (a) of this subsection, for a further period of one year, and so on for periods of one year at a time.

(3) Within the period of 2 months ending with the day on which a patient who is subject to guardianship under this Part of this Act would cease under this section to be so liable in default of the renewal of the authority for his guardianship—

(a) the responsible medical officer shall examine the patient or obtain from another medical practitioner a report on the condition of the patient; and, if it appears to him that the ground set out in section 36(a) of this Act continues to apply in relation to the patient, he shall furnish to such mental health officer as the local authority concerned may direct a report to that effect in the prescribed form along with the report first mentioned if such a report has been obtained; and

(b) that mental health officer shall consider whether the ground set out in section 36(b) of this Act continues to apply in relation to the patient; and, if it appears to him that it does continue so to apply, he shall furnish to the local authority concerned and to the Mental Welfare Commission a report to that effect in the prescribed form along with the report or reports furnished to him under paragraph (a) of this subsection.

(4) Subject to subsection (6) of this section and section 50(2) and (5) of this Act, where a report is duly furnished to a local authority under subsection (3) of this section, the authority for the guardianship of the patient shall be thereby renewed for the period prescribed in that case by subsection (2) of this section.

(5) Where a report under this section is furnished to them in respect of a patient, the local authority shall, unless they discharge the patient, cause him, his nearest relative and his guardian, to be informed.

(6) Any patient may within the period for which the authority for his guardianship is renewed by virtue of a report furnished in respect of him under this section appeal to the sheriff to order his discharge and the provisions of section 50(2) and (5) of this Act shall apply in relation to such an appeal.

48.—(1) If on the day on which, under this Part of this Act apart from this section, a patient would cease to be subject to guardianship, or within the period of one week ending with that day, the patient is absent without leave, he shall not cease to be so subject—

> (a) in any case, until the expiration of the period during which he can be taken into custody under section 44 of this Act, or the day on which he returns or is returned to the place where he ought to be, whichever is the earlier ; and
>
> (b) if he returns or is returned as aforesaid within the period first mentioned in the foregoing paragraph, until the expiration of the period of one week beginning with the day on which he is returned or returns as aforesaid.

(2) Where the period for which a patient is subject to guardianship is extended by virtue of this section, any examination and report to be made and furnished under section 47(3) of this Act may be made and furnished within that period as so extended.

(3) Where the authority for the guardianship of a patient is renewed by virtue of this section after the day on which, apart from this section, that authority would have expired under section 47 of this Act, the renewal shall take effect as from that day.

49.—(1) Where a patient who is subject to guardianship under this Part of this Act is detained in custody in pursuance of any sentence or order passed or made by a court in the United Kingdom (including an order committing or remanding him in custody) and is so detained for a period exceeding 6 months, he shall, at the end of that period, cease to be so subject.

(2) Where any such patient is detained in custody as aforesaid for a period not exceeding 6 months, or for successive periods that do not in the aggregate exceed 6 months, then—

> (a) if apart from this subsection the patient would have ceased to be subject as aforesaid on or before the day he is discharged from custody, he shall not cease to be so subject until the end of that day ; and
>
> (b) in any case, sections 44 and 48 of this Act shall apply in relation to the patient as if he had absented himself without leave on that day.

50.—(1) Subject to the provisions of this section and section 51 of this Act, a patient who is for the time being subject to guardianship under this Part of this Act shall cease to be so subject if an order in writing discharging him from guardianship (in this Act referred to as " an order for discharge ") is made in accordance with the following provisions of this section.

(2) An order for discharge may be made in respect of a patient by the responsible medical officer, the Mental Welfare Commission or, where an appeal has been taken under sections 47 or 51 of this Act, by the sheriff.

(3) The responsible medical officer or the Mental Welfare Commission shall make an order for discharge in respect of a patient where he is or they are satisfied that he is not suffering from mental disorder of a nature or degree which warrants his remaining under guardianship.

(4) The local authority concerned or the Mental Welfare Commission shall make an order for discharge where they are satisfied that it is not necessary in the interests of the welfare of the patient that he should remain under guardianship.

(5) Where an appeal is made to the sheriff by a patient under sections 47 or 51 of this Act, the sheriff shall order the discharge of the patient if he is satisfied that—

(a) the patient is not at the time of the hearing of the appeal suffering from mental disorder of a nature or degree which warrants his remaining under guardianship ; or

(b) it is not necessary in the interests of the welfare of the patient that he should remain under guardianship.

(6) Subject to the provisions of this section and section 51 of this Act, an order for discharge in respect of a patient may also be made by the nearest relative of the patient.

(7) A patient subject to guardianship shall cease to be so subject where the sheriff has approved under section 21 of this Act an application for his admission to a hospital.

51.—(1) An order for the discharge of a patient who is subject to guardianship shall not be made by his nearest relative except after giving not less than 14 days' notice in writing to the local authority concerned ; and within that period— *Restrictions on discharge by nearest relative: guardianship.*

(a) if it appears to the local authority that the ground set out in section 36(b) of this Act continues to apply in relation to the patient they shall inform the responsible medical officer of the notice given by the nearest relative ; and

(b) if it appears to the responsible medical officer that the ground set out in section 36(a) of this Act continues to apply in relation to the patient he shall inform the local authority ; and

(c) the local authority shall inform the nearest relative of the views taken by them and by the responsible medical officer, and in that event—

(i) any order for the discharge of the patient made by that relative in pursuance of the notice shall cease to have effect ; and

(ii) no further order for the discharge of the patient shall be made by that relative during the period of 6 months beginning with the date on which that relative is so informed.

(2) In any case where the local authority informs the nearest relative under subsection (1) of this section that relative may, within the period of 28 days beginning with the day on which he is so informed, appeal to the sheriff to order the discharge of the patient, and the provisions of section 50(2) and (5) of this Act shall apply in relation to such an appeal.

Appeals : guardianship

Appeals to
the sheriff:
guardianship.

52.—(1) Where an appeal lies to the sheriff under either of sections 47 or 51 of this Act, the local authority concerned shall when intimating that a report has been furnished in pursuance of the said section 47, or when informing the nearest relative under the said section 51, inform any person having a right so to appeal, whether the patient or his nearest relative, or both, of that right, and of the period within which it may be exercised.

(2) An appeal under either of the said sections shall be made by way of summary application to a sheriff of the sheriffdom within which the patient is resident at the time when the appeal is made.

(3) For the purpose of advising whether any appeal to the sheriff under either of the said sections should be made by or in respect of a patient who is subject to guardianship under this Part of this Act, or of furnishing information as to the condition of a patient for the purposes of such an appeal or of advising the nearest relative of any such patient as to the exercise of any power to order the discharge of the patient, any medical practitioner authorised by or on behalf of the patient or by the nearest relative of the patient, as the case may be, may, at any reasonable time, visit the patient and may examine him in private.

Functions of relatives of patients

Definition of
relative and
nearest
relative.

53.—(1) For the purposes of this section, " relative " means any of the following, that is to say—

(a) spouse ;

(b) child ;

(c) father or mother ;

(d) brother or sister ;

(e) grandparent ;

(f) grandchild ;

(g) uncle or aunt ;

(h) nephew or niece ;

(2) In deducing relationships for the purposes of this section, an illegitimate person shall be treated as the legitimate child of his mother.

(3) In this Act, subject to the provisions of this section and to the following provisions of this Part of this Act, the " nearest relative " means the person first listed in subsection (1) of this section who is caring for the patient, or was so caring immediately before the admission of the patient to a hospital or his reception into guardianship, failing whom the person first so listed, brothers and sisters of the whole blood being preferred to brothers and sisters of the half-blood, and the elder or eldest of two or more relatives listed in any paragraph of that subsection being preferred to the other or others of those relatives, regardless of sex.

(4) Where the person who, under subsection (3) of this section, would be the nearest relative of a patient—

(a) in the case of a patient ordinarily resident in the United Kingdom, the Channel Islands or the Isle of Man, is not so resident ; or

(b) being the husband or wife of the patient, is permanently separated from the patient, either by agreement or under an order of a court, or has deserted or has been deserted by the patient for a period and the spouse concerned is still in desertion ; or

(c) not being the husband, wife, father, or mother of the patient, is for the time being under 18 years of age,

the nearest relative of the patient shall be ascertained without regard to that person.

(5) In this section " spouse " includes a person who is living with the patient as if he or she were the husband or wife of the patient, as the case may be (or, if the patient is for the time being an in-patient in a hospital, was so living until the patient was admitted), and has been or had been so living for a period of not less than 6 months ; but a person shall not be treated by virtue of this subsection as the nearest relative of a married patient unless the husband or wife of the patient is disregarded by virtue of paragraph (b) of subsection (4) of this section.

(6) A person, other than a relative, with whom the patient ordinarily resides (or, if the patient is for the time being an in-

PART V

patient in a hospital, last ordinarily resided before he was admitted), and with whom he has or had been ordinarily residing for a period of not less than five years, shall be treated for the purposes of this Part of this Act as if he were a relative but—

    (a) shall be treated for the purposes of subsection (3) of this section as if mentioned last in subsection (1) of this section ; and

    (b) shall not be treated by virtue of this subsection as the nearest relative of a married patient unless the husband or wife of the patient is disregarded by virtue of paragraph (b) of subsection (4) of this section.

Children and young persons in care of local authority.

54. In any case where the rights and powers of a parent of a patient, being a child or young person, are vested in a local authority or other person by virtue of—

1968 c. 49.

    (a) section 17 of the Social Work (Scotland) Act 1968 (which relates to children in respect of whom parental rights have been assumed under section 16 of that Act) ; or

1980 c. 5.

    (b) section 3 of the Child Care Act 1980 (which makes corresponding provisions in England and Wales) ; or

    (c) section 10 of the said Act of 1980 (which relates to the powers and duties of local authorities in England and Wales with respect to persons committed to their care) ;

that authority or person shall be deemed to be the nearest relative of the patient in preference to any person except the husband or wife (if any) of the patient, and except, in a case where the said rights and powers are vested in a local authority by virtue of subsection (2) of the said section 17 or subsection (1) of the said section 3, any parent of the patient not being the person on whose account the resolution mentioned in that subsection was passed.

Nearest relative of child under guardianship etc.

55.—(1) Where a patient who has not attained the age of 18 years—

    (a) is, by virtue of an order made by a court in the exercise of jurisdiction (whether under any enactment or otherwise) in respect of the guardianship of children, or by virtue of a deed or will executed by his father or mother, under the guardianship of a person not being his nearest relative under the foregoing provisions of this Act, or is under the joint guardianship of two persons of whom one is such a person as aforesaid ; or (*b*) is, by virtue of an order made by a court in the exercise of such jurisdiction as aforesaid or in matrimonial proceedings, or by virtue of a separation agreement between his father and mother, in the custody of any such person,

the person or persons having the guardianship or custody of the patient shall, to the exclusion of any other person, be deemed to be his nearest relative.

(2) Section 53(4) of this Act shall apply in relation to a person who is, or who is one of the persons, deemed to be the nearest relative of a patient by virtue of this section as it applies in relation to a person who would be the nearest relative under subsection (3) of that section.

(3) A patient shall be treated for the purposes of this section as being in the custody or guardianship of another person if he would be in the custody or guardianship of that other person apart from section 41(2) of this Act.

(4) In this section " court " includes a court in England and Wales or Northern Ireland, and " enactment " includes an enactment of the Parliament of Northern Ireland, a measure of the Northern Ireland Assembly and an Order in Council under Schedule 1 to the Northern Ireland Act 1974.

1974 c. 28.

56.—(1) The sheriff may, upon application made in accordance with the provisions of this section in respect of a patient, by order direct that the functions under this Act of the nearest relative of the patient shall, during the continuance in force of the order, be exercisable by the applicant, or by any other person specified in the application, being a person who, in the opinion of the sheriff, is a proper person to act as the nearest relative of the patient, and who is willing to do so.

(2) An order under this section may be made on the application of—

(*a*) any relative (including the nearest relative) of the patient ;

(*b*) any other person with whom the patient is residing (or, if the patient is then an in-patient in a hospital, was last residing before he was admitted) ; or

(*c*) a mental health officer,

but in relation to an application made by such an officer subsection (1) of this section shall have effect as if for the words " the applicant " there were substituted the words " the local authority ".

PART V

(3) An application for an order under this section may be made upon any of the following grounds, that is to say—

(*a*) that the patient has no nearest relative within the meaning of this Act, or that it is not reasonably practicable to ascertain whether he has such a relative or who that relative is ;

(*b*) that the nearest relative of the patient is incapable of acting as such by reason of mental disorder or other illness ;

(*c*) where the application is made by the nearest relative of the patient, that he is unwilling or considers it undesirable to continue to act as such.

(4) While an order made under this section is in force, the provisions of this Part of this Act (other than this section and section 57 of this Act) shall apply in relation to the patient as if for any reference to the nearest relative of the patient there were substituted a reference to the person having the functions of that relative and (without prejudice to section 57 of this Act) shall so apply notwithstanding that the person who was the nearest relative of the patient when the order was made is no longer his nearest relative.

Discharge and variation of orders under s. 56.

57.—(1) An order made under section 56 of this Act in respect of a patient may be discharged by the sheriff upon application made—

(*a*) by the person having the functions of the nearest relative of the patient by virtue of the order ;

(*b*) by the nearest relative of the patient.

(2) An order made under the said section 56 in respect of a patient may be varied by the sheriff, on the application of the person having the functions of the nearest relative by virtue of the order or on the application of a mental health officer, by substituting for the first-mentioned person a local authority or any other person who, in the opinion of the sheriff, is a proper person to exercise those functions, being an authority or person who is willing to do so.

(3) If the person having the functions of the nearest relative of a patient by virtue of an order under the said section 56 dies, the foregoing provisions of this section shall apply as if for any reference to that person there were substituted a reference to any relative of the patient, and until the order is discharged or varied under those provisions the functions of the nearest relative under this Part of this Act shall not be exercisable by any person.

(4) An order under the said section 56 shall, unless previ-   PART V
ously discharged under subsection (1) of this section, cease to
have effect—

   (a) if the patient was on the date of the order liable to be
      detained in pursuance of an application for admission
      or subject to guardianship under this Part of this Act,
      or becomes so liable or so subject within the period of
      3 months beginning with that date, when he ceases to
      be so liable or so subject (otherwise than on being trans-
      ferred in pursuance of sections 29 or 45 of this Act) ;

   (b) if the patient was not on the date of the order and has
      not within the said period become so liable or so
      subject, at the expiration of that period.

(5) The discharge or variation under this section of an order
made under the said section 56 shall not affect the validity
of anything previously done in pursuance of the order.

Supplementary

58. The Secretary of State may make regulations for pres- Regulations
cribing anything which, under this Part of this Act, is required for purposes
or authorised to be prescribed. of Part V.

59.—(1) In this Part of this Act the expression " responsible Interpretation
medical officer " means— of Part V.

   (a) in relation to a patient who is liable to be detained in a
      hospital, any medical practitioner employed on the staff
      of that hospital who may be authorised by the mana-
      gers to act (either generally or in any particular case
      or class of case or for any particular purpose) as the
      responsible medical officer ;

   (b) in relation to a patient subject to guardianship, any med-
      ical practitioner authorised by the local authority to act
      (either generally or in any particular case or class of
      case or for any particular purpose) as the responsible
      medical officer.

(2) In relation to a patient who is subject to guardianship
under this Part of this Act, any reference in this Act to the local
authority concerned is a reference—

   (a) where a guardianship application is effective, to the local
      authority to whom that application is addressed ;

   (b) where the patient has been transferred to guardianship
      by the managers of a hospital under section 29(1) of
      this Act, to the local authority who received him into
      guardianship or approved his guardian.

(3) In this Act the expression " absent without leave " means absent from any hospital or other place and liable to be taken into custody and returned under section 28 or 44 of this Act, and kindred expressions shall be construed accordingly.

PART VI

DETENTION OF PATIENTS CONCERNED IN CRIMINAL PROCEEDINGS ETC. AND TRANSFER OF PATIENTS UNDER SENTENCE

Provisions for compulsory detention and guardianship of patients charged with offences etc.

Effect of hospital orders.

1975 c. 21.

60.—(1) A hospital order made under section 175 or 376 of the Criminal Procedure (Scotland) Act 1975 shall be sufficient authority—

(a) for a constable, a mental health officer, or any other person directed to do so by the court to convey the patient to the hospital specified in the order within a period of 28 days ; and

(b) for the managers of the hospital to admit him at any time within that period, and thereafter to detain him in accordance with the provisions of this Act.

(2) A patient who is admitted to a hospital in pursuance of a hospital order shall be treated for the purposes of Part V of this Act (other than section 23) as if he had been so admitted on the date of the order in pursuance of an application for admission, except that the power to order the discharge of the patient under section 33 of this Act shall not be exercisable by his nearest relative ; and accordingly the provisions of the said Part V specified in Part I of the Second Schedule to this Act shall apply in relation to him, subject to the exceptions and modifications set out in that Part and the remaining provisions of the said Part V shall not apply.

(3) Subject to the provisions of section 178(3) or 379(3) of the said Act of 1975, where a patient is admitted to a hospital in pursuance of a hospital order any previous application or hospital order by virtue of which he was liable to be detained in a hospital shall cease to have effect:

Provided that, if the order first-mentioned or the conviction to which it relates is quashed on appeal, this subsection shall not apply and section 32 of this Act shall have effect as if during any period for which the patient was liable to be detained under the order he had been detained in custody as mentioned in that section.

(4) If within the period of 28 days referred to in subsection (1) of this section it appears to the Secretary of State that by

reason of an emergency or other special circumstances it is not practicable for the patient to be received into the hospital specified in the order, he may give directions for the admission of the patient to such other hospital as appears to be appropriate in lieu of the hospital so specified ; and where such directions are given the Secretary of State shall cause the person having the custody of the patient to be informed, and the hospital order shall have effect as if the hospital specified in the directions were substituted for the hospital specified in the order.

61.—(1) A guardianship order made under section 175 or 376 of the Criminal Procedure (Scotland) Act 1975 shall confer on the authority or person therein named as guardian the like powers as a guardianship application effective under Part V of this Act.

Effect of guardianship orders.

1975 c. 21.

(2) A patient who is received into guardianship in pursuance of a guardianship order shall be treated for the purposes of Part V of this Act (other than section 42) as if he had been so received on the date of the order in pursuance of a guardianship application as aforesaid, except that the power to order the discharge of the patient under section 50 of this Act shall not be exercisable by his nearest relative ; and accordingly the provisions of the said Part V specified in Part III of the Second Schedule to this Act shall apply in relation to him subject to the exceptions and modifications set out therein, and the remaining provisions of the said Part V shall not apply.

(3) Where a patient is received into guardianship in pursuance of a guardianship order any previous application or order by virtue of which he was subject to guardianship shall cease to have effect :

> Provided that, if the order first-mentioned or the conviction to which it relates is quashed on appeal, this subsection shall not apply and section 49 of this Act shall have effect as if during any period for which the patient was subject to guardianship under the order he had been detained in custody as mentioned in that section.

62.—(1) The special restrictions applicable to a patient in respect of whom a restriction order made under section 178 or 379 of the Criminal Procedure (Scotland) Act 1975 is in force are as follows, that is to say—

Effect of restriction orders.

(a) none of the provisions of Part V of this Act relating to the duration, renewal and expiration of authority for the detention of patients shall apply, and the patient shall continue to be liable to be detained by virtue of the relevant hospital order until he is absolutely discharged under sections 63 to 68 of this Act ;

(*b*) the following powers shall be exercisable only with the consent of the Secretary of State, that is to say—

(i) power to grant leave of absence to the patient under section 27 of this Act ; and

(ii) power to transfer the patient under section 29 of this Act ;

and if leave of absence is granted under the said section 27 the power to recall the patient under that section shall be vested in the Secretary of State as well as in the responsible medical officer ; and

(*c*) the power to take the patient into custody and return him under section 28 of this Act may be exercised at any time,

and in relation to any such patient the provisions of the said Part V specified in Part II of the Second Schedule to this Act shall have effect subject to the exceptions and modifications set out in that Part and the remaining provisions of Part V shall not apply.

(2) While a person is a restricted patient within the meaning of section 63 of this Act or a person to whom section 67 (persons treated as restricted patients) of this Act applies, the responsible medical officer shall at such intervals (not exceeding one year) as the Secretary of State may direct examine and report to the Secretary of State on that person ; and every report shall contain such particulars as the Secretary of State may require.

(3) Without prejudice to the provisions of section 178(3) or 379(3) of the said Act of 1975, where a restriction order in respect of a patient ceases to have effect while the relevant hospital order continues in force, the provisions of section 60 of this Act and Part I of the Second Schedule to this Act shall apply to the patient as if he had been admitted to the hospital in pursuance of a hospital order (without a restriction order) made on the date on which the restriction order ceased to have effect.

Right of appeal of restricted patients etc.

63.—(1) In this section and in sections 64 to 67 of this Act—

" restricted patient " means a patient who is subject to a restriction order or to a restriction direction ;

" relevant hospital order " and " relevant transfer direction ", in relation to a restricted patient, mean the hospital order or transfer direction by virtue of which he is liable to be detained in a hospital.

(2) A restricted patient detained in a hospital may appeal by way of summary application to a sheriff of the sheriffdom within

which the hospital in which he is liable to be detained is
situated—

  (*a*) in the period between the expiration of 6 months and
    the expiration of 12 months beginning with the date
    of the relevant hospital order or transfer direction ;
    and

  (*b*) in any subsequent period of 12 months,

to order his discharge under section 64 or 65 of this Act.

(3) The provisions of section 35(3) and (4) of this Act shall
have effect in relation to an appeal under sections 63 to 67 of
this Act as they have in relation to an appeal under Part V
of this Act.

64.—(1) Where an appeal to the sheriff is made by a restric- Right of
ted patient who is subject to a restriction order, the sheriff shall appeal of
direct the absolute discharge of the patient if he is satisfied— patients
  subject to
  (*a*) that the patient is not, at the time of the hearing of the restriction
    appeal, suffering from mental disorder of a nature or orders.
    degree which makes it appropriate for him to be
    liable to be detained in a hospital for medical treat-
    ment ; or

  (*b*) that it is not necessary for the health or safety of the
    patient or for the protection of other persons that he
    should receive such treatment ; and (in either case)

  (*c*) that it is not appropriate for the patient to remain liable
    to be recalled to hospital for further treatment.

(2) Where in the case of any such patient as is mentioned in
subsection (1) of this section the sheriff is satisfied as to the matters referred to in paragraph (*a*) or (*b*) of that subsection but
not as to the matters referred to in paragraph (*c*) of that subsection he shall direct the conditional discharge of the patient.

(3) Where a patient is absolutely discharged under subsection (1) of this section he shall thereupon cease to be liable to
be detained by virtue of the relevant hospital order, and the
restriction order shall cease to have effect accordingly.

(4) Where a patient is conditionally discharged under subsection (2) of this section—

  (*a*) he may be recalled by the Secretary of State under sec-
    tion 68(3) of this Act as if he had been conditionally
    discharged under subsection (2) of that section ; and

  (*b*) he shall comply with such conditions (if any) as may
    be imposed at the time of discharge by the sheriff or
    at any subsequent time by the Secretary of State.

PART VI

(5) The Secretary of State may from time to time vary any condition imposed (whether by the sheriff or by him) under subsection (4) of this section.

(6) Where a restriction order in respect of a patient ceases to have effect after he has been conditionally discharged under subsection (2) of this section the patient shall, unless previously recalled, be deemed to be absolutely discharged on the date when the order ceases to have effect and shall cease to be liable to be detained by virtue of the relevant hospital order.

(7) The sheriff may defer a direction for the conditional discharge of a patient until such arrangements as appear to the sheriff to be necessary for that purpose have been made to his satisfaction ; and where by virtue of any such deferment no direction has been given on an appeal before the time when the patient's case comes before the sheriff on a subsequent appeal, the previous appeal shall be treated as one on which no direction under this section can be given.

(8) This section is without prejudice to section 68 of this Act.

Right of appeal of patients subject to restriction directions.

65.—(1) Where an appeal to the sheriff is made by a restricted patient who is subject to a restriction direction, the sheriff—

> (a) shall notify the Secretary of State if, in his opinion, the patient would, if subject to a restriction order, be entitled to be absolutely or conditionally discharged under section 64 of this Act ; and

> (b) if he notifies the Secretary of State that the patient would be entitled to be conditionally discharged, may recommend that in the event of the patient's not being released on licence or discharged under supervision under subsection 2(b)(ii) of this section he should continue to be detained in a hospital.

(2) If the sheriff notifies the Secretary of State—

> (a) that the patient would be entitled to be absolutely discharged, the Secretary of State shall—

>> (i) by warrant direct that the patient be remitted to any prison or other institution in which he might have been detained if he had not been removed to hospital, there to be dealt with as if he had not been so removed ; or

>> (ii) exercise any power of releasing the patient on licence or discharging the patient under supervision which would have been exercisable if the patient had been remitted to any prison or other institution in which he might have been detained if he had not been removed to hospital ;

(*b*) that the patient would be entitled to be conditionally discharged, the Secretary of State may—

> (i) by warrant direct that the patient be remitted to any prison or other institution in which he might have been detained if he had not been removed to hospital, there to be dealt with as if he had not been so removed ; or

> (ii) exercise any power of releasing the patient on licence or discharging the patient under supervision which would have been exercisable if the patient had been remitted to any prison or other institution in which he might have been detained if he had not been removed to hospital ; or

> (iii) decide that the patient should continue to be detained in a hospital,

and on his arrival in the prison or other institution or, as the case may be, his release or discharge as aforesaid, the transfer direction and the restriction direction shall cease to have effect.

66.—(1) Where a restricted patient has been conditionally Further consideration of case of conditionally discharged patient. discharged under sections 64 or 68(2) of this Act and is subsequently recalled under section 68(3) of this Act to hospital he may, within one month of the day on which he returns or is returned to hospital, appeal against such recall to a sheriff of the sheriffdom in which the hospital in which he is liable to be detained by virtue of the warrant under the said section 68(3) is situated.

(2) Where a restricted patient has been conditionally discharged as aforesaid but is not recalled to hospital he may appeal—

(*a*) in the period between the expiration of 12 months and the expiration of 2 years beginning with the date on which he was conditionally discharged ; and

(*b*) in any subsequent period of 2 years,

to a sheriff of the sheriffdom in which he resides.

(3) If in any appeal under subsection (1) or (2) of this section the sheriff is satisfied as mentioned in section 64(1) or (2) of this Act, he shall uphold the appeal and—

(*a*) where he is satisfied as mentioned in the said section 64(1), he shall direct the absolute discharge of the patient ;

PART VI

(*b*) where he is satisfied as mentioned in the said section 64(2), he shall direct, or (as the case may be) continue, the conditional discharge of the patient; and, in either case, he may vary any condition to which the patient is subject in connection with his discharge or impose any condition which might have been imposed in connection therewith.

(4) Where a patient is absolutely discharged in an appeal under subsection (1) or (2) of this section he shall thereupon cease to be liable to be detained by virtue of the relevant hospital order, and the restriction order shall cease to have effect accordingly.

Application of sections 63 to 66 to other persons treated as restricted patients.

1975 c. 21.

1983 c. 20.

67.—(1) Sections 63, 64 and 66 of this Act shall apply to a person who—

(*a*) is subject to—

　　(i) a direction which by virtue of section 69(3) of this Act; or

　　(ii) an order which by virtue of section 174(4) of the Criminal Procedure (Scotland) Act 1975,

has the like effect as a hospital order and a restriction order; or

(*b*) is treated as subject to a hospital order and a restriction order by virtue of section 80(2) of the Mental Health Act 1983 or section 81(2) of this Act,

as they apply to a restricted patient who is subject to a restriction order and references in the said sections 63, 64 and 66 to the relevant hospital order or restriction order shall be construed as references to the direction under section 69(1) of this Act or the order under section 174(3) of the Criminal Procedure (Scotland) Act 1975.

(2) Sections 63 and 65 of this Act shall apply to a person who is treated as subject to a transfer direction and a restriction direction by virtue of section 80(2) of the Mental Health Act 1983 or section 81(2) of this Act as they apply to a restricted patient who is subject to a restriction direction and references in the said sections 63 and 65 to the relevant transfer direction or the restriction direction shall be construed as references to the transfer direction or restriction direction to which that person is treated as subject by virtue of the said section 80(2) or 81(2).

68.—(1) If the Secretary of State is satisfied that a restriction order in respect of a patient is no longer required for the protection of the public from serious harm, he may direct that the patient shall cease to be subject to the special restrictions set out in section 62(1) of this Act; and, where the Secretary of State so directs, the restriction order shall cease to have effect and subsection (3) of that section shall apply accordingly.

(2) At any time while a restriction order is in force in respect of a patient, the Secretary of State may, if he thinks fit, by warrant discharge the patient from hospital, either absolutely or subject to conditions; and where a person is absolutely discharged under this subsection he shall thereupon cease to be liable to be detained by virtue of the relevant hospital order, and the restriction order shall cease to have effect accordingly.

(3) The Secretary of State may, at any time during the continuance in force of a restriction order in respect of a patient who has been conditionally discharged under subsection (2) of this section, and without prejudice to his further discharge as aforesaid, by warrant recall the patient to such hospital as may be specified in the warrant; and thereupon—

(a) if the hospital so specified is not the hospital from which the patient was conditionally discharged, the hospital order and the restriction order shall have effect as if the hospital specified in the warrant were substituted for the hospital specified in the hospital order;

(b) in any case, the patient shall be treated for the purposes of section 28 of this Act as if he had absented himself without leave from the hospital specified in the warrant, and if the restriction order was made for a specified period, that period shall not in any event expire until the patient returns to the hospital or is returned to the hospital under that section.

(4) If a restriction order ceases to have effect in respect of a patient after the patient has been conditionally discharged under this section, the patient shall, unless previously recalled under the last foregoing subsection, be deemed to be absolutely discharged on the date when the order ceases to have effect, and shall cease to be liable to be detained by virtue of the relevant hospital order accordingly.

(5) The Secretary of State may, if satisfied that the attendance at any place in Great Britain of a patient who is subject to a restriction order is desirable in the interests of justice or for the

PART VI

purposes of any public inquiry, direct him to be taken to that place; and where a patient is directed under this subsection to be taken to any place he shall, unless the Secretary of State otherwise directs, be kept in custody while being so taken, while at that place, and while being taken back to the hospital in which he is liable to be detained.

Persons
ordered to
be kept in
custody during
Her Majesty's
pleasure.

69.—(1) The Secretary of State may by warrant direct that any person who, by virtue of any enactment to which this subsection applies, is required to be kept in custody during Her Majesty's pleasure or until the directions of Her Majesty are known shall be detained in a State hospital or such other hospital as he may specify and, where that person is not already detained in the hospital, give directions for his removal there.

1968 c. 20.
1955 c. 18.
1955 c. 19.
1957 c. 53.

(2) The enactments to which subsection (1) of this section applies are section 16 of the Courts-Martial (Appeals) Act 1968, section 116 of the Army Act 1955, section 116 of the Air Force Act 1955, and section 63 of the Naval Discipline Act 1957.

1975 c. 21.

(3) A direction under this section in respect of any person shall have the like effect as an order referred to in section 174(3) of the Criminal Procedure (Scotland) Act 1975.

Transfer to hospital or guardianship of prisoners etc.

Removal to
hospital of
persons in
prison
awaiting
trial etc.

70.—(1) If in the case of a person committed in custody while awaiting trial or sentence it appears to the Secretary of State that the grounds are satisfied upon which an application may be made for his admission to a hospital under Part V of this Act he may apply to the sheriff for an order that that person be removed to and detained in such hospital (not being a private hospital) as may be specified in the order; and the sheriff, if satisfied by reports from 2 medical practitioners (complying with the provisions of this section) that the grounds are satisfied as aforesaid may make an order accordingly.

(2) An order under this section (in this Act referred to as " a transfer order ") shall cease to have effect at the expiration of the period of 14 days beginning with the date on which it is made, unless within that period the person with respect to whom it was made has been received into the hospital specified therein.

(3) A transfer order with respect to any person shall have the like effect as a hospital order made in his case together with a restriction order in respect of him made without limit of time.

(4) Of the medical practitioners whose reports are taken into account under subsection (1) of this section, at least one shall be a practitioner approved for the purposes of section 20 of this

Act by a Health Board as having special experience in the PART VI
diagnosis or treatment of mental disorder.

(5) A transfer order shall specify the form or forms of mental disorder, being mental illness or mental handicap or both, from which the patient is found by the sheriff to be suffering; and no such order shall be made unless the patient is described by each of the practitioners whose evidence is taken into account as aforesaid as suffering from the same form of mental disorder, whether or not he is also described by either of them as suffering from the other form.

71.—(1) If in the case of a person to whom this section Removal to applies the Secretary of State is satisfied by the like reports as hospital of are required for the purposes of section 70 of this Act that the persons grounds are satisfied upon which an application may be made serving for his admission to a hospital under Part V of this Act the sentences of Secretary of State may make a direction (in this Act referred to imprisonment as " a transfer direction ") in respect of him. and other prisoners.

(2) This section applies to the following persons, that is to say—

　　(a) persons serving sentences of imprisonment;
　　(b) civil prisoners, that is to say, persons committed by court to prison in respect of a civil debt;
　　(c) persons detained under the Immigration Act 1971.　　1971 c. 77.

(3) Subsections (2), (4) and (5) of section 70 of this Act shall apply for the purposes of this section and of any transfer direction given by virtue of this section as they apply for the purposes of that section and of any transfer order thereunder, with the substitution for any references to the sheriff of a reference to the Secretary of State.

(4) A transfer direction with respect to any person shall have the like effect as a hospital order made in his case.

(5) Where a transfer direction is given in respect of any person that person may, within one month of his transfer to a hospital thereunder, appeal to the sheriff to cancel the direction, and the sheriff shall cancel the direction unless he is satisfied that the grounds are satisfied upon which an application may be made for the admission of the person to a hospital under Part V of this Act; and, if a transfer direction is so cancelled, the Secretary of State shall direct that the person be remitted to any prison or other institution in which he might have been detained if he had not been removed to hospital, there to be dealt with as if he had not been so removed.

(6) Subsections (2), (3) and (4) of section 35 of this Act shall apply to an appeal under subsection (5) of this section in like manner as they apply to an appeal referred to in that section.

PART VI

1975 c. 21.

1952 c. 61.

(7) References in this section to a person serving a sentence of imprisonment include references—

(a) to a person detained in pursuance of any sentence or order for detention made by a court in criminal proceedings (other than an order under section 174 or 255 of the Criminal Procedure (Scotland) Act 1975, or under any enactment to which section 69 of this Act applies);

(b) to a person committed by a court to a prison or other institution to which the Prisons (Scotland) Act 1952, applies in default of payment of any fine to be paid on his conviction.

Restriction on discharge of prisoners removed to hospital.

72.—(1) Where a transfer direction is given in respect of any person, the Secretary of State, if he thinks fit, may by warrant direct that that person shall be subject to the special restrictions set out in section 62(1) of this Act.

(2) A direction under this section (in this Act referred to as " a restriction direction ") shall have the like effect as a restriction order in respect of the patient made under section 178 or 379 of the Criminal Procedure (Scotland) Act 1975.

Further provisions as to persons removed to hospital while awaiting trial etc.

73.—(1) Subject to the following provisions of this section any transfer order made in respect of a person under section 70(1) of this Act shall cease to have effect if the proceedings in respect of him are dropped or when his case is disposed of by the court to which he was committed, or by which he was remanded, but without prejudice to any power of that court to make a hospital order or other order under section 174A, 175, 178, 375A, 376 or 379 of the Criminal Procedure (Scotland) Act 1975 in his case.

(2) Where a transfer order has been made in respect of any such person as aforesaid, then, if the Secretary of State is notified by the responsible medical officer at any time before that person is brought before the court to which he was committed, or by which he was remanded, that he no longer requires treatment for mental disorder, the Secretary of State may by warrant direct that he be remitted to any place where he might have been detained if he had not been removed to hospital, there to be dealt with as if he had not been so removed, and on his arrival at the place to which he is so remitted the transfer order shall cease to have effect.

(3) Where a transfer order in respect of any person ceases to have effect under subsection (1) of this section, then unless his case has been disposed of by the court—

(a) passing a sentence of imprisonment (within the meaning of section 175(7) or 376(10) of the said Act of 1975) on him; or

(*b*) making a probation order under section 183, 184, 384
    or 385 of the said Act of 1975 in relation to him ; or
(*c*) making a hospital order or guardianship order in his
    case,

he shall continue to be liable to be detained in the hospital in
which he was detained under the transfer order as if he had been
admitted thereto, on the date on which that order ceased to have
effect, in pursuance of an application for admission made under
Part V of this Act, and the provisions of this Act shall apply
accordingly.

74.—(1) Where a transfer direction and a restriction direction   Further
have been given in respect of a person serving a sentence of   provisions as
imprisonment and the Secretary of State is satisfied—   to prisoners
under
(*a*) that the person is not suffering from mental disorder of   sentence.
    a nature or degree which makes it appropriate for him
    to be liable to be detained in a hospital for medical
    treatment ; or
(*b*) that it is not necessary for the health or safety of the
    person or for the protection of other persons that he
    should receive such treatment ; and (in either case)
(*c*) that it is not appropriate for the person to remain liable
    to be recalled to hospital for further treatment,

he shall—

(i) by warrant direct that the person be remitted to
any prison or other institution in which he might have
been detained if he had not been removed to hospital,
there to be dealt with as if he had not been so removed ; or

(ii) exercise any power of releasing the person on
licence or discharging the person under supervision,
which would have been exercisable if he had been
remitted to any prison or other institution in which
he might have been detained if he had not been removed to hospital,

and on his arrival in the prison or other institution, or as the
case may be his release or discharge as aforesaid, the transfer
direction and the restriction direction shall cease to have effect.

(2) Where in the case of any such person as is mentioned in
subsection (1) of this section the Secretary of State is satisfied
as to the matter referred to in paragraph (*a*) or (*b*) of that subsection but not as to the matters referred to in paragraph (*c*) of
that subsection he may—

(*a*) by warrant direct that the person be remitted to any
    prison or other institution in which he might have been

PART VI

detained if he had not been removed to a hospital, there to be dealt with as if he had not been removed ; or

(*b*) exercise any power of releasing the person on licence or discharging the person under supervision, which would have been exercisable if he had been remitted to any prison or other institution in which he might have been detained if he had not been removed to a hospital ; or

(*c*) decide that the person should continue to be detained in a hospital,

and on his arrival in the prison or other institution or, as the case may be, his release or discharge as aforesaid, the transfer direction and the restriction direction shall cease to have effect.

(3) A restriction direction given in respect of a person serving a sentence of imprisonment shall cease to have effect on the expiration of the sentence.

(4) Subject to the following provisions of this section, where a restriction direction ceases to have effect in respect of a person that person shall be discharged unless a report is furnished in respect of him under subsection (5) of this section.

(5) Within a period of 28 days before a restriction direction ceases to have effect in respect of a person, the responsible medical officer shall obtain from another medical practitioner a report on the condition of the patient in the prescribed form and thereafter shall assess the need for the detention of the patient to be continued ; and, if it appears to him that it is necessary in the interests of the health or safety of the patient or for the protection of other persons that the patient should continue to be liable to be detained in hospital, he shall furnish to the managers of the hospital where the patient is liable to be detained and to the Mental Welfare Commission a report to that effect in the prescribed form along with the report first mentioned.

(6) Where a report is duly furnished under subsection (5) of this section, the patient shall be treated as if he had been admitted to the hospital in pursuance of a hospital order (without a restriction order) made on the date on which the restriction direction ceased to have effect, but the provisions of section 30(5) and (6) and of section 35 of this Act shall apply to him in like manner as they apply to a patient the authority for whose detention in hospital has been renewed in pursuance of subsection (4) of the said section 30.

(7) Subject to subsection (8) of this section, references in this section to the expiration of a person's sentence are references to the expiration of the period during which he would have been

liable to be detained in a prison or other institution if the transfer direction had not been given and if he had not forfeited remission of any part of the sentence after his removal in pursuance of the direction.

(8) For the purposes of subsection (2) of section 37 of the Prisons (Scotland) Act 1952 (which subsection provides for discounting from the sentence of certain prisoners periods while they are unlawfully at large) a patient who, having been transferred in pursuance of a transfer direction from any such institution as is referred to in that subsection, is at large, in circumstances in which he is liable to be taken into custody under any provision of this Act, shall be treated as unlawfully at large and absent from that institution.

(9) In this section " prescribed " means prescribed by regulations made by the Secretary of State.

75.—(1) Subject to subsection (2) of this section, a transfer direction given in respect of any such person as is described in paragraph (*b*) or (*c*) of section 71(2) of this Act shall cease to have effect on the expiration of the period during which he would, but for his removal to a hospital, be liable to be detained in the place from which he was removed.

(2) Where a transfer direction and a restriction direction have been given in respect of any such person as is mentioned in subsection (1) of this section and the Secretary of State is satisfied—

(*a*) that the person is not suffering from mental disorder of a nature or degree which makes it appropriate for him to be liable to be detained in a hospital for medical treatment ; or

(*b*) that it is not necessary for the health or safety of the person or for the protection of other persons that he should receive such treatment ; and (in either case),

(*c*) that it is not appropriate for the person to remain liable to be recalled to hospital for further treatment,

he shall—

(i) by warrant direct that the person be remitted to any prison or other institution in which he might have been detained if he had not been removed to a hospital, there to be dealt with as if he had not been so removed ; or

(ii) exercise any power of releasing the person on licence or discharging the person under supervision, which would have been exercisable if he had been remitted to any prison or other institution in which he might have been detained if he had not been removed to a hospital,

and on his arrival in the prison or other institution, or as the case may be, his release or discharge as aforesaid, the transfer direction and the restriction direction shall cease to have effect.

(3) Where in the case of any such person as is mentioned in subsection (2) of this section the Secretary of State is satisfied as to the matters referred to in paragraph (*a*) or (*b*) of that subsection but not as to the matters referred to in paragraph (*c*) of that subsection he may—

> (*a*) by warrant direct that the person be remitted to any prison or other institution in which he might have been detained if he had not been removed to a hospital, there to be dealt with as if he had not been so removed ; or

> (*b*) exercise any power of releasing the person on licence or discharging the person under supervision, which would have been exercisable if he had been remitted to any prison or other institution in which he might have been detained if he had not been removed to hospital ; or

> (*c*) decide that the person should continue to be detained in hospital,

and on his arrival in the prison or other institution or, as the case may be, his release or discharge as aforesaid, the transfer direction and the restriction direction shall cease to have effect.

Supplementary

Interpretation
of Part VI.

76.—(1) In the following provisions of this Part of this Act, that is to say—

> (*a*) section 60(2) and (3) ;
> (*b*) section 61 ;
> (*c*) section 62(1) ; and
> (*d*) section 68

1975 c. 21.

and in section 178(3) or 379(3) of the Criminal Procedure (Scotland) Act 1975 any reference to a hospital order, a guardianship order or a restriction order in respect of a patient subject to a hospital order shall be construed as including a reference to any order or direction under this Part of this Act having the like effect as the first-mentioned order ; and the exceptions and modifications set out in the Second Schedule to this Act in respect of the provisions of Part V of this Act described in that Schedule accordingly include those which are consequential on the provisions of this subsection.

(2) References in this Part of this Act to persons serving a
sentence of imprisonment shall be construed in accordance with
section 71(7) of this Act.

PART VII

REMOVAL AND RETURN OF PATIENTS WITHIN
UNITED KINGDOM ETC.

Removal to and from England and Wales

77.—(1) If it appears to the Secretary of State, in the case of a   Removal of
patient who is for the time being liable to be detained or subject   patients to
to guardianship under this Act, that it is in the interests of the   England and
patient to remove him to England and Wales, and that arrange-   Wales.
ments have been made for admitting him to a hospital or, as the
case may be, for receiving him into guardianship there, the
Secretary of State may authorise his removal to England and
Wales and may give any necessary directions for his conveyance
to his destination.

(2) Where a patient who is liable to be detained under this
Act by virtue of an application, order or direction under any
enactment in force in Scotland is removed under this section and
admitted to a hospital in England and Wales, he shall be treated
as if on the date of his admission he had been so admitted in
pursuance of an application made, or an order or direction made
or given, on that date under the corresponding enactment in
force in England and Wales, and, where he is subject to an
order or direction under any enactment in this Act restricting
his discharge, as if he were subject to an order or direction under
the corresponding enactment in force in England and Wales.

(3) Where a patient who is subject to guardianship under this
Act by virtue of an application or order under any enactment in
force in Scotland is removed under this section and received into
guardianship in England and Wales, he shall be treated as if
on the date on which he arrives at the place where he is to
reside he had been so received in pursuance of an application or
order under the corresponding enactment in force in England
and Wales and as if the application had been accepted or, as the
case may be, the order had been made on that date.

(4) Where a patient removed under this section was immediately before his removal liable to be detained under this Act by
virtue of a transfer direction given while he was serving a sentence of imprisonment (within the meaning of section 71(7) of
this Act) imposed by a court in Scotland, he shall be treated as if
the sentence had been imposed by a court in England and Wales.

(5) Where a person so removed as aforesaid was immediately
before his removal subject to a restriction order or a restriction

PART VII

direction, being an order or direction of limited duration, the restriction order or restriction direction to which he is subject by virtue of subsection (2) of this section shall expire on the date on which the first-mentioned order or direction would have expired if he had not been so removed.

(6) In this section references to a hospital in England and Wales shall be construed as references to a hospital within the meaning of Part II of the Mental Health Act 1983.

1983 c. 20.

Position of nearest relative on removal to England and Wales.

78.—(1) Where a patient is removed from Scotland to England and Wales in pursuance of arrangements under this Part of this Act, and at the time of his removal there is in force an order under Part V of this Act directing that the functions of his nearest relative under this Act shall be exercisable by a person other than the nearest relative within the meaning of the said Part V, the order, so far as it so directs, shall, on the patient's admission to a hospital or reception into guardianship in England and Wales, have effect as if it were an order made by a county court under Part II of the Mental Health Act 1983, and accordingly may be discharged or varied by the county court under that Act and not by the sheriff under this Act.

(2) Where a patient is removed as aforesaid and the person who, apart from any such order, is treated by virtue of any of the provisions of sections 53 to 57 of this Act as the nearest relative within the meaning of Part V of this Act would not be treated by virtue of section 26 of the said Act of 1983 as the nearest relative within the meaning of Part II of that Act, that person shall, after the admission of the patient to a hospital or his reception into guardianship in England and Wales, be treated as the nearest relative within the meaning of Part II of the said Act of 1983, subject, however, to any order made or treated by the foregoing subsection as made, by the county court under section 29 of that Act and without prejudice to the operation of the other provisions of Part II of that Act with respect to the nearest relative of a patient.

(3) An order of the sheriff under section 56 of this Act may be proved by a certificate under the hand of the sheriff clerk.

Position of nearest relative on removal to Scotland.

79.—(1) Where a patient is removed from England and Wales to Scotland in pursuance of arrangements under the Mental Health Act 1983, and at the time of his removal there is in force an order under Part II of that Act directing that the functions of his nearest relative under that Act shall be exercisable by a person other than the nearest relative within the meaning of that Part of that Act, the order, so far as it so directs, shall, on his admission to a hospital or reception into guardianship in Scotland, have effect as if it were an order made by a sheriff under

Part V of this Act, and accordingly may be discharged or varied
by the sheriff under this Act and not by the county court under
that Act.

(2) Where a patient is removed as aforesaid and the person
who, apart from any such order, is treated by virtue of sections
26 to 28 of the said Act of 1983 as the nearest relative within the
meaning of Part II of that Act would not be treated by virtue
of section 53 of this Act as the nearest relative within the
meaning of Part V of this Act, that person shall, after the
admission of the patient to a hospital or his reception into
guardianship in Scotland, be treated as the nearest relative
within the meaning of Part V of this Act, subject, however, to
any order made, or treated by the foregoing subsection as made,
by the sheriff under section 56 of this Act and without prejudice
to the operation of the other provisions of Part V of this Act
with respect to the nearest relative of a patient.

(3) An entry made in a book or other document required to
be kept for the purposes of section 12 of the County Courts Act 1984 c. 28.
1984 (which relates to the keeping of records of proceedings of
county courts) and relating to an order of a county court under
section 29 or section 52 or 53 of the Mental Health Act 1959 or 1959 c. 72.
section 30 of the Mental Health Act 1983, or a copy of such an 1983 c. 20.
entry purporting to be signed and certified as a true copy by the
registrar of the county court, shall, in Scotland, be evidence of
the like matters and to the like extent as in England and Wales.

Removal to and from Northern Ireland

80.—(1) If it appears to the Secretary of State, in the case of Removal of
a patient who is for the time being liable to be detained or patients to
subject to guardianship under this Act, that it is in the interests Northern
of the patient to remove him to Northern Ireland, and that ar- Ireland.
rangements have been made for admitting him to a hospital or,
as the case may be, for receiving him into guardianship there,
the Secretary of State may authorise his removal to Northern
Ireland and may give any necessary directions for his conveyance to his destination.

(2) Subject to the provisions of subsection (4) of this section,
where a patient who is liable to be detained under this Act by
virtue of an application, order or direction under any enactment
in force in Scotland is removed under this section and admitted
to a hospital in Northern Ireland, he shall be treated as if on the
date of his admission he had been so admitted in pursuance of an
application made, or an order or direction made or given, on
that date under the corresponding enactment in force in Northern
Ireland, and, where he is subject to an order or direction under

PART VII
any enactment in this Act restricting his discharge, as if he were subject to an order or direction under the corresponding enactment in force in Northern Ireland.

(3) Where a patient who is subject to guardianship under this Act by virtue of an application or order under any enactment in force in Scotland is removed under this section and received into guardianship in Northern Ireland, he shall be treated as if on the date on which he arrives at the place where he is to reside he had been so received in pursuance of an application or order under the corresponding enactment in force in Northern Ireland, and as if the application had been accepted or, as the case may be, the order had been made on that date.

(4) Where a person removed under this section was immediately before his removal liable to be detained by virtue of an application for admission under this Act, he shall, on his admission to a hospital in Northern Ireland, be treated as if—

1961 c. 15
(N.I.).

    (*a*) he had been admitted thereto in pursuance of an application for admission under section 12 of the Mental Health Act (Northern Ireland) 1961, made on the date of his admission ; and

    (*b*) a medical report under section 19 of that Act had been made in respect of him on that date.

(5) Where a patient removed under this section was immediately before his removal liable to be detained under this Act by virtue of a transfer direction given while he was serving a sentence of imprisonment (within the meaning of section 71(7) of this Act) imposed by a court in Scotland, he shall be treated as if the sentence had been imposed by a court in Northern Ireland.

(6) Where a person removed under this section was immediately before his removal subject to a restriction order or a restriction direction, being an order or direction of limited duration, the order or direction to which he is subject by virtue of subsection (2) of this section shall expire on the date on which the first-mentioned order or direction would have expired if he had not been so removed.

(7) In this section " hospital " has the same meaning as in the Mental Health Act (Northern Ireland) 1961.

81.—(1) If it appears to the responsible authority, in the case of a patient who is for the time being liable to be detained or subject to guardianship under the Mental Health Act (Northern Ireland) 1961, that it is in the interests of the patient to remove him to Scotland, and that arrangements have been made for admitting him to a hospital or, as the case may be, for receiving him into guardianship there, the responsible authority may authorise his removal to Scotland and may give any necessary directions for his conveyance to his destination.

(2) Subject to the provisions of subsection (4) of this section, where a patient who is liable to be detained under this Act by virtue of an application, order or direction under any enactment in force in Northern Ireland is removed under this section and admitted to a hospital in Scotland, he shall be treated as if on the date of his admission he had been so admitted in pursuance of an application forwarded to the managers of the hospital, or an order or direction made or given, on that date under the corresponding enactment in force in Scotland and, where he is subject to an order or direction under any enactment in the Mental Health Act (Northern Ireland) 1961, restricting his discharge, as if he were subject to a restriction order or a restriction direction under the corresponding enactment in force in Scotland.

(3) Where a patient who is subject to guardianship under this Act by virtue of an application or order under any enactment in force in Northern Ireland is removed under this section and received into guardianship in Scotland, he shall be treated as if on the date on which he arrives at the place where he is to reside he had been so received in pursuance of an application or order under the corresponding enactment in force in Scotland and as if the application had been forwarded or, as the case may be, the order had been made on that date.

(4) Where a person removed under this section was immediately before his removal liable to be detained by virtue of an application for admission under section 12 of the Mental Health Act (Northern Ireland) 1961, he shall—

(*a*) if a report under section 19 of that Act has not been made in respect of him, be treated, on his admission to a hospital in Scotland, as if he had been admitted thereto in pursuance of an emergency recommendation made on the date of his admission;

(*b*) if a report under the said section 19 has been made in respect of him, be treated, on his admission to a hospital in Scotland, as if he had been admitted thereto in pursuance of an application for admission forwarded to the managers of that hospital on the date of his admission.

Part II   K

(5) Where a patient removed under this section was immediately before his removal liable to be detained under the Mental Health Act (Northern Ireland) 1961, by virtue of a transfer direction given while he was serving a sentence of imprisonment (within the meaning of section 58(6) of that Act) imposed by a court in Northern Ireland, he shall be treated as if the sentence had been imposed by a court in Scotland.

(6) Where a patient removed under this section was immediately before his removal subject to an order or direction restricting his discharge, being an order or direction of limited duration, the restriction order or restriction direction to which he is subject by virtue of subsection (2) of this section shall expire on the date on which the first-mentioned order or direction would have expired if he had not been so removed.

(7) In this section " the responsible authority " means the Department of Health and Social Services for Northern Ireland or, in relation to a patient who is subject to an order or direction restricting his discharge, the Secretary of State.

Other provisions as to removal

Removal of
certain
patients from
Channel
Islands and
Isle of Man
to Scotland.

82.—(1) The Secretary of State may by warrant direct that any offender found by a court in any of the Channel Islands or in the Isle of Man to be insane or to have been insane at the time of the alleged offence, and ordered to be detained during Her Majesty's pleasure, be removed to a hospital in Scotland.

(2) A patient removed under this section shall, on his reception into the hospital in Scotland, be treated as if he had been removed to that hospital in pursuance of an order under section 174 of the Criminal Procedure (Scotland) Act 1975.

1975 c. 21.

(3) The Secretary of State may by warrant direct that any patient removed under this section from any of the Channel Islands or from the Isle of Man be returned to the Island from which he was so removed, there to be dealt with according to law in all respects as if he had not been removed under this section.

Removal of
alien patients.

83. If it appears to the Secretary of State, in the case of any patient who is neither a British citizen nor a Commonwealth citizen having the right of abode in the United Kingdom by virtue of section 2(1)(*b*) of the Immigration Act 1971 and who is receiving treatment for mental illness as an in-patient in a hospital in Scotland, that proper arrangements have been made for the removal of that patient to a country or territory outside the United Kingdom, the Isle of Man and the Channel Islands and for his care or treatment there, and that it is in the interests of the patient to remove him, the Secretary of State may by

1971 c. 77.

warrant authorise the removal of the patient from the place where he is receiving treatment as aforesaid, and may give such directions as the Secretary of State thinks fit for the conveyance of the patient to his destination in that country or territory and for his detention in any place or on board any ship or aircraft until his arrival at any specified port or place in any such country or territory.

PART VII

Return of patients absent without leave

84.—(1) Subject to the provisions of this section, any person who, under section 28 or section 121 of this Act or under the said section 28 as applied by section 32 of this Act may be taken into custody in Scotland, may be taken into custody in, and returned to Scotland from, any other part of the United Kingdom or the Channel Islands or the Isle of Man.

Patients absent from hospitals in Scotland.

(2) For the purposes of the enactments referred to in subsection (1) of this section, in their application by virtue of this section to England and Wales, Northern Ireland, the Channel Islands or the Isle of Man, the expression " constable " includes an English constable, an officer or constable of the Royal Ulster Constabulary, a member of the police in Jersey, an officer of police within the meaning of section 43 of the Larceny (Guernsey) Law 1958, or any corresponding law for the time being in force, or a constable in the Isle of Man, as the case may be.

(3) For the purposes of the said enactments in their application by virtue of this section to England and Wales or Northern Ireland, any reference to a mental health officer shall be construed as including a reference—

(a) in England and Wales, to any approved social worker within the meaning of the Mental Health Act 1983,

1983 c. 20.

(b) in Northern Ireland, to any social worker within the meaning of the Mental Health Act (Northern Ireland) 1961.

1961 c. 15 (N.I.).

(4) This section shall not apply to any person who is subject to guardianship.

85. Any person (other than a person subject to guardianship) who—

Patients absent from hospitals in Northern Ireland.

(a) under section 30 or section 108 of the Mental Health Act (Northern Ireland) 1961 (which provide respectively for the retaking of patients absent without leave and for the retaking of patients escaping from custody) ; or

K 2

PART VII

     (*b*) under the said section 30 as applied by section 34 of the said Act of 1961 (which makes special provision as to persons sentenced to imprisonment);

may be taken into custody in Northern Ireland, may be taken into custody in, and returned to Northern Ireland from, Scotland by a mental health officer, by any constable or by any person authorised by or by virtue of the said Act of 1961 to take him into custody.

Supplementary

Regulations for purposes of Part VII.
1983 c. 20.

    86. Section 58 of this Act shall have effect as if references therein to Part V of this Act included references to this Part of this Act and to Part VI of the Mental Health Act 1983, so far as the said Parts apply to patients removed to Scotland thereunder.

General provisions as to patients removed from Scotland.

    87.—(1) Where a patient liable to be detained or subject to guardianship by virtue of an application, order or direction under Part V or Part VI of this Act is removed from Scotland in pursuance of arrangements under this Part of this Act, the application, order or direction shall cease to have effect when he is duly received into a hospital or other institution, or placed under guardianship, in pursuance of those arrangements.

    (2) The Secretary of State shall, where he authorises the removal from Scotland of a patient under any of the provisions of this Part of this Act, send notification of that authorisation to the Mental Welfare Commission and to the nearest relative of the patient not less than 7 days before the date of the removal of the patient.

Intimation of removal of patients to Scotland.

    88.—(1) Where a patient is admitted to a hospital in Scotland or received into guardianship there in pursuance of arrangements under this Part of this Act, or under Part VI of the Mental Health Act 1983, the responsible medical officer shall, within 28 days of such admission or reception as aforesaid, furnish to the managers of the hospital, or, as the case may be, the local authority concerned, a report in the prescribed form stating the form of mental disorder, being mental illness or mental handicap or both, from which, in the opinion of the responsible medical officer, the patient is suffering; and for the purposes of this Act the reason for his admission or reception as aforesaid, and for his being liable to detention or subject to guardianship, shall be that he is suffering from the form or forms of mental disorder so stated.

(2) Where a patient has been admitted to a hospital or received into guardianship as aforesaid, the managers of the hospital or the local authority concerned, as the case may be, shall send notification to the Mental Welfare Commission of that admission or reception together with a copy of the report relating to the patient, made in pursuance of the last foregoing subsection, within 7 days of the receipt by them of that report.

Part VII

89.—(1) Where a patient is treated by virtue of this Part of this Act as if he had been removed to a hospital in Scotland in pursuance of a direction under Part VI of this Act, that direction shall be deemed to have been given on the date of his reception into the hospital.

Interpretation of Part VII.

(2) In relation to a patient who has been received into guardianship in Scotland in pursuance of arrangements under this Part of this Act or under Part VI of the Mental Health Act 1959 or under Part VI of the Mental Health Act 1983, any reference in this Act to the local authority concerned shall be construed as a reference to the local authority for the place where he was received into guardianship as aforesaid.

1959 c. 72.
1983 c. 20.

Part VIII

State Hospitals

90.—(1) The Secretary of State shall provide such hospitals as appear to him to be necessary for persons subject to detention under this Act who require treatment under conditions of special security on account of their dangerous, violent or criminal propensities.

Provision of hospitals for patients requiring special security.

(2) Hospitals provided by the Secretary of State under this section are in this Act referred to as " State hospitals ".

91.—(1) Subject to the following provisions of this section, the State hospitals shall be under the control and management of the Secretary of State.

Administrative provisions.

(2) The Secretary of State may by order constitute in accordance with the provisions of Schedule 1 to this Act a committee to manage, on his behalf and subject to such directions as he may give, a State hospital; and a committee so constituted shall be called a State Hospital Management Committee.

(3) The Secretary of State may by order dissolve a State Hospital Management Committee and any such order may contain such provision as he considers necessary or expedient in connection with the dissolution of the Committee and the winding up

PART VIII   of its affairs including provision for the transfer of employment of staff, property, rights and liabilities.

(4) A State Hospital Management Committee may—

(a) pay to its members such remuneration; and

(b) make provision for the payment of such pensions, allowances or gratuities to or in respect of its members,

as the Secretary of State may, with the approval of the Treasury, determine; and such determination may make different provision for different cases or different classes of case.

(5) A State Hospital Management Committee may appoint such officers and servants on such terms as to remuneration and conditions of service as the Secretary of State may, with the approval of the Treasury, determine; and such determination may make different provision for different cases or different classes of case.

1978 c. 29.   (6) Section 79(1) of the National Health Service (Scotland) Act 1978 (which enables the Secretary of State to acquire land for the purposes of that Act) shall have effect as if the reference to the purposes of that Act included a reference to the purposes of this Part of this Act and as if the reference to any hospital vested in the Secretary of State included a reference to any State hospital.

PART IX

PROTECTION OF PROPERTY OF PATIENTS

Duties of local authority in relation to property.

92.—(1) Where a local authority is satisfied—

(a) that any person in their area is incapable, by reason of mental disorder, of adequately managing and administering his property and affairs;

(b) that a curator bonis ought to be appointed in respect of that person; and

(c) that no arrangements have been made or are being made in that behalf,

they shall petition the court for such appointment as aforesaid; and, where that person is a patient in a hospital or has been placed under guardianship, the authority shall, on the grant of any such petition, so inform the managers of the hospital or, as the case may be, the guardian within 28 days therefrom.

1948 c. 29.   (2) In relation to persons suffering from mental disorder, section 48 of the National Assistance Act 1948 (which imposes a duty on certain local authorities to provide protection for property of persons admitted to hospitals, etc.) shall have effect as if—

(*a*) in subsection (1) the reference to a person admitted as a patient to hospital included a reference to a person admitted to a private hospital within the meaning of this Act or subject to guardianship thereunder; and

(*b*) references to moveable property in subsections (1) and (2) included a reference to heritable property.

93. Where the Mental Welfare Commission are satisfied—   Power of Mental Welfare Commission to petition for appointment of curator bonis.

(*a*) that any person is incapable, by reason of mental disorder, of adequately managing and administering his property and affairs;

(*b*) that a curator bonis ought to be appointed in respect of that person; and

(*c*) that no arrangements have been made or are being made in that behalf,

they may petition the court for such appointment as aforesaid; and, where that person is a patient in a hospital or has been placed under guardianship, the Commission shall, on the grant of any such petition, so inform the managers of the hospital or, as the case may be, the local authority concerned within 28 days therefrom.

94.—(1) The managers of any hospital may receive and hold money and valuables on behalf of any person who is liable to be detained in that hospital under this Act or who is receiving treatment for mental disorder as a patient in that hospital, where the medical officer in charge of his treatment has stated that in his opinion that person is incapable, by reason of his mental disorder, of managing and administering his property and affairs; and a receipt or discharge given by the managers for any such money or valuables as aforesaid shall be treated as a valid receipt or discharge given by that person.   Powers of managers in relation to property of patients.

(2) The managers shall not, under subsection (1) of this section, receive or hold on behalf of any one person without the consent of the Mental Welfare Commission money or valuables exceeding in the aggregate such sums as the Secretary of State may from time to time direct.

(3) Where the managers of the hospital hold money or valuables on behalf of a person in pursuance of subsection (1) of this section, they may expend that money or dispose of those valuables for the benefit of that person and in the exercise of the

PART IX

powers conferred by this subsection the managers shall have regard to the sentimental value that any article may have for the patient, or would have but for his mental disorder.

(4) Without prejudice to the generality of subsection (3) of this section, where the managers of a hospital have received money on behalf of a person in pursuance of subsection (1) of this section, being either—

(*a*) money becoming payable to that person during his lifetime under an insurance policy on his life, or

(*b*) money becoming payable to him as proposer under an insurance policy following the death of the person insured,

they may arrange for part or all of the money to be used to refund premiums paid on the policy by another person on behalf of the first-mentioned person, if they are satisfied that such other person is legally entitled to such refund.

(5) The managers of a hospital may in pursuance of their functions under this section make application for a special death certificate for the purposes of the First Schedule to the Industrial Assurance and Friendly Societies Act 1948 and of Schedule 5 to the Friendly Societies Act 1974.

1948 c. 39.

1974 c. 46.

(6) The managers of a hospital shall not act on behalf of any person in pursuance of the foregoing provisions of this section where a curator bonis, tutor, judicial factor, committee, receiver or any person having the powers of a receiver or guardian has been appointed for that person under the law in force in Scotland, England and Wales or Northern Ireland, as the case may be ; and where such an appointment as aforesaid has been made the managers shall account for any intromission under this section to any such curator bonis, tutor, judicial factor, committee, receiver or any person having the powers of a receiver or guardian as aforesaid.

Reciprocal arrangements in relation to Northern Ireland as to exercise of powers.

95.—(1) Where a curator bonis, tutor or judicial factor has been appointed under the law in force in Scotland for any person suffering from mental disorder, the provisions of that law shall apply in relation to the property and affairs of that person in Northern Ireland unless a committee, receiver or guardian has been appointed for him in Northern Ireland.

(2) Where a committee, receiver or guardian has been appointed under the law in force in Northern Ireland for a person suffering from mental disorder, the provisions of that law shall apply in relation to the property and affairs of that person in Scotland unless a curator bonis, tutor or judicial factor has been appointed for him in Scotland.

(3) In this section references to property do not include references to land or interests in land:

Provided that this subsection shall not prevent the receipt of rent or other income arising from land or interests in land.

PART X

CONSENT TO TREATMENT

96.—(1) This Part of this Act applies to any patient liable to Preliminary. be detained under this Act except—

(a) a patient who is liable to be detained by virtue of an emergency recommendation;

(b) a patient who is liable to be detained by virtue of sections 25(2), 117 or 118 of this Act or section 177 or 378 of the Criminal Procedure (Scotland) Act 1975;   1975 c. 21.

(c) a patient who has been conditionally discharged under sections 64 or 68(2) of this Act and has not been recalled to hospital.

(2) Any certificate for the purposes of this Part of this Act shall be in such form as may be prescribed by regulations made by the Secretary of State.

97.—(1) This section applies to the following forms of medi- Treatment cal treatment for mental disorder— requiring consent and

(a) any surgical operation for destroying brain tissue or for a second destroying the functioning of brain tissue; and opinion.

(b) such other forms of treatment as may be specified for the purposes of this section by regulations made by the Secretary of State.

(2) Subject to section 102 of this Act, a patient shall not be given any form of treatment to which this section applies unless he has consented to it and—

(a) a medical practitioner (not being the responsible medical officer) appointed for the purposes of this Part of this Act by the Mental Welfare Commission and two other persons (not being medical practitioners) appointed for the purposes of this paragraph by the Commission have certified in writing that the patient is capable of understanding the nature, purpose and likely effects of the treatment in question and has consented to it; and

(b) the medical practitioner referred to in paragraph (a) of this subsection has certified in writing that, having regard to the likelihood of the treatment alleviating or preventing a deterioration of the patient's condition, the treatment should be given.

(3) Before giving a certificate under subsection (2)(b) of this section the medical practitioner concerned shall consult such person or persons who appear to him to be principally concerned with the patient's medical treatment.

(4) Where any person has given a certificate under subsection (2)(a) or (b) of this section he shall send a copy thereof to the Mental Welfare Commission within 7 days of the day on which the certificate was given.

(5) A medical practitioner or other person appointed as is mentioned in subsection (2)(a) of this section may, for the purpose of exercising his functions under this Part of this Act or (as the case may be) subsection (2)(a) of this section, at any reasonable time—

(a) in private visit and interview any patient; and

(b) in the case of a medical practitioner, examine any patient and require the production of and inspect any records relating to the treatment of the patient.

(6) Before making any regulations for the purposes of this section the Secretary of State shall consult such bodies as appear to him to be concerned.

Treatment requiring consent or a second opinion.
98.—(1) This section applies to the following forms of medical treatment for mental disorder—

(a) such forms of treatment as may be specified for the purposes of this section by regulations made by the Secretary of State; and

(b) the administration of medicine to a patient by any means (not being a form of treatment specified under paragraph (a) of this subsection or section 97 of this Act) at any time during a period for which he is liable to be detained as a patient to whom this Part of this Act applies if 3 months or more have elapsed since the first occasion in that period when medicine was administered to him by any means for his mental disorder.

(2) The Secretary of State may by order vary the length of the period mentioned in subsection (1)(b) of this section.

(3) Subject to section 102 of this Act, a patient shall not be
given any form of treatment to which this section applies unless—

    (a) he has consented to that treatment and either the respon-
sible medical officer or a medical practitioner appointed
for the purposes of this Part of this Act by the Mental
Welfare Commission has certified in writing that the
patient is capable of understanding its nature, purpose
and likely effects and has consented to it ; or

    (b) a medical practitioner (not being the responsible medical
officer) appointed as aforesaid has certified in writing
that the patient is not capable of understanding the
nature, purpose and likely effects of that treatment or
has not consented to it but that, having regard to
the likelihood of its alleviating or preventing a deterioration of his condition, the treatment should be given.

(4) Before giving a certificate under subsection (3)(b) of this
section the medical practitioner concerned shall consult such
person or persons who appear to him to be principally concerned
with the patient's medical treatment.

(5) Where any person has given a certificate under subsection
(3)(a) or (b) of this section he shall send a copy thereof to the
Mental Welfare Commission within 7 days of the day on which
the certificate was given.

(6) Before making any regulations for the purposes of this
section the Secretary of State shall consult such bodies as appear
to him to be concerned.

99.—(1) Where a patient is given treatment in accordance   Review of
with section 97(2) or 98(3)(b) of this Act a report on the treat-   treatment.
ment and the patient's condition shall be given by the responsible medical officer to the Mental Welfare Commission—

    (a) on the next occasion on which the responsible medical
officer furnishes a report in respect of the patient
under section 30 of this Act ; and

    (b) at any other time if so required by the Mental Welfare
Commission.

(2) The Mental Welfare Commission may at any time give
notice to the responsible medical officer directing that, subject to
section 102 of this Act, a certificate given in respect of a patient
under section 97(2) or 98(3)(b) of this Act shall not apply to
treatment given to him after a date specified in the notice, and
sections 97 and 98 of this Act shall then apply to any such
treatment as if that certificate had not been given.

Part X
Plans of
treatment.

100. Any consent or certificate under section 97 or 98 of this Act may relate to a plan of treatment under which the patient is to be given (whether within a specified period or otherwise) one or more of the forms of treatment to which that section applies.

Withdrawal
of consent.

101.—(1) Where the consent of a patient to any treatment has been given for the purposes of section 97 or 98 of this Act, the patient may, subject to section 102 of this Act, at any time before the completion of the treatment withdraw his consent, and those sections shall then apply as if the remainder of the treatment were a separate form of treatment.

(2) Without prejudice to the application of subsection (1) of this section to any treatment given under a plan of treatment to which a patient has consented, a patient who has consented to such a plan may, subject to section 102 of this Act, at any time withdraw his consent to further treatment, or to further treatment of any description, under the plan.

Urgent
treatment.

102.—(1) Sections 97 and 98 of this Act shall not apply to any treatment—

> (a) which is immediately necessary to save a patient's life; or
>
> (b) which (not being irreversible) is immediately necessary to prevent a serious deterioration of his condition; or
>
> (c) which (not being irreversible or hazardous) is immediately necessary to alleviate serious suffering by the patient; or
>
> (d) which (not being irreversible or hazardous) is immediately necessary and represents the minimum interference necessary to prevent the patient from behaving violently or being a danger to himself or to others.

(2) Sections 99(2) and 101 of this Act shall not preclude the continuation of any treatment or of treatment under any plan pending compliance with sections 97 and 98 of this Act if the responsible medical officer considers that the discontinuance of the treatment or of treatment under the plan would cause serious suffering to the patient.

(3) For the purposes of this section treatment is irreversible if it has unfavourable irreversible physical or psychological consequences and hazardous if it entails significant physical hazard.

(4) Where a patient is given treatment under this section the responsible medical officer shall, within 7 days of the day

on which the treatment is given, notify the Mental Welfare Commission as to—

    (*a*) which of paragraphs (*a*) to (*d*) of subsection (1) of this
section applied in relation to the patient ; and

    (*b*) the nature of the treatment given to the patient.

103. The consent of a patient shall not be required for any Treatment
medical treatment given to him for the mental disorder from not requiring
which he is suffering, not being treatment falling within section consent.
97 or 98 of this Act, if the treatment is given by or under the
direction of the responsible medical officer.

PART XI

MISCELLANEOUS AND GENERAL

Offences

104.—(1) Any person who makes any statement or entry which False
is false in a material particular in any application, recommen- statements.
dation, report, record or other document required or authorised
to be made for any of the purposes of this Act or, with intent to
deceive, makes use of any such entry or statement which he
knows to be false, shall be guilty of an offence.

    (2) Any person guilty of an offence under this section shall be
liable—

    (*a*) on summary conviction, to imprisonment for a term not
exceeding 6 months or to a fine not exceeding the
statutory maximum, or both; or

    (*b*) on conviction on indictment, to imprisonment for a
term not exceeding 2 years or to a fine, or both.

105.—(1) It shall be an offence for any person being an officer Ill-treatment
on the staff of or otherwise employed in a hospital or nursing of patients.
home, or being a manager of a hospital or a person carrying
on a nursing home—

    (*a*) to ill-treat or wilfully neglect a patient for the time being
receiving treatment for mental disorder as an in-patient
in that hospital or nursing home ; or

    (*b*) to ill-treat or wilfully neglect, on the premises of which
the hospital or nursing home forms part, a patient for
the time being receiving such treatment there as an out-
patient.

PART XI

(2) It shall be an offence for any individual to ill-treat or wilfully neglect a patient who is for the time being subject to his guardianship under this Act or otherwise in his custody or care.

(3) Any person guilty of an offence against this section shall be liable—

(a) on summary conviction, to imprisonment for a term not exceeding 6 months or to a fine not exceeding the statutory maximum or both ;

(b) on conviction on indictment, to imprisonment for a term not exceeding 2 years or to a fine, or both.

Protection of mentally handicapped females.

106.—(1) It shall be an offence, subject to the exception mentioned in this section,—

(a) for a man to have unlawful sexual intercourse with a woman who is protected by the provisions of this section ;

(b) for any person to procure or encourage any woman who is protected by the provisions of this section to have unlawful sexual intercourse ;

(c) for the owner or occupier of any premises or any person having or assisting in the management or control of premises to induce any woman who is protected by the provisions of this section to resort to or be upon such premises for the purpose of unlawful sexual intercourse with any man.

(2) A person shall not be guilty of an offence against this section if he did not know and had no reason to suspect that the woman in respect of whom he is charged was protected by the provisions of this section.

(3) Any person guilty of an offence under this section shall be liable on conviction on indictment to imprisonment for a term not exceeding 2 years or to a fine.

1976 c. 67.

(4) Section 18 of the Sexual Offences (Scotland) Act 1976 (which relates to warrants to search where there is reasonable cause to suspect that a woman or girl is being unlawfully detained for immoral purposes) shall apply in the case of a woman who is protected by the provisions of this section in the same manner as that section applies in the case of a girl who is under the age of 16 years.

(5) If on the trial of an indictment for rape the jury are satisfied that the accused is guilty of an offence against paragraph (a) of subsection (1) of this section, but are not satisfied that he is guilty of rape, the jury may acquit him of rape and find him guilty of such offence as aforesaid, and in that event he shall be

liable to be punished as if he had been convicted on an indictment for such offence as aforesaid.

(6) A woman is protected by the provisions of this section if she is suffering from a state of arrested or incomplete development of mind which includes significant impairment of intelligence and social functioning.

(7) In this section " woman " includes girl.

107.—(1) Without prejudice to the last foregoing section, it Protection of shall be an offence, subject to the exception mentioned in this patients. section,—

  (a) for a man who is an officer on the staff or is otherwise employed in a hospital or nursing home, or who is a manager of a hospital or who is a person carrying on a nursing home to have unlawful sexual intercourse with a woman who is for the time being receiving treatment for mental disorder as an in-patient in that hospital or nursing home, or to have such intercourse on the premises of which the hospital or nursing home forms part with a woman who is for the time being receiving such treatment there as an out-patient ;

  (b) for a man to have unlawful sexual intercourse with a woman suffering from mental disorder who is subject to his guardianship under this Act or is otherwise in his custody or care under this Act or in the care of a local authority under the Social Work (Scotland) Act 1968 or 1968 c. 49. resident in a house provided by a local authority under that Act.

(2) It shall not be an offence under this section for a man to have sexual intercourse with a woman if he does not know and has no reason to suspect her to be a person suffering from mental disorder.

(3) In this section any reference to having unlawful sexual intercourse with a woman shall include a reference to committing a homosexual act as defined in section 80(6) of the 1980 c. 62. Criminal Justice (Scotland) Act 1980.

(4) Any person guilty of an offence under this section shall be liable on conviction on indictment to imprisonment for a term not exceeding 2 years or to a fine.

108.—(1) Any person who induces or knowingly assists any Assisting other person— patients to
                                                              absent
  (a) being liable to be detained in a hospital or being sub- themselves
      ject to guardianship under this Act, to absent himself without leave
      without leave ; or etc.

(*b*) being in legal custody by virtue of section 120 of this Act, to escape from such custody,

shall be guilty of an offence.

(2) Any person who knowingly harbours a patient who is absent without leave or is otherwise at large and liable to be retaken under this Act, or gives him any assistance with intent to prevent, hinder or interfere with his being taken into custody or returned to the hospital or other place where he ought to be, shall be guilty of an offence.

(3) Any person guilty of an offence against this section shall be liable—

(*a*) on summary conviction, to imprisonment for a term not exceeding 6 months or to a fine not exceeding the statutory maximum or both ;

(*b*) on conviction on indictment, to imprisonment for a term not exceeding 2 years or to a fine, or both.

Obstruction.

109.—(1) Any person who refuses to allow the inspection of any premises, or without reasonable cause refuses to allow the visiting, interviewing or examination of any person, by a person authorised in that behalf by or under this Act, or to produce for the inspection of any person so authorised any document or record the production of which is duly required by him, or otherwise obstructs any such person in the exercise of his functions, shall be guilty of an offence.

(2) Without prejudice to the generality of the last foregoing subsection, any person who insists on being present when requested to withdraw by a person authorised as aforesaid to interview or examine a person in private, shall be guilty of an offence.

(3) Any person guilty of an offence against this section shall be liable on summary conviction to imprisonment for a term not exceeding 3 months or to a fine not exceeding level 3 on the standard scale, or both.

Miscellaneous provisions

Duty to give information to patients and nearest relatives.

110.—(1) The managers of a hospital in which a patient is detained under the provisions of this Act, or in the case of a patient subject to guardianship, the local authority concerned shall take such steps as are practicable to ensure that the patient understands—

(*a*) under which of those provisions he is for the time being detained or subject to guardianship and the effect of that provision ; and (*b*) what rights of appeal to the sheriff are available to him in respect of his detention or guardianship under that provision ; and

(*c*) that he may make representations to the Mental Welfare Commission,

and those steps shall be taken as soon as practicable after the commencement of the patient's detention or his reception into guardianship, or any renewal of the authority for his detention or guardianship.

(2) The managers of a hospital in which a patient is detained as aforesaid shall also take such steps as are practicable to ensure that the patient understands the effect, so far as relevant in his case, of—

(*a*) sections 33 and 34 of this Act ; and

(*b*) Part X and sections 115, 116 and 119 of this Act ;

and those steps shall be taken as soon as practicable after the commencement of the patient's detention in the hospital.

(3) The steps to be taken under this section shall include giving the requisite information both orally and in writing.

(4) The managers of a hospital in which a patient is detained as aforesaid or, as the case may be, the local authority concerned in relation to a patient subject to guardianship as aforesaid shall, except where the patient otherwise requests, take such steps as are practicable to furnish the person (if any) appearing to them to be his nearest relative with a copy of any information given to him in writing under subsection (1) and (2) above ; and those steps shall be taken when the information is given to the patient or within a reasonable time thereafter.

(5) Section 56(4) of this Act shall have effect as if subsection (4) of this section were contained in part V of this Act.

111.—(1) Where a patient liable to be detained in a hospital under this Act is to be discharged otherwise than by virtue of an order for discharge made by his nearest relative, the managers of the hospital shall, subject to subsection (2) of this section, take such steps as are practicable to inform the person (if any) appearing to them to be the nearest relative of the patient ; and that information shall, if practicable, be given at least seven days before the date of discharge.

(2) Subsection (1) of this section shall not apply if the patient or his nearest relative has requested that information about the patient's discharge should not be given under this section.

(3) Section 56(4) of this Act shall have effect as if this section were contained in Part V of this Act.

PART XI
Religious
persuasion of
patients.

112. In any arrangements that may be made for the detention of a patient or his reception into guardianship in pursuance of this Act, regard shall be had to the religious persuasion to which the patient belongs or appears to belong.

Duty of
sheriff to give
patient
opportunity
to be heard.

113.—(1) In any appeal to the sheriff under this Act, or in any proceedings relating to an application for admission to a hospital or for reception into guardianship, the sheriff shall give the patient an opportunity to be heard, either—

    (*a*) in person (unless cause to the contrary has been shown) : or

    (*b*) by means of a representative.

(2) Where it is established to the satisfaction of the sheriff that it would be prejudicial to the patient's health or treatment if he were present during any such appeal or proceedings, the sheriff may exclude the patient (but not his representative) from the whole or part of that appeal or those proceedings.

Provision for
personal
expenses of
in-patients
in hospital.

114.—(1) The Secretary of State may pay to persons who are receiving treatment as in-patients (whether liable to be detained or not) in any hospital, other than a private hospital, being a hospital wholly or mainly used for the treatment of persons suffering from mental disorder, such amounts as he thinks fit in respect of their occasional personal expenses where it appears to him that they would otherwise be without resources to meet those expenses.

1978 c. 29.

(2) For the purposes of the National Health Service (Scotland) Act 1978, the making of payments under this section to persons for whom services are provided under that Act shall be treated as included among those services.

Corres-
pondence
of patients.

115.—(1) Any postal packet addressed to any person by a patient detained in a hospital under this Act and delivered by him for dispatch may be withheld from the Post Office—

    (*a*) if that person has requested that communications addressed to him by the patient should be withheld ; or

    (*b*) subject to subsection (3) of this section, if the hospital is a State hospital and the managers of the hospital consider that the postal packet is likely—

        (i) to cause distress to the person to whom it is addressed or to any other person (not being a person on the staff of the hospital) ; or

        (ii) to cause danger to any person,

and any request for the purposes of paragraph (*a*) of this subsection shall be made by a notice in writing given to the managers
of the hospital, the responsible medical officer or the Secretary of
State.

(2) Subject to subsection (3) of this section a postal packet
addressed to a patient detained in a State hospital under this
Act may be withheld from the patient if, in the opinion of the
managers of the hospital, it is necessary to do so in the interests
of the safety of the patient or for the protection of other persons.

(3) Subsections (1)(*b*) and (2) of this section do not apply to
any postal packet addressed by a patient to, or sent to a
patient by or on behalf of—

> (*a*) any Minister of the Crown or member of either House
> of Parliament ;

> (*b*) the Mental Welfare Commission, any Commissioner
> thereof or any person appointed by them under section
> 3(9)(*b*) of this Act ;

> (*c*) the Parliamentary Commissioner for Administration, the
> Health Service Commissioner for Scotland, or the Com-
> missioner for Local Administration in Scotland ;

> (*d*) any judge or clerk of court ;

> (*e*) a Health Board, the Common Services Agency for the
> Scottish Health Service or a local council established
> under section 7 of the National Health Service (Scot- 1978 c. 29.
> land) Act 1978 ;

> (*f*) a local authority within the meaning of section 235
> of the Local Government (Scotland) Act 1973 ; 1973 c. 65.

> (*g*) the managers of the hospital in which the patient is
> detained ;

> (*h*) any legally qualified person instructed by the patient to
> act as his legal advisor ; or

> (*i*) the European Commission on Human Rights or the
> European Court of Human Rights.

(4) The managers of the hospital may open and inspect any
postal packet for the purpose of determining whether it is one to
which subsection (1) or (2) of this section applies and, if so,
whether or not it should be withheld under that subsection ; and
the power to withhold a postal packet under either of those
subsections includes power to withhold anything contained in it.

(5) Where a postal packet or anything contained in it is withheld under subsection (1) or (2) of this section the managers of
the hospital shall record that fact in writing and shall, within 7
days of the date on which they withheld the postal packet or

PART XI

anything contained in it, notify the Mental Welfare Commission of—

> (a) the name of the patient concerned ; and
>
> (b) the nature of the postal packet or contents withheld ; and
>
> (c) the reason for withholding the postal packet or contents.

(6) Where a postal packet or anything contained in it is withheld under subsection (1)(b) or (2) of this section the managers of the hospital shall within 7 days give notice of that fact to the patient and, in a case under subsection (2) of this section, to the person (if known) by whom the postal packet was sent ; and any such notice shall be in writing and shall contain a statement of the effect of section 116 of this Act.

(7) The functions of the managers of a hospital under this section shall be discharged on their behalf by a person on the staff of the hospital appointed by them for that purpose, and different persons may be appointed to discharge different functions.

(8) The Secretary of State may make regulations with respect to the exercise of the powers conferred by this section.

1953 c. 36.

(9) In this section and in section 116 of this Act " postal packet " has the same meaning as in the Post Office Act 1953 ; and the provisions of this section and section 116 of this Act shall have effect notwithstanding anything in section 56 of that Act.

Review of
decision to
withhold
postal
packet.

116.—(1) The Mental Welfare Commission shall review any decision to withhold a postal packet or anything contained in it under subsection (1)(b) or (2) of section 115 of this Act if an application in that behalf is made—

> (a) in a case under the said subsection (1)(b), by the patient ; or
>
> (b) in a case under the said subsection (2), either by the patient or by the person by whom the postal packet was sent ;

and any such application shall be made within 6 months of the receipt by the applicant of the notice referred to in subsection (6) of that section.

(2) On an application under subsection (1) of this section the Commission may direct that the postal packet or anything contained in it which is the subject of the application shall not be withheld and the managers of the hospital in which the patient is detained shall comply with any such direction.

(3) The Secretary of State may by regulations make provision with respect to the making and determination of applications under subsection (1) of this section, including provision for the production to the Mental Welfare Commission of any postal packet which is the subject of such an application.

117.—(1) Where a mental health officer or a medical commissioner has reasonable cause to believe that a person suffering from mental disorder—

(a) has been or is being ill-treated, neglected or kept otherwise than under control, in any place ; or

(b) being unable to care for himself, is living alone or uncared for in any place,

he may, on production of some duly authenticated document showing that he is so authorised, demand admission at all reasonable times and, if admission is not refused, may enter and inspect that place.

(2) If it appears to a justice of the peace on sworn information in writing by such officer or commissioner as aforesaid, that admission when demanded in pursuance of subsection (1) of this section has been refused or that a refusal of such admission is apprehended, he may issue a warrant authorising any constable named therein to enter, if need be by force, any premises specified in the warrant, and to remove, if it appears proper so to do, any person suffering from mental disorder to whom subsection (1) of this section applies to a place of safety with a view to the making of an application or emergency recommendation in respect of him under Part V of this Act, or of other arrangements for his treatment or care.

(3) If it appears to a justice of the peace on sworn information in writing by any constable or other person who is authorised by or under this Act or under section 88 of the Mental Health Act 1983, to take a patient to any place, or to take into custody or retake a patient who is liable to be so taken or retaken—

(a) that there is reasonable cause to believe that that patient is to be found on any premises ; and

(b) that admission to the premises has been refused or that a refusal of such admission is apprehended,

the justice may issue a warrant authorising any constable named therein to enter the premises, if need be by force, and to remove the patient.

(4) A patient who is removed to a place of safety in the execution of a warrant issued under this section may be detained there for a period not exceeding 72 hours.

Margin notes:

PART XI

Entry on premises and warrant to search for and remove patients.

1983 c. 20.

PART XI

(5) In the execution of a warrant issued under subsection (2) of this section, the constable to whom it is addressed shall be accompanied by a medical practitioner, and in the execution of a warrant issued under subsection (3) of this section the constable to whom it is addressed may be accompanied—

(*a*) by a medical practitioner ;

1983 c. 20.

(*b*) by any person authorised by or under this Act or section 88 of the Mental Health Act 1983, to take or retake the patient.

(6) It shall not be necessary in any information or warrant under subsection (2) of this section to name the person concerned.

(7) In this section—

(*a*) any reference to a justice of the peace includes a reference to the sheriff and to a stipendiary magistrate ; and

(*b*) " place of safety " means a hospital as defined by this Act or residential home for persons suffering from mental disorder or any other suitable place the occupier of which is willing temporarily to receive the patient ; but shall not include a police station unless by reason of emergency there is no place as aforesaid available for receiving the patient.

Mentally disordered persons found in public places.

118.—(1) If a constable finds in a place to which the public have access a person who appears to him to be suffering from mental disorder and to be in immediate need of care or control, the constable may, if he thinks it necessary to do so in the interests of that person or for the protection of other persons, remove that person to a place of safety within the meaning of the last foregoing section.

(2) A person removed to a place of safety under this section may be detained there for a period not exceeding 72 hours for the purpose of enabling him to be examined by a medical practitioner and of making any necessary arrangements for his treatment or care.

(3) Where a patient is removed as aforesaid, it shall, where practicable, be the duty of the constable who has so removed him without delay to inform some responsible person residing with the patient and the nearest relative of the patient of that removal.

Code of practice.

119.—(1) The Secretary of State shall prepare, and from time to time revise, a code of practice—

(*a*) for the guidance of medical practitioners, managers and staff of hospitals and mental health officers in relation to the detention and discharge of patients in and from hospitals under this Act ; and

(b) for the guidance of medical practitioners and members of other professions in relation to the medical treatment of patients suffering from mental disorder.

(2) Before preparing the code or making any alteration in it the Secretary of State shall consult such bodies as appear to him to be concerned.

(3) The Secretary of State shall lay copies of the code and of any alteration in the code before Parliament; and if either House of Parliament passes a resolution requiring the code or any alteration in it to be withdrawn the Secretary of State shall withdraw the code or alteration and, where he withdraws the code, shall prepare a code in substitution for the one which is withdrawn.

(4) No resolution shall be passed by either House of Parliament under subsection (3) of this section in respect of a code or alteration after the expiration of the period of 40 days beginning with the day on which a copy of the code or alteration was laid before that House ; but for the purposes of this subsection no account shall be taken of any time during which Parliament is dissolved or prorogued or during which both Houses are adjourned for more than four days.

(5) The Secretary of State shall publish the code as for the time being in force.

Supplementary

120.—(1) Any person required or authorised by or by virtue of this Act to be conveyed to any place or to be kept in custody or detained in a place of safety or at any place to which he is taken under section 68(5) of this Act shall, while being so conveyed, detained or kept, as the case may be, be deemed to be in legal custody.

Provisions as to custody, conveyance and detention.

(2) A constable or any other person required or authorised by or by virtue of this Act to take any person into custody, or to convey or detain any person shall, for the purposes of taking him into custody or conveying or detaining him, have all the powers, authorities, protection and privileges which a constable has within the area for which he acts as constable.

(3) In this section " convey " includes any other expression denoting removal from one place to another.

PART XI
Retaking of
patients
escaping from
custody.

121.—(1) If any person being in legal custody by virtue of section 120 of this Act escapes, he may, subject to the provisions of this section, be retaken—

    (*a*) in any case, by the person who had his custody immediately before the escape, or by any constable or mental health officer ;

    (*b*) if at the time of the escape he was liable to be detained in a hospital, or subject to guardianship under this Act, by any other person who could take him into custody under section 28 or 44 of this Act if he had absented himself without leave.

(2) A person who escapes as aforesaid when liable to be detained or subject to guardianship as mentioned in paragraph (*b*) of subsection (1) of this section (not being a person subject to a restriction order under Part VI of this Act or an order or direction having the like effect as such an order) shall not be retaken under this section after the expiration of the period within which he could be retaken under section 28 or 44 of this Act if he had absented himself without leave on the day of the escape ; and subsection (3) of the said section 28 and subsection (2) of the said section 44 shall apply, with the necessary modifications, accordingly.

(3) A person who escapes while being taken to or detained in a place of safety under section 117 or 118 of this Act shall not be retaken under this section after the expiration of the period of 72 hours beginning with the time when he escapes or the period during which he is liable to be so detained whichever expires first.

(4) This section, so far as it relates to the escape of a person liable to be detained in a hospital, shall apply in relation to a person who escapes—

    (*a*) while being taken to a hospital in pursuance of an application for admission approved by the sheriff ;

    (*b*) while being taken to or from a hospital in pursuance of section 29 of this Act, or of any order, direction or authorisation under Parts VI and VII of this Act ; or

    (*c*) while being taken to or detained in a place of safety in pursuance of an order under Part VI of this Act pending his admission to a hospital,

as if he were liable to be detained in that hospital and, if he had not previously been received therein, as if he had been so received.

(5) In computing for the purposes of sections 22 and 60 of this Act the periods therein mentioned relating to the removal,

admission or reception of patients, no account shall be taken of any time during which the patient is at large and liable to be retaken by virtue of this section.

(6) Section 31 (in the case of a patient who is liable to be detained in a hospital) and section 48 (in the case of a patient who is subject to guardianship) of this Act shall, with any necessary modifications, apply in relation to a patient who is at large and liable to be retaken by virtue of this section as it applies in relation to a patient who is absent without leave within the meaning of section 28 or section 44 of this Act respectively, and references therein to the said section 28 or the said section 44 (as the case may be) shall be construed accordingly.

122.—(1) No person shall be liable, whether on the ground of want of jurisdiction or on any other ground, to any civil or criminal proceedings to which he would have been liable apart from this section in respect of any act purporting to be done in pursuance of this Act or any regulations thereunder, unless the act was done in bad faith or without reasonable care.

Protection for acts done in pursuance of this Act.

(2) Outwith Scotland, section 139 of the Mental Health Act 1983 (which relates to protection for acts done in pursuance of that Act) shall apply in respect of any act purporting to be done in pursuance of this Act or any regulations thereunder as it applies in relation to an act purporting to be done in pursuance of that Act or any regulations or rules thereunder.

1983 c. 20.

123. The Secretary of State may cause an inquiry to be held in any case where he thinks it advisable to do so in connection with any matter arising under this Act, and subsections (2) to (9) of section 210 of the Local Government (Scotland) Act 1973 (which relates to the holding of local inquiries) shall apply to any inquiry held under this Act.

Inquiries.

1973 c. 65.

124.—(1) Any power of the Secretary of State to make regulations or orders under this Act shall be exercisable by statutory instrument.

General provisions as to regulations and orders.

(2) Any statutory instrument containing regulations made under this Act shall be subject to annulment in pursuance of a resolution of either House of Parliament.

125.—(1) In this Act, unless the context otherwise requires, the following expressions have the meanings hereby respectively assigned to them, that is to say—

Interpretation.

" absent without leave " has the meaning assigned to it by section 59 of this Act ;

PART XI

" application for admission " and " guardianship application " have the meanings respectively assigned to them by sections 18 and 37 of this Act ;

1978 c. 29.

" health service " has the meaning given by section 108(1) of the National Health Service (Scotland) Act 1978 ;

" hospital " means—

> (a) any hospital vested in the Secretary of State under the National Health Service (Scotland) Act 1978 ;
>
> (b) any private hospital registered under Part IV of this Act ; and
>
> (c) any State hospital ;

" hospital order " and " guardianship order " have the meanings respectively assigned to them by section 175 or 376 of the Criminal Procedure (Scotland) Act 1975 ;

1975 c. 21.
1968 c. 49.

" local authority " has the same meaning as in the Social Work (Scotland) Act 1968 ;

" managers of a hospital " means—

> (a) in relation to a hospital vested in the Secretary of State under the National Health Service (Scotland) Act 1978, the Health Board responsible for the administration of that hospital ;
>
> (b) in relation to a private hospital registered under Part IV of this Act, the person or persons carrying on the hospital ;
>
> (c) in relation to a State hospital, the Secretary of State or, if the Secretary of State has appointed a State Hospital Management Committee to manage that hospital, that Committee, or, if the management of that hospital has been delegated to a Health Board or to the Common Services Agency for the Scottish Health Service, that Board or Agency, as the case may be ;

1978 c. 30.

" medical practitioner " means a registered medical practitioner within the meaning of Schedule 1 to the Interpretation Act 1978 ;

" medical treatment " includes nursing, and also includes care and training under medical supervision ;

" mental health officer " means an officer of a local authority appointed to act as a mental health officer for the purposes of this Act ;

" nearest relative ", in relation to a patient, has the meaning assigned to it in Part V of this Act ;

" patient " (except in Part IX of this Act) means a person suffering or appearing to be suffering from mental disorder ;

" private hospital " has the meaning assigned to it in Part
    IV of this Act ;

" responsible medical officer " has the meaning assigned
    to it by section 59 of this Act ;

" restriction direction " has the meaning assigned to it
    by section 72 of this Act ;

" restriction order " means an order made under section
    178 or 379 of the Criminal Procedure (Scotland) Act 1975 c. 21.
    1975 ;

" standard scale " means the standard scale defined in sec-
    tion 75 of the Criminal Justice Act 1982 ;   1982 c. 48.

" State hospital " has the meaning assigned to it in Part
    VIII of this Act ;

" statutory maximum " means the statutory maximum de-
    fined in section 74(2) of the Criminal Justice Act 1982 ;

" transfer direction " has the meaning assigned to it by
    section 71 of this Act ;

" transfer order " has the meaning assigned to it by section
    70 of this Act ;

" voluntary organisation " means a body the activities of
    which are carried on otherwise than for profit, but does
    not include any public or local authority.

(2) Unless the context otherwise requires, any reference in
this Act to any other enactment is a reference thereto as amended, and includes a reference thereto as extended or applied
by or under any other enactment, including this Act.

(3) Without prejudice to the last foregoing subsection, any
reference in this Act to an enactment of the Parliament of
Northern Ireland, or to an enactment which that Parliament
has power to amend, shall be construed, in relation to Northern
Ireland, as a reference to that enactment as amended by any
Act of that Parliament, whether passed before or after this
Act.

(4) In relation to a person who is liable to be detained or
subject to guardianship by virtue of an order or direction under
Part VI of this Act or under section 174, 175, 178, 375, 376 or
379 of the Criminal Procedure (Scotland) Act 1975, any reference in this Act to any enactment contained in Part V of this
Act shall be construed as a reference to that enactment as it
applies to that person by virtue of the said Part VI or any of the
provisions of the said sections.

(5) Any reference, however expressed, in this Act to a patient
admitted to or detained in, or liable to be admitted to or
detained in, a hospital or received, or liable to be received,
into guardianship under this Act (other than under Part V

PART XI

1975 c. 21.

thereof) or under Part VI of this Act shall include a reference to a patient who is admitted to or detained in, or liable to be admitted to or detained in, a hospital or received or liable to be received into guardianship under the Criminal Procedure (Scotland) Act 1975.

Preservation of amendments.

1960 c. 61.

1938 c. 73.

126.—(1) Notwithstanding the repeal by this Act of the Mental Health (Scotland) Act 1960 (" the 1960 Act ")—

(a) the definition of " nursing home " in section 10 of the Nursing Homes Registration (Scotland) Act 1938 (which defines, *inter alia,* the expression " nursing home ") shall continue to have effect with the amendment made by section 15(2) of the 1960 Act (which substituted a new paragraph (ii) for paragraphs (ii) and (iii)) but subject to the amendment made to that definition, in consequence of this Act, by Schedule 3 to this Act ; and

(b) the amendments made by Schedule 4 of the 1960 Act shall, insofar as not otherwise repealed, continue to have effect but subject to any amendments made to them, in consequence of this Act, by Schedule 3 to this Act or by any other enactment.

1983 c. 39.

1973 c. 65.

(2) Notwithstanding the repeal by this Act of the Mental Health (Amendment) (Scotland) Act 1983 (" the 1983 Act ")—

(a) paragraph (bb) of section 64(5) of the Local Government (Scotland) Act 1973 (which was inserted by section 7(2) of the 1983 Act) shall continue to have effect but subject to the amendment made, in consequence of this Act, by Schedule 3 to this Act ;

(b) Sections 174, 174A, 175, 176, 178, 184, 280, 375A, 376, 377, 379, 385, 443, and 462 of, and paragraph 4(b) of Schedule 5 to, the Criminal Procedure (Scotland) Act 1975 shall continue to have effect with the amendments made by the 1983 Act but subject to any amendments made, in consequence of this Act, by Schedule 3 to this Act ;

1978 c. 44.

(c) paragraph 5 of Schedule 5 to the Employment Protection (Consolidation) Act 1978 (which was added by Schedule 2 to the 1983 Act) shall continue to have effect ; and

1983 c. 20.

(d) section 80 of the Mental Health Act 1983 shall continue to have effect with the amendments made by paragraph 1 of Schedule 2 to the 1983 Act.

Consequential and transitional provisions and repeals.

1978 c. 30.

127.—(1) Schedule 3 (consequential amendments) and Schedule 4 (transitional and saving provisions) to this Act shall have effect but without prejudice to the operation of sections 15 to 17 of the Interpretation Act 1978 (which relate to the effect of repeals).

(2) The enactments specified in Schedule 5 to this Act are hereby repealed to the extent mentioned in the third column of that Schedule.

PART XI

128. The following provisions of this Act shall extend to England and Wales, that is to say—

Application to England and Wales.

> section 10 ;
>
> section 68(5) ;
>
> section 77 ;
>
> section 78 ;
>
> section 84 and, so far as applied by that section, sections 28, 32 and 121 ;
>
> section 108, except so far as it relates to patients subject to guardianship ;
>
> section 120 ;
>
> section 122(2) ;
>
> section 127 and Schedules 2 and 5 so far as they relate to enactments extending to England and Wales ;

but except as aforesaid, and except so far as it relates to the interpretation or commencement of the said provisions, this Act shall not extend to England and Wales.

129. The following provisions of this Act shall extend to Northern Ireland, that is to say—

Application to Northern Ireland.

> sections 80 and 81 ;
>
> section 84 and, so far as applied by that section, sections 28, 32 and 121 ;
>
> section 85 ;
>
> section 95 ;
>
> section 108, except so far as it relates to patients subject to guardianship ;
>
> section 120 ;
>
> section 122(2) ;
>
> section 127 and Schedules 2 and 5 so far as they relate to enactments extending to Northern Ireland ;

but except as aforesaid, and except so far as it relates to the interpretation or commencement of the said provisions, this Act shall not extend to Northern Ireland.

130. This Act may be cited as the Mental Health (Scotland) Act 1984 and shall come into force on 30th September 1984.

Short title and commencement.

SCHEDULES

Section 91(2).

SCHEDULE 1

STATE HOSPITAL MANAGEMENT COMMITTEES

PART I

Constitution

1. A State Hospital Management Committee shall be a body corporate and shall have a common seal.

2. A State Hospital Management Committee shall consist of a chairman appointed by the Secretary of State and such number of other members so appointed as the Secretary of State thinks fit.

3. Not less than one half of the members of a State Hospital Management Committee shall be persons other than medical practitioners.

4. The application of the seal of a State Hospital Management Committee to any document shall be attested by at least one member of the Committee and by the person for the time being acting as secretary of the Committee.

5. Every document purporting to be an instrument issued by a State Hospital Management Committee and to be sealed and attested as aforesaid or to be duly signed on behalf of the Committee, shall be received in evidence and shall be deemed to be such an instrument without further proof, unless the contrary is shown.

PART II

Supplementary Provisions

6. Regulations may make provision—

    (*a*) as to the appointment, tenure and vacation of office of the chairman and other members of a State Hospital Management Committee ;

    (*b*) as to the delegation of functions to committees or sub-committees composed, as to a majority, of members of a State Hospital Management Committee ; and

    (*c*) as to the procedure of a State Hospital Management Committee, its committees and sub-committees.

7. The proceedings of a State Hospital Management Committee shall not be invalidated by any vacancy in membership or by any defect in the appointment of any member thereof.

1978 c. 29.

8. The following provisions of the National Health Service (Scotland) Act 1978 shall apply to a State Hospital Management Committee as they apply to a Health Board, that is to say—

    (*a*) section 77 (which gives default powers to the Secretary of State) ;

(*b*) section 78 (which gives emergency powers to the Secretary of State) ; SCH. 1

(*c*) sections 85(1), (2A), (4) and (6) (which contain provisions as to expenditure being met by the Secretary of State) ;

(*d*) sections 85A(1) and (3) (which impose financial duties) ; and

(*e*) section 86 (which provides for the auditing and examination of accounts).

SCHEDULE 2

APPLICATION OF PROVISIONS OF PART V TO PATIENTS SUBJECT TO HOSPITAL OR GUARDIANSHIP ORDERS   Sections 60, 61, 62, 76.

PART I

HOSPITAL ORDER WITHOUT RESTRICTION ORDER (SECTION 60(1)) ; TRANSFER FROM PRISON WITHOUT RESTRICTION (SECTION 71).

1. Sections 27, 31, 32, 53, 54, 55, 56 and 58 shall apply in relation to the patient without modification.

2. Sections 22, 28, 29, 30, 33, 35, 57 and 59 shall apply in relation to the patient with the modifications specified in paragraphs 3 to 10 of this Part of this Schedule.

3. In section 22—

(*a*) subsection (1) shall be omitted ; and

(*b*) in subsection (2) for the reference to an application for admission there shall be substituted a reference to the order or direction by virtue of which the patient is liable under Part VI of this Act to be detained.

4. In section 28 subsection (4) shall be omitted.

5. In section 29(3) for the words from " as follows " to the end of the subsection there shall be substituted the words " as if the order or direction by virtue of which he was liable under Part VI of this Act to be detained before being transferred were an order or direction for his admission or removal to the hospital to which he is transferred.".

6. In section 30—

(*a*) in subsection (1), for the words " an application for admission " and " day on which he was so admitted " there shall be substituted the words " an order or direction by virtue of which he is liable under Part VI of this Act to be detained " and " date of the relevant order or direction " respectively ; and (*b*) in subsection (3), for the words "this Part" there shall be substituted the words "Part VI".

7. In section 33—
   (*a*) in subsection (1), for the words "this Part" there shall be substituted the words "Part VI";
   (*b*) in subsection (4), for "26, 30 or 34" there shall be substituted "30"; and
   (*c*) in subsection (5) the words "by the nearest relative of the patient or" shall be omitted.

8. In section 35(1)—
   (*a*) the words "any of sections 26, 30 or 34 of" shall be omitted;
   (*b*) for the words "any of the said sections" there shall be substituted the words "Part V of this Act"; and
   (*c*) the words from "whether" to "both" shall be omitted.

9. In section 57(4) for paragraphs (*a*) and (*b*) there shall be substituted the words "on the date when the patient ceases to be liable to be detained in pursuance of the order or direction by virtue of which he was liable under Part VI of this Act to be detained (otherwise than on being transferred in pursuance of section 29(1)(*b*) or (*c*) of this Act.".

10. In section 59 subsections (1)(*b*) and (2) shall be omitted.

Part II

HOSPITAL ORDER WITH RESTRICTION ORDER, (SECTION 62) AND ORDERS OR DIRECTIONS HAVING THE LIKE EFFECT (SECTIONS 69, 70 AND 72).

1. Sections 53, 54, 56 and 58 shall apply in relation to the patient without modification.

2. Section 22, 27, 28, 29, 55, 57 and 59 shall apply in relation to the patient with the modifications specified in paragraphs 3 to 9 of this Part of this Schedule.

3. In section 22—
   (*a*) subsection (1) shall be omitted;
   (*b*) in subsection (2) for the words "application under this Part" there shall be substituted the words "order or direction by virtue of which he is liable under Part VI of this Act to be detained" and paragraph (*b*) shall be omitted;
   (*c*) subsections (3) and (4) shall be omitted.

4. In section 27—

 (*a*) in subsection (1) after the word "may" there shall be inserted the words "with the consent of the Secretary of State";

 (*b*) in subsection (2) the word "either" and the words from "or from any specified period" to the end of the subsection shall be omitted; and

 (*c*) in subsection (5) after the words "responsible medical officer" and after the words "that officer" there shall be inserted the words "or the Secretary of State".

5. In section 28 subsections (3) and (4) shall be omitted.

6. In section 29—

 (*a*) in subsection (1) after the word "may" there shall be inserted the words "with the consent of the Secretary of State" and paragraphs (*b*) and (*c*) shall be omitted;

 (*b*) in subsection (3) for the words from "as follows" to the end of the subsection there shall be substituted the words "as if the order or direction by virtue of which he was liable under Part VI of this Act to be detained before being transferred were an order or direction for his admission or removal to the hospital to which he is transferred.".

7. In section 55 subsection (3) shall be omitted.

8. In section 57(4) for paragraphs (*a*) and (*b*) there shall be substituted the words "on the date when the patient ceases to be liable to be detained in pursuance of the order or direction by virtue of which he was liable under Part VI of this Act to be detained (otherwise than on being transferred in pursuance of section 29(1)(*b*) or (*c*) of this Act.)".

9. In section 59, subsections (1)(*b*) and (2) shall be omitted.

PART III

GUARDIANSHIP ORDER (SECTION 61(2))

1. Sections 43, 44, 46, 48, 53, 55, 56 and 58 shall apply in relation to the patient without modification.

2. Sections 41, 45, 47, 49, 50, 52, 57 and 59 shall apply in relation to the patient with the modifications specified in paragraphs 3 to 10 of this Part of this Schedule.

3. In section 41—

 (*a*) in subsection (1) for the words "an application under this Part of this Act" and "the application" there shall be substituted the words "a guardianship order" and "the order" respectively; and

(b) in subsection (2) for the words from " Where " to " shall " and " named in the application " there shall be substituted the words " Where a guardianship order has been made in respect of a patient the order shall " and " named in the order " respectively.

4. In section 45(1) and (3) for the words " guardianship application " there shall be substituted the words " guardianship order ".

5. In section 47—

(a) in subsection (1) for the words " guardianship application " and " the day on which he was so received " there shall be substituted the words " guardianship order " and " the date of the order " respectively ;

(b) in subsection (3) for the words " this Part " there shall be substituted the words " Part VI ".

6. In section 49(1) for the words " this Part " there shall be substituted the words " Part VI ".

7. In section 50—

(a) in subsection (1) for the words " this Part " there shall be substituted the words " Part VI " ;

(b) in subsection (5) for the words " sections 47 or 51 " there shall be substituted the words " section 47 " ; and

(c) subsection (6) shall be omitted.

8. In section 52(1)—

(a) for the words " either of sections 47 or 51 " and " either of the said sections " there shall be substituted the words " section 47 " and " the said section " respectively ; and

(b) the words from " whether " to " both " shall be omitted.

9. In section 57(4) for paragraphs (a) and (b) there shall be substituted the words " on the date when the patient ceases to be subject to guardianship under this Act ".

10. In section 59(1)—

(a) in subsection (1) paragraph (a) shall be omitted ; and

(b) in subsection (2) for paragraphs (a) and (b) there shall be substituted the words " to the local authority to whose guardianship he is subject or who approved his guardian.".

Section 127(1).

SCHEDULE 3

CONSEQUENTIAL AMENDMENTS

The Improvement of Land Act 1864 (c. 114)

1. In section 68 for the words " Mental Health (Scotland) Act 1960 " there shall be substituted the words " Mental Health (Scotland) Act 1984 ".

2. In section 10(4)—

(*a*) in paragraph (*a*) for the words " section sixty-four of the Mental Health (Scotland) Act 1960 " there shall be substituted the words " section 69 of the Mental Health (Scotland) Act 1984 " ; and

(*b*) in paragraph (*b*) for the words " sixty-six " and " sixty-seven " there shall be substituted " 71 " and " 72 " respectively.

Nursing Homes Registration (Scotland) Act 1938 (*c.* 73)

3. In section 10(1)(ii) for the words " Mental Health (Scotland) Act 1960 " there shall be substituted the words " Mental Health (Scotland) Act 1984 ".

The Polish Resettlement Act 1947 (*c.* 19)

4. In section 11(3)(*b*) for the words " Mental Health (Scotland) Act 1960 " there shall be substituted the words " Mental Health (Scotland) Act 1984 ".

The Army Act 1955 (*c.* 18)

5. In section 116(7) for the words " section 64 of the Mental Health (Scotland) Act 1960 " there shall be substituted the words " section 69 of the Mental Health (Scotland) Act 1984 ".

The Air Force Act 1955 (*c.* 19)

6. In section 116(7) for the words " section 64 of the Mental Health (Scotland) Act 1960 " there shall be substituted the words " section 69 of the Mental Health (Scotland) Act 1984 ".

The Naval Discipline Act 1957 (*c.* 53)

7. In section 71(6) for the words " section 64 of the Mental Health (Scotland) Act 1960 " there shall be substituted the words " section 69 of the Mental Health (Scotland) Act 1984 ".

Local Government (Scotland) Act 1966 (*c.* 51)

8. In Part II of Schedule 4 in paragraph 25 for the words " section 15(4) of the Mental Health (Scotland) Act 1960 " there shall be substituted the words " Section 12(3) of the Mental Health (Scotland) Act 1984 ".

The Criminal Justice Act 1967 (*c.* 80)

9. In section 72—

    (*a*) in subsection (1)(*b*) for the words " section 36 or 106 of the Mental Health (Scotland) Act 1960 " there shall be substituted the words " section 28, 44 or 121 of the Mental Health (Scotland) Act 1984 " ;

    (*b*) in subsection (3) for the words " section 105 of the Mental Health (Scotland) Act 1960 " and " 1960 " there shall be substituted the words " section 120 of the Mental Health (Scotland) Act 1984 " and " 1984 " respectively ; and

    (*c*) in subsection (4) for the words " Part V of the Mental Health (Scotland) Act 1960 " and " or 1960 " there shall be substituted the words " Part VI of the Mental Health (Scotland) Act 1984 " and " or Part VI of the said Act of 1984 " respectively.

The Courts-Martial (Appeals) Act 1968 (*c.* 20)

10. In section 20(4) for the words " Part V of the Mental Health (Scotland) Act 1960 " there shall be substituted the words " Part VI of the Mental Health (Scotland) Act 1984 ".

11. In section 23(1) for the words " Section 64 of the Mental Health (Scotland) Act 1960 " there shall be substituted the words " section 69 of the Mental Health (Scotland) Act 1984 ".

12. In section 25(4) for the words " Mental Health (Scotland) Act 1960 " there shall be substituted the words " Mental Health (Scotland) Act 1984 ".

13. In section 43(4) for the words " Mental Health (Scotland) Act 1960 " there shall be substituted the words " Mental Health (Scotland) Act 1984 ".

The Social Work (Scotland) Act 1968 (*c.* 49)

14. In section 1(4)(*b*) for the words " Mental Health (Scotland) Act 1960 " there shall be substituted the words " Mental Health (Scotland) Act 1984 ".

15. In section 16(3) for the words " Mental Health (Scotland) Act 1960 " there shall be substituted the words " Mental Health (Scotland) Act 1984 ".

16. In section 46—

    (*a*) in subsection (1) for the words " Part IV of the Mental Health (Scotland) Act 1960 " there shall be substituted the words " Part V of the Mental Health (Scotland) Act 1984 " ; and (*b*) in subsection (2) for the words " section 23(3) of the said Act of 1960 " there shall be substituted the words " section 17(2) of the said Act of 1984 ".

17. In section 94(1)—

(*a*) in the definition of " hospital " for the words " Mental Health (Scotland) Act 1960" and " Part VII of the said Act of 1960" there shall be substituted the words " Mental Health (Scotland) Act 1984 " and " Part VIII of the said Act of 1984 " respectively ;

(*b*) in the definition of " mental disorder " for the words " section 6 of the Mental Health (Scotland) Act 1960 " there shall be substituted the words " section 1(2) of the Mental Health (Scotland) Act 1984 " ; and

(*c*) in the definition of " mental health officer " for the words " said Act of 1960 " there shall be substituted the words " said Act of 1984 ".

The Local Authority Social Services Act 1970 (*c.* 42)

18. In Schedule 1 for the words " Mental Health (Scotland) Act 1960 (c.61.) " there shall be substituted the words " Mental Health (Scotland) Act 1984 ".

Chronically Sick and Disabled Persons Act 1970 (*c.* 44)

19. In section 18(2) for the words " section 6 of the Mental Health (Scotland) Act 1960 " there shall be substituted the words " section 1(2) of the Mental Health (Scotland) Act 1984 ".

The Guardianship Act 1973 (*c.* 29)

20. In section 10(7) for the words " Mental Health (Scotland) Act 1960 " there shall be substituted the words " Mental Health (Scotland) Act 1984 ".

Local Government (Scotland) Act 1973 (*c.* 65)

21. In section 64(5) for paragraph (*bb*) there shall be substituted the following paragraph—

" (*bb*) section 9 of the Mental Health (Scotland) Act 1984 (appointment of mental health officers) ; ".

The Rehabilitation of Offenders Act 1974 (*c.* 53)

22. In section 5(7) for the words " Part V of the Mental Health (Scotland) Act 1960 " there shall be substituted the words " Part VI of the Mental Health (Scotland) Act 1984 ".

The Criminal Procedure (Scotland) Act 1975 (c. 21)

23. In section 13—

    (*a*) in subsection (1)(*b*) for the words " section 36 or 106 of the Mental Health (Scotland) Act 1960 " there shall be substituted the words " section 28, 44 or 121 of the Mental Health (Scotland) Act 1984 " ;

    (*b*) in subsection (3) for the words " section 105 of the Mental Health (Scotland) Act 1960 " and " 1960 " where it second appears there shall be substituted the words " section 120 of the Mental Health (Scotland) Act 1984 " and " 1984 " respectively ; and

    (*c*) in subsection (4) for the words " Part V of the Mental Health (Scotland) Act 1960 " there shall be substituted the words " Part VI of the Mental Health (Scotland) Act 1984 ".

24. In section 25(2) for the words " Part IV of the Mental Health (Scotland) Act 1960 " there shall be substituted the words " Part V of the Mental Health (Scotland) Act 1984 ".

25. In section 174A(1) for the words " section 6(1) of the Mental Health (Scotland) Act 1960 " there shall be substituted the words " Section 1(2) of the Mental Health (Scotland) Act 1984 ".

26. In section 175(1) for the words " 23(1) ", " 25(1A)(*a*) " and " Mental Health (Scotland) Act 1960 " there shall be substituted the words " 17(1) ", " 36(*a*) " and " Mental Health (Scotland) Act 1984 " respectively.

27. In section 176(1) for the words " section 27 of the Mental Health (Scotland) Act 1960 " there shall be substituted the words " section 20 or section 39 of the Mental Health (Scotland) Act 1984 ".

28. In section 178—

    (*a*) in subsection (1) for the words " section 60(3) of the Mental Health (Scotland) Act 1960 " there shall be substituted the words " section 62(1) of the Mental Health (Scotland) Act 1984 " ;

    (*b*) in subsection (2) for the words " section 27 of the Mental Health (Scotland) Act 1960 " there shall be substituted the words " section 20 or section 39 of the Mental Health (Scotland) Act 1984 " ; and

    (*c*) in subsection (3) for the words " section 58(4) of the Mental Health (Scotland) Act 1960 " there shall be substituted the words " section 60(4) of the Mental Health (Scotland) Act 1984 ".

29. In section 184—

    (*a*) in subsection (1) for the words " section 27 of the Mental Health (Scotland) Act 1960 " and " Part V of that Act " there

shall be substituted the words " section 20 or 39 of the
Mental Health (Scotland) Act 1984 " and " Part VI of that
Act " respectively ;

   (b) in subsection 2(a) for the words " Mental Health (Scotland)
   Act 1960 " there shall be substituted the words " Mental
   Health (Scotland) Act 1984 ".

30. In section 322—

   (a) in subsection (1)(b) for the words " section 36 or 106 of the
   Mental Health (Scotland) Act 1960 " there shall be substi-
   tuted the words " section 28, 44, or 121 of the Mental Health
   (Scotland) Act 1984 " ;

   (b) in subsection (3) for the words " section 105 of the Mental
   Health (Scotland) Act 1960 " and " 1960 " where it second
   occurs there shall be substituted the words " section 120 of
   the Mental Health (Scotland) Act 1984 " and " 1984 " respectively ; and

   (c) in subsection (4) for the words " Part V of the Mental Health
   (Scotland) Act 1960 " there shall be substituted the words
   " Part VI of the Mental Health (Scotland) Act 1984 ".

31. In section 330(2) for the words " Part IV of the Mental Health
(Scotland) Act 1960 " there shall be substituted the words " Part V of
the Mental Health (Scotland) Act 1984 ".

32. In section 375(A)(1) for the words " section 6(1) of the Mental
Health (Scotland) Act 1960 " there shall be substituted the words
" section 1(2) of the Mental Health (Scotland) Act 1984 ".

33. In section 376(1) for the words " 23(1) ", " 25(1)(a) " and " Mental Health (Scotland) Act 1960 " there shall be substituted the words
" 17(1) ", " 36(a) " and " Mental Health (Scotland) Act 1984 " respectively.

34. In section 377(1) for the words " section 27 of the Mental
Health (Scotland) Act 1960 " there shall be substituted the words
" section 20 or section 39 of the Mental Health (Scotland) Act 1984 ".

35. In section 379—

   (a) in subsection (1) for the words " section 60(3) of the Mental
   Health (Scotland) Act 1960 " there shall be substituted the
   words " section 62(1) of the Mental Health (Scotland) Act
   1984 " ;

   (b) in subsection (2) for the words " section 27 of the Mental
   Health (Scotland) Act 1960 " there shall be substituted the
   words " section 20 or section 39 of the Mental Health (Scotland) Act 1984 " ; and

   (c) in subsection (3) for the words " section 58(4) of the Mental
   Health (Scotland) Act 1960 " there shall be substituted the
   words " section 62(1) of the Mental Health (Scotland) Act
   1984 ".

36. In section 385—

   (*a*) in subsection (1) for the words " section 27 of the Mental Health (Scotland) Act 1960 " and " Part V of that Act " there shall be substituted the words " section 20 or 39 of the Mental Health (Scotland) Act 1984 " and " Part VI of that Act " respectively ;

   (*b*) in subsection 2(*a*) for the words " Mental Health (Scotland) Act 1960 " there shall be substituted the words " Mental Health (Scotland) Act 1984 ".

37. In section 462—

   (*a*) in the definition of " hospital " for the words " Part III of the Mental Health (Scotland) Act 1960 " there shall be substituted the words " Part IV of the Mental Health (Scotland) Act 1984 " ;

   (*b*) in the definition of " responsible medical officer " for the words " section 53 of the Mental Health (Scotland) Act 1960 " there shall be substituted the words " section 59 of the Mental Health (Scotland) Act 1984 " ; and

   (*c*) in the definition of " State hospital " for the words " Part VII of the Mental Health (Scotland) Act 1960 " there shall be substituted the words " Part VIII of the Mental Health (Scotland) Act 1984 ".

The Adoption (Scotland) Act 1978 (c. 28)

38. In section 32(3)(*c*) for the words " section 23 of the Mental Health (Scotland) Act 1960 " there shall be substituted the words " section 17 or 39 of the Mental Health (Scotland) Act 1984 ".

The National Health Service (Scotland) Act 1978 (c. 29)

39. In section 100(1) for the words " Mental Health (Scotland) Act 1960 " there shall be substituted the words " Mental Health (Scotland) Act 1984 ".

40. In section 102(1) for the words " Mental Health (Scotland) Act 1960 " there shall be substituted the words " Mental Health (Scotland) Act 1984 ".

41. In section 108(1) in the definitions of " illness " and " state hospital " for the words " Mental Health (Scotland) Act 1960 " there shall be substituted the words " Mental Health (Scotland) Act 1984 ".

42. In paragraph 7 of Schedule 14, for the words " Mental Health (Scotland) Act 1960 " there shall be substituted the words " Mental Health (Scotland) Act 1984 ".

The Child Care Act 1980 (c. 5)

43. In section 79(5)(*d*) for the words " Mental Health (Scotland) Act 1960 " there shall be substituted the words " Mental Health (Scotland) Act 1984 ".

The Reserve Forces Act 1980 (*c.* 9)

44. In paragraph (2)(*b*) of Schedule 2 for the words " Mental Health (Scotland) Act 1960 " there shall be substituted the words " Mental Health (Scotland) Act 1984 ".

The Concessionary Travel for Handicapped Persons (Scotland) Act 1980 (*c.* 29)

45. In section 2(1)(*a*) for the words " Mental Health (Scotland) Act 1960 " there shall be substituted the words " Mental Health (Scotland) Act 1984 ".

Solicitors (Scotland) Act 1980 (*c.* 46)

46. In section 18(1) for the words " Mental Health (Scotland) Act 1960 " there shall be substituted the words " Mental Health (Scotland) Act 1984 ".

Tenants' Rights, Etc. (Scotland) Act 1980 (*c.*52)

47. In section 1(10)(*o*) for the words " section 89 of the Mental Health (Scotland) Act 1960 " there shall be substituted the words " section 90 of the Mental Health (Scotland) Act 1984 ".

The Contempt of Court Act 1981 (*c.* 49)

48. In paragraph (10)(*b*) of Schedule 1 for the words " section 68(1) of the Mental Health (Scotland) Act 1960 " there shall be substituted the words " section 73(1) of the Mental Health (Scotland) Act 1984 ".

The Mental Health Act 1983 (*c.* 20)

49. In section 69(2)(*a*) for the words " section 73(2) of the Mental Health (Scotland) Act 1960 " there shall be substituted the words " section 77(2) of the Mental Health (Scotland) Act 1984 ".

50. In section 79(1)(*c*) for the words " section 73(2) of the Mental Health (Scotland) Act 1960 " there shall be substituted the words " section 77(2) of the Mental Health (Scotland) Act 1984 ".

51. In section 80, in subsections (4) and (7) for the words " Mental Health (Scotland) Act 1960 " there shall be substituted the words " Mental Health (Scotland) Act 1984 ".

52. In section 88(3)(*a*) for the words " Mental Health (Scotland) Act 1960 " there shall be substituted the words " Mental Health (Scotland) Act 1984 ".

53. In section 90 for the words " Part VI of the Mental Health (Scotland) Act 1960 " there shall be substituted the words " Part VII of the Mental Health (Scotland) Act 1984 ".

54. In section 92(3) for the words " Part VI of the Mental Health (Scotland) Act 1960 " there shall be substituted the words " Part VII of the Mental Health (Scotland) Act 1984 ".

55. In section 116(2) for the words "Mental Health (Scotland) Act 1960" there shall be substituted the words "Mental Health (Scotland) Act 1984".

56. In section 135—

    (*a*) in subsection (2) for the words "Mental Health (Scotland) Act 1960" there shall be substituted the words "Mental Health (Scotland) Act 1984".

    (*b*) in subsection (4) for the words "Mental Health (Scotland) Act 1960" there shall be substituted the words "Mental Health (Scotland) Act 1984".

Section 127(1).

SCHEDULE 4

TRANSITIONAL AND SAVINGS PROVISIONS

1. Where, apart from this paragraph, anything done under or in pursuance of, for the purposes of, any enactment which is repealed by this Act (in this Schedule referred to as "a repealed enactment") would cease to have effect by virtue of that repeal it shall have effect as if it had been done under, or in pursuance of, or for the purposes of, the corresponding provision of this Act.

2. Without prejudice to any express amendment by this Act, where any enactment or document refers either expressly or by implication, to a repealed enactment, the reference shall, except where the context otherwise requires, be construed as, or as including, a reference to the corresponding provision of this Act.

3. Where any period of time specified in a repealed enactment is current at the commencement of this Act, this Act shall have effect as if the corresponding provision of this Act had been in force when that period began to run.

4.—(1) Nothing in this Act shall affect a repealed enactment in its operation in relation to offences committed before the commencement of this Act.

(2) Where an offence, for the continuance of which a penalty was provided, has been committed under a repealed enactment proceedings may, in the same manner as if the offence had been committed under the corresponding provision of this Act, be taken under this Act in respect of the continuance, after the commencement of this Act, of the offence.

5. This Act shall apply in relation to any authority for the detention or guardianship of a person who was liable to be detained or subject to guardianship under the Mental Health (Scotland) Act 1960 immediately before 30th September 1984 as if the provisions of this Act which derive from provisions amended by section 5 of the Mental Health (Amendment) (Scotland) Act 1983 and any amend-

1960 c. 61.

1983 c. 39.

ments in Schedule 2 to that Act which are consequential on those sections were included in this Act in the form which the provisions from which they derive would take if those amendments were disregarded ; but this provision shall not apply to any renewal of that authority on or after that date.

6. This Act shall apply to any application made before 30th September 1984 as if the provisions of this Act which derive from provisions amended by sections 8(1) or (2) or (3*b*) or (3*c*) or 9 of the Mental Health (Amendment) (Scotland) Act 1983 and any amend- 1983 c. 39 ments in Schedule 2 to that Act which are consequential on those sections were included in this Act in the form which the provisions from which they derive would take if those amendments were disregarded.

7. Where on 30th September 1984 a person who has not attained the age of 16 years is subject to guardianship by virtue of a guardianship application the authority for his guardianship shall terminate on that day.

8. This Act shall apply to any emergency recommendation or admission following thereon made before 30th September 1984 as if the provisions of this Act which derive from provisions amended by section 12 of the Mental Health (Amendment) (Scotland) Act 1983 and the repeal in Schedule 3 to that Act which is consequential on that section were included in this Act in the form which the provisions from which they derive would take if those amendments were disregarded ; but, when the period during which a patient may be detained in pursuance of such an emergency recommendation expires, it shall not be competent for the patient to be further detained immediately thereafter under the said provisions of this Act in the form which they take as so amended.

9. This Act shall apply in relation to any renewal of authority made before 30th September 1984 as if the provisions of this Act which derive from provisions amended by section 16(*a*) to (*d*) of the Mental Health (Amendment) (Scotland) Act 1983 and any amendments in Schedule 2 to that Act which are consequential on that section were included in this Act in the form which the provisions from which they derive would take if those amendments were disregarded ; and, where an authority has been renewed before that date for a period of 2 years of which less than 16 months has expired on that date, that period shall expire at the end of 18 months from the date on which it began.

10. This Act shall apply in relation to the definition of " nearest relative " in any proceedings commenced before 30th September 1984 as if the provisions of this Act which derive from provisions amended by section 19 of the Mental Health (Amendment) (Scotland) Act 1983 and any amendments in Schedule 2 to that Act which are consequential on that section were included in this Act in the form which the provisions from which they derive would take if those amendments were disregarded.

11.—(1) Section 98(3) of this Act shall not apply to any treatment given to a patient in the period of 6 months beginning with 30th September 1984 if—

    (a) the detention of the patient began before the beginning of that period ; and

    (b) that subsection has not been complied with in respect of any treatment previously given to him in that period.

(2) The Secretary of State may by order reduce the length of the period mentioned in sub-paragraph (1) of this paragraph.

12. In the case of a patient who is detained at 30th September 1984 the steps to be taken under section 110 shall be taken as soon as practicable after that date, except where such steps have already been taken.

13. Section 113 of this Act shall not apply in relation to proceedings commenced before 30th September 1984.

SCHEDULE 5

REPEALS

Chapter	Short title	Extent of repeal
1960 c. 61.	The Mental Health (Scotland) Act 1960.	The whole Act.
1961 (N.I.) c. 15.	The Mental Health (Northern Ireland) Act 1961.	In Schedule 5, Part II.
1963 c. 39.	The Criminal Justice (Scotland) Act 1963.	In Schedule 5, the entry relating to the Mental Health (Scotland) Act 1960.
1967 c. 28.	The Superannuation (Miscellaneous Provisions) Act 1967.	Section 14.
1968 c. 20.	The Courts-Martial (Appeals) Act 1968.	In Schedule 4, the entry relating to the Mental Health (Scotland) Act 1960.
1968 c. 46.	The Health Services and Public Health Act 1968.	Section 75.
1968 c. 49.	The Social Work (Scotland) Act 1968.	In Schedule 8, paragraphs 50 to 59.
1969 c. 39.	The Age of Majority (Scotland) Act 1969.	In Schedule 1, Part 1, the entry relating to the Mental Health (Scotland) Act 1960.
1969 c. 54.	The Children and Young Persons Act 1969.	In Schedule 5, paragraphs 42 and 43.
1971 c. 77.	The Immigration Act 1971.	Section 30.
1972 c. 58.	The National Health Service (Scotland) Act 1972.	Section 52(1). In Schedule 6, paragraphs 105 to 117.
1974 c. 46.	The Friendly Societies Act 1974.	In Schedule 9, paragraph 17.
1975 c. 21.	The Criminal Procedure (Scotland) Act 1975.	In Schedule 9, paragraphs 17 to 29.
1976 c. 67.	The Sexual Offences (Scotland) Act 1976.	In Schedule 1, the entry relating to the Mental Health (Scotland) Act 1960.
1976 c. 83.	The Health Services Act 1976.	Section 19(3), (4)(c).
1978 c. 29.	The National Health Service (Scotland) Act 1978.	In Schedule 16, paragraphs 12 and 13.
1980 c. 5.	The Child Care Act 1980.	In Schedule 5, paragraphs 15 and 16.
1980 c. 44.	The Education (Scotland) Act 1980.	In Schedule 4, paragraph 2.
1980 c. 62.	The Criminal Justice (Scotland) Act 1980.	In section 80, subsection (4).
1982 c. 51.	The Mental Health (Amendment) Act 1982.	In Schedule 3 in Part I, paragraph 31.
1983 c. 20.	The Mental Health Act 1983.	In Schedule 4, paragraph 16.
1983 c. 39.	The Mental Health (Amendment) (Scotland) Act 1983.	The whole Act.

Child Abduction Act 1984

1984 CHAPTER 37

An Act to amend the criminal law relating to the abduction of children.   [12th July 1984]

B E IT ENACTED by the Queen's most Excellent Majesty, by and with the advice and consent of the Lords Spiritual and Temporal, and Commons, in this present Parliament assembled, and by the authority of the same, as follows:—

PART I

OFFENCES UNDER LAW OF ENGLAND AND WALES

Offence of abduction of child by parent, etc.

1.—(1) Subject to subsections (5) and (8) below, a person connected with a child under the age of sixteen commits an offence if he takes or sends the child out of the United Kingdom without the appropriate consent.

(2) A person is connected with a child for the purposes of this section if—

(a) he is a parent or guardian of the child ; or

(b) there is in force an order of a court in England or Wales awarding custody of the child to him, whether solely or jointly with any other person ; or

(c) in the case of an illegitimate child, there are reasonable grounds for believing that he is the father of the child.

(3) In this section " the appropriate consent ", in relation to a child, means—

(a) the consent of each person—

(i) who is a parent or guardian of the child ; or

> (ii) to whom custody of the child has been awarded (whether solely or jointly with any other person) by an order of a court in England or Wales ; or

(b) if the child is the subject of such a custody order, the leave of the court which made the order ; or

(c) the leave of the court granted on an application for a direction under section 7 of the Guardianship of Minors Act 1971 or section 1(3) of the Guardianship Act 1973.

1971 c. 3.

1973 c. 29.

(4) In the case of a custody order made by a magistrates' court, subsection (3)(b) above shall be construed as if the reference to the court which made the order included a reference to any magistrates' court acting for the same petty sessions area as that court.

(5) A person does not commit an offence under this section by doing anything without the consent of another person whose consent is required under the foregoing provisions if—

(a) he does it in the belief that the other person—

> (i) has consented ; or

> (ii) would consent if he was aware of all the relevant circumstances ; or

(b) he has taken all reasonable steps to communicate with the other person but has been unable to communicate with him ; or

(c) the other person has unreasonably refused to consent,

but paragraph (c) of this subsection does not apply where what is done relates to a child who is the subject of a custody order made by a court in England or Wales, or where the person who does it acts in breach of any direction under section 7 of the Guardianship of Minors Act 1971 or section 1(3) of the Guardianship Act 1973.

(6) Where, in proceedings for an offence under this section, there is sufficient evidence to raise an issue as to the application of subsection (5) above, it shall be for the prosecution to prove that that subsection does not apply.

(7) In this section—

(a) " guardian " means a person appointed by deed or will or by order of a court of competent jurisdiction to be the guardian of a child ; and

(b) a reference to a custody order or an order awarding custody includes a reference to an order awarding legal custody and a reference to an order awarding care and control.

(8) This section shall have effect subject to the provisions of the Schedule to this Act in relation to a child who is in the care of a local authority or voluntary organisation or who is committed to a place of safety or who is the subject of custodianship proceedings or proceedings or an order relating to adoption.

Offence of abduction of child by other persons.

2.—(1) Subject to subsection (2) below, a person not falling within section 1(2)(a) or (b) above commits an offence if, without lawful authority or reasonable excuse, he takes or detains a child under the age of sixteen—

(a) so as to remove him from the lawful control of any person having lawful control of the child ; or

(b) so as to keep him out of the lawful control of any person entitled to lawful control of the child.

(2) In proceedings against any person for an offence under this section, it shall be a defence for that person to show that at the time of the alleged offence—

(a) he believed that the child had attained the age of sixteen ; or

(b) in the case of an illegitimate child, he had reasonable grounds for believing himself to be the child's father.

Construction of references to taking, sending and detaining.

3. For the purposes of this Part of this Act—

(a) a person shall be regarded as taking a child if he causes or induces the child to accompany him or any other person or causes the child to be taken ;

(b) a person shall be regarded as sending a child if he causes the child to be sent ; and

(c) a person shall be regarded as detaining a child if he causes the child to be detained or induces the child to remain with him or any other person.

Penalties and prosecutions.

4.—(1) A person guilty of an offence under this Part of this Act shall be liable—

(a) on summary conviction, to imprisonment for a term not exceeding six months or to a fine not exceeding the statutory maximum, as defined in section 74 of the Criminal Justice Act 1982, or to both such imprisonment and fine ;

1982 c. 48.

(b) on conviction on indictment, to imprisonment for a term not exceeding seven years.

(2) No prosecution for an offence under section 1 above shall be instituted except by or with the consent of the Director of Public Prosecutions.

5. Except by or with the consent of the Director of Public Prosecutions no prosecution shall be instituted for an offence of kidnapping if it was committed—

(a) against a child under the age of sixteen ; and

(b) by a person connected with the child, within the meaning of section 1 above.

PART II

OFFENCE UNDER LAW OF SCOTLAND

6.—(1) Subject to subsections (4) and (5) below, a person connected with a child under the age of sixteen years commits an offence if he takes or sends the child out of the United Kingdom—

(a) without the appropriate consent if there is in respect of the child—

    (i) an order of a court in the United Kingdom awarding custody of the child to any person ; or

    (ii) an order of a court in England, Wales or Northern Ireland making the child a ward of court ;

(b) if there is in respect of the child an order of a court in the United Kingdom prohibiting the removal of the child from the United Kingdom or any part of it.

(2) A person is connected with a child for the purposes of this section if—

(a) he is a parent or guardian of the child ; or

(b) there is in force an order of a court in the United Kingdom awarding custody of the child to him (whether solely or jointly with any other person) ; or

(c) in the case of an illegitimate child, there are reasonable grounds for believing that he is the father of the child.

(3) In this section, the " appropriate consent " means—

(a) in relation to a child to whom subsection (1)(a)(i) above applies—

    (i) the consent of each person

        (a) who is a parent or guardian of the child ; or

        (b) to whom custody of the child has been awarded (whether solely or jointly with any other person) by an order of a court in the United Kingdom ; or

    (ii) the leave of that court ;

PART II

    (*b*) in relation to a child to whom subsection (1)(*a*)(ii) above applies, the leave of the court which made the child a ward of court;

Provided that, in relation to a child to whom more than one order referred to in subsection (1)(*a*) above applies, the appropriate consent may be that of any court which has granted an order as referred to in the said subsection (1)(*a*); and where one of these orders is an order referred to in the said subsection (1)(*a*)(ii) no other person as referred to in paragraph (*a*)(i) above shall be entitled to give the appropriate consent.

(4) In relation to a child to whom subsection (1)(*a*)(i) above applies, a person does not commit an offence by doing anything without the appropriate consent if—

    (*a*) he does it in the belief that each person referred to in subsection (3)(*a*)(i) above—

        (i) has consented; or

        (ii) would consent if he was aware of all the relevant circumstances; or

    (*b*) he has taken all reasonable steps to communicate with such other person but has been unable to communicate with him.

(5) In proceedings against any person for an offence under this section it shall be a defence for that person to show that at the time of the alleged offence he had no reason to believe that there was in existence an order referred to in subsection (1) above.

(6) For the purposes of this section—

    (*a*) a person shall be regarded as taking a child if he causes or induces the child to accompany him or any other person, or causes the child to be taken; and

    (*b*) a person shall be regarded as sending a child if he causes the child to be sent.

(7) In this section " guardian " means a person appointed by deed or will or by order of a court of competent jurisdiction to be the guardian of a child.

Power of arrest.

    7. A constable may arrest without warrant any person whom he reasonably suspects of committing or having committed an offence under this Part of this Act.

Penalties and prosecutions.

    8. A person guilty of an offence under this Part of this Act shall be liable—

    (*a*) on summary conviction, to imprisonment for a term not exceeding three months or to a fine not exceeding

the statutory maximum as defined in section 74(2) of
the Criminal Justice Act 1982, or both ; or

(b) on conviction on indictment, to imprisonment for a
term not exceeding two years or to a fine, or both.

PART II
1982 c. 48.

9.—(1) For the purposes of this Part of this Act, a document
duly authenticated which purports to be—

(a) an order or other document issued by a court of the
United Kingdom (other than a Scottish court) shall be
sufficient evidence of any matter to which it relates ;

(b) a copy of such an order or other document shall be
deemed without further proof to be a true copy unless
the contrary is shown, and shall be sufficient evidence
of any matter to which it relates.

(2) A document is duly authenticated for the purposes of—

(a) subsection (1)(a) above if it purports to bear the seal
of that court ;

(b) subsection (1)(b) above if it purports to be certified by
any person in his capacity as a judge, magistrate or
officer of that court to be a true copy.

Proof and
admissibility
of certain
documents.

10. In any proceedings in relation to an offence under this
Part of this Act it shall be presumed, unless the contrary is
shown, that the child named in the order referred to in section
6(1) above, or in any copy thereof, is the child in relation to whom
the proceedings have been taken.

Evidence.

PART III

SUPPLEMENTARY

11.—(1) At the end of paragraph 1(b) of the Schedule to the
Visiting Forces Act 1952 (definition of " offence against the
person "), there shall be inserted, appropriately numbered—

" ( ) the Child Abduction Act 1984.".

(2) After paragraph 2 of Schedule 1 to the Firearms Act
1968 there shall be inserted—

" 2A. Offences under Part I of the Child Abduction Act
1984 (abduction of children).".

Consequential
amendments
and repeals.
1952 c. 67.

1968 c. 27.

PART III
1978 c. 17.

(3) The reference to abduction in section 1(1) of the Internationally Protected Persons Act 1978 shall be construed as not including an offence under section 1 above or any corresponding provision in force in Northern Ireland or Part II of this Act.

1978 c. 26.

(4) In section 4(1)(a) of the Suppression of Terrorism Act 1978, after " 11,", there shall be inserted " 11B," ; and in Schedule 1 to that Act, after paragraph 11A, there shall be inserted—

> " 11B. An offence under section 2 of the Child Abduction Act 1984 (abduction of child by person other than parent etc.) or any corresponding provision in force in Northern Ireland.".

(5) The following provisions are hereby repealed—

1861 c. 100.

(a) section 56 of the Offences against the Person Act 1861 ;

1870 c. 52.

(b) in Schedule 1 to the Extradition Act 1870, the words " Child stealing " ;

1968 c. 27.

(c) in paragraph 2 of Schedule 1 to the Firearms Act 1968, the words " section 56 (child-stealing and abduction) ".

Enactment of corresponding provision for Northern Ireland.
1974 c. 28.

12. An Order in Council under paragraph 1(1)(b) of Schedule 1 to the Northern Ireland Act 1974 (legislation for Northern Ireland in the interim period) which contains a statement that it operates only so as to make for Northern Ireland provision corresponding to Part I of this Act—

(a) shall not be subject to paragraph 1(4) and (5) of that Schedule (affirmative resolution of both Houses of Parliament) ; but

(b) shall be subject to annulment in pursuance of a resolution of either House.

Short title, commencement and extent.

13.—(1) This Act may be cited as the Child Abduction Act 1984.

(2) This Act shall come into force at the end of the period of three months beginning with the day on which it is passed.

(3) Part I of this Act extends to England and Wales only, Part II extends to Scotland only and in Part III section 11(1) and (5)(a) and section 12 do not extend to Scotland and section 11(1), (2) and (5)(a) and (c) does not extend to Northern Ireland.

SCHEDULE

MODIFICATIONS OF SECTION 1 FOR CHILDREN IN CERTAIN CASES

Children in care of local authorities and voluntary organisations

1.—(1) This paragraph applies in the case of a child who is in the care of a local authority or voluntary organisation in England or Wales.

(2) Where this paragraph applies, section 1 of this Act shall have effect as if—

  (*a*) the reference in subsection (1) to the appropriate consent were a reference to the consent of the local authority or voluntary organisation in whose care the child is ; and

  (*b*) subsections (3) to (6) were omitted.

Children in places of safety

2.—(1) This paragraph applies in the case of a child who is committed to a place of safety in England or Wales in pursuance of—

  (*a*) section 40 of the Children and Young Persons Act 1933 ; or 1933 c. 12.

  (*b*) section 43 of the Adoption Act 1958 ; or 1958 c. 5 (7 & 8 Eliz. 2).

  (*c*) section 2(5) or (10), 16(3) or 28(1) or (4) of the Children and Young Persons Act 1969 ; or 1969 c. 54.

  (*d*) section 12 of the Foster Children Act 1980. 1980 c. 6.

(2) Where this paragraph applies, section 1 of this Act shall have effect as if—

  (*a*) the reference in subsection (1) to the appropriate consent were a reference to the leave of any magistrates' court acting for the area in which the place of safety is ; and

  (*b*) subsections (3) to (6) were omitted.

Adoption and custodianship

3.—(1) This paragraph applies in the case of a child—

  (*a*) who is the subject of an order under section 14 of the Children Act 1975 freeing him for adoption ; or 1975 c. 72.

  (*b*) who is the subject of a pending application for such an order ; or

  (*c*) who is the subject of a pending application for an adoption order ; or

  (*d*) who is the subject of an order under section 25 of the Children Act 1975 or section 53 of the Adoption Act 1958 relating to adoption abroad or of a pending application for such an order ; or

  (*e*) who is the subject of a pending application for a custodianship order.

(2) Where this paragraph applies, section 1 of this Act shall have effect as if—

(*a*) the reference in subsection (1) to the appropriate consent were a reference—

(i) in a case within sub-paragraph (1)(*a*) above, to the consent of the adoption agency which made the application for the order or, if the parental rights and duties in respect of the child have been transferred from that agency to another agency by an order under section 23 of the Children Act 1975, to the consent of that other agency ;

1975 c. 72

(ii) in a case within sub-paragraph (1)(*b*), (*c*) or (*e*) above, to the leave of the court to which the application was made ; and

(iii) in a case within sub-paragraph (1)(*d*) above, to the leave of the court which made the order or, as the case may be, to which the application was made ; and

(*b*) subsections (3) to (6) were omitted.

Cases within paragraphs 1 and 3

4. In the case of a child falling within both paragraph 1 and paragraph 3 above, the provisions of paragraph 3 shall apply to the exclusion of those in paragraph 1.

Interpretation

5.—(1) In this Schedule—

(*a*) subject to sub-paragraph (2) below, " adoption agency " has the same meaning as in section 1 of the Children Act 1975 ;

(*b*) " adoption order " means an order under section 8(1) of that Act ;

(*c*) " custodianship order " has the same meaning as in Part II of that Act ; and

1980 c. 5.

(*d*) " local authority " and " voluntary organisation " have the same meanings as in section 87 of the Child Care Act 1980.

(2) Until the coming into force of section 1 of the Children Act 1975, for the words " adoption agency " in this Schedule there shall be substituted " approved adoption society or local authority " ; and in this Schedule " approved adoption society " means an adoption society approved under Part I of that Act.

(3) In paragraph 3(1) above references to an order or to an application for an order are references to an order made by, or to an application to, a court in England or Wales.

(4) Paragraph 3(2) above shall be construed as if the references to the court included, in any case where the court is a magistrates' court, a reference to any magistrates' court acting for the same petty sessions area as that court.

Cycle Tracks Act 1984

1984 CHAPTER 38

An Act to amend the definition of " cycle track " in the Highways Act 1980 and to make further provision in relation to cycle tracks within the meaning of that Act. [12th July 1984]

BE IT ENACTED by the Queen's most Excellent Majesty, by and with the advice and consent of the Lords Spiritual and Temporal, and Commons, in this present Parliament assembled, and by the authority of the same, as follows:—

1.—(1) In section 329(1) of the Highways Act 1980 (referred to in this Act as " the 1980 Act "), in the definition of " cycle track " (which defines a cycle track as a way over which the public have a right of way on pedal cycles with or without a right of way on foot) after " pedal cycles " there shall be inserted " (other than pedal cycles which are motor vehicles within the meaning of the Road Traffic Act 1972) ". *Amendment of definition of " cycle track ". 1980 c. 66. 1972 c. 20.*

(2) Any way to which the said definition applied immediately before the commencement of subsection (1) above shall, as from that commencement, continue to be a cycle track within the meaning of the 1980 Act, but the public's right of way on pedal cycles over that way shall in accordance with that subsection no longer include a right to use pedal cycles which are motor vehicles.

2.—(1) Subject to the provisions of this section, any person who, without lawful authority, drives or parks a motor vehicle wholly or partly on a cycle track shall be guilty of an offence and liable, on summary conviction, to a fine not exceeding the third level on the standard scale (within the meaning of section 37 of the Criminal Justice Act 1982). *Prohibition of driving or parking on cycle tracks. 1982 c. 48.*

(2) A person shall not be convicted of an offence under subsection (1) above with respect to a vehicle if he proves to the satisfaction of the court—

(a) that the vehicle was driven or (as the case may be) parked in contravention of that subsection for the purpose of saving life, or extinguishing fire or meeting any other like emergency ; or

(b) that the vehicle was owned or operated by a highway authority or by a person discharging functions on behalf of a highway authority and was driven or (as the case may be) parked in contravention of that subsection in connection with the carrying out by or on behalf of that authority of any of the following, namely the cleansing, maintenance or improvement of the cycle track or its verges, or the maintenance or alteration of any structure or other work situated therein ; or

(c) that the vehicle was owned or operated by statutory undertakers and was driven or (as the case may be) parked in contravention of that subsection in connection with the carrying out by those undertakers of any works in relation to any apparatus belonging to or used by them for the purpose of their undertaking.

(3) In subsection (2)(c) above " statutory undertakers " means any body who are statutory undertakers within the meaning of the 1980 Act, any sewerage authority within the meaning of that Act or the operator of a telecommunications code system (as defined by paragraph 1(1) of Schedule 4 to the Telecommunications Act 1984), and in relation to any such sewerage authority " apparatus " includes sewers or sewerage disposal works.

1984 c. 12.

Conversion of footpaths into cycle tracks.

3.—(1) A local highway authority may in the case of any footpath for which they are the highway authority by order made by them and either—

(a) submitted to and confirmed by the Secretary of State, or

(b) confirmed by them as an unopposed order,

designate the footpath or any part of it as a cycle track, with the effect that, on such date as the order takes effect in accordance with the following provisions of this section, the footpath or part of the footpath to which the order relates shall become a highway which for the purposes of the 1980 Act is a highway maintainable at the public expense and over which the public have a right of way on pedal cycles (other than pedal cycles which are motor vehicles) and a right of way on foot.

(2) A local highway authority shall not make an order under this section designating as a cycle track any footpath or part

of a footpath which crosses any agricultural land unless every person having a legal interest in that land has consented in writing to the making of the order.

In this subsection " agricultural land " has the meaning given by section 1(2) of the Agricultural Holdings Act 1948 ; and 1948 c. 63 " legal interest " does not include an interest under a letting of land having effect as a letting for an interest less than a tenancy from year to year.

(3) An order made under this section by a local highway authority—

> (*a*) may be confirmed by the Secretary of State either in the form in which it was made or subject to such modifications as he thinks fit ;

> (*b*) may be confirmed by the authority as an unopposed order only in the form in which it was made.

(4) The Secretary of State may by regulations make provision with respect to the procedure to be followed in connection with the making, submission and confirmation of orders under this section ; and the Secretary of State shall by regulations under this subsection make such provision as he considers appropriate with respect to—

> (*a*) the publication of notice of the making of an order under this section and of its effect ;

> (*b*) the making and consideration of objections to any such order ; and

> (*c*) the publication of notice of the confirmation of any such order by the Secretary of State or by a local highway authority, and of the effect of the order as confirmed.

(5) Without prejudice to the generality of subsection (4) above, regulations under that subsection may in particular make provision—

> (*a*) for enabling the Secretary of State to cause a local inquiry to be held in connection with any order under this section submitted to him for confirmation ;

> (*b*) for the decision as to whether any such order should be confirmed, and, if so, as to the modifications (if any) subject to which it should be confirmed, to be made by a person appointed by the Secretary of State for the purpose instead of by the Secretary of State ;

> (*c*) for any decision made by any such person in pursuance of paragraph (*b*) above to be treated, for the purposes of any provision of the regulations or this section, as a decision of the Secretary of State ;

1972 c. 70. and subsections (2) to (5) of section 250 of the Local Government Act 1972 (giving of evidence at, and defraying of costs of, local inquiries) shall apply in relation to any local inquiry held in pursuance of paragraph (*a*) above as they apply in relation to a local inquiry which a Minister causes to be held under subsection (1) of that section.

(6) If a person aggrieved by an order under this section desires to question its validity on the ground that it is not within the powers of this section or on the ground that any requirement of regulations made under subsection (4) above has not been complied with in relation to the order, he may, within six weeks from the date on which any such notice as is mentioned in subsection (4)(*c*) above is first published, make an application for the purpose to the High Court.

(7) On any such application, the High Court—

    (*a*) may by interim order suspend the operation of the order, either wholly or to such extent as it thinks fit, until the final determination of the proceedings ; and

    (*b*) if satisfied that the order is not within the powers of this section or that the interests of the applicant have been substantially prejudiced by a failure to comply with any such requirement as aforesaid, may quash the order, either wholly or to such extent as it thinks fit.

(8) Subject to subsection (7) above, an order under this section shall not, either before or after it has been confirmed, be questioned in any legal proceedings whatever, and shall take effect on the date on which any such notice as is mentioned in subsection (4)(*c*) above is first published, or on such later date, if any, as may be specified in the order.

(9) A local highway authority may (subject to and in accordance with the provisions of subsections (3) to (8) above) by order made by them and either—

    (*a*) submitted to and confirmed by the Secretary of State, or

    (*b*) confirmed by them as an unopposed order,

revoke an order made by them under this section with the effect that, on such date as the order takes effect in accordance with those provisions, the way designated by the original order as a cycle track shall revert to being a footpath or a part of a footpath (as the case may be) and, as such, it shall only be maintainable at the public expense for the purposes of the 1980 Act if, prior to the original order taking effect, it constituted a highway so maintainable or, on the order under this subsection taking effect, it forms part of a highway so maintainable.

(10) A local highway authority shall have power to carry out any works necessary for giving effect to an order under this section ; and in so far as the carrying out of any such works, or any change in the use of land resulting from any such order, constitutes development within the meaning of the Town and Country Planning Act 1971, permission for that development shall be deemed to be granted under Part III of that Act.

1971 c. 78.

(11) The power to make regulations under subsection (4) above shall be exercisable by statutory instrument, which shall be subject to annulment in pursuance of a resolution of either House of Parliament.

4.—(1) A highway authority may provide and maintain in any cycle track such barriers as they think necessary for the purpose of safeguarding persons using the cycle track.

Provision of barriers in cycle tracks, etc.

(2) A highway authority may, in the case of any cycle track which is adjacent to a footpath or footway, provide and maintain such works as they think necessary for the purpose of separating, in the interests of safety, persons using the cycle track from those using the footpath or footway.

(3) A highway authority may alter or remove any works provided by them under subsection (1) or (2) above.

(4) Any reference in this section to a cycle track is a reference to a cycle track constituting or comprised in a highway maintainable at the public expense, and any reference to a footpath or a footway is a reference to a footpath constituting or a footway comprised in such a highway.

5.—(1) Where any person suffers damage by reason of the execution by a highway authority of any works under section 3(10) or 4 above, he shall be entitled to recover compensation in respect of that damage from that authority.

Compensation.

(2) Where in consequence of the coming into operation of an order under section 3 above any person suffers damage by the depreciation in value of any interest in land to which he is entitled, he shall be entitled to recover compensation in respect of that damage from the local highway authority which made the order ; but a person shall not be entitled to recover any compensation under this subsection in respect of any depreciation—

    (a) in respect of which compensation is recoverable by him under subsection (1) above ; or

    (b) which is attributable to the prospect of the execution of any such works as are referred to in that subsection.

(3) Subsections (1) to (3) of section 307 of the 1980 Act (disputes as to compensation to be referred to Lands Tribunal) shall apply in relation to any dispute arising on a claim for compensation under subsection (1) or (2) above as they apply in relation to any dispute arising as mentioned in subsection (1) of that section.

Application to Crown land.

6.—(1) In the case of any Crown land the appropriate authority and a highway authority may agree that any provisions of sections 3 and 4 above specified in the agreement shall apply to that land and, while the agreement is in force, those provisions shall apply to that land accordingly (subject, however, to the terms of the agreement).

(2) Any such agreement as is referred to in subsection (1) above may contain such consequential and incidental provisions, including provisions of a financial character, as appear to the appropriate authority to be necessary or equitable ; but provisions of a financial character shall not be included in an agreement made by a government department without the approval of the Treasury.

(3) In this section " Crown land " means land belonging to Her Majesty in right of the Crown or of the Duchy of Lancaster, or belonging to the Duchy of Cornwall, or belonging to a government department or held in trust for Her Majesty for the purposes of a government department, and " the appropriate authority " means—

(a) in the case of land belonging to Her Majesty in right of the Crown, the Crown Estate Commissioners or other government department having the management of the land in question ;

(b) in the case of land belonging to Her Majesty in right of the Duchy of Lancaster, the Chancellor of that Duchy ;

(c) in the case of land belonging to the Duchy of Cornwall, such person as the Duke of Cornwall, or the possessor for the time being of the Duchy of Cornwall, appoints ;

(d) in the case of land belonging to a government department or held in trust for Her Majesty for the purposes of a government department, that department.

(4) If any question arises as to what authority is the appropriate authority in relation to any Crown land that question shall be referred to the Treasury, whose decision shall be final.

Expenses.

7. There shall be paid out of money provided by Parliament—

(a) any expenses incurred by the Secretary of State under this Act ; and

(b) any increase attributable to this Act in the sums payable out of such money under any other Act.

8.—(1) In this Act—

    " the 1980 Act " means the Highways Act 1980 ; and

    " motor vehicle " means a motor vehicle within the meaning of the Road Traffic Act 1972.

(2) Except where the context otherwise requires, any expression used in this Act which is also used in the 1980 Act has the same meaning as in that Act.

9.—(1) This Act may be cited as the Cycle Tracks Act 1984.

(2) This Act shall come into force at the end of the period of two months beginning with the day on which it is passed.

(3) This Act extends to England and Wales only.

Interpretation.

1980 c. 66.

1972 c. 20.

Short title, commencement and extent.

Video Recordings Act 1984

1984 CHAPTER 39

An Act to make provision for regulating the distribution
of video recordings and for connected purposes.

[12th July 1984]

BE IT ENACTED by the Queen's most Excellent Majesty, by and
with the advice and consent of the Lords Spiritual and
Temporal, and Commons, in this present Parliament
assembled, and by the authority of the same, as follows:—

Preliminary

1.—(1) The provisions of this section shall have effect for the interpretation of terms used in this Act.

Interpretation of terms.

(2) " Video work " means any series of visual images (with or without sound)—

   (a) produced electronically by the use of information contained on any disc or magnetic tape, and

   (b) shown as a moving picture.

(3) " Video recording " means any disc or magnetic tape containing information by the use of which the whole or a part of a video work may be produced.

(4) " Supply " means supply in any manner, whether or not for reward, and, therefore, includes supply by way of sale, letting on hire, exchange or loan; and references to a supply are to be interpreted accordingly.

2.—(1) Subject to subsection (2) below, a video work is for the purposes of this Act an exempted work if, taken as a whole—

(*a*) it is designed to inform, educate or instruct ;

(*b*) it is concerned with sport, religion or music ; or

(*c*) it is a video game.

(2) A video work is not an exempted work for those purposes if, to any significant extent, it depicts—

(*a*) human sexual activity or acts of force or restraint associated with such activity ;

(*b*) mutilation or torture of, or other acts of gross violence towards, humans or animals ;

(*c*) human genital organs or human urinary or excretory functions ;

or is designed to any significant extent to stimulate or encourage anything falling within paragraph (*a*) or, in the case of anything falling within paragraph (*b*), is designed to any extent to do so.

3.—(1) The provisions of this section apply to determine whether or not a supply of a video recording is an exempted supply for the purposes of this Act.

(2) The supply of a video recording by any person is an exempted supply if it is neither—

(*a*) a supply for reward, nor

(*b*) a supply in the course or furtherance of a business.

(3) Where on any premises facilities are provided in the course or furtherance of a business for supplying video recordings, the supply by any person of a video recording on those premises is to be treated for the purposes of subsection (2) above as a supply in the course or furtherance of a business.

(4) Where a person (in this subsection referred to as the " original supplier ") supplies a video recording to a person who, in the course of a business, makes video works or supplies video recordings, the supply is an exempted supply—

(*a*) if it is not made with a view to any further supply of that recording, or

(*b*) if it is so made, but is not made with a view to the eventual supply of that recording to the public or is made with a view to the eventual supply of that recording to the original supplier.

For the purposes of this subsection, any supply is a supply to the public unless it is—

(i) a supply to a person who, in the course of a business, makes video works or supplies video recordings,

(ii) an exempted supply by virtue of subsection (2) above or subsections (5) to (10) below, or

(iii) a supply outside the United Kingdom.

(5) Where a video work—

(a) is designed to provide a record of an event or occasion for those who took part in the event or occasion or are connected with those who did so,

(b) does not, to any significant extent, depict anything falling within paragraph (a), (b) or (c) of section 2(2) of this Act, and

(c) is not designed to any significant extent to stimulate or encourage anything falling within paragraph (a) of that subsection or, in the case of anything falling within paragraph (b) of that subsection, is not designed to any extent to do so,

the supply of a video recording containing only that work to a person who took part in the event or occasion or is connected with someone who did so is an exempted supply.

(6) The supply of a video recording for the purpose only of the exhibition of any video work contained in the recording in premises other than a dwelling-house—

(a) being premises mentioned in subsection (7) below, or

(b) being an exhibition which in England and Wales or Scotland would be an exempted exhibition within the meaning of section 5 of the Cinematograph Act 1952 1952 c. 68. (cinematograph exhibition to which public not admitted or are admitted without payment), or in Northern Ireland would be an exempted exhibition within the meaning of section 5 of the Cinematograph Act (Northern 1959 c. 20 Ireland) 1959 (similar provision for Northern Ireland), (N.I.).

is an exempted supply.

(7) The premises referred to in subsection (6) above are—

(a) premises in respect of which a licence under section 2 of the Cinematograph Act 1909 is in force, 1909 c. 30.

(b) premises falling within section 7(2) of that Act (premises used only occasionally and exceptionally for cinematograph exhibitions), or

(c) premises falling within section 7(3) of that Act (building or structure of a movable character) in respect of which such a licence as is mentioned in paragraph (*a*) of that subsection has been granted.

(8) The supply of a video recording with a view only to its use for or in connection with—

    (*a*) broadcasting services provided by the British Broadcasting Corporation or the Independent Broadcasting Authority, or

1984 c. 12.

    (*b*) a service authorised by a licence granted or having effect as if granted under section 58 of the Telecommunications Act 1984 (power to license cable programme services) or, until the coming into force of that section, a system licensed under section 89 of the

1969 c. 48.

Post Office Act 1969 (licensing of programme distribution systems),

is an exempted supply.

(9) The supply of a video recording for the purpose only of submitting a video work contained in the recording for the issue of a classification certificate or otherwise only for purposes of arrangements made by the designated authority is an exempted supply.

(10) The supply of a video recording with a view only to its use—

    (*a*) in training for or carrying on any medical or related occupation,

    (*b*) for the purpose of—

1977 c. 49.
1978 c. 29.

        (i) services provided in pursuance of the National Health Service Act 1977 or the National Health Service (Scotland) Act 1978, or

S.I. 1972/1265
(N.I. 14).

        (ii) such of the services provided in pursuance of the Health and Personal Social Services (Northern Ireland) Order 1972 as are health services (within the meaning of that Order), or

    (*c*) in training persons employed in the course of services falling within paragraph (*b*) above,

is an exempted supply.

(11) For the purposes of subsection (10) above, an occupation is a medical or related occupation if, to carry on the occupation,

1960 c. 66.
1979 c. 36.
1983 c. 54.

a person is required to be registered under the Professions Supplementary to Medicine Act 1960, the Nurses, Midwives and Health Visitors Act 1979 or the Medical Act 1983.

(12) The supply of a video recording otherwise than for reward, being a supply made for the purpose only of supplying it to a person who previously made an exempted supply of the recording, is also an exempted supply.

Designated authority

4.—(1) The Secretary of State may by notice under this section designate any person as the authority responsible for making arrangements—

(a) for determining for the purposes of this Act whether or not video works are suitable for classification certificates to be issued in respect of them, having special regard to the likelihood of video works in respect of which such certificates have been issued being viewed in the home,

(b) in the case of works which are determined in accordance with the arrangements to be so suitable—

    (i) for making such other determinations as are required for the issue of classification certificates, and

    (ii) for issuing such certificates, and

(c) for maintaining a record of such determinations (whether determinations made in pursuance of arrangements made by that person or by any person previously designated under this section), including video recordings of the video works to which the determinations relate.

Authority to determine suitability of video works for classification.

(2) The power to designate any person by notice under this section includes power—

(a) to designate two or more persons jointly as the authority responsible for making those arrangements, and

(b) to provide that any person holding an office or employment specified in the notice is to be treated as designated while holding that office or employment.

(3) The Secretary of State shall not make any designation under this section unless he is satisfied that adequate arrangements will be made for an appeal by any person against a determination that a video work submitted by him for the issue of a classification certificate—

(a) is not suitable for a classification certificate to be issued in respect of it, or

(b) is not suitable for viewing by persons who have not attained a particular age,

or against a determination that no video recording containing the work is to be supplied other than in a licensed sex shop.

(4) The Secretary of State may at any time designate another person in place of any person designated under this section and, if he does so, may give directions as to the transfer of any record kept in pursuance of the arrangements referred to in

M 2

subsection (1) above; and it shall be the duty of any person having control of any such record or any part of it to comply with the directions.

(5) No fee shall be recoverable by the designated authority in connection with any determination falling within subsection (1)(a) or (b) above or the issue of any classification certificate unless the fee is payable in accordance with a tariff approved by the Secretary of State.

(6) The Secretary of State may for the purposes of subsection (5) above approve a tariff providing for different fees for different classes of video works and for different circumstances.

(7) Any notice under this section shall be published in the London, Edinburgh and Belfast Gazettes.

(8) In this Act, references to the designated authority, in relation to any transaction, are references to the person or persons designated under this section at the time of that transaction.

Parliamentary procedure for designation.

5.—(1) Where the Secretary of State proposes to make a designation under section 4 of this Act, he shall lay particulars of his proposal before both Houses of Parliament and shall not make the proposed designation until after the end of the period of forty days beginning with the day on which the particulars of his proposal were so laid.

(2) If, within the period mentioned in subsection (1) above, either House resolves that the Secretary of State should not make the proposed designation, the Secretary of State shall not do so (but without prejudice to his power to lay before Parliament particulars of further proposals in accordance with that subsection).

(3) For the purposes of subsection (1) above—

(a) where particulars of a proposal are laid before each House of Parliament on different days, the later day shall be taken to be the day on which the particulars were laid before both Houses;

(b) in reckoning any period of forty days, no account shall be taken of any time during which Parliament is dissolved or prorogued or during which both Houses are adjourned for more than four days.

Annual report.

6.—(1) The designated authority shall, as soon as it is reasonably practicable to do so after 31st December, make a report to the Secretary of State on the carrying out in the year ending with that date of the arrangements referred to in section 4(1) and

(3) of this Act (together with a statement of accounts) and on such other matters (if any) as the designated authority consider appropriate or the Secretary of State may require.

(2) The Secretary of State shall lay a copy of any report made to him under this section before each House of Parliament.

Classification and labelling

7.—(1) In this Act " classification certificate " means a certificate— Classification certificates.

   (*a*) issued in respect of a video work in pursuance of arrangements made by the designated authority ; and

   (*b*) satisfying the requirements of subsection (2) below.

(2) Those requirements are that the certificate must contain—

   (*a*) a statement that the video work concerned is suitable for general viewing and unrestricted supply (with or without any advice as to the desirability of parental guidance with regard to the viewing of the work by young children or as to the particular suitability of the work for viewing by children) ; or

   (*b*) a statement that the video work concerned is suitable for viewing only by persons who have attained the age (not being more than eighteen years) specified in the certificate and that no video recording containing that work is to be supplied to any person who has not attained the age so specified ; or

   (*c*) the statement mentioned in paragraph (*b*) above together with a statement that no video recording containing that work is to be supplied other than in a licensed sex shop.

8.—(1) The Secretary of State may, in relation to video works Requirements in respect of which classification certificates have been issued, by as to labelling, regulations require such indication as may be specified by the etc. regulations of any of the contents of any classification certificate to be shown in such a manner as may be so specified on any video recording containing the video work in respect of which the certificate was issued or any spool, case or other thing on or in which such a video recording is kept.

(2) Regulations under this section may make different provision for different video works and for different circumstances.

(3) The power to make regulations under this section shall be exercisable by statutory instrument which shall be subject to annulment in pursuance of a resolution of either House of Parliament.

M 3

Offences and penalties

Supplying
video
recording of
unclassified
work.

9.—(1) A person who supplies or offers to supply a video recording containing a video work in respect of which no classification certificate has been issued is guilty of an offence unless—

> (a) the supply is, or would if it took place be, an exempted supply, or
>
> (b) the video work is an exempted work.

(2) It is a defence to a charge of committing an offence under this section to prove that the accused believed on reasonable grounds—

> (a) that the video work concerned or, if the video recording contained more than one work to which the charge relates, each of those works was either an exempted work or a work in respect of which a classification certificate had been issued, or
>
> (b) that the supply was, or would if it took place be, an exempted supply by virtue of section 3(4) or (5) of this Act.

Possession of
video
recording of
unclassified
work for the
purposes of
supply.

10.—(1) Where a video recording contains a video work in respect of which no classification certificate has been issued, a person who has the recording in his possession for the purpose of supplying it is guilty of an offence unless—

> (a) he has it in his possession for the purpose only of a supply which, if it took place, would be an exempted supply, or
>
> (b) the video work is an exempted work.

(2) It is a defence to a charge of committing an offence under this section to prove—

> (a) that the accused believed on reasonable grounds that the video work concerned or, if the video recording contained more than one work to which the charge relates, each of those works was either an exempted work or a work in respect of which a classification certificate had been issued,
>
> (b) that the accused had the video recording in his possession for the purpose only of a supply which he believed on reasonable grounds would, if it took place, be an exempted supply by virtue of section 3(4) or (5) of this Act, or
>
> (c) that the accused did not intend to supply the video recording until a classification certificate had been issued in respect of the video work concerned.

11.—(1) Where a classification certificate issued in respect of a video work states that no video recording containing that work is to be supplied to any person who has not attained the age specified in the certificate, a person who supplies or offers to supply a video recording containing that work to a person who has not attained the age so specified is guilty of an offence unless the supply is, or would if it took place be, an exempted supply. Supplying video recording of classified work in breach of classification.

(2) It is a defence to a charge of committing an offence under this section to prove—

    (*a*) that the accused neither knew nor had reasonable grounds to believe that the classification certificate contained the statement concerned,

    (*b*) that the accused neither knew nor had reasonable grounds to believe that the person concerned had not attained that age, or

    (*c*) that the accused believed on reasonable grounds that the supply was, or would if it took place be, an exempted supply by virtue of section 3(4) or (5) of this Act.

12.—(1) Where a classification certificate issued in respect of a video work states that no video recording containing that work is to be supplied other than in a licensed sex shop, a person who at any place other than in a sex shop for which a licence is in force under the relevant enactment— Certain video recordings only to be supplied in licensed sex shops.

    (*a*) supplies a video recording containing the work, or

    (*b*) offers to do so,

is guilty of an offence unless the supply is, or would if it took place be, an exempted supply.

(2) It is a defence to a charge of committing an offence under subsection (1) above to prove—

    (*a*) that the accused neither knew nor had reasonable grounds to believe that the classification certificate contained the statement concerned,

    (*b*) that the accused believed on reasonable grounds that the place concerned was a sex shop for which a licence was in force under the relevant enactment, or

    (*c*) that the accused believed on reasonable grounds that the supply was, or would if it took place be, an exempted supply by virtue of section 3(4) of this Act or subsection (6) below.

(3) Where a classification certificate issued in respect of a video work states that no video recording containing that work is to be supplied other than in a licensed sex shop, a person who

M 4

has a video recording containing the work in his possession for the purpose of supplying it at any place other than in such a sex shop is guilty of an offence, unless he has it in his possession for the purpose only of a supply which, if it took place, would be an exempted supply.

(4) It is a defence to a charge of committing an offence under subsection (3) above to prove—

(*a*) that the accused neither knew nor had reasonable grounds to believe that the classification certificate contained the statement concerned,

(*b*) that the accused believed on reasonable grounds that the place concerned was a sex shop for which a licence was in force under the relevant enactment, or

(*c*) that the accused had the video recording in his possession for the purpose only of a supply which he believed on reasonable grounds would, if it took place, be an exempted supply by virtue of section 3(4) of this Act or subsection (6) below.

1982 c. 30.
1982 c. 45.
(5) In this section " relevant enactment " means Schedule 3 to the Local Government (Miscellaneous Provisions) Act 1982 or, in Scotland, Schedule 2 to the Civic Government (Scotland) Act 1982, and " sex shop " has the same meaning as in the relevant enactment.

(6) For the purposes of this section, where a classification certificate issued in respect of a video work states that no video recording containing that work is to be supplied other than in a licensed sex shop, the supply of a video recording containing that work—

(*a*) to a person who, in the course of a business, makes video works or supplies video recordings, and

(*b*) with a view to its eventual supply in sex shops, being sex shops for which licences are in force under the relevant enactment,

is an exempted supply.

Supply of
video
recording not
complying
with
requirements
as to labels,
etc.
13.—(1) A person who supplies or offers to supply a video recording or any spool, case or other thing on or in which the recording is kept which does not satisfy any requirement imposed by regulations under section 8 of this Act is guilty of an offence unless the supply is, or would if it took place be, an exempted supply.

(2) It is a defence to a charge of committing an offence under this section to prove that the accused—

(*a*) believed on reasonable grounds that the supply was, or would if it took place be, an exempted supply by virtue of section 3(4) or (5) of this Act, or

(*b*) neither knew nor had reasonable grounds to believe that the recording, spool, case or other thing (as the case may be) did not satisfy the requirement concerned.

14.—(1) A person who supplies or offers to supply a video recording containing a video work in respect of which no classification certificate has been issued is guilty of an offence if the video recording or any spool, case or other thing on or in which the recording is kept contains any indication that a classification certificate has been issued in respect of that work unless the supply is, or would if it took place be, an exempted supply.

Supply of video recording containing false indication as to classification.

(2) It is a defence to a charge of committing an offence under subsection (1) above to prove—

(*a*) that the accused believed on reasonable grounds—

(i) that a classification certificate had been issued in respect of the video work concerned, or

(ii) that the supply was, or would if it took place be, an exempted supply by virtue of section 3(4) or (5) of this Act, or

(*b*) that the accused neither knew nor had reasonable grounds to believe that the recording, spool, case or other thing (as the case may be) contained the indication concerned.

(3) A person who supplies or offers to supply a video recording containing a video work in respect of which a classification certificate has been issued is guilty of an offence if the video recording or any spool, case or other thing on or in which the recording is kept contains any indication that is false in a material particular of any statement falling within section 7(2) of this Act (including any advice falling within paragraph (*a*) of that subsection) contained in the certificate, unless the supply is, or would if it took place be, an exempted supply.

(4) It is a defence to a charge of committing an offence under subsection (3) above to prove—

(*a*) that the accused believed on reasonable grounds—

(i) that the supply was, or would if it took place be, an exempted supply by virtue of section 3(4) or (5) of this Act, or

(ii) that the certificate concerned contained the statement indicated, or

(b) that the accused neither knew nor had reasonable grounds to believe that the recording, spool, case or other thing (as the case may be) contained the indication concerned.

15.—(1) A person guilty of an offence under section 9 or 10 of this Act shall be liable, on summary conviction, to a fine not exceeding £20,000.

(2) In relation to England and Wales, Scotland or Northern Ireland, the Secretary of State may by order amend subsection (1) above so as to substitute for the sum specified in that subsection (whether at the passing of this Act or by a previous order made under this subsection) such other sum as appears to him to be justified by a change in the value of money appearing to him to have taken place since the passing of this Act or the date of the previous order made under this subsection, as the case may be.

(3) A person guilty of an offence under any other provision of this Act shall be liable, on summary conviction, to a fine not exceeding level 5 on the standard scale.

In this subsection " the standard scale " has the meaning given by section 75 of the Criminal Justice Act 1982.

(4) The power to make an order under subsection (2) above shall be exercisable by statutory instrument which shall be subject to annulment in pursuance of a resolution of either House of Parliament.

(5) An order under subsection (2) above shall not affect the punishment for an offence committed before that order comes into force.

Miscellaneous and supplementary

16.—(1) Where an offence under this Act committed by a body corporate is proved to have been committed with the consent or connivance of, or to be attributable to any neglect on the part of, any director, manager, secretary or other similar officer of the body corporate, or any person who was purporting to act in any such capacity, he as well as the body corporate shall be guilty of the offence and shall be liable to be proceeded against and punished accordingly.

(2) Where the affairs of a body corporate are managed by its members, subsection (1) above shall apply in relation to the acts and defaults of a member in connection with his functions of management as if he were a director of the body corporate.

17.—(1) If a justice of the peace is satisfied by information on oath that there are reasonable grounds for suspecting—

(a) that an offence under this Act has been or is being committed on any premises, and

(b) that evidence that the offence has been or is being committed is on those premises,

he may issue a warrant under his hand authorising any constable to enter and search the premises within one month from the date of issue of the warrant.

(2) A constable entering or searching any premises in pursuance of a warrant under subsection (1) above may use reasonable force if necessary and may seize anything found there which he has reasonable grounds to believe may be required to be used in evidence in any proceedings for an offence under this Act.

(3) In subsection (1) above—

(a) the reference to a justice of the peace is, in Scotland, a reference to the sheriff or a justice of the peace and, in Northern Ireland, a reference to a resident magistrate, and

(b) the reference to information is, in Scotland, a reference to evidence and, in Northern Ireland, a reference to a complaint.

18.—(1) If a constable has reasonable grounds for suspecting that a person has committed an offence under this Act, he may require him to give his name and address and, if that person refuses or fails to do so or gives a name and address which the constable reasonably suspects to be false, the constable may arrest him without warrant.

(2) This section does not extend to Scotland.

19.—(1) In any proceedings in England and Wales or North- ern Ireland for an offence under this Act, a certificate purporting to be signed by a person authorised in that behalf by the Secretary of State and stating—

(a) that he has examined—

(i) the record maintained in pursuance of arrangements made by the designated authority, and

(ii) a video work (or part of a video work) contained in a video recording identified by the certificate, and

(b) that the record shows that, on the date specified in the certificate, no classification certificate had been issued in respect of the video work concerned,

shall be admissible as evidence of the fact that, on that day, no classification certificate had been issued in respect of the video work concerned.

(2) A certificate under subsection (1) above may also state—

(a) that the video work concerned differs in such respects as may be specified from another video work examined by the person so authorised and identified by the certificate, and

(b) that the record shows that, on a date specified in the certificate under subsection (1) above, a classification certificate was issued in respect of that other video work ;

and, if it does so, shall be admissible as evidence of the fact that the video work concerned differs in those respects from the other video work.

(3) In any proceedings in England and Wales or Northern Ireland for an offence under this Act, a certificate purporting to be signed by a person authorised in that behalf by the Secretary of State and stating—

(a) that he has examined—

(i) the record maintained in pursuance of arrangements made by the designated authority, and

(ii) a video work (or part of a video work) contained in a video recording identified by the certificate, and

(b) that the record shows that, on the date specified in the certificate under this subsection, a classification certificate was issued in respect of the video work concerned and that a document identified by the certificate under this subsection is a copy of the classification certificate so issued,

shall be admissible as evidence of the fact that, on that date, a classification certificate in terms of the document so identified was issued in respect of the video work concerned.

(4) Any document or video recording identified in a certificate tendered in evidence under this section shall be treated as if it had been produced as an exhibit and identified in court by the person signing the certificate.

(5) This section does not make a certificate admissible as evidence in proceedings for an offence unless a copy of the certificate has, not less than seven days before the hearing, been

served on the person charged with the offence in one of the following ways—

 (a) by delivering it to him or to his solicitor, or

 (b) by addressing it to him and leaving it at his usual or last known place of abode or place of business or by addressing it to his solicitor and leaving it at his office, or

 (c) by sending it in a registered letter or by the recorded delivery service addressed to him at his usual or last known place of abode or place of business or addressed to his solicitor at his office, or

 (d) in the case of a body corporate, by delivering it to the secretary or clerk of the body at its registered or principal office or sending it in a registered letter or by the recorded delivery service addressed to the secretary or clerk of that body at that office.

20. At the end of Schedule 1 to the Criminal Justice (Scotland) Act 1980 there is added—

Evidence by certificate in Scotland.

1980 c. 62.

"The Video Recordings Act 1984 ss. 9 to 14 (offences relating to the supply and possession of video recordings in contravention of that Act).	A person authorised to do so by the Secretary of State, and who has— (a) in relation to the matters certified in paragraph (a) or (c) of Column 3, examined— (i) the record maintained in pursuance of arrangements made by the designated authority; and (ii) a video work (or part of a video work) contained in a video recording identified by the certificate; (b) in relation to the matters certified in paragraph (b) of Column 3 examined a video work other than the video work concerned in the proceedings.	In respect of a video work concerned in the proceedings— (a) that on the date specified in the certificate, no classification certificate had been issued; (b) where a certificate is given in respect of the matter referred to in paragraph (a) above, that the video work differs in such respects as may be specified from the other video work mentioned in paragraph (b) of Column 2; (c) that on the date specified in the certificate a classification certificate in terms of a document identified by the certificate as a copy of the classification certificate was issued."

21.—(1) Where a person is convicted of any offence under this Act, the court may order any video recording—

Forfeiture.

 (a) produced to the court, and

 (b) shown to the satisfaction of the court to relate to the offence,

to be forfeited.

(2) The court shall not order any video recording to be forfeited under subsection (1) above if a person claiming to be the owner of it or otherwise interested in it applies to be heard by the court, unless an opportunity has been given to him to show cause why the order should not be made.

(3) References in this section to a video recording include a reference to any spool, case or other thing on or in which the recording is kept.

(4) An order made under subsection (1) above in any proceedings in England and Wales or Northern Ireland shall not take effect until the expiration of the ordinary time within which an appeal may be instituted or, where such an appeal is duly instituted, until the appeal is finally decided or abandoned ; and for this purpose—

(a) an application for a case to be stated or for leave to appeal shall be treated as the institution of an appeal ; and

(b) where a decision on appeal is subject to a further appeal, the appeal is not finally decided until the expiration of the ordinary time within which a further appeal may be instituted or, where a further appeal is duly instituted, until the further appeal is finally decided or abandoned.

(5) An order made under subsection (1) above in any proceedings in Scotland shall not take effect until the expiration of the time within which, by virtue of any statute, an appeal may be instituted or, where such an appeal is duly instituted, until the appeal is finally disposed of or abandoned ; and for this purpose the lodging of an application for a stated case or note of appeal against sentence shall be treated as the institution of an appeal.

Other interpretation.

22.—(1) In this Act—

" business ", except in section 3(4), includes any activity carried on by a club ; and

" premises " includes any vehicle, vessel or stall.

(2) For the purposes of this Act, a video recording contains a video work if it contains information by the use of which the whole or a part of the work may be produced ; but where a video work includes any extract from another video work, that extract is not to be regarded for the purposes of this subsection as a part of that other work.

(3) Where any alteration is made to a video work in respect of which a classification certificate has been issued, the classification certificate is not to be treated for the purposes of this Act as issued in respect of the altered work.

In this subsection, " alteration " includes addition.

23.—(1) This Act may be cited as the Video Recordings Act 1984.

Short title, commencement and extent.

(2) This Act shall come into force on such day as the Secretary of State may by order made by statutory instrument appoint, and different days may be appointed for different provisions and for different purposes.

(3) This Act extends to Northern Ireland.

Animal Health and Welfare Act 1984

1984 CHAPTER 40

An Act to amend the provisions of the Animal Health Act 1981 relating to the seizure of things for the purpose of preventing the spread of disease, to powers of entry and declarations as to places infected with a disease and to enable certain orders under that Act to operate in or over territorial waters; to amend the Slaughter of Poultry Act 1967; to enable provision to be made for controlling the practice of artificial breeding of livestock; to repeal the Improvement of Live Stock (Licensing of Bulls) Act 1931 and the Horse Breeding Act 1958; to amend the Medicines Act 1968 in relation to feeding stuffs and veterinary drugs; and for connected purposes.   [12th July 1984]

B E IT ENACTED by the Queen's most Excellent Majesty, by and with the advice and consent of the Lords Spiritual and Temporal, and Commons, in this present Parliament assembled, and by the authority of the same, as follows:—

Animal Health Act 1981

1.—(1) In section 35(1) of the Animal Health Act 1981 (power of Ministers to provide for seizure, disposal etc. to prevent spread of disease)—

> (a) for paragraph (a) (seizure of carcases and other specified things) there is substituted—
>
> > " (a) for the seizure of anything, whether animate or inanimate, by or by means of which it appears to them that any disease to which this subsection applies might be carried or transmitted, and "; and

Seizure and disposal of things likely to spread disease.

1981 c. 22.

(*b*) for the words from " disease " to the end there is substituted " such disease ".

(2) After that subsection there is inserted—

" (1A) Subsection (1) above does not authorise provision for the seizure of any animal ; but such an order may provide for the seizure of carcases and of anything obtained from or produced by an animal.

In this subsection, ' animal ' includes anything that may, by virtue of an order under section 87 below, be included for any of the purposes of this Act in the definition of animals or of poultry contained in that section, and " carcases " is to be construed accordingly."

(3) In section 36 of that Act (compensation)—

(*a*) in subsection (1)(*b*) (duty to pay compensation for things seized under section 35(1), except carcases of animals or birds affected with disease) after the words " carcase of " there is inserted " or anything obtained from or produced by ", and

(*b*) in subsection (2) (power to pay compensation for such carcases) for the words " seized as mentioned above of " there is substituted " of, or things obtained from or produced by " and, at the end of that subsection, there is inserted " being carcases or things seized under an order made by virtue of section 35(1) above ".

Power of entry.   **2.**—(1) In section 63(9) of that Act (power of entry of Ministry inspectors in respect of pleuro-pneumonia, foot-and-mouth disease or swine fever), for the words from "for the purpose of ascertaining " to the end there is substituted " enter any land, building or other place, on or in which he has reasonable grounds for supposing that animals are or have been kept, for the purpose of ascertaining whether any disease exists there or has within 56 days existed there.

This subsection does not have effect in relation to poultry."

(2) In section 87(4) of that Act (application of Act to poultry), in the second sentence (provisions not so applied) for the words from " 7(2) " to the end there is substituted " 15(5), 32(4) and 63(9) ".

Exercise of certain powers in territorial zone.
1981 c. 22.

3. Where, apart from this section, any power to make provision by an order under the Animal Health Act 1981 does not include power to provide for its operation in or over territorial waters of the United Kingdom adjacent to Great Britain, it shall be treated as including such a power unless the context otherwise requires.

4. Section 17(4) of the Animal Health Act 1981 (power to declare defined part of port or aerodrome an infected place restricted to the Ministers) shall cease to have effect.

Removal of
restriction on
powers as to
infected
places.
1981 c. 22.

Slaughter of Poultry Act 1967

5.—(1) In section 1(1) of the Slaughter of Poultry Act 1967 (prohibition of slaughter of poultry for purposes of preparation for sale for human consumption, except by one of the methods mentioned), the words " for purposes of preparation for sale for human consumption " are omitted.

Extension of
scope of 1967
Act.
1967 c. 24.

(2) After subsection (2) of that section there is inserted—

" (2A) Subsection (1) of this section shall not apply to the slaughter of any bird—

(a) in pursuance of powers conferred by, or by any instrument made or having effect as if made under, the Animal Health Act 1981 ;

(b) in the course of an experiment in respect of which restrictions are imposed by the Cruelty to Animals Act 1876, being an experiment performed subject to any restrictions so imposed ; or

1876 c. 77.

(c) by a person registered in the register of veterinary surgeons or the supplementary veterinary register, or a person acting under his direction, where the person so registered is acting in the exercise of his profession.

(2B) The Ministers may, after consultation with such persons or bodies as seem to them representative of the interests concerned, by order approve subject to such conditions as they may think fit any method of slaughter as a method suitable for the slaughter of poultry chicks ; and where poultry chicks are slaughtered without the infliction of unnecessary suffering by any method so approved and in accordance with any conditions applicable to the approval—

(a) subsection (1) of this section shall not apply to their slaughter, and

(b) nothing done in the course of their slaughter shall be taken to be done in contravention of any prohibition or restriction imposed by or under any other enactment, being a prohibition or restriction of a kind described in the order.

In this subsection ' poultry chicks ' means birds to which this Act applies, not being more than 72 hours old.

(2C) The power conferred by subsection (2B) of this section to make orders shall be exercisable by statutory instrument which shall be subject to annulment in pursuance of a resolution of either House of Parliament."

Licences.

6. For section 3 of that Act (regulations for securing humane conditions of slaughter) there is substituted—

"Regulations for securing humane conditions of slaughter.

3.—(1) The Ministers may make regulations for the purpose of securing humane conditions and practices in connection with the slaughter of birds to which this Act applies.

(2) The regulations may—

(*a*) specify conditions to be observed in connection with the confinement and treatment of any such birds while awaiting slaughter and in connection with the slaughter of any such birds ;

(*b*) prohibit the slaughter of any such birds or any activity connected with their slaughter—

(i) on premises to which the regulations apply, or

(ii) by methods or in circumstances of any description specified in the regulations,

except under and in accordance with the terms of a licence under the regulations ;

(*c*) require occupiers of premises to which the regulations apply to secure that the provisions of the regulations are complied with on the premises ;

(*d*) make different provision for different cases ;

(*e*) provide, in the case of any contravention of any provision of the regulations, for the creation of offences and their punishment on summary conviction with a fine of an amount not exceeding that specified in the regulations.

(3) The regulations may include provision in respect of—

(*a*) the granting, modification, suspension and revocation of licences by local authorities and, in connection with those matters, the charging of such reasonable fees as the authority concerned may determine ;

(*b*) the requirements to be satisfied for the granting of licences and the conditions to which they are to be subject ; and

(*c*) the duration of licences.

(4) The amount that may be specified under subsection (2)(*e*) of this section is an amount not exceeding level 3 on the standard scale.

(5) Subsections (2) and (3) of this section are without prejudice to the generality of subsection (1) of this section.

(6) The Ministers shall, before making any regulations under this section, consult with such persons or bodies as seem to them representative of the interests concerned.

(7) The power to make regulations under this section shall be exercisable by statutory instrument which shall be subject to annulment in pursuance of a resolution of either House of Parliament."

7. After section 3 of that Act there is inserted—

"Codes of practice.

Codes of practice.

3A—(1) The Ministers may from time to time after consultation with such persons or bodies as seem to them representative of the interests concerned—

> (a) prepare and issue codes of practice for the purpose of providing practical guidance in respect of any provision of this Act or regulations under it ; and
>
> (b) revise any such code by revoking, varying, amending or adding to the provisions of the code.

(2) A code prepared in pursuance of this section and any alterations proposed to be made on a revision of such a code shall be laid before both Houses of Parliament, and the Ministers shall not issue the code or revised code, as the case may be, until after the end of the period of 40 days beginning with the day on which the code or the proposed alterations were so laid.

(3) If, within the period mentioned in subsection (2) of this section, either House resolves that the code be not issued or the proposed alterations be not made, as the case may be, the Ministers shall not issue the code or revised code (without prejudice to their power under that subsection to lay further codes or proposed alterations before Parliament).

(4) For the purposes of subsection (2) of this section—

> (a) where a code or proposed alterations are laid before each House of Parliament on different days, the later day shall be taken to be the day on which the code or the proposed alterations, as the case may be, were laid before both Houses ; and

(b) in reckoning any period of 40 days, no account shall be taken of any time during which Parliament is dissolved or prorogued or during which both Houses are adjourned for more than four days.

(5) The Ministers shall cause any code issued or revised under this section to be printed and distributed, and may make such arrangements as they think fit for its distribution, including causing copies of it to be put on sale to the public at such reasonable price as the Ministers may determine.

(6) A failure on the part of any person to follow any guidance contained in a code issued under this section shall not of itself render that person liable to proceedings of any kind.

(7) If, in proceedings against any person for an offence consisting of the contravention of any provision of this Act or of regulations under it, it is shown that, at any material time, he failed to follow any guidance contained in a code issued under this section, being guidance which was relevant to the provision concerned, that failure may be relied on by the prosecution as tending to establish his guilt."

Powers of entry under 1967 Act.

8. For section 4 of that Act (power to enter premises where slaughter for purposes of preparation for sale for human consumption takes place) there is substituted—

" Power of entry.

4.—(1) Where the power conferred by this subsection is exercisable in relation to any premises to which regulations under section 3 of this Act apply, a person authorised in that behalf by the Minister of Agriculture, Fisheries and Food or the Secretary of State or by the local authority within whose area the premises are situated may enter the premises for the purpose of ascertaining whether there is, or has been, on those premises any contravention of any provision of this Act or of any regulations made or code of practice issued under it.

(2) Where it is, or appears to the person so authorised to be, the case that the slaughter of birds to which this Act applies is in progress on the premises, the power conferred by subsection (1) of this section is exercisable at any time.

(3) Where it is, or appears to the person so authorised to be, the case that—

(a) the slaughter of such birds has within 48 hours been in progress on the premises, or

        (b) such birds are on the premises for the purpose of their being slaughtered,

the power conferred by subsection (1) of this section is exercisable at all reasonable hours.

(4) A person who intentionally obstructs a person in the exercise of his powers under subsection (1) of this section shall be guilty of an offence and liable on summary conviction to a fine not exceeding level 2 on the standard scale."

9. For section 6 of that Act (power to institute proceedings) there is substituted—

Enforcement of 1967 Act.

" Execution and enforcement.

      6.—(1) Every local authority shall execute and enforce in their area the provisions of this Act and of regulations under section 3 of this Act.

(2) In particular, every local authority shall, for the purpose of securing the execution of those provisions, make arrangements for the supervision by persons having such qualifications as may be specified in the regulations of any premises in their area to which the regulations apply.

(3) Arrangements under subsection (2) of this section shall comply with such directions as the Ministers may give from time to time.

(4) This section does not authorise a local authority in Scotland to institute proceedings for any offence."

Controls over Breeding of Livestock

10.—(1) The appropriate Minister may make regulations for controlling the practice of artificial breeding of livestock.

Artificial breeding of livestock.

In this section " artificial breeding " includes artificial insemination and transfer of ova or embryos.

(2) Regulations under this section—

    (a) may, for the purpose of controlling the use for artificial breeding of any specified kind of livestock or of semen, ova or embryos of such livestock, prohibit the carrying on of any specified activity in connection with such livestock or with such semen, ova or embryos except under the authority of a licence or approval issued under the regulations ;

    (b) may, for the purpose of controlling their use for artificial breeding, prohibit the importation of semen, ova or embryos of any specified kind of livestock except under the authority of such a licence ;

and, accordingly, the regulations may make such provision as appears to the appropriate Minister to be expedient in respect of the issue, modification, suspension and revocation of licences or approvals under the regulations including the conditions subject to which they may be issued.

(3) Regulations under this section may include provision—

(*a*) in respect of advertisements in connection with artificial breeding ;

(*b*) for the seizure and detention of anything imported in contravention of any provision of the regulations or any conditions of any licence under them or anything which appears to any person authorised in that behalf to have been so imported and for dealing with anything so imported (whether by requiring it to be destroyed or taken out of Great Britain or otherwise) ;

(*c*) for the payment of fees in connection with—

(i) the issue of licences or approvals under the regulations, and

(ii) tests or examinations carried out for the purposes of the regulations,

and, where the regulations provide for an appeal against a refusal to issue any such licence or approval, in connection with such an appeal, being (in all cases) fees determined with the approval of the Treasury ;

but subsection (2) above and this subsection are without prejudice to the generality of subsection (1) above.

(4) For the purpose of ascertaining whether the provisions of regulations under this section or the conditions of any licence or approval under them are being or have been contravened, a person authorised in writing in that behalf by the appropriate Minister may, on producing his authority, enter at all reasonable times—

(*a*) any premises used by the holder of a licence or approval under the regulations, being premises used for or in connection with any of the purposes authorised by the licence or approval ; and

(*b*) any premises on which he has reasonable grounds for suspecting that an offence under this section is being or has been committed ;

and may inspect the premises and any livestock or articles on them and carry out such test or other investigation as he thinks fit.

(5) For the purposes of any test or investigation under sub-section (4) above, the person so authorised may require any person on the premises to give such information as it is in his power to give.

(6) A person who—

(a) contravenes any provision of regulations under this section or any conditions of a licence or approval under such regulations ;

(b) intentionally obstructs any person in the exercise of the powers conferred on him by or under this section ; or

(c) refuses to give any such person any information which he is required to give under subsection (5) above ;

is guilty of an offence and liable on summary conviction to imprisonment for a term not exceeding three months or to a fine not exceeding level 3 on the standard scale, or both.

In this subsection " the standard scale " has the meaning given by section 75 of the Criminal Justice Act 1982. 　　1982 c. 48.

(7) It is a defence to a charge of committing an offence under subsection (6)(a) above to prove that the accused took all reasonable steps and exercised all due diligence to avoid committing the offence.

(8) In this section—

" appropriate Minister " means, in relation to England, the Minister of Agriculture, Fisheries and Food and, in relation to Scotland or to Wales, the Secretary of State ;

" contravention " includes failure to comply and " contravene " is to be construed accordingly ;

" livestock " includes any animal or bird not in the wild state ;

" premises " includes any description of vehicle ;

" specified " means specified in regulations under this section ;

and anything brought to Great Britain from a country out of Great Britain and landed here is imported for the purposes of this section.

11.—(1) Where an offence committed by a body corporate under section 10 of this Act is proved to have been committed with the consent or connivance of, or to be attributable to any neglect on the part of, any director, manager, secretary or other similar officer of the body corporate, or any person who was purporting to act in any such capacity, he as well as the body corporate shall be guilty of the offence, and shall be liable to be proceeded against and punished accordingly. Provisions supplementary to section 10.

(2) Where the affairs of a body corporate are managed by its members, subsection (1) above shall apply in relation to the acts and defaults of a member in connection with his functions of management as if he were a director of the body corporate.

1943 c. 16.

1978 c. 30.

(3) Section 17 of the Agriculture (Miscellaneous Provisions) Act 1943 (control of artificial insemination) shall cease to have effect but, without prejudice to section 17 of the Interpretation Act 1978 (repeal and re-enactment)—

> (a) in so far as regulations under section 17 of the Agriculture (Miscellaneous Provisions) Act 1943 could have been made under section 10 of this Act, they shall not be invalidated by the repeal but shall have effect as if so made and as if references in them to subsection (3) of the said section 17 were references to the corresponding provision (if any) of regulations under section 10 of this Act, and

> (b) if at the commencement of section 10 of this Act the importation of any semen is prohibited by regulations under that section except under the authority of a licence issued under the regulations then, in so far as any licence under subsection (3) of the said section 17 could have been issued under the regulations, it shall not be invalidated by the repeal but shall have effect as if so issued;

and references in section 10 of this Act to regulations under that section or licences or approvals under such regulations shall be interpreted accordingly.

(4) The power conferred by section 10 of this Act to make regulations shall be exercisable by statutory instrument which shall be subject to annulment in pursuance of a resolution of either House of Parliament.

Removal of
controls on
keeping of
bulls and
stallions.

1931 c. 43.

1958 c. 43.

12. The Improvement of Live Stock (Licensing of Bulls) Act 1931 (licence or permit required for keeping bulls which have attained prescribed age) and the Horse Breeding Act 1958 (similar requirement for stallions) shall cease to have effect.

Animal feeding stuffs and veterinary drugs

Medicated
animal
feeding stuffs.

1968 c. 67.

13.—(1) For section 40 of the Medicines Act 1968 (medicated animal feeding stuffs) there is substituted—

"Medicated animal feeding stuffs.   **40.**—(1) The Agriculture Ministers may by regulations prohibit the incorporation by any person, in the course of a business carried on by him, of a medicinal product of any description in an animal feeding stuff unless such of the conditions mentioned in subsection (2) of this section as may be specified in the regulations are satisfied.

(2) The conditions referred to in subsection (1) of this section are—

    (a) that it is incorporated in accordance with provisions relating to the incorporation of the medicinal product in animal feeding stuffs contained in a product licence or animal test certificate (whether held by him or by another person);

    (b) that it is incorporated in accordance with a written direction given by a veterinary surgeon or veterinary practitioner, being a written direction complying with such requirements as may be specified in the regulations;

    (c) that the person concerned is for the time being entered in a register kept for the purposes of the regulations by the registrar or the Northern Ireland enforcement authority.

(3) A condition imposed by virtue of subsection (2)(a) of this section shall be taken to be satisfied if the person incorporating the medicinal product in the animal feeding stuff—

    (a) is not the holder of a product licence or animal test certificate containing such provisions as are mentioned in that paragraph, but

    (b) believes, on reasonable grounds, that another person is the holder of such a licence or certificate containing such provisions and that the medicinal product is incorporated in accordance with those provisions.

(4) The Agriculture Ministers may by regulations prohibit—

    (a) the sale, offer for sale, supply or export by any person in the course of a business carried on by him of any animal feeding stuff in which a medicinal product has been incorporated, or

    (b) the importation by any person of any animal feeding stuff in which a medicinal product has been incorporated, unless such of the conditions mentioned in subsection (5) of this section as may be specified in the regulations are satisfied.

(5) The conditions referred to in subsection (4) of this section are—

    (*a*) that the medicinal product was not incorporated in the animal feeding stuff in contravention of any prohibition imposed by virtue of subsection (1) of this section ;

    (*b*) that the feeding stuff is sold, offered for sale, supplied, exported or imported (as the case may be) in accordance with a written direction given by a veterinary surgeon or veterinary practitioner, being a written direction complying with such requirements as may be specified in the regulations ;

    (*c*) that the person concerned is for the time being entered in a register kept for the purposes of the regulations by the registrar or the Northern Ireland enforcement authority.

(6) A condition imposed by virtue of subsection (5)(*a*) of this section shall be taken to be satisfied if the person selling, offering for sale, supplying, exporting or importing the animal feeding stuff—

    (*a*) did not incorporate the medicinal product in it, and

    (*b*) had no reasonable grounds to believe that it was incorporated in contravention of any prohibition imposed by virtue of subsection (1) of this section.

(7) Regulations under this section may impose such conditions as the Agriculture Ministers think fit in respect of the inclusion or retention of persons in a register kept for the purposes of the regulations, including conditions requiring the payment to the registrar or the Northern Ireland enforcement authority of fees of such amounts as the Agriculture Ministers may with the consent of the Treasury determine.

(8) In determining any such fees, the Agriculture Ministers may have regard to—

    (*a*) any costs incurred or to be incurred by the Pharmaceutical Society or the Northern Ireland enforcement authority in connection

with any duty to enforce any provision of
regulations under this section, and

(b) any costs incurred or to be incurred by any
other person for the purpose of maintaining
or improving standards among those engaged in the activities referred to in subsections (1) and (4) of this section.

(9) Any fees received by virtue of this section
for the inclusion or retention of any person in a
register kept for the purposes of the regulations shall,
if the Agriculture Ministers so determine, be applied
to such extent and in such manner as they may determine towards meeting any costs falling within subsection (8)(b) of this section ; subject to that, any such
fees received by the registrar shall be applicable for
the purposes of the Pharmaceutical Society.

(10) A person contravenes this section if he contravenes any prohibition imposed by virtue of subsection (1) or (4) of this section.

(11) References in this Act to the incorporation
of a medicinal product in an animal feeding stuff do
not include a reference to it being so incorporated in
the course of making a medicinal product ; but, subject to that, they include a reference to the incorporation—

(a) for a medicinal purpose of a substance or
article other than a medicinal product, or

(b) of a substance in which a medicinal product has been incorporated,

in an animal feeding stuff.

(12) In this section—

' the Northern Ireland enforcement authority '
means any Northern Ireland Department
having a duty to enforce any provision of
this section or of regulations under it ; and

' the registrar ' means any person appointed
under section 1 of the Pharmacy Act 1954 1954 c. 61
as registrar for the purposes of that Act."

(2) In section 130 of the Medicines Act 1968 (meaning of 1968 c. 67.
medicinal product and related expressions) after subsection (3)
there is inserted—

" (3A) An order made by the Agriculture Ministers may

provide that, for the purposes of this Act, any specified description or class of medicated feeding stuff—

> (a) is to be treated as a medicinal product (subject to the following provisions of this section), or
>
> (b) is not to be so treated (notwithstanding anything in subsection (1) of this section).

(3B) In subsection (3A) of this section 'medicated feeding stuff' means any substance which is manufactured, sold, supplied, imported or exported for use wholly or mainly in either or both of the following ways, that is to say—

> (a) use by being fed to one or more animals for a medicinal purpose or for purposes that include that purpose, or
>
> (b) use as an ingredient in the preparation of a substance which is to be fed to one or more animals for a medicinal purpose or for purposes that include that purpose.

(3C) No order shall be made under subsection (3A) of this section unless a draft of the order has been laid before Parliament and approved by resolution of each House of Parliament."

1968 c. 67.

(3) In section 132(1) of the Medicines Act 1968 (interpretation), after the definition of " animal " there is inserted—

> " ' animal feeding stuff ' means any substance which is intended for use either by being fed to one or more animals or as an ingredient in the preparation of such a substance, not being in either case a medicinal product ".

Registration of merchants in veterinary drugs.

14. In section 57 of the Medicines Act 1968 (power to extend or modify exemptions under sections 52 and 53, which regulate the sale or supply of medicinal products), after subsection (2) (power to impose conditions on any exemptions) there is inserted—

> " (2A) Without prejudice to the generality of subsection (2) of this section, an order under subsection (1) of this section providing for the exemption from section 52 of this Act of the sale, or offer or exposure for sale, by retail or the supply in circumstances corresponding to retail sale of veterinary drugs by any persons—
>
> > (a) may, as a condition of the exemption, require those persons to be entered for the time being in a register of merchants in veterinary drugs kept by the registrar or the Northern Ireland enforcement authority, and

(b) may impose such conditions as the appropriate Ministers think fit in respect of the inclusion or retention of persons in the register, including conditions requiring the payment to the registrar or the Northern Ireland enforcement authority of fees of such amounts as the appropriate Ministers may with the consent of the Treasury determine.

(2B) In determining any such fees, the appropriate Ministers may have regard to—

(a) any costs incurred or to be incurred by the Pharmaceutical Society or the Northern Ireland enforcement authority in connection with any power or duty to enforce any provisions of section 52 or of regulations under section 66 of this Act, so far as those powers or duties relate to veterinary drugs, and

(b) any costs incurred or to be incurred by any other person for the purpose of maintaining or improving standards among those engaged in the sale by retail of veterinary drugs or the supply of such drugs in circumstances corresponding to retail sale.

(2C) Any fees received by virtue of this section for the inclusion or retention of any person in a register of merchants in veterinary drugs shall, if the appropriate Ministers so determine, be applied to such extent and in such manner as they may determine towards meeting any costs falling within subsection (2B)(b) of this section; subject to that, any such fees received by the registrar shall be applicable for the purposes of the Pharmaceutical Society.

(2D) In the preceding provisions of this section—

' the Northern Ireland enforcement authority' means any Northern Ireland department having a duty to enforce any of the provisions referred to in subsection (2B)(a) of this section, being a duty relating to veterinary drugs; and

' the registrar' means the person appointed under section 1 of the Pharmacy Act 1954 as registrar for the purposes of that Act." 1954 c. 61.

15.—(1) In section 117 of the Medicines Act 1968 (special enforcement and sampling provisions relating to animal feeding stuffs), after subsection (5) there is inserted— Sampling of animal feeding stuffs.

" (5A) The power conferred by subsection (1) of this section to provide for the purposes there mentioned that any of the provisions of section 115 of this Act shall 1968 c. 67

have effect (with or without modifications) in relation to animal feeding stuffs includes power to provide in relation to animal feeding stuffs that, in place of all or any of those provisions, provisions specified in the regulations shall have effect, being provisions corresponding to any of those made by sections 75 and 78 of the Agriculture Act 1970."

1970 c. 40.

(2) At the end of subsection (6) of that section there is inserted " and the reference in subsection (2) of this section to the provisions of section 115 of this Act as modified by any such regulations shall be construed as including a reference to any provisions specified in the regulations in place of any of the provisions of section 115 of this Act."

Supplementary

Minor and consequential amendments and repeals.

16.—(1) Schedule 1 to this Act (which contains minor and consequential amendments) shall have effect.

(2) The enactments mentioned in Schedule 2 to this Act are repealed to the extent specified in the third column of that Schedule and the Slaughter of Poultry Act 1967 Extension Order 1978 is revoked.

S.I. 1978/201.

Short title, commencement and extent.

17.—(1) This Act may be cited as the Animal Health and Welfare Act 1984.

(2) Subject to subsection (3) below, this Act shall come into force at the end of the period of two months beginning with its passing.

(3) The following provisions of this Act, that is—

section 13,

paragraph 3 of Schedule 1, and

1968 c. 67.

so much of Schedule 2 as relates to the Medicines Act 1968, shall come into force on such day as the Agriculture Ministers may by order made by statutory instrument appoint, and different days may be appointed for different provisions and for different purposes.

In this subsection " the Agriculture Ministers " has the same meaning as in the Medicines Act 1968.

(4) Notwithstanding the repeal by this Act of the words " for purposes of preparation for sale for human consumption " in subsection (1) of section 1 of the Slaughter of Poultry Act 1967, that subsection shall not have effect in relation to the slaughter of poultry chicks within the meaning of subsection (2B) of that

1967 c. 24.

section until such day as the Ministers may by order made by statutory instrument appoint.

In this subsection " the Ministers " has the same meaning as in that Act.

(5) Except for—

(*a*) sections 13 to 15, and

(*b*) section 16 and Schedules 1 and 2 so far as relating to the Medicines Act 1968,   1968 c. 67.

this Act does not extend to Northern Ireland.

SCHEDULES

Section 16.

SCHEDULE 1

MINOR AND CONSEQUENTIAL AMENDMENTS

Slaughter of Poultry Act 1967 (c.24)

1.—(1) The Slaughter of Poultry Act 1967 shall be amended as follows.

(2) In section 1(1), for the words " turkey kept in captivity or domestic fowl so kept " there is substituted " bird to which this Act applies ".

(3) In section 1(3) (as originally enacted), for the words from " £50 " to the end there is substituted " level 3 on the standard scale ".

(4) In section 2 (as originally enacted)—

    (*a*) for the words " turkey kept in captivity or a domestic fowl so kept " there is substituted " bird to which this Act applies ",

    (*b*) the words " for purposes mentioned in section 1(1) above " are omitted,

    (*c*) for " £20 " there is substituted " level 2 on the standard scale " ;

and at the end of that section there is inserted—

    " (2) It is a defence to a charge of committing an offence under this section to prove that the accused took all reasonable steps and exercised all due diligence to avoid committing the offence ".

(5) In section 7(1), the words " for purposes mentioned in section 1(1) above " and the words " other than turkeys and domestic fowls " are omitted.

(6) In section 8—

    (*a*) before the definition of " local authority " there is inserted—

        " ' contravention ' includes failure to comply ", and

    (*b*) after the definition of " the Ministers " there is inserted—

1982 c. 48.

        " ' the standard scale ' has the meaning given by section 75 of the Criminal Justice Act 1982.

        (2) This Act applies to turkeys kept in captivity and domestic fowls, guinea fowls, ducks, geese and quails so kept ; and references in this Act to birds to which this Act applies shall be construed in accordance with this subsection and any order under section 7 above."

2. A person shall not, by virtue of paragraph 1(4)(*c*) above, be liable on conviction, after the time when this Act comes into force, of an offence committed before that time to any punishment by way of fine greater than that to which he would have been liable if convicted before that time.

Medicines Act 1968 (c. 67)

3.—(1) The Medicines Act 1968 shall be amended as follows.

(2) In section 28(3)(i), the words " or of any substance or article other than a medicinal product incorporated for a medicinal purpose " are omitted.

(3) Sections 41, 42 and 46(3) and (4) are omitted.

(4) In section 108(6)(*a*), after the word " sections " there is inserted " 40 " and after the word " Act " there is inserted " and of any regulations made under section 40 of this Act ".

(5) At the end of section 117 there is added—

" (8) References in subsections (1), (3) and (5A) of this section to animal feeding stuffs include a reference to any medicated feeding stuff, within the meaning of section 130(3A) of this Act."

(6) In section 126(1)(*a*), for " 40(1) " there is substituted " 40 ".

(7) In section 130(4), after the words " subsection (1) " there is inserted " or (3A) ".

(8) In section 130(6)—

    (*a*) after the words " subsection (1) " there is inserted " or (3B) ",

    (*b*) for the word " that " (where it first appears) there is substituted " the relevant ",

    (*c*) the words " (subject to the next following subsection) " are omitted, and

    (*d*) for the words " subsection (1) of this section " (in the second place where they appear) there is substituted " the relevant subsection ".

(9) Section 130(7) is omitted.

(10) In section 130(9), after the word " administering " (in both places) there is inserted " (or feeding) ".

(11) In paragraph 6 of Schedule 4, the words " section 42 " are omitted.

Animal Health Act 1981 (c. 22)

4. In section 63(3) of the Animal Health Act 1981, for the word " where " there is substituted " in respect of which ".

N 2

SCHEDULE 2

REPEALS

Chapter	Short Title	Extent of Repeal
1931 c. 43.	Improvement of Live Stock (Licensing of Bulls) Act 1931.	The whole Act.
1943 c. 16.	Agriculture (Miscellaneous Provisions) Act 1943	Section 17.
1944 c. 28.	Agriculture (Miscellaneous Provisions) Act 1944	In section 6, subsections (4) to (6).
1946 c. 26.	Emergency Laws (Transitional Provisions) Act 1946.	In Schedule 2, the entry relating to the Improvement of Live Stock (Licensing of Bulls) Act 1931.
1958 c. 43.	Horse Breeding Act 1958.	The whole Act.
1963 c. 11.	Agriculture (Miscellaneous Provisions) Act 1963	In section 16, subsection (4) and, in subsection (5), the words from " or containing " to " prescribing fees ".
1967 c. 24.	Slaughter of Poultry Act 1967.	In section 1(1), the words " for purposes of preparation for sale for human consumption " and, in sections 2 and 7(1), the words " for purposes mentioned in section 1(1) above ". In section 7(1), the words " other than turkeys and domestic fowls ".
1968 c. 67.	Medicines Act 1968.	In section 28(3)(i), the words " or of any substance or article other than a medicinal product incorporated for a medicinal purpose ". Sections 41 and 42. In section 46, subsections (3) and (4). In section 130(6), the words "(subject to the next following subsection) ". Section 130(7). In Schedule 4, in paragraph 6, the words " section 42 ".
1972 c. 62.	Agriculture (Miscellaneous Provisions) Act 1972	In section 8, subsections (1) to (4). Schedule 3.
1981 c. 22.	Animal Health Act 1981.	Section 17(4).

Agricultural Holdings Act 1984

1984 CHAPTER 41

An Act to amend the law with respect to agricultural holdings.   [12th July 1984]

B E IT ENACTED by the Queen's most Excellent Majesty, by and with the advice and consent of the Lords Spiritual and Temporal, and Commons, in this present Parliament assembled, and by the authority of the same, as follows:—

Rent

1. The following sections shall be substituted for section 8 of the 1948 Act—

Determination of rent of agricultural holding.

"Arbitration on terms of tenancies as to rent.

8.—(1) Subject to the provisions of this section, the landlord or the tenant of an agricultural holding may by notice in writing served on his tenant or landlord demand that the rent to be payable in respect of the holding as from the next termination date shall be referred to arbitration under this Act.

(2) On a reference under subsection (1) of this section the arbitrator shall determine what rent should be properly payable in respect of the holding at the date of the reference and accordingly shall, with effect from the next termination date following the date of the demand for arbitration, increase or reduce the rent previously payable or direct that it shall continue unchanged.

(3) For the purposes of the foregoing subsection the rent properly payable in respect of a holding shall be the rent at which the holding might reasonably be expected to be let by a prudent and willing landlord to a prudent and willing tenant, taking into account (subject to subsections (5) to (7) of this section) all relevant factors, including (in every case) the terms of the tenancy (including those relating to rent), the character and situation of the holding (including the locality in which it is situated), the productive capacity of the holding and its related earning capacity, and the current level of rents for comparable lettings, as determined in accordance with subsection (5) of this section.

(4) In subsection (3) of this section, in relation to the holding—

> (*a*) " productive capacity " means the productive capacity of the holding (taking into account fixed equipment and any other available facilities on the holding) on the assumption that it is in the occupation of a competent tenant practising a system of farming suitable to the holding ; and

> (*b*) " related earning capacity " means the extent to which, in the light of that productive capacity, a competent tenant practising such a system of farming could reasonably be expected to profit from farming the holding.

(5) In determining for the purposes of that subsection the current level of rents for comparable lettings the arbitrator shall take into account any available evidence with respect to the rents (whether fixed by agreement between the parties or by arbitration under this Act) which are, or (in view of rents currently being tendered) are likely to become, payable in respect of tenancies of comparable agricultural holdings on terms (other than terms fixing the rent payable) similar to those of the tenancy under consideration, but shall disregard—

> (*a*) any element of the rents in question which is due to an appreciable scarcity of comparable holdings available for letting on such terms compared with the number of persons seeking to become tenants of such holdings on such terms ;

(b) any element of those rents which is due to the fact that the tenant of, or a person tendering for, any comparable holding is in occupation of other land in the vicinity of that holding that may conveniently be occupied together with that holding ; and

(c) any effect on those rents which is due to any allowances or reductions made in consideration of the charging of premiums.

(6) On a reference under subsection (1) of this section the arbitrator shall disregard any increase in the rental value of the holding which is due to—

(a) tenant's improvements or fixed equipment other than improvements executed or equipment provided under an obligation imposed on the tenant by the terms of his contract of tenancy ; and

(b) landlord's improvements, in so far as the landlord has received or will receive grants out of moneys provided by Parliament or local government funds in respect of the execution of those improvements.

(7) On any such reference the arbitrator—

(a) shall also disregard any effect on the rent of the fact that the tenant who is a party to the arbitration is in occupation of the holding ; and

(b) shall not fix the rent at a lower amount by reason of any dilapidation or deterioration of, or damage to, buildings or land caused or permitted by the tenant.

(8) Subject to subsections (9) to (12) of this section, a demand for arbitration shall not be effective for the purposes of subsection (1) of this section if the next termination date following the date of the demand falls earlier than the end of three years from any of the following dates, that is to say—

(a) the commencement of the tenancy ; or

(b) the date as from which there took effect a previous increase or reduction of rent (whether made under this section or otherwise) ; or

(c) the date as from which there took effect a previous direction of an arbitrator under this section that the rent should continue unchanged.

(9) Subsection (10) of this section applies in any case where a tenancy of an agricultural holding ("the new holding") commences under a contract of tenancy between—

(a) a person who immediately before the date of the commencement of the tenancy was entitled to a severed part of the reversionary estate in an agricultural holding (" the original holding ") in which the new holding was then comprised ; and

(b) the person who immediately before that date was the tenant of the original holding ;

and where the rent payable in respect of the new holding at the commencement of the tenancy of that holding represents merely the appropriate portion of the rent payable in respect of the original holding immediately before the commencement of that tenancy.

(10) In any case to which this subsection applies—

(a) subsection (8)(a) of this section shall be read as referring to the commencement of the tenancy of the original holding ; and

(b) references to rent in subsection (8)(b) and (c) of this section shall be read as references to the rent payable in respect of the original holding ;

until the first occasion following the commencement of the tenancy of the new holding on which any such increase or reduction of, or direction with respect to, the rent of the new holding as is mentioned in subsection (8)(b) or (c) takes effect.

(11) Where under an agreement between the landlord and the tenant of the holding (not being an agreement expressed to take effect as a new contract of tenancy between the parties) provision is made for adjustment of the boundaries of the holding or for any other variation of the terms of the tenancy, exclusive of those relating to rent, then, unless the agreement otherwise provides—

(a) that provision shall for the purposes of subsection (8) of this section be treated as not operating to terminate the tenancy, and accordingly as not resulting in the commencement of a new contract of tenancy between the parties ; and

(*b*) any increase or reduction of rent solely attributable to any such adjustment or variation
as aforesaid shall be disregarded for the
purposes of paragraph (*b*) of that subsection.

(12) The following shall be disregarded for the
purposes of subsection (8)(*b*) of this section—

(*a*) an increase or reduction of rent under section
7(3) of this Act ;

(*b*) an increase of rent under section 9(1) of
this Act or such an increase as is referred
to in subsection (2) of that section, or any
reduction of rent agreed between the landlord and the tenant of the holding in consequence of any change in the fixed equipment
provided on the holding by the landlord ;

(*c*) a reduction of rent under section 10 of the
Agricultural Holdings (Notices to Quit) 1977 c.12.
Act 1977.

(13) A demand for arbitration under subsection (1)
of this section shall cease to be effective for the
purposes of that subsection on the next termination
date following the date of the demand unless before
the said termination date—

(*a*) an arbitrator has been appointed by agreement between the parties ; or

(*b*) an application has been made to the Minister
for the appointment of an arbitrator by
him.

Interpreta-
tion of
section 8.
8A.—(1) Section 8 of this Act applies in relation
to tenancies of agricultural holdings whenever
created.

(2) References in that section, in relation to a
demand for arbitration with respect to the rent of
any holding, to the next termination date following
the date of the demand are references to the next
day following the date of the demand on which the
tenancy of the holding could have been determined
by notice to quit given at the date of the demand.

(3) In subsection (6) of that section—

(*a*) " tenant's improvements " means any improvements which have been executed on
the holding, in so far as they were executed
wholly or partly at the expense of the

tenant (whether or not that expense has been or will be reimbursed by a grant out of moneys provided by Parliament or local government funds) without any equivalent allowance or benefit made or given by the landlord in consideration of their execution ;

(b) " tenant's fixed equipment " means fixed equipment provided by the tenant ; and

(c) " landlord's improvements " means improvements executed on the holding by the landlord.

(4) Where the tenant has held a previous tenancy of the holding, then—

(a) in the definition of " tenant's improvements " in subsection (3)(a) of this section, the reference to any such improvements as are there mentioned shall extend to improvements executed during that tenancy ; and

(b) in the definition of " tenant's fixed equipment " in subsection (3)(b), the reference to such equipment as is there mentioned shall extend to equipment provided during that tenancy ;

excluding, however, any improvement or fixed equipment so executed or provided in respect of which the tenant received any compensation on the termination of that (or any other) tenancy.

(5) For the purposes of subsection (3)(a) of this section, the continuous adoption by the tenant of a system of farming more beneficial to the holding—

(a) than the system of farming required by the contract of tenancy ; or

(b) in so far as no system is so required, than the system of farming normally practised on comparable agricultural holdings ;

shall be treated as an improvement executed at his expense."

Statutory succession to agricultural holdings

Abolition of statutory succession to agricultural holdings in the case of new tenancies.

2.—(1) Subject to subsection (2) below, section 18(1) of the 1976 Act (application of provisions of that Act for succession to agricultural holdings) shall not apply on the death of the sole (or sole surviving) tenant of an agricultural holding where the tenancy was granted on or after the date on which this Act is passed

(2) Section 18(1) of that Act shall nevertheless apply on the death of any such tenant of an agricultural holding as is mentioned in subsection (1) above if—

(a) the tenancy was obtained by virtue of a direction of the Agricultural Land Tribunal under section 20 of the 1976 Act ;

(b) the tenancy was granted (following such a direction) in circumstances within section 23(6) of that Act ;

(c) the tenancy was granted by a written contract of tenancy indicating (in whatever terms) that subsection (1) above is not to apply in relation to the tenancy ; or

(d) the tenancy was granted otherwise than as mentioned in the preceding provisions of this subsection to a person who, immediately before the date on which this Act is passed, was a tenant of the holding or of any agricultural holding which comprised the whole or a substantial part of the land comprised in the holding.

(3) In this section " tenant " has the same meaning as in section 18(1).

3.—(1) The following subsection shall be inserted in section 23 of the 1976 Act (effect of a direction under section 20) after subsection (1)—

Amendment of provisions relating to statutory succession in cases not excluded by section 2.

" (1A) Where the deceased's tenancy was not derived from the interest held by the landlord at the relevant time, the tenancy or joint tenancy deemed by virtue of subsection (1) above to be granted to, and accepted by, the person or persons so entitled shall be deemed to be granted by the person for the time being entitled to the interest from which the deceased's tenancy was derived, instead of by the landlord, with like effect as if the landlord's interest and any other supervening interest were not subsisting at the relevant time: but this provision shall not be read as affecting the rights and liabilities of the landlord under this Part of this Act.

The reference above to a supervening interest is a reference to any interest in the land comprised in the deceased's tenancy, being an interest created subsequently to that tenancy and derived (whether immediately or otherwise) from the interest from which that tenancy was derived and still subsisting at the relevant time."

(2) In section 18(2) of that Act (interpretation of the provisions of that Act relating to succession on death of tenant)—

(a) in paragraph (c) of the definition of " eligible person " (which excludes a person who is the occupier, other-

1967 c. 22.

wise than as a licensee, of a commercial unit of agricultural land within the meaning of Part II of the Agriculture Act 1967) the words from " within " to the end of the paragraph shall be omitted ; and

(b) at the end of that definition there shall be inserted the following words—

" but in the case of the deceased's wife the reference in paragraph (b) above to the survivor's agricultural work shall be read as a reference to agricultural work carried out by either the wife or the deceased (or both of them) ; ".

(3) After section 18(3) of that Act (attendance at educational institutions to count for the purposes of paragraph (b) of the definition of " eligible person " up to a limit of three years) there shall be inserted the following subsections—

" (3A) In paragraph (c) of that definition " commercial unit of agricultural land " means a unit of agricultural land which is capable, when farmed under competent management, of producing a net annual income of an amount not less than the aggregate of the average annual earnings of two full-time, male agricultural workers aged twenty or over ; and, in so far as any units of production for the time being prescribed by an order under subsection (3B) below are relevant to the assessment of the productive capacity of a unit of agricultural land when farmed as aforesaid, the net annual income which that unit is capable of producing for the purposes of this subsection shall be ascertained by reference to the provisions of that order.

(3B) The Minister shall by order made by statutory instrument subject to annulment in pursuance of a resolution of either House of Parliament—

(a) prescribe such units of production relating to agricultural land as he considers appropriate, being units framed by reference to any circumstances whatever and designed for the assessment of the productive capacity of such land ; and

(b) for any period of twelve months specified in the order, determine in relation to any unit of production so prescribed the amount which is to be regarded for the purposes of subsection (3A) above as the net annual income from that unit in that period.

(3C) Schedule 3A to this Act, which specifies—

(a) kinds of occupation that are to be disregarded for the purposes of paragraph (c) of the definition of " eligible person " in subsection (2) above ; and

(*b*) circumstances in which a person is deemed to be in occupation of land for those purposes ;
shall have effect."

(4) For section 18(6) of that Act (certificate of the Minister to be conclusive as to whether a particular agricultural unit is or would be a commercial unit within the meaning of Part II of the Agriculture Act 1967) there shall be substituted the follow- 1967 c. 22. ing subsections—

" (6) For the purposes of any proceedings under this Part of this Act in relation to the holding, the Minister shall—

(*a*) at the request of any of the following persons, namely any person falling within paragraphs (*a*) to (*d*) of subsection (1) above, the landlord or the secretary of the Tribunal ; and

(*b*) in relation to any relevant land ;

determine by reference to the provisions of any order for the time being in force under subsection (3B) above the net annual income which, in his view, the land is capable of producing for the purposes of subsection (3A) above, and shall issue a written statement of his view and the grounds for it to the person making the request.

In this subsection " relevant land " means agricultural land which is—

(*a*) occupied by any person falling within the said paragraphs (*a*) to (*d*) (whether he is, where the request is made by a person so falling, the person making the request or not) ; or

(*b*) the subject of an application made under section 20 of this Act by any such person.

(6A) Where—

(*a*) for the purposes of any proceedings under this Part of this Act the Minister has issued a statement to any person containing a determination under subsection (6) above made by reference to the provisions of an order under subsection (3B) above ; and

(*b*) before any hearing by the Tribunal in those proceedings is due to begin it appears to him that any subsequent order under that subsection has affected any matter on which that determination was based ;

he shall make a revised determination under subsection (6) above and shall issue a written statement of his view and the grounds for it to the person in question.

(6B) Any statement issued by the Minister in pursuance of subsection (6) or (6A) above shall be evidence of any facts stated in it as facts on which his view is based ; and any document purporting to be such a statement and to be signed by or on behalf of the Minister shall be taken to be such a statement unless the contrary is shown."

(5) Schedule 1 to this Act shall have effect for the purpose of making further minor amendments of the provisions of Part II of that Act as they apply in relation to cases not excluded by section 2 of this Act.

Nomination of successor by retiring tenant. **4.** Schedule 2 to this Act (under which a person nominated by the tenant of an agricultural holding may apply to the Agricultural Land Tribunal for a direction entitling him to a tenancy of the holding on the retirement of the tenant) shall have effect.

Notices to quit

Amendments with respect to length of notices to quit. **5.** The following subsections shall be added at the end of section 1 of the 1977 Act (length of notice to quit ordinarily needed to end tenancy of agricultural holding)—

" (5) Where on a reference under section 8(1) of the 1948 Act with respect to an agricultural holding the arbitrator determines that the rent payable in respect of the holding shall be increased, a notice to quit the holding given by the tenant at least six months before it purports to take effect shall not be invalid by virtue of subsection (1) above if it purports to terminate the tenancy at the end of the year of the tenancy beginning with the date as from which the increase of rent is effective.

(6) On an application made to the Tribunal with respect to an agricultural holding under subsection (4) of section 2 of this Act for the purposes of Case C in subsection (3) of that section, the Tribunal may, if they grant a certificate in accordance with the application, specify in the certificate a minimum period of notice for termination of the tenancy (not being a period of less than two months) and direct that that period shall apply instead of the period of notice required in accordance with subsection (1) above ; and in any such case a notice to quit the holding which states that the Tribunal have given a direction under this subsection shall not be invalid by virtue of subsection (1) above if the notice given is not less than the minimum notice specified in the certificate.

(7) A notice to quit within subsection (5) or (6) above shall not be invalid by virtue of any term of the contract of tenancy requiring a longer period of notice to terminate

the tenancy, and a notice to quit within subsection (6) shall not be invalid by reason of its terminating at a date other than the end of a year of the tenancy."

6.—(1) Section 2(3) of the 1977 Act (cases excepted from restriction on operation of notices to quit agricultural holdings) shall be amended as follows.

(2) Case A shall be omitted.

(3) In Case C, for the words from " on an application " to " so satisfied " there shall be substituted the words " not more than six months before the giving of the notice to quit, the Tribunal granted a certificate under subsection (4) below that the tenant of the holding was not fulfilling his responsibilities to farm in accordance with the rules of good husbandry ".

(4) In paragraph (i) of Case D, after the word " paragraph " there shall be inserted " (*a*) or ".

(5) In Case G—

(*a*) for the words from the beginning to " aforesaid " there shall be substituted the words " the notice to quit is given—

(*a*) following the death of a person who immediately before his death was the sole (or sole surviving) tenant under the contract of tenancy ; and

(*b*) not later than the end of the period of three months beginning with the date of any relevant notice ;

and it is stated in the notice to quit that it is given by reason of that person's death," ; and

(*b*) the following words shall be added at the end " and the reference to the date of any relevant notice shall be construed as a reference—

(i) to the date on which a notice in writing was served on the landlord by or on behalf of an executor or administrator of the tenant's estate informing the landlord of the tenant's death or the date on which the landlord was given notice by virtue of section 20(14) of the Agriculture (Miscellaneous Provisions) Act 1976 of any application with respect to the holding under section 20 or 21 of that Act ; or

(ii) where both of those events occur, to the date of whichever of them occurs first."

(6) The following Case shall be inserted after Case H—

" Case I—the holding is let as a smallholding by a

Margin notes:

Amendments with respect to cases excepted from restriction on operation of notices to quit.

1976 c. 55.

smallholdings authority or the Minister in pursuance of Part III of the Agriculture Act 1970 and was so let after the commencement of the Agricultural Holdings Act 1984, and—

(*a*) the tenant has attained the age of 65 ; and

(*b*) if the result of the notice to quit taking effect would be to deprive the tenant of living accommodation occupied by him under the tenancy, suitable alternative accommodation is available for him, or will be available for him when the notice takes effect ; and

(*c*) the instrument under which the tenancy was granted contains an acknowledgement signed by the tenant that the tenancy is subject to the provisions of this Case ;

and it is stated in the notice to quit that it is given by reason of the matter aforesaid.

Schedule 1A to this Act shall have effect for determining whether, for the purposes of paragraph (*b*) above, suitable alternative accommodation is or will be available for the tenant."

(7) The following subsection shall be inserted after section 2(3) of that Act—

" (3A) For the purposes of Case B no account shall be taken of any permission granted as mentioned in paragraph (*a*) of that Case if the permission—

(*a*) was granted on an application made by the National Coal Board ; and

(*b*) relates to the working of coal by opencast operations ; and

(*c*) was granted subject to a restoration condition and to an aftercare condition in which the use specified is use for agriculture or use for forestry.

In this subsection " restoration condition " and " aftercare condition " have the meaning given by section 30A(2) of the Town and Country Planning Act 1971."

(8) The following subsections shall be inserted after section 2(4) of that Act—

" (4A) In determining whether to grant a certificate under subsection (4) above the Tribunal shall disregard any practice adopted by the tenant in pursuance of any provision of the contract of tenancy, or of any other agreement with the landlord, which indicates (in whatever terms) that its object is the furtherance of one or more of the following purposes, namely—

    (*a*) the conservation of flora or fauna or of geological or physiographical features of special interest;

    (*b*) the protection of buildings or other objects of archaeological, architectural or historic interest;

    (*c*) the conservation or enhancement of the natural beauty or amenity of the countryside or the promotion of its enjoyment by the public.

(4B) For the purposes of Case D and Case E any provision such as is mentioned in subsection (4A) above shall (if it would not otherwise be so regarded) be regarded as a term or condition of the tenancy which is not inconsistent with the tenant's responsibilities to farm in accordance with the rules of good husbandry."

(9) In section 19 of the 1976 Act (restriction on operation of notices to quit within Case G), in paragraph (*a*), after the words " is made " there shall be inserted the words " (or has already at the time of the notice to quit been made) ".

7. In section 4(4) of the 1977 Act (additional restrictions on operation of notice to quit given by reason of tenant's non-compliance with notice to do work), for the words from " unless " to the end there shall be substituted the words " unless it appears to them, having regard— *Circumstances to be taken into account by Tribunal in cases of non-compliance with notice to do work.*

    (*a*) to the extent to which the tenant has failed to comply with the notice to do work;

    (*b*) to the consequences of his failure to comply with it in any respect; and

    (*c*) to the circumstances surrounding any such failure;

that a fair and reasonable landlord would not insist on possession."

Miscellaneous and supplemental

8.—(1) The functions of the Minister under the following provisions of the 1948 Act, namely— *Transfer of certain functions of Minister to President of R.I.C.S.*

    section 16(2) (appointment of person to make record of condition of holding);

    paragraph 1 of Schedule 6 (appointment of arbitrator);

    paragraph 5(*b*) of that Schedule (fixing of arbitrator's remuneration); and

    paragraph 13 of that Schedule (extension of time limited for making award);

shall be exercisable instead by the President of the Royal Institution of Chartered Surveyors (referred to in this section as " the President ").

(2) Accordingly any reference to the Minister in any of those provisions, or in any other provision of the 1948 Act relating to the appointment of an arbitrator by the Minister or to an arbitrator appointed by him, shall be construed, in relation to any time after the commencement of this section, as a reference to the President.

(3) No application may be made to the President—

(a) for a person to be appointed by him under section 16(2) of the 1948 Act ; or

(b) for an arbitrator to be appointed by him under paragraph 1 of Schedule 6 to that Act ;

unless the application is accompanied by the prescribed fee ; but once the prescribed fee has been paid in connection with any such application for the appointment of an arbitrator no further fee shall be payable in connection with any subsequent application for the President to exercise any function exercisable by him in relation to the arbitration by virtue of subsection (1) above (including an application for the appointment by him in an appropriate case of a new arbitrator).

(4) In subsection (3) above " the prescribed fee " means, in relation to any such application as is mentioned in paragraph (a) or (b) of that subsection, such fee as the Minister may by regulations made by statutory instrument prescribe as the fee for such an application ; but no regulations shall be made under this subsection unless a draft of the regulations has been laid before and approved by a resolution of each House of Parliament.

(5) Any instrument of appointment or other document purporting to be made in the exercise of any function exercisable by the President by virtue of subsection (1) above and to be signed by or on behalf of the President shall be taken to be such an instrument or document unless the contrary is shown.

Interpretation, etc.

1948 c. 63.

1976 c. 55.

1977 c. 12.

9.—(1) In this Act—

" the 1948 Act " means the Agricultural Holdings Act 1948 ;

" the 1976 Act " means the Agriculture (Miscellaneous Provisions) Act 1976 ; and

" the 1977 Act " means the Agricultural Holdings (Notices to Quit) Act 1977.

(2) Unless the context otherwise requires, expressions used in this Act and the 1948 Act have the same meaning in this Act as in that Act.

(3) Section 87(1) and (2) of the 1948 Act (Crown land) shall have effect as if references to that Act included references to this Act (except paragraph 30 of Schedule 3).

10.—(1) The enactments specified in Schedule 3 to this Act shall have effect subject to the amendments set out in that Schedule, being minor amendments and amendments consequential on the preceding provisions of this Act.

(2) The enactments specified in Schedule 4 to this Act (which include enactments which were spent before the passing of this Act or are no longer of practical utility) are repealed to the extent specified in the third column of that Schedule.

Minor and consequential amendments and repeals.

11.—(1) This Act may be cited as the Agricultural Holdings Act 1984.

(2) Subject to subsections (3) to (5) below, this Act shall come into force at the end of the period of two months beginning with the day on which it is passed; and references in this Act, and in any Act amended by this Act, to the commencement of this Act are references to the beginning of the day on which it so comes into force.

Short title, commencement, transitional provisions and extent.

(3) The following provisions shall come into force on the passing of this Act—

(a) sections 1, 2 and 9 and this section;

(b) paragraphs 5(3), 23 and 35 of Schedule 3 and section 10(1) so far as relating thereto;

(c) section 10(2) and Schedule 4 so far as relating to section 1(2) of the 1948 Act, section 2 of the Agriculture Act 1958 and Case H in section 2(3) of the 1977 Act; *1958 c. 71.*

(d) Schedule 5.

(4) Section 6(7) above shall be deemed to have come into force on 1st March 1984.

(5) The following provisions shall come into force on such day as the Minister may appoint by order made by statutory instrument—

(a) section 8;

(b) section 10(2) and Schedule 4 so far as relating to paragraph 28 of Schedule 6 to the 1948 Act.

(6) The transitional and saving provisions contained in Schedule 5 to this Act shall have effect.

(7) This Act extends to England and Wales only.

SCHEDULES

SCHEDULE 1

MINOR AMENDMENTS WITH RESPECT TO STATUTORY SUCCESSION

Definitions

1. In subsection (2) of section 18 of the 1976 Act (application of following sections of Part II)—

   (*a*) the following definition shall be inserted after the definition of " the 1977 Act "—

   " " agricultural land " has the meaning given by section 1(2) of the 1948 Act ; " ;

   (*b*) in the definition of " the holding ", the words " (except where the context otherwise requires) " shall be inserted after the words " the holding " ; and

   (*c*) the following definition shall be inserted after the definition of " eligible person "—

   " " related holding " means, in relation to the holding, any agricultural holding comprising the whole or a substantial part of the land comprised in the holding ; ".

Cases excluded from Part II of the 1976 *Act*

2.—(1) Subsection (4) of section 18 of that Act (cases where provisions of Part II of that Act do not apply) shall be amended as follows.

(2) In paragraph (*a*), the following sub-paragraph shall be substituted for sub-paragraph (ii)—

" (ii) the Tribunal consented before that date to its operation ; ".

(3) In paragraph (*c*)—

   (*a*) in sub-paragraphs (i) and (ii), for the words " that Act " there shall be substituted the words " the 1948 Act " ; and

   (*b*) the following sub-paragraph shall be substituted for sub-paragraph (iii)—

   " (iii) the Tribunal consented before that date to the operation of the notice ; ".

(4) In paragraph (*d*), sub-paragraph (ii) and the word " or " immediately preceding it shall be omitted.

(5) The following paragraph shall be substituted for paragraph (*e*)—

   " (*e*) without prejudice to subsection (5) below, if on each of the last two occasions when there died a sole (or sole surviving) tenant (within the meaning of subsection (1) above) of the holding or of a related holding there occurred one or other of the following things, namely—

(i) a tenancy of the holding or of a related holding was obtained by virtue of a direction of the Tribunal under section 20 of this Act, or such a tenancy was granted (following such a direction) in circumstances within section 23(6) of this Act ; or

(ii) a tenancy of the holding or of a related holding was granted by the landlord to a person who, being on that occasion a person falling within paragraphs (*a*) to (*d*) of subsection (1) above, was or had become the sole or sole remaining applicant for such a direction ; ".

(6) In paragraph (*f*), for the words from " and the " to the end of the paragraph there shall be substituted the words " (whether the tenancy was granted before or after the commencement of the said Part III) ; ".

(7) The following subsections shall be substituted for subsection (5) of that section—

" (5) If on any occasion prior to the date of death, as a result of an agreement between the landlord and the tenant for the time being of the holding or of a related holding, the holding or a related holding became let—

(*a*) under a tenancy granted by the landlord ; or

(*b*) by virtue of an assignment of the current tenancy ;

to a person who, if the said tenant had died immediately before the grant or assignment, would have fallen within paragraphs (*a*) to (*d*) of subsection (1) above, that occasion shall for the purposes of paragraph (*e*) of subsection (4) above be deemed to be an occasion such as is mentioned in that paragraph on which a tenancy of the holding or a related holding was obtained by virtue of a direction of the Tribunal under section 20 of this Act.

In this subsection " tenant " has the same meaning as in subsection (1) above ; and if any such tenancy was granted as aforesaid for a term commencing later than the date of the grant, the holding under that tenancy shall for the purposes of this subsection not be taken to have become let under that tenancy until the commencement of the term.

(5A) Subsections (4)(*e*) and (5) above—

(*a*) shall apply whether or not any tenancy granted or obtained (otherwise than by virtue of an assignment) as mentioned in those provisions related to the whole of the land held by the tenant on the occasion of whose death, or with whose agreement, the tenancy was so granted or obtained, as the case may be ; and

(*b*) shall apply where a joint tenancy is granted by the landlord to persons one of whom is a person such as is mentioned in either of those provisions as they apply where a tenancy is granted by the landlord to any such person alone :

and subsection (5) shall apply where a tenancy is assigned to joint tenants one of whom is a person such as is mentioned in that subsection as it applies where a tenancy is assigned to any such person alone."

Succession to part of a holding pursuant to a Tribunal direction

3.—(1) The following provisions of this paragraph have effect for the purpose of permitting a direction to be given under section 20 of the 1976 Act entitling the person or persons concerned to a tenancy (or a joint tenancy) of part of the agricultural holding to which an application under that section relates.

(2) In section 19 of that Act (restriction on operation of notice to quit given by reason of death of tenant), for paragraph (*b*) (ii) there shall be substituted the following—

　　" (ii) the Tribunal consent under section 22 of this Act to the operation of the notice to quit in relation to the whole or part of the holding ;

　　and where the Tribunal consent under that section to the operation of the notice in relation to part only of the holding the notice shall have effect accordingly as a notice to quit that part and shall not be invalid by reason that it relates only to part of the holding."

(3) In section 20 of that Act (applications for tenancy of the holding)—

　　(*a*) the words " subsection (9A) below and " shall be inserted after the words " subject to " in subsection (5) and after those words (in the second place where they occur) in subsection (6) ; and

　　(*b*) the following subsection shall be inserted after subsection (9)—

　　　　" (9A) Where the person or persons who would, subject to section 22 of this Act, be entitled to a direction under this section entitling him or them to a tenancy or (as the case may be) to a joint tenancy of the holding agree to accept instead a tenancy or joint tenancy of a part of the holding, any direction given by the Tribunal under subsection (5), (6) or (9) above shall relate to that part of the holding only."

(4) In section 22 of that Act (opportunity for landlord to obtain Tribunal's consent to operation of notice to quit)—

　　(*a*) the words " Subject to subsection (5) below " shall be inserted at the beginning of subsections (2) and (4) ; and

　　(*b*) the following subsection shall be added at the end—

　　　　" (5) Where in any case—

　　　　　　(*a*) a notice to quit to which section 19 of this Act applies has been given ; and

(b) section 20(9A) of this Act applies ;

the Tribunal shall give their consent to the operation of the notice to quit in relation to the part of the holding which would, in accordance with section 20(9A), be excluded from any direction given by the Tribunal with respect to the holding under section 20 ; and subsections (2) and (4) above shall not apply."

(5) The following subsection shall be added at the end of section 23 of that Act (effect of a direction under section 20)—

" (9) Where in accordance with section 20(9A) of this Act the tenancy to which a direction under that section entitles the person or persons concerned is a tenancy of part of the deceased's holding, references in this and the next following section to the holding shall be read as references to the whole of the deceased's holding or to the part of that holding to which the direction relates, as the context requires."

(6) In section 24 of that Act (arbitration on terms of new tenancy), the following words shall be added at the end of subsection (2)—

" and references to the holding shall be read in accordance with section 23(9) of this Act."

Continuing eligibility of applicant

4. In section 20(2) of that Act, for the words " that the applicant is an eligible person " there shall be substituted—

" (a) that the applicant was an eligible person at the date of death, and

(b) that he has not subsequently ceased to be such a person ; ".

Order of hearing of applications

5.—(1) In section 18(1) of that Act, after " 20(14) " there shall be inserted " and (15) ".

(2) In section 20 of that Act, the following subsection shall be added after subsection (14)—

" (15) If at the expiry of the period of three months beginning with the day after the date of the death of a tenant there are pending before such a tribunal separate applications made under this section by any person, or (as the case may be) by each one of a number of persons, in respect of more than one agricultural holding held by the tenant at that date, then, subject to and in accordance with the provisions of any order under the said section 73(3), those applications (together with, in each case, any associated application made under the following section) shall be heard and determined by the tribunal in such order as may be decided—

(a) where those applications were made by one person, by that person ;

(*b*) where those applications were made by two or more persons, by agreement between those persons or, in default of agreement, by the chairman of the tribunal ;

and any decision made by the chairman under paragraph (*b*) above shall be made according to the respective sizes of the holdings concerned so that any application in respect of any holding which is larger than any other of those holdings shall be heard and determined by the tribunal before any application in respect of that other holding."

Postponement of operative date of notice to quit

6. In section 22 of that Act, the following subsections shall be added after the subsection (5) added by paragraph 3(4)(*b*) above—

" (6) If on an application made in pursuance of subsection (1) above the Tribunal give their consent to the operation of a notice to quit—

(*a*) within the period of three months ending with the date on which the notice purports to terminate the tenancy (" the original operative date ") ; or

(*b*) at any time after that date ;

the Tribunal may, on the application of the tenant, direct that the notice shall have effect from a later date (" the new operative date ").

(7) The new operative date, in the case of a notice to quit, must be a date not later than the end of the period of three months beginning with—

(*a*) the original operative date ; or

(*b*) the date on which the Tribunal give their consent to the operation of the notice ;

whichever last occurs."

Postponement of " relevant time" etc.

7.—(1) The words " Subject to subsection (2A) below " shall be inserted at the beginning of section 23(2) of that Act.

(2) The following subsection shall be inserted after section 23(2)—

" (2A) Where the Tribunal give a direction under section 20(5), (6) or (9) of this Act in relation to the holding at any time after the beginning of the period of three months ending with the relevant time apart from this subsection (" the original relevant time "), then—

(*a*) if the direction is given within that period, the Tribunal may, on the application of the tenant, specify in the direction, as the relevant time for the purposes of this and the next following section, such a time falling within the period of three months immediately following the original relevant time as they think fit ;

(*b*) if the direction is given at any time after the original relevant time the Tribunal shall specify in the direction, as the relevant time for those purposes, such a time falling within the period of three months immediately following the date of the giving of the direction as they think fit ;

and any time so specified shall be the relevant time for those purposes accordingly."

(3) In section 24(2)—

(*a*) at the end of the definition of " the relevant time " there shall be inserted the words " or by section 23(2A) of this Act (as the case may require) " ; and

(*b*) in the definition of " the prescribed period " for the words from " and the " onwards there shall be substituted the words " and—

(*a*) the end of the three months immediately following the relevant time ; or

(*b*) the end of the three months immediately following the date of the giving of the direction ;

whichever last occurs."

Occupation of land

8. The following Schedule shall be inserted after Schedule 3 to that Act—

" SCHEDULE 3A

OCCUPATION OF LAND FOR PURPOSES OF STATUTORY SUCCESSION

Preliminary

1.—(1) In this Schedule " the occupancy condition " means paragraph (*c*) of the definition of " eligible person " in section 18(2) of this Act.

(2) For the purposes of this Schedule a body corporate is controlled by a survivor of the deceased if he or his spouse, or he and his spouse together, have the power to secure—

(*a*) by means of the holding of shares or the possession of voting power in or in relation to that or any other body corporate ; or

(*b*) by virtue of any powers conferred by the articles of association or other document regulating that or any other body corporate ;

that the affairs of that body corporate are conducted in accordance with his, her or their wishes, respectively.

(3) Any reference in this Schedule to the spouse of a survivor of the deceased does not apply in relation to any time when the survivor's marriage is the subject of a decree of judicial separation or a decree nisi of divorce or of nullity of marriage.

Excluded occupation

2.—(1) Occupation by a survivor of the deceased of any agricultural land shall be disregarded for the purposes of the occupancy condition if he occupies it only—

(a) under a tenancy approved by the Minister under section 2(1) of the 1948 Act or under such a tenancy relating to the use of land for grazing or mowing as is referred to in the proviso to that provision ;

(b) under a tenancy for more than one year but less than two years ;

(c) under a tenancy not falling within paragraph (a) or (b) above and not having effect as a contract of tenancy ;

(d) under a tenancy to which section 3 of the 1948 Act does not apply by virtue of section 3B of that Act ;

(e) as a licensee ; or

(f) as an executor, administrator, trustee in bankruptcy or person otherwise deriving title from another person by operation of law.

(2) Paragraphs (a) to (e) of sub-paragraph (1) above do not apply in the case of a tenancy or licence granted to a survivor of the deceased by his spouse or by a body corporate controlled by him.

(3) References in the following provisions of this Schedule to the occupation of land by any person do not include occupation under a tenancy, or in a capacity, falling within paragraphs (a) to (f) of that sub-paragraph.

Deemed occupation in case of Tribunal direction

3. Where a survivor of the deceased is, by virtue of a direction of the Tribunal under section 20 of this Act, for the time being entitled (whether or not with any other person) to a tenancy of the whole or part of any agricultural holding held by the deceased at the date of death other than the holding, he shall, for the purposes of the occupancy condition, be deemed to be in occupation of the land comprised in that holding or (as the case may be) in that part of that holding.

Joint occupation

4.—(1) Where any agricultural land is jointly occupied by a survivor of the deceased and one or more other persons as—

(a) beneficial joint tenants ;

(b) tenants in common ;

(c) joint tenants under a tenancy ; or

(d) joint licensees ;

the survivor shall be treated for the purposes of the occupancy condition as occupying the whole of the land.

(2) If, however, the Tribunal in proceedings under section 20 of this Act determine on the survivor's application that his appropriate share of the net annual income which the land is, or was at any time, capable of producing for the purposes of section 18(3A) of this Act is or was then less than the aggregate of the earnings referred to in that provision, then, for the purpose of determining whether the occupancy condition is or was then satisfied in his case, the net annual income which the land is, or (as the case may be) was, capable of so producing shall be treated as limited to his appropriate share.

(3) For the purposes of sub-paragraph (2) above the appropriate share of the survivor shall be ascertained—

(*a*) where he is a beneficial or other joint tenant or a joint licensee, by dividing the net annual income which the land is or was at the time in question capable of producing for the purposes of section 18(3A) by the total number of joint tenants or joint licensees for the time being ;

(*b*) where he is a tenant in common, by dividing the said net annual income in such a way as to attribute to him and to the other tenant or tenants in common shares of the income proportionate to the extent for the time being of their respective undivided shares in the land.

(4) Where by virtue of paragraph 3 above any land is deemed to be occupied by each of two or more survivors of the deceased as a result of a direction entitling them to a joint tenancy of the land, the preceding provisions of this paragraph shall apply to each of the survivors as if the land were jointly occupied by him and the other survivor or survivors as joint tenants under that tenancy.

Occupation by spouse or controlled company

5.—(1) For the purposes of the occupancy condition and of paragraph 4 above, occupation—

(*a*) by the spouse of a survivor of the deceased ; or

(*b*) by a body corporate controlled by a survivor of the deceased ;

shall be treated as occupation by the survivor.

(2) Where, in accordance with sub-paragraph (1) above, paragraph 4 above applies to a survivor of the deceased in relation to any time by virtue of the joint occupation of land by his spouse or a body corporate and any other person or persons, sub-paragraphs (2) and (3) of that paragraph shall apply to the survivor as if he were the holder of the interest in the land for the time being held by his spouse or the body corporate, as the case may be.

SCH. 1

Deemed occupation in case of tenancy or licence granted by survivor, spouse or controlled company

6.—(1) Where—

(a) any agricultural land is occupied by any person under such a tenancy as is mentioned in paragraphs (a) to (d) of paragraph 2(1) above or as a licensee ; and

(b) that tenancy or licence was granted by a survivor of the deceased or a connected person (or both), being at the time it was granted a person or persons entitled to occupy the land otherwise than under a tenancy, or in a capacity, falling within paragraphs (a) to (f) of paragraph 2(1) ;

then, unless sub-paragraph (2) below applies, the survivor shall, for the purposes of the occupancy condition, be deemed to be in occupation of the whole of the land.

(2) Where the tenancy or licence referred to in sub-paragraph (1) above was granted by the person or persons there referred to and one or more other persons who were at the time it was granted entitled to occupy the land as mentioned in paragraph (b) of that sub-paragraph, sub-paragraphs (2) and (3) of paragraph 4 above shall apply to the survivor as if the land were jointly occupied by him and the said other person or persons as holders of their respective interests for the time being in the land.

(3) In this paragraph " connected person ", in relation to a survivor of the deceased, means—

(a) the survivor's spouse ; or

(b) a body corporate controlled by the survivor ;

and for the purposes of sub-paragraph (2) above and the provisions of paragraph 4 there mentioned any interest in the land for the time being held by a connected person by whom the tenancy or licence was granted shall be attributed to the survivor.

Ministerial statements as to net annual income from land

7. The reference in the definition of " relevant land " in section 18(6) of this Act to agricultural land which is occupied by any such person as is mentioned in paragraph (a) of that definition includes a reference to any agricultural land which is deemed to be occupied by him by virtue of this Schedule."

Section 4.

SCHEDULE 2

STATUTORY SUCCESSION BY PERSON NOMINATED BY RETIRING TENANT

Application of Schedule

1.—(1) Where—

(a) an agricultural holding is held under a tenancy from year to year, being a tenancy granted before the date on which this Act is passed or on or after that date in circumstances within section 2(2) of this Act ; and

(*b*) a notice is given to the landlord by the tenant, or (in the case of a joint tenancy) by all the tenants, of the holding indicating (in whatever terms) that he or they wish a single eligible person named in the notice to succeed him or them as tenant of the holding as from a date specified in the notice, being a date on which the tenancy of the holding could have been determined by notice to quit given at the date of the notice and which falls not less than one year, but not more than two years, after the date of the notice ;

the principal paragraphs of this Schedule shall apply unless excluded by paragraph 2 below (and subject also to paragraph 3 below).

In this sub-paragraph " tenant " does not include an executor, administrator, committee of the estate, trustee in bankruptcy or other person deriving title from a tenant by operation of law.

(2) In this Schedule—

" agricultural land " has the meaning given by section 1(2) of the 1948 Act ;

" close relative " means—

(*a*) the wife or husband of the retiring tenant ;

(*b*) a brother or sister of the retiring tenant ;

(*c*) a child of the retiring tenant ;

(*d*) any person (not within (*b*) or (*c*) above) who, in the case of any marriage to which the retiring tenant has been at any time a party, has been treated by the latter as a child of the family in relation to that marriage ;

" eligible person " means (subject to sub-paragraph (3) below) a close relative in whose case the following conditions are satisfied—

(*a*) in the last seven years his only or principal source of livelihood throughout a continuous period of not less than five years, or two or more discontinuous periods together amounting to not less than five years, derived from his agricultural work on the holding or on an agricultural unit of which the holding forms part ; and

(*b*) he is not the occupier of a commercial unit of agricultural land ;

but in the case of the wife of the retiring tenant the reference in paragraph (*a*) above to the relative's agricultural work shall be read as a reference to agricultural work carried out by either the wife or the retiring tenant (or both of them) ;

" the holding " means the holding in respect of which the retirement notice is given ;

" the nominated successor " means the eligible person named in the retirement notice ;

" the principal paragraphs of this Schedule " means paragraphs 4 to 10 below (except paragraphs 5(10) and 6(6), which are of general application) ;

" the relevant period " means (subject to paragraphs 2(6) and 3(3) below) the period of one month beginning with the day after the date of the giving of the retirement notice ;

" the retirement date " means the date specified in the retirement notice as the date as from which the proposed succession is to take place ;

" the retirement notice " means the notice mentioned in sub-paragraph (1) above ;

" the retiring tenant " means the tenant by whom the retirement notice was given or, where it was given by joint tenants (and the context so permits), any one of those tenants, and " the retiring tenants " accordingly means those tenants ;

" the tenancy " means the tenancy of the holding ;

" the Tribunal " means the Agricultural Land Tribunal.

(3) For the purposes of paragraph (*a*) of the definition of " eligible person " in sub-paragraph (2) above any period during which a close relative was, in the period of seven years mentioned in that paragraph, attending a full-time course at a university, college or other establishment of further education shall be treated as a period throughout which his only or principal source of livelihood derived from his agricultural work on the holding ; but not more than **three** years in all shall be so treated by virtue of this sub-paragraph.

(4) For the purposes of paragraph (*b*) of that definition—

(*a*) " commercial unit of agricultural land " means a commercial unit of agricultural land as defined by subsection (3A) of section 18 of the 1976 Act (taken with subsection (3B) of that section) ;

(*b*) Schedule 3A to that Act (which provides for the disregarding of certain kinds of occupation as well as specifying circumstances in which a person is deemed to be in occupation of land) shall apply in relation to the nominated successor as it applies in relation to a survivor of a deceased tenant, but subject to the following modifications, namely—

(i) references to the occupancy condition shall be read as references to the said paragraph (*b*),

(ii) the reference in paragraph 4(2) to section 20 of that Act shall be read as a reference to paragraph 5 below, and

(iii) paragraphs 3, 4(4) and 7 shall be omitted ; and

(c) where the nominated successor is, by virtue of a direction of the Tribunal under paragraph 5(6) below, for the time being entitled to a tenancy of any agricultural holding held by the retiring tenant other than the holding he shall be deemed to be in occupation of that holding.

(5) For the purposes of any proceedings under this Schedule in relation to the holding the Minister shall—

(a) at the request of any of the following persons, namely the nominated successor, the landlord or the secretary of the Tribunal ; and

(b) in relation to any agricultural land which is occupied by the nominated successor ;

determine by reference to the provisions of any order for the time being in force under subsection (3B) of the said section 18 the net annual income which, in his view, the land is capable of producing for the purposes of subsection (3A) of that section (as applied by sub-paragraph (4)(a) above), and shall issue a written statement of his view and the grounds for it to the person making the request.

The reference above to any agricultural land which is occupied by the nominated successor includes a reference to any agricultural land which is deemed to be occupied by him by virtue of sub-paragraph (4)(b) or (c) above.

(6) Subsection (6A) of the said section 18 (revision of determinations) shall, with any necessary modifications, apply to a statement issued by the Minister in pursuance of sub-paragraph (5) above as it applies to one issued by him under subsection (6) of that section, and subsection (6B) of that section (evidential matters) shall apply also to any statement issued by him in pursuance of that or this sub-paragraph.

(7) Section 92 of the 1948 Act (service of notices) shall apply to a notice under sub-paragraph (1)(b) above as it applies to a notice under that Act.

Excluded cases

2.—(1) The principal paragraphs of this Schedule shall not apply—

(a) if on the date of the giving of the retirement notice the tenancy is the subject of a valid notice to quit to which subsection (1) of section 2 of the 1977 Act applies, being a notice given before that date in the case of which either—

(i) the month allowed by that subsection for serving a counter-notice thereunder expired before that date without such a counter-notice having been served ; or

(ii) the Tribunal consented before that date to its operation ;

(b) if on the date of the giving of the retirement notice the tenancy is the subject of a valid notice to quit given before that date and falling within Case C or F in subsection (3) of that section ;

(c) if on the date of the giving of the retirement notice the tenancy is the subject of a valid notice to quit given before that date and falling within Case B, D or E in subsection (3) of that section, and either—

(i) the time within which the tenant could have required any question arising in connection with the notice to quit to be determined by arbitration under the 1948 Act expired before that date without such a requirement having been made by the tenant, and the month allowed for serving any counter-notice in respect of the notice to quit expired before that date without any such counter-notice having been served ; or

(ii) questions arising in connection with the notice to quit were referred to arbitration under the 1948 Act before that date and were determined before that date in such a way as to uphold the operation of the notice to quit, and (where applicable) the month allowed for serving any counter-notice in respect of the notice to quit expired before that date without a counter-notice having been served ; or

(iii) the Tribunal consented before that date to the operation of the notice to quit ;

(d) if the retiring tenant has at any time given any other notice under paragraph 1(1)(b) above in respect of the holding or a related holding and an application to become the tenant of the holding or a related holding has been duly made by any person under paragraph 5 below in respect of that notice ;

(e) subject to sub-paragraph (3) below, if at the retirement date the retiring tenant will be under 65 ;

(f) if the holding consists of land held by a smallholdings authority or the Minister for the purposes of smallholdings within the meaning of Part III of the Agriculture Act 1970 (whether the tenancy was granted before or after the commencement of the said Part III) ;

(g) if the tenancy was granted by trustees in whom the land is vested on charitable trusts the sole or principal object of which is the settlement or employment in agriculture of persons who have served in any of Her Majesty's naval, military or air forces.

(2) In sub-paragraph (1)(d) above " related holding " means, in relation to the holding, any agricultural holding comprising the whole or a substantial part of the land comprised in the holding.

(3) The principal paragraphs of this Schedule are not excluded by sub-paragraph (1)(e) above if the retirement notice is given on the grounds that—

(a) the retiring tenant or (where the notice is given by joint tenants) each of the retiring tenants is or will at the retirement date be incapable, by reason of bodily or mental infirmity, of conducting the farming of the holding in such a way as to secure the fulfilment of the responsibilities of the tenant to farm in accordance with the rules of good husbandry ; and

(*b*) any such incapacity is likely to be permanent ;
and that fact is stated in the notice.

(4) The principal paragraphs of this Schedule shall not apply if, had a sole tenant of the holding died at the date of the giving of the retirement notice in circumstances falling within subsection (1) of section 18 of the 1976 Act, the application of the provisions of Part II of that Act referred to in that subsection would have been excluded in relation to the holding by paragraph (*e*) of subsection (4) of that section ; and the reference to that paragraph includes a reference to it as extended by subsection (5) of that section or by paragraph 10(1)(*b*) below in relation to a direction of the Tribunal under this Schedule.

(5) If on the date of the giving of the retirement notice the tenancy is the subject of a valid notice to quit given before that date and including a statement that it is given for any such reason as is referred to in Case B, D or E in section 2(3) of the 1977 Act (not being a notice to quit falling within sub-paragraph (1)(*c*) above), the principal paragraphs of this Schedule shall not apply unless one of the events referred to in sub-paragraph (6) below occurs.

(6) Those events are as follows—

(*a*) it is determined by arbitration under the 1948 Act that the notice to quit is ineffective for the purposes of section 2(3) on account of the invalidity of any such reason as aforesaid ; or

(*b*) where a counter-notice is duly served under section 4(2) or (3) of the 1977 Act—

    (i) the Tribunal withhold consent to the operation of the notice to quit, or

    (ii) the period for making an application to the Tribunal for such consent expires without such an application having been made ;

and where one of those events occurs the relevant period shall for the purposes of this Schedule be the period of one month beginning with the date on which the arbitrator's award is delivered to the tenant, with the date of the Tribunal's decision to withhold consent, or with the expiry of the said period for making an application (as the case may be).

Notices to quit restricting operation of Schedule

3.—(1) If the tenancy becomes the subject of a valid notice to quit given on or after the date of the giving of the retirement notice (but before the Tribunal have begun to hear any application by the nominated successor under paragraph 5 below in respect of the retirement notice) and the notice to quit—

(*a*) falls within Case C in section 2(3) of the 1977 Act and is founded on a certificate granted under section 2(4) of that Act in accordance with an application made before that date ; or

(*b*) falls within Case F in section 2(3);
the retirement notice shall be of no effect and no proceedings, or
(as the case may be) no further proceedings, shall be taken under
this Schedule in respect of it.

(2) If the tenancy becomes the subject of a valid notice to quit
given on or after the date of the giving of the retirement notice
(but before the Tribunal have begun to hear any application by the
nominated successor under paragraph 5 below in respect of the
retirement notice) and the notice to quit—

(*a*) includes a statement that it is given for any such reason
as is referred to in Case B in section 2(3) of the 1977
Act; or

(*b*) includes a statement that it is given for any such reason
as is referred to in Case D in section 2(3) and is founded
on a notice given for the purposes of that Case before
that date;

the retirement notice shall be of no effect and no proceedings, or
(as the case may be) no further proceedings, shall be taken under
this Schedule in respect of it unless one of the events referred to
in sub-paragraph (3) below occurs.

(3) Those events are as follows—

(*a*) it is determined by arbitration under the 1948 Act that
the notice to quit is ineffective for the purposes of section
2(3) on account of the invalidity of any such reason as
aforesaid; or

(*b*) where a counter-notice is duly served under section 4(2) or
(3) of the 1977 Act—

(i) the Tribunal withhold consent to the operation of
the notice to quit, or

(ii) the period for making an application to the
Tribunal for such consent expires without such an application having been made;

and where one of those events occurs, and the notice to quit was
given before the time when the relevant period would expire apart
from this sub-paragraph, that period shall for the purposes of this
Schedule expire at the end of the period of one month beginning
with the date on which the arbitrator's award is delivered to the
tenant, with the date of the Tribunal's decision to withhold consent,
or with the expiry of the said period for making an application
(as the case may be).

(4) For the purposes of this Schedule an application by the
nominated successor under paragraph 5 below which is invalidated
by sub-paragraph (1) or (2) above shall be treated as if it had
never been made.

Restriction on operation of certain notices to quit

4.—(1) This paragraph applies to any notice to quit the holding
or part of the holding given to the tenant thereof (whether before or

on or after the date of the giving of the retirement notice), not being a notice to quit falling within any provision of paragraph **2** or 3 above.

(2) A notice to quit to which this paragraph applies shall not, if it would otherwise be capable of so having effect, have effect—

(*a*) at any time during the relevant period ; or

(*b*) where an application to become the tenant of the holding is made by the nominated successor under paragraph 5 below within that period, at any time before the application has been finally disposed of by the Tribunal or withdrawn or abandoned ;

and shall in any event not have effect if any such application is disposed of by the Tribunal by the giving of a direction under sub-paragraph (6) of that paragraph.

Application for tenancy of the holding

5.—(1) The nominated successor may (subject to paragraph 8(2) below) apply to the Tribunal within the relevant period for a direction entitling him to a tenancy of the holding.

(2) Any such application—

(*a*) must be accompanied by a copy of the retirement notice ; and

(*b*) must be signed by both the nominated successor and the retiring tenant or, where the notice was given by joint tenants, by each of the retiring tenants.

(3) If the retirement notice includes a statement in accordance with paragraph 2(3) above that it is given on the grounds mentioned in that provision, then, before the nominated successor's application is further proceeded with under this paragraph, the Tribunal must be satisfied—

(*a*) that the retiring tenant or (as the case may be) each of the retiring tenants either is or will at the retirement date be incapable, by reason of bodily or mental infirmity, of conducting the farming of the holding in such a way as to secure the fulfilment of the responsibilities of the tenant to farm in accordance with the rules of good husbandry ; and

(*b*) that any such incapacity is likely to be permanent.

(4) If the Tribunal are satisfied—

(*a*) that the nominated successor was an eligible person at the date of the giving of the retirement notice ; and

(*b*) that he has not subsequently ceased to be such a person ;

the Tribunal shall determine whether he is in their opinion a suitable person to become the tenant of the holding.

(5) Before making a determination under sub-paragraph (4) above the Tribunal shall afford the landlord an opportunity of stating his

SCH. 2   views on the suitability of the nominated successor; and in making
any such determination the Tribunal shall have regard to all relevant matters, including—

    (*a*) the extent to which the nominated successor has been trained
in, or has had practical experience of, agriculture;

    (*b*) his age, physical health and financial standing;

    (*c*) the views (if any) stated by the landlord on his suitability.

(6) If the nominated successor is determined under that sub-paragraph to be in their opinion a suitable person to become the tenant
of the holding, the Tribunal shall, subject to sub-paragraph (7) below,
give a direction entitling him to a tenancy of the holding.

(7) The Tribunal shall not give such a direction if, on an application made by the landlord, it appears to the Tribunal that greater
hardship would be caused by giving the direction than by refusing the
nominated successor's application under this paragraph.

(8) If the Tribunal dispose of the nominated successor's application otherwise than by the giving of a direction under sub-paragraph
(6) above the retirement notice shall be of no effect (but without
prejudice to paragraph 2(1)(*d*) above).

(9) For the purposes of this Schedule an application by the nominated successor under this paragraph which is withdrawn or abandoned shall be treated as if it had never been made.

1947 c. 48.   (10) Provision shall be made by order under section 73(3) of the
Agriculture Act 1947 (procedure of Agricultural Land Tribunals)
for requiring any person making an application to such a tribunal
for a direction under this paragraph to give notice of the application
to the landlord of the agricultural holding to which the application
relates.

Effect of a direction under paragraph 5

6.—(1) Subject to the provisions of this and the following paragraph, a direction by the Tribunal under paragraph 5(6) above entitling the nominated successor to a tenancy of the holding shall
entitle him to a tenancy of the holding as from the relevant time on
the same terms as those on which the holding was let immediately
before it ceased to be let under the contract of tenancy under which
it was let at the date of the giving of the retirement notice; and
accordingly, subject as aforesaid, such a tenancy shall be deemed
to be at that time granted by the landlord to, and accepted by, the
nominated successor.

(2) Where the tenancy of the retiring tenant or (as the case may
be) of the retiring tenants was not derived from the interest held by
the landlord at the relevant time, the tenancy deemed by virtue of
sub-paragraph (1) above to be granted to, and accepted by, the
nominated successor shall be deemed to be granted by the
person for the time being entitled to the interest from which the
tenancy of the retiring tenant or tenants was derived, instead of by
the landlord, with like effect as if the landlord's interest and any
other supervening interest were not subsisting at the relevant time:

but this provision shall not be read as affecting the rights and liabilities of the landlord under this Schedule.

The reference above to a supervening interest is a reference to any interest in the land comprised in the tenancy of the retiring tenant or tenants, being an interest created subsequently to that tenancy and derived (whether immediately or otherwise) from the interest from which that tenancy was derived and still subsisting at the relevant time.

(3) If the terms of the tenancy to which the nominated successor is entitled by virtue of a direction such as is mentioned in sub-paragraph (1) above would not, apart from this sub-paragraph, include a covenant by the tenant not to assign, sub-let or part with possession of the holding or any part thereof without the landlord's consent in writing, sub-paragraph (1) above shall have effect as if those terms included that covenant.

(4) Any tenancy of the holding inconsistent with the tenancy to which the nominated successor is entitled by virtue of such a direction shall, if it would not cease at the relevant time apart from this sub-paragraph, cease at that time as if terminated at that time by a valid notice to quit given by the tenant.

(5) The rights conferred on any person by such a direction (as distinct from his rights under his tenancy of the holding after he has become the tenant thereof) shall not be capable of assignment.

(6) The Lord Chancellor may by regulations made by statutory instrument subject to annulment in pursuance of a resolution of either House of Parliament provide for all or any of the provisions of this Schedule (except this sub-paragraph) to apply, with such exceptions, additions or other modifications as may be specified in the regulations, in cases where the nominated successor, being entitled to a tenancy of the holding by virtue of such a direction, dies before the relevant time.

(7) In this paragraph " the relevant time " means the retirement date, except that—

(a) where such a direction is given within the period of three months ending with the retirement date, the Tribunal may, on the application of the tenant, specify in the direction, as the relevant time for the purposes of this paragraph, such a time falling within the period of three months immediately following the retirement date as they think fit ;

(b) where such a direction is given at any time after the retirement date, the Tribunal shall specify in the direction, as the relevant time for those purposes, such a time falling within the period of three months immediately following the date of the giving of the direction as they think fit ;

and any time so specified shall be the relevant time for those purposes accordingly.

Arbitration on terms of new tenancy

7.—(1) Where the Tribunal give a direction such as is mentioned in paragraph 6(1) above, subsections (3) to (8) of section 24 of the

1976 Act (provisions as to arbitration on terms of new tenancy)
shall have effect in relation to the tenancy which the nominated
successor is entitled to or has obtained by virtue of the direction,
but with the substitution—

    (*a*) in subsection (4) of a reference to paragraph 6(1) for the
reference to section 23(1) of that Act ;

    (*b*) in subsection (5)(*a*) of a reference to the tenancy of the
retiring tenant or (as the case may be) tenants for the
reference to the deceased's tenancy.

(2) In those provisions, as extended by sub-paragraph (1) above—

    " the landlord " means the landlord of the holding ;

    " the tenant " means the nominated successor ;

    " the relevant time " has the meaning given by paragraph 6(7)
above ;

    " the prescribed period " means the period between the giving
of the direction and—

        (*a*) the end of the three months immediately following
the relevant time ; or

        (*b*) the end of the three months immediately following
the date of the giving of the direction ;
whichever last occurs.

(3) Section 77 of the 1948 Act (arbitration under that Act) shall
have effect as if in subsection (1) the first reference to that Act included a reference to this Schedule.

Effect of death of retiring tenant on succession to the holding

8.—(1) Sub-paragraphs (2) to (4) below apply where the retiring
tenant, being the sole (or sole surviving) tenant of the holding,
dies after giving the retirement notice.

(2) If the tenant's death occurs at a time when no application
by the nominated successor has been made under paragraph 5 above
or such an application has not been finally disposed of by the Tribunal, the retirement notice shall be of no effect and no proceedings,
or (as the case may be) no further proceedings, shall be taken under
this Schedule in respect of it ; and accordingly, subject to section 2 of
this Act, section 18(1) of the 1976 Act shall apply on the tenant's
death in relation to the holding.

(3) If the tenant's death occurs at a time when any such application has been so disposed of by the giving of a direction such as is
mentioned in sub-paragraph (1) of paragraph 6 above, but before
the relevant time (within the meaning of that paragraph), that paragraph, paragraph 7 above and paragraphs 9 and 10 below shall continue to have effect in relation to the holding ; and accordingly
section 18(1) of the 1976 Act shall not apply on the tenant's death in
relation to the holding.

(4) If the tenant's death occurs at a time when any such application has been so disposed of otherwise than by the giving of any such

direction, section 18(1) of the 1976 Act shall, subject to section 2 of this Act, apply on the tenant's death in relation to the holding, but no application may be made on that occasion by the nominated successor under section 20 (or 21) of that Act in relation to the holding.

(5) Where the retirement notice was given by joint tenants and one of those tenants, not being the sole surviving tenant of the holding, dies, his death shall not affect any rights of the nominated successor under this Schedule.

Effect of direction on succession to other holdings under the 1976 Act

9. Where—

　(*a*) the retiring tenant, being the sole (or sole surviving) tenant of the holding, dies ; and

　(*b*) the nominated successor is for the time being entitled to a tenancy of the holding by virtue of a direction under paragraph 5(6) above,

then for the purpose of determining whether, in relation to any other agricultural holding held by the retiring tenant at the date of his death, the nominated successor is a person in whose case the condition specified in paragraph (*c*) of the definition of " eligible person " in subsection (2) of section 18 of the 1976 Act is satisfied, the nominated successor shall be deemed to be in occupation of the holding, and subsection (6) of that section shall have effect as if the reference in the definition of " relevant land " to agricultural land which is occupied as mentioned in paragraph (*a*) of that definition included a reference to agricultural land which is deemed to be occupied by the nominated successor by virtue of this paragraph.

Effect of succession of nominated successor on succession under the 1976 Act

10.—(1) Where the nominated successor obtains a tenancy of the holding by virtue of a direction under paragraph 5(6) above—

　(*a*) subsection (2) of section 2 of this Act shall apply to the tenancy as it applies to a tenancy obtained as mentioned in paragraph (*a*) of that subsection, and the reference in paragraph 1(1) above to that subsection accordingly includes a reference to it as applied by this paragraph ; and

　(*b*) that occasion shall for the purposes of subsection (4)(*e*) of section 18 of the 1976 Act (exclusion of Part II of that Act where two successions have already occurred), in its application on the death of a tenant of the holding or a related holding, be deemed to be an occasion on which there died a sole tenant (within the meaning of subsection (1) of that section) of the holding and a tenancy of the holding was obtained by virtue of a direction of the Tribunal under section 20 of that Act.

(2) In sub-paragraph (1)(*b*) above " related holding " means, in relation to the holding, any agricultural holding comprising land the whole or a substantial part of which is comprised in the holding.

Section 10(1).

Schedule 3

Minor and Consequential Amendments

The Agricultural Holdings Act 1948 (c. 63)

1.—(1) Section 1 of the 1948 Act (meaning of "agricultural holding") shall be amended as follows.

(2) In subsection (1), for the words "agricultural land comprised in a contract of tenancy" there shall be substituted the words "land (whether agricultural land or not) comprised in a contract of tenancy which is a contract for an agricultural tenancy".

(3) After that subsection there shall be inserted the following subsections—

"(1A) For the purposes of this section, a contract of tenancy relating to any land is a contract for an agricultural tenancy if, having regard to—

    (a) the terms of the tenancy ;

    (b) the actual or contemplated use of the land at the time of the conclusion of the contract and subsequently ; and

    (c) any other relevant circumstances ;

the whole of the land comprised in the contract, subject to such exceptions only as do not substantially affect the character of the tenancy, is let for use as agricultural land.

(1B) A change in user of the land concerned subsequent to the conclusion of a contract of tenancy which involves any breach of the terms of the tenancy shall be disregarded for the purpose of determining whether a contract which was not originally a contract for an agricultural tenancy has subsequently become one unless it is effected with the landlord's permission, consent or acquiescence."

2.—(1) In section 3 of that Act (tenancies for two years or more, unless terminated by notice, to continue as tenancies from year to year)—

    (a) at the beginning of subsection (1) there shall be inserted the words "Subject to sections 3A and 3B of this Act" ; and

    (b) at the beginning of subsection (4) there shall be inserted the words "Subject to section 3B of this Act".

(2) The following sections shall be inserted after that section—

"Restriction on continuation of tenancy where tenant dies before term expires.

3A.—(1) This section shall apply to any tenancy such as is referred to in section 3(1) of this Act granted after the commencement of the Agricultural Holdings Act 1984.

(2) If the person, or the survivor of the persons, to whom any such tenancy was granted dies one year or more before the date fixed for the expiration of the term

for which it was granted, the tenancy shall not continue as mentioned in section 3(1) and shall accordingly terminate on that date.

(3) If—

    (*a*) any such person dies at any other time before the expiration of the term, and

    (*b*) no notice effective to terminate the tenancy on the expiration of the term has been given under section 3(1),

any such tenancy shall, instead of continuing as mentioned in section 3(1), continue (as from the expiration of the term) for a further period of twelve months, but otherwise on the terms of the tenancy so far as applicable, and shall accordingly terminate on the first anniversary of the date fixed for the expiration of the term.

(4) For the purposes of the provisions of this Act with respect to compensation any tenancy terminating in accordance with subsection (2) or (3) of this section shall be deemed to terminate by reason of a notice to quit given by the landlord of the holding.

Exclusion of continuation of tenancy by agreement.

3B.—(1) This section shall apply to any tenancy of an agricultural holding for a term of not less than two, and not more than five, years.

(2) Where, before the grant of any such tenancy—

    (*a*) the persons who will be the landlord and the tenant in relation to the tenancy agree that section 3 of this Act shall not apply to the tenancy ; and

    (*b*) those persons make a joint application in writing to the Minister for his approval of that agreement ; and

    (*c*) the Minister notifies them of his approval ;

section 3 shall not apply to the tenancy if it satisfies the requirements of subsection (3) of this section.

(3) A tenancy satisfies the requirements of this subsection if the contract of tenancy is in writing and it, or a statement endorsed upon it, indicates (in whatever terms) that section 3 of this Act does not apply to the tenancy."

3.—(1) Section 5 of that Act (provisions for securing written tenancy agreements) shall be amended as follows.

(2) The following subsection shall be substituted for subsection (1)—

" (1) Where in respect of a tenancy of an agricultural holding (whether created before or after the commencement of this Act)—

    (*a*) there is not in force an agreement in writing embodying

SCH. 3

all the terms of the tenancy (including any terms established by the operation of regulations under section 6 of this Act) ; or

(b) such an agreement in writing is in force but the terms of the tenancy do not make provision for one or more of the matters specified in the First Schedule to this Act ;

the landlord or the tenant of the holding may, if he has requested his tenant or landlord to enter into an agreement in writing embodying all the terms of the tenancy and containing provision for all of the said matters but no such agreement has been concluded, refer the terms of the tenancy to arbitration under this Act."

(3) The following subsections shall be added at the end—

" (4) Where in respect of any such tenancy—

(a) the terms of the tenancy neither make provision for, nor make provision inconsistent with, the matter specified in paragraph 10 of the First Schedule to this Act ; and

(b) the landlord requests the tenant in writing to enter into such an agreement as is mentioned in subsection (1) of this section containing provision for all of the matters specified in that Schedule ;

the tenant may not without the landlord's consent in writing assign, sub-let or part with possession of the holding or any part of it during the period while the determination of the terms of the tenancy is pending.

(5) That period is the period beginning with the date of service of the landlord's request on the tenant and ending with the date on which an agreement is concluded in accordance with that request or (as the case may be) with the date on which the award of an arbitrator on a reference under this section relating to the tenancy takes effect.

(6) Any transaction entered into in contravention of subsection (4) of this section shall be void."

4. In section 7(5) of that Act (effect of award of arbitrator under section 5 or 6), after the words " having effect " there shall be inserted the words " (by way of variation of the agreement previously in force in respect of the tenancy) ".

5.—(1) Section 9 of that Act (increases of rent for certain improvements carried out by landlord) shall be amended as follows.

(2) In subsection (1)—

(a) the following provisions shall be omitted, namely—

(i) in paragraph (b), the words from the beginning to " or ",

(ii) paragraph (d) and the word " or " immediately preceding it, and

(iii) the words from " or, where " to " that day " ;

(*b*) for the words from " for the supply " to " the Minister " there shall be substituted the words " executed on the holding for the purpose of complying with the requirements of a notice under section 3 of the Agriculture (Safety, Health and Welfare Provisions) Act 1956 (provision of sanitary conveniences and washing facilities) " ; and

(*c*) in the proviso, after the words " moneys provided by Parliament " there shall be inserted the words " or local government funds ".

(3) The following subsection shall be substituted for subsection (2)—

" (2) No increase of rent shall be made under the foregoing subsection in respect of an improvement within paragraph (*a*) of that subsection if before the end of the period allowed under that subsection for the landlord to serve a notice requiring such an increase the landlord and tenant agree on any increase of rent or other benefit to the landlord in respect of the improvement."

(4) Subsections (3) and (5) shall be omitted.

6.—(1) Section 13 of that Act (tenant's right to remove fixtures and buildings) shall be amended as follows.

(2) In subsection (1), in paragraph (*a*), after the word " fixture " there shall be inserted the words " (of whatever description) ".

(3) The following subsections shall be inserted after subsection (4)—

" (4A) Subsection (1) of this section applies to a fixture whether it was affixed to the holding for the purposes of agriculture or not ; but this section shall not be taken as prejudicing any right to remove a fixture that subsists otherwise than by virtue of this section.

(4B) Any dispute between the landlord and the tenant with respect to the amount payable by the landlord under subsection (3) of this section in respect of any fixture or building shall be determined by arbitration under this Act."

7.—(1) Section 14 of that Act (tenant's right to, and measure of, compensation for damage by game, and indemnity to landlord) shall be amended as follows.

(2) In subsection (1)—

(*a*) for the words from " game, the " to " extends " there shall be substituted the words " any wild animals or birds, the right to kill and take which is vested in the landlord or anyone (other than the tenant himself) claiming under the landlord, being animals or birds which the tenant has not permission in writing to kill, he shall be entitled to compensation from his landlord for the damage: " ;

(*b*) in paragraph (*b*) of the proviso, for the words from " calendar year " to " therefor " there shall be substituted the word " year " ; and

(*c*) the following paragraph shall be added at the end—

" For the purposes of paragraph (*a*)(i) above, seed once sown shall be treated as a growing crop whether or not it has germinated ; and in paragraph (*b*) above " year " means any period of twelve months ending, in any year, with 29th September or with such other date as may by agreement between the landlord and tenant be substituted for that date."

(3) In subsection (3), for the word " game " there shall be substituted the words " wild animals or birds that did the damage ".

(4) Subsection (4) shall be omitted.

8. In section 16 of that Act (right of landlord or tenant to require making of record of condition of holding etc.)—

(*a*) in subsection (1), for the words from " the buildings " to " the holding " there shall be substituted the words " the fixed equipment on the holding and of the general condition of the holding itself (including any parts not under cultivation) " ; and

(*b*) at the end of subsection (2) there shall be added the words " ; and any person so appointed may, on production of evidence of his appointment, enter the holding at all reasonable times for the purpose of making any such record."

9.—(1) Section 34 of that Act (right to, and measure of, compensation for disturbance) shall be amended as follows.

(2) The following subsection shall be inserted after subsection (2)—

" (2A) Where—

(*a*) the tenant of an agricultural holding has sub-let the holding, and

(*b*) the sub-tenancy terminates by operation of law in consequence of the termination of the tenancy by reason of any such notice or counter-notice as is referred to in subsection (1)(*a*) or (*b*) of this section,

this section shall apply if the sub-tenant quits the holding in consequence of the termination of the sub-tenancy as mentioned in paragraph (*b*) above as it applies where a tenant quits a holding in consequence of any such notice or counter-notice as aforesaid."

(3) In subsection (4)—

(*a*) for the words " the notice given by the landlord " there shall be substituted the words " the notice to quit " ;

(*b*) for the words from " such " to " as is " there shall be substituted the words " relevant previous notice " ; and (*c*) the following paragraph shall be added at the end—

"In this subsection "relevant previous notice" means any notice to quit given by the same person who gave the current notice to quit or, where that person is a person entitled to a severed part of the reversionary estate in the holding, by that person or by any other person so entitled."

10. In section 37 of that Act (measure of compensation for old improvements), for the words from "such sum" to the end there shall be substituted the words "an amount equal to the increase attributable to the improvement in the value of the agricultural holding as a holding, having regard to the character and situation of the holding and the average requirements of tenants reasonably skilled in husbandry".

11. In section 53 of that Act (grants out of moneys provided by Parliament to be taken into account in assessing compensation for new improvements), after the words "moneys provided by Parliament" there shall be inserted the words "or local government funds".

12. In section 56(1) of that Act (right to, and measure of, compensation for continuous adoption of special system of farming), in proviso (ii), for the words from "the buildings" to the end there shall be substituted the words "the fixed equipment on the holding and of the general condition of the holding; ".

13. In section 57 of that Act (right to, and measure of, compensation for deterioration etc. of particular parts of holding)—

(*a*) at the beginning of subsection (2) there shall be inserted the words "Subject to subsection (4) of this section," ; and

(*b*) at the end of the section there shall be added the following subsection—

"(4) The amount of the compensation payable under subsection (1) of this section, or in accordance with subsection (3) of this section, shall in no case exceed the amount (if any) by which the value of the landlord's reversion in the holding is diminished owing to the dilapidation, deterioration or damage in question."

14. The existing provisions of section 60 of that Act (compensation provisions applicable to parts of holdings in certain cases) shall become subsection (1) of that section, and—

(*a*) the following paragraph shall be inserted after paragraph (*a*) of that subsection—

"(*aa*) by virtue of section 19 of the Agriculture (Miscellaneous Provisions) Act 1976; " ; and 1976 c. 55.

(*b*) the following subsections shall be added after that subsection—

"(2) Where a person entitled to a severed part of the

reversionary estate in an agricultural holding resumes possession of part of the holding by virtue of a notice to quit that part given to the tenant by virtue of section 140 of the Law of Property Act 1925 the provisions of this Act with respect to compensation shall apply to that part of the holding as if—

> (*a*) it were a separate holding which the tenant had quitted in consequence of the notice to quit; and

> (*b*) the person resuming possession were the landlord of that separate holding.

(3) References in this Act to the termination of the tenancy of or (as the case may be) of part of an agricultural holding include references to the resumption of possession of part of an agricultural holding in circumstances within subsection (1) or (2) above."

15. In section 61 of that Act (provisions as to compensation where holding is divided), for the words from the beginning of the section to " divided " there shall be substituted the words " Where the reversionary estate in an agricultural holding is for the time being vested in more than one person in several parts, the tenant shall be entitled, on quitting the entire holding, to require that any compensation payable to him under this Act shall be determined as if the reversionary estate were not so severed,".

16. In section 67 of that Act (effect of agreement to let or treat an agricultural holding as a market garden), the following paragraph shall be substituted for paragraph (*b*) of subsection (1)—

" (*b*) in section 13 of this Act—

> (i) the exception in subsection (1)(*b*) for a building in respect of which the tenant is entitled to compensation under this Act or otherwise shall not apply in relation to any building erected by the tenant on the holding, or acquired by him since 31st December 1900, for the purposes of his trade or business as a market gardener, and

> (ii) subsection (5)(*b*) shall not exclude that section from applying to any building acquired by him since that date for those purposes (whenever erected) ; ".

17. In section 68 of that Act (power of Tribunal in default of agreement to treat an agricultural holding as a market garden)—

> (*a*) in subsection (2) for the words " bankrupt or compounding with his creditors " and " bankruptcy or composition " there shall be substituted the words " insolvent " and " insolvency " respectively ; and

> (*b*) the following subsection shall be added at the end—

> " (6) For the purposes of subsection (2) of this section a person has become insolvent if any of the following events has occurred, namely—

>> (*a*) he has become bankrupt or has made a composition or arrangement with his creditors or a

receiving order has been made against him ; or

(*b*) where the tenant is a body corporate, a winding-up order has been made with respect to it or a resolution for voluntary winding-up has been passed with respect to it (other than a resolution passed solely for the purposes of its reconstruction or of its amalgamation with another body corporate) ;

and the reference in that subsection to the date of the insolvency is a reference to the date of the occurrence of the event in question."

18. In section 70 of that Act (settlement of claims between landlord and tenant on termination of tenancy)—

(*a*) in subsection (3), for the word " four " there shall be substituted the word " eight " and the words from " and the " to the end shall be omitted ;

(*b*) in subsection (4), the words from " and any extension " to " subsection " shall be omitted, and for the words from " cease " to the end there shall be substituted the words " be determined by arbitration under this Act ".

19.—(1) Section 77 of that Act (arbitrations under the Act) shall be amended as follows.

(2) In subsection (1), for the words " the Sixth Schedule to this Act " there shall be substituted the words " any order under this section, together with the provisions of the Sixth Schedule to this Act (as for the time being in force) ".

(3) The following subsections shall be substituted for subsections (2) to (4)—

" (2) The Lord Chancellor may by order make provision as to the procedure to be followed in, or in connection with, proceedings on arbitrations under this Act.

(3) An order under this section may in particular—

(*a*) provide for the provisions of the Sixth Schedule to this Act, exclusive of those mentioned in subsection (4) of this section, to have effect subject to such modifications as may be specified in the order ;

(*b*) prescribe forms for proceedings on arbitrations under this Act which, if used, shall be sufficient ;

(*c*) prescribe the form in which awards in such proceedings are to be made.

(4) An order under this section shall not make provision inconsistent with the following provisions of the Sixth Schedule, namely paragraphs 1 to 5 and 10 to 12, the proviso to paragraph 13, and paragraphs 17, 19, 20A, 20B and 24 to 28.

(5) The power to make an order under this section shall be exercisable by statutory instrument which shall be subject to

annulment in pursuance of a resolution of either House of Parliament.

(6) In this section " modifications " includes additions, omissions and amendments."

20. In section 83 of that Act (general provisions as to charges under the Act on holdings), the words " subsection (1) of " shall be omitted in subsections (3) and (4).

21. In section 92(1) of that Act (service of notices), at the end there shall be added the following words " or by the recorded delivery service ".

22. In section 93 of that Act (revocation and variation of orders)—

(*a*) after the word " sections " there shall be inserted the word " seventy-two " ; and

(*b*) the word " seventy-four " shall be omitted.

23. In section 94(1) of that Act (interpretation)—

(*a*) the following definition shall be inserted immediately after the definition of " livestock "—

" " local government funds " means, in relation to any grant in respect of an improvement executed by the landlord or tenant of an agricultural holding, the funds of any body which, under or by virtue of any enactment, has power to make grants in respect of improvements of the description in question within any particular area (whether or not it is a local authority for that area) ; " ; and

(*b*) the following definition shall be substituted for the definition of " the Minister "—

" " the Minister " means—

(*a*) in relation to England, the Minister of Agriculture, Fisheries and Food ; and

(*b*) in relation to Wales, the Secretary of State."

24. In Schedule 1 to that Act, paragraphs 6 and 7 (maintenance and repairing of fixed equipment and insurance against damage by fire etc., to be among the matters dealt with in a written tenancy agreement) shall cease to have effect.

25.—(1) In Part I of Schedule 3 to that Act (new improvements for which compensation is payable if consent of landlord is obtained for their execution)—

(*a*) in paragraph 2, the words " or works of irrigation " shall be omitted ; and

(*b*) the following paragraph shall be inserted after paragraph 7—

" 7A. Provision of underground tanks."

(2) In Part II of that Schedule (new improvements for which compensation is payable if consent of landlord or approval of Tribunal is obtained for their execution)—

(a) the following paragraph shall be inserted after paragraph 8—

"8A. The erection or construction of loading platforms, ramps, hard standings for vehicles or other similar facilities." ;

(b) in paragraph 13, for the words from "for the supply" to the end there shall be substituted the words "of works for the supply, distribution or use of water for such purposes (including the erection or installation of any structures or equipment which form part of or are to be used for or in connection with operating any such works)" ;

(c) the following paragraph shall be substituted for paragraph 22—

"22. Provision of facilities for the storage or disposal of sewage or farm waste." ; and

(d) the following paragraphs shall be substituted for paragraph 24—

"24. The grubbing up of orchards or fruit bushes.

25. Planting trees otherwise than as an orchard and bushes other than fruit bushes."

26. In Part II of Schedule 4 to that Act (matters for which compensation is payable without consent of landlord), the following words shall be added at the end of paragraph 9 "(including the growing of herbage crops for commercial seed production)".

27. The tenant of an agricultural holding shall not be entitled on quitting the holding to compensation—

(a) for any improvement specified in Part III of Schedule 2 to the 1948 Act ; or

(b) in the case of a holding to which section 67(1) of that Act applies, for any improvement deemed by virtue of paragraph (a) of that provision to be included in that Part of that Schedule and not being such an improvement as is specified in paragraph 5 of Schedule 5 to that Act.

28.—(1) Schedule 6 to that Act (provisions as to arbitrations under the Act) shall be amended as follows.

(2) The following sub-paragraph shall be inserted after paragraph 1(1)—

"(1A) Any such appointment by the Minister shall be made by him as soon as possible after receiving the application ; but where the application is referable to a demand for arbitration made under section 8 of this Act any such appointment shall in any event not be made by him earlier than four months before the next termination date following the date of the demand (as defined by section 8A(2) of this Act)."

(3) The following paragraph shall be inserted after paragraph 2—

" 2A. In relation to an arbitrator who is appointed in place of another arbitrator (whether under the foregoing paragraph or otherwise) the reference in section 8(2) of this Act to the date of the reference shall be construed as a reference to the date when the original arbitrator was appointed."

(4) At the end of paragraph 3 there shall be added the words " ; and his appointment shall not be revoked by the death of either party."

(5) In paragraph 5(*b*), after the words " as may be " there shall be inserted the words " agreed upon by him and the parties or, in default of agreement,".

(6) In paragraph 6, for the word " twenty-eight " in both places where it occurs there shall be substituted the word " thirty-five ".

(7) The following paragraphs shall be inserted after paragraph 20—

" *Reasons for award*

1971 c. 62.   20A. Section 12 of the Tribunals and Inquiries Act 1971 (reasons to be given for decisions of tribunals etc.) shall apply in relation to the award of an arbitrator appointed under this Schedule by agreement between the parties as it applies in relation to the award of an arbitrator appointed under this Schedule otherwise than by such agreement.

Interest on awards

20B. Any sum directed to be paid by the award shall, unless the award otherwise directs, carry interest as from the date of the award and at the same rate as a judgment debt."

(8) The following paragraph shall be substituted for paragraph 22—

" 22. On the application of either party any such costs shall be taxable in the county court according to such of the scales prescribed by county court rules for proceedings in the county court as may be directed by the arbitrator under the foregoing paragraph, or, in the absence of any such direction, by the county court."

(9) The following paragraph shall be inserted after paragraph 25—

" 25A.—(1) The county court may from time to time remit the award or any part of the award to the reconsideration of the arbitrator.

(2) In any case where it appears to the county court that there is an error of law on the face of the award the court may, instead of exercising its power of remission under the foregoing sub-paragraph, vary the award by substituting for so much of it as is affected by the error such award as the court considers that it would have been proper for the arbitrator to make in the circumstances ; and the award shall thereupon have effect as so varied.

(3) Where remission is ordered under that sub-paragraph, the arbitrator shall, unless the order otherwise directs, make and sign his award within thirty days after the date of the order.

(4) If the county court is satisfied that the time limited for making the said award is, for any good reason, insufficient, the court may extend or further extend that time for such period as it thinks proper."

(10) The following paragraph shall be added after paragraph 28—

" 29. For the purposes of this Schedule an arbitrator appointed by the Minister shall be taken to have been so appointed at the time when the Minister executed the instrument of appointment ; and in the case of any such arbitrator the periods mentioned in paragraphs 6 and 13 of this Schedule shall accordingly run from that time."

The Opencast Coal Act 1958 (c. 69)

29. In section 24(6) of the Opencast Coal Act 1958 (tenant's right to compensation for improvements etc.), in proviso (*b*), for each of the words " four " and " five " there shall be substituted the word " eight ".

The Agriculture Act 1958 (c. 71)

30. In section 4 of the Agriculture Act 1958 (rights of tenants as to provision of fixed equipment necessary to comply with statutory requirements), in the proviso to subsection (1), after the word " holding " (where it first occurs) there shall be inserted the word " continuously ".

The Agriculture (Miscellaneous Provisions) Act 1968 (c. 34)

31. In section 9 of the Agriculture (Miscellaneous Provisions) Act 1968 (additional payments to tenants quitting agricultural holdings), the following subsection shall be inserted after subsection (1)—

" (1A) This section applies where compensation for disturbance in respect of part of an agricultural holding becomes payable under that Act by a person entitled to a severed part of the reversionary estate in the holding to the tenant of the holding as it applies where such compensation becomes so payable by the landlord of an agricultural holding."

32.—(1) In section 10(1) of that Act (cases where tenant quitting an agricultural holding is not entitled to an additional payment of compensation)—

   (*a*) in paragraph (*b*), for the words " the said section 3(3) " there shall be substituted the words " section 3(3) of the Agricultural Holdings (Notices to Quit) Act 1977 " ; and 1977 c. 12

   (*b*) the following words shall be added at the end " ; or

        (*e*) the said section 2(1) does not apply to the relevant notice by virtue of Case I in the said section 2(3) (which relates to notices to quit smallholdings given where the tenant is over 65)."

Sch. 3

(2) In section 10(8) of that Act (construction, etc.), for the words "paragraphs (*a*) and " there shall be substituted the word "paragraph ".

33. In section 17(2) of that Act (interpretation of references to the termination of the tenancy of part of an agricultural holding), for the words from " by the landlord " to " holding " there shall be substituted the words " of possession of that part of the holding by the landlord or (as the case may be) by a person entitled to a severed part of the reversionary estate in the holding ".

The Agriculture (Miscellaneous Provisions) Act 1976 (*c.* 55)

34. In section 18(4) of the 1976 Act (cases where provisions for statutory succession to agricultural holdings do not apply), in paragraph (*b*), for " Case A, C " there shall be substituted " Case C ".

35. In section 24 of that Act (arbitration on terms of new tenancy), the following subsection shall be substituted for subsection (6)—

" (6) For the purposes of this section the rent properly payable in respect of the holding shall be the rent at which the holding might reasonably be expected to be let by a prudent and willing landlord to a prudent and willing tenant, taking into account all relevant factors, including (in every case) the terms of the tenancy or prospective tenancy (including those relating to rent) and any such other matters as are specifically referred to in subsection (3) of section 8 of the 1948 Act (read with subsections (4) and (5) of that section)."

The Agricultural Holdings (Notices to Quit) Act 1977 (*c.* 12)

36. In section 1(2) of the 1977 Act (cases where 12 months' notice to quit is not needed to end tenancy of agricultural holding), the following paragraph shall be submitted for paragraph (*a*)—

" (*a*) where the tenant is insolvent ; ".

37. In section 2(3) of that Act (cases where consent of Tribunal to operation of notice to quit is not required), in Case F, for the words " bankrupt or compounded with his creditors " there shall be substituted the word " insolvent ".

38. In section 5(1) of that Act (power of Lord Chancellor to provide by order for questions to be determined by arbitration, etc.)—

    (*a*) in paragraph (*a*)(i), after the words " section 2(2) and (3) above " there shall be inserted the words " (including any question arising under Schedule 1A to this Act) " ;

    (*b*) in paragraph (*a*)(ii), for the words from " any proceedings " to " taken " there shall be substituted the words " within which an arbitrator may be appointed by agreement between the parties, or (in default of such agreement) an application may be made under paragraph 1 of Schedule 6 to that Act for the appointment of an arbitrator, for the purposes of any such arbitration " ; and

(c) in paragraph (b), after the word "quit" there shall be inserted the words " until the expiry of any time fixed is pursuance of paragraph (a)(ii) above for the making of any such appointment by agreement or application as is there mentioned or, where any such appointment or application has been duly made,".

39. In section 8(2) of that Act (notice to quit part of agricultural holding not invalid in certain cases), the following paragraphs shall be substituted for paragraphs (a) and (b)—

" (a) the erection of cottages or other houses for farm labourers, whether with or without gardens ;

(b) the provision of gardens for cottages or other houses for farm labourers ; ".

40. In section 10 of that Act (reduction of rent where notice is given to quit part of holding)—

(a) in subsection (1), the words from " of an amount " to " Act " shall be omitted ;

(b) the following subsection shall be inserted after subsection (1)—

" (1A) The amount of any reduction of rent under this section shall, in default of agreement made after the landlord resumes possession of the part of the holding concerned, be determined by arbitration under the 1948 Act." ; and

(c) in subsection (2), after the word " above " there shall be inserted the words " that falls to be determined by arbitration under the 1948 Act ".

41. In each of subsections (3) and (4)(a) of section 11 of that Act (notice to quit where tenant is a service man), for " Cases A to G " there shall be substituted " Cases B to G ".

42. In section 12 of that Act (interpretation)—

(a) in subsection (1) for " " Case A ", " Case B " " " there shall be substituted " " Case B ", " Case C " " " ; and

(b) the following subsection shall be inserted after subsection (1)—

" (1A) For the purposes of this Act a tenant is insolvent if—

(a) he has become bankrupt or has made a composition or arrangement with his creditors or a receiving order is made against him ; or

(b) where the tenant is a body corporate, a winding-up order has been made with respect to it or a resolution for voluntary winding-up has been passed with respect to it (other than a resolution passed solely for the purposes of its reconstruction or of its amalgamation with another body corporate)."

SCH. 3   43. The following Schedule shall be inserted before Schedule 1 to that Act—

" SCHEDULE 1A

SUITABLE ALTERNATIVE ACCOMMODATION FOR PURPOSES OF CASE I

1. For the purposes of paragraph (*b*) of Case I, a certificate of the housing authority for the district in which the living accommodation in question is situated, certifying that the authority will provide suitable alternative accommodation for the tenant by a date specified in the certificate, shall be conclusive evidence that suitable alternative accommodation will be available for him by that date.

2. Where no such certificate as is mentioned in paragraph 1 above has been issued, accommodation shall be deemed to be suitable for the purposes of paragraph (*b*) of Case I if it consists of either—

1977 c. 42.

    (*a*) premises which are to be let as a separate dwelling such that they will then be let on a protected tenancy (within the meaning of the Rent Act 1977) ; or

    (*b*) premises to be let as a separate dwelling on terms which will afford to the tenant security of tenure reasonably equivalent to the security afforded by Part VII of that Act in the case of a protected tenancy ;

and the accommodation fulfils the conditions in paragraph 3 below.

3.—(1) The accommodation must be reasonably suitable to the needs of the tenant's family as regards proximity to place of work and either—

    (*a*) similar as regards rental and extent to the accommodation afforded by dwelling-houses provided in the neighbourhood by any housing authority for persons whose needs as regards extent are similar to those of the tenant and his family ; or

    (*b*) reasonably suitable to the means of the tenant and to the needs of the tenant and his family as regards extent and character.

(2) For the purposes of sub-paragraph (1)(*a*) above, a certificate of a housing authority stating—

    (*a*) the extent of the accommodation afforded by dwelling-houses provided by the authority to meet the needs of tenants with families of such number as may be specified in the certificate ; and

    (*b*) the amount of the rent charged by the authority for dwelling-houses affording accommodation of that extent ;

shall be conclusive evidence of the facts so stated.

(3) If any furniture was provided by the landlord for use

under the tenancy in question, furniture must be provided for use　SCH. 3
in the alternative accommodation which is either—

　　(*a*) similar to that so provided ; or

　　(*b*) reasonably suitable to the needs of the tenant and his
　　　family.

4. Accommodation shall not be deemed to be suitable to the
needs of the tenant and his family if the result of their occupation
of the accommodation would be that it would be an overcrowded
dwelling-house for the purposes of the Housing Act 1957.　　1957 c. 56.

5. Any document purporting—

　　(*a*) to be a certificate of a housing authority named therein
　　　issued for the purposes of this Schedule ; and

　　(*b*) to be signed by the proper officer of the authority ;

shall be received in evidence and, unless the contrary is shown,
shall be deemed to be such a certificate without further proof.

6.—(1) In this Schedule " housing authority " means a council
which is a local authority for the purposes of Part V of the
Housing Act 1957, and "district", in relation to such an authority,
means the district for supplying the needs of which the authority
has power under that Part of that Act.

(2) For the purposes of this Schedule a dwelling-house may
be a house or part of a house."

SCHEDULE 4　　　　　　　　Section 10(2).

ENACTMENTS REPEALED

Chapter	Short title	Extent of repeal
11 & 12 Geo. 6. c. 63.	The Agricultural Holdings Act 1948.	In section 1(2), the words from " of Agriculture " to " " the Minister ") ". In section 9(1), in paragraph (*b*) the words from the beginning to " or ", paragraph (*d*) and the word " or " immediately preceding it and the words from " or, where " to " that day ". Section 9(3) and (5). Section 14(4). Section 40. Section 42. Section 62. Section 66. In section 70, in subsection (3) the words from " and the " onwards, and in subsection (4) the words from " and any extension " to " subsection ". Section 74

Chapter	Short title	Extent of repeal
		In section 83(3) and (4), the words " subsection (1) of ". Section 91. In section 93, the word " seventy-four ". Sections 97 and 99. In section 100(2), the words " thirty " and " thirty-two ". In Schedule 1, paragraphs 6 and 7. In paragraph 2 of Schedule 3 the words " or works of irrigation ". In Schedule 6, paragraphs 15, 27 and 28.
14 & 15 Geo. 6. c. 18.	The Livestock Rearing Act 1951.	In section 1(2)(*b*), the words from " in paragraph " (where first occurring) to " 1948 ".
4 & 5 Eliz. 2. c. 49.	The Agriculture (Safety, Health and Welfare Provisions) Act 1956.	Section 3(10).
6 & 7 Eliz. 2. c. 71.	The Agriculture Act 1958.	Section 2.
1963 c. 11.	The Agriculture (Miscellaneous Provisions) Act 1963.	In section 20, in paragraph (*a*) the words from " paragraph 6 " to " 1948 and ", and in paragraph (ii) the words " the said paragraph 6 or ".
1968 c. 34.	The Agriculture (Miscellaneous Provisions) Act 1968.	Section 10(1)(*a*).
1976 c. 55.	The Agriculture (Miscellaneous Provisions) Act 1976.	In section 18, in subsection (2), in paragraph (*c*) of the definition of " eligible person " the words from " within " onwards, and in subsection (4) paragraph (*d*)(ii) and the word " or " immediately preceding it.
1977 c. 12.	The Agricultural Holdings (Notices to Quit) Act 1977.	In section 2(3), Case A, and in Case H the word " appropriate ", in the first two places where it occurs, and the words from " In this Case" onwards. Section 7. In section 10(1), the words from " of an amount " to "Act ". In Schedule 1, paragraphs 1(2) and (6) and 5(2), and in paragraph 5(3) the words from " for " section 25(1) " " to " and ".

SCHEDULE 5

TRANSITIONAL PROVISIONS AND SAVINGS

Arbitrations as to rent

1. In any case where—

(a) a demand has been made for arbitration under section 8(1) of the 1948 Act before the date on which this Act is passed, but

(b) an arbitrator has not been appointed before that date in pursuance of the demand,

the provisions substituted for section 8 by section 1 of this Act shall apply as if the demand had been made under section 8(1) as so substituted.

Succession to agricultural holdings

2.—(1) Nothing in the following provisions of this Act, namely section 3, Schedule 1 and the repeal in Schedule 4 which is consequential on that section, affects any application made under Part II of the 1976 Act before the commencement of this Act, and accordingly Part II of that Act shall have effect in relation to any such application, and sections 20 to 24 of that Act shall have effect in relation to any proceedings arising out of any such application or in relation to any direction given in any such proceedings, as if the said provisions of this Act had not been enacted.

(2) In section 18 of the 1976 Act, as amended by this Act—

(a) subsection (5) shall, in relation to any time before the commencement of this Act, have effect with the substitution for the words from "as a result" to "grant or assignment" of the words "the holding or a related holding became let under a new tenancy thereof granted by the landlord, with the agreement of the outgoing tenant, to a person who, if the outgoing tenant had died immediately before the grant," ; and

(b) subsection (5A) shall not apply in relation to any tenancy if—

(i) it was granted before the commencement of this Act ;

(ii) it was obtained by virtue of any such direction as is mentioned in sub-paragraph (1) above ; or

(iii) it was granted (following such a direction) in circumstances within section 23(6) of the 1976 Act.

Length of notices to quit and operation of such notices

3. In section 1 of the 1977 Act, as amended by section 5 of this Act—

(a) subsection (5) applies to notices to quit given after the commencement of this Act, whether the determination of the arbitrator was contained in an award made before or after that time ;

(b) subsection (6) does not apply to applications made under section 2(4) of the 1977 Act before the commencement of this Act.

4. In section 6 of this Act—

(a) subsection (3) and subsection (8), so far as relating to section 2(4A) of the 1977 Act, do not apply in relation to applications made as mentioned in paragraph 3(b) above ;

(b) subsection (5) applies to notices to quit given after the commencement of this Act, whether the death occurred before or after that time ;

(c) subsection (7) applies to notices to quit given after the commencement of that subsection, but does not affect any such notice which took effect before the date on which this Act is passed ;

(d) subsection (8), so far as relating to section 2(4B) of that Act, does not apply in relation to any act or omission by the tenant occurring before the commencement of this Act.

Transfer of functions of Minister

5. Neither section 8 of this Act nor the repeal in Schedule 4 to this Act of paragraph 28 of Schedule 6 to the 1948 Act applies in relation to the appointment of a person under section 16(2) of, or Schedule 6 to, the 1948 Act in pursuance of an application made before the commencement of the said provisions of this Act ; and Schedule 6 shall, in relation to any person appointed under that Schedule in pursuance of such an application, have effect as if the said provisions had not been enacted.

Rent increases reflecting improvements

6.—(1) Sub-paragraph (2)(c) of paragraph 5 of Schedule 3 does not apply in any case where a notice has been given by the landlord under section 9(1) of the 1948 Act before the commencement of this Act.

(2) Sub-paragraph (3) of that paragraph applies to agreements between landlord and tenant made on or after the date on which this Act is passed, whether the improvement was carried out before or after that date ; but that sub-paragraph does not affect paragraph (ii) of the proviso to subsection (3) of section 8 of the 1948 Act as it applies in relation to an arbitration under that Act in a case where the arbitrator was appointed before that date in pursuance of a demand made under subsection (1) of that section.

Right to remove fixtures

7. Paragraphs 6 and 16 of Schedule 3 to this Act do not apply in relation to an agricultural holding in any case where, before the commencement of this Act—

(a) the tenancy has terminated ; or

(b) the tenant has given a notice under section 13(2)(b) of the 1948 Act.

Compensation for damage by game

8. Nothing in paragraph 7 of that Schedule, and no repeal in Schedule 4 to this Act which is consequential on that paragraph, applies in relation to an agricultural holding in a case where before the commencement of this Act a notice has been given to the landlord under paragraph (*a*) of the proviso to section 14(1) of the 1948 Act.

Deductions in respect of grants

9. Paragraph 11 of Schedule 3 to this Act shall not affect any claim for compensation in respect of an improvement arising under the 1948 Act before the commencement of this Act.

Record of condition of holding

10. In paragraph (ii) of the proviso to section 56(1) of the 1948 Act the reference to a record made under section 16 of that Act shall include a reference to a record made under that section before the commencement of this Act.

Claims for dilapidations etc.

11. Paragraph 13 of Schedule 3 to this Act shall not affect any claim arising before the commencement of this Act under or in pursuance of any provision of section 57 of the 1948 Act.

Compensation on quitting part of holding

12. Paragraph 14(*b*) of that Schedule, so far as relating to section 60(2) of the 1948 Act, does not apply in relation to a notice to quit given before the commencement of this Act.

Settlement of claims

13. Nothing in paragraph 18 of that Schedule, and no repeal in Schedule 4 to this Act which is consequential on that paragraph, applies in relation to an agricultural holding in a case where the tenancy terminated before the commencement of this Act.

Forms for arbitrations

14. Any form specified in pursuance of paragraph 15 or 27 of Schedule 6 to the 1948 Act and in force immediately before the commencement of this Act shall have effect as if prescribed by an order under section 77 of that Act, as amended by paragraph 19 of Schedule 3 to this Act, and may be varied or revoked accordingly.

Arbitration procedure

15.—(1) In paragraph 1(1A) of Schedule 6 to the 1948 Act, as amended by paragraph 28(2) of Schedule 3 to this Act, the reference to an application which is referable to a demand for arbitra-

SCH. 5   tion made under section 8 of that Act shall not extend to an application made before the commencement of this Act.

(2) Sub-paragraphs (5) and (6) of paragraph 28 of Schedule 3 to this Act do not apply in relation to an arbitration under the 1948 Act in a case where the arbitrator has been appointed before the commencement of this Act, and sub-paragraph (10) of that paragraph does not affect the computation of any period of time for the purposes of any such arbitration.

Rights of tenant as to provision of fixed equipment

1958 c. 71.   16. Paragraph 30 of that Schedule applies in relation to applications made under section 4 of the Agriculture Act 1958 before the commencement of this Act as well as to those made thereafter.

Minor amendments etc. relating to notices to quit

1968 c. 34.   17. Nothing in Schedule 3 to this Act, or in the repeals made by this Act, so far as relating (in either case) to the 1977 Act or to the Agriculture (Miscellaneous Provisions) Act 1968 affects the operation of or otherwise applies in relation to a notice to quit an agricultural holding, or part of an agricultural holding, given before the commencement of this Act.

Arbitrations pursuant to s.24 of the 1976 Act

18. Paragraph 35 of that Schedule does not apply in relation to any arbitration under the 1948 Act in pursuance of a demand made under section 24(3) of the 1976 Act in any case where the arbitrator was appointed before the passing of this Act.

Matrimonial and Family Proceedings Act 1984

1984 CHAPTER 42

An Act to amend the Matrimonial Causes Act 1973 so far as it restricts the time within which proceedings for divorce or nullity of marriage can be instituted; to amend that Act, the Domestic Proceedings and Magistrates' Courts Act 1978 and the Magistrates' Courts Act 1980 so far as they relate to the exercise of the jurisdiction of courts in England and Wales to make provision for financial relief or to exercise related powers in matrimonial and certain other family proceedings; to make provision for financial relief to be available where a marriage has been dissolved or annulled, or the parties to a marriage have been legally separated, in a country overseas; to make related amendments in the Maintenance Orders (Reciprocal Enforcement) Act 1972 and the Inheritance (Provision for Family and Dependants) Act 1975; to make provision for the distribution and transfer between the High Court and county courts of, and the exercise in those courts of jurisdiction in, family business and family proceedings and to repeal and re-enact with amendments certain provisions conferring on designated county courts jurisdiction in matrimonial proceedings; to impose a duty to notify changes of address on persons liable to make payments under maintenance orders enforceable under Part II of the Maintenance Orders Act 1950 or Part I of the Maintenance Orders Act 1958; and for connected purposes.

[12th July 1984]

B E IT ENACTED by the Queen's most Excellent Majesty, by and with the advice and consent of the Lords Spiritual and Temporal, and Commons, in this present Parliament assembled, and by the authority of the same, as follows:—

PART I

TIME RESTRICTIONS ON PRESENTATION OF PETITIONS FOR DIVORCE OR NULLITY OF MARRIAGE

Bar on petitions for divorce within one year of marriage.
1973 c. 18.

1. For section 3 of the Matrimonial Causes Act 1973 (in this Part referred to as " the 1973 Act ") (which provides that no petition for divorce shall be presented within three years of marriage unless the leave of the court has been obtained) there shall be substituted the following section—

"Bar on petitions for divorce within one year of marriage.

3.—(1) No petition for divorce shall be presented to the court before the expiration of the period of one year from the date of the marriage.

(2) Nothing in this section shall prohibit the presentation of a petition based on matters which occurred before the expiration of that period."

Extension of period for proceedings for decree of nullity in respect of voidable marriage.

2.—(1) Section 13 of the 1973 Act (which imposes restrictions on the institution of proceedings for a decree of nullity in respect of a voidable marriage) shall be amended as follows.

(2) For subsection (2) of section 13 there shall be substituted the following subsection—

" (2) Without prejudice to subsection (1) above, the court shall not grant a decree of nullity by virtue of section 12 above on the grounds mentioned in paragraph (c), (d), (e) or (f) of that section unless—

(a) it is satisfied that proceedings were instituted within the period of three years from the date of the marriage, or

(b) leave for the institution of proceedings after the expiration of that period has been granted under subsection (4) below."

(3) At the end of section 13 there shall be added the following subsections—

"(4) In the case of proceedings for the grant of a decree of nullity by virtue of section 12 above on the grounds mentioned in paragraph (c), (d), (e) or (f) of that section, a judge of the court may, on an application made to him, grant leave for the institution of proceedings after the expiration of the period of three years from the date of the marriage if—

    (*a*) he is satisfied that the petitioner has at some time during that period suffered from mental disorder within the meaning of the Mental Health Act 1983, and

    (*b*) he considers that in all the circumstances of the case it would be just to grant leave for the institution of proceedings.

(5) An application for leave under subsection (4) above may be made after the expiration of the period of three years from the date of the marriage."

PART II

FINANCIAL RELIEF IN MATRIMONIAL PROCEEDINGS

Provisions relating to powers of the High Court and county courts

3. For section 25 of the Matrimonial Causes Act 1973 (in this Part referred to as "the 1973 Act") there shall be substituted the following sections—

Orders for financial relief after divorce etc.

1973 c. 18.

"*Matters to which court is to have regard in deciding how to exercise its powers under ss. 23, 24 and 24A.*

25.—(1) It shall be the duty of the court in deciding whether to exercise its powers under section 23, 24 or 24A above and, if so, in what manner, to have regard to all the circumstances of the case, first consideration being given to the welfare while a minor of any child of the family who has not attained the age of eighteen.

(2) As regards the exercise of the powers of the court under section 23(1)(*a*), (*b*) or (*c*), 24 or 24A above in relation to a party to the marriage, the court shall in particular have regard to the following matters—

    (*a*) the income, earning capacity, property and other financial resources which each of the parties to the marriage has or is likely to have in the foreseeable future, including in the case of earning capacity any increase in that capacity which it would in the opinion of the court be reasonable to expect a party to the marriage to take steps to acquire;

    (*b*) the financial needs, obligations and responsibilities which each of the parties to the marriage has or is likely to have in the foreseeable future;

    (c) the standard of living enjoyed by the family before the breakdown of the marriage ;

    (d) the age of each party to the marriage and the duration of the marriage ;

    (e) any physical or mental disability of either of the parties to the marriage ;

    (f) the contributions which each of the parties has made or is likely in the foreseeable future to make to the welfare of the family, including any contribution by looking after the home or caring for the family ;

    (g) the conduct of each of the parties, if that conduct is such that it would in the opinion of the court be inequitable to disregard it ;

    (h) in the case of proceedings for divorce or nullity of marriage, the value to each of the parties to the marriage of any benefit (for example, a pension) which, by reason of the dissolution or annulment of the marriage, that party will lose the chance of acquiring.

    (3) As regards the exercise of the powers of the court under section 23(1)(d), (e) or (f), (2) or (4), 24 or 24A above in relation to a child of the family, the court shall in particular have regard to the following matters—

    (a) the financial needs of the child ;

    (b) the income, earning capacity (if any), property and other financial resources of the child ;

    (c) any physical or mental disability of the child ;

    (d) the manner in which he was being and in which the parties to the marriage expected him to be educated or trained ;

    (e) the considerations mentioned in relation to the parties to the marriage in paragraphs (a), (b), (c) and (e) of subsection (2) above.

    (4) As regards the exercise of the powers of the court under section 23(1)(d), (e) or (f), (2) or (4), 24 or 24A above against a party to a marriage in favour of a child of the family who is not the child of that party, the court shall also have regard—

    (a) to whether that party assumed any responsibility for the child's maintenance, and, if so, to the extent to which, and the basis upon which, that party assumed such responsibility and to the length of time for which that party discharged such responsibility ;

(*b*) to whether in assuming and discharging such responsibility that party did so knowing that the child was not his or her own ;

(*c*) to the liability of any other person to maintain the child.

25A.—(1) Where on or after the grant of a decree of divorce or nullity of marriage the court decides to exercise its powers under section 23(1)(*a*), (*b*) or (*c*), 24 or 24A above in favour of a party to the marriage, it shall be the duty of the court to consider whether it would be appropriate so to exercise those powers that the financial obligations of each party towards the other will be terminated as soon after the grant of the decree as the court considers just and reasonable.

(2) Where the court decides in such a case to make a periodical payments or secured periodical payments order in favour of a party to the marriage, the court shall in particular consider whether it would be appropriate to require those payments to be made or secured only for such term as would in the opinion of the court be sufficient to enable the party in whose favour the order is made to adjust without undue hardship to the termination of his or her financial dependence on the other party.

(3) Where on or after the grant of a decree of divorce or nullity of marriage an application is made by a party to the marriage for a periodical payments or secured periodical payments order in his or her favour, then, if the court considers that no continuing obligation should be imposed on either party to make or secure periodical payments in favour of the other, the court may dismiss the application with a direction that the applicant shall not be entitled to make any further application in relation to that marriage for an order under section 23(1)(*a*) or (*b*) above."

4. In section 27 of the 1973 Act (financial provision in case of neglect to maintain) for subsection (3) there shall be substituted the following subsection—

" (3) Where an application under this section is made on the ground mentioned in subsection (1)(*a*) above, then, in deciding—

(*a*) whether the respondent has failed to provide reasonable maintenance for the applicant, and

(b) what order, if any, to make under this section in favour of the applicant,

the court shall have regard to all the circumstances of the case including the matters mentioned in section 25(2) above, and where an application is also made under this section in respect of a child of the family who has not attained the age of eighteen, first consideration shall be given to the welfare of the child while a minor."

Duration of orders for periodical payments and effect of remarriage.

5.—(1) In section 28(1) of the 1973 Act (duration of continuing financial provision orders in favour of party to a marriage), for the words from the beginning to " the following limits " there shall be substituted the words " Subject in the case of an order made on or after the grant of a decree of divorce or nullity of marriage to the provisions of sections 25A(2) above and 31(7) below, the term to be specified in a periodical payments or secured periodical payments order in favour of a party to a marriage shall be such term as the court thinks fit, except that the term shall not begin before or extend beyond the following limits ".

(2) After subsection (1) of the said section 28 there shall be inserted the following subsection—

" (1A) Where a periodical payments or secured periodical payments order in favour of a party to a marriage is made on or after the grant of a decree of divorce or nullity of marriage, the court may direct that that party shall not be entitled to apply under section 31 below for the extension of the term specified in the order ".

(3) In subsection (3) of the said section 28 (effect of remarriage on financial provision orders), after the word " remarries " there shall be inserted the words " whether at any time before or after the commencement of this Act ".

(4) In section 29(2) of the 1973 Act (duration of continuing financial provision orders in favour of children), in paragraph (a), for the words " unless the court thinks it right in the circumstances of the case to specify a later date " there shall be substituted the words " unless the court considers that in the circumstances of the case the welfare of the child requires that it should extend to a later date ".

Variation and discharge of orders for periodical payments.

6.—(1) Section 31 of the 1973 Act (variation and discharge of orders) shall be amended as follows.

(2) In subsection (1) after the words " subject to the provisions of this section " there shall be inserted the words " and of section 28(1A) above ".

(3) For subsection (7) there shall be substituted the following subsection—

" (7) In exercising the powers conferred by this section the court shall have regard to all the circumstances of the case, first consideration being given to the welfare while a minor of any child of the family who has not attained the age of eighteen, and the circumstances of the case shall include any change in any of the matters to which the court was required to have regard when making the order to which the application relates, and—

(a) in the case of a periodical payments or secured periodical payments order made on or after the grant of a decree of divorce or nullity of marriage, the court shall consider whether in all the circumstances and after having regard to any such change it would be appropriate to vary the order so that payments under the order are required to be made or secured only for such further period as will in the opinion of the court be sufficient to enable the party in whose favour the order was made to adjust without undue hardship to the termination of those payments ;

(b) in a case where the party against whom the order was made has died, the circumstances of the case shall also include the changed circumstances resulting from his or her death."

(4) After subsection (9) there shall be inserted the following subsection—

" (10) Where the court, in exercise of its powers under this section, decides to vary or discharge a periodical payments or secured periodical payments order, then, subject to section 28(1) and (2) above, the court shall have power to direct that the variation or discharge shall not take effect until the expiration of such period as may be specified in the order."

7. The following section shall be inserted after section 33 of the 1973 Act—

Consent orders for financial provision or property adjustment.

" *Consent orders*

Consent orders for financial provision or property adjustment.

33A.—(1) Notwithstanding anything in the preceding provisions of this Part of this Act, on an application for a consent order for finanical relief the court may, unless it has reason to think that there are other circumstances into which it ought to inquire, make an order in the terms agreed on the basis only of the prescribed information furnished with the application.

PART II

(2) Subsection (1) above applies to an application for a consent order varying or discharging an order for financial relief as it applies to an application for an order for financial relief.

(3) In this section—

'consent order', in relation to an application for an order, means an order in the terms applied for to which the respondent agrees ;

'order for financial relief' means an order under any of sections 23, 24, 24A or 27 above ; and

'prescribed' means prescribed by rules of court."

Restrictions imposed in divorce proceedings etc., on applications under Inheritance (Provision for Family and Dependants) Act 1975.

1975 c. 63.

8.—(1) For subsection (1) of section 15 of the Inheritance (Provision for Family and Dependants) Act 1975 (under which the court on the grant of a decree of divorce, nullity or judicial separation has power, if the parties to the marriage agree, to order that one party shall not on the death of the other party be entitled to apply for an order under section 2 of that Act) there shall be substituted the following subsection—

" (1) On the grant of a decree of divorce, a decree of nullity of marriage or a decree of judicial separation or at any time thereafter the court, if it considers it just to do so, may, on the application of either party to the marriage, order that the other party to the marriage shall not on the death of the applicant be entitled to apply for an order under section 2 of this Act.

In this subsection " the court " means the High Court or, where a county court has jurisdiction by virtue of Part V of the Matrimonial and Family Proceedings Act 1984, a county court."

(2) In section 25(1) of that Act (interpretation), in the definition of " the court " after the word " means " there shall be inserted the words " unless the context otherwise requires ".

Provisions relating to the powers of magistrates' courts

Orders for financial relief made by magistrates' courts in matrimonial proceedings.

1978 c. 22.

9.—(1) For section 3 of the Domestic Proceedings and Magistrates' Courts Act 1978 there shall be substituted the following section—

" Matters to which court is to have regard in exercising its powers under s.2.

3.—(1) Where an application is made for an order under section 2 of this Act, it shall be the duty of the court, in deciding whether to exercise its powers under that section and, if so, in what manner, to have regard to all the circumstances of the case, first consideration being given to the welfare while a minor of any child of the family who has not attained the age of eighteen.

(2) As regards the exercise of its powers under subsection (1)(*a*) or (*b*) of section 2, the court shall in particular have regard to the following matters—

   (*a*) the income, earning capacity, property and other financial resources which each of the parties to the marriage has or is likely to have in the foreseeable future, including in the case of earning capacity any increase in that capacity which it would in the opinion of the court be reasonable to expect a party to the marriage to take steps to acquire ;

   (*b*) the financial needs, obligations and responsibilities which each of the parties to the marriage has or is likely to have in the foreseeable future ;

   (*c*) the standard of living enjoyed by the parties to the marriage before the occurrence of the conduct which is alleged as the ground of the application ;

   (*d*) the age of each party to the marriage and the duration of the marriage ;

   (*e*) any physical or mental disability of either of the parties to the marriage ;

   (*f*) the contributions which each of the parties has made or is likely in the foreseeable future to make to the welfare of the family, including any contribution by looking after the home or caring for the family ;

   (*g*) the conduct of each of the parties, if that conduct is such that it would in the opinion of the court be inequitable to disregard it.

(3) As regards the exercise of its powers under subsection (1)(*c*) or (*d*) of section 2, the court shall in particular have regard to the following matters—

   (*a*) the financial needs of the child ;

   (*b*) the income, earning capacity (if any), property and other financial resources of the child ;

   (*c*) any physical or mental disability of the child ;

   (*d*) the standard of living enjoyed by the family before the occurrence of the conduct which is alleged as the ground of the application ;

   (*e*) the manner in which the child was being and in which the parties to the marriage expected him to be educated or trained ;

(*f*) the matters mentioned in relation to the parties to the marriage in paragraphs (*a*) and (*b*) of subsection (2) above.

(4) As regards the exercise of its powers under section 2 in favour of a child of the family who is not the child of the respondent, the court shall also have regard—

    (*a*) to whether the respondent has assumed any responsibility for the child's maintenance and, if he did, to the extent to which, and the basis on which, he assumed that responsibility and to the length of time during which he discharged that responsibility ;

    (*b*) to whether in assuming and discharging that responsibility the respondent did so knowing that the child was not his own child ;

    (*c*) to the liability of any other person to maintain the child."

(2) In section 5(2) of that Act (duration of periodical payments orders in favour of children), in paragraph (*a*), for the words " unless the court thinks it right in the circumstances of the case to specify a later date " there shall be substituted the words " unless the court considers that in the circumstances of the case the welfare of the child requires that it should extend to a later date ".

(3) In section 20(11) of that Act (variation and revocation of orders for periodical payments) for the words " including any change " there shall be substituted the words " first consideration being given to the welfare while a minor of any child of the family who has not attained the age of eighteen, and the circumstances of the case shall include any change ".

Orders for payments which have been agreed by the parties.

1978 c. 22.

10. For section 6 of the Domestic Proceedings and Magistrates' Courts Act 1978 there shall be substituted the following section—

" Orders for payments which have been agreed by the parties.

    6.—(1) Either party to a marriage may apply to a magistrates' court for an order under this section on the ground that either the party making the application or the other party to the marriage has agreed to make such financial provision as may be specified in the application and, subject to subsection (3) below, the court on such an application may, if—

        (*a*) it is satisfied that the applicant or the respondent, as the case may be, has agreed to make that provision, and (*b*) it has no reason to think that it would be contrary to the interests of justice to exercise its powers hereunder,

order that the applicant or the respondent, as the case may be, shall make the financial provision specified in the application.

(2) In this section " financial provision " means the provision mentioned in any one or more of the following paragraphs, that is to say—

(*a*) the making of periodical payments by one party to the other,

(*b*) the payment of a lump sum by one party to the other,

(*c*) the making of periodical payments by one party to a child of the family or to the other party for the benefit of such a child,

(*d*) the payment by one party of a lump sum to a child of the family or to the other party for the benefit of such a child,

and any reference in this section to the financial provision specified in an application made under subsection (1) above or specified by the court under subsection (5) below is a reference to the type of provision specified in the application or by the court, as the case may be, to the amount so specified as the amount of any payment to be made thereunder and, in the case of periodical payments, to the term so specified as the term for which the payments are to be made.

(3) Where the financial provision specified in an application under subsection (1) above includes or consists of provision in respect of a child of the family, the court shall not make an order under that subsection unless it considers that the provision which the applicant or the respondent, as the case may be, has agreed to make in respect of that child provides for, or makes a proper contribution towards, the financial needs of the child.

(4) A party to a marriage who has applied for an order under section 2 of this Act shall not be precluded at any time before the determination of that application from applying for an order under this section ; but if an order is made under this section on the application of either party and either of them has also made an application for an order under section 2 of this Act, the application made for the

order under section 2 shall be treated as if it had been withdrawn.

(5) Where on an application under subsection (1) above the court decides—

(*a*) that it would be contrary to the interests of justice to make an order for the making of the financial provision specified in the application, or

(*b*) that any financial provision which the applicant or the respondent, as the case may be, has agreed to make in respect of a child of the family does not provide for, or make a proper contribution towards, the financial needs of that child,

but is of the opinion—

(i) that it would not be contrary to the interests of justice to make an order for the making of some other financial provision specified by the court, and

(ii) that, in so far as that other financial provision contains any provision for a child of the family, it provides for, or makes a proper contribution towards, the financial needs of that child,

then if both the parties agree, the court may order that the applicant or the respondent, as the case may be, shall make that other financial provision.

(6) Subject to subsection (8) below, the provisions of section 4 of this Act shall apply in relation to an order under this section which requires periodical payments to be made to a party to a marriage for his own benefit as they apply in relation to an order under section 2(1)(*a*) of this Act.

(7) Subject to subsection (8) below, the provisions of section 5 of this Act shall apply in relation to an order under this section for the making of financial provision in respect of a child of the family as they apply in relation to an order under section 2(1)(*c*) or (*d*) of this Act.

(8) Where the court makes an order under this section which contains provision for the making of periodical payments and, by virtue of subsection (4) above, an application for an order under section 2 of this Act is treated as if it had been withdrawn, then the term which may be specified as the term for

which the payments are to be made may begin with the date of the making of the application for the order under section 2 or any later date.

(9) Where the respondent is not present or represented by counsel or solicitor at the hearing of an application for an order under subsection (1) above, the court shall not make an order under this section unless there is produced to the court such evidence as may be prescribed by rules of—

> (a) the consent of the respondent to the making of the order,
>
> (b) the financial resources of the respondent, and
>
> (c) in a case where the financial provision specified in the application includes or consists of provision in respect of a child of the family to be made by the applicant to the respondent for the benefit of the child or to the child, the financial resources of the child."

11. For section 20(2) of the Domestic Proceedings and Magistrates' Courts Act 1978 (under which the court can vary a consent order by ordering the payment of a lump sum if the consent order provided for the payment of a lump sum) there shall be substituted the following subsection—

Variation of consent orders by magistrates' courts.

1978 c. 22.

> " (2) Where a magistrates' court has made an order under section 6 of this Act for the making of periodical payments by a party to a marriage the court shall have power, on an application made under this section, to vary or revoke that order and also to make an order for the payment of a lump sum by that party either—
>
> (a) to the other party to the marriage, or
>
> (b) to a child of the family or to that other party for the benefit of that child."

PART III

FINANCIAL RELIEF IN ENGLAND AND WALES AFTER OVERSEAS DIVORCE ETC.

Applications for financial relief

12.—(1) Where—

> (a) a marriage has been dissolved or annulled, or the parties to a marriage have been legally separated, by means of judicial or other proceedings in an overseas country, and

Applications for financial relief after overseas divorce etc.

(*b*) the divorce, annulment or legal separation is entitled to be recognised as valid in England and Wales,

either party to the marriage may apply to the court in the manner prescribed by rules of court for an order for financial relief under this Part of this Act.

(2) If after a marriage has been dissolved or annulled in an overseas country one of the parties to the marriage remarries that party shall not be entitled to make an application in relation to that marriage.

(3) For the avoidance of doubt it is hereby declared that the reference in subsection (2) above to remarriage includes a reference to a marriage which is by law void or voidable.

(4) In this Part of this Act except sections 19, 23, and 24 " order for financial relief " means an order under section 17 or 22 below of a description referred to in that section.

Leave of the court required for applications for financial relief.

13.—(1) No application for an order for financial relief shall be made under this Part of this Act unless the leave of 'the court has been obtained in accordance with rules of court ; and the court shall not grant leave unless it considers that there is substantial ground for the making of an application for such an order.

(2) The court may grant leave under this section notwithstanding that an order has been made by a court in a country outside England and Wales requiring the other party to the marriage to make any payment or transfer any property to the applicant or a child of the family.

(3) Leave under this section may be granted subject to such conditions as the court thinks fit.

Interim orders for maintenance.

14.—(1) Where leave is granted under section 13 above for the making of an application for an order for financial relief and it appears to the court that the applicant or any child of the family is in immediate need of financial assistance, the court may make an interim order for maintenance, that is to say, an order requiring the other party to the marriage to make to the applicant or to the child such periodical payments, and for such term, being a term beginning not earlier than the date of the grant of leave and ending with the date of the determination of the application for an order for financial relief, as the court thinks reasonable.

(2) If it appears to the court that the court has jurisdiction to entertain the application for an order for financial relief by reason only of paragraph (*c*) of section 15(1) below the court shall not make an interim order under this section.

(3) An interim order under subsection (1) above may be
made subject to such conditions as the court thinks fit.

15.—(1) Subject to subsection (2) below, the court shall
have jurisdiction to entertain an application for an order for
financial relief if any of the following jurisdictional requirements are satisfied, that is to say—

(a) either of the parties to the marriage was domiciled in
England and Wales on the date of the application for
leave under section 13 above or was so domiciled on
the date on which the divorce, annulment or legal separation obtained in the overseas country took effect in
that country ; or

(b) either of the parties to the marriage was habitually resident in England and Wales throughout the period of
one year ending with the date of the application for
leave or was so resident throughout the period of one
year ending with the date on which the divorce, annulment or legal separation obtained in the overseas
country took effect in that country ; or

(c) either or both of the parties to the marriage had at the
date of the application for leave a beneficial interest
in possession in a dwelling-house situated in England
or Wales which was at some time during the marriage
a matrimonial home of the parties to the marriage.

(2) Where the jurisdiction of the court to entertain proceedings under this Part of this Act would fall to be determined by
reference to the jurisdictional requirements imposed by virtue
of Part I of the Civil Jurisdiction and Judgments Act 1982
(implementation of certain European conventions) then—

(a) satisfaction of the requirements of subsection (1) above
shall not obviate the need to satisfy the requirements
imposed by virtue of Part I of that Act ; and

(b) satisfaction of the requirements imposed by virtue of
Part I of that Act shall obviate the need to satisfy the
requirements of subsection (1) above ;

and the court shall entertain or not entertain the proceedings
accordingly.

16.—(1) Before making an order for financial relief the court
shall consider whether in all the circumstances of the case it
would be appropriate for such an order to be made by a court
in England and Wales, and if the court is not satisfied that it
would be appropriate, the court shall dismiss the application.

(2) The court shall in particular have regard to the following
matters—

(a) the connection which the parties to the marriage have
with England and Wales ;

PART III
(b) the connection which those parties have with the country in which the marriage was dissolved or annulled or in which they were legally separated ;

(c) the connection which those parties have with any other country outside England and Wales ;

(d) any financial benefit which the applicant or a child of the family has received, or is likely to receive, in consequence of the divorce, annulment or legal separation, by virtue of any agreement or the operation of the law of a country outside England and Wales ;

(e) in a case where an order has been made by a court in a country outside England and Wales requiring the other party to the marriage to make any payment or transfer any property for the benefit of the applicant or a child of the family, the financial relief given by the order and the extent to which the order has been complied with or is likely to be complied with ;

(f) any right which the applicant has, or has had, to apply for financial relief from the other party to the marriage under the law of any country outside England and Wales and if the applicant has omitted to exercise that right the reason for that omission ;

(g) the availability in England and Wales of any property in respect of which an order under this Part of this Act in favour of the applicant could be made ;

(h) the extent to which any order made under this Part of this Act is likely to be enforceable ;

(i) the length of time which has elapsed since the date of the divorce, annulment or legal separation.

Orders for financial provision and property adjustment

Orders for financial provision and property adjustment.
17.—(1) Subject to section 20 below, the court on an application by a party to a marriage for an order for financial relief under this section, may make any one or more of the orders which it could make under Part II of the 1973 Act if a decree of divorce, a decree of nullity of marriage or a decree of judicial separation in respect of the marriage had been granted in England and Wales, that is to say—

(a) any order mentioned in section 23(1) of the 1973 Act (financial provision orders) ;

(b) any order mentioned in section 24(1) of that Act (property adjustment orders).

(2) Subject to section 20 below, where the court makes a secured periodical payments order, an order for the payment of a lump sum or a property adjustment order under subsection (1) above, then, on making that order or at any time thereafter, the

court may make any order mentioned in section 24A(1) of the 1973 Act (orders for sale of property) which the court would have power to make if the order under subsection (1) above had been made under Part II of the 1973 Act.

18.—(1) In deciding whether to exercise its powers under section 17 above and, if so, in what manner the court shall act in accordance with this section.

(2) The court shall have regard to all the circumstances of the case, first consideration being given to the welfare while a minor of any child of the family who has not attained the age of eighteen.

(3) As regards the exercise of those powers in relation to a party to the marriage, the court shall in particular have regard to the matters mentioned in section 25(2)(*a*) to (*h*) of the 1973 Act and shall be under duties corresponding with those imposed by section 25A(1) and (2) of the 1973 Act where it decides to exercise under section 17 above powers corresponding with the powers referred to in those subsections.

(4) As regards the exercise of those powers in relation to a child of the family, the court shall in particular have regard to the matters mentioned in section 25(3)(*a*) to (*e*) of the 1973 Act.

(5) As regards the exercise of those powers against a party to the marriage in favour of a child of the family who is not the child of that party, the court shall also have regard to the matters mentioned in section 25(4)(*a*) to (*c*) of the 1973 Act.

(6) Where an order has been made by a court outside England and Wales for the making of payments or the transfer of property by a party to the marriage, the court in considering in accordance with this section the financial resources of the other party to the marriage or a child of the family shall have regard to the extent to which that order has been complied with or is likely to be complied with.

19.—(1) Notwithstanding anything in section 18 above, on an application for a consent order for financial relief the court may, unless it has reason to think that there are other circumstances into which it ought to inquire, make an order in the terms agreed on the basis only of the prescribed information furnished with the application.

(2) Subsection (1) above applies to an application for a consent order varying or discharging an order for financial relief as it applies to an application for an order for financial relief.

(3) In this section—

" consent order ", in relation to an application for an order, means an order in the terms applied for to which the respondent agrees ;

" order for financial relief " means an order under section 17 above ; and

" prescribed " means prescribed by rules of court.

Restriction of powers of court where jurisdiction depends on matrimonial home in England or Wales.

20.—(1) Where the court has jurisdiction to entertain an application for an order for financial relief by reason only of the situation in England or Wales of a dwelling-house which was a matrimonial home of the parties, the court may make under section 17 above any one or more of the following orders (but no other)—

(a) an order that either party to the marriage shall pay to the other such lump sum as may be specified in the order ;

(b) an order that a party to the marriage shall pay to such person as may be so specified for the benefit of a child of the family, or to such a child, such lump sum as may be so specified ;

(c) an order that a party to the marriage shall transfer to the other party, to any child of the family or to such person as may be so specified for the benefit of such a child, the interest of the first-mentioned party in the dwelling-house, or such part of that interest as may be so specified ;

(d) an order that a settlement of the interest of a party to the marriage in the dwelling-house, or such part of that interest as may be so specified, be made to the satisfaction of the court for the benefit of the other party to the marriage and of the children of the family or either or any of them ;

(e) an order varying for the benefit of the parties to the marriage and of the children of the family or either or any of them any ante-nuptial or post-nuptial settlement (including such a settlement made by will or codicil) made on the parties to the marriage so far as that settlement relates to an interest in the dwelling-house ;

(f) an order extinguishing or reducing the interest of either of the parties to the marriage under any such settlement so far as that interest is an interest in the dwelling-house ;

(g) an order for the sale of the interest of a party to the marriage in the dwelling-house.

(2) Where, in the circumstances mentioned in subsection (1) above, the court makes an order for the payment of a lump sum

by a party to the marriage, the amount of the lump sum shall not exceed, or where more than one such order is made the total amount of the lump sums shall not exceed in aggregate, the following amount, that is to say—

    (*a*) if the interest of that party in the dwelling-house is sold in pursuance of an order made under subsection (1)(*g*) above, the amount of the proceeds of the sale of that interest after deducting therefrom any costs incurred in the sale thereof ;

    (*b*) if the interest of that party is not so sold, the amount which in the opinion of the court represents the value of that interest.

(3) Where the interest of a party to the marriage in the dwelling-house is held jointly or in common with any other person or persons—

    (*a*) the reference in subsection (1)(*g*) above to the interest of a party to the marriage shall be construed as including a reference to the interest of that other person, or the interest of those other persons, in the dwelling-house, and

    (*b*) the reference in subsection (2)(*a*) above to the amount of the proceeds of a sale ordered under subsection (1)(*g*) above shall be construed as a reference to that part of those proceeds which is attributable to the interest of that party to the marriage in the dwelling-house.

21. The following provisions of Part II of the 1973 Act (financial relief for parties to marriage and children of family) shall apply in relation to an order made under section 14 or 17 above as they apply in relation to a like order made under that Part of that Act, that is to say—

Application to orders under ss. 14 and 17 of certain provisions of Part II of Matrimonial Causes Act 1973.

    (*a*) section 23(3) (provisions as to lump sums) ;

    (*b*) section 24A(2), (4), (5) and (6) (provisions as to orders for sale) ;

    (*c*) section 28(1) and (2) (duration of continuing financial provision orders in favour of party to marriage) ;

    (*d*) section 29 (duration of continuing financial provision orders in favour of children, and age limit on making certain orders in their favour) ;

    (*e*) section 30 (direction for settlement of instrument for securing payments or effecting property adjustment), except paragraph (*b*) ;

    (*f*) section 31 (variation, discharge etc. of certain orders for financial relief), except subsection (2)(*e*) and subsection (4) ;

(*g*) section 32 (payment of certain arrears unenforceable without the leave of the court) ;

(*h*) section 33 (orders for repayment of sums paid under certain orders) ;

(*i*) section 38 (orders for repayment of sums paid after cessation of order by reason of remarriage) ;

(*j*) section 39 (settlements etc. made in compliance with a property adjustment order may be avoided on bankruptcy of settlor) ; and

(*k*) section 40 (payments etc. under order made in favour of person suffering from mental disorder).

Orders for transfer of tenancies

Powers of the court in relation to certain tenancies of dwelling-houses.

1983 c. 19.

22. Where an application is made by a party to a marriage for an order for financial relief then, if—

(*a*) one of the parties to the marriage is entitled, either in his or her own right or jointly with the other party, to occupy a dwelling-house situated in England or Wales by virtue of such a tenancy as is mentioned in paragraph 1(1) of Schedule 1 to the Matrimonial Homes Act 1983 (certain statutory tenancies), and

(*b*) the dwelling-house has at some time during the marriage been a matrimonial home of the parties to the marriage,

the court may make in relation to that dwelling-house any order which it could make under Part II of that Schedule if a decree of divorce, a decree of nullity of marriage or a decree of judicial separation in respect of the marriage had been granted in England and Wales ; and the provisions of paragraphs 5 and 8(1) in Part III of that Schedule shall apply in relation to any order made under this section as they apply in relation to an order made under Part II of that Schedule.

Avoidance of transactions intended to prevent or reduce financial relief

Avoidance of transactions intended to defeat applications for financial relief.

23.—(1) For the purposes of this section " financial relief " means relief under section 14 or 17 above and any reference to defeating a claim by a party to a marriage for financial relief is a reference to preventing financial relief from being granted or reducing the amount of relief which might be granted, or frustrating or impeding the enforcement of any order which might be or has been made under either of those provisions at the instance of that party.

(2) Where leave is granted under section 13 above for the making by a party to a marriage of an application for an

order for financial relief under section 17 above, the court may, on an application by that party—

(a) if it is satisfied that the other party to the marriage is, with the intention of defeating the claim for financial relief, about to make any disposition or to transfer out of the jurisdiction or otherwise deal with any property, make such order as it thinks fit for restraining the other party from so doing or otherwise for protecting the claim ;

(b) if it is satisfied that the other party has, with that intention, made a reviewable disposition and that if the disposition were set aside financial relief or different financial relief would be granted to the applicant, make an order setting aside the disposition.

(3) Where an order for financial relief under section 14 or 17 above has been made by the court at the instance of a party to a marriage, then, on an application made by that party, the court may, if it is satisfied that the other party to the marriage has, with the intention of defeating the claim for financial relief, made a reviewable disposition, make an order setting aside the disposition.

(4) Where the court has jurisdiction to entertain the application for an order for financial relief by reason only of paragraph (c) of section 15(1) above, it shall not make any order under subsection (2) or (3) above in respect of any property other than the dwelling-house concerned.

(5) Where the court makes an order under subsection (2)(b) or (3) above setting aside a disposition it shall give such consequential directions as it thinks fit for giving effect to the order (including directions requiring the making of any payments or the disposal of any property).

(6) Any disposition made by the other party to the marriage (whether before or after the commencement of the application) is a reviewable disposition for the purposes of subsections (2)(b) and (3) above unless it was made for valuable consideration (other than marriage) to a person who, at the time of the disposition, acted in relation to it in good faith and without notice of any intention on the part of the other party to defeat the applicant's claim for financial relief.

(7) Where an application is made under subsection (2) or (3) above with respect to a disposition which took place less than three years before the date of the application or with respect to a disposition or other dealing with property which is about to take place and the court is satisfied—

(a) in a case falling within subsection (2)(a) or (b) above, that the disposition or other dealing would (apart from this section) have the consequence, or (*b*) in a case falling within subsection (3) above, that the disposition has had the consequence,

of defeating a claim by the applicant for financial relief, it shall be presumed, unless the contrary is shown, that the person who disposed of or is about to dispose of or deal with the property did so or, as the case may be, is about to do so, with the intention of defeating the applicant's claim for financial relief.

(8) In this section " disposition " does not include any provision contained in a will or codicil but, with that exception, includes any conveyance, assurance or gift of property of any description, whether made by an instrument or otherwise.

(9) The preceding provisions of this section are without prejudice to any power of the High Court to grant injunctions under section 37 of the Supreme Court Act 1981.

24.—(1) Where, on an application by a party to a marriage, it appears to the court—

    (*a*) that the marriage has been dissolved or annulled, or that the parties to the marriage have been legally separated, by means of judicial or other proceedings in an overseas country ; and

    (*b*) that the applicant intends to apply for leave to make an application for an order for financial relief under section 17 above as soon as he or she has been habitually resident in England and Wales for a period of one year ; and

    (*c*) that the other party to the marriage is, with the intention of defeating a claim for financial relief, about to make any disposition or to transfer out of the jurisdiction or otherwise deal with any property,

the court may make such order as it thinks fit for restraining the other party from taking such action as is mentioned in paragraph (*c*) above.

(2) For the purposes of an application under subsection (1) above—

    (*a*) the reference to defeating a claim for financial relief shall be construed in accordance with subsection (1) of section 23 above (omitting the reference to any order which has been made) ; and

    (*b*) subsections (7) and (8) of section 23 above shall apply as they apply for the purposes of an application under that section.

(3) The preceding provisions of this section are without prejudice to any power of the High Court to grant injunctions under section 37 of the Supreme Court Act 1981.

Financial provision out of estate of deceased party to marriage   PART III

25.—(1) The Inheritance (Provision for Family and Dependants) Act 1975 shall have effect with the following amendments, being amendments designed to give to persons whose marriages are dissolved or annulled overseas the same rights to apply for provision under that Act (as amended by section 8 of this Act) as persons whose marriages are dissolved or annulled under the 1973 Act.

(2) In section 25(1), for the definition of " former wife " and " former husband " there shall be substituted the following definition—

> " 'former wife' or 'former husband' means a person whose marriage with the deceased was during the lifetime of the deceased either—
>
> (*a*) dissolved or annulled by a decree of divorce or a decree of nullity of marriage granted under the law of any part of the British Islands, or
>
> (*b*) dissolved or annulled in any country or territory outside the British Islands by a divorce or annulment which is entitled to be recognised as valid by the law of England and Wales ; ".

(3) After section 15 (restriction in divorce proceedings etc. of applications under the Act) there shall be inserted the following section—

Extension of powers under Inheritance (Provision for Family and Dependants) Act 1975 in respect of former spouses.

1975 c. 63.

" Restriction imposed in proceedings under Matrimonial and Family Proceedings Act 1984 on application under this Act.

15A.—(1) On making an order under section 17 of the Matrimonial and Family Proceedings Act 1984 (orders for financial provision and property adjustment following overseas divorces, etc.) the court, if it considers it just to do so, may, on the application of either party to the marriage, order that the other party to the marriage shall not on the death of the applicant be entitled to apply for an order under section 2 of this Act.

In this subsection ' the court ' means the High Court or, where a county court has jurisdiction by virtue of Part V of the Matrimonial and Family Proceedings Act 1984, a county court.

(2) Where an order under subsection (1) above has been made with respect to a party to a marriage which has been dissolved or annulled, then, on the death of the other party to that marriage, the court shall not entertain an application under section 2 of this Act made by the first-mentioned party.

(3) Where an order under subsection (1) above has been made with respect to a party to a marriage the

parties to which have been legally separated, then, if the other party to the marriage dies while the legal separation is in force, the court shall not entertain an application under section 2 of this Act made by the first-mentioned party."

Recovery of maintenance in magistrates' courts after overseas divorce etc.

Extension of s. 28A of Maintenance Orders (Reciprocal) Enforcement Act 1972.

1972 c. 18.

26.—(1) Section 28A of the Maintenance Orders (Reciprocal Enforcement) Act 1972 (complaint by former spouse in convention country for recovery in England and Wales of maintenance from other spouse) shall have effect with the following amendments.

(2) For subsection (1) there shall be substituted the following subsection—

" (1) Where on an application under section 27(1) of this Act for the recovery of maintenance from a person who is residing in England and Wales—

(a) that person is a former spouse of the applicant in a convention country who is seeking to recover maintenance, and

(b) the marriage between the applicant and the former spouse has been dissolved or annulled in a country or territory outside the United Kingdom by a divorce or annulment which is recognised as valid by the law of England and Wales, and

(c) an order for the payment of maintenance for the benefit of the applicant or a child of the family has, by reason of the divorce or annulment, been made by a court in a convention country, and

(d) in a case where the order for the payment of maintenance was made by a court of a different country from that in which the divorce or annulment was obtained, either the applicant or his or her former spouse was resident in the convention country whose court made the maintenance order at the time the application for that order was made,

the application shall, notwithstanding that the marriage has been dissolved or annulled, be treated as a complaint for an order under section 2 of the Domestic Proceedings and Magistrates' Courts Act 1978, and the provisions of this section shall have effect."

(3) For subsection (4) there shall be substituted the following subsection—

" (4) A divorce or annulment obtained in a country or territory outside the United Kingdom shall be presumed for

the purposes of this section to be one the validity of which is
recognised by the law of England and Wales, unless the
contrary is proved by the defendant."

(4) Subsection (5) shall be omitted.

Interpretation

27. In this Part of this Act—   Interpretation
of Part III.
" the 1973 Act " means the Matrimonial Causes Act 1973 ;   1973 c. 18.

" child of the family " has the same meaning as in section
52(1) of the 1973 Act ;

" the court " means the High Court or, where a county
court has jurisdiction by virtue of Part V of this Act,
a county court ;

" dwelling-house " includes any building or part thereof
which is occupied as a dwelling, and any yard, garden,
garage or outhouse belonging to the dwelling-house
and occupied therewith ;

" order for financial relief " has the meaning given by section 12(4) above ;

" overseas country " means a country or territory outside
the British Islands ;

" possession " includes receipt of, or the right to receive,
rents and profits ;

" property adjustment order " means such an order as is
specified in section 24(1)(*a*), (*b*), (*c*) or (*d*) of the 1973
Act ;

" rent " does not include mortgage interest ;

" secured periodical payments order " means such an order
as is specified in section 23(1)(*b*) or (*e*) of the 1973 Act.

PART IV

FINANCIAL PROVISION IN SCOTLAND AFTER OVERSEAS DIVORCE ETC.

28.—(1) Where parties to a marriage have been divorced in an   Circumstances
overseas country, then, subject to subsection (4) below, if the   in which a
jurisdictional requirements and the conditions set out in sub-   Scottish court
sections (2) and (3) below respectively are satisfied, the court   may entertain
application
may entertain an application by one of the parties for an order   for financial
for financial provision.   provision.

(2) The jurisdictional requirements mentioned in subsection (1) above are that—

    (*a*) the applicant was domiciled or habitually resident in Scotland on the date when the application was made; and

    (*b*) the other party to the marriage—

        (i) was domiciled or habitually resident in Scotland on the date when the application was made; or

        (ii) was domiciled or habitually resident in Scotland when the parties last lived together as husband and wife; or

        (iii) on the date when the application was made, was an owner or tenant of, or had a beneficial interest in, property in Scotland which had at some time been a matrimonial home of the parties; and

    (*c*) where the court is the sheriff court, either—

        (i) one of the parties was, on the date when the application was made, habitually resident in the sheriffdom; or

        (ii) paragraph (*b*)(iii) above is satisfied in respect of property wholly or partially within the sheriffdom.

(3) The conditions mentioned in subsection (1) above are that—

    (*a*) the divorce falls to be recognised in Scotland;

    (*b*) the other party to the marriage initiated the proceedings for divorce;

    (*c*) the application was made within five years after the date when the divorce took effect;

    (*d*) a court in Scotland would have had jurisdiction to entertain an action for divorce between the parties if such an action had been brought in Scotland immediately before the foreign divorce took effect;

    (*e*) the marriage had a substantial connection with Scotland; and

    (*f*) both parties are living at the time of the application.

(4) Where the jurisdiction of the court to entertain proceedings under this Part of this Act would fall to be determined by reference to the jurisdictional requirements imposed by virtue

1982 c. 27. of Part I of the Civil Jurisdiction and Judgments Act 1982 (implementation of certain European conventions) then—

    (*a*) satisfaction of the requirements of subsection (2) above shall not obviate the need to satisfy the requirements imposed by virtue of Part I of that Act; and

(*b*) satisfaction of the requirements imposed by virtue of
Part I of that Act shall obviate the need to satisfy the
requirements of subsection (2) above ;

PART IV

and the court shall entertain or not entertain the proceedings
accordingly.

29.—(1) Subject to subsections (2) to (5) below, Scots law
shall apply, with any necessary modifications, in relation to
an application under section 28 above as it would apply if the
application were being made in an action for divorce in Scotland.

Disposal of application in Scotland.

(2) In disposing of an application entertained by it under the
said section 28, the court shall exercise its powers so as to place
the parties, in so far as it is reasonable and practicable to do
so, in the financial position in which they would have been if
the application had been disposed of, in an action for divorce
in Scotland, on the date on which the foreign divorce took effect.

(3) In determining what is reasonable and practicable for the
purposes of subsection (2) above, the court shall have regard in
particular to—

(*a*) the parties' resources, present and foreseeable at the
date of disposal of the application ;

(*b*) any order made by a foreign court in or in connection
with the divorce proceedings for the making of financial
provision in whatever form, or the transfer of property,
by one of the parties to the other ; and

(*c*) subsection (5) below.

(4) Except where subsection (5) below applies, the court may
make an order for an interim award of a periodical allowance
where—

(*a*) it appears from the applicant's averments that in the
disposal of the application an order for financial provision is likely to be made ; and

(*b*) the court considers that such an interim award is
necessary to avoid hardship to the applicant.

(5) Where but for section 28(2)(*b*)(iii) above the court would
not have jurisdiction to entertain the application, the court may
make an order—

(*a*) relating to the former matrimonial home or its furniture
and plenishings ; or

(*b*) that the other party to the marriage shall pay to the
applicant a capital sum not exceeding the value of
that other party's interest in the former matrimonial
home and its furniture and plenishings,

PART IV   but shall not be entitled to make any other order for financial provision.

Interpretation of Part IV.   **30.**—(1) In the foregoing provisions of this Part of this Act unless the context otherwise requires—

> " the court " means the Court of Session or the sheriff court:

1981 c. 59.   > " furniture and plenishings " has the meaning assigned by section 22 of the Matrimonial Homes (Family Protection) (Scotland) Act 1981 ;

> " matrimonial home " has the meaning assigned by the said section 22 ;

1976 c. 39.   > " order for financial provision " means any one or more of the orders specified in paragraphs (*a*) to (*c*) of section 5(1) of the Divorce (Scotland) Act 1976 (financial provision) or an order under section 13 of the Matrimonial Homes (Family Protection) (Scotland) Act 1981 (transfer of tenancy of matrimonial home) ;

> " overseas country " means a country or territory outside the British Islands ; and

> " tenant " has the meaning assigned by the said section 22.

(2) Any reference in the foregoing provisions of this Part of this Act to a party to a marriage shall include a reference to a party to a marriage which has been terminated.

Extension of s. 31 of Maintenance Orders (Reciprocal Enforcement) Act 1972.   **31.**—(1) Section 31(4) of the Maintenance Orders (Reciprocal Enforcement) Act 1972 (recovery of maintenance in Scotland from former spouse on order made in convention country) shall have effect with the following amendments.

1972 c. 18.   (2) In paragraph (i), for the words " granted in a convention country " there shall be substituted the words " obtained in a country or territory outside the United Kingdom ".

(3) For paragraph (ii) there shall be substituted the following paragraphs—

> " (ii) an order for the payment of maintenance for the benefit of the applicant as a divorced person has, in or by reason of, or subsequent to, the divorce proceedings, been made by a court in a convention country ;

> (ii*a*) in a case where the order mentioned in paragraph (ii) above was made by a court of a different country from that in which the divorce was obtained, either the applicant or the said former spouse was resident in that different country at the time the application for the order so mentioned was made ; and ".

PART V

FAMILY BUSINESS: DISTRIBUTION AND TRANSFER

Preliminary

32. In this Part of this Act— What is family business.

"family business" means business of any description which in the High Court is for the time being assigned to the Family Division and to no other Division by or under section 61 of (and Schedule 1 to) the Supreme Court 1981 c. 54. Act 1981 ;

"family proceedings" means proceedings which are family business ;

"matrimonial cause" means an action for divorce, nullity of marriage, judicial separation or jactitation of marriage ;

and "the 1973 Act" means the Matrimonial Causes Act 1973.   1973 c. 18.

Jurisdiction of county courts in matrimonial causes and matters

33.—(1) The Lord Chancellor may by order designate any Jurisdiction county court as a divorce county court and any court so desig- of county nated shall have jurisdiction to hear and determine any matri- courts in monial cause, except that it shall have jurisdiction to try such matrimonial a cause only if it is also designated in the order as a court of causes. trial.

In this Part of this Act "divorce county court" means a county court so designated.

(2) The jurisdiction conferred by this section on a divorce county court shall be exercisable throughout England and Wales, but rules of court may provide for a matrimonial cause pending in one such court to be heard and determined in another or partly in that and partly in another.

(3) Every matrimonial cause shall be commenced in a divorce county court and shall be heard and determined in that or another such court unless or except to the extent it is transferred to the High Court under section 39 below or section 41 of the County Courts Act 1984 (transfer to High Court by order of High 1984 c. 28. Court).

(4) The Lord Chancellor may by order designate a divorce county court as a court for the exercise of jurisdiction in matrimonial matters arising under Part III of this Act.

(5) The power to make an order under subsection (1) or (4) above shall be exercisable by statutory instrument.

PART V
Jurisdiction
of divorce
county courts
as respects
financial relief
and protection
of children.

34.—(1) Subject to subsections (2) and (3) below, a divorce county court shall have the following jurisdiction, namely—

(a) jurisdiction to exercise any power exercisable under Part II or Part III of the 1973 Act in connection with any petition, decree or order pending in or made by such a court and to exercise any power under section 27 or 35 of that Act;

(b) if designated by an order under section 33(4) above, jurisdiction to exercise any power under Part III of this Act.

(2) Any proceedings for the exercise of a power which a divorce county court has jurisdiction to exercise by virtue of subsection (1)(a) or (b) above shall be commenced in such divorce county court as may be prescribed by rules of court.

(3) A divorce county court shall not by virtue of subsection (1)(a) above have jurisdiction to exercise any power under section 32, 33, 36 or 38 of the 1973 Act; but nothing in this section shall prejudice the exercise by a county court of any jurisdiction conferred on county courts by any of those sections.

(4) Nothing in this section shall affect the jurisdiction of a magistrates' court under section 35 of the 1973 Act.

35. Any provision to be made by rules of court for the purposes of section 7 of the 1973 Act with respect to any power exercisable by the court on an application made before the presentation of a petition shall confer jurisdiction to exercise the power on divorce county courts.

36. The jurisdiction conferred by the preceding provisions of this Part of this Act on divorce county courts, so far as it is exercisable by judges of such courts, shall be exercised by such Circuit judges as the Lord Chancellor may direct.

Distribution and transfer of family business and proceedings

Directions
as to
distribution
and transfer
of family
business and
proceedings.

37. The President of the Family Division may, with the concurrence of the Lord Chancellor, give directions with respect to the distribution and transfer between the High Court and county courts of family business and family proceedings.

Transfer of
family
proceedings
from High
Court to
county court.

38.—(1) At any stage in any family proceedings in the High Court the High Court may, if the proceedings are transferable under this section, either of its own motion or on the application of any party to the proceedings, order the transfer of the whole or any part of the proceedings to a county court.

(2) The following family proceedings are transferable to a county court under this section, namely—

    (*a*) all family proceedings commenced in the High Court which are within the jurisdiction of a county court or divorce county court;

    (*b*) wardship proceedings, except applications for an order that a minor be made, or cease to be, a ward of court; and

    (*c*) all family proceedings transferred from a county court to the High Court under section 39 below or section 41 of the County Courts Act 1984 (transfer to High Court 1984 c. 28. by order of High Court).

(3) Proceedings transferred under this section shall be transferred to such county court or, in the case of a matrimonial cause or matter within the jurisdiction of a divorce county court only, such divorce county court as the High Court directs.

(4) The transfer shall not affect any right of appeal from the order directing the transfer, or the right to enforce in the High Court any judgment signed, or order made, in that Court before the transfer.

(5) Where proceedings are transferred to a county court under this section, the county court—

    (*a*) if it has no jurisdiction apart from this paragraph, shall have jurisdiction to hear and determine those proceedings;

    (*b*) shall have jurisdiction to award any relief which could have been awarded by the High Court.

39.—(1) At any stage in any family proceedings in a county court, the county court may, if the proceedings are transferable under this section, either of its own motion or on the application of any party to the proceedings, order the transfer of the whole or any part of the proceedings to the High Court.

Transfer of family proceedings to High Court from county court.

(2) The following family proceedings are transferable to the High Court under this section, namely—

    (*a*) all family proceedings commenced in a county court or divorce county court; and

    (*b*) all family proceedings transferred from the High Court to a county court or divorce county court under section 38 above.

Rules of court and fees

40.—(1) Subject to subsection (2) below, the power to make rules of court for the purposes of family proceedings in the High Court or county courts shall be exercisable by the Lord Chan-

Family proceedings rules.

cellor together with any four or more of the following persons, namely—

 (*a*) the President of the Family Division,

 (*b*) one puisne judge attached to that Division,

 (*c*) one registrar of the principal registry of that Division,

 (*d*) two Circuit Judges,

1984 c. 28. (*e*) one registrar appointed under the County Courts Act 1984,

 (*f*) two practising barristers, and

 (*g*) two practising solicitors, of whom one shall be a member of the Council of the Law Society and the other a member of the Law Society and also of a local law society.

(2) Subsection (1) above is without prejudice to the powers of the following authorities to make rules in respect of the matters referred to below and rules in respect of those matters shall continue to be made by those authorities and shall not be made by the authority constituted by subsection (1) above.

The rules and rule-making authorities are—

1958 c. 5.
1968 c. 53.
1976 c. 36.
 (*a*) adoption rules made by the Lord Chancellor under section 9(3) of the Adoption Act 1958, section 12(1) of the Adoption Act 1968 or section 66(1) of the Adoption Act 1976;

1981 c. 54.
 (*b*) probate rules made by the President of the Family Division with the concurrence of the Lord Chancellor under section 127 of the Supreme Court Act 1981.

(3) The persons to act in pursuance of subsection (1) above with the Lord Chancellor, other than the President of the Family Division, shall be appointed by the Lord Chancellor for such time as he may think fit.

(4) Rules made under this section may, in relation to county court rules, do anything which, as special rules, they are authorised by section 84 of the Supreme Court Act 1981 to do in relation to Supreme Court Rules and may—

 (*a*) modify or exclude the application of any provision of the County Courts Act 1984; and

 (*b*) provide for the enforcement in the High Court of orders made in a divorce county court.

1946 c. 36.
(5) Rules of court under this section shall be made by statutory instrument subject to annulment in pursuance of a resolution of either House of Parliament; and the Statutory Instruments Act 1946 shall apply to a statutory instrument containing such rules as if the rules had been made by a Minister of the Crown.

41. The fees to be taken in any family proceedings in the High Court or any county court shall be such as the Lord Chancellor with the concurrence of the Treasury may prescribe from time to time by order made by statutory instrument.

County court proceedings in principal registry

42.—(1) Sections 33 to 35 above shall not prevent the commencement of any proceedings in the principal registry except where rules of court under section 34(2) above otherwise provide ; and the following provisions of this section shall have effect for the purposes of enabling proceedings to be dealt with in that registry as in a divorce county court.

(2) The jurisdiction in matrimonial causes or matters conferred by sections 33, 34 and 35 above on divorce county courts shall be exercised in the principal registry—

(a) so far as it is exercisable by judges of such courts, at such sittings and in such places as the Lord Chancellor may direct ; and

(b) so far as it is exercisable by registrars of such courts, by such registrars or by registrars and other officers of the principal registry according as rules of court may provide ;

and rules of court may make provision for treating, for any purposes specified in the rules, matrimonial causes and matters pending in the registry with respect to which that jurisdiction is exercisable as pending in a divorce county court and for the application of section 74(3) of the Solicitors Act 1974 (costs) with respect to proceedings so treated.

(3) Where, by virtue of rules under subsection (2) above, a matrimonial cause is pending in the registry as in a divorce county court, any ancillary or related proceedings which could be taken in a divorce county court and which are not of a description excluded by the rules from the operation of this subsection may be taken and dealt with in the registry as in a divorce county court.

(4) The principal registry shall be treated as a divorce county court—

(a) for the purposes of any provision to be made by rules of court under section 33(2) above ;

(b) for the purpose of any provision to be made under section 34(2) above prescribing the county court in which any proceedings are to be commenced ; and

(c) for the purpose of any transfer of family proceedings under section 38 or 39 above between the High Court and a divorce county court.

PART V

(5) Rules of court shall make provision for securing, with respect to family proceedings dealt with under this section, that, as nearly as may be, the same consequences shall follow—

(*a*) as regards service of process, as if proceedings commenced in the principal registry had been commenced in a divorce county court; and

(*b*) as regards enforcement of orders, as if orders made in that registry in the exercise of the family jurisdiction conferred by sections 33, 34 and 35 above on divorce county courts were orders made by such a court.

(6) In this section " the principal registry " means the principal registry of the Family Division of the High Court and, for the purposes of subsection (3) above, proceedings are " ancillary " to a matrimonial cause if they are connected with the cause and are " related " to a matrimonial cause if they are for protecting or otherwise relate to any rights, or the exercise of any rights, of the parties to the marriage as husband and wife or any children of the family.

Distribution of business : proceedings under s. 17 of Married Women's Property Act 1882

Distribution of business: proceedings under s. 17 of Married Women's Property Act 1882.
1882 c. 75.

43. In section 17 of the Married Women's Property Act 1882 (which provides for the summary determination of property disputes between spouses and, as extended, former spouses and former engaged couples) for the words after " in a summary way " there shall be substituted the words " to the High Court or such county court as may be prescribed and the court may, on such an application (which may be heard in private), make such order with respect to the property as it thinks fit.

In this section " prescribed " means prescribed by rules of court and rules made for the purposes of this section may confer jurisdiction on county courts whatever the situation or value of the property in dispute.".

Magistrates' courts' domestic jurisdiction

Domestic proceedings in magistrates' courts to include applications to alter maintenance agreements.
1980 c. 43.

44. In section 65(1) of the Magistrates' Courts Act 1980 (which defines what proceedings are domestic proceedings) after paragraph (*e*) there shall be inserted the following paragraph—

" (*ee*) section 35 of the Matrimonial Causes Act 1973 ; "

Part VI

Miscellaneous and General

45.—(1) Section 29A of the Maintenance Orders (Reciprocal Enforcement) Act 1972 (complaint by former spouse in convention country for recovery in Northern Ireland of maintenance from other spouse) shall have effect with the following amendments.

Part VI

Extension of s. 29A of Maintenance Orders (Reciprocal Enforcement) Act 1972.
1972 c. 18.

(2) For subsection (1) there shall be substituted the following subsection—

" (1) Where on an application under section 27(1) of this Act for the recovery of maintenance from a person who is residing in Northern Ireland—

> (a) that person is a former spouse of the applicant in a convention country who is seeking to recover maintenance, and
>
> (b) the marriage between the applicant and the former spouse has been dissolved or annulled in a country or territory outside the United Kingdom by a divorce or annulment which is recognised as valid by the law of Northern Ireland, and
>
> (c) an order for the payment of maintenance for the benefit of the applicant or a child of the family has, by reason of the divorce or annulment, been made by a court in a convention country, and
>
> (d) in a case where the order for the payment of maintenance was made by a court of a different country from that in which the divorce or annulment was obtained, either the applicant or his or her former spouse was resident in the convention country whose court made the maintenance order at the time the application for that order was made,

the application shall, notwithstanding that the marriage has been dissolved or annulled, be treated as a complaint for an order under Article 4 of the Domestic Proceedings (Northern Ireland) Order 1980, and the provisions of this section shall have effect."

(3) For subsection (4) there shall be substituted the following subsection—

" (4) A divorce or annulment obtained in a country or territory outside the United Kingdom shall be presumed for the purposes of this section to be one the validity of which is recognised by the law of Northern Ireland unless the contrary is proved by the defendant."

(4) Subsection (5) shall be omitted.

PART VI
Amendments,
transitional
provisions and
repeals.

46.—(1) The enactments specified in Schedule 1 to this Act shall have effect subject to the amendments specified in that Schedule, being amendments consequential on the provisions of this Act or minor amendments relating to the enforcement of maintenance orders, the area of jurisdiction of magistrates' courts for purposes of altering maintenance agreements and the variation by magistrates' courts of certain existing maintenance, affiliation and other orders.

(2) The transitional provisions contained in Schedule 2 to this Act shall have effect.

(3) The enactments specified in Schedule 3 to this Act (which include some which are spent) are hereby repealed to the extent specified in the third column of that Schedule.

Commence-
ment.

47.—(1) The provisions of this Act other than this section and section 48 below shall come into force as follows—

(*a*) with the exception of section 10, Parts I and II and paragraphs 1 and 2 of Schedule 2 shall come into force at the expiry of the period of three months beginning with the day on which this Act is passed and that section shall come into force on such day as the Lord Chancellor appoints ;

(*b*) Part III shall come into force on such day as the Lord Chancellor appoints ;

(*c*) Schedule 1, except paragraphs 1(*b*), 6, 7 and 28 shall come into force on such day or days as the Lord Chancellor appoints ;

(*d*) Part IV and paragraphs 1(*b*), 6, 7 and 28 of Schedule 1 shall come into force on such day as the Lord Advocate appoints ; and

(*e*) Part V, section 45 above and paragraph 3 of Schedule 2 and the repeals specified in Schedule 3 shall come into force on such day or days as the Lord Chancellor appoints.

(2) The power to appoint days for the coming into force of provisions of this Act shall be exercised by order made by statutory instrument.

Short title
and extent.

48.—(1) This Act may be cited as the Matrimonial and Family Proceedings Act 1984.

(2) Parts I to III and V and Schedules 2 and 3 extend to England and Wales only, Part IV extends to Scotland only and section 45 above extends to Northern Ireland only.

(3) Where any enactment amended by Schedule 1 extends to any part of the United Kingdom, the amendment extends to that part.

SCHEDULES

SCHEDULE 1

Section 46(1).

MINOR AND CONSEQUENTIAL AMENDMENTS

Maintenance Orders Act 1950 (c. 37)

1. In section 16(2) of the Maintenance Orders Act 1950—

   (*a*) at the end of paragraph (*a*) (i) there shall be added the words " and section 14 or 17 of the Matrimonial and Family Proceedings Act 1984 " ; and

   (*b*) at the end of paragraph (*b*) (i) there shall be added the words " or section 29 of the Matrimonial and Family Proceedings Act 1984 ".

2. In section 18 of that Act, after subsection (2), there shall be inserted the following subsection—

   " (2A) Any person under an obligation to make payments under a maintenance order registered under this Part of this Act in a court of summary jurisdiction in England shall give notice of any change of address to the clerk of the court ; and any person who without reasonable excuse fails to give such a notice shall be liable on summary conviction to a fine not exceeding level 2 on the standard scale (as defined in section 75 of the Criminal Justice Act 1982)."

Matrimonial Causes (*Property and Maintenance*) *Act 1958*
(*c.35*)

3. In section 7 of the Matrimonial Causes (Property and Maintenance) Act 1958, for subsection (6), there shall be substituted the following subsection—

   " (6) Any power of a judge which is exercisable on an application under the said section seventeen shall be exercisable in relation to an application made under that section as extended by this section."

Maintenance Orders Act 1958 (c. 39)

4. In section 3 of the Maintenance Orders Act 1958, after subsection (3), there shall be inserted the following subsection—

   " (3A) Any person under an obligation to make payments under an order registered in a magistrates' court shall give notice of any change of address to the clerk of the court ; and any person who without reasonable excuse fails to give such a notice shall be liable on summary conviction to a fine not exceeding level 2 on the standard scale (as defined in section 75 of the Criminal Justice Act 1982)."

5. In section 4 of that Act, after subsection (6A) there shall be inserted the following subsection—

   " (6B) No application for any variation of a registered order shall be made to any court in respect of an order for periodical or other payments made under Part III of the Matrimonial and Family Proceedings Act 1984."

Succession (Scotland) Act 1964 (c. 41)

6. In section 33(2) of the Succession (Scotland) Act 1964, at the end there shall be added the words " or section 29 of the Matrimonial and Family Proceedings Act 1984 ".

Law Reform (Miscellaneous Provisions) (Scotland) Act 1966 (c. 19)

7. In section 8(1)(*c*) of the Law Reform (Miscellaneous Provisions) (Scotland) Act 1966, at the end there shall be added the words " or section 29 of the Matrimonial and Family Proceedings 1984 ".

Administration of Justice Act 1970 (c. 31)

8. In Schedule 8 to the Administration of Justice Act 1970 there shall be inserted at the end the following paragraph—

" 14. An order for periodical or other payments made under Part III of the Matrimonial and Family Proceedings Act 1984."

Maintenance Orders (Reciprocal Enforcement) Act 1972 (c. 18)

9. In section 28A(3)(*c*) of the Maintenance Orders (Reciprocal Enforcement) Act 1972, for the words " section 3(1) " there shall be substituted the words " section 3(2) and (3) ".

Matrimonial Causes Act 1973 (c. 18)

10. In section 1(4) of the Matrimonial Causes Act 1973 for the words " sections 3(3) and 5 " there shall be substituted the words " section 5 ".

11. In section 24A of that Act there shall be added at the end the following subsection—

" (6) Where a party to a marriage has a beneficial interest in any property, or in the proceeds of sale thereof, and some other person who is not a party to the marriage also has a beneficial interest in that property or in the proceeds of sale thereof, then, before deciding whether to make an order under this section in relation to that property, it shall be the duty of the court to give that other person an opportunity to make representations with respect to the order ; and any representations made by that other person shall be included among the circumstances to which the court is required to have regard under section 25(1) below.".

12. In section 27 of that Act—
   (*a*) in subsection (3A) for the words " section 25(1)(*a*) and (*b*) and (2)(*a*) to (*e*) " there shall be substituted the words " section 25(3)(*a*) to (*e*) " and for the words " section 25(3) " there shall be substituted the words " section 25(4) " ;

(*b*) in subsection (3B) for the words "section 25(1)(*c*)" there shall be substituted the words " section 25(2)(*c*) above " and for the words " section 25(2)(*d*) " there shall be substituted the words " section 25(2)(*c*) above (as it applies by virtue of section 25(3)(*e*) above) ".

13. In section 35 of that Act—

    (*a*) in subsection (2) for the words " section 25(3) " there shall be substituted the words " section 25(4) " ;

    (*b*) in subsection (3) for the words from " in the petty sessions area " to " for which the court acts " there shall be substituted the words " within the commission area (within the meaning of the Justices of the Peace Act 1979) for which the court is appointed ; ".

14. In section 45(2) of that Act for the words " county court rules " there shall be substituted the words " rules of court ".

15. In section 47(2) of that Act after paragraph (*d*) there shall be inserted the following paragraph—

    " (*dd*) an order under Part III of the Matrimonial and Family Proceedings Act 1984 ; ".

16. In section 52(1) of that Act, in the definition of " the court " for the words " the Matrimonial Causes Act 1967 " there shall be substituted the words " Part V of the Matrimonial and Family Proceedings Act 1984 ".

Domicile and Matrimonial Proceedings Act 1973 (c. 45)

17. In section 5(1) of the Domicile and Matrimonial Proceedings Act 1973, for the words " the Matrimonial Causes Act 1967 " there shall be substituted the words " Part V of the Matrimonial and Family Proceedings Act 1984 ".

Legal Aid Act 1974 (c. 4)

18. For section 10(2) of the Legal Aid Act 1974 there shall be substituted the following subsections—

    " (2) Subject to any rules of court under subsection (2A) below, the sums payable under subsection (1) above shall not exceed those allowed under Schedule 2 to this Act.

    (2A) Rules of court may provide that the sums payable under subsection (1) above to a solicitor or counsel acting in an undefended matrimonial cause (as defined in the rules) shall, at his election, be either—

        (*a*) such fixed amount specified in the rules as may be applicable under the rules ; or

        (*b*) an amount ascertained on taxation or assessment of costs as provided by Schedule 2 ;

and may provide for modifying that Schedule in relation to any proceedings which by virtue of any provision of Part V of the Matrimonial and Family Proceedings Act 1984 are at any stage treated as pending in a divorce county court (within the meaning of that Part)."

Children Act 1975 (c. 72)

19. In section 100 of the Children Act 1975—

    (*a*) in subsection (2)(*c*) for the words " section 75 of the County Courts Act 1984 " there shall be substituted the words " section 9(3) of the 1958 Act or section 40 of the Matrimonial and Family Proceedings Act 1984 " ; and

    (*b*) after subsection (9) there shall be inserted the following subsection—

        " (10) Any court to which the proceedings on an application are transferred under any enactment is, as regards the transferred proceedings, an authorised court if it is not an authorised court under the preceding provisions of this section."

Adoption Act 1976 (c. 36)

20. In section 62 of the Adoption Act 1976—

    (*a*) in subsection (2)(*c*) for the words " section 75 of the County Courts Act 1984 " there shall be substituted the words " section 66(1) of this Act ; " and

    (*b*) after subsection (6) there shall be inserted the following subsection—

        " (7) Any court to which the proceedings on an application are transferred under any enactment is, as regards the transferred proceedings, an authorised court if it is not an authorised court under the preceding provisions of this section."

Domestic Proceedings and Magistrates' Courts Act 1978 (c. 22)

21. In section 1 of the Domestic Proceedings and Magistrates' Courts Act 1978 the words " (in this Part of this Act referred to as " the respondent ") " shall be omitted.

22. In section 7(5) of that Act, for the words " subsection (1) " there shall be substituted the words " subsection (2)(*c*) ".

23. In section 11 of that Act—

    (*a*) in subsection (2), after the words " of this Act " there shall be inserted the words " on an application for an order under section 2 or 7 of this Act," ;

    (*b*) after subsection (2) there shall be inserted the following subsection—

        " (2A) Where by an order made under section 8(2) of this Act on an application for an order under section 6 of this Act, the right to the actual custody of a child is given to the party to the marriage who has agreed to make the financial provision specified in the application, the court may make one or both of the following orders, that is to say—

> (a) an order that the other party to the marriage shall make to that party for the benefit of the child or to the child such periodical payments, and for such term, as may be specified in the order ;
>
> (b) an order that the other party to the marriage shall pay to that party for the benefit of the child or to the child such lump sum as may be so specified." ;

(c) in subsection (5), after the words " subsection (2) " there shall be inserted " (2A) " and for the words " section 3(2) " there shall be substituted the words " section 3(3) " ;

(d) in subsection (6) after the words " subsection (2)(a) " there shall be inserted " (2A)(a) " ; and

(e) in subsection (7) after the words " subsection (2)(b) ", in both places where they occur, there shall be inserted " (2A)(b) ".

24. In section 19 of that Act, after subsection (3), there shall be inserted the following subsection—

" (3A) Where an application is made for an order under section 6 of this Act by the party to the marriage who has agreed to make the financial provision specified in the application—

> (a) subsection (1) shall apply as if the reference in paragraph (i) to the respondent were a reference to the applicant and the references to the applicant were references to the respondent ; and
>
> (b) subsections (2) and (3) shall apply accordingly."

25. In section 20(8) of that Act, after the word " respondent " there shall be inserted the words " or the applicant, as the case may be,".

26. In section 29 of that Act, at the end of subsection (2), there shall be added the words " or, in a case where there was made to the magistrates' court an application for an order under section 2 and an application under section 6 and the term of the periodical payments was or might have been ordered to begin on the date of the making of the application for an order under section 2, the date of the making of that application ".

27. In Schedule 1 to that Act—

> (a) in paragraph 2, after sub-paragraph (b), there shall be inserted the following sub-paragraph—
>
> " (bb) on a complaint after the coming into force of paragraph 27 of Schedule 1 to the Matrimonial and Family Proceedings Act 1984 for the variation, revival or revocation of the order, the court, in exercising its powers under the said section 8 in relation to any provision of

the order requiring the payment of money, shall have power to order that payments required to be made for the maintenance of a child of the family shall be made to the child himself." ; and

(*b*) in paragraph 3, at the end, there shall be added the words " but as respects enactments amended by this Act in their application in relation to orders made or decisions on applications for orders or for the variation, revival or revocation of orders made or having effect as if made under other Acts those enactments shall apply as amended by this Act ".

Land Registration (Scotland) Act 1979 (c. 33)

28. In section 12(3)(*b*) of the Land Registration (Scotland) Act 1979 after the word " 1976 " there shall be inserted the words " or by an order made by virtue of section 29 of the Matrimonial and Family Proceedings Act 1984 ".

County Courts Act 1984 (c. 28)

29. In section 40 of the County Courts Act 1984, the following shall be substituted for subsection (3)—

" (3) This section does not apply to proceedings which are family proceedings within the meaning of Part V of the Matrimonial and Family Proceedings Act 1984."

30. In section 41 of that Act there shall be added at the end of subsection (2) the words " but shall be exercised in relation to family proceedings (within the meaning of Part V of the Matrimonial and Family Proceedings Act 1984) in accordance with any directions given under section 37 of that Act (directions as to distribution and transfer of family business and proceedings)."

31. In section 42(3) of that Act for the words after " other than " there shall be substituted the words " proceedings which are family proceedings within the meaning of Part V of the Matrimonial and Family Proceedings Act 1984.".

Section 46(2).

SCHEDULE 2

Transitional Provisions

Time restrictions on petitions for divorce

1.—(1) Where at the coming into force of section 1 of this Act—

1973 c. 18.

(*a*) leave has been granted under section 3 of the Matrimonial Causes Act 1973 for the presentation of a petition for divorce or proceedings on an application for leave under that section are pending, and

(*b*) the period of one year from the date of the marriage has not expired.

nothing in section 1 of this Act shall prohibit the presentation of a petition for divorce before the expiration of that period ; and in relation to such a case sections 1(4) and 3 of that Act of 1973 as in force immediately before the coming into force of section 1 of this Act shall continue to apply.

(2) Where at the coming into force of section 1 of this Act—

(*a*) proceedings on an application for leave under section 3 of the Matrimonial Causes Act 1973 are pending, and

(*b*) the period of one year from the date of the marriage has expired,

the proceedings shall abate but without prejudice to the powers of the court as to costs.

Time restrictions on petitions for nullity

2. An application for leave under section 13(4) of the Matrimonial Causes Act 1973 to institute proceedings after the expiration of the period of three years from the date of the marriage may be made where that period expired before as well as where it expires after the coming into force of section 2 of this Act.

Scope of " matrimonial cause " for Part V purposes

3. For the purposes of Part V of this Act " matrimonial cause " shall, until the expiration of one year from the coming into force of section 1 of this Act, include an application under section 3 of the Matrimonial Causes Act 1973.

SCHEDULE 3

REPEALS

Chapter	Short title	Extent of repeal
1967 c. 56.	Matrimonial Causes Act 1967.	The whole Act.
1971 c. 3.	Guardianship of Minors Act 1971.	Section 16(1).
1971 c. 23.	Courts Acts 1971.	Section 45.
1973 c. 18.	Matrimonial Causes Act 1973.	Section 43(9). Section 44(6). Section 45(3). Sections 50 and 51. In Schedule 2, paragraphs 6 and 12.
1973 c. 45.	Domicile and Matrimonial Proceedings Act 1973.	Section 6(4)(*a*).
1975 c. 72.	Children Act 1975.	Section 101(1).
1976 c. 36.	Adoption Act 1976.	Section 63(1).
1978 c. 22.	Domestic Proceedings and Magistrates' Courts Act 1978.	In Schedule 2, paragraph 49.
1981 c. 24.	Matrimonial Homes and Property Act 1981.	Section 8(1).
1983 c. 19.	Matrimonial Homes Act 1983.	In Schedule 1, paragraph 8(3) and (4), and in paragraph 10(1), the definitions of " divorce county court " and " divorce registry ".
1984 c. 28.	County Courts Act 1984.	In section 147(1), the definition of " matrimonial cause ".

Finance Act 1984

1984 CHAPTER 43

An Act to grant certain duties, to alter other duties, and to amend the law relating to the National Debt and the Public Revenue, and to make further provision in connection with Finance.   [26th July 1984]

Most Gracious Sovereign,

WE, Your Majesty's most dutiful and loyal subjects, the Commons of the United Kingdom in Parliament assembled, towards raising the necessary supplies to defray Your Majesty's public expenses, and making an addition to the public revenue, have freely and voluntarily resolved to give and grant unto Your Majesty the several duties hereinafter mentioned; and do therefore most humbly beseech Your Majesty that it may be enacted, and be it enacted by the Queen's most Excellent Majesty, by and with the advice and consent of the Lords Spiritual and Temporal, and Commons, in this present Parliament assembled, and by the authority of the same, as follows:—

PART I

CUSTOMS AND EXCISE, VALUE ADDED TAX AND CAR TAX

CHAPTER I

CUSTOMS AND EXCISE

1.—(1) In section 5 of the Alcoholic Liquor Duties Act 1979 (excise duty on spirits) for " £15·19 " there shall be substituted " £15·48 ".

Duties on spirits, beer, wine, made-wine and cider.
1979 c. 4.

(2) In section 36 of that Act (excise duty on beer) for " £21·60 " and " £0·72 " there shall be substituted " £24·00 " and " £0·80 " respectively.

(3) For the provisions of Schedule 1 to that Act (rates of excise duty on wine) there shall be substituted the provisions of Schedule 1 to this Act.

(4) The rates of duty on made-wine shall be the same as those on wine and, accordingly, in section 55(1) of that Act for the words " Schedule 2 " there shall be substituted the words " Schedule 1 ".

(5) In section 62(1) of that Act (excise duty on cider) for " £9·69 " there shall be substituted " £14·28 " and in the definition of " cider " in section 1(6) of that Act for the words " less than 8·7 per cent." there shall be substituted the words " less than 8·5 per cent.".

(6) This section, and Schedule 1 to this Act, other than the paragraphs headed " Interpretation ", shall be deemed to have come into force on 14th March 1984.

Tobacco products. 1979 c. 7.

2.—(1) For the Table in Schedule 1 to the Tobacco Products Duty Act 1979 there shall be substituted—

" TABLE

1. Cigarettes	An amount equal to 21 per cent. of the retail price plus £24·97 per thousand cigarettes.
2. Cigars	£47·05 per kilogram.
3. Hand-rolling tobacco ...	£40·60 per kilogram.
4. Other smoking tobacco and chewing tobacco ...	£24·95 per kilogram."

(2) This section shall be deemed to have come into force on 16th March 1984.

Hydrocarbon oil. 1979 c. 5.

3.—(1) In section 6(1) of the Hydrocarbon Oil Duties Act 1979 (rates of duty on hydrocarbon oil) for " £0.1630 " (light oil) and " £0·1382 " (heavy oil) there shall be substituted " £0·1716 " and " £0·1448 " respectively.

(2) In section 11(1)(a) of that Act (rebate on kerosene, other than aviation turbine fuel) for the words " of £0·0022 a litre less than " there shall be substituted the words " equal to ".

(3) This section shall be deemed to have come into force at 6 o'clock in the evening of 13th March 1984.

4.—(1) The Vehicles (Excise) Act 1971 and the Vehicles (Excise) Act (Northern Ireland) 1972 shall be amended as follows.

(2) For the provisions of Part II of Schedules 1 to 5 to each of those Acts (annual rates of duty) there shall be substituted the provisions set out in Part I of Schedule 2 to this Act.

PART I
Vehicles
excise duty.
1971 c. 10.
1972 c. 10
(N.I.).

(3) The provisions of Part I of Schedule 4 to each of those Acts (annual rates of duty on goods vehicles: general provisions) shall have effect subject to the amendments made by Part II of Schedule 2 to this Act.

(4) In section 16 of the Act of 1971 (rates of duty for trade licences)—

   (*a*) in subsection (5), including that subsection as set out in paragraph 12 of Part I of Schedule 7 to that Act, for " £42 " and " £8·50 " there shall be substituted, respectively, " £44 " and " £9 " ; and

   (*b*) in subsection (8) the following definition shall be inserted at the appropriate place—

      " ' disabled vehicle ' includes a vehicle which has been abandoned or is scrap ; ".

(5) In section 16 of the Act of 1972 (rates of duty for trade licences)—

   (*a*) in subsection (6), including that subsection as set out in paragraph 12 of Part I of Schedule 9 to that Act, for " £42 " and " £8·50 " there shall be substituted, respectively, " £44 " and " £9 " ; and

   (*b*) in subsection (10) the following definition shall be inserted at the appropriate place—

      " ' disabled vehicle ' includes a vehicle which has been abandoned or is scrap ; ".

(6) The provisions of this section other than subsections (4)(*b*) and (5)(*b*) apply in relation to licences taken out after 13th March 1984.

5.—(1) Section 7 of the Vehicles (Excise) Act 1971 and section 7 of the Vehicles (Excise) Act (Northern Ireland) 1972 (exemption from vehicles excise duty) shall have effect with the following amendments.

Vehicles
excise duty:
recipients of
mobility
supplement.

(2) In subsection (2) of that section of each Act (by virtue of which vehicles used by or for the purposes of persons in receipt of a mobility allowance are exempt from duty and vehicles are deemed to be registered in the names of such persons in certain circumstances)—

   (*a*) after the words " mobility allowance ", in both places, there shall be inserted the words " or a mobility supplement " ; and

(*b*) for the words from " a person appointed " to " powers " and the words " a person so appointed " there shall in each case be substituted the words " an appointee ".

(3) After subsection (2) of section 7 of the 1971 Act there shall be inserted —

" (2A) In subsection (2) above—

' mobility supplement ' means a mobility supplement under—

1939 c. 82.

(*a*) a scheme made under the Personal Injuries (Emergency Provisions) Act 1939, or

(*b*) an Order in Council made under section 12 of the Social Security (Miscellaneous Provisions) Act 1977,

1977 c. 5.

or any payment appearing to the Secretary of State to be of a similar kind and specified by him by order made by statutory instrument ; and

' appointee ' means—

(i) a person appointed pursuant to regulations under the Social Security Act 1975 to exercise any of the rights or powers of a person in receipt of a mobility allowance, or

1975 c. 14.

(ii) a person to whom a mobility supplement is paid for application for the benefit of another person in receipt of the supplement.

(2B) An order under subsection (2A) above may provide that it shall be deemed to have come into force on any date after 20th November 1983.".

(4) After subsection (2A) of section 7 of the 1972 Act there shall be inserted—

" (2AA) In subsection (2)—

' mobility supplement ' means a mobility supplement under—

(*a*) a scheme made under the Personal Injuries (Emergency Provisions) Act 1939, or

(*b*) an Order in Council made under section 12 of the Social Security (Miscellaneous Provisions) Act 1977,

or any payment appearing to the Secretary of State to be of a similar kind and specified by him by order made by statutory instrument ; and

' appointee ' means—

(i) a person appointed pursuant to regulations under the Social Security (Northern Ire-

1975 c. 15
(N.I.).

land) Act 1975 to exercise any of the rights or powers of a person in receipt of a mobility allowance, or

(ii) a person to whom a mobility supplement is paid for application for the benefit of another person in receipt of the supplement.

(2AB) An order under subsection (2AA) above may provide that it shall be deemed to have come into force on any date after 20th November 1983.".

(5) This section shall be deemed to have come into force on 21st November 1983.

6.—(1) In section 14 of the Betting and Gaming Duties Act 1981 (rate of gaming licence duty), for the Table set out in subsection (1) there shall be substituted the following Table—

Gaming licence duty. 1981 c. 63.

" TABLE

Part of gross gaming yield	Rate
The first £375,000	2½ per cent.
The next £1,875,000 ...	12½ per cent.
The next £2,250,000 ...	25 per cent.
The remainder	33⅓ per cent."

(2) This section shall have effect in relation to gaming licences for any period beginning after 31st March 1984.

7.—(1) For the purpose of providing for gaming machine licences to be granted, in certain circumstances, in respect of gaming machines instead of in respect of premises and of providing for whole-year gaming machine licences granted in respect of premises to run from different dates in different parts of Great Britain, the Betting and Gaming Duties Act 1981 shall have effect subject to the amendments set out in Schedule 3 to this Act.

Gaming machine licence duty.

(2) The amendments made by Part I of Schedule 3 shall not have effect in relation to any licence granted for a period beginning before 1st October 1984 ; and the Act of 1981 shall have effect subject to Part II of Schedule 3 (which makes transitional provision in relation to certain licences first having effect after 30th September 1984 but before 1st February 1986).

8. The provisions set out in Part I of Schedule 4 to this Act (which provide for special areas, to be known as free zones, to be designated for customs and excise purposes) shall be inserted in the Customs and Excise Management Act 1979 after Part VIII as a new Part VIIIA, and that Act shall have effect with the amendments specified in Part II of that Schedule (which also relate to free zones).

Free zones. 1979 c. 2.

PART I
Entry of
goods on
importation.
1979 c. 2.

9.—(1) The Customs and Excise Management Act 1979 shall have effect with the amendments specified in Schedule 5 to this Act, being amendments relating to the entry of goods on importation.

(2) Paragraph 1 of that Schedule shall come into force on 1st January 1985.

CHAPTER II

VALUE ADDED TAX

Zero-rating.
1983 c. 55.

10.—(1) Schedule 5 to the Value Added Tax Act 1983 (zero-rating) shall have effect subject to the modifications in Schedule 6 to this Act.

(2) In Schedule 6 to this Act—

(a) Part I has effect with respect to supplies made on or after 1st May 1984 ; and

(b) Parts II and III have effect with respect to supplies made on or after 1st June 1984.

Refund of
tax to
Government
departments
etc. in certain
cases.

11. After subsection (2) of section 27 of the Value Added Tax Act 1983 (application of value added tax legislation to the Crown) there shall be inserted the following subsections—

" (2A) Where tax is chargeable on the supply of goods or services to, or on the importation of goods by, a Government department and the supply or importation is not for the purpose—

(a) of any business carried on by the department, or

(b) of a supply by the department which, by virtue of a direction under subsection (2) above, is treated as a supply in the course or furtherance of a business,

then, if and to the extent that the Treasury so direct and subject to subsection (2B) below, the Commissioners shall, on a claim made by the department at such time and in such form and manner as the Commissioners may determine, refund to it the amount of the tax so chargeable.

(2B) The Commissioners may make the refunding of any amount due under subsection (2A) above conditional upon compliance by the claimant with requirements with respect to the keeping, preservation and production of records relating to the supply or importation in question."

12.—(1) In paragraph 5 of Schedule 1 to the Value Added Tax Act 1983 (discretionary registration subject to conditions imposed by the Commissioners) after sub-paragraph (1) there shall be inserted the following sub-paragraph—

PART I
Conditions imposed on discretionary registration.
1983 c. 55.

" (1A) Conditions under sub-paragraph (1) above—

> (*a*) may be imposed wholly or partly by reference to, or without reference to, any conditions prescribed for the purposes of this paragraph ; and
>
> (*b*) may (whenever imposed) be subsequently varied by the Commissioners."

(2) In paragraph 11 of Schedule 1 (discretionary registration subject to conditions imposed by the Commissioners) after sub-paragraph (2) there shall be inserted the following sub-paragraph—

" (2A) Conditions under sub-paragraph (1)(*b*) above—

> (*a*) may be imposed wholly or partly by reference to, or without reference to, any conditions prescribed for the purposes of this paragraph ; and
>
> (*b*) may (whenever imposed) be subsequently varied by the Commissioners."

13. In section 16 of the Value Added Tax Act 1983 (zero-rating) in subsection (5) (certain supplies outside the United Kingdom and other transactions to be treated as supplies of goods or services in the United Kingdom) the words " of a supply of goods or services outside the United Kingdom or " and " supply or " shall be omitted.

Certain zero-rated supplies and transactions.

CHAPTER III

MISCELLANEOUS

14.—(1) For section 7 of the Customs and Excise Duties (General Reliefs) Act 1979 (relief from customs or excise duty on imported legacies) there shall be substituted—

Reliefs from duty and value added tax in respect of imported legacies.

" Power to provide for reliefs from duty and value added tax in respect of imported legacies.

7.—(1) The Commissioners may by order make provision for conferring reliefs from duty and value added tax in respect of goods imported into the United Kingdom by or for any person who has become entitled to them as legatee.

1979 c. 3.

(2) Any such relief may take the form either of an exemption from payment of duty and tax or of a provision whereby the sum payable by way of duty or tax is less than it would otherwise be.

(3) The Commissioners may by order make provision supplementing any Community relief, in such manner as they think necessary or expedient.

(4) An order under this section—

(a) may make any relief for which it provides or any Community relief subject to conditions, including conditions which are to be complied with after the importation of the goods to which the relief applies ;

(b) may, in relation to any relief conferred by order made under this section, contain such incidental and supplementary provisions as the Commissioners think necessary or expedient ; and

(c) may make different provision for different cases.

(5) In this section—

" Community relief " means any relief which is conferred by a Community instrument and is of a kind, or of a kind similar to that, which could otherwise be conferred by order made under this section ;

" duty " means customs or excise duty chargeable on goods imported into the United Kingdom and, in the case of excise duty, includes any addition to the duty by virtue of section 1 of the Excise Duties (Surcharges or Rebates) Act 1979 ;

1979 c. 8.

" legatee " means any person taking under a testamentary disposition or donatio mortis causa or on an intestacy ; and

" value added tax " means value added tax chargeable on the importation of goods.".

1979 c. 3.

(2) In section 17 of the Customs and Excise Duties (General Reliefs) Act 1979 (parliamentary control of orders and regulations), in subsection (3), after the figure " 4 " there shall be inserted " 7 ".

(3) This section shall be deemed to have come into force on 1st July 1984.

Extension to certain Community reliefs of power to make supplementary provision.

15.—(1) Section 13 of the Customs and Excise Duties (General Reliefs) Act 1979 (orders providing for personal reliefs from duties etc.) shall be amended as provided by subsections (2) to (5) below.

(2) After subsection (1) there shall be inserted the following subsection—

" (1A) The Commissioners may by order make provision supplementing any Communuity relief, in such manner as they think necessary or expedient.".

(3) In subsection (3)(*a*), after the word " provides " there shall be inserted the words ", or any Community relief,".

(4) In subsection (3)(*b*), after the word " may " there shall be inserted the words ", in relation to any relief conferred by order made under this section,".

(5) In subsection (4) there shall be inserted at the appropriate place—

> " ' Community relief ' means any relief which is conferred by a Community instrument and is of a kind, or of a kind similar to that, which could otherwise be conferred by order made under this section ; ".

(6) In section 17 of the Customs and Excise Duties (General 1979 c. 3. Reliefs) Act 1979 (parliamentary control of orders and regulations), in subsection (4), after the figure " 13 " there shall be inserted " (1) ".

(7) In the Isle of Man Act 1979— 1979 c. 58.

> (*a*) in section 8 (removal of goods from Isle of Man to United Kingdom), in subsection (3), the words " or under any Community instrument " shall be inserted after the words " imported goods) " and the words " or under the Community instrument in question " shall be added at the end ; and

> (*b*) in section 9 (removal of goods from United Kingdom to Isle of Man), in subsection (5), the words " or under any Community instrument " shall be added at the end.

(8) This section shall be deemed to have come into force on 31st March 1984.

16.—(1) In paragraph 3(2)(*a*) and (*b*) of Schedule 1 to the Unpaid car Car Tax Act 1983 and in paragraph 6(4)(*a*) and (*b*) of Schedule tax and 7 to the Value Added Tax Act 1983 (power by regulation to value added make provision for distress and poinding in connection with un- and poinding. paid tax) there shall be inserted, after the word " regulations " 1983 c. 53. the words " and for the imposition and recovery of costs, charges, 1983 c. 55. expenses and fees in connection with anything done under the regulations ".

(2) Regulations 58 and 59 of the Value Added Tax (General) S.I. 1980/1536. Regulations 1980 shall, so far as they relate to costs, charges, expenses and fees in connection with any distraining or poinding occurring after the commencement of this section, have effect as if paragraph 6(4) of Schedule 7 to the Act of 1983 and this section had been in force when those regulations were made.

Part II

Income Tax, Corporation Tax and Capital Gains Tax etc.

Chapter I

General

Charge of
income tax
for 1984–85.

17.—(1) Income tax for the year 1984-85 shall be charged at the basic rate of 30 per cent.; and in respect of so much of an individual's total income as exceeds the basic rate limit (£15,400) at such higher rates as are specified in the Table below:

TABLE

Higher rate bands	*Higher rate*
The first (£2,800)	40 per cent.
The second (£4,900)	45 per cent.
The third (£7,500)	50 per cent.
The fourth (£7,500)	55 per cent.
The fifth	60 per cent.

1971 c. 68.

and paragraphs (a) and (b) of subsection (1) of section 32 of the Finance Act 1971 (charge of tax at the basic and higher rates) shall have effect accordingly.

(2) The provisions of Schedule 7 to this Act shall have effect with respect to the additional rate for the year 1984-85 and subsequent years of assessment.

1973 c. 51.
1974 c. 30.

(3) In accordance with the provisions of Schedule 7 to this Act, for the year 1984-85 any sum which, by virtue of any provision of Part III of the Finance Act 1973 or Chapter I of Part III of the Finance Act 1974, is chargeable at the additional rate, as defined for the purposes of that provision, shall be charged to income tax at the additional rate of 15 per cent.

Corporation
tax for
financial
years 1983
to 1986:
charge,
rates and
consequential
provisions.
1972 c. 41.

18.—(1) Corporation tax shall be charged for each of the financial years specified in the first column of the table in subsection (3) below at the rate specified in the second column of that table.

(2) The fraction by which, under section 93(2) of the Finance Act 1972, chargeable gains are to be reduced before they are for the purposes of corporation tax included in the profits of a company shall, for each of the financial years specified in the first column of the table in subsection (3) below, be the fraction specified in the third column of that table (instead of the fraction specified in section 10(1)(a) of the Finance Act 1974).

(3) The table referred to in subsections (1) and (2) above is as follows:—

TABLE

Financial year		Rate of tax	Reducing fraction
1983	... ...	50 per cent.	Two-fifths
1984	... ...	45 per cent.	One-third
1985	... ...	40 per cent.	One-quarter
1986	... ...	35 per cent.	One-seventh

(4) In section 310 of the Taxes Act, subsections (1), (2) and (4) (relief for insurance companies where rate of corporation tax exceeds 37.5 per cent.) shall not have effect with respect to the financial year 1986 or any subsequent financial year.

(5) After subsection (6) of the said section 310 there shall be inserted the following subsection:—

" (7) For the purposes of subsection (6) above, ' unrelieved income ' means income which has not been excluded from charge to tax by virtue of any provision and against which no relief has been allowed by deduction or set-off ".

(6) With respect to the financial year 1986 and subsequent financial years, in paragraph 2(4) of Schedule 18 to the Finance Act 1972 (which refers to a particular part of unrelieved income) for the words from " subsection (4) " onwards there shall be substituted the words " subsection (7) of that section) from investments held in connection with the company's life assurance business ". 1972 c. 41.

19. The rate of advance corporation tax for the financial year 1984 shall be three-sevenths. Rate of advance corporation tax for financial year 1984.

20.—(1) The small companies rate for each of the financial years 1983 to 1986 shall be 30 per cent. Corporation tax: other rates and fractions.

(2) For each of the financial years specified in the first column of the table set out below the fraction mentioned in subsection (2) of section 95 of the Finance Act 1972 (marginal relief for small companies) shall be the fraction specified in the second column of that table:—

TABLE

Financial year	Marginal relief fraction
1983	One-twentieth
1984	Three-eightieths
1985	One-fortieth
1986	One-eightieth.

(3) In section 10(3) of the Finance Act 1974 (which fixed for the purposes of section 96 of the Finance Act 1972 the special rate for certain industrial and provident societies, housing associations and building societies) after the words " subsequent years " there shall be inserted the words " up to and including the financial year 1984 "; and the said section 96 shall not have effect with respect to the financial year 1985 or any subsequent financial year.

(4) In any case where the said section 96 has effect in relation to one part of an accounting period of a body to which that section applies but, by virtue of subsection (3) above, does not have effect with respect to the other part—

(a) those parts of that accounting period shall be treated for the purposes of that section as if they were separate accounting periods ; and

(b) the income of the body for that period (as defined in that section) shall be apportioned between those parts.

21.—(1) Section 24(5) of the Finance Act 1980 (increase of personal reliefs) shall not apply for the year 1984-85.

(2) In section 8 of the Taxes Act (personal reliefs)—

(a) in subsection (1)(a) (married) for " £2,795 " there shall be substituted " £3,155 ";

(b) in subsection (1)(b) (single) and (2) (wife's earned income relief) for " £1,785 " there shall be substituted " £2,005 ";

(c) in subsection (1A) (age allowance) for " £3,755 " and " £2,360 " there shall be substituted " £3,955 " and " £2,490 " respectively ; and

(d) in subsection (1B) (income limit for age allowance) for " £7,600 " there shall be substituted " £8,100 ".

22.—(1) In paragraph 5 of Schedule 1 to the Finance Act 1974 (limit on relief for interest on certain loans for the purchase or improvement of land)—

(a) in sub-paragraph (1), for the words from " that is to say " to " reduced " there shall be substituted the words " that is to say, the qualifying maximum for the year of assessment, reduced "; and

(b) in paragraph (b) of that sub-paragraph, for the words from " below " to " more " there shall be substituted the words " below is equal to or exceeds the qualifying maximum for the year of assessment "; and

(c) after that sub-paragraph there shall be inserted the following sub-paragraph: —

"(1A) In this Schedule references to the qualifying maximum for any year of assessment are references to such sum as Parliament may determine for the purpose for that year."

(2) In paragraph 6 of that Schedule (continuing relief for an existing home loan where the borrower raises a new loan to purchase another home in which he takes up residence) after sub-paragraph (1) there shall be inserted the following sub-paragraph: —

"(1A) Where Part I of Schedule 9 to the Finance Act 1972 c. 41. 1972 continues to apply to a loan by virtue of sub-paragraph (1)(a) above, paragraph 5 above shall also continue to have effect in relation to the loan as if that Part applied to it by virtue of paragraph 4(1)(a) above."

(3) In paragraph 24 of that Schedule (loans to purchase life annuities), in sub-paragraph (3), for the amounts of money there specified (which, by virtue of section 3(2) of the Finance (No. 2) 1983 c. 49. Act 1983, are £30,000 for the year 1983-84) there shall be substituted in both places the words "the qualifying maximum for the year of assessment".

(4) For the year 1984-85 the qualifying maximum referred to in paragraphs 5(1) and 24(3) of Schedule 1 to the Finance Act 1974 c. 30. 1974 shall be £30,000.

(5) Subsections (1) to (3) above have effect with respect to the year 1984-85 and subsequent years of assessment.

23.—(1) If, in a case where subsection (1) of section 28 of the Variation of Finance Act 1982 applies (variation of combined payments terms of where loan interest payable under deduction of tax),— repayment of certain loans

(a) on or after the date on which this Act is passed, the 1982 c. 39. qualifying lender concerned gives notice to the qualifying borrower under subsection (2)(a) of that section, and

(b) the qualifying borrower gives a notice under subsection (2)(b) of that section,

then subsection (4)(b) of that section (which determines the maximum amount of each combined payment where the qualifying borrower has given such a notice) shall have effect subject to the modifications in subsection (2) below.

(2) The modifications of the said subsection (4)(b) referred to in subsection (1) above are—

(a) for the words "first combined payment payable by the borrower after the date referred to in subsection (1)(c) above " there shall be substituted the words " combined payment payable by the borrower on the effective date of the notice under subsection (2)(*a*) above " ; and

(*b*) for the words " year 1983-84 " there shall be substituted the words " year of assessment in which that effective date falls ".

(3) After subsection (4) of the said section 28 there shall be inserted the following subsection :—

" (4A) For the purposes of subsection (4)(*b*) above, the effective date of a notice under subsection (2)(*a*) above is the date which, in accordance with regulations, is the due date for the first combined payment which, in consequence of that notice and the notice under subsection (2)(*b*) above, is a net payment for the purposes of subsection (3)(*b*) above."

(4) In subsection (1) above " qualifying lender ", " qualifying borrower " and " combined payment " have the same meaning as in section 28 of the Finance Act 1982.

24.—(1) Paragraph 10D of Schedule 1 to the Finance Act 1974 (loans applied in investing in employee-controlled companies) shall be amended as follows.

(2) In sub-paragraph (2), for the words " at least 75 per cent." there shall be substituted the words " more than 50 per cent.".

(3) In sub-paragraph (3), for the words " 5 per cent. " there shall be substituted the words " 10 per cent.".

(4) After sub-paragraph (3) there shall be inserted the following sub-paragraph—

" (3A) Where an individual and his spouse are both fulltime employees of the company, sub-paragraph (3) above shall apply in relation to them with the omission of the words ' or he and his spouse together own beneficially'.".

(5) Paragraph 10D shall have effect as if the amendments made by this section had been incorporated in that paragraph as originally enacted.

25.—(1) In paragraph 4A of Schedule 1 to the Finance Act 1974 (restrictions on relief for loans for purchase etc. of land: persons living in job-related accommodation) after sub-paragraph (3) there shall be inserted the following sub-paragraphs : —

" (3A) Subject to sub-paragraph (3B) below, living accommodation is also job-related for a person if, under a contract entered into at arm's length and requiring him or his spouse to carry on a particular trade, profession or vocation, he or his spouse is bound—

(*a*) to carry on that trade, profession or vocation on premises or other land provided by another person (whether under a tenancy or otherwise) ; and (*b*) to live either on those premises or on other premises provided by that other person.

(3B) Sub-paragraph (3A) above does not apply if the living accommodation concerned is, in whole or in part, provided by—

(*a*) a company in which the borrower or his spouse has a material interest ; or

(*b*) any person or persons together with whom the borrower or his spouse carries on a trade or business in partnership."

(2) The amendment effected by subsection (1) above has effect—

(*a*) with respect to interest paid on or after 6th April 1983 ; and

(*b*) so far as (by virtue of section 101(8) of the Capital Gains Tax Act 1979) it relates to relief from tax on capital gains, with respect to residence on and after that date in living accommodation which is job-related within the meaning of the said paragraph 4A.

1979 c. 14.

26.—(1) In the year 1984-85 and in every subsequent year of assessment the Treasury shall by order made by statutory instrument determine a rate which shall, for the following year of assessment, be—

(*a*) the reduced rate for the purposes of section 343 of the Taxes Act (building societies) ; and

(*b*) the composite rate for the purposes of section 27 of this Act.

Determination of reduced rate for building societies and composite rate for banks etc.

(2) The order made under subsection (1) above in each year of assessment shall—

(*a*) be made before 31st December in that year ; and

(*b*) be based only on information relating to periods before the end of the year of assessment in which the order is made.

(3) Whenever they exercise their powers under this section the Treasury shall aim at securing that (assuming for the purposes of this subsection that the amounts payable by building societies under section 343 of the Taxes Act and by deposit-takers under section 27 of this Act are income tax) the total income tax becoming payable to, and not being repayable by, the Crown is (when regard is had to the operation of those sections) as nearly as may be the same in the aggregate as it would have been if those sections had not been enacted.

(4) In relation to the exercise of their powers under this section at any time before the year 1988-89, the Treasury may

regard subsection (3) above as directed only to amounts payable by building societies under section 343 and to the operation of that section.

(5) In section 343(1) of the Taxes Act, the proviso and in paragraph (*a*) the words from " which takes " to " this section " shall cease to have effect as from 6th April 1985.

(6) An order under this section shall be subject to annulment in pursuance of a resolution of the Commons House of Parliament.

(7) For the purposes of enabling the Treasury to comply with the requirements of subsection (3) above, the Board may by notice in writing require any deposit-taker (within the meaning of paragraph 2 of Schedule 8 to this Act) or building society to furnish to the Board such information about its depositors as the Board may reasonably require for those purposes ; and may so require any deposit-taker at any time before the year 1988-89 notwithstanding subsection (4) above.

1970 c. 9.
(8) The Table in section 98 of the Taxes Management Act 1970 (penalties) shall be amended by inserting at the end of the first column—

" Section 26 of the Finance Act 1984.".

(9) In subsection (7) above " depositors ", in relation to a building society, includes shareholders.

Interest paid
on deposits
with banks
etc.
27.—(1) Any deposit-taker making a payment of interest in respect of any relevant deposit shall be liable to account for and pay an amount representing income tax on that payment, calculated by applying the composite rate (determined in accordance with section 26 of this Act) to the grossed-up amount of the payment, that is to say to the amount which after deduction of tax at the composite rate would be equal to the amount actually paid.

(2) Any payment of interest within subsection (1) above shall be treated as not being within section 54 of the Taxes Act (annual interest).

(3) Schedule 8 to this Act shall have effect for the purpose of supplementing this section.

(4) Subject to paragraph 6(1) of Schedule 8, this section applies in relation to payments made after 5th April 1985.

Accommodation
allowances
and
expenditure
of MPs.
28.—(1) An allowance—

    (*a*) which is paid to a Member of the Commons House of Parliament in respect of any period after 31st March **1984, and** (*b*) for which provision is made by Resolution of that House, and

(*c*) which is expressed to be in respect of additional expenses necessarily incurred by the Member in staying overnight away from his only or main residence for the purpose of performing his parliamentary duties, either in the London area, as defined in such a Resolution, or in his constituency,

shall not be regarded as income for any income tax purpose.

(2) For the year 1984-85 and subsequent years of assessment,—

(*a*) no deduction shall be made under section 189 of the Taxes Act (relief for necessary expenses) in respect of expenditure incurred by a Member of the Commons House of Parliament in, or in connection with, the provision or use of residential or overnight accommodation to enable him to perform his duties as such a Member in or about the Palace of Westminster or his constituency ; and

(*b*) no allowance shall be made under Chapter I of Part III of the Finance Act 1971 (capital allowances) in respect of any expenditure so incurred.

1971 c. 68.

29.—(1) Grants made under section 3 of the European Assembly (Pay and Pensions) Act 1979 (resettlement grants to persons ceasing to be Representatives) and payments under section 13 of the Parliamentary Pensions etc. Act 1984 (grants to persons ceasing to hold certain Ministerial and other offices) shall be exempt from income tax under Schedule E as emoluments, but without prejudice to their being taken into account, to the extent permitted by section 188(3) of the Taxes Act, under section 187 of that Act.

Terminal grants to Representatives to the Assembly of the European Communities etc.
1979 c. 50.
1984 c. 60.

(2) This section applies to grants and payments whenever made.

30.—(1) Paragraphs 2 and 3 of Schedule 7 to the Finance Act 1977 (relief from income tax under Case I of Schedule E in relation to short or intermittent absences abroad and foreign employments) shall cease to apply in relation to years of assessment after the year 1984-85 ; and in relation to the year 1984-85 those paragraphs shall have effect with the substitution for the words " one-quarter " of the words " one-eighth ".

Reduction and abolition of reliefs in relation to foreign earnings and emoluments etc.
1977 c. 36.

(2) Section 27 of the Finance Act 1978 (relief from income tax under Case I or Case II of Schedule D in relation to short or intermittent absences abroad) shall cease to apply in relation to years of assessment after the year 1984-85 ; and in relation to the year 1984-85 paragraph 4 of Schedule 4 to that

1978 c. 42.

Act shall have effect with the substitution for the words " one-quarter " of the words " one-eighth ".

(3) Subject to subsection (4) below, section 23(3) of the Finance Act 1974 (relief from income tax in respect of trade, profession or vocation carried on abroad) shall cease to apply in relation to any year of assessment after the year 1984-85.

(4) Section 23(3) of the Finance Act 1974 shall continue to have effect in relation to losses sustained before the year 1983-84 and capital allowances for any year of assessment before 1984-85 and shall have effect—

(a) in relation to losses sustained in the year 1983-84, and capital allowances for the year 1984-85, with the substitution for the words " three-quarters " of the words " seven-eighths " ;

(b) in relation to losses sustained after 5th April 1984, with the omission of the restriction of the relief given by subsection (2) of section 23 ; and

(c) in relation to any charge to tax for the year 1984-85, with the substitution for the words " one-quarter " of the words " one-eighth ".

(5) Paragraph 35 of Schedule 9 to the Finance Act 1981 (reduction of stock relief where relief from income tax given under section 23(3) of the Finance Act 1974) shall have effect in relation to any relief under that Schedule for which the relevant year of assessment is the year 1984-85—

(a) with the omission of the words " of one-quarter of the amount of that income " ; and

(b) with the substitution for the words " three-quarters " of the words " seven-eighths " ;

and where by virtue of that paragraph any relief is reduced in the year which is the relevant year of assessment for that relief, it shall be so reduced in any subsequent year in which effect is given to it.

(6) For the purposes of subsection (4) above, any reference to capital allowances for a year of assessment shall be construed as a reference to those falling to be made in taxing the trade, profession or vocation for that year but excluding any part of the allowances carried forward from an earlier year.

(7) Subject to subsection (8) below, section 188(2)(a) of the Taxes Act (relief from income tax in relation to payments on retirement or removal from certain foreign offices and employments) shall cease to apply in any case where the relevant date (within the meaning of section 188) falls after 13th March 1984.

(8) Subsection (7) above does not apply where the payment is made before 1st August 1984 in pursuance of an obligation incurred before 14th March 1984.

(9) Subject to subsection (10) below, paragraph 3 of Schedule 2 to the Finance Act 1974 (relief from income tax in relation to foreign emoluments chargeable under Case I or Case II of Schedule E) shall cease to apply in relation to years of assessment after the year 1983-84.

(10) Subsection (9) above does not apply in relation to any year of assessment, before the year 1989-90, in which—

(a) the conditions mentioned in subsection (11) below are satisfied in relation to the holder of the office or employment in question ; and

(b) the deduction from emoluments would (by virtue of paragraph 3(2) of Schedule 2 and disregarding this section) be one-half.

(11) The conditions referred to in subsection (10) above are—

(a) that the person in question either held a foreign employment at any time in the period beginning with 6th April 1983 and ending with 13th March 1984 or did not hold a foreign employment in that period but, in fulfilment of an obligation incurred before 14th March 1984, performed duties of a foreign employment in the United Kingdom before 1st August 1984 ; and

(b) that he has held a foreign employment in the year 1984-85 and in each subsequent year of assessment.

In this subsection " foreign employment " means an office or employment the emoluments of which are foreign emoluments chargeable under Case I or Case II of Schedule E.

(12) Where by virtue of subsection (10) above paragraph 3(2) of Schedule 2 to the Finance Act 1974 continues to have effect in relation to the year 1987-88 or the year 1988-89, it shall do so with the substitution for the words " one-half " of the words " one-quarter ".

(13) In section 23(4) of the Act of 1974, for the words from " in the charging " to " this section " there shall be substituted the words " falling within subsection (1) above ".

(14) In section 31(2) of the Finance Act 1977—

(a) the words from the beginning to " emoluments) ; and " shall cease to have effect ; and

(b) for the words " the said Schedule 2 " there shall be substituted the words " Schedule 2 to the Finance Act 1974 ".

(15) Subsections (13) and (14) above shall have effect in relation to the year 1985-86 and subsequent years of assessment.

31.—(1) In subsection (3) of section 62A of the Finance Act 1976 (scholarships)—

(a) after paragraph (b) there shall be inserted—" ; and

    (*c*) which would not be regarded, for the purposes of this Chapter, as provided by reason of a person's employment were subsection (2) above and section 72(3) below to be disregarded ; " ; and

    (*b*) for the words from " so held " to the end there shall be substituted the words " held as mentioned in paragraph (*b*) above is attributable to relevant scholarships.".

(2) In subsection (4) of section 62A—

    (*a*) after the word " section " where it first occurs, there shall be inserted—

       " 'relevant scholarship' means a scholarship which is provided by reason of a person's employment (whether or not that employment is director's or higher-paid employment) ; and " ; and

    (*b*) at the end there shall be inserted—

       " For the purposes of the definition of relevant scholarship, ' employment ' includes an office or employment whose emoluments do not fall to be assessed under Schedule E but would fall to be so assessed if the employee were resident, and ordinarily resident, and all the duties of the employment were performed wholly, in the United Kingdom.".

1983 c. 28.

    (3) In section 20 of the Finance Act 1983 (which inserts section 62A into the Act of 1976 and specifies the payments to which it applies), for subsection (3)(*c*) there shall be substituted—

       " (*c*) in relation to payments made after 5th April 1989, the person holding the scholarship is receiving full-time instruction at the university, college, school or other educational establishment at which he was receiving such instruction on—

          (i) 15th March 1983, in a case where the first payment in respect of the scholarship was made before that date ; or

          (ii) the date on which the first such payment was made, in any other case.

    (3A) For the purposes of subsection (3)(*c*) above, a payment made before 6th April 1989 in respect of any period beginning on or after that date shall be treated as made at the beginning of that period.".

    (4) The amendments made by subsections (1) and (2) above shall have effect in relation to payments made on or after 6th April 1984 and those made by subsection (3) shall be deemed to have been incorporated in section 20 of the Finance Act 1983 as originally enacted.

32.—(1) In paragraph 5(4) of Schedule 16 to the Finance Act 1972 (minimum amount on which an individual is to be assessed to income tax by virtue of apportionment), in paragraph (*a*), for the words " £200 " there shall be substituted the words " £1,000 ". PART II
Apportion-
ment of
income etc. of
close
companies.
1972 c. 41.

(2) This section has effect in relation to accounting periods ending on or after 6th April 1984.

33. Section 28 of the Finance Act 1983 (relief in cases where a company seconds an employee to a charity) shall have effect and be deemed always to have had effect with the insertion, after subsection (2), of the following subsections:— Employees
seconded to
charities:
extension of
relief to
individual
traders etc.
1983 c. 28.

" (2A) In any case where a person (" the employer ") who is not a company makes available to a charity, on a basis which is expressed and intended to be of a temporary nature, the services of a person who is in his employment for the purposes of a trade carried on by the employer, subsections (1) and (2) above apply as if references therein to a company were references to the employer.

(2B) This section applies in relation to a profession or vocation as it applies in relation to a trade, taking the reference in subsection (2) above to Case I of Schedule D as a reference to Case II of that Schedule."

34.—(1) In paragraph (iii) of the proviso to subsection (3) of section 343 of the Taxes Act (arrangements for payment of income tax on interest etc. paid by building societies) after the words " certificate of deposit " there shall be inserted the words " or on any qualifying time deposit ". Building
societies:
interest to be
payable gross
on certain
deposits.

(2) After subsection (8A) of that section there shall be inserted the following subsection—

" (8B) In subsection (3) above " qualifying time deposit " means a deposit which is made with the society concerned by way of loan and which—

(*a*) is in sterling and for an amount which is not less than £50,000 ;

(*b*) is made on terms requiring repayment of the loan at the end of a specified period which expires before the end of the period of twelve months beginning on the date on which the deposit is made ; and

(*c*) is not made on terms which make provision for the transfer of the right to repayment."

(3) This section has effect in relation to interest on qualifying time deposits (as defined above) which is or was payable after 30th September 1983.

35.—(1) Section 54 of the Taxes Act (deduction of income tax from certain interest payments) shall not apply to interest paid on any quoted Eurobond where—

    (a) the person by or through whom the payment is made is not in the United Kingdom ; or

    (b) the payment is made by or through a person who is in the United Kingdom but either of the conditions mentioned in subsection (2) below is satisfied.

(2) The conditions are—

    (a) that it is proved, on a claim in that behalf made to the Board, that the person who is the beneficial owner of the quoted Eurobond and is entitled to the interest is not resident in the United Kingdom ;

    (b) that the quoted Eurobond is held in a recognised clearing system.

(3) In a case falling within subsection (1)(b) above, the person by or through whom the payment is made shall deliver to the Board—

    (a) on demand by the Board, an account of the amount of any such payment ; and

    (b) not later than 12 months after making any such payment, and unless within that time he delivers an account with respect to the payment under paragraph (a) above, a written statement specifying his name and address and describing the payment.

(4) In section 248 of the Taxes Act (allowance of charges on company's income), the following paragraph shall be inserted after paragraph (a) of subsection (4)—

    " (aa) by virtue of section 35 of the Finance Act 1984 (interest on quoted Eurobonds), section 54 of this Act does not apply to the payment ; or ".

(5) Where by virtue of any provision of the Tax Acts interest paid on any quoted Eurobond is deemed to be income of a person other than the person who is the beneficial owner of the quoted Eurobond, subsection (2)(a) above shall apply as if it referred to that other person.

(6) Subsections (3) to (6) of section 159 of the Taxes Act (assessment and charge to tax etc. in respect of foreign dividends) shall apply in relation to interest on quoted Eurobonds as they apply in relation to foreign dividends but with the following modifications—

    (a) subsection (4) shall apply as if it required a claim to have been made on or before the event by virtue of which tax would otherwise be chargeable ; and (*b*) paragraph 6 of Schedule 5 to that Act shall apply with the omission of paragraphs (*a*) and (*b*).

(7) In this section—

" quoted Eurobond " means a security which—

      (*a*) is issued by a company ;

      (*b*) is quoted on a recognised stock exchange (within the meaning of section 535 of the Taxes Act) ;

      (*c*) is in bearer form ; and

      (*d*) carries a right to interest ; and

" recognised clearing system " means any system for clearing quoted Eurobonds which is for the time being designated for the purposes of this section, by order made by the Board, as a recognised clearing system.

(8) An order under subsection (7) above—

(*a*) may contain such transitional and other supplemental provisions as appear to the Board to be necessary or expedient ; and

(*b*) may be varied or revoked by a subsequent order so made.

(9) In the Table in section 98 of the Taxes Management Act 1970 c. 9. 1970, at the end of the second column there shall be inserted—

" Section 35(3) of the Finance Act 1984.".

(10) This section has effect in relation to payments of interest made after the passing of this Act.

36.—(1) Schedule 9 to this Act shall have effect with respect Deep discount to the treatment, for the purposes of income tax, corporation securities. tax and capital gains tax, of deep discount securities.

(2) For the purposes of this section—

" the amount payable on redemption " does not include any amount payable by way of interest ;

" a deep discount ", in relation to any redeemable security, means a discount which—

      (*a*) represents more than 15 per cent. of the amount payable on redemption of that security ; or

      (*b*) is 15 per cent. or less, but exceeds half Y per cent., of the amount so payable (where Y is the number of complete years between the date of issue of the security and the redemption date) ;

" a deep discount security " means any redeemable security which has been issued by a company at a deep discount, other than—

      (*a*) a share in the company ;

     (*b*) a security in respect of which the amount payable on redemption is determined by reference to the movement of the retail prices index (within the meaning of section 24 of the Finance Act 1980) or any similar general index of prices which is published by, or by an agent of, the government of any territory outside the United Kingdom ; or

     (*c*) a security, the whole or any part of which falls, by virtue of section 233(2)(*c*) of the Taxes Act, within the meaning of " distribution " in the Corporation Tax Acts ;

" a discount " means any amount by which the issue price of a redeemable security is less than the amount payable on redemption of that security ; and

" the redemption date " in relation to any redeemable security, means the earliest date on which, under the terms on which the security is issued, the holder of the security will be entitled to require it to be redeemed by the company which issued it.

(3) Where securities which were issued on or before 13th March 1984 have been exchanged, at any time after that date, for new securities which would be deep discount securities but for this subsection, the new securities shall not be treated as deep discount securities it—

     (*a*) the old securities would not have been deep discount securities if they had been issued after 13th March 1984 ;

     (*b*) the date which is the redemption date in relation to the new securities is not later than the date which was the redemption date in relation to the old securities ; and

     (*c*) the amount payable on redemption of the new securities does not exceed the amount which would have been payable on redemption of the old securities.

(4) For the purposes of this section, a security comprised in any letter of allotment or similar instrument shall be treated as issued unless the right to the security conferred by the letter or instrument remains provisional until accepted, and there has been no acceptance.

(5) Subject to paragraph 3(8) of Schedule 9 to this Act, this section shall have effect in relation to securities issued after 13th March 1984.

37.—(1) In paragraph 6(2) of Schedule 5 to the Finance Act 1983 (trades which are excluded from being qualifying trades for purposes of business expansion scheme) there shall be added, at the end, the words " or of farming ".

(2) After that paragraph there shall be inserted— Part II

" (2A) A trade shall not be treated as failing to comply with this paragraph by reason only of its consisting to a substantial extent of receiving royalties or licence fees if—

    (a) the company carrying on the trade is engaged throughout the relevant period in the production of films ; and

    (b) all royalties and licence fees received by it in that period are in respect of films produced by it or sound recordings in relation to such films or other products arising from such films.

(2B) In this paragraph—

    ' film ' means an original master negative of a film, an original master film disc or an original master film tape ; and

    ' sound recording ' means, in relation to a film, its sound track, original master audio disc or, as the case may be, original master audio tape.".

(3) Subsection (1) of this section has effect in relation to shares issued after 13th March 1984.

38.—(1) The provisions of this section shall apply where, on Approved or after 6th April 1984, an individual obtains a right to acquire share option shares in a body corporate— schemes.

    (a) by reason of his office or employment as a director or employee of that or any other body corporate ; and

    (b) in accordance with the provisions of a scheme approved under Schedule 10 to this Act.

(2) Subject to subsection (5) below, tax shall not be chargeable under any provision of the Tax Acts in respect of the receipt of the right.

(3) If the conditions mentioned in subsection (4) below are satisfied and he exercises the right in accordance with the provisions of the scheme at a time when it is approved under Schedule 10—

    (a) tax shall not be chargeable under any provision of the Tax Acts in respect of the exercise nor under section 79(4) of the Finance Act 1972 in respect of an increase 1972 c. 41. in the market value of the shares ;

    (b) section 29A(1) of the Capital Gains Tax Act 1979 1979 c. 14. (assets deemed to be acquired at market value) shall not apply in calculating the consideration for the acquisition of the shares by him or for any corresponding disposal of them to him.

(4) The conditions are that—

   (*a*) the period beginning with his obtaining the right and ending with his exercising it is not less than three, nor greater than ten, years ;

   (*b*) the right is not exercised within three years of the date on which he last exercised (in circumstances in which paragraphs (*a*) and (*b*) of subsection (3) above apply) any right obtained under the scheme or under any other scheme approved under Schedule 10 (any such right exercised on the same day as the right in question being disregarded).

(5) Where the aggregate of—

   (*a*) the amount or value of any consideration given by him for obtaining the right ; and

   (*b*) the price at which he may acquire the shares by exercising the right ;

is less than the market value, at the time he obtains the right, of the same quantity of issued shares of the same class, he shall be chargeable to tax under Schedule E for the year of assessment in which he obtains the right on the amount of the difference ; and the amount so chargeable shall be treated as earned income, whether or not it would otherwise fall to be so treated.

1979 c. 14.

(6) For the purposes of section 32(1)(*a*) of the Capital Gains Tax Act 1979 (computation of chargeable gains: allowable expenditure), the consideration given for shares acquired in the exercise of the right shall be taken to have included that part of any amount on which income tax is payable in accordance with subsection (5) above which is attributable to the shares disposed of.

This subsection applies whether or not the exercise is in accordance with the provisions of the scheme and whether or not the scheme is approved at the time of the exercise.

(7) Subsections (8) and (9) below apply where he is chargeable to tax under subsection (5) above on any amount (" the amount of the discount ") and subsequently, in circumstances in which subsection (3) above does not apply—

   (*a*) is chargeable to tax under section 186 of the Taxes Act (directors and employees of companies granted rights to acquire shares: charge to tax under Schedule E) ; or

1976 c. 40.

   (*b*) is treated by virtue of section 67 of the Finance Act 1976 (benefits in kind: employee shareholdings) as having had the benefit of a notional interest-free loan.

(8) In a case falling within subsection (7)(*a*) above the amount of the gain on which he is chargeable to tax under section 186

shall be reduced by that part of the amount of the discount which is attributable to the shares in question.

(9) In a case falling within subsection (7)(*b*) above the amount of the notional loan initially outstanding shall be reduced by that part of the amount of the discount which is attributable to the shares in question.

(10) The Table in section 98 of the Taxes Management Act 1970 (penalties) shall be amended by inserting at the end of the first column— 1970 c. 9.

" Paragraph 14 of Schedule 10 to the Finance Act 1984.".

39.—(1) In section 47(1)(*b*)(ii) of the Finance Act 1980 (section 29A(1) of the Capital Gains Tax Act 1979 not to apply in calculating consideration for acquisition of shares under savings-related share option scheme), the words " by him or any corresponding disposal of them to him " shall be added at the end. Share options 1980 c. 48. 1979 c. 14.

(2) In Schedule 10 to that Act, in paragraph 1(1) (conditions for approval of such schemes) the following paragraphs shall be inserted after paragraph (*a*)—

" (*aa*) if they are satisfied that there are no features of the scheme (other than any which are included to satisfy requirements of this Schedule) which have or would have the effect of discouraging any of the persons who fulfil the conditions in paragraph 20(1)(*a*) to (*c*) below from actually participating in the scheme ; and

(*ab*) where the company concerned is a member of a group of companies, if they are satisfied that the scheme does not and would not have the effect of conferring benefits wholly or mainly on directors of companies in the group or on those employees of companies in the group who are in receipt of the higher or highest levels of remuneration ; and ".

(3) In paragraph 1 of that Schedule the following sub-paragraph shall be inserted after sub-paragraph (1):—

" (1A) In sub-paragraph (1)(*ab*) above, a group of companies means a company and any other companies of which it has control."

(4) In paragraph 3(1) of that Schedule, for the words from " any of the conditions " to " ceases to be satisfied " there shall be substituted the words " they cease to be satisfied as mentioned in paragraph 1 above ".

R 2

(5) In paragraph 13 the words " (not exceeding £50 monthly) " shall be omitted and at the end there shall be inserted—

" (2) Subject to sub-paragraph (3) below, the scheme must not—

(*a*) permit the aggregate amount of a person's contributions under certified contractual savings schemes linked to schemes approved under this Schedule to exceed £100 monthly, nor

(*b*) impose a minimum on the amount of a person's contributions which exceeds £10 monthly.

(3) The Treasury may by order made by statutory instrument, which shall be subject to annulment in pursuance of a resolution of the Commons House of Parliament, amend sub-paragraph (2) above by substituting for any amount for the time being specified in that sub-paragraph such amount as may be specified in the order."

(6) In paragraph 20 of that Schedule (conditions as to persons eligible to participate)—

(*a*) at the end of sub-paragraph (1) there shall be added the words " and those who do participate in the scheme must actually do so on similar terms " ; and

(*b*) at the end of sub-paragraph (2) there shall be added the words " or do not actually do so ".

(7) In section 40 of the Finance Act 1982 (share options), subsections (4) and (5) (payment of tax by instalments) shall cease to have effect in relation to any right to acquire shares which is obtained after 5th April 1984.

(8) In relation to any such right which is obtained before 6th April 1984 and exercised after 5th April 1983, section 40 of the Act of 1982 shall be amended as follows—

(*a*) in subsections (4) and (5) (payment of tax by instalments)—

(i) for the word " three ", in each place where it occurs, there shall be substituted the word " five " ; and

(ii) for the word " third ", in each place where it occurs, there shall be substituted the word " fifth " ; and

(*b*) for paragraph (*c*) of subsection (4) there shall be substituted the following paragraph :—

" (*c*) the second, third and fourth instalments shall be due on such dates as will secure, so far as may be, that the interval between any two consecutive instalments is the same ".

(9) Subsection (1) above shall apply to acquisitions and disposals made after 14th November 1980, subsection (5) above shall come into force on such day as the Treasury may by order made by statutory instrument appoint for the purposes of this subsection, and the amendments made by this section to Schedule 10 to the 1980 Act shall apply in relation to schemes whenever approved.

40.—(1) In section 79 of the Finance Act 1972 (share incentive schemes) in subsection (2) (exemptions from the income tax charge on increase in value) at the end of paragraph (*b*) there shall be inserted the following paragraph:—

> " (*bb*) the acquisition was an acquisition of an interest in shares and that interest consists of shares in an authorised unit trust (hereafter in this section referred to as " units ") and—
>
>> (i) prior to the acquisition the unit trust was approved by the Board for the purposes of this section and, at the time of the acquisition, continues to be so approved, and
>>
>> (ii) the condition in subsection (2B) below is fulfilled with respect to the body corporate (in that subsection referred to as " the relevant company "), directorship of or employment by which gave rise to the right or opportunity by virtue of which the acquisition was made ; or "

Share
incentive
schemes:
shares in
authorised
unit trusts.
1972 c. 41.

(2) After subsection (2A) of that section there shall be inserted the following subsection:—

> " (2B) The condition referred to in subsection (2)(*bb*) above is fulfilled with respect to the relevant company if, for no continuous period of one month or more, throughout which any director or employee of the relevant company either—
>
>> (*a*) has, by virtue of his office or employment, any such right or opportunity as is referred to in subsection (1) above to acquire units in the unit trust, or
>>
>> (*b*) retains any beneficial interest in any units in the unit trust which he acquired in pursuance of such a right or opportunity,
>
> do investments in the relevant company and in any other company in relation to which the relevant company is an associated company make up more than 10 per cent. by value of the investments subject to the trusts of the unit trust."

PART **II**

(3) After subsection (4) of that section there shall be inserted the following subsection: —

" (4A) In any case where subsection (4) above applies and the acquisition was an acquisition of units,—

    (*a*) any reference in that subsection or in subsections (5), (6), (9) and (11) below to shares shall be construed as a reference to units ; and

    (*b*) any reference in those subsections to an interest in shares shall be omitted."

1972 c. 41.

(4) In Part VII of Schedule 12 to the Finance Act 1972 (provisions supplementary to sections 77 to 79 of that Act) after paragraph 3 there shall be inserted the following paragraph: —

" 3A. The Board may by notice in writing require the managers or trustees of any unit trust scheme which is an authorised unit trust approved by the Board for the purposes of section 79 of this Act to furnish to the Board, within such time as they may direct (but not being less than thirty days), such information as the Board think necessary for the purposes of enabling them—

    (*a*) to determine whether the condition in subsection (2B) of that section is being or has at any time been fulfilled ; and

    (*b*) to determine the liability to tax of any unit holder whose rights were acquired as mentioned in subsection (1) of that section."

(5) In paragraph 6 of that Schedule (interpretation) after the definition of " associated company " there shall be inserted—

" ' authorised unit trust ' and ' unit holder ' have the meaning assigned to them by section 358 of the Taxes Act ; ".

1970 c. 9.

(6) In section 98 of the Taxes Management Act 1970 (penalty for failure to furnish information etc.) in the entry in the second column which begins " Paragraph 3 of Part VII of Schedule 12 to the Finance Act 1972 " after the words " Paragraph 3 " there shall be inserted the words " or paragraph 3A ".

(7) This section applies to acquisitions on or after 6th April 1984.

Share incentive schemes: exemption for certain acquisitions.

41.—(1) After subsection (1) of section 79 of the Finance Act 1972 (share incentive schemes) there shall be inserted—

" (1A) Where—

    (*a*) a director or employee of a body corporate acquires shares in pursuance of an opportunity to acquire shares of that class offered to directors and employees of the body in their capacity as such ('the discount offer'); and

(b) the discount offer is made in conjunction with an offer to the public ('the main offer') under which shares of the same class may be acquired on the same terms, except that a discount in price is offered to directors and employees; and

(c) the director or employee is chargeable to tax under Schedule E on an amount equal to the discount in the price of the shares acquired by him; and

(d) at least 75 per cent. of the aggregate number of shares of the class in question which are acquired in pursuance of the discount offer and the main offer taken together are shares acquired in pursuance of the main offer,

he shall be treated for the purposes of subsection (1) above as acquiring the shares in pursuance of an offer to the public.

(1B) Where a director or an employee acquires an interest in shares, subsection (1A) above shall apply as if the references in that subsection to the acquisition of shares were references to the acquisition of an interest in shares.".

(2) In paragraph 3 of Part VII of Schedule 12 to that Act (furnishing of information) there shall be inserted at the end—

" (2) For the purposes of this paragraph subsections (1A) and (1B) of section 79 shall be disregarded."

42.—(1) This section applies in any case where—

(a) a bill of exchange drawn by a company is or was accepted by a bank and discounted by that or any other bank or by a discount house; and

(b) the bill becomes or became payable on or after 1st April 1983; and

(c) the discount suffered by the company is not (apart from this section) deductible in computing the company's profits or any description of those profits for purposes of corporation tax.

Discounts on bills of exchange drawn by trading companies etc.

(2) Subject to subsection (3) below, in computing, in a case where this section applies, the corporation tax chargeable for the accounting period of the company in which the bill of exchange is paid, an amount equal to the discount referred to in subsection (1)(c) above shall be allowed as a deduction against the total profits for the period as reduced by any relief other than group relief and, except for the purposes of

R 4

an allowance under section 248(1) of the Taxes Act, that amount shall be treated for the purposes of the Corporation Tax Acts as a charge on income.

(3) Subsection (2) above shall not apply if the discount is not ultimately suffered by the company and shall not apply unless—

> (*a*) the company exists wholly or mainly for the purpose of carrying on a trade ; or
>
> (*b*) the bill is drawn to obtain funds which are wholly and exclusively expended for the purposes of a trade carried on by the company ; or
>
> (*c*) the company is an investment company, as defined by section 304(5) of the Taxes Act.

(4) Where an amount falls to be allowed as mentioned in subsection (2) above, there may be deducted, in computing the profits or gains of the company to be charged under Case I of Schedule D, the incidental costs incurred on or after 1st April 1983 in securing the acceptance of the bill by the bank ; and those incidental costs shall be treated for the purposes of section 304 of the Taxes Act as expenses of management.

(5) For the purposes of subsection (4) above " incidental costs " means fees, commission and any other expenditure wholly and exclusively incurred for the purpose of securing the acceptance of the bill.

(6) In this section " bank " means a bank carrying on a bona fide banking business in the United Kingdom and " discount house " means a person bona fide carrying on the business of a discount house in the United Kingdom.

Incidental costs of obtaining loan finance.

1980 c. 48.

43.—(1) In section 38 of the Finance Act 1980 (incidental costs of obtaining loan finance)—

> (*a*) at the beginning of subsection (1) there shall be inserted the words " Subject to subsection (3B) below " ;
>
> (*b*) in subsection (2) for the words " Subject to subsection (3) " there shall be substituted the words " Subject to subsections (3) and (3A) " ;   and
>
> (*c*) at the beginning of subsection (3) there shall be inserted the words " Except as provided by subsection (3A) below ".

(2) After subsection (3) of that section there shall be inserted the following subsections : —

> "(3A) A loan or loan stock—
>
> > (*a*) which carries such a right as is referred to in subsection (3) above, and

(*b*) which, by virtue of that subsection, is not a qualifying loan or qualifying loan stock,

shall, nevertheless be regarded as a qualifying loan or qualifying loan stock, as the case may be, if the right is not, or is not wholly, exercised before the expiry of the period of three years from the date when the loan was obtained or the stock was issued.

(3B) For the purposes of the application of subsection (1) above in relation to a loan or loan stock which is a qualifying loan or qualifying loan stock by virtue of subsection (3A) above—

(*a*) if the right referred to in paragraph (*a*) of subsection (3A) above is exercised as to part of the loan or stock within the period referred to in that subsection, only that proportion of the incidental costs of obtaining finance which corresponds to the proportion of the stock in respect of which the right is not exercised within that period shall be taken into account ; and

(*b*) in so far as any of the incidental costs of obtaining finance are incurred before the expiry of the period referred to in subsection (3A) above they shall be treated as incurred immediately after that period expires."

(3) The amendments effected by this section have effect in relation to expenditure incurred on or after 1st April 1983.

44.—(1) For the purposes of sections 256 to 264 (group income and group relief) and 272 to 281 (groups of companies) of the Taxes Act, a trustee savings bank as defined in section 54(1) of the Trustee Savings Banks Act 1981 shall be deemed to be a body corporate.   Trustee savings banks.

1981 c. 65.

(2) In section 272(2) of the Taxes Act (meaning of " company " in provisions relating to transfer of assets within a group of companies) the following shall be added at the end—

" ; and

(*d*) a trustee savings bank as defined in section 54(1) of the Trustee Savings Banks Act 1981.".

(3) Subsection (1) above, so far as it applies to sections 256 and 257 of the Taxes Act, has effect in relation to dividends paid, and other payments made, after the passing of this Act and, so far as it applies to sections 258 to 264 of that Act, has effect in relation to any accounting period of the surrendering company ending on or after 20th November 1982.

PART II

(4) Subsection (2) above, and subsection (1) above so far as it applies to sections 272 to 281, shall be deemed to have come into force on 21st November 1982.

Pension funds etc.: extension of tax exemptions to dealings in financial futures and traded options.

45.—(1) For the purpose of each of the enactments specified in subsection (2) below (which confer on certain pension funds and schemes either exemption from income tax in respect of income derived from investments or exemption from capital gains tax in respect of gains accruing on the disposal of investments) a contract entered into in the course of dealing in financial futures or traded options shall be regarded as an investment.

(2) The enactments referred to in subsection (1) above are—

(*a*) sections 211(2), 214(2), 216(2), 217(2), and 226(6) of the Taxes Act;

1970 c. 24.

(*b*) subsections (2) and (7) of section 21 of the Finance Act 1970; and

1980 c. 48.

(*c*) subsections (2)(*a*) and (3) of section 36 of the Finance Act 1980.

(3) In this section " traded option " means an option which is for the time being quoted on a recognised stock exchange, within the meaning of section 535 of the Taxes Act, or on the London International Financial Futures Exchange.

Consortia: group income and relief.

46.—(1) With respect to dividends and other payments paid or made after 31st December 1984, in section 256 of the Taxes Act (group income) in subsection (6)(*c*) (which provides that, for the purposes of that section, a company is owned by a consortium if, among other conditions, three-quarters of the company's ordinary share capital is beneficially owned by five or fewer companies resident in the United Kingdom) the words " five or fewer " shall be omitted.

(2) In section 258 of the Taxes Act (group relief) for subsection (8) (company owned by a consortium) there shall be substituted the following subsection:—

" (8) For the purposes of this and the following sections of this Chapter, a company is owned by a consortium if three-quarters or more of the ordinary share capital of the company is beneficially owned between them by companies of which none beneficially owns less than one-twentieth of that capital, and those companies are called the members of the consortium."

(3) Subject to subsections (4) and (5) below, subsection (2) above has effect with respect to accounting periods of the surrendering company (within the meaning of the said section 258) ending after the passing of this Act.

(4) In any case where, immediately before the passing of this Act,—

  (*a*) for the purposes of sections 258 onwards of Chapter I of Part XI of the Taxes Act, a company was owned by a consortium, and

  (*b*) any of the members of that consortium beneficially owned less than one-twentieth of the ordinary share capital of the company,

then, as respects accounting periods of the company ending on or before 31st March 1986, if and so long as all the ordinary share capital of the company continues to be beneficially owned between them by five or fewer companies which include a member falling within paragraph (*b*) above, the ordinary share capital which is beneficially owned by that member shall be deemed for the purposes of subsection (8) of section 258 of the Taxes Act (as set out in subsection (2) above) to constitute not less than one-twentieth of that capital.

(5) In any case where section 258(8) of the Taxes Act is relevant to the question whether two companies are associated with one another for the purposes of Part II of the Oil Taxation 1975 c. 22. Act 1975 (by virtue of the definition in section 19(3) of that Act), without prejudice to subsection (4) above, subsection (2) above has effect in relation to any allowance or distribution made, interest paid or other thing done after the passing of this Act.

47.—(1) In section 262 of the Taxes Act (companies joining Group relief: or leaving group or consortium) subsection (2) (true accounting apportion-period to be treated as two or more separate accounting periods ment. with profits and losses etc. apportioned) shall be amended as follows : —

  (*a*) in paragraph (*a*), the words " on a time basis according to their lengths " shall be omitted ; and

  (*b*) in paragraph (*b*), the word " so " shall be omitted ; and

  (*c*) at the end there shall be added the words " and an apportionment under this subsection shall be on a time basis according to the respective lengths of the component accounting periods except that, if it appears that that method would work unreasonably or unjustly, such other method shall be used as appears just and reasonable."

(2) At the end of subsection (4) of the said section 262 (application of subsections (2) and (3) to consortia) there shall be added the words " except that in a case where—

  (*a*) the surrendering company is owned by a consortium and two or more members of the consortium claim relief in respect of losses or other amounts of the surrendering company, or (*b*) the claimant company is owned by a consortium and claims relief in respect of losses or other amounts of two or more members of the consortium,

the basis of apportionment which is adopted under subsection (2) above in relation to the losses or other amounts or, as the case may be, the total profits of the true accounting period of the company owned by the consortium shall be the same on each of the claims."

(3) Subsections (1) and (2) above apply in any case where—

(*a*) the occasion giving rise to the apportionment under subsection (2) of the said section 262 occurs after 13th March 1984 ; and

(*b*) the true accounting period referred to in that subsection begins after 7th November 1983.

Ending of
stock relief.
1981 c. 35.

48.—(1) No relief shall be given and no charge shall be made under Schedule 9 to the Finance Act 1981 in respect of any period of account beginning after 12th March 1984.

(2) The following provisions of that Schedule shall have effect as if any period of account beginning on or before and ending after 12th March 1984 ended on that date—

(*a*) paragraph 3(1), (2) and (4) (entitlement to relief from income tax) ;

(*b*) paragraph 4(1), (3) and (4) (recovery of income tax relief on cessation of trade etc.) ;

(*c*) paragraph 12(1), (2) and (4) (entitlement to relief from corporation tax) ;

(*d*) paragraph 13(1) and (3) (recovery of corporation tax relief on cessation of trade etc.) ;

(*e*) paragraph 19 (new businesses) ;

(*f*) paragraph 20 (successions: transfers between related traders) ;

and accordingly no relief shall be given or charge made under those provisions in respect of any such period of account by virtue of any event occurring after that date.

(3) Subsection (2) above shall not affect the date on which trading stock is to be valued for the purposes of sub-paragraph (2)(*a*) of paragraph 19 of that Schedule.

(4) No obligation shall arise under paragraph 1 of that Schedule to prepare and publish the all stocks index for any month after March 1984.

(5) Where there is a change in the persons carrying on a trade, profession or vocation after 12th March 1984 and (apart from

this subsection) sub-paragraph (2) of paragraph 21 of that Schedule (successions: changes in persons carrying on trades) would apply—

  (*a*) sub-paragraphs (1) to (4) of that paragraph shall not apply ; and

  (*b*) sub-paragraph (5) shall apply with the omission of paragraph (*a*).

(6) An election for the herd basis made under paragraph 2 of Schedule 6 to the Taxes Act after the passing of this Act but not later than two years after the end of the first period of account of the person making the election commencing on or after 13th March 1984 shall be valid notwithstanding that it is not made within the time required by paragraph 2(3) or 6(2) of that Schedule.

(7) An election which is valid by virtue only of subsection (6) above shall have effect only for the first relevant chargeable period and for subsequent chargeable periods.

(8) For the purposes of subsection (7) above the first relevant chargeable period is—

  (*a*) in a case where the election so specifies, the first chargeable period for which the profits or gains or losses of the trade in question are computed by reference to the facts of the period of account commencing on or before and ending after 12th March 1984, or

  (*b*) in any other case, the first chargeable period for which that computation is by reference to the facts of the first period of account commencing on or after 13th March 1984.

(9) In this section " period of account " means any period for which an account is made up for the trade, profession or vocation in question.

49.—(1) This section applies in any case where—

Stock relief: houses taken in part-exchange.

  (*a*) a person carrying on a trade which consists of or includes the construction or substantial reconstruction of dwelling-houses (in this section referred to as a " builder ") disposes to an individual or two or more individuals of his interest in a dwelling-house, and

  (*b*) immediately before the disposal, that interest formed part of the builder's trading stock, otherwise than by virtue of this section, and

  (*c*) the consideration which the builder receives for the disposal consists of or includes an interest in another dwelling-house which, immediately before the disposal, was occupied by the individual or, as the case may be, at least one of the individuals referred to in paragraph (*a*) above or by a relative, and

(*d*) the individual or individuals referred to in paragraph (*a*) above intends or intend that the dwelling-house should be occupied by himself or, as the case may be, by at least one of them or by a relative.

1981 c. 35. (2) Notwithstanding anything in paragraph 28(2) of Schedule 9 to the Finance Act 1981 (which provides that land cannot be trading stock unless it is developed by the person carrying on the trade) in a case where this section applies, the interest referred to in subsection (1)(*c*) above shall form part of the builder's trading stock.

(3) In this section—

(*a*) " dwelling-house " means a building or part of a building which is used or intended to be used as a dwelling ;

(*b*) " relative " means—

(i) the husband or wife of a relevant individual, or

(ii) the parent or remoter forebear, child or remoter issue, or brother or sister of a relevant individual or of the husband or wife of a relevant individual,

" relevant individual " meaning, for this purpose, the individual referred to in subsection (1)(*a*) above or, as the case may be, one of the individuals there referred to ; and

(*c*) " trading stock " has the same meaning as in Schedule 9 to the Finance Act 1981.

(4) This section applies in any case where the disposal referred to in subsection (1)(*a*) above occurred or occurs on or after 15th March 1983.

Furnished holiday lettings. **50.**—(1) Schedule 11 to this Act shall have effect with respect to the treatment for the purposes of income tax, corporation tax and capital gains tax of the commercial letting of furnished holiday accommodation in the United Kingdom.

(2) For the purposes of this section a letting—

(*a*) is a commercial letting if it is on a commercial basis and with a view to the realisation of profits ; and

(*b*) is of furnished accommodation if the tenant is entitled to the use of furniture.

(3) Accommodation shall not be treated as holiday accommodation for the purposes of this section unless—

   (a) it is available for commercial letting to the public generally as holiday accommodation for periods which amount, in the aggregate, to not less than 140 days ;

   (b) the periods for which it is so let amount, in the aggregate, to at least 70 days ; and

   (c) for a period comprising at least seven months (which need not be continuous but includes any months in which it is let as mentioned in paragraph (b) above) it is not normally in the same occupation for a continuous period exceeding 31 days.

(4) Any question whether accommodation let by any person other than a company is, at any time in a year of assessment, holiday accommodation shall be determined—

   (a) if the accommodation was not let by him as furnished accommodation in the preceding year of assessment but is so let in the following year of assessment, by reference to the 12 months beginning with the date on which he first so let it in the year of assessment ;

   (b) if the accommodation was let by him as furnished accommodation in the preceding year of assessment but is not so let in the following year of assessment, by reference to the 12 months ending with the date on which he ceased so to let it in the year of assessment ; and

   (c) in any other case, by reference to the year of assessment.

(5) Any question whether accommodation let by a company is at any time in an accounting period holiday accommodation shall be determined—

   (a) if the accommodation was not let by it as furnished accommodation in the period of 12 months immediately preceding the accounting period but is so let in the period of 12 months immediately following the accounting period, by reference to the 12 months beginning with the date in the accounting period on which it first so let it ;

   (b) if the accommodation was let by it as furnished accommodation in the period of 12 months immediately preceding the accounting period but is not so let by it in the period of 12 months immediately following the accounting period, by reference to the 12 months ending with the date in the accounting period on which it ceased so to let it ; and

(c) in any other case, by reference to the period of 12 months ending with the last day of the accounting period.

(6) Where, in any year of assessment or accounting period, a person lets furnished accommodation which is treated as holiday accommodation for the purposes of this section in that year or period (" the qualifying accommodation "), he may make a claim under this subsection, within two years after that year or period, for averaging treatment to apply for that year or period to that and any other accommodation specified in the claim which was let by him as furnished accommodation during that year or period and would fall to be treated as holiday accommodation in that year or period if paragraph (b) of subsection (3) were satisfied in relation to it.

(7) Where a claim is made under subsection (6) above in respect of any year of assessment or accounting period, any such other accommodation shall be treated as being holiday accommodation in that year or period if the number of days for which the qualifying accommodation and any other such accommodation was let by the claimant as mentioned in paragraph (a) of subsection (3) above during the year or period amounts on average to at least 70.

(8) Qualifying accommodation may not be specified in more than one claim in respect of any one year of assessment or accounting period.

(9) For the purposes of this section a person lets accommodation if he permits another person to occupy it, whether or not in pursuance of a lease ; and " letting " and " tenant " shall be construed accordingly.

(10) This section has effect—

(a) for the purposes of income tax for the year 1982-83 and subsequent years of assessment ;

(b) for the purposes of capital gains tax and corporation tax on chargeable gains—

(i) in so far as it applies in relation to sections 115 to 120 of the Capital Gains Tax Act 1979, where the acquisition of, or of the interest in, the new assets takes place on or after 6th April 1982, and

(ii) otherwise, in relation to disposals made on or after that date ; and

(c) for the purposes of corporation tax, otherwise than on chargeable gains, in relation to accounting periods commencing in the financial year 1982 and subsequent periods.

1979 c. 14.

51.—(1) In section 92 of the Taxes Act, after subsection (3) (meaning of " occupier " for purposes of Schedule B), there shall be inserted the following subsection—

" (4) A person who, in connection with any trade carried on by him, has the use of any woodlands wholly or mainly for the purpose of—

    (a) felling, processing or removing timber ; or

    (b) clearing or otherwise preparing the lands, or any part of them, for replanting ;

shall not be treated as an occupier of the lands for the purposes of Schedule B and subsections (1) and (2) above.".

(2) This section has effect in relation to any use commencing after 13th March 1984.

52.—(1) In section 85 of the Finance Act 1972 (payments of advance corporation tax to be set against a company's liability to corporation tax), in subsection (3), for the words " two years ", in the second place where they occur, there shall be substituted the words " six years ".

(2) Subject to subsection (3) below, subsection (1) above has effect with respect to accounting periods ending on or after 1st April 1984 in which there is an amount of surplus advance corporation tax.

(3) Notwithstanding the amendment made by subsection (1) above, if a company claims under subsection (3) of the said section 85 to have any surplus advance corporation tax of an accounting period (in this subsection referred to as " the basis period ") treated for the purposes of that section as if it were advance corporation tax paid in respect of distributions made by the company in an accounting period—

    (a) which ends before 1st April 1984, and

    (b) which begins outside the two years preceding the basis period,

the amount of that surplus advance corporation tax which may be so treated shall be limited to so much of that surplus as was paid by the company (and not repaid) in respect of distributions actually made in the basis period.

53.—(1) In section 100 of the Finance Act 1972 (double taxation relief) in subsection (3) for the words " to (6) " there shall be substituted the words " and (5) "; in subsection (4) for the words " subsections (5) and (6) " there shall be substituted the words " subsection (5) "; and in subsection (6), for paragraphs (a) and (b) and the following words, there shall be substituted the following : —

" (a) so far as that liability relates to the relevant income, it shall be taken to be reduced by the amount of the credit for foreign tax attributable to that income, as determined in accordance with subsections (4) and (5) above ; and

(*b*) subject to paragraph (*c*) below, the company may for the purposes of this section allocate that advance corporation tax in such amounts and to the corporation tax attributable for that period as it thinks fit ; and

(*c*) the amount of advance corporation tax which may be allocated to the corporation tax attributable to the relevant income shall not exceed the amount of corporation tax which remains so attributable after the reduction under paragraph (*a*) above ;

and if the limit which is imposed by paragraph (*c*) above on the amount of advance corporation tax which may be set against the company's liability to corporation tax on its relevant income is lower than the limit which would apply under section 85(2) above if the relevant income were the company's only income for the relevant accounting period, the limit in paragraph (*c*) above shall apply in relation to the relevant income and section 85(2) above shall have effect in relation only to so much of the income of the company chargeable to corporation tax for that period as does not include the relevant income."

(2) In section 85(3) of that Act (surplus advance corporation tax) after the words " subsection (2) above " there shall be inserted the words " or section 100(6) below ".

(3) This section applies to accounting periods ending on or after 1st April 1984.

Exemption from tax of regional development grants.

54.—(1) A regional development grant—

(*a*) which is made to a person carrying on a trade, and

(*b*) which, apart from this subsection, would be taken into account as a receipt in computing the profits of that trade,

shall not be taken into account as a receipt in computing the profits of the trade which are chargeable under Case I of Schedule D.

(2) A regional development grant which is made to an investment company as defined in subsection (5) of section 304 of the Taxes Act—

(*a*) shall not be taken into account as a receipt in computing its profits under Case VI of Schedule D ; and

(*b*) shall not be deducted, by virtue of the proviso to subsection (1) of that section, from the amount treated as expenses of management.

(3) In this section " regional development grant " means a PART II payment by way of grant under Part II of the Industrial Devel- 1982 c. 52. opment Act 1982 (regional development grants).

(4) This section applies in relation to a profession or vocation as it applies to a trade, taking the reference in subsection (1) above to Case I of Schedule D as a reference to Case II of that Schedule.

55.—(1) In section 42 of the Finance Act 1980 (certain pay- Grants to ments by way of grant to be taken into account as receipts in assist industry computing profits) in subsection (2), at the end of paragraph in Northern Ireland. (*b*) there shall be inserted " or 1980 c. 48.

> (*c*) any of Articles 7, 9 and 30 of the Industrial Develop- S.I. 1982/1083
> ment (Northern Ireland) Order 1982 " ; (N.I. 15).

and at the end of the subsection there shall be added the words " and other than a grant falling within subsection (3) below ".

(2) At the end of the said section 42 there shall be added the following subsection : —

> " (3) A payment by way of grant which is made—
>
> > (*a*) under Article 7 of the Order referred to in sub-section (2)(*c*) above, and
> >
> > (*b*) in respect of a liability for corporation tax (in-cluding a liability which has already been met),
>
> shall not be taken into account as mentioned in subsection (1) above, whether by virtue of this section or otherwise."

(3) This section has effect with respect to payments made on or after 1st April 1984.

56.—(1) Section 341A of the Taxes Act (tax exemptions for Certain reliefs self-build societies) shall extend to Northern Ireland and in sub- extended to section (11) (definitions) after the words " Part I of the Housing Northern Ireland Act 1974 " there shall be inserted the words " or, in Northern housing Ireland, Part VII of the Housing (Northern Ireland) Order associations 1981 " and at the end of the section there shall be added the and societies. following subsection : — 1974 c. 44.

> " (12) In the application of this section to Northern S.I. 1981/1561
> Ireland— (N.I. 3).
>
> > (*a*) any reference in subsections (4) to (6) above to the Secretary of State shall be construed as a reference to the Department of the Environment for Northern Ireland ;
> >
> > (*b*) the reference in subsection (4)(*a*) to the Industrial 1965 c. 12.
> > and Provident Societies Act 1965 shall be con-

PART II
1969 c. 24
(N.I.).

S.I. 1979/1573
(N.I. 12).

1954 c. 33
(N.I.).

strued as a reference to the Industrial and Provident Societies Act (Northern Ireland) 1969 ; and

(c) in subsection (6) any reference to a statutory instrument shall be construed as a reference to a statutory rule for the purposes of the Statutory Rules (Northern Ireland) Order 1979 and for the words from " annulment " onwards there shall be substituted the words " negative resolution within the meaning of section 41(6) of the Interpretation Act (Northern Ireland) 1954 "."

1982 c. 39.

(2) In consequence of the amendments effected by subsection (1) above, in section 29 of the Finance Act 1982 (supplementary regulations as to deduction of tax from certain loan interest) subsection (1)(b) (self-build societies) shall be amended as follows : —

S.I. 1981/1561
(N.I. 3).

(a) after the words " Part I of the Housing Act 1974 " there shall be added the words " or, in Northern Ireland, Part VII of the Housing (Northern Ireland) Order 1981 " ; and

(b) at the end there shall be added the words " or Northern Ireland ".

(3) After section 342A of the Taxes Act there shall be inserted the following section—

" Disposals by Northern Ireland housing associations.

342B.—(1) In any case where—

(a) a registered Northern Ireland housing association disposes of any land to another such association, or

(b) in pursuance of a direction of the Department of the Environment for Northern Ireland given under Chapter II of Part VII of the Housing (Northern Ireland) Order 1981 requiring it to do so, a registered Northern Ireland housing association disposes of any of its property, other than land, to another such association,

both parties to the disposal shall be treated for the purposes of corporation tax in respect of chargeable gains as if the land or property disposed of were acquired from the association making the disposal for a consideration of such an amount as would secure that on the disposal neither a gain nor a loss accrued to that association.

(2) In subsection (1) above " registered Northern Ireland housing association " means a registered housing association within the meaning of Part VII of the Order referred to in paragraph (b) of that subsection."

(4) Subsection (1) above has effect for the year 1984-85 and subsequent years of assessment and subsection (3) above has effect with respect to disposals on or after 6th April 1984.

57.—(1) In section 65 of the Taxes Management Act 1970 (recovery of assessed tax in magistrates' courts)—

(a) in subsection (1) for " £50 " in each place where it occurs there shall be substituted " £250 " ;

(b) in subsection (4) for the words from " in the manner " to the end there shall be substituted the words " in proceedings under Article 62 of the Magistrates' Courts (Northern Ireland) Order 1981 " ; and

(c) at the end of that section there shall be added the following subsection—

" (5) The Treasury may by order made by statutory instrument increase the sums specified in subsection (1) above ; and any such statutory instrument shall be subject to annulment in pursuance of a resolution of the Commons House of Parliament."

(2) In section 66 of that Act (recovery of assessed tax in county courts) for subsection (2) there shall be substituted the following subsection—

" (2) An officer of the Board who is authorised by the Board to do so may address the court in any proceedings under this section in a county court in England and Wales."

PART II

Proceedings in magistrates' courts and county courts.
1970 c. 9.

S.I. 1981/1675 (N.I. 26).

CHAPTER II

CAPITAL ALLOWANCES

58.—(1) Each of the following allowances in respect of capital expenditure, namely,—

(a) initial allowances under section 1 of the Capital Allowances Act 1968 (industrial buildings and structures),

(b) first-year allowances under section 41 of the Finance Act 1971 (machinery and plant), and

(c) initial allowances under Schedule 12 to the Finance Act 1982 (dwelling-houses let on assured tenancies),

shall be progressively withdrawn in accordance with Part I of Schedule 12 to this Act.

(2) Part II of Schedule 12 to this Act shall have effect—

(a) to provide transitional relief in respect of certain capital expenditure incurred in connection with projects in development areas and Northern Ireland ; and

Withdrawal of initial and first-year allowances.
1968 c. 3.
1971 c. 68.

1982 c. 39.

(*b*) with respect to the treatment of certain capital expenditure incurred in the financial years 1984 and 1985 under contracts entered into after 13th March 1984 and on or before 31st March 1986.

(3) In paragraph 8 of Schedule 8 to the Finance Act 1971 (special rules for new ships) in sub-paragraph (2)(*b*) for the words " the expenditure to which the allowance relates " there shall be substituted the words " so much of the expenditure as is equal to the whole allowance."

(4) Nothing in subsection (1)(*a*) above or in paragraph 1 of Schedule 12 to this Act affects the continuing operation of—

(*a*) paragraph 1 of Schedule 6 to the Finance Act 1978 (20 per cent. initial allowance for capital expenditure in respect of hotels) ; or

(*b*) paragraph 1 of Schedule 13 to the Finance Act 1980 (100 per cent. initial allowance for capital expenditure in respect of industrial buildings etc. in enterprise zones and for capital expenditure incurred before 27th March 1985 in respect of small workshops) ;

and paragraph 5 of Schedule 12 to this Act does not apply to expenditure in respect of which the rate of initial allowance is determined by the provision referred to in paragraph (*b*) above.

59.—(1) In section 44 of the Finance Act 1971 (writing-down allowances in respect of expenditure on machinery or plant) after subsection (2) there shall be inserted the following subsection :—

" (2A) For any chargeable period ending after 13th March 1984 for which a company has qualifying expenditure, the company may, by notice in writing given to the inspector not later than two years after the end of that period, either disclaim a writing-down allowance or require that the allowance be reduced to an amount specified in that behalf in the notice " ;

and, in subsection (4) of that section, after " (2) " there shall be inserted " (2A) ".

(2) With respect to expenditure incurred after 13th March 1984, sub-paragraph (1) of paragraph 8 of Schedule 8 to the Finance Act 1971 (special rules for new ships) shall be amended by substituting for the words from " require the postponement " onwards the words—

" (*a*) require the postponement of the whole allowance or, in the case of a company, disclaim it, or

(*b*) require that the amount of the allowance be reduced to an amount specified in the notice, or

(c) require the postponement of so much of the allowance as is so specified,

and a notice which contains a requirement under paragraph (b) above may also contain a requirement under paragraph (c) above with respect to the reduced amount of the allowance ".

(3) In consequence of the amendment made by subsection (2) above, the said paragraph 8 shall also be amended, with respect to expenditure incurred after 13th March 1984, as follows—

(a) in sub-paragraph (2) for the words " in respect " there shall be substituted the words " requiring the postponement of the whole or part " ; and

(b) at the end there shall be added the following sub-paragraph : —

" (6) In any case where a notice under sub-paragraph (1) above contains requirements under both paragraphs (b) and (c) of that sub-paragraph, any reference in sub-paragraphs (2) to (5) above to the first-year allowance is a reference to the reduced amount of that allowance as specified in the notice."

(4) In any case where—

(a) after 13th March 1984, a company carrying on a trade incurs capital expenditure on the provision of machinery or plant for the purposes of the trade, and

(b) apart from any disclaimer of the allowance, a first-year allowance would fall to be made for any chargeable period in respect of that expenditure, and

(c) the company disclaims the allowance by notice under section 41(3) of the Finance Act 1971 or (in the case 1971 c. 68. of new ships) under paragraph 8(1)(a) of Schedule 8 to that Act,

then, for the purposes of section 44 of that Act, that expenditure shall not, by virtue of sub-paragraph (ii) of paragraph (a) of subsection (4) of that section, be excluded from the capital expenditure referred to in that paragraph.

(5) In any case where—

(a) after 13th March 1984, a person carrying on a trade, but not being a company, incurs capital expenditure on the provision of machinery or plant for the purposes of the trade, and

(b) if a claim were made in that behalf, a first-year allowance would fall to be made in respect of that expenditure for the chargeable period related to the incurring of it, and

(c) no claim is so made but, by notice in writing given to the inspector not later than two years after the end of that chargeable period, the person concerned elects that this subsection shall apply,

then, for the purposes of section 44 of the Finance Act 1971, that expenditure shall not, by virtue of sub-paragraph (ii) of paragraph (a) of subsection (4) of that section, be excluded from the capital expenditure referred to in that paragraph.

(6) In any case where—

(a) after 13th March 1984, a person (whether a company or not) carrying on a trade has incurred capital expenditure on the provision of machinery or plant for the purposes of the trade, and

(b) a first-year allowance falls to be made to that person in respect of that expenditure (and, in the case of a person other than a company, a claim is made for that allowance), and

(c) for the chargeable period related to the incurring of that expenditure, the amount of that first-year allowance or, as the case may be, the aggregate amount of that and other first-year allowances which fall to be made to that person is required to be reduced by virtue of section 41(3) of the Finance Act 1971 or (in the case of new ships) paragraph 8(1)(b) of Schedule 8 to that Act,

then, for the purposes of section 44 of that Act, an amount equal to the relevant portion of so much of the expenditure giving rise to the first-year allowance or allowances referred to in paragraph (c) above as was incurred after 13th March 1984 shall be treated as expenditure in respect of which no first-year allowance is or could be made for the chargeable period in question.

(7) In subsection (6) above " the relevant portion " of expenditure giving rise to a first-year allowance or allowances and incurred after 13th March 1984 is that which bears to the whole of that expenditure the same proportion as the amount of the reduction mentioned in paragraph (c) of that subsection bears to what the amount of the allowance or allowances would have been apart from that reduction.

(8) Subsections (2) to (7) above shall be construed as if they were contained in Chapter I of Part III of the Finance Act 1971.

60.—(1) This section shall have effect in relation to any transfer of assets made pursuant to a direction under section 11 of the Oil and Gas (Enterprise) Act 1982 by the British Gas Corporation or any relevant subsidiary, within the meaning of that section, other than a transfer of assets made on any transfer of a trade to which section 252 of the Taxes Act applies.

(2) The transfer shall not give rise to any allowance or charge provided for by Chapter I of Part III of the Finance Act 1971 (capital allowances and charges in respect of machinery and plant) or the Capital Allowances Act 1968. 1971 c. 68.

1968 c. 3.

(3) Paragraph 3 of Schedule 8 to the 1971 Act and section 78 of, and Schedule 7 to, the 1968 Act (special rules for sales between connected persons) shall not apply in relation to the transfer.

(4) In respect of any chargeable period beginning after the transfer there shall be made in accordance with the provisions mentioned in subsection (2) above all such further allowances and charges in respect of the assets transferred by the transfer as would have fallen to be made if—

(a) everything done to or by the transferor in relation to the assets (other than the transfer) had been done to or by the transferee ;

(b) the trade carried on by the transferee, in relation to which the assets are first used by it after the transfer, were the same trade as the trade in relation to which the transferor used the assets at the time of the transfer ; and

(c) that trade had been carried on by the transferee since the transferor began to carry it on.

(5) This section has effect in relation to transfers whenever made.

61.—(1) In section 43(3) of the Finance Act 1971 (by virtue of which restrictions on the making of first-year allowances for vehicles do not apply to vehicles provided wholly or mainly for the use of persons in receipt of certain mobility allowances) and in subsection (12) of section 64 of the Finance Act 1980 (by virtue of which the provisions of that section excluding such allowances for certain leased assets do not apply to such vehicles)— First-year
allowances:
recipients of
mobility
supplement.
1980 c. 48.

(a) the words from " a mobility allowance " onwards shall become paragraph (a) ; and

(b) after that paragraph there shall be inserted—

" (b) a mobility supplement under a scheme made under the Personal Injuries (Emergency Provisions) Act 1939 ; or 1939 c. 82.

(c) a mobility supplement under an Order in Council made under section 12 of the Social Security (Miscellaneous Provisions) Act 1977 ; or 1977 c. 5.

      (*d*) any payment appearing to the Treasury to be of a similar kind and specified by them by order made by statutory instrument.

An order made under paragraph (*d*) above may provide that it has effect in relation to expenditure incurred on or after 21st November 1983 (expenditure being taken to be incurred for this purpose on the date when the sums in question become payable).".

(2) The amendment made by paragraph (*b*) of subsection (1) above applies in relation to expenditure incurred on or after 21st November 1983 and for the purposes of this subsection expenditure is incurred on the date when the sums in question become payable.

Expenditure
on production
or acquisition
of films etc.
1982 c. 39.

    62.—(1) Section 72 of the Finance Act 1982 (expenditure on production and acquisition of films etc.) shall be amended in accordance with the provisions of this section.

(2) In subsection (3) (expenditure to be allocated to relevant periods in accordance with subsection (4)) for the words " subsection (4) ", in both places where they occur, there shall be substituted the words " subsections (4) to (4B) " and at the beginning of subsection (4) there shall be inserted the words " Subject to subsection (4A) below ".

(3) After subsection (4) there shall be inserted the following subsections : —

" (4A) In addition to any expenditure which is allocated to a relevant period in accordance with subsection (4) above, if a claim is made in that behalf not later than two years after the end of that period, there shall also be allocated to that period so much of the unallocated expenditure as is specified in the claim and does not exceed the difference between—

    (*a*) the amount allocated to that period in accordance with subsection (4) above ; and

    (*b*) the value of the film, tape or disc which is realised in that period (whether by way of income or otherwise).

(4B) As respects any relevant period, ' the unallocated expenditure ' referred to in subsection (4A) above is that expenditure falling within subsection (3) above—

    (*a*) which does not fall to be allocated to that period in accordance with subsection (4) above ; and

    (*b*) which has not been allocated to any earlier relevant period in accordance with subsection (4) or subsection (4A) above."

(4) In subsection (5) (exclusion of trading stock) for the words "and (4)" there shall be substituted the words "to (4B)".

(5) In subsection (7) (which, as amended by section 32(1) of the Finance Act 1983, provides transitional relief for certain expenditure incurred on or before 31st March 1987) the words "on or before 31st March 1987" shall cease to have effect.

(6) In subsection (8) (conditions for certification) after the words "this section" there shall be inserted the words "unless, by notice in writing given by the person incurring the expenditure, he is requested to do so and".

CHAPTER III

CAPITAL GAINS

63.—(1) In the Capital Gains Tax Act 1979,—

(*a*) section 6 (gains accruing to an individual on gifts of assets not exceeding £100 in any year not to be chargeable gains), and

(*b*) sections 8 and 9 (postponement of payment of tax),

shall cease to have effect.

(2) In section 107 of that Act (small part disposals of land) in each of paragraphs (*a*) and (*b*) of subsection (3) (the monetary limits) for "£10,000" there shall be substituted "£20,000".

(3) In section 80 of the Finance Act 1980 (exemption for gains on letting of private residences) in subsection (1)(*b*) (the monetary limit) for "£10,000" there shall be substituted "£20,000".

(4) In section 124 of the Capital Gains Tax Act 1979 (relief for transfer of business on retirement) in subsection (3) (the monetary limits)—

(*a*) in paragraph (*a*) for "£50,000", there shall be substituted "£100,000"; and

(*b*) in paragraph (*b*) for "£10,000", in each place where it occurs, there shall be substituted "£20,000".

(5) Subsection (1) above has effect with respect to disposals on or after 6th April 1984 and subsections (2) to (4) above have effect with respect to disposals on or after 6th April 1983.

64.—(1) Part I of Schedule 13 to this Act shall have effect for the purpose of—

(*a*) providing, in relation to qualifying corporate bonds, an exemption from capital gains tax and corporation tax on chargeable gains similar to that provided in relation to gilt-edged securities by Part IV of the Capital Gains Tax Act 1979 ; and

(b) making corresponding amendments of other enactments.

(2) For the purposes of this section, a " corporate bond " is a security, as defined in section 82(3)(b) of the Capital Gains Tax Act 1979,—

(a) which, from the time of its issue, has been quoted on a recognised stock exchange in the United Kingdom or dealt in on the Unlisted Securities Market or which was issued by a body of which, at the time of the issue, any other share, stock or security was so quoted or dealt in ; and

(b) the debt on which represents and has at all times represented a normal commercial loan, as defined in paragraph 1(5) of Schedule 12 to the Finance Act 1973 ; and

(c) which is expressed in sterling and in respect of which no provision is made for conversion into, or redemption in, a currency other than sterling.

(3) For the purposes of subsection (2)(c) above,—

(a) a security shall not be regarded as expressed in sterling if the amount of sterling falls to be determined by reference to the value at any time of any other currency or asset ; and

(b) a provision for redemption in a currency other than sterling but at the rate of exchange prevailing at redemption shall be disregarded.

(4) Subject to subsection (6) below, for the purposes of this section and Schedule 13 to this Act, a corporate bond—

(a) is a " qualifying " corporate bond if it is issued after 13th March 1984 ; and

(b) becomes a " qualifying " corporate bond if, having been issued on or before that date, it is acquired by any person after that date and that acquisition is not as a result of a disposal which is excluded for the purposes of this subsection.

(5) Where a person disposes of a corporate bond which was issued on or before 13th March 1984 and, before the disposal, the bond had not become a qualifying corporate bond, the disposal is excluded for the purposes of subsection (4) above if, by virtue of any enactment,—

(a) the disposal is treated for the purposes of the Capital Gains Tax Act 1979 as one on which neither a gain nor a loss accrues to the person making the disposal ; or (*b*) the consideration for the disposal is treated for the purposes of that Act as reduced by an amount equal to the held-over gain on that disposal, as defined for the purposes of section 126 of that Act or section 79 of the Finance Act 1980.

(6) A security which is issued by a member of a group of companies to another member of the same group is not a qualifying corporate bond for the purposes of this section or Schedule 13 to this Act ; and references in this subsection to a group of companies or to a member of a group shall be construed in accordance with section 272 of the Taxes Act.

(7) Part II of Schedule 13 to this Act shall have effect in any case where a transaction occurs of such a description that, apart from the provisions of that Schedule,—

(*a*) sections 78 to 81 of the Capital Gains Tax Act 1979 would apply by virtue of any provision of Chapter II of Part IV of that Act ; and

(*b*) either the original shares would consist of or include a qualifying corporate bond and the new holding would not, or the original shares would not and the new holding would consist of or include such a bond ;

and in paragraph (*b*) above " the original shares " and " the new holding " have the same meaning as they have for the purposes of the said sections 78 to 81.

(8) For the purposes of this section, in any case where—

(*a*) a security is comprised in a letter of allotment or similar instrument, and

(*b*) the right to the security thereby conferred remains provisional until accepted,

the security shall not be treated as issued until there has been acceptance.

65.—(1) In section 137(4)(*aa*) of the Capital Gains Tax Act Traded 1979 (abandonment of traded option to buy or sell shares in a options. company) and section 138(1)(*aa*) of that Act (restriction of allowable expenditure in relation to such an option) the words " to buy or sell shares in a company " shall be omitted.

(2) At the end of section 137(9) of that Act (definition of " traded option ") there shall be added the words " or on the London International Financial Futures Exchange ".

(3) This section has effect in relation to any abandonment or other disposal on or after 6th April 1984.

PART II
Disposals and
acquisitions
treated as
made at
market value:
removal of
certain
exceptions.
1979 c. 14.

66.—(1) In section 29A of the Capital Gains Tax Act 1979 (certain disposals and acquisitions treated as made at market value) in subsection (2) (which, among other things, excludes certain acquisitions where the corresponding disposal is made by an excluded person) the words " Except in the case specified in subsection (4) below " and, in paragraph (*a*), the words " or the corresponding disposal is made by an excluded person " shall be omitted.

(2) For subsections (3) and (4) of the said section 29A there shall be substituted the following subsections:—

" (3) In any case where—

(*a*) apart from this subsection, subsection (1) above would apply to the acquisition of an asset, and

(*b*) the condition in subsection (2)(*b*) above is fulfilled with respect to the acquisition, and

(*c*) the corresponding disposal is made on or after 6th April 1983 and before 6th April 1985, and

(*d*) the corresponding disposal is made by an excluded person who is within the charge to capital gains tax or corporation tax in respect of any chargeable gain accruing to him on the disposal,

then, if the person acquiring the asset and the excluded person so elect by notice in writing given to the Board within the period of two years beginning at the end of the chargeable period in which the corresponding disposal is made, subsection (1) above shall not apply to the acquisition or the corresponding disposal.

(4) There shall be made all such adjustments of capital gains tax or corporation tax (in respect of chargeable gains), whether by way of assessment or by way of discharge or repayment of tax, as may be required in consequence of the making of an election under subsection (3) above."

(3) Subsections (5) and (6) of section 32 of the Capital Gains Tax Act 1979 (special rules as to sums allowable on account of expenditure in certain cases of disposals by non-residents) shall not apply where the disposal by the person who is neither resident nor ordinarily resident in the United Kingdom is made on or after 6th April 1985.

(4) Subsections (1) and (2) above have effect in relation to acquisitions and disposals on or after 6th April 1983.

Parallel
pooling.
1983 c. 28.

67.—(1) Schedule 6 to the Finance Act 1983 (election for pooling) shall have effect, and be deemed always to have had effect, with the amendments set out in the following provisions of this section.

(2) In paragraph 1 (interpretation) at the end of sub-paragraph (2) (which excludes certain assets from being qualifying securities for the purposes of that Schedule) there shall be added the words " nor

> (c) securities which are, or have at any time after the expiry of the period which, in relation to a disposal of them, would be the qualifying period, been material interests in a non-qualifying offshore fund, within the meaning of Chapter VII of Part II of the Finance Act 1984 ".

(3) In sub-paragraph (5) of paragraph 3 (effect of election: time when the holding comes into being) in paragraph (b) for the words " on 1st April 1982 " there shall be substituted the words " immediately before 1st April 1982 ".

(4) In paragraph 9 (transfers on a no gain/no loss basis) for sub-paragraphs (2) and (3) there shall be substituted the following sub-paragraphs: —

> " (2) The disposal referred to in sub-paragraph (1) above shall be regarded for the purposes of this Schedule as an operative event.

> (3) Notwithstanding anything in paragraph 2 of Schedule 13 to the 1982 Act, the amount which, on the disposal referred to in sub-paragraph (1) above, is to be regarded as the consideration given by the second company for the acquisition of the securities (and, accordingly, the amount which is to be added to that company's unindexed pool of expenditure on the disposal) shall not include the indexation allowance on that disposal.

> (4) Nothing in sub-paragraph (3) above affects the amount which, by virtue of paragraph 2(3) of Schedule 13 to the 1982 Act, is to be treated as the consideration received by the first company on the disposal referred to in sub-paragraph (1) above, and it shall be that amount (rather than the smaller amount referred to in sub-paragraph (3) above) which, on that disposal, shall be added to the second company's indexed pool of expenditure.

> (5) Paragraph 3 of Schedule 13 to the 1982 Act shall not apply on any subsequent disposal of the holding in which the securities referred to in sub-paragraph (1) above are comprised."

68. In consequence of the operation of section 79 of the Finance Act 1980 (general relief for gifts) section 148 of the Capital Gains Tax Act 1979 (specific relief in the case of certain disposals relating to maintenance funds for historic buildings) shall cease to have effect with respect to disposals made on or after 6th April 1984.

Maintenance funds for historic buildings.
1980 c. 48.
1979 c. 14.

69.—(1) At the end of subsection (4) of section 18 of the Capital Gains Tax Act 1979 (location of assets) there shall be added the following paragraph—

" (*j*) a debt which—

    (i) is owed by a bank, and

    (ii) is not in sterling, and

    (iii) is represented by a sum standing to the credit of an account in the bank of an individual who is not domiciled in the United Kingdom,

is situated in the United Kingdom if and only if that individual is resident in the United Kingdom and the branch or other place of business of the bank at which the account is maintained is itself situated in the United Kingdom."

(2) Subsection (1) above shall be deemed to have come into force on 6th April 1983.

Postponement
of tax due
from
beneficiaries
on gains of
non-resident
trustees.

70.—(1) The provisions of Schedule 14 to this Act have effect in any case where,—

    (*a*) before 6th April 1981, a chargeable gain accrued to the trustees of a settlement in such circumstances that section 17 of the Capital Gains Tax Act 1979 (non-resident trust) applies as respects that chargeable gain ; and

    (*b*) by virtue of that section a beneficiary under the settlement is treated for the purposes of that Act as if, in the year 1983-84 or any earlier year of assessment, an amount determined by reference to the chargeable gain which accrued to the trustees or, as the case may be, the whole or part of that gain had been a chargeable gain accruing to the beneficiary ; and

    (*c*) at 29th March 1983 some or all of the capital gains tax payable in respect of the chargeable gain accruing to the beneficiary had not been paid.

(2) In subsection (3)(*b*) of the said section 17 (which relates to capital payments which are made in the exercise of a discretion, which are received at any time and which represent a chargeable gain to which that section applies) after the words " after the chargeable gain accrues " there shall be inserted the words " but before 6th April 1984 ".

(3) In consequence of the amendment made by subsection (2) above, in section 80 of the Finance Act 1981 (new provisions as to gains of non-resident settlements) in subsection (8) (which, among other things, excludes from the scope of that section payments received on or after 10th March 1981 so far as they re-

present chargeable gains accruing to the trustees before 6th
April 1981) after the words " received on or after that date "
there shall be inserted the words " and before 6th April 1984 ".

(4) In this section and Schedule 14 to this Act " settlement ",
" settlor " and " settled property " have the same meaning as in
section 17 of the Capital Gains Tax Act 1979.   1979 c. 14.

71.—(1) At the end of section 83 of the Finance Act 1981   Non-resident
(definitions etc. for provisions relating to gains of non-resident   settlements:
settlements) there shall be added the following subsection—   definition of
     " settlement "

    " (7) In sections 80 to 82 above and in the preceding   and " settlor ".
    provisions of this section—   1981 c. 35.

     " settlement " and " settlor " have the meaning given
       by section 454(3) of the Taxes Act and " settlor "
       includes, in the case of a settlement arising under
       a will or intestacy, the testator or intestate ; and
    " settled property " shall be construed accordingly."

(2) This section has effect for the year 1984-85 and subsequent years of assessment.

CHAPTER IV

INSURANCE

72.—(1) Relief shall not be granted under section 19 of the   Withdrawal
Taxes Act (premium relief on post-1916 life policies etc.) in   of life
respect of premiums payable under any policy issued in respect   assurance
of an insurance made after 13th March 1984, except where the   premium
relief relates to part only of any such payment as falls within   relief.
paragraph 11 of Schedule 3 to the Finance Act 1978 (part pay-   1978 c. 42.
ments to friendly societies).

(2) A policy which was issued in the course of industrial
assurance business, within the meaning of the Industrial Assurance Act 1923 or, as the case may be, the Industrial Assurance   1923 c. 8.
(Northern Ireland) Order 1979, and which was so issued in res-   S.I. 1979/1574
pect of an insurance made after 13th March 1984 shall be   (N.I. 13).
treated for the purposes of this section as issued in respect of
an insurance made on or before that date if—

    (a) the proposal form for the policy was completed on or
       before that date, and

    (b) on or before 31st March 1984 the policy was prepared
       for issue by the company or society concerned, and

    (c) on or before 31st March 1984 and in accordance with
       the normal business practice of the company or soc-
       iety a permanent record of the preparation of the
       policy was made in any book or by any other means

kept or instituted by the company or society for the purpose.

(3) For the purposes of subsection (1) above, a policy of life insurance which was issued in respect of an insurance made on or before 13th March 1984 shall be treated as issued in respect of an insurance made after that date if the policy is varied after that date so as to increase the benefits secured or to extend the term of the insurance.

(4) If a policy of life insurance which was issued as mentioned in subsection (3) above confers on the person to whom it was issued an option to have another policy substituted for it or to have any of its terms changed, then, for the purposes of that subsection and subsection (1) above, any change in the terms of the policy which is made in pursuance of the option shall be deemed to be a variation of the policy.

1975 c. 7.

(5) In subsection (8) of section 7 of the Finance Act 1975 (early surrender or conversion of life policies), after the word " apply " in the second place where it occurs, and in subsection (5) of section 8 of that Act (surrender etc. of policies after four years), after the word " apply ", there shall be inserted—

" (a) to a policy in respect of the premiums on which relief under section 19 of that Act is not available, by virtue of section 72 of the Finance Act 1984 ; or

(b) ".

(6) In any case where—

(a) one policy is replaced by another in such circumstances that the provisions of subsection (1) of section 34 of the

1982 c. 39.

Finance Act 1982 apply (variation in life or lives assured), and

(b) the earlier policy was issued in respect of an insurance made on or before 13th March 1984, and

(c) the later policy confers on the life or lives assured thereby benefits which are substantially equivalent to those which would have been enjoyed by the life or lives assured under the earlier policy, if that policy had continued in force,

then, for the purposes of subsection (1) above, the insurance in respect of which the later policy is issued shall be deemed to have been made before 13th March 1984 ; and in this subsection " the earlier policy " and " the later policy " have the same meaning as in the said section 34.

(7) In any case where—

(a) there is a substitution of policies falling within subparagraph (1) or sub-paragraph (3) of paragraph 2 of Schedule 15 to this Act, and

(b) the old policy was issued in respect of an insurance
made on or before 13th March 1984,

then, for the purposes of subsection (1) above, the insurance in respect of which the new policy is issued shall be deemed to have been made before 13th March 1984 ; and in this subsection " the old policy " and " the new policy " have the same meaning as in paragraph 9 of Schedule 1 to the Taxes Act.

(8) In any case where, before the passing of this Act—

    (a) an individual, in exercise of the right conferred on him by paragraph 5(a) of Schedule 4 to the Finance Act 1976 c. 40. 1976, has deducted an amount from a payment in respect of a premium falling within subsection (1) above, and

    (b) in accordance with paragraphs 4(1) and 5(b) of that Schedule, the Board have made good to the person to whom that payment was made the deficiency arising from that deduction,

then, without prejudice to any other power of the Board to recover sums which have been paid to make good any such deficiency (being a deficiency which would not have arisen if this Act had been in force on the date referred to in subsection (1) above), those sums may be recovered by the Board by deduction from any further sums which, after the passing of this Act, fall to be paid to the person concerned in accordance with the said paragraphs 4(1) and 5(b).

(9) The aggregate of any amounts which, as mentioned in subsection (8)(a) above, an individual has deducted from payments in respect of premiums falling within subsection (1) above may be recovered by the person to whom those payments were made as if it were an additional premium due under the policy on 5th August 1984 ; but no account shall be taken of that additional premium—

    (a) in determining whether the policy is a qualifying policy within the meaning of Schedule 1 to the Taxes Act ; or

    (b) for the purposes of section 334 of that Act (conditions for tax exempt business) ; or

    (c) for the purposes of section 395 of that Act or paragraph 9 of Schedule 2 to the Finance Act 1975 (chargeable 1975 c. 7. events legislation).

73.—(1) In relation to registered friendly societies, references Insurance to tax exempt life or endowment business, as defined in section business of 337(3) of the Taxes Act, shall be construed in accordance with registered subsections (2) and (3) below. friendly societies.

(2) In so far as the profits of a registered friendly society from life or endowment business relate to contracts made after

PART II

13th March 1984, the references in subsections (2) and (3) of section 332 of the Taxes Act (business exempt from income tax and corporation tax) to £500 and £104 (the basic limits for gross sums assured and annuities) shall have effect as references to £750 and £156 respectively.

(3) Subsection (5) of the said section 332 (which, in the case of certain registered friendly societies, increases the tax exempt limits in subsections (2) and (3) of that section to £2,000 and £416) shall not have effect with respect to sums assured or annuities granted under contracts made after 13th March 1984.

1970 c. 31.
(N.I.).
1974 c. 46.

(4) In consequence of the preceding provisions of this section and subsection (5) below, in section 1 of the Friendly Societies Act (Northern Ireland) 1970 and section 7 of the Friendly Societies Act 1974 (societies which may be registered),—

(*a*) paragraph (*a*) of subsection (3), and

(*b*) subsection (3A),

shall not have effect with respect to benefits secured by contracts made after 13th March 1984.

(5) In the following enactments which specify, in relation to tax exempt life or endowment business, maximum benefits which may be provided for members, and persons claiming through members, of registered friendly societies, namely,—

(*a*) subsection (1) of section 55 of the Friendly Societies Act (Northern Ireland) 1970 ; and

(*b*) subsection (1) of section 64 of the Friendly Societies Act 1974,

in paragraph (*a*) for " £2,000 " there shall be substituted " £750 " and in paragraph (*b*) for " £416 " there shall be substituted " £156 ".

(6) The amendments made by subsection (5) above have effect—

(*a*) in relation to benefits secured by contracts made after 13th March 1984 ; and

(*b*) in relation to the aggregate of the benefits secured by contracts made after that day and those secured by contracts made on or before that day.

(7) If, after 13th March 1984, the committee of a registered society or branch whose rules make provision for it to carry on life or endowment business resolve to accept, in respect of any contract falling within subsection (8) below, premiums of amounts arrived at by deducting 15 per cent. from the premiums provided for by the rules of the society or branch (that is to say by deducting the same amount as, apart from section 72 above,

would have been deductible by way of relief under section 19 of the Taxes Act),—

   (*a*) the resolution shall be deemed to be permitted by the principal Act and the rules of the society or branch; and

   (*b*) nothing in the principal Act shall require the registration of the resolution; and

   (*c*) together with the annual return of the society or branch for the year of account ending 31st December 1984, the society or branch shall send a copy of the resolution to the registrar.

(8) Subsection (7) above applies to any contract entered into by a registered society or branch—

   (*a*) which is for the assurance under life or endowment business of any gross sum; and

   (*b*) which is entered into pursuant to a proposal received by the society or branch on or before 13th March 1984; and

   (*c*) which is one which the society might lawfully have entered into on that date; and

   (*d*) which is entered into after 13th March 1984 and before 1st May 1984.

(9) In subsection (7) above " the principal Act " means, according to the enactment under which the society or branch is registered,—

   (*a*) the Friendly Societies Act (Northern Ireland) 1970; or 1970 c. 31.

   (*b*) the Friendly Societies Act 1974; (N.I.).

and subsections (7) and (8) shall be construed as one with 1974 c. 46. the principal Act.

74.—(1) In section 30 of the Finance Act 1980 (in this section Disqualifica- referred to as the " principal section ")— tion of

   (*a*) in subsection (1) (certain life insurance policies not to certain life
insurance be qualifying policies) for the words " the terms of policies. which " there shall be substituted the words " and 1980 c. 48. the terms of either policy "; and

   (*b*) in subsection (3) (definition of " policy " by reference to ordinary long-term insurance business) for the words from " ordinary " to " and " there shall be substituted the words " long term business, as defined in section 1 of the Insurance Companies Act 1982, and ". 1982 c. 50.

(2) Subsections (6) and (7) of the principal section (commencement) shall have effect in relation to the principal section as amended by subsection (1) above as if for the words " 26th

March 1980 ", in each place where they occur, there were substituted the words " 23rd August 1983 " ; but nothing in this subsection affects the operation of the principal section in relation to a policy to which it would have applied apart from subsection (1) above.

(3) In any case where payments made—

(a) after 22nd August 1983, and

(b) by way of premium or other consideration in respect of a policy issued in respect of an insurance made before that date,

exceed £5 in any period of twelve months, the policy shall be treated for the purposes of the principal section as if it were issued in respect of an insurance made after 22nd August 1983 ; but nothing in that section shall apply with respect to any premium paid in respect of it before that date.

(4) In subsections (2) and (3) above " policy " means a policy issued in the course of ordinary long-term insurance business
1982 c. 50.   as defined in section 96(1) of the Insurance Companies Act 1982 and includes any such policy issued outside the United Kingdom.

Life policies: chargeable events.   75.—(1) In section 394 of the Taxes Act (chargeable events in relation to life policies) in subsection (3) (maturity of a policy not a chargeable event in certain cases where a new policy is issued in the exercise of an option conferred by the maturing policy) for the words from " if " to " unless " there shall be substituted the words " if—

(a) a new policy is issued in consequence of the exercise of an option conferred by the maturing policy, and

(b) the whole of the sums becoming payable under the maturing policy are retained by the company with whom the insurance was made and applied in the payment of one or more premiums under the new policy,

unless the circumstances are such that ".

(2) Subsection (1) above has effect, and shall be deemed to have had effect, in any case where the option concerned is exercised after 13th March 1984.

Insurance policies issued outside the United Kingdom.   76.—(1) After paragraph 1 of Schedule 2 to the Finance Act 1975 (certification of qualifying insurance policies) there shall be inserted the paragraph set out in Part I of Schedule 15 to this Act.

1975 c. 7.   (2) In connection with the amendment made by subsection (1) above, Schedule 1 to the Taxes Act and Schedule 2 to the

Finance Act 1975 shall have effect subject to the modifications
set out in Part II of Schedule 15 to this Act.

(3) In paragraph 9(3)(*a*) of Schedule 1 to the Taxes Act
(circumstances in which a policy substituted for a policy issued
outside the United Kingdom may be a qualifying policy) for
the words " person in respect of whom the new insurance is
made " there shall be substituted the words " policy holder
under the new policy ".

(4) The provisions of Chapter III of Part XIV of the Taxes
Act (additional charges to tax on chargeable events in relation
to life insurance policies etc.) shall have effect subject to the
modifications set out in Part III of Schedule 15 to this Act,
being modifications in relation to—

   (*a*) insurance policies affected by the amendment made by
        subsection (1) above ; and

   (*b*) new offshore capital redemption policies, as defined in
        subsection (5) below.

(5) In subsection (4)(*b*) above and Part III of Schedule 15
to this Act, a " new offshore capital redemption policy " means
a capital redemption policy, as defined in section 393(3) of the
Taxes Act, which—

   (*a*) is issued in respect of an insurance made after 22nd
        February 1984 ; and

   (*b*) is so issued by a company resident outside the United
        Kingdom.

(6) Subsection (3) above applies where the new policy referred
to in paragraph 9(2)(*c*) of Schedule 1 to the Taxes Act is issued
after 22nd February 1984.

CHAPTER V

OIL AND GAS INDUSTRY

77.—(1) No advance corporation tax shall be repaid to a com-   Termination
pany under section 17(3) of the Oil Taxation Act 1975 (advance   of repayments
corporation tax which cannot be set off in an accounting period   of ACT
because the income limit has been reduced by the deduction of   under Oil
payments of petroleum revenue tax) if it is advance corporation   Taxation
tax paid by the company in respect of a distribution made in an   1975 c. 22.
accounting period of the company ending on or after 1st April
1984.

(2) The reference in subsection (1) above to advance corporation tax paid by the company in respect of a distribution in a
particular accounting period is a reference to—

   (*a*) advance corporation tax which is actually paid by the
        company in respect of such a distribution ; and

    (*b*) advance corporation tax which, by virtue of section 85(4) or section 92(2) of the Finance Act 1972 (tax carried forward or surrendered to a subsidiary), is treated as paid by the company in respect of such a distribution.

78.—(1) This section applies where,—

    (*a*) there is, for the purposes of Schedule 17 to the Finance Act 1980, a transfer by a participator in an oil field of the whole or part of his interest in the field ; and

    (*b*) in pursuance of that transfer, the old participator disposes of, and the new participator acquires, machinery or plant used, or expected to be used, in connection with the field, or a share in such machinery or plant.

(2) In the application of Chapter I of Part III of the Finance Act 1971 (capital allowances) to expenditure incurred by the new participator in the acquisition referred to in subsection (1)(*b*) above, there shall be disregarded so much (if any) of that expenditure as exceeds—

    (*a*) the disposal value to be brought into account by the old participator under section 44 of that Act (balancing adjustments etc.) by reason of the disposal ; or

    (*b*) if subsection (2) of section 41 of that Act applies in relation to the old participator (machinery or plant disposed of before being brought into use), the amount of the expenditure in respect of which, but for that subsection, a first year allowance would have been made (and not withdrawn).

(3) In this section—

    (*a*) " machinery or plant " has the same meaning as in Chapter I of Part III of the Finance Act 1971 (capital allowances) ;

    (*b*) subsection (7) of section 50 of that Act applies to any reference to a share in machinery or plant ; and

    (*c*) " the old participator " and " the new participator " have the same meaning as in Schedule 17 to the Finance Act 1980 ;

and, subject thereto, expressions used in subsection (1) above have the same meaning as in Part I of the Oil Taxation Act 1975 and expressions used in subsection (2) above have the same meaning as in Chapter I of Part III of the Finance Act 1971.

(4) Nothing in this section affects the operation of paragraph 3 of Schedule 8 to the Finance Act 1971 (which restricts allowable expenditure on sales between connected persons etc.).

(5) This section applies where the acquisition referred to in subsection (1)(*b*) above occurs on or after 13th March 1984.

79.—(1) This section applies where, on or after 13th March 1984 and in pursuance of a transfer by a participator in an oil field of the whole or part of his interest in the field, there is—

> (*a*) a disposal of an interest in oil to be won from the oil field ; or
>
> (*b*) a disposal of an asset used in connection with the field ;

and section 12 of the Oil Taxation Act 1975 (interpretation of Part I of that Act) applies for the interpretation of this subsection and the reference to the transfer by a participator in an oil field of the whole or part of his interest in the field shall be construed in accordance with paragraph 1 of Schedule 17 to the Finance Act 1980.

(2) In this section " disposal " has the same meaning as in the Capital Gains Tax Act 1979 and " material disposal " means—

> (*a*) a disposal falling within paragraph (*a*) or paragraph (*b*) of subsection (1) above ; or
>
> (*b*) the sale of an asset referred to in subsection (3) of section 278 of the Taxes Act (company ceasing to be a member of a group: notional sale and repurchase of asset acquired from another member) where the asset was acquired by the chargeable company (within the meaning of that section) on a disposal falling within one of those paragraphs.

(3) For any chargeable period (within the meaning of the Taxes Act) in which a chargeable gain or allowable loss accrues to any person (in the following provisions of this section referred to as " the chargeable person ") on a material disposal (whether taking place in that period or not), subject to subsection (7) below there shall be aggregated—

> (*a*) the chargeable gains accruing to him in that period on such disposals, and
>
> (*b*) the allowable losses accruing to him in that period on such disposals,

and the lesser of the two aggregates shall be deducted from the other to give an aggregate gain or, as the case may be, an aggregate loss for that chargeable period.

(4) For the purposes of capital gains tax and corporation tax in respect of capital gains,—

> (*a*) the several chargeable gains and allowable losses falling within paragraphs (*a*) and (*b*) of subsection (3) above shall be left out of account ; and

(*b*) the aggregate gain or aggregate loss referred to in that subsection shall be treated as a single chargeable gain or allowable loss accruing to the chargeable person in the chargeable period concerned on the notional disposal of an asset ; and

(*c*) if in any chargeable period there is an aggregate loss, then, except as provided by subsection (6) below, it shall not be allowable as a deduction against any chargeable gain arising in that or any later period, other than an aggregate gain treated as accruing in a later period by virtue of paragraph (*b*) above (so that the aggregate gain of that later period shall be reduced or extinguished accordingly) ; and

(*d*) if in any chargeable period there is an aggregate gain, no loss shall be deducted from it except in accordance with paragraph (*c*) above ; and

(*e*) without prejudice to any indexation allowance which was taken into account in determining an aggregate gain or aggregate loss under subsection (3) above, no further indexation allowance shall be allowed on a notional disposal referred to in paragraph (*b*) above.

(5) Where, in accordance with subsection (3) above, the chargeable person has an aggregate gain, that gain (reduced in the case of companies in accordance with section 93 of the Finance Act 1972) and his ring fence income (if any) for the chargeable period concerned together constitute, for the purposes of this section, his ring fence profits for that period and, in relation to the chargeable person, in subsections (2), (3) and (5) of section 13 and in section 15 of the Oil Taxation Act 1975 (limitations on losses and charges etc. to be set against income) any reference to income arising from oil extraction activities or from oil rights shall be construed, except in relation to relief under section 168 of the Taxes Act and section 71 of the Capital Allowances Act 1968, as a reference to his ring fence profits.

1972 c. 41.

1975 c. 22.

1968 c. 3.

(6) In any case where—

(*a*) by virtue of subsection (4)(*b*) above, an aggregate loss is treated as accruing to the chargeable person in any chargeable period, and

(*b*) before the expiry of the period of two years beginning at the end of the chargeable period concerned, the chargeable person makes a claim under this subsection,

the whole, or such portion as is specified in the claim, of the aggregate loss shall be treated for the purposes of capital gains tax or corporation tax, as the case may be, as an allowable loss arising in that chargeable period otherwise than on a material disposal.

(7) In any case where a loss accrues to the chargeable person on a material disposal made to a person who is connected with him (within the meaning of section 63 of the Capital Gains Tax Act 1979)—

    (*a*) the loss shall be excluded from those referred to in paragraph (*b*) of subsection (3) above and, accordingly, shall not be aggregated under that subsection ; and

    (*b*) except as provided by subsection (8) below, section 62 of that Act shall apply in relation to the loss as if, in subsection (3) of that section (losses on disposals to a connected person to be set only against gains on disposals made to the same person at a time when he is a connected person), any reference to a disposal were a reference to a disposal which is a material disposal ; and

    (*c*) to the extent that the loss is set against a chargeable gain by virtue of paragraph (*b*) above, the gain shall be excluded from those referred to in paragraph (*a*) of subsection (3) above and, accordingly, shall not be aggregated under that subsection.

(8) In any case where—

    (*a*) the losses accruing to the chargeable person in any chargeable period on material disposals to a connected person exceed the gains accruing to him in that chargeable period on material disposals made to that person at a time when they are connected persons, and

    (*b*) before the expiry of the period of two years beginning at the end of the chargeable period concerned, the chargeable person makes a claim under this subsection,

the whole, or such part as is specified in the claim, of the excess referred to in paragraph (*a*) above shall be treated for the purposes of section 62 of the Capital Gains Tax Act 1979 as if it were a loss accruing on a disposal in that chargeable period, being a disposal which is not a material disposal and which is made by the chargeable person to the connected person referred to in paragraph (*a*) above.

(9) Where a claim is made under subsection (6) or subsection (8) above, all such adjustments shall be made, whether by way of discharge or repayment of tax (including capital gains tax) or otherwise, as may be required in consequence of the operation of that subsection.

(10) In subsection (5) above " ring fence income " means income arising from oil extraction activities or oil rights, within the meaning of Part II of the Oil Taxation Act 1975.

PART II
Replacement
of business
assets used in
connection
with oil
fields.
1979 c. 14.

80.—(1) If the consideration which a person obtains on a material disposal is applied, in whole or in part, as mentioned in subsection (1) of section 115 or section 116 of the Capital Gains Tax Act 1979 (replacement of business assets), that section shall not apply unless the new assets are taken into use, and used only, for the purposes of the ring fence trade.

(2) Subsection (1) above has effect notwithstanding subsection (7) of the said section 115 (which treats two or more trades as a single trade for certain purposes).

(3) Where the said section 115 or the said section 116 applies in relation to any of the consideration on a material disposal, the asset which constitutes the new assets for the purposes of that section shall be conclusively presumed to be a depreciating asset, and section 117 of the Capital Gains Tax Act 1979 (special rules for depreciating assets) shall have effect accordingly, except that—

    (a) the reference in subsection (2)(b) of that section to a trade carried on by the claimant shall be construed as a reference solely to his ring fence trade ; and

    (b) subsections (3) to (6) of that section shall be omitted.

(4) In any case where sections 115 to 117 of the Capital Gains Tax Act 1979 have effect in accordance with the preceding provisions of this section, the operation of section 276 of the Taxes Act (replacement of business assets by members of a group) shall be modified as follows :—

    (a) only those members of a group which actually carry on a ring fence trade shall be treated for the purposes of those sections as carrying on a single trade which is a ring fence trade ; and

    (b) only those activities which, in relation to each individual member of the group, constitute its ring fence trade shall be treated as forming part of that single trade.

(5) In this section—

    (a) " material disposal " has the meaning assigned to it by section 79 above ; and

    (b) " ring fence trade " means a trade consisting of either or both of the activities mentioned in paragraphs (a) and (b) of subsection (1) of section 13 of the Oil Taxation Act 1975.

1975 c. 22.

Disposals by
non-residents
etc. of assets
used in con-
nection with
exploration
and
exploitation
activities.
1973 c. 51.

81.—(1) Section 38 of the Finance Act 1973 (territorial extension of charge to income tax, capital gains tax and corporation tax) shall be amended in accordance with this section.

(2) After subsection (3) there shall be inserted the following subsections :—

    " (3A) Gains accruing on the disposal of—

        (a) exploration or exploitation assets which are situated in a designated area, or (*b*) unquoted shares deriving their value or the greater PART II part of their value directly or indirectly from exploration or exploitation assets situated in the United Kingdom or a designated area or from such assets and exploration or exploitation rights taken together,

shall be treated for the purposes of the Capital Gains Tax 1979 c. 14. Act 1979 as gains accruing on the disposal of assets situated in the United Kingdom.

(3B) For the purposes of this section, an asset disposed of is an exploration or exploitation asset if either—

(*a*) it is not a mobile asset and it is being or has at some time within the period of two years ending at the date of the disposal been used in connection with exploration or exploitation activities carried on in the United Kingdom or a designated area ; or

(*b*) it is a mobile asset which, at some time within the period of two years ending at the date of the disposal, has been used in connection with exploration or exploitation activities so carried on and is dedicated to an oil field in which the person making the disposal, or a person connected with him within the meaning of section 533 of the Taxes Act, is or has been a participator ;

and expressions used in paragraphs (*a*) and (*b*) above have the same meaning as if those paragraphs were included in Part I of the Oil Taxation Act 1975. 1975 c. 22.

(3C) In paragraph (*b*) of subsection (3A) above " unquoted shares " means shares other than those which are quoted on a recognised stock exchange (within the meaning of the Corporation Tax Acts) ; and references in subsections (4) and (5) below to exploration or exploitation assets include references to unquoted shares falling within that paragraph."

(3) In subsection (4) (which, among other things, provides that certain gains are to be treated as gains accruing on the disposal of trade assets) after the words " such rights " there shall be inserted the words " or of exploration or exploitation assets ".

(4) In subsection (5) (inter-company disposals) after the word " rights " there shall be inserted the words " or exploration or exploitation assets ".

(5) This section has effect in relation to disposals on or after 13th March 1984.

PART II

CHAPTER VI

CONTROLLED FOREIGN COMPANIES

Imputation of
chargeable
profits and
creditable tax
of controlled
foreign
companies.

82.—(1) If the Board have reason to believe that in any accounting period a company—

(a) is resident outside the United Kingdom, and

(b) is controlled by persons resident in the United Kingdom, and

(c) is subject to a lower level of taxation in the territory in which it is resident,

and the Board so direct, the provisions of this Chapter shall apply in relation to that accounting period.

(2) A company which falls within paragraphs (a) to (c) of subsection (1) above is in this Chapter referred to as a " controlled foreign company ".

(3) Where, by virtue of a direction under subsection (1) above, the provisions of this Chapter apply in relation to an accounting period of a controlled foreign company, the chargeable profits of that company for that period and its creditable tax (if any) for that period shall each be apportioned in accordance with section 87 below among the persons (whether resident in the United Kingdom or not) who had an interest in that company at any time during that accounting period.

(4) Where, on such an apportionment of a controlled foreign company's chargeable profits for an accounting period as is referred to in subsection (3) above, an amount of those profits is apportioned to a company resident in the United Kingdom then, subject to subsection (5) below,—

(a) a sum equal to corporation tax at the appropriate rate on that apportioned amount of profits, less the portion of the controlled foreign company's creditable tax for that period (if any) which is apportioned to the resident company, shall be assessed on and recoverable from the resident company as if it were an amount of corporation tax chargeable on that company ; and

(b) if, apart from this paragraph, section 478 of the Taxes Act would deem any sum forming part of the company's chargeable profits for that accounting period to be the income of an individual for the purposes of the Income Tax Acts, that section shall not apply to such portion of that sum as corresponds to the portion of those chargeable profits which is apportioned to companies which are resident in the United Kingdom and which, by virtue of paragraph (a) above, have a liability to tax in respect thereof ;

and for the purposes of paragraph (a) above " the appropriate rate " means the rate of corporation tax applicable to profits of that accounting period of the resident company in which ends the accounting period of the controlled foreign company to which the direction under subsection (1) above relates or, if there is more than one such rate, the average rate over the whole of that accounting period of the resident company.

(5) Tax shall not, by virtue of subsection (4) above, be assessed on and recoverable from a company resident in the United Kingdom unless, on the apportionment in question, the aggregate of—

(a) the amount of the controlled foreign company's chargeable profits for the accounting period in question which is apportioned to the resident company, and

(b) any amounts of those chargeable profits which are apportioned to persons who are connected or associated with the resident company,

is at least 10 per cent. of the total of those chargeable profits.

(6) In relation to a company resident outside the United Kingdom—

(a) any reference in this Chapter to its chargeable profits for an accounting period is a reference to the amount which, on the assumptions in Schedule 16 to this Act, would be the amount of the total profits of the company for that period on which, after allowing for any deductions available against those profits, corporation tax would be chargeable; and

(b) any reference in this Chapter to profits does not include a reference to chargeable gains but otherwise (except as provided by paragraph (a) above) has the same meaning as it has for the purposes of corporation tax.

83.—(1) No direction may be given under section 82(1) above with respect to an accounting period of a controlled foreign company if— Limitations on direction-making power.

(a) in respect of that period the company pursues, within the meaning of Part I of Schedule 17 to this Act, an acceptable distribution policy; or

(b) throughout that period the company is, within the meaning of Part II of that Schedule, engaged in exempt activities; or

(c) the public quotation condition set out in Part III of that Schedule is fulfilled with respect to that period; or

(d) the chargeable profits of the accounting period do not exceed £20,000 or, if the accounting period is less than twelve months, a proportionately reduced amount.

(2) Without prejudice to any right of appeal, nothing in subsection (1) above prevents the Board from giving a direction with respect to an accounting period after the end of that period

but before it is known whether the company has paid such **a** dividend as establishes that it is pursuing an acceptable distribution policy in respect of the profits arising in that period.

(3) Notwithstanding that none of paragraphs (*a*) to (*d*) of subsection (1) above applies to an accounting period of a controlled foreign company, no direction may be given under section 82(1) above with respect to that accounting period if it appears to the Board that—

> (*a*) in so far as any of the transactions the results of which are reflected in the profits arising in that accounting period, or any two or more of those transactions taken together, achieved a reduction in United Kingdom tax, either the reduction so achieved was minimal or it was not the main purpose or one of the main purposes of that transaction or, as the case may be, of those transactions taken together to achieve that reduction, and
>
> (*b*) it was not the main reason or, as the case may be, one of the main reasons for the company's existence in that accounting period to achieve a reduction in United Kingdom tax by a diversion of profits from the United Kingdom,

and Part IV of Schedule 17 to this Act shall have effect with respect to the preceding provisions of this subsection.

Residence and interests.

84.—(1) Subject to subsections (2) and (4) below, in any accounting period in which a company is resident outside the United Kingdom, it shall be regarded for the purposes of this Chapter as resident in that territory in which, throughout that period, it is liable to tax by reason of domicile, residence or place of management.

(2) If, in the case of any company, there are in any accounting period two or more territories falling within subsection (1) above, the company shall in that accounting period be regarded for the purposes of this Chapter as resident in only one of them, namely,—

> (*a*) if, throughout the accounting period, the company's place of effective management is situated in one of those territories only, in that territory; and
>
> (*b*) if, throughout the accounting period, the company's place of effective management is situated in two or more of those territories, in that one of them in which, at the end of the accounting period, the greater amount of the company's assets is situated; and
>
> (*c*) if neither paragraph (*a*) nor paragraph (*b*) above applies, in that one of the territories falling within subsection (1) above in which, at the end of the accounting period, the greater amount of the company's assets is situated; and

(*d*) if paragraph (*a*) above does not apply and neither paragraph (*b*) nor paragraph (*c*) above produces one, and only one, of those territories, in that one of them which may be specified in a direction under section 82(1) above relating to that accounting period.

(3) If, in the case of any company, there is in any accounting period no territory falling within subsection (1) above, then, for the purposes of this Chapter, it shall be conclusively presumed that the company is in that accounting period resident in a territory in which it is subject to a lower level of taxation.

(4) In any case where it becomes necessary for the purposes of subsection (2) above to determine in which of two or more territories the greater amount of a company's assets is situated at the end of an accounting period, account shall be taken only of those assets which, immediately before the end of that period, are situated in those territories and the amount of them shall be determined by reference to their market value at that time.

(5) For the purposes of this Chapter, the following persons have an interest in a controlled foreign company,—

(*a*) any person who possesses, or is entitled to acquire, share capital or voting rights in the company,

(*b*) any person who possesses, or is entitled to acquire, a right to receive or participate in distributions of the company or any amounts payable by the company (in cash or in kind) to loan creditors by way of premium on redemption,

(*c*) any person who is entitled to secure that income or assets (whether present or future) of the company will be applied directly or indirectly for his benefit, and

(*d*) any other person who, either alone or together with other persons, has control of the company,

and for the purposes of paragraph (*b*) above the definition of " distribution " in Part X of the Taxes Act shall be construed without any limitation to companies resident in the United Kingdom.

(6) References in subsection (5) above to being entitled to do anything apply where a person is presently entitled to do it at a future date, or will at a future date be entitled to do it; but a person whose entitlement to secure that any income or assets of the company will be applied as mentioned in paragraph (*c*) of that subsection is contingent upon a default of the company or any other person under any agreement shall not be treated as falling within that paragraph unless the default has occurred.

(7) Without prejudice to subsection (5) above, the Board may, if they think it appropriate, treat a loan creditor of a controlled foreign company as having an interest in the company for the purposes of this Chapter.

85.—(1) Without prejudice to subsection (3) of section 84 above, a company which, by virtue of subsection (1) or subsection (2) of that section, is to be regarded as resident in a particular territory outside the United Kingdom shall be considered to be subject to a lower level of taxation in that territory if the amount of tax (in this section referred to as " the local tax ") which is paid under the law of that territory in respect of the profits of the company which arise in any accounting period is less than one half of the corresponding United Kingdom tax on those profits.

(2) For the purposes of this Chapter, the amount of the corresponding United Kingdom tax on the profits arising in an accounting period of a company resident outside the United Kingdom is the amount of corporation tax which, on the assumptions set out in Schedule 16 to this Act and subject to subsection (3) below, would be chargeable in respect of the chargeable profits of the company for that accounting period.

(3) In determining the amount of corporation tax which, in accordance with subsection (2) above, would be chargeable in respect of the chargeable profits of an accounting period of a company resident outside the United Kingdom—

(a) it shall be assumed for the purposes of Schedule 16 to this Act—

(i) that a direction has been given under section 82(1) above in respect of that period ; and

(ii) that the Board have made any declaration which they could have made under sub-paragraph (3) of paragraph 11 of that Schedule and of which they gave notice in writing as mentioned in that sub-paragraph ; and

(b) there shall be disregarded so much of any relief from corporation tax in respect of income as would be attributable to the local tax and would fall to be given by virtue of any provision of Part XVIII of the Taxes Act (double taxation relief) other than section 515 (postponement of capital allowances to secure relief) ; and

(c) there shall be deducted from what would otherwise be the amount of that corporation tax—

(i) any amount which (on the assumptions set out in Schedule 16 to this Act) would fall to be set off against corporation tax by virtue of section 240(5) of the Taxes Act (sums received under deduction of income tax) ; and

(ii) any amount of income tax or corporation tax actually charged in respect of any of those chargeable profits.

(4) The references in subsection (3)(*c*) above to an amount falling to be set off or an amount actually charged do not include so much of any such amount as has been or falls to be repaid to the company whether on the making of a claim or otherwise.

86.—(1) For the purposes of this Chapter, an accounting Accounting period of a company resident outside the United Kingdom shall periods and begin— creditable tax.

    (*a*) whenever the company comes under the control of persons resident in the United Kingdom ;

    (*b*) whenever the company, not being the subject of an earlier direction under section 82(1) above, commences to carry on business ; and

    (*c*) whenever an accounting period of the company ends without the company then ceasing either to carry on business or to have any source of income whatsoever ;

and for the purposes of paragraph (*a*) above a company which is under the control of persons resident in the United Kingdom immediately before this Chapter comes into force shall be treated as coming under their control immediately after it comes into force.

(2) For the purposes of this Chapter, an accounting period of a company resident outside the United Kingdom shall end if and at the time when—

    (*a*) the company ceases to be under the control of persons resident in the United Kingdom ; or

    (*b*) the company becomes, or ceases to be, liable to tax in a territory ; or

    (*c*) the company ceases to have any source of income whatsoever ;

and for the purposes of paragraph (*b*) above " liable to tax " means liable to tax by reason of domicile, residence or place of management.

(3) Without prejudice to subsections (1) and (2) above, subsections (3), (5) and (7) of section 247 of the Taxes Act (end of accounting periods and provisions as to winding up) shall apply for the purposes of this Chapter as they apply for the purposes of corporation tax, but with the omission of so much of those provisions as relates to a company coming or ceasing to be within the charge to corporation tax.

(4) Where it appears to the Board that the beginning or end of any accounting period of a company resident outside the United Kingdom is uncertain, a direction under section 82(1) above may specify as an accounting period of the company such period, not exceeding twelve months, as appears to the Board to be appropriate, and that period shall be treated for the

purposes of this Chapter as an accounting period of the company unless the direction is subsequently amended under subsection (5) below.

(5) If, on further facts coming to the knowledge of the Board after the making of a direction (including facts emerging on an appeal against notice of the making of the direction), it appears to the Board that any accounting period specified in the direction is not the true accounting period, the Board shall amend the direction so as to specify the true period.

(6) In this Chapter, in relation to an accounting period of a controlled foreign company in respect of which a direction is given under section 82(1) above, the creditable tax means the aggregate of—

>   (a) the amount of any relief from corporation tax in respect of income which (on the assumptions set out in Schedule 16 to this Act and assuming the company to be liable for corporation tax on the chargeable profits of that accounting period) would fall to be given to the company by virtue of any provision of Part XVIII of the Taxes Act (double taxation relief) in respect of foreign tax attributable to any income which is brought into account in determining those chargeable profits ; and

>   (b) any amount which (on those assumptions) would fall to be set off against corporation tax on those chargeable profits by virtue of section 240(5) of the Taxes Act (sums received under deduction of income tax) ; and

>   (c) the amount of any income tax or corporation tax actually charged in respect of the chargeable profits of that accounting period, less any of that tax which has been or falls to be repaid to the company, whether on the making of a claim or otherwise.

Apportionment of chargeable profits and creditable tax.

87.—(1) Where a direction has been given under section 82(1) above in respect of an accounting period of a controlled foreign company, then, subject to subsections (2) and (3) below, the apportionment of the company's chargeable profits and creditable tax (if any) for that period shall be made among, and according to the respective interests of, the persons who at any time during that period had interests in the company.

(2) In determining for the purposes of this Chapter the respective interests of persons who (in accordance with section 84

above) have interests in a controlled foreign company, the Board may, if it seems to them just and reasonable to do so, attribute to each of those persons an interest corresponding to his interest in the assets of the company available for distribution among those persons in the event of a winding up or in any other circumstances.

(3) Where the controlled foreign company is not a trading company, the Board may, if it seems to them just and reasonable to do so, treat a loan creditor as having for the purposes of this section an interest in the company to the extent to which the income of the company has been, or is available to be, expended in redemption, repayment or discharge of the loan capital or debt (including any premium thereon) in respect of which he is a loan creditor.

(4) Subject to subsections (5) and (7) below, as between persons each of whom has an unvarying holding of shares of the same class throughout a particular accounting period of a controlled foreign company, the amount of the company's chargeable profits and creditable tax which is apportioned to each of them by virtue of his holding of those shares shall be in direct proportion to the numbers of shares comprised in each of their holdings; and similar principles shall apply in relation to an apportionment among other persons each of whom holds an interest of the same description in the controlled foreign company.

(5) Where the same interest in a controlled foreign company is held directly by one person and indirectly by another or others (as in a case where one company has a shareholding in the controlled foreign company and the first company is controlled by a third company or by two or more persons together) then, subject to subsection (6) below, the Board, in apportioning the company's chargeable profits and creditable tax, may treat that interest as held solely by a person who holds that interest indirectly or, as the case may be, by two or more persons (in this subsection referred to as " holders ") who, taken together, hold that interest indirectly and, in particular, if that person or one or more of those holders is resident in the United Kingdom, may treat the interest as held solely by that person or, as the case may be, those holders.

(6) In a case where the same interest is held directly by one person and indirectly by another and the circumstances are as set out in any of paragraphs (*a*) to (*c*) below, the Board shall treat the interest as held solely by the company which is des-scribed in the paragraph concerned as " the assessable company "—

> (*a*) where the interest is held directly by a company resident in the United Kingdom, that company is the assessable company; and
>
> (*b*) where the interest is held directly by a person resident outside the United Kingdom and indirectly by only

one company resident in the United Kingdom, that company is the assessable company ; and

(c) where the interest is held directly by a person resident outside the United Kingdom and indirectly by two or more companies resident in the United Kingdom, the assessable company is that one of those companies which so holds the interest by virtue of holding directly an interest in a foreign holding company ;

and for the purposes of paragraph (c) above a foreign holding company is a company resident outside the United Kingdom which holds directly or indirectly the interest in the controlled foreign company.

(7) Without prejudice to subsection (5) above, in any case where an interest in a controlled foreign company is held in a fiduciary or representative capacity in such circumstances that there is or are an identifiable beneficiary or beneficiaries, the Board may treat the interest as held by that beneficiary or, as the case may be, as apportioned among those beneficiaries ; and any such apportionment shall be made on such basis as seems to the Board to be just and reasonable.

(8) Subject to the preceding provisions of this section, the apportionment of the chargeable profits and creditable tax of a controlled foreign company for any accounting period shall be made on such basis as seems to the Board to be just and reasonable.

88.—(1) Where the Board have given a direction under section 82(1) above with respect to an accounting period of a controlled foreign company, notice of the making of the direction shall be given to every company resident in the United Kingdom which appears to the Board to have had an interest in the controlled foreign company at any time during that period.

(2) A notice under subsection (1) above shall—
  (a) specify the date on which the direction was made and the controlled foreign company to which it relates ;
  (b) specify the accounting period to which the direction relates and the amount of the chargeable profits and creditable tax computed for that period ;
  (c) specify the reliefs (if any) which it has been assumed that the company has claimed by virtue of paragraph 4(1) of Schedule 16 to this Act ;
  (d) specify, in a case where paragraph (d) of subsection (2) of section 84 above applies, the territory which, by virtue of that paragraph, was specified in the direction and, in any other case, specify the territory (if any) in which, by virtue of that section, the Board consider that the company is to be regarded as resident for the purposes of this Chapter ;

(*e*) inform the recipient of the notice of the right of appeal conferred on him by subsection (4) below and of the right to give notice under paragraph 4(2) of Schedule 16 to this Act; and

(*f*) specify any declaration with respect to the accounting period concerned which was made prior to or at the same time as the notice by virtue of paragraph 11(3) of Schedule 16 to this Act or paragraph 3(2) of Schedule 17 to this Act;

and, in the case of a notice given after the direction concerned has been amended by virtue of section 86(5) above, the notice shall specify the date of the amendment and (so far as paragraphs (*b*) and (c) above are concerned) shall relate to the position resulting from the amendment.

(3) Where, by virtue of section 86(5) above, the Board have amended a direction so as to specify a revised accounting period, notice of the making of the amendment shall be given to every company which was previously given notice of the making of the direction; and a notice under this subsection—

(*a*) shall identify the direction which is amended and state the effect of the amendment, including the extent to which the matters specified in the notice of the making of the direction are superseded; and

(*b*) shall contain the provisions required, by virtue of paragraphs (*b*) to (*f*) of subsection (2) above, to be included in a notice under subsection (1) above.

(4) Any company to which notice is given under subsection (1) or subsection (3) above may, by giving notice of appeal in writing to the Board within sixty days of the date of the notice given to the company, appeal to the Special Commissioners against that notice on all or any of the following grounds,—

(*a*) that the direction should not have been given or, where the direction has been amended, that the amendment should not have been made;

(*b*) that the amount of chargeable profits or creditable tax specified in the notice is incorrect;

(*c*) that the company did not have an interest in the controlled foreign company concerned at any time during the accounting period in question;

(*d*) that, if the notice specifies a declaration made by virtue of sub-paragraph (3) of paragraph 11 of Schedule 16 to this Act, the condition for the making of that declaration in sub-paragraph (5) of that paragraph was not fulfilled; and (*e*) that, if the notice specifies a declaration made by virtue of paragraph 3(2) of Schedule 17 to this Act, the condition for the making of that declaration was not fulfilled ;

and the notice of appeal shall specify the grounds of appeal, but on the hearing of the appeal the Special Commissioners may allow the appellant to put forward any ground not specified in the notice and take it into consideration if satisfied that the omission was not wilful or unreasonable.

(5) If, after the time at which notice is given under subsection (1) above with respect to an accounting period of a controlled foreign company, the Board make a declaration by virtue of—

(*a*) paragraph 11(3) of Schedule 16 to this Act, or

(*b*) paragraph 3(2) of Schedule 17 to this Act,

then, unless the effect of the declaration is such that a notice (which, among other matters, will specify the declaration) will be required to be given under subsection (3) above, the Board shall give notice specifying the declaration to every company which was previously given notice of the making of the direction ; and subsection (4) above shall apply in relation to a notice under this subsection as it applies in relation to a notice under subsection (3) above, but with the omission of paragraphs (*a*) to (*c*).

(6) If it appears to the inspector that the amount of the chargeable profits or creditable tax specified in a notice under subsection (1) or subsection (3) above is incorrect, he shall give notice of the revised amount to every company to which notice was given under subsection (1) or subsection (3) above and, except where the revised amount results from—

(*a*) an appeal under this section, or

(*b*) a notice given to the Board under paragraph 4(2) of Schedule 16 to this Act or by virtue of paragraph 13 of that Schedule,

any company to which notice is given under this subsection may, by giving notice of appeal in writing to the Board within sixty days of the date of the notice given to the company, appeal to the Special Commissioners against the revised amount specified in the notice.

(7) The jurisdiction of the Special Commissoners on an appeal under this section shall include jurisdiction to review any decision of the Board or the inspector which is relevant to a ground of the appeal.

(8) The Board may make regulations—

(*a*) as respects the conduct of appeals under this section ;

(*b*) entitling any person who has received, or is connected or associated with a person who has received, a notice under subsection (1) above with respect to a particular accounting period of a controlled foreign company to appear on an appeal brought by another person who has received such a notice ; and

(*c*) with respect to the joinder of appeals brought by different persons with respect to the same direction or the same amount of chargeable profits or creditable tax ;

and any such regulations shall be made by statutory instrument subject to annulment in pursuance of a resolution of the Commons House of Parliament.

89.—(1) Subject to the following provisions of this section, the provisions of section 82(4)(*a*) above relating to assessment and recovery of a sum as if it were an amount of corporation tax shall be taken as applying, subject to the provisions of the Taxes Acts, and to any necessary modifications, all enactments applying generally to corporation tax, including those relating to the assessing, collecting and receiving of corporation tax, those conferring or regulating a right of appeal and those concerning administration, penalties, interest on unpaid tax and priority of tax in cases of insolvency under the law of any part of the United Kingdom.

Assessment, recovery and postponement of tax.

(2) For the purposes of the Taxes Acts, any sum assessable and recoverable under section 82(4)(*a*) above shall be regarded as corporation tax which falls to be assessed for the accounting period in which ends that one of the controlled foreign company's accounting periods the chargeable profits of which give rise to that sum ; and a notice of assessment relating to such a sum shall (in addition to any other matter required to be contained in such a notice) specify separately—

(*a*) the total amount of those chargeable profits and of any creditable tax which has been apportioned to persons falling within each of paragraphs (*a*) to (*d*) of subsection (5), or within subsection (7), of section 84 above, and

(*b*) where there is more than one class of shares in the controlled foreign company, the total amount apportioned to persons holding shares of each class,

but such a notice shall not identify any particular person (other than the person assessed) as having an interest of any description in the controlled foreign company.

(3) In subsection (3) of section 31 of the Taxes Management Act 1970 (appeals to Special Commissioners) after paragraph (c) there shall be inserted " or

> (d) is an assessment to tax under section 82(4)(a) of the Finance Act 1984 ";

and, on an appeal against an assessment to tax under section 82(4)(a) above, the jurisdiction of the Special Commissioners shall include jurisdiction to review any relevant decision taken by the Board under section 87 above in connection with the apportionment of chargeable profits or creditable tax.

(4) No appeal may be brought against an assessment to tax under section 82(4)(a) above on a ground on which an appeal has or could have been brought under subsection (4) or subsection (6) of section 88 above.

(5) At the end of subsection (1) of section 55 of the Taxes Management Act 1970 (recovery of tax not postponed) there shall be added the following paragraph—

> " (g) a notice under subsection (1) or subsection (3) of section 88 of the Finance Act 1984 where, before the appeal is determined, the appellant is assessed to tax under section 82(4)(a) of that Act by reference to an amount of chargeable profits specified in that notice ".

(6) Where an appeal is brought against an assessment to tax under section 82(4)(a) above as well as against a notice under subsection (1) or subsection (3) of section 88 above, section 55 of the Taxes Management Act 1970 shall have effect as follows : —

> (a) an application under subsection (3) of that section may relate to matters arising on both appeals and, in determining the amount of tax the payment of which should be postponed, the Commissioners shall consider matters so arising together ; and
>
> (b) if the Commissioners have determined the amount of tax the payment of which should be postponed solely in relation to one of the appeals, the bringing of the other appeal shall be taken to be a change of circumstances falling within subsection (4) of that section ; and
>
> (c) any reference in that section to the determination of the appeal shall be construed as a reference to the determination of the two appeals, but the determination of one before the other shall be taken to be a change of circumstances falling within subsection (4) of that section.

(7) Schedule 18 to this Act shall have effect with respect to the reliefs which may be claimed by a company resident in the United Kingdom which has a liability for tax in respect of an amount of chargeable profits ; and no reliefs other than those provided for by that Schedule shall be allowed against any such liability.

(8) In any case where—

  (*a*) the whole or any part of the tax assessed on a company (in this section referred to as the " assessable company ") by virtue of section 87(6) above is not paid before the date on which it is due and payable in accordance with the Taxes Act or, as the case may be, the Taxes Management Act 1970, and

  (*b*) the Board serve a notice of liability to tax under this subsection on another company (in this section referred to as the " responsible company ") which is resident in the United Kingdom and holds or has held (whether directly or indirectly) the same interest in the controlled foreign company as is or was held by the assessable company,

the tax assessed on the assessable company or, as the case may be, so much of it as remains unpaid shall be payable by the responsible company upon service of the notice.

(9) Where a notice of liability is served under subsection (8) above,—

  (*a*) any interest due on the tax assessed on the assessable company and not paid, and

  (*b*) any interest accruing due on that tax after the date of service,

shall be payable by the responsible company.

(10) In any case where—

  (*a*) a notice of liability is served on the responsible company under subsection (8) above, and

  (*b*) the relevant tax and any interest payable by the responsible company under subsection (9) above is not paid by that company before the expiry of the period of three months beginning on the date of service of the notice,

that tax and interest may, without prejudice to the right of recovery from the responsible company, be recovered from the assessable company.

(11) In this section " the Taxes Acts " has the same meaning as in the Taxes Management Act 1970.

PART II
Information
relating to
controlled
foreign
companies.

90.—(1) Where it appears to the Board that a company resident outside the United Kingdom (in this section referred to as a " foreign subsidiary ") may be a controlled foreign company, the Board may, by notice in writing given to any company which appears to them to be a controlling company of the foreign subsidiary, require that company to give to the Board, within such time (not being less than thirty days) as may be specified in the notice, such particulars (which may include details of documents) as may be so specified with respect to any matter concerning the foreign subsidiary, being particulars required by the Board for the purposes of this Chapter as being relevant to the affairs of the controlling company, the foreign subsidiary or any connected or associated company.

(2) In this section " controlling company ", in relation to a foreign subsidiary or any other company, means a company which is resident in the United Kingdom and has, alone or together with other persons so resident, control of the foreign subsidiary or, as the case may be, that other company.

(3) The Board may by notice in writing given to a company which appears to them to be a controlling company in relation to a foreign subsidiary require that company to make available for inspection any relevant books, accounts or other documents or records whatsoever of the company itself or, subject to subsection (6) below, of any other company, including the foreign subsidiary, in relation to which it appears to the Board to be a controlling company.

(4) In subsection (3) above " relevant " means relevant to—

(a) the computation of any profits of the foreign subsidiary ; or

(b) the question whether a direction should be given under section 82(1) above with respect to the foreign subsidiary or a connected or associated company or whether any such direction should be amended ; or

(c) any question as to the amount of the chargeable profits or creditable tax for any accounting period of the foreign subsidiary or a connected or associated company ; or

(d) any question as to the sum which, in accordance with section 82(4)(a) above, should be assessed on and recoverable from any person.

(5) In subsections (1) and (4) above " connected or associated company " means a controlled foreign company with which the foreign subsidiary or the controlling company is connected or associated.

(6) In any case where—

    (*a*) under subsection (3) above a company is by notice required to make available for inspection any books, accounts, documents or records of a company other than itself, and

    (*b*) it appears to the Board, on the application of the company, that the circumstances are such that the requirement ought not to have effect,

the Board shall direct that the company need not comply with the requirement.

(7) If, on an application under subsection (6) above, the Board refuse to give a direction under that subsection, the company concerned may, by notice in writing given to the Board within thirty days after the refusal, appeal to the Special Commissioners who, if satisfied that the requirement in question ought in the circumstances not to have effect, may determine accordingly.

(8) In the Table in section 98 of the Taxes Management Act 1970 (penalties), at the end of the first column there shall be added—

    " Section 90 of the Finance Act 1984."

1970 c. 9.

91.—(1) In this Chapter " trading company " means a company whose business consists wholly or mainly of the carrying on of a trade or trades.

(2) For the purposes of this Chapter—

    (*a*) section 533 of the Taxes Act (connected persons) applies ; and

    (*b*) subsection (10) of section 494 of that Act (associated persons) applies as it applies for the purposes of that section.

(3) The following provisions of Chapter III of Part XI of the Taxes Act (close companies) apply for the purposes of this Chapter as they apply for the purposes of that Chapter,—

    (*a*) section 302 (meaning of " control ") ; and

    (*b*) subsections (7) and (8) of section 303 (meaning of " loan creditor ") ;

but, in the application of subsection (6) of section 302 for the purposes of this Chapter, for the words " five or fewer participators " there shall be substituted the words " persons resident in the United Kingdom ".

(4) This Chapter shall be deemed to have come into force on 6th April 1984.

Interpretation, construction and commencement of Chapter VI.

Chapter VII

Offshore Funds

Material interests in non-qualifying funds

Disposal of
material
interests in
non-qualifying
offshore
funds.

92.—(1) This Chapter applies to a disposal by any person of an asset if—

(*a*) the disposal occurs on or after 1st January 1984 and, at the time of the disposal, the asset constitutes a material interest in an offshore fund which is or has at any material time been a non-qualifying offshore fund ; or

(*b*) paragraph (*a*) above does not apply but the disposal occurs on or after 1st January 1985 and the conditions in subsection (7) below are fulfilled.

(2) Subject to the following provisions of this section and section 93 below, there is a disposal of an asset for the purposes of this Chapter if there would be such a disposal for the purposes of the Capital Gains Tax Act 1979 (in this Chapter referred to as " the principal Act ").

1979 c. 14.

(3) Notwithstanding anything in subsection (1)(*b*) of section 49 of the principal Act (general provisions applicable on death: no deemed disposal by the deceased) where a person dies on or after 1st January 1984 and the assets of which he was competent to dispose include an asset which is or has at any time been a material interest in a non-qualifying offshore fund, then, for the purposes of this Chapter, other than section 93 below,—

(*a*) immediately before the acquisition referred to in subsection (1)(*a*) of that section, that interest shall be deemed to be disposed of by the deceased for such a consideration as is mentioned in that subsection ; but

(*b*) nothing in this subsection affects the determination, in accordance with subsection (1) above, of the question whether that deemed disposal is one to which this Chapter applies.

(4) Subject to subsection (3) above, section 49 of the principal Act applies for the purposes of this Chapter as it applies for the purposes of that Act, and the reference in subsection (3) above to the assets of which a deceased person was competent to dispose shall be construed in accordance with subsection (10) of that section.

(5) Notwithstanding anything in section 85 of the principal Act (exchange of securities for those in another company) in any case where—

(*a*) the company which is company B for the purposes of subsection (1) of that section is or was at a material time a non-qualifying offshore fund and the company which is company A for those purposes is not such a fund, or

   (*b*) under section 86 of that Act (reconstruction or amalgamation involving issue of securities) persons are to be treated, in consequence of an arrangement, as exchanging shares, debentures or other interests in or of an entity which is or was at a material time a non-qualifying offshore fund for assets which do not constitute interests in such a fund,

then, unless the exchange or arrangement is effected before 1st January 1985 and the shares, debentures or interests which are acquired as a result of the exchange or arrangement are shares, debentures or interests in or of a company resident in the United Kingdom, subsection (3) of the said section 85 (which applies provisions of that Act treating transactions as not being disposals and equating original shares with a new holding in certain cases) shall not apply for the purposes of this Chapter.

(6) In any case where, apart from subsection (5) above, section 85(3) of the principal Act would apply, the exchange concerned of shares, debentures or other interests in or of a non-qualifying offshore fund shall for the purposes of this Chapter constitute a disposal of interests in the offshore fund for a consideration equal to their market value at the time of the exchange.

(7) The conditions referred to in subsection (1)(*b*) above are—

   (*a*) that at the time of the disposal the asset constitutes an interest in a company resident in the United Kingdom or in a unit trust scheme, as defined in section 26(1) of the Prevention of Fraud (Investments) Act 1958, the trustees of which are at that time resident in the United Kingdom ; and 1958 c. 45.

   (*b*) that at a material time after 31st December 1984 the company or unit trust scheme was a non-qualifying offshore fund and the asset constituted a material interest in that fund ;

and for the purpose of determining whether the asset disposed of falls within paragraph (*b*) above, section 78 of the principal Act (equation of original shares and new holding) shall have effect as it has effect for the purposes of that Act.

(8) For the purposes of this section, a material time, in relation to the disposal of an asset, is any time on or after 1st January 1984 or, if it is later, the earliest date on which any relevant consideration was given for the acquisition of the asset ; and for this purpose " relevant consideration " means consideration which, assuming the application to the disposal of Chapter II of Part II of the principal Act, would fall to be taken into

account in determining the amount of the gain or loss accruing on the disposal, whether that consideration was given by or on behalf of the person making the disposal or by or on behalf of a predecessor in title of his whose acquisition cost represents, directly or indirectly, the whole or any part of the acquisition cost of the person making the disposal.

Offshore fund operating equalisation arrangements.

93.—(1) For the purposes of this Chapter, an offshore fund operates equalisation arrangements if, and at a time when, arrangements are in existence which have the result that where—

(a) a person acquires by way of initial purchase a material interest in the fund at some time during a period relevant to the arrangements, and

(b) the fund makes a distribution for a period which begins before the date of his acquisition of that interest,

the amount of that distribution which is paid to him (assuming him still to retain that interest) will include a payment of capital which is debited to an account maintained under the arrangements (in this Chapter referred to as " the equalisation account ") and which is determined by reference to the income which had accrued to the fund at the date of his acquisition.

(2) For the purposes of this section, a person acquires an interest in an offshore fund by way of initial purchase if—

(a) his acquisition is by way of subscription for or allotment of new shares, units or other interests issued or created by the fund ; or

(b) his acquisition is by way of direct purchase from the persons concerned with the management of the fund and their sale to him is made in their capacity as managers of the fund.

(3) Without prejudice to section 92(1) above, this Chapter applies, subject to the following provisions of this section, to a disposal by any person of an asset if—

(a) the disposal occurs on or after 6th April 1984 and, at the time of the disposal, the asset constitutes a material interest in an offshore fund which at the time of the disposal is operating equalisation arrangements ; and

(b) the fund is not and has not at any material time, within the meaning of section 92 above, been a non-qualifying offshore fund ; and

(c) the proceeds of the disposal do not fall to be taken into account as a trading receipt.

(4) This Chapter does not, by virtue of subsection (3) above, apply to a disposal if—

(a) it takes place during such a period as is mentioned in subsection (1)(a) above, and

(*b*) throughout so much of that period as precedes the   Part II
disposal, the income of the offshore fund concerned
has been of such a nature as is referred to in paragraph 3(1) of Schedule 19 to this Act.

(5) An event which, apart from section 78 of the principal
Act (re-organisations etc.), would constitute a disposal of an
asset shall constitute such a disposal for the purpose of determining whether, by virtue of subsection (3) above, there is a
disposal to which this Chapter applies.

(6) The reference in subsection (5) above to section 78 of the
principal Act includes a reference to that section as applied
by section 85 of that Act (exchange of securities) but not as
applied by section 82 of that Act (conversion of securities).

94.—(1) In this Chapter references to a material interest in an Material
offshore fund are references to such an interest in any of the interests in
following, namely— offshore
funds.
    (*a*) a company which is resident outside the United King-
dom ;
    (*b*) a unit trust scheme, as defined in section 26(1) of the
Prevention of Fraud (Investments) Act 1958, the trus- 1958 c. 45.
tees of which are not resident in the United Kingdom ;
and
    (*c*) any arrangements which do not fall within paragraph
(*a*) or paragraph (*b*) above, which take effect by virtue
of the law of a territory outside the United Kingdom
and which, under that law, create rights in the nature
of co-ownership (without restricting that expression to
its meaning in the law of any part of the United Kingdom) ;
and any reference in this Chapter to an offshore fund is a reference to any such company, unit trust scheme or arrangements in
which any person has an interest which is a material interest.

(2) Subject to the following provisions of this section, a
person's interest in a company, unit trust scheme or arrangements is a material interest if, at the time when he acquired the
interest, it could reasonably be expected that, at some time during the period of seven years beginning at the time of his acquisition, he would be able to realise the value of the interest
(whether by transfer, surrender or in any other manner).

(3) For the purposes of subsection (2) above, a person is at
any time able to realise the value of an interest if at that time he
can realise an amount which is reasonably approximate to that
portion which the interest represents (directly or indirectly) of
the market value at that time of the assets of the company or, as
the case may be, of the assets subject to the scheme or arrangements.

(4) For the purposes of subsections (2) and (3) above—

    (a) a person is able to realise a particular amount if he is able to obtain that amount either in money or in the form of assets to the value of that amount ; and

    (b) if at any time an interest in an offshore fund has a market value which is substantially greater than the portion which the interest represents, as mentioned in subsection (3) above, of the market value at that time of the assets concerned, the ability to realise such a market value of the interest shall not be regarded as an ability to realise such an amount as is referred to in that subsection.

(5) An interest in a company, scheme or arrangements is not a material interest if—

    (a) it is an interest in respect of any loan capital or debt issued or incurred for money which, in the ordinary course of a business of banking, is lent by a person carrying on that business ; or

    (b) it is a right arising under a policy of insurance.

(6) Shares in a company falling within subsection (1)(a) above (in this subsection referred to as an " overseas company ") do not constitute a material interest if—

    (a) the shares are held by a company and the holding of them is necessary or desirable for the maintenance and development of a trade carried on by the company or a company associated with it ; and

    (b) the shares confer at least 10 per cent. of the total voting rights in the overseas company and a right, in the event of a winding-up, to at least 10 per cent. of the assets of that company remaining after the discharge of all liabilities having priority over the shares ; and

    (c) not more than ten persons hold shares in the overseas company and all the shares in that company confer both voting rights and a right to participate in the assets on a winding-up ; and

    (d) at the time of its acquisition of the shares, the company had such a reasonable expectation as is referred to in subsection (2) above by reason only of the existence of—

        (i) an arrangement under which, at some time within the period of seven years beginning at the time of acquisition, that company may require the other participators to purchase its shares ; or

        (ii) provisions of either an agreement between the participators or the constitution of the overseas company under which the company will be wound up within a period which is, or is reasonably expected to be, shorter than the period referred to in subsection (2) above ; or

  (iii) both such an arrangement and such provisions ;

and in this paragraph " participators " means the persons holding shares falling within paragraph (c) above.

(7) For the purposes of subsection (6)(a) above, a company is associated with another company if one of them has control of the other within the meaning of section 302 of the Taxes Act or both of them are under the control, within the meaning of that section, of the same person or persons.

(8) An interest in a company falling within subsection (1)(a) above is not a material interest at any time when the following conditions are satisfied, namely,—

  (a) that the holder of the interest has the right to have the company wound up ; and

  (b) that, in the event of a winding up, the holder is, by virtue of the interest and any other interest which he then holds in the same capacity, entitled to more than 50 per cent. of the assets remaining after the discharge of all liabilities having priority over the interest or interests concerned.

(9) The market value of any asset for the purposes of this Chapter shall be determined in like manner as it would be determined for the purposes of the principal Act except that, in the case of an interest in an offshore fund for which there are separate published buying and selling prices, subsection (4) of section 150 of that Act (meaning of " market value " in relation to rights of unit holders in a unit trust scheme) shall apply with any necessary modifications for determining the market value of the interest for the purposes of this Chapter.

95.—(1) For the purposes of this Chapter, an offshore fund is a non-qualifying fund except during an account period of the fund in respect of which the fund is certified by the Board as a distributing fund.

(2) An offshore fund shall not be certified as a distributing fund in respect of any account period unless, with respect to that period, the fund pursues a full distribution policy, within the meaning of Part I of Schedule 19 to this Act.

(3) Subject to Part II of Schedule 19 to this Act, an offshore fund shall not be certified as a distributing fund in respect of any account period if, at any time in that period,—

(*a*) more than 5 per cent. by value of the assets of the fund consists of interests in other offshore funds ; or

(*b*) subject to subsections (4) and (5) below, more than 10 per cent. by value of the assets of the fund consists of interests in a single company ; or

(*c*) the assets of the fund include more than 10 per cent. of the issued share capital of any company or of any class of that share capital ; or

(*d*) subject to subsection (6) below, there is more than one class of material interest in the offshore fund and they do not all receive proper distribution benefits, within the meaning of subsection (7) below.

(4) For the purposes of subsection (3)(*b*) above, in any account period the value, expressed as a percentage of the value of all the assets of an offshore fund, of that portion of the assets of the fund which consists of an interest in a single company shall be determined as at the most recent occasion (whether in that account period or an earlier one) on which the fund acquired an interest in that company for consideration in money or money's worth ; but for this purpose there shall be disregarded any occasion—

(*a*) on which the interest acquired constituted the " new holding " for the purposes of section 78 of the principal Act (equation of original shares and new holding), including that section as applied by any later provision of Chapter II of Part IV of that Act (reorganisation of share capital, conversion of securities, etc.) ; and

(*b*) on which no consideration fell to be given for the interest acquired, other than the interest which constituted the " original shares " for the purposes of the said section 78.

(5) Except for the purpose of determining the total value of the assets of an offshore fund, an interest in a company shall be disregarded for the purposes of subsection (3)(*b*) above if—

(*a*) the company carries on (in the United Kingdom or elsewhere) a banking business providing current or deposit account facilities in any currency for members of the public and bodies corporate ; and

(*b*) the interest consists of a current or deposit account provided in the normal course of the company's banking business.

(6) There shall be disregarded for the purposes of subsection (3)(*d*) above any interests in an offshore fund—

(*a*) which are held solely by persons employed or engaged in or about the management of the assets of the fund ; and (*b*) which carry no right or expectation to participate directly or indirectly, in any of the profits of the fund ; and

(*c*) which, on a winding up or on redemption, carry no right to receive anything other than the return of the price paid for the interests.

(7) If in any account period of an offshore fund there is more than one class of material interests in the fund, the classes of interest do not, for the purposes of subsection (3)(*d*) above, all receive proper distribution benefits unless, were each class of interests and the assets which that class represents interests in and assets of a separate offshore fund, each of those separate funds would, with respect to that period, pursue a full distribution policy, within the meaning of Part I of Schedule 19 to this Act.

(8) For the purposes of this Chapter, an account period of an offshore fund shall begin—

(*a*) whenever the fund begins to carry on its activities or, if it is later, on 1st January 1984 ; and

(*b*) whenever an account period of the fund ends without the fund then ceasing to carry on its activities.

(9) For the purposes of this Chapter, an account period of an offshore fund shall end on the first occurrence of any of the following—

(*a*) the expiration of twelve months from the beginning of the period ;

(*b*) an accounting date of the fund or, if there is a period for which the fund does not make up accounts, the end of that period ; and

(*c*) the fund ceasing to carry on its activities.

(10) For the purposes of this Chapter,—

(*a*) an account period of an offshore fund which is a company falling within section 94(1)(*a*) above shall end if, and at the time when, the company ceases to be resident outside the United Kingdom ; and

(*b*) an account period of an offshore fund which is a unit trust scheme falling within section 94(1)(*b*) above shall end if, and at the time when, the trustees of the scheme become resident in the United Kingdom.

(11) The provisions of Part III of Schedule 19 to this Act shall have effect with respect to the procedure for and in connection with the certification of an offshore fund as a distributing fund, and the supplementary provisions in Part IV of that Schedule shall have effect.

Charge to tax of offshore income gains

96.—(1) If a disposal to which this Chapter applies gives rise, in accordance with section 93 above or Schedule 20 to this Act, to an offshore income gain, then, subject to the provisions of this section, the amount of that gain shall be treated for all the purposes of the Tax Acts as income arising at the time of the disposal to the person making the disposal and as constituting profits or gains chargeable to tax under Case VI of Schedule D for the chargeable period in which the disposal is made.

(2) Subject to subsection (3) below, sections 2 and 12 of the principal Act (persons chargeable to tax in respect of chargeable gains) and section 246(2)(b) of the Taxes Act (chargeable gains accruing to certain companies not resident in the United Kingdom) shall have effect in relation to income tax or corporation tax in respect of offshore income gains as they have effect in relation to capital gains tax or corporation tax in respect of chargeable gains.

(3) In the application of section 12 of the principal Act in accordance with subsection (2) above, paragraphs (a) and (b) of subsection (1) of that section (which define the assets on the disposal of which chargeable gains are taxable) shall have effect with the omission of the words " situated in the United Kingdom and ".

(4) In a case where section 12 of the principal Act has effect as modified by subsection (3) above, section 246 of the Taxes Act shall have effect as if, in subsection (2)(b), the words " situated in the United Kingdom " were omitted.

(5) In the case of individuals resident or ordinarily resident but not domiciled in the United Kingdom, section 14 of the principal Act (which provides for taxation on a remittance basis) shall have effect in relation to income tax chargeable by virtue of subsection (1) above on an offshore income gain as it has effect in relation to capital gains tax in respect of gains accruing to such individuals from the disposal of assets situated outside the United Kingdom.

(6) Section 360(2) of the Taxes Act (exemption for charities from tax on chargeable gains by reference to section 145 of the principal Act) shall apply in relation to income tax chargeable by virtue of subsection (1) above on an offshore income gain as it applies in relation to tax on chargeable gains.

(7) In any case where—

(a) a disposal to which this Chapter applies is a disposal of settled property, within the meaning of the principal Act, and

(b) for the purposes of the principal Act, the general administration of the trusts is ordinarily carried on
outside the United Kingdom and the trustees or a
majority of them for the time being are not resident
or not ordinarily resident in the United Kingdom,

PART II

subsection (1) above shall not apply in relation to any offshore
income gain to which the disposal gives rise.

(8) In Schedule 10 to the Finance Act 1975 (capital transfer
tax: valuation) in paragraph 9 (value transferred on death) at
the end of sub-paragraph (1) there shall be added the words
" and

1975 c. 7.

(e) allowance shall be made for a liability for income tax
in respect of an offshore income gain, within the meaning of Chapter VII of Part II of the Finance Act 1984,
arising on a disposal which is deemed to occur on
the death by virtue of section 92(3) of that Act."

97.—(1) Section 15 of the principal Act (chargeable gains
accruing to certain non-resident companies) shall have effect in
relation to offshore income gains subject to the following modifications—

Offshore
income gains
accruing to
persons
resident or
domiciled
abroad.

(a) for any reference to a chargeable gain there shall be
substituted a reference to an offshore income gain ;

(b) for the reference in subsection (7) to capital gains tax
there shall be substituted a reference to income tax
or corporation tax ; and

(c) paragraphs (b) and (c) of subsection (5) and subsection
(8) shall be omitted.

(2) Subject to subsections (3) and (4) below, sections 80 to 84
of the Finance Act 1981 (gains of non-resident settlements) shall
have effect in relation to offshore income gains subject to the
following modifications,—

1981 c. 35.

(a) for any reference to chargeable gains, other than the
reference in section 80(5), there shall be substituted
a reference to offshore income gains ;

(b) in section 80(2) for the words " tax under section 4(1)
of the Capital Gains Tax Act 1979 " there shall be
substituted the words " income tax by virtue of section
96 of the Finance Act 1984 " ;

1979 c. 14.

(c) in section 80(6) the reference to tax shall be construed
as a reference to income tax or corporation tax ; and

(d) sections 80(8) and 83(6) shall be omitted.

(3) In subsection (5) of section 80 of the Finance Act 1981,
both as originally enacted and as applied by subsection (2)

above, the reference to chargeable gains shall be construed as including a reference to offshore income gains.

(4) If, in any year of assessment,—

    (*a*) under subsection (3) of section 80 of the Finance Act 1981, as originally enacted, a chargeable gain falls to be attributed to a beneficiary, and

    (*b*) under that subsection, as applied by subsection (2) above, an offshore income gain also falls to be attributed to him,

subsection (4) of that section (gains attributed in proportion to capital payments received) shall have effect as if it required offshore income gains to be attributed before chargeable gains.

(5) Subject to subsection (6) below, for the purpose of determining whether an individual ordinarily resident in the United Kingdom has a liability for income tax in respect of an offshore income gain which arises on a disposal to which this Chapter applies where the disposal is made by a person resident or domiciled outside the United Kingdom, the following enactments (which relate to the avoidance of tax by the transfer of assets abroad)—

    (*a*) section 478 of the Taxes Act, and

    (*b*) section 45 of the Finance Act 1981,

shall apply as if the offshore income gain arising to the person resident or domiciled outside the United Kingdom constituted income becoming payable to him and, accordingly, any reference in those enactments to income of (or payable or arising to) such a person includes a reference to the offshore income gain arising to him by reason of the disposal to which this Chapter applies.

(6) To the extent that an offshore income gain is treated, by virtue of subsection (1) or subsection (2) above, as having accrued to any person resident or ordinarily resident in the United Kingdom, that gain shall not be deemed to be the income of any individual for the purposes of—

    (*a*) either of the enactments referred to in subsection (5) above ; or

    (*b*) any provision of Part XVI of the Taxes Act (settlements).

Deduction of offshore income gain in determining capital gain.
    98.—(1) The provisions of this section apply where a disposal to which this Chapter applies gives rise to an offshore income gain ; and, if that disposal also constitutes the disposal of the interest concerned for the purposes of the principal Act, then that disposal is in the following provisions of this section referred to as " the 1979 Act disposal ".

(2) So far as relates to an offshore income gain which arises on a material disposal, within the meaning of Part I of Schedule 20 to this Act, subsections (3) and (4) below shall have effect in relation to the 1979 Act disposal in substitution for section 31(1) of the principal Act (deduction of consideration chargeable to tax on income).

(3) Subject to the following provisions of this section, in the computation under Chapter II of Part II of the principal Act of any gain accruing on the 1979 Act disposal, a sum equal to the offshore income gain shall be deducted from the sum which would otherwise constitute the amount or value of the consideration for the disposal.

(4) Where the 1979 Act disposal is of such a nature that, by virtue of section 35 of the principal Act (part disposals) an apportionment falls to be made of certain expenditure, no deduction shall be made by virtue of subsection (3) above in determining, for the purposes of the fraction in subsection (2) of that section, the amount or value of the consideration for the disposal.

(5) If the 1979 Act disposal forms part of a transfer to which section 123 of the principal Act applies (roll-over relief on transfer of business in exchange wholly or partly for shares) then, for the purposes of subsection (4) of that section (determination of the amount of the deduction from the gain on the old assets) " B " in the fraction in that subsection (the value of the whole of the consideration received by the transferor in exchange for the business) shall be taken to be what it would be if the value of the consideration other than shares so received by the transferor were reduced by a sum equal to the offshore income gain.

(6) Where the disposal to which this Chapter applies constitutes such a disposal by virtue of section 92(6) or section 93(5) above, the principal Act shall have effect as if an amount equal to the offshore income gain to which the disposal gives rise were given (by the person making the exchange concerned) as consideration for the new holding, within the meaning of section 79 of that Act (consideration given or received for new holding on a reorganisation).

(7) In any case where—

    (*a*) a disposal to which this Chapter applies by virtue of subsection (3) of section 93 above is made otherwise than to the offshore fund concerned or the persons referred to in subsection (2)(*b*) of that section, and

    (*b*) subsequently, a distribution which is referable to the asset disposed of is paid ether to the person who made the disposal or to a person connected with him, and

PART II

(c) the disposal gives rise (in accordance with Part II of Schedule 20 to this Act) to an offshore income gain,

then, for the purposes of the Tax Acts, the amount of the first distribution falling within paragraph (b) above shall be taken to be reduced or, as the case may be, extinguished by deducting therefrom an amount equal to the offshore income gain referred to in paragraph (c) above and, if that amount exceeds the amount of that first distribution, the balance shall be set against the second and, where necessary, any later distribution falling within paragraph (b) above, until the balance is exhausted.

(8) Section 533 of the Taxes Act (connected persons) applies for the purposes of subsection (7)(b) above.

Offshore income gains of insurance companies.

99.—(1) An offshore income gain accruing to an insurance company carrying on life assurance business shall, if it accrues in respect of investments held in connection with that business, be treated for the purposes of sections 310 (rate relief: investment income reserved for policy holders) and 315 (foreign life assurance funds) of the Taxes Act as if it were income from investments held in connection with that business.

(2) Income attributable to offshore income gains shall be left out of account in computing under section 312 of the Taxes Act (general annuity business and pension business: separate charge on profits) the profits arising to an insurance company from general annuity business and, accordingly, in subsection (2)(a) of section 313 of the Taxes Act (general annuity business) after the words " development gains " there shall be inserted the words " or offshore income gains, within the meaning of Chapter VII of Part II of the Finance Act 1984 ".

(3) In section 316 of the Taxes Act (overseas life insurance companies: charge on investment income) in subsection (1A) (exclusion of income attributable to development gains) after the words " development gains " there shall be inserted the words " or offshore income gains, within the meaning of Chapter VII of Part II of the Finance Act 1984 ".

(4) Section 323 of the Taxes Act (interpretation of Chapter II of Part XII of that Act) has effect in relation to this section as if it were included in that Chapter.

Offshore income gains of trustees.

100.—(1) Income arising in a year of assessment by virtue of section 96(1) above to trustees shall be chargeable to income tax at a rate equal to the sum of the basic rate and the additional rate for that year.

1973 c. 51.

(2) In section 17 of the Finance Act 1973 (payments under discretionary trusts), in subsection (3) (amounts to be set against

tax assessable on trustees in connection with such payments), at the end of paragraph (*e*) there shall be inserted the words " and

    (*f*) the amount of any tax on income arising to the trustees by virtue of section 96(1) of the Finance Act 1984 (offshore income gains) and charged at a rate equal to the sum of the basic rate and the additional rate by virtue of section 100(1) of that Act ".

(3) Where an offshore income gain accrues in respect of a disposal of assets made by a person holding them as trustee for a person who would be absolutely entitled as against the trustee but for being an infant, the income which by virtue of section 96(1) above is treated as arising by reference to that gain shall for the purposes of Chapter II of Part XVI of the Taxes Act (settlements on children) be deemed to be paid to the infant; and in this subsection " infant ", in relation to Scotland, means a pupil or minor.

PART III

CAPITAL TRANSFER TAX

101.—(1) Section 91(1) of the Finance Act 1982 (indexation of Reduction rate bands) shall not apply to chargeable transfers made in the of tax. year beginning with 6th April 1984.   1982 c. 39.

(2) For the Tables in section 37(3) of the Finance Act 1975 1975 c. 7. there shall be substituted the Tables set out below.

FIRST TABLE

Portion of value		Rate of tax
Lower limit £	Upper limit £	Per cent.
0	64,000	Nil
64,000	85,000	30
85,000	116,000	35
116,000	148,000	40
148,000	185,000	45
185,000	232,000	50
232,000	285,000	55
285,000	—	60

Second Table

Portion of value		Rate of tax
Lower limit £	Upper limit £	Per cent.
0	64,000	Nil
64,000	85,000	15
85,000	116,000	17½
116,000	148,000	20
148,000	185,000	22½
185,000	232,000	25
232,000	285,000	27½
285,000	—	30

(3) Subsection (2) above applies to any chargeable transfer made on or after 13th March 1984.

Special
discretionary
trusts:
excluded
property.
1982 c. 39.
102.—(1) In section 113 of the Finance Act 1982 (charge to tax in respect of property leaving temporary charitable trusts), the following subsection shall be inserted after subsection (6) and will accordingly be applied by sections 114 (accumulation and maintenance trusts), 116 (property leaving employee trusts and newspaper trusts) and 118 (protective trusts and trusts for disabled persons) of that Act—

" (6A) Where the whole or part of the amount on which tax is charged under this section is attributable to property which was excluded property at any time during the relevant period then, in determining the rate at which tax is charged under this section in respect of that amount or part, no quarter throughout which that property was excluded property shall be counted.".

(2) In subsection (7) of section 113 (which defines " relevant period " for the purposes of subsection (6)) for the words " subsection (6) " there shall be substituted the words " subsections (6) and (6A) ".

(3) This section has effect in relation to events on or after 9th March 1982.

Discretionary
trusts:
distributions
made within
two years
of testator's
death.
1975 c. 7.
103.—(1) After subsection (1A) of section 47 of the Finance Act 1975 (certain distributions made within two years of testator's death to be treated as made under his will) there shall be inserted the following subsection—

" (1AA) This Part of this Act shall also apply as mentioned in subsection (1A)(*b*) above in any case where the circumstances are as mentioned in subsection (1A) but the

event in question is one on which tax would be so chargeable apart from—

> (a) section 115 of the Finance Act 1982 (property
> becoming subject to employee trusts);
>
> (b) section 119 of that Act (property becoming held
> for charitable purposes or by exempt bodies); or
>
> (c) paragraph 1(1) of Schedule 16 to that Act (pro-
> perty becoming comprised in maintenance funds
> for historic buildings)."

(2) This section has effect in relation to deaths occurring on
or after 13th March 1984.

104.—(1) In section 121 of the Finance Act 1982 (property   Property
moving between settlements), the following subsection shall be   moving
added at the end—   between
settlements.

> " (3) Subsection (1) above does not apply where a re-
> versionary interest in the property expectant on the termina-
> tion of a qualifying interest in possession subsisting under
> the first settlement was settled on the trusts of the other
> settlement before 10th December 1981.".

(2) In paragraph 3 of Schedule 7 to the Finance Act 1975   1975 c. 7.
(certain government securities to be excluded property if person
beneficially entitled is domiciled and ordinarily resident abroad)
the following sub-paragraph shall be inserted after sub-paragraph
(2A)—

> " (2AA) Sub-paragraph (2A) above does not apply where
> a reversionary interest in the property expectant on the
> termination of a qualifying interest in possession subsisting
> under the first settlement was settled on the trusts of the
> second settlement before 10th December 1981.".

(3) This section has effect in relation to events on or after
15th March 1983.

105.—(1) In paragraph 23(3) of Schedule 4 to the Finance Act   Adjustment
1975 (adjustment of tax in cases of fraud, wilful default or   of tax.
neglect), for the words " a person liable for the tax, the period "
there shall be substituted the words " any of the following—

> (a) a person liable for the tax; and
>
> (b) in the case of tax chargeable under Chapter II of Part
> IV of the Finance Act 1982, the person who is the   1982 c. 39.
> settlor in relation to the settlement;

the period ".

(2) With effect from 1st April 1983, subsection (8) of section 114 of the Finance Act 1976 (transfers reported late) shall cease to have effect.

(3) Subsection (1) above has effect in relation to any fraud, wilful default or neglect coming to the knowledge of the Board on or after 1st April 1983.

Recovery of tax.
1975 c. 7.

1971 c. 58.

106.—(1) In Schedule 4 to the Finance Act 1975, after paragraph 22 there shall be inserted—

" 22A.—In Scotland, tax and interest on tax may, without prejudice to any other remedy, and if the amount of the tax and interest does not exceed the sum for the time being specified in section 35(1)(a) of the Sheriff Courts (Scotland) Act 1971, be sued for and recovered in the sheriff court.

22B. An officer of the Board who is authorised by the Board to do so may address the court in any proceedings in a county court or sheriff court for the recovery of tax or interest on tax."

(2) After paragraph 36 of that Schedule there shall be inserted—

" 36A. In any proceedings for the recovery of tax or interest on tax, a certificate by an officer of the Board—

(a) that the tax or interest is due, or

(b) that, to the best of his knowledge and belief, it has not been paid,

shall be sufficient evidence that the sum mentioned in the certificate is due or, as the case may be, unpaid ; and a document purporting to be such a certificate shall be deemed to be such a certificate unless the contrary is proved."

Relief for stud farms.
1981 c. 35.

107.—(1) For the purposes of Schedule 14 to the Finance Act 1981 (capital transfer tax: relief for agricultural property) the breeding and rearing of horses on a stud farm and the grazing of horses in connection with those activities shall be taken to be agriculture and any buildings used in connection with those activities to be farm buildings.

(2) In paragraph 12 of Schedule 10 to the Finance Act 1975 (farm cottages) the existing provisions shall become sub-paragraph (1) and at the end there shall be inserted—

" (2) Expressions used in sub-paragraph (1) above and in Schedule 14 to the Finance Act 1981 have the same meaning in that sub-paragraph as in that Schedule."

(3) In section 97 of the Finance Act 1981 (grant of tenancies PART III of agricultural property) for subsection (2) there shall be sub- 1981 c. 35. stituted—

" (2) Expressions uscd in subsection (1) abovc and in Schedule 14 to this Act have the same meaning in that subsection as in that Schedule."

(4) This section has effect in relation to transfers of value and other events occurring on or after 10th March 1981.

108. Schedule 21 to this Act (which contains amendments Pre-designed to facilitate, or otherwise desirable in connection with, consolidation the consolidation of the law relating to capital transfer tax) amendments. shall have effect.

PART IV

STAMP DUTY

109.—(1) In subsection (1) of section 55 of the Finance Act Reduction 1963 and subsection (1) of section 4 of the Finance Act (Northern of stamp duty Ireland) 1963 for paragraphs (a) to (e) there shall be substituted on conveyances the following paragraphs : — and transfers.

1963 c. 25.

" (a) where the amount or value of the consideration is 1963 c. 22 £30,000 or under and the instrument is certified, as (N.I.). described in section 34(4) of the Finance Act 1958, at 1958 c. 56. £30,000, nil ;

(b) where paragraph (a) above does not apply and the amount or value of the consideration does not exceed £500, the rate of 50p for every £50 or part of £50 of the consideration ; and

(c) where paragraph (a) above does not apply and the amount or value of the consideration exceeds £500, the rate of £1 for every £100 or part of £100 of the consideration " ;

and in subsection (2) of each of those sections for the words from " as if " onwards there shall be substituted the words " as if paragraph (a) and, in paragraphs (b) and (c), the words " paragraph (a) above does not apply and " were omitted ".

(2) Part III of Schedule 11 to the Finance Act 1974 (saving 1974 c. 30. for certain transfers of stock or marketable securities) shall cease to have effect.

(3) Subject to subsection (4) below, subsections (1) and (2) above apply—

(a) to instruments executed on or after 20th March 1984 ; **and** (*b*) to instruments executed on or after 13th March 1984 which are stamped on or after 20th March 1984 ;

and, for the purposes of section 14(4) of the Stamp Act 1891 (instruments not to be given in evidence etc. unless stamped in accordance with the law in force at the time of first execution), the law in force at the time of execution of an instrument falling within paragraph (*b*) above shall be deemed to be that as varied in accordance with subsections (1) and (2) above.

(4) In the case of an instrument giving effect to a stock exchange transaction, as defined in section 4 of the Stock Transfer Act 1963, subsections (1) to (3) above do not apply unless the transaction takes place on or after 12th March 1984 and is one in respect of which settlement is due on or after 13th March 1984.

(5) This section shall be deemed to have come into force on 20th March 1984.

110.—(1) Section 107 of the Finance Act 1981 (sales of houses at discount by local authorities etc.) shall be amended in accordance with the following provisions of this section.

(2) At the end of subsection (3) of that section (which lists the bodies a conveyance or transfer by which is affected by the section) there shall be added the following paragraph : —

" (*n*) the United Kingdom Atomic Energy Authority ".

(3) After subsection (3) of that section there shall be added the following subsection : —

" (3A) This section also applies to any conveyance or transfer on sale of a dwelling house where the conveyance or transfer is made pursuant to a sub-sale made at a discount by a body falling within subsection (3)(*f*) above."

(4) Subsections (2) and (3) above have effect with respect to instruments—

(*a*) executed on or after 20th March 1984, or

(*b*) executed on or after 13th March 1984 and stamped on or after 20th March 1984,

and, for the purposes of section 14(4) of the Stamp Act 1891 (instruments not to be given in evidence etc. unless stamped in accordance with the law in force at the time of first execution), the law in force at the time of execution of an instrument falling within paragraph (*b*) above shall be deemed to be that as varied in accordance with subsections (2) and (3) above.

(5) With respect to instruments executed on or after the passing of this Act, at the end of subsection (3) of that section,

and after the paragraph inserted by subsection (2) above, there shall be added the following paragraph: —

"(*o*) such other body as the Treasury may, by order made by statutory instrument, prescribe for the purposes of this section ".

111.—(1) In section 75 of the Stamp Act 1891 (agreements for leases for terms not exceeding 35 years to be stamped as if they were leases) in subsection (1) the words " not exceeding thirty-five years " shall be omitted and for subsection (2) (5 pence stamp on lease in conformity with duly stamped agreement) there shall be substituted the following subsection: —

" (2) Where duty has been duly paid on an agreement for a lease or tack and, subsequent to that agreement, a lease or tack is granted which either—

(*a*) is in conformity with the agreement, or

(*b*) relates to substantially the same property and term as the agreement,

then the duty which would otherwise be charged on the lease or tack shall be reduced (or, as the case may be, extinguished) by the deduction therefrom of the duty paid on the agreement."

(2) In any case where—

(*a*) an interest in land is conveyed or transferred subject to an agreement for a lease or tack for a term exceeding 35 years, or

(*b*) a lease or tack is granted subject to an agreement for a lease or tack for a term exceeding 35 years,

then, whether or not the conveyance, transfer, lease or tack is expressed to be so subject, it shall not be taken to be duly stamped unless there is denoted upon the conveyance, transfer, lease or tack the duty paid on the agreement; and section 11 of the Stamp Act 1891 shall have effect for this purpose as if the duty chargeable on the conveyance, transfer, lease or tack depended on the duty paid on the agreement.

(3) For the purposes of subsection (2) above, an interest conveyed or transferred or, as the case may be, a lease or tack granted is not to be regarded as subject to an agreement for a lease or tack if that agreement is directly enforceable against another interest in the land in relation to which the interest conveyed or transferred or, as the case may be, the lease or tack granted is a superior interest.

(4) In section 15 of the Stamp Act 1891 (stamping of instruments after execution) in the Table following paragraph (*d*) of subsection (2) (instruments as to which certain special provisions

PART IV

apply), after the entry beginning " lease or tack ", there shall be inserted: —

| " Agreement for lease or tack chargeable under section 75. | The person contracting for the lease or tack to be granted to him or another." |

(5) This section applies to any agreement for a lease or tack entered into on or after 20th March 1984 and shall be deemed to have come into force on that date.

Sub-sales.
1891 c. 39.

112.—(1) In subsection (4) of section 58 of the Stamp Act 1891 (in case of a sub-sale to a single purchaser, duty chargeable only on consideration moving from the sub-purchaser) after the words " conveyed immediately to the sub-purchaser " there shall be inserted the words " then, except where—

(a) the chargeable consideration moving from the sub-purchaser is less than the value of the property immediately before the contract of sale to him, and

1981 c. 35.

(b) the conveyance is not one to which section 107 of the Finance Act 1981 (sales of houses at discount by local authorities etc.) applies ".

(2) In subsection (5) of section 58 of the Stamp Act 1891 (in case of a sub-sale in parts or parcels to different sub-purchasers, each conveyance chargeable with duty only on consideration moving from the sub-purchaser) after the words " to different persons in parts or parcels " there shall be inserted the words " then, except where the aggregate of the chargeable consideration for the sale of all such parts or parcels is less than the value of the whole of the property immediately before the contract for their sale or, as the case may be, the first contract for the sale of any of them ".

(3) At the end of the said section 58 there shall be inserted the following subsection: —

" (7) Any reference in subsection (4) or subsection (5) of this section to chargeable consideration is a reference to consideration which falls to be brought into account in determining the duty (if any) chargeable on the conveyance to the sub-purchaser or, as the case may be, on the conveyance of each of the parts or parcels in question ; and in any case where it is necessary for the purposes of either of those subsections to determine the value of any property, that value shall be determined as for the purposes of section 74 of the Finance (1909-10) Act 1910 (gifts inter vivos)."

1910 c. 8.

(4) This section applies where the contract for the sub-sale or, as the case may be, the first contract for sub-sale of a part or parcel is entered into on or after 20th March 1984, and shall be deemed to have come into force on that date.

PART V

OIL TAXATION

113.—(1) Subject to subsection (3) below, in determining Restriction whether any abortive exploration expenditure or exploration on PRT and appraisal expenditure is allowable in the case of a partici- reliefs. pator in an oil field under section 5 or section 5A of the principal Act, no account shall be taken of any expenditure incurred before his qualifying date.

(2) Subject to subsection (3) below, in determining whether any unrelievable field losses are allowable in the case of a participator in an oil field under section 6 of that Act, no account shall be taken of any allowable loss which, in the case of any other oil field from which the winning of oil has permanently ceased, has accrued as mentioned in subsection (1) of that section unless the date on which the winning of oil from that other field permanently ceased fell on or after his qualifying date.

(3) Subsections (1) and (2) above do not apply in the case of a participator in an oil field if his qualifying date falls before 14th September 1983 or before the end of the first chargeable period in relation to the field.

(4) In this section " qualifying date ", in relation to a partici- pator in an oil field, means whichever of the following dates is applicable in his case or (if there is more than one) the ear- liest of them—

(*a*) the date on which the participator first qualified in respect of any licensed area, being an area which is wholly or partly included in the field ;

(*b*) if the participator is a company, the date on which another company first satisfied both of the following conditions, that is to say—

(i) it qualified in respect of any licensed area, being an area which is wholly or partly included in the field ; and

(ii) it was connected with the participator ; and

(*c*) if he is a participator in the field by reason of an ar- rangement between him and another company, being an arrangement to which paragraph 5 of Schedule 3 to the principal Act applies (transfer of rights etc. to associated company), the date on which the arrange- ment was made or, if later, the date on which that other company first qualified in respect of any licensed area, being an area which is wholly or partly included in the field.

(5) For the purposes of subsection (4) above, a person qualifies in respect of a licensed area when, in respect of that area—

> (*a*) he is, or is one of those, entitled to the benefit of a licence, or
>
> (*b*) he enjoys rights under an agreement, being an agreement which has been approved by the Board and certified by the Secretary of State to confer on him rights which are the same as, or similar to, those conferred by a licence.

(6) Where (apart from this section) expenditure would be allowable under section 5 or section 5A of the principal Act in the case of a participator in an oil field (in this subsection referred to as " the new participator ") by virtue only of paragraph 16 or paragraph 16A of Schedule 17 to the Finance Act 1980 (transfers of interests in oil fields) then, for the purpose of determining whether the expenditure is allowable in his case in accordance with this section, the date which was the qualifying date in relation to the old participator (within the meaning of that Schedule) is an applicable date to be taken into account for the purposes of subsection (4) above in the case of the new participator.

(7) For the purposes of subsection (2) above the date on which the winning of oil from an oil field has permanently ceased is the date stated in a decision (whether of the Board or on appeal from the Board) under Schedule 8 to the principal Act to be that date.

(8) For the purposes of this section, one company is connected with another if—

> (*a*) one is a 51 per cent. subsidiary of the other and the other is not a 51 per cent. subsidiary of any company ; or
>
> (*b*) each of them is a 51 per cent. subsidiary of a third company which is not itself a 51 per cent. subsidiary of any company ;

and section 532 of the Taxes Act (subsidiaries) applies for the purposes of this subsection.

(9) In this section—

> (*a*) " company " means any body corporate ; and
>
> (*b*) any reference to the winning of oil from an oil field permanently ceasing includes a reference to the permanent cessation of operations for the winning of oil from the field.

(10) This section shall have effect in relation to any expenditure or losses in respect of which a claim is made after 13th September 1983.

114.—(1) This section applies only in relation to oil consisting of gas and references in the following provisions of this section to oil shall be construed accordingly.

PART V

Sales of gas: treatment of certain payments.

(2) In any case where, under a contract for the sale of oil won from an oil field, the consideration includes any sum—

    (*a*) which is payable by the buyer in respect of a quantity of oil to be delivered at a specified time or in a specified period, and

    (*b*) which is payable whether or not the buyer takes delivery of the whole of the oil at that time or in that period, and

    (*c*) which, in the event that the buyer does not take delivery of the whole of the oil, entitles the buyer to delivery of oil free of charge at a later time or in a later period,

then, to the extent that the sum is payable in respect of oil which is not delivered at the time or in the period in question, the sum shall be treated for the purposes of the principal Act as an advance payment for the oil to be delivered free of charge and, accordingly, that oil shall be treated for those purposes as sold for a price which (subject to any additional element arising under the following provisions of this section) is equal to that advance payment.

(3) Where, in a case falling within subsection (2) above, an amount of oil is delivered free of charge in pursuance of the entitlement referred to in paragraph (*c*) of that subsection, the proportion of the advance payment referred to in that subsection which is to be attributed to that amount of oil shall be that which that amount of oil bears to the total quantity of oil of which the buyer is entitled to delivery free of charge by virtue of the payment of the sum in question.

(4) In any case where—

    (*a*) by virtue of subsection (2) above a sum falls to any extent to be treated as an advance payment for oil to be delivered free of charge, but

    (*b*) at the latest date at which oil could be delivered free of charge in pursuance of the entitlement referred to in paragraph (*c*) of that subsection, the whole or any part of the oil to which that entitlement relates has not been so delivered,

then at that latest date, one tonne of oil shall be deemed to be delivered as mentioned in paragraph (*b*) above and so much of the advance payment as has not, under subsection (3) above, been attributed to oil actually delivered shall be attributed to that one tonne.

(5) Where, under a contract for the sale of oil won from an oil field, the consideration includes any sums (in this section referred to as " capacity payments ")—

    (*a*) which are payable by the buyer at specified times or in respect of specified periods, and

    (*b*) which, though they may vary in amount by reference to deliveries of oil or other factors, are payable whether or not oil is delivered under the contract at particular times or in particular periods, and

    (*c*) which do not, under the terms of the contract or by virtue of subsection (2) above, fall to be treated, in whole or in part, as advance payments for oil to be delivered at some time after the times or periods at or in respect of which the sums are payable,

then, in so far as they would not do so apart from this subsection, the capacity payments shall be treated for the purposes of the principal Act as an additional element of the price received or receivable for the oil sold under the contract.

(6) For the purpose of determining, in a case where there are capacity payments under a contract for the sale of oil won from an oil field, the assessable profit or allowable loss accruing in a particular chargeable period to the participator by whom oil is sold under the contract, each capacity payment shall be treated as an additional element of the price received or receivable for the oil delivered by him under the contract in the chargeable period in which the capacity payment is paid or payable ; and if no oil is in fact so delivered in a chargeable period in which a capacity payment is paid or payable, one tonne of oil shall be deemed to be so delivered in that period and, accordingly, the capacity payment shall be treated for the purposes of the principal Act as the price for which that tonne is sold.

(7) If, by virtue of subsection (4) or subsection (6) above, one tonne of oil is deemed to be delivered in any chargeable period of the oil field referred to in subsection (2) or, as the case may be, subsection (5) above, a return for that period by the participator concerned under paragraph 2 of Schedule 2 to the principal Act shall give the like information in relation to that tonne as in relation to any other oil falling within sub-paragraph (2)(*a*) of that paragraph.

Information relating to sales at arm's length and market value of oil.

115.—(1) The Board may, by notice in writing given to a company which is or has been a participator in an oil field, require that company to give to the Board, within such time (not being less than thirty days) as may be specified in the notice, such particulars (which may include details of relevant documents) as may be so specified of any related transaction which appears to the Board to be relevant for the purpose of—

(a) determining whether a disposal of any oil is a sale at arm's length, or

(b) ascertaining the market value of any oil.

(2) For the purposes of a notice under subsection (1) above a transaction is a related transaction if, but only if, it is one to which the company to whom the notice is given or a company associated with that company was a party ; and for the purposes of this subsection two companies are associated with one another if—

(a) one is under the control of the other ; or

(b) both are under the control of the same person or persons ;

and in this subsection " control " has the meaning given by section 534 of the Taxes Act.

(3) In any case where a company (in this subsection and subsection (4) below referred to as " the participator company ") is or has been a participator in an oil field and—

(a) the participator company is a 51 per cent. subsidiary of another company, or

(b) another company is a 51 per cent. subsidiary of the participator company, or

(c) the participator company and another company are both 51 per cent. subsidiaries of a third company,

the Board may, by notice in writing given to any company referred to in paragraphs (a) to (c) above which is resident in the United Kingdom, require it to make available for inspection any relevant books, accounts or other documents or records whatsoever of the company itself or, subject to subsection (5) below, of any other company which is its 51 per cent. subsidiary.

(4) In subsection (3) above " relevant " means relating to any transaction which is relevant for the purpose of—

(a) determining whether a disposal of any oil by the participator company is a sale at arm's length ; or

(b) ascertaining the market value of oil won by the participator company.

(5) In any case where—

(a) under subsection (3) above a company is by notice required to make available for inspection any books, accounts, documents or records of one of its 51 per cent. subsidiaries which is resident outside the United Kingdom, and (*b*) it appears to the Board, on the application of the company, that the circumstances are such that the requirement ought not to have effect,

the Board shall direct that the company need not comply with the requirement.

(6) If, on an application under subsection (5) above, the Board refuse to give a direction under that subsection, the company concerned may, by notice in writing given to the Board within thirty days after the refusal, appeal to the Special Commissioners who, if satisfied that the requirement in question ought in the circumstances not to have effect, may determine accordingly.

(7) In this section—

" company " means any body corporate ; and

" 51 per cent. subsidiary " shall be construed in accordance with section 532 of the Taxes Act (subsidiaries).

Offences
relating to
section 115.

116.—(1) Where a company has been required by notice under subsection (1) or subsection (3) of section 115 above to give any particulars or, as the case may be, to make available for inspection any books, accounts, documents or records and fails to comply with the notice, the company shall be liable, subject to subsection (3) below—

(*a*) to a penalty not exceeding £500 ; and

(*b*) if the failure continues after it has been declared by the court or the Commissioners before whom proceedings for the penalty have been commenced, to a further penalty not exceeding £100 for each day on which the failure so continues.

(2) Where a company fraudulently or negligently furnishes, gives, produces or makes any incorrect information, document or record of a kind mentioned in subsection (1) or subsection (3) of section 115 above, the company shall be liable to a penalty not exceeding £2,500 or, in the case of fraud on its part, £5,000.

(3) A company shall not be liable to any penalty incurred under subsection (1) above for failure to comply with a notice if the failure is remedied before proceedings for the recovery of the penalty are commenced.

(4) In this section " company " has the same meaning as in section 115 above.

Part VI

Miscellaneous and Supplementary

National insurance surcharge

117. The surcharge payable under the National Insurance Surcharge Act 1976 is hereby abolished— Abolition of national insurance surcharge. 1976 c. 85.

    (*a*) with respect to earnings paid on or after 6th April 1985, in the case of secondary Class 1 contributions payable by any of the bodies mentioned in section 143(4) of the Finance Act 1982 ; and 1982 c. 39.

    (*b*) with respect to earnings paid on or after 1st October 1984, in any other case.

Development land tax

118. With respect to financial years ending after 31st March 1984, in the following provisions of the Development Land Tax Act 1976 (which provide for, or relate to, the exemption for the first £50,000 of realised development value) for " £50,000 ", in each place where it occurs, there shall be substituted " £75,000 "— Increase of exemption from £50,000 to £75,000. 1976 c. 24.

    (*a*) section 12 (the exemption itself) ; and

    (*b*) in Part II of Schedule 8 (notification) paragraphs 35(1) and 38(3).

119.—(1) In section 19A of the Development Land Tax Act 1976 (which, in the case of certain deemed disposals before 1st April 1984, defers liability to tax in relation to development for the owner's use) the words " and before 1st April 1984 " shall be omitted. Deferred liability.

(2) In section 27 of that Act (deferred liability for tax) in subsection (2), at the beginning of paragraph (*b*) (liability to arise at the time of the operative disposal) there shall be inserted the words " except as provided by subsection (2A) below ".

(3) After subsection (2) of the said section 27 there shall be inserted the following subsection : —

    " (2A) If the operative disposal does not fall within the period of twelve years beginning on the date of the deemed disposal, any liability for development land tax on the accrued development value shall be extinguished with effect from the expiry of that period."

(4) At the end of the said section 27 there shall be added the following subsection : —

    " (8) The extinguishment of any deferred liability for development land tax on the accrued development value shall not affect the operation of any enactment (whether passed before or after this Act) which, before the liability was extinguished, had effect in relation to that liability or the accrued development value."

(5) In Schedule 8 to that Act, after paragraph 38 there shall be inserted the following paragraph:—

" 38A. A person who becomes chargeable to development land tax by virtue of a disposal—

    (*a*) which is the operative disposal for the purposes of section 27 of this Act or which is a further disposal falling within subsection (5) of that section, and

    (*b*) of which he is not required to give notice by virtue of any of the preceding provisions of this Part of this Schedule,

shall give notice of it to the Board not later than the end of the financial year following that in which the disposal occurred."

(6) In that Schedule, in paragraph 41 (penalties) in sub-paragraph (1)(*a*), after the words " 35(1) or " there shall be inserted the words " paragraph 38A or ".

Extension of relief for Housing Corporation and registered housing associations.
1976 c. 24.

120.—(1) In section 26 of the Development Land Tax Act 1976 (provisions relating to the Housing Corporation and certain housing associations) in subsection (1) (exemption from tax on realised development value accruing on deemed disposals by approved co-operative housing associations and self-build societies) for paragraphs (*a*) and (*b*) there shall be substituted—

" (*a*) the Housing Corporation, or

    (*b*) a registered housing association, or

    (*c*) an approved co-operative housing association not falling within paragraph (*b*) above, or

    (*d*) an unregistered self-build society " ;

and for the words " by that association or society " there shall be substituted the words " by that body ".

(2) In consequence of the amendments made by subsection (1) above, subsection (2) of the said section 26 (cases where tax liability was deferred) and, in subsection (3) of that section, the words " or subsection (2) " shall be omitted.

(3) This section has effect with respect to deemed disposals on or after 13th March 1984.

Deduction of tax from consideration for disposals by non-residents.

121.—(1) Section 40 of the Development Land Tax Act 1976 (deduction on account of tax from consideration for disposals by non-residents) shall be amended in accordance with this section.

(2) In subsection (1) the words " which, at that time, is development land " shall be omitted.

(3) In subsection (2) (no deduction where consideration does not exceed £50,000) for " £50,000 " there shall be substituted " £75,000 or such other limit as may be specified by regulations under subsection (7) below ".

(4) In subsection (3) (the amount of the deduction) for the words " one half " there shall be substituted the words " subject to any provision made by regulations under subsection (7) below, two fifths ".

(5) In subsection (7) (regulations of the Board) in paragraph (*b*) after the word " vary " there shall be inserted the words " the limit in subsection (2) above or " and after the word " section " there shall be inserted the words " either generally or ".

(6) Subsection (8) (meaning of " development land ") shall be omitted.

(7) Except in so far as relates to the making of regulations—

    (*a*) subsection (3) above has effect in relation to any disposal on or after 1st April 1984 ; and

    (*b*) the other provisions of this section have effect in relation to any disposal on or after 6th August 1984.

122. In section 47 of the Development Land Tax Act 1976 (interpretation) in subsection (1A) (which was inserted by section 14 of the Finance (No. 2) Act 1983 and provides that " development " does not include certain operations relating to telecommunications which are begun on or before 31st December 1984) the words " are begun on or before 31st December 1984 and " shall be omitted.

Operations relating to telecommunications
1976 c. 24.
1983 c. 49.

123.—(1) For the purpose of extending the period during which development land tax may, in certain cases, be paid by instalments from eight to ten years and of restricting those instalments to annual instalments, the following amendments shall be made in Schedule 8 to the Development Land Tax Act 1976—

Payment by instalments and postponement.

    (*a*) the word " ten " shall be substituted for the word " eight ", in each of paragraphs 45(5) and (7)(*b*) and 50(1) and (4), and for the words from " eight " onwards in paragraph 45(2)(*b*) ;

    (*b*) in paragraph 45(3)(*c*), for the word " nine " there shall be substituted the word " eleven " ; and

    (*c*) in paragraph 44(1) for the words from " instalments " onwards there shall be inserted the words " yearly instalments ".

(2) In section 114(6)(*b*) of the Finance Act 1980 (application of paragraph 45 of Schedule 8 to the Act of 1976 in relation to advance assessment of tax on deemed disposals), for the words from " nine years " onwards there shall be substituted the words " ' eleven years ' there were substituted the words ' ten years ' ".

(3) In paragraph 52 of Schedule 8 to the Act of 1976 (postponement of tax on incorporation disposal), in sub-paragraphs (4) and (6) for the word " eight " there shall be substituted the word " ten ".

(4) In section 86A of the Taxes Management Act 1970 (interest on development land tax unpaid on reckonable date)—

> (*a*) in subsection (1), for the words " and (3) " there shall be substituted the words " (3) and (3A) " ; and
>
> (*b*) after subsection (3) there shall be inserted the following subsection—
>
>> " (3A) Subsection (1) above shall have effect, in relation to any tax postponed under paragraph 52 of Schedule 8 to the Act of 1976 (postponement on incorporation disposal) as if the reference to the reckonable date were a reference to the date determined in accordance with sub-paragraphs (4) to (6) of paragraph 52."

(5) This section has effect in relation to disposals made, and events occurring, on or after 6th August 1983 ; but where, in relation to any such disposal made, or event occurring, before the commencement of this section a person has duly elected to pay development land tax by half-yearly instalments he shall be entitled to continue to pay by such instalments and the Act of 1976 shall have effect accordingly.

Miscellaneous

124.—(1) In paragraph 4 of Schedule 15 to the Finance Act 1973 (provisions supplementing the territorial extension of charge to tax under section 38 of that Act), after sub-paragraph (2) there shall be inserted the following sub-paragraph—

> " (3) A payment in pursuance of a notice under this paragraph shall not be allowed as a deduction in computing any income, profits or losses for any tax purposes."

(2) After that paragraph, there shall be inserted the following paragraph—

> " 4A.—(1) Subject to the following provisions of this Schedule, the power of the Board under paragraph 4 above to serve a notice in respect of tax remaining unpaid as there mentioned shall also apply where—
>
>> (*a*) tax is assessed on any person not resident in the United Kingdom as mentioned in paragraph 4(1)

(*a*) or (*b*) but more than one licence under the Petroleum (Production) Act 1934 is the basis for the assessment ; or

(*b*) tax assessed on any such person includes, but is not limited to, tax assessed on him as so mentioned (whether by reference to one or to more than one such licence) ;

but in any such case the amount the holder of any licence in question may be required to pay by a notice under that paragraph shall be the amount of the tax remaining unpaid under the assessment which is attributable to the profits or gains in respect of which that licence was the basis for the assessment, together with a corresponding proportion of any interest due as mentioned in paragraph 4(1).

(2) For the purposes of sub-paragraph (1) above the amount of the tax remaining unpaid under the assessment which is attributable to the profits or gains in respect of which any licence in question was the basis for the assessment is such part of the total amount of that tax as bears to that total amount the same proportion as the proportion borne by the amount of the profits or gains in respect of which that licence was the basis for the assessment to the total amount of the profits or gains in respect of which the assessment was made."

(3) In paragraph 6 of that Schedule, after the word " apply " there shall be inserted the words " in relation to the holder of any licence ".

(4) In paragraph 7 of that Schedule, at the end there shall be added the words " or, if the certificate is cancelled under paragraph 8 below, to any such tax which becomes due after the cancellation of the certificate in respect of profits or gains arising while the certificate is in force (referred to below in this Schedule as pre-cancellation profits or gains) ".

(5) After paragraph 7 of that Schedule, there shall be inserted the following paragraph—

" 7A.—(1) Paragraph 7 above is subject to the following provisions of this paragraph in any case where—

(*a*) after the cancellation of a certificate issued to the holder of a licence under that paragraph tax is assessed as mentioned in paragraph 4(1)(*a*) or (*b*) above on the person who applied for the certificate ; and

(*b*) the relevant profits or gains include (but are not limited to) pre-cancellation profits or gains.

(2) In this paragraph " the relevant profits or gains " means—

(*a*) in a case where the amount of the tax remaining unpaid under the assessment which, but for paragraph 7 above, the holder of the licence could be required to pay by a notice under paragraph 4 above (referred to below in this paragraph as the amount otherwise applicable in his case) is the whole of the amount remaining unpaid, all the profits or gains in respect of which the assessment was made ; or

(*b*) in a case where the amount otherwise applicable in his case falls under paragraph 4A above to be determined by reference to profits or gains in respect of which the licence was the basis for the assessment, the profits or gains in question.

(3) In any case to which this paragraph applies, the amount the holder of the licence may be required to pay by a notice under paragraph 4 shall be the amount otherwise applicable in his case reduced by the amount of the tax remaining unpaid under the assessment which is attributable to the pre-cancellation profits or gains, together with a corresponding proportion of any interest due as mentioned in paragraph 4(1).

(4) For the purposes of sub-paragraph (3) above the amount of the tax remaining unpaid under the assessment which is attributable to the pre-cancellation profits or gains is such part of the amount otherwise applicable in the case of the holder of the licence as bears to the whole of the amount otherwise so applicable the same proportion as the proportion borne by the amount of the pre-cancellation profits or gains to the total amount of the relevant profits or gains."

(6) After paragraph 8 of that Schedule, there shall be inserted the following paragraph—

" 8A.—(1) For the purposes of paragraphs 4A and 7A above and this paragraph, profits or gains in respect of which an assessment is made as mentioned in paragraph 4(1)(*a*) or (*b*) above are profits or gains in respect of which any licence in question was the basis for the assessment if those profits or gains fall within paragraph 4(1)(*a*) or (*b*) by reference to that licence.

(2) In determining—

(*a*) for the purposes of paragraph 4A(2) or 7A(4) above, the amount of the profits or gains in res-

pect of which any licence was the basis for an
assessment ; or

(*b*) for the purposes of paragraph 7A(4) above, the
amount of any pre-cancellation profits or gains ;

the Board shall compute that amount as if for the purposes
of making a separate assessment in respect of those profits
or gains on the person on whom the assessment was made,
making all such allocations and apportionments of receipts,
expenses, allowances and deductions taken into account or
made for the purposes of the actual assessment as appear
to the Board to be just and reasonable in the circumstances.

(3) A notice under paragraph 4 above as it applies by
virtue of paragraph 4A or 7A above shall give particulars
of the manner in which the amount required to be paid was
determined.

(4) References in paragraphs 4A, 7 and 7A above and in
this paragraph to profits or gains include chargeable
gains."

(7) In section 3(4) of the Oil Taxation Act 1975 (items ex- 1975 c. 22.
cluded from allowable expenditure under that section for any
oil field)—

(*a*) the word " or " at the end of paragraph (*d*) shall be
omitted ; and

(*b*) after paragraph (*e*) there shall be inserted the following
words—

" or

(*f*) any payment made in pursuance of a notice under paragraph 4 of Schedule 15 to the Finance Act 1973 (pro- 1973 c. 51.
visions supplementing the territorial extension of charge
to tax under section 38 of that Act)."

(8) Schedule 15 to the Finance Act 1973 shall apply as
modified by subsections (2) and (3) above in any case where a
period of thirty days relevant for the purposes of the service of
a notice under paragraph 4 of that Schedule in relation to any
tax expires on or after 12th March 1984.

125.—(1) For section 4 of the National Loans Act 1968 Local loans.
(power to make local loans) there shall be substituted the follow- 1968 c. 13.
ing section—

"Limit for   4.—(1) The aggregate of—
local loans.

(*a*) any commitments of the Loan Commissioners outstanding in respect of undertakings entered into by them to grant local
loans ; and

(b) any amount outstanding in respect of the principal of any local loans ;

shall not at any time exceed £28,000 million or such other (lower or higher) sum, not exceeding £35,000 million, as the Treasury may from time to time specify by order made by statutory instrument.

(2) No order shall be made under this section unless a draft of it has been laid before and approved by a resolution of the Commons House of Parliament."

(2) In section 3 of that Act—

(a) in subsection (5), the words from " and " to " future Act " shall be omitted ; and

(b) in subsection (11), for the words from the beginning to "those " there shall be substituted the words " Subject to the limit in this Act, the Loan Commissioners may make loans of the descriptions ".

Tax exemptions in relation to designated international organisations.

126.—(1) Where—

(a) the United Kingdom or any of the Communities is a member of an international organisation ; and

(b) the agreement under which it became a member provides for exemption from tax, in relation to the organisation, of the kind for which provision is made by this section ;

the Treasury may, by order made by statutory instrument, designate that organisation for the purposes of this section.

(2) Where an organisation has been so designated, the provisions mentioned in subsection (3) below shall, with the exception of any which may be excluded by the designation order, apply in relation to that organisation.

(3) The provisions are—

(a) a person not resident in the United Kingdom shall not be liable to income tax in respect of income from any security issued by the organisation if he would not be liable but for the fact that—

(i) the security or income is issued, made payable or paid in the United Kingdom or in sterling ; or

(ii) the organisation maintains an office or other place of business in the United Kingdom ;

(b) any security issued by the organisation shall be taken, for the purposes of capital transfer tax and capital gains tax, to be situated outside the United Kingdom ; and

(c) no stamp duty shall be chargeable under the heading "Bearer Instrument" in Schedule 1 to the Stamp Act 1891 on the issue of any instrument by the organisation or on the transfer of the stock constituted by, or transferable by means of, any instrument issued by the organisation.

PART VI
1891 c. 39.

127.—(1) Schedule 22 to this Act shall have effect for the purpose of making provision in relation to the Special and General Commissioners.

(2) This section and Part XIII of Schedule 23 to this Act shall come into operation on such day as the Lord Chancellor may by order made by statutory instrument appoint, and different days may be so appointed for different provisions and for different purposes.

Special and General Commissioners.

128.—(1) This Act may be cited as the Finance Act 1984.

(2) In this Act "the Taxes Act" means the Income and Corporation Taxes Act 1970.

(3) Part II of this Act, so far as it relates to income tax, shall be construed as one with the Income Tax Acts, so far as it relates to corporation tax, shall be construed as one with the Corporation Tax Acts and, so far as it relates to capital gains tax, shall be construed as one with the Capital Gains Tax Act 1979.

(4) Part III of this Act shall be construed as one with Part III of the Finance Act 1975.

(5) Part V of this Act shall be construed as one with Part I of the Oil Taxation Act 1975 and references in Part V of this Act to the principal Act are references to that Act.

(6) The enactments specified in Schedule 23 to this Act are hereby repealed to the extent specified in the third column of that Schedule, but subject to any provision at the end of any Part of that Schedule.

Short title, interpretation, construction and repeals.
1970 c. 10.
1979 c. 14.
1975 c. 7.
1975 c. 2.

SCHEDULES

SCHEDULE 1

WINE AND MADE-WINE

Description of wine or made-wine	Rates of duty per hectolitre
	£
Wine or made-wine of a strength of less than 15 per cent. and not being sparkling	90·50
Sparkling wine or sparkling made-wine of a strength of less than 15 per cent	149·40
Wine or made-wine of a strength of not less than 15 per cent. but not exceeding 18 per cent	157·50
Wine or made-wine of a strength exceeding 18 per cent. but not exceeding 22 per cent	183·30
Wine or made-wine of a strength exceeding 22 per cent	183·30 plus £15·48 for every 1 per cent. or part of 1 per cent. in excess of 22 per cent.

Interpretation

1.—(1) Subject to sub-paragraph (3) below, for the purposes of this Act, wine or made-wine which is for the time being in a closed container is sparkling if, due to the presence of carbon dioxide or any other gas, the pressure in the container, measured at a temperature of 20° C, is not less than 1 bar in excess of atmospheric pressure.

(2) For the purposes of this Act, wine or made-wine which is not for the time being in a closed container is sparkling if it has characteristics similar to those of wine or made-wine which has been removed from a closed container and which, before removal, fell within sub-paragraph (1) above.

(3) Notwithstanding anything in sub-paragraph (1) above, wine or made-wine which is for the time being in a closed container shall not be regarded as sparkling for the purposes of the rates of duty set out above, if—

    (a) the container does not have a mushroom-shaped stopper (whether solid or hollow) held in place by a tie or fastening ; and

    (b) the pressure in the container, measured at a temperature of 20° C, is less than 3 bars in excess of atmospheric pressure.

2. For the purposes of this Act, wine or made-wine shall be regarded as having been rendered sparkling if—

(*a*) as a result of aeration, fermentation or any other process, it either falls within paragraph 1(1) above or takes on such characteristics as are referred to in paragraph 1(2) above ; or

(*b*) being sparkling wine or made-wine which, by virtue only of paragraph 1(3) above, was not chargeable to duty as sparkling wine or made-wine, it is transferred into a closed container which has a mushroom-shaped stopper (whether solid or hollow) held in place by a tie or fastening.

SCHEDULE 2

Section 4.

VEHICLES EXCISE DUTY

PART I

PROVISIONS SUBSTITUTED IN PART II OF SCHEDULES 1 TO 5 TO THE VEHICLES (EXCISE) ACT 1971 AND THE VEHICLES (EXCISE) ACT (NORTHERN IRELAND) 1972

1971 c. 10.
1972 c. 10
(N.I.).

1. The following are the provisions substituted in the Act of 1971 and the Act of 1972 for Part II of Schedule 1—

Description of vehicle	Rate of duty
	£
1. Bicycles and tricycles of which the cylinder capacity of the engine does not exceed 150 cubic centimetres	9·00
2. Bicycles of which the cylinder capacity of the engine exceeds 150 cubic centimetres but does not exceed 250 cubic centimetres; tricycles (other than those in the foregoing paragraph) and vehicles (other than mowing machines) with more than three wheels, being tricycles and vehicles neither constructed nor adapted for use nor used for the carriage of a driver or passenger	18·00
3. Bicycles and tricycles not in the foregoing paragraphs ...	36·00

2. The following are the provisions substituted in the Act of 1971 and the Act of 1972 for Part II of Schedule 2—

Description of vehicle	Rate of duty
Hackney carriages	£ 45·00 with an additional 90p for each person above 20 (excluding the driver) for which the vehicle has seating capacity.

3. The following are the provisions substituted in the Act of 1971 and the Act of 1972 for Part II of Schedule 3—

1. Description of vehicle	Weight unladen of vehicle		Rate of duty	
	2. Exceeding	3. Not exceeding	4. Initial	5. Additional for each ton or part of a ton in excess of the weight in column 2
			£	£
1. Agricultural machines; digging machines; mobile cranes; works trucks; mowing machines; fishermen's tractors.	—	—	15·00	—
2. Haulage vehicles, being showmen's vehicles.	—	7¼ tons	144·00	—
	7¼ tons	8 tons	172·00	—
	8 tons	10 tons	203·00	—
	10 tons	—	203·00	31·00
3. Haulage vehicles, not being showmen's vehicles.	—	2 tons	171·00	—
	2 tons	4 tons	308·00	—
	4 tons	6 tons	445·00	—
	6 tons	7¼ tons	581·00	—
	7¼ tons	8 tons	710·00	—
	8 tons	9 tons	831·00	—
	9 tons	10 tons	951·00	—
	10 tons	11 tons	1,088·00	—
	11 tons	—	1,088·00	136·00

4. The following are the provisions substituted in the Act of 1971 and the Act of 1972 for Part II of Schedule 4—

TABLE A

RATES OF DUTY ON RIGID GOODS VEHICLES EXCEEDING 12 TONNES PLATED GROSS WEIGHT

GENERAL RATES

Plated gross weight of vehicle		Rate of duty		
1. Exceeding	2. Not exceeding	3. Two axle vehicle	4. Three axle vehicle	5. Four or more axle vehicle
tonnes	tonnes	£	£	£
12	13	410	320	320
13	14	530	340	340
14	15	640	340	340
15	17	850	340	340
17	19	—	460	340
19	21	—	610	340
21	23	—	780	490
23	25	—	1,250	690
25	27	—	—	930
27	29	—	—	1,200
29	30·49	—	—	2,100

TABLE A(1)

RATES OF DUTY ON RIGID GOODS VEHICLES EXCEEDING 12 TONNES PLATED GROSS WEIGHT

RATES FOR FARMERS' GOODS VEHICLES

Plated gross weight of vehicle		Rate of duty		
1. Exceeding	2. Not exceeding	3. Two axle vehicle	4. Three axle vehicle	5. Four or more axle vehicle
tonnes	tonnes	£	£	£
12	13	140	125	125
13	14	150	125	125
14	15	155	125	125
15	17	195	135	125
17	19	—	145	125
19	21	—	160	135
21	23	—	170	145
23	25	—	230	160
25	27	—	—	190
27	29	—	—	225
29	30·49	—	—	360

U 3

TABLE A(2)

RATES OF DUTY ON RIGID GOODS VEHICLES EXCEEDING 12 TONNES PLATED GROSS WEIGHT

RATES FOR SHOWMEN'S GOODS VEHICLES

Plated gross weight of vehicle		Rate of duty		
1. Exceeding	2. Not exceeding	3. Two axle vehicle	4. Three axle vehicle	5. Four or more axle vehicle
tonnes	tonnes	£	£	£
12	13	140	125	125
13	14	150	125	125
14	15	155	125	125
15	17	195	135	125
17	19	—	145	130
19	21	—	170	145
21	23	—	185	170
23	25	—	270	190
25	27	—	—	230
27	29	—	—	280
29	30·49	—	—	455

TABLE B

SUPPLEMENTARY RATES OF DUTY ON RIGID GOODS VEHICLES OVER 12 TONNES USED FOR DRAWING TRAILERS EXCEEDING 4 TONNES PLATED GROSS WEIGHT

GENERAL RATES

Gross weight of trailer		Duty supplement
Exceeding	Not exceeding	
tonnes	tonnes	£
4	8	75
8	10	95
10	12	120
12	14	170
14	—	330

TABLE B(1)

SUPPLEMENTARY RATES OF DUTY ON RIGID GOODS VEHICLES
OVER 12 TONNES USED FOR DRAWING TRAILERS EXCEEDING
4 TONNES PLATED GROSS WEIGHT

RATES FOR FARMERS' GOODS VEHICLES

Gross weight of trailer		Duty supplement
Exceeding	Not exceeding	
tonnes	tonnes	£
4	8	75
8	10	95
10	12	120
12	14	170
14	—	330

TABLE B(2)

SUPPLEMENTARY RATES OF DUTY ON RIGID GOODS VEHICLES
OVER 12 TONNES USED FOR DRAWING TRAILERS EXCEEDING
4 TONNES PLATED GROSS WEIGHT

RATES FOR SHOWMEN'S GOODS VEHICLES

Gross weight of trailer		Duty supplement
Exceeding	Not exceeding	
—	—	£ 75

TABLE C

RATES OF DUTY ON TRACTOR UNITS EXCEEDING 12 TONNES
PLATED TRAIN WEIGHT AND HAVING ONLY 2 AXLES

GENERAL RATES

Plated train weight of tractor unit		Rate of duty		
1.	2.	3.	4.	5.
Exceeding	Not exceeding	For a tractor unit to be used with semi-trailers with any number of axles	For a tractor unit to be used only with semi-trailers with not less than two axles	For a tractor unit to be used only with semi-trailers with not less than three axles
tonnes	tonnes	£	£	£
12	14	470	420	420
14	16	590	440	440
16	18	690	440	440
18	20	810	440	440
20	22	940	550	440
22	23	1,000	620	440
23	25	1,150	780	440
25	26	1,150	870	530
26	28	1,150	1,090	720
28	29	1,210	1,210	820
29	31	1,680	1,680	1,050
31	33	2,450	2,450	1,680
33	34	2,450	2,450	2,250
34	36	2,750	2,750	2,750
36	38	3,100	3,100	3,100

TABLE C(1)

RATES OF DUTY ON TRACTOR UNITS EXCEEDING 12 TONNES
PLATED TRAIN WEIGHT AND HAVING ONLY 2 AXLES

RATES FOR FARMERS' GOODS VEHICLES

Plated train weight of tractor unit		Rate of duty		
1.	2.	3.	4.	5.
Exceeding	Not exceeding	For a tractor unit to be used with semi-trailers with any number of axles	For a tractor unit to be used only with semi-trailers with not less than two axles	For a tractor unit to be used only with semi-trailers with not less than three axles
tonnes	tonnes	£	£	£
12	14	145	140	140
14	16	160	140	140
16	18	170	140	140
18	20	175	140	140
20	22	185	145	140
22	23	190	155	140
23	25	210	165	145
25	26	210	170	155
26	28	210	190	175
28	29	210	205	185
29	31	280	280	220
31	33	395	395	320
33	34	750	750	750
34	36	905	905	905
36	38	1,020	1,020	1,020

TABLE C(2)

RATES OF DUTY ON TRACTOR UNITS EXCEEDING 12 TONNES PLATED TRAIN WEIGHT AND HAVING ONLY 2 AXLES

RATES FOR SHOWMEN'S GOODS VEHICLES

Plated train weight of tractor unit		Rate of duty		
1. Exceeding	2. Not exceeding	3. For a tractor unit to be used with semi-trailers with any number of axles	4. For a tractor unit to be used only with semi-trailers with not less than two axles	5. For a tractor unit to be used only with semi-trailers with not less than three axles
tonnes	tonnes	£	£	£
12	14	145	140	140
14	16	160	140	140
16	18	170	140	140
18	20	180	155	155
20	22	205	165	165
22	23	220	170	170
23	25	250	190	175
25	26	250	205	185
26	28	250	240	215
28	29	260	260	230
29	31	355	355	275
31	33	495	495	405
33	34	925	925	925
34	36	1,125	1,125	1,125
36	38	1,265	1,265	1,265

TABLE D

RATES OF DUTY ON TRACTOR UNITS EXCEEDING 12 TONNES PLATED TRAIN WEIGHT AND HAVING 3 OR MORE AXLES

GENERAL RATES

Plated train weight of tractor unit		Rate of duty		
1. Exceeding	2. Not exceeding	3. For a tractor unit to be used with semi-trailers with any number of axles	4. For a tractor unit to be used only with semi-trailers with not less than two axles	5. For a tractor unit to be used only with semi-trailers with not less than three axles
tonnes	tonnes	£	£	£
12	14	420	420	420
14	20	440	440	440
20	22	550	440	440
22	23	620	440	440
23	25	780	440	440
25	26	870	440	440
26	28	1,090	440	440
28	29	1,210	520	440
29	31	1,680	640	440
31	33	2,450	970	440
33	34	2,450	1,420	550
34	36	2,450	2,030	830
36	38	2,730	2,730	1,240

Table D(1)

Rates of Duty on Tractor Units exceeding 12 Tonnes Plated Train Weight and having 3 or more Axles

Rates for Farmers' Goods Vehicles

Plated train weight of tractor unit		Rate of duty		
1. Exceeding	2. Not exceeding	3. For a tractor unit to be used with semi-trailers with any number of axles	4. For a tractor unit to be used only with semi-trailers with not less than two axles	5. For a tractor unit to be used only with semi-trailers with not less than three axles
tonnes	tonnes	£	£	£
12	20	140	140	140
20	22	145	140	140
22	23	150	140	140
23	25	165	140	140
25	26	170	145	140
26	28	190	170	155
28	29	205	180	165
29	31	280	215	195
31	33	395	315	230
33	34	470	470	285
34	36	670	670	430
36	38	900	900	650

TABLE D(2)

RATES OF DUTY ON TRACTOR UNITS EXCEEDING 12 TONNES
PLATED TRAIN WEIGHT AND HAVING 3 OR MORE AXLES

RATES FOR SHOWMEN'S GOODS VEHICLES

Plated train weight of tractor unit		Rate of duty		
1. Exceeding	2. Not exceeding	3. For a tractor unit to be used with semi-trailers with any number of axles	4. For a tractor unit to be used only with semi-trailers with not less than two axles	5. For a tractor unit to be used only with semi-trailers with not less than three axles
tonnes	tonnes	£	£	£
12	18	140	140	140
18	20	145	145	140
20	22	165	160	140
22	23	170	165	140
23	25	190	170	155
25	26	205	180	165
26	28	240	210	180
28	29	260	225	200
29	31	355	270	240
31	33	495	395	290
33	34	580	580	355
34	36	830	830	540
36	38	1,115	1,115	805

5. The following are the provisions substituted in the Act of 1971 and the Act of 1972 for Part II of Schedule 5—

Description of vehicle	Rate of duty
	£
1. Any vehicle first registered under the Roads Act 1920 before 1st January 1947, or which, if its first registration for taxation purposes had been effected in Northern Ireland, would have been so first registered under the Act as in force in Northern Ireland	60·00
2. Other vehicles	90·00

PART II

AMENDMENT OF PART I OF SCHEDULE 4 TO THE VEHICLES (EXCISE) ACT 1971 AND THE VEHICLES (EXCISE) ACT (NORTHERN IRELAND) 1972

1971 c. 10

1972 c. 10 (N.I.).

AMENDMENTS MADE IN BOTH ACTS

6.—(1) Part I of Schedule 4 to the Act of 1971 and the Act of 1972 (annual rates of duty on goods vehicles: general provisions) shall be amended as follows.

(2) In paragraph 1(1), for " £150 " there shall be substituted " £130 ".

(3) In paragraph 2, for " £320 " there shall be substituted " £290 ".

(4) In paragraph 6(1), for " £63 " there shall be substituted " £67 ".

(5) In paragraph 7, for " £85 " there shall be substituted " £90 ".

Section 7.

SCHEDULE 3

GAMING MACHINE LICENCE DUTY

Part I

Special Licences and Staggered Starting Dates for Whole-Year Licences in Respect of Premises

1981 c. 63.

1. The Betting and Gaming Duties Act 1981 shall be amended as follows.

2. For section 21 there shall be substituted—

" Gaming machine licences.

21.—(1) Except in the cases specified in Part I of Schedule 4 to this Act, no gaming machine (other than a two-penny machine) shall be provided for gaming on any premises situated in Great Britain unless there is for the time being in force—

　　(*a*) a licence granted under this Part of this Act with respect to the premises ; or

　　(*b*) a licence so granted with respect to the machine.

(2) A licence of either kind granted under this Part of this Act shall be known as a gaming machine licence ; and in this Part " ordinary licence " means a licence falling within subsection (1)(*a*) above and " special licence " means one falling within subsection (1)(*b*).

(3) A special licence may be a whole-year or half-year licence and an ordinary licence may be a whole-year, half-year or quarter-year licence ; and the period for which a gaming machine licence is to be granted shall be determined by reference to the following Table.

Table

Type of licence	Period for which licence is to be granted
1. Whole-year special licence ...	Twelve months beginning with 1st October.
2. Half-year special licence ...	Six months beginning with 1st April or 1st October.
3. Whole-year ordinary licence in respect of premises situated in—	
(*a*) The first region ...	Twelve months beginning with 1st December.

Type of licence	Period for which licence is to be granted	
(b) The second region ...	Twelve months beginning with 1st February.	SCH. 3
(c) The third region ...	Twelve months beginning with 1st June.	
(d) The fourth region ...	Twelve months beginning with 1st August.	
4. Half-year ordinary licence ...	Six months beginning with 1st April or 1st October.	
5. Quarter-year ordinary licence	Three months beginning with 1st January, 1st April, 1st July or 1st October.	

In this Table any reference to a named region is a reference to that part of Great Britain which has been designated by the Commissioners, for the purposes of this Act, as that named region.

(4) For the purposes of this Part of this Act, any premises which consist of a means of transport shall be treated as being situated in the fourth region except in any case where the Commissioners direct that they are to be treated as being situated in another named region.".

3. After section 21 there shall be inserted the following section—

"Special licences.   21A.—(1) No special licence shall authorise more than one machine.

(2) An application for a special licence shall only be granted if—

    (a) the Commissioners are satisfied that at least nine other special licences will be granted to the applicant, for the period to which that application relates, on applications made together with that application ; or

    (b) at least ten special licences, granted for that period and for the time being in force, are held by the applicant.

(3) A special licence shall be taken not to be in force with respect to a gaming machine at any time when either that machine is provided for gaming on premises which are not at that time treated by section 22 below as having local authority approval under the Gaming Acts or the licence is not displayed in such manner as may be prescribed by regulations made by the Commissioners.".

4. In section 22(1), for paragraphs (a) and (b) there shall be substituted—

"(a) in the case of an ordinary licence—

    (i) to whether the premises in respect of which the licence is granted have or have not local authority approval under the Gaming Acts ; and

(ii) to the number of machines which it authorises ; and

(b) in any case, to whether the licence authorises the provision of machines chargeable at the lower or higher rate.".

5. In section 23(1)(a), after the word " apply " there shall be inserted " to special licences and shall apply to ordinary licences ".

6. In section 24—

(a) subsection (1) shall cease to have effect ;

(b) in subsection (2), for the words " gaming machine " there shall be substituted " whole-year ordinary licence, one half-year ordinary licence and one quarter-year " and after the word " one ", in the second and fourth place, there shall be inserted " of each such " ;

(c) in subsection (3), after the word " licence " there shall be inserted " or licences " and at the end there shall be added " ; but any gaming machine with respect to which there is in force a special licence shall be disregarded for the purposes of this subsection." ;

(d) in subsection (4), there shall be added at the end " or there are special licences in force with respect to those machines " ;

(e) in subsections (5) and (6), in each case after the words " contravention of " there shall be inserted " section 21(1) above or " ; and

(f) in subsection (6)(a)(ii), for the words " gaming machine " there shall be substituted " ordinary ".

7.—(1) Part II of Schedule 4 shall be amended as follows.

(2) In paragraphs 6 and 8(2), the words " in respect of any premises " shall, in each case, be omitted.

(3) For sub-paragraph (3) of paragraph 7 there shall be substituted—

"(3) A gaming machine licence shall expire at the end of the period for which it is granted.".

(4) In paragraph 8(1), for the words from " transfer " to the end there shall be substituted—

"(a) transfer an ordinary licence in respect of any premises to a successor in title to the interest in those premises of the person to whom the licence was granted ; and

(b) where—

(i) a person holding special licences so requests ; and

(ii) the proper officer is satisfied that it is appropriate to do so and will not result in any person holding any number of special licences less than ten,

transfer such number of special licences to such other person, as may be specified in the request.".

(5) In paragraph 9—

(*a*) for the words " a gaming machine " there shall be substituted " an ordinary " ;

(*b*) in paragraph (*a*), after the word " licence " there shall be inserted " or, in the case of a whole-year licence, substituting premises in a different named region (within the meaning of section 21(3) of this Act) " ; and

(*c*) in paragraph (*b*), for the word " licence ", where it first occurs, there shall be substituted " ordinary licence for the same period " and for the word " the ", where it last occurs, there shall be substituted " any such ".

(6) In paragraph 10, in sub-paragraph (1), for the words " a gaming machine " there shall be substituted " an ordinary " and in sub-paragraph (3) the words from " except " to the end shall be omitted.

(7) For sub-paragraphs (1) and (2) of paragraph 11 there shall be substituted the following sub-paragraphs—

"(1) Where the holder of a gaming machine licence surrenders it to the proper officer at a time when the licence has at least three months to run, he shall, subject to any provision made by regulations under paragraph 11A below, be entitled to a repayment of duty equal to the appropriate fraction of the duty paid on the grant of the licence, the appropriate fraction being—

(*a*) in the case of a half-year licence, 5/11ths ;

(*b*) in the case of a whole-year licence surrendered not more than three months after the date on which the period for which it was granted began, 7/10ths ;

(*c*) in the case of a whole-year licence surrendered more than three, but not more than six, months after that date, 9/20ths ; and

(*d*) in the case of a whole-year licence surrendered more than six months after that date, 3/20ths.

(2) A special licence shall not be surrendered unless the Commissioners are satisfied that, if it is surrendered, its holder will (having regard to any other licences surrendered at the same time) hold at least ten, or cease to hold any, special licences.".

(8) In sub-paragraph (3) of paragraph 11 for the words " Sub-paragraph (2) " there shall be substituted " Sub-paragraph (1) " and for the words " that section " there shall be substituted the words " section 21(1) or 24 of this Act ".

(9) After paragraph 11 there shall be inserted—

"Reduction of duty in certain cases

11A.—(1) For the purpose of giving credit, on the taking out of a gaming machine licence in certain circumstances where duty has been paid on one or more previous licences, the Commissioners may make regulations providing that, in prescribed cases, the amount of duty payable on a gaming machine licence shall, subject to prescribed conditions, be reduced by a prescribed amount.

(2) Regulations under this paragraph may make provision modifying, or excluding, the application of paragraph 11 above in cases in which duty is reduced in accordance with the regulations.".

(10) In paragraph 12, for the words "a gaming machine" there shall be substituted ", an ordinary".

(11) In paragraph 13, for the words from "gaming machines provided" to "in force" there shall be substituted—

"(a) gaming machines provided on any premises in respect of which an ordinary licence is in force ; and

(b) gaming machines in respect of which special licences are in force".

(12) In paragraph 17(1), for the words "section 24" there shall be substituted "section 21(1) or 24".

(13) In paragraph 18, for the words from "either" to the end of paragraph (b) there shall be substituted "the officer is satisfied, having regard to the number and description of—

(a) those machines which are authorised by the ordinary licence or licences produced to him ; and

(b) those machines displaying special licences ;

that there has been a contravention of section 21(1) or 24 of this Act,".

PART II

TRANSITIONAL PROVISIONS

Whole-year licences during transitional period

8.—(1) A whole-year ordinary licence in respect of any premises shall, if first having effect after 30th September 1984 but before the latest date specified (in relation to the region in which the premises are situated) in the second column of the following Table, be granted for a period determined by reference to the Table.

Region in which premises are situated	Date on which licence first has effect	Period for which licence is to be granted
1. First.	(*a*) Before 1st May 1985.	Seven months beginning with 1st October 1984.
	(*b*) After 30th April 1985 but before 1st December 1985.	Seven months beginning with 1st May 1985.
2. Second.	(*a*) Before 1st June 1985.	Eight months beginning with 1st October 1984.
	(*b*) After 31st May 1985 but before 1st February 1986.	Eight months beginning with 1st June 1985.
3. Third.	Before 1st June 1985.	Eight months beginning with 1st October 1984.
4. Fourth.	Before 1st August 1985.	Ten months beginning with 1st October 1984.

References in this Table to named regions shall be construed as in section 21 of the Betting and Gaming Duties Act 1981.

1981 c. 63.

(2) Where, by virtue of sub-paragraph (1) above, a whole-year licence is granted for a period of 7, 8 or 10 months, the duty payable on the licence shall be 7/12ths, 8/12ths or, as the case may be, 10/12ths of the appropriate amount set out in the relevant Table in section 23 of the Act of 1981.

(3) In relation to a whole-year licence falling within sub-paragraph (1) above, paragraph 11 of Schedule 4 to the Act of 1981 shall have effect as if—

(*a*) in a case falling within paragraph 11(1)(*b*), the appropriate fraction were 17/35ths for a seven-month licence, 11/20ths for an eight-month licence and 16/25ths for a ten-month licence ;

(*b*) in a case falling within paragraph 11(1)(*c*), the appropriate fraction were 2/35ths for a seven-month licence, 7/40ths for an eight-month licence and 17/50ths for a ten-month licence ; and

(*c*) in a case falling within paragraph 11(1)(*d*), no provision were made for repayment of duty.

SCHEDULE 4

Section 8.

FREE ZONES

Part I

Provisions inserted in Customs and Excise Management Act 1979 as Part VIIIA

1979 c. 2.

" Part VIIIA

Free Zones

100A.—(1) The Treasury may by order designate any area in the United Kingdom as a special area for customs purposes.

Designation of free zones.

SCH. 4

(2) An area so designated shall be known as a " free zone ".

(3) An order under subsection (1) above—

(a) shall have effect for such period as shall be specified in the order ;

(b) may be made so as to take effect, in relation to the area or any part of the area designated by a previous order under this section, on the expiry of the period specified in the previous order ;

(c) shall appoint one or more persons as the responsible authority or authorities for the free zone ;

(d) may impose on any responsible authority such conditions or restrictions as may be specified ; and

(e) may be revoked if the Commissioners are satisfied that there has been a failure to comply with any condition or restriction.

(4) The Treasury may by order—

(a) from time to time vary—

(i) the conditions or restrictions imposed by a designation order ; or

(ii) with the agreement of the responsible authority, the area designated ; or

(b) appoint one or more persons as the responsible authority or authorities for a free zone either in addition to or in substitution for any person appointed as such by a designation order.

(5) In this Act " designation order " means an order made under subsection (1) above.

(6) Any order under this section shall be made by statutory instrument.

Free zone regulations.

100B.—(1) The Commissioners may by regulations (in this Act referred to as " free zone regulations ") make provision with respect to the movement of goods into, and the removal of goods from, any free zone and the keeping, securing and treatment of goods which are within a free zone.

(2) Subject to any provision of the regulations, references in this Act to " free zone goods " are references to goods which are within a free zone.

Free zone goods: customs duties, etc.

100C.—(1) Subject to any contrary provision made by any directly applicable Community provision, goods which are chargeable with any customs duty or agricultural levy, or in respect of which any negative monetary compensatory amount is payable, may be moved into a free zone and may remain as free zone goods without payment of that duty, levy or amount.

(2) Except in such cases as may be specified in free zone regulations, subsection (1) above shall not apply in relation to goods which are chargeable with any excise duty unless that duty has been paid and not repaid.

(3) Without prejudice to the generality of section 100B above, free zone regulations may make provision—

(a) for enabling the Commissioners to allow goods to be removed from a free zone without payment of customs duty, agricultural levy, or any negative monetary compensatory amount, in such circumstances and subject to such conditions as they may determine ;

(b) for determining, where any customs duty, agricultural levy or negative monetary compensatory amount becomes payable in respect of goods which cease to be free zone goods—

(i) the rates of any duty, levy or monetary compensatory amount applicable ; and

(ii) the time at which those goods cease to be free zone goods ;

(c) for determining, for the purpose of enabling customs duty or agricultural levy to be charged or any negative monetary compensatory amount to be paid in respect of free zone goods in a case where a person wishes to pay that duty or levy or to receive the negative monetary compensatory amount notwithstanding that the goods will continue to be free zone goods, the rate of duty, levy or negative monetary compensatory amount to be applied ; and

(d) permitting free zone goods to be destroyed without payment of any customs duty, agricultural levy or negative monetary compensatory amount in such circumstances and subject to such conditions as the Commissioners may determine.

(4) Without prejudice to the generality of section 100B above, free zone regulations may make provision—

(a) for relief from the whole or part of any value added tax chargeable on the importation of goods into the United Kingdom in such circumstances as they may determine ;

(b) in place of, or in addition to, any provision made by section 4 or 5 of the Value Added Tax Act 1983 or any other 1983 c. 55. enactment, for determining the time when a supply of goods which are or have been free zone goods is to be treated as taking place for the purposes of the charge to value added tax ; and

(c) as to the treatment, for the purposes of value added tax, of goods which are manufactured or produced within a free zone from other goods or which have other goods incorporated in them while they are free zone goods.

(5) In this section—

" agricultural levy " means any tax or charge, not being a customs duty, provided for under the common agricultural policy or under any special arrangements which, pursuant to Article 235 of the EEC Treaty, are applicable to goods resulting from the processing of agricultural products ;

"negative monetary compensatory amount" means an amount granted on importation under the Regulation of the Commission of the European Communities dated 19th May 1981 No. 1371/81 or any Community provision for the time being amending or replacing that Regulation.

100D.—(1) Without prejudice to the generality of section 100B above, free zone regulations may make provision—

(a) specifying the circumstances in which goods which are within a free zone are to be treated, for the purposes of this Act and the regulations, as not being free zone goods ;

(b) specifying the circumstances in which goods which are not within a free zone are to be treated, for those purposes, as being within a free zone ;

(c) requiring any goods which are within a free zone to be produced to, or made available for inspection by, an officer on request by him ;

(d) imposing, or providing for the Commissioners to impose by direction, conditions and restrictions to which free zone goods are to be subject ;

(e) prohibiting the carrying out on free zone goods of operations other than those prescribed by, or allowed under, the regulations ;

(f) requiring any permitted operations to be carried out in such manner and subject to such conditions and restrictions as may be imposed by or under the regulations ;

(g) imposing, or providing for the Commissioners to impose by direction, obligations on responsible authorities in relation to the security of free zones and in respect of conditions and restrictions imposed by designation orders ;

(h) enabling the Commissioners to recover from any responsible authority expenditure incurred by the Commissioners in consequence of any failure by that authority to comply with any requirements imposed by or under the regulations ;

(i) imposing, or providing for the Commissioners to impose by direction, requirements on the occupier of any premises, or proprietor of any goods, within a free zone to keep and preserve records relating to his business as such an occupier or proprietor and to produce them to an officer when required to do so for the purpose of allowing him—

(i) to inspect them ;

(ii) to copy or take extracts from them ; or

(iii) to remove them at a reasonable time and for a reasonable period ;

(j) imposing, or providing for the Commissioners to impose by direction, on the responsible authority requirements in connection with any provision made by virtue of paragraph (*i*) above ;

(*k*) providing for the Commissioners to specify by direction the information which must be given to them in connection with free zone goods and the form in which, persons by whom and time within which, it must be given ;

(*l*) for the forfeiture of goods in the event of non-compliance with any condition or restriction imposed by virtue of paragraph (*f*) above or in the event of the carrying out of any operation on free zone goods which is not by virtue of paragraph (*e*) above permitted to be carried out on such goods.

(2) Free zone regulations may make different provision for goods or services of different classes or descriptions or for goods or services of the same class or description in different circumstances.

(3) If any person fails to comply with any free zone regulation or with any condition, restriction or requirement imposed under a free zone regulation he shall be liable on summary conviction to a penalty of level 3 on the standard scale together with a penalty of £20 for each day on which the failure continues.

100E.—(1) No person shall carry on any trade or business in a free zone unless he is authorised to do so by the Commissioners. Control of trading in free zones.

(2) An authorisation under this section may be granted for such period and subject to such conditions as the Commissioners consider appropriate.

(3) The Commissioners may at any time for reasonable cause revoke, or vary the terms of, any authorisation under this section.

(4) If any person—

(*a*) contravenes subsection (1) above, or

(*b*) fails to comply with any condition imposed under subsection (2) above,

he shall be liable on summary conviction to a penalty of level 3 on the standard scale.

100F.—(1) Any person entering or leaving a free zone shall answer such questions as any officer may put to him with respect to any goods and shall, if required by the officer, produce those goods for examination at such place as the Commissioners may direct. Powers of search.

(2) At any time while a vehicle is entering or leaving a free zone, any officer may board the vehicle and search any part of it.

(3) Any officer may at any time enter upon and inspect a free zone and all buildings and goods within the zone.".

PART II

FURTHER AMENDMENTS OF 1979 ACT

1. In section 1 (interpretation) the following definitions shall be inserted at the appropriate places—

> " ' designation order ' has the meaning given by section 100A(5) ;
>
> ' free zone ' has the meaning given by section 100A(2) ;
>
> ' free zone goods ' has the meaning given by section 100B(2) ;
>
> ' free zone regulations ' has the meaning given by section 100B(1) ; ".

2. In section 31(1) (power to make regulations controlling the movement of goods)—

> (a) in paragraph (a) after the words " clearance out of charge of such goods " there shall be inserted the words ", a free zone " ; and
>
> (b) after paragraph (a) there shall be inserted—
>
> > " (aa) the movement of goods between—
> >
> > > (i) a free zone and a place approved by the Commissioners for the clearance out of charge of such goods,
> > >
> > > (ii) such a place and a free zone, and
> > >
> > > (iii) a free zone and another free zone ; ".

3. In section 37 (entry of goods on importation)—

> (a) in subsection (2), the following paragraph shall be inserted after paragraph (a)—
>
> > " (aa) free zone goods (other than goods which are chargeable with any excise duty) ; " ;
>
> (b) in subsection (3), the following paragraph shall be inserted after paragraph (a)—
>
> > " (aa) in the case of goods which are chargeable with any excise duty, as free zone goods ; ".

4. In section 119(1) (delivery of imported goods on giving of security for duty) after " warehouse " there shall be inserted the words " or free zone ".

5. In section 159 (power to examine and take account of goods), in subsection (1) there shall be inserted after paragraph (b)—

> " (bb) which are in a free zone ; or ".

6. In section 164 (power to search persons) in subsection (4) there shall be inserted after paragraph (e)—

> " (ee) any person in, entering or leaving a free zone ; ".

SCHEDULE 5

ENTRY ON IMPORTATION:

AMENDMENT OF CUSTOMS AND EXCISE MANAGEMENT 1979 c. 2. ACT 1979

1. In paragraph (*d*) of subsection (3) of section 37 (entry of goods on importation for inward processing) after the words " inward processing " there shall be inserted the words " or other processing under Community arrangements ".

2. The following sections shall be inserted after section 37—

" Initial and supplementary entries.

37A.—(1) Without prejudice to section 37 above, a direction under that section may—

> (*a*) provide that where the importer is authorised for the purposes of this section, the entry may consist of an initial entry and a supplementary entry ; and

> (*b*) may make such supplementary provision in connection with entries consisting of initial and supplementary entries as the Commissioners think fit.

(2) Where an initial entry of goods has been accepted the goods may, on the importer giving security by deposit of money or otherwise to the satisfaction of the Commissioners for payment of the unpaid duty, be delivered without payment of any duty chargeable in respect of the goods, but any such duty shall be paid within such time as the Commissioners may direct.

(3) An importer who makes an initial entry shall complete the entry by delivering the supplementary entry within such time as the Commissioners may direct.

(4) For the purposes of the customs and excise Acts an entry of goods shall be taken to have been delivered when an initial entry of the goods has been delivered, and accepted when an initial entry has been accepted.

Postponed entry.

37B.—(1) The Commissioners may, if they think fit, direct that where—

> (*a*) such goods as may be specified in the direction are imported by an importer authorised for the purposes of this subsection ;

> (*b*) the importer has delivered a document relating to the goods to the proper officer, in such form and manner, containing such particulars and accompanied by such documents as the Commissioners may direct ; and

> (*c*) the document has been accepted by the proper officer,

the goods may be delivered before an entry of them has been delivered or any duty chargeable in respect of them has been paid.

(2) The Commissioners may, if they think fit, direct that where—

(a) such goods as may be specified in the direction are imported by an importer authorised for the purposes of this subsection ;

(b) the goods have been removed from the place of importation to a place approved by the Commissioners for the clearance out of charge of such goods ; and

(c) the conditions mentioned in subsection (3) below have been satisfied,

the goods may be delivered before an entry of them has been delivered or any duty chargeable in respect of them has been paid.

(3) The conditions are that—

(a) on the arrival of the goods at the approved place the importer delivers to the proper officer a notice of the arrival of the goods in such form and containing such particulars as may be required by the directions ;

(b) within such time as may be so required the importer enters such particulars of the goods and such other information as may be so required in a record maintained by him at such place as the proper officer may require ; and

(c) the goods are kept secure in the approved place for such period as may be required by the directions.

(4) The Commissioners may direct that the condition mentioned in subsection (3)(a) above shall not apply in relation to any goods specified in the direction and such a direction may substitute another condition.

(5) No goods shall be delivered under this section unless the importer gives security by deposit of money or otherwise to the satisfaction of the Commissioners for the payment of any duty chargeable in respect of the goods which is unpaid.

(6) Where goods of which no entry has been made have been delivered under this section, the importer shall deliver an entry of the goods under section 37(1) above within such time as the Commissioners may direct.

(7) For the purposes of section 43(2)(a) below such an entry shall be taken to have been accepted—

(a) in the case of goods delivered by virtue of a direction under subsection (1) above, on the date on which the document mentioned in that subsection was accepted ; and (*b*) in the case of goods delivered by virtue of a direction under subsection (2) above, on the date on which particulars of the goods were entered as mentioned in subsection (3)(*b*) above.

Provisions supplementary to ss. 37A and 37B.

37C.—(1) The Commissioners may, if they think fit—

(*a*) authorise any importer for the purposes of section 37A, or 37B(1) or (2) above ; and

(*b*) suspend or cancel the authorisation of any importer where it appears to them that he has failed to comply with any requirement imposed on him by or under this Part of this Act or that there is other reasonable cause for suspension or cancellation.

(2) The Commissioners may give directions—

(*a*) imposing such requirements as they think fit on any importer authorised under this section ; or

(*b*) varying any such requirements previously imposed.

(3) If any person without reasonable excuse contravenes any requirement imposed by or under section 37A, 37B or this section he shall be liable on summary conviction to a penalty of level 4 on the standard scale."

3. In section 171 (general provisions as to offences and penalties) after subsection (2) there shall be inserted the following subsection—

" (2A) In this Act " the standard scale " has the meaning assigned to it by section 75 of the Criminal Justice Act 1982 and for the purposes of this subsection— 1982 c. 48.

(*a*) section 37 of that Act ; and

(*b*) an order under section 143 of the Magistrates' Courts Act 1980 which alters the sums specified in subsection (2) of section 37, 1980 c. 43.

shall extend to Northern Ireland, and section 75 of the 1982 Act shall have effect as if after the words " England and Wales " there were inserted the words " or Northern Ireland ".

SCHEDULE 6

Section 10.

MODIFICATIONS OF SCHEDULE 5 TO VALUE ADDED TAX ACT 1983

1983 c. 55.

PART I

FOOD

1. In Group 1 (Food), in Note (3) (which provides that a supply in the course of catering includes a supply for consumption on the premises) after the word " includes " there shall be inserted " (*a*) " and at the end of the Note there shall be added " and

Sch. 6   (*b*) any supply of hot food for consumption off those premises ; and for the purpose of paragraph (*b*) above ' hot food ' means food which, or any part of which,—

> (i) has been heated for the purpose of enabling it to be consumed at a temperature above the ambient air temperature ; and
>
> (ii) is at the time of the supply above that temperature ".

Part II

Construction of buildings etc.

2. Group 8 (construction of buildings etc.) shall be amended in accordance with this Part of this Schedule.

3. In item 2 (supply of services in the course of certain operations relating to buildings and civil engineering works), for paragraphs (*a*) and (*b*) there shall be substituted the words " in the course of the construction or demolition of ".

4. In item 3 (supply, by a person supplying services within item 2 and in connection with those services, of certain materials etc. and services relating to them) after the words " item 2 " there shall be inserted the words " of this Group or of Group 8A below ".

5. After Note (1) there shall be inserted the following Note :—

> " (1A) Any reference in item 2 or the following Notes to the construction of any building or the construction of any civil engineering work does not include a reference to the conversion, reconstruction, alteration or enlargement of any existing building or civil engineering work, and the reference in item 1 to a person constructing a building shall be construed accordingly."

6.—(1) In Note (2) (matters excluded from item 2), for paragraph (*a*) (which excluded repair or maintenance and is rendered unnecessary by the removal from item 2 of the reference to alteration) there shall be substituted the following paragraph :—

> " (*a*) the supply of any services in the course of the construction of any building (" the secondary building ") within the grounds or garden of another building (" the main building ") which is used or to be used wholly or mainly as a private residence except—
>
> > (i) where the secondary building is itself to be so used ; or
> >
> > (ii) where the secondary building is a garage which is to be used and occupied together with another building which is being constructed at the same time as the secondary building and which is either the main building or another secondary building which is to be used wholly or mainly as a private residence."

(2) In that Note—

(*a*) in paragraph (*b*), the words " or alteration ", and

(*b*) paragraph (*c*) (supply of services otherwise than in the course
  or furtherance of a business),

shall be omitted.

7. After Note (2) there shall be inserted the following Note:—

" (2A) In item 3, the goods referred to in paragraph (*a*) do not include—

(*a*) finished or prefabricated furniture, other than furniture designed to be fitted in kitchens ; or

(*b*) materials for the construction of fitted furniture, other than kitchen furniture ; or

(*c*) domestic electrical or gas appliances, other than those designed to provide space heating or water heating or both."

PART III

PROTECTED BUILDINGS

8. After Group 8 there shall be inserted the following—

" GROUP 8A—PROTECTED BUILDINGS

Item No.

1. The granting, by a person substantially reconstructing a protected building, of a major interest in, or in any part of, the building or its site.

2. The supply, in the course of an approved alteration of a protected building, of any services other than the services of an architect, surveyor or any person acting as consultant or in a supervisory capacity.

Notes

(1) ' Protected building ' means a building which is—

(*a*) a listed building, within the meaning of—

  (i) the Town and Country Planning Act 1971 ; or 1971 c. 78.

  (ii) the Town and Country Planning (Scotland) Act 1972 c. 52. 1972 ; or

  (iii) the Planning (Northern Ireland) Order 1972 ; S.I. 1972/1634 or (N.I.17).

(*b*) a scheduled monument, within the meaning of—

  (i) the Ancient Monuments and Archaeological 1979 c. 46. Areas Act 1979 ; or

  (ii) the Historic Monuments Act (Northern Ire- 1971 c. 17. land) 1971. (N.I.).

(2) For the purposes of item 1, a protected building shall not be regarded as substantially reconstructed unless the recon-

SCH. 6

struction is such that at least one of the following conditions is fulfilled when the reconstruction is completed—

(a) that, of the works carried out to effect the reconstruction, at least three-quarters, measured by reference to cost, are of such a nature that the supply of services (other than excluded services) materials and other items to carry out the works, would, if supplied by a taxable person, be within either item 2 of this Group or item 3 of Group 8 above, as it applies to a supply by a person supplying services within item 2 of this Group ; and

(b) that the reconstructed building incorporates no more of the original building (that is to say, the building as it was before the reconstruction began) than the external walls, together with other external features of architectural or historic interest ;

and in paragraph (a) above 'excluded services' means the services of an architect, surveyor or other person acting as consultant or in a supervisory capacity.

(3) 'Approved alteration' means,—

(a) in the case of a protected building which is an ecclesiastical building which is for the time being used for ecclesiastical purposes or would be so used but for the works in question, any works of alteration ; and

1971 c. 17.
(N.I.).

(b) in the case of a protected building which is a scheduled monument within the meaning of the Historic Monuments Act (Northern Ireland) 1971 and in respect of which a protection order, within the meaning of that Act, is in force, works of alteration for which consent has been given under section 10 of that Act ; and

(c) in any other case, works of alteration which may not, or but for the existence of a Crown interest or Duchy interest could not, be carried out unless authorised under, or under any provision of,—

1971 c. 78.

(i) Part IV of the Town and Country Planning Act 1971,

1972 c. 52.

(ii) Part IV of the Town and Country Planning (Scotland) Act 1972,

S.I. 1972/1634
(N.I.17).

(iii) Part V of the Planning (Northern Ireland) Order 1972, or

1979 c. 46.

(iv) Part I of the Ancient Monuments and Archaeological Areas Act 1979,

and for which, except in the case of a Crown interest or Duchy interest, consent has been obtained under any provision of that Part ;

and in paragraph (c) above 'Crown interest' and 'Duchy interest' have the same meaning as in section 50 of the said Act of 1979.

(4) For the purposes of paragraph (a) of Note (3), a building used or available for use by a minister of religion wholly or

mainly as a residence from which to perform the duties of his   Sch. 6
office shall be treated as not being an ecclesiastical building.

(5) Where the benefit of the consideration for the grant of a
major interest as described in item 1 accrues to the person substantially reconstructing the protected building but that person
is not the grantor, he shall be treated for the purposes of that
item as the person making the grant.

(6) In item 2 ' alteration ' does not include repair or maintenance ; and where any work consists partly of an approved
alteration and partly of other work, an apportionment shall be
made to determine the supply which falls within item 2.

(7) Note (2) to Group 8 above applies in relation to item 2
of this Group as it applies in relation to item 2 of that Group."

SCHEDULE 7   Section 17.

THE ADDITIONAL RATE

1. In subsection (1) of section 32 of the Finance Act 1971, for 1971 c. 68.
the words following paragraph (b) there shall be substituted the
words " and, in relation to any year of assessment, any reference in
the Income Tax Acts to the additional rate is a reference to a rate
determined by subtracting the basic rate for that year from the rate
of tax which, for that year, is applicable to the second higher rate
band ".

2.—(1) In the definition of " excess liability " or, as the case
may be, " excess amount " wherever it appears in the enactments
specified in sub-paragraph (2) below, the words " or additional "
shall be omitted.

(2) The enactments referred to in sub-paragraph (1) above are the
following, namely—

    (a) sections 30(3), 36(1), 403(1), 424(c), 430(1), 457(1) and 458(1)
        of the Taxes Act ;

    (b) section 87(6) of and paragraph 5(6A) of Schedule 16 to the
        Finance Act 1972 ; and   1972 c. 41.

    (c) paragraph 19(1A) of Schedule 2 to the Finance Act 1975.   1975 c. 7.

3.—(1) In the Taxes Act, in section 38(2), the words from " and
in determining " to " investment income " shall be omitted.

(2) In the Finance Act 1971, sections 32(3) and (4) and 34(4)
and, in paragraph 2(2) of Schedule 7, the words " or additional "
shall be omitted.

(3) In the Finance Act 1973, in section 44, the words " or addi- 1973 c. 51.
tional " and, in section 59(2), the words from " the additional rate "
to " them, and " shall be omitted.

(4) In the Finance Act 1974, there shall be omitted—   1974 c. 36.
    (a) section 15 ;

SCH. 7

(b) in section 16(1), the words following "subsection (2) below";

(c) in section 43(1), the words from "In this subsection" onwards; and

(d) in Schedule 7, paragraph 1 and, in paragraph 9(5), the words from "and" onwards.

1980 c. 48.

(5) In section 24(3) of the Finance Act 1980, for the word "amounts" there shall be substituted the word "amount"; and the words from "or over which" to "additional rate", the word "respectively", where it first occurs, and the words "and the investment income threshold" shall be omitted.

Section 27(3).

SCHEDULE 8

INTEREST PAID ON DEPOSITS WITH BANKS ETC.

General

1.—(1) In this Schedule "the principal section" means section 27 of this Act.

(2) Any amount which is credited as interest in respect of a relevant deposit shall, for the purposes of the principal section and this Schedule, be treated as a payment of interest.

Meaning of "deposit-taker"

2.—(1) In the principal section and in this Schedule "deposit-taker" means any of the following—

(a) the Bank of England;

(b) any recognised bank, licensed institution or municipal bank (within the meaning of the Banking Act 1979);

1979 c. 37.

(c) the Post Office;

1981 c. 65.

(d) any trustee savings bank within the meaning of the Trustee Savings Banks Act 1981;

1819 c. 62.

(e) any bank formed under the Savings Bank (Scotland) Act 1819; and

(f) any person or class of person which receives deposits in the course of his business or activities and which is for the time being prescribed by order made by the Treasury by statutory instrument for the purposes of this section.

(2) Where the Treasury makes an order under sub-paragraph (1)(f) above, the order shall have effect from the beginning of the first year of assessment which begins after the date on which the order is made.

(3) An order under sub-paragraph (1)(f) above shall be subject to annulment in pursuance of a resolution of the Commons House of Parliament.

Meaning of " deposit " and " relevant deposit "

3.—(1) In the principal section and in this Schedule " deposit " means a sum of money paid on terms under which it will be repaid with or without interest and either on demand or at a time or in circumstances agreed by or on behalf of the person making the payment and the person to whom it is made.

(2) For the purposes of the principal section and this Schedule, a deposit is a " relevant deposit " if, but only if—

   (*a*) the person who is beneficially entitled to any interest in re-spect of the deposit is an individual or, where two or more persons are so entitled, all of them are individuals ; or

   (*b*) the person entitled to any such interest receives it as a per-sonal representative in his capacity as such ;

and the deposit is not prevented from being a relevant deposit by sub-paragraph (3) below.

(3) A deposit is not a relevant deposit if—

   (*a*) a qualifying certificate of deposit has been issued in respect of it or it is a qualifying time deposit ;

   (*b*) it is a debt on a debenture (" debenture " having the meaning given in section 455 of the Companies Act 1948) issued by the deposit-taker ; 1948 c. 38.

   (*c*) it is a loan made by a deposit-taker in the ordinary course of his business or activities ;

   (*d*) it is a debt on a security which is listed on a recognised stock exchange (within the meaning of section 535 of the Taxes Act) ;

   (*e*) it is made by a Stock Exchange money broker (recognised by the Bank of England) in the course of his business as such a broker ;

   (*f*) in the case of a deposit-taker resident in the United King-dom for the purposes of income or corporation tax, it is held at a branch of his situated outside the United King-dom ;

   (*g*) in the case of a deposit-taker who is not so resident, it is held otherwise than at a branch of his situated in the United Kingdom ; or

   (*h*) the appropriate person has declared in writing to the deposit-taker liable to pay interest in respect of the deposit that—

      (i) at the time when the declaration is made, the person who is beneficially entitled to the interest is not, or, as the case may be, all of the persons who are so entitled are not, ordinarily resident in the United Kingdom ;

      (ii) in a case falling within sub-paragraph (2)(*b*) above, the deceased was, immediately before his death, not or-dinarily resident in the United Kingdom.

(4) A declaration under sub-paragraph (3)(*h*)(i) shall contain an undertaking by the person making it that if the person, or any of the persons, in respect of whom it is made becomes ordinarily resident in the United Kingdom he will notify the deposit-taker accordingly.

SCH. 8

(5) A deposit-taker shall, on being so required by notice given to him in writing by an inspector, make all declarations which have been made to him under sub-paragraph (3) above available for inspection by the inspector or by a named officer of the Board.

(6) Where a notice has been given to a deposit-taker under sub-paragraph (5) above, the declarations shall be made available within such time as may be specified in the notice; and the person to whom they are to be made available may take copies of, or extracts from, them.

(7) A deposit-taker shall treat every deposit made with him as a relevant deposit unless satisfied that it is not a relevant deposit; but where he has satisfied himself that a deposit is not a relevant deposit he shall be entitled to continue to so treat it until such time as he is in possession of information which can reasonably be taken to indicate that the deposit is, or may be, a relevant deposit.

(8) In sub-paragraph (3) above—

" appropriate person ", in relation to a deposit, means any person who is beneficially entitled to any interest in respect of the deposit or entitled to receive any such interest as a personal representative in his capacity as such or to whom any such interest is payable ;

1968 c. 44.
" qualifying certificate of deposit " means a certificate of deposit, as defined in section 55(3) of the Finance Act 1968, which is issued by a deposit-taker and under which—

(a) the amount payable by the deposit-taker, exclusive of interest, is not less than £50,000 (or, for a deposit denominated in foreign currency, not less than the equivalent of £50,000 at the time when the deposit is made) ; and

(b) the obligation of the deposit-taker to pay that amount arises after a period of not less than 28 days beginning with the date on which the deposit is made ; and

" qualifying time deposit " means a deposit which is made by way of loan for an amount which is not less than £50,000 (or, for a deposit denominated in foreign currency, not less than the equivalent of £50,000 at the time when the deposit is made) and on terms which—

(a) prevent repayment of the deposit before the expiry of the period of 28 days beginning with the date on which the deposit is made, but which require repayment at the end of a specified period ;

(b) do not make provision for the transfer of the right to repayment ; and

(c) prevent partial withdrawals of, or additions to, the deposit.

(9) For the purposes of sub-paragraph (3)(f) and (g) above, a deposit is held at a branch of a deposit-taker if it is recorded in his books as a liability of that branch.

Assessments to income tax etc.

4.—(1) Where in relation to any payment of interest (the "payment") a deposit-taker is liable to account for and pay an amount under the principal section—

    (*a*) subject to sub-paragraph (2) below, no assessment to income tax shall be made on, and no repayment of income tax shall be made to, the person receiving or entitled to the payment in respect of it ;

    (*b*) the payment shall, in computing the total income of the person entitled to it, be treated as income for that year received by him after deduction of income tax at the basic rate from a corresponding gross amount ; and

    (*c*) the payment (and no more) shall, in applying sections 52 and 53 of the Taxes Act to other payments be treated as profits or gains which have been brought into charge to income tax.

(2) Sub-paragraph (1)(*a*) above shall not prevent an assessment in respect of income tax at a rate other than the basic rate.

(3) For the purpose of determining whether any or what amount of tax is, by virtue of sub-paragraph (1)(*b*) above, to be taken into account as having been deducted from a gross amount in the case of an individual whose total income is reduced by any deductions, so much only of that gross amount shall be taken into account as is part of his total income as so reduced.

Collection

5.—(1) Any payment of interest in respect of which an amount is payable under the principal section shall be a relevant payment for the purposes of Schedule 20 to the Finance Act 1972 (collection 1972 c. 41. of income tax on company payments which are not distributions) whether or not the deposit-taker making the payment is resident in the United Kingdom.

(2) Schedule 20 to that Act shall apply in relation to any payment which is a relevant payment by virtue of sub-paragraph (1) above—

    (*a*) with the substitution for any reference to a company of a reference to a deposit-taker ;

    (*b*) as if any amount payable under the principal section were payable as income tax ;

    (*c*) as if paragraph 5 (set-off of income tax on deposit-taker's income against liability under the principal section) applied only in relation to payments received by the deposit-taker after 5th April 1985 and falling to be taken into account in computing his income chargeable to corporation tax ; and

    (*d*) as if in paragraph 7 (amounts set-off under paragraph 5 not to be set-off also under section 240(5) of the Taxes Act) the reference to section 240(5) included a reference to sections 53 and 246(3) of that Act.

SCH. 8

(3) In relation to any deposit-taker who is not a company Schedule 20 shall have effect as if—

(*a*) paragraph 5 were omitted ; and

(*b*) references to accounting periods were references to periods for which the deposit-taker makes up his accounts.

Transitional provisions

6.—(1) Any deposit denominated in a foreign currency shall not be treated, at any time before 6th April 1986, as a relevant deposit.

1968 c. 44.

(2) A certificate of deposit, as defined in section 55(3) of the Finance Act 1968, which was issued before 13th March 1984 on terms which provide for interest to be payable on the deposit at any time after 5th April 1985 (whether or not interest is payable on it before that date) shall, if it is not a qualifying certificate of deposit, be treated for the purposes of paragraph 3(3) of this Schedule as if it were a qualifying certificate of deposit.

(3) Any deposit which was made before 6th July 1984 but which is not a qualifying time deposit shall, where it is made on terms which—

(*a*) do not make provision for the transfer of the right to repayment ;

(*b*) prevent partial withdrawals of, or additions to, the deposit ; and

(*c*) require—

(i) the deposit-taker to repay the sum at the end of a specified period which ends after 5th April 1985 ; or

(ii) in a case where interest is payable only at the time of repayment of the deposit, the deposit-taker to repay the sum on demand or on notice ;

be treated, for the purposes of paragraph 3(3) of this Schedule, as if it were a qualifying time deposit.

1970 c. 9.

(4) A declaration made before 6th July 1984 under section 17(4) of the Taxes Management Act 1970 which contains an undertaking of the kind referred to in sub-paragraph (4) of paragraph 3 of this Schedule shall, at all times before 6th April 1988, be treated as a declaration made for the purposes of that paragraph.

(5) Where a deposit which is a source of income of any person (the " lender ") is not a composite rate deposit but at any time becomes such a deposit, section 121 of the Taxes Act (special rules where source of income ceases) shall apply as if the deposit were a source of income which the lender ceased to possess immediately before it became a composite rate deposit.

(6) Where a deposit becomes a composite rate deposit on 6th April 1985, section 121 of the Taxes Act shall apply in relation to it with the omission from subsection (1)(*b*) of the words from " and shall " to " this provision ".

(7) Where a deposit which is a source of income of any person ceases to be a composite rate deposit, section 120(3) of the Taxes Act

shall apply as if the deposit were a new source of income acquired by him immediately after it ceased to be a composite rate deposit.

(8) For the purposes of sub-paragraphs (5) to (7) above a deposit is at any time a composite rate deposit if, were the person holding it to make a payment of interest in respect of it at that time, he would be liable to account for and pay an amount on that payment under the principal section.

Penalties

7. The Table in section 98 of the Taxes Management Act 1970 (penalties) shall be amended by inserting at the end of the first column— 1970 c. 9.

" Paragraph 3(3)(*h*) and (5) of Schedule 8 to the Finance Act 1984 ".

SCHEDULE 9

Section 36(1).

DEEP DISCOUNT SECURITIES

Charge to tax

1.—(1) On the disposal by any person of any deep discount security—

(*a*) an amount which represents the accrued income attributable to the period between his acquisition and disposal of the security (the " period of ownership ") shall be treated as income chargeable to tax under Case III or, as may be, Case IV of Schedule D ;

(*b*) the tax shall (notwithstanding anything in sections 119 to 121 or, as may be, 122 to 124 of the Taxes Act but subject to sub-paragraph (5) below) be computed on the income so arising from any disposal made in the year of assessment ; and

(*c*) in computing the gain accruing on the disposal for the purposes of capital gains tax—

(i) section 31 of the Capital Gains Tax Act 1979 shall not apply but the consideration for the disposal shall be treated as reduced by the amount mentioned in paragraph (*a*) above ; and 1979 c. 14.

(ii) where that amount exceeds the consideration for the disposal, the amount of the excess shall be treated as expenditure within section 32(1)(*b*) of that Act incurred by him on the security immediately before the disposal.

(2) The amount which represents the accrued income attributable to any period of ownership is the aggregate of the income elements for each income period or part of an income period in the period of ownership.

(3) In relation to any security, the income element for any income period shall be determined by applying the formula—

$$\left(\frac{A \times B}{100}\right) - C$$

where A is the adjusted issue price ;

B is the yield to maturity ; and

C is the amount of interest (if any) attributable to the income period.

(4) The income element for any period (the " short period ") falling within an income period shall be determined by applying the formula—

$$\frac{P}{Y} \times I$$

where I is the income element for the income period in which the short period falls ;

P is the number of days in the short period ; and

Y is the number of days in that income period.

(5) Where—

(a) by virtue of sub-paragraph (1) above income tax is chargeable under Case IV of Schedule D, and

(b) the person making the disposal satisfies the Board, on a claim in that behalf, that he is not domiciled in the United Kingdom, or that, being a British subject or a citizen of the Republic of Ireland, he is not ordinarily resident in the United Kingdom,

the tax shall be computed on the amounts, if any, received in the United Kingdom in the year of assessment in question in respect of the sum mentioned in sub-paragraph (1)(a) above (any such amounts being treated as income arising when they are received in the United Kingdom).

(6) For the purposes of subsection (5) above—

(a) there shall be treated as received in the United Kingdom all amounts paid, used or enjoyed in, or in any manner or form transmitted or brought to, the United Kingdom ; and

(b) subsections (4) to (7) of section 122 of the Taxes Act shall apply as they apply for the purposes of subsection (3) of that section.

(7) In this Schedule—

" adjusted issue price ", in relation to any security in a particular income period, is the aggregate of the issue price of the security and the income elements for all previous income periods ;

" income period " means—

(a) in the case of a security carrying a right to interest, any period to which a payment of interest which falls to be made in respect of the security is attributable : and

(*b*) in any other case, any year ending immediately
before the anniversary of the issue of the security or any
period of less than a year which begins on such an
anniversary and ends on the redemption date ;

" yield to maturity ", in relation to any security, means a rate
(expressed as a percentage) such that if a sum equal to the
issue price of the security were to be invested at that rate
on the assumption that—

(*a*) the rate would be applied on a compounding basis
at the end of each income period ; and

(*b*) the amount of any interest attributable to an income
period would be deducted after applying the rate,

the value of that sum at the redemption date would be
equal to the amount payable on redemption of the security.

(8) Every company which issues deep discount securities shall
cause to be shown on the certificate of each such security the income
element for each income period between the date of issue of the
security and the redemption date.

(9) Sections 52 to 54 of the Taxes Act (deduction of income tax
by persons making certain payments) and section 159 of that Act
(foreign dividends) shall not apply to so much of the proceeds of
redemption of a deep discount security as represents income chargeable to tax under Case III or, as may be, Case IV of Schedule D.

Meaning of " disposal "

2.—(1) Subject to sub-paragraph (2) and paragraph 8 below, there
is a disposal of a deep discount security for the purposes of this
Schedule if there would be such a disposal for the purposes of the
Capital Gains Tax Act 1979.

(2) Notwithstanding anything in section 49(1)(*b*) of the Act of
1979 (no deemed disposal on death), where the assets of which a
deceased person was competent to dispose include any deep discount
security that security shall, for the purposes of this Schedule, be
deemed to have been disposed of by the deceased immediately before
his death.

Deduction of income element from total profits of company and allowance as charge on income

3.—(1) In computing the corporation tax chargeable for any
accounting period of a company which has issued any deep discount
security, the income element in respect of that security for any
income period ending in or with that accounting period shall be
allowed as a deduction against the total profits of the company for
the accounting period as reduced by any relief other than group
relief.

(2) The income element for any income period ending in or with
an accounting period of a company which has issued a deep discount
security shall be treated for the purposes of the Corporation Tax
Acts, other than those of section 248(1) of the Taxes Act (which
makes provision, in relation to charges, similar to that made by

X 4

sub-paragraph (1) above) as a charge on income paid by the company in the accounting period.

(3) No income element in respect of any deep discount security shall be so allowed or treated unless—

(a) the cost of paying so much of the amount payable on redemption as represents the discount is ultimately borne by the company ;

(b) the income element would not otherwise be deductible in computing the issuing company's profits or any description of those profits for purposes of corporation tax ; and

(c) one or more of the conditions mentioned in sub-paragraph (4) below are satisfied.

(4) The conditions are that—

(a) the company exists wholly or mainly for the purpose of carrying on a trade ;

(b) the deep discount security was issued wholly and exclusively to raise money for purposes of a trade carried on by the company ;

(c) the company is an investment company, as defined by section 304(5) of the Taxes Act.

(5) Where, on redemption of any deep discount security any part of the amount payable on redemption is, by virtue of section 233(2)(d) of the Taxes Act, a distribution of the company for the purposes of the Corporation Tax Acts, sub-paragraphs (1) and (2) above shall not apply to any income element in respect of that security.

(6) Without prejudice to its application apart from this paragraph section 38 of the Finance Act 1980 (incidental costs of obtaining loan finance to be deductible in computing profits or gains to be charged under Case I or Case II of Schedule D and to be treated for certain purposes as expenses of management) shall apply in relation to any qualifying security as it applies in relation to loan stock the interest on which is deductible as mentioned in subsection (2) of that section.

(7) In sub-paragraph (6) above, " qualifying security " means any deep discount security in respect of which the income elements are deductible under sub-paragraph (1) above in computing the total profits of the company by which the incidental costs in question are incurred.

(8) Sub-paragraphs (6) and (7) above shall have effect in relation to expenditure incurred after 13th March 1984.

(9) Relief shall not be given under any provision of the Tax Acts in respect of any income element if (at any time) a scheme has been effected or arrangements have been made such that the sole or main benefit that might be expected to accrue to the company from the issue of the security in question is the obtaining of a reduction in tax liability by means of that relief.

(10) Subsections (2) and (3) of section 38 of the Finance Act 1976 (restriction of relief for payment of interest) shall apply in relation to sub-paragraph (9) above as they apply in relation to subsection (1) of that section.

4.—(1) Section 15 of the Oil Taxation Act 1975 (oil extraction SCH. 9
activities etc. ; charges on income) shall apply in relation to income 1975 c. 22.
elements in respect of deep discount securities and paragraph 3 above
as it applies in relation to interest and section 248 of the Taxes Act
(allowance of charges on income).

(2) In the application of section 15 to any deep discount security,
subsection (2)(*b*) shall have effect as if the references to the rate at
which interest was payable were references to the aggregate of the
rate of interest payable and the amount of any income element in
respect of the security for the period in question.

*Securities issued and owned by associated companies or companies
belonging to same group*

5.—(1) Where a deep discount security issued by a company is at
any time beneficially owned by another company which is—

  (*a*) an associated company (within the meaning of section 302
     of the Taxes Act) of the issuing company ; or

  (*b*) a member of a group of companies of which the issuing com-
     pany is also a member ;

sub-paragraphs (1) and (2) of paragraph 3 of this Schedule shall
apply to any linked income element with the addition, after the words
" the accounting period ", of the words " in which the security is
redeemed ".

(2) In this paragraph " linked income element " means the income
element in respect of the security in question for any income period
in which the security is at any time beneficially owned by the other
company.

(3) For the purposes of this paragraph, two companies shall be
deemed to be members of a group of companies if one is a 51 per
cent. subsidiary of the other or both are 51 per cent. subsidiaries of
a third company.

Close companies

6.—(1) Where a deep discount security issued by a close company
is at any time beneficially owned by—

  (*a*) a participator in the company ;

  (*b*) an associate of such a participator ; or

  (*c*) a company of which such a participator has control,

sub-paragraphs (1) and (2) of paragraph 3 of this Schedule shall
apply to any linked income element with the addition, after the
words " the accounting period ", of the words " in which the security
is redeemed ".

(2) In sub-paragraph (1) above " linked income element " means
the income element in respect of the security in question for any
income period in which the security is at any time beneficially owned
by a person mentioned in that sub-paragraph.

(3) Any amount which a close company is allowed, by virtue
of paragraph 3(1) of this Schedule, to deduct from its total profits
for any accounting period shall be treated for the purposes of

paragraph 3A of Schedule 16 to the Finance Act 1972 (apportionment amongst participators of interest paid by close company as if it were income of the company) as if it were interest paid by the company in that period.

(4) In this paragraph—

" associate " has the meaning given in section 303(3) of the Taxes Act ;

" control " shall be construed in accordance with section 302(2) to (6) of that Act ; and

" participator " means a person who is, in relation to a company, a participator for the purposes of Chapter III of Part XI of the Taxes Act (by virtue of section 303 of that Act) other than a person who is a participator for those purposes by virtue only of his holding a deep discount security issued by the company.

(5) In determining whether a person who carries on a business of banking is a participator in a company for the purposes of this paragraph, there shall be disregarded any securities of the company acquired by him in the ordinary course of his business.

Early redemption

7.—(1) Where any deep discount security is redeemed before the redemption date by the company which issued it, the preceding paragraphs shall have effect subject to the provisions of this paragraph.

(2) The accrued income attributable to the period between the acquisition of the security by the person who, immediately before its redemption, was the beneficial owner of the security and its redemption shall be the amount paid to him on redemption of the security less the issue price of the security or, in a case where he did not acquire it on its issue, less the aggregate of—

(*a*) the issue price ; and

(*b*) the accrued income attributable to the period beginning with the issue, and ending with his acquisition, of the security.

(3) The deduction allowed under paragraph 3(1) above in relation to the accounting period in which the deep discount security is redeemed shall be the amount paid by the company on redemption less the aggregate of—

(*a*) the issue price of the security ; and

(*b*) the accrued income attributable to the period beginning with the issue of the security and ending with the last income period to end in or with the accounting period of the company which precedes that in which the security is redeemed.

(4) Where paragraph 5 or 6 above has applied to the deep discount security at any time, the amount mentioned in sub-paragraph (3)(*b*) above shall not include any linked income element (within the meaning of that paragraph).

(5) Where the aggregate mentioned in sub-paragraph (3) above SCH. 9
exceeds the amount paid by the company on redemption of the
security, the amount of the excess or, if it is less, the amount mentioned in paragraph (*b*) of that sub-paragraph shall be treated as
income of the company—

    (*a*) arising in the accounting period in which the security is
        redeemed ; and

    (*b*) chargeable to tax under Case VI of Schedule D.

(6) Where a resolution is passed, an order made or any other act
takes place for the winding up of a company which has issued a deep
discount security before the security is redeemed, this paragraph
shall have effect in relation to any payment made in respect of the
security in the course of the winding up as if the payment were made
on redemption.

Reorganisations, conversions, reconstructions and amalgamations

8.—(1) This paragraph applies where—

    (*a*) there is a conversion of securities to which section 82 of the
        Capital Gains Tax Act 1979 applies and those securities 1979 c. 14.
        include deep discount securities ; or

    (*b*) securities including deep discount securities are exchanged
        (or by virtue of section 86(1) of that Act are treated as
        exchanged) for other securities in circumstances in which
        section 85(3) of that Act applies.

(2) Where this paragraph applies—

    (*a*) the securities converted or exchanged shall (subject to sub-
        paragraph (3) below and notwithstanding section 78 of the
        Act of 1979) be treated for the purposes of the charge to tax
        under paragraph 1 of this Schedule as having been disposed
        of immediately before the time of the conversion, or, as the
        case may be, exchange, by the person who was the bene-
        ficial owner of the securities at that time ;

    (*b*) sub-paragraph (1)(c) of that paragraph and section 31 of the
        Act of 1979 shall not apply, but any sum payable to the
        beneficial owner of the deep discount securities by way of
        consideration for their disposal (in addition to his new
        holding) shall be treated for the purposes of capital gains
        tax as reduced by the amount of the accrued income on
        which he is chargeable to income tax by virtue of para-
        graph (*a*) above ; and

    (*c*) where that amount exceeds any such sum, the excess shall
        be treated as expenditure within section 32(1)(b) of that Act
        incurred by him on the security immediately before that
        time.

(3) Where a person would (but for this sub-paragraph) be treated
by sub-paragraph (2)(*a*) above as having, for the purposes of paragraph 1 of this Schedule, disposed of deep discount securities which
are converted into, or exchanged for, other deep discount securities—

    (*a*) he shall not be so treated—

            (i) if the date which is the redemption date in relation

to the new securities is not later than the date which was the redemption date in relation to the converted or exchanged securities ; and

(ii) no consideration is given for the conversion or exchange other than the new securities ; but

(*b*) the amount of the accrued income attributable to his period of ownership of the converted or exchanged securities (including any amount added by virtue of the previous operation of this paragraph) shall be added to the amount of the accrued income attributable to his period of ownership of the new securities.

Disposals on a no-gain/no-loss basis

9. Where a disposal of a deep discount security is to be treated for the purposes of capital gains tax as one on which neither a gain nor a loss accrues to the person making the disposal, the consideration for which the person acquiring the security would, apart from this paragraph, be treated for the purposes of capital gains tax as having acquired the security shall be increased by the amount mentioned in paragraph 1(1)(*a*) of this Schedule.

Time of disposal and acquisition where securities disposed of under contract

10.—(1) Where any deep discount security is disposed of and acquired under a contract, the time at which the disposal and acquisition is made is the time at which the contract is made (and not, if different, the time at which the security is transferred).

(2) If the contract is conditional (and in particular if it is conditional on the exercise of an option) the time at which the disposal and acquisition is made is the time when the condition is satisfied.

Identification of securities disposed of

1982 c. 39.

11.—(1) The rules contained in section 88 and 89 of the Finance Act 1982 (identification, for the purposes of capital gains tax, of securities disposed of) shall apply for the purposes of this Schedule as they apply for the purposes of capital gains tax.

1938 c. 28.

(2) In paragraph 1(2) of Schedule 6 to the Finance Act 1983 (exclusion of certain securities from provisions relating to election for pooling for purposes of capital gains tax), there shall be added, after paragraph (*a*)—

" ; nor

(*aa*) deep discount securities (within the meaning of section 36 of the Finance Act 1984) ".

Exemption for charities

12. Section 360(2) of the Taxes Act (exemption for charities from tax on chargeable gains) shall apply in relation to tax chargeable by virtue of paragraph 1 above as it applies in relation to tax on chargeable gains.

Consequential amendments

13. In section 254 of the Taxes Act (losses and charges etc. for which claim to set-off against surplus of franked investment income may be made), the words " or paragraph 3 of Schedule 9 to the Finance Act 1984 " shall be inserted—

(*a*) at the end of paragraph (*b*) in subsection (2) ; and

(*b*) after the words " 248 of this Act " in subsection (7)(*b*).

14. In Schedule 10 to the Finance Act 1975 (capital transfer tax : 1975 c. 7. valuation) in paragraph 9 (value transferred on death) at the end of sub-paragraph (1) there shall be added the words " and

(*f*) allowance shall be made for any liability to income tax aris-ing under paragraph 1 of Schedule 9 to the Finance Act 1984 (deep discount securities) on a disposal which is deemed to occur by virtue of paragraph 2(2) of that Schedule."

SCHEDULE 10

APPROVED SHARE OPTION SCHEMES

Approval of schemes

1.—(1) On the application of a body corporate (in this Schedule referred to as " the grantor ") which has established a share option scheme, the Board shall approve the scheme if they are satisfied that it fulfils the requirements of this Schedule ; but shall not ap-prove it if it appears to them that there are features of the scheme which are neither essential nor reasonably incidental to the purpose of providing for employees and directors benefits in the nature of rights to acquire shares.

(2) An application under sub-paragraph (1) above shall be made in writing and contain such particulars and be supported by such evidence as the Board may require.

(3) Where the grantor has control of another company or com-panies, the scheme may be expressed to extend to all or any of the companies of which it has control and in this Schedule a scheme which is expressed so to extend is referred to as a " group scheme ".

(4) In relation to a group scheme the expression " participating company " means the grantor or any other company to which for the time being the scheme is expressed to extend.

(5) Where the provisions of a scheme are approved in pursuance of an application made under this paragraph before 1st January 1985, section 38 of this Act shall apply in relation to any right obtained before 1st July 1985 as if the scheme containing those provisions had always been approved.

2.—(1) If, at any time after the Board have approved a scheme, any of the requirements of this Schedule cease to be satisfied or the grantor fails to provide information requested by the Board under paragraph 14 below, the Board may withdraw the approval with effect from that time or such later time as the Board may specify.

(2) If an alteration is made in the scheme at any time after the Board have approved the scheme, the approval shall not have effect after the date of the alteration unless the Board have approved the alteration.

3. If the grantor is aggrieved by—

(*a*) the failure of the Board to approve the scheme or to approve an alteration in the scheme ; or

(*b*) the withdrawal of approval ;

it may, by notice in writing given to the Board within thirty days from the date on which it is notified of the Board's decision, require the matter to be determined by the Special Commissioners, and the Special Commissioners shall hear and determine the matter in like manner as an appeal.

Eligibility

4.—(1) The scheme must not provide for any person to be eligible to participate in it, that is to say to obtain and exercise rights under it—

(*a*) unless he is a full-time director or qualifying employee of the grantor or, in the case of a group scheme, of a participating company ;

(*b*) at any time when he has, or has within the preceding twelve months had, a material interest in a close company within the meaning of Chapter III of Part XI of the Taxes Act, which is—

(i) a company the shares of which may be acquired pursuant to the exercise of rights obtained under the scheme ; or

(ii) a company which has control of such a company or is a member of a consortium which owns such a company.

(2) Notwithstanding sub-paragraph (1)(*a*) above, the scheme may provide that a person may exercise rights obtained under it despite having ceased to be a full-time director or qualifying employee.

(3) In determining whether a company is a close company for the purposes of sub-paragraph (1) above, section 282(1)(*a*) of the Taxes Act (exclusion of companies not resident in United Kingdom) and section 283 of that Act (exclusion of certain companies with quoted shares) shall be disregarded.

(4) In determining for the purposes of this paragraph whether a person has or has had a material interest in a company, subsection (6) of section 285 of the Taxes Act (interest paid to directors and directors' associates) and paragraph (ii) of the proviso to section 303 (3) of that Act (meaning of " associate ") shall have effect with the substitution for the references in those provisions to 5 per cent. of references to 10 per cent.

Limitation of rights

5.—(1) The scheme must provide that no person shall obtain rights under it which would, at the time they are obtained, cause the aggregate market value of the shares which he may acquire in pursuance of rights obtained under the scheme or under any other scheme approved under this Schedule and established by the grantor or by any associated company of the grantor (and not exercised) to exceed or further exceed the appropriate limit.

(2) The appropriate limit is the greater of—

   (*a*) £100,000 ; or

   (*b*) four times the amount of the relevant emoluments for the current or preceding year of assessment (whichever of those years gives the greater amount).

(3) Where there were no relevant emoluments for the preceding year of assessment, sub-paragraph (2) above shall apply with the following paragraph substituted for paragraph (*b*)—

   " (*b*) four times the amount of the relevant emoluments for the period of twelve months beginning with the first day during the current year of assessment in respect of which there are relevant emoluments ".

(4) For the purposes of sub-paragraph (1) above, the market value of shares shall be calculated as at the time when the rights in relation to those shares were obtained or, in a case where an agreement relating to them has been made under paragraph 13 below, such earlier time or times as may be provided in the agreement.

(5) For the purposes of sub-paragraph (2) above the relevant emoluments are such of the emoluments of the office or employment by virtue of which the person in question is eligible to participate in the scheme as are liable to be paid under deduction of tax pursuant to section 204 of the Taxes Act (pay-as-you-earn), after deducting from them amounts included by virtue of Chapter II of Part III of the Finance Act 1976.

1976 c. 40.

Scheme shares

6. The scheme must provide for directors and employees to obtain rights to acquire shares (in this Schedule referred to as " scheme shares ") which satisfy the requirements of paragraphs 7 to 11 below.

7. Scheme shares must form part of the ordinary share capital of—

   (*a*) the grantor ; or

   (*b*) a company which has control of the grantor ; or

   (*c*) a company which either is, or has control of, a company which—

   (i) is a member of a consortium owning either the grantor or a company having control of the grantor ; and

   (ii) beneficially owns not less than three twentieths of the ordinary share capital of the company so owned.

8. Scheme shares must be—

    (*a*) shares of a class quoted on a recognised stock exchange ; or

    (*b*) shares in a company which is not under the control of another company ; or

    (*c*) shares in a company which is under the control of a company (other than a company which is, or would if resident in the United Kingdom be, a close company within the meaning of section 282 of the Taxes Act) whose shares are quoted on a recognised stock exchange.

9. Scheme shares must be—

    (*a*) fully paid up ;

    (*b*) not redeemable ; and

    (*c*) not subject to any restrictions other than restrictions which attach to all shares of the same class.

10.—(1) In determining for the purposes of paragraph 9(*c*) above whether scheme shares which are or are to be acquired by any person are subject to any restrictions, there shall be regarded as a restriction attaching to the shares any contract, agreement, arrangement or condition by which his freedom to dispose of the shares or of any interest in them or of the proceeds of their sale or to exercise any right conferred by them is restricted or by which such a disposal or exercise may result in any disadvantage to him or to a person connected with him.

(2) Sub-paragraph (1) above does not apply to so much of any contract, agreement, arrangement or condition as contains provisions similar in purpose and effect to any of the provisions of the Model Rules set out in the Model Code for Securities Transactions by Directors of Listed Companies issued by the Stock Exchange in April 1981.

11. Except where scheme shares are in a company whose ordinary share capital consists of shares of one class only, the majority of the issued shares of the same class must be held by persons other than—

    (*a*) persons who acquired their shares in pursuance of a right conferred on them or an opportunity afforded to them as a director or employee of the grantor or any other company and not in pursuance of an offer to the public ;

    (*b*) trustees holding shares on behalf of persons who acquired their beneficial interests in the shares as mentioned in paragraph (*a*) above ; and

    (*c*) in a case where the shares fall within sub-paragraph (*c*) and do not fall within sub-paragraph (*a*) of paragraph 8 above, companies which have control of the company whose shares are in question or of which that company is an associated company.

Transfer of rights

12.—(1) The scheme must not permit any person obtaining rights under it to transfer any of them but may provide that if such a person dies before exercising them, they may be exercised after, but not later than one year after, the date of his death.

(2) Where the scheme contains the provision permitted by sub-paragraph (1) above and any rights are exercised—

   (*a*) after the death of the person who obtained them ; but

   (*b*) before the expiry of the period of ten years beginning with his obtaining them ;

subsection (3) of section 38 of this Act shall apply with the omission of the reference to the conditions mentioned in subsection (4).

Share price

13. The price at which scheme shares may be acquired by the exercise of a right obtained under the scheme must be stated at the time the right is obtained and must not be manifestly less than the market value of shares of the same class at that time or, if the Board and the grantor agree in writing, at such earlier time or times as may be provided in the agreement, but the scheme may provide for such variation of the price so stated as may be necessary to take account of any variation in the share capital of which the scheme shares form part.

Information

14. The Board may by notice in writing require any person to furnish them, within such time as the Board may direct (not being less than thirty days), with such information as the Board think necessary for the performance of their functions under this Schedule, and as the person to whom the notice is addressed has or can reasonably obtain, including in particular information—

   (*a*) to enable the Board to determine—

      (i) whether to approve a scheme or withdraw an approval already given ; or

      (ii) the liability to tax, including capital gains tax, of any person who has participated in a scheme ; and

   (*b*) in relation to the administration of a scheme and any alteration of the terms of a scheme.

Interpretation

15.—(1) In this Schedule—

"associated company" has the same meaning as in section 302 of the Taxes Act ;

"control" has the same meaning as in section 534 of the Taxes Act ;

"grantor" has the meaning given by paragraph 1(1) ;

"group scheme" and, in relation to such a scheme, "participating company" have the meanings given by paragraph 1 ;

"market value" has the same meaning as in Part VIII of the Capital Gains Tax Act 1979 ;   1979 c. 14.

"qualifying employee" in relation to a company, means an employee of the company (other than one who is a director of the company or, in the case of a group scheme, of a participating company) who is required, under the terms of his employment, to work for the company for at least twenty hours a week ;

" scheme shares " has the meaning given by paragraph 6 ; and

" shares " includes stock.

(2) Section 303(3) of the Taxes Act (meaning of " associate ") shall have effect in a case where the scheme is a group scheme, with the substitution of a reference to all the participating companies for the first reference to the company in paragraph (ii) of the proviso to that subsection.

(3) Section 533 of the Taxes Act (connected persons) shall apply for the purposes of this Schedule.

(4) For the purposes of this Schedule a company is a member of a consortium owning another company if it is one of a number of companies which between them beneficially own not less than three-quarters of the other company's ordinary share capital and each of which beneficially owns not less than one-twentieth of that capital.

Section 50(1).

SCHEDULE 11

FURNISHED HOLIDAY LETTINGS

Treatment of lettings as a trade for certain purposes

1.—(1) Subject to the provisions of this Schedule, for the purposes of the provisions mentioned in sub-paragraph (2) below—

(*a*) the commercial letting of furnished holiday accommodation in respect of which the profits or gains are chargeable under Case VI of Schedule D shall be treated as a trade ; and

(*b*) all such lettings made by a particular person or partnership or body of persons shall be treated as one trade.

(2) The provisions mentioned in sub-paragraph (1) above are—

(*a*) section 4(2) of the Taxes Act (payment of income tax in two equal instalments) ;

(*b*) sections 168 to 175 and 177 to 178 of the Taxes Act and section 30 of the Finance Act 1978 (relief for losses) ;

1978 c. 42.

(*c*) subsection (9)(*c*) of section 226 of the Taxes Act (retirement annuity contracts) ;

(*d*) subsection (1)(*c*) of section 530 of that Act (earned income) ;

1971 c. 68.

(*e*) Chapter I of Part III of the Finance Act 1971 (capital allowances) ;

1979 c. 14.

(*f*) sections 115 to 120 of the Capital Gains Tax Act 1979 (roll-over relief for replacement of business assets) ;

(*g*) section 124 of that Act (transfer of business on retirement) ;

(*h*) section 126 of that Act (relief for gifts of business assets) ;

(*i*) section 136 of that Act (relief in respect of loans to traders) ;   Sch. 11
and

(*j*) section 39 of the Finance Act 1980 (relief for pre-trading ex- 1980 c. 48.
penditure).

Losses and pre-trading expenditure

2.—(1) In their application by virtue of paragraph 1 above section
175(1) of the Taxes Act (treatment of interest as a loss for purposes
of carry-forward and carry-back) and section 39(1) of the Finance
Act 1980 shall have effect as if for the references in those sections to
Case I of Schedule D there were substituted references to Case VI of
that Schedule.

(2) No relief shall be given to an individual under section 30 of the
Finance Act 1978, as it applies by virtue of paragraph 1 above, in 1978 c. 42.
respect of a loss sustained in any year of assessment, if any of the
accommodation in respect of which the trade is carried on in that
year was first let by him as furnished accommodation more than three
years before the beginning of that year of assessment.

(3) Relief shall not be given for the same loss or the same portion
of a loss both under any of the provisions mentioned in paragraph
1(2)(*b*) above, as they apply by virtue of this Schedule, and under
any other provision of the Tax Acts.

Expenditure

3. In computing the profits or gains arising from the commercial
letting of furnished holiday accommodation which are chargeable
to tax under Case VI of Schedule D, such expenditure may be deducted as would be deductible if the letting were a trade and those
profits or gains were accordingly to be computed in accordance with
the rules applicable to Case I of that Schedule.

Capital gains tax

4.—(1) Subject to sub-paragraph (2) below, for the purposes of
the provisions mentioned in sub-paragraph (2)(*f*) to (*i*) of paragraph
1 above as they apply by virtue of that paragraph, where in any
year of assessment a person makes a commercial letting of furnished
holiday accommodation—

(*a*) the accommodation shall be taken to be used in that year
only for the purposes of the trade of making such lettings ;
and

(*b*) that trade shall be taken to be carried on throughout that
year.

(2) Sub-paragraph (1) above does not apply to any period in a year
of assessment during which the accommodation is neither let com-
mercially nor available to be so let unless it is prevented from being
so let or available by any works of construction or repair.

5. Where—

(*a*) a gain to which section 101 of the Capital Gains Tax Act 1979 c. 14.
1979 (relief on disposal of private residence) applies accrues
to any individual on the disposal of an asset ; and

(*b*) by virtue of paragraph 1 above the amount or value of the consideration for the acquisition of the asset is treated as reduced under section 115 or 116 of that Act,

the gain to which section 101 applies shall be reduced by the amount of the reduction mentioned in paragraph (*b*) above.

Power to make apportionments

6. Where there is a letting of accommodation only part of which is holiday accommodation such apportionments shall be made for the purposes of this Schedule as appear to the inspector, or on appeal the Commissioners, to be just and reasonable.

Adjustments of tax charged

7. Where a person has been charged to income tax, corporation tax or capital gains tax otherwise than in accordance with the provisions of this Schedule, such assessment, reduction or discharge of an assessment or, where a claim for repayment is made, such repayment, shall be made as may be necessary to give effect to those provisions.

Section 58.

SCHEDULE 12

INITIAL ALLOWANCES AND FIRST-YEAR ALLOWANCES

Part I

Withdrawal of Allowances

Initial allowances for industrial buildings and structures

1968 c. 3.   1.—(1) In section 1(2) of the Capital Allowances Act 1968 (rate of initial allowances for capital expenditure on the construction of industrial buildings or structures) for the words " three-quarters " there shall be substituted,—

(*a*) with respect to capital expenditure incurred after 13th March 1984 and before 1st April 1985, the words " one half " ; and

(*b*) with respect to capital expenditure incurred on or after 1st April 1985 and before 1st April 1986, the words " one quarter " ;

and no initial allowance shall be made in respect of expenditure incurred on or after 1st April 1986.

(2) Nothing in sub-paragraph (1) above applies to capital expenditure which—

(*a*) is incurred after 13th March 1984 and before 1st April 1987 ; and

(*b*) consists of the payment of sums under a contract entered into on or before 13th March 1984 by the person incurring the expenditure.

(3) Sub-paragraphs (1) and (2) above shall be construed as if
they were contained in Part I of the Capital Allowances Act 1968
except that—

    (*a*) expenditure shall not be treated for the purposes of those
sub-paragraphs as having been incurred after the date on
which it was in fact incurred by reason only of section
1(6) of that Act (expenditure incurred before a trade begins) ;
and

    (*b*) expenditure falling within subsection (1)(*b*) of section 5 of
that Act (purchase price of building or structure bought
unused) shall be treated for the purposes of those sub-
paragraphs as having been incurred at the latest time when
any expenditure falling within subsection (1)(*a*) of that
section (expenditure on the construction of the building or
structure) was incurred.

First-year allowances for machinery and plant

2.—(1) In section 42(1) of the Finance Act 1971 (rate of first-year
allowance for capital expenditure incurred on provision of machinery
or plant) for the words " the whole " there shall be substituted,—

    (*a*) with respect to capital expenditure incurred after 13th March
1984 and before 1st April 1985, the words "three-quarters" ;
and

    (*b*) with respect to capital expenditure incurred on or after 1st
April 1985 and before 1st April 1986, the words " one
half " ;

and no first-year allowance shall be made in respect of expenditure
incurred on or after 1st April 1986.

(2) Nothing in sub-paragraph (1) above applies to capital expenditure which—

    (*a*) is incurred after 13th March 1984 and before 1st April 1987 ;
and

    (*b*) consists of the payment of sums under a contract entered
into on or before 13th March 1984 by the person incurring
the expenditure or by a person whose contractual obligations that person has assumed with a view to entering into
leasing arrangements.

(3) For the purposes of sub-paragraph (2)(*b*) above, a person incurring expenditure on the provision of machinery or plant (in this
sub-paragraph referred to as " the lessor ") shall be taken to have
assumed, with a view to entering into leasing arrangements, the contractual obligations of a person who entered into a contract for the
provision of that machinery or plant (in this sub-paragraph referred
to as " the lessee ") if, and only if,—

    (*a*) arrangements exist under which the lessor will lease the
machinery or plant to the lessee ; and

    (*b*) the obligations of the lessee under the contract either have
been taken over by the lessor or have been discharged on
the lessor's entering into a new contract for the provision
of the machinery or plant concerned ;

and, where there is such a new contract as is referred to in paragraph (*b*) above, sums paid under that contract shall be treated for the purposes of sub-paragraph (2)(*b*) above and Part II of this Schedule as paid under the contract referred to in that sub-paragraph.

(4) Sub-paragraphs (1) to (3) above shall be construed as if they were contained in Chapter I of Part III of the Finance Act 1971, except that expenditure shall not be treated for the purposes of those sub-paragraphs as having been incurred after the date on which it was in fact incurred by reason only of so much of section 50(4) of that Act as relates to expenditure incurred before a trade begins.

Initial allowances in respect of dwelling-houses let on assured tenancies

3.—(1) In paragraph 1(2) of Schedule 12 to the Finance Act 1982 (rate of initial allowance in respect of qualifying dwelling-house on the construction of which capital expenditure is incurred) for the words " three-quarters " there shall be substituted,—

(*a*) with respect to capital expenditure incurred after 13th March 1984 and before 1st April 1985, the words " one half " ; and

(*b*) with respect to capital expenditure incurred on or after 1st April 1985 and before 1st April 1986, the words " one quarter " ;

and no initial allowance shall be made in respect of expenditure incurred on or after 1st April 1986.

(2) Nothing in sub-paragraph (1) above applies to capital expenditure which—

(*a*) is incurred after 13th March 1984 and before 1st April 1987 ; and

(*b*) consists of the payment of sums under a contract entered into on or before 13th March 1984 by the person incurring the expenditure.

(3) Sub-paragraphs (1) and (2) above shall be construed as if they were contained in Schedule 12 to the Finance Act 1982 except that expenditure falling within sub-paragraph (1)(*b*) of paragraph 8 of that Schedule (purchase price of building bought unused) shall be treated for the purposes of those sub-paragraphs as having been incurred at the latest time when any expenditure falling within sub-paragraph (1)(*a*) of that paragraph (expenditure on the construction of the building) was incurred.

Part II

Supplementary

Transitional relief for regional projects

4.—(1) The provisions of Part I of this Schedule do not apply to so much of any expenditure as is certified by the Secretary of State for the purposes of this paragraph to be expenditure which, in his

opinion, qualifies for a regional development grant or a grant under   SCH. 12
Part IV of the relevant Order and consists of the payment of sums on
a project—

    (*a*) either in an area which on 13th March 1984 was a develop-
        ment area, within the meaning of the Industrial Develop- 1982 c. 52.
        ment Act 1982, or in Northern Ireland ; and

    (*b*) in respect of which a written offer of financial assistance
        under section 7 or section 8 of that Act was made on behalf
        of the Secretary of State in the period beginning on 1st
        April 1980 and ending on 13th March 1984 or in respect of
        which a written offer of financial assistance was made in
        that period by the Highlands and Islands Development
        Board.

(2) The provisions of Part I of this Schedule do not apply to so
much of any expenditure as is certified by the Department of
Economic Development in Northern Ireland for the purposes of this
paragraph to be expenditure which, in the opinion of that Department, qualifies for a grant under Part IV of the relevant Order and
consists of the payment of sums on a project—

    (*a*) in Northern Ireland ; and

    (*b*) in respect of which a written offer of financial assistance
        under Article 7 or Article 8 of the relevant Order was made
        on behalf of a Department of the Government of Northern
        Ireland in the period beginning on 1st April 1980 and
        ending on 13th March 1984 or in respect of which a written
        offer of financial assistance was made in that period by the
        Local Enterprise Development Unit.

(3) In this paragraph—

    " regional development grant " means a grant under Part II
of the Industrial Development Act 1982 ;

    " the relevant Order " means the Industrial Development S.I. 1982/1083
(Northern Ireland) Order 1982 ;   (N.I. 15).

and any reference to a particular provision of that Act or Order includes a reference to the corresponding provision of any Act or Order
which was in force before and repealed by the said Act or Order of
1982.

Spreading of expenditure under certain contracts

5.—(1) Where in circumstances falling within paragraph 8 below
a person incurs such capital expenditure as is referred to in section
1 of the Capital Allowances Act 1968 under a contract—   1968 c. 3.

    (*a*) which is entered into after 13th March 1984 and on or before
        31st March 1986, and

    (*b*) which either specifies no date on or by which the contractual
        obligations must be fully performed or specifies such a date
        which is after 31st March 1985,

Chapter I of Part I of that Act shall have effect in relation to the
capital expenditure so incurred subject to the following provisions
of this paragraph.

(2) In this Part of this Schedule, in relation to a contract falling within sub-paragraph (1) above,—

" the contract date " means the date on which the contract is entered into ;

" the contract price " means the total capital expenditure on the construction of the building or structure concerned which the person referred to in sub-paragraph (1) above is to incur pursuant to the contract ;

" the completion date " means the date specified as mentioned in sub-paragraph (1)(*b*) above or, if no date is so specified, 31st March 1987 ; and

" the maximum allowable expenditure " shall be construed in accordance with paragraph 9 below.

(3) In respect of capital expenditure incurred in either of the financial years 1984 and 1985 under a contract falling within sub-paragraph (1) above, the initial allowance under section 1 of the Capital Allowances Act 1968 shall not exceed the fraction appropriate under paragraph 1 above of the maximum allowable expenditure for that year.

(4) So much (if any) of the capital expenditure incurred in the financial year 1984 under a contract falling within sub-paragraph (1) above as exceeds the maximum allowable expenditure for that year shall be deemed for all purposes of Chapter I of Part I of the Capital Allowances Act 1968 to be incurred on 1st April 1985.

(5) So much (if any) of the aggregate of—

(*a*) the capital expenditure incurred in the financial year 1985 under a contract falling within sub-paragraph (1) above, and

(*b*) any excess relating to that contract which, by virtue of sub-paragraph (4) above, is deemed to be incurred in that financial year,

as exceeds the maximum allowable expenditure for that financial year shall be deemed for all purposes of Chapter I of Part I of the Capital Allowances Act 1968 to be incurred on 1st April 1986.

(6) This paragraph shall be construed as if it were contained in Chapter I of Part I of the Capital Allowances Act 1968 except that—

(*a*) expenditure shall not be treated for the purposes of this paragraph as having been incurred after the date on which it was in fact incurred by reason only of section 1(6) of that Act ; and

(*b*) expenditure falling within subsection (1)(*b*) of section 5 of that Act shall be treated for the purposes of this paragraph as having been incurred at the latest time when any expenditure falling within subsection (1)(*a*) of that section was incurred.

6.—(1) Where in circumstances falling within paragraph 8 below a person carrying on a trade incurs capital expenditure on the provision of machinery or plant for the purposes of that trade under a contract—

(*a*) which is entered into after 13th March 1984 and on or before 31st March 1986, and

(*b*) which provides that he shall or may become the owner of the machinery or plant on or before the performance of the contract, and

(*c*) which either specifies no date on or by which the contractual obligations must be fully performed or specifies such a date which is after 31st March 1985,

Chapter I of Part III of the Finance Act 1971 shall have effect in relation to the capital expenditure so incurred subject to the following provisions of this paragraph.

(2) In this Part of this Schedule, in relation to a contract falling within sub-paragraph (1) above,—

" the contract date " means the date on which the contract is entered into ;

" the contract price " means the total capital expenditure on the provision of the machinery or plant which the person referred to in sub-paragraph (1) above is to incur pursuant to the contract ;

" the completion date " means the date specified as mentioned in sub-paragraph (1)(*c*) above or, if no date is so specified, 31st March 1987 ; and

" the maximum allowable expenditure " shall be construed in accordance with paragraph 9 below.

(3) The provisions of this paragraph do not apply in relation to capital expenditure to which section 45(1)(*b*) of the Finance Act 1971 (machinery and plant on hire-purchase etc.) applies.

(4) In respect of capital expenditure incurred in either of the financial years 1984 and 1985 under a contract falling within sub-paragraph (1) above, the first-year allowance under section 42(1) of the Finance Act 1971 shall not exceed the fraction appropriate under paragraph 2 above of the maximum allowable expenditure for that year.

(5) So much (if any) of the capital expenditure incurred in the financial year 1984 under a contract falling within sub-paragraph (1) above as exceeds the maximum allowable expenditure for that year shall be deemed for all purposes of Chapter I of Part III of the Finance Act 1971 to be incurred on 1st April 1985.

(6) So much (if any) of the aggregate of—

(*a*) the capital expenditure incurred in the financial year 1985 under a contract falling within sub-paragraph (1) above, and

(*b*) any excess relating to that contract which, by virtue of sub-paragraph (5) above, is deemed to be incurred in that financial year, as exceeds the maximum allowable expenditure for that financial year shall be deemed for all purposes of Chapter I of Part III of the Finance Act 1971 to be incurred on 1st April 1986.

(7) This paragraph shall be construed as if it were contained in Chapter I of Part III of the Finance Act 1971 except that expenditure shall not be treated for the purposes of this paragraph as having been incurred after the date on which it was in fact incurred by reason only of so much of section 50(4) of that Act as relates to expenditure incurred before a trade began.

7.—(1) Where in circumstances falling within paragraph 8 below an approved body incurs such capital expenditure as is referred to in paragraph 1(1) of Schedule 12 to the Finance Act 1982 under a contract—

(a) which is entered into after 13th March 1984 and on or before 31st March 1986, and

(b) which either specifies no date on or by which the contractual obligations must be fully performed or specifies such a date which is after 31st March 1985,

that Schedule shall have effect in relation to the capital expenditure so incurred subject to the following provisions of this paragraph.

(2) In this Part of this Schedule, in relation to a contract falling within sub-paragraph (1) above,—

" the contract date " means the date on which the contract was entered into ;

" the contract price " means the total capital expenditure on the construction of the building concerned which the approved body referred to in sub-paragraph (1) above is to incur pursuant to the contract ;

" the completion date " means the date specified as mentioned in sub-paragraph (1)(b) above or, if no date is so specified, 31st March 1987 ; and

" the maximum allowable expenditure " shall be construed in accordance with paragraph 9 below.

(3) In respect of capital expenditure incurred in either of the financial years 1984 and 1985 under a contract falling within sub-paragraph (1) above, the initial allowance under paragraph 1 of Schedule 12 to the Finance Act 1982 shall not exceed the fraction appropriate under paragraph 3 above of the maximum allowable expenditure for that year.

(4) So much (if any) of the capital expenditure incurred in the financial year 1984 under a contract falling within sub-paragraph (1) above as exceeds the maximum allowable expenditure for that year shall be deemed for all purposes of Schedule 12 to the Finance Act 1982 to be incurred on 1st April 1985.

(5) So much (if any) of the aggregate of—

(a) the capital expenditure incurred in the financial year 1985 under a contract falling within sub-paragraph (1) above, and

(b) any excess relating to that contract which, by virtue of sub-paragraph (4) above, is deemed to be incurred in that financial year, as exceeds the maximum allowable expenditure for that financial year shall be deemed for all purposes of Schedule 12 to the Finance Act 1982 to be incurred on 1st April 1986.

(6) This paragraph shall be construed as if it were contained in Schedule 12 to the Finance Act 1982 except that expenditure falling within sub-paragraph (1)(*b*) of paragraph 8 of that Schedule shall be treated for the purposes of this paragraph as having been incurred at the latest time when any expenditure falling within sub-paragraph (1)(*a*) of that paragraph was incurred.

8.—(1) The circumstances referred to in sub-paragraph (1) of each of paragraphs 5 to 7 above is that the sole or main benefit which (apart from this Part of this Schedule) might have been expected to be gained by incurring the expenditure at the time at which it was incurred was either—

(*a*) the securing of an initial allowance or first-year allowance in respect of the expenditure, rather than a writing-down allowance ; or

(*b*) the securing of a higher rate of initial or first-year allowance in respect of the expenditure.

(2) In sub-paragraph (1) above—

" initial allowance " means an initial allowance under section 1 of the Capital Allowances Act 1968 or Schedule 12 to the Finance Act 1982 ; and

" first-year allowance " means a first-year allowance under section 41 of the Finance Act 1971.

9.—(1) References in paragraphs 5 to 7 above to the maximum allowable expenditure for each of the financial years 1984 and 1985 shall be construed in accordance with this paragraph.

(2) For each contract falling within sub-paragraph (1) of any of paragraphs 5 to 7 above, the maximum allowable expenditure shall be that fraction of the contract price of which—

(*a*) the numerator,—

(i) for the financial year 1984, is the number of complete months in the period beginning on the contract date and ending on 31st March 1985 ; and

(ii) for the financial year 1985, is 12 or, if it is less, the number of complete months in the period beginning on the contract date and ending on 31st March 1986 ; and

(*b*) the denominator is the number of complete months in the period beginning on the contract date and ending on the completion date or, if it is earlier, 31st March 1987.

10.—(1) Where, by virtue of paragraph 5(4), paragraph 6(5) or paragraph 7(4) above, a portion of any expenditure which is incurred by any person in the financial year 1984 is deemed to be incurred on 1st April 1985, so much of that expenditure as is not deemed to be incurred on that date shall be apportioned to the chargeable periods or their basis periods which begin or end in the financial year 1984 on a time basis according to the respective lengths of those periods which fall within that financial year.

(2) Where, by virtue of paragraph 5(5), paragraph 6(6) or paragraph 7(5) above, a portion of the aggregate of any capital expenditure incurred and deemed to be incurred by any person in the financial year 1985 is deemed to be incurred on 1st April 1986, so much of that aggregate expenditure as is not deemed to be incurred on that date shall be apportioned to the chargeable periods or their basis periods which begin or end in the financial year 1985 on the like time basis as is specified in sub-paragraph (1) above.

Section 64.

SCHEDULE 13

QUALIFYING CORPORATE BONDS

PART I

APPLICATION OF PROVISIONS RELATING TO GILT-EDGED SECURITIES

1979 c. 14

Capital Gains Tax Act 1979

1. In section 64 of the Capital Gains Tax Act 1979 (interpretation provisions relating to shares and securities) after the definition of " gilt-edged securities " there shall be inserted—

" ' qualifying corporate bonds ' has the meaning given by section 64 of the Finance Act 1984 ".

2. In section 67(1) of that Act after the words " gilt-edged securities " there shall be added the words " or qualifying corporate bonds ".

3.—(1) In section 70 of that Act, in subsection (1) after the words " gilt-edged securities " there shall be inserted the words " or, subject to subsection (1A) below, qualifying corporate bonds ".

(2) After subsection (1) of that section there shall be inserted the following subsection:—

1975 c. 45.

" (1A) This section does not apply in relation to a disposal of qualifying corporate bonds if the disposal is such that section 58 of the Finance (No. 2) Act 1975 applies but, subject to that, any reference in the following provisions of this section to gilt-edged securities includes a reference to qualifying corporate bonds."

Other enactments

4. In section 270(3) of the Taxes Act (groups of companies: gilt-edged securities) after the words " specified securities " there shall be inserted the words " or qualifying corporate bonds as defined in section 64 of the Finance Act 1984 ".

1973 c. 51.

5. In Schedule 16 to the Finance Act 1973 (underwriters) at the end of paragraph 7 (exclusion of gilt-edged securities) there shall be added the words " or of qualifying corporate bonds as defined in section 64 of the Finance Act 1984 ".

6. In Schedule 6 to the Finance Act 1983 (election for pooling) SCH. 13 in paragraph 1(2) (definition of qualifying securities) after para- 1983 c. 28. graph (*a*) there shall be inserted—

"(*aa*) qualifying corporate bonds, as defined in section 64 of the Finance Act 1984 ; nor ".

PART II
REORGANISATIONS, CONVERSIONS, RECONSTRUCTIONS ETC.

7.—(1) In this Part of this Schedule " relevant transaction " means a reorganisation, conversion of securities or other transaction such as is mentioned in subsection (7) of section 64 of this Act.

(2) Where the qualifying corporate bond referred to in paragraph (*b*) of that subsection would constitute the original shares for the purposes of sections 78 to 81 of the principal Act, it is in this Part of this Schedule referred to as " the old asset " and the shares or securities which would constitute the new holding for those purposes are referred to as " the new asset ".

(3) Where the qualifying corporate bond referred to in section 64(7)(*b*) of this Act would constitute the new holding for the purposes of sections 78 to 81 of the principal Act, it is in this Part of this Schedule referred to as " the new asset " and the shares or securities which would constitute the original shares for those purposes are referred to as " the old asset ".

(4) In this Part of this Schedule " the principal Act " means the Capital Gains Tax Act 1979. 1979 c. 14.

8.—(1) So far as the relevant transaction relates to the old asset and the new asset, sections 78 to 81 of the principal Act shall not apply in relation to it.

(2) In accordance with sub-paragraph (1) above, the new asset shall not be treated as having been acquired on any date other than the date of the relevant transaction or, subject to sub-paragraphs (3) and (4) below, for any consideration other than the market value of the old asset as determined immediately before that transaction.

(3) If, on the relevant transaction, the person concerned receives, or becomes entitled to receive, any sum of money which, in addition to the new asset, is by way of consideration for the old asset, that sum shall be deducted from the consideration referred to in sub-paragraph (2) above.

(4) If, on the relevant transaction, the person concerned gives any sum of money which, in addition to the old asset, is by way of consideration for the new asset, that sum shall be added to the consideration referred to in sub-paragraph (2) above.

9. In any case where—

(*a*) the old asset consists of a qualifying corporate bond, and

(*b*) the relevant transaction takes place at such a time that, if there were then a disposal of the old asset, it would be a disposal within section 67 of the principal Act, then, so far as it relates to the old asset and the new asset, the relevant transaction shall be treated for the purposes of that Act as a disposal of the old asset and an acquisition of the new asset.

10.—(1) Except in a case falling within paragraph 9 above, so far as it relates to the old asset and the new asset, the relevant transaction shall be treated for the purposes of the principal Act as not involving any disposal of the old asset but—

(a) there shall be calculated the chargeable gain or allowable loss that would have accrued if, at the time of the relevant transaction, the old asset had been disposed of for a consideration equal to its market value immediately before that transaction ; and

(b) subject to paragraph 11 below, the whole or a corresponding part of the chargeable gain or allowable loss mentioned in paragraph (a) above shall be deemed to accrue on a subsequent disposal of the whole or part of the new asset (in addition to any gain or loss that actually accrues on that disposal) ; and

(c) if that subsequent disposal is within section 67 of the principal Act, that section shall have effect only in relation to any gain or loss that actually accrues and not in relation to any gain or loss which is deemed to accrue by virtue of paragraph (b) above.

(2) Paragraphs (b) and (c) of sub-paragraph (1) above shall not apply to any disposal falling within the provisions of—

(a) section 44(1) of the principal Act (disposals between husband and wife) ; or

(b) section 49(4) of that Act (disposals by personal representatives to legatees) ; or

(c) section 273(1) of the Taxes Act (disposals within a group of companies) ;

but a person who has acquired the new asset on a disposal falling within those provisions (and without there having been a previous disposal falling within those provisions or a devolution on death) shall be treated for the purposes of paragraphs (b) and (c) of sub-paragraph (1) above as if the new asset had been acquired by him at the same time and for the same consideration as, having regard to paragraph 8 above, it was acquired by the person making the disposal.

11.—(1) In any case where—

(a) on the calculation under paragraph 10(1)(a) above, a chargeable gain would have accrued, and

(b) the consideration for the old asset includes such a sum of money as is referred to in paragraph 8(3) above,

then, subject to sub-paragraph (2) below, the proportion of that chargeable gain which that sum of money bears to the market value of the old asset immediately before the relevant transaction shall be deemed to accrue at the time of that transaction.

(2) If the inspector is satisfied that the sum of money referred to in sub-paragraph (1)(*b*) above is small, as compared with the market value of the old asset immediately before the relevant transaction, and so directs, sub-paragraph (1) above shall not apply.

(3) In a case where sub-paragraph (1) above applies, the chargeable gain which, apart from this paragraph, would by virtue of paragraph 10(1)(*b*) above be deemed to accrue on a subsequent disposal of the whole or part of the new asset shall be reduced or, as the case may be, extinguished by deducting therefrom the amount of the chargeable gain which, by virtue of sub-paragraph (1) above, is deemed to accrue at the time of the relevant transaction.

SCHEDULE 14

BENEFICIARY'S LIABILITY FOR TAX ON GAINS OF
NON-RESIDENT TRUSTEES

Interpretation

1.—(1) In this Schedule—

" attributed gain ", in relation to the beneficiary, means the chargeable gain which, as mentioned in paragraph (*b*) of subsection (1) of the principal section, is treated as accruing to him ;

" the beneficiary " means the beneficiary referred to in that paragraph and paragraph (*c*) of that subsection ;

" claim " means a claim under paragraph 2(1) below ;

" close relative ", in relation to any person, means his spouse or a child or remoter descendant of his ;

" ineligible gain " shall be construed in accordance with paragraph 2(3) below ;

" offshore income gain " has the same meaning as in Chapter VII of Part II of this Act ;

" the principal Act " means the Capital Gains Tax Act 1979 ;

" the principal section " means section 70 of this Act ;

" related settlement " shall be construed in accordance with paragraph 5(6) below ;

" relevant benefit " shall be construed in accordance with paragraph 5 below ; and

" the relevant year of assessment ", in relation to an attributed gain, means the year of assessment in which the gain is treated as accruing to the beneficiary.

(2) Subject to subsection (4) of the principal section, section 83 of the Finance Act 1981 (meaning of " capital payment " etc.) applies for the purposes of this Schedule as it applies for the purposes of sections 80 to 82 of that Act.

(3) In any case where the beneficiary is a married woman, any reference in the following provisions of this Schedule to the payment of capital gains tax by the beneficiary shall be construed as including

a reference to the payment by her husband of capital gains tax which, under subsection (1) of section 45 of the principal Act, is assessed and charged on him.

Claims for postponement of tax

2.—(1) Subject to sub-paragraph (3) below, in a case falling within the principal section, the provisions of this Schedule have effect to determine whether, on a claim made to the Board, payment of any of the capital gains tax referable to an attributed gain may be postponed and, if so, to what extent and for how long.

(2) A claim must be made before 1st July 1985 or, if it is later, the expiry of the period of thirty days beginning with the date of the issue of a notice of assessment requiring the payment of an amount of capital gains tax assessed, in whole or in part, by reason of an attributed gain to which the claim relates.

(3) The provisions of this Schedule do not have effect to allow postponement of the payment of the capital gains tax referable to an attributed gain if the capital gains tax chargeable on the gain—

(*a*) has previously been postponed under section 17(4)(*b*) of the principal Act (pre-6th April 1965 settlements) ; or

1970 c. 9.

(*b*) subject to sub-paragraph (4) below, carries interest, by virtue of section 88(1) of the Taxes Management Act 1970 (interest on tax recovered to make good tax lost due to fraud, wilful default or neglect), from the date on which the tax ought to have been paid until payment ;

and an attributed gain falling within paragraph (*a*) or paragraph (*b*) above is in this Schedule referred to as an ineligible gain.

(4) Sub-paragraph (3)(*b*) above does not apply where the tax carries interest by reason only of the neglect of any person and that neglect is remedied before 1st July 1985.

(5) In relation to a claim, any reference in this Schedule to an attributed gain to which the claim relates is a reference to such a gain—

(*a*) which is specified in the claim, and

(*b*) which is not an ineligible gain, and

(*c*) in respect of which the claim is not out of time by virtue of sub-paragraph (2) above,

and any reference to the settlement to which the claim relates is a reference to the settlement under which the beneficiary is a beneficiary and to the trustees of which accrued the chargeable gain which gives rise to the attributed gain or gains to which the claim relates.

(6) In a case where a claim relates to attributed gains accruing to the beneficiary by virtue of more than one settlement, the provisions of this Schedule shall have effect as if there were separate claims, each relating to the attributed gain or gains accruing by virtue of a single settlement.

(7) Without prejudice to the application of sub-paragraph (2) above
in a case where the personal representatives of the beneficiary receive
a notice of assessment requiring the payment by them of an amount
of capital gains tax assessed, in whole or in part, by reason of an
attributed gain, if—

    (*a*) before his death the beneficiary or, where paragraph 1(3)
        above applies, the beneficiary's husband received a notice
        of assessment requiring the payment by him of such an
        amount of capital gains tax, and

    (*b*) at the time of his death the period within which he might
        make a claim in respect of any of the tax assessed by that
        notice had not expired,

a claim by his personal representatives relating to that tax may be
made at any time before the expiry of the period of six months
beginning on the date of the death of the beneficiary or, as the case
may be, her husband (or, if it is later, before 1st July 1985).

(8) In relation to any claim by the personal representatives of the
beneficiary, references in this Schedule to the postponement of the
payment of any tax shall be construed as references to the discharge
of that tax and, accordingly, paragraphs 11 and 12 below do not
apply where a claim is made by the personal representatives.

Tax referable to attributed gains

3. Any reference in this Schedule to the tax referable to an
attributed gain is a reference to the amount determined by multiplying the total capital gains tax on chargeable gains accruing to the
beneficiary in the relevant year of assessment by a fraction—

    (*a*) of which the numerator is the amount of the attributed
        gain ; and

    (*b*) the denominator is the total of the chargeable gains accruing
        to the beneficiary in the relevant year of assessment.

Initial calculations relevant to tax which may be postponed

4.—(1) Where a claim is made, the determination referred to in
paragraph 2(1) above shall, in the first instance, be made (in accordance with paragraph 6 below) by reference to—

    (*a*) the amount defined in sub-paragraph (4) below as the unpaid
        tax ;

    (*b*) the amount defined in sub-paragraph (5) below as the tax
        already paid ; and

    (*c*) the aggregate value of any relevant benefits which, by
        virtue of paragraph 5 below, fall to be taken into account
        in relation to the claim.

(2) Subject to sub-paragraph (3) below, in this paragraph and
paragraph 5 below " the base year " means the year of assessment
which precedes the relevant year of assessment in relation to the
attributed gain or, as the case may be, the earliest of the attributed
gains to which the claim relates.

(3) Where the relevant year of assessment referred to in sub-paragraph (2) above is the year 1965-66, the base year is also that year of assessment.

(4) In relation to a claim, "the unpaid tax" means the amount of tax—

(a) which is referable to the attributed gain (or attributed gains) to which the claim relates ; and

(b) which remains unpaid at the date of the claim.

(5) In relation to a claim, "the tax already paid" means the amount of tax—

(a) which has been paid at the date of the claim, excluding any tax which was so paid, or is or was otherwise borne, by the trustees of the settlement to which the claim relates ; and

(b) which is referable to any attributed gains—

(i) which have accrued to the beneficiary by virtue of the settlement to which the claim relates ; and

(ii) for which the relevant year of assessment is, or is later than, the base year ; and

(iii) which are not ineligible gains.

Relevant benefits

5.—(1) The provisions of this paragraph have effect to determine what are the relevant benefits to be taken into account (as mentioned in paragraph 4(1)(c) above) in relation to a claim ; and in the following provisions of this paragraph "the calculation period" means the period beginning at the beginning of the base year and ending on 9th March 1981.

(2) Subject to sub-paragraph (3) below, if, under or by reference to the settlement to which the claim relates or a related settlement, the beneficiary received a capital payment from the trustees of the settlement—

(a) at any time in the calculation period, or

(b) after the end of that period but before 6th April 1984, in so far as that payment represented a chargeable gain which, before 6th April 1981, accrued to the trustees of the settlement to which the claim relates,

the amount of that capital payment is a relevant benefit.

(3) In any case where, apart from this sub-paragraph, sub-paragraph (2) above would bring into account, as a relevant benefit in relation to a claim, a capital payment received under or by reference to a related settlement, and either—

(a) on a claim relating to the related settlement, the payment falls to be taken into account under this paragraph as a relevant benefit, or

(b) it appears to the Board to be likely that the payment will fall to be so taken into account on a claim relating to the related settlement, the payment shall not be taken into account as a relevant benefit in relation to the claim referred to in sub-paragraph (2) above except to the extent that it constitutes a surplus benefit by virtue of paragraph 6(5) below.

(4) If, at any time in the period beginning at the beginning of the base year and ending at the beginning of the year of assessment in which the claim is made, the beneficiary disposed of his interest in the settlement to which the claim relates in circumstances such that, by virtue of section 58(1) of the principal Act, no chargeable gain could accrue on the disposal, then the amount or value of the consideration for the disposal is a relevant benefit.

(5) Where the disposal referred to in sub-paragraph (4) above was made before 6th April 1984, the reference in that sub-paragraph to the consideration for the disposal shall be construed as a reference only to such consideration (if any) as was actually given for the disposal.

(6) For the purposes of this Schedule, a settlement is a related settlement in relation to the settlement to which a claim relates if, by the exercise in the base year or later (whether before or after the making of the claim) of a power conferred by one of the settlements, or by the combination of such an exercise and any other transactions, property of any description forming part of the settled property of one of the settlements is at any time appointed to the other settlement or otherwise dealt with so as to increase the value of the settled property of the other settlement.

The basic rules as to postponement

6.—(1) Unless on a claim the aggregate of—

    (*a*) the unpaid tax (as defined in paragraph 4(4) above), and

    (*b*) the tax already paid (as defined in paragraph 4(5) above),

exceeds 30 per cent. of the aggregate of the relevant benefits referred to in paragraph 4(1)(*c*) above, there is no postponement of the payment of any of the capital gains tax referable to the attributed gains to which the claim relates.

(2) Subject to the following provisions of this Schedule, the amount of capital gains tax payment of which is, on a claim, postponed by virtue of this Schedule is whichever is the smaller of—

    (*a*) the unpaid tax ; and

    (*b*) the amount of the excess referred to in sub-paragraph (1) above ;

and, where the amount in paragraph (*b*) above is the smaller, payment of tax assessed for a later year shall be postponed in priority to payment of tax assessed for an earlier year.

(3) Without prejudice to paragraph 2(8) above, if at any time after a claim is made the beneficiary dies, any tax the payment of which would, by virtue of this Schedule, still be postponed at the date of his death shall be discharged on that date.

(4) Notwithstanding anything in Part IX of the Taxes Management Act 1970 (interest on overdue tax), where payment of an amount of capital gains tax is postponed by virtue of this Schedule none of that tax shall carry interest (or be taken to have carried interest) for any period before the time when the tax becomes payable in accordance with paragraph 11 below.

(5) In any case where, by virtue of sub-paragraph (1) above, there is on a claim no postponement of the payment of capital gains tax, there shall be determined—

(*a*) whether there would still be no postponement if there were left out of account all relevant benefits (if any) referable to capital payments received under or by reference to a related settlement, and

(*b*) if so, what is the excess of all the other relevant benefits over $3\frac{1}{3}$ times the aggregate of the tax referred to in paragraphs (*a*) and (*b*) of sub-paragraph (1) above,

and so much of those other relevant benefits as are referable to capital payments falling within sub-paragraph (2) of paragraph 5 above and equal (or do not exceed) that excess shall be regarded as a surplus benefit for the purposes of sub-paragraph (3) of that paragraph.

Effect of subsequent capital payments received by the beneficiary

7.—(1) The provisions of this paragraph apply if—

(*a*) on a claim there would, in accordance with paragraph 6(2) above, be an amount of capital gains tax payment of which is postponed by virtue of this Schedule ; but

(*b*) before the beginning of the year of assessment in which the claim is made, the beneficiary has received from the trustees of the settlement to which the claim relates or a related settlement a capital payment which is not a relevant benefit and has not been brought into account under subsections (3) and (4) of section 80 of the Finance Act 1981 (new provisions as to gains of non-resident settlements) in determining whether chargeable gains or offshore income gains should be attributed to the beneficiary by reference to any trust gains for any previous year of assessment.

(2) If the amount of capital gains tax referred to in paragraph (*a*) of sub-paragraph (1) above exceeds 30 per cent. of the aggregate of the amount of the capital payments which fall within paragraph (*b*) of that sub-paragraph, then, subject to paragraph 9 below, the amount of capital gains tax payment of which is postponed by virtue of this Schedule is an amount equal to that excess.

(3) If the amount of capital gains tax referred to in paragraph (*a*) of sub-paragraph (1) above is less than or equal to 30 per cent. of the aggregate of the amount of the capital payments which fall within paragraph (*b*) of that sub-paragraph, then there is no postponement of the payment of any of that capital gains tax.

(4) In any case where—

    (*a*) the amount of capital gains tax referred to in sub-paragraph (1)(*a*) above equals or exceeds 30 per cent. of the aggregate of those capital payments falling within sub-paragraph (1)(*b*) above which the beneficiary has received from the trustees of the settlement to which the claim relates, and

    (*b*) apart from this paragraph, those capital payments would fall to be brought into account under subsections (3) and (4) of section 80 of the Finance Act 1981 (new provisions as to gains of non-resident settlements) in determining whether chargeable gains or offshore income gains should be attributed to the beneficiary by reference to any trust gains for the year of assessment in which the claim is made,

then, as respects that year of assessment and any subsequent year, those capital payments shall be left out of account for the purposes of the said subsections (3) and (4).

(5) In any case where—

    (*a*) the condition in sub-paragraph (4)(*a*) above is not fulfilled, but

    (*b*) the condition in sub-paragraph (4)(*b*) above is fulfilled,

then, as respects the year of assessment in which the claim is made and any subsequent year, so much of the capital payments referred to in sub-paragraph (4) above as is equal to $3\frac{1}{3}$ times the amount of capital gains tax referred to in sub-paragraph (1)(*a*) above shall be left out of account for the purposes of subsections (3) and (4) of section 80 of the Finance Act 1981.

(6) Where, by virtue of sub-paragraph (4) or sub-paragraph (5) above, the whole or any part of a capital payment falls to be left out of account as mentioned in that sub-paragraph,—

    (*a*) the payment shall to the same extent be left out of account for the purposes of the application on any other occasion of any provision of paragraphs 7 to 12 of this Schedule ; and

    (*b*) section 45 of the Finance Act 1981 (transfer of assets abroad : liability of non-transferors) shall have effect in relation to a benefit received by the beneficiary which, in whole or in part, consists of that payment as if, in the year of assessment in which the claim is made, chargeable gains equal to so much of that payment as falls to be so left out of account were, by reason of that payment, treated under section 80 of that Act as accruing to the beneficiary.

(7) Where any capital payments falling within sub-paragraph (1)(*b*) above which the beneficiary has received from the trustees of the settlement to which the claim relates are not such as are referred to in sub-paragraph (4)(*b*) above, sub-paragraph (6)(*a*) above shall apply to each of those payments in like manner as if it had been such a payment as is referred to in sub-paragraph (4)(*b*) above and the amount of it to be left out of account had been determined accordingly under sub-paragraph (4) or sub-paragraph (5) above.

8.—(1) The provisions of this paragraph apply if, in a case where paragraph 7 above applies, the amount of capital gains tax referred to in sub-paragraph (1)(a) of that paragraph exceeds 30 per cent. of the aggregate of those capital payments falling within sub-paragraph (1)(b) of that paragraph which the beneficiary has received from the trustees of the settlement to which the claim relates.

(2) In the following provisions of this paragraph—

(a) the capital payments falling within sub-paragraph (1)(b) of paragraph 7 above which the beneficiary has received other-wise than from the trustees of the settlement to which the claim relates are referred to as " related payments " ; and

(b) any of those related payments which, apart from this para-graph, would fall to be brought into account as mentioned in sub-paragraph (4)(b) of paragraph 7 above is referred to as a " related section 80 payment ".

(3) If sub-paragraph (2) of paragraph 7 above applies, then—

(a) as respects the year of assessment in which the claim is made and any subsequent year, any related section 80 pay-ment shall be left out of account for the purposes of sub-paragraphs (3) and (4) of section 80 of the Finance Act 1981 ; and

1981 c. 35.

(b) all the related payments shall be left out of account for the purposes of the application on any other occasion of any provision of paragraphs 7 to 12 of this Schedule.

(4) If sub-paragraph (3) of paragraph 7 above applies, then—

(a) as respects the year of assessment in which the claim is made and any subsequent year, so much of any related section 80 payment as is equal to $3\frac{1}{3}$ times the amount of capital gains tax released by that payment shall be left out of account for the purposes of subsections (3) and (4) of sec-tion 80 of the Finance Act 1981 ; and

(b) so much of each of the related payments as is equal to $3\frac{1}{3}$ times the amount of capital gains tax released by the pay-ment shall be left out of account for the purposes mentioned in sub-paragraph (3)(b) above.

(5) For the purposes of sub-paragraph (4) above, the amount of capital gains tax released by a related payment shall be determined by the formula—

$$(A—B) \times \frac{C}{D}$$

where—

" A " is the capital gains tax referred to in sub-paragraph (1)(a) of paragraph 7 above ;

" B " is an amount equal to 30 per cent. of the aggregate of those capital payments falling within sub-paragraph (1)(b) of that paragraph which the beneficiary has received from the trustees of the settlement to which the claim relates ;

" C " is the related payment in question ; and

" D " is the aggregate of all the related payments.

(6) Where, by virtue of sub-paragraph (3)(*a*) or sub-paragraph (4)(*a*) above, the whole or any part of a related section 80 payment falls to be left out of account as mentioned in that sub-paragraph, section 45 of the Finance Act 1981 shall have effect in relation to the 1981 c. 35. benefit received by the beneficiary which, in whole or in part, consists of that payment as if, in the year of assessment in which the claim is made, chargeable gains equal to so much of that payment as falls to be so left out of account were, by reason of that payment, treated under section 80 of that Act as accruing to the beneficiary.

Effect of related benefits derived from payments received by close relatives of the beneficiary

9.—(1) The provisions of this paragraph apply if,—

   (*a*) on a claim, payment of an amount of capital gains tax determined in accordance with paragraph 6(2) or paragraph 7(2) above would, apart from this paragraph, be postponed by virtue of this Schedule ; and

   (*b*) as a result of a capital payment received by a close relative of the beneficiary, there is, in accordance with paragraph 10 below, a related benefit which falls to be taken into account in relation to the claim.

(2) If the amount of capital gains tax referred to in sub-paragraph (1)(*a*) above exceeds 30 per cent. of the aggregate of the related benefits which fall to be taken into account in relation to the claim, then the amount of capital gains tax payment of which is postponed by virtue of this Schedule is an amount equal to that excess.

(3) If the amount of capital gains tax referred to in sub-paragraph (1)(*a*) above is less than or equal to 30 per cent. of the aggregate of the related benefits which fall to be taken into account in relation to the claim, then there is no postponement of the payment of any of that capital gains tax.

Related benefits

10.—(1) The provisions of this paragraph have effect to determine what are, in relation to a claim, the related benefits which are to be taken into account under paragraph 9 above.

(2) If, on or after 6th April 1984 and before the beginning of the year of assessment in which the claim is made, a close relative of the beneficiary has received from the trustees of the settlement to which the claim relates or a related settlement a capital payment which has not been brought into account under subsections (3) and (4) of section 80 of the Finance Act 1981 in determining whether chargeable gains or offshore income gains should be attributed to the close relative by reference to any trust gains for any previous year

SCH. 14   of assessment, then, subject to sub-paragraphs (3) and (4) below, that capital payment is a related benefit which falls to be taken into account in relation to the claim.

(3) A capital payment falling within sub-paragraph (2) above is not a related benefit which falls to be taken into account as mentioned in that sub-paragraph to the extent that it has already been taken into account on any previous operation of sub-paragraph (4) or sub-paragraph (5) of paragraph 7 above on the occasion of a claim in respect of which the close relative himself or a close relative of his or a person whose close relative he is was the beneficiary.

(4) A capital payment falling within sub-paragraph (2) above is not a related benefit which falls to be taken into account as mentioned in that sub-paragraph if the Board so direct on the grounds that it appears likely that the payment will fall to be taken into account, either as giving rise to a relevant benefit or under paragraph 7 above, in relation to such a claim as is referred to in sub-paragraph (3) above.

(5) Sub-paragraphs (3) to (6) of paragraph 8 above shall have effect for the purposes of this paragraph—

(a) as if any reference to a provision of paragraph 7 above were a reference to the corresponding provision of paragraph 9 above ; and

(b) as if any reference to a related payment were a reference to a related benefit which falls to be taken into account as mentioned in sub-paragraph (2) above ; and

(c) as if any reference to a related section 80 payment were a reference to a related benefit which falls to be taken into account as mentioned in sub-paragraph (2) above and which, apart from this paragraph, would fall to be taken into account under sub-paragraphs (3) and (4) of section 80 of the Finance Act 1981 in determining whether chargeable gains or offshore income gains should be attributed to the close relative concerned by reference to any trust gains for the year of assessment in which is made the claim referred to in sub-paragraph (2) above ; and

1981 c. 35.

(d) as if " B " in the formula in sub-paragraph (5) were nil ; and

(e) as if any reference in sub-paragraph (6) to the beneficiary were a reference to the close relative concerned.

Time when postponed tax becomes payable

11.—(1) The provisions of this paragraph apply where, as a result of a claim, payment of an amount of capital gains tax, determined in accordance with paragraphs 6 to 9 above, is postponed by virtue of this Schedule ; and, subject to sub-paragraph (6) below, any reference in the following provisions of this paragraph to postponed tax is a reference to tax the payment of which is so postponed.

(2) Postponed tax shall become payable in accordance with sub-paragraph (5) below if, at any time in the year of assessment in which the claim is made or any later year, the beneficiary disposes of his interest in the settlement to which the claim relates in circumstances such that, by virtue of section 58(1) of the principal Act, no chargeable gain could accrue on the disposal; and in sub-paragraph (5) below " the relevant consideration " means the amount or value of the consideration for such a disposal.

(3) Subject to paragraph 12 below, postponed tax shall become payable in accordance with sub-paragraph (5) below if, in the year of assessment in which the claim is made or any later year, the beneficiary or a close relative of his receives a capital payment from the trustees of the settlement to which the claim relates or a related settlement.

(4) In the following provisions of this paragraph and paragraph 12 below, any reference to a material year of assessment is a reference to one in which the beneficiary disposes of his interest as mentioned in sub-paragraph (2) above or in which sub-paragraph (3) above applies.

(5) For any material year of assessment, so much of the postponed tax as does not exceed 30 per cent. of the aggregate of—

> (*a*) the relevant consideration in respect of any disposal in that year, and
>
> (*b*) subject to paragraph 12 below, the capital payments received in that year as mentioned in sub-paragraph (3) above,

shall become payable as if it were capital gains tax assessed in respect of gains accruing in that year.

(6) If, for any material year of assessment, the amount of the postponed tax exceeds 30 per cent. of the aggregate referred to in sub-paragraph (5) above, only the excess shall continue after the end of that year to be postponed tax for the purposes of this paragraph, but without prejudice to the subsequent operation of this paragraph in relation to a later year of assessment which is a material year.

(7) Where part, but not the whole, of any postponed tax becomes payable in accordance with sub-paragraph (5) above, tax assessed for an earlier year shall be regarded as becoming so payable before tax assessed for a later year.

Balance of capital payments

12.—(1) If any capital payments received in any year of assessment as mentioned in paragraph 11(3) above fall to be brought into account for that year for the purposes of subsections (3) and (4) of section 80 of the Finance Act 1981, those capital payments shall 1981 c. 35. be disregarded for the purposes of sub-paragraph (5) or, as the case may be, sub-paragraph (6) of paragraph 11 above except to the extent that the aggregate of those payments exceeds the chargeable gains and offshore income gains which in that year are treated under the said section 80 as accruing to the beneficiary or, as the case may be, the close relative ; and any such excess is in the following provisions of this paragraph referred to as the balance of section 80 payments for that year.

(2) Subject to the following provisions of this paragraph, as respects any year of assessment subsequent to a material year of assessment for which there is a balance of section 80 payments there shall be left out of account for the purposes of subsections (3) and
(4) of section 80 of the Finance Act 1981 so much of the capital payments as made up that balance.

(3) If paragraph 11(6) above did not apply for any material year of assessment for which there is a balance of section 80 payments then, as respects years of assessment subsequent to that year, sub-paragraph (2) above shall apply only to so much of the capital payments mentioned therein as is equal to $3\frac{1}{3}$ times the amount of postponed tax released by that balance.

(4) For any material year of assessment, the amount of postponed tax released by a balance of section 80 payments for that year shall be determined by the formula :—

$$(E{-}F) \times \frac{G}{H}$$

where

"E" is the postponed tax, within the meaning of paragraph 11 above ;

"F" is an amount equal to 30 per cent. of any consideration for that year which falls within sub-paragraph (5)(*a*) of that paragraph ;

"G" is the balance of the section 80 payments for that year ; and

"H" is the aggregate of the capital payments (including that balance) taken into account under sub-paragraph (5)(*b*) of that paragraph for that year.

(5) If, in a case where sub-paragraph (2) above applies in accordance with sub-paragraph (3) above, there were, for the material year of assessment concerned,—

(*a*) a balance of section 80 payments derived from payments received by the beneficiary, and

(*b*) another such balance derived from payments received by a close relative of his,

sub-paragraph (2) above shall apply (in accordance with sub-paragraph (3) above) to the capital payments which made up the balance derived from payments received by the beneficiary in priority to capital payments which made up the other balance.

(6) Subject to sub-paragraph (5) above, where there is more than one capital payment to which sub-paragraph (2) above applies, the proportion of each of them which is left out of account as mentioned in that sub-paragraph shall be the same.

(7) Where, by virtue of the preceding provisions of this paragraph, SCH. 14 the whole or any part of a capital payment falls to be left out of account as mentioned in sub-paragraph (2) above, section 45 of the Finance Act 1981 shall have effect in relation to a benefit which is 1981 c. 35. received by the beneficiary or, as the case may be, a close relative of his and which, in whole or in part, consists of that payment as if, in the material year of assessment concerned, chargeable gains equal to so much of that payment as falls to be so left out of account were, by reason of that payment, treated under section 80 of that Act as accruing to the beneficiary or, as the case may be, the close relative.

13.—(1) Where, by virtue of sub-paragraph (2) of paragraph 12 above, the whole or any part of a capital payment falls to be left out of account as mentioned in that sub-paragraph, it shall to the same extent be left out of account for the purposes of the application on any other occasion of any provision of paragraphs 7 to 12 of this Schedule.

(2) Where sub-paragraph (6) of paragraph 11 above applies for any material year of assessment, any capital payments which—

(a) fall to be taken into account under sub-paragraph (5)(b) of that paragraph for that year, and

(b) are not such as to fall within paragraph 12(1) above,

shall be left out of account for the purposes referred to in sub-paragraph (1) above.

(3) Where sub-paragraph (6) of paragraph 11 above does not apply for any material year of assessment, so much of any capital payment falling within paragraphs (a) and (b) of sub-paragraph (2) above as is equal to $3\frac{1}{3}$ times the amount of postponed tax released by that payment shall be left out of account for the purposes referred to in sub-paragraph (1) above.

(4) The amount of postponed tax released by a capital payment shall be determined for the purposes of sub-paragraph (3) above by the formula in paragraph 12(4) above, except that, in applying that formula for those purposes, " G " shall be the amount of the capital payment in question.

(5) In this paragraph, " material year of assessment " shall be construed in accordance with paragraph 11(4) above.

Second and later claims

14.—(1) This paragraph applies where—

(a) as a result of a claim (in this paragraph referred to as " the earlier claim "), payment of an amount of capital gains tax (in this paragraph referred to as " the original tax "), determined in accordance with paragraph 6 or paragraph 7 above, is or was postponed by virtue of this Schedule ; and

(b) after the making of the earlier claim, another claim (in this paragraph referred to as " the later claim ") is made in relation to an attributed gain to which the earlier claim did not relate ; and

(c) the settlement to which the earlier and the later claims relate is the same.

(2) If the year of assessment which is the relevant year of assessment in relation to any attributed gain to which the later claim relates is earlier than the earliest year of assessment which is the relevant year of assessment in relation to any attributed gain to which the earlier claim related, then,—

> (a) the earlier claim and the postponement resulting from it shall be set aside ; and
>
> (b) the provisions of this Schedule shall have effect as if (notwithstanding paragraph 2(2) above) the attributed gains to which the later claim relates included the attributed gains to which the earlier claim related.

(3) Where sub-paragraph (2) above does not apply and, at the time the later claim is made, payment of any of the original tax remains postponed by virtue of this Schedule, then, subject to sub-paragraph (4) below,—

> (a) paragraphs 4 to 10 above shall not apply in relation to the later claim ; and
>
> (b) payment of the tax referable to the attributed gain or gains to which the later claim relates shall be postponed by virtue of this Schedule ; and
>
> (c) paragraphs 11 and 12 above shall apply as if the payment of that tax had been postponed as a result of the earlier claim and, accordingly, that tax shall be added to the original tax.

(4) If, in a case where sub-paragraph (3) above applies, the relevant year of assessment in relation to an attributed gain (in this sub-paragraph referred to as " the later gain ") to which the later claim relates is the same as the relevant year of assessment in relation to an attributed gain to which the earlier claim related,—

> (a) paragraph 3 above shall not apply in relation to the later gain ; and
>
> (b) in relation to the later gain, the references in sub-paragraph (3) above to the tax referable to the gain shall be construed as references to the capital gains tax assessed by reason of the gain.

(5) Where sub-paragraph (2) above does not apply and, at the time the later claim is made, there is no longer any postponement of the payment of any of the original tax, then, in the application of the provisions of this Schedule in relation to the later claim, paragraph 4(2) above shall not apply and " the base year " for the purposes of paragraphs 4 and 5 above shall be that year of assessment which was the base year in relation to the earlier claim.

Information

15.—(1) The Board may by notice in writing require any person to furnish them, within such time as they may direct, not being less than twenty-eight days, with such particulars as they think necessary for the purposes of section 70 of this Act and this Schedule.

(2) Subsections (2) to (5) of section 481 of the Taxes Act shall have effect in relation to sub-paragraph (1) above as they have effect in relation to subsection (1) of that section ; but, in the application of those subsections by virtue of this sub-paragraph, references to Chapter III of Part XVII of the Taxes Act shall be construed as references to section 70 of this Act and this Schedule.

(3) In any case where—

    (*a*) a claim has been made, and

    (*b*) as a result of the claim, payment of an amount of capital gains tax was postponed by virtue of this Schedule, and

    (*c*) at a time when any of that tax remains unpaid, there is a disposal to which paragraph 11(2) above applies or the beneficiary or a close relative of his receives such a capital payment as is referred to in paragraph 11(3) above,

then, not later than three months after the end of the year of assessment in which the disposal occurs or the payment is received, the beneficiary shall inform the Board of the disposal or receipt, as the case may be.

(4) The Table in section 98 of the Taxes Management Act 1970 (penalties for failure to comply with notices, furnish information etc.) shall be amended as follows—   1970 c. 9.

    (*a*) at the end of the first column there shall be inserted—

        " Paragraph 15(1) of Schedule 14 to the Finance Act 1984 " ; and

    (*b*) at the end of the second column there shall be inserted—

        " Paragraph 15(3) of Schedule 14 to the Finance Act 1984 ".

Consequential relief from C.T.T.

16. In any case where—

    (*a*) payment of an amount of capital gains tax is postponed by virtue of this Schedule, and

    (*b*) any of that tax becomes payable in accordance with paragraph 11 above by reason of the receipt of a capital payment by a close relative of the beneficiary, as mentioned in sub-paragraph (3) of that paragraph, and

    (*c*) all or part of the tax becoming so payable is paid by the close relative,

the payment by the close relative shall be treated for the purposes of capital transfer tax as made in satisfaction of a liability of his.

SCHEDULE 15

OFFSHORE LIFE ASSURANCE: NEW NON-RESIDENT POLICIES

PART I

PARAGRAPH TO BE INSERTED IN PART I OF SCHEDULE 2 TO FINANCE ACT 1975

" 1A.—(1) The provisions of this paragraph apply to a policy of life insurance—

    (*a*) which is issued in respect of an insurance made after 17th November 1983 ; and

    (*b*) which is so issued by a company resident outside the United Kingdom ;

and in the following provisions of this paragraph such a policy is referred to as a " new non-resident policy " and the company by which it is issued is referred to as " the issuing company ".

(2) Notwithstanding anything in paragraph 1 above—

    (*a*) a new non-resident policy shall not be certified under sub-paragraph (1)(*a*) of that paragraph, and

    (*b*) a new non-resident policy which conforms with such a form as is mentioned in sub-paragraph (1)(*b*) of that paragraph shall not be a qualifying policy,

until such time as the conditions in either sub-paragraph (3) or sub-paragraph (4) below are fulfilled with respect to it.

(3) The conditions first referred to in sub-paragraph (2) above are—

    (*a*) that the issuing company is lawfully carrying on in the United Kingdom life assurance business (as defined in section 323(2) of the Taxes Act) ; and

    (*b*) that the premiums under the policy are payable to a branch in the United Kingdom of the issuing company, being a branch through which the issuing company carries on its life assurance business ; and

    (*c*) the premiums under the policy form part of those business receipts of the issuing company which arise through that branch.

(4) The conditions secondly referred to in sub-paragraph (2) above are—

    (*a*) that the policy holder is resident in the United Kingdom ; and

    (*b*) that the income of the issuing company from the investments of its life assurance fund is, by virtue of section 316 of the Taxes Act, charged to corporation tax under Case III of Schedule D ;

and expressions used in paragraph (*b*) above have the same
meaning as in subsection (1) of the said section 316."

PART II

MODIFICATIONS OF PROVISIONS RELATING TO QUALIFYING POLICIES

1. In this Part of this Schedule—

" Schedule 1 " means Schedule 1 to the Taxes Act (qualifying conditions etc.) ;

" Schedule 2 " means Schedule 2 to the Finance Act 1975 1975 c. 7. (certification of qualifying policies etc.) ; and

" the old policy " and " the new policy " have the same meaning as in paragraph 9 of Schedule 1.

2.—(1) In the application of paragraph 9 of Schedule 1 (substitutions) in any case where—

(*a*) the old policy was issued in respect of an insurance made after 17th November 1983 and could not be a qualifying policy by virtue of paragraph 1A of Schedule 2, and

(*b*) the new policy is not a new non-resident policy, as defined in the said paragraph 1A,

the rules for the determination of the question whether the new policy is a qualifying policy shall apply with the modifications in sub-paragraph (2) below.

(2) The modifications referred to in sub-paragraph (1) above are as follows : —

(*a*) if, apart from paragraph 1A of Schedule 2, the old policy and any related policy (within the meaning of sub-paragraph (2)(*b*) of paragraph 9 of Schedule 1) of which account falls to be taken would have been, or would have been capable of being certified as, a qualifying policy under paragraph 1 of Schedule 2, that policy shall be assumed to have been a qualifying policy for the purposes of paragraph 9(2) of Schedule 1 ; and

(*b*) if, apart from this paragraph, the new policy would be, or would be capable of being certified as, a qualifying policy, it shall not be such a policy or, as the case may be, be capable of being so certified unless the circumstances are as specified in paragraph 9(3) of Schedule 1 ; and

(*c*) in paragraph 9(3)(*b*) of Schedule 1 the words " either by a branch or agency of theirs outside the United Kingdom or " shall be omitted.

(3) In the application of paragraph 9 of Schedule 1 in any case where—

> (*a*) the old policy is a qualifying policy which was issued in respect of an insurance made on or before 17th November 1983 but, if the insurance had been made after that date, the policy could not have been a qualifying policy by virtue of paragraph 1A of Schedule 2, and
>
> (*b*) the new policy is issued after 17th November 1983 and is not a new non-resident policy, as defined in the said paragraph 1A,

the rules for the determination of the question whether the new policy is a qualifying policy shall apply with the modification in sub-paragraph (2)(*c*) above.

3. If, in the case of a substitution of policies falling within sub-paragraph (1) or sub-paragraph (3) of paragraph 2 above, the new policy confers such an option as results in the application to it of sub-paragraph (3) of paragraph 3 of Schedule 2 (amendment of qualifying conditions) the new policy shall be treated for the purposes of that sub-paragraph as having been issued in respect of an insurance made on the same day as that on which was made the insurance in respect of which the old policy was issued.

4.—(1) For the purposes of Schedule 1 and Part I of Schedule 2, a policy of life insurance which was issued—

> (*a*) in respect of an insurance made on or before 17th November 1983, and
>
> (*b*) by a company resident outside the United Kingdom,

shall be treated as issued in respect of an insurance made after that date if the policy is varied after that date so as to increase the benefits secured or to extend the term of the insurance.

(2) If a policy of life insurance which was issued as mentioned in paragraphs (*a*) and (*b*) of sub-paragraph (1) above confers on the person to whom it is issued an option to have another policy substituted for it or to have any of its terms changed, then for the purposes of that sub-paragraph any change in the terms of the policy which is made in pursuance of the option shall be deemed to be a variation of the policy.

PART III

MODIFICATIONS OF CHARGEABLE EVENTS LEGISLATION

5. In this Part of this Schedule—

> (*a*) " chargeable event " has, subject to paragraph 6 below, the meaning assigned to it by section 394 of the Taxes Act (life policies) or, as the case may be, section 398 of that Act (capital redemption policies) ; and

(*b*) " new non-resident policy " has the meaning assigned to Sch. 15 it by paragraph 1A of Schedule 2 to the Finance Act 1975 c. 7. 1975.

6. If, in the case of a substitution of policies falling within sub-paragraph (1) or sub-paragraph (3) of paragraph 2 above, the new policy is a qualifying policy, section 394 of the Taxes Act shall have effect with the following modifications: —

(*a*) the surrender of the rights conferred by the old policy shall not be a chargeable event ; and

(*b*) the new policy shall be treated as having been issued in respect of an insurance made on the day referred to in paragraph 3 above.

7. If at any time neither the conditions in sub-paragraph (3) nor the conditions in sub-paragraph (4) of paragraph 1A of Schedule 2 to the Finance Act 1975 are fulfilled with respect to a new non-resident policy which has previously become a qualifying policy, then, from that time onwards, Chapter III of Part XIV of the Taxes Act shall apply in relation to the policy as if it did not fall within subsection (2) of section 394 of that Act (qualifying policies).

8.—(1) On the happening of a chargeable event in relation to a new non-resident policy or a new offshore capital redemption policy, the amount which, apart from this paragraph, would by virtue of section 395 of the Taxes Act be treated as a gain arising in connection with the policy shall be reduced by multiplying it by a fraction of which—

(*a*) the denominator is the number of days in the period for which the policy has run before the happening of the chargeable event ; and

(*b*) the numerator is the number of days in the period referred to in paragraph (*a*) above on which the policy holder was resident in the United Kingdom.

(2) The calculation of the number of days in the period referred to in sub-paragraph (1) above shall be made in like manner as is provided in the second paragraph of subsection (3) of section 400 of the Taxes Act (substituting a reference to the number of days for the reference in that paragraph to the number of years).

9.—(1) Subject to sub-paragraph (2) below, where, under section 395 of the Taxes Act, a gain (reduced in accordance with paragraph 8 above) is to be treated as arising in connection with a new non-resident policy or a new offshore capital redemption policy—

(*a*) section 399 of that Act shall have effect, in relation to the gain, as if subsection (4) were omitted ; and

(*b*) the gain shall be chargeable to tax under Case VI of **Schedule D** ;

but any relief under section 400 of the Taxes Act shall be computed as if this paragraph had not been enacted.

(2) Paragraphs (*a*) and (*b*) of sub-paragraph (1) above do not apply to a gain arising in connection with a new non-resident policy if the conditions in either sub-paragraph (3) or sub-paragraph (4) of paragraph 1A of Schedule 2 to the Finance Act 1975 are fulfilled at all times between the date on which the policy was issued and the date on which the gain is treated as arising.

10. Where a claim is made under section 400 of the Taxes Act in respect of the amount of a gain treated as arising in connection with a new non-resident policy or a new offshore capital redemption policy (with or without other amounts), the " appropriate fraction " which, in accordance with subsection (2) of that section, is to be applied to that amount shall be modified by deducting from the number of complete years referred to in subsection (3) of that section any complete years during which the policy holder was not resident in the United Kingdom.

11. Paragraph 18 of Schedule 2 to the Finance Act 1975 (which modifies the operation of section 400(3) of the Taxes Act when there is more than one chargeable event of a particular description) shall not apply in relation to a new non-resident policy or a new offshore capital redemption policy.

SCHEDULE 16

ASSUMPTIONS FOR CALCULATING CHARGEABLE PROFITS, CREDITABLE TAX AND CORRESPONDING UNITED KINGDOM TAX OF FOREIGN COMPANIES

General

1.—(1) The company shall be assumed to be resident in the United Kingdom.

(2) Nothing in sub-paragraph (1) above requires it to be assumed that there is any change in the place or places at which the company carries on its activities.

(3) For the avoidance of doubt, it is hereby declared that, if any sums forming part of the company's profits for an accounting period have been received by the company without any deduction of or charge to tax by virtue of section 99 or section 100 of the Taxes Act (securities held by non-residents), the effect of the assumption in sub-paragraph (1) above is that those sums are to be brought within the charge to tax for the purposes of calculating the company's chargeable profits or corresponding United Kingdom tax.

(4) In any case where—

(*a*) it is at any time necessary for any purpose of this Act to determine the chargeable profits of the company for an accounting period, and

(b) at that time no direction has been given under section 82(1) of this Act with respect to that or any earlier accounting period of the company,

it shall be assumed, for the purpose of any of the following provisions of this Schedule which refer to the first accounting period in respect of which a direction is given under that section, that such a direction has been given for that period (but not for any earlier period).

(5) Nothing in this Schedule affects any liability for, or the computation of, corporation tax in respect of a trade which is carried on by a company resident outside the United Kingdom through a branch or agency in the United Kingdom.

2.—(1) The company shall be assumed to have become resident in the United Kingdom (and, accordingly, within the charge to corporation tax) at the beginning of the first accounting period in respect of which a direction is given under section 82(1) of this Act and that United Kingdom residence shall be assumed to continue throughout subsequent accounting periods of the company (whether or not a direction is given in respect of all or any of them) until the company ceases to be controlled by persons resident in the United Kingdom.

(2) Except in so far as the following provisions of this Schedule otherwise provide, for the purposes of calculating a company's chargeable profits or corresponding United Kingdom tax for any accounting period which is not the first such period referred to in sub-paragraph (1) above (and, in particular, for the purpose of applying any relief which is relevant to two or more accounting periods), it shall be assumed that a calculation of chargeable profits or, as the case may be, corresponding United Kingdom tax has been made for every previous accounting period throughout which the company was, by virtue of sub-paragraph (1) above, assumed to have been resident in the United Kingdom.

3. The company shall be assumed not to be a close company.

4.—(1) Subject to sub-paragraph (2) below, where any relief under the Corporation Tax Acts is dependent upon the making of a claim or election, the company shall be assumed to have made that claim or election which would give the maximum amount of relief and to have made that claim or election within any time limit applicable to it.

(2) If, by notice in writing given to the Board at any time not later than the expiry of the time for the making of an appeal under section 88 of this Act or within such longer period as the Board may in any particular case allow, the United Kingdom resident company which has or, as the case may be, any two or more

SCH. 16   United Kingdom resident companies which together have, a majority interest in the company so request, the company shall be assumed—

(*a*) not to have made any claim or election specified in the notice ; or

(*b*) to have made a claim or election so specified, being different from one assumed by sub-paragraph (1) above but being one which (subject to compliance with any time limit) could have been made in the case of a company within the charge to corporation tax ; or

(*c*) to have disclaimed or required the postponement, in whole or in part, of an allowance if (subject to compliance with any time limit) a company within the charge to corporation tax could have disclaimed the allowance or, as the case may be, required such a postponement.

(3) For the purposes of this paragraph, a United Kingdom resident company has, or two or more United Kingdom resident companies together have, a majority interest in the company if on the apportionment of the company's chargeable profits for the relevant accounting period under subsection (3) of section 82 of this Act, more than half of the profits—

(*a*) which are apportioned to United Kingdom resident companies, and

(*b*) which give rise to an assessment on any such companies under subsection (4)(*a*) of that section,

are apportioned to the United Kingdom resident company or companies concerned.

(4) In sub-paragraph (3) above " the relevant accounting period " means the accounting period or, as the case may be, the first accounting period in which the relief in question is or would be available in accordance with sub-paragraph (1) above.

Group relief, etc.

5. The company shall be assumed to be neither a member of a group of companies nor a member of a consortium for the purposes of any provision of the Tax Acts.

6.—(1) In relation to section 256 of the Taxes Act (group income) it shall be assumed—

(*a*) that the conditions for the making of an election under subsection (1) are not fulfilled with respect to dividends paid or received by the company ; and

(*b*) that the conditions for the making of an election under subsection (2) are not fulfilled with respect to payments made or received by the company.

(2) References in sub-paragraph (1) above to dividends or payments received by the company apply to any received by another person on behalf of or in trust for the company, but not to any received by the company on behalf of or in trust for another person.

7. The company shall be assumed not to be a subsidiary to which the benefit of any advance corporation tax may be surrendered under section 92 of the Finance Act 1972.

Company reconstructions

8. Without prejudice to the operation of section 252 of the Taxes Act (company reconstructions without change of ownership) in a case where the company is the predecessor, within the meaning of that section, and a company resident in the United Kingdom is the successor, within the meaning of that section, the assumption that the company is resident in the United Kingdom shall not be regarded as requiring it also to be assumed that the company is within the charge to tax in respect of a trade for the purposes of section 252 of the Taxes Act and, accordingly, except in so far as the company is actually within that charge (by carrying on the trade through a branch or agency in the United Kingdom), it shall be assumed that the company can never be the successor, within the meaning of that section, to another company (whether resident in the United Kingdom or not).

Losses in pre-direction accounting periods

9.—(1) Subject to sub-paragraph (2) below, this paragraph applies in any case where the company incurred a loss in a trade in an accounting period—

(a) which precedes the first accounting period in respect of which a direction is given under section 82(1) of this Act (in this paragraph referred to as " the starting period ") ; and

(b) which ended less than six years before the beginning of the starting period ; and

(c) in which the company was not resident in the United Kingdom ;

and in this paragraph any such accounting period is referred to as a " pre-direction period ".

(2) This paragraph does not apply in any case where a declaration is made under paragraph 11(3) below specifying an accounting period of the company which begins before, or is the same as, the first pre-direction period in which the company incurred a loss as mentioned in sub-paragraph (1) above.

(3) If a claim is made for the purpose by the United Kingdom resident company or companies referred to in paragraph 4(2) above, the chargeable profits (if any) of the company for accounting periods beginning with that pre-direction period which is specified in the claim and in which a loss is incurred as mentioned in sub-paragraph (1) above shall be determined (in accordance with the provisions of this Schedule other than this paragraph) on the assumption that that pre-direction period was the first accounting period in respect of which a direction was given under section 82(1) of this Act.

(4) A claim under sub-paragraph (3) above shall be made by notice in writing given to the Board within sixty days of the date

of the notice under subsection (1) or subsection (3) of section 88 of this Act relating to the starting period or within such longer period as the Board may in any particular case allow.

(5) For the purposes of a claim under sub-paragraph (3) above, it shall be assumed that Chapter VI of Part II of this Act was in force before the beginning of the first of the pre-direction periods.

(6) In determining for the purposes of this paragraph which accounting period of the company is the starting period, no account shall be taken of the effect of any declaration under paragraph 11(3) below.

Capital allowances

10.—(1) Subject to paragraphs 11 and 12 below, if, in an accounting period falling before the beginning of the first accounting period in respect of which a direction is given under section 82(1) of this Act, the company incurred any capital expenditure on the provision of machinery or plant for the purposes of its trade, that machinery or plant shall be assumed, for the purposes of section 44 of the Finance Act 1971 (writing-down allowances and balancing adjustments), not to have been brought into use for the purposes of that trade until the beginning of that first accounting period, and paragraph 7 of Schedule 8 to that Act (expenditure treated as equivalent to market value at the time the machinery or plant is brought into use) shall apply accordingly.

(2) This paragraph shall be construed as one with Chapter I of Part III of the Finance Act 1971.

11.—(1) This paragraph applies in any case where it appears to the Board that the reason why no direction was given under section 82(1) of this Act in respect of an accounting period which precedes the starting period was that the effect of any allowance which would be assumed for that preceding period by virtue of this Schedule would be such that—

(a) the company would not have been considered to be subject in that accounting period to a lower level of taxation in the territory in which it was resident ; or

(b) the company would have had no chargeable profits for that accounting period ; or

(c) the chargeable profits of the company for that accounting period would not have exceeded £20,000 or such smaller amount as was appropriate in accordance with section 83(1)(d) of this Act.

(2) In this paragraph " the starting period " means the first accounting period in respect of which a direction is given under section 82(1) of this Act and, in a case where a claim is made under sub-paragraph (3) of paragraph 9 above, no account shall be taken of the effect of that sub-paragraph in determining which accounting period is the starting period for the purposes of this paragraph.

(3) If, in a case where this paragraph applies, the Board so declare by notice in writing given to every company to which, in accordance

with section 88(1) of this Act, notice of the making of the direction relating to the starting period is required to be given, the chargeable profits of that period and every subsequent accounting period and the corresponding United Kingdom tax for every subsequent accounting period shall be determined (in accordance with the provisions of this Schedule other than this paragraph) on the assumption that the accounting period specified in the declaration was the first accounting period in respect of which a direction was given and, accordingly, as if allowances had been assumed in respect of that accounting period and any subsequent accounting period which precedes the starting period.

(4) Nothing in sub-paragraph (3) above affects the operation of paragraph 9(3) above in a case where the accounting period specified in a claim under the said paragraph 9(3) begins before the period specified in a declaration under sub-paragraph (3) above.

(5) Subject to sub-paragraph (6) below, the Board shall not make a declaration under sub-paragraph (3) above with respect to an accounting period which precedes the starting period unless the facts are such that—

    (*a*) assuming the company to have been subject in that period to a lower level of taxation in the territory in which it was resident, and

    (*b*) assuming the company to have had in that period chargeable profits of such an amount that the condition in section 83(1)(*d*) of this Act would not be fulfilled,

a direction could have been given in respect of that period under section 82(1) of this Act.

(6) In its application to a company falling within section 84(3) of this Act, sub-paragraph (5) above shall have effect with the omission of paragraph (*a*).

(7) In this paragraph " allowance " means an allowance under Chapter I of Part I of the Capital Allowances Act 1968 or Chapter I of Part III of the Finance Act 1971.

1968 c. 3.
1971 c. 68.

12.—(1) Notwithstanding anything in the preceding provisions of this Schedule, if it appears that the transaction by which an asset was acquired by the company had as its sole or main purpose the reduction of the amount of the company's chargeable profits or, as the case may be, corresponding United Kingdom tax for any accounting period (by virtue of the assumption of a relevant allowance in respect of that asset), it shall be assumed that no relevant allowance is available to the company in respect of expenditure incurred on the acquisition of that asset.

(2) In sub-paragraph (1) above " relevant allowance " means—

    (*a*) an initial allowance under Chapter I of Part I of the Capital Allowances Act 1968 (industrial buildings and structures) ; or

    (*b*) a first-year allowance, as defined in section 41 of the Finance Act 1971.

Unremittable overseas income

13. For the purposes of the application of section 418 of the Taxes Act (relief for unremittable income) to the company's income it shall be assumed—

(*a*) that any reference in paragraph (*a*) or paragraph (*b*) of subsection (1) of that section to the United Kingdom is a reference to both the United Kingdom and the territory in which the company is in fact resident ; and

(*b*) that a notice under subsection (2) of that section (expressing a wish to be assessed in accordance with that subsection) may be given on behalf of the company by the United Kingdom resident company or companies referred to in paragraph 4(2) above.

Section 83.

SCHEDULE 17

CASES EXCLUDED FROM DIRECTION-MAKING POWERS

Part I

Acceptable Distribution Policy

1. The provisions of this Part of this Schedule have effect for the purposes of paragraph (*a*) of subsection (1) of section 83 of this Act.

2.—(1) Subject to sub-paragraph (2) below, a controlled foreign company pursues an acceptable distribution policy in respect of a particular accounting period if, and only if—

(*a*) a dividend which is not paid out of specified profits is paid for that accounting period or for some other period which, in whole or in part, falls within that accounting period ; and

(*b*) the dividend is paid during, or not more than eighteen months after the expiry of, the period for which it is paid or at such later time as the Board may in any particular case allow ; and

(*c*) the proportion of the dividend or, if there is more than one, of the aggregate of those dividends which is paid to persons resident in the United Kingdom represents at least 50 per cent. of the company's available profits for the accounting period referred to in paragraph (*a*) above or, where sub-paragraph (4) or sub-paragraph (5) below applies, of the appropriate portion of those profits ;

and for the purposes of this sub-paragraph a dividend which is not paid for a specified period shall be treated as paid for the period or periods the profits of which are, in relation to the dividend, the relevant profits for the purposes of section 506 of the Taxes Act (computation of underlying tax on dividends).

(2) In the case of a controlled foreign company which is not a trading company, sub-paragraph (1) above shall have effect with the substitution of 90 per cent. for 50 per cent.

(3) For the purposes of this Part of this Schedule, a dividend represents those profits of the controlled foreign company in question which in relation to that dividend are the relevant profits for the purposes of section 506 of the Taxes Act and, accordingly, where those profits are the profits of a period which falls partly within and partly outside an accounting period of that company, the necessary apportionment shall be made to determine what proportion of those profits is attributable to that accounting period.

(4) This sub-paragraph applies where—

(a) throughout the accounting period in question all the issued shares of the controlled foreign company are of a single class, and

(b) at the end of that accounting period some of those shares are held by persons resident outside the United Kingdom, and

(c) at no time during that accounting period does any person have an interest in the company other than an interest derived from the issued shares of the company,

and in a case where this sub-paragraph applies the appropriate portion for the purposes of sub-paragraph (1)(c) above is the fraction of which the denominator is the total number of the issued shares of the company at the end of the accounting period in question and, subject to sub-paragraph (8) below, the numerator is the number of those issued shares by virtue of which persons resident in the United Kingdom have interests in the company at that time.

(5) This sub-paragraph applies where—

(a) throughout the accounting period in question there are only two classes of issued shares of the controlled foreign company and, of those classes, one (in this paragraph referred to as " non-voting shares ") consists of non-voting fixed-rate preference shares and the other (in this paragraph referred to as " voting shares ") consists of shares which carry the right to vote in all circumstances at general meetings of the company, and

(b) at the end of that accounting period some of the issued shares of the company are held by persons resident outside the United Kingdom, and

(c) at no time during that accounting period does any person have an interest in the company other than an interest derived from non-voting shares or voting shares,

and in a case where this sub-paragraph applies the appropriate portion of the profits referred to in sub-paragraph (1)(c) above is the amount determined in accordance with sub-paragraph (6) below.

(6) The amount referred to in sub-paragraph (5) above is that given by the formula—

$$\frac{P \times Q}{R} + \frac{(X - P) \times Y}{Z}$$

where—

P is the amount of any dividend falling within paragraphs (a) and (b) of sub-paragraph (1) above which is paid in respect of the non-voting shares or, if there is more than one such dividend, of the aggregate of them ;

Q is, subject to sub-paragraph (8) below, the number of the non-voting shares by virtue of which persons resident in the United Kingdom have interests in the company at the end of the accounting period in question ;

R is the total number at that time of the issued non-voting shares ;

X is the available profits for the accounting period in question ;

Y is, subject to sub-paragraph (8) below, the number of voting shares by virtue of which persons resident in the United Kingdom have interests in the company at the end of that accounting period ; and

Z is the total number at that time of the issued voting shares.

(7) For the purposes of sub-paragraph (5)(a) above, non-voting fixed-rate preference shares are shares—

(a) which are fixed-rate preference shares as defined in paragraph 1 of Schedule 12 to the Finance Act 1973 ; and

(b) which either carry no right to vote at a general meeting of the company or carry such a right which is contingent upon the non-payment of a dividend on the shares and which has not in fact become exercisable at any time prior to the payment of a dividend for the accounting period in question.

(8) In any case where the immediate interests held by persons resident in the United Kingdom who have indirect interests in a controlled foreign company at the end of a particular accounting period do not reflect the proportion of the shares or, as the case may be, shares of a particular class in the company by virtue of which they have those interests (as in a case where they hold, directly or indirectly, part of the shares in a company which itself holds, directly or indirectly, some or all of the shares in the controlled foreign company) the number of those shares shall be treated as reduced for the purposes of sub-paragraph (4) or, as the case may be, sub-paragraph (6) above to such number as may be appropriate having regard to—

(a) the immediate interests held by the persons resident in the United Kingdom ; and

(b) any intermediate shareholdings between those interests and the shares in the controlled foreign company.

(9) The definition of " profits " in section 82(6)(*b*) of this Act does not apply to any reference in this paragraph to specified profits or to relevant profits for the purposes of section 506 of the Taxes Act.

3.—(1) Subject to sub-paragraph (2) below, for the purposes of this Part of this Schedule, the available profits of a controlled foreign company for any accounting period shall be ascertained, subject to sub-paragraph (5) below, by—

(*a*) determining what would be the relevant profits of that period for the purposes of section 506 of the Taxes Act if a dividend were paid for that period ; and

(*b*) deducting so much of those relevant profits as consists of an excess of capital profits over capital losses.

(2) If, for any accounting period of the controlled foreign company which—

(*a*) is of less than twelve months' duration, and

(*b*) is not an accounting period which, but for the coming into operation of this Chapter on 6th April 1984, would have begun before that date and been of at least twelve months' duration,

the available profits, as ascertained under sub-paragraph (1) above, are less than the chargeable profits (determined on the additional assumptions in section 85(3)(*a*) of this Act), then, if the Board so declare, for the purposes of this Part of this Schedule the available profits for the accounting period shall be those chargeable profits.

(3) The definition of " profits " in section 82(6)(*b*) of this Act does not apply to the reference in sub-paragraph (1)(*a*) above to relevant profits for the purposes of section 506 of the Taxes Act.

(4) In sub-paragraph (1)(*b*) above " capital profits " means gains—

(*a*) which accrue on the disposal of assets ; and

(*b*) which, if the company were within the charge to corporation tax in respect of the activities giving rise to those disposals, would not be taken into account as receipts in computing the company's income or profits or gains or losses for the purposes of the Income Tax Acts ;

and the expression " capital losses " shall be construed accordingly.

(5) In any case where—

(*a*) a controlled foreign company pays a dividend for any period out of specified profits, and

(*b*) those specified profits represent dividends received by the company, directly or indirectly, from another controlled foreign company,

so much of those specified profits as is equal to the dividend referred to in paragraph (*a*) above shall be left out of account in determining, for the purposes of this Part of this Schedule, the available profits of the controlled foreign company referred to in that paragraph for any accounting period.

4.—(1) For the purposes of this Part of this Schedule, where—

(a) a controlled foreign company pays a dividend (in this paragraph referred to as "the initial dividend") to another company which is also not resident in the United Kingdom, and

(b) that other company or another company which is related to it pays a dividend (in this paragraph referred to as "the subsequent dividend") to a United Kingdom resident, and

(c) the subsequent dividend is paid out of profits which are derived, directly or indirectly, from the whole or part of the initial dividend,

so much of the initial dividend as is represented by the subsequent dividend shall be regarded as paid to the United Kingdom resident.

(2) For the purposes of this paragraph, one company is related to another if the other—

(a) controls directly or indirectly, or

(b) is a subsidiary of a company which controls directly or indirectly,

at least 10 per cent. of the voting power in the first-mentioned company ; and where one company is so related to another and that other is so related to a third company, the first company is for the purposes of this paragraph related to the third, and so on where there is a chain of companies, each of which is related to the next.

PART II

EXEMPT ACTIVITIES

5.—(1) The provisions of this Part of this Schedule have effect for the purposes of paragraph (b) of subsection (1) of section 83 of this Act.

(2) In the case of a controlled foreign company—

(a) which is, by virtue of section 84(3) of this Act, presumed to be resident in a territory in which it is subject to a lower level of taxation, and

(b) the business affairs of which are, throughout the accounting period in question, effectively managed in a territory outside the United Kingdom other than one in which companies are liable to tax by reason of domicile, residence or place of management,

references in the following provisions of this Part of this Schedule to the territory in which that company is resident shall be construed as references to the territory falling within paragraph (b) above or, if there is more than one, to that one of them which may be notified to the Board by the United Kingdom resident company or companies referred to in paragraph 4(2) of Schedule 16 to this Act.

6.—(1) Throughout an accounting period a controlled foreign company is engaged in exempt activities if, and only if, each of the following conditions is fulfilled,—

> (*a*) that, throughout that accounting period, the company has a business establishment in the territory in which it is resident ; and

> (*b*) that, throughout that accounting period, its business affairs in that territory are effectively managed there ; and

> (*c*) that any of sub-paragraphs (2) to (4) below applies to the company.

(2) This sub-paragraph applies to a company if,—

> (*a*) at no time during the accounting period in question does the main business of the company consist of either—
>> (i) investment business, or
>> (ii) dealing in goods for delivery to or from the United Kingdom or to or from connected or associated persons ; and

> (*b*) in the case of a company which is mainly engaged in wholesale, distributive or financial business in that accounting period, less than 50 per cent. of its gross trading receipts from that business is derived directly or indirectly from connected or associated persons.

(3) This sub-paragraph applies to a company which is a holding company if at least 90 per cent. of its gross income during the accounting period in question is derived directly from companies which it controls and which, throughout that period,—

> (*a*) are resident in the territory in which the holding company is resident ; and

> (*b*) are not themselves holding companies, but otherwise are, in terms of this Schedule, engaged in exempt activities ;

and a holding company to which this sub-paragraph applies is in this Part of this Schedule referred to as a " local holding company ".

(4) This sub-paragraph applies to a company which is a holding company, but not a local holding company, if at least 90 per cent. of its gross income during the accounting period in question is derived directly from companies which it controls and which, throughout that period,—

> (*a*) are local holding companies ; or

> (*b*) are not themselves holding companies (whether local or not), but otherwise are, in terms of this Schedule, engaged in exempt activities.

(5) Any reference in sub-paragraph (3) or sub-paragraph (4) above to a company which a holding company controls includes a reference to a trading company in which the holding company holds the maximum amount of ordinary share capital which is permitted under the law of the territory—

> (*a*) in which the trading company is resident ; and

(*b*) from whose laws the trading company derives its status as a company.

(6) The following provisions of this Part of this Schedule have effect in relation to sub-paragraphs (1) to (4) above.

7.—(1) For the purposes of paragraph 6(1)(*a*) above, a " business establishment ", in relation to a controlled foreign company, means premises—

    (*a*) which are, or are intended to be, occupied and used with a reasonable degree of permanence ; and

    (*b*) from which the company's business in the territory in which it is resident is wholly or mainly carried on.

(2) For the purposes of sub-paragraph (1) above, the following shall be regarded as premises,—

    (*a*) an office, shop, factory or other building or part of a building ; or

    (*b*) a mine, an oil or gas well, a quarry or any other place of extraction of natural resources ; or

    (*c*) a building site or the site of a construction or installation project ;

but such a site as is referred to in paragraph (*c*) above shall not be regarded as " premises " unless the building work or the project, as the case may be, has a duration of at least twelve months.

8.—(1) Subject to sub-paragraph (4) below, the condition in paragraph 6(1)(*b*) above shall not be regarded as fulfilled unless—

    (*a*) the number of persons employed by the company in the territory in which it is resident is adequate to deal with the volume of the company's business ; and

    (*b*) any services provided by the company for persons resident outside that territory are not in fact performed in the United Kingdom.

(2) For the purposes of sub-paragraph (1)(*a*) above, persons who are engaged wholly or mainly in the business of the company and whose remuneration is paid by a person connected with, and resident in the same territory as, the company shall be treated as employed by the company.

(3) In the case of a holding company, sub-paragraph (2) above shall apply with the omission of the words " wholly or mainly ".

(4) For the purposes of sub-paragraph (1)(*b*) above, no account shall be taken—

    (*a*) of services provided through a branch or agency of the controlled foreign company if the profits or gains of the business carried on through the branch or agency are within the charge to tax in the United Kingdom ; or

    (*b*) of services provided through any other person whose profits or gains from the provision of the services are within the charge to tax in the United Kingdom and who provides the services for a consideration which is, or which is not dissimilar from what might reasonably be expected to be, determined under a contract entered into at arm's length ; or

(c) of services which are no more than incidental to services provided outside the United Kingdom.

9.—(1) Subject to sub-paragraph (3) below, for the purposes of paragraph 6(2)(a)(i) above, each of the following activities constitutes investment business,—

(a) the holding of securities, patents or copyrights ;

(b) dealing in securities, other than in the capacity of a broker ;

(c) the leasing of any description of property or rights ; and

(d) the investment in any manner of funds which would otherwise be available, directly or indirectly, for investment by or on behalf of any person (whether resident in the United Kingdom or not) who has, or is connected or associated with a person who has, control, either alone or together with other persons, of the controlled foreign company in question.

(2) In sub-paragraph (1)(b) above " broker " includes any person offering to sell securities to, or purchase securities from, members of the public generally.

(3) For the purposes of paragraph 6(2) above, in the case of a company which is mainly engaged in banking or any similar business falling within paragraph 11(1)(c) below, nothing in sub-paragraph (1) above shall require the main business of the company to be regarded as investment business.

10. Goods which are actually delivered into the territory in which the controlled foreign company is resident shall not be taken into account for the purposes of paragraph 6(2)(a)(ii) above.

11.—(1) For the purposes of paragraph 6(2)(b) above, each of the following activities constitutes wholesale, distributive or financial business,—

(a) dealing in any description of goods wholesale rather than retail ;

(b) the business of shipping or air transport, as defined in section 514(1) of the Taxes Act ;

(c) banking or any similar business involving the receipt of deposits, loans or both and the making of loans or investments ;

(d) the administration of trusts ;

(e) dealing in securities in the capacity of a broker, as defined in paragraph 9(2) above ;

(f) dealing in commodity or financial futures ; and

(g) insurance business which is long-term business or general business, as defined in section 1 of the Insurance Companies Act 1982.

1982 c. 50.

SCH. 17

(2) In a case where the gross trading receipts of a company include an amount in respect of the proceeds of sale of any description of property or rights, the cost to the company of the purchase of that property or those rights shall be a deduction in calculating the company's gross trading receipts for the purposes of paragraph 6(2)(*b*) above.

(3) In the case of a controlled foreign company engaged in a banking or other business falling within sub-paragraph (1)(*c*) above, no payment of interest received from a company resident in the United Kingdom shall be regarded for the purposes of paragraph 6(2)(*b*) above as a receipt derived directly or indirectly from connected or associated persons, but it shall be conclusively presumed that the condition in paragraph 6(2)(*b*) above is not fulfilled if, at any time during the accounting period in question, the amount by which the aggregate value of the capital interests in the company held directly or indirectly by—

(*a*) the persons who have control of the company, and

(*b*) any person connected or associated with those persons,

exceeds the value of the company's fixed assets is 15 per cent. or more of the amount by which the company's outstanding capital exceeds that value.

(4) For the purposes of this paragraph, in relation to a controlled foreign company,—

(*a*) " capital interest " means an interest in the issued share capital or reserves of the company or in a loan to or deposit with the company or the liability of a guarantor under a guarantee given to or for the benefit of the company ;

(*b*) except in the case of the liability of a guarantor, the value of a capital interest is its value as shown in the company's accounts ;

(*c*) in the case of the liability of a guarantor, the value shall be taken to be the market value of the benefit which the controlled foreign company derives from the provision of the guarantee ;

(*d*) the value of the company's fixed assets means the value, as shown in the company's accounts, of the plant, premises and trade investments employed in the company's business ; and

(*e*) " outstanding capital " means the total value of all the capital interests in the company, less the value, as shown in the company's accounts, of any advances made by the company to persons resident outside the United Kingdom and falling within paragraph (*a*) or paragraph (*b*) of sub-paragraph (3) above.

(5) For the purposes of sub-paragraph (4) above—

(*a*) " trade investments ", in relation to a controlled foreign company, means securities any profit on the sale of which would not be brought into account as a trading receipt in computing the chargeable profits of an accounting period in which that profit arose ; and

(b) the reference in paragraph (e) to advances made to a person by the controlled foreign company includes, in the case of a company which is a person resident outside the United Kingdom and falling within paragraph (a) or paragraph (b) of sub-paragraph (3) above, any securities of that company which are held by the controlled foreign company but are not trade investments, as defined in paragraph (a) above ;

and in this sub-paragraph " securities " includes stocks and shares.

(6) In the application of paragraph 6(2)(b) above in the case of a controlled foreign company engaged in insurance business of any kind—

(a) the reference to gross trading receipts which are derived directly or indirectly from connected or associated persons is a reference to those which, subject to sub-paragraph (7) below, are attributable, directly or indirectly, to liabilities undertaken in relation to any of those persons or their property ;

(b) the only receipts to be taken into account are commissions and premiums received under insurance contracts ;

(c) so much of any such commission or premium as is returned is not to be taken into account ; and

(d) when a liability under an insurance contract is reinsured, in whole or in part, the amount of the premium which is attributable, directly or indirectly, to that liability shall be treated as reduced by so much of the premium under the reinsurance contract as is attributable to that liability.

(7) In determining, in relation to a controlled foreign company to which sub-paragraph (6) above applies, the gross trading receipts referred to in paragraph (a) of that sub-paragraph, there shall be left out of account any receipts under a local reinsurance contract which are attributable to liabilities which—

(a) are undertaken under an insurance contract made in the territory in which the company is resident ; and

(b) are not reinsured under any contract other than a local reinsurance contract ; and

(c) relate either to persons who are resident in that territory and are neither connected nor associated with the company or to property which is situated there and belongs to persons who are not so connected or associated ;

and in paragraph (a) above " insurance contract " does not include a reinsurance contract.

(8) In sub-paragraph (7) above " local reinsurance contract " means a reinsurance contract—

(a) which is made in the territory in which the controlled foreign company is resident ; and

(b) the parties to which are companies which are resident in that territory.

Z

(9) For the purposes of sub-paragraphs (7) and (8) above, any question as to the territory in which a company is resident shall be determined in accordance with section 84 of this Act and, where appropriate, paragraph 5(2) above ; and, for the purpose of the application of those provisions in accordance with this sub-paragraph, the company shall be assumed to be a controlled foreign company.

12.—(1) Subject to sub-paragraph (2) below, in paragraphs 6 and 8(3) above and sub-paragraphs (4) and (5) below " holding company " means—

(a) a company the business of which consists wholly or mainly in the holding of shares or securities of companies which are either local holding companies and its 90 per cent. subsidiaries or trading companies and either its 51 per cent. subsidiaries or companies falling within paragraph 6(5) above ; or

(b) a company which would fall within paragraph (a) above if there were disregarded so much of its business as consists in the holding of property or rights of any description for use wholly or mainly by companies which it controls and which are resident in the territory in which it is resident.

(2) In determining whether a company is a holding company for the purposes of paragraph 6(3) above (and, accordingly, whether the company is or may be a local holding company), sub-paragraph (1) above shall have effect with the omission from paragraph (a) thereof of the words " either local holding companies and its 90 per cent. subsidiaries or ".

(3) In its application for the purposes of this paragraph, section 532 of the Taxes Act shall have effect with the omission—

(a) from subsection (1)(a) of the words " or indirectly " ; and

(b) of subsection (2).

(4) For the purposes of sub-paragraph (3) or, as the case may be sub-paragraph (4) of paragraph 6 above, as it applies in relation to a holding company part of whose business consists of activities other than the holding of shares or securities or the holding of property or rights as mentioned in paragraph (a) or paragraph (b) of sub-paragraph (1) above, the company's gross income during any accounting period shall be determined as follows—

(a) there shall be left out of account so much of what would otherwise be the company's gross income as is derived from any activity which, if it were the business in which the company is mainly engaged, would be such that paragraph 6(2) above would apply to the company ; and

(b) to the extent that the receipts of the company from any other activity include receipts from the proceeds of sale of any description of property or rights, the cost to the company of the purchase of that property or those rights shall (to the extent that the cost does not exceed the receipts) be a deduction in calculating the company's gross income, and no other deduction shall be made in respect of that activity.

(5) For the purposes of sub-paragraphs (3) and (4) of paragraph 6 above, so much of the income of a holding company as—

(*a*) is derived directly from another company which it controls and which is not a holding company but otherwise is, in terms of this Schedule, engaged in exempt activities, and

(*b*) was or could have been paid out of any non-trading income of that other company which is derived directly or indirectly from a third company connected or associated with it,

shall be treated, in relation to the holding company, as if it were not derived directly from companies which it controls.

(6) The reference in sub-paragraph (5) above to the non-trading income of a company is a reference to so much of its income as, if the company were carrying on its trade in the United Kingdom, would not be within the charge to corporation tax under Case I of Schedule D.

Pᴀʀᴛ III

Tʜᴇ Pᴜʙʟɪᴄ Qᴜᴏᴛᴀᴛɪᴏɴ Cᴏɴᴅɪᴛɪᴏɴ

13.—(1) The provisions of this Part of this Schedule have effect for the purposes of paragraph (*c*) of subsection (1) of section 83 of this Act.

(2) Subject to paragraph 14 below, a controlled foreign company fulfils the public quotation condition with respect to a particular accounting period if—

(*a*) shares in the company carrying not less than 35 per cent. of the voting power in the company (and not being shares entitled to a fixed rate of dividend, whether with or without a further right to participate in profits) have been allotted unconditionally to, or acquired unconditionally by, the public and, throughout that accounting period, are beneficially held by the public ; and

(*b*) within the period of twelve months ending at the end of the accounting period, any such shares have been the subject of dealings on a recognised stock exchange situated in the territory in which the company is resident ; and

(*c*) within that period of twelve months the shares have been quoted in the official list of such a recognised stock exchange.

14.—(1) The condition in paragraph 13(2) above is not fulfilled with respect to an accounting period of a controlled foreign company if at any time in that period the total percentage of the voting power in the company possessed by all of the company's principal members exceeds 85 per cent.

Z 2

(2) For the purposes of paragraph 13(2) above, shares in a controlled foreign company shall be deemed to be beneficially held by the public if they are held by any person other than—

(*a*) a person connected or associated with the company ; or

(*b*) a principal member of the company ;

and a corresponding construction shall be given to the reference to shares which have been allotted unconditionally to, or acquired unconditionally by, the public.

15.—(1) References in this Part of this Schedule to shares held by any person include references to any shares the rights or powers attached to which could, for the purposes of section 302 of the Taxes Act (meaning of " control ") be attributed to that person under subsection (5) of that section (nominees).

(2) For the purposes of this Part of this Schedule—

(*a*) a person is a principal member of a controlled foreign company if he possesses a percentage of the voting power in the company of more than 5 per cent. and,—

(i) where there are more than five such persons, if he is one of the five persons who possess the greatest percentages, or

(ii) if, because two or more persons possess equal percentages of the voting power in the company, there are no such five persons, he is one of the six or more persons (so as to include those two or more who possess equal percentages) who possess the greatest percentages ; and

(*b*) a principal member's holding consists of the shares which carry the voting power possessed by him.

(3) In arriving at the voting power which a person possesses, there shall be attributed to him any voting power which, for the purposes of section 302 of the Taxes Act, would be attributed to him under subsection (5) or subsection (6) of that section (nominees, controlled companies and associates).

(4) In this Part of this Schedule " share " includes stock.

PART IV

REDUCTIONS IN UNITED KINGDOM TAX AND DIVERSION OF PROFITS

16.—(1) The provisions of this Part of this Schedule have effect for the purposes of subsection (3) of section 83 of this Act.

(2) Any reference in paragraphs 17 and 18 below to a transaction—

(*a*) is a reference to a transaction reflected in the profits arising in an accounting period of a controlled foreign company ; and

(b) includes a reference to two or more such transactions taken together.

17.—(1) A transaction achieves a reduction in United Kingdom tax if, had the transaction not been effected, any person—

(a) would have been liable for any such tax or for a greater amount of any such tax ; or

(b) would not have been entitled to a relief from or repayment of any such tax or would have been entitled to a smaller relief from or repayment of any such tax.

(2) In this Part of this Schedule and section 83(3) of this Act " United Kingdom tax " means income tax, corporation tax or capital gains tax.

18. It is the main purpose or one of the main purposes of a transaction to achieve a reduction in United Kingdom tax if this is the purpose or one of the main purposes—

(a) of the controlled foreign company concerned ; or

(b) of a person who has an interest in that company at any time during the accounting period concerned.

19.—(1) The existence of a controlled foreign company achieves a reduction in United Kingdom tax by a diversion of profits from the United Kingdom in an accounting period if it is reasonable to suppose that, had neither the company nor any company related to it been in existence,—

(a) the whole or a substantial part of the receipts which are reflected in the controlled foreign company's profits in that accounting period would have been received by a company or individual resident in the United Kingdom ; and

(b) that company or individual or any other person resident in the United Kingdom either—

(i) would have been liable for any United Kingdom tax or for a greater amount of any such tax ; or

(ii) would not have been entitled to a relief from or repayment of any such tax or would have been entitled to a smaller relief from or repayment of any such tax.

(2) For the purposes of sub-paragraph (1) above, a company is related to a controlled foreign company if—

(a) it is resident outside the United Kingdom ; and

(b) it is connected or associated with the controlled foreign company ; and

(c) in relation to any company or companies resident in the United Kingdom, it fulfils or could fulfil, directly or indirectly, substantially the same functions as the controlled foreign company.

Z 3

(3) Any reference in sub-paragraph (1) above to a company resident in the United Kingdom includes a reference to such a company which, if the controlled foreign company in question were not in existence, it is reasonable to suppose would have been established.

Section 89(7)

SCHEDULE 18

RELIEFS AGAINST LIABILITY FOR TAX IN RESPECT OF CHARGEABLE PROFITS

Trading losses and group relief etc.

1.—(1) In any case where—

(*a*) an amount of chargeable profits is apportioned to a company resident in the United Kingdom, and

(*b*) the company is entitled, or would on the making of a claim be entitled, in computing its profits for the appropriate accounting period, to a deduction in respect of any relevant allowance, and

(*c*) for the appropriate accounting period the company has no profits against which a deduction could be made in respect of that allowance or, as the case may be, the amount of that allowance exceeds the profits against which a deduction falls to be made in respect of it,

then, on the making of a claim, a sum equal to corporation tax at the appropriate rate on so much of the relevant allowance or, as the case may be, of the excess of it referred to in paragraph (*c*) above as is specified in the claim shall be set off against the company's liability to tax under section 82(4)(*a*) of this Act in respect of the chargeable profits apportioned to it.

(2) In this paragraph—

(*a*) " the appropriate accounting period " means the accounting period for which, by virtue of section 89(2) of this Act, the company is regarded as assessed to corporation tax in respect of the chargeable profits concerned ; and

(*b*) " the appropriate rate " means the rate of corporation tax applicable to profits of the appropriate accounting period or, if there is more than one such rate, the average rate over the whole accounting period.

(3) In this paragraph " relevant allowance " means—

(*a*) any loss to which section 177(2) of the Taxes Act applies ;

(*b*) any charge on income to which section 248(1) of that Act applies ;

(*c*) any expenses of management to which section 304(1) of that Act applies ;

1968 c. 3.

(*d*) so much of any allowance to which section 74 of the Capital Allowances Act 1968 applies as falls within subsection (3) of that section ; and

(*e*) any amount available to the company by way of group
relief.

(4) In any case where, for the appropriate accounting period, an amount would have been available to the company by way of group relief if a claim had been made under section 264 of the Taxes Act, such a claim may be made for the purposes of this paragraph at any time before the end of the accounting period following that in which the assessment under section 82(4)(*a*) of this Act is made, notwithstanding that the period of two years referred to in section 264(1)(*c*) of the Taxes Act has expired.

(5) Where, by virtue of sub-paragraph (1) above, a sum is set off against a liability to tax, so much of the relevant allowance as gives rise to the amount set off shall be regarded for the purposes of the Tax Acts as having been allowed as a deduction against the company's profits in accordance with the appropriate provisions of those Acts.

(6) In its application to a claim under this paragraph, section 43 of the Taxes Management Act 1970 (time limit for making claims) 1970 c. 9. shall have effect as if, in subsection (2),—

(*a*) any reference to an assessment to income tax were a reference to an assessment under section 82(4)(*a*) of this Act; and

(*b*) any reference to a year of assessment were a reference to an accounting period.

Advance corporation tax

2.—(1) In any case where—

(*a*) an amount of chargeable profits is apportioned to a company resident in the United Kingdom, and

(*b*) the company has an amount of advance corporation tax which, apart from this paragraph, would, in relation to the appropriate accounting period, be surplus advance corporation tax for the purposes of subsection (3) of section 85 of the Finance Act 1972,   1972 c. 41.

then, on the making of a claim, so much of that advance corporation tax as is specified in the claim and does not exceed the relevant maximum shall be set against the company's liability to tax under section 82(4)(*a*) of this Act in respect of the chargeable profits apportioned to it, to the extent that that liability has not or could not have been relieved by virtue of paragraph 1 above.

(2) So much of any advance corporation tax as, by virtue of this paragraph, is set against the company's liability to tax under section 82(4)(*a*) of this Act in respect of chargeable profits shall be regarded for the purposes of the Tax Acts as not being surplus advance corporation tax within the meaning of section 85 of the Finance Act 1972.

(3) In this paragraph " the appropriate accounting period " has the same meaning as in paragraph 1 above and " the relevant maximum ", in relation to the liability to tax referred to in sub-paragraph (1)

above, is the amount of advance corporation tax that would have been payable (apart from section 89 of the Finance Act 1972) in respect of a distribution made at the end of the appropriate accounting period of an amount which, together with the advance corporation tax in respect of it, is equal to—

    (*a*) that amount of the chargeable profits apportioned to the company on which it is chargeable to corporation tax for that accounting period,

less

    (*b*) any amount which, for that accounting period, is to be regarded, by virtue of paragraph 1(5) above, as having been allowed as a deduction against the company's profits.

Gains on disposal of shares in controlled foreign company etc.

3.—(1) This paragraph applies in any case where—

    (*a*) a direction has been given under section 82(1) of this Act in respect of an accounting period of a controlled foreign company (in this paragraph referred to as " the direction period ") ; and

    (*b*) the company's chargeable profits for the direction period have been apportioned among the persons referred to in section 82(3) of this Act ; and

    (*c*) a company resident in the United Kingdom (in this section referred to as " the claimant company ") disposes of—

        (i) shares in the controlled foreign company, or

        (ii) shares in another company which, in whole or in part, give rise to the claimant company's interest in the controlled foreign company,

    being, in either case, shares acquired before the end of the direction period ; and

    (*d*) by virtue of the apportionment referred to in paragraph (*b*) above, under section 82(4)(*a*) of this Act a sum is assessed on and recoverable from the claimant company as if it were an amount of corporation tax ; and

    (*e*) the claimant company makes a claim for relief under this paragraph ;

and in this paragraph the disposal mentioned in paragraph (*c*) above is referred to as " the relevant disposal ".

(2) Subject to the following provisions of this section, in the computation under Chapter II of Part II of the Capital Gains Tax Act 1979 of the gain accruing on the relevant disposal, the appropriate fraction of the sum referred to in sub-paragraph (1)(*d*) above shall be allowable as a deduction ; but to the extent that any sum has been allowed as a deduction under this sub-paragraph it shall not again be allowed as a deduction on any claim under this paragraph (whether made by the claimant company or another company).

(3) In relation to the relevant disposal, the appropriate fraction means that of which the numerator is the average market value in

the direction period of the shares disposed of and the denominator is the average market value in that period of the interest in the controlled foreign company which, in the case of the claimant company, was taken into account in the apportionment referred to in sub-paragraph (1)(*b*) above.

(4) Where, before the relevant disposal,—

    (*a*) a dividend is paid by the controlled foreign company, and

    (*b*) the profits out of which the dividend is paid are those from which the chargeable profits referred to in sub-paragraph (1)(*b*) above are derived, and

    (*c*) at least one of the two conditions in sub-paragraph (5) below is fulfilled,

this paragraph does not apply in relation to a sum assessed and recoverable in respect of so much of the chargeable profits as corresponds to the profits which the dividend represents.

(5) The conditions referred to in sub-paragraph (4)(*c*) above are—

    (*a*) that the effect of the payment of the dividend is such that the value of the shares disposed of by the relevant disposal is less after the payment than it was before it ; and

    (*b*) that, in respect of a dividend paid or payable on the shares disposed of by the relevant disposal, the claimant company is, by virtue of paragraph 4(2) below, entitled under Part XVIII of the Taxes Act to relief (by way of underlying tax) by reference to sums which include the sum referred to in sub-paragraph (1)(*d*) above.

(6) A claim for relief under this paragraph shall be made before the expiry of the period of three months beginning—

    (*a*) at the end of the accounting period in which the relevant disposal occurs ; or

    (*b*) if it is later, on the date on which the assessment to tax for which the claimant company is liable by virtue of section 82(4)(*a*) of this Act becomes final and conclusive.

(7) In identifying for the purposes of this paragraph shares in a company with shares of the same class which are disposed of by the relevant disposal, shares acquired at an earlier time shall be deemed to be disposed of before shares acquired at a later time.

Dividends from the controlled foreign company

4.—(1) This paragraph applies in any case where—

    (*a*) a direction has been given under section 82(1) of this Act in respect of an accounting period of a controlled foreign company, and

    (*b*) the company's chargeable profits for that period have been apportioned among the persons referred to in section 82(3) of this Act, and

    (*c*) the controlled foreign company pays a dividend in whole or in part out of the total profits from which (in accordance with section 82(6)(*a*) of this Act) those chargeable profits are derived.

(2) Subject to paragraphs 5 and 6 below, where this paragraph applies, the aggregate of the sums assessed on and recoverable from companies resident in the United Kingdom in accordance with section 82(4)(*a*) of this Act in respect of the chargeable profits referred to in sub-paragraph (1)(*b*) above shall be treated for the purposes of Part XVIII of the Taxes Act (double taxation relief) as if it were an amount of tax paid in respect of the profits concerned under the law of the territory in which the controlled foreign company was resident and, accordingly, as underlying tax for the purposes of Chapter II of that Part.

(3) In the following provisions of this paragraph and in paragraphs 5 and 6 below the aggregate of the sums which, under sub-paragraph (2) above, fall to be treated as underlying tax is referred to as the " gross attributed tax ".

(4) If, in the case of a person who receives the dividend, section 504 or section 505 of the Taxes Act (limit on credit) has the effect of reducing the amount which (apart from that section) would have been the amount of the credit for foreign tax which is to be allowed to that person, then, for the purposes of sub-paragraph (5) below, the amount of that reduction shall be determined and so much of it as does not exceed the amount of the foreign tax, exclusive of underlying tax, for which credit is to be allowed in respect of the dividend is in that sub-paragraph referred to as " the wasted relief ".

(5) Except for the purpose of determining the amount of the wasted relief, the gross attributed tax shall be treated as reduced by the aggregate of the wasted relief arising in the case of all the persons falling within sub-paragraph (4) above and, on the making of a claim by any of the companies referred to in sub-paragraph (2) above,—

> (*a*) the sum assessed on and recoverable from the company in accordance with section 82(4)(*a*) of this Act in respect of the chargeable profits referred to in sub-paragraph (1)(*b*) above shall, where appropriate, be reduced ; and

> (*b*) all such adjustments (whether by repayment of tax or otherwise) shall be made as are appropriate to give effect to any reduction under paragraph (*a*) above.

5.—(1) In so far as any provision of—

> (*a*) arrangements having effect by virtue of section 497 of the Taxes Act (relief by agreement with other countries), or

> (*b*) section 498 of that Act (unilateral relief),

makes relief which is related to foreign dividends received by a company resident in the United Kingdom conditional upon that company either having a particular degree of control of the company paying the dividend or being a subsidiary of another company which has that degree of control, that condition shall be treated as fulfilled in considering whether any such company is by virtue of paragraph 4(2) above entitled to relief under Part XVIII of that Act in respect of any of the gross attributed tax.

(2) Notwithstanding anything in paragraph 4(2) above, in section

503(2)(*b*) of the Taxes Act (income from dividends treated as increased by underlying tax) the expression " underlying tax " does not include gross attributed tax.

(3) In a case where the controlled foreign company pays a dividend otherwise than out of specified profits and, on the apportionment referred to in paragraph 4(1) above, less than the whole of the chargeable profits of the controlled foreign company concerned is apportioned to companies which are resident in the United Kingdom and liable for tax thereon as mentioned in section 82(4)(*a*) of this Act,—

  (*a*) the gross attributed tax shall be regarded as attributable to a corresponding proportion of the profits in question, and in this sub-paragraph the profits making up that proportion are referred to as " taxed profits " ;

  (*b*) so much of the dividend as is received by, or by a successor in title of, any such company shall be regarded as paid primarily out of taxed profits ; and

  (*c*) so much of the dividend as is received by any other person shall be regarded as paid primarily out of profits which are not taxed profits.

(4) The reference in sub-paragraph (3)(*b*) above to a successor in title of a company resident in the United Kingdom is a reference to a person who is such a successor in respect of the whole or any part of that interest in the controlled foreign company by virtue of which an amount of its chargeable profits was apportioned to that company.

6.—(1) In any case where—

  (*a*) on a claim for relief under paragraph 3 above, the whole or any part of any sum has been allowed as a deduction on a disposal of shares in any company, and

  (*b*) that sum forms part of the gross attributed tax in relation to a dividend paid by that company, and

  (*c*) a person receiving the dividend in respect of the shares referred to in paragraph (*a*) above (in this paragraph referred to as " the primary dividend ") or any other relevant dividend is, by virtue of paragraph 4(2) above, entitled under Part XVIII of the Taxes Act to relief (by way of underlying tax) by reference to the whole or any part of the gross attributed tax,

the amount which, apart from this paragraph, would be available by way of such relief to the person referred to in paragraph (*c*) above shall be reduced or, as the case may be, extinguished by deducting therefrom the amount allowed by way of relief as mentioned in paragraph (*a*) above.

(2) For the purposes of sub-paragraph (1)(*c*) above, in relation to the primary dividend, another dividend is a relevant dividend if—

  (*a*) it is a dividend in respect of shares in a company which is resident outside the United Kingdom ; and (*b*) it represents profits which, directly or indirectly, consist of or include the primary dividend.

Section 95.

SCHEDULE 19

DISTRIBUTING FUNDS

Part I

The Distribution Test

Requirements as to distributions

1.—(1) For the purposes of this Chapter, an offshore fund pursues a full distribution policy with respect to an account period if—

(*a*) a distribution is made for that account period or for some other period which, in whole or in part, falls within that account period ; and

(*b*) subject to Part II of this Schedule, the amount of the distribution which is paid to the holders of material and other interests in the fund—

(i) represents at least 85 per cent. of the income of the fund for that period, and

(ii) is not less than 85 per cent. of the fund's United Kingdom equivalent profits for that period ; and

(*c*) the distribution is made during that account period or not more than six months after the expiry of it ; and

(*d*) the form of the distribution is such that, if any sum forming part of it were received in the United Kingdom by a person resident there and did not form part of the profits of a trade, profession or vocation, that sum would fall to be chargeable to tax under Case IV or Case V of Schedule D ;

and any reference in this sub-paragraph to a distribution made for an account period includes a reference to any two or more distributions so made or, in the case of paragraph (*b*), the aggregate of them.

(2) Subject to sub-paragraph (3) below, with respect to any account period for which—

(*a*) there is no income of the fund, and

(*b*) there are no United Kingdom equivalent profits of the fund,

the fund shall be treated as pursuing a full distribution policy notwithstanding that no distribution is made as mentioned in sub-paragraph (1) above.

(3) For the purposes of this Chapter, an offshore fund shall be regarded as not pursuing a full distribution policy with respect to an account period for which the fund does not make up accounts.

(4) For the purposes of this paragraph—

> (*a*) where a period for which an offshore fund makes up accounts includes the whole or part of two or more account periods of the fund, then, subject to paragraph (*c*) below, income shown in those accounts shall be apportioned between those account periods on a time basis according to the number of days in each period which are comprised in the period for which the accounts are made up ;

> (*b*) where a distribution is made for a period which includes the whole or part of two or more account periods of the fund, then, subject to sub-paragraph (5) below, the distribution shall be apportioned between those account periods on a time basis according to the number of days in each period which are comprised in the period for which the distribution is made ;

> (*c*) where a distribution is made out of specified income but is not made for a specified period, that income shall be attributed to the account period of the fund in which it in fact arose and the distribution shall be treated as made for that account period ; and

> (*d*) where a distribution is made neither for a specified period nor out of specified income, then, subject to sub-paragraph (5) below, it shall be treated as made for the last account period of the fund which ended before the distribution was made.

(5) If, apart from this sub-paragraph, the amount of a distribution made, or treated by virtue of sub-paragraph (4) above as made, for an account period would exceed the income of that period, then, for the purposes of this paragraph,—

> (*a*) if the amount of the distribution was determined by apportionment under sub-paragraph (4)(*b*) above, the excess shall be re-apportioned, as may be just and reasonable, to any other account period which, in whole or in part, falls within the period for which the distribution was made or, if there is more than one such period, between those periods ; and

> (*b*) subject to paragraph (*a*) above, the excess shall be treated as an additional distribution or series of additional distributions made for preceding account periods in respect of which the distribution or, as the case may be, the aggregate distributions would otherwise be less than the income of the period, applying the excess to later account periods before earlier ones, until it is exhausted.

(6) In any case where—

> (*a*) for a period which is or includes an account period, an offshore fund is subject to any restriction as regards the making of distributions, being a restriction imposed by the law of any territory outside the United Kingdom, and

> (*b*) the fund is subject to that restriction by reason of an excess of losses over profits (applying the concepts of " profits " and " losses " in the sense in which and to the extent to which they are relevant for the purposes of the law in question),

Sch. 19   then, in determining, for the purposes of the preceding provisions of this paragraph, the amount of the fund's income for that account period, there shall be allowed as a deduction any amount which, apart from this sub-paragraph, would form part of the income of the fund for that account period and which cannot be distributed by virtue of the restriction.

Funds operating equalisation arrangements

2.—(1) In the case of an offshore fund which throughout any account period operates equalisation arrangements, on any occasion in that period when there is a disposal to which this sub-paragraph applies, the fund shall be treated for the purposes of this Part of this Schedule as making a distribution of an amount equal to so much of the consideration for the disposal as, in accordance with this paragraph, represents income accrued to the date of the disposal.

(2) Sub-paragraph (1) above applies to a disposal—

    (*a*) which is a disposal of a material interest in the offshore fund concerned ; and

    (*b*) which is a disposal to which this Chapter applies (whether by virtue of subsection (3) of section 93 of this Act or otherwise) or is one to which this Chapter would apply if subsections (5) and (6) of that section applied generally and not only for the purpose of determining whether, by virtue of subsection (3) of that section, there is a disposal to which this Chapter applies ; and

    (*c*) which is not a disposal with respect to which the conditions in subsection (4) of that section are fulfilled ; and

    (*d*) which is a disposal to the fund itself or to the persons concerned with the management of the fund (in this paragraph referred to as " the managers ") in their capacity as such.

(3) On a disposal to which sub-paragraph (1) above applies, the part of the consideration which represents income accrued to the date of the disposal is, subject to sub-paragraph (4) and paragraph 4(4) below, the amount which would be credited to the equalisation account of the offshore fund concerned in respect of accrued income if, on the date of the disposal, the material interest which is disposed of were acquired by another person by way of initial purchase.

(4) If, after the beginning of the period by reference to which the accrued income referred to in sub-paragraph (3) above is calculated, the material interest disposed of by a disposal to which sub-paragraph (1) above applies was acquired by way of initial purchase (whether or not by the person making the disposal), there shall be deducted from the amount which, in accordance with sub-paragraph (3) above, would represent income accrued to the date of the disposal, the amount which on that acquisition was credited to the equalisation account of the fund in respect of accrued income ; and if in that period there has been more than one such acquisition of that material interest by way of initial purchase, the deduction to be made under this sub-paragraph shall be the amount so credited to the equalisation account on the latest such acquisition prior to the disposal in question.

(5) Where, by virtue of this paragraph, an offshore fund is treated for the purposes of this Part of this Schedule as making a distribution on the occasion of a disposal, the distribution shall be treated for those purposes—

(a) as complying with paragraph 1(1)(d) above ; and

(b) as made out of the income of the fund for the account period in which the disposal occurs ; and

(c) as paid, immediately before the disposal, to the person who was then the holder of the interest disposed of.

(6) In any case where—

(a) a distribution in respect of an interest in an offshore fund is made to the managers of the fund, and

(b) their holding of that interest is in their capacity as such, and

(c) at the time of the distribution, the fund is operating equalisation arrangements,

the distribution shall not be taken into account for the purposes of paragraph 1(1) above except to the extent that the distribution is properly referable to that part of the period for which the distribution is made during which that interest has been held by the managers of the fund in their capacity as such.

(7) Subsection (2) of section 93 applies for the purposes of this paragraph as it applies for the purposes of that section.

Income taxable under Case IV or Case V of Schedule D

3.—(1) Sub-paragraph (2) below applies if any sums which form part of the income of an offshore fund falling within paragraph (b) or paragraph (c) of subsection (1) of section 94 of this Act are of such a nature that—

(a) the holders of interests in the fund who are either companies resident in the United Kingdom or individuals domiciled and resident there—

(i) are chargeable to tax under Case IV or Case V of Schedule D in respect of such of those sums as are referable to their interests ; or

(ii) if any of that income is derived from assets within the United Kingdom, would be so chargeable had the assets been outside the United Kingdom ; and

(b) the holders of interests who are not such companies or individuals would be chargeable as mentioned in sub-paragraph (i) or sub-paragraph (ii) above if they were resident in the United Kingdom or, in the case of individuals, if they were domiciled and both resident and ordinarily resident there.

(2) To the extent that sums falling within sub-paragraph (1) above do not actually form part of a distribution complying with paragraphs 1(1)(c) and 1(1)(d) above, they shall be treated for the purposes of this Part of this Schedule—

(a) as a distribution complying with those paragraphs and made out of the income of which they form part ; and (*b*) as paid to the holders of the interests to which they are referable.

Commodity income

4.—(1) To the extent that the income of an offshore fund for any account period includes profits from dealing in commodities, one half of those profits shall be left out of account in determining for the purposes of paragraphs 1(1)(*b*) above and 5 below—

(*a*) the income of the fund for that period ; and

(*b*) the fund's United Kingdom equivalent profits for that period ;

but in any account period in which an offshore fund incurs a loss in dealing in commodities the amount of that loss shall not be varied by virtue of this paragraph.

(2) In this paragraph, " dealing in commodities " shall be construed as follows—

(*a*) " commodities " does not include currency, securities, debts or other assets of a financial nature but, subject to that, means tangible assets which are dealt with on a commodity exchange in any part of the world ; and

(*b*) " dealing " includes dealing by way of futures contracts and traded options.

(3) Where the income of an offshore fund for any account period consists of profits from dealing in commodities and other income then,—

(*a*) in determining whether the condition in paragraph 1(1)(*b*) above is fulfilled with respect to that account period, the expenditure of the fund shall be apportioned in such manner as is just and reasonable between the profits from dealing in commodities and the other income ; and

(*b*) in determining whether, and to what extent, any expenditure is deductible under section 304 of the Taxes Act (management expenses of investment companies) in computing the fund's United Kingdom equivalent profits for that period, so much of the business of the fund as does not consist of dealing in commodities shall be treated as a business carried on by a separate company.

(4) Where there is a disposal to which sub-paragraph (1) of paragraph 2 above applies, then, to the extent that any amount which was or would be credited to the equalisation account in respect of accrued income, as mentioned in sub-paragraph (3) or sub-paragraph (4) of that paragraph, represents profits from dealing in commodities, one half of that accrued income shall be left out of account in determining under those sub-paragraphs the part of the consideration for the disposal which represents income accrued to the date of the disposal.

United Kingdom equivalent profits

5.—(1) Any reference in this Schedule to the United Kingdom equivalent profits of an offshore fund for an account period is a reference to the amount which, on the assumptions in sub-paragraph

(3) below, would be the total profits of the fund for that period on which, after allowing for any deductions available against those profits, corporation tax would be chargeable.

(2) In this paragraph the expression "profits" does not include chargeable gains.

(3) The assumptions referred to in sub-paragraph (1) above are—

(*a*) that the offshore fund is a company which, in the account period in question, but not in any other account period, is resident in the United Kingdom ; and

(*b*) that the account period is an accounting period of that company ; and

(*c*) that any dividends or distributions which, by virtue of section 239 of the Taxes Act (dividends and distributions of companies resident in the United Kingdom), should be left out of account in computing income for corporation tax purposes are nevertheless to be brought into account in that computation in like manner as if they were dividends or distributions of a company resident outside the United Kingdom.

(4) Without prejudice to any deductions available apart from this sub-paragraph, the deductions referred to in sub-paragraph (1) above include—

(*a*) a deduction equal to any amount which, by virtue of paragraph 1(6) above, is allowed as a deduction in determining the income of the fund for the account period in question ; and

(*b*) a deduction equal to any amount of tax (paid under the law of a territory outside the United Kingdom) which was taken into account as a deduction in determining the income of the fund for the account period in question but which, because it is referable to capital rather than income, does not fall to be taken into account by virtue of section 516 of the Taxes Act.

(5) For the avoidance of doubt it is hereby declared that, if any sums forming part of the offshore fund's income for any period have been received by the fund without any deduction of or charge to tax by virtue of section 99 or section 100 of the Taxes Act (securities held by non-residents), the effect of the assumption in sub-paragraph (3)(*a*) above is that those sums are to be brought into account in determining the total profits referred to in sub-paragraph (1) above.

Part II

Modifications of Conditions For Certification in Certain Cases

Exclusion of investments in distributing offshore funds

6.—(1) In any case where—

(*a*) in an account period of an offshore fund (in this Part of

this Schedule referred to as the " primary fund "), the assets
of the fund consist of or include interests in another offshore
fund, and

   (b) those interests (together with other interests which the primary fund may have) are such that, by virtue of paragraph
(a) of subsection (3) of section 95 of this Act or, if the
other fund concerned is a company, by virtue of paragraph
(b) or paragraph (c) of that subsection, the primary fund
could not, apart from this paragraph, be certified as a distributing fund in respect of that account period, and

   (c) without regard to the provisions of this paragraph, that
other fund could be certified as a distributing fund in respect of its account period or, as the case may be, each of
its account periods which comprises the whole or any part
of the account period of the primary fund,

then, in determining whether anything in paragraphs (a) to (c) of the
said subsection (3) prevents the primary fund being certified as mentioned in paragraph (b) above, the interests of the primary fund in
that other fund shall be left out of account except for the purpose
of determining the total value of the assets of the primary fund.

(2) In this Part of this Schedule an offshore fund falling within
sub-paragraph (1)(c) above is referred to as a " qualifying fund ".

(3) In a case falling within sub-paragraph (1) above—

   (a) paragraphs (a) to (c) of subsection (3) of section 95 of this
Act shall have effect in relation to the primary fund with
the modification in paragraph 7 below (in addition to that
provided for by sub-paragraph (1) above) ; and

   (b) Part I of this Schedule shall have effect in relation to the
primary fund with the modification in paragraph 8 below.

7. The modification referred to in paragraph 6(3)(a) above is that,
in any case where—

   (a) at any time in the account period referred to in paragraph
6(1) above, the assets of the primary fund include an interest
in an offshore fund or in any company (whether an offshore
fund or not), and

   (b) that interest falls to be taken into account in determining
whether anything in paragraphs (a) to (c) of subsection (3) of
section 95 of this Act prevents the primary fund being certified as a distributing fund in respect of that account period,
and

   (c) at any time in that account period the assets of the qualifying
fund include an interest in the offshore fund or company
referred to in paragraph (a) above,

for the purpose of the application in relation to the primary fund
of the provisions referred to in paragraph (b) above, at any time when
the assets of the qualifying fund include the interest referred to in
paragraph (c) above, the primary fund's share of that interest shall
be treated as an additional asset of the primary fund.

8.—(1) The modification referred to in paragraph 6(3)(*b*) above is that, in determining whether the condition in paragraph 1(1)(*b*)(ii) above is fulfilled with respect to the account period of the primary fund referred to in paragraph 6(1) above, the United Kingdom equivalent profits of the primary fund for that period shall be treated as increased by the primary fund's share of the excess income (if any) of the qualifying fund which is attributable to that period.

(2) For the purposes of this paragraph, the excess income of the qualifying fund for any account period of that fund is the amount (if any) by which its United Kingdom equivalent profits for that account period exceed the amount of the distributions made for that period, as determined for the purposes of the application of paragraph 1(1) above to the qualifying fund.

(3) If an account period of the qualifying fund coincides with an account period of the primary fund, then the excess income (if any) of the qualifying fund for that period is the excess income which is attributable to that period of the primary fund.

(4) In a case where sub-paragraph (3) above does not apply, the excess income of the qualifying fund which is attributable to an account period of the primary fund is the appropriate fraction of the excess income (if any) of the qualifying fund for any of its account periods which comprises the whole or any part of the account period of the primary fund and, if there is more than one such account period of the qualifying fund, the aggregate of the excess income (if any) of each of them.

(5) For the purposes of sub-paragraph (4) above, the appropriate fraction is that of which—

(*a*) the numerator is the number of days in the account period of the primary fund which are also days in an account period of the qualifying fund ; and

(*b*) the denominator is the number of days in that account period of the qualifying fund or, as the case may be, in each of those account periods of that fund which comprises the whole or any part of the account period of the primary fund.

9.—(1) The references in paragraphs 7 and 8(1) above to the primary fund's share of—

(*a*) an interest forming part of the assets of the qualifying fund, or

(*b*) the excess income (as defined in paragraph 8 above) of the qualifying fund,

shall be construed as references to the fraction specified in sub-paragraph (2) below of that interest or excess income.

(2) In relation to any account period of the primary fund, the fraction referred to in sub-paragraph (1) above is that of which—

(*a*) the numerator is the average value of the primary fund's holding of interests in the qualifying fund during that **period ; and** (*b*) the denominator is the average value of all the interests in the qualifying fund held by any persons during that period.

Offshore funds investing in trading companies

10.—(1) In any case where the assets of an offshore fund for the time being include an interest in a trading company, as defined in sub-paragraph (2) below, the provisions of subsection (3) of section 95 of this Act have effect subject to the modifications in sub-paragraphs (3) and (4) below.

(2) In this paragraph " trading company " means a company whose business consists wholly of the carrying on of a trade or trades and does not to any extent consist of—

> (*a*) dealing in commodities, as defined in paragraph 4(2) above, or dealing, as so defined, in currency, securities, debts or other assets of a financial nature ; or
>
> (*b*) banking or money-lending.

(3) In the application of section 95(3)(*b*) of this Act to so much of the assets of an offshore fund as for the time being consists of interests in a single trading company, for the words " 10 per cent. " there shall be substituted the words " 20 per cent."

(4) In the application of section 95(3)(*c*) of this Act to an offshore fund the assets of which for the time being include any issued share capital of a trading company or any class of that share capital, for the words " more than 10 per cent." there shall be substituted the words " 50 per cent. or more ".

Offshore funds with wholly-owned subsidiaries dealing in commodities

11.—(1) In relation to an offshore fund which has a wholly-owned subsidiary—

> (*a*) which is a company, and
>
> (*b*) the business of which consists wholly or mainly of dealing in commodities, as defined in paragraph 4(2) above,

the provisions of subsection (3) of section 95 of this Act and Part I of this Schedule have effect subject to the modifications in sub-paragraph (3) below.

(2) For the purposes of this paragraph, a company is a wholly-owned subsidiary of an offshore fund if and so long as the whole of the issued share capital of the company is,—

> (*a*) in the case of an offshore fund falling within section 94(1)(*a*) of this Act, directly and beneficially owned by the fund ; and
>
> (*b*) in the case of an offshore fund falling within section 94(1)(*b*) of this Act, directly owned by the trustees of the fund for the benefit of the fund ; and
>
> (*c*) in the case of an offshore fund falling within section 94(1)(*c*) of this Act, owned in a manner which, as near as may be, corresponds either to paragraph (*a*) or paragraph (*b*) above.

(3) The modifications referred to in sub-paragraph (1) above are that, for the purposes of the provisions referred to in that sub-paragraph,—

- (*a*) the receipts, expenditure, assets and liabilities of the subsidiary shall be regarded as the receipts, expenditure, assets and liabilities of the fund ; and
- (*b*) there shall be left out of account the interest of the fund in the subsidiary and any distributions or other payments made by the subsidiary to the fund or by the fund to the subsidiary.

Offshore funds with interests in dealing and management companies

12.—(1) Section 95(3)(*c*) of this Act shall not apply to so much of the assets of an offshore fund as consists of issued share capital of a company which is either—

- (*a*) a wholly-owned subsidiary of the fund which falls within sub-paragraph (2) below, or
- (*b*) a subsidiary management company of the fund, as defined in sub-paragraph (3) below.

(2) A company which is a wholly-owned subsidiary of an offshore fund is one to which sub-paragraph (1)(*a*) above applies if—

- (*a*) the business of the company consists wholly of dealing in material interests in the offshore fund for the purposes of and in connection with the management and administration of the business of the fund ; and
- (*b*) the company is not entitled to any distribution in respect of any material interest for the time being held by it ;

and paragraph 11(2) above shall apply to determine whether a company is, for the purposes of this paragraph, a wholly-owned subsidiary of an offshore fund.

(3) A company in which an offshore fund has an interest is for the purposes of sub-paragraph (1)(*b*) above a subsidiary management company of the fund if—

- (*a*) the company carries on no business other than providing services falling within sub-paragraph (4) below either for the fund alone or for the fund and for any other offshore fund which has an interest in the company ; and
- (*b*) the company's remuneration for the services which it provides to the fund is not greater than it would be if it were determined at arm's length between the fund and a company in which the fund has no interest.

(4) The services referred to in sub-paragraph (3) above are—

- (*a*) holding property (of any description) which is occupied or used in connection with the management or administration of the fund ; and
- (*b*) providing administrative management and advisory services to the fund.

(5) In determining, in accordance with sub-paragraph (3) above, whether a company in which an offshore fund has an interest is a subsidiary management company of that fund,—

(a) every business carried on by a wholly-owned subsidiary of the company shall be treated as carried on by the company ; and

(b) no account shall be taken of so much of the company's business as consists of holding its interests in a wholly-owned subsidiary ; and

(c) any reference in sub-paragraph (3)(b) above to the company shall be taken to include a reference to a wholly-owned subsidiary of the company.

(6) Any reference in sub-paragraph (5) above to a wholly-owned subsidiary of a company is a reference to another company the whole of the issued share capital of which is for the time being directly and beneficially owned by the first company.

PART III

CERTIFICATION PROCEDURE

Application for certification

13.—(1) The Board shall, in such manner as they think appropriate, certify an offshore fund as a distributing fund in respect of an account period if—

(a) an application in respect of that period is made under this paragraph ; and

(b) the application is accompanied by the accounts of the fund for, or for a period which includes, the account period to which the application relates ; and

(c) there is furnished to the Board such information as they may reasonably require for the purpose of determining whether the fund should be so certified ; and

(d) they are satisfied that nothing in subsection (2) or subsection (3) of section 95 of this Act prevents the fund being so certified.

(2) An application under this paragraph shall be made to the Board by the fund or by a trustee or officer thereof on behalf of the fund and may be so made—

(a) before the expiry of the period of six months beginning at the end of the account period to which the application relates ; or

(b) if it is later, before 1st January 1985 ; or

(c) at such later time as the Board may in any particular case allow.

(3) In any case where, on an application under this paragraph, the Board determine that the offshore fund concerned should not be

certified as a distributing fund in respect of the account period to   Sᴄʜ. 19
which the application relates, they shall give notice in writing of
that fact to the fund.

(4) If at any time it appears to the Board that the accounts accompanying an application under this paragraph in respect of any account
period of an offshore fund or any information furnished to the Board
in connection with such an application is or are not such as to
make full and accurate disclosure of all facts and considerations
relevant to the application, they shall give notice to the fund
accordingly, specifying the period concerned.

(5) Where a notice is given by the Board under sub-paragraph
(4) above, any certification by them in respect of the account period
in question shall be void.

Appeals

14.—(1) An appeal to the Special Commissioners—

    (*a*) against such a determination as is referred to in paragraph
        13(3) above, or

    (*b*) against a notification under paragraph 13(4) above,

may be made by the offshore fund or by a trustee or officer thereof
on behalf of the fund, and shall be so made by notice in writing
specifying the grounds of appeal and given to the Board within 90
days of the date of the notice under paragraph 13(3) or, as the case
may be, paragraph 13(4) above.

(2) The jurisdiction of the Special Commissioners on an appeal
under this paragraph shall include jurisdiction to review any decision
of the Board which is relevant to a ground of the appeal.

Pᴀʀᴛ IV

Sᴜᴘᴘʟᴇᴍᴇɴᴛᴀʀʏ

Assessment : effect of non-certification

15. No appeal may be brought against an assessment to tax on
the ground that an offshore fund should have been certified as a
distributing fund in respect of an account period of the fund.

16.—(1) Without prejudice to paragraph 15 above, in any case
where no application has been made under paragraph 13 above in
respect of an account period of an offshore fund, any person who is
assessed to tax for which he would not be liable if the offshore fund
were certified as a distributing fund in respect of that period may by
notice in writing require the Board to take action under this paragraph with a view to determining whether the fund should be so
certified.

(2) Subject to sub-paragraphs (3) and (5) below, if the Board
receive a notice under sub-paragraph (1) above, they shall, by notice

Sch. 19   in writing, invite the offshore fund concerned to make an application under paragraph 13 above in respect of the period in question.

(3) Where sub-paragraph (2) above applies, the Board shall not be required to give notice under that sub-paragraph before the expiry of the account period to which the notice is to relate nor if an application under paragraph 13 above has already been made ; but where notice is given under that sub-paragraph, an application under paragraph 13 above shall not be out of time under paragraph 13(2)(*a*) or paragraph 13(2)(*b*) above if it is made within 90 days of the date of that notice.

(4) If an offshore fund to which notice in writing is given under sub-paragraph (2) above does not, within the time allowed by sub-paragraph (3) above or, as the case may be, paragraph 13(2)(*a*) or paragraph 13(2)(*b*) above, make an application under paragraph 13 above in respect of the account period in question, the Board shall proceed to determine the question of certification in respect of that period as if such an application had been made.

(5) Where the Board receive more than one notice under sub-paragraph (1) above with respect to the same account period of the same offshore fund, their obligations under sub-paragraphs (2) and (4) above shall be taken to be fulfilled with respect to each of those notices if they are fulfilled with respect to any one of them.

(6) Notwithstanding anything in sub-paragraph (5) above, for the purpose of a determination under sub-paragraph (4) above with respect to an account period of an offshore fund, the Board shall have regard to accounts and other information furnished by all persons who have given notice under sub-paragraph (1) above with respect to that account period ; and paragraph 13 above shall apply as if accounts and information so furnished had been furnished in compliance with sub-paragraph (1) of that paragraph.

(7) Without prejudice to sub-paragraph (5) above, in any case where—

(*a*) at a time after the Board have made a determination under sub-paragraph (4) above that an offshore fund should not be certified as a distributing fund in respect of an account period, notice is given under sub-paragraph (1) above with respect to that period, and

(*b*) the person giving that notice furnishes the Board with accounts or information which had not been furnished to the Board at the time of the earlier determination,

the Board shall reconsider their previous determination in the light of the new accounts or information and, if they consider it appropriate, may determine to certify the fund accordingly.

(8) Where any person has given notice to the Board under sub-paragraph (1) above with respect to an account period of an offshore

fund and no application has been made under paragraph 13 above SCH. 19
with respect to that period,—

(*a*) the Board shall notify that person of their determination
with respect to certification under sub-paragraph (4) above ;
and

(*b*) paragraph 14 above shall not apply in relation to that determination.

*Postponement of tax pending determination of question as to
certification*

17.—(1) In any case where—

(*a*) an application has been made under paragraph 13 above with
respect to an account period of an offshore fund and that
application has not been finally determined, or

(*b*) paragraph (*a*) above does not apply but notice has been
given under paragraph 16(1) above in respect of an account
period of an offshore fund and the Board have not yet
given notice of their decision as to certification under paragraph 16(4) above,

any person who has been assessed to tax and considers that, if the
offshore fund were to be certified as a distributing fund in respect of
the account period in question, he would be overcharged to tax by
the assessment may, by notice in writing given to the inspector within
30 days after the date of the issue of the notice of assessment, apply
to the General Commissioners for a determination of the amount of
tax the payment of which should be postponed pending the determination of the question whether the fund should be so certified.

(2) A notice of application under sub-paragraph (1) above shall
state the amount in which the applicant believes that he is overcharged to tax and his grounds for that belief.

(3) Subsections (3A) onwards of section 55 of the Taxes Manage- 1970 c. 9.
ment Act 1970 (recovery of tax not postponed) shall apply with any
necessary modifications in relation to an application under sub-
paragraph (1) above as if it were an application under subsection
(3) of that section and as if the determination of the question as to
certification (whether by the Board or on appeal) were the determination of an appeal.

Information as to decisions on certification etc.

18. No obligation as to the secrecy imposed by statute or otherwise
shall preclude the Board or an inspector from disclosing to any
person appearing to have an interest in the matter—

(*a*) any determination of the Board or (on appeal) the Special
Commissioners whether an offshore fund should or should
not be certified as a distributing fund in respect of any
account period ; or

(*b*) the content and effect of any notice given by the Board under
paragraph 13(4) above.

Section 96.

SCHEDULE 20

COMPUTATION OF OFFSHORE INCOME GAINS

PART I

DISPOSALS OF INTERESTS IN NON-QUALIFYING FUNDS

Interpretation

1. In this Part of this Schedule—

1979 c. 14.

     " the principal Act " means the Capital Gains Tax Act 1979 ;

     " the principal section " means section 96 of this Act ; and

     " material disposal " means a disposal to which Chapter VII of Part II of this Act applies, otherwise than by virtue of section 93(3) of this Act.

Calculation of unindexed gain

2.—(1) Where there is a material disposal, there shall first be determined for the purposes of this Part of this Schedule the amount (if any) which, in accordance with the provisions of this paragraph, is the unindexed gain accruing to the person making the disposal.

(2) Subject to subsections (3) to (6) of section 92 of this Act and paragraph 3 below, the unindexed gain accruing on a material disposal is the amount which would be the gain on that disposal for the purposes of the principal Act if it were computed—

     (*a*) without regard to any charge to income tax or corporation tax by virtue of the principal section ; and

     (*b*) without regard to any indexation allowance on the disposal under Chapter III of Part III of the Finance Act 1982.

1982 c. 39.

3.—(1) If the amount of any chargeable gain or allowable loss which (apart from section 98 of this Act) would accrue on the material disposal would fall to be determined in a way which, in whole or in part, would take account of the indexation allowance on an earlier disposal to which paragraph 2 of Schedule 13 to the Finance Act 1982 applies (disposals on a no-gain/no-loss basis), the unindexed gain on the material disposal shall be computed as if—

     (*a*) no indexation allowance had been available on any such earlier disposal ; and

     (*b*) subject to that, neither a gain nor a loss had accrued to the person making such an earlier disposal.

(2) If the material disposal forms part of a transfer to which section 123 of the principal Act applies (roll-over relief on transfer of business), the unindexed gain accruing on the disposal shall be computed without regard to any deduction which falls to be made under that section in computing a chargeable gain.

1980 c. 48.

(3) If the material disposal is made otherwise than under a bargain at arm's length and a claim for relief is made in respect of that disposal under section 79 of the Finance Act 1980 (relief for gifts), that section shall not affect the computation of the unindexed gain accruing on the disposal.

(4) Where, in the case of an insurance company carrying on life assurance business, a profit arising from general annuity business and attributable to a material disposal falls (or would but for section 99(2) of this Act fall) to be taken into account in the computation under section 312 of the Taxes Act (general annuity business and pension business: separate charge on profits), the unindexed gain, if any, accruing to the company on the disposal shall be computed as if section 31(1) of the principal Act (computation of chargeable gains: exclusion of sums taken into account in computing income) did not apply.

(5) Notwithstanding section 29 of the principal Act (losses to be determined in like manner as gains) if, apart from this sub-paragraph, the effect of any computation under the preceding provisions of this Part of this Schedule would be to produce a loss, the unindexed gain on the material disposal shall be treated as nil ; and, accordingly, for the purposes of this Part of this Schedule no loss shall be treated as accruing on a material disposal.

(6) Section 323 of the Taxes Act (interpretation of Chapter II of Part XII of that Act) has effect in relation to sub-paragraph (4) above as if it were included in that Chapter.

Gains since 1st January 1984

4.—(1) This paragraph applies where—

- (a) the interest in the offshore fund which is disposed of by the person making a material disposal was acquired by him before 1st January 1984 ; or

- (b) he is treated by virtue of any provisions of sub-paragraphs (3) and (4) below as having acquired the interest before that date.

(2) Where this paragraph applies, there shall be determined for the purposes of this Part of this Schedule the amount which would have been the gain on the material disposal—

- (a) on the assumption that, on 1st January 1984, the interest was disposed of and immediately reacquired for a consideration equal to its market value at that time ; and

- (b) subject to that, on the basis that the gain is computed in like manner as, under paragraphs 2 and 3 above, the unindexed gain on the material disposal is determined ;

and that amount is in paragraph 5 below referred to as the "post-1983 gain" on the material disposal.

(3) Where the person making the material disposal acquired the interest disposed of on or after 1st January 1984 and in such circumstances that, by virtue of any enactment other than section 86(5) of or Schedule 13 to the Finance Act 1982 (indexation provisions), he 1982 c. 39. and the person from whom he acquired it (in this sub-paragraph and sub-paragraph (4) below referred to as " the previous owner ") fell to be treated for the purposes of the principal Act as if his acquisition were for a consideration of such an amount as would secure that, on the disposal under which he acquired it, neither a gain nor a loss

Sch. 20   accrued to the previous owner, the previous owner's acquisition of the interest shall be treated as his acquisition of it.

(4) If the previous owner acquired the interest disposed of on or after 1st January 1984 and in circumstances similar to those referred to in sub-paragraph (3) above, his predecessor's acquisition of the interest shall be treated for the purposes of this paragraph as the previous owner's acquisition, and so on back through previous acquisitions in similar circumstances until the first such acquisition before 1st January 1984 or, as the case may be, until an acquisition on a material disposal on or after that date.

The offshore income gain

5.—(1) Subject to sub-paragraph (2) below, a material disposal gives rise to an offshore income gain of an amount equal to the unindexed gain on that disposal.

(2) In any case where—

     (a) paragraph 4 above applies, and

     (b) the post-1983 gain on the material disposal is less than the unindexed gain on the disposal,

the offshore income gain to which the disposal gives rise is an amount equal to the post-1983 gain.

Part II

Disposals Involving an Equalisation Element

6.—(1) Subject to paragraph 7 below, a disposal to which Chapter VII of Part II of this Act applies by virtue of section 93(3) of this Act gives rise to an offshore income gain of an amount equal to the equalisation element relevant to the asset disposed of.

(2) Subject to sub-paragraphs (4) to (6) below, the equalisation element relevant to the asset disposed of by a disposal falling within sub-paragraph (1) above is the amount which would be credited to the equalisation account of the offshore fund concerned in respect of accrued income if, on the date of the disposal, the asset which is disposed of were acquired by another person by way of initial purchase.

(3) In the following provisions of this Part of this Schedule, a disposal falling within sub-paragraph (1) above is referred to as a " disposal involving an equalisation element ".

(4) Where the asset disposed of by a disposal involving an equalisation element was acquired by the person making the disposal after the beginning of the period by reference to which the accrued income referred to in sub-paragraph (2) above is calculated, the amount which, apart from this sub-paragraph, would be the equalisation element relevant to that asset shall be reduced by the following amount, that is to say,—

     (a) if that acquisition took place on or after 1st January 1984, the amount which, on that acquisition, was credited to the equalisation account of the offshore fund concerned in respect of accrued income or, as the case may be, would have been so credited if that acquisition had been by way of initial purchase ; and

(b) in any other case, the amount which would have been credited to that account in respect of accrued income if that acquisition had been an acquisition by way of initial purchase taking place on 1st January 1984.

(5) In any case where—

(a) the asset disposed of by a disposal involving an equalisation element was acquired by the person making the disposal at or before the beginning of the period by reference to which the accrued income referred to in sub-paragraph (2) above is calculated, and

(b) that period began before 1st January 1984 and ends after that date,

the amount which, apart from this sub-paragraph, would be the equalisation element relevant to that asset shall be reduced by the amount which would have been credited to the equalisation account of the offshore fund concerned in respect of accrued income if the acquisition referred to in paragraph (a) above had been an acquisition by way of inital purchase taking place on 1st January 1984.

(6) Where there is a disposal involving an equalisation element, then, to the extent that any amount which was or would be credited to the equalisation account of the offshore fund in respect of accrued income, as mentioned in any of sub-paragraphs (2) to (5) above, represents profits from dealing in commodities, within the meaning of paragraph 4 of Schedule 19 to this Act, one half of that accrued income shall be left out of account in determining under those sub-paragraphs the equalisation element relevant to the asset disposed of by that disposal.

7.—(1) For the purposes of this Part of this Schedule, there shall be determined, in accordance with paragraph 8 below, the Part I gain (if any) on any disposal involving an equalisation element.

(2) Notwithstanding anything in paragraph 6 above,—

(a) if there is no Part I gain on a disposal involving an equalisation element, that disposal shall not give rise to an offshore income gain ; and

(b) if, apart from this paragraph, the offshore income gain on a disposal involving an equalisation element would exceed the Part I gain on that disposal, the offshore income gain to which that disposal gives rise shall be reduced to an amount equal to that Part I gain.

8.—(1) On a disposal involving an equalisation element, the Part I gain is the amount (if any) which, by virtue of Part I of this Schedule (as modified by the following provisions of this paragraph), would be the offshore income gain on that disposal if it were a material disposal within the meaning of that Part.

SCH. 20

(2) For the purposes only of the application of Part I of this Schedule to determine the Part I gain (if any) on a disposal involving an equalisation element, subsections (5) and (6) of section 93 of this Act shall have effect as if, in subsection (5), the words " by virtue of subsection (3) above " were omitted.

1982 c. 39.
1979 c. 14.

(3) If a disposal involving an equalisation element is one which, by virtue of any enactment other than section 86(5)(*b*) of or Schedule 13 to the Finance Act 1982 (indexation), is treated for the purposes of the Capital Gains Tax Act 1979 as one on which neither a gain nor a loss accrues to the person making the disposal, then, for the purpose only of determining the Part I gain (if any) on the disposal, that enactment shall be deemed not to apply to it (but without prejudice to the application of that enactment to any earlier disposal).

1983 c. 28.

(4) In any case where a disposal involving an equalisation element is made by a company which has made an election under Schedule 6 to the Finance Act 1983 (indexation: election for pooling) and the asset disposed of consists of or includes securities which, by virtue of paragraph 3(3) of that Schedule, are to be regarded for the purposes of the principal Act as a single asset or part of a single asset, then, for the purpose only of determining the Part I gain (if any) on the disposal,—

(*a*) the reference in paragraph 2(2)(*b*) above to an indexation allowance under Chapter III of Part III of the Finance Act 1982 shall be construed as including a reference to an indexation allowance under Schedule 6 to the Finance Act 1983 ; and

(*b*) if some of the securities comprised in the asset disposed of were acquired by the company making the disposal before 1st January 1984 and some were not, paragraph 4(2) above shall not apply and paragraph 5 above shall have effect with the omission of sub-paragraph (2) (and the reference to that sub-paragraph in sub-paragraph (1)).

(5) The reference in sub-paragraph (4)(*b*) above to securities acquired before 1st January 1984 includes a reference to securities which, by virtue of any provisions of paragraph 4 above, are treated as so acquired.

Section 108.

SCHEDULE 21

CAPITAL TRANSFER TAX: PRE-CONSOLIDATION AMENDMENTS

The Finance Act 1975

1975 c. 7.

1. In section 22(4) of the Finance Act 1975 (in this Schedule referred to as " the 1975 Act ")—

(*a*) for the words from the beginning to " his death " there shall be substituted the words " In determining for the purposes

of this Part of this Act the value of the estate, immediately
before his death, of a person whose spouse (or former
spouse) died before 13th November 1974 " ; and

(*b*) for the words " that death " there shall be substituted the
words " the later death ".

2. In section 25(10) of the 1975 Act, after the word " section "
there shall be inserted the words " (except subsection (8)) ".

3. In section 26(2) of the 1975 Act—

(*a*) the words from the beginning to " respectively, and " shall
cease to have effect ; and

(*b*) at the end, there shall be added the words " or by virtue of
paragraph 24(2) of Schedule 5 to this Act ".

4. In section 45(1) of the 1975 Act, after the words " as domiciled
in the United Kingdom " there shall be inserted the words " (and
not elsewhere) " ; and section 51(3) of that Act shall cease to have
effect.

5. In section 51(1) of the 1975 Act—

(*a*) the definition of " enactment " shall cease to have effect ;
and

(*b*) after the definition of " Inland Revenue charge " there shall
be inserted—

" ' land ' includes buildings and other structures, land
covered with water, and any estate, interest, easement,
servitude or right in or over land ; but does not include
any estate, interest or right by way of mortgage or other
security ; ".

6. In paragraph 6(6) of Schedule 4 to the 1975 Act, for the words
following " including references " there shall be substituted the words
" to—

(*a*) disposals on which tax is chargeable under paragraph 2 of
Schedule 9 to this Act,

(*b*) chargeable events by reference to which tax is chargeable
under section 78 of the Finance Act 1976, 1976 c. 40.

(*c*) occasions on which tax is chargeable under section 82 of
the Finance Act 1976 or under Chapter II of Part IV
of the Finance Act 1982, 1982 c. 39.

or to the amounts on which tax is then chargeable."

7. In paragraph 14(2) of Schedule 4 to the 1975 Act, for the words
" value of an interest " there shall be substituted the words " net
value of an interest ".

8. In paragraph 19(4) of Schedule 4 to the 1975 Act, the words
" to any person " and the words " of that person " shall cease to have
effect.

9. Paragraph 44 of Schedule 4 to the 1975 Act shall cease to have
effect.

10. In paragraph 1(8) of Schedule 5 to the 1975 Act, for the words " and section 25(3)(*d*) of this Act " there shall be substituted the words " , sections 22(2) and (3), 24(3) and 25(3)(*d*) of this Act and sections 93 and 94 ".

11. In paragraph 4(7) of Schedule 5 to the 1975 Act, after the words " surviving spouse " there shall be inserted the words " (or surviving former spouse) ".

12. In paragraph 17(3)(*b*) of Schedule 5 to the 1975 Act, for the words " this Schedule and of Chapter II of Part IV of the Finance Act 1982 " there shall be substituted the words " this Part of this Act (except subsection (3) of section 23 and section 20(4) so far as relating to that subsection) ".

13. In paragraph 22(1) of Schedule 5 to the 1975 Act, for the words " this Schedule " there shall be substituted the words " this Part of this Act ".

14.—(1) Paragraph 24 of Schedule 5 to the 1975 Act shall be amended as follows.

(2) In sub-paragraph (1), for paragraph (*a*) there shall be substituted the following paragraphs—

> " (*a*) the reference in subsection (2) of that section to subsection (1) shall have effect as including a reference to sub-paragraph (2) below ;
> (*aa*) subsection (3) of that section shall apply in relation to tax chargeable by virtue of sub-paragraph (2) below as it applies in relation to tax chargeable under subsection (1) of that section ; ".

(3) In sub-paragraph (5), for the words " this Schedule and of Chapter II of Part IV of the Finance Act 1982 " there shall be substituted the words " this Part of this Act (except subsection (3) of section 23 and section 20(4) so far as relating to that subsection) ".

15. In paragraph 4(2)(*b*) of Schedule 7 to the 1975 Act, for the words " which is, or forms part of, a colony, protectorate, protected state or United Kingdom trust territory " there shall be substituted the words " which, at the time when the fund was established, was, or formed part of, a colony (within the meaning of Schedule 1 to the

Interpretation Act 1978), protectorate, protected state or United Kingdom trust territory ".

16. In paragraph 1(1) of Schedule 10 to the 1975 Act, for the words " a transferor's estate " there shall be substituted the words " a person's estate ".

17. In paragraph 5(1)(*b*) of Schedule 10 to the 1975 Act, for the word " by " there shall be substituted the word " for ".

The Development Land Tax Act 1976

18.—(1) Section 34 of the Development Land Tax Act 1976 shall be amended as follows.

(2) In subsection (3), for paragraph (*d*) there shall be substituted   Sᴄʜ. 21
the following paragraph—

    " (*d*) ' a CTT transfer ' means an event which is—

        (i) a transfer of value, for the purposes of capital transfer tax, giving rise to liability for that tax,

        (ii) an occasion on which capital transfer tax is chargeable under Chapter II of Part IV of the Finance Act 1982, 1982 c. 39. or

        (iii) a capital distribution (within the meaning of section 51(1) of the Finance Act 1975 as it has effect in 1975 c. 7. relation to events before 9th March 1982),

    and on the occurrence of which an interest in land is acquired by any person."

(3) For subsection (5) there shall be substituted the following subsection—

    " (5) In any case where the whole or any part of the land in which the interest referred to in paragraph (*d*) of subsection (3) above subsists—

        (*a*) is designated under section 77 of the Finance Act 1976 1976 c. 40. (conditional exemption) in relation to a conditionally exempt transfer (as defined in section 76 of that Act) made on a death, or

        (*b*) is designated as property to which section 34 of the Finance Act 1975 applies (conditional exemption on death before 7th April 1976),

    it shall be assumed for the purpose only of determining whether the transfer of value in question falls within sub-paragraph (i) of subsection (3)(*d*) above that the transfer of value was not a conditionally exempt transfer or, as the case may be, that section 34 of the Finance Act 1975 never applied to the property."

19. In paragraph 18(2) of Schedule 6 to the Development Land 1976 c. 24. Tax Act 1976—

    (*a*) for the words from " as property " to " death) " there shall be substituted the words " under section 34 of that Act or under section 77 of the Finance Act 1976 (conditional exemption) " ; and

    (*b*) in paragraph (*a*) after the words " Act 1975 " there shall be inserted the words " or under section 78 of the Finance Act 1976 ".

The Finance Act 1976

20. In section 76(3)(*b*) of the Finance Act 1976, the words from " or the value " to the end shall cease to have effect.

21. In section 105 of the Finance Act 1976, subsections (3) and (4) shall cease to have effect.

22. In section 123(2) of the Finance Act 1976, after the words " shall carry interest " there shall be inserted the words " (which shall not constitute income for any tax purposes) ".

The Finance Act 1980

23. In Schedule 15 to the Finance Act 1980—

(*a*) in paragraphs 2A, 5 and 6, for the word " previous " there shall be substituted the word " other " ; and

(*b*) in paragraphs 5 and 6, after the words " by that reduction " there shall be inserted the words " (or by the most recent of those reductions) ".

The Finance Act 1982

24. In section 94(6) of the Finance Act 1982, the words from " and, in " to the end shall cease to have effect.

25. In sections 120(1), 121(1) and (2) and 123 of the Finance Act 1982, after the words " for the purposes of this Chapter " there shall be inserted the words ", of sections 93 and 94 above and of sections 81, 82 and 82A of the Finance Act 1976 ".

26. In sections 122(1) and 124 of the Finance Act 1982, after the words " for the purposes of this Chapter " there shall be inserted the words " and of sections 93 and 94 above ".

SCHEDULE 22

SPECIAL AND GENERAL COMMISSIONERS

Appointment of Special Commissioners

1. For section 4 of the Taxes Management Act 1970 (appointment of Special Commissioners) there shall be substituted—

" Special Commissioners.

4.—(1) The Lord Chancellor shall, after consultation with the Lord Advocate, appoint such persons as he thinks fit as " Commissioners for the special purposes of the Income Tax Acts " (in the Taxes Acts referred to as " Special Commissioners ") and shall designate one of the Special Commissioners as the Presiding Special Commissioner.

(2) No person shall be appointed under subsection (1) above unless he is a barrister, advocate or solicitor of not less than ten years' standing.

(3) If the Presiding Special Commissioner is temporarily absent or unable to act or there is a vacancy in his office, the Lord Chancellor may designate another Special Commissioner to act as deputy Presiding Special Commissioner and the Commissioner so designated shall, when so acting, have all the functions of the Presiding Special Commissioner.

(4) The Lord Chancellor may, if he thinks fit, and after consultation with the Lord Advocate, remove a Special Commissioner from office on the grounds of incapacity or misbehaviour.

(5) By virtue of their appointment the Special Commissioners shall have authority to execute such powers, and to perform such duties, as are assigned to them by any enactment.

(6) Such sums shall be allowed to Special Commissioners in respect of salary and incidental expenses and such pensions (including allowances and gratuities) shall be paid to, or in respect of, them as the Lord Chancellor may, with the approval of the Treasury, determine.

(7) Officers and staff may be appointed under section 27 of the Courts Act 1971 (court staff) for carrying out the administrative work of the Special Commissioners.

SCH. 22

1971 c. 23.

Deputy Special Commissioners.

4A.—(1) If it appears to the Lord Chancellor expedient to do so in order to facilitate the performance of any functions of the Special Commissioners, he may, after consultation with the Lord Advocate, appoint a person to be a deputy Special Commissioner during such period or on such occasions as the Lord Chancellor thinks fit.

(2) A person shall not be qualified for appointment as a deputy Special Commissioner unless he is qualified for appointment as a Special Commissioner.

(3) A deputy Special Commissioner while acting under this section shall have all the jurisdiction and functions of a Special Commissioner and any reference to a Special Commissioner in the following provisions of this Act or in any other enactment or any instrument made under any enactment (whenever passed or made) shall include a reference to a deputy Special Commissioner.

(4) The duty under section 6(1) below shall only apply to a deputy Special Commissioner on his first appointment to that office.

(5) Notwithstanding the expiry of any period for which a person is appointed under this section, he may continue to act under the appointment for the purpose of continuing to deal with any matter with which he was concerned during that period.

(6) The Lord Chancellor may pay to any person appointed under this section such remuneration and allowances as he may, with the approval of the Treasury, determine."

Special Commissioners : quorum

2.—(1) Section 45 of the Act of 1970 (quorum of Special Commissioners) shall be amended as follows.

(2) In subsection (1), for the word "may" there shall be substituted the words "shall, except in any case where the Presiding Special Commissioner directs otherwise," and the words "or any two or more Special Commissioners" shall be omitted.

(3) In subsection (3), after the word " brought " there shall be inserted the words " , in accordance with a direction of the Presiding Special Commissioner ".

(4) Subsections (2) and (4) to (6) shall be omitted.

Elections to bring appeals before Special Commissioners

3.—(1) In section 31 of the Act of 1970 (appeals against assessments) the following subsections shall be inserted after subsection (5)—

" (5A) An election under subsection (4) above shall be disregarded if—

(a) the appellant and the inspector or other officer of the Board agree in writing, at any time before the determination of the appeal, that it is to be disregarded ; or

(b) the General Commissioners have given a direction under subsection (5C) below and have not revoked it.

(5B) At any time before the determination of an appeal in respect of which an election has been made under subsection (4) above, the inspector or other officer of the Board after giving notice to the appellant may refer the election to the General Commissioners.

(5C) On any such reference the Commissioners shall, unless they are satisfied that the appellant has arguments to present or evidence to adduce on the merits of the appeal, direct that the election be disregarded.

(5D) If, at any time after the giving of a direction under subsection (5C) above (but before the determination of the appeal) the General Commissioners are satisfied that the appellant has arguments to present or evidence to adduce on the merits of the appeal, they shall revoke the direction.

(5E) Any decision to give a direction under subsection (5C) above or revoke such a direction under subsection (5D) above shall be final.".

(2) In Schedule 2 to the Act of 1970 (appeals against decisions on claims), in paragraph 1, the following sub-paragraphs shall be inserted after sub-paragraph (1)—

" (1A) An election under sub-paragraph (1) above shall be disregarded if—

(a) the appellant and the inspector or other officer of the Board agree in writing, at any time before the determination of the appeal, that it is to be disregarded ; or

(b) the General Commissioners have given a direction under sub-paragraph (1C) below and have not revoked it.

(1B) At any time before the determination of an appeal in respect of which an election has been made under sub-paragraph

(1) above, the inspector or other officer of the Board after giving notice to the appellant may refer the election to the General Commissioners.

(1C) On any such reference the Commissioners shall, unless they are satisfied that the appellant has arguments to present or evidence to adduce on the merits of the appeal, direct that the election be disregarded.

(1D) If, at any time after the giving of a direction under sub-paragraph (1C) above (but before the determination of the appeal) the General Commissioners are satisfied that the appellant has arguments to present or evidence to adduce on the merits of the appeal, they shall revoke the direction.

(1E) Any decision to give a direction under sub-paragraph (1C) or revoke such a direction under sub-paragraph (1D) above shall be final.".

Procedural rules

4. After section 57A of the Act of 1970 there shall be inserted the following section—

"Commissioners: procedural rules.

57B—(1) The Lord Chancellor may, with the consent of the Lord Advocate, make rules—

(a) as to the procedure of the Special Commissioners and the procedure in connection with the bringing of matters before them ;

(b) as to the time within which matters may be brought before the Special Commissioners ; and

(c) providing for appeals which have been heard by the Special Commissioners in the absence of the appellant to be reheard, in such circumstances and subject to such conditions, as the rules may prescribe.

(2) Rules under this section may make such consequential provision (including the amendment of any enactment or instrument made under any enactment) as the Lord Chancellor considers necessary.

(3) Rules under this section shall be made by statutory instrument subject to annulment in pursuance of a resolution of either House of Parliament."

Transfer of appeals from General to Special Commissioners

5. In section 44 of the Act of 1970 (jurisdiction of General Commissioners) the following subsection shall be inserted after subsection (3)—

" (3A) Where in any case (including one in which proceedings may be brought as mentioned in subsection (3) above)—

(a) an appeal has been brought before the General Commissioners ; and

(b) those Commissioners consider that, because of the complexity of the appeal or the length of time likely to be required for hearing it, the appeal should be brought before the Special Commissioners ;

the General Commissioners may, with the agreement of the Special Commissioners, and having considered any representations made to them by the parties, arrange for the transfer of the proceedings to the Special Commissioners.".

Fee for statement of case

6. In section 56(3) of the Act of 1970 and paragraph 10(2) of Schedule 4 to the Finance Act 1975 (fee for statement of case for opinion of High Court) for " £1 " there shall be substituted " £25 ".

Statement of case from Special Commissioners to Court of Appeal

7. In the Act of 1970, the following section shall be inserted after section 56 (statement of case for opinion of High Court)—

" Statement of case: Special Commissioners to Court of Appeal. **56A.**—(1) The Lord Chancellor may by order provide that—

(*a*) in such classes of appeal in England and Wales as may be prescribed by the order ; and

(*b*) subject to the consent of the parties and to such other conditions as may be so prescribed ;

a case stated by the Special Commissioners under section 56 above, for the opinion of the High Court, shall be referred to the Court of Appeal.

(2) An order under this section—

(*a*) may provide that section 56 above shall have effect, in relation to any appeal to which the order applies, with such modifications as may be specified in the order ; and

(*b*) shall be made by statutory instrument subject to annulment in pursuance of a resolution of either House of Parliament.".

Saving

8. Nothing in this Schedule shall affect the appointment of any person who, immediately before the passing of this Act, held office as a Special Commissioner.

SCHEDULE 23

REPEALS

PART I

MADE-WINE

Chapter	Short title	Extent of repeal
1979 c. 4.	The Alcoholic Liquor Duties Act 1979.	Schedule 2.
1982 c. 39.	The Finance Act 1982.	Section 1(4). Schedule 2.
1983 c. 28.	The Finance Act 1983.	Section 1(4). Schedule 2.

PART II

GAMING MACHINE LICENCE DUTY

Chapter	Short title	Extent of repeal
1981 c. 63.	The Betting and Gaming Duties Act 1981.	Section 24(1). In Schedule 4, in paragraphs 6 and 8(2), the words " in respect of any premises " and in paragraph 10(3) the words from " except " to the end.
1982 c. 39.	The Finance Act 1982.	In Schedule 6, paragraphs 6 to 8 and 16.

These repeals do not affect licences granted for periods beginning before 1st October 1984.

PART III

VALUE ADDED TAX

Chapter	Short title	Extent of repeal
1983 c. 55.	The Value Added Tax Act 1983.	In section 16(5) the words " of a supply of goods or services outside the United Kingdom or " and " supply or ". In Schedule 5, in Group 8, in Note (2), in paragraph (*b*), the words " or alteration " and paragraph (*c*).

PART IV

CUSTOMS AND EXCISE: MISCELLANEOUS

Chapter	Short title	Extent of repeal
1979 c. 58.	The Isle of Man Act 1979.	In Schedule 1, paragraph 25.
1982 c. 39.	The Finance Act 1982.	Section 2.
1983 c. 28.	The Finance Act 1983.	Section 2.
1983 c. 55.	The Value Added Tax Act 1983.	In section 24(3)(*b*) the figure " 7 ".

PART V

INCOME TAX AND CORPORATION TAX: GENERAL

Chapter	Short title	Extent of repeal
1970 c. 10.	The Income and Corporation Taxes Act 1970.	Section 310(1), (2) and (4). In section 343(1), in paragraph (*a*), the words from " which takes " to " this section " and the proviso.
1972 c. 41.	The Finance Act 1972.	Section 96. In Schedule 18, paragraph 2(1).
1974 c. 30.	The Finance Act 1974.	Section 10(3). In paragraph 14(1)(*a*) of Schedule 1, the words " employee-controlled company ", in both places.
1975 c. 22.	The Oil Taxation Act 1975.	Section 17(3).
1980 c. 48.	The Finance Act 1980.	Section 58. In Schedule 10, in paragraph 13, the words " (not exceeding £50 monthly) ".
1982 c. 39.	The Finance Act 1982.	Section 35(3). Section 40(4) and (5). In section 72(7), the words " on or before 31st March 1987 ".
1982 c. 50.	The Insurance Companies Act 1982.	In Schedule 5, paragraph 24.
1983 c. 28.	The Finance Act 1983.	Section 20(4).

1. The repeals in section 310 of the Income and Corporation Taxes Act 1970 and in Schedule 18 to the Finance Act 1972 do not have effect with respect to any financial year ending before 1st April 1986.

2. The repeals in section 343 of the Income and Corporation Taxes Act 1970 and section 58 of the Finance Act 1980 have effect from 6th April 1985.

3. The repeals in section 96 of the Finance Act 1972 and section 10(3) of the Finance Act 1974 do not have effect with respect to any financial year ending before 1st April 1985.

4. The repeals in Schedule 1 to the Finance Act 1974 have effect in relation to payments of interest made after the passing of this Act.

5. The repeal of section 17(3) of the Oil Taxation Act 1975 has effect with respect to any advance corporation tax which is, within the meaning of section 77 of this Act, advance corporation tax paid by a company in respect of distributions made in an accounting period of the company ending on or after 1st April 1984.

6. The repeal in paragraph 13 of Schedule 10 to the Finance Act 1980 has effect from the day appointed under section 39(9) of this Act.

7. The repeal in section 40 of the Finance Act 1982 has effect in relation to any right to acquire shares which is obtained after 5th April 1984.

8. The repeal in section 20(4) of the Finance Act 1983 has effect in relation to payments made on or after 6th April 1984.

Part VI

Income Tax: The Additional Rate

Chapter	Short title	Extent of repeal
1970 c. 10.	The Income and Corporation Taxes Act 1970.	In section 30(3), the words " or additional ". In section 36(1), the words " or additional ". In section 38(2) the words from " and in determining " to " investment income ". In sections 403(1), 424(*c*), 430(1), 457(1) and 458(1) the words " or additional ".
1971 c. 68.	The Finance Act 1971.	Section 32(3) and (4). Section 34(4). In Schedule 7, in paragraph 2(2), the words " or additional ".
1972 c. 41.	The Finance Act 1972.	In section 87(6), the words " or additional ". In Schedule 16, in paragraph 5(6A), the words " or additional ".
1973 c. 51.	The Finance Act 1973.	In section 44, the words " or additional ". In section 59(2), the words from " the additional rate " to " them and ".
1974 c. 30.	The Finance Act 1974.	Section 15. In section 16(1), the words following " subsection (2) below ". In section 43(1), the words from " In this subsection " onwards. In Schedule 7, paragraph 1 and, in paragraph 9(5), the words from " and " onwards.

Chapter	Short title	Extent of repeal
1975 c. 7.	The Finance Act 1975.	In Schedule 2, in paragraph 19(1A) the words " or additional ".
1980 c. 48.	The Finance Act 1980.	In section 24(3), the words from " or over which " to " additional rate ", the word " respectively ", where it first occurs, and the words " and the investment income threshold ".

The repeal in subsection (6) of section 87 of the Finance Act 1972 does not have effect for the purpose of determining whether a person has paid tax in respect of excess liability, within the meaning of that subsection, for the year 1983–84 or any earlier year of assessment or the amount so paid.

PART VII

FOREIGN EARNINGS AND EMOLUMENTS

Chapter	Short title	Extent of repeal
1970 c. 10.	The Income and Corporation Taxes Act 1970.	In section 188(2), the words from " in respect of one-half " to " charged " and paragraph (*a*). In Schedule 8, in paragraph 12, the words " (2) or ". In Part III of Schedule 12, in paragraph 2(3) the words " (3) and ".
1974 c. 30.	The Finance Act 1974.	Section 23(3). In Schedule 2, paragraph 3.
1975 c. 14.	The Social Security Act 1975.	In Schedule 2, in paragraph 3(2), paragraph (*cc*).
1975 c. 15.	The Social Security (Northern Ireland) Act 1975.	In Schedule 2, in paragraph 3(2), paragraph (*cc*).
1977 c. 36.	The Finance Act 1977.	In section 31(2), the words from the beginning to " emoluments); and ". In Schedule 7, paragraphs 2, 3, 4(3), (4) and 5, in paragraph 9 the words " or 2 ", and paragraph 10.
1978 c. 42.	The Finance Act 1978.	Section 27. Schedule 4.

1. The repeals in subsection (2) of section 188 of, and in Schedule 8 to, the Taxes Act have effect where the relevant date (within the meaning of that section) falls after 13th March 1984 but subject to subsection (8) of section 30 of this Act.

2. The repeal of section 23(3) of the Finance Act 1974 and the repeal in Schedule 12 of the Taxes Act have effect in relation to the year 1985–86 and subsequent years of assessment but subject to subsection (4) of section 30 of this Act.

3. The repeal in Schedule 2 of the Finance Act 1974 has effect in relation to the year 1989–90 and subsequent years of assessment.

4. The repeals in the Acts of 1975, section 31(2) of, and Schedule 7 to, the Finance Act 1977 and the Finance Act 1978 have effect for the year 1985–86 and subsequent years of assessment.

PART VIII

CAPITAL GAINS

Chapter	Short title	Extent of repeal
1979 c. 14.	The Capital Gains Tax Act 1979.	Section 6. Sections 8 and 9. In section 29A, in subsection (2), the words " Except in the case specified in subsection (4) below " and, in paragraph (*a*), the words " or the corresponding disposal is made by an excluded person ". Section 32(5) and (6). In sections 137(4)(*aa*) and 138(1)(*aa*), the words " to buy or sell shares in a company ". Section 148.
1980 c. 48.	The Finance Act 1980.	Section 82.
1982 c. 39.	The Finance Act 1982.	Section 85.

1. The repeal of sections 6, 8, 9 and 148 of the Capital Gains Tax Act 1979 and of section 82 of the Finance Act 1980 and section 85 of the Finance Act 1982 has effect with respect to disposals on or after 6th April 1984.

2. The repeals in section 29A of the Capital Gains Tax Act 1979 have effect in relation to disposals and acquisitions on or after 6th April 1983.

3. The repeals in section 32 of that Act have effect where the disposal by the person who is neither resident nor ordinarily resident in the United Kingdom is made on or after 6th April 1985.

4. The repeals in sections 137(4)(*aa*) and 138(1)(*aa*) of that Act have effect in relation to any abandonment or other disposal on or after 6th April 1984.

Part IX

Capital Transfer Tax

Chapter	Short title	Extent of repeal
1975 c. 7.	The Finance Act 1975.	In section 26(2), the words from the beginning to "respectively, and ". In section 51(1), the definition of " enactment ". Section 51(3). In Schedule 4, in paragraph 19(4), the words " to any person " and the words " of that person ". In Schedule 4, paragraph 44.
1976 c. 40.	The Finance Act 1976.	In section 76(3)(*b*), the words from " or the value " onwards. Section 105(3) and (4). Section 114(8). In Schedule 11, paragraph 2.
1982 c. 39.	The Finance Act 1982.	In section 94(6), the words from " and, in " onwards. In Schedule 17, paragraphs 9, 18 and 28.

The repeal of section 114(8) of the Finance Act 1976 has effect as from 1st April 1983.

Part X

Stamp Duty

Chapter	Short title	Extent of repeal
1891 c. 39.	The Stamp Act 1891.	In section 75(1), the words " not exceeding thirty-five years ".
1963 c. 25.	The Finance Act 1963.	In Schedule 11, Part I.
1974 c. 30.	The Finance Act 1974.	In Schedule 11, in Part I, paragraphs 3 and 4, in Part II, paragraphs 13 and 14 and Part III.
1980 c. 48.	The Finance Act 1980.	Section 95(1).
1982 c. 39.	The Finance Act 1982.	Section 128(1).

PART XI

NATIONAL INSURANCE SURCHARGE

Chapter	Short title	Extent of repeal
1976 c. 85.	The National Insurance Surcharge Act 1976.	The whole Act.
1977 c. 36.	The Finance Act 1977.	Section 57.
1978 c. 42.	The Finance Act 1978.	Section 75.
1980 c. 48.	The Finance Act 1980.	In section 118(4), the words from " and section 57 " to " surcharge) ".
1982 c. 39.	The Finance Act 1982.	Section 143.
1982 c. 55.	The National Insurance Surcharge Act 1982.	The whole Act.
1983 c. 28.	The Finance Act 1983.	Section 42. In section 46(4), the words from " and section 57 " to " surcharge) ".

These repeals have effect with respect to earnings paid on or after 6th April 1985.

PART XII

DEVELOPMENT LAND TAX

Chapter	Short title	Extent of repeal
1976 c. 24.	The Development Land Tax Act 1976.	In section 19A(1), the words " and before 1st April 1984 ". In section 26, subsection (2) and, in subsection (3), the words " or subsection (2) ". In section 40, in subsection (1), the words " which, at that time, is development land " and subsection (8). In section 47(1A), the words " are begun on or before 31st December 1984 and ". In Schedule 8, in paragraph 45(1), (3), (4), (5) and (7)(*b*), the words " or half-yearly ".

Part XIII

Special and General Commissioners

Chapter	Short title	Extent of repeal
1970 c. 9.	The Taxes Management Act 1970.	In section 45, in subsection (1) the words " or any two or more Special Commissioners ", and subsections (2), (4), (5) and (6). In section 55(11) the words from the beginning to " and ".

Part XIV

Miscellaneous

Chapter	Short title	Extent of repeal
1968 c. 13.	The National Loans Act 1968.	In section 3(5), the words from " and " to " future Act ".
1972 c. 41.	The Finance Act 1972.	Section 132.
1975 c. 7.	The Finance Act 1975.	Section 55.
1975 c. 22.	The Oil Taxation Act 1975.	In section 3(4), the word " or " at the end of paragraph (*d*).
1978 c. 42.	The Finance Act 1978.	Section 78.
1982 c. 39.	The Finance Act 1982.	Section 154.

Appropriation Act 1984

1984 CHAPTER 44

An Act to apply a sum out of the Consolidated Fund to the service of the year ending on 31st March 1985, to appropriate the supplies granted in this Session of Parliament, and to repeal certain Consolidated Fund and Appropriation Acts.   [26th July 1984]

Most Gracious Sovereign,

WE, Your Majesty's most dutiful and loyal subjects the Commons of the United Kingdom in Parliament assembled, towards making good the supply which we have cheerfully granted to Your Majesty in this Session of Parliament, have resolved to grant unto Your Majesty the sum hereinafter mentioned; and do therefore most humbly beseech Your Majesty that it may be enacted, and be it enacted by the Queen's Most Excellent Majesty, by and with the advice and consent of the Lords Spiritual and Temporal, and Commons, in this present Parliament assembled, and by the authority of the same, as follows:—

GRANT OUT OF THE CONSOLIDATED FUND

1. The Treasury may issue out of the Consolidated Fund of the United Kingdom and apply towards making good the supply granted to Her Majesty for the service of the year ending on 31st March 1985 the sum of £51,611,104,000.

Issue out of the Consolidated Fund for the year ending 31st March 1985.

APPROPRIATION OF GRANTS

Appropriation of sums voted for supply services.

2. All sums granted by this Act and the other Acts mentioned in Schedule (A) annexed to this Act out of the said Consolidated Fund towards making good the supply granted to Her Majesty amounting, as appears by the said schedule, in the aggregate, to the sum of £93,298,575,449·27 are appropriated, and shall be deemed to have been appropriated as from the date of the passing of the Acts mentioned in the said Schedule (A), for the services and purposes expressed in Schedule (B) annexed hereto.

The abstract of schedules and schedules annexed hereto, with the notes (if any) to such schedules, shall be deemed to be part of this Act in the same manner as if they had been contained in the body thereof.

1891 c. 24.

In addition to the said sums granted out of the Consolidated Fund, there may be applied out of any money directed, under section 2 of the Public Accounts and Charges Act 1891, to be applied as appropriations in aid of the grants for the services and purposes specified in Schedule (B) annexed hereto the sums respectively set forth in the last column of the said schedule.

Repeals.

3. The enactments mentioned in Schedule (C) annexed to this Act are hereby repealed.

Short title.

4. This Act may be cited as the Appropriation Act 1984.

ABSTRACT

OF

SCHEDULES (A) and (B) to which this Act refers

SCHEDULE (A)

Grants out of the Consolidated Fund　...　...　...　...　...　...　£93,298,575,449·27　　Section 2.

SCHEDULE (B)—APPROPRIATION OF GRANTS　　Section 2.

	Supply Grants	Appropriations in Aid
	£	£
1982–83 and 1983–84		
Part 1. Defence and Civil (Excesses), 1982–83	135,693,449·27	436,483·83
Part 2. Supplementary, 1983–84	2,566,290,000·00	130,181,000·00
	2,701,983,449·27	130,617,483·83

SCHEDULE (B)—APPROPRIATION OF GRANTS—*continued*

1984-85		Supply Grants £	Appropriations in Aid £
Part 3.	Class I	16,796,775,000·00	1,676,874,000·00
Part 4.	Class II	1,856,915,000·00	45,072,000·00
Part 5.	Class III	939,680,000·00	209,095,000·00
Part 6.	Class IV	6,780,512,000·00	1,359,577,000·00
Part 7.	Class V	228,998,000·00	6,000·00
Part 8.	Class VI	2,183,344,000·00	114,806,000·00
Part 9.	Class VII	1,837,216,000·00	—
Part 10.	Class VIII	726,875,000·00	30,429,000·00
Part 11.	Class IX	2,993,243,000·00	237,026,000·00
Part 12.	Class X	2,917,416,000·00	9,059,000·00
Part 13.	Class XI	11,501,298,000·00	1,711,479,000·00
Part 14.	Class XII	16,891,807,000·00	657,526,000·00
Part 15.	Class XIII	1,710,787,000·00	119,614,000·00

Part 16.	Class XIIIA	·	·	·	·	·	·	·	·	·	17,394,000·00	145,000·00
Part 17.	Class XIIIB	·	·	·	·	·	·	·	·	·	10,099,000·00	2,567,000·00
Part 18.	Class XIV	·	·	·	·	·	·	·	·	·	2,196,537,000·00	412,547,000·00
Part 19.	Class XV -	·	·	·	·	·	·	·	·	·	3,150,851,000·00	226,473,000·00
Part 20.	Class XVI	·	·	·	·	·	·	·	·	·	1,262,668,000·00	106,437,000·00
Part 21.	Class XVII	·	·	·	·	·	·	·	·	·	1,218,051,000·00	3,200,000·00
Part 22.	Class XVIII	·	·	·	·	·	·	·	·	·	15,376,126,000·00	1,783,316,000·00
TOTAL	· · ·	·	·	·	·	·	·	·	·	·	90,596,592,000·00	8,705,248,000·00
GRAND TOTAL	·	·	·	·	·	·	·	·	·	·	93,298,575,449·27	8,835,865,483·83

SCHEDULE (A)

GRANTS OUT OF THE CONSOLIDATED FUND

	£
For the service of the year ended 31st March 1983—	
Under Act 1984 c. 1	135,693,449·27
For the service of the year ended 31st March 1984—	
Under Act 1983 c. 57	1,172,383,000·00
Under Act 1984 c. 1	1,393,907,000·00
For the service of the year ending on 31st March 1985—	
Under Act 1983 c. 57	38,985,488,000·00
Under this Act	51,611,104,000·00
TOTAL	93,298,575,449·27

SCHEDULE (B)—PART 1

DEFENCE AND CIVIL (EXCESSES), 1982–83

Defence and
Civil (Excesses),
1982–83.

SUMS granted, and sums which may be applied as appropriations in aid in addition thereto, to make good excesses on certain grants for Defence and Civil Services for the year ended 31st March 1983, viz.:—

Vote	Supply Grants £	Surplus receipts available to be applied as Appropriations in Aid £
CLASS I		
3. DEFENCE: ARMED FORCES RETIRED PAY, PENSIONS, ETC - - - - -	1,089,456·70	151,309·93
4 DEFENCE ACCOMMODATION SERVICES, ETC - - - - -	4,896,379·55	285,173·90
CLASS II		
2. OVERSEAS REPRESENTATION: ACCOMMODATION SERVICES, ETC (PSA OF THE DEPARTMENT OF THE ENVIRONMENT) - - - - -	242,650·29	—
CLASS IV		
1. REGIONAL AND SELECTIVE ASSISTANCE, ETC (DEPARTMENT OF INDUSTRY) - -	81,037,324·99	—
CLASS VIII		
4. ROYAL PALACES, ROYAL PARKS, HISTORIC BUILDINGS, ANCIENT MONUMENTS AND THE NATIONAL HERITAGE (DEPARTMENT OF THE ENVIRONMENT) - - - -	189,367·91	—

Class XII

	Supply Grants	Surplus receipts available to be applied as Appropriations in Aid
	£	£
1. Pension Benefits (Non-Contributory) · · · · ·	11,874,533·51	—
2. Supplementary Benefits · · · · · ·	36,363,736·32	—
Total, Defence and Civil (Excesses) 1982–83 · ·	135,693,449·27	436,483·83

SCHEDULE (B)—PART 2

SUPPLEMENTARY, 1983–84

SCHEDULE OF SUPPLEMENTARY SUMS granted, and of the sums which may be applied as appropriations in aid in addition thereto, to defray the charges for the Services herein particularly mentioned for the year ended 31st March 1984, viz.:—

Vote	Supply Grants £	Appropriations in Aid £
CLASS I		
1. For expenditure by the Ministry of Defence on pay, allowances etc of the Armed Forces and their Reserves and Cadet Forces etc, pay etc of Defence Ministers and of certain civilian staff employed by the Ministry of Defence; on movements; certain stores; supplies and services; plant and machinery; charter and contract repair of ships; certain research; lands and buildings; sundry grants; payments abroad including contributions and subscriptions to international organisations; and grants in aid - - - - -	1,000	39,505,000
2. For expenditure by the Procurement Executive of the Ministry of Defence in operating its Headquarters and Establishments and for its other common services; for research etc by contract; lands and buildings; for development by contract, production, repair etc and purchases for sale abroad of sea systems, land systems, air systems and associated equipment; for reservation of capacity in Royal Ordnance Factories; for certain contingent liabilities, and for sundry other Procurement Executive services including those on repayment terms to non-exchequer customers - -	1,000	4,423,000
3. For expenditure by the Ministry of Defence on retired pay, pensions etc - -	17,051,000	240,000

Supplementary, 1983–84.

CLASS I—*continued*

	Supply Grants £	Appropriations in Aid £
Vote		
4. For expenditure including loans by the Property Services Agency of the Department of the Environment on public building work and certain accommodation services etc for defence purposes - - - -	17,004,000	*—9,357,000
5. For operating the Royal Dockyards and for the repair of ships by contract including work undertaken on repayment terms for exchequer and non-exchequer customers	1,000	243,000
CLASS II		
1. For expenditure by the Foreign and Commonwealth Office on the salaries, building and other accommodation services, and administration of H.M. Diplomatic Service, official information services, military aid, certain grants in aid and sundry other grants, services and loans	2,000	2,627,000
2. For expenditure by the Foreign and Commonwealth Office on grants and subscriptions, etc, to certain international organisations, special payments and assistance, a loan to Yugoslavia and sundry other grants and services - - -	1,769,000	907,000
4. For expenditure by the Foreign and Commonwealth Office on a grant in aid of the British Council - - - -	1,412,000	—
8. For expenditure by the Foreign and Commonwealth Office (Overseas Development Administration) on the official United Kingdom aid programme including pensions and allowances in respect of overseas service, assistance to certain refugee students, grants in aid, certain subscriptions to international organisations and certain payments under the Commonwealth Scholarship and Fellowship Plan -	2,000	559,000

* Deficit.

10. For payments to the Budget of the European Communities not covered by direct charges on the Consolidated Fund under Section 2(3) of the European Communities Act 1972 - - - - - - -	436,008,000	—
CLASS III		
1. For expenditure by the Intervention Board for Agricultural Produce in giving effect in the United Kingdom to the agricultural support provisions of the Common Agricultural Policy of the European Community and to Community food aid measures and for certain other services - - -	1,000	14,349,000
3. For expenditure by the Ministry of Agriculture, Fisheries and Food on educational, advisory, research and development services, livestock services, plant health and pest control, food services and assistance to marketing and processing, land management and smallholdings, emergency and strategic food services, some central, special and other services; including grants in aid and subscriptions to certain international organisations - - - -	1,000	—
4. For expenditure by the Intervention Board for Agricultural Produce on central administration and miscellaneous services -	253,000	9,000
5. For expenditure by the Ministry of Agriculture, Fisheries and Food on assistance to the fishing industry, research and development, protective and other services including subscriptions to certain international organisations -	1,505,000	—
CLASS IV		
1. For expenditure by the Department of Trade and Industry on regional development grants, selective assistance to industry, certain other services including the provision of public dividend capital to the National Enterprise Board, UK contributions to the funding of buffer stock operations of international commodity agreements, a strategic mineral stockpile, and on investment grants	1,000	14,250,000

CLASS IV—*continued*

	Supply Grants £	Appropriations in Aid £
Vote		
2. For expenditure by the Department of Trade and Industry on provision of land and buildings, assistance for publicity, other support services including grants in aid and promotion of tourism - - -	2,350,000	1,723,000
3. For expenditure by the Department of Energy on assistance to the coal industry including grants to the National Coal Board and payments to redundant workers	289,952,000	*470,000
4. For expenditure by the Department of Trade and Industry on promotion of tourism, export promotion, trade co-operation, protection of innovation, regulation of trading practices and consumer protection, standards, central and miscellaneous services, shipping and civil aviation, wireless and telegraphy and other services including grants in aid, international subscriptions and other grants -	1,000	580,000
5. For expenditure by the Department of Energy in connection with the energy industries including related research and development, selective assistance to industry, energy conservation, oil storage, and certain other services including grants in aid and an international subscription -	1,000	9,000
6. For expenditure by the Department of Trade and Industry on the Department's Research establishments; industrial research and development and other support; general research and developments on civil aeronautics and aeroengines and associated equipment; national and international space technology programmes; standards; loans, grants in aid, international subscriptions and a grant to the National Research Development Corporation and certain other grants -	1,000	537,000
8. For expenditure by the Department of Trade and Industry on support for the aerospace, shipbuilding, steel and vehicle manufacturing industries, including loans, grants and the purchase of assets, and assistance to redundant steel workers -	91,506,000	2,207,000

* Deficit

10. For expenditure by the Export Credits Guarantee Department in connection with export credits guarantees, including an international subscription, special guarantees, refinancing and financing arrangements made for facilitating trade with other countries and assistance towards the cost of financing export credits, the purchase of securities, overseas investment insurance and cost escalation guarantees -	100,177,000	*—20,045,000
13. For expenditure by the Department of Employment on general labour market services, on services for seriously disabled people and on an international subscription -	20,141,000	—
15. For expenditure by the Department of Employment as a grant in aid to the Advisory, Conciliation and Arbitration Service -	160,000	—
17. For expenditure by the Department of Employment on the administration of benefit services and on central and miscellaneous services -	1,000	—
18. For expenditure by the Department of Trade and Industry on central and miscellaneous services, on services provided by the Ministry of Defence (Procurement Executive) Headquarters, on international subscriptions, on British Telecommunications Civil Defence, on fund for sub-postmasters and on the World Communication year -	1,000	2,215,000
24. For expenditure by Her Majesty's Treasury in connection with the sale of Ordinary shares in the British Petroleum Company plc -	1,000	24,999,000
25. For expenditure by the Department of Trade and Industry in connection with the sale of shares in British Telecommunications plc -	750,000	—
26. For expenditure by Her Majesty's Treasury in connection with the sale of Ordinary shares in Cable and Wireless plc -	1,000	12,599,000

* Deficit

	Supply Grants	Appropriations in Aid
	£	£
CLASS V		
Vote		
1. For Government investment in the British Steel Corporation and British Shipbuilders -	305,000,000	—
CLASS VI		
2. For expenditure by the Department of Transport on assistance to local transport; shipping; civil aviation; central administration; certain licensing and testing schemes including privatisation of vehicle testing; research and development; and certain other transport services including civil defence, a grant in aid and international subscriptions -	1,000	5,966,000
3. For expenditure by the Department of Transport on support to nationalised transport industries and assistance to local transport and ports - -	42,241,000	—
6. For expenditure by the Department of Transport in connection with the sales of shares in British Airways - - - -	50,000	—
CLASS VII		
1. For expenditure by the Department of the Environment on subsidies, the option mortgage scheme, improvements and investment, grants to housing associations and the Housing Corporation and sundry other housing services - -	183,842,000	—
CLASS VIII		
1 For expenditure by the Department of the Environment on assistance to the construction industry, other water supply, conservation and sewerage, local authority and other environmental services including recreation - -	894,000	—

2.	For expenditure by the Department of the Environment on other environmental services including grants in aid and international subscriptions, on grants in aid to the British Waterways Board and Development Fund, on bridgeworks, on certain categories of derelict land and on Civil Defence water services - -	500,000
3.	For expenditure by the Department of the Environment on town and country planning (including compensation), certain categories of derelict land, and other local services	20,020,000
4.	For expenditure by the Department of the Environment on royal palaces etc, royal parks etc, historic buildings, ancient monuments and certain public buildings, the national heritage, on grants in aid, other grants and on payments to Inland Revenue covering assets accepted in lieu of tax, and on the administration of those activities -	9,413,000
7.	For expenditure by the Department of the Environment on grants-in-aid to Urban Development Corporations - - - - -	28,179,000

CLASS IX

3.	For expenditure by the Departments of the Director of Public Prosecutions and the Treasury Solicitor on Crown Prosecutions and other legal services - -	1,000
6.	For expenditure by the Home Office on court services, compensation for criminal injuries, including a grant in aid, and probation and after-care - -	1,000
9.	For expenditure by the Home Office on police, fire, control of immigration and nationality, and of gaming and other protective services, and civil defence, including grants in aid and international subscriptions - - - -	1,000
10.	For expenditure by the Home Office on grants to local and police authorities and the Metropolitan Police Fund for police and community services and for police and fire services superannuation payments - - - -	1,000

Column totals at top of page: 142,000 and 127,000 and 700,000

	Supply Grants £	Appropriations in Aid £
CLASS IX—continued		
Vote		
12. For expenditure by the Departments of the Director of Public Prosecutions, the Law Officers and the Treasury Solicitor on central and certain other services -	161,000	*—142,000
14. For expenditure by the Northern Ireland Court Service on legal aid and court services	2,500,000	—
CLASS X		
2. For expenditure by the Department of Education and Science on the assisted places scheme, students' awards and in respect of compensation payments to redundant teachers and staff of certain institutions - - - - -	40,685,000	2,000
3. For expenditure by the Department of Education and Science on universities and certain other institutions, grants for higher and further education, grants in aid and a subscription to an international organisation - - - -	1,000	—
4. For expenditure by the Department of Education and Science and the University Grants Committee on administration - - - -	2,000	180,000
21. For certain grants and services for the benefit of the arts, for grants in aid to the Arts Council and certain other institutions and for a grant in aid to the National Heritage Memorial Fund and for payments to the Inland Revenue covering assets accepted in lieu of tax, and for expenditure on the Government Art Collection - -	2,411,000	—
23. For expenditure by the Office of Arts and Libraries on central administration - -	2,000	68,000

* Deficit.

CLASS XI

1. For expenditure by the Department of Health and Social Security on the provision of services under the national health service in England, on other health and personal social services including certain services in relation to the United Kingdom, and on research, exports, services for the disabled and certain other services; including grants in aid and international subscriptions -	14,681,000	1,000
2. For expenditure by the Department of Health and Social Security on the provision of services under the national health service in England, on other health and personal social services, on welfare food and certain other services including grants under Section 8 of the Industry Act 1972 -	9,308,000	175,711,000

CLASS XII

1. For expenditure by the Department of Health and Social Security on non-contributory retirement pensions, Christmas bonus payments to pensioners, pensions etc for disablement or death arising out of war or service in the armed forces after 2 September 1939 and on certain associated services, on attendance allowances, invalid care allowance, non-contributory invalidity pensions and mobility allowance, etc. -	—	35,000,000
2. For expenditure by the Department of Health and Social Security on supplementary pensions and allowances -	—	413,000,000
3. For expenditure by the Department of Health and Social Security on child benefit, one parent benefit, family income supplements and non-contributory maternity grants -	—	45,000,000
4. For expenditure by the Department of Health and Social Security for the payment of rate rebate, rent rebate and rent allowance subsidies to rating, housing and local authorities respectively and the additional costs incurred by these authorities in operating the housing benefit scheme -	—	169,000,000

Vote	Supply Grants £	Appropriations in Aid £
CLASS XIII		
1. For the expenditure of the House of Lords - - - -	311,000	32,000
2. For expenditure of the House of Commons on members' salaries, allowances, pensions, etc, financial assistance to opposition parties and a grant in aid - -	4,416,000	—
7. For the expenditure of the Inland Revenue Department on life assurance premium relief and mortgage interest relief - - - - -	10,000,000	—
8. For the expenditure of the Department of the Comptroller and Auditor General, including an international subscription - - -	1,000	238,000
12. For expenditure by the Management and Personnel Office on the central management of the Civil Service, on the Office of the Parliamentary Counsel and certain other services including grants in aid - - - -	1,000	85,000
16. For the expenditure of the Office of Population Censuses and Surveys, including a grant in aid - - - - -	1,000	330,000
18. For the expenditure of the Charity Commission for England and Wales - -	1,000	98,000
19. For the expenditure of the Cabinet Office, the Chancellor of the Duchy of Lancaster and grants in aid to international organisations - - - -	1,000	—
CLASS XIIIB		
1. For the expenditure of the National Audit Office - - -	238,000	—

Part II

CLASS XIV

2.	For expenditure by the Property Services Agency of the Department of the Environment on administration and certain other services - - - -	—	5,559,000

CLASS XV

1.	For expenditure by the Department of Agriculture and Fisheries for Scotland on price guarantees, production grants and subsidies, grants and loans for capital and other improvements, support for agriculture in special areas and certain other services including services relating to livestock diseases	—	8,935,000
2.	For expenditure by the Department of Agriculture and Fisheries for Scotland on educational, advisory, livestock services, plant health and pest control, assistance to marketing and processing, administration, land management and land settlement, the Royal Botanic and associated gardens, assistance to crofters, assistance to the Scottish fishing industry, protective and certain other services including research and development and special services -	—	1,000
5.	For expenditure by the Industry Department for Scotland on selective assistance to industry; on compensation to private industry and on state owned harbours -	*—3,180,000	4,280,000
8.	For expenditure by the Scottish Development Department on subsidies, the option mortgage scheme, improvements and investment, certain rent registration expenses, capital grants to housing associations, loans and grants to first-time purchasers and sundry other housing services - - -	—	23,695,000
9.	For expenditure by the Industry Department for Scotland on grants to New Town Development Corporations in connection with housing and other services -	—	1,498,000
10.	For expenditure by the Scottish Development Department in connection with water supply, sewerage, land drainage and flood protection, town and country planning (including compensation), recreation, land reclamation, coast protection, urban programme and other local environmental services -	—	482,000

* Deficit.

2 B

Vote	Supply Grants £	Appropriations in Aid £
CLASS XV—*continued*		
11. For expenditure by the Scottish Courts Administration on court services, the Scottish Law Commission and certain other legal services, including grants in aid -	1,000	249,000
14. For expenditure by the Scottish Home and Health Department on legal aid administration, certain services relating to crime, prisons, treatment of offenders, civil defence (including grants), and on fire and police services (excluding grants and superannuation), on the provision of services under the national health service, on other health services, on research, services for the disabled and certain other services including a grant in aid -	2,000	—
17. For expenditure by the National Library of Scotland, including a purchase grant in aid - - - -	57,000	*—65,000
20. For expenditure by the Scottish Home and Health Department on the provision of services under the national health service in Scotland, on welfare food and certain other services - - -	6,340,000	1,450,000
23. For the expenditure of the Department of the Registers of Scotland - -	1,000	674,000
CLASS XVI		
1. For expenditure by the Welsh Office on tourism; roads and certain associated services including road safety; housing subsidies and administration; historic buildings and ancient monuments, other environmental services; schools, higher and further education, grants in aid of the National Library of Wales and the National Museum of Wales, miscellaneous educational services and other arts; services under the national health service, other health and personal social services, services for the disabled; civil defence (including grants); grants in aid, other grants and certain other services including research - - -	10,450,000	951,000

* Deficit

	£	£
2. For expenditure by the Welsh Office on production grants and subsidies, grants and loans for capital and other improvements, support for agriculture in special areas, assistance to marketing and processing, animal health and support services, land drainage and certain other services - - - - -	4,295,000	150,000
3. For expenditure by the Welsh Office on selective assistance to industry in assisted areas, and special assistance to rural areas - - - -	2,531,000	—
5. For expenditure by the Welsh Office on assistance to marketing and processing, pest control, land management and smallholdings, research, support to the fishing industry, protective and other services to the fishing industry, special assistance for rural and highland areas, on the Welsh Development Agency and some special and other services including grants in aid - - -	1,000	—
8. For expenditure by the Welsh Office in connection with water supply, sewerage, town and country planning (including compensation), recreation, other local services, including clean air grants, coast protection, urban programme, schools, student awards, miscellaneous educational services, services under the national health service, on other health and personal social services, including welfare food -	7,162,000	580,000

CLASS XVII

	£	£
1. For expenditure by the Northern Ireland Office on crown prosecutions and other legal services, services related to crime, compensation schemes, prisons, probation, training schools and after-care etc, police, central and miscellaneous services, a grant in aid to the Police Complaints Board and to Co-operation North, and certain other grants - - - - - -	2,000	—
2. For expenditure by the Northern Ireland Office on a grant in aid of the Northern Ireland Consolidated Fund and other transfers - - -	1,000	—

CLASS XVIII

	Supply Grants	Appropriations in Aid
Vote	£	£
1. For rate support grants in England (including adjustments between England and Wales for pooled education expenditure) - - - - - -	1,000	—
2. For rate support grants for Wales - - - - - - -	2,000	545,000
10. For sums payable out of the Consolidated Fund to the National Insurance Fund -	22,000,000,000	—
11. For expenditure by the Department of Education and Science on superannuation allowances and gratuities, etc, in respect of teachers, and the widows, children and dependants of deceased teachers - - - - - - -	1,000	4,903,000
16. For transitional relief under the Finance Acts, 1965 and 1972, for companies with an overseas source of trading income - - - - - - - -	350,000	—
TOTAL, SUPPLEMENTARY 1983–84 -	£2,566,290,000	130,181,000

SCHEDULE (B).—PART 3

CLASS I

SCHEDULE OF SUMS granted, and of the sums which may be applied as appropriations in aid in addition thereto, to defray the charges of the several Services herein particularly mentioned, which will come in course of payment during the year ending on 31st March 1985, including provision for numbers of personnel as set out hereunder, viz.:—

	Sums not exceeding	
	Supply Grants £	Appropriations in Aid £
Vote 1. For expenditure by the Ministry of Defence on pay, allowances etc of the Armed Forces and their Reserves and Cadet Forces etc, (including provision for Naval Service to a number not exceeding 74,500, provision for Army Service to a number not exceeding 190,500, for the Individual Reserves to a number not exceeding 125,000, for the Territorial Army to a number not exceeding 86,000, for the Home Service Force to a number not exceeding 5,000, and for the Ulster Defence Regiment to a number not exceeding 12,600, and provision for Air Force Service to a number not exceeding 96,600, for RAF Reserves to a number not exceeding 11,675, and for the Royal Auxiliary Air Force to a number not exceeding 4,550); pay etc of Defence Ministers and of certain civilian staff employed by the Ministry of Defence; on movements; certain stores; supplies and services; plant and machinery; charter and contract repair of ships; certain research; lands and buildings; sundry grants; payments abroad including contributions and subscriptions to international organisations; and grants in aid (Revised sum) - - - - - - -	6,367,775,000	874,082,000

Class 1
1984-85

Vote		Sums not exceeding	
		Supply Grants £	Appropriations in Aid £
2.	For expenditure by the Procurement Executive of the Ministry of Defence in operating its Headquarters and Establishments and for its other common services; for research etc by contract; lands and buildings; for development by contract, production, repair etc and purchases for sale abroad of sea systems, land systems, air systems and associated equipment; for reservation of capacity in Royal Ordnance Factories; for certain contingent liabilities, and for sundry other Procurement Executive services including those on repayment terms to non-exchequer customers (Revised sum) -		8,078,907,000	613,477,000
3.	For expenditure by the Ministry of Defence on retired pay, pensions etc -		831,245,000	1,738,000
4.	For expenditure including loans by the Property Services Agency of the Department of the Environment on public building work and certain accommodation services etc for defence purposes (Revised sum) -		1,058,476,000	185,016,000
5.	For operating the Royal Dockyards (and certain tasks of the Portsmouth Fleet Maintenance Base) and for the repair of ships by contract including work undertaken on repayment terms for exchequer and non-exchequer customers (Revised sum) -		460,372,000	2,561,000
	TOTAL, CLASS I - £		16,796,775,000	1,676,874,000

Class II,
1984-85

SCHEDULE (B).—Part 4

Class II

Schedule of Sums granted, and of the sums which may be applied as appropriations in aid in addition thereto, to defray the charges of the several Services herein particularly mentioned, which will come in course of payment during the year ending on 31st March 1985, viz.:—

	Sums not exceeding	
Vote	Supply Grants £	Appropriations in Aid £
1. For expenditure by the Foreign and Commonwealth Office on the salaries, building and other accommodation services, and administration of Her Majesty's Diplomatic Service, official information services, military aid, certain grants in aid, and sundry other grants, services and loans (Revised sum) - - - - -	373,968,000	31,672,000
2. For expenditure by the Foreign and Commonwealth Office on grants and subscriptions, etc, to certain international organisations, special payments and assistance, and sundry other grants and services (Revised sum) - - - - -	74,960,000	2,631,000
3. For expenditure by the Foreign and Commonwealth Office on grants in aid of the British Broadcasting Corporation for external broadcasting and monitoring services (Revised sum) - - - - - - -	78,544,000	1,358,000
4. For expenditure by the Foreign and Commonwealth Office on a grant in aid of the British Council - - - - - - - - -	44,021,000	—
5. For a grant in aid of the Commonwealth War Graves Commission - - -	9,603,000	—

SCHEDULE (B).—PART 4—*continued*

Vote		Sums not exceeding	
		Supply Grants	Appropriations in Aid
		£	£
6.	For Her Majesty's foreign and other secret services - - - - -	76,000,000	—
7.	For expenditure by the Foreign and Commonwealth Office (Overseas Development Administration) on pensions and superannuation payments etc in respect of overseas service, pensions in respect of service with the Cotton Research Corporation and sundry other services and expenses - - - - - -	112,338,000	3,329,000
8.	For expenditure by the Foreign and Commonwealth Office (Overseas Development Administration) on the official United Kingdom aid programme including pensions and allowances in respect of overseas service, assistance to certain refugee students, grants in aid, certain subscriptions to international organisations and certain payments under the Commonwealth Scholarship and Fellowship Plan (Revised sum)	1,061,561,000	6,002,000
9.	For expenditure by the Foreign and Commonwealth Office (Overseas Development Administration) on administration - - - - - - - - -	25,920,000	80,000
	TOTAL, CLASS II - - - - - - - - - - £	1,856,915,000	45,072,000

SCHEDULE (B).—PART 5

CLASS III

SCHEDULE OF SUMS granted, and of the sums which may be applied as appropriations in aid in addition thereto, to defray the charges of the several Services herein particularly mentioned, which will come in course of payment during the year ending on 31st March 1985, viz.:—

Vote		Sums not exceeding	
		Supply Grants £	Appropriations in Aid £
1.	For expenditure by the Intervention Board for Agricultural Produce in giving effect in the United Kingdom to the agricultural support provisions of the Common Agricultural Policy of the European Community and to Community food aid measures and for certain other services - - - - - - -	326,822,000	163,026,000
2.	For expenditure by the Intervention Board for Agricultural Produce on central administration and miscellaneous services (including a Supplementary sum of £380,000)	19,481,000	432,000
3.	For expenditure by the Ministry of Agriculture, Fisheries and Food on market regulation and production support, grants and loans for capital and other improvements, support for agriculture in special areas, animal health, land drainage, flood protection and water supply, and certain other services - - - - - -	195,116,000	28,431,000
4.	For expenditure by the Ministry of Agriculture, Fisheries and Food on research and development, education and training services, botanical services, assistance to production, marketing and processing, support for the fishing industry, emergency and strategic food services, protective, agency and other services, including grants in aid and international subscriptions (including a Supplementary sum of £1,386,000) -	143,545,000	7,830,000

SCHEDULE (B).—PART 5—*continued*

Vote		Sums not exceeding	
		Supply Grants	Appropriations in Aid
		£	£
5.	For expenditure by the Ministry of Agriculture, Fisheries and Food on departmental research, advisory services and administration and certain other services (Revised sum) - - - - - - - - - - -	199,522,000	9,376,000
6.	For a grant in aid of the Forestry Fund (Revised sum) - - - - - - - - - -	55,194,000	—
	TOTAL, CLASS III - - - - - - -£	939,680,000	209,095,000

SCHEDULE (B).—PART 6

Class IV

SCHEDULE OF SUMS granted, and of the sums which may be applied as appropriations in aid in addition thereto, to defray the charges of the several Services herein particularly mentioned, which will come in course of payment during the year ending on 31st March 1985, viz.:—

Vote		Sums not exceeding	
		Supply Grants £	Appropriations in Aid £
1.	For expenditure by the Department of Trade and Industry on regional development grants, selective assistance to industry, certain other services including U.K. contributions to the funding of buffer stock operations of international commodity agreements and a strategic mineral stockpile (Revised sum) - - - -	565,107,000	23,879,000
2.	For expenditure by the Department of Trade and Industry on provision of land and buildings, inward investment promotion, other support services, promotion of tourism and standards, including grants in aid - - - - - -	85,728,000	200,000
3.	For expenditure by the Department of Energy on assistance to the coal industry including grants to the National Coal Board and payments to redundant workers (including a Supplementary sum of £393,562,000) - - - -	1,303,887,000	23,000,000
4.	For expenditure by the Department of Trade and Industry on export promotion, trade co-operation, protection of innovation, regulation of trading practices and consumer protection, radio regulation, standards, and other services including grants in aid and international subscriptions, and other grants (Revised sum) -	49,290,000	82,913,000

SCHEDULE (B).—PART 6—*continued*

Vote		Sums not exceeding	
		Supply Grants £	Appropriations in Aid £
5.	For expenditure by the Department of Energy in connection with the energy industries including related research and development, selective assistance to industry, energy efficiency, oil storage, and certain other services including grants in aid and an international subscription - - - -	97,869,000	20,020,000
6.	For expenditure by the Department of Trade and Industry on the Department's research establishments; industrial research and development and other support; general research and development on civil aeronautics and aeroengines and associated equipment; national and international space technology programmes; standards; loans, grants in aid, international subscriptions and certain other grants (Revised sum) - - - - -	378,178,000	25,097,000
7.	For expenditure by the Department of Energy in connection with nuclear energy including a grant in aid to the United Kingdom Atomic Energy Authority, subscriptions and contributions to international organisations and projects, grants in aid, loans, guarantees, and for sundry other services (Revised sum) -	199,954,000	—
8.	For expenditure by the Department of Trade and Industry on support for the aerospace, shipbuilding, steel and vehicle manufacturing industries, including loans, grants, and the purchase of assets, and assistance to redundant steel workers (including a Supplementary sum of £72,000,000) - - - -	193,943,000	32,212,000
9.	For expenditure by the Export Credits Guarantee Department on administration -	26,269,000	203,000

10. For expenditure by the Export Credits Guarantee Department in connection with export credits guarantees including an international subscription, special guarantees, refinancing and financing arrangements made for facilitating trade with other countries and assistance towards the cost of financing export credits, the purchase of securities, overseas investment insurance and cost escalation guarantees - - -	451,316,000	509,252,000
11. For expenditure by the Registry of Friendly Societies - - -	2,197,000	356,000
12. For expenditure by the Office of Fair Trading - - - -	7,204,000	—
13. For expenditure by the Department of Employment on general labour market services, on services for seriously disabled people and on an international subscription (Revised sum) - - - - -	692,622,000	1,000
14. For expenditure by the Department of Employment on demand determined measures to promote and preserve employment opportunities, compensation to persons for certain dismissals, payments towards expenses of trade union ballots and compensation for persons disabled by pneumoconiosis, byssinosis and diffuse mesothelioma - - - -	387,618,000	25,000
15. For expenditure by the Department of Employment on a grant in aid to the Advisory, Conciliation and Arbitration Service - - - -	13,180,000	—
16. For expenditure by the Department of Employment on a grant in aid to the Manpower Services Commission (Revised sum) - - - -	1,212,879,000	222,588,000
17. For expenditure by the Department of Employment on the administration of benefit services and on central and miscellaneous services (Revised sum) - - -	232,298,000	72,917,000
18. For expenditure by the Department of Trade and Industry on central and miscellaneous services, on services provided by the Ministry of Defence (Procurement Executive) Headquarters, on international subscriptions, on British Telecommunications Civil Defence, on the fund for sub-postmasters and on setting up costs of the Office of Telecommunications (Revised sum) - - - -	140,545,000	5,243,000

SCHEDULE (B).—PART 6—*continued*

Vote		Sums not exceeding	
		Supply Grants	Appropriations in Aid
		£	£
19.	For expenditure by the Department of Energy on salaries and other services - -	22,348,000	4,477,000
20.	For refunds and repayments of petroleum licensing proceeds, and other payments in connection with such proceeds, to be made by the Department of Energy out of income received from application fees; from annual and other payments for exploration, production, mining and methane drainage licences; from royalty; and from the disposal of petroleum taken as royalty in kind - - -	1,000	332,590,000
21.	For expenditure by the Department of Energy to meet expenses incurred in transferring to the private sector oil interests of the British Gas Corporation (BGC) -	1,000	799,000
22.	For expenditure by the Department of Employment as a grant in aid to the Health and Safety Commission (Revised sum) - - - -	90,298,000	—
23.	For Government investment in the British Steel Corporation and British Shipbuilders (including a Supplementary sum of £45,000,000) - - - -	626,000,000	—
24.	For expenditure by the Department of Trade and Industry in connection with the sale of shares in British Telecommunications plc - - - -	1,000	1,276,000
25.	For remanet expenditure by Her Majesty's Treasury in connection with the sale in 1983–84 of ordinary shares in the British Petroleum Company plc- - -	1,242,000	—

26. For remanet expenditure by Her Majesty's Treasury in connection with the sale in 1983–84 of ordinary shares in Cable and Wireless plc - - - - -	536,000	—
27. For expenditure by the Office of Telecommunications - - - -	1,000	2,529,000
TOTAL, CLASS IV - - - - - - - - -£	6,780,512,000	1,359,577,000

SCHEDULE (B).—PART 7

CLASS V

SCHEDULE OF SUMS granted, and of the sums which may be applied as appropriations in aid in addition thereto, to defray the charges of the several Services herein particularly mentioned, which will come in course of payment during the year ending on 31st March 1985, viz.:—

Vote		Sums not exceeding	
		Supply Grants	Appropriations in Aid
		£	£
1.	For expenditure of the British Museum including a purchase grant in aid	12,865,000	—
2.	For expenditure of the Imperial War Museum including a purchase grant in aid	4,383,000	—
3.	For expenditure of the National Gallery including a purchase grant in aid	7,024,000	—
4.	For the expenditure of the National Maritime Museum including a purchase grant in aid	4,304,000	—
5.	For the expenditure of the National Portrait Gallery including a purchase grant in aid	1,866,000	—
6.	For the expenditure of the Science Museum including purchase grants in aid	8,492,000	—
7.	For the expenditure of the Tate Gallery including a purchase grant in aid	5,595,000	—
8.	For the expenditure of the Victoria and Albert Museum including purchase grants in aid	11,397,000	—

9. For the expenditure of the Wallace Collection - - - - - - -	823,000	—
10. For certain grants and services for the benefit of the arts, for grants in aid to the Arts Council and certain other institutions, payments in respect of Public Lending Right, for a grant in aid to the National Heritage Memorial Fund and for payments to the Inland Revenue covering assets accepted in lieu of tax, and for expenditure on the Government Art Collection - - - - - -	123,900,000	5,000
11. For grants in aid to the British Library and certain other institutions and for the expenses of the Royal Commission on Historical Manuscripts - - -	47,300,000	—
12. For expenditure by the Office of Arts and Libraries on administration - -	1,049,000	1,000
TOTAL, CLASS V - - - - - - - - -£	228,998,000	6,000

SCHEDULE (B).—PART 8

CLASS VI

Class VI,
1984–85.

SCHEDULE OF SUMS granted, and of the sums which may be applied as appropriations in aid in addition thereto, to defray the charges of the several Services herein particularly mentioned, which will come in course of payment during the year ending on 31st March 1985, viz.:—

	Sums not exceeding	
	Supply Grants	Appropriations in Aid
	£	£
Vote		
1. For expenditure by the Department of Transport on roads and certain associated services including lighting and road safety, including a grant in aid, and certain grants - - - - - -	806,788,000	18,050,000
2. For expenditure by the Department of Transport on assistance to local transport; shipping; civil aviation; central administration; certain licensing and testing schemes; research and development; and certain other transport services including civil defence; a grant in aid and international subscriptions (Revised sum) -	145,628,000	88,167,000
3. For expenditure by the Department of Transport on support to nationalised transport industries and assistance to local transport and ports (Revised sum) - -	1,130,102,000	303,000
4. For expenditure by the Department of Transport in connection with driver and motor vehicle registration and licensing and the collection of revenue (Revised sum) -	100,462,000	5,536,000
5. For expenditure by the Department of Transport in connection with the sale of shares in Associated British Ports (Revised sum) - - - - - -	114,000	2,750,000

6. For expenditure by the Department of Transport in connection with the sale of shares in British Airways (Supplementary sum) - - - - - - - - - - - - - - -	250,000	—
TOTAL, CLASS VI - - - - - - - -£	2,183,344,000	114,806,000

Class **VII**,
1984–85.

SCHEDULE (B).—PART 9

Class VII

SCHEDULE OF SUMS granted, and of the sums which may be applied as appropriations in aid in addition thereto, to defray the charges of the several Services herein particularly mentioned, which will come in course of payment during the year ending on 31st March 1985, viz.:—

	Sums not exceeding	
	Supply Grants	Appropriations in Aid
	£	£
Vote 1. For expenditure by the Department of the Environment on subsidies, the option mortgage scheme, improvements and investment, grants to housing associations and the Housing Corporation and sundry other housing services (including a Supplementary sum of £184,000,000) - - - - - - - - - - -	1,837,216,000	—
TOTAL, CLASS VII - - - - - - -£	1,837,216,000	—

Class VIII,
1984–85.

SCHEDULE (B).—PART 10

CLASS VIII

SCHEDULE OF SUMS granted, and of the sums which may be applied as appropriations in aid in addition thereto, to defray the charges of the several Services herein particularly mentioned, which will come in course of payment during the year ending on 31st March 1985, viz.:—

Vote		Sums not exceeding	
		Supply Grants £	Appropriations in Aid £
1.	For expenditure by the Department of the Environment on assistance to the construction industry, other water supply, conservation and sewerage, local authority and other environmental services including recreation - - - -	32,515,000	—
2.	For expenditure by the Department of the Environment on other environmental services including grants in aid and international subscriptions, on grants in aid to the British Waterways Board and Development Commission, on bridgeworks and on developing Civil Defence water supply services (Revised sum) - -	126,887,000	19,000
3.	For expenditure by the Department of the Environment on town and country planning (including compensation), derelict land reclamation and other local services - -	77,975,000	—
4.	For expenditure by the Department of the Environment on royal palaces, etc, royal parks, etc, historic buildings, ancient monuments and certain public buildings, the national heritage, on grants in aid, other grants and on payments to Inland Revenue covering assets accepted in lieu of tax, and on the administration of those activities (Revised sum) - - - - - - - - -	92,641,000	8,834,000

SCHEDULE (B).—PART 10—*continued*

| | Sums not exceeding | |
	Supply Grants	Appropriations in Aid
	£	£
Vote		
5. For expenditure by the Department of the Environment on housing administration; central administration including royal commissions, committees etc; privatisation of hydraulics research station; the audit commission; payments in connection with licence fees; building construction and civil engineering research and environmental research and surveys (Revised sum) - - - - - -	171,995,000	21,576,000
6. For expenditure by the Department of the Environment on the urban programme -	150,000,000	—
7. For expenditure by the Department of the Environment on grants in aid to Urban Development Corporations - - - - - - - - -	74,862,000	—
TOTAL, CLASS VIII - - - - - - - - - -£	726,875,000	30,429,000

Class IX,
1984–85.

SCHEDULE (B).—PART 11

CLASS IX

SCHEDULE OF SUMS granted, and of the sums which may be applied as appropriations in aid in addition thereto, to defray the charges of the several Services herein particularly mentioned, which will come in course of payment during the year ending on 31st March 1985, viz.:—

	Sums not exceeding	
Vote	Supply Grants £	Appropriations in Aid £
1. For expenditure by the Lord Chancellor's Department on court services, the Law Commission, Legal Aid Administration, the Public Trustee Office and certain other legal services (Revised sum) - - - - -	85,640,000	105,417,000
2. For expenditure by the Northern Ireland Court Service on court services, certain other legal services including a grant in aid, accommodation services, and legal aid administration in Northern Ireland - - - -	7,639,000	3,283,000
3. For expenditure by the Departments of the Director of Public Prosecutions, and the Treasury Solicitor on Crown prosecutions and other legal services - -	6,621,000	635,000
4. For grants to the Legal Aid Fund and for expenditure by the Lord Chancellor's Department on legal aid in criminal cases, court services, and costs paid from central funds - - - - -	356,581,000	5,400,000
5. For expenditure by the Crown Office on crown prosecutions and certain other legal services - - - - - - -	2,872,000	3,000

SCHEDULE (B).—PART 11—*continued*

Vote		Sums not exceeding	
		Supply Grants £	Appropriations in Aid £
6.	For expenditure by the Home Office on court services, compensation for criminal injuries, including a grant-in-aid, probation, police, community services, and superannuation payments for police and fire services	1,612,826,000	8,904,000
7.	For expenditure by the Home Office on court services, other services related to crime, probation and aftercare, police, fire, civil defence, control of immigration and nationality, issue of passports etc, other protective services and community services and other miscellaneous services including grants in aid and international subscriptions; and on administrative and operational staff (excluding prisons) and central services (Revised sum)	304,452,000	77,489,000
8.	For expenditure by the Home Office on prisons (including central administrative staff) and associated stores in England and Wales, and the Parole Board (Revised sum)	584,940,000	34,956,000
9.	For expenditure by the Departments of the Director of Public Prosecutions, the Law Officers and the Treasury Solicitor on central and certain other services (Revised sum)	12,062,000	888,000
10.	For expenditure by the Lord Advocate's Departments on central and miscellaneous services including grants in aid	13,168,000	51,000
11.	For expenditure by the Northern Ireland Court Service on legal aid and court services	6,442,000	—
	TOTAL, CLASS IX —£	2,993,243,000	237,026,000

SCHEDULE (B).—PART 12

CLASS X

SCHEDULE OF SUMS granted, and of the sums which may be applied as appropriations in aid in addition thereto, to defray the charges of the several Services herein particularly mentioned, which will come in course of payment during the year ending on 31st March 1985, viz.:—

Vote	Sums not exceeding		Appropriations in Aid
	Supply Grants		
	£		£
1. For expenditure by the Department of Education and Science on schools, further education, teacher training, adult education, miscellaneous educational services and research, including grants in aid and international subscriptions - - -	190,239,000		5,360,000
2. For expenditure by the Department of Education and Science on the assisted places scheme, student awards and compensation payments to redundant teachers and staff of certain institutions - - - - - -	668,386,000		13,000
3. For expenditure by the Department of Education and Science on universities and certain other institutions, grants for higher and further education, grants in aid and a subscription to an international organisation - - - - - -	1,463,239,000		1,388,000
4. For expenditure by the Department of Education and Science and the University Grants Committee on administration (Revised sum) - - - - - -	49,991,000		2,298,000
5. For a grant in aid of the Agricultural and Food Research Council - - -	46,538,000		—

SCHEDULE (B).—Part 12—*continued*

Vote		Sums not exceeding	
		Supply Grants	Appropriations in Aid
		£	£
6.	For grants in aid of the Medical Research Council including subscriptions to certain international organisations - - - - -	117,152,000	—
7.	For a grant in aid of the Natural Environment Research Council - - - -	65,853,000	—
8.	For grants in aid of the Science and Engineering Research Council including subscriptions to certain international organisations - - - - -	278,827,000	—
9.	For a grant in aid of the Economic and Social Research Council - - - -	21,979,000	—
10.	For the expenditure of the British Museum (Natural History), including a purchase grant in aid - - - - - - -	9,751,000	—
11.	For grants in aid of the Royal Society and the Fellowship of Engineering - - - -	5,461,000	—
	Total, Class X	£2,917,416,000	9,059,000

SCHEDULE (B).—PART 13

CLASS XI

Class XI,
1984–85.

SCHEDULE OF SUMS granted, and of the sums which may be applied as appropriations in aid in addition thereto, to defray the charges of the several Services herein particularly mentioned, which will come in course of payment during the year ending on 31st March 1985, viz.:—

	Sums not exceeding	
	Supply Grants £	Appropriations in Aid £
Vote		
1. For expenditure by the Department of Health and Social Security on the provision of services under the national health service in England, on other health and personal social services including certain services in relation to the United Kingdom, and on research, exports, services for the disabled and certain other services; including grants in aid and international subscriptions (Revised sum) - - -	8,839,637,000	1,377,941,000
2. For expenditure by the Department of Health and Social Security on the provision of services under the national health service in England, on other health and personal social services, on welfare food and certain other services including grants under Section 8 of the Industry Act 1972 (Revised sum) - - - - - - -	2,661,661,000	333,538,000
TOTAL, CLASS XI - - - - - - - - - -£	11,501,298,000	1,711,479,000

Class XII,
1984–85.

SCHEDULE (B).—PART 14

CLASS XII

SCHEDULE OF SUMS granted, and of the sums which may be applied as appropriations in aid in addition thereto, to defray the charges of the several Services herein particularly mentioned, which will come in course of payment during the year ending on 31st March 1985, viz.:—

Vote		Sums not exceeding	
		Supply Grants £	Appropriations in Aid £
1.	For expenditure by the Department of Health and Social Security on non-contributory retirement pensions, Christmas bonus payments to pensioners, pensions etc for disablement or death arising out of war or service in the armed forces after 2 September 1939 and on certain associated services, on attendance allowances, invalid care allowance, non-contributory invalidity pensions and severe disablement allowance, and mobility allowance - - - - -	1,727,000,000	—
2.	For expenditure by the Department of Health and Social Security on supplementary pensions and allowances - - - - - -	6,157,000,000	96,000,000
3.	For expenditure by the Department of Health and Social Security on child benefit, one parent benefit, family income supplements and non-contributory maternity grants	4,562,000,000	—
4.	For expenditure by the Department of Health and Social Security for the payment of rate rebate, rent rebate and rent allowance subsidies, to rating, housing and local authorities respectively and subsidies towards the administrative costs incurred by these authorities in operating the housing benefit scheme and development costs incurred in 1982–83 and claimed in 1983–84 but not paid until 1984–85 -	3,725,700,000	—

5. For expenditure by the Department of Health and Social Security on administration and certain other services including an international subscription (Revised sum) -	720,107,000	561,526,000
Total, Class XII - · · · · · · · -£	16,891,807,000	657,526,000

SCHEDULE (B).—PART 15

CLASS XIII

SCHEDULE OF SUMS granted, and of the sums which may be applied as appropriations in aid in addition thereto, to defray the charges of the several Services herein particularly mentioned, which will come in course of payment during the year ending on 31st March 1985, viz.:—

	Sums not exceeding		Class XIII, 1984–85.
	Supply Grants	Appropriations in Aid	
	£	£	
Vote			
1. For the expenditure of the House of Lords - - - - -	8,700,000	232,000	
2. For the expenditure of the House of Commons on members' salaries, allowances, pensions, etc, financial assistance to opposition parties and a grant in aid -	30,084,000	—	
3. For the expenditure of the Department of Her Majesty's Most Honourable Privy Council - - - - - - -	1,130,000	15,000	
4. For expenditure by the Treasury on the management of the economy, and for certain other services including grants in aid to certain parliamentary bodies and others (Revised sum) - - - - - - - - -	43,370,000	2,486,000	
5. For expenditure by the Customs and Excise Department including the expenses of value added tax tribunals and an international subscription (Revised sum) -	342,202,000	7,823,000	
6. For the expenditure of the Inland Revenue Department (Revised sum) - -	793,529,000	41,610,000	

7. For the expenditure of the Inland Revenue Department on life assurance premium relief and mortgage interest relief (Revised sum)	92,000,000	—
8. For the expenditure of the Department of the Comptroller and Auditor General	7,206,000	—
9. For the expenditure of the National Debt Office, Pensions Commutation Board and Public Works Loan Commission	1,000	1,015,000
10. For the expenditure of the Department for National Savings (Revised sum)	148,972,000	1,350,000
11. For expenditure by the Treasury in connection with the manufacture, storage and distribution of coinage for use in the United Kingdom	22,000,000	1,914,000
12. For the expenditure by the Management and Personnel Office on the central management of the civil service, on the Office of the Parliamentary Counsel, and certain other services, including grants in aid	34,649,000	527,000
13. For expenditure by the Central Computer and Telecommunications Agency (Treasury) in connection with computers and general telecommunications including an international subscription	16,660,000	19,961,000
14. For the expenditure of the Civil Service Catering Organisation (Treasury) in connection with the provision of catering services	211,000	1,558,000
15. For the expenditure of the Public Record Office	9,355,000	438,000
16. For the expenditure of the Office of Population Censuses and Surveys, including a grant in aid	25,805,000	7,117,000
17. For the expenditure of the Land Registry (Revised sum)	79,292,000	82,000
18. For the expenditure of the Charity Commission for England and Wales	4,762,000	110,000

SCHEDULE (B).—PART 15—*continued*

Vote		Sums not exceeding	
		Supply Grants	Appropriations in Aid
		£	£
19.	For the expenditure of the Cabinet Office, the Chancellor of the Duchy of Lancaster and grants in aid to international organisations - -	14,870,000	5,382,000
20.	For the expenditure of the Office of the Parliamentary Commissioner for Administration and the Health Service Commissioners for England, Scotland and Wales, including an international subscription - - - - - -	1,855,000	—
21.	For expenditure by the Controller of Her Majesty's Stationery Office to compensate the HMSO Trading Fund for the provision of reports of parliamentary debates at less than full cost, and for the price concessions to public libraries -	6,509,000	—
22.	For expenditure by the Controller of Her Majesty's Stationery Office on the reimbursement of the HMSO trading fund in respect of stationery and printing supplied to the Houses of Parliament and to United Kingdom members of the European Assembly - - - - - - - - - -	10,756,000	122,000
23.	For expenditure by the Ordnance Survey on the survey of Great Britain and other mapping services (Revised sum) - - - - - - - -	16,519,000	27,872,000
24.	To repay to the Contingencies Fund certain miscellaneous advances - - -	350,000	—
	TOTAL, CLASS XIII -	£ 1,710,787,000	119,614,000

SCHEDULE (B).—Part 16

Class XIIIA

Schedule of Sums granted, and of the sums which may be applied as appropriations in aid in addition thereto, to defray the charges of the several Services herein particularly mentioned, which will come in course of payment during the year ending on 31st March 1985, viz.:—

	Sums not exceeding	
	Supply Grants	Appropriations in Aid
	£	£
Vote 1. For the expenditure of the House of Commons Commission	17,394,000	145,000
Total, Class XIIIA - £	17,394,000	145,000

Class XIIIB,
1984-85.

SCHEDULE (B).—PART 17

CLASS XIIIB

SCHEDULE OF SUMS granted, and of the sums which may be applied as appropriations in aid in addition thereto, to defray the charges of the several Services herein particularly mentioned, which will come in course of payment during the year ending on 31st March 1985, viz.:—

	Sums not exceeding	
	Supply Grants	Appropriations in Aid
	£	£
Vote 1. For the expenditure of the National Audit Office including an international subscription - - - - - - - - - - - - -	10,099,000	2,567,000
TOTAL, CLASS XIIIB - - - - - - - - -£	10,099,000	2,567,000

Class XIV,
1984-85.

SCHEDULE (B).—PART 18

CLASS XIV

SCHEDULE OF SUMS granted, and of the sums which may be applied as appropriations in aid in addition thereto, to defray the charges of the several Services herein particularly mentioned, which will come in course of payment during the year ending on 31st March 1985, viz.:—

	Sums not exceeding	
	Supply Grants	Appropriations in Aid
Vote	£	£
1. For expenditure (partly recoverable), including loans, by the Property Services Agency of the Department of the Environment on acquisitions, public building work and accommodation services, etc, for civil purposes in the United Kingdom (Revised sum) - - - - - -	531,981,000	61,311,000
2. For expenditure by the Property Services Agency of the Department of the Environment on administration and certain other services (Revised sum) - -	351,630,000	11,000,000
3. For expenditure by the Central Office of Information on home and overseas publicity	67,750,000	—
4. For expenditure by the Paymaster General's Office on the superannuation of civil servants, pensions, etc, in respect of former members of the Royal Irish Constabulary and other pensions and non-recurrent payments; and for certain other services -	1,139,835,000	75,000,000
5. For rates and contributions in lieu of rates paid by the Rating of Government Property Department in respect of property occupied by the Crown and premises occupied by representatives of commonwealth and foreign countries and international **organisations** - - - - - - -	92,300,000	264,300,000

2 C 2

SCHEDULE (B).—PART 18—*continued*

	Sums not exceeding	
	Supply Grants	Appropriations in Aid
	£	£
Vote		
6. For the expenditure of the Department of the Government Actuary (Revised sum)	1,145,000	536,000
7. For expenditure by the Paymaster General's Office	11,896,000	400,000
TOTAL, CLASS XIV　　-£	2,196,537,000	412,547,000

SCHEDULE (B).—PART 19

CLASS XV

SCHEDULE OF SUMS granted, and of the sums which may be applied as appropriations in aid in addition thereto, to defray the charges of the several Services herein particularly mentioned, which will come in course of payment during the year ending on 31st March 1985, viz.:—

	Sums not exceeding	
Vote	Supply Grants £	Appropriations in Aid £
1. For expenditure by the Department of Agriculture and Fisheries for Scotland on price guarantees, production grants and subsidies, grants and loans for capital and other improvements, support for agriculture in special areas and certain other services including services relating to livestock diseases - - - - -	57,465,000	15,107,000
2. For expenditure by the Department of Agriculture and Fisheries for Scotland on educational, advisory services, botanical services, assistance to marketing and processing, administration, land management and land settlement, livestock services, assistance to crofters, assistance to the Scottish fishing industry, protective and certain other services including research and development and special services -	61,235,000	5,276,000
3. For expenditure by the Industry Department for Scotland on grants in aid to the Scottish Development Agency and to the Highlands and Islands Development Board; on the promotion of tourism, including a grant in aid; on financial assistance to nationalised industries; on employment services in Scotland; on consumer protection, and on sundry other services in connection with trade and industry -	138,362,000	2,451,000

SCHEDULE (B).—PART 19—*continued*

Vote		Sums not exceeding	
		Supply Grants	Appropriations in Aid
		£	£
4.	For expenditure by the Industry Department for Scotland on a contribution to the Department of Employment towards the grant in aid to the Manpower Services Commission in relation to activities in Scotland (Revised sum) - - -	138,134,000	—
5.	For expenditure by the Industry Department for Scotland on selective assistance to industry; on compensation to private industry and on state owned harbours -	28,060,000	3,094,000
6.	For expenditure by the Scottish Development Department in connection with acquisition of land and related services, on roads and certain associated services, including lighting and road safety, on assistance to local transport, on support for transport services in the Highlands and Islands, piers and harbours and on certain other transport services and grants, on housing subsidies, Royal Palaces and Royal Parks, historic buildings and ancient monuments, other central environmental services and grants in aid - - - - - - -	144,986,000	5,224,000
7.	For expenditure by the Scottish Development Department on assistance to local transport, and on piers and harbours - - - - -	9,362,000	58,000
8.	For expenditure by the Scottish Development Department on subsidies, the option mortgage scheme, improvements and investment, certain rent registration expenses, capital grants to housing associations, loans and grants to first time purchasers and sundry other housing services - - - - - -	232,098,000	1,000
9.	For expenditure by the Industry Department for Scotland on grants to New Town Development Corporations in connection with housing and other services - -	40,448,000	—

No.	For expenditure		
10.	For expenditure by the Scottish Development Department in connection with water supply and sewerage, land drainage and flood protection, town and country planning (including compensation), recreation, land reclamation, coast protection, urban programme and other local environmental services - - -	37,138,000	—
11.	For expenditure by the Scottish Courts Administration on court services, the Scottish Law Commission and certain other legal services, including a grant in aid -	7,660,000	5,650,000
12.	For expenditure by the Scottish Home and Health Department on legal aid and criminal injuries compensation (excluding administration), on police and fire services superannuation and police grant - - - -	174,940,000	940,000
13.	For expenditure by the Scottish Courts Administration on costs and fees in connection with legal proceedings - - - -	2,150,000	—
14.	For expenditure by the Scottish Home and Health Department on legal aid administration, certain services relating to crime, prisons, treatment of offenders, civil defence (including grants) and on fire and police services (excluding grants and superannuation), on the provision of services under the national health service, on other health services, on research, services for the disabled and certain other services including a grant in aid (Revised sum) - - -	1,424,657,000	140,197,000
15.	For expenditure by the Scottish Education Department on schools, and certain grants to local authorities, higher and further education, libraries, miscellaneous educational services including compensation payments for redundant staff at colleges of education, research and administration, the Royal Scottish Museum, certain grants for the arts, including purchase grants in aid, sport, social work and other grants in aid - - - -	118,821,000	10,000
16.	For expenditure by the Scottish Education Department on awards to students receiving higher and further education - - -	106,900,000	—

2 C 4

SCHEDULE (B).—PART 19 *continued*

Vote		Sums not exceeding	
		Supply Grants	Appropriations in Aid
		£	£
17.	For expenditure by the National Library of Scotland, including a purchase grant in aid	3,121,000	144,000
18.	For the expenditure of the National Gallery of Scotland, the Scottish National Gallery of Modern Art, the Scottish National Portrait Gallery and the Department of Prints and Drawings, including purchase grants in aid	2,809,000	—
19.	For the expenditure of the National Museum of Antiquities of Scotland, including a purchase grant in aid	922,000	—
20.	For expenditure by the Scottish Home and Health Department on the provision of services under the National Health Service in Scotland, on welfare food and certain other services (Revised sum)	319,730,000	34,881,000
21.	For the expenditure of the Scottish Record Office and on certain other services including a grant in aid	1,655,000	313,000
22.	For the expenditure of the General Register Office for Scotland	2,925,000	789,000
23.	For the expenditure of the Department of the Registers of Scotland	1,000	9,019,000
24.	For expenditure by the Scottish Office on administration, Royal Commissions and certain other services (Revised sum)	97,272,000	3,319,000
	TOTAL, CLASS XV -£	3,150,851,000	226,473,000

Class XVI,
1984-85.

SCHEDULE (B).—PART 20

CLASS XVI

SCHEDULE OF SUMS granted, and of the sums which may be applied as appropriations in aid in addition thereto, to defray the charges of the several Services herein particularly mentioned, which will come in course of payment during the year ending on 31st March 1985, viz.:—

	Sums not exceeding	
	Supply Grants	Appropriations in Aid
	£	£
Vote		
1. For expenditure by the Welsh Office on civil defence (including grants); tourism; roads and certain associated services including road safety; housing administration; historic buildings and ancient monuments; other environmental services; education grants; libraries and museums; services under the national health service; other health and personal social services; grants in aid, other grants and certain other services including research (Revised sum) -	743,978,000	69,895,000
2. For expenditure by the Welsh Office on market regulation and production support, grants and loans for capital and other improvements, support for agriculture in special areas, animal health and support services, land drainage, flood protection and certain other services - - - - - - - -	43,066,000	9,562,000
3. For expenditure by the Welsh Office on selective assistance to industry in assisted areas, and special assistance to rural areas - - - - - - - -	13,881,000	4,900,000
4. For expenditure by the Welsh Office on a contribution to the Department of Employment towards the grant in aid to the Manpower Services Commission in relation to activities in Wales (Revised sum) - - - - - - -	81,378,000	—

SCHEDULE (B).—PART 20—*continued*

	Sums not exceeding	
	Supply Grants £	Appropriations in Aid £
Vote		
5. For expenditure by the Welsh Office on other assistance to agricultural production, food processing and marketing, certain other services including research, land management, assistance to the Welsh fishing industry including protective and other services, special assistance for rural and highland areas, on the Welsh Development Agency and some special and other services including grants in aid -	48,979,000	19,000
6. For expenditure by the Welsh Office on subsidies, the option mortgage scheme, improvements, investment, grants to housing associations, and sundry other housing services - - - - -	104,267,000	—
7. For expenditure by the Welsh Office on central administration and certain other services (Revised sum) - - - -	31,723,000	1,193,000
8. For expenditure by the Welsh Office in connection with water supply, sewerage, town and country planning (including compensation), recreation, other local services including clean air grants, coast protection, urban programme, services under the national health service, on other health and personal social services, including welfare food (Revised sum) - - - - - - -	195,396,000	20,868,000
Total, Class XVI - - - £	1,262,668,000	106,437,000

Class XVII,
1984-85.

SCHEDULE (B).—PART 21

CLASS XVII

SCHEDULE OF SUMS granted, and of the sums which may be applied as appropriations in aid in addition thereto, to defray the charges of the several Services herein particularly mentioned, which will come in course of payment during the year ending on 31st March 1985, viz.:—

	Sums not exceeding	
	Supply Grants	Appropriations in Aid
	£	£
Vote 1. For expenditure by the Northern Ireland Office on crown prosecutions and other legal services, services related to crime, compensation schemes, prisons, probation, training schools and after-care, etc., police, central and miscellaneous services, a grant in aid to the Police Complaints Board and Co-operation North and certain other grants (Revised sum) - - - - - - -	403,051,000	3,200,000
2. For expenditure by the Northern Ireland Office on a grant in aid of the Northern Ireland Consolidated Fund and other transfers - - - - - - - -	815,000,000	—
TOTAL, CLASS XVII - - - - -£	1,218,051,000	3,200,000

SCHEDULE (B).—PART 22

CLASS XVIII

SCHEDULE OF SUMS granted, and of the sums which may be applied as appropriations in aid in addition thereto, to defray the charges of the several Services herein particularly mentioned, which will come in course of payment during the year ending on 31st March 1985, viz.:—

	Sums not exceeding	
	Supply Grants	Appropriations in Aid
	£	£
Vote		
1. For rate support grants in England (including adjustments between England and Wales for pooled education expenditure) (Revised sum) - - - -	8,848,000,000	—
2. For rate support grants for Wales (Revised sum) - - -	803,350,000	—
3. For national parks supplementary grants to county councils in Wales - - -	5,500,000	—
4. For national parks supplementary grants to county councils in Wales - - -	1,900,000	—
5. For rate support grants in Scotland - - - - - -	1,713,200,000	—
6. For rate rebates and domestic rate relief grants to local authorities in England and for additional rate support grants and payments of compensation for loss of rates to local authorities in England and Wales (including a Supplementary sum of £11,540,000) - - - - -	89,075,000	—
7. For rate rebate grants in Wales - - - - -	4,700,000	—

8. For rate rebate grants to local authorities in Scotland - - -	10,160,000	—
9. For expenditure by the Home Office on grants to the British Broadcasting Corporation for home broadcasting and sundry other services	779,700,000	—
10. For sums payable out of the Consolidated Fund to the National Insurance Fund -	2,523,000,000	—
11. For expenditure by the Department of Education and Science on superannuation allowances and gratuities, etc, in respect of teachers, and the widows, children and dependants of deceased teachers (Revised sum) -	136,304,000	834,584,000
12. For the expenditure by the Scottish Home and Health Department on superannuation allowances and gratuities, etc, in respect of teachers, and the widows and dependants of deceased teachers - - - - -	29,292,000	91,092,000
13. For expenditure by the Department of Health and Social Security on pensions, allowances, gratuities, etc, to or in respect of persons engaged in health services or in other approved employment - - - -	1,000	727,296,000
14. For expenditure by the Scottish Home and Health Department on pensions, allowances, gratuities, etc, to or in respect of persons engaged in health services or in other approved employment - - - -	1,000	92,475,000
15. For the salaries of the Commissioners of the Crown Estate and the expenses of their Office - - - - - -	842,000	—
16. For transitional relief under the Finance Acts, 1965 and 1972, for companies with an overseas source of trading income - - - -	100,000	—
17. For payment of pensions, etc, to members of the United Kingdom Atomic Energy Authority's superannuation schemes and other related expenditure - -	1,000	37,869,000

SCHEDULE (B).—PART 22—*continued*

| | Sums not exceeding | |
	Supply Grants	Appropriations in Aid
	£	£
Vote		
18. For supplementary grants for transport purposes to county councils in England and the Greater London Council - - - - - - -	400,000,000	—
19. For supplementary grants for transport purposes to county councils in Wales - - - - - - - -	31,000,000	—
TOTAL, CLASS XVIII - - - - - - -£	15,376,126,000	1,783,316,000

Section 3.

SCHEDULE (C)

ENACTMENTS REPEALED

Chapter	Short title
1982 c. 8	Consolidated Fund Act 1982.
1982 c. 40	Appropriation Act 1982.
1983 c. 1	Consolidated Fund Act 1983.

Prescription and Limitation (Scotland) Act 1984

1984 CHAPTER 45

An Act to make new provision for Scotland with respect to the extinction of obligations to make contributions between wrongdoers; to amend the law relating to the time-limits for bringing actions which consist of or include a claim of damages in respect of personal injuries or a person's death; to make provision relating to the application of rules of law of a country other than Scotland in respect of the extinction of obligations or the limitation of time within which proceedings may be brought to enforce obligations; and for connected purposes.   [26th July 1984]

B E IT ENACTED by the Queen's most Excellent Majesty, by and with the advice and consent of the Lords Spiritual and Temporal, and Commons, in this present Parliament assembled, and by the authority of the same, as follows:—

Extinction of obligations to make contributions between wrongdoers.

1. After section 8 of the Prescription and Limitation (Scotland) Act 1973 (in this Act referred to as " the principal Act ") there shall be inserted the following section—

" Extinction of obligations to make contributions between wrongdoers.
1940 c. 42.

8A.—(1) If any obligation to make a contribution by virtue of section 3(2) of the Law Reform (Miscellaneous Provisions) (Scotland) Act 1940 in respect of any damages or expenses has subsisted for a continuous period of 2 years after the date on which the right to recover the contribution became enforceable by the creditor in the obligation—

(*a*) without any relevant claim having been made in relation to the obligation ; and

(b) without the subsistence of the obligation having been relevantly acknowledged;

then as from the expiration of that period the obligation shall be extinguished.

(2) Subsections (4) and (5) of section 6 of this Act shall apply for the purposes of this section as they apply for the purposes of that section.".

2. For sections 17 to 19 of the principal Act there shall be substituted the following sections— Limitation of actions.

" Actions in respect of personal injuries not resulting in death.

17.—(1) This section applies to an action of damages where the damages claimed consist of or include damages in respect of personal injuries, being an action (other than an action to which section 18 of this Act applies) brought by the person who sustained the injuries or any other person.

(2) Subject to subsection (3) below and section 19A of this Act, no action to which this section applies shall be brought unless it is commenced within a period of 3 years after—

(a) the date on which the injuries were sustained or, where the act or omission to which the injuries were attributable was a continuing one, that date or the date on which the act or omission ceased, whichever is the later; or

(b) the date (if later than any date mentioned in paragraph (a) above) on which the pursuer in the action became, or on which, in the opinion of the court, it would have been reasonably practicable for him in all the circumstances to become, aware of all the following facts—

(i) that the injuries in question were sufficiently serious to justify his bringing an action of damages on the assumption that the person against whom the action was brought did not dispute liability and was able to satisfy a decree;

(ii) that the injuries were attributable in whole or in part to an act or omission; and

(iii) that the defender was a person to whose act or omission the injuries were attributable in whole or in part or the employer or principal of such a person.

(3) In the computation of the period specified in subsection (2) above there shall be disregarded any time during which the person who sustained the injuries was under legal disability by reason of nonage or unsoundness of mind.

Actions where death has resulted from personal injuries.

18.—(1) This section applies to any action in which, following the death of any person from personal injuries, damages are claimed in respect of the injuries or the death.

(2) Subject to subsections (3) and (4) below and section 19A of this Act, no action to which this section applies shall be brought unless it is commenced within a period of 3 years after—

    (*a*) the date of death of the deceased ; or

    (*b*) the date (if later than the date of death) on which the pursuer in the action became, or on which, in the opinion of the court, it would have been reasonably practicable for him in all the circumstances to become, aware of both of the following facts—

        (i) that the injuries of the deceased were attributable in whole or in part to an act or omission ; and

        (ii) that the defender was a person to whose act or omission the injuries were attributable in whole or in part or the employer or principal of such a person.

(3) Where the pursuer is a relative of the deceased, there shall be disregarded in the computation of the period specified in subsection (2) above any time during which the relative was under legal disability by reason of nonage or unsoundness of mind.

(4) Subject to section 19A of this Act, where an action of damages has not been brought by or on behalf of a person who has sustained personal injuries within the period specified in section 17(2) of this Act and that person subsequently dies in consequence of those injuries, no action to which this section applies shall be brought in respect of those injuries or the death from those injuries.

1976 c. 1.

(5) In this section " relative " has the same meaning as in Schedule 1 to the Damages (Scotland) Act 1976.".

3. For section 22 of the principal Act there shall be substituted the following section—

" Interpretation of Part II and supplementary provisions. Provisions supplementary to section 2.

    22.—(1) In this Part of this Act—

        " the court " means the Court of Session or the sheriff court ; and

        " personal injuries " includes any disease and any impairment of a person's physical or mental condition.

    (2) Where the pursuer in an action to which section 17 or 18 of this Act applies is pursuing the action by virtue of the assignation of a right of action, the reference in subsection (2)(*b*) of the said section 17 or, as the case may be, 18 to the pursuer in the action shall be construed as a reference to the assignor of the right of action.

    (3) For the purposes of the said subsection (2)(*b*) knowledge that any act or omission was or was not, as a matter of law, actionable, is irrelevant.

    (4) An action which would not be entertained but for the said subsection (2)(*b*) shall not be tried by jury.".

4. At the beginning of Part III of the principal Act there shall be inserted the following section—

Private international law application.

" Private international law application.   23A.—(1) Where the substantive law of a country other than Scotland falls to be applied by a Scottish court as the law governing an obligation, the court shall apply any relevant rules of law of that country relating to the extinction of the obligation or the limitation of time within which proceedings may be brought to enforce the obligation to the exclusion of any corresponding rule of Scots law.

    (2) This section shall not apply where it appears to the court that the application of the relevant foreign rule of law would be incompatible with the principles of public policy applied by the court.

    (3) This section shall not apply in any case where the application of the corresponding rule of Scots law has extinguished the obligation, or barred the bringing of proceedings prior to the coming into force of the Prescription and Limitation (Scotland) Act 1984.".

5.—(1) Section 2 of this Act shall have effect as regards rights of action accruing both before and after the coming into force of this Act.

Transitional provisions.

(2) Section 4 of this Act shall not have effect as regards any proceedings commenced before the coming into force of this Act.

(3) The amendment to section 7(2) of the principal Act specified in paragraph 2 of Schedule 1 to this Act shall have effect as regards any obligation which has not been extinguished before the coming into force of this Act.

Minor and consequential amendments and repeals.

6.—(1) The enactments mentioned in Schedule 1 to this Act shall have effect subject to the amendments respectively specified in that Schedule, being minor amendments and amendments consequential on the provisions of this Act.

(2) The enactments set out in Schedule 2 to this Act are hereby repealed to the extent specified in column 3 of that Schedule.

Short title, commencement and extent.

7.—(1) This Act may be cited as the Prescription and Limitation (Scotland) Act 1984.

(2) This Act shall come into force at the end of a period of 2 months beginning with the date on which it is passed.

(3) This Act extends to Scotland only.

SCHEDULES

SCHEDULE 1

MINOR AND CONSEQUENTIAL AMENDMENTS

The Limitation (Enemies and War Prisoners) Act 1945 (c. 16)

1. In subsection (1) of section 1, as substituted for Scotland by paragraph (*a*) of section 4, in the list of enactments appended to the subsection for the words " sections 17 and 20(1) of the Prescription and Limitation (Scotland) Act 1973 " there shall be substituted the words " sections 8A and 17 of the Prescription and Limitation (Scotland) Act 1973 ".

The Prescription and Limitation (Scotland) Act 1973 (c. 52)

2. At the end of section 7(2) there shall be added the words " or an obligation to make reparation in respect of personal injuries within the meaning of Part II of this Act or in respect of the death of any person as a result of such injuries."

3. In section 9—

    (*a*) in subsection (1) for the words " and 7 " in both places where they occur there shall be substituted the words " 7 and 8A " ;

    (*b*) in subsection (3) for the words " or 8 " there shall be substituted the words " 8 or 8A ".

4. In section 10, for the words " and 7 " wherever they occur there shall be substituted the words " 7 and 8A ".

5. In section 13, for the words " or 8 " there shall be substituted the words " 8 or 8A ".

6. In section 14(1)(*b*) for the words " section 6(4) " there shall be substituted the words ' subsection (4) of section 6 of this Act including that subsection as applied by section 8A of this Act ".

7. In section 15(1), in the definition of " prescriptive period " for the words " or 8 " there shall be substituted the words " 8 or 8A ".

8. In section 19A—

    (*a*) in subsection (1) for the words " (as read with sections 18 and 19) " there shall be substituted the words " or section 18 " ;

    (*b*) after subsection (3) there shall be added the following subsection—

        " (4) An action which would not be entertained but for this section shall not be tried by jury.".

Section 6(2).

SCHEDULE 2

Repeals

Chapter	Short title	Extent of repeal
1973 c. 52.	The Prescription and Limitation (Scotland) Act 1973.	In section 11(4) the words from " and in the " to the end. Sections 20 and 21. In section 25, in subsection (2) the words " Subject to subsection (3) below ", and subsection (3). In Part II of Schedule 4, the entry relating to the Limitation (Enemies and War Prisoners) Act 1945.
1980 c. 55.	The Law Reform (Miscellaneous Provisions) (Scotland) Act 1980.	In section 23, paragraphs (*b*), (*c*) and (*d*).

Cable and Broadcasting Act 1984

1984 CHAPTER 46

An Act to provide for the establishment and functions of a Cable Authority and to make other provision with respect to cable programme services; to amend the Broadcasting Act 1981, to provide for the establishment and functions of a Satellite Broadcasting Board and to make other provision with respect to broadcasting services; and for connected purposes. [26th July 1984]

B E IT ENACTED by the Queen's most Excellent Majesty, by and with the advice and consent of the Lords Spiritual and Temporal, and Commons, in this present Parliament assembled, and by the authority of the same, as follows:—

PART I

CABLE PROGRAMME SERVICES

Introductory

1.—(1) There shall be an authority to be called the Cable Authority (in this Part referred to as " the Authority ") for the purpose of performing the functions assigned to the Authority by this Part. The Cable. Authority.

(2) The Authority shall consist of—

    (*a*) a chairman and deputy chairman ; and

    (*b*) such number of other members, not being less than three nor more than ten, as the Secretary of State may from time to time determine.

(3) Schedule 1 to this Act shall have effect with respect to the Authority.

2.—(1) In this Act " cable programme service " means a service which consists wholly or mainly in the sending by any person, by means of a telecommunication system (whether run by him or by any other person), of sounds or visual images or both either—

(a) for reception, otherwise than by wireless telegraphy, at two or more places in the United Kingdom, whether they are so sent for simultaneous reception or at different times in response to requests made by different users of the service ; or

(b) for reception, by whatever means, at a place in the United Kingdom for the purpose of their being presented there either to members of the public or to any group of persons.

(2) In this Part " licensable service " means a cable programme service which consists wholly or mainly in the sending by any person, by means of a telecommunication system (whether run by him or by any other person), of sounds or visual images or both either—

(a) for simultaneous reception, otherwise than by wireless telegraphy, in two or more dwelling-houses in the United Kingdom ; or

(b) for reception, by whatever means, at a place in the United Kingdom for the purpose of their being presented there either to members of the public or to a group of persons some or all of whom do not have a business interest in hearing or seeing them.

(3) In this Part—

" diffusion service " means a service falling within subsection (2)(a) above ;

" prescribed diffusion service " means a diffusion service of such a description as the Secretary of State after consultation with the Authority may by order made by statutory instrument prescribe ;

" restricted service " means a service falling within subsection (2)(b) above.

(4) Subsections (1) and (2) above do not apply in relation to a service which consists wholly or mainly in the sending of sounds or visual images or both by any person if it is an essential feature of the service that, while they are being conveyed, there will or may be sent from each place of reception, by means of the telecommunication system or (as the case may be) the part of it by means of which they are conveyed, sounds or visual images or both for reception by that person.

(5) References in subsections (2) and (4) above to sounds are references to speech or music or both except that they do not

include, in relation to any telecommunication system, speech
providing information for the purposes of facilitating the use
of a telecommunication service provided by means of that
system.

(6) References in subsections (2) and (4) above to visual
images are references to visual images which are such that
sequences of them may be seen as moving pictures.

(7) References in this section to a telecommunication system
do not include references to a telecommunication system the
running of which does not require to be licensed under Part II
of the Telecommunications Act 1984 (in this Act referred to 1984 c. 12.
as " the 1984 Act ").

(8) For the purposes of this section a person has a business
interest in hearing sounds or seeing visual images if he has an
interest in hearing or seeing them for the purposes of his business, trade, profession or employment.

(9) In this section " dwelling-house " includes a hotel, inn,
boarding house or other similar establishment.

Licensing of services by Authority

3.—(1) Subject to any exceptions for which the Secretary of Prohibition on
State after consultation with the Authority may by order pro- unlicensed
vide, a person who provides a licensable service shall be guilty services.
of an offence unless he is authorised to provide the service by a
licence granted under section 4 below (in this Part referred to
as a licence).

(2) A person guilty of an offence under this section shall be
liable—

    (a) on summary conviction, to a fine not exceeding the
        statutory maximum ;

    (b) on conviction on indictment, to a fine.

(3) No proceedings in respect of an offence under this section
shall be instituted—

    (a) in England and Wales, except by or with the consent
        of the Director of Public Prosecutions ;

    (b) in Northern Ireland, except by or with the consent of
        the Director of Public Prosecutions for Northern
        Ireland.

(4) Without prejudice to subsection (2) above, compliance
with this section shall be enforceable by civil proceedings by
the Crown for an injunction or interdict or for any other appropriate relief.

(5) An order under this section shall be made by statutory instrument which shall be subject to annulment in pursuance of a resolution of either House of Parliament.

Power to
license
services.

4.—(1) A licence may be granted by the Authority for the provision of such a licensable service as is specified in the licence or is of a description so specified.

(2) A licence shall be in writing and, subject to subsections (3) and (8) and section 17 below, shall continue in force for such period as may be specified in the licence.

(3) A licence for the provision of a prescribed diffusion service (whether as originally granted or as varied under subsection (8) below) shall not continue in force for a period exceeding the relevant maximum period.

(4) For the purposes of subsection (3) above the relevant maximum period is—

(*a*) fifteen years in the case of a licence for the provision of a prescribed diffusion service in an area—

(i) in which such a service has not previously been provided ; or

(ii) in which such a service has previously been so provided, but only in so much of it as in the opinion of the Authority does not amount to a substantial part of it ; and

(*b*) eight years in every other case.

(5) A licence may include—

(*a*) such conditions as appear to the Authority to be requisite or expedient having regard to the duties imposed on them by this Part and, in the case of a licence for the provision of a prescribed diffusion service, to the information included in the application in pursuance of section 6(1) below ;

(*b*) conditions requiring the rendering to the Authority of a payment on the grant of the licence or payments during the currency of the licence or both of such amount or amounts as may be determined by or under the licence ; and

(*c*) conditions requiring the holder of the licence to furnish to the Authority, in such manner and at such times as they may reasonably require, such information as they may require for the purpose of exercising the functions assigned to them by or under this Part.

(6) Without prejudice to the generality of paragraph (*a*) of subsection (5) above, conditions included in a licence by virtue of that paragraph may require the holder of the licence—

    (*a*) to comply with any direction given by the Authority as to such matters as are specified in the licence or are of a description so specified ; and

    (*b*) except in so far as the Authority consent to his doing or not doing them, not to do or to do such things as are specified in the licence or are of a description so specified.

(7) The payment or payments required to be rendered to the Authority by conditions included in a licence by virtue of subsection (5)(*b*) above shall be such as to represent what appears to the Authority to be the appropriate contribution of the holder of the licence towards meeting the sums which the Authority regard as necessary in order to discharge their duty under section 18(1) below.

(8) The Authority may vary a licence by notice in writing served on the holder of the licence if—

    (*a*) in the case of a variation of the period for which the licence is to continue in force, the holder consents ; or

    (*b*) in any other case, the holder has been given a reasonable opportunity of making representations.

(9) Subject to the provisions of this Part, it shall be the duty of the Authority to exercise the powers conferred on them by this section in the manner which they consider is best calculated—

    (*a*) to promote the provision of prescribed diffusion services ; and

    (*b*) subject to paragraph (*a*) above, to promote the provision, by means of telecommunication systems, of services other than telecommunication services.

5.—(1) This section applies where the Authority propose to Publicity etc. grant a licence for the provision of a prescribed diffusion service with respect to in any area. certain licences.

(2) The Authority shall publish, in such manner as they consider appropriate, a notice—

    (*a*) stating that they propose to grant a licence for the provision of such a service in the area ;

    (*b*) inviting applications for the licence ; and

    (*c*) stating the fee (if any) which will be payable on each application.

(3) The Authority shall also publish, in such manner as they consider appropriate, as regards each application received—

    (*a*) the name and address of the applicant ; and

    (*b*) such of the information included in the application in pursuance of section 6(1) below as they consider appropriate.

(4) The Authority shall take such steps as they consider appropriate—

    (*a*) to ascertain the opinions of the public in the area about the prescribed diffusion service and any related services proposed to be provided there ; and

    (*b*) to encourage the making of comments and suggestions about those services by members of the public in the area,

and shall take account of those opinions and any such comments and suggestions received by them.

(5) In this section and section 7 below " related service ", in relation to a prescribed diffusion service, means a service (other than a telecommunication service) provided by means of the same telecommunication system.

Applications for licences and prior consultation.

6.—(1) An application for a licence must be in writing and, in the case of a licence for the provision of a prescribed diffusion service, must be accompanied by the fee (if any) stated in the notice under section 5(2) above and must contain information as the matters mentioned in section 7(2) below.

(2) Before deciding whether or to whom to grant a licence, the Authority shall consult with—

    (*a*) the licensing authorities for the purposes of Part II of the 1984 Act ; and

    (*b*) in the case of a licence for the provision of a prescribed diffusion service in any area, every local authority whose area consists of or includes the whole or any part of that area.

Matters to be taken into account.

7.—(1) In deciding whether or to whom to grant a licence, the Authority shall take into account all matters appearing to them to be relevant.

(2) Without prejudice to the generality of subsection (1) above, in deciding whether or to whom to grant a licence for the provision of a prescribed diffusion service in any area, the Authority shall take into account the extent to which the applicant or each applicant proposes to do the following things, namely—

    (*a*) to include a range and diversity of programmes ;

(b) to include in the programmes matter which originates within the European Economic Community and is performed by nationals of member States ;

(c) to include in the programmes an increasing proportion of such matter ;

(d) to include programmes of an educational nature, programmes calculated to appeal specially to the taste and outlook of persons living in the area and programmes in which such persons are given an opportunity to participate ;

(e) to include programmes provided otherwise than by himself or by associates of his ;

(f) to include programmes provided by local voluntary associations and to assist such organisations in the preparation and production of programmes ;

(g) to include in the programmes matter which is calculated to promote the understanding or enjoyment of programmes by persons who are deaf ;

(h) to provide, or secure the provision of, related services.

(3) In this section " local voluntary organisation " includes a local branch of a national voluntary organisation.

8.—(1) The Authority shall do all that they can to secure that none of the following becomes or remains the holder of a licence for the provision of a diffusion service to which this section applies, that is to say— Restrictions on the holding of licences.

(a) an individual who is neither—

(i) a national of a member State who is ordinarily resident within the European Economic Community ; nor

(ii) ordinarily resident in the United Kingdom, the Isle of Man or the Channel Islands ;

(b) a body corporate which is neither—

(i) a body formed under the law of a member State which has its registered or head office or principal place of business within the European Economic Community ; nor

(ii) a body incorporated under the law of the Isle of Man or the Channel Islands ;

(c) a local authority ;

(d) a body whose objects are wholly or mainly of a religious or political nature ;

(e) an individual who is an officer of a body falling within paragraph (d) above ; and

(f) a body corporate which is under the control of a person falling within any of the foregoing paragraphs, or any two or more such persons together.

(2) The Authority shall do all that they can to secure that a person who is, or is an associate of,—

(*a*) a programme contractor for the provision of television programmes for any area ;

(*b*) a programme contractor for the provision of local sound broadcasts for reception in any locality ; or

(*c*) the proprietor of a local newspaper circulating wholly or mainly in any area,

does not become or remain the holder of a licence for the provision in any part of that area or locality of a diffusion service to which this section applies.

(3) The Authority shall do all that they can to secure that a body corporate in which—

(*a*) any of the persons mentioned in subsection (4) below is a participant ; or

(*b*) any of the persons mentioned in subsection (5) below is a principal participant,

does not become or remain the holder of a licence for the provision of a diffusion service to which this section applies if, in the opinion of the Authority, that person's participation in that body corporate has led, is leading or is likely to lead to results which are adverse to the public interest.

(4) The persons referred to in subsection (3)(*a*) above are—

(*a*) a local authority ;

(*b*) a body whose objects are wholly or mainly of a religious or political nature ;

(*c*) the BBC, the IBA and the Welsh Authority ; and

(*d*) a body corporate which is under the control of a person falling within paragraph (*a*), (*b*) or (*c*) above.

(5) The persons referred to in subsection (3)(*b*) above are—

(*a*) a person who is a principal participant in another body corporate which is the holder of a licence for the provision of a diffusion service to which this section applies ;

(*b*) a programme contractor, the proprietor of a newspaper and an advertising agent ;

(*c*) a person carrying on a business which consists (wholly or partly) of—

(i) the production, distribution or exhibition of cinematograph films ;

(ii) the manufacture of records or the publication of musical works ; or

(iii) promoting the broadcasting of sound recordings or the broadcasting or performance of musical works ;

(d) an associate of a person falling within paragraph (a),
(b) or (c) above ;

(e) a person who has control over a body corporate falling within paragraph (a), (b), (c) or (d) above ; and

(f) a body corporate which is under the control of a person falling within paragraph (a), (b), (c) or (d) above.

(6) This section applies to any diffusion service in the case of which programmes are included otherwise than by the reception and immediate re-transmission of broadcasts made by a broadcasting authority.

(7) In this section—

" participant ", in relation to a body corporate, means a person who (whether alone or jointly with one or more other persons, and whether directly or through one or more nominees) holds or is beneficially entitled to shares, or possesses voting power, in that body corporate ;

" principal participant ", in relation to a body corporate, means a person who (whether alone or jointly with one or more other persons, and whether directly or through one or more nominees) holds or is beneficially entitled to not less than one-twentieth of the shares, or possesses not less than one-twentieth of the voting power, in that body corporate.

(8) In this section " cinematograph film ", " record " and " sound recording " have the same meanings as in the Copyright 1956 c. 74. Act 1956 (in this Act referred to as " the 1956 Act ") ; and references to the publication, broadcasting or performance of musical works shall be construed as if they were contained in the 1956 Act.

9.—(1) Where the Authority grant a licence for the provision Information of a service other than a prescribed diffusion service, the Auth- as to licences ority shall, on request made by any person and on payment and by him of such sum (if any) as the Authority may reasonably for licences. require, furnish to that person a copy of that licence.

(2) Where the Authority grant a licence for the provision of a prescribed diffusion service, the Authority shall, on request by any person and on payment by him of such sum (if any) as the Authority may reasonably require, furnish to that person such of the following as may be specified in the request, that is to say—

(a) a copy of that licence ;

(b) a statement of the number of applications received by the Authority for that licence ; and (*c*) a copy of so much of the licensee's application for that licence as related to the matters mentioned in section 7(2) above.

Duties of Authority

General provisions as to programmes.   **10.**—(1) The Authority shall do all that they can to secure that every licensed service complies with the following requirements, that is to say—

(*a*) that nothing is included in the programmes which offends against good taste or decency or is likely to encourage or incite to crime or to lead to disorder or to be offensive to public feeling ;

(*b*) that the programmes do not include any technical device which, by using images of very brief duration or by any other means, exploits the possibility of conveying a message to, or otherwise influencing the minds of, members of an audience without their being aware, or fully aware, of what has been done ;

(*c*) that all news given (in whatever form) in programmes which originate in the United Kingdom is presented with due accuracy and impartiality ; and

(*d*) that there are included in the programmes proper proportions of recorded and other matter which originates within the European Economic Community and is performed by nationals of member States.

(2) References in this section and section 11 below to programmes do not include programmes which are included in a licensed service by the reception and immediate re-transmission of broadcasts made by a broadcasting authority.

Programmes other than advertisements.   **11.**—(1) The Authority shall draw up, and from time to time review, a code giving guidance—

(*a*) as to the rules to be observed in regard to the showing of violence, and in regard to the inclusion in sound programmes of sounds suggestive of violence, particularly in circumstances such that large numbers of children and young persons may be expected to be watching or listening to the programmes ;

(*b*) as to the rules to be observed in regard to the inclusion in programmes of appeals for donations ; and

(*c*) as to such other matters concerning standards and practice for programmes as the Authority may consider suitable for inclusion in the code ;

and the Authority shall do all that they can to secure that the provisions of the code are observed in the provision of licensed services.

(2) In considering what other matters ought to be included in the code in pursuance of subsection (1)(*c*) above, the Authority shall have special regard to programmes included in a licensed service in circumstances such that large numbers of children and young persons may be expected to be watching or listening to the programmes.

(3) The Authority shall do all that they can to secure that every licensed diffusion service complies with the following requirements, that is to say—

(*a*) that undue prominence is not given in the programmes to the views and opinions of particular persons or bodies on religious matters or matters of political or industrial controversy or relating to current public policy ; and

(*b*) that there are excluded from the programmes all expressions of the views and opinions of the person providing the service on religious matters or on matters (other than the provision of diffusion services) which are of political or industrial controversy or relate to current public policy.

(4) In applying subsection (3)(*a*) above, the programmes included in a licensed diffusion service shall be taken as a whole.

(5) References in this section to programmes do not include advertisements.

12.—(1) It shall be the duty of the Authority—

(*a*) after consultation with the IBA and such other bodies and persons concerned with standards of conduct in advertising as the Authority think fit, to draw up, and from time to time review, a code governing standards and practice in advertising (including in particular the sponsoring of programmes) and prescribing the advertisements and methods of advertising to be prohibited, or prohibited in particular circumstances ; and

(*b*) to do all that they can to secure that the provisions of the code are observed in the provision of licensed services.

(2) The Authority shall do all that they can to secure that, subject to such exceptions as may be prescribed by order made by the Secretary of State, no licensed service includes an advertisement which—

(*a*) is inserted by or on behalf of any body whose objects are wholly or mainly of a political nature ; or (*b*) is directed towards any political end or has any relation to any industrial dispute.

(3) The Authority shall do all that they can to secure that the amount of time which is given to advertisements in any hour or other period in any particular circumstances does not exceed—

    (*a*) in the case of so much of a licensed diffusion service as appears to the Authority, after consultation with the IBA, calculated to appeal to tastes and interests which are generally catered for by ITV, the maximum amount of time which could be so given if that service were ITV ; and

    (*b*) in the case of so much of a licensed diffusion service as appears to the Authority, after consultation with the IBA, calculated to appeal to tastes and interests which are generally catered for by local sound broadcasting services, the maximum amount of time which could be so given if that service were a local sound broadcasting service.

(4) It shall also be the duty of the Authority—

    (*a*) to consult from time to time with the Secretary of State as to the classes and descriptions of advertisements which must not be included in licensed services and the methods of advertising which must not be employed in the provision of such services ; and

    (*b*) to carry out any directions which he may give to them in those respects.

(5) The committee referred to in paragraph (*b*) of subsection (2) of section 16 (general advisory council and specialist advisory committees etc.) of the Broadcasting Act 1981 (in this Act referred to as " the 1981 Act ") and the panel referred to in subsection (5) of that section shall also have the function of advising the Authority ; and that section shall accordingly have effect as if—

1981 c. 68.

    (*a*) the first reference to the IBA in subsection (2), so far as relating to the committee referred to in paragraph (*b*) of that subsection, the first reference to the IBA in that paragraph and any reference to the IBA in subsections (3) to (7) included a reference to the Authority ;

    (*b*) any reference to the programmes broadcast by the IBA in paragraph (*b*) of subsection (2) were, in relation to the Authority, a reference to licensed services ;

    (*c*) any reference to the code under section 9 of that Act in subsections (3) and (6) were, in relation to the Authority, a reference to the code under this section ; and

    (*d*) the duty imposed on the Authority by subsection (7) were a duty to do all that they can to secure that,

before the first occasion on which a licensed service includes an advertisement which in their opinion falls
under paragraph (*a*), (*b*) or (*c*) of subsection (5), the
advertisement is referred as mentioned in subsection (7).

(6) An order under this section shall be made by statutory
instrument; but no such order shall be made unless a draft of
the order has been laid before and approved by a resolution of
each House of Parliament.

(7) References in this section to advertisements do not include
advertisements which are included in a licensed service by the
reception and immediate re-transmission of broadcasts made by
a broadcasting authority.

13.—(1) The Authority shall do all that they can to secure Inclusion of
that, subject to any exceptions for which the Secretary of State, certain
after consultation with the Authority and both broadcasting broadcasts.
authorities, may by order made by statutory instrument provide,
every licensed diffusion service provided by any person in any
area includes, by the reception and immediate re-transmission of
the broadcasts, the programmes included in each television or
sound broadcasting service provided by a broadcasting authority
for reception in that area.

(2) Where a television broadcasting service provided by a
broadcasting authority for reception in an area in which a
licensed diffusion service is provided consists in the broadcasting for simultaneous reception of programmes contained in two
or more programme schedules, then, so far as relating to that
television broadcasting service, the duty in subsection (1) above
shall be subject to the limitation in whichever of subsections
(3) and (4) below is applicable.

(3) Where the programmes contained in one of the programme schedules are broadcast for reception in a greater part
of the area than the programmes contained in the other schedule
or any of the other schedules, the said duty so far as so relating
shall extend only to the programmes contained in the first-
mentioned schedule.

(4) Where subsection (3) above does not apply, the said duty
so far as so relating shall extend only to the programmes contained in such one of the programme schedules as the broadcasting authority may determine.

(5) Where the programmes in a DBS service or additional
teletext service provided by a broadcasting authority fall to be
included in a licensed diffusion service provided by any person,
they shall be so included on such terms as to—

(*a*) the recovery by that person on behalf of that authority
or, as the case may require, the programme or tele-

text contractors of any charges made by them for the reception of the programmes ;

(b) any payments to be made by one party to another ; and

(c) any other matter for which provision requires to be made,

as may be agreed between the parties or, in default of agreement, determined by a person appointed for the purpose by the Secretary of State ; and any fee or other sum charged by a person so appointed in respect of a determination made under this subsection shall be paid by the parties in such proportions as he may determine.

(6) In this section—

" additional teletext service ", in relation to a broadcasting authority, means a teletext service (other than a DBS service) which is additional to those already provided by that authority ;

" DBS service " means a television broadcasting service provided by means of the technique known as direct broadcasting by satellite or DBS ;

" programme " includes a teletext transmission.

14.—(1) The Authority shall do all that they can to secure that no licensed service provided by any person includes a programme which consists of or includes the whole or any part of a listed event, unless the Authority are satisfied that both broadcasting authorities have been given an opportunity to acquire broadcasting rights in respect of that event on terms comparable to those on which that person acquired the right to include it in that service ; and for the purposes of this subsection an opportunity given to the Welsh Authority, the IBA's subsidiary or a programme contractor to acquire broadcasting rights in respect of a listed event shall be treated as given to the IBA.

(2) The Authority shall do all that they can to secure that—

(a) no licensed diffusion service includes on pay-per-view terms ; and

(b) no licensed restricted service includes,

a programme which consists of or includes the whole or any part of a listed or protected event.

(3) In this section—

" listed event " means a sporting or other event of national interest which is for the time being included in a list maintained by the Secretary of State for the purposes of this section and published by him in such manner as he considers appropriate for bringing it to the attention of the Authority and of persons providing licensed services ;

" national interest " includes interest within England, Scotland, Wales or Northern Ireland ;

" protected event " means a sporting or other event which, in the opinion of the Authority, is one of a series of similar events the whole or any part of which—

> (*a*) it was at the commencement of this section the practice of a broadcasting authority to broadcast ; and

> (*b*) but for the acquisition of rights to include the whole or any part of events in that series in licensed services, it would still be the practice of that authority to broadcast ;

and for the purposes of this subsection anything broadcast by either of the broadcasting authorities shall be treated as broadcast by each of them.

(4) For the purposes of this section a programme is included in a licensed diffusion service on pay-per-view terms if any payments falling to be made by subscribers to that service will or may vary according as that programme is or is not actually received by them.

(5) Neither subsection (1) nor (2) above shall apply in relation to the inclusion in such a service as is mentioned in that subsection of a programme which consists of or includes a record of the whole or any part of any such event as is so mentioned where the programme is so included more than 24 hours after the original recording was made.

Powers of Authority

15.—(1) The Authority may give directions, which may be, to any degree, either general or specific and qualified or unqualified, with respect to— Power to give directions.

> (*a*) the exclusion of any programme from a licensed service ;

> (*b*) the classes and descriptions of advertisements and methods of advertising to be excluded, or to be excluded in particular circumstances, from licensed services ; or

> (*c*) the exclusion of a particular advertisement from licensed services, or its exclusion from such services in particular circumstances.

(2) References in this section and section 16 below to programmes or advertisements do not include programmes or advertisements which are included in a licensed service by the reception and immediate re-transmission of broadcasts made by a broadcasting authority.

16.—(1) Where the Authority have served on a person authorised by a licence to provide a diffusion service a written notice applying this subsection to programmes specified or of a description specified in the notice, they may, within such period as—

(a) begins with the inclusion in that service of any programme to which the notice relates ; and

(b) is of a length (not exceeding two months) specified in the notice,

direct that person to produce to them for examination or reproduction a visual or sound record of any matter included in that programme.

(2) If the Authority are satisfied that a person authorised by a licence to provide a diffusion service has failed to comply with any condition of that licence or with any direction given by the Authority, the Authority may serve a written notice on that person—

(a) stating that the Authority are so satisfied ;

(b) stating the effect of subsection (3) below ; and

(c) specifying for the purposes of that subsection a period not exceeding twelve months ;

and the Authority shall publish any notice under this subsection in such manner as they consider appropriate.

(3) If the Authority are satisfied that, at any time during the period specified in a notice under subsection (2) above, the person concerned has failed to comply with any condition of the licence or any direction given by the Authority, the Authority may direct that person—

(a) to provide the Authority in advance with such scripts and particulars of the programmes to be included in the diffusion service as may be specified in the direction ; and

(b) in respect of such of those programmes as will consist of or include recorded matter, to produce to the Authority in advance for examination or reproduction such visual or sound records of that matter as may be so specified ;

and a direction under this subsection shall have effect for such period, not exceeding six months, as may be specified in the direction.

(4) Nothing done under or in pursuance of a notice or direction given under this section shall—

(a) constitute an infringement of the copyright in any work, sound recording, cinematograph film or television or sound broadcast ; or

(b) constitute an offence under any of the provisions of the Performers' Protection Acts 1958 to 1972.

(5) Expressions used in this section which are also used PART I
in the 1956 Act have the same meanings as in that Act.

17.—(1) Every licence authorising a person to provide a Power to
licensable service shall contain all such provisions as the Auth- revoke
ority consider requisite or expedient to ensure that— licenses.

- (a) if, in view of any failure by that person to comply with any condition of the licence or any direction given by the Authority, the Authority consider it necessary to do so in the public interest ; or
- (b) where the licence authorises the provision of a diffusion service, if the Authority consider it necessary to do so for the purpose of complying with section 8 above ; or
- (c) where that person is a body corporate, if any change affecting the nature or characteristics of the body corporate, or any change in the persons having control over or interests in the body corporate, takes place after the granting of the licence which, if it had occurred before the granting of the licence, would have induced the Authority to refrain from granting the licence,

the Authority may by notice in writing to that person, taking
effect forthwith or on a date specified in the notice, revoke the
licence.

(2) Before revoking a licence under a provision included in
the licence in pursuance of subsection (1) above, the Authority
shall—

- (a) give the person concerned a reasonable opportunity of making representations with respect to the matter ; and
- (b) consult with the licensing authorities for the purposes of Part II of the 1984 Act.

Other provisions with respect to Authority

18.—(1) It shall be the duty of the Authority so to conduct Finances of
their affairs as to secure that their revenues become at the earliest Authority.
possible date, and continue thereafter, at least sufficient to enable
them to meet their obligations and to discharge their functions
under this Part.

(2) Any excess of the Authority's revenues for any financial
year over the sums required by them for that year for meeting
their obligations and discharging their functions under this Part
shall be applied by the Authority in such manner as the Secretary of State, with the approval of the Treasury and after consultation with the chairman (or in his absence the deputy chairman) of the Authority, may direct.

2 D 4

(3) A direction under subsection (2) above may require the whole or any part of any excess of the revenues of the Authority to be paid into the Consolidated Fund.

Advances to
Authority.

19.—(1) For the purposes of furnishing the Authority with working capital, the Secretary of State may with the consent of the Treasury make advances to the Authority out of money provided by Parliament.

(2) The aggregate amount outstanding by way of principal in respect of sums advanced to the Authority under this section shall not at any time exceed £2 million.

(3) Any sums advanced under this section shall be repaid to the Secretary of State at such times and by such methods, and interest on those sums shall be paid to him at such times and at such rates, as he may from time to time direct with the consent of the Treasury.

(4) Any sums received by the Secretary of State in pursuance of subsection (3) above shall be paid into the Consolidated Fund.

Accounts and
audit.

20.—(1) The Authority shall keep proper accounts and proper records in relation to the accounts, and shall prepare in respect of each financial year a statement of accounts in such form as the Secretary of State with the approval of the Treasury may direct, being a form which shall conform with the best commercial standards.

(2) The accounts of the Authority shall be audited by auditors to be appointed by the Authority with the approval of the Secretary of State.

(3) A person shall not be qualified to be appointed as an auditor in pursuance of subsection (2) above unless he is a member of one or more of the following bodies—

the Institute of Chartered Accountants in England and Wales;

the Institute of Chartered Accountants of Scotland;

the Association of Certified Accountants;

the Institute of Chartered Accountants in Ireland;

any other body of accountants established in the United Kingdom and for the time being recognised for the purposes of section 161(1)(a) of the Companies Act 1948 by the Secretary of State,

1948 c. 38.

but a Scottish firm may be so appointed if each of the partners in the firm is qualified to be so appointed.

(4) The Authority shall at all reasonable times upon demand made by the Secretary of State or by any persons authorised by him in that behalf—

(*a*) afford to him or them full liberty to examine the accounts of the Authority ; and

(*b*) furnish him or them with all forecasts, estimates, information and documents which he or they may require with respect to the financial transactions and engagements of the Authority.

21.—(1) As soon as may be after the end of every financial year, the Authority shall prepare a general report of their proceedings during that year, and transmit it to the Secretary of State who shall consider it and lay copies of it before each House of Parliament. Annual reports.

(2) The report shall have attached to it the statement of accounts for the year and a copy of any report made by the auditor on that statement, and shall include such information (including information relating to the financial position of the Authority) as the Secretary of State may from time to time direct.

(3) The report shall also include an account of the way in which the Authority have discharged their duty under section 10(1)(*d*) above and a general account of—

(*a*) any complaints received by the Authority about the discharge of their duties under sections 10 and 11 above ; and

(*b*) the action taken by the Authority in relation to those complaints.

Copyright

22. After section 14 of the 1956 Act there shall be inserted the following section— Copyright in cable programmes.

" Copyright in cable programmes.   **14A.**—(1) Copyright shall subsist, subject to the provisions of this Act, in every cable programme which is included in a cable programme service provided by a qualified person in the United Kingdom or in any other country to which this section extends.

(2) Copyright shall not subsist in a cable programme by virtue of this section if the programme is included in the cable programme service by the reception and immediate re-transmission of a television broadcast or a sound broadcast.

(3) Subject to the provisions of this Act, a person providing a cable programme service shall be entitled to any copyright subsisting in a cable programme included in that service and any such copy-

right shall continue to subsist until the end of the period of fifty years from the end of the calendar year in which the cable programme is so included, and shall then expire.

(4) In so far as a cable programme is a repetition (whether the first or any subsequent repetition) of a cable programme previously included as mentioned in subsection (1) of this section—

    (*a*) copyright shall not subsist therein by virtue of this section if it is so included after the end of the period of fifty years from the end of the calendar year in which it was previously so included ; and

    (*b*) if it is so included before the end of that period any copyright subsisting therein by virtue of this section shall expire at the end of that period.

(5) The acts restricted by the copyright in a cable programme are—

    (*a*) in so far as it consists of visual images, making, otherwise than for private purposes, a cinematograph film of it or a copy of such a film ;

    (*b*) in so far as it consists of sounds, making, otherwise than for private purposes, a sound recording of it or a record embodying such a recording ;

    (*c*) causing it, in so far as it consists of visual images, to be seen in public, or, in so far as it consists of sounds, to be heard in public, if it is seen or heard by a paying audience ;

    (*d*) broadcasting it or including it in a cable programme service.

(6) The restrictions imposed by virtue of the last preceding subsection in relation to a cable programme shall apply whether the act in question is done by the reception of the programme or by making use of any record, print, negative, tape or other article on which the programme has been recorded.

(7) In relation to copyright in cable programmes, in so far as they consist of visual images, the restrictions imposed by virtue of subsection (5) of this section shall apply to any sequence of images sufficient to be seen as a moving picture ; and accordingly, for the purpose of establishing an infringement of such

copyright, it shall not be necessary to prove that the
act in question extended to more than such a sequence of images.

(8) For the purposes of subsection (5) of this section a cinematograph film or a copy thereof, or a
sound recording or a record embodying a recording,
shall be taken to be made otherwise than for private
purposes if it is made for the purposes of the doing
by any person of any of the following acts, that is to
say,—

(*a*) the sale or letting for hire of any copy of the
     film, or, as the case may be, of any record
     embodying the recording;

(*b*) broadcasting the film or recording or includ-
     ing it in a cable programme service;

(*c*) causing the film or recording to be seen or
     heard in public.

(9) For the purposes of paragraph (*c*) of subsection
(5) of this section, a cable programme shall be taken
to be seen or heard by a paying audience if it is seen
or heard by persons who either—

(*a*) have been admitted for payment to the place
     where the programme is to be seen or heard,
     or have been admitted for payment to a
     place of which that place forms part, or

(*b*) have been admitted to the place where the
     programme is to be seen or heard in cir-
     cumstances where goods or services are sup-
     plied there at prices which exceed the prices
     usually charged at that place and are partly
     attributable to the facilities afforded for
     seeing or hearing the programme;

     Provided that for the purposes of para-
     graph (*a*) of this subsection no account
     shall be taken—

     (i) of persons admitted to the place in
     question as residents or inmates therein,
     or

     (ii) of persons admitted to that place as
     members of a club or society, where
     payment is only for membership of the
     club or society and the provision of facili-
     ties for seeing or hearing cable pro-
     grammes is only incidental to the main
     purposes of the club or society.

(10) The copyright in a cable programme is not infringed by anything done in relation to the programme for the purposes of a judicial proceeding.

(11) In this Act—

' cable programme ' means a programme which is included, after the commencement of section 22 of the Cable and Broadcasting Act 1984, in a cable programme service ;

' cable programme service ' means a cable programme service within the meaning of the said Act of 1984 or a service provided outside the United Kingdom which would be such a service if subsection (7) of section 2 of that Act and references in subsection (1) of that section to the United Kingdom were omitted ;

' programme ', in relation to a cable programme service, includes any item included in that service.

(12) The foregoing provisions of this section shall have effect as if references in those provisions and in section 12(9) of this Act to sounds included references to signals serving for the impartation of matter otherwise than in the form of sounds or visual images."

Inclusion of broadcasts in cable programmes.

23.—(1) At the end of paragraph (*d*) of subsection (4) and paragraph (*b*) of subsection (7) of section 14 of the 1956 Act (copyright in television and sound broadcasts) there shall be added the words " or including it in a cable programme ".

(2) After subsection (8) of that section there shall be inserted the following subsection—

" (8A) The copyright in a television broadcast or sound broadcast is not infringed by any person who, by the reception and immediate re-transmission of the broadcast, includes a programme in a cable programme service—

(*a*) if the programme is so included in pursuance of a requirement imposed under subsection (1) of section 13 of the Cable and Broadcasting Act 1984 ; or

(*b*) where the broadcast is made otherwise than in a DBS service (as defined in subsection (6) of that section) or an additional teletext service (as so defined), if and to the extent that it is made for reception in the area in which the cable programme service is provided."

(3) After section 27A of that Act there shall be inserted the following section—

" Exercise of jurisdiction of tribunal in relation to inclusion of broadcasts in cable programmes.

27B.—(1) On a reference to the tribunal under this Part of this Act relating to licences to broadcast works or sound recordings for reception in any area, the tribunal shall exercise its powers under this Part of this Act so as to secure that the charges payable for the licences adequately reflect the extent to which the works or recordings will be included, in pursuance of requirements imposed under section 13(1) of the Cable and Broadcasting Act 1984, in cable programme services provided in areas parts of which fall outside that area.

(2) The preceding subsection shall have effect, with the necessary modifications, in relation to applications under this Part of this Act as it has effect in relation to references thereunder."

(4) For subsection (3) of section 40 of that Act (broadcast of sound recordings and cinematograph films and diffusion of broadcast programmes) there shall be substituted the following subsections—

" (3) Where a television broadcast or sound broadcast is made by the Corporation or the Authority and the broadcast is an authorised broadcast, then, subject to subsection (3A) below, any person who, by the reception and immediate re-transmission of the broadcast, includes a programme in a cable programme service, being a programme comprising a literary, dramatic or musical work, or an adaptation of such a work, or an artistic work, or a sound recording or cinematograph film, shall be in the like position, in any proceedings for infringement of the copyright (if any) in the work, recording or film, as if he had been the holder of a licence granted by the owner of that copyright to include the work, adaptation, recording or film in any programme so included in that service.

(3A) Subsection (3) above applies only—

(*a*) if the programme is included in the service in pursuance of a requirement imposed under section 13(1) of the Cable and Broadcasting Act 1984 ; or

(*b*) if and to the extent that the broadcast is made for reception in the area in which the service is provided."

PART I
Inclusion
of sound
recordings and
cinematograph
films in
cable
programmes.

24.—(1) At the end of paragraph (c) of section 12(5) of the 1956 Act (copyright in sound recordings) there shall be added the words " or including it in a cable programme."

(2) In section 13(5) of that Act (copyright in cinematograph films) for paragraph (d) there shall be substituted the following paragraph—

" (d) including the film in a cable programme."

(3) After section 40 of that Act there shall be inserted the following section—

" Inclusion
of sound
recordings
and
cinemato-
graph films
in cable
pro-
grammes.

40A.—(1) Where a cable programme is sent and a person, by the reception of that programme, causes a sound recording to be heard in public, he does not thereby infringe the copyright (if any) in that recording under section 12 of this Act.

(2) Where a cable programme is sent and the programme is an authorised programme, any person who, by the reception of the programme, causes a cinematograph film to be seen or heard in public shall be in the like position, in any proceedings for infringement of copyright (if any) in the film under section 13 of this Act, as if he had been the holder of a licence granted by the owner of that copyright to cause the film to be seen or heard in public by the reception of the programme.

(3) If, in the circumstances mentioned in the last preceding subsection, a person causing a cinematograph film to be seen or heard infringes the copyright in the film by reason that the cable programme was not an authorised programme—

> (a) no proceedings shall be brought against that person under this Act in respect of his infringement of that copyright, but

> (b) it shall be taken into account in assessing damages in any proceedings against the person sending the programme, in so far as that copyright was infringed by him in sending the programme.

(4) For the purposes of this section, a cable programme shall be taken, in relation to a cinematograph film, to be an authorised programme if, but only if, it is sent by, or with the licence of, the owner of the copyright in the film."

Obscenity

Obscene
programmes.

25.—(1) Subject to the following provisions of this section, if—

> (a) the inclusion of a programme in a cable programme

service involves the publication of an obscene article;
or

(b) a programme included in such a service is such that, if any matter included in it were recorded matter, the inclusion of the programme would involve the publication of such an article,

the person providing that service shall be guilty of an offence.

(2) A person guilty of an offence under this section shall be liable—

(a) on summary conviction, to a fine not exceeding the statutory maximum or to imprisonment for a term not exceeding six months;

(b) on conviction on indictment, to a fine or to imprisonment for a term not exceeding three years or both.

(3) Subsection (1) above shall not apply in relation to a programme which is included in a cable programme service by the reception and immediate re-transmission of a broadcast made by a broadcasting authority.

(4) Proceedings for an offence under this section shall not be commenced more than two years after the commission of the offence.

(5) Proceedings for an offence under this section shall not be instituted—

(a) in England and Wales, except by or with the consent of the Director of Public Prosecutions;

(b) in Northern Ireland, except by or with the consent of the Director of Public Prosecutions for Northern Ireland.

(6) A person shall not be proceeded against for an offence at common law—

(a) in respect of a programme included in a cable programme service or anything said or done in the course of such a programme, where it is of the essence of the common law offence that the programme or, as the case may be, what was said or done was obscene, indecent, offensive, disgusting or injurious to morality; or

(b) in respect of an agreement to cause a programme to be included in a cable programme service or to cause anything to be said or done in course of such a programme so included, where the common law offence consists of conspiring to corrupt public morals or to do any act contrary to public morals or decency.

(7) A person shall not be convicted of an offence under this section if he proves that he did not know and had no reason

to suspect that the programme in question would be such that its inclusion in a cable programme service would make him liable to be convicted of an offence under this section.

(8) A person shall not be convicted of an offence under this section if he proves that the inclusion in a cable programme service of the programme in question was justified as being for the public good on the ground that it was in the interests of drama, opera, ballet or any other art, or of literature or learning.

(9) It is hereby declared that the opinion of experts as to the artistic, literary or other merits of a programme may be admitted in any proceedings under this section either to establish or negative the said ground.

1959 c. 66.

(10) In this section expressions used in the Obscene Publications Act 1959 have the same meanings as in that Act.

(11) This section does not extend to Scotland.

Obscene programmes in Scotland. 1982 c. 45.

26.—(1) Section 51 of the Civic Government (Scotland) Act 1982 (offences in respect of obscene material) shall be amended as follows—

 (a) in subsection 6(a) for the words from " a programme transmitted " to " Secretary of State " there shall be substituted the words " or any such broadcast which is received and immediately re-transmitted by a cable programme service ";

 (b) in the said subsection (8) at the end of the definition of " material " there shall be added " and any matter included in a programme transmitted as part of a cable programme service "; and

 (c) in the said subsection (8), after the words " the reference to publishing includes a reference to " there shall be inserted the word " showing,".

(2) This section extends to Scotland only.

Miscellaneous

Incitement to racial hatred.

27.—(1) Subject to the following provisions of this section, if a programme involving the use of threatening, abusive or insulting words is included in a cable programme service in a case where, having regard to the circumstances in which the programme is so included, hatred is likely to be stirred up against any racial group in the United Kingdom by the words in question, each of the persons mentioned in subsection (2) below shall be liable—

 (a) on summary conviction, to a fine not exceeding the statutory maximum or to imprisonment for a term not exceeding six months or both;

(*b*) on conviction on indictment, to a fine or to imprisonment for a term not exceeding two years or both.

(2) The said persons are—

(*a*) the person providing the cable programme service ;

(*b*) any person by whom the programme is produced or directed ; and

(*c*) any person by whom the offending words are used.

(3) In any proceedings for an offence under this section alleged to have been committed by a person falling within subsection (2)(*a*) or (*b*) above, it shall be a defence for the accused to prove—

(*a*) that he did not know and had no reasonable cause to suspect that the programme would involve the use of the offending words ; and

(*b*) that, having regard to the circumstances in which the programme was included in the cable programme service, it was not reasonably practicable for him to secure the removal of those words before the programme was so included.

(4) In any proceedings for an offence under this section alleged to have been committed by a person falling within subsection (2)(*b*) above, it shall be a defence for the accused to prove that he did not know and had no reasonable cause to suspect—

(*a*) that the programme would be included in a cable programme service ; or

(*b*) that the circumstances in which the programme would be so included would be such that hatred would be likely to be stirred up against any racial group in the United Kingdom by the offending words.

(5) In any proceedings for an offence under this section alleged to have been committed by a person falling within subsection (2)(*c*) above, it shall be a defence for the accused to prove that he did not know and had no reasonable cause to suspect—

(*a*) that a programme involving the use of the offending words would be included in a cable programme service ; or

(*b*) that the circumstances in which a programme involving the use of those words would be so included, or a programme so included would involve the use of those words, would be such that hatred would be likely to be stirred up against any racial group in the United Kingdom by those words.

(6) Subsection (1) above does not apply in relation to a programme which is included in a cable programme service by the

PART I

reception and immediate re-transmission of broadcasts made by a broadcasting authority.

(7) Subsection (1) above does not apply in relation to a programme in so far as it contains—

(*a*) a fair and accurate report of proceedings publicly heard before any court or tribunal exercising judicial authority, being a report which is published contemporaneously with those proceedings or, if it is not reasonably practicable or would be unlawful to publish a report of them contemporaneously, is published as soon as publication is reasonably practicable and (if previously unlawful) lawful ; or

(*b*) a fair and accurate report of proceedings in Parliament.

(8) Proceedings for an offence under this section shall not be instituted—

(*a*) in England and Wales, except by or with the consent of the Attorney General ;

(*b*) in Northern Ireland, except by or with the consent of the Attorney General for Northern Ireland.

(9) In this section " racial group " means a group of persons defined by reference to colour, race, nationality or ethnic or national origins, and in this definition " nationality " includes citizenship.

(10) In this section and section 28 below " words " includes pictures, visual images, gestures and other methods of signifying meaning.

Amendment of law of defamation.

28.—(1) For the purposes of the law of libel and slander (including the law of criminal libel so far as it relates to the publication of defamatory matter) the publication of words in the course of a programme included in a cable programme service shall be treated as publication in permanent form.

(2) Subsection (1) above shall apply for the purposes of section 3 of each of the Defamation Acts (slander of title etc.) as it applies for the purposes of the law of libel and slander.

(3) Section 7 of each of those Acts (qualified privilege of newspapers) shall apply in relation to reports or matters included in a cable programme service which is or does not require to be licensed, and in relation to any inclusion in such a service of any such report or matter, as it applies in relation to reports and matters published in a newspaper and to publication in a newspaper ; and subsection (2) of that section shall have effect, in relation to any such inclusion, as if for the words " in the newspaper in which " there were substituted the words " in the matter in which ".

(4) In this section " the Defamation Acts " means the Defamation Act 1952 and the Defamation Act (Northern Ireland) 1955.

(5) Subsections (1) and (2) above do not extend to Scotland.

29. The Broadcasting Complaints Commission shall also have the function of considering and adjudicating upon complaints of—

> (a) unjust or unfair treatment in programmes actually included in a licensed service after the commencement of this section otherwise than by the reception and immediate re-transmission of broadcasts made by a broadcasting authority ; or
>
> (b) unwarranted infringement of privacy in, or in connection with the obtaining of material included in, programmes actually so included ;

and Part III of the 1981 Act (which relates to that Commission) shall accordingly have effect with the amendments made by Schedule 2 to this Act.

30.—(1) The Secretary of State shall, for the financial year which includes the commencement of this section and each subsequent financial year, notify to the Authority the total sum which he considers to be the appropriate contribution of persons providing licensed services towards the expenses of the Broadcasting Complaints Commission.

(2) The Authority shall do all that they can to secure that persons providing licensed services make to the Authority in respect of every financial year payments representing what appear to the Authority to be the appropriate contributions of those persons towards meeting the sum notified to the Authority for that year under subsection (1) above.

(3) The payments made to the Authority by virtue of subsection (2) above shall not form part of the revenue of the Authority and, when received by the Authority, shall be paid to the Secretary of State.

(4) All sums received by the Secretary of State under subsection (3) above shall be paid into the Consolidated Fund.

31.—(1) Where a service to which this section applies which is provided in any area includes, by the reception and immediate re-transmission of the broadcasts, the programmes included in any television or sound broadcasting service provided by a broadcasting authority for reception in that area, any apparatus which, for the purpose of enabling any person to receive any

PART I

1949 c. 54.

of the programmes included in the service to which this section applies, is connected (within the meaning of the 1984 Act) to the telecommunication system by means of which that service is provided shall be deemed for the purposes of the Wireless Telegraphy Act 1949 to be apparatus for wireless telegraphy.

(2) This section applies to any cable programme service and any service which would be such a service if subsection (7) of section 2 above were omitted.

Supplemental

Entry and search of premises.

32.—(1) If a justice of the peace is satisfied by information on oath—

> (*a*) that there is reasonable ground for suspecting that an offence under section 3 above has been or is being committed on any premises specified in the information ; and

> (*b*) that evidence of the commission of the offence is to be found on those premises,

he may grant a search warrant conferring power on any person or persons authorised in that behalf by the Authority and named in the warrant to enter and search the premises specified in the information at any time within one month from the date of the warrant.

(2) A person who intentionally obstructs a person in the exercise of powers conferred on him under this section shall be guilty of an offence and liable on summary conviction to a fine not exceeding level 5 on the standard scale.

(3) A person who discloses, otherwise than for the purposes of any legal proceedings or of a report of any such proceedings, any information obtained by means of an exercise of powers conferred by this section, shall be guilty of an offence and liable—

> (*a*) on summary conviction, to a fine not exceeding the statutory maximum ;

> (*b*) on conviction on indictment, to imprisonment for a term not exceeding two years or to a fine or to both.

(4) In the application of this section to Scotland, for the reference to a justice of the peace there shall be substituted a reference to the sheriff and for any reference to information on oath there shall be substituted a reference to evidence on oath.

(5) In the application of this section to Northern Ireland, for the reference to a justice of the peace there shall be substituted a reference to a resident magistrate and for any reference to information on oath there shall be substituted a reference to complaint on oath.

33.—(1) Where a programme included in a cable programme
service was based on a script, then, in any proceedings for a
relevant offence alleged to have been committed in respect of
that programme—

    (*a*) an actual script on which that programme was based
shall be evidence of what was included in the programme and of the manner in which the programme
or any part of it was performed ; and

    (*b*) if such a script is given in evidence on behalf of any
party to the proceedings then, except in so far as the
contrary is shown, whether by evidence given on behalf
of the same or any other party, the programme shall
be taken to have been performed in accordance with
that script.

(2) In this section and section 34 below—

" relevant offence " means an offence under section 27
above or—

    (*a*) in relation to England and Wales and Northern
Ireland, an offence under section 25 above ; or

    (*b*) in relation to Scotland, an offence under sec-
tion 51 of the Civic Government (Scotland) Act
1982 ;

" script ", in relation to a programme, means the text of
the programme (whether expressed in words or in
musical or other notation) together with any directions
for its performance, whether contained in a single
document or not.

34.—(1) If a police officer of or above the rank of superintendent has reasonable grounds for suspecting—

    (*a*) that a relevant offence has been committed by any per-
son in respect of a programme included in a cable
programme service ; or

    (*b*) that a programme is to be so included and that a rele-
vant offence is likely to be committed by any person
in respect of that programme,

he may make an order in writing under this section relating to
that person and that programme.

(2) Every order made under this section shall be signed by the
person by whom it is made, shall name the person to whom it
relates, and shall describe the programme to which it relates in-
a manner sufficient to enable that programme to be identified.

(3) Where an order under this section has been made, any
police officer, on production if so required of the order may

require the person named in the order to produce, if such a thing exists—

 (*a*) an actual script on which the programme was or, as the case may be, will be based ; or

 (*b*) a visual or sound record of any matter which was or, as the case may be, will be included in the programme,

and if such a script or record is produced to him, may require the person so named to afford him an opportunity of causing a copy thereof to be made.

(4) Any person who without reasonable excuse fails to comply with a requirement under subsection (3) above shall be liable on summary conviction to a fine not exceeding level 3 on the standard scale.

(5) Where, in the case of a programme based on a script, a copy of an actual script on which that programme was based has been made by or on behalf of a police officer by virtue of an order under this section relating to that programme, section 33 above shall apply in relation to that copy as it applies in relation to an actual script on which the programme was based.

(6) In the application of this section to Scotland, for the reference to a police officer of or above the rank of superintendent having reasonable grounds there shall be substituted a reference to the procurator fiscal being satisfied, on receiving a report from a police officer, that there are reasonable grounds.

Availability of visual and sound records.

35.—(1) The Authority shall do all that they can to secure that, if an order is made under section 34 above in relation to a person providing a licensed service and a programme included in that service, that person will be able to comply with a requirement under subsection (3)(*b*) of that section made within 14 days of the inclusion of that programme.

(2) Nothing done under or in pursuance of a condition included in a licence by virtue of this section shall—

 (*a*) constitute an infringement of the copyright in any work, sound recording, cinematograph film or television or sound broadcast ; or

 (*b*) constitute an offence under any of the provisions of the Performers' Protection Acts 1958 to 1972.

(3) Expressions used in this section which are also used in the 1956 Act have the same meanings as in that Act.

Interpretation of Part I.

36.—(1) In this Part—

 " the Authority " means the Cable Authority ;

 " broadcasting authority " means the BBC or the IBA ;

" diffusion service " has the meaning given by section 2(3) above ;

" licence " means a licence under section 4 above and " licensed " shall be construed accordingly ;

" licensable service " has the meaning given by section 2(2) above ;

" local authority "—

> (*a*) in relation to England and Wales, means any of the following, that is to say, the council of a county, district or London borough, the Greater London Council, the Common Council of the City of London and the Council of the Isles of Scilly ;

> (*b*) in relation to Scotland, means a regional, islands or district council ; and

> (*c*) in relation to Northern Ireland, means a district council ;

" national ", in relation to the United Kingdom, has the meaning given by section 20(7) of the 1981 Act ;

" prescribed diffusion service " has the meaning given by section 2(3) above ;

" restricted service " has the meaning given by section 2(3) above.

(2) For the purposes of this Part section 63(3) of the 1981 Act (meaning of " advertising agent ") shall have effect as if the reference to the selection and purchase of advertising space or time for persons wishing to advertise included a reference to the sale of advertising space or time to such persons.

Part II

Broadcasting Services

Provision by IBA of DBS services

37.—(1) This section and sections 38 to 41 below have effect for the purpose of facilitating, or making special provision in connection with, the provision by the IBA, by means of the technique known as direct broadcasting by satellite or DBS, of television broadcasting services additional to those already provided by them under the 1981 Act.

Provision of DBS services.

(2) The following provisions of the 1981 Act, namely—

> (*a*) in section 2(2) (duty of IBA), paragraph (*c*) and so much of paragraph (*b*) as relates to the maintenance by the programmes broadcast by the IBA of a proper balance and a wide range in their subject matter ;

(b) in section 4(1) (general provisions as to programmes), paragraph (d) and so much of paragraph (b) as relates to the giving of a sufficient amount of time in the programmes to news and news features ;

(c) in section 20 (programme contractors), subsections (1), (2)(b) and (3) ;

(d) section 22 (provision for news broadcasts) ; and

(e) section 24 (buying and selling of programmes by programme contractors),

shall not apply in relation to the provision of DBS services or, as the case may be, to DBS programme contractors.

(3) In this Part and in the 1981 Act—

" DBS service " means any such additional television broadcasting service as is referred to in subsection (1) above ;

" DBS programme contractor " means a person whose contract as a programme contractor gives him the right and the duty to provide programmes or parts of programmes for broadcasting in a DBS service ;

" DBS teletext contractor " means a person whose contract as a teletext contractor gives him the right and the duty to provide material for inclusion in teletext transmissions broadcast in a DBS service.

Contracts for programmes.

38.—(1) In subsection (2) of section 19 of the 1981 Act (duration of programme contracts etc.) there shall be inserted after paragraph (a) the following paragraph—

" (aa) twelve years in the case of a contract for the provision of television programmes for broadcasting in a DBS service ; and ".

(2) Every contract between the IBA and a DBS programme contractor shall contain all such provisions as the IBA think necessary or expedient to ensure that the financial and other arrangements for the provision of the satellite transponder are made by the contractor.

Charges for reception of programmes.

39.—(1) For the purpose of enabling a DBS programme or teletext contractor to make charges for the reception of programmes provided by him or transmissions containing material so provided, the IBA may, notwithstanding anything in the 1981 Act, broadcast the programmes or transmissions in such a form (whether scrambled, encoded or otherwise) as will prevent any person from receiving them unless he obtains from the contractor the means of doing so.

(2) Where under the power conferred by subsection (1) above the IBA broadcast programmes or transmissions in such a

form as is mentioned in that subsection, nothing in the 1981
Act shall be taken as requiring the IBA to permit advertisements to be included in the programmes or transmissions.

40.—(1) In subsection (6) of section 32 of the 1981 Act   Rental
(rental payments by programme contractors) for the words " TV   payments.
programme contractor ", in each place where they occur, there
shall be substituted the words " TV or DBS programme contractor ".

(2) For paragraphs (ii) and (iii) of subsection (9) of that section
there shall be substituted the following paragraphs—

" (ii) only in relation to persons who are DBS programme
  contractors (including persons who are both DBS programme contractors and teletext contractors) ; or

(iii) only in relation to persons who are teletext contractors
  (other than DBS teletext contractors) but are not TV
  or DBS programme contractors ; or

(iv) only in relation to persons who are DBS teletext contractors but are not TV or DBS programme contractors ; or

(v) differently in relation to persons within paragraphs (i),
  (ii), (iii) and (iv) respectively."

(3) In relation to any time before the making under subsection
(8) of section 32 of the 1981 Act of an order amending subsection (4) of that section in relation to—

(*a*) persons who are DBS programme contractors (including persons who are both DBS programme contractors and teletext contractors) ; or

(*b*) persons who are DBS teletext contractors,

the said subsection (4) shall have effect in relation to such
persons as if the relevant rate were nil.

41.—(1) For the purposes of this section—   Finances of
                                                  IBA.
(*a*) so much of the television branch of the IBA's undertaking as consists of the provision by them of DBS
  services ; and

(*b*) so much of that branch as consists of the provision by
  them of other television broadcasting services,

shall be regarded as separate parts of that branch.

(2) Except in so far as the Secretary of State on the application
of the IBA otherwise directs, for each part of the television
branch of their undertaking, it shall be the duty of the IBA so
to conduct their affairs as to secure that their revenues from that

part become at the earliest possible date, and thereafter continue, at least sufficient—

    (a) to meet all sums properly chargeable to revenue account in respect of that part of that branch (including sums which, for the purposes of that part, are required for the repayment of loans and interest thereon, for provision for depreciation and for the maintenance of so much of the reserve fund for that branch as is attributable to that part) ; and

    (b) to make provision towards, and as soon as practicable for, necessary capital expenditure for the purposes of that part of that branch.

(3) Any direction given under this section may be varied or revoked by a subsequent direction so given.

(4) A copy of every direction given under this section shall be laid before each House of Parliament.

The Satellite Broadcasting Board

The Board.
    42.—(1) There shall be a Board to be called the Satellite Broadcasting Board (in this Part referred to as " the Board ") whose function it shall be to provide, by means of the said technique known as direct broadcasting by satellite or DBS, television broadcasting services of high quality (both as to the transmission and as to the matter transmitted) for the United Kingdom, the Isle of Man and the Channel Islands.

(2) The Board shall consist of six members, of whom three shall be appointed from among the governors of the BBC and three from among the members of the IBA.

(3) It shall be the duty of the BBC and the IBA to supply to the Board (on commercial terms) such services as the Board may reasonably require.

(4) The Board, unless previously dissolved, shall cease to function at the end of the period of ten years beginning with the day on which the Board begin to provide their first television broadcasting service.

(5) Schedule 3 to this Act shall have effect with respect to the Board.

Provision of
programmes.
    43.—(1) Without prejudice to the powers conferred on the Board by this Part, the programmes broadcast by the Board shall be provided not by the Board but by a person (in this Part referred to as " the programme provider ") who—

    (a) is approved for the purposes of this section by the Secretary of State after consultation with the IBA ; and (*b*) under a contract with the Board, has the right and the duty to provide programmes to be broadcast by the Board, which may include advertisements.

(2) The Secretary of State may after consultation with the Board withdraw an approval under this section if a relevant change takes place which, if it had occurred before the giving of the approval, would have induced the Secretary of State to refrain from giving the approval.

(3) The Board shall do all that they can to secure that—

(*a*) no person who is a disqualified person, and no body corporate over which a disqualified person has control, becomes or continues as the programme provider (whether alone or in partnership) ; and

(*b*) no body corporate in which a disqualified person participates becomes or continues as the sole programme provider.

(4) The contract between the Board and the programme provider shall—

(*a*) contain all such provisions as the Board think necessary or expedient to ensure that the financial and other arrangements for the provision of the satellite transponder are made by the programme provider ; and

(*b*) provide for the payment by the programme provider to the Board of such sums as the Board consider appropriate for enabling them to meet their reasonable outgoings.

(5) For the purpose of enabling the programme provider to make charges for the reception of programmes provided by him, the Board may, notwithstanding anything in this Part, transmit the programmes in such a form (whether scrambled, encoded or otherwise) as will prevent any person from receiving them unless he obtains from the programme provider the means of doing so.

(6) In this section—

" disqualified person " has the meaning given by section 20(6) of the 1981 Act ;

" programme " includes a teletext transmission ;

" relevant change "—

(*a*) in relation to an approval of two or more persons in partnership, means any change affecting the rights and duties of those persons in relation to the partnership ; and

(*b*) in relation to an approval of a body corporate (whether alone or in partnership), means any change affecting participation in, or the nature and characteristics of, that body corporate or any other body corporate which participates in that body corporate.

(7) For the purposes of this section and section 44 below a person participates in a body corporate if (whether alone or jointly with one or more other persons, and whether directly or through nominees) he holds or is beneficially entitled to shares, or possesses voting power, in the body corporate.

Application of 1981 Act and other enactments.

44.—(1) Subject to subsection (2) below, the provisions of the 1981 Act specified in Schedule 4 to this Act shall apply in relation to the Board, television broadcasting services provided by the Board and the programme provider as they apply in relation to the IBA, ITV, TV programme contractors and teletext contractors.

(2) In its application to the Board, subsection (2) of section 43 of the 1981 Act (annual reports) shall have effect as if it required the report for any financial year to include an account of the extent to which the programmes broadcast by the Board have been supplied to the programme provider by persons other than those mentioned in subsection (3) below.

(3) The persons referred to in subsection (2) above are—

(a) where a body corporate is the programme provider in partnership with other persons, an associate of that body corporate, a person who has control over that body corporate and a body corporate which is under the control of such a person ; and

(b) where a body corporate is the sole programme provider, a person who participates in that body corporate, an associate of such a person and a body corporate which is under the control of such a person.

(4) Part III of the 1981 Act (the Broadcasting Complaints Commission) shall have effect as if—

(a) any reference in section 53 to the IBA, or to a member, officer or employee of the IBA, included a reference to the Board, or to a member, officer or employee of the Board ; and

(b) any reference in that Part to a broadcasting body included a reference to the Board.

(5) The Secretary of State may by order provide that any other enactments (including provisions of this Act) which apply in relation to the IBA, ITV, TV programme contractors or teletext contractors shall apply in relation to the Board, television broadcasting services provided by the Board or the programme provider with such modifications, if any, as may be specified in the order.

(6) An order under this section shall be made by statutory PART II instrument which shall be subject to annulment in pursuance of a resolution of either House of Parliament.

Miscellaneous

45.—(1) In subsection (1) of section 2 of the 1981 Act (which Extension of makes it the function of the IBA to provide television and local duration of sound broadcasting services until 31st December 1996) for the IBA's words " 31st December 1996 " there shall be substituted the function. words " 31st December 2001 ".

(2) In subsection (5) of that section (power of Secretary of State to extend the duration of the function of the IBA) for the words " any date not later than 31st December 2001 " there shall be substituted the words " any later date ".

46.—(1) The IBA need not comply with subsection (4) of No need for section 19 of the 1981 Act (prior consultation etc.) in relation IBA to invite to any contract for the provision of television programmes which applications is entered into on the expiration (by effluxion of time) of a entering into contract to which subsection (2) below applies. certain
contracts.

(2) This subsection applies to any contract for the provision of television programmes which was entered into before the commencement of this section.

(3) In this section " television programme " includes a teletext transmission.

47.—(1) If the IBA provide additional teletext services, then, Provision of for the purpose of enabling a teletext contractor to make charges additional for the reception of transmissions containing material provided services. by him and broadcast in such a service, the IBA may, notwithstanding anything in the 1981 Act, broadcast the transmissions in such a form (whether scrambled, encoded or otherwise) as will prevent any person from receiving them unless he obtains from the contractor the means of doing so.

(2) In this section and in the 1981 Act " additional teletext service " means a teletext service (other than a DBS service) which is additional to those already provided by the IBA under the 1981 Act.

48.—(1) With a view to the provision by the IBA of a Provision of national sound broadcasting service the IBA shall have power transmitting to do all such things as are in their opinion necessary or equipment for expedient for the purposes of equipping themselves to transmit sound the programmes included in such a service. broadcasting
service.

(2) Without prejudice to the generality of the power conferred by subsection (1) above, the IBA shall have power for the purpose there mentioned—

    (*a*) to establish and install stations for wireless telegraphy (within the meaning of the Wireless Telegraphy Act 1949) ; and

    (*b*) to arrange for the provision and equipment of or, if need be, themselves to provide and equip studios and other premises for sound broadcasting purposes.

(3) Without prejudice to the generality of the preceding provisions of this section and subsection (3) of section 3 of the 1981 Act (extent of IBA's powers), that subsection shall be construed as applying in relation to activities undertaken and in relation to property or rights acquired or held by the IBA for the purposes of this section.

(4) The aggregate amount outstanding in respect of the principal of any sums borrowed by the IBA by virtue of this section shall not exceed £2,500,000 or such greater sum as the Secretary of State may from time to time with the consent of the Treasury specify.

(5) Any property or rights acquired or liabilities incurred by the IBA for the purposes of this section shall be treated for financial purposes as property or rights acquired or liabilities incurred by the IBA for the purposes of the branch of their undertaking consisting of the provision of local sound broadcasting services.

(6) The reference in paragraph 4(1) of Schedule 1 to the 1981 Act (capacity of the IBA as a statutory corporation) to the powers of the IBA under that Act shall be construed as including a reference to the powers of the IBA under this section.

(7) Nothing in this section shall be construed as authorising the IBA to do, otherwise than under and in accordance with a licence under section 1 of the Wireless Telegraphy Act 1949 or section 7 of the 1984 Act, anything for the doing of which such a licence is requisite under those Acts respectively.

49.—(1) This section applies where—

    (*a*) the broadcasts in a television or sound broadcasting service are made from a place outside the United Kingdom for reception in the United Kingdom ; and

    (*b*) programmes are proposed to be broadcast in that service by the reception and re-transmission (whether immediately or after an interval) of material sent by means of a telecommunication system licensed under Part II of the 1984 Act.

(2) If it appears to the Secretary of State, after consultation with both broadcasting authorities, that it is requisite or expedient to do so in the interests of public service broadcasting in the United Kingdom, he may by a direction under this section prohibit any person from sending material either for programmes generally, for programmes of a particular description or for particular programmes.

(3) Without prejudice to the generality of subsection (2) above, the Secretary of State may give a direction under this section if it appears to him, after such consultation as aforesaid, that any of the programmes—

    (a) would consist of or include the whole or any part of listed or protected events ; or

    (b) would be such that they could not be included in a television or sound broadcasting service provided by the IBA.

(4) A direction under this section shall be published in such manner as the Secretary of State considers appropriate.

(5) A person who knowingly contravenes a direction under this section shall be liable—

    (a) on summary conviction, to a fine not exceeding the statutory maximum ;

    (b) on conviction on indictment, to a fine.

(6) Without prejudice to subsection (5) above, compliance with a direction under this section shall be enforceable by civil proceedings by the Crown for an injunction or interdict or for any other appropriate relief.

(7) So much of section 14(10) of the 1956 Act as relates to the place from which a broadcast is to be treated as made shall apply for the purposes of this section as it applies for the purposes of that Act.

(8) In this section—

    " broadcasting authority " means the BBC or the IBA ;

    " listed event " has the same meaning as in section 14 above ;

    " material " means sounds or visual images or both ;

    " programme " includes a teletext transmission ;

    " protected event " means a sporting or other event which, in the opinion of the Secretary of State, is one of a series of similar events the whole or any part of which—

        (a) it was at the commencement of this section the practice of a broadcasting authority to broadcast ; and (*b*) but for the acquisition of rights to include the whole or any part of events in that series in external broadcasting services, it would still be the practice of that authority to broadcast;

and for the purposes of this subsection anything broadcast by either of the broadcasting authorities shall be treated as broadcast by each of them.

50. Section 25(1) of the 1981 Act (wages and conditions of employment of persons employed by programme contractors to be as favourable as those under a contract complying with the requirements of any resolution of the House of Commons for the time being in force applicable to contracts of Government departments) shall cease to have effect.

Supplemental

51.—(1) Subject to subsection (2) below, the Secretary of State shall by order repeal sections 42 to 44 above and Schedules 3 and 4 to this Act as from the date on which the Board cease to function in accordance with section 42(4) above.

(2) The Secretary of State may by order repeal those provisions as from an earlier date if he is satisfied that there is no suitable person able and willing to become or continue as the programme provider.

(3) An order under this section may, if the Secretary of State thinks fit, also repeal section 46 above.

(4) An order under this section may include such incidental, supplemental and transitional provisions as the Secretary of State thinks fit, and in particular may make provision for keeping the Board temporarily in existence for purposes connected with their activities and finances prior to the repeal effected by the order and for winding up the affairs of, and dissolving, the Board.

(5) An order under this section shall be made by statutory instrument which shall be subject to annulment in pursuance of a resolution of either House of Parliament.

52. In this Part—

" the Board " means the Satellite Broadcasting Board;

" DBS service ", " DBS programme contractor " and " DBS teletext contractor " have the meanings given by section 37(3) above;

" the programme provider " has the meaning given by section 43(1) above.

PART III

MISCELLANEOUS AND GENERAL

53.—(1) A person who dishonestly receives a programme included in a service to which this section applies with intent to avoid payment of any charge applicable to the reception of that programme shall be liable on summary conviction to a fine not exceeding level 5 on the standard scale.

Fraudulently receiving certain programmes.

(2) This section and section 54 below apply to—

(*a*) any cable programme service ;

(*b*) any television or sound broadcasting service provided by the BBC or the IBA ; and

(*c*) any service (other than a television or sound broadcasting service) which consists wholly or mainly in the sending, by means of a telecommunication system, of sounds or visual images or both and is provided for a person providing a service falling within paragraph (*a*) or (*b*) above ;

and for the purposes of this subsection a service provided for the Welsh Authority, the IBA's subsidiary or a programme contractor shall be treated as provided for the IBA.

(3) Her Majesty may by Order in Council make provision, in the case of any country specified in the Order, for applying this section and section 54 below to—

(*a*) any service provided in that country which would be a cable programme service if subsection (7) of section 2 above and references in subsection (1) of that section to the United Kingdom were omitted ;

(*b*) any television or sound broadcasting service provided in that country by an organisation constituted in, or under the laws of, that country ; and

(*c*) any service provided in that country (other than a television or sound broadcasting service) which consists wholly or mainly in the sending, by means of a telecommunication system, of sounds or visual images or both and is provided for a person providing a service falling within paragraph (*a*) or (*b*) above.

(4) Her Majesty shall not make an Order in Council under subsection (3) above in the case of any country unless Her Majesty is satisfied that provision has been or will be made under the laws of that country whereby adequate protection will be given to persons making charges for programmes included in services falling within subsection (2) above.

(5) Any statutory instrument containing an Order in Council under subsection (3) above shall be subject to annulment in pursuance of a resolution of either House of Parliament.

Proprietary rights in respect of certain programmes.

54.—(1) Every person who makes charges for the reception of programmes included in a service to which this section applies shall be entitled to the proprietary rights conferred by this section.

(2) The rights conferred by this section are infringed by the manufacture, importation, sale or letting on hire of any apparatus or device which is designed or adapted, or the publication of any information which is calculated, to enable or assist persons to receive the programmes without payment.

(3) Subject to subsection (5) below, infringements of the rights conferred by this section on any person shall be actionable at the suit of that person ; and in any proceedings for such an infringement all such relief, by way of damages, injunction, interdict, account or otherwise, shall be available as is available in any corresponding proceedings in respect of infringements of other proprietary rights.

(4) Where rights conferred by this section on any person have been infringed by the manufacture, importation, sale or letting on hire of any apparatus or device, then, subject to subsection (5) below, that person shall be entitled in respect of the conversion by any other person of the apparatus or device to all such relief, by way of an order for its delivery or otherwise, as he would be entitled to if he were its owner and had been its owner since the time of the infringement.

(5) A person shall not be entitled to recover damages from another person by virtue of this section if, at the time of the infringement or conversion, that other person was not aware, and had no reasonable grounds for suspecting, that the rights conferred by this section on the first-mentioned person would be or had been infringed.

1981 c. 54.
1978 c. 23.

(6) Section 72 of the Supreme Court Act 1981 and section 94A of the Judicature (Northern Ireland) Act 1978 (withdrawal of privilege against incrimination of self or spouse in certain proceedings) shall each have effect as if the proceedings to which subsection (1) of that section applies included proceedings in the High Court brought by virtue of this section.

(7) In the application of this section to Scotland, for any reference to the conversion by any person of any apparatus or device there shall be substituted a reference to an intromission by any person with any apparatus or device.

55.—(1) Where a body corporate is guilty of an offence under this Act and that offence is proved to have been committed with the consent or connivance of, or to be attributable to any neglect on the part of, any director, manager, secretary or other similar officer of the body corporate or any person who was purporting to act in any such capacity he, as well as the body corporate, shall be guilty of that offence and shall be liable to be proceeded against and punished accordingly.

(2) Where the affairs of a body corporate are managed by its members, subsection (1) above shall apply in relation to the acts and defaults of a member in connection with his functions of management as if he were a director of the body corporate.

Part III

Offences by bodies corporate.

56.—(1) Unless the contrary intention appears, expressions used in this Act which are also used in the 1981 Act have the same meanings as in that Act.

General interpretation.

(2) In this Act and, unless the contrary intention appears, in any enactment amended by this Act—

" the 1956 Act " means the Copyright Act 1956 ;   1956 c. 74.

" the 1981 Act " means the Broadcasting Act 1981 ;   1981 c. 68.

" the 1984 Act " means the Telecommunications Act 1984 ;   1984 c. 12.

" cable programme service " has the meaning given by section 2(1) above ;

" the IBA's subsidiary " means the subsidiary mentioned in section 12(2) of the 1981 Act ;

" licensable cable programme service " has the same meaning as " licensable service " has in Part I of this Act ;

" licensed ", in relation to a cable programme service, means licensed under section 4 above ;

" programme ", in relation to a cable programme service, includes any item included in that service ;

" standard scale " has the meaning given by section 75 of the Criminal Justice Act 1982 ;   1982 c. 48.

" statutory maximum " has the meaning given by section 74 of that Act ;

" telecommunication service " and " telecommunication system " have the same meanings as in the 1984 Act.

57.—(1) The enactments mentioned in Schedule 5 to this Act shall have effect subject to the amendments there specified (being minor amendments or amendments consequential on the provisions of this Act).

Amendments and repeals.

(2) The enactments mentioned in Schedule 6 to this Act are hereby repealed to the extent specified in the third column of that Schedule.

PART III
Transitional
provisions.

58.—(1) An order made, or having effect as if made, under section 57 of the 1984 Act shall have effect as if made under section 3 of this Act; and the provisions of this Act and the enactments amended by this Act shall have effect accordingly.

(2) A licence granted, or having effect as if granted, by the Secretary of State under section 58 of the 1984 Act shall have effect as if granted by the Cable Authority under section 4 of this Act; and the provisions of this Act and the enactments amended by this Act shall have effect accordingly.

Short title,
extent and
commence-
ment.

59.—(1) This Act may be cited as the Cable and Broadcasting Act 1984.

(2) This Act extends to Northern Ireland.

(3) Her Majesty may by Order in Council direct that all or any of the provisions of this Act shall extend to the Isle of Man or any of the Channel Islands with such adaptations and modifications, if any, as may be specified in the Order.

(4) This Act shall come into force on such day as the Secretary of State may by order made by statutory instrument appoint; and different days may be so appointed for different provisions or for different purposes.

SCHEDULES

SCHEDULE 1

THE AUTHORITY: SUPPLEMENTARY PROVISIONS

Status and capacity

1.—(1) The Authority shall be a body corporate.

(2) The Authority shall not be treated for the purposes of the enactments and rules of law relating to the privileges of the Crown as a body exercising functions on behalf of the Crown.

(3) It shall be within the capacity of the Authority as a statutory corporation to do such things and enter into such transactions as are incidental or conducive to the exercise of their functions under this Part, including the borrowing of money.

Appointment of members

2.—(1) All the members of the Authority (including the chairman and deputy chairman who shall be appointed as such) shall be appointed by the Secretary of State.

(2) A person shall be disqualified for being appointed or being a member of the Authority so long as he is a governor of the BBC or a member of the IBA or the Welsh Authority.

(3) Before appointing a person to be a member of the Authority, the Secretary of State shall satisfy himself that that person will have no such financial or other interest as is likely to affect prejudicially the discharge by him of his functions as member of the Authority ; and the Secretary of State shall also satisfy himself from time to time with respect to every member of the Authority that he has no such interest.

(4) Any person who is, or whom the Secretary of State proposes to appoint to be, a member of the Authority shall, whenever requested by the Secretary of State to do so, furnish to him such information as the Secretary of State considers necessary for the performance by him of his duties under sub-paragraph (3) above.

Tenure of office

3.—(1) Subject to the following provisions of this Schedule, a person shall hold and vacate office as a member or as chairman or deputy chairman of the Authority in accordance with the terms of his appointment.

(2) A person shall not be appointed as a member of the Authority for more than five years at a time.

(3) A person may at any time resign his office as a member or as chairman or deputy chairman.

Remuneration and pensions of members

4.—(1) The Authority may pay to each member such remuneration and allowances as the Secretary of State may determine.

(2) The Authority may pay or make provision for paying to or in respect of any member such sums by way of pensions, allowances or gratuities as the Secretary of State may determine.

(3) Where a person ceases to be a member otherwise than on the expiry of his term of office and it appears to the Secretary of State that there are special circumstances which make it right for him to receive compensation, the Authority may make to him a payment of such amount as the Secretary of State may determine.

(4) The approval of the Treasury shall be required for any determination under this paragraph.

Disqualification of members of Authority for House of Commons and Northern Ireland Assembly

1975 c. 24.   5. In Part II of Schedule 1 to the House of Commons Disqualification Act 1975 (bodies of which all members are disqualified) there shall be inserted (at the appropriate place in alphabetical order) the following entry—

" The Cable Authority " ;

and the like insertion shall be made in Part II of Schedule 1 to
1975 c. 25.   the Northern Ireland Assembly Disqualification Act 1975.

Proceedings

6.—(1) The quorum of the Authority and the arrangements relating to their meetings shall be such as the Authority may determine.

(2) The arrangements may, with the approval of the Secretary of State, provide for the discharge, under the general directions of the Authority, of any of the Authority's functions by a committee or by one or more of the members, officers or employees of the Authority.

7.—(1) A member of the Authority who is in any way directly or indirectly interested in a licence granted or proposed to be granted by the Authority shall, as soon as possible after the relevant circumstances have come to his knowledge, disclose the nature of his interest at a meeting of the Authority.

(2) Any disclosure under sub-paragraph (1) above shall be recorded in the minutes of the Authority, and the member shall not take part after the disclosure in any deliberation or decision of the Authority with respect to the licence.

8. The validity of any proceedings of the Authority shall not be affected by any vacancy among the members or by any defect in the appointment of a member or by any failure to comply with the requirements of paragraph 7 above.

Officers and employees of Authority

9.—(1) The Authority may appoint a secretary and such other officers, and take into their employment such other persons, as they may determine.

(2) The Authority shall, as regards any officers or persons employed in whose case it may be determined by the Authority so to do, pay to or in respect of them such pensions, allowances or gratuities, or provide and maintain for them such pension schemes (whether contributory or not), as may be so determined.

(3) If any officer of or other person employed by the Authority, being a participant in any pension scheme applicable to his office or employment, becomes a member of the Authority, he may, if the Secretary of State so determines, be treated for the purposes of the pension scheme as if his service as a member of the Authority were service as an officer of or person employed by the Authority.

Authentication of Authority's seal

10. The application of the seal of the Authority shall be authenticated by—

 (a) the signature of the chairman or deputy chairman of the Authority or some other member of the Authority authorised by the Authority to authenticate the application of their seal ; and

 (b) the signature of the secretary of the Authority or some other officer of the Authority authorised by the Authority to act in that behalf.

Presumption of authenticity of documents issued by Authority

11. Any document purporting to be an instrument issued by the Authority and to be sealed as aforesaid or to be signed on behalf of the Authority shall be received in evidence and shall be deemed to be such an instrument without further proof unless the contrary is shown.

SCHEDULE 2

AMENDMENTS OF PART III OF 1981 ACT

1. In section 53(3) of the 1981 Act (disqualification for membership of Broadcasting Complaints Commission) after the words " the IBA ", in the first place where they occur, there shall be inserted the words " or the Cable Authority " and for the words from " the preparation " to the end there shall be substituted the words—

 " (i) the preparation or provision of programmes for broadcasting by the BBC or the IBA (including, in the case of the IBA, programmes consisting of advertisements) ; and

 (ii) the provision of a licensed cable programme service or the preparation or provision of programmes for inclusion in such a service."

2.—(1) For paragraph (*b*) of subsection (1) of section 54 of that Act (functions of Commission) there shall be substituted the following paragraphs—

" (*b*) unjust or unfair treatment in programmes actually included in a licensed cable programme service after the commencement of section 29 of the Cable and Broadcasting Act 1984 otherwise than by the reception and immediate re-transmission of broadcasts made by a broadcasting body ; or

(*c*) unwarranted infringement of privacy in, or in connection with the obtaining of material included in, sound or television programmes actually so broadcast or programmes actually so included."

(2) For the definitions of " complaint " and " participant " in subsection (3) of that section there shall be substituted the following definitions—

" ' broadcasting complaint ' means a complaint in the case of which the relevant programme was broadcast by a broadcasting body ;

' cable programme complaint ' means a complaint in the case of which the relevant programme was included in a licensed cable programme service otherwise than by the reception and immediate re-transmission of broadcasts made by a broadcasting body ;

' complaint ' means a complaint to the Commission of any such unjust or unfair treatment or unwarranted infringement of privacy as is mentioned in subsection (1) ;

' participant ', in relation to a programme, means a person who appeared, or whose voice was heard, in the programme ; ".

3.—(1) In subsection (4) of section 55 of that Act (making and entertaining of complaints) after the words " relevant programme " there shall be inserted the words " or its inclusion in a licensed cable programme service ".

(2) At the end of subsection (5) of that section there shall be added the words " or included in a licensed cable programme service ".

(3) In subsection (6) of that section after the word " broadcast " there shall be inserted the words " or included in a licensed cable programme service ".

4.—(1) For paragraphs (*b*) and (*c*) of subsection (2) of section 56 of that Act (consideration of complaints) there shall be substituted the following paragraphs—

" (*b*) in the case of a broadcasting complaint, the broadcasting body by whom the relevant programme was broadcast ;

(*c*) in the case of a cable programme complaint, the Cable Authority and every person providing a licensed cable programme service in which the relevant programme was included ; and (*d*) in either case, any person not falling within the foregoing paragraphs who appears to the Commission to have been responsible for the making or provision of the relevant programme."

(2) For subsection (3) of that section there shall be substituted the following subsection—

" (3) Before they proceed to consider a complaint the Commission shall—

(*a*) in the case of a broadcasting complaint, send a copy of it to the broadcasting body by whom the relevant programme was broadcast ; and

(*b*) in the case of a cable programme complaint, send a copy of it to the Cable Authority."

(3) In subsection (4) of that section after the words " broadcasting body " there shall be inserted the words " or the Cable Authority " and after the words " that body ", in each place where they occur, there shall be inserted the words " or Authority ".

(4) For subsections (5) and (6) of that section there shall be substituted the following subsections—

" (5) Where a broadcasting body or the Cable Authority receive from the Commission a copy of a complaint, it shall be the duty of that body or Authority, if so required by the Commission, to arrange for one or more of the governors, members or officers of that body or Authority to attend and assist the Commission in their consideration of the complaint.

(6) Where a broadcasting body or the Cable Authority receive from the Commission a copy of a complaint and, in connection with the complaint, the Commission make to any person (other than that body or Authority) a request to which this subsection applies, it shall be the duty of that body or Authority to take such steps as they reasonably can to ensure that the request is complied with."

5.—(1) In subsection (1) of section 57 of that Act (publication of Commission's findings) for the words from " to the broadcasting body " to " so specified " there shall be substituted the words " directions requiring the publication, in any manner specified in the directions and within such period as may be so specified, of ".

(2) For subsection (2) of that section there shall be substituted the following subsections—

" (2) Directions under subsection (1) shall, in the case of a broadcasting complaint, be given to the broadcasting body by whom the relevant programme was broadcast ; and it shall be the duty of a broadcasting body to comply with any directions so given.

(2A) Directions under subsection (1) shall, in the case of a cable programme complaint, be given to every person providing a licensed cable programme service in which the relevant programme was included ; and it shall be the duty of the Cable Authority to take such steps as they reasonably can to ensure that any directions so given are complied with."

(3) In subsection (5) of that section for the words " or programme contractor " there shall be substituted the words " , programme contractor or person providing a licensed cable programme service ".

6.—(1) In section 58 of that Act (duty to publicise Commission) for the word " complaints " there shall be substituted the words " broadcasting complaints ".

(2) That section as so amended shall be renumbered as subsection (1) of that section and after that provision as so renumbered there shall be inserted the following subsection—

" (2) It shall be the duty of the Cable Authority to take such steps as they reasonably can to secure the publication (by means of licensed cable programme services or otherwise) of regular announcements publicising the Commission and their function of considering and adjudicating upon cable programme complaints."

7. At the end of section 59(3) of that Act (annual report of Commission) there shall be added the words " and to the Cable Authority and every person providing a licensed cable programme service ".

SCHEDULE 3

THE BOARD: SUPPLEMENTARY PROVISIONS

Status and capacity

1.—(1) The Board shall be a body corporate.

(2) The Board shall not be treated for the purposes of the enactments and rules of law relating to the privileges of the Crown as a body exercising functions on behalf of the Crown.

(3) It shall be within the capacity of the Board as a statutory corporation to do such things and enter into such transactions as are incidental or conducive to the exercise of their functions under this Part, including the borrowing of money.

Appointment of members

2—(1) All the members of the Board shall be appointed by the Secretary of State after consultation with the BBC and the IBA.

(2) Before appointing a person to be a member of the Board, the Secretary of State shall satisfy himself that that person will have no such financial or other interest as is likely to affect prejudicially the discharge by him of his functions as member of the Board ; and the Secretary of State shall also satisfy himself from time to time with respect to every member of the Board that he has no such interest.

(3) Any person who is, or whom the Secretary of State proposes to appoint to be, a member of the Board shall, whenever requested by the Secretary of State to do so, furnish to him such information as the Secretary of State considers necessary for the performance by him of his duties under sub-paragraph (2) above.

Chairman

3. The Board shall elect a chairman from among their members.

Tenure of office

4.—(1) Subject to the following provisions of this Schedule, a person shall hold and vacate office as a member of the Board in accordance with the terms of his appointment.

(2) A person shall not be appointed as a member of the Board for more than five years at a time.

(3) A person may at any time resign his office as a member or as chairman.

Remuneration and pensions of members

5.—(1) The Board may pay to each member such remuneration and allowances as the Secretary of State may determine.

(2) The Board may pay or make provision for paying to or in respect of any member such sums by way of pensions, allowances or gratuities as the Secretary of State may determine.

(3) Where a person ceases to be a member otherwise than on the expiry of his term of office and it appears to the Secretary of State that there are special circumstances which make it right for him to receive compensation, the Board may make to him a payment of such amount as the Secretary of State may determine.

(4) The approval of the Treasury shall be required for any determination under this paragraph.

Proceedings

6.—(1) The quorum of the Board and the arrangements relating to their meetings shall be such as the Board may determine.

(2) The arrangements may, with the approval of the Secretary of State, provide for the discharge, under the general directions of the Board, of any of the Board's functions by a committee or by one or more of the members, officers or employees of the Board.

7. The validity of any proceedings of the Board shall not be affected by any vacancy among the members or by any defect in the appointment of a member.

Officers and employees of Board

8.—(1) The Board may appoint a secretary and such other officers, and take into their employment such other persons, as they may determine.

(2) The Board shall, as regards any officers or persons employed in whose case it may be determined by the Board so to do, pay to or in respect of them such pensions, allowances or gratuities, or provide and maintain for them such pension schemes (whether contributory or not), as may be so determined.

(3) If any officer of or other person employed by the Board, being a participant in any pension scheme applicable to his office or employment, becomes a member of the Board, he may, if the Secretary of State so determines, be treated for the purposes of the pension scheme as if his service as a member of the Board were service as an officer of or person employed by the Board.

Authentication of Board's seal

9. The application of the seal of the Board shall be authenticated by—

(a) the signature of the chairman of the Board or some other member of the Board authorised by the Board to authenticate the application of their seal ; and

(b) the signature of the secretary of the Board or some other officer of the Board authorised by the Board to act in that behalf.

Presumption of authenticity of documents issued by Board

10. Any document purporting to be an instrument issued by the Board and to be sealed as aforesaid or to be signed on behalf of the Board shall be received in evidence and shall be deemed to be such an instrument without further proof unless the contrary is shown.

Section 44(1).

SCHEDULE 4

PROVISIONS OF 1981 ACT APPLIED BY SECTION 44(1)

Provision	*Subject-matter*
In section 2(2), so much of paragraph (a) as relates to the provision by the IBA of broadcasting services as a public service for disseminating information and entertainment and so much of paragraph (b) as relates to the maintenance by the programmes broadcast by the IBA of a high general standard in all respects (and in particular in respect of their content and quality).	Duty of IBA to provide broadcasting services as a public service.
Section 3(1)(a) and (b), (3), (4) and (7).	Powers of IBA.

Section 4 except paragraph (*d*) of subsection (1) and so much of paragraph (*b*) of that subsection as relates to the giving of a sufficient amount of time in the programmes to news and news features.	General provisions as to programmes.	Sch. 4
Sections 5 to 7.	Code for programmes other than advertisements, submission of programme schedules for IBA's approval and programme prizes.	
Sections 8 and 9.	Advertisements and code for advertisements.	
Section 14(1)	Provision of teletext services by IBA.	
Section 15.	Code for teletext transmissions.	
Section 16(1).	Advisory committees and general advisory council.	
Section 21(1), (6)(*a*) and (*b*) and (7).	Provisions to be included in contracts for programmes.	
Sections 28 to 30.	Government control over IBA as to hours of broadcasting and as to certain other matters and prevention of exclusive arrangements for broadcasting events of national interest.	
Section 42.	Accounts and audit.	
Section 43 (1) and (2).	Annual reports.	
Sections 61 and 62.	Approvals by IBA and variation and revocation of directions and notices.	
Schedule 2.	Rules as to advertisements.	

SCHEDULE 5

Section 57(1).

Minor and Consequential Amendments

The Parliamentary Papers Act 1840

1840 c. 9.

1. Section 3 of the Parliamentary Papers Act 1840 (which confers protection in respect of proceedings for printing extracts from or abstracts of parliamentary papers) shall have effect as if the reference to printing included a reference to inclusion in a cable programme service which is or does not require to be licensed.

The Law of Libel Amendment Act 1888

2. Section 3 of the Law of Libel Amendment Act 1888 (which relates to contemporary reports of proceedings before courts exercising judicial authority) shall apply in relation to reports or matters included in a cable programme service which is or does not require to be licensed, and in relation to any inclusion in such a service of any such report or matter, as it applies in relation to reports and matters published in a newspaper and to publication in a newspaper.

The Cinematograph Act 1909

3.—(1) In section 1(3) of the Cinematograph Act 1909 (provision against cinematograph exhibition except in licensed premises) the words " under Part IV of the Telecommunications Act 1984 " shall be omitted.

(2) This paragraph does not extend to Northern Ireland.

The Children and Young Persons Act 1933

4.—(1) In subsection (2)(*a*) of section 28 of the Children and Young Persons Act 1933 (powers of entry) after the words " broadcasting studio " there shall be inserted the words " a cable programme studio " and after the word " broadcast " there shall be inserted the words " in a cable programme ".

(2) After subsection (3) of that section there shall be inserted the following subsection—

" (4) In this section ' cable programme ' means a programme included in a cable programme service and ' cable programme studio ' shall be construed accordingly."

(3) Sections 39 and 49 of that Act (which restrict newspaper reports of court proceedings involving children and young persons) shall with the necessary modifications apply in relation to reports or matters included in a cable programme service as they apply in relation to newspapers.

The Children and Young Persons (Scotland) Act 1937

5.—(1) In subsection (2)(*a*) of section 36 of the Children and Young Persons (Scotland) Act 1937 (powers of entry) after the words " broadcasting studio " there shall be inserted the words " a cable programme studio " and after the word " broadcast ", there shall be inserted the words " in a cable programme ".

(2) After subsection (3) of that section there shall be inserted the following subsection—

" (4) In this section ' cable programme ' means a programme included in a cable programme service and ' cable programme studio ' shall be construed accordingly."

(3) Section 46 of that Act (which restricts newspaper reports of court proceedings involving children and young persons) shall with the necessary modifications apply in relation to reports or matters included in a cable programme service as it applies in relation to newspapers.

The Copyright Act 1956

6.—(1) In the proviso to subsection (3) of section 2 of the 1956 Act (copyright in literary, dramatic and musical works) the word " and " immediately preceding paragraph (*d*) shall be omitted and after that paragraph there shall be inserted the following paragraph—

" (*e*) the inclusion of the work in a cable programme,".

(2) In subsection (5) of that section for paragraph (*e*) there shall be substituted the following paragraph—

" (*e*) including the work in a cable programme ; ".

(3) In section 3(5) of that Act (copyright in artistic works) for paragraph (*d*) there shall be substituted the following paragraph—

" (*d*) including the work in a cable programme."

(4) In section 6(9) of that Act (general exceptions from protection of literary, dramatic and musical works) for the words " caused to be transmitted to subscribers to a diffusion service " there shall be substituted the words " included in a cable programme ".

(5) In section 7(8) of that Act (special exceptions as regards libraries and archives) for the words " causes it to be transmitted to subscribers to a diffusion service " there shall be substituted the words " includes it in a cable programme ".

(6) In section 9(11) of that Act (general exceptions from protection of artistic works) for the words " television programme which is caused to be transmitted to subscribers to a diffusion service " there shall be substituted the words " cable programme ".

(7) In subsection (10) of section 14 of that Act (copyright in television broadcasts and sound broadcasts) for the words from " the visual images or sounds " to the end there shall be substituted the following paragraphs—

" (*a*) the visual images or sounds in question, or both, as the case may be, are broadcast ; or

(*b*) in the case of a television broadcast or sound broadcast made by the technique known as direct broadcasting by satellite, the visual images or sounds in question, or both, as the case may be, are transmitted to the satellite transponder."

(8) After that subsection there shall be inserted the following subsection—

" (11) The foregoing provisions of this section shall have effect as if references in those provisions and in section 12(9) of this Act to sounds included references to signals serving for the impartation of matter otherwise than in the form of sounds or visual images."

(9) In subsection (1) of section 16 of that Act (supplementary provisions for purposes of Part II) for the words " and sound broadcasts " there shall be substituted the words " sound broadcasts and cable programmes ".

(10) In subsection (6) of that section after the word " broadcast " there shall be inserted the words " cable programme ".

(11) In section 18(3) of that Act (right of owner of copyright in respect of infringing copies etc.) for the words " a sound broadcast " there shall be substituted the words " a sound broadcast or a cable programme " and for the words " or broadcast " there shall be substituted the words " broadcast or programme ".

(12) In section 24(2) of that Act (general provisions as to jurisdiction of tribunal) for the words " cause the work or an adaptation thereof to be transmitted to subscribers to a diffusion service " there shall be substituted the words " include the work or an adaptation thereof in a cable programme " and for the words " or to broadcast it " there shall be substituted the words " to broadcast it or to include it in a cable programme ".

(13) In subsection (1) of section 28 of that Act (exercise of jurisdiction of tribunal in relation to diffusion of foreign broadcasts) for the words " cause works to be transmitted to subscribers to a diffusion service " there shall be substituted the words " include works or sound recordings in a cable programme service provided ", for the word " distributing ", in the first place where it occurs, there shall be substituted the words " including in such a service ", after the word " works ", in the second place where it occurs, there shall be inserted the words " or recordings " and for the words " distributing those programmes " there shall be substituted the words " including those programmes in a cable programme service ".

(14) In subsection (2) of that section after the words " the works ", in both places where they occur, there shall be inserted the words " or recordings ", for the words " cause those works to be transmitted to subscribers to diffusion services " there shall be substituted the words " include those works or recordings in cable programme services provided " and for the words " cause those works to be so transmitted " there shall be substituted the words " so include those works or recordings ".

(15) In subsection (4) of that section after the word " works ", in the first place where it occurs, there shall be inserted the words " or sound recordings ".

(16) At the end of section 31(3) of that Act (extension of Act to Isle of Man, Channel Islands, colonies and dependencies) there shall be added the words " or—

(e) in the case of a cable programme, it was sent from a place in that country."

(17) At the end of section 32(1) of that Act (application of Act to countries to which it does not extend) there shall be added the following paragraph—

" (f) apply in relation to cable programmes sent from places in that country as they apply in relation to cable programmes sent from places in the United Kingdom."

(18) In subsection (4) of section 40 of that Act (broadcasts of sound recordings and cinematograph films and diffusion of broadcast programmes) for the words " the programme to be transmitted "

there shall be substituted the words "including the programme in a cable programme service".

(19) In subsection (5) of that section after the words "a work" there shall be inserted the words "or sound recording" and after the words "the work" there shall be inserted the words "or recording".

(20) In section 41(5) of that Act (use of copyright material for education) for the words "and television broadcasts" there shall be substituted the words "television broadcasts and cable programmes".

(21) In section 43(2)(*d*) of that Act (false attribution of authorship) for the words "or broadcasts" there shall be substituted the words "broadcasts or includes in a cable programme".

(22) In subsection (1) of section 48 of that Act (interpretation) after the definition of "building" there shall be inserted the following definition—

"'cable programme', 'cable programme service' and 'programme' have the meanings assigned to them by section 14A of this Act;".

(23) For subsection (3) of that section there shall be substituted the following subsections—

"(3) References in this Act to the inclusion of a programme in a cable programme service are references to its inclusion in such a service by the person providing that service.

(3A) For the purposes of this Act no account shall be taken of a cable programme service if, and to the extent that, it is provided for—

(*a*) a person providing another such service;

(*b*) the Corporation; or

(*c*) the Authority;

and for the purposes of this subsection a cable programme service provided for the Welsh Fourth Channel Authority, the subsidiary mentioned in section 12(2) of the Broadcasting Act 1981 or a programme contractor within the meaning of that Act shall be treated as provided for the Authority.

(3B) For the purposes of this Act no account shall be taken of a cable programme service which is only incidental to a business of keeping or letting premises where persons reside or sleep, and is operated as part of the amenities provided exclusively or mainly for residents or inmates therein."

(24) In subsection (5) of that section for the words "the causing of a work or other subject matter to be transmitted to subscribers to a diffusion service" there shall be substituted the words "including a work or other subject matter in a cable programme".

(25) In paragraph 36(3) of Schedule 7 to that Act (transitional provisions) for paragraph (*c*) there shall be substituted the following paragraph—

"(*c*) including the work or an adaptation thereof in a cable programme."

The Dramatic and Musical Performers' Protection Act 1958

7.—(1) In section 6 of the Dramatic and Musical Performers' Protection Act 1958 (special defences) for the word " transmission ", in each place where it occurs, there shall be substituted the words " cable programme " and after the word " made " there shall be inserted the words " or included ".

(2) In section 7 of that Act (consent on behalf of performers) for the word " transmission ", in each place where it occurs, there shall be substituted the words " cable programme ", after the word " made " there shall be inserted the words " or included " and after the word " making ", in both places where it occurs, there shall be inserted the words " or including ".

(3) In subsection (1) of section 8 of that Act (interpretation), after the definition of " broadcast " there shall be inserted the following definitions—

" ' cable programme ' means a programme included in a cable programme service, and references to the inclusion of a cable programme shall be construed accordingly ;

' cable programme service ' means a cable programme service within the meaning of the Cable and Broadcasting Act 1984 or a service provided outside the United Kingdom which would be such a service if subsection (7) of section 2 of that Act and references in subsection (1) of that section to the United Kingdom were omitted ; ".

(4) Also in that subsection after the definition of " performers " there shall be inserted the following definition—

" ' programme ', in relation to a cable programme service, includes any item included in that service ; ".

(5) After subsection (2) of that section there shall be inserted the following subsection—

" (3) Section 48(3) of the Copyright Act 1956 (which explains the meaning of references in that Act to the inclusion of a programme in a cable programme service) shall apply for the purposes of this Act as it applies for the purposes of that Act."

The Obscene Publications Act 1959

8.—(1) Proceedings for an offence under section 2 of the Obscene Publications Act 1959 (prohibition of publication of obscene matter) for publishing an obscene article—

(a) shall not be instituted in any case where the relevant publication took place in the course of including a programme in a cable programme service ; and

(b) shall not be instituted except by or with the consent of the Director of Public Prosecutions in any case where the only other publication which followed from the relevant publication took place in the course of including a programme in such a service ;

and in this sub-paragraph " the relevant publication " means the
publication in respect of which the defendant would be charged if
the proceedings were brought.

(2) It is hereby declared that a person who has an obscene article
in his ownership, possession or control with a view to its being shown,
played or projected in the course of a cable programme service shall
be taken for the purposes of subsection (1) of that section to have
that article for publication for gain.

(3) Proceedings for an offence under that section for having an
obscene article for publication for gain shall not be instituted except
by or with the consent of the Director of Public Prosecutions in any
case where the relevant publication or the only other publication
which could reasonably have been expected to follow from the
relevant publication was to take place in the course of including a
programme in a cable programme service ; and in this sub-paragraph
" the relevant publication " means the publication which, if the
proceedings were brought, the defendant would be alleged to have
had in contemplation.

(4) Without prejudice to the duty of a court to make an order
for the forfeiture of an article under section 1(4) of the Obscene 1964 c. 74.
Publications Act 1964 (orders on conviction), in a case where by
virtue of sub-paragraph (3) above proceedings under the said section
2 for having an article for publication for gain could not be instituted
except by or with the consent of the Director of Public Prosecutions,
no order for the forfeiture of the article shall be made under
section 3 of the said Act of 1959 (power of search and seizure) unless
the warrant under which the article was seized was issued on an
information laid by or on behalf of the Director of Public Prosecutions.

(5) In this paragraph expressions used in the said Act of 1959
have the same meanings as in that Act.

The Public Bodies (Admission to Meetings) Act 1960

1960 c. 67.

9. In section 1(7) of the Public Bodies (Admissions to Meetings)
Act 1960 (admission of public to meetings of local authorities and
other bodies) after the word " broadcasts " there shall be inserted
the words " or for programmes to be included in a cable programme
service which is or does not require to be licensed ".

The Betting, Gaming and Lotteries Act 1963

1963 c. 2.

10. For paragraphs (*a*) and (*b*) of paragraph 5 of Schedule 4 to
the Betting, Gaming and Lotteries Act 1963 (exclusion of facilities
for seeing or hearing certain broadcasts) there shall be substituted
the following paragraphs—

　　" (*a*) seeing any television programme which is broadcast by
　　　　wireless telegraphy within the meaning of the Wireless
　　　　Telegraphy Act 1949 or is included in a cable programme
　　　　service ; or

(*b*) hearing any sound programme which is so broadcast or so included and which—

    (i) is intended to be received by the general public; or

    (ii) comprises matter other than information relating to events in connection with which betting transactions may be or have been effected on the licensed premises,".

The Protection of Depositors Act 1963

11. In section 26(3) of the Protection of Depositors Act 1963 (definition of " advertisement ") after the word " television " there shall be inserted the words " or by inclusion in a cable programme service ".

The Children and Young Persons Act 1963

12. For paragraph (*d*) of section 37(2) of the Children and Young Persons Act 1963 (restriction on persons under 16 taking part in certain performances) there shall be substituted the following paragraphs—

" (*d*) any performance included in a cable programme service;

    (*e*) any performance recorded (by whatever means) with a view to its use in a broadcast or such a service or in a film intended for public exhibition; ".

The Performers' Protection Act 1963

13.—(1) In section 3(1) of the Performers' Protection Act 1963 (relaying of performances) after the word " reception " there shall be inserted the words " and immediate re-transmission " and for the words from " causes " to " public " there shall be substituted the words " includes a performance to which the principal Act applies, or any part of such performance, in a cable programme without the consent in writing of the performers ".

(2) In section 4(1)(*a*) of that Act (giving of consent without authority) for the words " broadcast or transmission is made " there shall be substituted the words " or broadcast is made or a cable programme is included "

The Licensing Act 1964

14. In section 182(1) of the Licensing Act 1964 (relaxation, with respect to licensed premises, of law relating to music and dancing licences) after the word " broadcasts " there shall be inserted the words " or by the use of a cable programme service which is or does not require to be licensed ".

The Protection of Depositors Act (Northern Ireland) 1964

15. In section 26(3) of the Protection of Depositors Act (Northern Ireland) 1964 (definition of " advertisement ") after the word " television " there shall be inserted the words " or by inclusion in a cable programme service ".

The Private Places of Entertainment (Licensing) Act 1967   1967 c. 19.

16. At the end of section 2(3) of the Private Places of Entertainment (Licensing) Act 1967 (certain private places of entertainment to require licences) there shall be inserted the words " or of being included in a cable programme service which is or does not require to be licensed ".

The Wireless Telegraphy Act 1967   1967 c. 72.

17. In section 6(1) of the Wireless Telegraphy Act 1967 (interpretation of Part I)—

(*a*) after the definition of " television dealer " there shall be inserted the following definition—

" ' television programme ' means a television programme broadcast for general reception or included in a licensable cable programme service " ; and

(*b*) in the definition of " television set " the words " wireless telegraphy " and " broadcast for general reception " shall be omitted.

The London Cab Act 1968   1968 c. 7.

18. In section 4(5) of the London Cab Act 1968 (restrictions on advertising in connection with private hire-cars) after the word " television " there shall be inserted the words " or by inclusion in a cable programme service ".

The Trade Descriptions Act 1968   1968 c. 29.

19. In section 39(2) of the Trade Descriptions Act 1968 (interpretation) after the word " broadcast " there shall be inserted the words " or in a programme included in a cable programme service ".

The Social Work (Scotland) Act 1968   1968 c. 49.

20. In section 58(1) of the Social Work (Scotland) Act 1968 (prohibition of publication of proceedings in a children's hearing) after the word " broadcast " in both places where it occurs there shall be inserted the words " or a programme included in a cable programme service ".

The Theatres Act 1968   1968 c. 54.

21.—(1) In subsection (2)(*b*)(iii) of section 7 of the Theatres Act 1968 (exceptions for performances given in certain circumstances) for the words " transmitted to subscribers to a diffusion service " there shall be substituted the words " included in a cable programme service which is or does not require to be licensed ".

(2) In subsection (3) of that section the words from " and section " to the end shall be omitted.

Sch. 5
1968 c. 65.

The Gaming Act 1968

22. In section 42(8) of the Gaming Act 1968 (definition of " advertisement ") after the word " television " there shall be inserted the words " or by inclusion in a cable programme service ".

1968 c. 67.

The Medicines Act 1968

23.—(1) In subsection (1) of section 92 of the Medicines Act 1968 (definition of " advertisement ") after the word " television " there shall be inserted the words " or by inclusion in a cable programme service ".

(2) In subsection (2)(*b*) of that section for the words " transmitted to subscribers to a diffusion service " there shall be substituted the words " included in a cable programme service ".

(3) In subsection (6) of that section the words from " and section " to the end shall be omitted.

1968 c. 34
(N.I.).

The Children and Young Persons Act (Northern Ireland) 1968

24.—(1) For paragraph (*d*) of section 40(2) of the Children and Young Persons Act (Northern Ireland) 1968 (restriction on persons under 16 taking part in certain performances) there shall be substituted the following paragraphs—

" (*d*) any performance included in a cable programme service ;

(*e*) any performance recorded (by whatever means) with a view to its use in a broadcast or such a service or in a film intended for public exhibition ; ".

(2) In subsection (2)(*a*) of section 45 of that Act (powers of entry) after the words " broadcasting studio " there shall be inserted the words " a cable programme studio " and after the word " broadcast " there shall be inserted the words " in a cable programme ".

(3) At the end of that section there shall be added the following subsection—

" (5) In this section ' cable programme ' means a programme included in a cable programme service and ' cable programme studio ' shall be construed accordingly."

(4) Sections 59 and 68 of that Act (which restrict newspaper reports of court proceedings involving children and young persons) shall with the necessary modifications apply in relation to reports or matters included in a cable programme service as they apply in relation to newspapers.

1972 c. 9 (N.I.).

The Local Government Act (Northern Ireland) 1972

25. In section 148 of the Local Government Act (Northern Ireland) 1972 (interpretation) at the end of the definition of " newspaper " there shall be added the words " or for programmes to be included in a cable programme service which is or does not require to be licensed ".

The Education and Libraries (Northern Ireland) Order 1972

26. In Article 2(2) of the Education and Libraries (Northern Ireland) Order 1972 (interpretation) at the end of the definition of " newspaper " there shall be added the words " or for programmes to be included in a cable programme service which is or does not require to be licensed ".

S.I. 1972/1263 (N.I.12).

The Employment Agencies Act 1973

27. In section 13(4) of the Employment Agencies Act 1973 (interpretation) the word " or " immediately following paragraph (*b*) shall be omitted and after paragraph (*c*) there shall be inserted the words " or

(*d*) to providing a licensable cable programme service."

1973 c. 35.

The Northern Ireland Constitution Act 1973

28. In paragraph 14 of Schedule 3 to the Northern Ireland Constitution Act 1973 (minimum reserved matters) for the words " including sound broadcasting and television " there shall be substituted the words " (including sound broadcasting and television) and the provision of cable programme services ".

1973 c. 36.

The Fair Trading Act 1973

29. In Part I of Schedule 7 to the Fair Trading Act 1973 (goods and services wholly excluded from section 50 of that Act) after paragraph 8 there shall be inserted the following paragraph—

" 9. The provision of a licensed cable programme service."

1973 c. 41.

The Criminal Procedure (Scotland) Act 1975

30. In subsection (2) of sections 169 and 374 of the Criminal Procedure (Scotland) Act 1975 (restrictions on reporting of criminal proceedings involving persons under 16) after the word " broadcasts " there shall be inserted the words " and any programme included in a cable programme service ".

1975 c. 21.

The Industry Act 1975

31.—(1) At the end of subsection (1) of section 9 of the Industry Act 1975 (the National Enterprise Board and the media) there shall be added the words " or

(*c*) provide a licensed cable programme service ".

(2) At the end of subsection (3) of that section there shall be added the words " or

(iii) activities connected with the provision of a licensed cable programme service ".

(3) After subsection (9) of that section there shall be inserted the following subsection—

" (9A) If the Board or any of the Board's subsidiaries acquire any of the share capital of a body corporate which

1975 c. 68.

provides a licensed cable programme service, they shall consult the Cable Authority as to the steps that they are to take with regard to that share capital and obey any direction given by that Authority."

The Scottish Development Agency Act 1975

32. In section 17 of the Scottish Development Agency Act 1975 (the Scottish Development Agency and the media) after " 1975 " there shall be inserted the words " as amended by the Cable and Broadcasting Act 1984 ".

The Welsh Development Agency Act 1975

33.—(1) At the end of subsection (1) of section 19 of the Welsh Development Agency Act 1975 (the Welsh Development Agency and the media) there shall be added the words " or

(c) provide a licensed cable programme service ".

(2) At the end of subsection (3) of that section there shall be added the words " or

(iii) activities connected with the provision of a licensed cable programme service ".

(3) After subsection (9) of that section there shall be inserted the following subsection—

" (9A) If the Agency or any of the Agency's subsidiaries acquire any of the share capital of a body corporate which provides a licensed cable programme service, they shall consult the Cable Authority as to the steps that they are to take with regard to that share capital and obey any direction given by that Authority."

The Sexual Offences (Amendment) Act 1976

34.—(1) In subsection (1) of section 4 of the Sexual Offences (Amendment) Act 1976 (anonymity of complainant in rape etc. cases) after the word " broadcast " there shall be inserted the words " or included in a cable programme ".

(2) In subsection (5) of that section for the words " or broadcast " there shall be substituted the words " broadcast or included in a cable programme ", the word " and " immediately following paragraph (b) shall be omitted and after paragraph (c) there shall be inserted the words " and

(d) in the case of an inclusion in a cable programme, any body corporate which sends or provides the programme and any person having functions in relation to the programme corresponding to those of an editor of a newspaper,".

(3) In subsection (6) of that section after the definition of " a broadcast " there shall be inserted—

" ' cable programme ' means a programme included in a cable programme service ; ".

(4) In subsection (7) of that section for the words " or broadcasting " there shall be substituted the words " broadcasting or inclusion in a cable programme " and for the words " or broadcast " there shall be substituted the words " broadcast or inclusion in a cable programme ".

(5) In section 5(5) of that Act (provisions supplementary to section 4) for the words " or broadcast " there shall be substituted the words " broadcast or cable programme ".

(6) In section 6(1) of that Act (anonymity of defendants in rape etc. cases) after the word " broadcast " there shall be inserted the words " or included in a cable programme ".

The Sexual Offences (Northern Ireland) Order 1978

S.I. 1978/460 (N.I. 5).

35.—(1) In paragraph (1) of Article 6 of the Sexual Offences (Northern Ireland) Order 1978 (anonymity of complainant in rape etc. cases) after the word " broadcast " there shall be inserted the words " or included in a cable programme ".

(2) In paragraph (5) of that Article for the words " or broadcast " there shall be substituted the words " broadcast or included in a cable programme ", the word " and " immediately following sub-paragraph (*b*) shall be omitted and after sub-paragraph (*c*) there shall be inserted the words " and—

    (*d*) in the case of an inclusion in a cable programme, any body corporate which sends or provides the programme and any person having functions in relation to the programme corresponding to those of an editor of a newspaper."

(3) In paragraph (6) of that Article after the definition of " a broadcast " there shall be inserted—

    " ' cable programme ' means a programme included in a cable programme service ; ".

(4) In paragraph (7) of that Article for the words " or broadcasting " there shall be substituted the words " broadcasting or inclusion in a cable programme " and for the words " or broadcast " there shall be substituted the words " broadcast or inclusion in a cable programme ".

(5) In Article 7(3) of that Order (provisions supplementary to Article 6) for the words " or broadcast " there shall be substituted the words " broadcast or cable programme ".

(6) In Article 8(1) of that Order (anonymity of defendants in rape etc. cases) after the word " broadcast " there shall be inserted the words " or included in a cable programme ".

The Banking Act 1979

1979 c. 37.

36. In section 34(4) of the Banking Act 1979 (definition of " advertisement ") after the word " television " there shall be inserted the words " or by inclusion in a cable programme service ".

Sch. 5
1980 c. 43.

The Magistrates' Courts Act 1980

37.—(1) In subsection (1) of section 8 of the Magistrates' Courts Act 1980 (restrictions on reports of committal proceedings) after the word " broadcast " there shall be inserted the words " or include in a cable programme ".

(2) In subsections (2B), (4), (5) and (8) of that section for the words " or broadcast ", in each place where they occur, there shall be substituted the words " broadcast or included in a cable programme ".

(3) In subsection (3) of that section for the words " or broadcast ", in each place where they occur, there shall be substituted the words " broadcast or include in a cable programme ".

(4) After paragraph (c) of subsection (5) of that section there shall be inserted the following paragraph—

" (d) in the case of an inclusion of a report in a cable programme, any body corporate which sends or provides the programme and any person having functions in relation to the programme corresponding to those of an editor of a newspaper,".

(5) In subsection (10) of that section after the definition of " broadcast " there shall be inserted—

" cable programme " means a programme included in a cable programme service ; ".

1981 c. 42.

The Indecent Displays (Control) Act 1981

38. In section 1(4)(a) of the Indecent Displays (Control) Act 1981 (indecent displays) for the words from " transmitted " to " State " there shall be substituted the words " included in a cable programme service which is or does not require to be licensed ".

1981 c. 49.

The Contempt of Court Act 1981

39.—(1) In section 2(1) of the Contempt of Court Act 1981 (limitation of scope of strict liability) after the word " broadcast " there shall be inserted the words " cable programme ".

(2) In section 19 of that Act (interpretation) immediately before the definition of " court " there shall be inserted the following definition—

" ' cable programme ' means a programme included in a cable programme service ; ".

1981 c. 68.

The Broadcasting Act 1981

40.—(1) For paragraph (c) of section 3(1) of the 1981 Act (powers of Authority) there shall be substituted the following paragraph—

" (c) by arrangements made for the purpose with persons providing cable programme services, to provide for the inclusion in the services of programmes broadcast by the Authority."

(2) In section 9(1) of that Act (code for advertisements), at the beginning of paragraph (*a*) there shall be inserted the words " after consultation with the Cable Authority ".

(3) In subsection (3) of section 14 of that Act (provision of teletext services) for the words " TV programme contractor " there shall be substituted the words " TV or DBS programme contractor ".

(4) In subsections (2) and (3) of section 33 of that Act (provisions supplementary to section 32), for the words " from stations ", in each place where they occur, there shall be substituted the words " for reception in areas or localities " and for the word " stations ", in the third place where it occurs in subsection (2) and in the fourth place where it occurs in subsection (3), there shall be substituted the words " areas or localities ".

(5) For subsection (2) of section 42 of that Act (accounts and audit) there shall be substituted the following subsections—

" (2) The accounts of the Authority shall be audited by auditors to be appointed by the Authority with the approval of the Secretary of State.

(2A) A person shall not be qualified to be appointed as an auditor in pursuance of subsection (2) above unless he is a member of one or more of the following bodies—

the Institute of Chartered Accountants in England and Wales ;

the Institute of Chartered Accountants of Scotland ;

the Association of Certified Accountants ;

the Institute of Chartered Accountants in Ireland ;

any other body of accountants established in the United Kingdom and for the time being recognised for the purposes of section 161(1)(*a*) of the Companies Act 1948 by the Secretary of State ;   1948 c. 38.

but a Scottish firm may be so appointed if each of the partners in the firm is qualified to be so appointed."

(6) In section 63(1) of that Act (interpretation) after the definition of " local sound broadcast " there shall be inserted the following definition—

" ' programme ', in relation to a television or sound broadcasting service, includes any item broadcast in that service ; ".

(7) After paragraph 1 of Schedule 4 to that Act (rental payments) there shall be inserted the following paragraph—

" 1A. In the principal sections (other than section 33(1)) and the following provisions of this Schedule references to advertising receipts—

(*a*) in relation to a DBS programme contractor, and in relation to any period, include references to payments received or to be received by that contractor in respect of charges made for the reception of programmes provided by him and broadcast in a DBS service in that period ; and (*b*) in relation to a teletext contractor, and in relation to any period, include references to payments received or to be received by that contractor in respect of charges made for the reception of programmes provided by him and broadcast in a DBS or additional teletext service in that period."

(8) In paragraph 2 of that Schedule—

(*a*) after sub-paragraph (5) there shall be inserted the following sub-paragraph—

"(5A) Without prejudice to the generality of sub-paragraph (5) "relevant expenditure" includes, in relation to a DBS programme contractor, any expenditure incurred by the contractor in connection with the provision of the satellite transponder." ; and

(*b*) in sub-paragraph (7) for the words "the provisions of paragraph 1" there shall be substituted the words "the foregoing provisions of this Schedule" ; and

(*c*) in sub-paragraph (8) after the words "in the case of" there shall be inserted the words "a DBS programme contractor, of".

(9) In paragraph 3(2) of that Schedule after the words "TV programme contractors," there shall be inserted the words "DBS programme contractors,".

(10) At the end of paragraph 8(2) of Schedule 7 to that Act (the Broadcasting Complaints Commission: supplementary provisions) there shall be inserted the words "but a Scottish firm may be so appointed if each of the partners in the firm is qualified to be so appointed".

S.I. 1981/839
(N.I. 20).

The Employment (Miscellaneous Provisions) (Northern Ireland)
Order 1981

41. In Article 11(4) of the Employment (Miscellaneous Provisions) (Northern Ireland) Order 1981 (interpretation) the word "or" immediately following sub-paragraph (*b*) shall be omitted and after sub-paragraph (*c*) there shall be inserted the words "or

(*d*) to providing a licensable cable programme service".

1982 c. 33.

The Cinematograph (Amendment) Act 1982

42. In section 1 of the Cinematograph (Amendment) Act 1982 (extension of Cinematograph Act 1909 to certain other exhibitions of moving pictures) the words "under Part IV of the Telecommunications Act 1984" shall be omitted.

1982 c. 50.

The Insurance Companies Act 1982

43. In section 72(6) of the Insurance Companies Act 1982 (definition of "advertisement") after the word "television" there shall be inserted the words "or by inclusion in a cable programme service".

The Representation of the People Act 1983

1983 c. 2.

44.—(1) In section 75(1)(i) of the Representation of the People Act 1983 (prohibition of expenses not authorised by election agent) after the word " Authority " there shall be inserted the words " or in a programme included in a cable programme service which is or does not require to be licensed ".

(2) At the end of section 93 of that Act (broadcasting during elections) there shall be added the following subsection—

" (3) References in this section to items being broadcast from a television or other wireless telegraphy transmitting station in the United Kingdom include references to items being included in a cable programme service ; and references in this section to the making of broadcasts shall be construed accordingly ".

The Telecommunications Act 1984

1984 c. 12.

45.—(1) After subsection (10) of section 7 of the 1984 Act (power to licence telecommunication systems) there shall be inserted the following subsections—

" (10A) Before the Secretary of State or the Director decides whether to grant or revoke a licence under this section which authorises the running of a telecommunication system to which subsection (10B) below applies, he shall consult with the Cable Authority.

(10B) A telecommunication system is one to which this subsection applies if—

    (*a*) any person proposes to provide or is providing, by means of the system, a licensable cable programme service ; and

    (*b*) notice of that fact has been given to the Secretary of State or the Director."

(2) In subsection (1) of section 42 of that Act (fraudulent use of telecommunication system) for the words " service provided by means of a licensed telecommunication system " there shall be substituted the words " service to which this subsection applies ".

(3) In subsection (2) of that section for the words " In this section ' licensed telecommunication system ' means " there shall be substituted the words " Subsection (1) above applies to any service (other than a service to which section 53 of the Cable and Broadcasting Act 1984 applies) which is provided by means of ".

(4) In section 43(2) of that Act (improper use of public telecommunication system) the words " (within the meaning of Part IV of this Act) " shall be omitted.

The Video Recordings Act 1984

1984 c. 39.

46. For paragraph (*b*) of section 3(8) of the Video Recordings Act 1984 (exempted supplies) there shall be substituted the following paragraph—

" (*b*) a cable programme service which is or does not require to be licensed."

Section 57(2).

SCHEDULE 6

REPEALS

Chapter	Short title	Extent of repeal
9 Edw. 7. c. 30.	The Cinematograph Act 1909.	In section 1(3), the words " under Part IV of the Tele-communications Act 1984 ".
12, 13 & 14 Geo. 6. c. 54.	The Wireless Telegraphy Act 1949.	In section 19(1), the proviso.
15 & 16 Geo. 6 & 1 Eliz. 2. c. 66.	The Defamation Act 1952.	Section 16(4).
1955 c. 11. (N.I.).	The Defamation Act (Northern Ireland) 1955.	Section 14(3).
4 & 5 Eliz. 2. c. 74.	The Copyright Act 1956.	In section 2(3), the word " and " immediately preceding paragraph (d).
1963 c. 53.	The Performers' Protection Act 1963.	Section 3(2).
1967 c. 72.	The Wireless Telegraphy Act 1967.	In section 6(1), in the definition of " television set ", the words " wireless telegraphy " and " broadcast for general reception ".
1968 c. 54.	The Theatres Act 1968.	In section 7(3), the words from " and section " to the end.
1968 c. 67.	The Medicines Act 1968.	In section 92(6), the words from " and section " to the end.
1969 c. 48.	The Post Office Act 1969.	In Schedule 4, paragraph 53.
1973 c. 35.	The Employment Agencies Act 1973.	In section 13(4), the word " or " immediately following paragraph (b).
1976 c. 82.	The Sexual Offences (Amendment) Act 1976.	In section 4(5), the word " and " immediately following paragraph (b).
S.I. 1978/460 (N.I. 5).	The Sexual Offences (Northern Ireland) Order 1978.	In Article 6(5), the word " and " immediately following sub-paragraph (b).
1981 c. 68.	The Broadcasting Act 1981.	In section 25, subsections (1) to (3) and (5). In section 63(1) the definition of " broadcast relay station ". In Schedule 3, in Part I, the entry relating to section 63(1).
S.I. 1981/839 (N.I. 20).	The Employment (Miscellaneous Provisions) (Northern Ireland) Order 1981.	In Article 11(4), the word " or " immediately following sub-paragraph (b).
1982 c. 33.	The Cinematograph (Amendment) Act 1982.	In section 1, the words " under Part IV of the Telecommunications Act 1984 ".

Chapter	Short title	Extent of repeal
1984 c. 12.	The Telecommunications Act 1984.	In section 43(2), the words " (within the meaning of Part IV of this Act) ". Section 92(3). Part IV. In Schedule 4, paragraphs 30 and 32.

The repeal in the Cinematograph Act 1909 does not extend to Northern Ireland.

Repatriation of Prisoners Act 1984

1984 CHAPTER 47

An Act to make provision for facilitating the transfer between the United Kingdom and places outside the British Islands of persons for the time being detained in prisons, hospitals or other institutions by virtue of orders made in the course of the exercise by courts and tribunals of their criminal jurisdiction. [26th July 1984]

B E IT ENACTED by the Queen's most Excellent Majesty, by and with the advice and consent of the Lords Spiritual and Temporal, and Commons, in this present Parliament assembled, and by the authority of the same, as follows:—

1.—(1) Subject to the following provisions of this section, where— *Issue of warrant for transfer.*

   (*a*) the United Kingdom is a party to international arrangements providing for the transfer between the United Kingdom and a country or territory outside the British Islands of persons to whom subsection (7) below applies, and

   (*b*) the Secretary of State and the appropriate authority of that country or territory have each agreed to the transfer under those arrangements of a particular person (in this Act referred to as " the prisoner "), and

   (*c*) the prisoner has consented to being transferred in accordance with those arrangements,

the Secretary of State shall issue a warrant providing for the transfer of the prisoner into or out of the United Kingdom.

(2) The Secretary of State shall not issue a warrant under this Act, and, if he has issued one, shall revoke it, in any case where after the duty under subsection (1) above has arisen and before the transfer in question takes place circumstances arise, or are brought to the Secretary of State's attention, which in his opinion make it inappropriate that the transfer should take place.

(3) The Secretary of State shall not issue a warrant under this Act providing for the transfer of any person into the United Kingdom unless—

    (*a*) that person is a British citizen ; or

    (*b*) the transfer appears to the Secretary of State to be appropriate having regard to any close ties which that person has with the United Kingdom ; or

    (*c*) it appears to the Secretary of State that the transfer is such a transfer for the purpose of the temporary return of the prisoner to the United Kingdom as may be provided for by virtue of section 4(1)(*b*) below.

(4) The Secretary of State shall not issue a warrant under this Act, other than one superseding an earlier warrant, unless he is satisfied that all reasonable steps have been taken to inform the prisoner in writing in his own language—

    (*a*) of the substance, so far as relevant to the prisoner's case, of the international arrangements in accordance with which it is proposed to transfer him,

    (*b*) of the effect in relation to the prisoner of the warrant which it is proposed to issue in respect of him under this Act,

    (*c*) in the case of a transfer into the United Kingdom, of the effect in relation to the prisoner of the law relating to his detention under that warrant (including the effect of any enactment or instrument under which he may be released earlier than provided for by the terms of the warrant),

    (*d*) in the case of a transfer out of the United Kingdom, of the effect in relation to the prisoner of so much of the law of the country or territory to which he is to be transferred as has effect with respect to transfers under those arrangements, and

    (*e*) of the powers of the Secretary of State under section 6 of this Act ;

and, the Secretary of State shall not issue a warrant superseding an earlier warrant under this Act unless the requirements of this subsection were fulfilled in relation to the earlier warrant.

(5) The Secretary of State shall not issue a warrant under this Act unless he is satisfied that the consent given for the purposes of subsection (1)(*c*) above was given in a manner

authorised by the international arrangements in accordance with which the prisoner is to be transferred and was so given either—

(*a*) by the prisoner himself ; or

(*b*) in circumstances where it appears to the Secretary of State inappropriate by reason of the physical or mental condition or the youth of the prisoner for the prisoner to act for himself, by a person appearing to the Secretary of State to be an appropriate person to have acted on the prisoner's behalf.

(6) A consent given for the purposes of subsection (1)(*c*) above shall not be capable of being withdrawn after a warrant has been issued in respect of the prisoner ; and, accordingly, a purported withdrawal of that consent after that time shall not affect the validity of the warrant, or of any provision which by virtue of section 6 below subsequently supersedes provisions of that warrant, or of any direction given in relation to the prisoner under section 2(3) below.

(7) This subsection applies to a person if he is for the time being required to be detained in a prison, a hospital or any other institution either—

(*a*) by virtue of an order made in the course of the exercise by a court or tribunal in the United Kingdom, or in any country or territory outside the British Islands, of its criminal jurisdiction ; or

(*b*) under the provisions of this Act or any similar provisions of the law of any part of the United Kingdom or of the law of any country or territory outside the British Islands.

(8) In subsection (7)(*b*) above the reference to provisions similar to the provisions of this Act shall be construed as a reference to any provisions which have effect with respect to the transfer between different countries and territories (or different parts of a country or territory) of persons who are required to be detained in prisons, hospitals or other institutions by virtue of orders made in the course of the exercise by courts and tribunals of their criminal jurisdiction.

2.—(1) The effect of a warrant providing for the transfer of the prisoner out of the United Kingdom shall be to authorise— Transfer out of the United Kingdom.

(*a*) the taking of the prisoner to any place in any part of the United Kingdom and his delivery, at a place of departure from the United Kingdom, into the custody of a person representing the appropriate authority of the country or territory to which the prisoner is to be transferred ; and

(*b*) the removal of the prisoner by the person to whom he is so delivered to a place outside the United Kingdom.

2F 2

(2) Subject to subsections (3) to (5) below, the order by virtue of which the prisoner is required to be detained at the time such a warrant is issued in respect of him shall continue to have effect after his removal from the United Kingdom so as to apply to him if he is again in the United Kingdom at any time when under that order he is to be, or may be, detained.

(3) If, at any time after the removal of the prisoner from the United Kingdom, it appears to the Secretary of State appropriate to do so in order that effect may be given to the international arrangements in accordance with which the prisoner was transferred, the Secretary of State may give a direction varying the order referred to in subsection (2) above or providing for that order to cease to have effect.

(4) The power by direction under subsection (3) above to vary the order referred to in subsection (2) above shall include power by direction—

(a) to provide for how any period during which the prisoner is, by virtue of a warrant under this Act, out of the part of the United Kingdom in which that order has effect is to be treated for the purposes of that order ; and

(b) to provide for the prisoner to be treated as having been—

(i) released on licence under section 60 or 61 of the Criminal Justice Act 1967 (release on licence of, respectively, persons serving determinate sentences and persons sentenced to imprisonment for life etc.) ; or

1967 c. 80.

(ii) released on licence under section 206(2) of the Criminal Procedure (Scotland) Act 1975 (release on licence of children convicted on indictment) or released under section 58A(3) of the Children and Young Persons (Scotland) Act 1937 (release of children committed for residential training) ; or

1975 c. 21.

1937 c. 37.

(iii) released on licence under section 23 of the Prison Act (Northern Ireland) 1953 or discharged on licence under section 73 of the Children and Young Persons Act (Northern Ireland) 1968 (release and discharge on licence of, respectively, persons serving imprisonment for life and young persons in detention for grave crimes) ; or

1953 c. 18 (N.I.).

1968 c. 34 (N.I.).

(iv) for the purposes of Part II of the Treatment of Offenders (Northern Ireland) Order 1976 (conviction within certain period after discharge), discharged from prison or a young offenders centre in pursuance of rules made under section 13 of the said Act of 1953.

S.I. 1976/226 (N.I. 4).

(5) Except in relation to any period during which a restriction order is in force in respect of the prisoner, subsection (2) above shall not apply in relation to a hospital order; and, accordingly, a hospital order shall cease to have effect in relation to the prisoner—

(a) at the time of his removal from the United Kingdom if no restriction order is in force in respect of him at that time; and

(b) if at that time a restriction order is in force in respect of him, as soon after his removal as the restriction order ceases to have effect.

(6) In subsection (5) above—

" hospital order " means an order made under section 37 of the Mental Health Act 1983, section 175 or 376 of the Criminal Procedure (Scotland) Act 1975 or section 48 of the Mental Health Act (Northern Ireland) 1961 or any order or direction made under another enactment but having the same effect as an order made under one of those sections; and

" restriction order " means an order made under section 41 of the said Act of 1983, section 178 or 379 of the said Act of 1975 or section 53 of the said Act of 1961 or any order or direction made under another enactment but having the same effect as an order made under one of those sections.

1983 c. 20.

1975 c. 21.

1961 c. 13 (N.I.).

(7) References in this section to the order by virtue of which the prisoner is required to be detained at the time a warrant under this Act is issued in respect of him include references to any order by virtue of which he is required to be detained after the order by virtue of which he is required to be detained at that time ceases to have effect.

3.—(1) The effect of a warrant providing for the transfer of the prisoner into the United Kingdom shall be to authorise—

(a) the bringing of the prisoner into the United Kingdom from a place outside the United Kingdom;

(b) the taking of the prisoner to such place in any part of the United Kingdom, being a place at which effect may be given to the provisions contained in the warrant by virtue of paragraph (c) below, as may be specified in the warrant; and

(c) the detention of the prisoner in any part of the United Kingdom in accordance with such provisions as may be contained in the warrant, being provisions appearing to the Secretary of State to be appropriate for giving

Transfer into the United Kingdom.

2F 3

effect to the international arrangements in accordance with which the prisoner is transferred.

(2) Subject to section 4(2) to (4) below, a provision shall not be contained by virtue of subsection (1)(c) above in a warrant under this Act unless it satisfies the following two conditions, that is to say—

   (a) it is a provision with respect to the detention of a person in a prison, a hospital or any other institution ; and

   (b) it is a provision which at the time the warrant is issued may be contained in an order made either—

      (i) in the course of the exercise of its criminal jurisdiction by a court in the part of the United Kingdom in which the prisoner is to be detained ; or

      (ii) otherwise than by a court but for the purpose of giving effect to an order made as mentioned in sub-paragraph (i) above.

(3) In determining for the purposes of paragraph (c) of subsection (1) above what provisions are appropriate for giving effect to the international arrangements mentioned in that paragraph, the Secretary of State shall, to the extent that it appears to him consistent with those arrangements to do so, have regard to the inappropriateness of the warrant's containing provisions which—

   (a) are equivalent to more than the maximum penalties (if any) that may be imposed on a person who, in the part of the United Kingdom in which the prisoner is to be detained, commits an offence corresponding to that in respect of which the prisoner is required to be detained in the country or territory from which he is to be transferred ; or

   (b) are framed without reference to the length—

      (i) of the period during which the prisoner is, but for the transfer, required to be detained in that country or territory ; and

      (ii) of so much of that period as will have been, or be treated as having been, served by the prisoner when the said provisions take effect.

(4) Subject to subsection (6) below and the Schedule to this Act, a provision contained by virtue of subsection (1)(c) above in a warrant under this Act shall for all purposes have the same effect as the same provision contained in an order made as mentioned in sub-paragraph (i) or, as the case may be, sub-paragraph (ii) of subsection (2)(b) above.

(5) A provision contained by virtue of subsection (1)(*c*) above in a warrant under this Act shall take effect with the delivery of the prisoner to the place specified in the warrant for the purposes of subsection (1)(*b*) above.

(6) Subsection (4) above shall not confer any right of appeal on the prisoner against provisions contained by virtue of subsection (1)(*c*) above in a warrant under this Act.

(7) The Schedule to this Act shall have effect, subject to section 4(4) below, with respect to the operation of certain enactments in relation to provisions contained by virtue of subsection (1)(*c*) above in a warrant under this Act.

(8) For the purposes of determining whether at any particular time any such order as is mentioned in subsection (2)(*b*) above could have been made as so mentioned, there shall be disregarded both—

(*a*) any requirement that certain conditions must be satisfied before the order is made ; and

(*b*) any restriction on the minimum period in respect of which the order may be made.

4.—(1) A single warrant under this Act may provide for the Temporary transfer of the prisoner both out of and into (or into and out of) return. the United Kingdom if it appears to the Secretary of State that the transfers are to be for the purpose of the temporary return of the prisoner either—

(*a*) from the United Kingdom to a country or territory outside the British Islands from which he has previously been transferred into the United Kingdom under this Act or any other enactment ; or

(*b*) to the United Kingdom from a country or territory outside the British Islands to which he has previously been transferred from the United Kingdom under this Act.

(2) The provisions contained by virtue of section 3(1)(*c*) above in a warrant under this Act issued for the purpose of the temporary return of the prisoner to a country or territory outside the British Islands may, where the prisoner is required when that warrant is issued to be detained in accordance with provisions so contained in an earlier warrant under this Act, require the prisoner to continue, after his return to the part of the United Kingdom in which the provisions contained in the earlier warrant have effect, to be detained in accordance with those earlier provisions.

(3) A warrant issued under this Act containing, with respect to provisions contained in an earlier warrant, any such requirement as is referred to in subsection (2) above, shall provide that any period during which the prisoner is out of the part of the United Kingdom in which the provisions contained in the earlier warrant have effect and is in custody is to be treated (except to such extent as may be specified in the warrant in order that effect may be given to the international arrangements in question) as a period during which the prisoner is detained under the provisions contained in the earlier warrant.

(4) The provisions contained by virtue of section 3(1)(c) above in a warrant under this Act issued for the purpose of the temporary return of the prisoner to the United Kingdom may require the prisoner to be detained in accordance with any order which on his return will apply in respect of him in pursuance of section 2(2) above ; and the Schedule to this Act shall not apply in relation to the provisions so contained in such a warrant.

Operation of warrant and retaking prisoners.

5.—(1) Where a warrant has been issued under this Act the following provisions of this section shall have effect for the purposes of the warrant, except (without prejudice to section 3(4) above or any enactment contained otherwise than in this Act) in relation to any time when the prisoner is required to be detained in accordance with provisions contained in the warrant by virtue of section 3(1)(c) above.

(2) The prisoner shall be deemed to be in the legal custody of the Secretary of State at any time when, being in the United Kingdom or on board a British ship, a British aircraft or a British hovercraft, he is being taken under the warrant to or from any place, or being kept in custody under the warrant.

(3) The Secretary of State may, from time to time, designate any person as a person who is for the time being authorised for the purposes of the warrant to take the prisoner to or from any place under the warrant, or to keep the prisoner in custody under the warrant.

(4) A person authorised by or for the purposes of the warrant to take the prisoner to or from any place or to keep the prisoner in custody shall have all the powers, authority, protection and privileges—

(a) of a constable in any part of the United Kingdom in which that person is for the time being ; or

(b) if he is outside the United Kingdom, of a constable in the part of the United Kingdom to or from which the prisoner is to be taken under the warrant.

(5) If the prisoner escapes or is unlawfully at large, he may be arrested without warrant by a constable and taken to any place to which he may be taken under the warrant under this Act.

(6) In subsection (2) above—

" British aircraft " means a British-controlled aircraft within the meaning of section 92 of the Civil Aviation Act 1982 (application of criminal law to aircraft), or one of Her Majesty's aircraft ; 1982 c. 16.

" British hovercraft " means a British-controlled hovercraft within the meaning of the said section 92 as applied in relation to hovercraft by virtue of provision made under the Hovercraft Act 1968, or one of Her Majesty's hovercraft ; and 1968 c. 59.

" British ship " means a British ship within the meaning of the Merchant Shipping Act 1894, or one of Her Majesty's ships ; 1894 c. 60.

and in this subsection references to Her Majesty's aircraft, hovercraft or ships are references to the aircraft, hovercraft or, as the case may be, ships which belong to, or are exclusively employed in the service of, Her Majesty in right of the government of the United Kingdom.

(7) In subsection (5) above " constable ", in relation to any part of the United Kingdom, means any person who is a constable in that or any other part of the United Kingdom or any person who, at the place in question has, under any enactment (including subsection (4) above), the powers of a constable in that or any other part of the United Kingdom.

6.—(1) Subject to section 1(4) above, if at any time it appears to the Secretary of State appropriate, in order that effect may be given to any such arrangements as are mentioned in section 1(1)(*a*) above or in a case falling within section 1(2) above, for a warrant under this Act to be revoked or varied, he may, as the case may require— Revocation etc. of warrants.

(*a*) revoke that warrant ; or

(*b*) revoke that warrant and issue a new warrant under this Act containing provision superseding some or all of the provisions of the previous warrant.

(2) Subject to subsection (3)(*c*) below, the provision that may be contained in a new warrant issued by virtue of subsection (1)(*b*) above shall be any provision that could have been contained in the previous warrant.

(3) A new warrant issued by virtue of subsection (1)(*b*) above may provide—

   (*a*) that a provision contained in it is to be treated as having taken effect when the provisions which that provision supersedes took effect ;

   (*b*) that things done under or for the purposes of the superseded provisions are, accordingly, to be treated as having been done under or for the purposes of the provision contained in the new warrant ; and

   (*c*) that an enactment in force at the time the new warrant is issued is, for the purposes of subsection (2) above or this subsection, to be treated as having been in force when the superseded provisions took effect.

(4) The powers conferred by this section shall be exercisable notwithstanding any defect in the warrant which is revoked.

Expenses.

7.—(1) Subject to subsection (2) below, any expenses incurred by the Secretary of State for the purposes of this Act shall be defrayed out of money provided by Parliament.

(2) Subject to subsections (3) and (4) below, it shall be the duty of the Secretary of State, in the case of the transfer of a person into the United Kingdom under this Act, to secure the payment to him by that person, or from some other source, of the amount of any expenses incurred by him in connection with the conveyance of that person to the United Kingdom ; and for this purpose the Secretary of State shall have the same power as in any other case where he assists the return of a person to the United Kingdom to require a person to give an undertaking to pay the Secretary of State the whole or any part of that amount, to enforce such an undertaking and to make such other arrangements for recovering that amount as he thinks fit.

(3) Subsection (2) above shall not apply to the extent that in any case it appears to the Secretary of State that it would be unreasonable for him to exercise any of the powers conferred by that subsection either because of the exceptional circumstances of the case or because the means of the prisoner are insufficient to meet the expenses and their recovery, whether immediately or at some future time, from the prisoner or from any other source is impracticable.

(4) The expenses mentioned in subsections (2) and (3) above shall not include—

   (*a*) any expenses of providing an escort for a person transferred into the United Kingdom under this Act ; or

   (*b*) any expenses of the conveyance of such a person beyond the place at which he first arrives in the United Kingdom.

(5) The Secretary of State shall pay any sums received by him by virtue of subsection (2) above into the Consolidated Fund.

8.—(1) In this Act, except in so far as the context otherwise requires— Interpretation and certificates.

" international arrangements " includes any arrangements between the United Kingdom and a colony ;

" order " includes any sentence, direction, warrant or other means of giving effect to the decision of a court or tribunal ; and

" the prisoner " has the meaning given by section 1(1)(*b*) above.

(2) In this Act a reference to criminal jurisdiction, in relation to a court or tribunal in a country or territory outside the British Islands, includes a reference to any jurisdiction which would be a criminal jurisdiction but for the age or incapacity of the persons in respect of whom it is exercised.

(3) In any proceedings, the certificate of the Secretary of State—

(*a*) that a particular country or territory is a party to any such international arrangements as are mentioned in section 1(1)(*a*) above,

(*b*) that the appropriate authority of a country or territory which is such a party has agreed to the transfer of a particular person in accordance with any such arrangements, or

(*c*) that, for the purposes of any provision of this Act, a particular person is or represents the appropriate authority of any country or territory,

shall be conclusive of the matter certified.

9.—(1) This Act may be cited as the Repatriation of Prisoners Act 1984. Short title, commencement and extent.

(2) This Act shall come into force on such day as the Secretary of State may by order made by statutory instrument appoint.

(3) This Act extends to Northern Ireland.

(4) Her Majesty may by Order in Council make provision for extending the provisions of this Act, with such exceptions, adaptations and modifications as may be specified in the Order, to any of the Channel Islands, to the Isle of Man or to any colony.

SCHEDULE

OPERATION OF CERTAIN ENACTMENTS IN RELATION TO THE PRISONER

Application of Schedule

1. This Schedule applies where a warrant is issued under this Act providing for the transfer of the prisoner into the United Kingdom ; and in this Schedule " the relevant provisions " means the provisions contained in the warrant by virtue of section 3(1)(c) of this Act or, in the case of a warrant which contains such a requirement as is referred to in section 4(2) of this Act, the provisions in accordance with which the prisoner continues, in pursuance of that requirement, to be detained.

Release on licence

1967 c. 80.

2.—(1) In determining for the purposes of section 60 of the Criminal Justice Act 1967 (release on licence) whether the prisoner has at any time served one third of his sentence or the specified period mentioned in subsection (1) of that section the prisoner's sentence shall, subject to sub-paragraph (2) below, be deemed to begin with the day on which the relevant provisions take effect.

(2) If the warrant specifies a period to be taken into account for the purposes of this paragraph the prisoner's sentence and the amount he has served shall, so far only as the question whether he has served one third of his sentence is concerned, be deemed to be increased by that period.

Life imprisonment

3. Where the relevant provisions include provision equivalent to a sentence in relation to which section 61 of the Criminal Justice Act 1967 (release on licence, on the recommendation of the Parole Board and after consultation with the Lord Chief Justice or Lord Justice General and with the trial judge if available, of person sentenced to life imprisonment etc.) applies, subsection (1) of that section shall be deemed to have effect in relation to the prisoner as if the words " together with the trial judge if available " were omitted.

Persons under the age of 21

1982 c. 48.

4.—(1) Where the prisoner has not attained the age of 21 years at the time the warrant containing the relevant provisions is issued and the relevant provisions include provision equivalent to a sentence under section 6 or 8 of the Criminal Justice Act 1982 (youth custody and custody for life)—

    (*a*) subsections (1) to (7) of section 12 of that Act (accommodation of persons sentenced under section 6 or 8) shall not apply in relation to the prisoner ; and

    (*b*) the prisoner may be detained—

        (i) in a youth custody centre,

        (ii) in a remand centre, or

        (iii) in a prison,

    as the Secretary of State may from time to time direct.

(2) Where—

    (*a*) at the time the warrant containing the relevant provisions is issued the prisoner is not less than 16 years of age but has not attained the age of 21 years, and

    (*b*) the relevant provisions include provision equivalent to an order imposing detention under section 207 or 415 of the Criminal Procedure (Scotland) Act 1975 (restriction on detention of persons under 21 years of age),   1975 c. 21.

the provisions of those sections which require that, in certain circumstances, a person shall be detained in a specified type of institution shall not apply in relation to the prisoner, and the prisoner may be detained—

    (i) in a young offenders institution, or

    (ii) in a prison,

as the Secretary of State may from time to time direct.

Mental health legislation

5.—(1) References in—

    (*a*) the Mental Health Act 1983, and   1983 c. 20.

    (*b*) the Mental Health Act (Northern Ireland) 1961,   1961 c. 15. (N.I.).

to the date of an order under either of those Acts shall have effect, in relation to any of the relevant provisions which is equivalent to such an order, as references to the day on which the relevant provisions take effect.

(2) Where the relevant provisions include provision equivalent to a hospital order within the meaning of the said Act of 1983 or such an order and a restriction order within the meaning of that Act, the prisoner may (in addition to any application he may make under that Act) apply to a Mental Health Review Tribunal at any time in the period of six months beginning with the day on which the relevant provisions take effect.

(3) References howsoever expressed in—

    (*a*) the Mental Health (Scotland) Act 1984, and   1984 c. 36.

    (*b*) the Criminal Procedure (Scotland) Act 1975,   1975 c. 21.

to the date of an order of the type referred to in the definition of hospital order or restriction order in section 2(6) of this Act shall have effect, in relation to any of the relevant provisions which is equivalent to such an order, as a reference to the day on which the relevant provisions take effect.

(4) Where the relevant provisions include provisions equivalent in Scotland to such an order, the prisoner may at any time in the period of six months beginning with the day on which the relevant provisions take effect, appeal to the Sheriff to order his discharge ; and (without prejudice to section 3(4) of this Act) in any appeal under this paragraph the provisions of the said Act of 1984 in respect of appeals by a patient subject to such an order apply to an appeal by the prisoner where he is subject to any such equivalent provision as they apply to a patient who is subject to such an order.

Rehabilitation of offenders

6. The relevant provisions shall be disregarded for the purposes of the application, in relation to any offence of which the prisoner was convicted in a country or territory outside the British Islands, of—

1974 c. 53.

    (*a*) the Rehabilitation of Offenders Act 1974, except section 1(2) (person not rehabilitated unless he serves sentence etc.); and

S.I. 1978/1908 (N.I. 27).

    (*b*) the Rehabilitation of Offenders (Northern Ireland) Order 1978, except Article 3(2) (person not rehabilitated unless he serves sentence etc.).

1981 c. 34.

The Representation of the People Act 1981

7. For the purposes of section 1 of the Representation of the People Act 1981 (disqualification of certain offenders for membership of the House of Commons), the prisoner shall, while detained in accordance with the relevant provisions, be deemed to be detained in pursuance of the order in pursuance of which, at the time of his transfer into the United Kingdom, he was required to be detained in the country or territory from which he was transferred.

S.I. 1981/155 (N.I. 2).

The Firearms (Northern Ireland) Order 1981

8. Where the relevant provisions include provision equivalent to such a sentence as is mentioned in paragraph (2) of Article 22 of the Firearms (Northern Ireland) Order 1981 (possession of firearm by person previously convicted of crime), that paragraph shall apply in relation to the prisoner as if for the reference in that paragraph to the period of eight years from the date so mentioned there were substituted a reference to the period of eight years from the day on which the relevant provisions take effect.

Health and Social Security Act 1984

1984 CHAPTER 48

An Act to amend the Opticians Act 1958; to make amendments of the National Health Service Act 1977 and the National Health Service (Scotland) Act 1978 in relation to general ophthalmic services, finance in the National Health Service and certain functions of the Secretary of State; to make amendments of the National Health Service Act 1977 in relation to Family Practitioner Committees; to make provision for the reimbursement of the cost of certain treatment in the European Economic Community; to amend the law relating to social security, statutory sick pay and contracted-out occupational pension schemes; and for connected purposes.   [26th July 1984]

BE IT ENACTED by the Queen's most Excellent Majesty, by and with the advice and consent of the Lords Spiritual and Temporal, and Commons, in this present Parliament assembled, and by the authority of the same, as follows:

PART I

HEALTH

Optical appliances

1.—(1) In section 21 of the Opticians Act 1958 (restriction on sale and supply of optical appliances)—

    (*a*) at the end of subsection (3) (exemptions) there shall be added " or

Supply etc. of optical appliances.
1958 c. 32.

(f) in accordance with an order under subsection (3A) below." ;

(b) the following subsections shall be inserted after that subsection—

" (3A) An order under this subsection is an order made by the Privy Council and specifying—

(a) optical appliances to which it applies ; and

(b) conditions subject to which their sale is exempted from the requirements of subsection (1) above.

(3B) Any such order relating to optical appliances consisting of or including one or more lenses shall specify as a condition subject to which the sale of any such appliance is so exempted the condition that the appliance must be in accordance with a written prescription which—

(a) has been given by a registered medical practitioner or registered ophthalmic optician following a testing of sight by him ; and

(b) bears a date not more than such time as is specified in the order before the prescription is presented to the proposed seller of the appliance.

(3C) An order under subsection (3A) above may not specify as appliances to which it applies—

(a) contact lenses ; or

(b) any optical appliance for a person under 16 years of age.

(3D) An order under subsection (3A) above shall be made by statutory instrument which shall be subject to annulment in pursuance of a resolution of either House of Parliament.".

(2) The following subsections shall be substituted for subsection (5) of section 25 of that Act (rules)—

" (5) Rules under this section shall not come into force until approved by order of the Privy Council.

(6) The Privy Council—

(a) may approve rules under subsection (1)(a) above either as submitted to them or subject to such modifications as appear to them requisite ; and

(b) after consulting the General Optical Council, may by order vary or revoke any rules made under that paragraph and previously approved by them (whether the approval was before or after the commencement of this subsection).

(7) Where the Privy Council propose to approve any such rules subject to modifications, they shall notify to the General Optical Council the modifications they propose to make and consider any observations of the General Optical Council thereon.

(8) The power to make an order under this section shall be exercisable by statutory instrument which, subject to the following provisions of this section, shall be subject to annulment in pursuance of a resolution of either House of Parliament.

(9) No order to which this subsection applies shall be made unless a draft of the order has been laid before and approved by resolution of each House of Parliament.

(10) Subsection (9) above applies to an order—

(a) which is made by virtue of paragraph (a) of subsection (6) above and approves rules subject to modifications ; or

(b) which is made by virtue of paragraph (b) of that subsection,

unless it is contained in a statutory instrument that states that the General Optical Council have indicated their consent to the terms of the order either in the course of consultations under subsection (6)(b) above or in observations under subsection (7) above.".

(3) In section 38 of the National Health Service Act 1977 (arrangements for general ophthalmic services) for the words from " ophthalmic ", in the first place where it occurs, to the end of the first paragraph there shall be substituted the words " and ophthalmic opticians for securing the testing of sight by them.". 1977 c. 49.

(4) In paragraph (c) of section 39 of that Act (regulations as to arrangements for general ophthalmic services) the words " and the ophthalmic or dispensing optician who is to supply the appliances " shall cease to have effect.

(5) The following provisions of section 26 of the National Health Service (Scotland) Act 1978 (arrangements for provision of general ophthalmic services) shall cease to have effect— 1978 c. 29.

(a) subsection (1)(b) ; and

(b) in subsection (2)(c), the words " and the ophthalmic or dispensing optician who is to supply the appliances ".

(6) The amendments of the National Health Service Act 1977 contained in Part I of Schedule 1 to this Act shall have effect in consequence of subsections (3) and (4) above.

(7) The amendments of the National Health Service (Scotland) Act 1978 contained in Part II of that Schedule shall have effect in consequence of subsection (5) above.

2.—(1) The following section shall be inserted after section 20 of the Opticians Act 1958—

"Restrictions on fitting of contact lenses.

20A.—(1) Subject to the following provisions of this section, a person who is not a registered medical practitioner or registered optician shall not fit contact lenses.

(2) The foregoing subsection shall not apply to the fitting of contact lenses by a person recognised by a medical authority as a medical student, if carried out as part of a course of instruction approved by that authority for medical students or as part of an examination so approved.

(3) The General Optical Council may by rules exempt from subsection (1) of this section the fitting of contact lenses by persons training as opticians, or any prescribed class thereof, in such cases and subject to compliance with such conditions as may be prescribed by the rules.

(4) Rules under the last foregoing subsection shall not come into force until approved by order of the Privy Council, and the power to make any such order shall be exercisable by statutory instrument.

(5) Any person who contravenes subsection (1) of this section shall be liable on summary conviction to a fine of an amount not exceeding level 4 on the standard scale, as defined in section 75 of the Criminal Justice Act 1982.".

(2) The following subsections shall be inserted after section 25(3) of that Act—

" (3A) The General Optical Council may make rules specifying requirements which registered opticians, enrolled bodies corporate or employees of registered opticians or enrolled bodies corporate must meet if they are to prescribe, fit or supply contact lenses.

(3B) The power conferred by subsection (3A) above is a power—

   (a) in relation to registered opticians or employees of registered opticians or of enrolled bodies corporate, to specify qualifications which they must have ; and

   (b) in relation to enrolled bodies corporate, to specify conditions which they must satisfy.".

Other amendments of Opticians Act 1958

3.—(1) In section 22 of the Opticians Act 1958 (penalty for pretending to be registered, etc.) the words " or the title of optometrist " shall be inserted after the words " ophthalmic optician " in subsections (1)(a) and (2)(a).

Taking and use of titles.

1958 c. 32.

(2) The following subsections shall be inserted after subsection (1) of that section—

   " (1A) On any prosecution for an offence under subsection (1)(b) of this section the taking or use of the title of optician (either alone or in combination with any other words) by a person to whom this subsection applies is to be taken to imply that he is registered in one of the registers, but the implication may be rebutted if the defendant proves that he took or, as the case may be, used the title in circumstances where it would have been unreasonable for people to believe, in consequence of his taking or, as the case may be, use of it, that he was in fact registered in one of the registers.

   (1B) Subject to the following subsection, subsection (1A) of this section applies to a person who carries on the business—

   (a) of selling optical appliances ; or

   (b) of supplying optical appliances in pursuance of arrangements made as mentioned in section 21(2) of this Act.

   (1C) Subsection (1A) of this section does not apply to a person who sells or supplies optical appliances only as mentioned in section 21(3)(a) to (e) of this Act.".

(3) The following subsections shall be inserted after subsection (2) of that section—

   " (2A) On any prosecution for an offence under subsection (2)(b) of this section the taking or use of the title of optician (either alone or in combination with any other words) by a body corporate to which this subsection applies is to be taken to imply that it is enrolled in one of the lists, but the implication may be rebutted if the body corporate proves that it took or, as the case may be, used the title in circumstances where it would have been unreasonable for people to believe, in consequence of its taking or, as the case may be, use of it, that it was in fact enrolled in either of the lists.

(2B) Subject to the following subsection, subsection (2A) of this section applies to a body corporate which carries on the business—

(*a*) of selling optical appliances ; or

(*b*) of supplying optical appliances in pursuance of arrangements made as mentioned in section 21(2) of this Act.

(2C) Subsection (2A) of this section does not apply to a body corporate which sells or supplies optical appliances only as mentioned in section 21(3)(*a*) to (*e*) of this Act.".

4. Schedule 2 to this Act—

(*a*) Part I of which inserts new sections in the Opticians Act 1958 giving the Disciplinary Committee of the General Optical Council power—

(i) to suspend the registration of a registered optician or the enrolment of a body corporate carrying on business as an ophthalmic optician or a dispensing optician instead of erasing the name of the registered optician or the body corporate from the register or list ; and

(ii) to impose financial penalties on registered opticians and on such bodies corporate instead of or in addition to erasure or suspension ; and

(*b*) Part II of which makes minor and consequential amendments to that Act in connection with the disciplinary powers of the Committee,

shall have effect.

National Health Service

5.—(1) The following section shall be substituted for section 10 of the National Health Service Act 1977—

" Family
Practitioner
Committees.

10.—(1) It is the duty of the Secretary of State by order to establish, in accordance with Part II of Schedule 5 to this Act, authorities to be called Family Practitioner Committees.

(2) Family Practitioner Committees shall be known by such names, in addition to that title, as the order may specify.

(3) When the Secretary of State makes an order under subsection (1) above establishing a Family Practitioner Committee, he shall also (either in the same or another instrument) make an order in rela-

tion to that Committee specifying a locality for which the Committee is to act.

(4) The Secretary of State may by order—

   (a) vary a Committee's locality;

   (b) abolish a Committee;

   (c) establish a new one.

(5) The Secretary of State shall so exercise his powers under subsections (3) and (4) above as to secure—

   (a) that the localities for which Family Practitioner Committees are at any time acting together comprise the whole of England and Wales; but

   (b) that none of them extends both into England and into Wales.

(6) Without prejudice to the generality of section 126(4) below, the power to make incidental or supplemental provision conferred by that subsection includes, in its application to orders under this section, power to make provision for the transfer of staff, property, rights and liabilities.

(7) It is the Secretary of State's duty before he makes an order under subsection (4) above to consult with respect to the order—

   (a) such bodies as he may recognise as representing officers who in his opinion are likely to be affected by the order; and

   (b) such other bodies as he considers are concerned with the order.".

(2) In subsection (1) of section 15 of that Act (duty of Family Practitioner Committee) the following paragraph shall be substituted for paragraph (a)—

   " (a) to administer the arrangements made in pursuance of this Act for the provision of general medical services, general dental services, general ophthalmic services and pharmaceutical services for their locality; ".

(3) In Part III of Schedule 1 to the House of Commons Disqualification Act 1975 (disqualifying offices), in the entry beginning " Chairman in receipt of remuneration of any Regional Health Authority " after the words " District Health Authority " there shall be inserted the words " Family Practitioner Committee ". 1975 c. 24.

(4) Schedule 3 to this Act shall have effect.

(5) The Secretary of State shall by order specify a date not later than 1st April 1985 on which Family Practitioner Committees established by orders under section 10(1) of the National Health Service Act 1977 are to begin to act for their localities.

(6) Notwithstanding the substitution made by subsection (1) above, Family Practitioner Committees established or adopted by District Health Authorities shall continue to discharge their functions until the date specified by an order under subsection (5) above but shall cease to exist on that date.

(7) The Secretary of State may by order make such repeals in or other modifications of any enactment or instrument as appear to him to be necessary or expedient in consequence of subsection (1), (2) or (4) above.

(8) An order under subsection (5) or (7) above shall be made by statutory instrument which shall be subject to annulment in pursuance of a resolution of either House of Parliament.

Finance in National Health Service.

6.—(1) The following subsection shall be inserted after subsection (2) of section 97 of the National Health Service Act 1977 (means of meeting expenditure of health authorities)—

" (2A) The date on which an allotment to an authority under subsection (1) or (2) above (including an allotment increasing or reducing an allotment previously made) takes effect is the date on which the authority are notified of its amount by the Secretary of State or, as the case may be, the Regional Health Authority.".

(2) The following subsection shall be inserted after subsection (2) of section 98 of that Act (accounts and audit)—

" (2A) The accounts prepared and transmitted by a District Health Authority in pursuance of subsection (2) above shall include annual accounts of a Community Health Council if—

(a) the Council is established for the Authority's district ; or

(b) the Authority is the prescribed Authority in relation to the Council.".

1978 c. 29.

(3) The following subsection shall be inserted after subsection (1) of section 85 of the National Health Service (Scotland) Act 1978 (expenses)—

" (1A) The date on which an allotment under subsection (1) above (including an allotment increasing or reducing an allotment previously made) takes effect is the date on which the body receiving the allotment are notified of its amount by the Secretary of State.".

(4) In subsection (11) of section 121 of the Mental Health Act 1983 (Mental Health Act Commission) for the words " sub-paragraphs (4) and (5) were omitted " there shall be substituted the words " the reference to a member in sub-paragraph (4) included a reference to the chairman ".

PART I
1983 c. 20.

7.—(1) The following shall be inserted after section 43 of the National Health Service Act 1977—

Professional remuneration in National Health Service.
1977 c. 49.

" *Remuneration for services*

Regulations as to remuneration.

43A.—(1) Regulations shall make provision as to the remuneration to be paid to persons who provide general medical services, general dental services, general ophthalmic services or pharmaceutical services under this Part of this Act.

(2) Subject to sections 29(4) and 35(2) above, remuneration under the regulations may consist of payments by way of—

(*a*) salary ;

(*b*) fees ;

(*c*) allowances ;

(*d*) reimbursement (in full or in part) of expenses incurred or expected to be incurred in connection with the provision of the services,

and the regulations may provide that the remuneration shall be determined from time to time by such authority as may be specified.

(3) If section 10 of the National Health Service Act 1966 is brought into operation, upon the date of its commencement the words " section 10 of the National Health Service Act 1966 and section " shall be substituted for the words " sections 29(4) and " in subsection (2) above.".

1966 c. 8.

(2) The following shall be inserted after section 28 of the National Health Service (Scotland) Act 1978—

1978 c. 29.

" *Remuneration for services*

Regulations as to remuneration.

28A.—(1) Regulations shall make provision as to the remuneration to be paid to persons who provide general medical services, general dental services, general ophthalmic services or pharmaceutical services under this Part of this Act.

(2) Subject to sections 19(3) and 25(3), remuneration under the regulations may consist of payments by way of—

(*a*) salary ;

(*b*) fees ;

(*c*) allowances ;

(*d*) reimbursement (in full or in part) of expenses incurred or expected to be incurred in connection with the provision of the services,

and the regulations may provide that the remuneration shall be determined from time to time by such authority as may be specified.

(3) If section 10 of the National Health Service Act 1966 is brought into operation, upon the date of its commencement the words " section 10 of the National Health Service Act 1966 and section " shall be substituted for the words " sections 19(3) and " in subsection (2) above.".

(3) The following section shall be added after each of the sections inserted by subsections (1) and (2) above, as section 43B of the National Health Service Act 1977 and section 28B of the National Health Service (Scotland) Act 1978—

"Remuneration—supplementary.

(1) The authority specified in regulations under the preceding section may be the Secretary of State or some other person or persons and is referred to in this section as a " determining authority ".

(2) The power conferred by the preceding section includes power to make regulations providing for a determination in more than one stage and by more than one determining authority.

(3) Regulations under the preceding section shall provide—

(*a*) that a determination may be made with respect either to any of the descriptions of services mentioned in subsection (1) of the preceding section generally or to any category of services falling within such a description ;

(*b*) that, before making such a determination, the determining authority shall consult—

(i) a prescribed body established to provide advice in connection with the matters to be determined ; or

(ii) an organisation appearing to the Secretary of State to be representative of persons to whose remuneration the determination would relate,

or both such a body and such an organisation.

(4) Regulations under the preceding section may provide—

   (*a*) that a determination such as is mentioned in subsection (3) above shall have effect in relation to remuneration in respect of a period beginning on or after a date specified in the determination, which may be the date of the determination or an earlier or later date, but may be an earlier date only if, taking the determination as a whole, it is not detrimental to the persons to whose remuneration it relates ; and

   (*b*) that any such determination which does not specify such a date shall have effect in relation to remuneration in respect of a period beginning—

      (i) if it is required to be published, on the date of publication ;

      (ii) if it is not so required, on the date on which it is made.

(5) Regulations under the preceding section may provide—

   (*a*) for determinations of the remuneration of particular persons or descriptions of persons for particular items of service or in particular circumstances ;

   (*b*) that a determining authority shall have a discretion, when making a determination by virtue of this subsection,—

      (i) as to the amount of remuneration to be paid ; and

      (ii) as to the persons to whom and conditions on which it is to be paid ; and

   (*c*) that a determination made by virtue of this subsection may be revised—

      (i) to correct an error ; or

      (ii) where it appears to the determining authority that it was made in ignorance of or under a mistake as to a relevant fact.

(6) Regulations under the preceding section may provide—

   (*a*) that determinations may be made by reference to any of the following—

      (i) rates or conditions of remuneration of any persons or any descriptions of persons which are fixed or determined, or to be fixed or determined, otherwise than by way of a determination under the regulations ;

(ii) scales, indices or other data of any description specified in the regulations ; and

(b) that any determination which in accordance with regulations made by virtue of paragraph (a)(ii) above falls to be made by reference to a scale or an index or to any other data may be made not only by reference to that index or scale or those data in the form current at the time of the determination but also by reference to the scale, index or data in any subsequent form attributable to amendment or revision taking effect after that time or to any other cause.

(7) Any determination under regulations under the previous section shall be made after taking into account all the matters which are considered to be relevant by the determining authority and, without prejudice to the generality of this subsection, such matters may include—

(a) the amount or estimated amount of expenses (taking into account any discounts) incurred in the past or likely to be incurred in the future (whether or not by persons to whose remuneration the determination will relate) in connection with the provision of services of a kind to which the determination will relate ;

(b) the amount or estimated amount of any remuneration paid or likely to be paid to persons providing such services ;

(c) the amount or estimated amount of any other payments or repayments or other benefits received or likely to be received by any such persons ;

(d) the extent to which it is desirable to encourage the provision of particular descriptions of services either generally or in particular localities ;

(e) the desirability of promoting services which are—

(i) economic and efficient ; and

(ii) of an appropriate standard.".

(4) Any determination in relation to remuneration in respect Part I
of services under Part II of the National Health Service Act 1977 c. 49.
1977 or Part II of the National Health Service (Scotland) Act 1978 c. 29.
1978 which was made—

    (*a*) before the passing of this Act ; or

    (*b*) after it but at a time before the coming into force of a
        provision inserted by this section,

shall be deemed to be validly made if regulations authorising such
a determination could have been made had that provision been
in force at that time.

8. In section 6(3) of the National Health Service Act 1966 Increase in
(which limits the aggregate amount which may be outstanding in borrowing
respect of the principal of money borrowed by the General powers of
Practice Finance Corporation to £40 million or such greater Practice
amount not exceeding £100 million as the Secretary of State may Finance
by order specify) for the words " £40 million " and " £100 mil- Corporation.
lion " there shall be substituted, respectively, the words " £150 1966 c. 8.
million " and " £250 million ".

9.—(1) The following subsection shall be added after section Holidays for
5(2A) of the National Health Service Act 1977— patients etc.

    " (2B) The Secretary of State's functions may be per-
formed outside England and Wales, in so far as they relate—

    (*a*) to holidays for patients ;

    (*b*) to the transfer of patients to or from Scotland,
        Northern Ireland, the Isle of Man or the Channel
        Islands ; or

    (*c*) to the return of patients who have received treat-
        ment in England and Wales to countries or terri-
        tories outside the British Islands.".

(2) The following section shall be added after section 99 of
the National Health Service (Scotland) Act 1978—

" Holidays   99A. The Secretary of State's functions may be
for patients performed outside Scotland, in so far as they relate—
etc.

    (*a*) to holidays for patients ;

    (*b*) to the transfer of patients to or from Eng-
        land, Wales, Northern Ireland, the Isle of
        Man or the Channel Islands ; or

    (*c*) to the return of patients who have received
        treatment in Scotland to countries or terri-
        tories outside the British Islands.".

Reimburse-
ment of cost
of medical
and maternity
treatment in
member States
of European
Economic
Community.

Treatment in European Economic Community

10.—(1) The Secretary of State may pay to a competent institution in a member State the cost of treatment to which this
section applies provided by that institution under the social
security scheme of that State for a person who, at the relevant
time—

(a) was ordinarily resident in Great Britain ; and

(b) was a national of a member State or a dependant of such
a national.

(2) The Secretary of State may only make a payment under
this section of the cost of treatment—

(a) which is given to a person during a temporary stay in
a member State because his condition required immediate treatment ;

(b) which—

(i) is given in continuance of treatment commenced in the United Kingdom ; and

(ii) follows an agreement between the Secretary of
State and the person treated that, on his subsequent
return to, or transfer of residence to, the member
State, his treatment for the same condition would be
at the expense of the Secretary of State for a period
agreed with the Secretary of State ; or

(c) which is given following an agreement between the
Secretary of State and the person treated that he should
go to the member State to receive treatment to which
this section applies appropriate to his condition.

(3) This section applies—

(a) to treatment for sickness or injury ; and

(b) to treatment in connection with pregnancy or maternity,

which is given to a person to whom the 1971 Community regulation did not apply at the relevant time.

(4) In this section—

" competent institution " has the meaning assigned to it by
the 1971 Community regulation ;

" the 1971 Community regulation " means Council Regulation (EEC) No. 1408/71 as it has effect from time to
time ; and

" the relevant time " means the time when treatment was
given.

PART II

SOCIAL SECURITY

11.— (1) The following section shall be substituted for section 36 of the Social Security Act 1975—

" Severe
disablement
allowance.

36.—(1) Subject to the provisions of this section, a person shall be entitled to a severe disablement allowance for any day (" the relevant day ") if he satisfies—

(a) the conditions specified in subsection (2) below ; or

(b) the conditions specified in subsection (3) below.

(2) The conditions mentioned in subsection (1)(a) above are that—

(a) on the relevant day he is incapable of work ; and

(b) he has been incapable of work for a period of not less than 196 consecutive days—

(i) beginning not later than the day on which he attained the age of 20 ; and

(ii) ending immediately before the relevant day.

(3) The conditions mentioned in subsection (1)(b) above are that—

(a) on the relevant day he is both incapable of work and disabled ; and

(b) he has been both incapable of work and disabled for a period of not less than 196 consecutive days ending immediately before the relevant day.

(4) A person shall not be entitled to a severe disablement allowance if—

(a) he is under the age of 16 ; or

(b) he is receiving full-time education ; or

(c) he does not satisfy the prescribed conditions—

(i) as to residence in Great Britain ; or

(ii) as to presence there ; or

(d) he has attained pensionable age and was not entitled to a severe disablement allowance immediately before he attained it and is not treated by regulations as having been so entitled immediately before he attained it.

(5) A person is disabled for the purposes of this section if he suffers from loss of physical or mental faculty such that the assessed extent of the resulting disablement amounts to not less than 80 per cent.

(6) A severe disablement allowance shall be paid at the weekly rate specified in relation thereto in Schedule 4, Part III, paragraph 2.

(7) Regulations—

(*a*) may direct that persons who—

(i) have attained retiring age ; and

(ii) were entitled to a severe disablement allowance immediately before they attained it,

shall continue to be so entitled notwithstanding that they do not satisfy the conditions specified in subsection (2) or (3) above ;

(*b*) may direct—

(i) that persons who have previously been entitled to a severe disablement allowance shall be entitled to such an allowance notwithstanding that they do not satisfy the conditions specified in subsection (2)(*b*) or (3)(*b*) above ;

(ii) that those paragraphs shall have effect in relation to such persons subject to such modifications as may be specified in the regulations ;

(*c*) may prescribe the circumstances in which a person is or is not to be treated—

(i) as incapable of work ; or

(ii) as receiving full-time education ; and

(*d*) may provide for disqualifying a person from receiving a severe disablement allowance for such period not exceeding 6 weeks as may be determined in accordance with sections 97 to 104 below if—

(i) he has become incapable of work through his own misconduct ; or

               (ii) he fails without good cause to attend for, or to submit himself to, such medical or other examination or treatment as may be required in accordance with the regulations, or to observe any prescribed rules of behaviour.

(8) In this section—

    " assessed " means assessed in accordance with Schedule 8 to this Act ; and

    " retiring age " means, in the case of a man, 70 and, in the case of a woman, 65.".

(2) Schedule 4 to this Act, which makes amendments to other enactments consequential on subsection (1) above, shall have effect.

12. The following section shall be inserted after section 45 of the Social Security Act 1975—

" Pension increase (husband).

    45A.—(1) Where a Category A retirement pension is payable to a woman for any period—

    (a) which began immediately upon the termination of a period for which the pensioner was entitled to an increase in unemployment benefit, sickness benefit or invalidity pension by virtue of section 44(3)(a) or 47(1) (a) of this Act (increases in respect of adult dependants) ; and

    (b) during which the conditions specified in subsection (2) below are satisfied (without interruption),

then the weekly rate of the pensioner's Category A retirement pension shall be increased by the amount specified in relation thereto in Schedule 4, Part IV, column 3 (" the specified amount ").

    (2) The conditions referred to in subsection (1) (b) above are—

    (a) that the pensioner is residing with her husband or is contributing to his maintenance at a weekly rate not less than the specified amount ; and

    (b) that the pensioner's husband is not engaged in any one or more employments from which his weekly earnings exceed the specified amount.".

PART II
Dependent
children.
1975 c. 14.
1975 c. 16.

13. Schedule 5 to this Act, which makes amendments to the Social Security Act 1975 and the Industrial Injuries and Diseases (Old Cases) Act 1975 in relation to increases in benefits payable in respect of dependent children, shall have effect.

14. In the Social Security Act 1975—

Earnings to
include
occupational
pensions for
purposes of
benefits in
respect of
dependants.

(*a*) the following section shall be inserted after section 47A—

" Earnings
to include
occupational
pensions for
purposes of
benefits.

47B.—(1) Except as may be prescribed—

    (*a*) in section 41 and sections 44 to 47 above any reference to earnings includes a reference to payments by way of occupational pension ; and

    (*b*) in sections 44, 45, 45A and 47 above any reference to a period during which a person is not engaged in any employment includes a reference to a period in respect of which a person is not entitled to any payment by way of occupational pension.

(2) For the purposes of the provisions mentioned in subsection (1) above, the Secretary of State may by regulations provide, in relation to cases where payments by way of occupational pension are made otherwise than weekly, that any necessary apportionment of the payments shall be made in such manner and on such basis as may be prescribed." ; and

(*b*) the following section shall be inserted after section 66—

" Earnings
to include
occupational
pensions for
purposes of
disablement
pension.

66A.—(1) Except as may be prescribed, any reference to earnings in section 64 or 66 above includes a reference to payments by way of occupational pension.

(2) For the purposes of those sections, the Secretary of State may by regulations provide, in relation to cases where payments by way of occupational pension are made otherwise than weekly, that any necessary apportionment of the payments shall be made in such manner and on such basis as may be prescribed.".

Attendance
allowance:
daily
entitlement.
S.I. 1975/560.
S.I. 1977/1361.

15.—(1) In this section—

    " the 1975 Regulations " means the Social Security (Claims and Payments) Regulations 1975 ;

    " the 1977 amendment Regulations " means the Social Security (Attendance Allowance) Amendment Regulations 1977 ;

"the 1979 Regulations" means the Social Security (Claims Part II
and Payments) Regulations 1979; S.I. 1979/628.

"the 1980 amendment Regulations" means the Social Security (Attendance Allowance) Amendment Regulations S.I. 1980/1136.
1980;

"regulation 16A" means regulation 16A of the 1975 Regulations, which was added by regulation 9 of the 1977 amendment Regulations;

"regulation 18" means regulation 18 of the 1979 Regulations, both as originally made and as substituted by regulation 6(2) of the 1980 amendment Regulations;

"appropriate pay day" means a day for payment under regulation 15(7) of the 1975 Regulations or regulation 16(7) of the 1979 Regulations of weekly sums on account of an attendance allowance; and

"13 week period" means the period mentioned in regulation 16A or regulation 18.

(2) Regulation 16A and regulation 18 shall be deemed always to have had effect as if—

(*a*) the words "Notwithstanding anything in the foregoing provisions of these regulations" were inserted at the beginning;

(*b*) any reference to attendance allowance being payable for a period were a reference to attendance allowance which would have been payable for that period but for—

　　(i) regulation 15(9) or (10) of the 1975 Regulations; or

　　(ii) regulation 16(10) or (11) of the 1979 Regulations; and

(*c*) in relation to any case where a 13 week period does not end on an appropriate pay day, any reference to a 13 week period in paragraph (1) were a reference to that period together with any days after its end but before the next appropriate pay day.

Constitution of panels for social security appeal tribunals.

16. In the Social Security Act 1975—

(*a*) the following subsection shall be substituted for subsections (2A) and (2B) of section 97—

1975 c. 14.

　　"(2A) Members of a social security appeal tribunal other than the chairman shall be drawn from the appropriate panel constituted under Schedule 10 to this Act."; and (*b*) the following sub-paragraphs shall be substituted for paragraph 1(2) to (5) of Schedule 10—

" (2) The panel for an area shall be composed of persons appearing to the President to have knowledge or experience of conditions in the area and to be representative of persons living or working in the area.

(2A) Before appointing members of a panel, the President shall take into consideration any recommendations from such organisations or persons as he considers appropriate.".

Late Paid
Class 2
contributions.
1975 c. 14.

17.—(1) In subsection (1) of section 7 (Class 2 contributions) of the Social Security Act 1975 after the word " section " there shall be inserted the words " and section 7A below ".

(2) The following section shall be inserted after that section—

" Late paid
Class 2
contributions.

7A.—(1) This section applies to any Class 2 contribution paid in respect of a week falling within a tax year (" the contribution year ") earlier than the tax year in which it is paid (" the payment year ").

(2) Subject to subsections (3) to (5) below, the amount of a contribution to which this section applies shall be the amount which the earner would have had to pay if he had paid the contribution in the contribution year.

(3) Subject to subsections (4), (5) and (6) below, in any case where—

(*a*) the earner pays an ordinary contribution to which this section applies after the end of the tax year immediately following the contribution year ; and

(*b*) the weekly rate of ordinary contributions for the contribution year differs from the weekly rate for the payment year,

the amount of the contribution shall be computed by reference to the weekly rate of ordinary Class 2 contributions for the payment year.

(4) The Secretary of State may by regulations direct that subsection (3) above shall have effect in relation to a higher-rate contribution to which this section applies subject to such modifications as may be prescribed.

(5) Subject to subsection (6) below, for the purposes of proceedings in any court relating to an earner's failure to pay Class 2 contributions, the

amount of each contribution which he is to be
treated as having failed to pay is the amount which
he would have paid in accordance with subsections
(1) to (3) above or regulations under subsection
(6) below if he had paid that contribution on the
date on which the proceedings commenced.

(6) The Secretary of State may by regulations provide that the amount of any contribution which,
apart from the regulations, would fall to be computed
in accordance with subsection (3) or (5) above shall
instead be computed by reference to a tax year not
earlier than the contribution year but earlier—

> (a) in a case falling within subsection (3) above,
> than the payment year ; and

> (b) in a case falling within subsection (5) above,
> than the tax year in which the proceedings
> commenced.

(7) For the purposes of this section—

> (a) proceedings in the High Court or a county
> court commence when an action commen-
> ces ; and

> (b) proceedings under section 146 below com-
> mence when an information is laid.

(8) In this section—

> " ordinary contribution " means a contribution
> under subsection (1) of section 7 above ;
> and

> " higher-rate contribution " means a contribution
> under regulations made under subsection (4)
> of that section.".

18.—(1) In section 8 of the Social Security Act 1975 (Class 3
contributions)—

Class 3 contributions.

1975 c. 14.

> (a) in subsection (1), after the word " and ", in the second
> place where it occurs, there shall be inserted the words
> " , subject to the following provisions of this section," ;

> (b) the following subsection shall be inserted after sub-
> section (2)—

> > " (2A) The amount of a Class 3 contribution in
> > respect of a tax year earlier than the tax year in
> > which it is paid shall be the same as if it had
> > been paid in the earlier year and in respect of that
> > year.".

(2) Subsection (1) above shall be deemed to have come into
force on 6th April 1975.

(3) At the end of the subsection inserted by subsection (1)(*b*) above there shall be added—

", unless it falls to be calculated in accordance with subsection (2C) below or regulations under subsection (2D) below.

(2B) In this section—

"the payment year" means the tax year in which a contribution is paid; and

"the contribution year" means the earlier year mentioned in subsection (2A) above.

(2C) Subject to the following provisions of this section, in any case where—

(*a*) a Class 3 contribution is paid after the end of the next tax year but one following the contribution year; and

(*b*) the amount of a Class 3 contribution in respect of the contribution year differs from the amount in respect of the payment year,

the amount of the contribution shall be computed by reference to the amount of a Class 3 contribution for the payment year.

(2D) The Secretary of State may by regulations provide that the amount of a contribution which apart from the regulations would fall to be computed in accordance with subsection (2C) above shall instead be computed by reference to the amount of a Class 3 contribution for a tax year earlier than the payment year but not earlier than the contribution year.".

Accrued rights and entitlement to benefits under occupational pension schemes.

1975 c. 60.

19.—(1) The following subsections shall be substituted for section 38(1) and (2) of the Social Security Pensions Act 1975—

" (1) Regulations may prescribe circumstances in which and conditions subject to which—

(*a*) an earner's accrued rights to the requisite benefits under a contracted-out scheme; or

(*b*) the liability for the payment of such benefits to or in respect of any person who has become entitled to them,

may be transferred to another occupational pension scheme.

(1A) Any such regulations may be made so as to apply to earners who are not in employment at the time of the transfer.

(1B) Regulations under subsection (1) above may provide that any provision of this Part of this Act shall have effect, where there has been a transfer to which they apply, subject to such modifications as may be specified in the regulations.

(1C) Regulations under subsection (1) above shall have effect in relation to transfers whenever made unless they provide that they are only to have effect in relation to transfers which take place after they come into force.

(1D) The power conferred by subsection (1) above is without prejudice to the generality of section 166(2) of the principal Act.".

(2) In section 44 of that Act (premium on termination of contracted-out scheme)—

> (a) the following subsections shall be inserted after subsection (1)—
>
> > " (1A) Regulations may provide that any provision of this Part of this Act shall have effect where the Occupational Pensions Board have approved arrangements under subsection (1) above subject to such modifications as may be specified in the regulations.
> >
> > (1B) Any such regulations shall have effect in relation to arrangements whenever approved, unless they provide that they are only to have effect in relation to arrangements approved after they come into force." ; and
>
> (b) the following subsection shall be inserted after subsection (9)—
>
> > " (10) Any reference to earners in this section includes, in relation to any particular time, not only a reference to earners who are in employment at that time but also a reference to earners who are not in employment at that time but who have been in employment before it or will be in employment after it.".

20. The Social Security Pensions Act 1975 shall be amended in accordance with Schedule 6 to this Act for the purpose of protecting pensions under occupational pension schemes which are or have been contracted-out.

Protection of pensions.
1975 c. 60.

21. The enactments specified in Schedule 7 to this Act shall have effect subject to the amendments there specified.

Miscellaneous social security amendments.

2 G 3

PART II
Regulations.
1980 c. 30.
1975 c. 14.

22.—(1) Section 10(1) of the Social Security Act 1980 (reference of regulations etc. to Social Security Advisory Committee) shall not apply to regulations—

(a) made under section 36 of the Social Security Act 1975 before the expiry of the period of six months beginning with the commencement of section 11 above ;

(b) made under any enactment before the expiry of the period of six months beginning with the commencement of section 11 above and contained in a statutory instrument which states that it contains only provisions consequential on that section or such provisions and regulations made under section 36 of the Social Security Act 1975 ;

(c) made under any enactment before the expiry of the period of six months beginning with the commencement of Schedule 4 to this Act and contained in a statutory instrument which states that it contains only provisions consequential on that Schedule ;

(d) made under section 47B or 66A of the Social Security Act 1975 before the expiry of the period of six months beginning with the commencement of section 14 above ;

(e) made under any enactment before the expiry of the period of six months beginning with the commencement of section 14 above and contained in a statutory instrument which states that it contains only provisions consequential on that section or such provisions and regulations made under section 47B or 66A of the Social Security Act 1975 ;

(f) made under section 7A of the Social Security Act 1975 before the expiry of the period of six months beginning with the commencement of section 17 above ;

(g) made under section 129(1) of the Social Security Act 1975 before the expiry of that period and contained in a statutory instrument which states that it contains only provisions modifying section 7A of that Act ;

(h) made under section 8(2D) of the Social Security Act 1975 before the expiry of the period of six months beginning with the commencement of section 18(3) above ;

(j) made under section 28 below or under that section as extended by paragraph 17 of Schedule 4 to this Act ;

(k) made under any enactment before the expiry of the period of six months beginning with the commencement of Schedule 5 to this Act and contained in a statutory instrument which states that it contains only provisions consequential on that Schedule ;

(*l*) made under section 4(1) of the Social Security Pensions
Act 1975 before the expiry of the period of six months
beginning with the commencement of paragraph 3 of
Schedule 7 to this Act ;

(*m*) made under any enactment before the expiry of that
period and contained in a statutory instrument which
states that it contains only provisions consequential
on such regulations as are mentioned in paragraph (*l*)
above ;

(*n*) made under any enactment before the expiry of that
period and contained in a statutory instrument which
states that it contains only provisions consequential
on paragraph 3(*b*) of Schedule 7 to this Act ;

(*o*) made under section 4 of the Social Security and Housing
Benefits Act 1982 by virtue of the power contained
in the words inserted in that section by paragraph 7
of Schedule 7 to this Act and before the expiry of the
period of six months beginning with the commencement
of that paragraph.

(2) If an order under section 27 below appoints different days
for different purposes of the same provision of this Act, references to commencement in subsection (1) above or subsection
(4) below are to be construed, in relation to that provision, as
references to the day on which it first comes into force for any
purpose.

(3) Section 141(2) of the Social Security Act 1975 (references
of regulations to Industrial Injuries Advisory Council) shall not
apply to regulations within subsection (1)(*k*) above.

(4) Section 61(2) of the Social Security Pensions Act 1975
(reference of regulations to Occupational Pensions Board) shall
not apply to regulations—

(*a*) made under section 38 or 44(1A) or (1B) of the Social
Security Pensions Act 1975 before the expiry of the
period of six months beginning with the commencement
of section 19 above ;

(*b*) made under any enactment before the expiry of the
period of six months beginning with the commencement of section 19 above and contained in a statutory
instrument which states that it contains only provisions
consequential on that section or such provisions and
regulations made under section 38 or 44(1A) or (1B) of
the Social Security Pensions Act 1975 ;

(*c*) made under section 41C or 41E of that Act before the
expiry of the period of six months beginning with the
commencement of Schedule 6 to this Act ; or

2 G 4

PART II

(d) made under any enactment before the expiry of the period of six months beginning with the commencement of that Schedule and contained in a statutory instrument which states that it contains only provisions consequential on that Schedule or such provisions and regulations made under section 41C or 41E of the Social Security Pensions Act 1975.

1975 c. 60.

PART III

SUPPLEMENTARY

Expenses.

23. Any expenses of the Secretary of State incurred in consequence of the provisions of this Act, including any increase attributable to those provisions in sums provided under any other Act, shall be defrayed out of money provided by Parliament.

Repeals.

24. The enactments specified in Schedule 8 to this Act are repealed to the extent specified in the third column of that Schedule.

Northern
Ireland.
1974 c. 28.

25.—(1) An Order in Council under paragraph 1(1)(*b*) of Schedule 1 to the Northern Ireland Act 1974 (legislation for Northern Ireland in the interim period) which states that it is made only for purposes to which this section applies—

    (a) shall not be subject to paragraph 1(4) and (5) of that Schedule (affirmative resolution of both Houses of Parliament) ; but

    (b) shall be subject to annulment in pursuance of a resolution of either House.

(2) The purposes to which subsection (1) above applies are purposes corresponding to those—

    (a) of section 1(3), (4) and (6) above ;

    (b) of section 7(1), (3) and (4) above ;

    (c) of Part II above ; and

    (d) of this Part.

Extent.

26.—(1) The following provisions of this Act—

section 1(3), (4) and (6) ;

section 5, except subsection (3), and Schedule 3 ;

section 6(1), (2) and (4) ;

in section 7—

        (a) subsection (1) ; and

        (b) subsections (3) and (4), so far as they relate to the National Health Service Act 1977 ;

1977 c. 49.

section 9(1),
extend to England and Wales only.

(2) The following provisions of this Act—
   section 1(5) and (7);
   section 6(3);
   in section 7—
> (*a*) subsection (2); and
> (*b*) subsections (3) and (4), so far as they relate to the National Health Service (Scotland) Act 1978;   1978 c. 29.

   section 9(2),
extend to Scotland only.

(3) Section 25 above extends to Northern Ireland only.

(4) The following provisions of this Act—
   section 8;
   section 10; and
   Part II, except the provisions mentioned in subsection (5) below,
extend to England and Wales and Scotland.

(5) Section 11(2) above, so far as it relates to paragraph 2 of Schedule 4, and section 21 above, so far as it relates to paragraph 6 of Schedule 7, extend to England and Wales, Scotland and Northern Ireland.

(6) The following provisions of this Act also extend to England and Wales, Scotland and Northern Ireland—
   section 1(1) and (2);
   sections 2 to 4 and Schedule 2;
   section 5(3);
   section 23;
   this section;
   sections 27 to 29.

(7) Where any enactment repealed by this Act extends to any part of the United Kingdom, the repeal extends to that part.

27.—(1) Subject to the following provisions of this section, the provisions of this Act shall come into force on such day as the Secretary of State may by order made by statutory instrument appoint, and different days may be so appointed for different purposes.

(2) The following provisions of this Act shall come into force on the day this Act is passed—
   section 6(4);
   section 7(4);

Commence-
ment.

PART III

section 9 ;

section 10 ;

section 15 ;

section 18(1) and (2) ;

section 21, so far as it relates to paragraph 6 or 8 of Schedule 7 ;

sections 22 and 23 ;

sections 25 and 26 ;

this section ;

sections 28 and 29.

(3) The following provisions of this Act shall come into force at the end of the period of two months beginning with the day on which this Act is passed—

section 8 ;

section 16 ;

section 19 ;

section 21, so far as it relates to paragraphs 4, 5, 7 and 9 of Schedule 7 ;

1975 c. 60.

section 24, so far as it relates to section 38 of the Social Security Pensions Act 1975.

Transitional.

28.—(1) The Secretary of State may by regulations made by statutory instrument make such transitional provision or saving as he considers necessary or expedient in connection with the coming into force of any provision of this Act or the operation of any enactment which is repealed or amended by a provision of this Act during any period when the repeal or amendment is not wholly in force.

(2) Without prejudice to the generality of subsection (1) above, regulations under this section may provide that references to dispensing opticians in the National Health Service Act 1977 or the National Health Service (Scotland) Act 1978 shall be treated as including suppliers of optical appliances who are not dispensing opticians as defined in those Acts.

1977 c. 49.
1978 c. 29.

(3) Section 126(4) of the National Health Service Act 1977 and section 105(7) of the National Health Service (Scotland) Act 1978 shall have effect in relation to the power to make regulations under this section containing any such provision as is mentioned in subsection (2) above as if that subsection were contained in each of those Acts.

(4) Regulations under this section shall be subject to annulment in pursuance of a resolution of either House of Parliament.

29.—(1) This Act may be cited as the Health and Social Security Act 1984.

(2) Part II of this Act and section 24 above, so far as it relates to Part II of Schedule 8 to this Act, may be cited together with the Social Security Acts 1975 to 1982 as the Social Security Acts 1975 to 1984.

PART III
Citation.

SCHEDULES

SCHEDULE 1

OPTICAL APPLIANCES

PART I

AMENDMENTS OF NATIONAL HEALTH SERVICE ACT 1977

1. In section 39 of the National Health Service Act 1977 (regulations as to arrangements for general ophthalmic services)—

    (*a*) in paragraph (*a*), for the words " ophthalmic opticians and dispensing " there shall be substituted the words " and ophthalmic " ;

    (*b*) in paragraph (*b*), for the words " ophthalmic optician or dispensing " there shall be substituted the words " or ophthalmic " ; and

    (*c*) in paragraph (*d*), for the words " ophthalmic opticians or dispensing " there shall be substituted the words " or ophthalmic ".

2. In sub-paragraph (1) of paragraph 2 of Schedule 12 to that Act (regulations for the making and recovery of charges), the following entry shall be substituted for the words from " Glasses " to " cost ", in the first place where it occurs—

    " Glasses.   Such sum as may be determined by or in accordance with directions given by the Secretary of State.".

3. The following paragraph shall be inserted after that paragraph—

" 2A.—(1) It shall be the duty of the Secretary of State to provide by regulations for payments to be made by him or by any authority established under this Act to meet, or to contribute towards, the cost incurred (whether by way of charge under this Act or otherwise) for the supply of optical appliances for which a prescription has been given in consequence of a testing of sight under this Act—

    (*a*) for a child ;

    (*b*) for a person whose resources fall to be treated under the regulations as being less than his requirements ; or

    (*c*) for a person of such other description as may be prescribed.

(2) In sub-paragraph (1) above " child " means—

    (*a*) a person who is under the age of 16 years ; or

    (*b*) a person who is under the age of 19 years and receiving qualifying full-time education.

(3) Regulations under this paragraph may direct how a person's resources and requirements are to be calculated and,

without prejudice to the generality of this sub-paragraph, may direct that they shall be calculated—

  (a) by reference—

  (i) to any enactment ; or

  (ii) to the person's being or having been entitled to payments under any enactment,

  either as it has effect at the time when the regulations are made or as amended subsequently ; or

  (b) by reference to a scale or an index or to any other data either in the form current when the regulations are made or in any subsequent form attributable to amendment or revision taking effect after that time or to any other cause.

(4) If regulations under this paragraph provide for payments to be made by an authority established under this Act, it shall be the duty of the Secretary of State to pay to the authority, in respect of each financial year, the sum attributable to the authority's disbursements under the regulations.

(5) Sums falling to be paid in pursuance of regulations made under this paragraph shall be payable subject to compliance with such conditions as to records, certificates or otherwise as the Secretary of State may determine.".

PART II

AMENDMENTS OF NATIONAL HEALTH SERVICE (SCOTLAND) ACT 1978

1. In subsection (1) of section 26 (general ophthalmic services) of the National Health Service (Scotland) Act 1978, for the words " with ophthalmic opticians and with dispensing opticians " there shall be substituted the words " and with ophthalmic opticians ".

2. In subsection (2)(a) of the said section, for the words " , ophthalmic opticians and dispensing opticians " there shall be substituted the words " and ophthalmic opticians ".

3. In subsection (2)(b), for the words " any ophthalmic optician or any dispensing optician " there shall be substituted the words " or any ophthalmic optician ".

4. In subsection (2)(d)—

  (a) for the words " ophthalmic opticians or dispensing opticians " there shall be substituted the words " or ophthalmic opticians " ; and

  (b) for the words " ophthalmic optician or dispensing optician " there shall be substituted the words " or ophthalmic optician ".

5. In sub-paragraph (1) of paragraph 2 of Schedule 11 to that Act (charges for dental or optical appliances) the following entry shall be substituted for the words from " Glasses " to the end—

" Glasses.	Such sum as may be determined by or in accordance with directions given by the Secretary of State.".

6. In paragraph 2 of Schedule 11, in sub-paragraph (7), for the words from the beginning to "testing" there shall be substituted—

" (7) In sub-paragraph (4), " the relevant time " means—

(*a*) in relation to a dental appliance supplied otherwise than under Part II, the time of the examination leading to the supply of the appliance, or the first such examination ; ".

7. The following paragraph shall be inserted after that paragraph—

" 2A.—(1) It shall be the duty of the Secretary of State to provide by regulations for payments to be made by him or by a Health Board to meet, or to contribute towards, the cost incurred (whether by way of charge under this Act or otherwise) for the supply of optical appliances for which a prescription has been given in consequence of a testing of sight under this Act—

(*a*) for a child ;

(*b*) for a person whose resources fall to be treated under the regulations as being less than his requirements ; or

(*c*) for a person of such other description as may be prescribed.

(2) In sub-paragraph (1) above " child " means—

(*a*) a person who is under the age of 16 years ; or

(*b*) a person who is under the age of 19 years and receiving qualifying full-time education.

(3) Regulations under this paragraph may direct how a person's resources and requirements are to be calculated and, without prejudice to the generality of this sub-paragraph, may direct that they shall be calculated—

(*a*) by reference—

(i) to any enactment ; or

(ii) to the person's being or having been entitled to payments under any enactment,

either as it has effect at the time when the regulations are made or as amended subsequently ; or

(*b*) by reference to a scale or an index or to any other data either in the form current when the regulations are made or in any subsequent form attributable to amendment or revision taking effect after that time or to any other cause.

(4) If regulations under this paragraph provide for payments to be made by a Health Board, it shall be the duty of the Secretary of State to pay to the Board, in respect of each financial year, the sum attributable to the Board's disbursements under the regulations.

(5) Sums falling to be paid in pursuance of regulations made under this paragraph shall be payable subject to compliance with such conditions as to records, certificates or otherwise as the Secretary of State may determine.".

SCHEDULE 2

DISCIPLINARY PROVISIONS OF OPTICIANS ACT 1958

PART I

NEW SECTIONS

1. The following sections shall be inserted after section 10 of the 1958 c. 32. Opticians Act 1958—

" Disciplinary orders.

10A. In this Act—

" disciplinary order " means—

(*a*) an erasure order ;

(*b*) a suspension order ;

(*c*) a penalty order ;

" erasure order " means—

(*a*) in relation to a registered optician, an order that his name shall be erased from the register ; and

(*b*) in relation to an enrolled body corporate, an order that its name shall be erased from the list in which it is enrolled ;

" suspension order " means—

(*a*) in relation to a registered optician, an order that his registration shall be suspended for a period specified in the order ; and

(*b*) in relation to an enrolled body corporate, an order that its enrolment in the list in which it is enrolled shall be suspended for a period specified in the order ; and

" penalty order " means an order that a registered optician or an enrolled body corporate shall pay to the General Optical Council a sum specified in the order.

Suspension orders.

10B.—(1) The period specified in a suspension order shall not exceed twelve months.

(2) While the registration of a person in the register is suspended by virtue of a suspension order he shall be treated as not being registered, notwithstanding that his name still appears in the register.

(3) While the enrolment of a body corporate is suspended by virtue of a suspension order it shall be treated as not being enrolled, notwithstanding that its name still appears in the list.

(4) Where a suspension order is made against a person or body corporate the registrar shall make in the register or list a note of that fact and of the period for which the registration or enrolment is to be suspended ; and the registrar shall erase the note at such time as the order for any reason ceases to have effect.

Penalty
orders.

10C.—(1) A penalty order may specify any sum not exceeding the maximum penalty.

(2) In this section "the maximum penalty" means £1,000 or such sum as is for the time being substituted in this definition by an order in force under subsection (3) below.

(3) If it appears to the Privy Council that there has been a change in the value of money since the last occasion when the maximum penalty was fixed, whether by the coming into force of this section, or by order under this section, the Privy Council may by order substitute for the sum specified in subsection (2) above such other sum as appears to them justified by the change.

(4) An order under subsection (3) above—

    (*a*) shall be made by statutory instrument subject to annulment in pursuance of a resolution of either House of Parliament ; and

    (*b*) shall not affect the punishment for an offence committed before that order comes into force.

(5) A penalty order shall specify a period within which the sum specified in it is to be paid.

(6) The General Optical Council may recover the sum specified in a penalty order from the person or body against whom the order was made if that person or body does not pay it within the period specified in the order.

(7) The General Optical Council shall pay a sum paid under a penalty order or recovered under subsection (6) above into the Consolidated Fund.".

2. The following section shall be substituted for section 11—

" Powers of
Disciplinary
Committee.

11.—(1) If any registered optician—

    (*a*) is convicted by any court in the United Kingdom of any criminal offence ; or

    (*b*) is judged by the Disciplinary Committee to have been guilty of serious professional misconduct,

the Committee may make a disciplinary order against him.

(2) If—

    (*a*) an enrolled body corporate is convicted of an offence under this Act, or of aiding, abetting, counselling or procuring the commission of, or inciting another person to commit, such an offence ; or

    (*b*) in the case of a body corporate which is for the time being enrolled by virtue of paragraph (*a*), (*c*) or (*d*) of subsection (2) of section four of this Act, the Disciplinary Committee is of opinion that the condition, or any of the conditions, for the enrolment of the body corporate under that subsection is no longer satisfied,

the Committee may make a disciplinary order against that body corporate.

(3) Where a registered optician dies while he is either a director of an enrolled body corporate or the manager of that part of the business of an enrolled body corporate which consists of the testing of sight or the fitting and supply of optical appliances, he shall be deemed, for the purposes of subsection (2) of this section, to have continued to be a director of that body or a manager of that part of its business, as the case may be, until the expiration of the three months beginning with the date of his death or until a director or manager is appointed in his place, whichever occurs first.

(4) If it appears to the Disciplinary Committee that a registered optician or an enrolled body corporate—

(*a*) has contravened or failed to comply with any rules made under section twenty-five of this Act ; or

(*b*) has failed to pay the sum specified in a penalty order within the period there specified,

the Committee may make a disciplinary order against the optician or body corporate.

(5) If it appears to the Disciplinary Committee that—

(*a*) a registered optician or enrolled body corporate is engaged in the fitting and supply of optical appliances ; and

(*b*) that the arrangements made by the optician or body corporate for carrying on his practice or his or its business are not such as to secure that the fitting and supply of optical appliances in the course of that practice or business are carried out by, or under the supervision of, an ophthalmic optician registered in the register of ophthalmic opticians engaged or proposing to engage both in the testing of sight and in the fitting and supply of optical appliances or a registered dispensing optician,

the Committee may make a disciplinary order against that optician or body corporate.

(6) Where—

(*a*) a disciplinary order is made against a director of an enrolled body corporate ; or

SCH. 2

(*b*) a responsible officer of an enrolled body corporate is convicted of an offence under this Act ; or

(*c*) a disciplinary order is made against a registered optician employed by an enrolled body corporate and the act or omission constituting the ground on which the order was made was instigated or connived at by a responsible officer of the body corporate, or, if the act or omission was a continuing act or omission, a responsible officer of the body corporate had or reasonably ought to have had knowledge of its continuance,

the Disciplinary Committee may make a disciplinary order against the body corporate.

(7) In a case—

(*a*) where—

(i) an enrolled body corporate is convicted of an offence under this Act ; and

(ii) the offence was instigated or connived at by a responsible officer of the body corporate, or, if the offence was a continuing offence, a responsible officer of the body corporate had or reasonably ought to have had knowledge of its continuance ; or

(*b*) where—

(i) a disciplinary order is made against an enrolled body corporate ; and

(ii) the act or omission constituting the ground on which the order was made was instigated or connived at by a responsible officer of the body corporate, or, if the act or omission was a continuing act or omission, a responsible officer of the body corporate had or reasonably ought to have had knowledge of its continuance,

the Disciplinary Committee may, if the responsible officer is a registered optician, make a disciplinary order against him.

(8) The Disciplinary Committee shall not take a case into consideration during any period within which proceedings by way of appeal may be brought which may result in subsection (6) or (7) of this section being rendered inapplicable in that case or while any such proceedings are pending.

(9) Where it appears to the Disciplinary Committee—

(*a*) that a body corporate which carries on business as an ophthalmic or dispensing optician at more than one set of premises is liable to have a disciplinary order made against it ; and (*b*) that the events giving rise to the liability were confined, or substantially confined, to a particular set of premises,

the Committee may, instead of making a disciplinary order against the body corporate, direct that the body corporate shall not use the title of optician, ophthalmic optician, dispensing optician, registered optician, enrolled optician or optometrist in connection with that set of premises ; and if at any time thereafter it appears to the Committee that the body corporate has contravened a direction in force under this subsection, the Committee may make a disciplinary order against the body corporate.

(10) A direction under subsection (9) of this section shall remain in force until revoked, on an application made to them in that behalf, by the Disciplinary Committee.

(11) When the Disciplinary Committee—

(*a*) make a disciplinary order against an individual or body corporate ; or

(*b*) direct that a body corporate shall not use any of the titles specified in subsection (9) of this section in connection with a set of premises,

the registrar shall serve on that individual or body a notification of the order or direction.

(12) Any power conferred by this section to make a disciplinary order is a power to make—

(*a*) an erasure order ;

(*b*) a suspension order ;

(*c*) a penalty order ; or

(*d*) an erasure order or suspension order together with a penalty order.

(13) In this Act " responsible officer " means any director, manager, secretary or other similar officer of a body corporate, or of a branch or department of a body corporate, or any person purporting to act in any such capacity.".

Part II

Minor and Consequential Amendments

3. The Opticians Act 1958 shall also have effect subject to the amendments specified in the following paragraphs of this Schedule. 1958 c. 32.

4. In subsection (1) of section 9 (preliminary investigations), for the words from " his " to " eleven " there shall be substituted the words " made against him or it a disciplinary order or an order under section thirteen ".

5.—(1) In subsection (1) of section 12 of that Act (restoration to register), for the words from " the name " to " direction " there shall be substituted the words " an erasure order has been made against an individual or body corporate ".

(2) In subsection (2)(*b*) of that section, after the word " of " there shall be inserted the words " the Committee's decision on ".

6. The following section shall be inserted after section 13—

" Service of   13A.—(1) A notification under section 11 or 13 above
notifications. which is required to be served on a person may be served by being delivered personally, or being sent by post in a registered letter or by the recorded delivery service.

(2) For the purposes of this section, and of section 7 of the Interpretation Act 1978 (which defines " service by post ") in its application to this section, a letter to a person other than a body corporate containing such a notification shall be deemed to be properly addressed if it is addressed to him at his address in the register or at his last known address if that address differs from his address in the register and it appears to the registrar that the notification is more likely to reach him at his last known address.

(3) A notification which is required to be served on a body corporate shall be duly served if it is served on the secretary or clerk of that body.

(4) For the purposes of this section, and of section 7 of the Interpretation Act 1978 in its application to this section, the proper address of a person, in the case of a body corporate or the secretary or clerk of a body corporate, shall be its address in the list or the address of its registered or principal office if that address differs from its address in the list and it appears to the registrar that the notification is more likely to reach the body corporate or its secretary or clerk there.".

7.—(1) In subsection (1) of section 14 (appeals), for the words from " that ", in the first place where it occurs, to " premises " there shall be substituted the words " in relation to an individual or body corporate under section 11 or 13 of this Act ".

(2) In subsection (3) of that section, for the words from the beginning to " the ", in the first place where it occurs, there shall be substituted the words " Where no appeal is brought against—

(*a*) a disciplinary order ; or

(*b*) a direction under subsection (9) of section eleven of this Act ; or

(*c*) a direction under section thirteen of this Act,

or where such an appeal is brought but withdrawn or struck out for want of prosecution, the order or ".

(3) In subsection (4) of that section, for the words " direction under either of those sections, the direction " there shall be substituted the words " any such order or direction, it ".

8. In subsection (2) of section 15 (procedure)—

(*a*) in paragraph (*a*), for the words " his or its name erased from the register or list " there shall be substituted the words

" a disciplinary order or a direction under section thirteen of this Act made against him or it " ;

(*b*) in paragraph (*e*), for the words " infamous conduct in a professional respect " there shall be substituted the words " serious professional misconduct " ;

(*c*) in paragraph (*f*), for the words " his " to " (4) " there shall be substituted the words " a disciplinary order made against him or it under subsection (4) or (5) " ; and

(*d*) in the proviso, for " (6) " there shall be substituted " (9) ".

9. In subsection (3) of section 23 (death or bankruptcy of registered optician), for the words " any direction that the name of a body corporate shall be erased from the list " there shall be substituted the words " a disciplinary order ".

10. In section 24 (offences by bodies corporate), for the words from " director " to " capacity " there shall be substituted the words " responsible officer of the body corporate ".

11. In subsection (1) of section 27 (expenses and accounts of General Optical Council), after the word " money " there shall be inserted the words " , other than a sum paid under a penalty order or recovered under section 10C(6) above,".

12. In subsection (1) of section 29 (powers of Privy Council), for the words " directions to erase names from the register or list " there shall be substituted the words " disciplinary orders or directions under section 13 above ".

13. In subsection (1) of section 30—

(*a*) the following definition shall be inserted after the definition of " disciplinary case "—

  " " disciplinary order " has the meaning assigned to it by section 10A of this Act ; " ;

(*b*) the following definition shall be inserted after the definition of " enrolled "—

  " " erasure order " has the meaning assigned to it by section 10A of this Act ; " ;

(*c*) the following definition shall be inserted after the definition of " optical appliance "—

  " " penalty order " has the meaning assigned to it by section 10A of this Act ; " ; and

(*d*) the following definitions shall be inserted after the definition of "registered dispensing optician "—

  " " responsible officer " has the meaning assigned to it by subsection (13) of section 11 of this Act ;
  " suspension order " has the meaning assigned to it by section 10A of this Act.".

SCHEDULE 3

FAMILY PRACTITIONER COMMITTEES

1. The National Health Service Act 1977 shall have effect subject to the following amendments.

2. The following section shall be substituted for section 17—

"Directions   17.—(1) The Secretary of State may give directions with
as to   respect to the exercise of any functions exercisable by
exercise of   virtue of sections 13 to 16 above ; and, subject to any
functions.   directions given by the Secretary of State by virtue of this
               section, a Regional Health Authority may give directions
               with respect to the exercise by a District Health Authority
               of which the district is included in its region, of any
               functions exercisable by the District Health Authority
               by virtue of section 14 above.

(2) It shall be the duty of a body to whom directions are given under subsection (1) above to comply with the directions.".

3. In section 22 (co-operation between health authorities and local authorities)—

    (*a*) in subsection (1), after the words " health authorities " there shall be inserted the words ", Family Practitioner Committees " ;

    (*b*) in subsection (2), for the words from " advise " to " below " there shall be substituted the words " bodies represented on them " ;

    (*c*) in the Table at the end of that subsection, the following paragraph shall be inserted in the second column at the end of each of the three two-column entries—

        " Any Family Practitioner Committee whose locality is wholly or partly in the District Health Authority's district." ;

  and

    (*d*) in section (4)(*b*), after the word " Authority "—

        (i) in the first place where it occurs, there shall be inserted the words " or a Family Practitioner Committee " ; and

        (ii) in the second place where it occurs, there shall be added the words " or the locality of the Family Practitioner Committee".

4. The following subsection shall be inserted after subsection (1) of section 30 (applications to provide general medical services)—

" (1A) No medical practitioner who is a national of a member State and is registered by virtue of a qualification granted in a member State shall be entitled to have his application for the inclusion of his name in the list kept by any Family Practitioner Committee referred to the Medical Practices Committee unless he satisfies the Family Practitioner Committee that he has that knowledge of English which, in the interests of himself and his patients, is necessary for the provision of general medical services in the Committee's locality ; and where a Family Practitioner Committee is not so satisfied with respect to any applicant the Family Practitioner Committee shall not refer his application to the Medical Practices Committee.".

5.—(1) Section 36 (regulations as to arrangements for general dental services) shall be re-numbered so as to become section 36(1).

(2) At the end of the resulting subsection (1) there shall be added as subsection (2)—

" (2) No dental practitioner who is a national of a member State and is registered by virtue of a qualification granted in a member State shall be entitled to have his name included in the list kept by any Family Practitioner Committee unless he satisfies the Committee that he has that knowledge of English which, in the interests of himself and his patients, is necessary for the provision of general dental services in the Committee's locality.".

6. In subsection (1) of section 44 (recognition of local representative committees)—

(a) for the words from " area ", in the first place where it occurs, to " Authority ", in the second place where it occurs, there shall be substituted the words " locality of any Family Practitioner Committee " ;

(b) the word " locality " shall be substituted for the words " area or district ", in each place where they occur.

7. In section 45 (functions of local representative committees)—

(a) in subsection (1), for the words " the area of an Area Health Authority or for the district of a District Health Authority " there shall be substituted the words " a locality " ;

(b) in subsection (2)—

(i) for the words " area or district " there shall be substituted the word " locality " ; and

(ii) the words " with the Secretary of State's approval " shall be omitted ; and

(c) in subsection (3), the words " with the Secretary of State's approval " shall be omitted.

8. The following paragraph shall be substituted for paragraph (i) of section 56 (inadequate services)—

" (i) he may authorise the Family Practitioner Committee to make such other arrangements as he may approve, or may himself make such other arrangements, and ".

9. In section 97 (means of meeting expenditure of health authorities out of public funds)—

(a) the following paragraph shall be substituted for subsection (1)(b)—

" (b) to each Family Practitioner Committee—

(i) sums not exceeding the amount allotted by him to the Committee for that year towards meeting

SCH. 3

the expenditure attributable to the performance by the Committee of their functions in that year ;

(ii) sums equal to the expenditure by them in that year which is attributable to disbursements to persons providing services in pursuance of Part II of this Act ; " ;

(b) the following subsection shall be substituted for subsection (3)—

" (3) The Secretary of State may give directions to a Regional Health Authority or Family Practitioner Committee or to a District Health Authority whose district is in Wales with respect to the application of sums paid to them under subsection (1) above." ; and

(c) in subsection (5), after the words " health authority " there shall be inserted the words " or Family Practitioner Committee ".

10. The following section shall be inserted after section 97A—

" Financial duties of Family Practitioner Committees.

97B.—(1) It is the duty of every Family Practitioner Committee, in respect of each financial year, so to perform their functions as to secure that the expenditure attributable to the performance of those functions in that year, other than expenditure attributable to disbursements to persons providing services in pursuance of Part II of this Act, in respect of their provision of such services, does not exceed the aggregate of—

(a) the amounts allotted to the Committee for that year under section 97(1) above ;

(b) any other sums received by the Committee under this Act in that year ; and

(c) any sums received otherwise than under this Act in that year by the Committee for the purpose of enabling the Committee to defray any such expenditure.

(2) The Secretary of State may give such directions to a Family Practitioner Committee as appear to him to be requisite to secure that the Committee comply with the duty imposed on them by subsection (1) above and it shall be the duty of the Committee to comply with the direction.

(3) Directions under subsection (2) above may be specific in character.

(4) The Secretary of State may, by directions, determine—

(a) whether sums of a description specified in the directions are or are not to be treated for the purposes of this section as being receivable under this Act by a Family Practitioner Committee for the purposes of their functions ;

(b) whether expenditure of a description specified Sch. 3
in the directions is or is not to be treated for
the purposes of this section as being attributable to a Family Practitioner Committee's performance of their functions; or

(c) the extent to which and the circumstances in
which sums received but not yet spent by a
Family Practitioner Committee under section
97(1) above are to be treated for the purposes
of this section as part of the expenditure of the
Committee attributable to the performance of
their functions and to which financial year's
expenditure in the performance of such functions they are to be attributed.".

11. In section 128(1) (interpretation and construction) the following definition shall be substituted for the definition of " health
authority "—

" " health authority " means a Regional or District Health Authority or a special health authority but does not include a
Family Practitioner Committee ; ".

12. For Part II of Schedule 5 there shall be substituted the following Part—

" PART II

FAMILY PRACTITIONER COMMITTEES

6.—(1) Subject to paragraph 7 below, a Family Practitioner
Committee shall consist of a chairman and 30 other members.

(2) The chairman shall be appointed by the Secretary of State.

(3) The other members shall be appointed by the Secretary of
State, as follows—

(a) 8 shall be appointed from persons nominated by the
Local Medical Committee for the locality of the Family
Practitioner Committee, and one of them must be, but
not more than one of them shall be, a medical practitioner having the qualifications prescribed in pursuance
of section 38 above ;

(b) 3 shall be appointed from persons nominated by the
Local Dental Committee for that locality ;

(c) 2 shall be appointed from persons nominated by the
Local Pharmaceutical Committee for that locality ;

(d) 1 shall be an ophthalmic optician appointed from persons nominated by such members of the Local Optical
Committee for that locality as are ophthalmic opticians ;

(e) 1 shall be a dispensing optician appointed from persons
nominated by such members of the Local Optical
Committee as are dispensing opticians ;

(f) 4 shall be appointed from persons nominated by local
authorities any part of whose area is in the locality of
the Family Practitioner Committee ;

      (*g*) 4 shall be appointed from persons nominated by District Health Authorities any part of whose district is in the locality of the Family Practitioner Committee ; and

      (*h*) 7 shall be appointed after such consultations with such bodies as the Secretary of State considers appropriate.

(4) One member must be a person who—

      (*a*) is registered in the register of qualified nurses, midwives and health visitors—

            (i) as a nurse recorded in the register as having an additional qualification in district nursing ;

            (ii) as a midwife ; or

            (iii) as a health visitor ; and

      (*b*) has recent experience of providing services to patients (other than patients resident in hospital) in any such capacity.

(5) If a nomination required for the purposes of sub-paragraph (3) above is not made before such date as the Secretary of State may determine, he may appoint a member without waiting any longer for the nomination.

(6) No person—

      (*a*) shall be nominated for appointment to a Family Practitioner Committee under sub-paragraph (3)(*f*) or (*g*) above or sub-paragraph (5) above ; or

      (*b*) shall be appointed to such a Committee under sub-paragraph (3)(*f*), (*g*) or (*h*) above,

if he is—

      (i) a medical practitioner ;

      (ii) a dental practitioner ;

      (iii) an ophthalmic optician ;

      (iv) a dispensing optician ;

      (v) a registered pharmacist ; or

      (vi) a person conducting a business providing any service for the purposes of Part II of this Act.

(7) If a Local Medical Committee so require, the Secretary of State shall appoint from among medical practitioners having the qualifications prescribed in pursuance of section 38 above and nominated by the Local Medical Committee under sub-paragraph (3)(*a*) above a medical practitioner to be the deputy of such a practitioner appointed from among persons nominated by them under sub-paragraph (3)(*a*) above.

(8) If a Local Optical Committee so require, the Secretary of State shall appoint from among ophthalmic opticians nominated by the Committee under sub-paragraph (3)(*d*) above an ophthalmic optician to be the deputy of such an optician appointed from among persons nominated by them under sub-paragraph (3)(*d*) above.

(9) If a Local Optical Committee so require, the Secretary of State shall appoint from among dispensing opticians nominated by the Committee under sub-paragraph (3)(*e*) above a dispensing

optician to be the deputy of such an optician appointed from among persons nominated by them under sub-paragraph (3)(*e*) above.

(10) A deputy may, while the member for whom he is deputy is absent from any meeting of the relevant Family Practitioner Committee, act as a member of that Committee in the place of the absent member.

(11) The Committee shall appoint one of their members to be vice-chairman.

7.—(1) If it appears to the Secretary of State that, by reason of special circumstances affecting a locality, it is appropriate that the Family Practitioner Committee for that locality should not be in accordance with paragraph 6 above, he may by order provide that that paragraph shall apply in relation to the Committee for that locality with such modifications as are specified in the order.

(2) Subject to sub-paragraph (3) below, it is the Secretary of State's duty, before he makes an order under sub-paragraph (1) above, to consult the Family Practitioner Committee for the locality and any District Health Authority any part of whose district is in the locality of the Family Practitioner Committee with respect to the order.

(3) It shall also be his duty, in making any such order, to have regard to the desirability of maintaining, so far as practicable, the same numerical proportion as between members falling to be appointed in pursuance of paragraph 6 above as there would be if no modification were made.

7A.—(1) Any member of a Family Practitioner Committee appointed by virtue of paragraph 6(3)(*e*) above shall cease to be a member of the Committee on the day on which the repeal of that paragraph by section 24 of the Health and Social Security Act 1984 comes into force.

(2) The following paragraph shall be substituted on that day for paragraph 6(3)(*e*) above—

" (*e*) 1 shall be appointed from persons nominated—

(i) by the Local Medical Committee for the locality of the Family Practitioner Committee ;

(ii) by the Local Dental Committee for that locality ;

(iii) by the Local Pharmaceutical Committee for that locality ; or

(iv) by the Local Optical Committee for that locality ; "."

13. In paragraph 9 of Schedule 5 (pay and allowances of chairmen of certain authorities)—

(*a*) in sub-paragraph (1) the words " other than a Family Practitioner Committee " shall cease to have effect ; and

(*b*) in sub-paragraphs (2) and (3) the words " other than such a Committee " shall cease to have effect.

14. In paragraph 10(1) of that Schedule (employment of officers by certain authorities) (as amended by paragraph 3(1) of Schedule 6 to the Health and Social Services and Social Security Adjudications Act 1983) the words " (other than a Family Practitioner Committee) " shall cease to have effect.

15. The following sub-paragraphs shall be substituted for paragraph 2(*d*) to (*g*) of Schedule 7 (additional provisions as to Community Health Councils)—

" (*d*) the consultation of Councils by District Health Authorities or relevant Family Practitioner Committees with respect to such matters, and on such occasions, as may be prescribed ;

(*e*) the furnishing of information to Councils by such Authorities and Committees, and the right of members of Councils to enter and inspect premises controlled by such Authorities ;

(*f*) the consideration by Councils of matters relating to the operation of the health service within their districts, and the giving of advice by Councils to such Authorities and Committees on such matters ;

(*g*) the preparation and publication of reports by Councils on such matters, and the furnishing and publication by such Authorities or Committees of comments on the reports ; and ".

16. In paragraph 3(*d*) of that Schedule, for the words " Area or District Health Authority " there shall be substituted the words " District Health Authority or Family Practitioner Committee ".

17. The following paragraph shall be added at the end of that Schedule—

" 8. A Family Practitioner Committee is a relevant Family Practitioner Committee in relation to a Council's district if any part of the Committee's locality is in that district, but is only a relevant Committee in relation to that Council to the extent that the Council performs its functions in relation to that part.".

SCHEDULE 4

Severe Disablement Allowance

Part I

Consequential Amendments

Law Reform (Personal Injuries) Act 1948 (c.41)

1. In section 2(1) of the Law Reform (Personal Injuries) Act 1948 after the words " non-contributory invalidity pension " there shall be inserted the words " severe disablement allowance ".

Income and Corporation Taxes Act 1970 (c.10)

2. In section 219(1)(*a*) of the Income and Corporation Taxes Act 1970 after the words " non-contributory invalidity pension " there shall be inserted the words " severe disablement allowance ".

Social Security Act 1975 (c.14)

3. In the following provisions of the Social Security Act 1975—
   section 34(1)(*b*) ;
   section 49(*a*) ;
   section 79(3)(*a*) and (*d*) ;
   section 135(2)(*b*) ; and
   paragraph 2 of Part III of Schedule 4 and paragraph 9 of Part IV of that Schedule,
for the words " non-contributory invalidity pension " there shall be substituted the words " severe disablement allowance ".

4. At the end of each of the following provisions of that Act—
   section 98(2)(*b*) ;
   section 100(3)(*b*) ;
   section 102(2) ;
   section 103(1)(*b*) ; and
   section 104(1)(*c*)(ii),
there shall be added the words " or severe disablement allowance ".

5. In section 108(1) of that Act—
   (*a*) after the words " industrial injuries benefit " there shall be inserted the words " and severe disablement allowance " ;
   (*b*) at the beginning of paragraph (*a*) there shall be inserted the words " in relation to industrial injuries benefit," ; and
   (*c*) at the beginning of paragraph (*b*) there shall be inserted the words " in relation to both benefits,".

6. At the end of section 108(2) of that Act there shall be added the words " or, in such cases relating to severe disablement allowance as may be prescribed, by an adjudication officer.".

7. In section 109(1) of that Act after the words " disablement benefit " there shall be inserted the words " or severe disablement allowance ".

8. In section 110 of that Act—
   (*a*) in subsection (6), after the words " and in particular may " there shall be inserted the words " in any case relating to disablement benefit " ; and
   (*b*) in subsection (7), after the words " disablement benefit " there shall be inserted the words " or severe disablement allowance, as the case may be,".

9. In section 112(1)(*b*) of that Act after the words " relevant accident " there shall be inserted the words " or, in a case relating to severe disablement allowance, at the prescribed time ".

10. In Schedule 8 to that Act—
    (*a*) in paragraph 1—
        (i) for the words " section 57 " there shall be substituted the words " section 36 or 57 " : and

(ii) in sub-paragraph (*b*) at the beginning there shall be inserted the words " except in the case of an assessment for the purposes of section 36," ;

(*b*) after paragraph 4 there shall be inserted the following paragraph—

" 4A. Paragraph 4 above shall not apply in the case of an assessment of any person's disablement for the purposes of section 36 but the period to be taken into account for any such assessment shall be the period during which that person has suffered and may be expected to continue to suffer from the relevant loss of faculty beginning not later than—

(*a*) the first claim day if his entitlement to benefit falls to be determined in accordance with section 36(3)(*b*) as modified by regulations under section 36(7)(*b*) ;

(*b*) where his disablement has previously been assessed for the purposes of section 36 at a percentage which is not less than 80 per cent.—

(i) if the period taken into account for that assessment was or included the period of 196 days ending immediately before the first claim day, the first claim day, or

(ii) if the period so taken into account included any day falling within that period of 196 days, the day immediately following that day or, if there is more than one such day, the last such day ;

(*c*) in any other case, 196 days before the first claim day ;

and, in any case, ending not later than the day on which that person, if a woman, attains the age of 65 or, if a man, attains the age of 70.

In this paragraph " the first claim day " means the first day in respect of which the person concerned has made the claim in question for a severe disablement allowance " ; and

(*c*) after paragraph 5 there shall be inserted the following paragraph—

" 5A. Paragraph 5 above shall not apply in relation to an assessment of any person's disablement for the purposes of section 36 but—

(*a*) any such assessment shall state the degree of disablement in the form of a percentage and shall specify the period taken into account by the assessment ; and

(*b*) for the purposes of any such assessment—

(i) a percentage which is not a whole number shall be rounded to the nearest whole number or if it falls equally near two whole numbers shall be rounded up to the higher; and

(ii) a percentage between 5 and 100 which is not a multiple of 10 shall be treated, if it is a multiple of 5, as being the next higher percentage which is a multiple of 10 and, in any other case, as being the nearest percentage which is a multiple of 10 ; and

(c) if on the assessment the person's disablement is found to be less than 5 per cent. that degree of disablement shall for the purposes of section 36 be disregarded and, accordingly, the assessment shall state that he is not disabled.".

11. In Schedule 20 to that Act—

(a) the following entry shall be inserted after the entry relating to " Long-term benefit "—

" " Loss of physical faculty ".   Includes disfigurement whether or not accompanied by any actual loss of faculty." ;

and

(b) at the end of the entry relating to " relevant loss of faculty " there shall be added the words " or, in a case within section 36, the loss of faculty which results in disablement ".

Child Benefit Act 1975 (c.61)

12. In section 17(5) and (6) of the Child Benefit Act 1975, after the words " non-contributory invalidity pension " there shall be inserted the words " or severe disablement allowance ".

13. In paragraph 5 of Schedule 1 to that Act, for the words " non-contributory invalidity pension " there shall be substituted the words " severe disablement allowance ".

Pensioners' Payments and Social Security Act 1979 (c. 48)

14. In section 2(1)(a) of the Pensioners' Payments and Social Security Act 1979, the following sub-paragraph shall be substituted for sub-paragraph (iv)—

" (iv) a severe disablement allowance ; ".

Social Security and Housing Benefits Act 1982 (c. 24)

15. In the Social Security and Housing Benefits Act 1982—

(a) the following paragraph shall be substituted for section 18(1)(e)—

" (e) a severe disablement allowance." ; and

(b) in paragraph 5(1)(a) of Schedule 1, after the words " in validity pension " there shall be inserted the words " or a severe disablement allowance ".

Part II

Transitional

16. Without prejudice to the generality of section 27 above, different days may be appointed under that section for the purposes—

(*a*) of section 11 above ; and

(*b*) of this Schedule,

in relation to persons of different ages, but where different days are so appointed, no person shall be entitled to non-contributory invalidity pension in respect of any day on or after the first such day.

17. Without prejudice to the generality of section 28 above, regulations under that section may include provision for any person who, immediately before the day appointed under section 27 for the purposes of section 11 above or, if more than one such day is appointed, the first such day, is entitled to non-contributory invalidity pension to be entitled for that day and subsequent days to a severe disablement allowance, whether or not—

1975 c. 14.

(*a*) he is disabled within the meaning of section 36(5) of the Social Security Act 1975 (as substituted by section 11 above) ; or

(*b*) where more than one such day is appointed, the first day so appointed was appointed in relation to persons of his age.

Section 13.

SCHEDULE 5

Dependent Children

975 c. 16.

1. The Social Security Act 1975 and the Industrial Injuries and Diseases (Old Cases) Act 1975 shall have effect subject to the amendments specified in the following paragraphs of this Schedule.

2. In section 12(1) of the Social Security Act 1975 (description of contributory benefits)—

(*a*) in paragraphs (*a*) and (*b*), after the word " and " there shall be inserted the words " , where the beneficiary is over pensionable age," ; and

(*b*) in paragraph (*d*), the words " and child " shall cease to have effect.

3. In section 41 of that Act (increases in benefits payable in respect of dependent children)—

(*a*) in subsection (2)(*a*) and (*b*), after the word " benefit " there shall be added the words " where the beneficiary is over pensionable age " ;

(*b*) subsections (2)(*d*) and (3) shall cease to have effect ; and

(*c*) the following subsections shall be inserted after subsection (2)—

" (2A) Where—

(*a*) a beneficiary is one of two persons who are—

(i) spouses residing together ; or

(ii) an unmarried couple ; and

(b) the other person had earnings in any week,

the beneficiary's right to payment of increases for the following week under subsection (1) above shall be determined in accordance with subsection (2B) below.

(2B) No such increase shall be payable—

(a) in respect of the first child where the earnings were £80 or more ; and

(b) in respect of a further child for each complete £10 by which the earnings exceeded £80.

(2C) The Secretary of State may by order substitute larger amounts for the amounts for the time being specified in subsection (2B) above.

(2D) In this section—

"unmarried couple " means a man and a woman who are not married to each other but are living together as husband and wife ; and

"week " means such period of 7 days as may be prescribed by regulations made for the purposes of this section.".

4. In section 64 of that Act (increases in disablement pension payable in respect of dependent children) the following subsections shall be inserted after subsection (1)—

" (1A) Where—

(a) a beneficiary is one of two persons who are—

(i) spouses residing together ; or

(ii) an unmarried couple ; and

(b) the other person had earnings in any week,

the beneficiary's right to payment of increases for the following week under this section shall be determined in accordance with subsection (1B) below.

(1B) No such increase shall be payable—

(a) in respect of the first child where the earnings were £80 or more ; and

(b) in respect of a further child for each complete £10 by which the earnings exceeded £80.

(1C) The Secretary of State may by order substitute larger amounts for the amounts for the time being specified in subsection (1B) above.

(1D) In this section " week " means such period of 7 days as may be prescribed by regulations made for the purposes of this section.".

5. The following section shall be substituted for section 70 of that Act—

" Children of deceased's family.   70.—(1) Subject to Schedule 9 (limits on benefit payable on death), where at his death the deceased was entitled to child benefit in respect of a child or children, then,

SCH. 5

for any period for which—

(a) the widow of the deceased is entitled—

(i) to death benefit (other than a gratuity) under sections 67 and 68 of this Act ; and

(ii) to child benefit in respect of that child or one or more of those children ; or

(b) such other person as may be prescribed is entitled to child benefit in respect of that child or one or more of those children ;

the widow or, as the case may be, the person so prescribed shall be entitled in respect of that child, or in respect of each respectively of those children, to death benefit by way of an allowance at the weekly rate specified in Schedule 4, Part V, paragraph 15.

(2) Section 65(1) and (2) of this Act apply in relation to an allowance under this section as they apply in relation to an increase of benefit under section 64.".

6. The following paragraph shall be substituted for paragraph 15 of Part V of Schedule 4 to that Act—

| " 15. Weekly rate of allowance under section 70 in respect of children. | In respect of each qualifying child   ...   £7·60 " |

7. In Schedule 20 to that Act—

(a) in the definition of " week ", for the words " and 45(3) " there shall be substituted the words " 41, 45(3) and 64 " ; and

(b) after the definition of " unemployability supplement " there shall be inserted the following definition—

" " Unmarried couple " See section 41 ".

1975 c. 16.

8. In the Industrial Injuries and Diseases (Old Cases) Act 1975—

(a) the following paragraph shall be substituted for section 7(3)(c)—

" (c) where the person is entitled to child benefit in respect of a child or children, and is in receipt of an allowance which comprises such an increase as is mentioned in paragraph (a) above, by an amount equal to any increase which would be payable under section 64 of that Act in respect of that child or those children if he were entitled to disablement pension plus unemployability supplement ; " ; and

(b) the following subsection shall be substituted for section 7(4)—

" (4) Where under this section an allowance comprises such an increase as is mentioned in paragraph (a) of subsection (3) above, that subsection shall have effect as if for paragraph (d) there were substituted the following paragraph—

" (d) where the person is treated under the provisions of the scheme as residing with his wife or contributing at a weekly rate of not less than the relevant amount towards her maintenance, by the relevant amount (that is to say an amount equal to any increase which would be payable under section 66 of that Act in respect of her if he were entitled to disablement pension plus unemployability supplement).".".

SCH. 5

SCHEDULE 6

Section 20.

PROTECTION OF PENSIONS

The following provisions shall be inserted after section 41 of the Social Security Pensions Act 1975—

1975 c. 60.

" Protection of pensions

41A.—(1) If—

(*a*) there is an interval between—

(i) the date on which an earner ceases to be in employment which is contracted-out by reference to an occupational pension scheme (" the termination of employment date ") ; and

(ii) the date on which his guaranteed minimum pension under that scheme commences (" the commencement of payment date ") ;

(*b*) the relevant sum exceeds his guaranteed minimum on the day after the termination of employment date ; and

(*c*) on the commencement of payment date or at any time thereafter his guaranteed minimum pension under the scheme exceeds the amount of his guaranteed minimum under it on the day after the termination of employment date,

the weekly rate on the commencement of payment date and at any time thereafter of the pension payable to him under the scheme shall be an amount not less than the aggregate of the following—

(i) the relevant sum ;

(ii) the excess mentioned in paragraph (*c*) above ; and

(iii) any amount which is an appropriate addition at that time.

(2) In subsection (1) above " appropriate addition " means—

(*a*) where a scheme provides that part of an earner's pension shall accrue after the termination of employment date by reason of employment after that date, an amount equal to the part which has so accrued ; and

(*b*) where a scheme provides that an earner's pension which has accrued before that date shall be enhanced after it if payment of the pension is postponed, the amount by which the excess of the pension on the day after the termination of

Earners' pensions.

2 H 2

employment date over the earner's guaranteed minimum on the day after the termination of employment date has been enhanced by reason of the postponement.

(3) Subject to subsections (6) to (8) below, in this section " the relevant sum " means—

    (a) if the earner reaches normal pension age on or before the termination of employment date, an amount equal to the weekly rate of his pension on the day after the termination of employment date ; and

    (b) if he reaches normal pension age after the termination of employment date, an amount equal to the weekly rate of—

        (i) any short service benefit which has accrued to him on the termination of employment date ; or

        (ii) where no short service benefit has then accrued to him, any other benefit to which this paragraph applies and which has then accrued to him.

(4) The benefit other than short service benefit to which subsection (3)(b) above applies is benefit—

    (a) which would have been provided as either the whole or part of the earner's short service benefit ; or

    (b) of which the earner's short service benefit would have formed part,

if paragraph 6(1) of Schedule 16 to the Social Security Act 1973 had effect with the substitution—

    (i) in paragraph (a), of a reference to the earner's age on the termination of employment date (as defined in subsection (1)(a)(i) above) for the reference to the age of 26 ; and

    (ii) in paragraph (b), of a reference to the service which the earner had on that date for the reference to 5 years' qualifying service.

(5) Any such benefit is only to be included in the relevant sum to the extent that it does not exceed the amount which the scheme would have had to provide as short service benefit if paragraph 6(1) of Schedule 16 to the Social Security Act 1973 had effect as mentioned in subsection (4) above.

(6) To the extent that amounts attributable to transfer credits have accrued by reason of any transfer before the commencement of this section they are to be disregarded for the purposes of subsection (1)(c) and (ii) above.

(7) If any part of the earner's pension is postponed beyond the termination of employment date, the relevant sum is an amount equal to what would have been the weekly rate of his pension on the day after the termination of employment date if there had been no such postponement.

(8) If—

    (a) an earner's employment ceases to be contracted-out by reference to an occupational pension scheme but the scheme continues to apply to it ; or

(b) an earner transfers from employment which is contracted-
out by reference to an occupational pension scheme to employment to which the scheme applies but which is not
contracted-out by reference to it,

the amount of any short service or other benefit which has accrued
to the earner shall be computed for the purposes of subsection
(3)(b) above as it would be computed if he had ceased on the
termination of employment date to be in employment to which the
scheme applies.

(9) An earner shall be treated for the purposes of this section
as if benefit under a scheme had accrued to him—

   (a) if—

   (i) one of the events mentioned in subsection (8) above
   occurs before he has attained the age at which, if he
   had attained it, that benefit would have accrued to him ;
   and

   (ii) he continues to be in employment to which the
   scheme applies until he attains that age ; or

   (b) if—

   (i) one of those events occurs before he has a particular
   period of service ; and

   (ii) that benefit would have accrued to him if he had
   that period ; and

   (iii) he continues to be in employment to which the
   scheme applies until he has it.

(10) Nothing in this section shall be construed as entitling an
earner who has not reached normal pension age to any portion of
a pension under a scheme to which he would not otherwise be
entitled.

(11) In this section, " short service benefit " is to be construed in
accordance with Schedule 16 to the Social Security Act 1973.   1973 c. 38.

41B.—(1) If—
   (a) there is an interval between the earner's termination of
   employment date and whichever of the following is the
   earlier—

   (i) the date of his death ;

   (ii) his commencement of payment date ; and

   (b) the relevant sum exceeds one half of the earner's guaranteed
   minimum on the day after the termination of employment
   date ; and

   (c) at any time when a pension under the occupational pension
   scheme is required to be paid to his widow her guaranteed
   minimum pension under the scheme exceeds one half of his
   guaranteed minimum on the day after the termination of
   employment date,

2 H 3

the weekly rate of the pension to be paid to her at that time shall be an amount not less than the aggregate of the following—

    (i) the relevant sum ;

    (ii) the excess mentioned in paragraph (*c*) above ; and

    (iii) any amount which is an appropriate addition at that time.

(2) In subsection (1) above " appropriate addition " means—

    (*a*) where a scheme provides that part of a widow's pension shall accrue after the termination of employment date by reason of the earner's employment after that date, an amount equal to the part which has so accrued ; and

    (*b*) where a scheme provides that a widow's pension which has accrued before that date shall be enhanced after it if payment of the earner's pension is postponed, the amount by which the excess of the widow's pension on the day after the termination of employment date over one half of the earner's guaranteed minimum on the day after the termination of employment date has been enhanced by reason of the postponement.

(3) Subject to subsection (5) below, in this section " the relevant sum " means an amount equal to the weekly rate at which, on the assumption specified in subsection (4) below, a pension would have commenced to be paid to the widow if she had satisfied the conditions for entitlement to a pension which are specified in the scheme.

(4) The assumption mentioned in subsection (3) above is that the earner died on the day after the termination of employment date, and no other assumption which is contrary to the facts is to be made for the purpose of calculating the relevant sum in a particular case.

(5) To the extent that amounts attributable to transfer credits have accrued by reason of any transfer before the commencement of this section they are to be disregarded for the purposes of subsection (1)(*c*) and (ii) above.

Provisions
supplementary
to sections
41A and 41B.

41C.—(1) Subject to subsection (2) below, sections 41A and 41B above override any provision of a scheme to the extent that it conflicts with them.

(2) Sections 41A and 41B above do not override a protected provision of a scheme.

(3) In subsection (2) above " protected provision " means—

    (*a*) any provision contained in a scheme by virtue of—

1973 c. 38.

        (i) paragraph 9(2), 15(2), (3) or (4), 16(2), (3) or (4), 17(2) or 18 of Schedule 16 to the Social Security Act 1973 ; or

        (ii) section 36(7), (8) or (9) or 39 above ; and

    (*b*) any provision of a scheme to the extent that it deals with priorities on a winding-up ; and

(c) any provision of a scheme which is included in it for the
purpose of effecting a transfer of rights or liabilities authorised by regulations under section 38(1) above.

SCH. 6

(4) In making any calculation for the purposes of section 41A or
41B above—

    (a) any commutation, forfeiture or surrender of the whole or
part of a pension ;

    (b) any charge or lien on the whole or part of a pension ; and

    (c) any set-off against the whole or part of a pension,

shall be disregarded.

(5) Any reference in section 41A or 41B above to the weekly rate
of a pension is to be construed, in relation to a pension payable
otherwise than weekly, as a reference to the weekly sum which would
be payable in respect of a pension of that amount payable weekly.

(6) Sections 41A and 41B above do not apply to a pension to which
an earner or his widow is entitled in respect of employment if before
the commencement of this section—

    (a) he left the employment, or left it for the last time ; or

    (b) the employment ceased, or ceased for the last time, to be
contracted-out in relation to him.

(7) The Secretary of State may by regulations direct that sections
41A and 41B above and this section shall have effect, in such cases
as he may specify in the regulations, subject to such modifications
as he may there specify.

(8) In subsection (7) above " modification " includes, without prejudice to the generality of that subsection, addition, omission and
amendment.

41D. The Occupational Pensions Board may at any time, and shall
if requested by the trustees or managers of an occupational pension
scheme, advise on any question whether or not any provision of section 41A or 41B above (including, without prejudice to section 20(2)
of the Interpretation Act 1978, any such provision as modified by
regulations under section 41C(7) above) does or does not override
any provision of the scheme.

Advice of
Occupational
Pensions Board
on questions
whether section
41A or 41B
overrides
provisions of
schemes.
1978 c. 30.

41E.—(1) On an application made to them in respect of an occupational pension scheme (other than a public service pension
scheme) by persons competent to make such an application in respect
of it, the Occupational Pensions Board shall issue a determination
on any such question as is mentioned in section 41D above.

Determination
of questions
whether
schemes
conform with
sections 41A
to 41C.

(2) The persons competent to make an application under this section in respect of a scheme are—

    (a) the trustees or managers of the scheme ;

    (b) any person other than the trustees or managers who has
power to alter any of the rules of the scheme ;

    (c) any person who is an employer of persons in service in an employment to which the scheme applies ;

    (d) any member or prospective member of the scheme ;

    (e) such other persons as regulations may specify, in relation to any category of schemes into which the scheme falls, as being proper persons to make an application for the purposes of this section in respect of a scheme of that category.".

Section 21.

SCHEDULE 7

Miscellaneous Social Security Amendments

Social Security Act 1975 (c.14)

1. In subsection (2) of section 48 of the Social Security Act 1975 (pension increases: supplementary provisions), " 45A " shall be inserted after " 45 ".

2. In Schedule 20 to that Act (glossary of expressions) the following definition shall be inserted after the definition of " The Old Cases Act "—

1980 c. 39.

" " Payments by way of occupational pension "	Has the same meaning as in section 5 of the Social Security (No. 2) Act 1980.".

Social Security Pensions Act 1975 (c.60)

3. In section 4(1) of the Social Security Pensions Act 1975 (exemption from liability to pay primary Class 1 contributions on earnings in respect of periods after pensionable age)—

    (a) at the beginning there shall be inserted the words " Except as may be prescribed ", and

    (b) the words " in respect of any period " shall cease to have effect.

4. The following subsection shall be inserted after section 43(2) of that Act—

    " (2A) For the purposes of this Act any period of an earner's service in an employment is linked qualifying service in relation to a later period of service (whether in the same or another employment) if—

        (a) under the rules of a scheme applying to him in the earlier period of service there was made a transfer of his accrued rights under that scheme to another scheme applying to him in the later period of service ; and

        (b) in consequence of that transfer, there are (or were) allowed to him transfer credits under the rules of that other scheme,

    except that, for any service to be taken into account as linked qualifying service, it must be actual service and no regard shall be had to any scheme rule which provides for service to be treated for any purposes of benefit or otherwise as longer or shorter than it actually was.".

5. In section 66(1) of that Act (interpretation)—

SCH. 7

    (*a*) in the definition of " linked qualifying service " for " 38(4) " there shall be substituted " 43(2A) " ; and

    (*b*) the following definition shall be substituted for the definition of " transfer credits "—

        " " transfer credits " means rights allowed to an earner under the rules of an occupational pension scheme by reference to a transfer to that scheme of his accrued rights from another scheme.".

Social Security Act 1980 (c.30)

6. In section 9(7) of the Social Security Act 1980 (definition of relevant enactments regulations under which are to be referred to the Social Security Advisory Committee) for the words " the Social Security Acts 1975 to 1979 ", in both places where they occur, there shall be substituted the words " the Social Security Acts 1975 to 1984.".

Social Security and Housing Benefits Act 1982 (c.24)

7. In section 4(2) of the Social Security and Housing Benefits Act 1982 (qualifying days) for the words " as may be agreed " there shall be substituted the words " as may, subject to regulations, be agreed ".

8. The following section shall be inserted after section 23 of that Act—

"Deductions from statutory sick pay.

    23A.—(1) It is hereby declared for the avoidance of doubt that an agreement between an employer and an employee authorising any deductions from any statutory sick pay which the employer is liable to pay the employee in respect of any period shall not be void by reason only of section 1(2)(*a*) of this Act if the employer—

        (*a*) is authorised by that or another agreement to make the same deductions from any contractual remuneration which he is liable to pay in respect of the same period ; or

        (*b*) would be so authorised if he were liable to pay contractual remuneration in respect of that period.

    (2) The Truck Act 1896 shall apply in relation to an agreement between an employer and a workman (within the meaning of that Act) for the deduction of any amount from statutory sick pay as it applies to a contract for any deduction from the sum contracted to be paid by an employer to a workman ; and, accordingly, any reference in that Act to such a contract shall include a reference to such an agreement and any reference to the sum contracted to be paid shall include a reference to a payment of statutory sick pay.".

1896 c. 44.

Health and Social Services and Social Security Adjudications Act
1983 (c.41)

9. In Schedule 8 to the Health and Social Services and Social
Security Adjudications Act 1983 (social security adjudications)—

(*a*) in sub-paragraph (1) of paragraph 31 (transitional regulations) for the words " and this Schedule " there shall be
substituted the words " this Schedule and section 16 of the
Health and Social Security Act 1984 " ; and

(*b*) in sub-paragraph (3), for the words from " and this Schedule ", in the first place where they occur, to the end of the
sub-paragraph there shall be substituted the words " this
Schedule and section 16 of the Health and Social Security
Act 1984 and before the expiry of the period of six months
beginning with their commencement ".

SCHEDULE 8   Section 24.

REPEALS

PART I

HEALTH

Chapter	Short title	Extent of repeal
6 & 7 Eliz. 2 c. 32.	Opticians Act 1958.	In section 13(3), the words from " and " onwards.
1971 c. 62.	Tribunals and Inquiries Act 1971.	In Schedule 1, in paragraph 17(*a*) the words from " or established " to " 1980 ".
1977 c. 49.	National Health Service Act 1977.	In section 12(*b*), the words " or under section 2 of the Health Services Act 1980 ".
		In section 15, in subsection (1), the words from " This subsection " to the end and subsection (2).
		In section 19(1)(*e*), the words " and dispensing ".
		In section 39(*c*), the words " and the ophthalmic or dispensing optician who is to supply the appliances ".
		In section 44(1)(*c*), the words " and dispensing opticians ".
		In section 45(2) and (3), the words " with the Secretary of State's approval ".
		Section 46(1)(*e*).
		In section 72(5)(*a*), the words " or dispensing ".
		In section 81(*b*), the words " or general ophthalmic services " and the words " or optical ".
		In section 82(*b*), the words " or general ophthalmic services " and the words " or optical ".
		In section 83(*b*), the words " or the general ophthalmic services ".
		In section 97(1)(*a*) and (*c*) and (2), the words " or further allotted ".
		In section 98(2), the second paragraph.
		In section 128(1), the definition of " dispensing optician ".
		In Schedule 5, in paragraph 1(2)(*c*), the words " and dispensing ", in paragraph 2(2)(*a*), the words " and dispensing ", in paragraph 6, as originally enacted, sub-paragraph (1)(*g*) and in sub-paragraph (3)(*a*), the words " or, as the case may be, a dispensing ", in paragraph 6, as substituted by para-

SCH. 8

Chapter	Short title	Extent of repeal
		graph 12 of Schedule 3 above, sub-paragraph (3)(*e*), sub-paragraph (5)(iv) and sub-paragraph (8), in paragraph 9, in sub-paragraph (1), the words " other than a Family Practitioner Committee " and in sub-paragraphs (2) and (3), the words " other than such a Committee " and in paragraph 10, the words " other than a Family Practitioner Committee ".
		In Schedule 9, paragraph 4(*e*).
		In Schedule 12, in paragraph 2(1), the words from " In this sub-paragraph " to the end, in paragraph 2, sub-paragraph (2)(iii), sub-paragraph (5), in sub-paragraph (6), the words " or sub-paragraph (5) " and in sub-paragraph (7), the words " and (5) ", in paragraph (*a*), the words " or to an optical appliance supplied under this Act ", the words " or testing of sight " and the words " or testing " and in sub-paragraph (8), the words " or lenses " and in paragraph 5, the words " or optical ".
1978 c. 29.	National Health Service (Scotland) Act 1978.	In section 9(1)(*e*), the words " and dispensing ".
		In section 26, subsection (1)(*b*) and the word " and " immediately preceding it and in subsection (2)(*c*), the words " and the ophthalmic or dispensing optician who is to supply the appliances ".
		In section 29(1), paragraph (*e*).
		In section 64(5)(*a*), the words " or dispensing ".
		In section 73(*b*), the words " or general ophthalmic services " and the words " or optical ".
		In section 74(*b*), the words " or general ophthalmic services " and the words " or optical ".
		In section 75(*b*), the words " or the general ophthalmic services ".
		In section 85(1), the words " or further allotted ".
		In section 108(1), the definition of " dispensing optician ".
		In Schedule 8, paragraph 5(*e*).

Chapter	Short title	Extent of repeal	
		In Schedule 11, in paragraph 2, sub-paragraph (2)(iii), sub-paragraph (5), in sub-paragraph (6), the words " or sub-paragraph (5) " and in sub-paragraph (8), the words " or lenses ", and in paragraph 5, the words " or optical ".	SCH. 8
1980 c. 53.	Health Services Act 1980.	In section 1, in subsection (6) the words " Subject to section 2 below ". Section 2. Section 18. In Schedule 1, paragraph 30, in paragraph 35, the words from " and in subsection (2) " to the end, paragraph 37, paragraphs 56 and 57, in paragraph 69, sub-paragraph (b) and the word " and " immediately preceding it, paragraph 77(b), paragraph 79, paragraph 82(2) and (3), and paragraphs 87 to 99. In Schedule 5, paragraph 2(2) and (4) and paragraph 6(2) and (4).	

PART II
SOCIAL SECURITY

Chapter	Short title	Extent of repeal
1975 c. 14.	Social Security Act 1975.	In section 12(1)(d), the words " and child ". Section 41(2)(d) and (3). Section 57(2). In Schedule 4, Part IV, in paragraph 1(a) and (c) and in paragraph 3, the entries relating to increases for qualifying children.
1975 c. 60.	Social Security Pensions Act 1975.	In section 4(1), the words " in respect of any period ". In section 38, in subsection (3), the definition of " transfer credits " and subsection (4).
1975 c. 61.	Child Benefit Act 1975.	In Schedule 4, paragraph 25.
1977 c. 5.	Social Security (Miscellaneous Provisions) Act 1977.	In section 22(2), the words " 36(2)(b) ".
1980 c. 30.	Social Security Act 1980.	Section 3(5).
1982 c. 24.	Social Security and Housing Benefits Act 1982.	In Schedule 4, paragraph 18(4).

Trade Union Act 1984

1984 CHAPTER 49

An Act to make provision for election to certain positions in trade unions and with respect to ballots held in connection with strikes or other forms of industrial action; to require trade unions to compile and maintain registers of members' names and addresses; to amend the law relating to expenditure by trade unions and unincorporated employers' associations on political objects; and to amend sections 1 and 2 of the Employment Act 1980.   [26th July 1984]

B E IT ENACTED by the Queen's most Excellent Majesty, by and with the advice and consent of the Lords Spiritual and Temporal, and Commons, in this present Parliament assembled, and by the authority of the same, as follows:—

PART I

SECRET BALLOTS FOR TRADE UNION ELECTIONS

1.—(1) Subject to the following provisions of this Part of this Act, it shall be the duty of every trade union (notwithstanding anything in its rules) to secure—

Duty of trade union to hold elections for certain positions.

    (a) that every person who is a voting member of the principal executive committee of the union holds that position by virtue of having been elected as such a member at an election in relation to which section 2 of this Act has been satisfied ; and

(b) that no person remains such a member for a period of more than five years without being re-elected at such an election.

(2) Where a person is a voting member of the principal executive committee of a trade union by virtue of holding some other position in that union, subsection (1) above shall apply as if references to a voting member of that committee were references to the holder of that other position.

(3) Where a person—

(a) was a voting member of the principal executive committee of a trade union immediately before an election ; and

(b) is not elected at that election as such a member or, as the case may be, as the holder of a position in the union by virtue of which the holder is such a member ;

nothing in this section shall be taken to require the union to prevent him from continuing to be such a member, or continuing to hold that position, at any time before the expiry of such period (not exceeding six months) as may reasonably be required for effect to be given to the result of the election.

(4) Any term or condition upon which a person is employed by a trade union shall be disregarded in so far as it would otherwise prevent the union from complying with any provision of this Part.

(5) In this section " principal executive committee ", in relation to a trade union, means the principal committee of the trade union exercising executive functions, by whatever name it is known.

(6) Nothing in this Part shall affect the validity of anything done by the principal executive committee of a trade union.

(7) For the purposes of this section a person is a voting member of the principal executive committee of a trade union if he is entitled in his own right to attend meetings of the committee and to vote on matters on which votes are taken by the committee (whether or not he is entitled to attend all such meetings or to vote on all such matters or in all circumstances).

Requirements to be satisfied in relation to elections.

2.—(1) Entitlement to vote at the election must be accorded equally to all members of the trade union in question other than those who belong to a class—

(a) which is, or which falls within, one or other of the classes mentioned in subsection (2) below ; and (*b*) all the members of which are excluded by the rules of the union from voting at the election.

(2) The classes are—

(*a*) members who are not in employment ;

(*b*) members who are in arrears in respect of any subscription or contribution due to the union ;

(*c*) members who are apprentices, trainees or students or new members of the union.

(3) Where the conditions mentioned in subsection (4) below are satisfied, nothing in subsection (1) above shall be taken to prevent a trade union from restricting entitlement to vote at an election to members of the union who fall within—

(*a*) a class determined by reference to any trade or occupation ;

(*b*) a class determined by reference to any geographical area ;

(*c*) a class which is by virtue of the rules of the union treated as a separate section within the union ; or

(*d*) a class determined by reference to any combination of the matters mentioned in paragraphs (*a*), (*b*) and (*c*) above.

(4) The conditions are that—

(*a*) entitlement to vote is restricted by the rules of the union ;

(*b*) no member of the union is denied entitlement to vote at all elections held for the purposes of this Part otherwise than by virtue of belonging to a class mentioned in subsection (1) above.

(5) The method of voting must be by the marking of a voting paper by the person voting.

(6) Every person who is entitled to vote at the election must—

(*a*) be allowed to vote without intereference from, or constraint imposed by, the union or any of its members, officials or employees ; and

(*b*) so far as is reasonably practicable, be enabled to do so without incurring any direct cost to himself.

(7) So far as is reasonably practicable, every person who is entitled to vote at the election must—

(*a*) have sent to him, at his proper address and by post, a voting paper which either lists the candidates at the election or is accompanied by a separate list of those candidates ; and

(*b*) be given a convenient opportunity to vote by post.

(8) The ballot shall be conducted so as to secure that—

(a) so far as is reasonably practicable, those voting do so in secret ;

(b) the result of the election is determined solely by counting the number of votes cast directly for each candidate at the election by those voting (nothing in this paragraph being taken to prevent the system of voting used for the election being the single transferable vote) ; and

(c) the votes given at the election are fairly and accurately counted (any inaccuracy in counting being disregarded for the purposes of this paragraph if it is accidental and on a scale which could not affect the result of the election).

(9) No member of the trade union in question shall be unreasonably excluded from standing as a candidate at the election.

(10) No candidate at the election shall be required, whether directly or indirectly, to be a member of a political party.

(11) A member of a trade union shall not be taken to have been unreasonably excluded from standing as a candidate at the election if he has been excluded on the ground that he belongs to a class all the members of which are excluded by the rules of the union.

(12) For the purposes of subsection (11) above, any rule which provides for a class to be determined by reference to those members which the union chooses to exclude from so standing shall be disregarded.

(13) A trade union which has overseas members may choose whether or not to accord any of those members entitlement to vote at the election ; and nothing in the preceding provisions of this section shall apply in relation to any overseas member or in relation to any vote cast by such a member.

(14) Nothing in this section shall be taken to require a ballot to be held at an uncontested election.

Modification of section 2 requirements.

3.—(1) Where a trade union proposes to hold an election and is satisfied that there are no reasonable grounds for believing that the requirements of section 2 of this Act would not be satisfied in relation to that election if subsection (7) of that section were to apply as modified by this section, it may proceed as if for paragraphs (a) and (b) of subsection (7) there were substituted—

" (a) have made available to him—

(i) immediately before, immediately after, or during his working hours ; and

(ii) at his place of work or at a place which is more convenient for him ;

or be supplied with, a voting paper which either lists the candidates at the election or is accompanied by a separate list of those candidates ; and

(*b*) be given—

(i) a convenient opportunity to vote by post (but no other opportunity to vote) ;

(ii) an opportunity to vote immediately before, immediately after, or during, his working hours and at his place of work or at a place which is more convenient for him (but no other opportunity) ; or

(iii) as alternatives, both of those opportunities (but no other opportunity).

4.—(1) It shall be the duty of every trade union—

(*a*) to compile, by the date appointed under section 22(3) of this Act, and thereafter maintain a register of the names and proper addresses of its members ; and

(*b*) to secure, so far as is reasonably practicable, that the entries in the register are accurate and are kept up-to-date.

Register of members' names and addresses.

(2) The register may be kept by means of a computer.

(3) Any duty falling upon a branch under this section by reason of its being a trade union shall be treated as having been discharged to the extent to which the union of which it is a branch has discharged that duty instead of the branch.

5.—(1) Any person who claims that a trade union has failed to comply with one or more of the provisions of this Part may apply to the Certification Officer or to the court for a declaration to that effect if—

Remedy for failure to comply with Part I.

(*a*) in a case where the application relates to an election which has been held, he was a member of the trade union at the date when the election was held and is such a member at the time when the application is made ; and

(*b*) in any other case, he is a member of the union at the time when the application is made.

(2) An application relating to an election which has been held must be made before the expiry of the period of one year beginning with the date on which the result of the election is announced by the trade union.

(3) On an application under this section the Certification Officer or, as the case may be, the court may make or refuse to make the declaration asked for.

(4) A declaration made under this section shall specify the provisions with which the trade union has failed to comply.

(5) Where the court makes such a declaration it shall also make an enforcement order unless it considers that to do so would be inappropriate.

(6) In this section " enforcement order " means an order which imposes on the trade union one or more of the requirements mentioned in subsection (7) below.

(7) The requirements are—

(a) to secure the holding of such an election as may be specified in the order ;

(b) to take such other steps to remedy the declared failure as may be so specified ;

(c) to abstain from such acts as may be so specified with a view to securing that a failure of the same, or any similar, kind as that of the declared failure does not arise on the part of the trade union.

(8) In making an enforcement order which requires the union to hold a fresh election, in any case where the application relates to an election which has been held, the court shall (unless it considers that it would be inappropriate to do so in the particular circumstances of the case) require the fresh election to be conducted—

(a) in accordance with such provisions as may be made by the order ; and

(b) with a postal ballot (that is to say, as if section 3 were omitted from this Part).

(9) An enforcement order under this section which imposes requirements by virtue of paragraph (a) or (b) of subsection (7) above shall be so expressed as to require the trade union to comply with those requirements before the expiry of such period as the court considers appropriate.

(10) The remedy of any person for a failure of a trade union to comply with one or more of the provisions of this Part shall be by way of application under this section and not otherwise.

(11) Where an enforcement order has been made, any person who satisfies the requirements of subsection (12) below shall be entitled to enforce obedience to the order as if he had made the application in pursuance of which the order was made.

(12) The requirements are that—

    (*a*) he is a member of the union at the time when the proceedings to enforce obedience to the order are begun ; and

    (*b*) he was such a member at the time when the order was made.

(13) The court having jurisdiction for the purposes of this section shall be the High Court or, in Scotland, the Court of Session.

6.—(1) Where the Certification Officer makes a declaration under section 5 of this Act and is satisfied that—

    (*a*) steps have been taken by the union with a view to remedying the declared failure or securing that a failure of the same, or any similar, kind as that of the declared failure does not arise on the part of the union ; or

    (*b*) the union has agreed to take such steps ;

the Certification Officer shall, in making the declaration, specify those steps.

(2) On an application to him under section 5, the Certification Officer (whether or not he makes a declaration) shall give reasons for his decision in writing ; and any such reasons may be accompanied by written observations on any matter arising from, or connected with, the proceedings.

(3) The making of an application to the Certification Officer under section 5 shall not be taken to prevent the applicant, or any other person, from making a subsequent application to the court under that section in respect of the same matter.

(4) Where such a subsequent application is made, the court shall have due regard to any declaration, reasons or observations of the Certification Officer in the proceedings before him which are brought to the notice of the court in the proceedings before it.

(5) On an application made to him under section 5, the Certification Officer shall—

    (*a*) make such enquiries as he thinks fit ; and

    (*b*) where he considers it appropriate, give the applicant and the trade union an opportunity to be heard.

(6) The Certification Officer may regulate the procedure to be followed on applications to him under section 5.

(7) In exercising his functions under this section the Certification Officer shall ensure, so far as is reasonably practicable, that every application made to him under section 5 is determined within six months.

(8) Where the Certification Officer requests any person to furnish information to him in connection with enquiries made by him under this section, he shall specify the date by which that information is to be furnished and shall, unless he considers that in all the circumstances of the case it would be inappropriate to do so, proceed with his determination of the application notwithstanding that the information has not been furnished to him by the specified date.

7.—(1) This Part does not apply to any trade union which—

(a) falls within section 28(1)(b) of the 1974 Act (unions which consist wholly or mainly of, or of representatives of, constituent or affiliated organisations) ; and

(b) has no members (other than such representatives) who are individuals.

(2) Subsection (1)(b) above shall not apply where—

(a) a trade union has members ("special members") who are individuals but who are not such representatives as are mentioned in subsection (1)(a) above ; and

(b) the conditions mentioned in subsection (3) below are satisfied.

(3) The conditions are that—

(a) all of the special members are merchant seamen ;

(b) a majority of the special members are ordinarily resident outside the United Kingdom.

(4) This Part does not apply to a trade union at any time when the conditions mentioned in subsection (5) below are satisfied in relation to it.

(5) The conditions are that—

(a) the trade union was formed after the commencement of this Part ; and

(b) not more than one year has elapsed since its formation.

(6) In subsection (5) above "formed" includes formed by amalgamation under the 1964 Act.

(7) Where a trade union is formed otherwise than by amalgamation under the 1964 Act, the date of its formation shall be taken, for the purposes only of this section, to be the date on which the first members of its principal executive committee are first appointed or, as the case may be, elected to that committee.

(8) Where one trade union (the "transferring union") has transferred its engagements to another trade union (the "re-

ceiving union ") then, during the period of one year beginning
with the date of the transfer, this Part shall not apply in relation
to any person who—

(a) was a member of the principal executive committee of
the transferring union immediately before the transfer ;
and

(b) became a member of the principal executive committee
of the receiving union in accordance with the instrument of transfer.

8.—(1) Section 1(1)(b) of this Act does not apply to any   Exemption for
voting member of the principal executive committee of a trade   certain persons
union at any time when the conditions mentioned in subsection   nearing
(2) below are satisfied in relation to him.   retirement.

(2) The conditions are that—

(a) he holds his position as such a member by virtue of
having been elected (whether as such a member or as
the holder of another position in the union) at an election in relation to which section 2 of this Act has been
satisfied ;

(b) he is—

(i) in the case of a person who has been elected
as such a member, a full-time employee of the union
by virtue of being such a member ; or

(ii) in the case of a person who has been elected
as the holder of another position in the union by
virtue of which he is such a member, a full-time employee of the union by virtue of holding that other
position ;

(c) he will reach retirement age within five years ;

(d) he is entitled under the rules of the union to continue
as the holder of the position in question until retirement
age without standing for re-election ;

(e) he has been a full-time employee of the union for a
period (which need not be continuous) of at least ten
years ; and

(f) the period between the day on which the election referred
to in paragraph (a) above took place and the day immediately preceding that on which paragraph (c) above is
first satisfied does not exceed five years.

(3) For the purposes of this section " retirement age ", in
relation to any person, means the earlier of—

(a) the age fixed by, or in accordance with, the rules of the
union for him to retire from the position in question ;
or

(b) the age which is for the time being pensionable age for
the purpose of the Social Security Act 1975.   1975 c. 14.

(4) Where the election referred to in paragraph (*a*) of subsection (2) above was held before the commencement of this Part, that paragraph shall apply as if it did not require section 2 of this Act to be satisfied in relation to that election.

Interpretation
of Part I and
transitional
provision.

1964 c. 24.
1974 c. 52.

1975 c. 71.

9.—(1) In this Part—

" the 1964 Act " means the Trade Union (Amalgamations, etc.) Act 1964 ;

" the 1974 Act " means the Trade Union and Labour Relations Act 1974 ;

" the Certification Officer " means the officer appointed under section 7 of the Employment Protection Act 1975 ;

" merchant seaman " means a person whose employment, or the greater part of it, is carried out on board seagoing ships ;

" offshore worker " means any person in employment to which section 127 of the Employment Protection Act 1975 (employment for purposes of activities in territorial or other offshore waters) applies, other than one who is in such employment in any area where the law of Northern Ireland applies ;

" overseas member ", in relation to a trade union, means a member of the union (other than a merchant seaman or offshore worker) who is outside Great Britain throughout the period during which votes may be cast ;

" post " means a postal service which—

1981 c. 38.

(*a*) is provided by the Post Office or under a licence granted under section 68 of the British Telecommunications Act 1981 ; or

(*b*) does not infringe the exclusive privilege conferred on the Post Office by section 66(1) of that Act only by virtue of an order made under section 69 of that Act ;

" principal executive committee " has the meaning given in section 1(5) of this Act ;

" proper address ", in relation to any member of a trade union, means his home address or any other address which he has requested the union in writing to treat as his postal address ;

" section ", in relation to a trade union, includes any part of the union which is itself a trade union ;

" single transferable vote " means a vote capable of being—

(*a*) given so as to indicate the voter's order of preference for the candidates ; and

(*b*) transferred to the next choice—
　(i) when it is not required to give a prior choice the necessary quota of votes ; or
　(ii) when, owing to the deficiency in the number of votes given for a prior choice, that choice is eliminated from the list of candidates ;

" trade union " has the same meaning as it has in the 1974 Act by virtue of section 28 ;

" voting member " shall be construed in accordance with section 1(7) of this Act ; and

" working hours ", in relation to an employee, means any time when, in accordance with his contract of employment, he is required to be at work.

(2) For the purposes of this Part, the date on which a contested election is held is, in the case of a ballot in which votes may be cast on more than one day, the last of those days.

(3) Where a voting member of the principal executive committee of a trade union was elected as such a member, or as the case may be as the holder of a relevant position, at an election held within the period of five years ending with the commencement of this Part—

　(*a*) section 1(1)(*a*) of this Act shall have effect, as if it did not require section 2 of this Act to be satisfied in relation to that election ; and

　(*b*) the period of five years mentioned in section 1(1)(*b*) shall be calculated from the date of that election.

(4) In subsection (3) above " relevant position " means a position in the union by virtue of which the holder is a voting member of the principal executive committee of the union.

PART II

SECRET BALLOTS BEFORE INDUSTRIAL ACTION

10.—(1) Nothing in section 13 of the 1974 Act shall prevent an act done by a trade union without the support of a ballot from being actionable in tort (whether or not against the trade union) on the ground that it induced a person to break his contract of employment or to interfere with its performance.

(2) Nothing in section 13 of the 1974 Act shall prevent an act done by a trade union from being actionable in tort (whether or not against the trade union) on the ground that it induced a person to break a commercial contract or to interfere with its performance where—

　(*a*) one of the facts relied upon for the purpose of establishing liability is that the union induced another

person to break his contract of employment or to interfere with its performance ; and

(b) by virtue of subsection (1) above, nothing in section 13
of the 1974 Act would prevent the act of inducement
referred to in paragraph (a) above from being actionable in tort.

(3) For the purposes of subsection (1) above, an act shall be
taken as having been done with the support of a ballot if, but
only if—

(a) the trade union has held a ballot in respect of the strike
or other industrial action in the course of which the
breach or interference referred to in subsection (1)
above occurred ;

(b) the majority of those voting in the ballot have answered
" Yes " to the appropriate question ;

(c) the first authorisation or endorsement of any relevant
act, and in the case of an authorisation the relevant
act itself, took place after the date of the ballot and
before the expiry of the period of four weeks beginning
with that date ; and

(d) section 11 of this Act has been satisfied in relation to the
ballot.

(4) In subsection (3)(b) above " appropriate question "
means—

(a) where the industrial action mentioned in subsection
(3)(a) above is, or includes, a strike, the question referred to in subsection (4)(a) of section 11 ; and

(b) in any other case, that referred to in subsection (4)(b) of
that section.

(5) In this Part—

1974 c. 52.
" the 1974 Act " means the Trade Union and Labour
Relations Act 1974 ;

" authorisation or endorsement " means an authorisation or
endorsement of an act which, by virtue of section 15
1982 c. 46.
of the Employment Act 1982, causes the act to be
taken, for the purposes mentioned in that section, to
have been done by the trade union ;

" commercial contract " means any contract which is not a
contract of employment ;

" contract of employment " has the same meaning as it has
in the 1974 Act by virtue of section 30 ;

" the date of the ballot " means, in the case of a ballot in
which votes may be cast on more than one day, the
last of those days ;

"relevant act" means an act (done in the course of the action mentioned in subsection (3)(*a*) above) of inducing a person to break his contract of employment or to interfere with its performance;

"tort", as respects Scotland, means delict;

"trade union" has the same meaning as it has in the 1974 Act by virtue of section 28;

and any reference to a breach or interference occurring in the course of a strike or other industrial action includes a reference to a breach or interference which, taken together with any corresponding action relating to other contracts of employment, constitutes that action.

11.—(1) Entitlement to vote in the ballot must be accorded—

    (*a*) equally, to all those members of the trade union who it is reasonable at the time of the ballot for the union to believe will be called upon in the strike or other industrial action in question to act in breach of, or to interfere with the performance of, their contracts of employment or, as the case may be, to continue so to act; and

    (*b*) to no others.

(2) Where a person who was a member of a trade union at the time when a ballot was held for the purposes of this Part—

    (*a*) was denied entitlement to vote in the ballot; and

    (*b*) is induced by the union, in the course of the action in respect of which the ballot was held, to break his contract of employment or to interfere with its performance ("in the course of" having the same meaning as in section 10 of this Act);

this section shall be taken not to have been satisfied in relation to that ballot.

(3) The method of voting in the ballot must be by the marking of a voting paper by the person voting.

(4) The voting paper must contain at least one of the following questions—

    (*a*) a question (however framed) which requires the voter to say, by answering "Yes" or "No", whether he is prepared to take part, or as the case may be to continue to take part, in a strike involving him in a breach of his contract of employment;

    (*b*) a question (however framed) which requires the voter to say, by answering "Yes" or "No", whether he is prepared to take part, or as the case may be to continue to take part, in industrial action falling short of a strike but involving him in a breach of his contract of employment.

(5) Every person who is entitled to vote in the ballot must—

(a) be allowed to vote without interference from, or constraint imposed by, the union or any of its members, officials or employees ; and

(b) so far as is reasonably practicable, be enabled to do so without incurring any direct cost to himself.

(6) So far as is reasonably practicable, every person who is entitled to vote in the ballot must—

(a) have made available to him—

(i) immediately before, immediately after, or during his working hours ; and

(ii) at his place of work or at a place which is more convenient for him ;

or be supplied with, a voting paper ; and

(b) be given—

(i) a convenient opportunity to vote by post (but no other opportunity to vote) ;

(ii) an opportunity to vote immediately before, immediately after, or during, his working hours and at his place of work or at a place which is more convenient for him (but no other opportunity) ; or

(iii) as alternatives, both of those opportunities (but no other opportunity).

(7) The ballot shall be conducted so as to secure that—

(a) so far as is reasonably practicable, those voting do so in secret ; and

(b) the votes given in the ballot are fairly and accurately counted (any inaccuracy in counting being disregarded for the purposes of this paragraph if it is accidental and on a scale which could not affect the result of the ballot).

(8) As soon as is reasonably practicable after the holding of the ballot, the trade union shall take such steps as are reasonably necessary to ensure that all persons entitled to vote in the ballot are informed of the number of—

(a) votes cast in the ballot ;

(b) individuals voting " Yes " ;

(c) individuals voting " No " ; and

(d) spoiled voting papers.

(9) A trade union which has overseas members may choose whether or not to accord any of those members entitlement

to vote in a ballot ; and nothing in subsections (1) to (7) above
shall apply in relation to any overseas member or in relation
to any vote cast by any such member.

(10) Where overseas members have voted in the ballot, subsection (8) above shall be read as requiring the information in
question to be provided to all those entitled to vote in the ballot
other than overseas members and to distinguish between overseas members and other members.

(11) In this section—

    " overseas member " has the same meaning as is given
      in section 9(1) of this Act ;

    " post " means a postal service which—

       (*a*) is provided by the Post Office or under a licence
         granted under section 68 of the British Telecom-   1981 c. 38.
         munications Act 1981 ; or

       (*b*) does not infringe the exclusive privilege con-
         ferred on the Post Office by section 66(1) of that Act
         only by virtue of an order made under section 69 of
         that Act ;

    " working hours ", in relation to an employee, means any
      time when, in accordance with his contract of employ-
      ment, he is required to be at work ; and

    " strike " means any concerted stoppage of work.

PART III

POLITICAL FUNDS AND OBJECTS

Resolutions under 1913 *Act*

12.—(1) In this Part of this Act references to a " resolution " Political fund
are to a resolution under section 3 of the 1913 Act (restriction resolutions:
on application of trade union funds for certain political pur- periodical
poses). ballots.

(2) A resolution shall, if it has not previously been rescinded,
cease to have effect—

    (*a*) on the expiry of the period of ten years beginning with
      the date (whether before or after the commencement
      date) of the ballot on which it was passed ; or

    (*b*) if a ballot is held before the expiry of that period and
      the result of the ballot is that a new resolution is not
      passed, on the expiry of the period of two weeks begin-
      ning with the date of the ballot.

(3) For the purposes of this section, any resolution which—

    (*a*) is in force on the commencement date ; and

(*b*) was passed more than nine years before that date ;

shall be deemed to have been passed nine years before that date.

(4) Where a trade union holds a ballot at a time when a resolution (the " old resolution ") is in force in respect of that union and the result of the ballot is that a new resolution is passed, the old resolution shall be treated as rescinded on the passing of the new resolution.

(5) Where two or more trade unions have amalgamated under the 1964 Act and by virtue of section 5(4) of that Act the amalgamated union is treated as having passed a resolution immediately after the amalgamation, that resolution shall, for the purposes of this section, be treated as having been passed on the date of the earliest of the ballots on which the resolutions in force immediately before the amalgamation with respect to the amalgamating unions were passed.

Ballots: supplementary provisions.

13.—(1) In section 4(1) of the 1913 Act (ballots to be in accordance with rules approved by the Certification Officer) for the words from " every member " to the end there shall be substituted " the requirements of subsections (1A) to (1F) below would be satisfied in relation to a ballot taken by the union in accordance with those rules."

(2) After subsection (1) of section 4 of the 1913 Act there shall be inserted the following subsections—

" (1A) Entitlement to vote in the ballot must be accorded equally to all members of the trade union.

(1B) The method of voting must be by the marking of a voting paper by the person voting.

(1C) Every person who is entitled to vote in the ballot must—

(*a*) be allowed to vote without interference from, or constraint imposed by, the union or any of its members, officials or employees ; and

(*b*) so far as is reasonably practicable, be enabled to do so without incurring any direct cost to himself.

(1D) So far as is reasonably practicable, every person who is entitled to vote in the ballot must—

(*a*) have made available to him—

(i) immediately before, immediately after, or during, his working hours ; and

(ii) at his place of work or at a place which is more convenient for him ;

or be supplied with, a voting paper ; and

(*b*) be given—

(i) a convenient opportunity to vote by post (but no other opportunity to vote) ;

(ii) an opportunity to vote immediately before, immediately after, or during, his working hours and at his place of work or at a place which is more convenient for him (but no other opportunity) ; or

(iii) as alternatives, both of those opportunities (but no other opportunity).

(1E) The ballot must be conducted so as to secure that—

(*a*) so far as is reasonably practicable, those voting do so in secret ; and

(*b*) the votes given in the ballot are fairly and accurately counted (any inaccuracy in counting being disregarded for the purposes of this paragraph if it is accidental and on a scale which could not affect the result of the ballot).

(1F) In this section—

" post " means a postal service which—

(*a*) is provided by the Post Office or under a licence granted under section 68 of the British 1981 c. 38. Telecommunications Act 1981 ; or

(*b*) does not infringe the exclusive privilege conferred on the Post Office by section 66(1) of that Act only by virtue of an order made under section 69 of that Act ; and

" working hours ", in relation to an employee, means any time when, in accordance with his contract of employment, he is required to be at work."

(3) Where it is proposed to hold a ballot, section 4(1) of the 1913 Act shall have effect so as to require the rules of the trade union to be approved in relation to the proposed ballot notwithstanding that approval has been given under that section in relation to a ballot previously held by that union.

(4) If the Certification Officer is satisfied, and certifies, that rules made for the purposes of complying with the provisions of section 4(1) or section 5(1) of that Act (rules relating to giving to members of notice of right to be exempt from contributing to political fund) have been approved by the principal executive committee of a trade union, those rules shall have effect as rules of the trade union for the purposes of section 4(1) or, as the case may be, 5(1) as it applies in relation to the first review, notwithstanding that the provisions of the rules of the union as to

the alteration of rules or the making of new rules have not been complied with.

(5) Subsection (4) above applies only where a resolution was in force with respect to the union at the commencement date.

(6) In subsection (4) above "first review" means a ballot which—

(a) is held before the expiry of the period of one year beginning with the commencement date ; and

(b) is the first ballot held during that period.

(7) Where a resolution is in force with respect to a trade union—

(a) rules made by the union for the purpose of complying with section 4(1) of the 1913 Act in relation to a proposed ballot may provide for overseas members of the union not to be accorded entitlement to vote in the ballot ; and

(b) rules made by the union for the purpose of complying with section 5(1) of the 1913 Act may provide for notice not to be given by the union to its overseas members.

(8) Where subsection (7) above applies—

(a) in a case where rules have been made by virtue of paragraph (a) of subsection (7), the Certification Officer shall not withhold his approval under section 4(1) of the 1913 Act on the ground that the rule in question makes such provision in relation to overseas members of the union as is mentioned in subsection (7) ; and

(b) in a case where rules have been made by virtue of paragraph (b) of subsection (7), section 5(1) of the 1913 Act shall be taken not to require notice to be given by the union to its overseas members.

(9) Where, following a notice given by a trade union under subsection (1) of section 5 of the 1913 Act on the passing of a new resolution, a member of the union gives notice of his objection to contribute to the political fund of the union, subsection (2) of that section (effective date of exemption) shall have effect as if the words from " or, in the case " to the end were omitted.

(10) In this section—

" new resolution ", in relation to a trade union, means a resolution passed on a ballot held at a time when a resolution is in force in respect of that union ; and

" overseas member " has the same meaning as is given in section 9(1) of this Act.

14.—(1) At any time when there is a resolution in force with respect to a trade union, no property shall be added to the union's political fund other than— PART III
Assets and
liabilities of
political fund.

    (*a*) sums representing contributions made to the fund by members of the union or by any person other than the union itself ; and

    (*b*) property which accrues to the fund in the course of administering the assets of the fund.

(2) At any time when there is no resolution in force with respect to a trade union which has a political fund—

    (*a*) subject to section 15(5) of this Act, no property shall be added to the fund other than that which accrues to the fund in the course of administering the assets of the fund ;

    (*b*) no rule of the union shall be taken to require any member of the union to contribute to the fund ;

    (*c*) the union may, notwithstanding any of its rules or any trusts on which the political fund is held, transfer the whole or any part of the fund to such other fund of the union as it thinks fit.

(3) No liability of a political fund shall be discharged out of any other fund of the trade union (whether or not any asset of that other fund has been charged in connection with that liability).

(4) Subsection (3) above shall have effect notwithstanding any term or condition on which any liability was incurred, but shall not have effect in relation to any liability incurred before the passing of this Act.

(5) In section 6 of the 1913 Act, the words from " and in that case ", where they first occur, to " that fund " (which are superseded by subsection (1) above) are hereby repealed.

15.—(1) Where on the holding of a ballot a resolution has ceased to have effect by virtue of subsection (2) of section 12 of this Act, in the circumstances mentioned in paragraph (*b*) of that subsection, the trade union may at any time before the expiry of the period of six months beginning with the date of the ballot make payments out of the political fund as if the resolution were still in force. Position where
resolution has
ceased to have
effect.

(2) Nothing in subsection (1) above shall be taken to authorise any payment which would cause the political fund to be in deficit or would increase any deficit in the fund.

(3) On a resolution ceasing to have effect, the trade union—

   (*a*) shall take such steps as are necessary to ensure that the collection of contributions to the political fund is discontinued as soon as is reasonably practicable ; and

   (*b*) may, notwithstanding any of its rules, pay any such contribution which is received by it after the date of cessation into any of its other funds.

(4) Where a resolution has ceased to have effect but the trade union has continued to collect contributions to the political fund from any of its members, it shall pay to any member who applies to it for a refund of his contribution the amount collected from him by way of such a contribution after the date of cessation.

(5) Where a resolution has ceased to have effect, any contributions to the political fund paid to the union or to any person on behalf of the union, before the date of cessation, may be paid into the political fund notwithstanding section 14(2)(*a*) of this Act.

(6) Where a resolution has ceased to have effect, any provision made by any rule of the trade union for the purpose of complying with the 1913 Act shall cease to have effect—

   (*a*) in a case where the resolution has ceased to have effect by virtue of subsection (2) of section 12 of this Act in the circumstances mentioned in paragraph (*b*) of that subsection, on the date on which the period of six months beginning with the date of the ballot expires ; and

   (*b*) in any other case, on the date of cessation.

(7) Nothing in subsection (6) above shall be taken to affect—

   (*a*) any provision made by any rule of the union which is required to enable the union's political fund to be administered at a time when there is no resolution in force with respect to the union ;

   (*b*) the operation of section 3(2) of the 1913 Act (complaint to Certification Officer in respect of breach of rules) in relation to any breach occurring before the date on which the rule in question ceased to have effect.

(8) Where a resolution has ceased to have effect, no member of the trade union who has at any time been exempt from the obligation to contribute to the political fund of the union shall, by reason of his having been so exempt be—

   (*a*) excluded from any benefits of the union ; or

(*b*) placed in any respect either directly or indirectly under any disability or at any disadvantage as compared with other members of the union (except in relation to the control or management of the political fund).

(9) Where, at any time after a resolution has ceased to have effect—

(*a*) the trade union holds a ballot ; and

(*b*) the result of the ballot is that a new resolution is passed ;

no property which immediately before the date of the ballot was held by or on behalf of the union otherwise than in its political fund, and no sums representing any such property, shall be added to that fund.

(10) Where a resolution ceases to have effect but immediately afterwards there is a new resolution in force with respect to the trade union, the cessation of the old resolution shall be disregarded for the purposes of this section.

(11) In this section " date of cessation " means the date on which the resolution which was last in force ceased to have effect.

16.—(1) Any person who claims that a trade union has failed to comply with section 15(3)(*a*) of this Act may apply to the court for a declaration to that effect if he is a member of the union at the time when the application is made. Remedy for failure to comply with s. 15(3)(*a*).

(2) Where, on an application under this section, the court is satisfied that a trade union has failed to comply with section 15(3)(*a*) it may, if it considers it appropriate to do so in order to secure that the collection of contributions to the political fund is discontinued, make an order requiring the union to take, within such time as may be specified in the order, such steps as may be so specified.

(3) Where an order has been made under this section, any person who satisfies the requirements of subsection (4) below shall be entitled to enforce obedience to the order as if he had made the application in pursuance of which the order was made.

(4) The requirements are that—

(*a*) he is a member of the union at the time when proceedings to enforce obedience to the order are begun ; and

(*b*) he was such a member at the time when the order was made.

(5) The remedy of any person for a failure of a trade union to comply with section 15(3)(*a*) of this Act shall be by way of application under this section and not otherwise ; but nothing in

this subsection shall be taken to prejudice the right of any person to recover any sum payable to him by the union under section 15(4) of this Act.

(6) The court having jurisdiction for the purposes of this section shall be the High Court or, in Scotland, the Court of Session.

Political objects

Political objects.

17.—(1) For subsection (3) of section 3 of the 1913 Act (which defines the political objects expenditure on which must be met out of the political fund of the trade union) there shall be substituted—

" (3) The political objects to which this section applies are the expenditure of money—

(*a*) on any contribution to the funds of, or on the payment of any expenses incurred directly or indirectly by, a political party ;

(*b*) on the provision of any service or property for use by or on behalf of any political party ;

(*c*) in connection with the registration of electors, the candidature of any person, the selection of any candidate or the holding of any ballot by the union in connection with any election to a political office ;

(*d*) on the maintenance of any holder of a political office ;

(*e*) on the holding of any conference or meeting by or on behalf of a political party or of any other meeting the main purpose of which is the transaction of business in connection with a political party ;

(*f*) on the production, publication or distribution of any literature, document, film, sound recording or advertisement the main purpose of which is to persuade people to vote for a political party or candidate or to persuade them not to vote for a political party or candidate.

(3A) Where a person attends a conference or meeting as a delegate or otherwise as a participator in the proceedings, any expenditure incurred in connection with his attendance as such shall, for the purposes of subsection (3)(*e*) above, be taken to be expenditure incurred on the holding of the conference or meeting.

(3B) In determining, for the purposes of subsection (3) above, whether a trade union has incurred expenditure of a

kind mentioned in that subsection, no account shall be
taken of the ordinary administrative expenses of the union.

(3C) In this section—

" candidate " means a candidate for election to a political office and includes a prospective candidate ;

" contribution ", in relation to the funds of a political party, includes any fee payable for affiliation to, or membership of, the party and any loan made to the party ;

" electors " means electors at any election to a political office ;

" film " has the same meaning as in section 38 of the Films Act 1960 ;   1960 c. 57.

" local authority " means a local authority within the meaning of section 270 of the Local Government 1972 c. 70. Act 1972 or section 235 of the Local Govern- 1973 c. 65. ment (Scotland) Act 1973 ; and

" political office " means the office of member of Parliament, member of the Assembly of the European Communities or member of a local authority or any position within a political party."

(2) Where a resolution is in force with respect to a trade union at the commencement date, that resolution and any rule of the union made in pursuance of section 3 of the 1913 Act which is in force at that date shall have effect as if for any reference to the political objects to which that section applied immediately before the commencement date there were substituted a reference to those objects as amended by this section.

(3) Section 1(2) of the 1913 Act (which defines " statutory objects " and which is spent in consequence of this section) is hereby repealed.

Union dues

18.—(1) Where any person who is a member of a trade union Collection of which has a political fund has certified in writing to his employer union dues by that, or to the effect that, he—   employers.

(a) is exempt from the obligation to contribute to that fund ; or

(b) has, in accordance with the 1913 Act, notified the union in writing of his objection to contributing to it ;

the employer to whom the certificate was given shall ensure that no amount representing a contribution to the political fund of the union is deducted by him from emoluments payable to the member.

(2) Subsection (1) above does not apply—

(*a*) before the first day, following the giving of the certificate, on which it is reasonably practicable for the employer to comply with it ; or

(*b*) after the certificate is withdrawn.

(3) Where an employer—

(*a*) refuses (otherwise than to the extent required by sub-section (1) above) to deduct any union dues from emoluments payable to any person who has given a certificate to him under this section ; but

(*b*) continues to deduct union dues from emoluments payable to other members of the union ;

he shall be taken to have failed to comply with this section unless he satisfies the court that his refusal is not attributable to the giving of that certificate or otherwise connected with the duty imposed by subsection (1) above.

(4) Where, on an application made by a person who claims that his employer has failed to comply with this section in deducting or refusing to deduct any amount from emoluments payable to him, the court is satisfied that there has been such a failure it shall make a declaration to that effect.

(5) Where the court makes such a declaration it may, if it considers it appropriate to do so in order to secure that the failure is not repeated, make an order requiring the employer to take, within such time as may be specified in the order, such steps in relation to emoluments payable by him to the applicant as may be so specified.

(6) The court having jurisdiction for the purposes of this section shall be the county court or, in Scotland, the sheriff court.

(7) This section has effect (with the omission of subsection (5)) in relation to employment under or for the purposes of a government department or any officer or body exercising on behalf of the Crown any functions conferred by any enactment as it has effect in relation to other employment.

Interpretation

Interpretation of Part III.

19.—(1) Expressions used in this Part and in the 1913 Act have the same meaning in this Part as they have in that Act.

(2) In this Part—

1913 c. 30.

1964 c. 24.

" the 1913 Act " means the Trade Union Act 1913 ;

" the 1964 Act " means the Trade Union (Amalgamations, etc.) Act 1964 ;

" the date of the ballot " means, in the case of a ballot in which votes may be cast on more than one day, the last of those days ;

" the commencement date " means the date on which this Part comes into force ;

" principal executive committee ", in relation to a trade union, means the principal committee of the trade union exercising executive functions, by whatever name it is known ; and

" resolution " has the meaning given by section 12(1) of this Act.

(3) References in this Part to the holding of a ballot (other than the reference in section 17(1)) are to the holding of a ballot for the purposes of the 1913 Act.

(4) This Part applies, with the necessary modifications, in relation to unincorporated employers' associations as it applies in relation to trade unions.

PART IV

SUPPLEMENTARY

20.—(1) Section 1 of the Employment Act 1980 (payments in respect of secret ballots) shall have effect as amended by subsections (2) to (4) below.

Amendment of ss. 1 and 2 of Employment Act 1980.

(2) In subsection (3) (ballots to which the section applies)—

1980 c. 42.

(a) in paragraph (b) (election provided for by union's rules) at the end there shall be inserted the words " or in relation to which section 2 of the Trade Union Act 1984 is required to be satisfied " ; and

(b) after paragraph (e) there shall be inserted—

" (f) obtaining a decision on a resolution for the purposes of section 3 of the Trade Union Act 1913 ".

(3) After subsection (3) there shall be inserted the following subsection—

" (3A) Notwithstanding anything in subsections (2) and (3) above, this section does not apply to any ballot held by a trade union, if—

(a) the purpose of any question to be voted upon is the obtaining of a decision of the kind mentioned in paragraph (f) of subsection (3) ; and

(b) the ballot is held at a time when there is no resolution in force in respect of that union under section 3 of the Act of 1913."

PART IV

(4) In subsection (5) (ballots to be conducted so as to secure that those voting may do so in secret) the word " may ", where it last occurs, shall be omitted.

(5) In section 2(2)(*b*) of the Act of 1980 (ballots to which section 2 applies to be conducted so as to secure that those voting may do so in secret), the word " may " shall be omitted.

Expenses.

1980 c. 42.

21. There shall be defrayed out of money provided by Parliament any increase attributable to this Act in the sums payable out of money so provided under section 1 of the Employment Act 1980 (payments in respect of secret ballots).

Short title, commencement and extent.

22.—(1) This Act may be cited as the Trade Union Act 1984.

(2) Section 4 shall come into force on the day on which this Act is passed.

(3) Save as aforesaid, Part I shall come into force on such day as the Secretary of State may by order made by statutory instrument appoint.

(4) Part II shall come into force on the expiry of the period of two months beginning with the day on which this Act is passed.

(5) Part III shall come into force on 31st March 1985.

(6) Parts I and II and sections 18 and 20 of this Act do not extend to Northern Ireland and Part III does not apply in relation to any trade union which has its head or main office in Northern Ireland.

INDEX

TO THE

PUBLIC GENERAL ACTS

AND

GENERAL SYNOD MEASURE 1984

A

S

AGRICULTURE (AMENDMENT) ACT: 1984 c. 20   ...   ...   I, pp. 327, 328

§ 1. Amendment of Agriculture Act 1967: " co-operative marketing business ",
       I, p. 327.
   2. Amendments of Agricultural Statistics Act 1979, I, p. 328.
   3. Short title and commencement, I, p. 328.

ANATOMY ACT: 1984 c. 14 ...   .   I, p. 287

Introductory
§ 1. Definitions, and scope of Act, I, p. 287.

Anatomical examination
   2. Control of examinations and possession, I, p. 288.
   3. Licences, I, p. 288.
   4. Lawful examinations, I, p. 289.

Possession after examination
   5. Control of possession after examination, I, p. 291.
   6. Lawful possession, I, p. 292.

Miscellaneous
   7. Licences: general provisions, I, p. 292.
   8. Regulations, I, p. 293.
   9. Inspectors of anatomy, I, p. 294.
  10. Power to inspect records and premises, I, p. 294.
  11. Offences, I, p. 295.
General
  12. Finance, I, p. 297.
  13. Short title, etc., I, p. 297.

ANIMAL HEALTH AND WELFARE ACT: 1984 c. 40 ...   .   II, p. 1351

Animal Health Act 1981
§ 1. Seizure and disposal of things likely to spread disease, II, p. 1351.
   2. Power of entry, II, p. 1352.
   3. Exercise of certain powers in territorial zone, II, p. 1352.
   4. Removal of restriction on powers as to infected places, II, p. 1353.

Slaughter of Poultry Act 1967
   5. Extension of scope of 1967 Act, II, p. 1353.
   6. Licences, II, p. 1354.
   7. Codes of Practice, II, p. 1355.
   8. Powers of entry under 1967 Act, II, p. 1356.
   9. Enforcement of 1967 Act, II, p. 1357.

Controls over Breeding of Livestock
  10. Artificial breeding of livestock, II, p. 1357.
  11. Provisions supplementary to section 10, II, p. 1359.
  12. Removal of controls on keeping of bulls and stallions, II, p. 1360.

Animal feeding stuffs and veterinary drugs
  13. Medicated animal feeding stuffs, II, p. 1360.
  14. Registration of merchants in veterinary drugs, II, p. 1364.
  15. Sampling of animal feeding stuffs, II, p. 1365.

Supplementary
16 and schedules 1, 2.   Minor and consequential amendments and repeals, II, p. 1366.
  17. Short title, commencement and extent, II, p. 1366.
Schedule 1.   Minor and consequential amendments, II, p. 1368.
Schedule 2.   Repeals, II, p. 1370.

APPEALS. Under—

Building Act (c. 55, ss. 20(5), 22(4), 27(2), 28(2), 39–42, 55, 68(3), 69(4) 73(2), 75, 85(3), 86, 102)

    III, pp. 2479, 2482, 2486, 2487, 2493–2496, 2510, 2520, 2521, 2526, 2528, 2538, 2545

Capital Transfer Tax Act (c. 51, s. 222) ... ... III, p. 2176

Data Protection Act (c. 35, ss. 13, 14) ... ... II, p. 1176

Dentists Act (c. 24, s. 29) ... ... I, p. 426

Finance Act (c. 43, s. 88(4)) ... ... II, p. 1549

Food Act (c. 30, ss. 24, 104, 105, sch. 2 para. 4)... I, pp. 894, 942, 963

Foster Children (Scotland) Act (c. 56, s 11(1)) ... ... III, p. 2587

Housing and Building Control Act (c. 29, s. 47) ... ... I, p. 817

Mental Health (Scotland) Act (c. 36, ss. 26(6), 30(6), 34(2), 35, 47(6), 51(2), 52, 63(2), 64, 65, 66, 67)

    II, pp. 1299, 1232, 1235, 1243, 1246, 1254–1258

Police and Criminal Evidence Act (c. 60, s. 103) (substituting s. 37 of, and sch. 5 to, the Police Act 1964 c. 48) ... ... III, p. 2827

Public Health (Control of Disease) Act (c. 22, s. 67(2)) ... I, p. 366

Rating and Valuation (Amendment) (Scotland) Act (c. 31, s. 5) (adding s. 5(7) and s. 6(5A) to the Rating (Disabled Persons) Act 1978 c. 40) ...

    II, p. 986

Rating and Valuation (Amendment) (Scotland) Act (c. 31, s. 11) (adding s. 3(2A)(2B) to the Local Government (Scotland) Act 1975 c. 30)

    II, p. 991

Registered Homes Act (c. 23, ss. 15, 34) ... ... I, pp. 385, 397

Road Traffic Regulation Act (c. 27, sch. 4 para. 14) ... ... I, p. 614

Roads (Scotland) Act (c. 54, s. 21(6)) ... ... III, p. 2285

See also COUNTY COURTS ACT, PART IV.

APPROPRIATION ACT: 1984 c. 44 ... ... II, pp. 1733–1797

    § 1. Issue out of the Consolidated Fund for the year ending 31st March 1985, II, p. 1733.
    2 and schedules (A) and (B). Appropriation of sums voted for supply services, II, p. 1734.
    3 and schedule (C). Repeals, II, p. 1734.
    4. Short title, II, p. 1734.

ARBITRATION. References to, under—

Agricultural Holdings Act (c 41, s. 1) (substituting s. 8 of the Agricultural Holdings Act 1948 c. 63) ... ... II, p. 1371

Building Act (c. 55, s. 111) ... ... III, p. 2549

Food Act (c. 30, ss. 108(*b*), 109) ... ... I, pp. 943, 944

Merchant Shipping Act (c. 5, s. 4) ... ... I, p. 11

Roads (Scotland) Act (c. 54, ss. 16(3), 17(4), 84, 112(7), 114(5)) III, pp. 2281, 2284, 2322, 2341, 2343

B

PART II

SUPERVISION OF BUILDING WORK ETC. OTHERWISE
THAN BY LOCAL AUTHORITIES

Supervision of plans and work by approved inspectors

Supervision of their own work by public bodies

Supplementary

C

CABLE AND BROADCASTING ACT: 1984 c. 46 ... ... II, p. 1805

PART I

CABLE PROGRAMME SERVICES

Introductory

Part I

General

Main charges and definitions

§ 1. Charge on transfers, III, p. 2033.
2. Chargeable transfers and exempt transfers, III, p. 2033.
3. Transfers of value, III, p. 2034.
4. Transfers on death, III, p. 2034.
5. Meaning of estate, III, p. 2034.
6. Excluded property, III, p. 2035.

Rates

7 and schedule 1. Rates, III, p. 2036.
8. Indexation of rate bands, III, p. 2036.
9 and schedule 2. Transitional provisions on reduction of tax, III, p. 2037.

Dispositions that are not transfers of value

10. Dispositions not intended to confer gratuitous benefit, III, p. 2037.
11. Dispositions for maintenance of family, III, p. 2037.
12. Dispositions allowable for income tax or conferring retirement benefits, III, p. 2039.
13. Dispositions by close companies for benefit of employees, III, p. 2039.
14. Waiver of remuneration, III, p. 2041.
15. Waiver of dividends, III, p. 2041.
16. Grant of tenancies of agricultural property, III, p. 2041.
17. Changes in distribution of deceased's estate, etc., III, p. 2041.

Part II

Exempt Transfers

Chapter I

General

18. Transfers between spouses, III, p. 2042.
19. Annual exemption, III, p. 2042.
20. Small gifts, III, p. 2043.
21. Normal expenditure out of income, III, p. 2043.
22. Gifts in consideration of marriage, III, p. 2044.
23. Gifts to charities, III, p. 2045.
24. Gifts to political parties, III, p. 2046.
25 and schedule 3. Gifts for national purposes, etc., III, p. 2047.
26. Gifts for public benefit, III, p. 2047.
27 and schedule 4. Maintenance funds for historic buildings, etc., III, p. 2049.
28. Employee trusts, III, p. 2049.
29. Loans—modifications of exemptions, III, p. 2050.

PART V

MISCELLANEOUS RELIEFS

CHAPTER I

BUSINESS PROPERTY

CHAPTER II

AGRICULTURAL PROPERTY

CHAPTER III

WOODLANDS

CHAPTER IV

TRANSFER WITHIN THREE YEARS BEFORE DEATH

CHAPTER V

MISCELLANEOUS

Successive charges

141. Two or more transfers within five years, III, p. 2123.

Changes in distribution of deceased's estate, etc.

142. Alteration of dispositions taking effect on death, III, p. 2125.
143. Compliance with testator's request, III, p. 2126.
144. Distribution etc. from property settled by will, III, p. 2126.
145. Redemption of surviving spouse's life interest, III, p. 2127.
146. Inheritance (Provision for Family and Dependants) Act 1975, III, p. 2127.
147. Scotland: legitim, III, p. 2128.

Mutual and voidable transfers

148. Mutual transfers: exemption for donee's gift, III, p. 2130.
149. Mutual transfers: relief for donor's gift, III, p. 2130.
150. Voidable transfers, III, p. 2132.

Pension schemes, etc.

151. Treatment of pension rights, etc., III, p. 2133.
152. Cash options, III, p. 2133.
153. Overseas pensions, III, p. 2134.

Armed forces

154. Death on active service, etc., III, p. 2135.
155. Visiting forces, etc., III, p. 2136.

Apsley House and Chevening Estate

156. Apsley House and Chevening Estate, III, p. 2137.

Non-residents' bank accounts

157. Non-residents' bank accounts, III, p. 2137.

Double taxation relief

158. Double taxation conventions, III, p. 2138.
159. Unilateral relief, III, p. 2139.

PART VI

VALUATION

CHAPTER I

GENERAL

160. Market value, III, p. 2141.
161. Related property, III, p. 2141.
162. Liabilities, III, p. 2142.
163. Restriction on freedom to dispose, III, p. 2142.
164. Transferor's expenses, III, p. 2143.
165. Tax on capital gains, III, p. 2143.
166. Creditors' rights, III, p. 2144.
167. Life policies, etc., III, p. 2144.
168. Unquoted shares and securities, III, p. 2145.
169. Farm cottages, III, p. 2145.
170. Leases for life, etc., III, p. 2146.

CHAPTER II

ESTATE ON DEATH

171. Changes occurring on death, III, p. 2146.
172. Funeral expenses, III, p. 2146.
173. Expenses incurred abroad, III, p. 2146.
174. Income tax and unpaid capital transfer tax, III. 2146.
175. Liability to make future payments, etc., III, p. 2147.
176. Related property etc.—sales, III, p. 2147.
177. Scottish agricultural leases, III, p. 2148.

PART II

OFFENCE UNDER LAW OF SCOTLAND

6. Offence in Scotland of parent, etc. taking or sending child out of United Kingdom, II, p. 1319.
7. Power of arrest, II, p. 1320.
8. Penalties and prosecutions, II, p. 1320.
9. Proof and admissibility of certain documents, II, p. 1321.
10. Evidence, II, p. 1321.

PART III

SUPPLEMENTARY

11. Consequential amendments and repeals, II, p. 1321.
12. Enactment of corresponding provision for Northern Ireland, II, p. 1322.
13. Short title, commencement and extent, II, p. 1322.
Schedule. Modifications of section 1 for children in certain cases, II, p. 1323.

COMPENSATION. Under—

COMPULSORY PURCHASE. *See* LAND.

§ 1. Issue out of the Consolidated Fund for the year ending 31st March 1983, I, p. 1.
2. Issue out of the Consolidated Fund for the year ending 31st March 1984, I, p. 1.
3. Short title, I, p. 1.

§ 1. Issue out of the Consolidated Fund for the year ending 31st March 1985, III, p. 2872.
2. Issue out of the Consolidated Fund for the year ending 31st March 1986, III, p. 2872.
3. Short title, III, p. 2872.

CONSOLIDATION ACTS. *See* BUILDING ACT (c. 55); CAPITAL TRANSFER TAX ACT (c. 51); COUNTY COURTS ACT (c. 28); DENTISTS ACT (c. 24); FOOD ACT (c. 30); FOSTER CHILDREN (SCOTLAND) ACT (c. 56); MENTAL HEALTH (SCOTLAND) ACT (c. 36); PUBLIC HEALTH (CONTROL OF DISEASE) ACT (c. 22); REGISTERED HOMES ACT (c. 23); RENT (SCOTLAND) ACT (c. 58); ROAD TRAFFIC REGULATION ACT (c. 27).

PART I

CO-OPERATIVE DEVELOPMENT AGENCY

§ 1. Increase in limit on grants to Agency, III, p. 2597.
2. Extension of functions and control of Agency, III, p. 2598.
3. Power to dissolve Agency, III, p. 2599.

PART III

PROCEDURE

Parties

D

DIRECTOR OF PUBLIC PROSECUTIONS. *See* PUBLIC PROSECUTOR.

E

EDUCATION (AMENDMENT) (SCOTLAND) ACT: 1984 c. 6 ... ... I, p. 21

§ 1. Secretary of State's power to control use of dangerous materials or apparatus in educational establishments, I, p. 21.
  2. Short title and commencement, I, p. 21.

EDUCATION (GRANTS AND AWARDS) ACT: 1984 c. 11 ... ... I, pp. 57–60

PART I

EDUCATION SUPPORT GRANTS

§ 1. Education support grants, I, p. 57.
  2. Limit on expenditure approved for grant purposes, I, p. 58.
  3. Regulations, I, p. 59.

PART II

AWARDS

4. Amendment of s. 1(3)(*d*) of Education Act 1962, I, p. 60.

PART III

GENERAL

5. Expenses of Secretary of State, I, p. 60.
6. Short title, commencement and extent, I, p. 60.

ENTRY. Powers of under—

Anatomy Act (c. 14, s. 10(2)–(5)) ... ... I, p. 295
Building Act (c. 55, ss. 95, 96) ... ... III, pp. 2542, 2543
Cable and Broadcasting Act (c. 46, s. 32) ... ... II, p. 1834
Data Protection Act (c. 35, s. 16, sch. 4) ... ... II, pp. 1204–1206
Food Act (c. 30, ss. 87–89) ... ... I, pp. 930–932
Inshore Fishing (Scotland) Act (c. 26, s. 5(2)(7)(*a*)) ... I, pp. 471, 472
Mental Health (Scotland) Act (c. 36, s. 117) ... ... II, p. 1291
Public Health (Control of Diseases) Act (c. 22, ss. 50, 61) I, pp. 359, 364
Registered Homes Act (c. 23, ss. 17, 27(*d*), 35(1)) ... I, pp. 387, 394, 398
Telecommunications Act (c. 12, ss. 37–39, 59) ... ... I, pp. 101–103, 116
Road Traffic Regulation Act (c. 27, s. 71) ... ... I, p. 546
Roads (Scotland) Act (c. 54, ss. 121(1), 140) ... ... III, pp. 2346, 2355
Video Recordings Act (c. 39, s. 17(1)) ... ... II, p. 1345
See also POLICE AND CRIMINAL EVIDENCE ACT, PART II.

EVIDENCE. Provisions under—

See also POLICE AND CRIMINAL EVIDENCE ACT, PARTS VII, VIII.

F

PART I

CUSTOMS AND EXCISE, VALUE ADDED TAX AND CAR TAX

CHAPTER I

CUSTOMS AND EXCISE

CHAPTER II

VALUE ADDED TAX

CHAPTER III

MISCELLANEOUS

PART II

INCOME TAX, CORPORATION TAX AND CAPITAL GAINS TAX ETC.

CHAPTER I

GENERAL

CHAPTER II
CAPITAL ALLOWANCES

CHAPTER III
CAPITAL GAINS

T

T 2

G

H

Other amendments of Opticians Act 1958

3. Taking and use of titles, II, p. 1897.
4 and schedule 2.   Disciplinary provisions, II, p. 1898.

National Health Service

5 and schedule 3.   Family Practitioner Committees, II, p. 1898.
6. Finance in National Health Service, II, p. 1900.
7. Professional remuneration in National Health Service, II, p. 1901.
8. Increase in borrowing powers of General Practice Finance Corporation, II, p. 1905.
9. Holidays for patients etc., II, p. 1905.

Treatment in European Economic Community

10. Reimbursement of cost of medical and maternity treatment in member States of European Economic Community, II, p. 1906.

Part II

Social Security

11 and schedule 4.   Severe disablement allowance, II, p. 1907.
12. Pension increase in respect of husbands, II, p. 1909.
13 and schedule 5.   Dependent children, II, p. 1910.
14. Earnings to include occupational pensions for purposes of benefits in respect of dependants, II, p. 1910.
15. Attendance allowance: daily entitlement, II, p. 1910.
16. Constitution of panels for social security appeal tribunals, II, p. 1911.
17. Late paid Class 2 contributions, II, p. 1912.
18. Class 3 contributions, II, p. 1913.
19. Accrued rights and entitlement to benefits under occupational pension schemes, II, p. 1914.
20 and schedule 6.   Protection of pensions, II, p. 1915.
21 and schedule 7. Miscellaneous social security amendments, II, p. 1915.
22. Regulations, II, p. 1916.

Part III

Supplementary

23. Expenses, II, p. 1918.
24 and schedule 8.   Repeals, II, p. 1918.
25. Northern Ireland, II, p. 1918.
26. Extent, II, p. 1918.
27. Commencement, II, p. 1919.
28. Transitional, II, p. 1920.
29. Citation, II, p. 1921.
Schedule 1.   Optical appliances, II, p. 1922.
    Part I.   Amendments of National Health Service Act 1977, II, p. 1922.
    Part II.   Amendments of National Health Service (Scotland) Act 1978, II, p. 1923.
Schedule 2.   Disciplinary provisions of Opticians Act 1958, II, p. 1925.
    Part I.   New sections, II, p. 1925.
    Part II.   Minor and consequential amendments, II, p. 1929.
Schedule 3.   Family Practitioner Committees, II, p. 1932.
Schedule 4.   Severe disablement allowance, II, p. 1938.
    Part I.   Consequential amendments, II, p. 1938.
    Part II.   Transitional, II, p. 1942.
Schedule 5.   Dependent children, II, p. 1942.
Schedule 6.   Protection of pensions, II, p. 1945.
Schedule 7.   Miscellaneous social security amendments, II, p. 1950.
Schedule 8.   Repeals, II, p. 1953.
    Part I.   Health, II, p. 1953.
    Part II.   Social Security, II, p. 1955.

PART II

SUPERVISION OF BUILDING WORK ETC., OTHERWISE THAN BY LOCAL AUTHORITIES

Supervision of plans and work by approved inspectors

Supervision of their own work by public bodies

Supplemental

PART III

MISCELLANEOUS AMENDMENTS RELATING TO BUILDING WORK

Exemptions and relaxations for public bodies

Approved documents giving practical guidance

Certification and reports

Miscellaneous

PART IV

MISCELLANEOUS AND GENERAL

I

N

O

ORDNANCE FACTORIES AND MILITARY SERVICES ACT: 1984 c. 59... III, p. 2717

Ordnance factories: transfer schemes

§ 1. Transfer schemes, III, p. 2717.
  2. Property, rights and liabilities, III, p. 2719.
  3 and schedule 1. Operation of schemes, III, p. 2720.
  4 and schedule 2. Employment, III, p. 2721.

Ordnance factories: supplementary

  5. Government investment, III, p. 2721.
  6. Secretary of State's nominees, III, p. 2722.
  7. Government investment limit, III, p. 2722.
  8. Vested liabilities on winding up, III, p. 2724.
  9. Trustee investments in successor company, III, p. 2725.
 10. Extinguishment of certain liabilities, III, p. 2725.
 11 and schedule 3. Special constables, III, p. 2726.
 12. Building and planning contraventions, III, p. 2726.
 13. Stamp duty, III, p. 2727.
 14. Interpretation, III, p. 2727.
 15. Repeal, III, p. 2728.

Military services

 16. Military services, III, p. 2729.

General

 17. Finance: general, III, p. 2729.
 18. Short title, etc., III, p. 2729.
Schedule 1. Operation of schemes, III, p. 2730.
Schedule 2. Employment, III, p. 2731.
Schedule 3. Special constables, III, p. 2733.

P

PARLIAMENT.

Draft Orders, regulation, reports etc. to be laid before Parliament for approval
under, or by virtue of:
Prevention of Terrorism (Temporary Provisions) Act (c. 8, s. 14(10))
                                                                    I, p. 37
Education (Grants and Awards) Act (c. 11, s. 3(2))   ...   I, p. 59
Dentists Act (c. 24, ss. 45(9), 46(5))   ...   ...   I, pp. 439, 440
Betting, Gaming and Lotteries (Amendment) Act (c. 25, s. 1(1)) I, p. 466
Road Traffic Regulation Act (c. 27, ss. 88(8), 95(5), 97(1), 106(6), 134(5),
    sch. 9 para. 15(2))   ...   .   I, pp. 558, 562, 575, 598, 639
County Courts Act (c. 28, ss. 112(8), 145(3))   ...   I, pp. 732, 743
Food Act (c. 30, s. 120(3)(4))   ...   .   I, p. 951
London Regional Transport (c. 32, ss. 36(7), 47(10))   II, pp. 1044, 1060
Rates Act (c. 33, s. 9(3))   ...   .   II, p. 1139
Data Protection Act (c. 35, s. 40(4))   ...   .   II, p. 1194
Animal Health and Welfare Act (c. 40, s. 13(2))   ...   ...   II, p. 1363
Agricultural Holdings Act (c. 41, s. 8(4))   ...   .   II, p. 1384
Cable and Broadcasting Act (c. 46, s. 12(6))   ...   .   II, p. 1817
Health and Social Security Act (c. 48, s. 1(2))   ...   ...   II, p. 1894
Housing Defects Act (c. 50, s. 24(2))   ...   .   III, p. 2013
Local Government (Interim Provisions) Act (c. 53, s. 1(4))   ...   III, p. 2258
Co-operative Development Agency and Industrial Development Act (c. 57,
    s. 3(5), sch. 1 Pt. I)   ...   .   III, pp. 2599, 2603
Police and Criminal Evidence Act (c. 60, s. 67(3), 100(5), 113(5)
                                            III, pp. 2800, 2824, 2838
Roads (Scotland) Act (c. 54, s. 143(2)(b))   ...   .   III, p. 2359

Draft Orders, regulations, reports etc. to be laid before House of Commons
for approval under, or by virtue of:
London Regional Transport Act (c. 32, ss. 13(9), 22(4))

           II, pp. 1025, 1032

Rates Act (c. 33, ss. 4(5), 11(4))   ...   .   II, pp. 1135, 1140
Finance Act (c. 43, s. 125(1)) ...   .   II, p. 1589
Housing Defects Act (c. 50, s. 19(4)) ...   .   III, p. 2009
Capital Transfer Tax Act (c. 51, s. 158(4)) ...   .   III, p. 2139
Ordnance Factories and Military Services Act (c. 59, ss. 15(2), 16(3))

           III, pp. 2728, 2729

Orders, regulations, reports etc. to be laid before Parliament under, or by
virtue of:
Prevention of Terrorism (Temporary Provisions) Act (c. 8, s. 14(11))

           I, p. 37

Telecommunications Act (c. 12, ss. 9(2), 55(3), 94(4), Sch. 5 para. 39(6))

           I, pp. 72, 114, 148, 267

Dentists Act (c. 24, sch. 1 para. 7(2)) ...   .   I, p. 448
Road Traffic Regulation Act (c. 27, s. 20(4), 43(15, 81(2))

           I, pp. 494, 517, 553

County Courts Act (c. 28, ss. 2(2), 128(2))   ...   I, pp. 674, 737
Food Act (c. 30, s. 68(5))   ...   .   I, p. 921
Rating and Valuation (Amendment) (Scotland) Act (c. 31, s. 12(1), sch. 1)

           II, pp. 991, 1005

London Regional Transport Act (c. 32, ss. 19(5), 20(2), 34(4), 40(10))

           II, pp. 1031, 1043, 1049

Data Protection Act (c. 35, ss. 36(5), 40(6), sch. 2 para. 7(2))

           II, pp. 1191, 1194, 1201

Mental Health (Scotland) Act (c. 36, ss. 3(7), 119(3))   II, pp. 1211, 1293
Video Recordings Act (c. 39, ss. 5(1), 6(2)) ...   ...   II, pp. 1338, 1339
Animal Health and Welfare Act (c. 40, s. 7)   ...   ...   II, p. 1355
Cable and Broadcasting Act (c. 46, ss. 21(1), 41(4))   II, pp. 1823, 1840
Co-operative Development Agency and Industrial Development Act (c. 57,
s. 5(4)) ...   .   III, p. 2600
Rent (Scotland) Act (c. 58, ss. 53(2), 64(5), 95(3))

           III, pp. 2650, 2658, 2676

Ordnance Factories and Military Services Act (c. 59, s. 3(9))   III, p. 2721
Police and Criminal Evidence Act (c. 60, ss. 97(5), 103(2), sch. 4 para. 13(2))

           III, pp. 2822, 2828, 2854

Orders, regulations, reports etc. to be laid before House of Commons under,
or by virtue of:
Rating and Valuation (Amendment) (Scotland) Act (c. 31, ss.   2(1), 3,
15, sch. 1)   ...   .   II, pp. 984, 993, 998
Rates Act (c. 33, 5. 2(1))   ...   .   II, p. 1132

Orders, regulations, etc, subject to annulment in pursuance of a resolution of
either House of Parliament under, or by virtue of:
Prevention of Terrorism (Temporary Provisions) Act (c. 8, s. 14(9))

           I, p. 37

Education (Grants and Awards) Act (c. 11, s. 3(3)) ...   ...   I, p. 60
Telecommunications Act (c. 12, ss. 58(9), 104(1))   ...   I, pp. 116, 156
Anatomy Act (c. 14, ss. 3(6), 4(11), 5(7), 8(4))   I, pp. 289, 291, 292, 294
Tenants' Rights, Etc. (Scotland) Amendment Act (c. 18, ss. 2(2), 7)

           I, pp. 310, 313

Orders, regulations etc. subject to annulment in pursuance of a resolution of the House of Commons under, or by virtue of:

Rating and Valuation (Amendment) (Scotland) Act (c. 31, sch. 1)
II, p. 998

Rates Act (c. 33, ss. 2(4), 6(4), 10(6)) ...   ...   II, pp. 1133, 1137, 1139
Finance Act (c. 43, ss. 26(6), 39(5), 57(1), 88(8), sch. 8 para. 2(3))
II, pp. 1486, 1498, 1515, 1551, 1622
Housing Defects Act (c. 50, s. 24(5)) ...   . III, p. 2013
Capital Transfer Tax Act (c. 51, ss. 50(4), 233(4), 256(4))   ... III, pp. 2065
2184, 2194

Resolution of each House of Parliament required for approval of Orders, regulations etc. under, or by virtue of:

Prevention of Terrorism (Temporary Provisions) Act (c. 8, s. 14(10)(11))
I, p. 37
Education (Grants and Awards) Act (c. 11, s. 3(2))   ...   I, p. 59
Dentists Act (c. 24, ss. 45(9), 46(5)) ...   .   I, pp. 439, 440
Betting, Gaming and Lotteries (Amendment) Act (c. 25, s. 1(1))   I, p. 466
Road Traffic Regulation Act (c. 27, ss. 20(4), 81(2), 86(2)(3), 88(8), 95(5), 106(6), 134(4)(5), 140(1), sch. 9 para. 15(2))
I, pp. 494, 553, 558, 562, 575, 598, 603, 639
County Courts Act (c. 28, ss. 112(8), 145(3))   ...   I, pp. 732, 743
Food Act (c. 30, s. 120(3))   ...   .   I, p. 951
Rating and Valuation (Amendment) (Scotland) Act (c. 31, s. 12(1), sch. 1)
II, pp. 991, 998
London Regional Transport Act (c. 32, ss. 36(7), 47(10))
II, pp. 1044, 1060
Rates Act (c. 33, s. 9(3), sch. 1 para. 5)   ...   II, pp. 1139, 1145
Data Protection Act (c. 35, s. 40(4)) ...   . II, p. 1194
Animal Health and Welfare Act (c. 40, s. 13(2))   ...   ... II, p. 1363
Agricultural Holdings Act (c. 41, s. 8(4))   ...   . II, p. 1384
Cable and Broadcasting Act (c. 46, s. 12(6)) ...   . II, p. 1817
Health and Social Security Act (c. 48, s. 1(2))   ...   ... II, p. 1894
Housing Defects Act (c. 50, s. 24(2)) ...   . III, p. 2013
Local Government (Interim Provisions) Act (c. 53, s. 1(4))... III, p. 2258
Roads (Scotland) Act (c. 54, s. 143(2)(*b*))   ...   ... III, p. 2359
Co-operative Development Agency and Industrial Development Act (c. 57, ss. 3(5), 5(4), sch. 1 Pt. I)   ...   ...   III, pp. 2599, 2600, 2603
Rent (Scotland) Act (c. 58, ss. 53(2), 64(5), 95(3))
III, pp. 2650, 2658, 2676
Police and Criminal Evidence Act (c. 60, ss. 67(5), 100(5))
III, pp. 2800, 2824

Resolution of House of Commons required for approval of Orders, regulations, reports, salaries etc. under, or by virtue of:

Rating and Valuation (Amendment) (Scotland) Act (c. 31, ss. 2(1), 3, 15, sch. 1) ...   . II, pp. 984, 998
London Regional Transport Act (c. 32, ss. 13(9), 22(4)) II, pp. 1025, 1032
Rates Act (c. 33, ss. 4(5), 11(4))   ...   ... II, pp. 1135, 1140
Data Protection Act (c. 35, sch. 2 para. 3(1))   ...   ... II, p. 1199
Finance Act (c. 43, s. 125(1)) ...   . II, p. 1589
Housing Defects Act (c. 50, s. 19(4)) ...   . III, p. 2009
Capital Transfer Tax Act (c. 51, s. 158(4))   ...   ... III, p. 2139
Ordnance Factories and Military Services Act (c. 59, ss. 15(2), 16(3))
III, pp. 2728, 2729

*Index to the Public General Acts
and General Synod Measures 1984*

PRESCRIPTION AND LIMITATION (SCOTLAND) ACT: 1984 c. 45   ...   II, p. 1799

PREVENTION OF TERRORISM (TEMPORARY PROVISIONS) ACT: 1984 c. 8   I, p. 25

PART I

PROSCRIBED ORGANISATIONS

PART II

EXCLUSION ORDERS

PART III

MISCELLANEOUS OFFENCES

PART IV

ARREST, DETENTION AND PORT POWERS

R

U

Part III

Protection against Harassment and Eviction
without due process of Law

Part IV

Rents under Regulated Tenancies

Part V

Registration of Rents under Regulated Tenancies

PART VI

RENT LIMIT FOR DWELLING-HOUSES LET BY HOUSING
ASSOCIATIONS AND THE HOUSING CORPORATION

PART VII

PART VII CONTRACTS

PART VIII

PREMIUMS, ETC.

PART IX

HERITABLE SECURITIES

PART X

MISCELLANEOUS AND GENERAL

REPATRIATION OF PRISONERS ACT: 1984 c. 47   ...   .   II, p. 1879

RESTRICTIVE TRADE PRACTICES (STOCK EXCHANGE) ACT: 1984 c. 2   I, pp. 2, 3

ROAD TRAFFIC (DRIVING INSTRUCTION) ACT: 1984 c. 13...   I, pp. 283–286

ROAD TRAFFIC REGULATION ACT: 1984 c. 27   ...   .   I, p. 479

PART I

GENERAL PROVISIONS FOR TRAFFIC REGULATION

Outside Greater London

In Greater London

Experimental traffic schemes

PART II

TRAFFIC REGULATION IN SPECIAL CASES

PART III

CROSSINGS AND PLAYGROUNDS

Pedestrian crossings

School crossings

ROADS (SCOTLAND) ACT: 1984 c. 54   ...   .   III, p. 2265

PART I

PUBLIC ROADS

General powers and duties of roads authorities

Trunk roads

Special roads

Classification of roads

Supplementary

PART II

PRIVATE ROADS

PART III

NEW ROADS

PART X

MISCELLANEOUS

PART XI

OFFENCES

PART XII

STATUTORY UNDERTAKERS

PART XIII

GENERAL

Notices

Inquiries

Powers of entry etc.

Regulations, orders and schemes

Crown application

Financial provisions

S

T